ISBN 978-0-428-61476-8
PIBN 11211386

1 MONTH OF
FREE
READING

at

www.ForgottenBooks.com

By purchasing this book you are eligible for one month membership to ForgottenBooks.com, giving you unlimited access to our entire collection of over 1,000,000 titles via our web site and mobile apps.

To claim your free month visit:

www.forgottenbooks.com/free1211386

English
Français
Deutsche
Italiano
Español
Português

www.forgottenbooks.com

Mythology Photography **Fiction**
Fishing Christianity **Art** Cooking
Essays Buddhism Freemasonry
Medicine **Biology** Music **Ancient**
Egypt Evolution Carpentry Physics
Dance Geology **Mathematics** Fitness
Shakespeare **Folklore** Yoga Marketing
Confidence Immortality Biographies
Poetry **Psychology** Witchcraft
Electronics Chemistry History **Law**
Accounting **Philosophy** Anthropology
Alchemy Drama Quantum Mechanics
Atheism Sexual Health **Ancient History**
Entrepreneurship Languages Sport
Paleontology Needlework Islam
Metaphysics Investment Archaeology
Parenting Statistics Criminology
Motivational

OF

PERSONAL INJURIES ON RAILROADS

BY

EDW. J. WHITE

AUTHOR OF "MINES AND MINING REMEDIES," "PERSONAL INJURIES IN MINES,"
EDITOR THIRD EDITION "TIEDEMAN ON REAL PROPERTY," ETC.

IN TWO VOLUMES

VOL. I. INJURIES TO EMPLOYEES
VOL. II. INJURIES TO PASSENGERS, LICENSEES AND
TRESPASSERS

VOL. II.

PUBLISHED BY
THE F. H. THOMAS LAW BOOK CO.
ST. LOUIS, MO.

INJURIES TO PASSENGERS, LICENSEES AND TRESPASSERS.

TABLE OF CONTENTS

VOLUME I.
INJURIES TO EMPLOYEES.

CHAPTER I.

GENERAL CONSIDERATIONS IN ACTIONS FOR PERSONAL INJURIES.

CHAPTER II.

PROXIMATE CAUSE OF INJURY.

CHAPTER III.

JURISDICTION OF ACTION.

LAW OF PLACE.

CHAPTER IV.

PARTIES TO ACTIONS FOR DEATH.

CHAPTER V.

EVIDENCE IN RAILWAY ACCIDENT CASES.

TABLE OF CONTENTS.

CHAPTER VI.

DEMONSTRATIVE EVIDENCE OF NEGLIGENCE — RULE RES IPSA LOQUITUR.

CHAPTER VII.

ISSUES FOR THE COURT ALONE.

CHAPTER VIII.

JURY ISSUES IN RAILROAD ACCIDENTS

CHAPTER IX.

ELEMENTS AND COMPUTATION OF DAMAGES.

CHAPTER X.

GENERALLY OF EMPLOYER AND EMPLOYEE, IN PERSONAL IN-
JURY ACTIONS.

CHAPTER XI.

THE VARIOUS DUTIES OF THE EMPLOYER.

xiv

CHAPTER XII.

NEGLIGENCE OF INDEPENDENT CONTRACTORS.

CHAPTER XIII.

INJURIES TO INFANT EMPLOYEES.

CHAPTER XIV.

RISKS ASSUMED BY EMPLOYEES.

CHAPTER XV.

RISKS NOT ASSUMED BY EMPLOYEES.

CHAPTER XVI.

CONTRIBUTORY NEGLIGENCE OF EMPLOYEES.

xviii

CHAPTER XVII.

COMPARATIVE NEGLIGENCE.

CHAPTER XVIII.

COEMPLOYEES AT COMMON LAW.

CHAPTER XIX.

STATUTES ABOLISHING THE COMMON LAW.

VOLUME II.

INJURIES TO PASSENGERS, LICENSEES, AND TRESPASSERS.

CHAPTER XX.

THE RELATION OF CARRIER AND PASSENGER, GENERALLY.

CHAPTER XXI.

DUTIES AND LIABILITIES OF PASSENGER CARRIERS.

CHAPTER XXII.

THE ROADBED AND TRACK.

CHAPTER XXIII.

STATIONS AND APPROACHES.

CHAPTER XXIV.

CARS, ENGINES AND APPLIANCES.

CHAPTER XXV.

NEGLIGENCE IN THE EQUIPMENT AND OPERATION OF TRAINS.

CHAPTER XXVI.

INJURIES IN BOARDING TRAINS.

CHAPTER XXVII.

INJURIES IN ALIGHTING FROM TRAINS.

CHAPTER XXVIII.

INJURIES TO PASSENGERS BY EMPLOYEES.

CHAPTER XXIX.

INJURIES BY FELLOW PASSENGERS.

CHAPTER XXX.

WRONGFUL ACTS OF STRANGERS.

CHAPTER XXXI.

CONTRIBUTORY NEGLIGENCE OF PASSENGERS.

CHAPTER XXXVII.

INJURIES AT GRADE CROSSINGS.

CHAPTER XXXVIII.

INJURIES AT OVERHEAD CROSSINGS AND SUBWAYS.

CHAPTER XXXIX.

INJURIES AT DEFECTIVE CROSSINGS.

CHAPTER XL.

MAINTENANCE OF GATES AND SIGNS.

CHAPTER XLI.

MAINTENANCE OF FLAGMEN AND WATCHMEN.

CHAPTER XXXVII.

INJURIES AT GRADE CROSSINGS.

CHAPTER XXXVIII.

INJURIES AT OVERHEAD CROSSINGS AND SUBWAYS.

CHAPTER XXXIX.

INJURIES AT DEFECTIVE CROSSINGS.

CHAPTER XL.

MAINTENANCE OF GATES AND SIGNS.

CHAPTER XLI.

MAINTENANCE OF FLAGMEN AND WATCHMEN.

CHAPTER XLV.

THE DOCTRINE OF IMPUTED NEGLIGENCE.

CHAPTER XLVI.

WHO DEEMED TRESPASSERS GENERALLY.

TABLE OF CONTENTS.

CHAPTER XLV.

THE DOCTRINE OF IMPUTED NEGLIGENCE.

xxxvi

CHAPTER XLVI.

WHO DEEMED TRESPASSERS GENERALLY.

CHAPTER XLVII.

DUTIES AND LIABILITIES TOWARD TRESPASSERS.

CHAPTER XLVIII.

CONTRIBUTORY NEGLIGENCE OF TRESPASSERS.

THE LAW

OF

PERSONAL INJURIES ON RAILROADS.

VOLUME II.

INJURIES TO PASSENGERS, LICENSEES, AND TRESPASSERS.

CHAPTER XX.

THE RELATION OF CARRIER AND PASSENGER, GENERALLY.

§ 551. **Who considered passenger carrier.**— A company engaged in transporting passengers for hire, upon a railroad

827

operated by it, is denominated by the law, a common carrier of passengers.[1]   A common carrier of passengers, therefore, is one who undertakes, for hire, to carry all persons, indifferently, who may apply for passage.[2]

To constitute a common carrier of passengers, it is necessary that the carrier should hold itself, or himself, out to the general public as such and this may be done not only by advertisement, but by actually engaging in the business, and continuously pursuing the occupation of a carrier of passengers, as a permanent employment.[3]

But it is not every carrier of passengers for hire that will constitute such carrier a common carrier of passengers.   One having the conveniences for carrying persons for hire, may do so in many instances, at the instance and for the accommodation of passengers, but the responsibility of a common carrier will not result, unless the business is regularly followed, as such.[4]

Contractors building a railroad for another company and with no intention of carrying passengers regularly for hire, may occasionally carry persons for hire, as an accommodation, without incurring the responsibility of a common carrier of passengers and in such case the passenger will assume the ordinary risks incident to the known method of conveyance used and the only duty imposed upon the carrier will be that of ordinary prudence, used by reasonably careful persons engaged in the same business.[5]

If a private corporation, however, regularly engages in the

---

[1] Davis v. Button, 78 Cal. 247; 18 Pac. Rep. 133; 20 Pac. Rep. 545.

[2] Nashville, etc., R. Co. v. Messine, 1 Sneed (Tenn.) 220; Gillingham v. Ohio River R. Co., 35 W. Va. 588; 14 S. E. Rep. 243; 14 L. R. A. 798; 51 Am. & Eng. R. Cas. 222.

[3] Nashville, etc., R. Co. v. Messine, *supra*.

[4] Nashville, etc., R. Co. v. Messine, *supra*.

[5] Shoemaker v. Kingsbury, 12 Wall. (U. S.) 369.

business of carrying passengers, for hire, although not organized specially for that purpose, and one taking passage by the means of conveyance furnished, sustains an injury while enroute, damages can be recovered from the carrier and it cannot avoid liability, on the ground that the act of carrying such passenger was *ultra vires,* as it is no defense to a company receiving and carrying persons for hire, that it had no legal right to do so, since the law charges the carrier with responsibility for wrongs coming to those who commit their personal safety to it, for a remuneration and who suffer injury from its negligence or misconduct.[6] Besides, it is generally no defense to legal proceedings in tort, that the tort was *ultra vires.*[7]

§ 552. **Who deemed passenger, in law.**— A " passenger," in the legal acceptation of the term, is one who travels in some public conveyance, by virtue of a contract, express or implied, with the carrier, for the payment of fare, or the acceptance of something equivalent therefor.[8]

No person will become a passenger, except by the consent, express or implied, of the carrier.[9]

The existence of the relation of passenger and carrier, by railroad, is only to be implied from circumstances such as will warrant the implication that the one has offered himself to be carried and that the other has accepted the offer and has received the proposed passenger, to be properly cared for, until the trip is begun and then to be carried over the railroad of the carrier.[10] The relation depends, primarily, upon

[6] Gruber v. Washington, etc., R. Co., 92 N. Car. 1; 21 Am. & Eng. R. Cas. 438.

[7] Green's Brice's *Ultra Vires* 265.

[8] Pennsylvania R. Co. v. Price, 96 Pa. St. 256.

[9] Hoar v. Maine Central R. Co., 70 Me. 65.

[10] Webster v. Fitchburg, etc., R. Co., 161 Mass. 289; 37 N. E. Rep.

the existence of a contract, express or implied. This being so, the passenger must, in some manner, indicate his purpose of becoming a passenger and place himself or' herself, in charge of the carrier. If a person, instead of waiting in the carrier's station, for a given train, stays at a boarding house, off the carrier's property several hundred feet, until the arrival of the train and then endeavors to get on the train, while it is in motion, as a result of which injuries are sustained, the relation of passenger and carrier does not exist.[11]

But an actual entry into the cars of the railroad company is not always essential to create the relation of passenger and carrier,[12] and if a person is waiting in the waiting-room of a railroad company, with the intention of becoming a passenger and taking passage on its cars, this will just as effectually constitute such person a passenger, as if he had actually entered within the body of one of the company's cars.[13]

165; 58 Am. & Eng. R. Cas. 1; Dodge v. Boston, etc., Co., 148 Mass. 207; 37 Am. & Eng. R. Cas. 67.

[11] Spannagle v. Chicago, etc., R. Co., 31 Ill. App. 460.

[12] Allender v. Chicago, etc., R. Co., 37 Iowa 264; Gordon v. Grand St. R. Co., 40 Barb. (N. Y.) 546; Norfolk, etc., R. Co. v. Galligher, 89 Va. 639; Warren v. Fitchburg, etc., R. Co., 8 Allen (Mass.) 227; Baltimore, etc., R. Co. v. State, 63 Md. 135; Murphy v. St. Louis, etc., R. Co., 43 Mo. App. 342.

[13] Central, etc., R. Co. v. Perry, 58 Ga. 461; 16 Am. Ry. Rep. 122; Gordon v. Grand St. R. Co., 40 Barb. (N. Y.) 546.

A carrier owes no duty whatever to a person intending to become a passenger, until she has become a passenger by either getting on, or attempting to get on, the car after it has stopped for the purpose of permitting her to board it. Lexington Ry. Co. v. Herring (Ky. 1906), 96 S. W. Rep. 558.

The relation of passenger and carrier does not exist where it does not appear that the party claiming to be a passenger has placed himself in charge of the carrier for transportation, and where it does not appear that the carrier has expressly or impliedly accepted such party for carriage. Illinois Cent. R. Co. v. McMillion, 129 Ill. App. 27, 37.

A person having a permit to ride in the caboose of a freight train

§ 553. **Presumption that one is a passenger.**— Every one riding in a railroad car is presumed, *prima facie,* to be there lawfully as a passenger, having paid, or being liable, when

cannot recover for injuries sustained by him while on his way to board the caboose without proof of negligence on the part of the company in the construction or maintenance of its station or yards which is the proximate cause of the injury.　Chicago & L. Ry. Co. v. Mann. (Neb. 1907), 111 N. W. Rep. 379.

Ordinarily when one goes to a railroad's station to take the next train, he becomes in contemplation of the law a passenger, whether he has actually bought a ticket or not, provided he goes within a reasonable time before the schedule time for the departure of the train, and, where his arrival is not within such reasonable time, the carrier owes him no duty, save such as it owes to a licensee.　Texas Midland R. Co. v. Griggs (Tex. Civ. App. 1907), 106 S. W. Rep. 411.

It has very recently been held by the Supreme Court of Oregon in the case of Gray v. Columbia River & O. R. R. Co. (88 Pac. Rep. 297), that the plaintiff was a passenger upon defendant's railroad under the following circumstances: During the spring and summer of 1905 the defendant company was engaged in the construction of a railroad in the State of Oregon.

The conductor permitted the plaintiff to ride without objection.　On the way down to Rock Creek, the engine and front wheels of the tank car left the track owing as it was alleged to the unsafe and unfinished condition of the track and to the excessive and dangerous rate of speed at which the train was moving.　The plaintiff was thrown from the car and injured.

The defendant gave in evidence a rule of the company which provided that "freight conductors must allow none but train crew to ride on freight cars," and it was contended by the defendant that by reason of this rule the conductor of the train on which plaintiff was riding at the time of his injury had no authority to bind the defendant by receiving him thereon as a passenger.　But the court held that the conductor was not a freight conductor and that plaintiff was on the car in the performance of a duty he owed his employers and was being carried in pursuance of a contract between such employers and the defendant company and consequently was a passenger. In the course of its opinion, the court said:

"This is not a case of a stranger riding on a train of a railway company after the road has been completed and is under the sole charge of the operating department after it has been completed, but it is that of an employee of a contractor on an uncompleted road being called on, to pay his railroad fare.[14]   One traveling by a passenger train and shown not to be connected with the railroad company, is therefore legally presumed to be a passenger and traveling for a consideration,[15] and if such a person sustains an injury while traveling, it is the presumption of law that he has all the rights of any other passenger.[16]

But this presumption, like all other presumptions, which are indulged in, in the absence of a showing as to the facts, is subject to rebuttal.[17]   No presumption of law or of fact arises where the person is found on a car not ordinarily used for the accommodation of passengers and in such a case, it is for the jury to determine, under all the facts and circumstances, whether such a person, is or is not a passenger.[18]   If a person, by his own solicitation, or consent, is carried on a vehicle or conveyance which is not used for the purpose of passenger carriage, there is no legal presumption that he is a passenger on such vehicle, although the owner may be a common carrier of passengers by means of other convey-

carried in discharge of his duty in pursuance of an agreement between his employer and the company."

Considering that tne tank car was in no wise adapted for passengers, and that it was at the request of plaintiff's employers that he was allowed to ride on it; that there was a passenger coach where he could have ridden in safety; that the road was uncompleted; that the conductor had no authority to allow plaintiff to ride upon the tank car and that plaintiff was there for the sole purpose of looking after his employer's property, which apparently could have been transported in the freight car, it may well be doubted whether the court's opinion will bear very close scrutiny.

[14] Gillingham v. Ohio River R. Co., 35 W. Va. 558; 14 S. E. Rep. 243; 14 L. R. A. 798; 51 Am. & Eng. R. Cas. 222; Pennsylvania R. Co. v. Books, 57 Pa. St. 339; 98 Am. Dec. 234; Anderson v. Missouri Pacific Ry. Co., 196 Mo. 442, by Judge Fox; 93 S. W. Rep. 394.

[15] Creed v. Pennsylvania R. Co., 86 Pa. St. 139.

[16] Atchison, etc., R. Co. v. Headland, 18 Colo. 477; 33 Pac. Rep. 185; 58 Am. & Eng. R. Cas. 4.

[17] People v. Douglas, 87 Cal. 281; 25 Pac. Rep. 417.

[18] People v. Douglas, *supra*.

ances, devoted exclusively to passenger carriage.[19]   The presumption that one riding on a passenger train, is a passenger, does not apply to a person riding on a freight train,[20] and the fact that a person was found in a caboose attached to a freight train is not, of itself, sufficient to warrant a court in assuming that the railroad company had undertaken the duties and assumed the obligations toward such a person, as a passenger, but, in the absence of proof to the contrary, the legal presumption would be that he was not a passenger.[21]

§ 554. **How the relation is created.**— The relation of carrier and passenger arises out of contract. It need not necessarily be an express contract, but may be implied in law from the facts and circumstances connected with the status of the parties. But the relation is always based upon a contract of the one kind or the other.[22]

And the contract must be that of the railroad company as distinguished from the personal undertaking of an unauthorized agent; for while the railroad company can only lawfully contract through the medium of its agents, the contract would not be the company's but that of an employee, if the individual, instead of contracting with an authorized agent of the railroad company, entered into a private arrangement with an unauthorized agent and one known to have no authority to make such a contract.[23]

If there was no contract between the railroad company and the individual, there would be no relation sufficient to estab-

[19] Snyder v. Natchez, etc., R. Co., 42 La. Ann. 302; 7 So. Rep. 582; 44 Am. & Eng. R. Cas. 278.

[20] Atchison, etc., R. Co. v. Headland, 18 Colo. 477; 33 Pac. Rep. 185; 58 Am. & Eng. R. Cas. 4.

[21] Atchison, etc., R. Co. v. Headland, *supra*.

[22] Dovey v. St. Louis Transit Co., 192 Mo. 197; 91 S. W. Rep. 140; O'Donnell v. Kansas City, etc., R. Co., 197 Mo. 110, 117; 95 S. W. Rep. 196.

[23] O'Donnell v. Kansas City, etc., R. Co., *supra*.

lish a liability as a carrier of passengers, toward such an individual, and it would be immaterial that such a person entered the company's train, under an agreement with its brakeman, with the consent of the conductor of the train.[24] An employee who has no authority to enter into contracts of carriage, for a railroad company, cannot bind it by such a contract and one riding on the invitation of such an employee is not a passenger, but a trespasser.[25]

One who fraudulently attempts to ride gratuitously, is not a passenger, toward whom the railroad company owes any duty, as such,[26] and if a person knowingly induces a conductor of a train to violate a known rule, to carry him without charge, he is guilty of a fraud on the railroad company and cannot claim to be entitled to the rights of a passenger.[27]

§ 555. **Payment of fare or purchase of ticket.**— The actual payment of fare is not an essential prerequisite to the status of a passenger on a railroad train,[28] for if one, although he

[24] O'Donnell v. Kansas City, etc., R. Co., *supra.*

[25] Drogmund v. Metropolitan R. Co., 122 Mo. App. 154; 98 S. W. Rep. 1091.

[26] Louisville, etc., R. Co. v. Thompson, 107 Ind. 442; 8 N. E. Rep. 18; 57 Am. Rep. 120; 27 Am. & Eng. R. Cas. 88.

[27] McVeety v. St. Paul, etc., R. Co., 45 Minn. 268; 47 N. W. Rep. 809; 47 Am. & Eng. R. Cas. 47. But see, Wagner v. Missouri Pacific R. Co., 97 Mo. 512; 10 S. W. Rep. 486; 3 L. R. A. 156.

In discussing the elements that must exist to constitute the relation of passenger and carrier, Mr. Hutchinson, in his work on Carriers, uses this language: " Unless some contract, express or implied from the circumstances, can be shown, it is difficult to see how the relation can be held to be established. The mere intention to take passage upon the carrier's vehicle ought not, certainly, to have that effect under any circumstances." 2 Hutchinson on Carriers (3 ed.), § 1015, p. 1168.

[28] Florida Southern R. Co. v. Hirst, 30 Fla. 1; 11 So. Rep. 506; 52 Am. & Eng. R. Cas. 409; Murphy v. St. Louis, etc., R. Co., 43 Mo.

has paid no fare, is on a train with the knowledge or permission of the person in charge thereof, he is a passenger, in law, and is entitled to the same care and protection as if he had paid his fare.[29]

Regardless of the question of compensation to the carrier, a person lawfully on a car and entitled to transportation, is a passenger and in case such a person was injured by the negligence of the carrier or its employees, if the injury occurred without fault on his part, he would be entitled to recover damages,[30] as it is sufficient to fix the liability of the carrier, for injuries occasioned by the negligence of its employees, that the passenger was lawfully on the train, whether by reason of having paid his fare, or by the permission or invitation of the officers or agents of the railroad company.[31]

Neither is the actual purchase of a ticket, before entering a railroad train, a necessary prerequisite to constitute the relation of passenger and to place upon the railroad company that degree of care which a common carrier is held to owe to a passenger.[32] The possession of a ticket is but evidence of the terms and conditions of the contract, but it is not essential to constitute the relation, and where the person was properly and lawfully on a train, with the knowledge of the agents or employees of the railroad company, for the purpose of being transported, he is, to all intents and pur-

App. 342; Pennsylvania R. Co. v. Price, 96 Pa. St. 256; 1 Am. & Eng. R. Cas. 234.

[29] Muelhausen v. St. Louis, etc., R. Co., 91 Mo. 332; 2 S. W. Rep. 315; 28 Am. & Eng. R. Cas. 157; Sherman v. Hannibal, etc., R. Co., 72 Mo. 65; Buck v. Peoples, etc., R. Co., 46 Mo. App. 555; Reynolds v. St. Louis Transfer Co., 189 Mo. 408; 88 S. W. Rep. 50; Anderson v. Missouri Pacific Ry. Co., 196 Mo. 442; 93 S. W. Rep. 394.

[30] Gulf, etc., R. Co. v. Wilson, 79 Texas 371; 15 S. W. Rep. 280.

[31] Prince v. International, etc., R. Co., 64 Texas 144; 21 Am. & . Eng. R. Cas. 152.

[32] Allender v. Chicago, etc., R. Co., 37 Iowa 264; Norfolk, etc., R. Co. v. Groseclose, 88 Va. 267; 13 S. E. Rep. 454.

poses a passenger, although he had not purchased a ticket, before entering the train.[33]

§ 556. When relation of passenger begins.

— It is not always essential that a person should have actually paid his fare or bought a ticket, to establish the relation of passenger and carrier between such person and the railroad company, but to lay down any precise rule for determining just the instant the relation begins, is not possible. If one applies to a station agent for a ticket and is referred to a

[33] Secord v. St. Paul, etc., R. Co., 5 McCrary (U. S.) 515; 18 Fed. Rep. 221.

"It is the duty of a passenger to supply himself with a ticket before getting on the train." McCook v. Dublin, etc., R. Co. (Ga. App. 1907), 58 S. E. Rep. 491.

"Though plaintiff boarded a train without the intention of paying fare, and hence did not become a passenger, the conductor was not entitled to put him off, regardless of the place or manner of his removal or the injuries he might receive." Gates v. Quincy, etc., Ry. Co. (Mo. App. 1907), 102 S. W. Rep. 50.

"While one who has no ticket and who willfully refuses to pay fare is not a passenger, yet, if he intends to pay fare and has the ability to do so, he is entitled to a reasonable time to get the money after demand, and does not become a trespasser on the very instant of failure or refusal." St. Louis Southwestern Ry. Co. v. Fussell (Tex. Civ. App. 1906), 97 S. W. Rep, 332.

"One who fails to provide himself with a ticket before entering a car, or who fails to tender enough money to pay fare when requested, is a trespasser, and not a passenger." Louisville & N. R. Co. v. Cottengim, 104 S. W. Rep. 280; 31 Ky. Law Rep. 871.

"As to what would be a reasonable time to allow a passenger to produce his ticket or pay his fare depends on the circumstances of each case." Seaboard Air Line Ry. v. Scarborough (Fla. 1906), 42 So. Rep. 706.

"Whether a passenger was given a reasonable time in which to produce his ticket or pay his fare is ordinarily a question of fact for the jury." Seaboard Air Line Ry. v. Scarborough (Fla. 1906), 42 So. Rep. 706.

"It is not essential to establish the status of a passenger to show that fare was either paid or intended to be paid." Wabash R. Co. v. Jellison, 124 Ill. App. 652.

freight conductor of the train on which passage is desired, such a person is held to be a passenger, in Iowa.[34] A person who, in good faith goes to a station to buy a ticket and takes passage on a passenger train, is held to be a passenger, even though the agent refuses to sell him a ticket.[35] Likewise, it is not necessary that fare should be paid, to constitute the relation, but it is ordinarily sufficient that it is understood between the parties that fare is to be paid.[36] Carriers may demand the prepayment of fare, but if they do not and permit persons to go into their cars without prepayment of fare, such persons are passengers, within the legal definition of the term, before payment of fare.[37] One who has purchased a ticket and is present at the regular point of departure of a train to take passage, is held to be a passenger and entitled to protection as such, though he has not entered the cars.[38]

After a person enters the car of a railroad company to take passage thereon, he is a passenger, whether he has purchased a ticket or not, and if the company permits persons to enter its cars at other than regular stations, after actually entering the cars at such a place, all persons will be considered passengers, the same as though the cars had been entered at a regular station of the railroad company.[39]

[34] Allender v. Chicago, etc., R. Co., 37 Iowa 264; 8 Am. Ry. Rep. 115.

[35] Grimes v. Pennsylvania R. Co., 36 Fed. Rep. 72; Norfolk, etc., R. Co. v. Galligher, 89 Va. 639.

[36] Gordon v. Grand Street, etc., R. Co., 40 Barb. (N. Y.) 546; Nashville, etc., R. Co. v. Messine, 1 Sneed (Tenn.) 220.

[37] Hurt v. Southern R. Co., 40 Miss. 391.

[38] Baltimore, etc., R. Co. v. State, 63 Md. 135; 21 Am. & Eng. R. Cas. 202; Warren v. Fitchburg, etc., R. Co., 8 Allen (Mass.) 227; Central, etc., R. Co. v. Perry, 58 Ga. 461; 16 Am. Ry. Rep. 122.

[39] Lake Erie, etc., R. Co. v. Mays, 4 Ind. App. 413; 30 N. E. Rep. 1106; Bellman v. New York, etc., R. Co., 5 N. Y. S. R. 153; 42 Hun 130; 122 N. Y. 671; 34 N. Y. S. R. 1015; Shannon v. Boston, etc., R.

But when fare is demanded, the instant that a person refuses to pay his fare, or otherwise comply with the reasonable
regulations of the carrier, such person becomes a trespasser,
in law, and can be dealt with as such.[40]   A person enroute
to a passenger station, intending to take passage on a train
after arrival, will not be considered a passenger, until he
arrives at the station and submits himself to the control of
the carrier.[41]   One who signals a passenger train to stop at
a point not a regular station and in attempting to board
the train at such a place, is injured, is not a passenger, although the conductor, subsequent to such injury, collects a
fare from such injured person.[42]   Nor does a person become
a passenger, who gets on a train after it has started to move,
until he actually reaches a place of safety inside the car and
no action can be maintained by his representatives, if he falls
off the platform and is killed, in attempting to get on such
train.[43]

Co., 78 Me. 52; 2 Atl. Rep. 678; 23 Am. & Eng. R. Cas. 511; Dewire
v. Boston, etc., R. Co., 148 Mass. 343; 19 N. E. Rep. 523; 2 L. R. A.
166; 37 Am. & Eng. R. Cas. 57.

[40] Lake Erie, etc., R. Co. v. Mays, 4 Ind. App. 413; 30 N. E. Rep.
1106.

[41] June v. Boston, etc., R. Co., 153 Mass. 79; 26 N. E. Rep. 238.
But see, where person rides to depot in stage furnished by railroad
company, Buffet v. New York, etc., R. Co., 40 N. Y. 169, affirming 36
Barb. 420.

[42] Georgia Pacific R. Co. v. Robinson, 68 Miss. 643; 10 So. Rep. 60.

[43] Merrill v. Eastern R. Co., 139 Mass. 238; 1 N. E. Rep. 548; 52
Am. Rep. 705.

For rule that relation of passenger and carrier does not obtain,
until the person of the passenger has been placed under the control of
the carrier, either upon the premises or vehicle of the latter. See, 3
Thompson on Neg., § 2641, citing Webster v. Fitchburg R. Co., 161
Mass. 298; 37 N. E. Rep. 165; 24 L. R. A. 521. But see, also, where
the passenger has brought himself within the rule, by purchasing a
ticket and entering upon the premises of the carrier. Young v.
New York, etc., R. Co., 171 Mass. 33; 50 N. E. Rep. 455; 41 L. R. A.
193.

§ 557. **When the relation terminates.**— The duty of a railroad company under its contract to carry a passenger, does not terminate until he has alighted from its cars. The transit cannot be considered as ended until the passenger has left the car and a passenger on a railroad car continues to be such while rightfully leaving the car at the station at which it has stopped.[44] The liability of the carrier ends, only when the passenger has safely alighted from the car. If the train stops long enough for the passengers to get off safely, then the carrier has done its full duty, but if, by sudden jerks, a passenger is injured in the act of alighting, the railroad company is liable for such an injury.[45] The railroad company's liability toward a passenger continues until the train arrives at the passenger's place of destination, and he has had notice of such arrival and then for a reasonable time, to enable him to alight.[46] The period allowed a passenger to alight from a train, after arrival at his place of destination, is said to be the time within which a person of ordinary prudence, under similar circumstances, would take to alight.[47] Nor does the responsibility of the carrier cease immediately upon the passenger's exit from the train, at the place of destination, but the relation continues until the passenger has had a reasonable opportunity to leave the company's premises in the di-

[44] McKimble v. Boston, etc., R. Co., 139 Mass. 542; 2 N. E. Rep. 97; 21 Am. & Eng. R. Cas. 213; Pennsylvania R. Co. v. Marion, 104 Ind. 239; 27 Am. & Eng. R. Cas. 132; Texas, etc., R. Co. v. Miller, 79 Texas 78; 15 S. W. Rep. 264; St. Louis, etc., R. Co. v. Finley, 79 Texas 85; 15 S. W. Rep. 266.

[45] Central R. Co. v. Whitehead, 74 Ga. 441; Timpson v. Manhattan R. Co., 24 N. Y. S. R. 629; 52 Hun 489; 5 N. Y. Supp. 684; Pittsburg, etc., R. Co. v. Krouse, 30 Ohio St. 222; 15 Am. Ry. Rep. 298; Knight v. Portland R. Co., 56 Me. 234; Ormond v. Hays, 60 Texas 180.

[46] Imhoff v. Chicago, etc., R. Co., 20 Wis. 344; Jeffersonville, etc., R. Co. v. Parmalee, 51 Ind. 42.

[47] Chicago, etc., R. Co. v. Barrett, 16 Ill. App. 17; Imhoff v. Chicago, etc., R. Co., 20 Wis. 344; Allerton v. Boston, etc., R. Co., 146 Mass. 241; 15 N. E. Rep. 621; 34 Am. & Eng. R. Cas. 563.

rection ordinarily taken, and it is the additional duty of the
railroad company to keep the way of egress used by passengers
reasonably safe for the purpose of leaving the carrier's
premises.[48]   And if the passenger leaves the train on the
wrong side of the car, the responsibility still continues, unless he has been advised of the proper side to get off on.[49]

If a passenger, by a mistake of his own, however, has entered the wrong train, the liability of the railroad company is
at an end when such passenger voluntarily leaves the train,
at a place provided for him to alight.[50]   And when a passenger has safely alighted and left the station, the railroad
company owes him no further duty, regardless of whether he
is sober or intoxicated.[51]

But a passenger does not lose his status by alighting at an
intermediate or transfer station, in the course of his journey,
where he does so with the express or implied consent of the
carrier, but if he goes out of sight or leaves the car without
the consent of the carrier, he takes upon himself the responsibility of his own movements.[52]   The same duty is imposed
upon carriers, toward passengers who, while on a continuous
journey, go to and return from the eating houses, provided

[48] Burnham v. Wabash R. Co., 91 Mich. 523; 52 N. W. Rep. 14;
Gaynor v. Old Colony R. Co., 100 Mass. 208; Ormund v. Hays, 60 Texas
180.

[49] McKimble v. Boston, etc., R. Co., 139 Mass. 542; 2 N. E. Rep. 97;
21 Am. & Eng. R. Cas. 213, and note, p. 215.

[50] Cincinnati, etc., R. Co. v. Carper, 112 Ind. 26; 13 N. E. Rep. 122;
21 Am. & Eng. R. Cas. 36.

[51] Rozwadosfski v. International, etc., R. Co., 1 Texas Civ. App.
487; 20 S. W. Rep. 872.

[52] State v. Grand Trunk R. Co., 58 Mo. 176; Parsons v. New York,
etc., R. Co., 113 N. Y. 355; 21 N. E. Rep. 145; 22 N. Y. S. R. 697;
48 Hun 615; 3 L. R. A. 683; Dice v. Williamette, etc., Co., 8 Oregon
60; DeKay v. Chicago, etc., R. Co., 41 Minn. 178; 43 N. W. Rep. 182;
4 L. R. A. 632; 39 Am. & Eng. R. Cas. 463; Missouri Pacific Ry. Co,
v. Foreman, 73 Texas 311; 11 S. W. Rep. 326,

by the carrier for the accommodation of its passengers.[53] The relation and obligation of the carrier continues at transfer stations, while the transfer is being made;[54] during the time that a passenger is being transferred to another train, on account of a washout on the line, he is still a passenger and entitled to protection as such.[55] And this is generally true, whenever he leaves the car, before the termination of his journey, with the consent of the carrier, or its employees or authorized agents.[56]

But the contract of transportation is ordinarily regarded as an entirety and the law does not compel the railroad company to continuously exert itself to keep its passengers aboard, and if a passenger, without stop-over privileges, gets off the train at an intermediate station or at any other place, without the consent of the carrier, he thereby voluntarily terminates the relation of passenger and carrier and could not recover for an injury thus received while off the train on his own private business.[57]

[53] Atchison, etc., R. Co. v. Shean, 18 Colo. 368; 33 Pac. Rep. 108; 58 Am. & Eng. R. Cas. 360; Jeffersonville, etc., R. Co. v. Riley, 39 Ind. 568.

[54] Baltimore, etc., R. Co. v. State, 60 Md. 449; 12 Am. & Eng. R. Cas. 149; Knight v. Portland, etc., R. Co., 56 Me. 234.

[55] Dwinnelle v. New York, etc., R. Co., 120 N. Y. 117; 24 N. E. Rep. 319; 30 N. Y. S. R. 578; 8 L. R. A. 224; 44 Am. & Eng. R. Cas. 384.

[56] State v. Grand Trunk R. Co., 58 Me. 176; Wandell v. Corbin, 17 N. Y. S. R. 718; 1 N. Y. Supp. 795.

[57] Stone v. Chicago, etc., R. Co., 47 Iowa 82; 17 Am. Ry. Rep. 461; Drew v. Central Pacific R. Co., 51 Cal. 425; 12 Am. Ry. Rep. 222. "A passenger during his journey may alight from the car without losing his status as a passenger. Order (Sup. 1906), 99 N. Y. S. 936, reversed." Zeccardi v. Yonkers R. Co., 83 N. E. Rep. 31. "A passenger having made known to the conductor his desire to alight to get a lunch during the time the train stopped, and the conductor having informed him that he would have time to do so and consented to his alighting for that purpose, the passenger, on alighting, continued to sustain that relation." Missouri, K. & T. Ry. Co. v. Price (Tex. Civ. App.), 106 S. W. Rep. 700.

The relation of passenger does not necessarily cease as soon as one leaves the car, especially when he is seeking to return to obtain his property on the car. Flynn v. St. Louis Transit Co., 113 Mo. App. 185; 87 S. W. Rep. 560.

The relation continues until the passenger is safely off the car. Senf v. St. Louis, etc., R. Co., 112 Mo. App. 74; 86 S. W. Rep. 887; Cramer v. Springfield, etc., R. Co., 112 Mo. App. 350; 87 S. W. Rep. 24.

It is the duty to stop trains at stations long enough to allow passengers, acting expeditiously, to leave the train in safety. Gross v. Missouri Pacific Ry. Co., 109 Mo. App. 716; 84 S. W. Rep. 122.

If a passenger from mere curiosity leaves a train at an intermediate station, on a dark night, where only a short stop is made and on the train pulling out, sustains an injury, in attempting to overtake it, the railroad company is not liable therefor. Laub v. Chicago, etc., R. Co., 118 Mo. App. 488; 94 S. W. Rep. 550.

" A passenger having through railroad transportation and a check evidencing his right to occupy a through sleeping car, was directed to leave his car at an intermediate point and there board another car. After alighting from the car, he was directed to go to the depot, and while walking on the depot platform he fell and was injured. *Held*, that the failure of the sleeping car company to fulfill its contract for continuous passage was not the proximate cause of the injury." Pullman Co. v. Stearn (Miss. 1906), 41 So. Rep. 383.

" A passenger having made known to the conductor his desire to alight to get a lunch during the time the train stopped, and the conductor having informed him that he would have time to do so, and consented to his alighting for that purpose and the passenger having alighted, it was the duty of the conductor to hold the train in accordance with his answer; the passenger not having boarded the train sooner." Missouri, K. & T. Ry. Co. v. Price (Tex. Civ. App. 1908), 106 S. W. Rep. 700.

" A train regularly stopped twice at a town; the second stop being near a restaurant, where the train stopped for 20 minutes to allow passengers to procure supper. A passenger mistakenly left the train at its first stop at the town through the negligent misdirection of a brakeman. Before learning of the mistake, the train left him. There was no servant of the railroad present to guide him, and the passenger had no knowledge of the way to take to reach the train. A conductor of an independent carrier directed the passenger, who, while obeying the direction, was injured in consequence of a defect at the end of the platform where the train stopped. *Held*, that the proximate cause of the injury was the negligent misdirection of the brakeman, rendering the railroad company liable." Laub v. Chicago, etc., Ry. Co. (Mo. App. 1906), 94 S. W. Rep. 550.

§ 558. **Passenger reaching first destination, remaining on train.**— While the liability of a carrier for injuries to a passenger is generally only held to continue until the train arrives at the passenger's destination and he has been so notified and then for such a length of time as would enable a person of ordinary care and prudence to alight from the

" The court cannot say as a matter of law that the relation of carrier and passenger ceases after the expiration of four minutes after the arrival of the train at the point of destination." Hodges v. Southern Pac. Co. (Cal. App. 1906), 86 Pac. Rep. 620.

" A carrier is bound to use proper care to see that a passenger alighting from a train at a station has a safe way of exit from the station grounds, and the relation of carrier and passenger continues until such exit is completed." Legge v. New York & H. R. Co. (Mass. 1908), 83 N. E. Rep. 367.

" A carrier having offered a reasonable opportunity for passengers to alight and being without knowledge or reason to know of the perilous position of a passenger then attempting to alight, is entitled to act upon the presumption that passengers will exercise due care to avoid perilous positions." Central Ry. Co. v. McNab (Ala. 1907), 43 So. Rep. 222.

" The rule that, where a passenger has reached his destination and alighted, he is still entitled to protection as a passenger until he has had a reasonable time to leave the station premises, applies strictly to injuries resulting from any instrumentality or agency under the carrier's control." Taylor v. Atlantic Coast Line R. Co. (S. C. 1907), 59 S. E. Rep. 641.

" A passenger who shows that the car stopped at a crossing to permit passengers to alight, and that he, while alighting, was thrown from the car by reason of the sudden starting thereof, establishes his right to recover." Ghio v. Metropolitan St. Ry. Co. (Mo. App. 1907), 103 S. W. Rep. 142.

" Whether a person who has alighted from a standing train at a station and is crossing the tracks by planked way provided by the company after the train from which he has alighted has moved out is still a passenger entitled to cross without looking or listening, is a question of fact for the jury, where reasonable men may differ as to whether he was proceeding to a place of safety within a reasonable time after he had alighted from the train." Atlantic City R. Co. v. Kiefer (N. J. Sup. 1907), 66 Atl. Rep. 930.

" A passenger on a railroad train alighted in the night at the town where he resided. The station, the town, and his home were

train, under similar circumstances,[58] this rule would not apply, in case the passenger, after reaching his destination, remained on the car, with a view of traveling further, for in

all on the west side of the track, and the doors of the cars, which were vestibuled, were opened on that side. After his train had departed, he was killed by another train on a track to the eastward. *Held,* that he had ceased to be a passenger prior to his death, and the company at that time owed no duty to him as such." Payne v. Illinois Cent. R. Co. (U. S., C. C. A., Tenn. 1907), 155 Fed. Rep. 73.

"Where a carrier has made proper arrangements for the exit by passengers from its station grounds, a passenger must use the ways provided, and where he knowingly fails to do so, and without invitation makes his exit in some other way, he ceases to be a passenger, and becomes at most a mere licensee; and it makes no difference that he goes where others, with the knowledge of the carrier, have gone before him, unless there is some invitation on the part of the carrier, and knowledge of such use does not of itself amount to such invitation." Legge v. New York & H. R. Co. (Mass. 1908), 83 N. E. Rep. 367.

"Where plaintiff paid his fare from T. to S., which also entitled him to a transfer to B., which the conductor promised him at a certain point, but at the point named plaintiff did not see the conductor, and at S., where it was necessary for him to change cars, he asked for the transfer, and the conductor requested him to get out of the way of the other passengers, and he got off the car, whereupon a dispute arose over the transfer, and plaintiff was assaulted by the conductor, *held,* that the relation of passenger and carrier had not terminated." Blomsness v. Puget Sound Ry. Co. (Wash. 1907), 92 Pac. Rep. 414.

It is held in the following cases that if a passenger, at an intermediate station, voluntarily leaves a train and stays away, without notice to the railway company, he thereby terminates the relation of passenger and carrier. DeKay v. Chicago, etc., R. Co., 41 Minn. 178; 43 N. W. Rep. 182; 4 L. R. A. 632; State v. Grand Trunk R. Co., 58 Me. 176; 4 Am. Rep. 258; Bullock v. Houston, etc., R. Co. (Texas), 55 S. W. Rep. 184.

But persons carried by their stations and brought back thereto by the railroad company (Rosenberg v. Third Ave. R. Co., 61 N. Y. S. 1052), and persons delayed by accidents, remain passengers until their voyage is terminated. Dwinelle v. New York, etc., R. Co., 120 N. Y. 117; 24 N. E. Rep. 319; 2 L. R. A. 224; Wilsie v. Louisville, etc., R. Co., 83 Ky. 511.

[58] Imhoff v. Chicago, etc., R. Co., 20 Wis. 344; Jeffersonville, etc.,

such case the relation of passenger and carrier will continue until the trip is finally ended.[59]

This identical question was recently before the Supreme Court of Missouri,[60] for decision, and after reviewing the facts, the court observed: " There is no rule of law which requires a passenger, if he has only paid his fare to a certain point of destination, to leave the train at that point; but, if he desires to continue his journey, it is manifestly his right to remain on the car, and when demanded of him, pay his fare to the place of destination. It is but common knowledge that persons traveling upon railroad trains very frequently do not alight and stop at the place of destination originally contemplated, when they entered the car, but proceed to some other point, where business may call them, and under such circumstances, they simply remain on the train and proceed with their journey."

§ 559. **Children riding without payment of fare.**— A person getting on a train of cars for the honest purpose of taking transportation is generally held to be a passenger,[61] and

R. Co. v. Parmerlee, 51 Ind. 42; Chicago, etc., R. Co. v. Barrett, 16 Ill. App. 17.

" A passenger who fails to alight from the train at the destination to which he purchased a ticket is not a trespasser, and if he remain on the train, which is one on which passengers are entitled to ride, it must be presumed that he intends to pay the proper fare, and, until this presumption is overcome by evidence that he intends to be carried without payment of fare, he is entitled to the protection of a passenger." Forbes v. Chicago, etc., Ry. Co. (Iowa 1907), 113 N. W. Rep. 477.

[59] Anderson v. Missouri Pacific Ry. Co., 196 Mo. 442; 93 S. W. Rep. 394.

[60] Anderson v. Missouri Pacific Ry. Co., 196 Mo. 442; 93 S. W. Rep. 394. In this case the court held that it was not necessary to show that the passenger purposed to continue on to his home, after arrival at the station to which he had paid his fare, as this purpose could be inferred from the facts and circumstances in evidence if they, in the estimation of the jury, authorized such an inference.

[61] Cross v. Kansas City, etc., R. Co., 56 Mo. App. 674.

since the purchase of a ticket or payment of railroad fare is not essential to constitute the relation of passenger and carrier,[62] but the railroad company may if it elects, insist upon the prepayment of fare, or otherwise, and it will be held to recognize, by implication, the status of a person lawfully upon its train, as that of a passenger, with the corresponding obligations to which the relation subjects it.[63] If a small child, for whom a ticket has not been procured, is permitted to enter the train, in company with an older person, it is generally held to be rightfully on the train and entitled to the privileges of any other passenger.[64]

In a recent Missouri case,[65] Judge Broaddus, for the Kansas City Court of Appeals, used this language: " In view of the general custom of railroad carriers, to permit small children like the plaintiff, to ride on their cars, free of charge, when accompanied by some older person, who pays fare, it is reasonable to presume that plaintiff was a passenger, in good faith, especially so as no objection was made to him, as a passenger, for want of prepayment of fare, and no demand and refusal to make such payment was shown. This entering the car, under the circumstances, constituted him a passenger, with all the rights of such."

But if the child is over age to bring it within the rule or custom, or its fare is refused,[66] or it voluntarily rides on a hand car, at the request of the employees of the railroad company, or in any other prohibited manner, the relation of carrier and passenger will not arise, merely because of the infancy of the child.[67]

[62] Fetter, Carriers of Passengers, § 221.
[63] Central, etc., R. Co. v. Huggins, 89 Ga. 494.
[64] Austin v. Great Western R. Co., L. R. 2 Q. B. 442; 8 B. & S. 327; 36 L. J. Q. B. 201; 15 W. R. 863; 16 L. T. 320.
[65] Rawlings v. Wabash Ry. Co., 97 Mo. App. 515, 518.
[66] Beckwith v. Cheshire, etc., Ry. Co., 143 Mass. 68; 8 N. E. Rep. 875; 27 Am. & Eng. R. Cas. 192.
[67] Gulf, etc., R. Co. v. Dawkins, 77 Texas 228; 13 S. W. Rep. 982.

§ 560. **Persons riding on wrong train.**— A passenger has no right on a train which, under the rules of the railroad company, does not stop at the station for which he has purchased a ticket,[68] and the failure of those in charge of a train on which he has wrongfully taken passage, to warn him to get off, cannot be construed into a permission by the railroad company to become a passenger on that train.[69]

The status of such person, when on the wrong train, and whether he will be regarded in law as a passenger or a trespasser, will depend, generally, upon the reasonable belief of such a person that he had boarded the right train, justified by some conduct on the part of the railroad company's officers or agents, having control of the movements of the train.[70]

It is held, in Texas,[71] that a person who, by mistake, gets on a different train from the one he intended taking passage on, is a passenger on the train he boards and the relation of passenger and carrier exists between him and the railroad company. And in Indiana[72] it is held that where a person

"The fact that no fare was paid for a child by the person in charge of him upon the train did not deprive him of the character of a passenger, where he was riding with the knowledge of and without objection by the conductor." Southern Ry. Co. v. Lee (Ky. 1907), 101 S. W. Rep. 307.

"Where plaintiff refused to pay fare for her son, nine years of age, though he was of such age as to require payment of fare, the conductor was authorized to require plaintiff and the child to leave the train." Ft Worth, etc., Ry. Co. v. Gribble (Tex. Civ. App. 1907), 102 S. W. Rep. 157.

[68] Chicago, etc., R. Co. v. Bills, 104 Ind. 13; 3 N. E. Rep. 611.

[69] Brown v. Scarboro, 97 Ala. 316; 12 So. Rep. 289; 58 Am. & Eng. R. Cas. 364.

[70] Brown v. Scarboro, *supra.*

[71] International, etc., R. Co. v. Gilbert, 64 Texas 536; 22 Am. & Eng. R. Cas. 405.

[72] Cincinnati, etc., R. Co. v. Carper, 112 Ind. 26; 13 N. E. Rep. 122; 31 Am. & Eng. R. Cas. 36; Columbus, etc., R. Co. v. Powell, 40 Ind. 37.

bought a ticket and by mistake took passage on the wrong train, he is a passenger so far as to entitle him to protection against the negligence of the employees of the railroad company.

§ 561. **Employee's permission to enter train.**— Since the relation of passenger and carrier, in its inception, depends upon the existence of a contract express or implied, it would seem, upon principle, that no employee could bind the carrier to such a relation, unless the employee possessed the requisite authority, as no contract can exist, by agency, without the requisite authority to make the contract, on the part of the alleged agent. It is accordingly held, in a well-considered Missouri case,[73] that if an invitation to travel upon a conveyance, on which the person invited would otherwise have no right, is given by an employee without authority to permit persons to ride on the car, and the invitation or permission is not in any sense in the interest of the carrier, or in the course of its employment, a person so traveling does not become a passenger. And if the train is not of the char-

"Where a car bore the sign 'Not in Service,' but was stopped at a crossing and the doors were open, plaintiff, if she entered the car in good faith, was a passenger on the car and continued to be such until she was given a reasonable opportunity to alight." Ahern v. Minneapolis Ry. Co. (Minn. 1907), 113 N. W. Rep. 1019.

"One who takes his position upon the steps of the platform of a car, having no intention of becoming a passenger and not presenting himself to the carrier as such, does not acquire the rights of a passenger." Chicago, etc., Ry. Co. v. Moran, 129 Ill. App. 38.

"One who attempts to board a rapidly moving train does not become a passenger, though he may have a ticket for it." Illinois Cent. R. Co. v. Cotter (Ky. 1907), 103 S. W. Rep. 279.

"One who gets on the train, mistaking it for that of another road and attempts to alight, but changes his mind, and decides to pay his fare, is not, while on the car steps, a passenger." DeVane v. Atlanta & A. R. Co., Ga., 60 S. E. Rep. 1079.

73 Snyder v. Hannibal, etc., R. Co., 60 Mo. 413.

acter from which it could be presumed that the employee in charge had authority to carry persons thereon, an invitation by such an employee in charge of such a train, is held, in New York,[74] not to create the relation of passenger and carrier, between the railroad operating the train and a person riding thereon, at the invitation of the conductor.

But it is held, in some States, that if a person is riding in a place which is not adapted for passengers, by the invitation of the person in charge of the car, he is not a trespasser and the railroad company will be responsible to him for injuries sustained as a result of the negligence of its employees,[75] and if a person entitled to transportation is requested by employees in charge of a switch engine, to get upon the engine and be transported to his destination, it is held, in Illinois, that such person is entitled to the same degree of care, on the part of the railroad company's employees, that the law would exact toward a passenger, and the decision of the issue as to the exact status of such a person, would be a proper question for the jury.[76] It is held, however, in the same State, that if a person wrongfully gets upon an engine, without consent of the employees in charge of it, or in violation of the rules of the employer, with the intention of evading the payment of his fare, the legal relation of passenger and carrier does not exist.[77]

[74] Eaton v. Delaware, etc., R. Co., 57 N. Y. 382; 15 Am. Rep. 513.
[75] Wilson v. Middlesex R. Co., 107 Mass. 108; 125 Mass. 130.
[76] Lake Shore, etc., R. Co. v. Brown, 31 Am. & Eng. R. Cas. 61.
[77] Chicago, etc., R. Co. v. Michie, 83 Ill. 427.

One riding upon a construction train, by permission of the conductor, was held to be a passenger, in St. Joseph, etc., R. Co. v. Wheeler (Kan.), 26 Am. & Eng. R. Cas. 173; Lucas v. Milwaukee, etc., R. Co., 33 Wis. 41. And one wantonly assaulted, on a freight train, is held to occupy the status of a passenger, although no consent to his presence had been given by the employees, in Western, etc., R. Co. v. Turner (Ga.), 28 Am. & Eng. R. Cas. 455.

Although a person entered a freight train, without the consent of

§ 562. **Persons riding freight trains or hand cars.**— A person who enters a freight train which habitually carries passengers and at the time receives no notice that he cannot ride thereon, becomes a passenger, the same as if he had entered a regular passenger train, and the mere fact that the train has not stopped at the station or that the ticket office was not opened before its departure, will not be sufficient to charge the passenger with notice that such train does not carry pas-

the conductor, if he is permitted to remain, after his presence is discovered, he is held to be a passenger, in Brennan v. Fair Haven, etc., R. Co., 45 Conn. 284; Mulhausen v. St. Louis, etc., R. Co., 91 Mo. 332; 2 S. W. Rep. 315; 28 Am. & Eng. R. Cas. 157; Sherman v. Hannibal, etc., R. Co., 72 Mo. 62; 37 Am. Rep. 423; 4 Am. & Eng. R. Cas. 589; Secord v. St. Paul, etc., R. Co., 18 Fed. Rep. 221.

One whose ticket or fare is accepted on a freight train, is held to be a passenger, in Dunn v. Grand Trunk R. Co., 58 Me. 187; International, etc., R. Co. v. Irvine (Texas), 23 Am. & Eng. R. Cas. 518.

A person knowingly violating a rule by riding on a train without payment of fare, although with consent of the employees, in charge thereof, is held not to be a passenger, in Houston, etc., R. Co. v. Moore, 49 Texas 31; 30 Am. Rep. 98; Higgins v. Cherokee, etc., R. Co. (Ga.), 27 Am. & Eng. R. Cas. 218.

The engineer is held to have no authority to carry a person as a passenger on the engine, in Chicago, etc., R. Co. v. Michie, 83 Ill. 427; Robertson v. New York, etc., R. Co., 22 Barb. (N. Y.) 91.

A fireman is held to have no authority to invite a person to ride as a passenger, on the engine. Flower v. Pennsylvania R. Co., 69 Pa. St. 210.

Nor has a baggage master, to permit persons to ride in the baggage car, as his guests. Reary v. Louisville, etc., R. Co. (La. Ann.), 34 Am. & Eng. R. Cas. 277.

"A contract by a brakeman of a freight train to allow a person to ride on the train in consideration of his rendering assistance in the loading and unloading of freight was outside the scope of the brakeman's authority, not binding the railroad company, and the person so riding was a trespasser." O'Donnell v. Kansas City, etc., R. Co. (Mo. 1906), 95 S. W. Rep. 196; Doyle v. Same, id., 200.

"Plaintiff boarded defendant's local freight train, and asked the conductor in charge if he could come back with him the next day on his train. The conductor replied that he could, and that he was to help unload and load freight. Plaintiff boarded the train on the

sengers.[78] Where the railroad company has adopted the custom of carrying passengers on freight trains, a person who goes upon such train, in good faith, supposing it to be a train carrying passengers, is entitled to all the rights of a passenger, at least until notice to him that passengers are not carried on the train.[79] The question of liability, in such case, does not depend upon the uses to which the train is usually put; and where there are no rules of the company forbidding it, or if there are such rules and the officers making such rules relax or dispense with them, and persons are taken on freight trains and fares accepted for the privilege of riding thereon, or when they are permitted to enter such trains with the expectation of paying fares, when demanded, they are then lawfully on the train and the company owes them the duty that passengers are entitled to receive.[80]

next day, was discovered by some of the train men, and was injured by the explosion of the engine shortly thereafter. *Held*, that the conductor had no authority to employ plaintiff as a servant or permit him to work his passage on the train, and hence the carrier owed plaintiff no duty as a passenger." Vassor v. Atlantic Coast Line R. Co. (N. C. 1906), 54 S. E. Rep. 849.

"Where a conductor allows a person without a ticket to board a train and pay cash fare to any particular point, a valid contract arises between the carrier and such person, under which he is entitled to be transported as a passenger to the station of the company at the place to which fare is paid." Williamson v. Central Ry. Co. (Ga. 1906), 56 S. E. Rep. 119.

[78] Burke v. Missouri Pacific Ry. Co., 51 Mo. App. 491; Lucas v. Milwaukee, etc., R. Co., 33 Wis. 41.

[79] Secord v. St. Paul, etc., R. Co., 5 McCrary (U. S.) 515; 18 Fed. Rep. 221; Lucas v. Milwaukee, etc., R. Co., 33 Wis. 41.

[80] Prince v. International, etc., R. Co., 64 Texas 144; 21 Am. & Eng. R. Cas. 152; Creed v. Pennsylvania R. Co., 86 Pa. St. 139; McGee v. Missouri Pacific Ry. Co., 92 Mo. 208; 4 S. W. Rep. 739; 31 Am. & Eng. R. Cas. 1; Dunn v. Grand Trunk R. Co., 58 Me. 187; Lake Shore, etc., R. Co. v. Brown, 123 Ill. 162; 14 N. E. Rep. 197; 31 Am. & Eng. R. Cas. 61; Everett v. Oregon, etc., R. Co., 9 Utah 340; 34 Pac. Rep. 289; Boggess v. Chesapeake, etc., R. Co., 37 W. Va. 297; 16 S. E. Rep. 525.

But a person riding unlawfully upon a freight train is not a passenger,[81] and if a person gets on a freight train, after having been refused permission to ride, by the conductor, he does not become a passenger,[82] and a person who enters a freight car against the rules of the railroad company and in violation of the conductor's orders, cannot recover for an injury received, although the brakeman may have told him he could ride on such train.[83]   Likewise, if the railroad company only permits its employees to ride on freight trains, or hand cars, no liability will attach for an injury received by one unlawfully riding on such vehicles, though ignorant of the railroad company's rules, if the permission to ride is not by the authorized agents of the railroad company, but by those employees employed to work with such appliances.[84]

[81] Planz v. Boston, etc., R. Co., 157 Mass. 377; 32 N. E. Rep. 356; Smith v. Louisville, etc., R. Co., 124 Ind. 394; 24 N. E. Rep. 753; O'Donnell v. Kansas City, etc., R. Co., 197 Mo. 110; 95 S. W. Rep. 196.

[82] Atchison, etc., R. Co. v. Headland, 18 Colo. 477; 33 Pac. Rep. 185; 58 Am. & Eng. R. Cas. 4.

[83] Gulf, etc., R. Co. v. Campbell, 76 Texas 174; 13 S. W. Rep. 19; 41 Am. & Eng. R. Cas. 100.

[84] Gulf, etc., R. Co. v. Dawkins, 77 Texas 228; 13 S. W. Rep. 982; O'Donnell v. Kansas City, etc., R. Co., 197 Mo. 110; 95 S. W. Rep. 196.

"A passenger on a freight train does not lose his character as a passenger by leaving the train to talk with an acquaintance during the time cars are being switched at a station." Arkansas Cent. R. Co. v. Bennett (Ark. 1907), 102 S. W. Rep. 198.

"A railway company, admitting a passenger into a caboose attached to a freight train, incurs the same liability for his safety as though he had taken passage on a regular passenger train." Southern Ry. Co. v. Burgess (Ala. 1905), 42 So. Rep. 35.

"A railroad assuming to carry passengers on its freight trains is bound to exercise the same degree of care as is required in the operation of passenger trains; the difference being that a passenger submits himself to the inconvenience and danger necessarily attending that mode of conveyance." Hawk v. Chicago, etc., Ry. Co. (Mo. App. 1908), 108 S. W. Rep. 1119.

"Where a railroad undertook for hire to carry a person as a passenger on a freight train, it was required to use the same degree of care

§ 563. Mail agents held to be passengers.— A railroad company is quite generally held to owe the same degree of care to postal clerks and mail agents, riding in mail cars, that it owes to passengers,[85] and this is held to be true, in England, although they may be carried pursuant to an obligation imposed upon the railroad company by statute.[86] In a comparatively recent decision by the Supreme Court of Missouri,[87] *in banc*, it was decided that, " A United States postal agent, riding on a railroad train, in the discharge of his duties, under contract between the government and the rail-

as was required in the operation of its regular passenger trains; the passenger submitting himself to the inconvenience and danger necessarily attending that mode of conveyance." Bussell v. Quincy, C. R. Co. (Mo. App. 1907), 102 S. W. Rep. 613.

" One holding a permit to ride on a freight train while on his way to the yards of a company to board a caboose which does not carry passengers except by special permission is not a passenger being transported over the road within Cobbey's Ann. St. 1903, § 10,039 and the duty which the company owes to him is only that of ordinary care." Chicago, etc., Ry. Co. v. Mann. (Neb. 1907), 111 N. W. Rep. 379.

" The test as to negligence in case of a passenger on a freight train is the same as that on a passenger train; and the carrier is held to the exercise of the highest reasonable degree of care." Herring v. Galveston, etc., Ry. Co. (Tex. Civ. App. 1908), 108 S. W. Rep. 977.

85 Gulf, etc., R. Co. v. Wilson, 79 Texas 371; 15 S. W. Rep. 280; Arrowsmith v. Nashville, etc., R. Co., 57 Fed. Rep. 165; Cleveland, etc., R. Co. v. Ketchum, 133 Ind. 346; 33 N. E. Rep. 116; Libby v. Maine Central R. Co., 85 Me. 34; 26 Atl. Rep. 943; Magoffin v. Missouri Pacific Ry. Co., 102 Mo. 540; 15 S. W. Rep. 76; 47 Am. & Eng. R. Cas. 489; Mellor v. Missouri Pacific Ry. Co., 105 Mo. 455; 16 S. W. Rep. 849; 47 Am. & Eng. R. Cas. 450; Nolton v. Western R. Co., 15 N. Y. 444; 10 Hun 97; Seybolt v. New York, etc., R. Co., 95 N. Y. 562; 31 Hun 100; 47 Am. Rep. 75; 18 Am. & Eng. R. Cas. 162; Hammond v. North Eastern R. Co., 6 So. Car. 130; Houston, etc., R. Co. v. Hampton, 64 Texas 427; 22 Am. & Eng. R. Cas. 291; Collett v. London, etc., R. Co., 16 Q. B. 984; 15 Jur. 1053; 20 L. J. Q. B. 411.

86 Collett v. London, etc., R. Co., *supra*.

87 Mellor v. Missouri Pacific Ry. Co., 105 Mo. 455; 16 S. W. Rep. 849; 10 L. R. A. 36, same case, before Division 1, 14 S. W. Rep. 758.

853

road company, occupies the position of a passenger, with respect to the company's liability for its negligence."

The fact that the government has contracted for the transportation of such an employee, along with its mails, to take charge of the mails, will not constitute him any the less a passenger, nor diminish the duty which the railroad company owes him, to carry him safely, for privity of contract is not essential in such cases.[88]

But a postal clerk, traveling upon a train in the regular discharge of his duties, is not a passenger, within the meaning of the Pennsylvania statute, exempting railroad companies from liability for injuries to persons, engaged upon or about the cars of the company but who are not employed by it; [89] nor will the federal statutes providing for the employment and directing the service of mail route agents, change the legal status of a postal clerk, under the Pennsylvania statute, into that of a passenger, as the government statutes do not attempt to establish such relation.[90]

And, no doubt, strictly speaking, the relation of passenger and carrier does not exist between the employees carried under contract with the government as mail clerks, as this is not the intention of such contracts, entered into by railroad companies and the relation can only exist, by contract, express or implied.[91] Such employees assume the ordinary risks of the service in which they are engaged, not arising from the negligence of the railroad company, but the com-

[88] This is practically Judge Sherwood's language in Magoffin v. Missouri Pacific Ry. Co. (Mo.), 47 Am. & Eng. R. Cas. 491.

[89] Pennsylvania R. Co. v. Price, 96 Pa. St. 256; 1 Am. & Eng. R. Cas. 243.

[90] Price v. Pennsylvania R. Co., 113 U. S. 218; 18 Am. & Eng. R. Cas. 273.

[91] Price v. Pennsylvania R. Co., *supra;* Hammons v. North Eastern R. Co., *supra;* Nolton v. Western R. Co., 15 N. Y. 444; New York, etc., R. Co. v. Seylott, 18 Am. & Eng. R. Cas. 162; Blair v. Erie R. Co., 66 N. Y. 313; Union Pacific R. Co. v. Nichols, 8 Kansas 505.

pany owes a certain measure of duty toward them and in case of injury through its negligence, an action is clearly maintainable.[92]

[92] *Ante idem;* Gleeson v. Virginia Midland R. Co., 140 U. S. 435; 35 L. Ed. 458; 11 Sup. Ct. Rep. 859; Cleveland, etc., R. Co. v. Ketchum, 133 Ind. 346; 33 N. E. Rep. 116; 19 L. R. A. 339.

In Schaeffer v. St. Louis, etc., R. Co. (128 Mo. 64; 30 S. W. Rep. 331), it was held that the relation of carrier and passenger could never exist in the absence of a contract, express or implied, establishing such relation.

In Price v. Pennsylvania R. Co. (113 U. S. 218; 18 Am. & Eng. R. Cas. 273), the court said: " The person thus to be carried with the mail matter, without extra charge, is no more a passenger, because he is in charge of the mail, nor because no other compensation is made for his transportation, than if he had no such charge; nor does the fact that he is in the employment of the United States and that defendant is bound by contract with the government to carry him, affect the question."

In Mellor v. Missouri Pacific Ry. Co. (105 Mo. 460), the court said: " There is no foundation on which to predicate a defense that plaintiff's injury arose from any negligence of fellow servants. The train operatives were clearly not such, as to him. Defendant's duty to him, *so far as concerned safe transportation, was as a passenger.*"

In Gulf, etc., R. Co. v. Wilson (75 S. W. Rep. 280), the Supreme Court of Texas said, " We are of opinion that essentially the relation of carrier and passenger exists in every case in which the carrier receives and agrees to transport another, not in its employment, whether this be by contract between them, or between the carrier and some other person in whose employment the person is to be carried. * * * It is enough that he is lawfully on the car, and entitled to transportation, to give to him the character of passenger and to entitle him to recover for an injury resulting from the negligence of the carrier. * * * It may be held that a mail agent assumes the risk of danger necessarily arising from the position of the mail car in the train; but he does not assume the risk of danger that may result from the negligence of the carrier."

But in recognizing that the contract would impose any assumption of risk upon such an employee, the court necessarily admits that the technical relation of passenger and carrier does not exist, and so far as not assuming the negligence of the railroad company goes, no employee assumes such risks, as they are not within the implied contract of employment.

" A postal clerk in the service of the United States who is in charge

§ 564. **Express messengers.**— Where an express company hires its freight transported by a railroad company and hires an agent to take charge of such freight, whose passage is paid for in the contract between the express company and the railroad company, such agent is held to occupy the relation of an ordinary passenger, with reference to the liability of the railroad company for injuries he may receive, resulting from the negligence of its employees.[93]   And the same duty to provide for the safety of such an employee is held to obtain, on the part of the railroad company, where it undertakes to carry an express messenger, in a car provided for the use of the express company, in the absence of an express contract for the carriage of the express company's agent.[94]

of mail on a train and who is carried on the train as a postal clerk is a passenger." Malott v. Central Trust Co. of Greencastle (Ind. 1906), 79 N. E. Rep. 369.

" A railway postal clerk, in the discharge of his duties on a railroad, is a passenger." Illinois Cent. R. Co. v. Porter (Tenn. 1906), 94 S. W. Rep. 666.

" A mail clerk in the employ of the United States government is a passenger of the defendant carrier as well while in transit as during the ensuing period, when he, pursuant to a long-continued custom, remained in the yards of the defendant at work in his car." Wabash R. Co. v. Jellison, 124 Ill. App. 652.

" A railway mail clerk in the service of the United States, and as such having charge of the mails carried in a mail car by a railroad company, is a passenger on the mail car, and the railroad company owes him the same duty that it would a passenger for hire therein." Decker v. Chicago & St. P. Ry. Co. (Minn. 1907), 112 N. W. Rep. 901.

" In the carriage of postal clerks of the United States, charged with duties respecting the protection and proper distribution of the mails carried under contracts in accordance with law, a carrier is under the same obligation to them, as regards suitable and safe carriage, that it is to its ordinary passengers." Lindsey v. Pennsylvania R. Co. (D. C. 1906), 26 App. D. C. 503.

[93] Fordyce v. Jackson, 56 Ark. 594; 20 S. W. Rep. 528, 597; Yeomans v. Contra Costa, etc., Co., 44 Cal. 71; Blair v. Erie R. Co., 66 N. Y. 313; Pennsylvania R. Co. v. Woodworth, 26 Ohio St. 585; Jennings v. Grand Trunk R. Co., 15 Ont. App. 477.

[94] Fordyce v. Jackson, *supra*.

Where there is no express exemption by contract, the railroad company is liable for the consequences of its employees' negligence to employees of express companies traveling upon its trains, to the same extent as to passengers, although no extra charge is exacted for their railroad fare.[95] And notwithstanding a contract between the companies that the agents of the express company shall not hold the railroad company liable for injuries from the negligence of the employees of the railroad company, unless the express company brings the details of the contract home to its employees, or the express messenger in some way assents thereto, the liability of the railroad company for injuries from its negligence will not be affected by the existence of such a contract, but an employee of the express company would be entitled to damages for an injury due to the negligence of the railroad company.[96] Where, however, the express agent assents to the terms of a contract, exempting the railroad company from liability in case of injury to the express company's agent, such contract will be enforced,[97] in the absence of a statute rendering the same void,[98] or at least such is the opinion of

[95] Blair v. Erie R. Co., 66 N. Y. 313; 23 Am. Rep. 55.

[96] Chamberlain v. Pierson, 87 Fed. Rep. 420; 31 C. C. A. 157; 59 U. S. App. 55; Kenney v. New York, etc., R. Co., 125 N. Y. 422; 26 N. E. Rep. 626; Brewer v. New York, etc., R. Co., 124 N. Y. 59; 26 N. E. Rep. 324; 11 L. R. A. 483.

[97] Baltimore, etc., R. Co. v. Voigt, 176 U. S. 498; Bates v. Old Colony R. Co., 147 Mass. 255; 18 N. E. Rep. 633; Hosmer v. Old Colony R. Co., 156 Mass. 506; 31 N. E. Rep. 652; Louisville, etc., R. Co. v. Keefer, 146 Ind. 21; 44 N. E. Rep. 796; 38 L. R. A. 93; Pittsburg, etc., R. Co. v. Mahoney, 148 Ind. 196; 46 N. E. Rep. 917; 47 N. E. Rep. 464; 40 L. R. A. 101; Blank v. Illinois, etc., R. Co., 182 Ill. 332; 55 N. E. Rep. 332; 80 Ill. App. 475.

[98] O'Brien v. Chicago, etc., R. Co., 116 Fed. Rep. 502.

In the case of O'Brien v. Chicago & N. W. Ry. Co. (116 Fed. Rep. 502), which involved the statute of Iowa, making such contracts invalid, the court said:

"That while such contracts would be effective to protect the railroad company from liability at common law, under such statutory provisions,

the Supreme Court of the United States, and the holding in many well-considered cases of different State courts.

§ 565. Employees of sleeping car company.— Since the porter or other employees of a sleeping car company, whose

declaratory of the public policy of the State, they were invalid, and constituted no defense to an action against it for the death of the messenger occurring in the State of Iowa by reason of the wrecking of the express car in which he was employed, through the negligence and want of ordinary care of defendant or its servants, whether the messenger be regarded as an employee of the defendant or not."

In Baltimore, etc., R. Co. v. Voigt (176 U. S. 498), the court said, speaking of a contract exempting the carrier from liability for injury to the agent of the express company: "It is manifest that the relation existing between express messengers and transportation companies, under such contracts as existed in the present case, is widely different from that of ordinary passengers, and that to relieve the defendant in error from the obligation of his contract, would require us to give a much wider extension of the doctrine of public policy than was justified by the facts and reasoning in the Lockwood case." 176 U. S. 514.

New York, etc., R. Co. v. Lockwood (17 Wall. 357; 21 L. Ed. 627), was a decision construing the validity of a contract exempting the railroad company from liability for injury to a passenger — a stock drover, accompanying his stock — and the court held that it would be contrary to public policy to uphold such a contract.

The same distinction drawn between the Lockwood case and the case of an express messenger, participating in the business of the transportation company, is noted in Bates v. Old Colony R. Co. (147 Mass. 255; 17 N. E. Rep. 633), and Hosmer v. Old Colony R. Co. (156 Mass. 506; 31 N. E. Rep. 652), in the former of which the court said: "The question of the right of carriers to limit their liability for negligence in the discharge of their duties as carriers by contract with their customers and passengers in regard to such duties, does not arise under this contract, as construed in this case. * * * The consideration of the plaintiff's agreement was not the performance of anything by the defendant which it was under any obligation to do, or which the plaintiff had any right to have done. It was a privilege granted to the plaintiff. * * *

"His duties were substantially the same as those of the baggage master in the same car; the latter relating to merchandise carried for passengers, and the former to merchandise carried for the express

cars are carried, with its employees therein, over the line of a railroad company, cannot be said to have either a common employer, a common director, nor a common service with the employees of the railroad company, such employees, in a Missouri case, are held not to be employees of a railroad company, but to occupy the status of passengers toward the railroad company, so as to charge it for damages, in case of an injury, due to the negligence of the employees of the railroad company, in operating the train.[99]

Speaking of the status occupied by the injured porter of a sleeping car, injured by the negligence of the engineer and fireman of an engine, pulling the car in which he was em-

company. * * * It does not seem that a contract between the express company and the plaintiff on the one hand and the defendant on the other, that the express messenger in performing his duties, should take the same risk of injury from the negligence of the railroad engaged in the transportation that he would take, if employed by the railroad to perform the same duties, would be void as unreasonable or as against public policy."

It was held, in Baltimore, etc., R. Co. v. McCamey (12 Ohio C. C. 543), that a person acting in the dual capacity of baggage agent and express messenger, could not claim to be a passenger.

Nor is a party, riding in the express car, to learn the duties of the place, entitled to be regarded as a passenger. Union Pacific R. Co. v. Nichols, 8 Kansas 505; 12 Am. Rep. 475.

But one taking the place of a regular messenger is held to stand in his place, as passenger, in Blair v. Erie R. Co., 66 N. Y. 313. See, also, Florida Southern R. Co. v. Hirst (30 Fla. 1; 11 So. Rep. 506; 52 Am. & Eng. R. Cas. 409), where a former employee of the express company was passed by the conductor, as a passenger and it was held that it could not be said that he did not occupy, at same time, that relation toward the defendant.

"A contract whereby a railroad company undertook to transport the express matter and messengers of an express company, the latter assuming all risk of accidents happening to its messengers and agreeing to indemnify the railroad company against all claims made by its messengers for injuries received, was valid." Robinson v. St. Johnsbury & L. C. R. Co. (Vt. 1907), 66 Atl. Rep. 814.

[99] Jones v. St. Louis, etc., Ry. Co., 125 Mo. 666; 28 S. W. Rep. 883; 46 Am. St. Rep. 514; 26 L. R. A. 718.

ployed, the Missouri court said: "Plaintiff was transported over defendant's road under a contract which was supported by a sufficient consideration and he was entitled to the rights of a passenger, in respect to the careful running and management of the train." [1]

But in the performance of duties common to employees of the sleeping car company and those of the railroad company, this rule would not obtain, and it has been held that employees of the sleeping car company will be treated as the employees of the railroad company, in all matters pertaining to the safety and security of passengers being transported in the sleeping cars, or on the railroad train where an injury may occur, and such employees are so far regarded as employees of the railroad company, as to render the railroad company liable to passengers injured by the negligence of the sleeping car company's employees.[2] The relation of employer and employee, in such cases, and the liability of the railroad company, is placed upon the ground of the obligation of a carrier and though in direct violation of a contract between the two companies, for the law will not permit a carrier to evade its duty toward a passenger, by means of a contract with some third person.[3]

[1] Jones v. St. Louis, etc., R. Co., 125 Mo., pp. 675, 676.

[2] Pennsylvania R. Co. v. Roy, 102 U. S. 451; 26 L. Ed. 141; Williams v. Car Company, 40 La. Ann. 417; Kinsley v. Boston, etc., R. Co., 125 Mass. 54; Dwinnell v. New York, etc., R. Co., 120 N. Y. 117; Cincinnati, etc., R. Co. v. Walrath, 38 Ohio St. 461; Louisville, etc., . R. Co. v. Katzenberger, 16 Lea (Tenn.) 380; 26 Am. St. Rep. 334.

[3] Jones v. St. Louis, etc., R. Co., 125 Mo. 666; 28 S. W. Rep. 883; 46 Am. St. Rep. 514; 26 L. R. A. 718.

The rule stated in the text, that an employee of a sleeping car was to be regarded as a passenger, was held not to apply, in the sense that the railway company was answerable for any less than the highest degree of care toward such an employee, nor will the rule *res ipsa loquitur* apply to such an employee from the mere fact of an accident and an injury resulting therefrom. Hughson v. Richmond, etc., R. Co., 2 App. (D. C.) 98; 22 Wash. L. Rep. 815.

§ 566. **News agents and fruit venders.**— The legal status of news agents and other similar employees, employed by third persons, to sell newspapers and periodicals, or fruit and such commodities on a railroad train, is analogous to that of mail clerks and express agents or messengers, whose employers provide for their transportation, on the train of the railroad company, to enable such employees to perform the services for which they are engaged by their employers.

Where a common carrier rents a room to a person for the sale of liquors and cigars, at a stipulated rental, and contracts to carry him and board him as a part of the agreement, he is held to occupy the legal relation of a passenger, on the conveyance of the carrier, and not that of an employee.[4] And where a railroad company, in consideration of the payment of a fixed sum of money, and of an agreement to supply passengers on its train with ice water, issues season tickets to a person and permits him to sell pop corn and such commodities on the train, such person is held not to be an employee of the railroad company, but to occupy the legal status of a passenger and entitled to all the rights of one.[5]

But a news agent who has no right to regular transportation, but is extended a simple license to go on and off the trains of a railroad company, for the purpose of selling newspapers, does not occupy the relation of a passenger of the railroad company and while the company would be held liable for a wanton injury inflicted upon such a person, it would be under no obligation to care for his safety, since there is no relation upon which such a duty could be predicated.[6]

[4] Yeomans v. Contra Costa Nav. Co., 44 Cal. 71.

[5] Commonwealth v. Vermont, etc., R. Co., 108 Mass. 7.

[6] Fleming v. Brooklyn City R. Co., 1 Abb. N. Cas. (N. Y.) 433.

In Wennecker v. Missouri & C. R. Co. (169 Mo. 592), the licensee had business relations with the defendant's conductor, but none with

§ 567. **Drover traveling with stock.**— It may be stated as a general proposition that a drover, traveling upon a pass, for the purpose of taking care of stock shipped over a railroad, is regarded in the same light as any other passenger for hire.[7] In considering the legal status of a person riding on a stock pass, accompanying stock shipped, under contract with the railroad company, wherein the transportation of such person was stipulated for, as a part of the consideration of the contract, Justice Bradley, in one of his characteristically strong decisions,[8] said, for the United States Supreme Court: " It may be assumed, *in limine*, that the case was one of carriage for hire; for though the pass certifies that

the defendant itself, and in considering what, if any, duty was created from this relation with its own conductor, the Supreme Court said: " The deceased's business being with the conductor and *not with the defendant*, in our opinion, the facts fail to show that defendant owed him any other duty than as before indicated, and was under no obligation to notify him, as he approached the car, of the danger to be apprehended by him ' by the running out of the slack in the train ' but if any such duty was imposed by law upon any one, it was upon Conductor Stone, for whose benefit and with whose knowledge he was on his way to the car with the lunch when he met him on the platform of the depot. This being the case, the fact that deceased was only about eleven years of age at the time of his unfortunate death, is of no significance." 169 Mo. 600, 601; 70 S. W. Rep. 145.

In the recent case of Smallwood v. Baltimore, etc., R. Co. (20 Am. Neg. Rep. 718), the Pennsylvania court held that a railroad company was not liable for the death of a news agent, killed in a wreck, due to an employee's negligence, as such news agent was not a passenger.

The court distinguishes the case of Rowdin v. Pennsylvania R. Co. (208 Pa. St. 623; 57 Atl. Rep. 1125), in which it held that a postal clerk is a passenger, but it is held that a news agent. does not come within the same rule as laid down in Pennsylvania R. Co. v. Price, 96 Pa. St. 256; 10 Am. Neg. Cas. 218.

[7] Pennsylvania R. Co. v. Henderson, 51 Pa. St. 315; Missouri Pacific R. Co. v. Ivey (Texas), 37 Am. & Eng. R. Cas. 46; Lawson v. Chicago, etc., R. Co. (Wis.), 21 Am. & Eng. R. Cas. 249.

[8] New York, etc., R. Co. v. Lockwood, 17 Wall. 357; 84 U. S. 349–362; 21 L. Ed. 627.

the plaintiff was entitled to pass free, yet his passage was one of the mutual terms of the arrangement for carrying his cattle."

In answering the contention of the railroad company that a drover, accompanying his stock, on a railroad train, was an employee of the railroad company, the Missouri court,[9] in discussing the status of such a person, said: "He received no wages, performed and was to perform no service, unless it was in looking after the stock of which he was the owner and his death did not occur while he was engaged in that behalf. He performed no duty upon the train, and was not connected, in any manner, with its management and operation and was not subject to the defendant's orders in that behalf and owed it no obedience, at least in the sense in which said duties and relations commonly exist."

It is the carrier's duty to use due care for the safety of the shipper, or his employee, while riding in a car specially provided for the shipper, and the carrier will be liable for an injury to the shipper or his employee, due to the negligence of its employees to the same extent that it is liable to any other passenger.[10] Nor is it considered just or reasonable, in the law, for a common carrier to stipulate for exemption from liability for the negligence of itself or its employees, in case of a resulting injury to a drover traveling on a stock train, on a free pass, to look after his cattle and in case of an injury to such a person, the railroad company is generally held responsible, notwithstanding a stipulation in the pass, exempting it from such liability.[11]

[9] Carroll v. Missouri Pacific Ry. Co., 88 Mo. 239, 245; 57 Am. Rep. 382.

[10] Baker v. Boston, etc., R. Co. (N. H.), 65 Atl. Rep. 386.

[11] Carroll v. Missouri Pacific Ry. Co., 88 Mo. 239; 57 Am. Rep. 382; New York, etc., R. Co. v. Lockwood, 17 Wall. 357; 21 L. Ed. 627; Cleveland, etc., R. Co. v. Curran, 19 Ohio St. 1; 2 Am. Rep. 362; Ohio, etc., Ry. Co. v. Selby, 47 Ind. 471; 17 Am. Rep. 719; Brennan v.

But this rule does not apply, in England, under the earlier decisions, and a railroad company was not liable for an injury to one riding on a drover's pass, where, by the express conditions of the pass, the railroad company was exempted from liability for such an injury.[12]

Fairhaven, etc., R. Co., 45 Conn. 284; 29 Am. Rep. 679; Lemon v. Chansler, 68 Mo. 340; 30 Am. Rep. 799.

[12] Gallin v. London, etc., Ry. Co., 10 Q. B. 212; 12 Moak's Eng. 268; Alexander v. Toronto, etc., Ry. Co., 35 U. C. Q. B. 453; McCawley v. Ry. Co., 4 Moak's Eng. 218; L. R. 8 Q. B. 57.

"Where plaintiff, who had shipped his horses in a freight car, on purchasing a ticket in order to ride with the horses, was informed by the ticket agent that he would arrive at his destination at 5 p. m. and shortly before 5 p. m. the car reached a junction, where it remained all night, whereby he sustained injuries from exposure to cold in the car, and he testified that ' every minute ' he thought the train would start, the delay was the proximate cause of the injury though there was a station house at the junction in which plaintiff could have passed the night." Green v. Missouri, etc., Ry. Co. (Mo. App. 1906), 121 Mo. App. 720; 97 S. W. Rep. 646.

"It is a carrier's duty to use due care for the safety of a shipper's employee while riding in a car specially provided for the shipper, the consideration for the employee's passage being services rendered in caring for the shipper's property, or the transportation charge paid by the shipper, and the carrier is liable for injuries to the employee due to negligence of itself or its employees." Baker v. Boston, etc., R. Co. (N. H. 1906), 65 Atl. Rep. 386.

If a drover sustains injury by voluntarily taking a dangerous place on a train, the carrier would not be liable for his injury. Atchison, etc., Ry. Co. v. Lindsey (Kansas), 41 Am. & Eng. R. Cas. 72; McCorkle v. Chicago, etc., Ry. Co. (Iowa), 18 Am. & Eng. R. Cas. 156; Little Rock, etc., R. Co. v. Miles (Ark.), 13 Am. & Eng. R. Cas. 10.

But, see where shipper goes on top of train, on order of the conductor. Indianapolis, etc., Ry. Co. v. Horst, 93 U. S. 291.

"One who, being the agent of the owner of horses, rode on the freight train on which they were shipped, was a passenger, and did not assume the risk of injury from negligence of the carrier." Southern Ry. Co. v. Roach (Ind. App. 1906), 78 N. E. Rep. 201.

"One who under contract with a railroad company accompanies a shipment of live stock is not a passenger, within Cobbey's Ann. St. 1903, § 10,039, and in an action for injuries received, the common-law

§ 568. **Employees riding to and from work.**— Persons in the employ of a railroad company who travel back and forth from their residences to their places of work, upon the cars of the railroad company, where their transportation is furnished free of charge, are not regarded as passengers, but

and not the statutory rule of liability, applies." Riley v. Chicago, etc., Ry. Co. (Neb. 1907), 111 N. W. Rep. 847.

" A railway company is not only liable for injuries sustained by a caretaker accompanying stock by reason of defects in the walks in the yards of which it has actual knowledge, but also by reason of a patent defect which has existed so long that notice of it may be reasonably inferred." Atchison, T. & S. F. Ry. Co. v. Allen, 88 Pac. Rep. 966.

" In an action against a railway company for personal injury to plaintiff while in charge of a car of horses, etc., being shipped by him, testimony that four successive conductors in charge of the train did not object to his riding in the car, and at least three knew that he was so riding, was sufficient to show a waiver of a provision of the contract of shipment requiring him to ride in the caboose; there being no showing of want of the conductor's authority to permit him to ride in the car." Chicago, etc., Ry. Co. v. Burns (Tex. Civ. App. 1907), 104 S. W. Rep. 1081.

" While the duty of feeding and watering stock in transit devolves on the railway company, the caretakers accompanying the stock have a right to follow and inspect it and ascertain whether they are being given proper care, and the railway company is bound to exercise reasonable care for their safety." Atchison, etc., Ry. Co. v. Allen (Kan. 1907), 88 Pac. Rep. 966.

" One authorized by contract to accompany cattle while in transport is a passenger, and his status as such is not changed by the fact that while accompanying the same he rides on an engine, there being no more suitable place available." Southern Ry. Co. v. Cullen, 122 Ill. App. 293; 77 N. E. Rep. 470; 221 Ill. 392.

" A shipper's contract with a carrier by which the carrier was indemnified against claims for personal injuries to the shipper's employees by reason of carrying such employees free on cars specially provided for the shipper is void, where the carrier refused to furnish such special cars unless the shipper would furnish men to handle and care for the shipper's goods, and transportation according to the carrier's public duty is not afforded the shipper as an alternative, and no reduction of rates is made." Baker v. Boston & M. R. Co. (N. H. 1906), 65 Atl. Rep. 386.

II—3 .

as employees of the railroad company, and for injuries received, while so traveling, the railroad company would not be liable, unless under the circumstances surrounding the injury, it would be responsible as for any other injury to one of its employees.[13]

But whether a given employee of a railroad company, riding on a train of his employer, will or will not be regarded as a passenger, depends upon whether he is being carried for his own convenience or about his own business, or upon business of his employer, or he is going to or from his place of work, as an incident of his employment. If he is engaged upon his own business, or riding for his own convenience, he is generally held to be a passenger, while he is held to occupy the relation of an employee to the railroad company, if he is

[13] Moss v. Johnson, 22 Ill. 633; Abend v. Terre Haute, etc., R. Co. (Ill.), 17 Am. & Eng. R. Cas. 614; Capper v. Louisville, etc., R. Co. (Ind.), 21 Am. & Eng. R. Cas. 525; McQueen v. Central Branch R. Co. (Kan.), 15 Am. & Eng. R. Cas. 226; Kansas Pacific R. Co. v. Salmon, 11 Kansas 83; Gillshannon v. Stony Brook R. Co., 10 Cush. (Mass.) 228; Seaver v. Boston, etc., R. Co., 14 Gray (Mass.) 466; New York, etc., R. Co. v. Vick (N. Y.), 17 Am. & Eng. R. Cas. 609; Russell v. Hudson River R. Co., 17 N. Y. 134; Ross v. New York, etc., R. Co., 5 Hun 488; 74 N. Y. 617; Manville v. Cleveland, etc., R. Co., 11 Ohio St. 417; Ryan v. Cumberland Valley R. Co., 23 Pa. St. 284; Hutchison v. New York, etc., R. Co., 5 Exch. 343; Howland v. Milwaukee, etc., R. Co. (Wis.), 5 Am. & Eng. R. Cas. 578; Higgins v. Hannibal, etc., R. Co., 36 Mo. 418; Martin v. Atchison, etc., R. Co., 166 U. S. 399; 41 L. Ed. 1051; 17 Sup. Ct. Rep. 603; McGuirk v. Shattuck, 160 Mass. 45; 35 N. E. Rep. 110; 39 Am. St. Rep. 454; Ionnone v. New York, etc., R. Co., 21 R. I. 452; 44 Atl. Rep. 592; 79 Am. Rep. 812; 46 L. R. A. 730; Indianapolis, etc., R. Co. v. Foreman, 162 Ind. 85; 69 N. E. Rep. 669; 102 Am. St. Rep. 185; O'Neill v. Pittsburg, etc., R. Co., 130 Fed. Rep. 204; Fletcher v. Baltimore, etc., R. Co., 168 U. S. 135; 42 L. Ed. 411; 18 Sup. Ct. Rep. 35; Ewald v. Chicago, etc., R. Co., 70 Wis. 420; 36 N. W. Rep. 12; 5 Am. St. Rep. 178; Noe v. Rapid R. Co., 133 Mich. 152; 94 N. W. Rep. 743; St. Clair v. St. Louis, etc., R. Co., 122 Mo. App. 519; 99 S. W. Rep. 775.

engaged upon the employer's work, or is riding to or from his work, as an incident thereof.[14]

And if an employee of a railroad company is carried on the company's cars, to and from his work, as a part of his contract of employment and in consideration of a reduction in his wages or for any other consideration, he would occupy the position of a regular passenger upon the train and would not be prevented from a recovery for an injury received while so traveling, by the fact that the injury sustained resulted from the negligence of the railroad company's employees.[15]

[14] St. Clair v. St. Louis, etc., R. Co., 122 Mo. App. 519.

[15] Haas v. St. Louis, etc., R. Co., 111 Mo. App. 706; 90 S. W. Rep. 1155; St. Clair v. St. Louis, etc., R. Co., 122 Mo. App. 519; 99 S. W. Rep. 775; Enos v. Rhode Island R. Co. (R. I.), 67 Atl. Rep. 5; 12 L. R. A. (N. S.) 244; Dickinson v. West End R. Co., 177 Mass. 365; 59 N. E. Rep. 60; 83 Am. St. Rep. 284; 52 L. R. A. 326; McNulty v. Pennsylvania R. Co., 182 Pa. St. 479; 38 Atl. Rep. 524; 61 Am. St. Rep. 721; 38 L. R. A. 376; Chattanooga, etc., R. Co. v. Venable, 105 Tenn. 460; 58 S. W. Rep. 861; 51 L. R. A. 886; Vick v. New York, etc., R. Co., 95 N. Y. 267; 47 Am. Rep. 36; O'Donnell v. Allegheny Valley R. Co., 59 Pa. St. 239; Ohio, etc., R. Co. v. Muhling, 30 Ill. 1; Washburn v. Nashville, etc., R. Co., 3 Head (Tenn.) 638.

Mere proof that the conductor received and treated an employee as a passenger does not determine his relation. Texas, etc., R. Co. v. Scott, 64 Texas 549.

A bookkeeper who had nothing to do with running trains was held to be a passenger, while riding on a train, in Chicago, etc., R. Co. v. Keefe, 47 Ill. 108.

An employee riding on a train, for his own business, was held a passenger, in Louisville, etc., R. Co. v. Stacker, 86 Tenn. 343; 6 S. W. Rep. 737; 6 Am. St. Rep. 840.

An employee riding on a train, for his own business, was held to be a passenger, in McDaniel v. Highland, etc., R. Co., 90 Ala. 64; 8 So. Rep. 41; Rosenbaum v. St. Paul, etc., R. Co., 38 Minn. 173; 36 N. W. Rep. 447; 34 Am. & Eng. R. Cas. 274.

An employee of a contractor getting out timbers for a railroad company, who knowingly rides on a train carrying only company employees, is held not to be a passenger, but a mere licensee, in McCauley v. Tennessee, etc., R. Co., 93 Ala. 356; 9 So. Rep. 611; 47

§ 569. **Passenger assisting carrier's employees.**— It frequently occurs, in the transportation of passengers, by rail, that emergencies will arise when the employees of the carrier require the assistance of passengers, before the journey

Am. & Eng. R. Cas. 580. See, also, Graham v. Toronto, etc., R. Co., 23 U. C. C. P. 541; Sherman v. Toronto, etc., R. Co., 34 U. C. Q. B. 451; Torpey v. Grand Trunk R. Co., 20 U. C. Q. B. 446.

"A railroad flagman, who received as compensation for his services a weekly sum of money and transportation tickets on the railroad to convey him to and from his work, was a passenger while riding home on one of the tickets after his day's work had been fully completed." Enos v. Rhode Island Suburban Ry. Co., 67 Atl. Rep. 5; 28 R. I. 291.

"In an action to recover for the death of plaintiff's husband, who, after securing an appointment of locomotive engineer, was traveling on a locomotive for the purpose of informing himself more particularly as to the character of the road, and was killed by the train leaving the tracks, owing to the negligence of the engineer in charge, whether deceased was or was not a passenger was for the jury." Wilkes v. Buffalo, etc., Ry. Co. (Pa. 1907), 65 Atl. Rep. 787.

An employee riding on a car, under orders of his foreman, was held to be a passenger, in Haas v. St. Louis, etc., R. Co., 111 Mo. App. 706; 90 S. W. Rep. 1155.

"A section hand, riding to work on a freight train, is not a 'passenger' within the common meaning of the term, but the railroad owes him the duty of exercising ordinary care for his protection." St. Louis, etc., Ry. Co. v. Harmon (Ark. 1908), 109 S. W. Rep. 295.

Whether an employee is a passenger or not, depends upon whether he is being carried for his own convenience, or business, or to or from his work, as an incident of his employment. If the former, he is a passenger, but if the latter, he is an employee. St. Clair v. St. Louis, etc., R. Co., 122 Mo. App. 519; 99 S. W. Rep. 775.

A toolhouse foreman, riding in a caboose, under orders from his superior, was held to be a passenger, in St. Clair v. St. Louis, etc., R. Co., 122 Mo. App. 519; 99 S. W. Rep. 775.

Where a section hand, employed to handle wood, boarded a train to go some distance down the track to dinner, which was the usual mode of going to dinner and which was adopted with the consent of the foreman, to save time, he was not in the position of a trespasser or licensee, but the company, his employer, was bound to use ordinary care to protect him from injuries. Boss v. Northern Pac. R. Co., 5 Dak. 308; 40 N. W. Rep. 590.

can be safely completed. A passenger who voluntarily, or on the invitation of the employees of the carrier, leaves a car to render such assistance as he may be able to render, in case of a derailment or otherwise, does not lose his status as a passenger, and if he receives an injury while so engaged, he is held entitled to recover, the same as any other passenger, if the injury is due to the negligence of the employees of the carrier.[16]

A passenger upon a street car, who was assisting the driver to push the car back to a switch which had been inadvertently passed, who was injured by the carelessness of the driver of another car, in striking him while so engaged, was held entitled to recover, as a passenger, for the injury so received,[17] and a passenger on a railroad train, who was assisting the railroad company's employees to carry a sick passenger back to a caboose, when he fell between the cars and was injured, was held not to lose his status as a passenger by the assistance he was rendering to the company's employees, but to retain this relation, while so engaged.[18]

§ 570. Persons accompanying passengers on train.— A person accompanying a passenger, to assist him in entering the train, such as friends or relatives of the passenger, though not a passenger himself, is not a trespasser nor bare licensee, as he has at least a tacit invitation from the carrier, by virtue of the relation between it and the passenger, and the carrier, as to such a person, is held to the rule of exercising ordinary care to avoid injuring him, by defective station facilities or approaches thereto,[19] or by negligent movement of the train,

---

[16] 2 Hutchinson on Carriers (3 ed.), § 1013, p. 1167, and cases cited.

[17] McIntire, etc., Ry. Co. v. Bolton, 43 Ohio St. 224.

[18] Cincinnati, etc., Ry. Co. v. Salzman, 52 Ohio St. 558; 40 N. E. Rep. 891; 49 Am. St. Rep. 745; 31 L. R. A. 261.

[19] Chesapeake, etc., Ry. Co. v. Paris' Admr. (Va.), 59 S. E. Rep. 398;

when such a person is entering or leaving it.[20]   It is held, in Missouri,[21] that where a carrier permits a person to assist a passenger to carry baggage on the train, or to enter the train with a passenger, though the relation of passenger and carrier does not exist as to such person, the carrier owes him reasonable care to avoid injuring him and to this end is bound to hold the train stationary, until the guest, in the exercise of reasonable care, can safely alight.   It is also said that where reasonable minds would differ as to whether or not such a person was negligent in alighting from a moving train, it would be a jury issue, although the person attempted to alight in the face of a caution from an employee of the railroad company not to do so.[22]   This rule, applied by the Kansas City Court of Appeals, of Missouri,[23] is not believed to be the general rule of law upon this subject, and, indeed, the Supreme Court of the same State has held in several cases, that it was negligence as matter of law for a person to attempt to alight from a moving train, where there was a caution from an employee not to do so.[24]

This would seem to be the better rule, for if a railroad com-

Galveston, etc., R. Co. v. Hewitt, 67 Texas 473; 3 S. W. Rep. 705; Texas, etc., R. Co. v. Best, 66 Texas 116; Hamilton v. Texas, etc., R. Co., 64 Texas 251; Stiles v. Atlanta, etc., R. Co., 65 Ga. 370; 8 Am. & Eng. R. Cas. 195; Coleman v. Georgia, etc., R. Co., 84 Ga. 1; 10 S. E. Rep. 498; 40 Am. & Eng. R. Cas. 690.

[20] Bond v. Chicago, etc., R. Co., 122 Mo. App. 207; 99 S. W. Rep. 30; 110 Mo. App. 131; 84 S. W. Rep. 124.

[21] Bond v. Chicago, etc., Ry. Co., supra; Doss v. Missouri, etc., Ry. Co., 59 Mo. 27; 21 Am. Rep. 371; 8 Am. Ry. Rep. 462; Yarnell v. Kansas City, etc., Ry. Co., 113 Mo. 570; 21 S. W. Rep. 1; 18 L. R. A. 599; Saxton v. Missouri Pacific Ry. Co., 98 Mo. App. 494; 72 S. W. Rep. 717.

[22] Bond v. Chicago, etc., R. Co., 122 Mo. App. 207; 99 S. W. Rep. 30; 110 Mo. App. 131; 84 S. W. Rep. 124.

[23] Bond v. Chicago, etc., Ry. Co., supra.

[24] Behen v. Transit Co., 186 Mo. 430; 85 S. W. Rep. 346; Fulks v. St. Louis, etc., Ry. Co., 111 Mo. 335; 19 S. W. Rep. 818.

pany is to be held negligent for an act of a third person, toward whom it has assumed no obligations, other than such as the law would imply, when such person acts in direct violation of the company's orders, given to protect him, then it is making the company liable for the rash act of a stranger, acting in pursuance to his own judgment, in a matter wherein the railroad company could not be said to be at fault. This is not the trend of the decisions and it is also held, quite generally, that to render the railroad company liable, in any case, for an injury to one accompanying a passenger on its train, it must have had notice that such person was on the train, or consented to his presence, for otherwise it is not bound to hold its trains for the accommodation of such a person, toward whom it has assumed no direct obligations.[25] And if a person, without notice to the carrier, boards a train, to accompany a passenger and attempts to leave it while it is in motion, under circumstances such as to make it a dangerous proceeding, he assumes the risk of injury and cannot hold the carrier, if he is hurt.[26]

[25] Yarnell v. Kansas City, etc., Ry. Co., 113 Mo. 570; 21 S. W. Rep. 1; Griswold v. Chicago, etc., R. Co., 64 Wis. 652; 23 Am. & Eng. R. Cas. 463; Coleman v. Georgia, etc., R. Co., 84 Ga. 1; 40 Am. & Eng. R. Cas. 690; Little Rock, etc., R. Co. v. Lawton, 55 Ark. 428; 18 S. W. Rep. 543; 52 Am. & Eng. R. Cas. 260; Lucas v. New Bedford R. Co., 6 Gray (Mass.) 64; Imhoff v. Chicago, etc., Ry. Co., 20 Wis. 344.

[26] Keokuk, etc., Co. v. Henry, 50 Ill. 264; Lucas v. New Bedford R. Co., 6 Gray (Mass.) 64; Central, etc., R. Co. v. Letcher (Ala.), 12 Am. & Eng. R. Cas. 115; Coleman v. Georgia, etc., R. Co., 84 Ga. 1; 10 S. E. Rep. 498; 40 Am. & Eng. R. Cas. 690.

It is held, in Illinois, by the Appellate Court, that a railroad company is not bound to hold a train for one going with a passenger on a car. Spannagle v. Chicago, etc., R. Co., 31 Ill. App. 460.

One getting on a fast mail train, with the intention of alighting, is not entitled to notice to do so. Coleman v. Georgia, etc., R. Co., 84 Ga. 1; 10 S. E. Rep. 498; 40 Am. & Eng. R. Cas. 690.

There is no duty to hold a freight train, for the accommodation of a person bidding some one traveling thereon, good-bye. Dowd v.

, § 571. **Persons obtaining transportation by fraud.**— Where a person by stealth obtains a ride upon a railroad train, as where he secretes himself upon a train, without the knowledge of the railroad company's employees, or if he induces the em-

Chicago, etc., R. Co., 84 Wis. 105; 54 N. W. Rep. 24; 58 Am. & Eng. R. Cas. 18.

In Stiles v. Atlanta, etc., Ry. Co. (65 Ga. 370; 8 Am. & Eng. R. Cas. 195), plaintiff had gone to defendant's station to meet his wife. The station grounds were dark and he fell in a hole and sued the railway company for the resulting injuries. It was held that it was not liable to him.

In Griswold v. Chicago, etc., Ry. Co. (64 Wis. 652; 26 N. W. Rep. 101; 23 Am. & Eng. R. Cas. 463), plaintiff went to a depot to meet his wife, and after the passengers had left the train, he went on the train and into a sleeping car, looking for her. He passed out of this car into another car, where he received injuries by the jerking of the car. It was held that the railroad company was not liable to him.

Where a conductor knew that a person had gone on the train to assist a sick passenger on, it was held, in Indiana, that the railroad company owed him the same duty it did a passenger, to hold the train, until he could safely alight. Louisville, etc., R. Co. v. Crank, 119 Ind. 542; 21 N. E. Rep. 31; 41 Am. & Eng. R. Cas. 158.

But, see where such a person attempts to leave a moving train, notwithstanding no notice was given him. Lucas v. New Bedford R. Co., 6 Gray (Mass.) 64; Gavett v. Manchester, etc., R. Co., 16 Gray (Mass.) 501.

"A person accompanying passengers to assist them in entering a train, though not a passenger, is not a trespasser, nor bare licensee, as he has at least a tacit invitation from the carrier by virtue of the relation between it and the passenger, and the carrier must exercise at least ordinary care to avoid injuring him by defective stational facilities or approaches thereto." Chesapeake, etc., Ry. Co. v. Paris' Adm'r (Va. 1907), 59 S. E. Rep. 398.

"In an action against a carrier by one entering a train to assist a passenger, for injuries sustained in leaving the moving train, evidence *held* sufficient to take to the jury the question whether the carrier had notice of plaintiff's intention to disembark." Cooper v. Atlantic Coast Line R. Co. (S. C. 1907), 59 S. E. 704.

"Where plaintiff went to defendant's station to accompany his wife and children, who intended to become passengers on defendant's train, and plaintiff was injured by the premature starting of the train while he was endeavoring to place his wife's baggage aboard, plaintiff was on

ployees of the railroad company to violate a rule of the company and carry him without charge, he is guilty of such a fraud upon the railroad company as will prevent him from claiming the rights of a passenger, since one of the essential elements of the relation, the consent of the carrier, is lacking.[27]   The same result follows upon the use of unauthorized transportation and one guilty of such a fraud cannot claim advantage of his own wrong, to the extent of claiming to occupy a relation that his fraud alone would entitle him to occupy.   A person representing himself to be the holder

defendant's premises by its implied invitation, and defendant was therefore bound to exercise ordinary care for his safety." Chesapeake & O. Ry. Co. v. Fortune (Va. 1907), 59 S. E. Rep. 1095.

" Where a train stopped its usual length of time at a station, during which plaintiff, with baggage in her hand and without explaining her purpose, got on the train to assist her grandchildren, who were with her and were to be passengers, there was no notice to the train men that she did not intend to remain on the train." Louisville & N. R. Co. v. Wilson (Ky. 1907), 100 S. W. Rep. 290.

" A person who accompanies a passenger onto a train to render her assistance, in conformity with a custom acquiesced in by the carrier, is not a trespasser, and, if the carrier has notice of his intention to disembark, it must hold the train a reasonable time to allow him to leave it." Cooper v. Atlantic Coast Line R. Co. (S. C. 1907), 59 S. E. Rep. 704.

" Where a brakeman in good faith makes an unsuccessful attempt to prevent one who had assisted a passenger to board a train from alighting after it had started, the railroad is not liable for the person's injury, although he might have alighted in safety had the brakeman not interfered; the brakeman's acting being one in an emergency, which will not create a liability on the master's part, though the result shows it to have been a mistake." Chesapeake & O. Ry. Co. v. Paris' Admr. (Va. 1907), 59 S. E. Rep. 398.

" Though a person assisting a passenger in boarding a train has a right to enter the train in conformity with a practice acquiesced in by the carrier, he should inform those in charge of his purpose; and, where they have no actual or constructive notice that he intends to disembark, they are not bound to hold the train, nor to notify him before it starts." Chesapeake & O. Ry. Co. v. Paris' Admr (Va. 1907), 59 S. E. Rep. 398.

[27] Toledo, etc., R. Co. v. Brooks, 81 Ill. 245.

of a nontransferable free pass, issued to another [28] or a person who, by false representations, obtains a ticket or pass, as the owner of property which would give him the right of transportation,[29] cannot claim the rights of a passenger, for the fraud will vitiate the contract and the ticket or pass obtained by such means will not entitle the holder to claim any rights thereunder.

But a person, who, in good faith, uses a ticket or pass, which he believes will rightfully entitle him to transportation, if his right to travel on such transportation is recognized by the carrier's agents, will be entitled to the rights of a passenger. It is accordingly held, that where a person was induced to believe, by the conduct and language of the company's employees, that he was entitled to ride upon the transportation presented, that he would be entitled to all the rights of a passenger,[30] and where a person presented a commutation ticket, issued to another, in the belief that he was rightfully entitled to ride upon such ticket, and he was recognized as having the right to transportation upon such a ticket, by the employees of the railroad company, he would be regarded as a passenger although the ticket was not, in fact, transferable.[31]

[28] Toledo, etc., R. Co. v. Beggs, 85 Ill. 80.

[29] Brown v. Missouri, etc., R. Co., 64 Mo. 536; Gardner v. New Haven, etc., R. Co. (Conn.), 18 Am. & Eng. R. Cas. 170. But a mother who does not represent that her child is less than three, in order to obtain a ride, where the conductor carries the child without such representation, is held not to prevent the child from recovering for an injury received while being transported by the carrier, although the child is over the age when it could be carried free, in England. Austin v. Great Western R. Co., 2 Q. B. 442.

[30] Russ v. The War Eagle, 14 Iowa 363.

[31] Robestelli v. New York, etc., R. Co., 34 Am. & Eng. R. Cas. 515; Great Northern R. Co. v. Harrison, 10 Exch. 376.

"Where one boards a railroad train without any intention to pay fare for his transportation, he does not become a passenger." Gates v. Quincy, etc., Ry. Co. (Mo. App. 1907), 102 S. W. Rep. 50.

" Rev. Laws, ch. 111, § 228, provides that a railroad may make contracts for the conveyance of passengers at such reduced rates of fare as the parties may agree on. *Held*, that one riding on a ticket procured at a reduced rate by false representations to the effect that she was a student at a certain school was not a passenger." Fitzmaurice v. New York & H. R. Co. (Mass. 1906), 78 N. E. Rep. 418.

CHAPTER XXI.

§ 572. **Obligations arising by implication of law.**— The obligation of a carrier, for the safe transportation of a passenger, is one arising by contract establishing the relation, to which the law imposes the duty of using the utmost care to see that the passenger is carried without fault or negligence.[1] The duty of exercising care in the transportation of passengers is not dependent wholly upon the contract establishing

[1] Leslie v. Wabash R. Co., 88 Mo. 50; 26 Am. & Eng. R. Cas. 229; Baltimore, etc., R. Co. v. Breinig, 25 Md. 378.

876

the relation but it also arises from the hazardous character of the business and the fact that human life is imperiled by it.[2]

By its acceptance of a passenger, a carrier comes under the obligation to take due and reasonable care for his safe carriage, which obligation arises by implication of law and independent of contract, so that it may exist, although the contract of carriage is illegal, or even where there is no express contract of carriage at all.[3]

For a negligent injury to a passenger, an action lies against the carrier, although there is no contract and the service being rendered is wholly gratuitous, for whether the action is brought under contract, or for a failure to perform the duty imposed by the law, the liability is the same, for the obligation is not made to rest upon contract alone, but is annexed to the relation, to preserve, as far as may be, the lives and safety of citizens.[4]

§ 573. Carrier not liable as insurer.— A passenger carrier is not an insurer of the safety of the traveler, nor required to use means to prevent injuries which shall necessarily and in all cases be sufficient, efficient or effective against probable accidents.[5]

The railway company is an insurer of the safety of its passengers only against those risks which are caused or increased solely by reason of the carrier's negligence or that of its employees, or, in other words, it does not promise absolute safety, nor is this exacted of it, by the law, but it only guarantees transportation free from the risks of injuries resulting from negligence.[6]

[2] Galveston, etc., R. Co. v. Hewitt, 67 Texas 473; 3 S. W. Rep. 705.
[3] New York, etc., R. Co. v. Ball, 53 N. J. L. 283; 21 Atl. Rep. 1052.
[4] Carroll v. Staten Island R. Co., 58 N. Y. 126; 65 Barb. 32.
[5] Chicago, etc., R. Co. v. Fisher, 49 Kansas 460; 30 Pac. Rep. 462.
[6] Grand Rapids, etc., R. Co. v. Boyd, 65 Ind. 526.

It is a familiar expression of the courts that a railway company engaged in the carriage of passengers, cannot be held liable as an insurer of the absolute safety of the passengers during their transportation.[7]   And, indeed, if the liability of an insurer were to be placed upon railroad companies, along with the rapidly increasing responsibilities imposed by legislative acts and decisions of the courts, and such companies were held to the responsibility of warranting the safety of their passengers against all accidents and at all events, it is doubtful if the business of such carriers would be sufficient to enable them to exist against the burdens which such a rule of liability would impose, in addition to those already borne by such public service corporations.[8]

[7] Grand Rapids, etc., R. Co. v. Huntley, 38 Mich. 537; Chicago, etc., R. Co. v. Carroll, 5 Ill. App. 201; Louisville, etc., R. Co. v. Pedigo, 108 Ind. 481; 8 N. E. Rep. 627; 27 Am. & Eng. R. Cas. 310; Gillingham v. Ohio River R. Co., 35 W. Va. 588; 14 S. E. Rep. 243; 14 L. R. A. 798; 51 Am. & Eng. R. Cas. 222; International, etc., R. Co. v. Halloren, 53 Texas 46; 37 Am. Rep. 744; 3 Am. & Eng. R. Cas. 434; Sawyer v. Hannibal, etc., R. Co., 37 Mo. 241; Leslie v. Wabash R. Co., 88 Mo. 50; 26 Am. & Eng. R. Cas. 229; O'Connell v. St. Louis, etc., R. Co., 106 Mo. 482; 17 S. W. Rep. 494; Baltimore, etc., R. Co. v. State, 60 Md. 449; 12 Am. & Eng. R. Cas. 149; Chicago, etc., R. Co. v. Arnold, 114 Ill. 261; 33 N. E. Rep. 264; 58 Am. & Eng. R. Cas. 411; Chicago, etc. R. Co. v. Lewis, 145 Ill. 67; 33 N. E. Rep. 960; 58 Am. & Eng. R. Cas. 126; Hazard v. Chicago, etc., R. Co., 1 Biss. (U. S.) 503.

[8] Nagle v. California Southern R. Co., 88 Cal. 86; 25 Pac. Rep. 1106; Baltimore, etc., R. Co. v. Leonhardt, 66 Md. 70; 27 Am. & Eng. R. Cas. 194; 5 Atl. Rep. 346.

"A carrier, though held to strict care in the safe transportation of passengers, is not an insurer of their safety, and is only responsible for its own negligence in causing injury to a passenger." Reiss v. Wilmington City Ry. Co. (Del. Super. 1907), 67 Atl. Rep. 153.

"While a carrier of passengers is required to use the utmost diligence and care in providing reasonably safe cars, such carrier is not an insurer of the absolute safety of its passengers, but has discharged its duty in respect to its cars and trains when it has supplied the best instrumentalities that a highly prudent person would have supplied in the same business in the then known condition of the art and busi-

§ 574. **Negligence essential to liability.**— Carriers of passengers are only liable for injuries resulting from actual negligence or that of their employees and while they are responsible for the least degree of negligence — if any degrees can be said to exist — they are only liable for negligence or carelessness, and the existence of negligence is always essential to a liability.[9]

It is said, in an Arkansas case, that two things are essential to establish the liability of a railway company, as a passenger carrier — that the company is guilty of some negligence or omission, which mediately or immediately produced or enhanced the injury, and that the passenger was not, himself, guilty of any want of ordinary care, contributing to produce the injury.[10]

In other words, it may be stated that a carrier of passengers, for hire, is liable for all injuries resulting from the misconduct of the carrier or its employees,[11] while a passenger upon a train takes all the risks attending that mode of travel, except such as are caused or increased solely by the negligence of the carrier.[12]

§ 575. **What constitutes negligence toward passenger.**—

ness." Ozanne v. Illinois Cent. R. Co. (U. S. C. C., Ky. 1907), 151 Fed. Rep. 900.

" A carrier is not an insurer of the safety of passengers, but must exercise towards them such a high degree of care as a highly prudent person would exercise under the same or similar circumstances." Gilmore v. Houston Electric Co. (Tex. Civ. App. 1907), 102 S. W. Rep. 168.

[9] Grand Rapids, etc., R. Co. v. Huntley, 38 Mich. 537; Jeffersonville R. Co. v. Hendricks, 26 Ind. 228; Tennery v. Pippinger, 1 Phila. (Pa.) 543.

[10] George v. St. Louis, etc., R. Co., 34 Ark. 613; 1 Am. & Eng. R. Cas. 294.

[11] Springer Trans. Co. v. Smith, 16 Lea (Tenn.) 498; 1 S. W. Rep. 280.

[12] Grand Rapids, etc., R. Co, v. Boyd, 65 Ind. 526.

In an Indiana case,[13] the negligence for which the carrier for hire was held answerable to a passenger was said to be want of care concerning the condition of the road, the character of its machinery, the quality of the cars used, the sufficiency of the equipment, the conduct of the railway company's agents and employees and every other thing necessary for the safety of a passenger, who is not himself at fault.

In a West Virginia case,[14] it was said that " where the common experience of mankind and the common consensus of prudent persons have recognized that to do or omit to do certain acts is prolific of danger, we may call the doing or omission of them ' negligence *per se*,' or ' legal negligence.' " The omission of a duty enjoined by law for the protection and safety of the public by a common carrier or the doing of an act by such a carrier, which by the common experience or consensus of prudent persons would create dangers to passengers, is legal negligence.

Of course the exposure of a passenger to a danger which the exercise of a reasonable foresight might have anticipated and due care avoided, is held to be negligence on the part of the carrier.[15]

If a railway company, for instance, has notice that a passenger has fallen from a rapidly moving train onto the railroad track, and is there exposed to other trains being operated on the same track, it would be negligence to leave the passenger so exposed in such condition and in case of his being injured or killed by another train of the same company, it would be held liable for his injury or death.[16]   But where a rail-

---

[13] Grand Rapids, etc., R. Co. v. Boyd, 65 Ind. 526.

[14] Carrico v. West Virginia, etc., R. Co., 35 W. Va. 389; 14 S. E. Rep. 12; 52 Am. & Eng. R. Cas. 393.

[15] Lehr v. Steinway, etc., R. Co., 118 N. Y. 556; 44 Hun 627; 23 N. E. Rep. 889.

[16] Cincinnati, etc., R. Co. v. Kassen, 49 Ohio St. 230; 31 N. E. Rep. 282; 16 L. R. A. 674; 52 Am. & Eng. R. Cas. 427.

way company removes a drunken passenger, who has failed
and refused to pay his fare, to a reasonably safe distance from
the railroad track, it could not be held answerable for negligence in not foreseeing that he would subsequently wander
back onto the track, where he would be struck by another engine of the company and if he sustained such an injury, it
would not be answerable therefor, as no negligence could
be predicated on the acts of its employees.[17]

§ 576. **Presumption of negligence in actions by passengers.**
— In accordance with the rule *res ipsa loquitur,* already explained,[18] a presumption of negligence arises on the part of
the carrier for hire, in every case of injury to a passenger,
caused by a defect in the roadway, track, or appliances of
the carrier, or any failure to discharge their duty, on the
part of its employees, and the passenger makes out a *prima
facie* case of negligence by proof of the relation and the injury sustained by reason of some defect in the roadway,
track, appliances or vehicles of the carrier, or by some act
on the part of its employees, without specifying the act or
defect occasioning the injury.[19]   Where the passenger is injured by an accident due either to a collision, or some defect
in the roadway, track or cars, on which he is being trans-

[17] McClellan v. Louisville, etc., R. Co., 94 Ind. 276; 18 Am. & Eng.
R. Cas. 260; Indianapolis, etc., R. Co. v. Pitzer, 109 Ind. 179; 58
Am. Rep. 387; 25 Am. & Eng. R. Cas. 313.

[18] See chapter *Demonstrative Evidence of Negligence, rule res ipsa
loquitur.*

[19] Ohio, etc., R. Co. v. Voight, 122 Ind. 288; 23 N. E. Rep. 774; White
v. Boston, etc., R. Co., 144 Mass. 404; 11 N. E. Rep. 552; George v. St.
Louis, etc., R. Co., 34 Ark. 613; Gleason v. Virginia, etc., R. Co., 140
U. S. 435; 35 L. Ed. 458; Madden v. Missouri, etc., R. Co., 50 Mo.
App. 666; Och v. Missouri, etc., R. Co., 130 Mo. 27; 31 S. W. Rep.
962; 36 L. R. A. 442; 2 Am. & Eng. R. Cas. (N. S.) 343; Terre Haute,
etc., R. Co. v. Sheets, 155 Ind. 74; 56 N. E. Rep. 434; Pennsylvania
R. Co. v. Lyons, 129 Pa. St. 113; 18 Atl. Rep. 759; 41 Am. & Eng.
R. Cas. 154.

ported, he is only required to establish the fact of the accident during the existence of his relation as a passenger and the nature of the resulting injury and he then establishes a *prima facie* case and the burden is cast upon the carrier to disprove the negligence which the law implies from the facts thus established. The law presumes that the injury was due to the carrier's negligence and it must overcome this presumption, by showing that the injury resulted from an unavoidable accident, or something against which human prudence could not provide, or the passenger will be entitled to recover damages.[20]

But this presumption will not be indulged in when the facts of the injury show the cause thereof to be one for which the railroad company is not responsible,[21] as the presumption is based upon the *cause* of the injury and not upon the fact of the injury itself. The presumption does not obtain when the passenger has equal knowledge of the defect or cause of the accident with the carrier, and does not advise the carrier or its employees thereof, or voluntarily enters upon the relation with such notice and subsequently sustains injury.[22] The presumption does not apply when the fact of the accident illustrates that it would not have occurred, but for the voluntary act of the passenger, which, in part occasions the injury.[23] Nor does it obtain, where the act causing the injury is that of some third person, or passenger, or other cause,

[20] Meier v. Pennsylvania R. Co., 64 Pa. St. 225; Walker v. Erie R. Co., 63 Barb. (N. Y.) 260; Philadelphia, etc., R. Co. v. Anderson, 94 Pa. St. 351; 39 Am. Rep. 787.

[21] Holbrook v. Utica R. Co., 12 N. Y. 266; Shearm. & Redf. on Neg., § 280; 3 Thompson on Neg., § 2756; Fleming v. Pittsburg, etc., R. Co., 158 Pa. St. 130; 27 Atl. Rep. 858; 22 L. R. A. 351; Chicago, etc., R. Co. v. Rood, 163 Ill. 477; 45 N. E. Rep. 238.

[22] Carpue v. London, etc., R. Co., 5 Ad. & El. (N. S.) 747; 3 Thompson on Neg., § 2763, and cases cited.

[23] Connor v. Concord, etc., R. Co., 67 N. H. 311; 30 Atl. Rep. 1121; 3 Thompson on Neg., § 2764, and cases cited.

not subject to the control of the carrier, such as the act of God,[24] for in all such cases the proof of the fact of the accident would supply the existence of the evidence necessary to rebut the presumption, in showing the cause of the injury to be one for which the carrier was not answerable.

In the absence of such explanatory cause of the injury, however, either by the evidence of the passenger, or of evidence thereof, on the part of the carrier, the presumption would carry the passenger's cause to the jury and in the absence of evidence consistent with the exercise of the high care which the law exacts of the passenger carrier, a recovery would be permitted by the carrier, based alone on such a presumption.[25]

[24] St. Louis, etc., R. Co. v. Burrows (Kansas), 61 Pac. Rep. 439.

[25] Union, etc., R. Co. v. Harris, 158 U. S. 326; 39 L. Ed. 1003; 15 Sup. Ct. Rep. 843.

"Where, in an action for injuries, it is shown that the accident which caused the injury occurred while the plaintiff was a passenger, the burden of proof is on the defendant to explain the cause of the accident, and to show, if that be the defense, that the plaintiff was negligent, and his negligence caused or contributed to the injury." Washington, etc., Ry. Co. v. Chapman (D. C. 1906). 26 App. D. C. 472.

"In an action for death of a passenger on a railroad train by a collision, an instruction that the burden of showing that the collision occurred by no fault of defendant, and from some inevitable casualty or unavoidable accident or cause beyond the power of human care or foresight to prevent, was on the defendant, merely required the carrier to comply with Civ. Code, § 2100, providing that carriers shall use the utmost care and diligence for the safe carriage of passengers, and was not objectionable as requiring too high a degree of care." Valente v. Sierra Ry. Co. (Cal. 1907), 91 Pac. Rep. 481.

"Proof that plaintiff was a passenger upon a car of defendant, that she was in her seat and that while there she was struck by another car of the defendant and injured, makes a *prima facie* case." Chicago City Ry. Co. v. Pural, 127 Ill. App. 652, judgment affirmed, 79 N. E. Rep. 686; 224 Ill. 324.

"In an action for death of a passenger by the alleged negligence of a carrier's servants, evidence that plaintiff was a passenger, and that her death resulted from an accident to the train, was sufficient to

§ 577. Negligence must be proximate cause of injury.—
As in the case of injuries to employees, it is always essential
to a recovery by a passenger for negligence, that the carelessness of the carrier should be the proximate cause of the in-

establish a *prima facie* case of the carrier's negligence." Hopper v.
Denver & R. G. R. Co. (U. S. C. C. A., Colo., 1907), 155 Fed. Rep. 273.

" A passenger, suing for injuries, establishes a *prima facie* case of
negligence by showing the derailment of the train and the consequent
injury." Illinois Cent. R. Co. v. Porter (Tenn. 1906), 94 S. W.
Rep. 666.

" Where a passenger on defendant's train was thrown against one of
the seats and injured by a sudden stoppage of the train, such evidence,
in the absence of explanation by defendant, was *prima facie* to be
attributed to defendant's negligence, under the doctrine *res ipsa
loquitur.*" Todd v. Missouri Pac. Ry. Co. (Mo. App. 1907), 105 S.
W. Rep. 671.

" Where, in an action for injuries to a passenger, it appeared that
the car came to a sudden stop and that a piece of iron came up
through the seat on which she was seated, in the absence of any explanation tending to show that the accident occurred without negligence
on the part of the defendant, a finding of a want of proper care was
justified." Hebblethwaite v. Old Colony St. Ry. Co. (Mass. 1906),
78 N. E. Rep. 477.

" Where proof of an accident to a passenger made a *prima facie*
case of negligence on the part of the carrier is ordinarily presented,
but the carrier can explain the same from the passenger's own evidence
if it can, and, if on that evidence different minds might reach different
conclusions as to its conduct, it is for the jury to say whether a recovery of damages is warranted." Metropolitan St. Ry. Co. v. Warren
(Kan. 1906), 86 Pac. Rep. 131.

" In an action for injuries to a passenger on a freight train, where
it was proved that the injury was caused by the sudden and violent
stopping of the train, a *prima facie* case was made out against the
carrier which cast upon it the burden to show that the accident was not
the result of a want of care and skill which the law imposes upon a
common carrier." Bussell v. Quincy, O. & K. C. R. Co. (Mo. App.
1907), 102 S. W. Rep. 613.

" Where it was shown that plaintiff was a passenger on defendant's
train and was injured by a derailment of a part of the train, the burden
of proof was on the carrier to show that the casualty to the train was
not the result of its negligence." Bowlin v. Union Pac. R. Co. (Mo.
App. 1907), 102 S. W. Rep. 631.

jury. Carriers are liable for the natural, ordinary and proximate consequences of their acts, but not for such as are remote or extraordinary.[26]

The railway company is not necessarily responsible for any act that a passenger may do in consequence of some breach of duty on the part of its employees, but it is only liable for such results as are natural or probable consequences of such breach of duty. The railway employees are not chargeable with notice of a passenger's peculiar " intelligence and experience in life," but they are authorized to act upon appearances before them and if they have no notice of other facts putting them upon inquiry, making it necessary to bestow especial care upon a given passenger, the company would not be responsible for a failure to bestow such especial care.[27]

" In an action against a carrier for injuries to a passenger, the burden of proof of negligence is on the plaintiff, and cannot be shifted to the defendant without showing that the injury in question was caused by some person or thing connected with the carrier's railroad or business of transportation." Pennsylvania R. Co. v. McCaffrey (U. S. C. C. A., N. J. 1907), 149 Fed. Rep. 404.

" Though, where a passenger is injured by reason of a defect in an appliance, the presumption of negligence of the carrier arises, where the plaintiff's evidence showed, not only that the wheels of the car were broken and defective, but also that the defect was such that it could not have been detected by precaution, the court properly sustained a demurrer to the evidence." Ferguson v. St. Louis & S. F. R. Co. (Mo. App. 1907), 100 S. W. Rep. 537.

" Where the derailment of a train, injuring a passenger, is unexplained, negligence of the carrier is presumed." Galveston, H. & S. A. Ry. Co. v. Garcia (Tex. Civ. App. 1907), 100 S. W. Rep. 198.

" Where, in an action for injuries to a passenger by the derailment of a train, it was shown that the derailment was caused by a cyclone, the presumption of negligence arising therefrom did not obtain, and the burden was on plaintiff to prove defendant's negligence." Galveston, etc., R. Co. v. Crier, 100 S. W. Rep. 1178.

[26] Francis v. St. Louis, etc., R. Co., 5 Mo. App. 7; Pennsylvania R. Co. v. Aspell, 23 Pa. St. 147; Conroy v. Pennsylvania R. Co., 1 Pittsb. (Pa.), 440.

[27] Spohn v. Missouri Pacific Ry. Co., 101 Mo. 417; 14 S. W. Rep. 880.

Merely carrying a passenger by his station and putting him off at the next station, cannot be said to be the proximate cause of an injury by the passenger's being subsequently struck by a passing train, while he was walking on the railroad track, as the railroad company could not, by reasonable care, have foreseen that he would walk back upon its railroad track.[28] A passenger injured by jumping from a moving train, crossing a public street, cannot predicate a right of recovery on the company's failure to ring the bell or sound the whistle for such street crossing,[29] for in neither of these cases was the negligence of the carrier the proximate cause of the injury to the passenger.

But if a train is side-tracked at a station and the same is started up without notice to the passengers, who have been permitted to alight at the intermediate station, and a passenger is injured while stepping from a car platform to his own coach, which has been uncoupled from the other car and an employee standing near when he mounted the front car had failed to notify him of such fact, he is held entitled to recover, as the negligence of the carrier's employee in the latter case is the proximate cause of his injury.[30]

§ 578. **Highest degree of care exacted.**— While it is not strictly accurate to speak of care or negligence as having any degrees, but the terms are necessarily relative and without degrees, it is customary for the courts to speak of that care

[28] Benson v. Central Pacific R. Co., 98 Cal. 45; 32 Pac. Rep. 809; 54 Am. & Eng. R. Cas. 126; Lewis v. Flint, etc., R. Co., 54 Mich. 55; 19 N. W. Rep. 744; 52 Am. Rep. 790; 18 Am. & Eng. R. Cas. 263.

[29] Central R. Co. v. Harris, 76 Ga. 501.

[30] Andrist v. Union Pacific R. Co., 30 Fed. Rep. 345.

"In an action for injuries to a passenger, plaintiff could not recover if the negligence of defendant was not the proximate cause of the injury, or if by ordinary care he himself could have avoided the injury." Central of Georgia Ry. Co. v. Clay (Ga. App. 1907), 59 S. E. Rep. 843.

which is exacted of the carrier for hire toward the passenger, as being the "highest degree of care and diligence" for the safety of the passenger.[31]

Of course public policy requires that a carrier for hire should be held to the greatest possible care and diligence and that the personal safety of passengers should not be left to the sport of chance or the negligence of careless employees.[32] The carrier has no right to experiment at the risk of those it carries, and the duty of the carrier is to exercise the utmost care and caution.[33] The care and circumspection required of a railroad company, with respect to passengers in its charge is the utmost which can be exercised, under the circumstances, short of a warranty of their safety.[34]

In other words, a carrier is bound, in the management of its trains and the care of its tracks, to exercise the highest degree of care which it reasonably can, to prevent such in-

[31] Waller v. Hannibal, etc., R. Co., 83 Mo. 608; Higgins v. Hannibal, etc., R. Co., 36 Mo. 418; Knight v. Portland, etc., R. Co., 56 Mo. 234; Mathew v. Wabash R. Co., 115 Mo. App. 468; Wabash R. Co. v. Mathew (same case), 199 U. S. 605; 50 L. Ed. 329; Estes v. Missouri Pacific R. Co., 110 Mo. App. 725; 111 Mo. App. 1; 85 S. W. Rep. 627 and 85 S. W. Rep. 909; Atchison, etc., R. Co. v. Shean, 18 Colo. 368; 33 Pac. Rep. 108; Lambeth v. North Carolina R. Co., 66 N. Car. 494; Georgia R. Co. v. Homer, 73 Ga. 251; 27 Am. & Eng. R. Cas. 186; Raymond v. Burlington, etc., R. Co., 65 Iowa 152; 17 N. W. Rep. 923; 18 Am. & Eng. R. Cas. 217; Baltimore, etc., R. Co. v. State, 60 Md. 449; 12 Am. & Eng. R. Cas. 149; Little Rock, etc., R. Co. v. Miles, 40 Ark. 298; 48 Am. Rep. 10; 13 Am. & Eng. R. Cas. 10; Louisville, etc., R. Co. v. Snyder, 117 Ind. 435; 20 N. E. Rep. 284; 3 L. R. A. 434; 37 Am. & Eng. R. Cas. 137; Cleveland, etc., R. Co. v. Manson, 30 Ohio St. 451; St. Louis, etc., R. Co. v. Finley, 79 Texas 85; 15 S. W. Rep. 266.

[32] Bryan v. Missouri Pacific Ry. Co., 32 Mo. App. 228.

[33] Barrett v. Third Avenue R. Co., 45 N. Y. 628; 8 Abb. Pr. N. S. 205; 1 Sweeny 568.

[34] International, etc., R. Co. v. Welsh, 86 Texas 204; 24 S. W. Rep. 390; 58 Am. & Eng. R. Cas. 70.

juries to its passengers as human care and forethought can prevent.[35]

These are the oft repeated standards erected by the courts, for gauging the liability of common carriers of passengers and any less measure of accountability would not be consistent with a sound policy on the part of the State, for the protection of the lives and limbs of its citizens, on the part of those to whom it has delegated important rights and franchises.

[35] White v. Fitchburg, etc., R. Co., 136 Mass. 321; 18 Am. & Eng. R. Cas. 140. See, also, Denver, etc., R. Co. v. Hodgson, 18 Colo. 117; 31 Pac. Rep. 954; George v. St. Louis, etc., R. Co., 34 Ark. 613; 1 Am. & Eng. R. Cas. 294; Nagle v. California Southern R. Co., 88 Cal. 86; 25 Pac. Rep. 1106; Kellow v. Central Iowa R. Co., 68 Iowa 470; 23 N. W. Rep. 740; 21 Am. & Eng. R. Cas. 485; Eureka Springs R. Co. v. Timmons, 51 Ark. 459; 11 S. W. Rep. 690; Yerkes v. Keokuk, etc., Co., 7 Mo. App. 265.

"Carriers are held to the highest degree of care for the safety of passengers." Farrell v. Great Northern Ry. Co. (Minn. 1907), 111 N. W. Rep. 388.

"A carrier is bound to use the highest degree of care in the management of its trains, because in that respect a passenger can do nothing to insure his own personal safety." St. Louis, etc., Ry. Co. v. Green (Ark. 1908), 107 S. W. Rep. 168.

"A carrier is bound to exercise the utmost diligence to secure the safety of the passenger." Interurban Ry. & Terminal Co. v. Hancock (Ohio 1906), 78 N. E. Rep. 964; Chicago, etc., Ry. Co. v. Stibbs (Okla. 1906), 87 Pac. Rep. 293.

"After a person pays his fare to the conductor, the carrier is bound to extraordinary diligence in the protection of his life and person until the relation of passenger and carrier ceases to exist." Williamson v. Central of Georgia Ry. Co. (Ga. 1906), 56 S. E. Rep. 119.

"A carrier of passengers must exercise the highest degree of care for their safety and transportation, and is liable for any injury sustained by them in the course of transportation through failure to exercise such care." Bonnea v. North Shore R. Co. (Cal. 1907), 93 Pac. Rep. 106.

"A carrier is held to the highest degree of care to prevent injury to its passengers." Texas Midland R. Co. v. Griggs (Texas 1907) 106 S. W. Rep. 411.

§ 579. **Exceptions to the rule of extraordinary care.**— The rule imposing upon the carrier of passengers the highest degree of care, is held to apply only to the means and measures for safety which the passenger must, of necessity, trust wholly to the carrier. It is generally applicable only to the period during which the carrier is in a sense the bailee of the person of the passenger [36] and does not apply to precautions to prevent passengers from being left, where full and fair opportunity has been afforded them to take their places in the cars of the carrier.[37]

A carrier is never bound to adopt the highest possible precaution suggested by the greatest scientific skill, according to speculative evidence, in the adoption of its appliances, but only such high degree of care as that bestowed by practical, cautious men in the same business; [38] the carrier is not responsible for the wrongful acts of third persons or strangers, unless it was remiss in not discovering them in time to have avoided the accident resulting in the injury to its passengers; [39] nor is the degree of care exacted in any case to be determined by looking back upon the occurrence and determining what would have avoided the accident, but it is to be determined by reference to the care that a cautious man would take, without knowledge that an accident might occur in the manner in which it later did occur.[40]

[36] Texas, etc., R. Co. v. Miller, 79 Texas 78; 15 S. W. Rep. 264.

[37] Central, etc., R. Co. v. Perry, 58 Ga. 461; 16 Am. Ry. Rep. 122.

[38] Ford v. London, etc., R. Co., 2 F. & F. 730.

[39] Fredericks v. Northern, etc., R. Co., 157 Pa. St. 103; 27 Atl. Rep. 689; 58 Am. & Eng. R. Cas. 91.

[40] Bowen v. New York, etc., R. Co., 18 N. Y. 408; Griffith v. Utica, etc., R. Co., 43 N. Y. S. R. 835.

In Kelly v Manhattan R. Co. (112 N. Y. 443; 21 N. Y. S. R. 507; 20 N. E. Rep. 383; 3 L. R. A. 74), it is held that a less degree of care is required as to stations and approaches thereto, than in the management and operation of trains, as ordinary care alone is exacted as to the former, while extraordinary care is required in the latter

§ 580. **More than ordinary care required.**— Of course the care required of a passenger carrier is greater toward a passenger than the railroad company would owe to a mere trespasser or licensee, for toward a passenger the carrier is bound by considerations of public policy to the highest degree of care, while as to others the carrier is only bound to use reasonable care, after danger to such others is discovered.[41] In a number of cases the rule is said to be that the carrier is bound to a passenger in more than a mere ordinary duty and should consequently use more than ordinary care and diligence for the protection of the passenger.[42]

In other words, carriers are liable for a want of ordinary care in all cases, both in the case of injuries to employees and third persons, due to such want of ordinary care, but in the case of injuries to passengers, the courts hold the carriers to a higher responsibility and they are held liable for an injury to a passenger resulting from a failure to use extraordinary care for the protection of the passenger.[43] This expression is not of universal application in the United States, but some courts use the expression " such reasonable care as the circumstances demand," for the protection of the passenger and the carrier is not held to " extraordinary care," even in the case of injuries to passengers,[44] but no less measure of accounta-

instance. See, also, Robertson v. Wabash R. Co., 152 Mo. 382; 53 S. W. Rep. 1082; Knight v. Portland, etc., R. Co., 56 Me. 234; Pennsylvania R. Co. v. Hammill, 56 N. J. L. 370; 29 Atl. Rep. 151; 24 L. R. A. 531; Chicago, etc., R. Co. v. Scates, 90 Ill. 586; Trinity, etc., R. Co. v. O'Brien, 18 Texas Civ. App. 690; 46 S. W. Rep. 389.

[41] Carrico v. West Virginia, etc., R. Co., 35 W. Va. 389; 14 S. E. Rep. 12; 52 Am. & Eng. R. Cas. 393.

[42] Franklin v. Southern R. Co., 85 Cal. 63; 24 Pac. Rep. 723; Carrico v. West Virginia R. Co., 35 W. Va. 389; 14 S. E. Rep. 12; 52 Am. & Eng. R. Cas. 393; Libbey v. Maine Central R. Co., 85 Me. 34; 26 Atl. Rep. 943; 58 Am. & Eng. R. Cas. 81; Spellman v. Lincoln, etc., R. Co., 36 Neb. 890; 55 N. W. Rep. 270; 58 Am. & Eng. R. Cas. 297.

[43] Savannah, etc., R. Co. v. Stewart, 71 Ga. 427.

[44] Gadsden, etc., R. Co. v. Causler, 97 Ala. 235; 12 So. Rep. 439;

bility than that of ordinary care is exacted in any case, and some courts that recognize the rule of ordinary care, hold that in case the danger to the passenger is augmented, then a higher degree of care is required.[45] The use of every possible precaution is not the true rule, but the carrier must adopt such precautions of known value as are sanctioned by experience and secure such skilled labor as it can reasonably procure.[46]

§ 581. Liable for slight negligence.— Since the rule is applied to carriers of passengers that the carrier is held to the duty of using extraordinary care, for the protection of the passenger, it follows that for a failure to use such care, or for an injury due to the slight negligence of the carrier, it is responsible to the passenger.[47] The cases are numerous which hold that carriers of passengers by steam are responsible for the smallest or slightest negligence.[48] If an injury

58 Am. & Eng. R. Cas. 258, where a charge that the carrier was bound to use extraordinary care in the employment of its employees, or to employ men of extraordinary skill, was held to be error.

[45] Curtis v. Central R. Co., 6 McLean (U. S.) 401; Chicago, etc., R. Co. v. Hazzard, 26 Ill. 373; Chicago, etc., R. Co. v. Pillsbury, 123 Ill. 9; 14 N. E. Rep. 22; 31 Am. & Eng. R. Cas. 24; Klein v. Jewett, 26 N. J. Eq. 474; 27 N. J. Eq. 550.

[46] International, etc., R. Co. v. Halloren, 53 Texas 46; 37 Am. Rep. 744; 3 Am. & Eng. R. Cas. 343.

"An instruction that it is the duty of a railroad company to use the highest degree of care and caution consistent with a practical operation of its road to provide for the safety and security of passengers while being transported was not erroneous as requiring more care than was 'reasonably' consistent with the practical operation of the road." Chicago City Ry. Co. v Pural, 79 N. E. Rep. 686; 224 Ill. 324.

[47] Hulenkamp v. Citizens R. Co., 37 Mo. 537; Furnish v. Missouri Pacific Ry. Co., 102 Mo. 438; 13 S. W. Rep. 1044; Boss v. Providence, etc., R. Co., 15 R. I. 149; 1 Atl. Rep. 9; 21 Am. & Eng. R. Cas. 364; Barrett v. Third Avenue R. Co., 45 N. Y. 628; Central R. Co. v. Thompson, 76 Ga. 770; Bryan v. Missouri Pacific Ry. Co., 32 Mo. App. 228; Seymour v. Chicago, etc., R. Co., 3 Biss. (U. S.) 43.

[48] Little Rock, etc., R. Co. v. Miles, 40 Ark. 298; 48 Am. Rep. 10;

occurs to a passenger by reason of the slightest omission in regard to the perfection of all the appliances of transportation used by the carrier, or the mode or management of the train, at the time of the injury, the railroad company is liable,[49] for the carrier is bound to use the utmost care and diligence and it is liable for an injury resulting from the slightest negligence, if human prudence and foresight might have guarded against it.[50]

But while held to a strict degree of care and skill for the protection of the passenger, carriers of passengers are not liable for an injury to a passenger in the absence of some negligence on the part of the carrier or its employees.[51] The carrier is not responsible if the passenger is guilty of any negligence that contributed to produce the injury and the passenger assumes the risk of injury attending the mode of travel adopted and the carrier is only liable for injuries due proximately to its negligence.[52]

§ 582. **Care such as used by prudent persons.**— Where the carrier's liability is not restricted by special contract,[53] the rule is that it is bound to use such care and skill as prudent,

13 Am. & Eng. R. Cas. 10; Jeffersonville, etc., R. Co. v. Hendricks, 26 Ind. 228; Spellman v. Transit Co., 36 Neb. 890; 55 N. W. Rep. 270; 58 Am. & Eng. R. Cas. 297; Taylor v. Grand Trunk R. Co., 48 N. H. 304; Schultz v. Pacific R. Co., 36 Mo. 13; Eureka Springs R. Co. v. Timmonds, 51 Ark. 459; 11 S. W. Rep. 690; 40 Am. & Eng. R. Cas. 698; Pershing v. Chicago, etc., R. Co., 71 Iowa 561; 32 N. W. Rep. 488; 34 Am. & Eng. R. Cas. 405; Jamison v. San Jose, etc., R. Co., 55 Cal. 593; 3 Am & Eng. R. Cas. 350.

[49] George v. St. Louis, etc., R. Co., 34 Ark. 613; 1 Am. & Eng. R. Cas. 294.

[50] Treadwell v. Whittier, 80 Cal. 574; 22 Pac. Rep. 266.

[51] Grand Rapids, etc., R. Co. v. Huntley, 38 Mich. 537; George v. St. Louis, etc., R. Co., 34 Ark. 613; 1 Am. & Eng. R. Cas. 294.

[52] Grand Rapids, etc., R. Co. v. Boyd, 65 Ind. 526.

[53] Thayer v. St. Louis, etc., R. Co., 22 Ind. 26.

cautious men are accustomed to use under similar circumstances, toward its passengers for hire.[54]

Care and negligence are both relative terms and the degree of caution required of carriers of passengers is to be estimated in a measure, by the hazard to the passenger, but such care and vigilance is always exacted as reasonably prudent persons would exercise under similar circumstances, or the highest care and caution that capable and faithful railroad men would exercise in like circumstances toward passengers.[55]

The rule is not that the measure of accountability is alone that ordinary care and caution used by reasonably prudent men in the same business,[56] but the passenger has a right to expect of the carrier more care than reasonably prudent men would ordinarily use under the circumstances, or such high degree of care as very prudent and cautious men would exercise.[57]

But the rule of caution required of very prudent persons, or that of extraordinary care toward passengers, is not of universal application, and in a well-considered Michigan

[54] Bowen v. New York, etc., R. Co., 18 N. Y. 408; Gilson v. Jackson County R. Co., 76 Mo. 282; 12 Am. & Eng. R. Cas. 132; Boss v. Providence, etc., R. Co., 15 R. I. 149; 1 Atl. Rep. 9; 21 Am. & Eng. R. Cas. 364; Fuller v. Nangatuck, etc., R. Co., 21 Conn. 557; Mackey v. Missouri Pacific Ry. Co., 5 McCrary (U. S.) 538.

[55] Dougherty v. Missouri Pacific Ry. Co., 81 Mo. 325; 9 Mo. App. 478; 51 Am. Rep. 239; 21 Am. & Eng. R. Cas. 497; Louisville Southern R. Co. v. Minogue, 90 Ky. 369; 14 S. W. Rep. 357.

[56] Smith v. Chicago, etc., R. Co., 108 Mo. 243; 18 S. W. Rep. 971; 52 Am. & Eng. R. Cas. 483; Wheaton v. North Beach R. Co., 36 Cal. 590; Richmond City R. Co. v. Scott, 86 Va. 902; 11 S. E. Rep. 404; 44 Am. & Eng. R. Cas. 418; Franklin v. Southern California R. Co., 85 Cal. 63; 24 Pac. Rep. 723.

[57] Louisville, etc., R. Co. v. Snyder, 117 Ind. 435; 20 N. E. Rep. 284; 3 L. R. A. 434; 37 Am. & Eng. R. Cas. 137; O'Connell v. St. Louis, etc., R. Co., 106 Mo. 482; 17 S. W. Rep. 494; Nagle v. California Southern R. Co., 88 Cal. 86; 25 Pac. Rep. 1106; Libbey v. Maine Central R. Co., 85 Me. 34; 26 Atl. Rep. 943; 58 Am. & Eng. R. Cas. 81.

case,[58] as well as in other cases,[59] it was held to be error to charge that more care than that required by reasonably prudent men engaged in the same business, was necessary on the part of a carrier toward a passenger for hire, but that railroads were only held to the duty of being prudent and to the diligence embraced by the common ordinary rules of good railroad management.

§ 583. **Care proportionate to mode of conveyance adopted.** — The degree of care which is exacted by the law of carriers of passengers is subject to the reasonable limitation that it is not the utmost and highest absolutely, but the highest degree of care that is consistent with the nature of the business and the due regard to its necessary requirements.[60]

The true rule in regard to the degree of care required of railroad companies is that the carrier shall do all that human care, vigilance and foresight can reasonably do, consiste with the mode of conveyance adopted by the passenger a the practical operation of the railroad by the carrier.[61]

To state this rule in another way, carriers of passen

58 Michigan Central R. Co. v. Coleman, 28 Mich. 440; 12 An Rep. 59.

59 Franklin v. Southern California R. Co., 85 Cal. 63; 24 Pa 723.

"A common carrier is required to exercise towards passen high degree of care that a very cautious and prudent person w under similar circumstances." International, etc., Co. v. Huj Civ. App. 1907), 100 S. W. Rep. 1000.

"A street car company as a carrier of passengers is bo\ ercise the highest care and skill for the safety of passeng prudent man would exercise in a like business and und(cumstances." O'Gara v. St. Louis Transit Co. (Mo. 1907) Rep. 54.

60 Philadelphia, etc., R. Co. v. Anderson, 72 Md. 519; 2; 44 Am. & Eng. R. Cas. 345.

61 Pittsburg, etc., R. Co. v. Thompson, 56 Ill. 138; 3 454; Carr v. Eel River R. Co., 98 Cal. 366; 33 Pac. Rep. '

are only held to the utmost degree of care and vigilance which is consistent with the mode of transportation adopted by the passenger.[62]

A railroad company in operating freight trains carrying passengers is not held to the utmost skill and diligence which human foresight can effect, but is required to use the highest degree of practical care, skill and diligence that is consistent with the operation of its railroad and that will not render the business of carrying passengers impractical.[63]   Carriers are not required to adopt on freight or mixed trains, all the appliances for the comfort and convenience of the passengers, that are used on passenger trains, but are only required to use the highest degree of care, consistent with the practical operation of such class of trains and the passengers on such trains assume the risks resulting from the mode of conveyance used on such trains.[64]

[62] Mobile, etc., R. Co. v. Klein, 43 Ill. App. 63; North Chicago, etc. R. Co. v. Cook, 145 Ill. 551; 33 N. E. Rep. 958; Libbey v. Maine Central R. Co., 85 Me. 34; 26 Atl. Rep. 943; Chicago, etc., R. Co. v. Lewis, 145 Ill. 67; 33 N. E. Rep. 960; 58 Am. & Eng. R. Cas. 126.

[63] St. Louis, etc., R. Co. v. Sweet, 57 Ark. 287; 21 S. W. Rep. 587; Arkansas Midland R. Co. v. Cannon, 52 Ark. 524.

[64] Oviatt v. Dakota, etc., R. Co., 43 Minn. 300; 45 N. W. Rep. 436.

" It is the duty of a common carrier of passengers to do all that human vigilance and foresight can, under the circumstances, considering the character and mode of conveyance, to prevent accidents to passengers." Pomroy v. Bangor & Aroostook R. Co. (Me. 1907), 67 Atl. Rep. 561.

" A carrier must exercise the strictest vigilance and the highest degree of care in receiving, conveying, and discharging passengers that the means of conveyance employed and the circumstances permit." Southern Ry. Co. v. Cunningham (Ala. 1907), 44 So. Rep. 658.

" A railway company assuming to carry passengers for hire upon its freight trains is bound to exercise the same degree of care as is required in the operation of regular passenger trains; the difference being that a passenger submits himself to the inconvenience and danger necessarily attending that mode of conveyance." Guffey v. Railway, 53 Mo. App. 462. See, also, Hawk v. Chicago, etc., Ry. Co. (Mo. App.), 108 S. W. Rep. 1119.

§ 584. **When ordinary care sufficient.**— As to the means and measures for the passenger's safety, which he is not compelled to rely wholly upon the carrier to adopt, or in the care to be bestowed upon the passenger before or after the bailment of the person of the passenger, only ordinary care is generally exacted of the carrier, for the reason that the same rule for the application of the greater degree of care does not then exist.[65].

The degree of care required of a railroad company in transporting passengers is that which a person of great prudence would exercise under the same circumstances, and is not affected by the character of the train upon which the passenger is carried, except that the liability of the carrier would not extend to increased risks necessarily incident to riding upon a freight train, since such increased risks are assumed by the passenger when he selects that mode of travel. Missouri, K. & T. Ry. Co. v. Schroeder, 100 S. W. Rep. 808.

" An instruction, in an action for injuries to a passenger on a freight train, that a carrier owes to its passengers the duty to exercise the highest degree of diligence known to diligent persons engaged in like business, does not require too high a degree of care in the carriage of passengers on freight trains." Southern Ry. Co. v. Burgess (Ala. 1905), 42 So. Rep. 35.

" It is the duty of a railroad company, when it carries passengers in the car attached to a local freight train, to use the highest possible degree of care to protect the passengers to which such train is susceptible, considering its construction, equipment, and use as a carrier of freight." Chicago, etc., Ry. Co. v. Ralston (Kan. 1908), 93 Pac. Rep. 592.

" In taking passage on a freight train, a passenger assumes the usual risks incident to traveling on such trains when managed by prudent men in a careful manner." Marable v. Southern Ry. Co. (N. C. 1906), 55 S. E. Rep. 355.

" A carrier must exercise such reasonable diligence for the safety of a passenger as the nature of the business allows." Chaffe v. Consolidated Ry. Co. (Mass. 1907), 82 N. E. Rep. 497.

" It is a carrier's duty to use a very high degree of care to safely transport its passengers, doing all that human care, vigilance, and foresight can reasonably do, in view of the character and mode of conveyance adopted, consistent with the practical operation of its cars." Chicago City Ry. Co. v. Shreve, 80 N. E. Rep. 1049; 226 Ill. 530.

[65] Texas, etc., R. Co. v. Miller, 79 Texas 78; 15 S. W. Rep. 264; Central, etc., R. Co. v. Perry, 58 Ga. 461; 16 Am. Ry. Rep. 122.

In duties touching the convenience or accommodation of passengers, waiting at the ordinary place of departure, to take a train, the carrier is held only to ordinary care and diligence.[66]   A carrier is only held to reasonable or ordinary care to prevent an injury to a passenger by the accidental falling of baggage from a car truck or rack, and not to a higher degree of care in providing safe means of transportation.[67]   And so, likewise a carrier is only answerable for a want of ordinary care or caution in preventing injuries to one passenger by another, and not to the utmost care, which is required in the construction of the railroad track or the management of the train, for the care of the passenger who may cause such an injury or the regulation of his conduct is not within the control of the carrier, except in so far as it may expel him for conduct which would constitute him a trespasser.[68]

§ 585. Carrier only held to ordinary care, in England.— The rule in the United States that the carrier of passengers is held liable to the highest degree of care, does not obtain in England, but in that country the carrier, like others against whom negligence is charged, is answerable only for a want of ordinary or reasonable care, or such care as reasonably prudent persons in the same business would exercise, under the same or similar circumstances.[69]

[66] Central, etc., R. Co. v. Perry, 58 Ga. 461; 16 Am. Ry. Rep. 122.

[67] Morris v. New York, etc., R. Co., 106 N. Y. 678; 13 N. E. Rep. 455, reversing 36 Hun 647. See, also, Keep v. Indianapolis, etc., R. Co., 3 McCrary (U. S.) 208; 9 Fed. Rep. 625.

[68] Buck v. Manhattan R. Co., 32 N. Y. S. R. 51; 10 N. Y. Supp. 107.

"Ordinary care under the circumstances must be exercised by a carrier of passengers at all times, whether during transit, at stations, upon platforms, or in waiting rooms." Pomroy v. Bangor & Aroostook R. Co. (Me. 1907), 67 Atl. Rep. 561.

[69] Metropolitan R. Co. v. Jackson, L. R. 3 App. Cas. 193; Withers

In one English case,[70] where a passenger was injured by
a derailment caused by an unusually hard rain, which washed
out the roadbed, and the question was presented whether or
not, by reasonable care, the carrier should have anticipated
the rain and guarded the track, accordingly, the court held
that the carrier, like any other reasonably careful person,
was only bound to anticipate that which could be known by
the exercise of ordinary care and diligence and if a reasonably prudent man, under the same circumstances could not
be held negligent, in not foreseeing the rain storm and guarding against its consequences, then the carrier could not be
held answerable for an injury due to such a cause.   This
case may be said to fairly present the law of England on
this subject, and other cases under various other circumstances connected with the cause of the injury, present the
law in the same way.[71]

§ 586. **Duty toward sick or insane passengers.**— Persons
who are ill have the same right to be carried by a passenger
carrier that those in good health have to insist upon being
transported by such carriers and a carrier has no right to
refuse to transport a person merely because of the illness of
such a person offering himself to be carried by the carrier,
for this would be inconsistent with the general duties toward
the public, which the law annexes to the business of such
public carriers.[72]

v. North Kent R. Co., 27 L. J. (Exch.) 3; Bird v. Great Northern R.
Co. (by Pollock, C. B.), 28 L. J. (Exch.) 3.

[70] Withers v. North Kent R. Co. (by Bramwell, B.), 27 L. J.
(Exch.) 417.

[71] Great Western R. Co. v. Baird, 1 Moo. P. C. C. (N. S.) 101.   But
the rule *res ipsa loquitur* is held to apply, in England, as well as in
the United States, in the case of an injury to a passenger in a collision.
Carpue v. London, etc., R. Co., 5 Ad. & El. (N. S.) 751; 3 Thompson
on Negligence, §§ 2744 and 2745, and cases cited.

[72] Pullman Palace Car Co. v. Barber, 4 Colo. 344.

But passenger carriers are not held answerable to sick persons for any greater degree of care than they owe other passengers offering themselves to be carried, but the increased risks of a journey, in so far as they arise from the passenger's condition of health, and the passenger's fitness for the journey, as ordinarily conducted, must be assumed by the passenger, especially where no notice of the condition of the passenger is specially brought home to the employees or agents of the carrier.[73]

.The law does not require a passenger carrier to receive and carry an insane, or drunken person, or one with an infectious disease, or whose physical or mental condition is such that his presence may cause injury or discomfort to other passengers and the carrier may rightfully refuse to carry such persons.[74] Nor is it compelled to accept disabled or sick persons, traveling without an attendant or nurse, where due care toward such persons would require an attendant or nurse to properly look after the welfare of such a passenger.[75] Where the carrier voluntarily accepts such a person as a passenger,

"In the exercise of care commensurate with the circumstances and danger to be apprehended, a railway company is required to give greater attention to its aged and infirm passengers than to passengers of younger years and greater physical capacity. The fact that a man was so old and feeble as to require the assistance of a conductor and others to enter one of its cars and be placed in a seat, coupled with his request to the conductor that the latter afford him sufficient time to alight, is notice to an interurban railway company which will render it liable for starting its car without affording him reasonable time to alight in safety." Toledo, etc., Traction Co. v. McFall, 28 Ohio Cir. Ct. R. 362.

[73] Pullman Palace Car Co. v. Barber, 4 Colo. 344.

[74] Thurston v. Union Pacific R. Co., 4 Dill. (U. S.) 321; Meyer v. St. Louis, etc., R. Co., 54 Fed. Rep. 116; 10 U. S. App. 677; 4 C. C. A. 221; 58 Am. & Eng. R. Cas. 111; Pearson v. Duane, 4 Wall. (U. S.) 605. And the same rule applies as to a drunken passenger. Pittsburg, etc., R. Co. v. Van Dyke, 57 Ind. 576; 18 Am. Ry. Rep. 454.

[75] Croom v. Chicago, etc., R. Co., 52 Minn. 296; 53 N. W. Rep. 1128.

however, if special care is necessary to be bestowed for the protection of such a person, the carrier will be held negligent if it fails to bestow such care and in case of the injury to such a passenger, by the neglect of this additional duty, made necessary because of the physical condition of the passenger so accepted, the carrier would be liable in damages therefor[76]

§ 587. ·Care toward women and children.— While a railroad company is required to bestow the highest degree ·of care and caution toward all its passengers, without regard to who they are, it must not be understood that the carrier owes precisely the same care to all of its passengers, without respect

[76] Croom v. Chicago, etc., R. Co., *supra.*

" A carrier knowingly accepting as a passenger a person physically unable to take care of herself, must render to her such special assistance as her condition requires, so that she may be safely transported." Williams v. Louisville & N. R. Co. (Ala. 1907), 43 So. Rep. 576.

" A carrier is bound to render reasonable assistance to a passenger whose inability to take care of himself is made known to the carrier." Horn v. Southern Ry. (S. C. 1907), 58 S. E. Rep. 963.

Persons so infirm as to be unable to care for themselves, who travel on railroad trains, must provide assistance and it is not the duty of the employees of the carrier, in the absence of positive instructions to that effect, to render such assistance. Louisville, etc., R. Co. v. Fleming, 14 Lea (Tenn.) 128; 18 Am. & Eng. R. Cas. 347; New Or-. leans, etc., R. Co. v. Statham, 42 Miss. 607; Sheridan v. Brooklyn, etc., R. Co., 36 N. Y. 39.

When advised of a passenger's dimness of vision, it is the duty of the carrier to use such care in putting the passenger off, as to prevent his injury. Columbus, etc., R. Co. v. Powell, 40 Ind. 37.

If an unattended passenger becomes unconscious, sick, or insane it is the carrier's duty to put him off the train, and provide for his care, until he is able to continue the journey. Atchison, etc., R. Co. v. Weber, 33 Kansas 543; 6 Pac. Rep. 877; 21 Am. & Eng. R. Cas. 418; Indianapolis, etc., R. Co. v. Pitzer, 109 Ind. 179; 58 Am. Rep. 387; 25 Am. & Eng. R. Cas. 313; Croom v. Chicago, etc., R. Co., 52 Minn. 296; 53 N. W. Rep. 1128; Meyer v. St. Louis, etc., R. Co., 54 Fed. Rep. 116; 10 U. S. App. 677; 4 C. C. A. 221.

to the age, sex or bodily infirmity of the passenger, for although the degree of care toward all is the same, what would be proper care to bestow upon a healthy male adult would not be such care as would be due to one physically less able to care for himself or herself, such as a child of tender years, or a female of feeble health.[77]   Hence, it is that the measure of care in such cases which the carrier is required to bestow upon passengers of feeble health or small children, who are not able to look out for their own protection, is greater than is required in other cases where no such physical disability exists, and the law recognizes on the part of the employees of the carrier, a higher duty toward such persons than it does toward healthy male passengers of years sufficient to enable them to protect themselves, and if women of feeble health or children are permitted to go into places of danger without proper assistance, the carrier will be liable, whenever it has notice of the danger to such persons, during the relation of passenger and carrier.[78]

§ 588. **Care toward intoxicated passengers.**—While the carrier is held to the same high degree of care toward a drunken passenger that it owes to a sober passenger, it is held in a New York case,[79] that no higher degree of care is required to be bestowed upon the one than upon the other. The law does not compel a carrier to place a guard over a passenger who voluntarily becomes intoxicated, to prevent

[77] St. Louis, etc., R. Co. v. Finley, 79 Texas 85; 15 S. W. Rep. 266.

[78] Cleveland, etc., R. Co. v. Manson, 30 Ohio St. 451.

Notice to the conductor of a train that a passenger is feeble and will need assistance in leaving the train, is sufficient notice to the carrier of this fact, and it is not necessary to notify all other conductors that may take charge of the train, or all other employees in charge thereof, of the fact. Foss v. Boston, etc., R. Co. (N. H.), 47 Am. & Eng. R. Cas. 566.

[79] Milliman v. New York, etc., R. Co., 66 N. Y. 642; 4 Hun 409; 6 T. & C. 585.

him from injuring himself, or placing himself in a place of danger.[80]

And if the railroad company's employees do not know that a passenger has been drinking, they are only bound to use toward him that care and caution to prevent his injury that they would be compelled to bestow upon a sober passenger.[81]

But a degree of intoxication that would render a passenger unconscious, or incapable of caring for himself, when brought home to the carrier, would impose the duty of caring for the passenger, or looking after his present protection or comfort, and for a failure to adopt reasonable precautions for the protection of such a passenger, the carrier would be liable.[82]

And if a passenger is riding upon the platform of a car in such a state of intoxication as to be careless of the danger to which he is exposed, it is the duty of the carrier, after notice of the fact to its employees, to use ordinary precautions for his safety, such as calling his attention to his danger and the rules of the railroad company forbidding such exposure and inviting him to enter the car and for a failure to discharge such duty, in case of the injury to such a passenger, the company would be liable.[83]

However, in case of an injury to an intoxicated passenger, in leaving the train, if his intoxication interfered at all with his care in leaving the train, or lessened his prudence in getting off, and this effect, however slight, contributed to pro-

[80] St. Louis, etc., R. Co. v. Carr, 47 Ill. App. 353.

[81] Strand v. Chicago, etc., R. Co., 67 Mich. 380; 34 N. W. Rep. 712; 31 Am. & Eng. R. Cas. 54.

[82] Atchison, etc., R. Co. v. Weber, 33 Kansas 543; 6 Pac. Rep. 877; 21 Am. & Eng. R. Cas. 418.

[83] Fisher v. West Virginia R. Co. (W. Va.) 19 S. E. Rep. 578; 58 Am. & Eng. R. Cas. 337; McClelland v. Louisville, etc., R. Co., 94 Ind. 276; 18 Am. & Eng. R. Cas. 260.

duce his injury, he is not entitled to recover from the railroad company therefor.[84]

§ 589. **Duty to employ competent employees.**— The negligence for which a carrier is responsible to a passenger, includes that of its employees and for a want of skill on the part of the employees or any incompetency that effects an injury to a passenger, the carrier is liable.[85] The railroad company is responsible for the unskillfulness or incompetency of its employees, and in case of an injury to a passenger by an incompetent conductor, the railroad company is liable [86] and it not only engages with passengers, for the competent skill of its employees, in the first instance, but for the faithful and continued application of skill and competency.[87]

[84] Strand v. Chicago, etc., R. Co., 67 Mich. 380; 34 N. W. Rep. 712; 31 Am. & Eng. R. Cas. 54.

As to the carrier's right to expel an intoxicated passenger, see Vinton v. Middlesex R. Co., 11 Allen (Mass.) 304; Atchison, etc., R. Co. v. Weber, 33 Kansas 543; 6 Pac. Rep. 877; 21 Am. & Eng. R. Cas. 418. ·

"A passenger's intoxication at the time he was injured by being thrown from the train was not material unless it contributed to the injury." Midland Valley R. Co. v. Hamilton (Ark. 1907), 104 S. W. Rep. 540.

"A carrier receiving a helpless, imbecile, or drunken person as a passenger, when unattended, owes him a duty commensurate with his condition, and must give him such care as will insure a safe passage to some proper destination, and cannot lawfully put him off or permit him to get off at a place where there is danger of his perishing or coming to harm, even though such place would be reasonably safe for one in a normal condition." Sullivan v. Seattle Electric Co. (Wash. 1906), 86 Pac. Rep. 786.

[85] Grand Rapids, etc., R. Co. v. Boyd, 65 Ind. 526.

[86] Alexander v. Louisville, etc., R. Co., 83 Ky. 589; 25 Am. & Eng. R. Cas. 458.

[87] Gillenwater v. Madison, etc., R. Co., 5 Ind. 339; Montgomery, etc., R. Co. v. Mallette, 92 Ala. 209; 9 So. Rep. 363; International, etc., R. Co. v. Halloren, 53 Texas 46; 37 Am. Rep. 744; 3 Am. & Eng. R. Cas. 343.

But while the law exacts of railroad companies, carrying passengers for hire, the employment of ordinarily skillful and competent employees and agents, it is not bound to engage only employees of extraordinary skill in the business of railroading and in an action by a passenger for an injury while being transported by a railroad, a charge to the jury that the company was liable if it failed to employ men of extraordinary care, skill and diligence in the business is erroneous, as placing too great a degree of care on the part of the carrier.[88]

§ 590. **Negligence of employees.**— The duty of the carrier is to protect the passenger as far as possible from danger, through the efforts of the carrier or its employees. The employees of the railroad company stand in its place and all their acts, so far as they are connected with the duty which the carrier owes to the passenger, are regraded in the same light as those of the carrier itself.[89]

The carrier cannot exonerate itself from liability for an injury to a passenger, caused by the negligence of its own employees, by showing that they acted through mistake, but it is liable for any injury due to the neglect or carelessness of its employees, resulting in an injury to a passenger.[90]

[88] Gadsden, etc., R. Co. v. Causler, 97 Ala. 235; 12 So. Rep. 439; 58 Am. & Eng. R. Cas. 258.
"Though the obligation of a carrier is not that of an insurer, it must exercise the highest degree of care, and is bound to protect its passengers from the negligence of its employees." Louisville & N. R. Co. v. Moulder (Ala. 1906), 42 So. Rep. 742.

[89] Chicago, etc., R. Co. v. Flexman, 9 Ill. App. 250; Kansas City, etc., R. Co. v. Saunders, 98 Ala. 293; 13 So. Rep. 57; 58 Am. & Eng. R. Cas. 140; Louisville, etc., R. Co. v. Ballard, 85 Ky. 307; 3 S. W. Rep. 530; 7 Am. St. Rep. 600; 28 Am. & Eng. R. Cas. 135; Nashville, etc., R. Co. v. Messino, 1 Sneed (Tenn.) 220; Hanson v. Mansfield, etc., R. Co., 38 La. Ann. 111; 58 Am. Rep. 162.

[90] Gillenwater v. Madison, etc., R. Co., 5 Ind. 339; Baltimore, etc.,

And in case of an injury to a passenger, due to the negligence of an employee of the carrier, the carrier is liable, although the employee was not acting strictly within the line of his duties, as same were delegated to him by the employer, for in such case a distinction is recognized between the status of a passenger and a mere licensee, and if the employee was acting within the scope of his employment, the carrier would be liable for an injury negligently inflicted, although the employee causing the injury was not strictly within the line of his duty at the time of the commission of the wrongful act.[91]

But while responsible for the acts of their employees within the scope of their employment, in case of an injury to a passenger, railroad companies are not liable for the acts of employees of other companies, carried on their trains, under an arrangement whereby certain duties are rendered to their employers, and transportation furnished by the railroad company, for in case of the negligent injury of a passenger, due to a wrongful act of a person, such as a postal clerk, not in the employ of the carrier, the carrier would not be responsible, unless it or its employees acted in concert with such a person in causing the injury, as the rule of *respondeat superior* is confined to acts done by the employees or agents of the superior.[92]

R. Co. v. Blocher, 27 Md. 277; Gillingham v. Ohio River R. Co., 35 W. Va. 588; 14 S. E. Rep. 243; 14 L. R. A. 798; 51 Am. & Eng. R. Cas. 222.

[91] Lakin v. Oregon, etc., R. Co., 15 Oregon 220; 15 Pac. Rep. 641; 34 Am. & Eng. R. Cas. 500; Grand Rapids, etc., R. Co. v. Ellison, 117 Ind. 234; 20 N. E. Rep. 135; 39 Am. & Eng. R. Cas. 480; Terre Haute, etc., R. Co. v. Jackson, 81 Ind. 19; 6 Am. & Eng. R. Cas. 178.

[92] Muster v. Chicago, etc., R. Co., 61 Wis. 325; 21 N. W. Rep. 223; 49 Am. Rep. 41; 18 Am. & Eng. R. Cas. 113; Poling v. Ohio River R. Co., 38 W. Va. 645; 18 S. E. Rep. 782. Nor is the carrier liable for the wrongful act of a stranger. Chicago, etc., R. Co. v. Scates, 90 Ill. 586; Thomas v. Philadelphia, etc., R. Co., 148 Pa. St. 180; 23 Atl. Rep. 989; Reibel v. Cincinnati, etc., R. Co., 114 Ind. 476; 17 N. E. Rep. 107;

§ 591. **Negligence of strangers — Missile thrown through window.** — The courts, while placing the highest degree of care on the carrier of passengers, will not adopt a construction that will render the carrier liable for the wrongful acts of strangers, unless the carrier was negligent in failing to discover the wrongful act on the part of the third person, in time to have avoided the injury to its passengers, for any less rule would make the carrier liable regardless of the question of its negligence and render it practically an insurer of the safety of its passengers.[93]

In an Indiana case,[94] the carrier is held not responsible to a passenger who is injured by another person, on alighting from its train, running against the passenger and throwing him under the train, and a like rule is applied to one injured. by having a door in the carrier's station shut against his hand by the wrongful act of a stranger in the station.[95]

And where a passenger on a train, sitting near the car window, was injured by a missile, the nature and origin of which was unknown and there was nothing to connect the accident with any defect in the vehicles or appliances of the carrier, or any negligence on the part of its employees, there can be no recovery against the railroad company.[96]

Graeff v. Philadelphia, etc., R. Co. (Pa.), 28 Atl. Rep. 1107; 58 Am. & Eng. R. Cas. 431.

[93] Fredericks v. Northern, etc., R. Co., 157 Pa. St. 103; 27 Atl. Rep. 689; 58 Am. & Eng. R. Cas. 91.

[94] Reibel v. Cincinnati, etc., R. Co., 114 Ind. 476; 17 N. E. Rep. 107.

[95] Graeff v. Philadelphia, etc., R. Co. (Pa.), 28 Atl. Rep. 1107; 58 Am. & Eng. R. Cas. 431. And see, also, Ellinger v. Philadelphia, etc., R. Co., 153 Pa. St. 215; 25 Atl. Rep. 1132; 58 Am. & Eng. R. Cas. 429.

[96] Thomas v. Philadelphia, etc., R. Co., 148 Pa. St. 180; 23 Atl. Rep. 989.

"In an action for injuries to a passenger by a missile coming through an open car window, plaintiff's evidence was that the missile entered through an open window on the side next to a passing freight train; that it was a bolt with a nut on the end of it, and

§ 592. Inevitable accident or act of God.— A carrier of passengers is not obliged to foresee and provide against casualties which have not been known to occur before and which may not be reasonably expected to happen again. If it has availed itself of the best known and most extensively used appliances as safeguards against danger, it has done all that the law requires and its liability is not to be ascertained by what appears for the first time after the disaster to be a proper precaution against its recurrence, but by what was to have been anticipated by judging the future by the past, before the occurrence of the casualty.[97]

that such bolts were largely used in constructing ordinary freight cars, while, on the other hand, there was evidence that the missile was thrown through an open window on the opposite side of the car by one of several boys who were pelting the train as it went by them. *Held*, that the evidence as to whether the missile came from a source for which the carrier was responsible was insufficient to justify a verdict against it, and that a verdict should, therefore, have been directed in its favor." Pennsylvania R. Co. v. McCaffrey (U. S. C. C. A., N. J. 1907), 149 Fed. Rep. 404.

"A railroad company is bound to use extraordinary care to protect its passengers from violence or outrage by third persons, which protection must be afforded by the conductor to the extent of all the power with which he is clothed by the company or by the law." Hillman v. Georgia R. & Banking Co., 56 S. E. Rep. 68; 126 Ga. 814.

"A carrier is not liable for injuries to a passenger from the conduct of third persons on the station premises, unless it knew of the existence of the danger or of circumstances from which the danger might have been reasonably anticipated." Taylor v. Atlantic Coast Line R. Co. (S. C. 1907), 59 S. E. Rep. 641.

"While a carrier is not an insurer of its passenger's safety, it is its duty to use extraordinary care to protect a passenger from injuries by third persons, and it is bound to use extreme caution to anticipate an injury to a passenger by third persons or fellow passengers." Grimsley v. Atlantic Coast Line R. Co. (Ga. App. 1907), 57 S. E. Rep. 943.

"A carrier of passengers must exercise a high, if not the highest, degree of diligence to protect its passengers from employees, fellow passengers, and strangers." St. Louis, I. M. & S. Ry. Co. v. Hatch (Tenn. 1906), 94 S. W. Rep. 671.

[97] Higgins v. Cherokee R. Co., 73 Ga. 149; 27 Am. & Eng. R. Cas.

Railroad companies are not responsible for mere accidents or misadventures, any more than for the act of God, or the public enemy, or for any sudden convulsion of nature, or an unknown or unforeseen destruction, or an unknowable insufficiency in some part of the track or roadbed. Before they will be liable for injuries from such sources, there must be, in addition to such a cause of accident, some want of diligence or foresight, or some actual negligence on the part of the railroad company or its employees, contributing to effect the injury.[98]

Illustrative of this rule of law, it is held that a railroad company is not liable for an injury to a passenger, caused by the derailment of a train, due to the sudden breaking of a sound rail, caused by the extreme cold, which no amount of foresight could foresee would cause such an injury.[99] Nor is the carrier to anticipate or guard against storms of such extraordinary and unusual violence as have not, within practical experience, been known in the locality where the storm occurred.[1] And in anticipating such accidents it is held that the carrier is not bound to the highest degree of foresight but only to such care as an ordinarily prudent man would use under the same or similar circumstances.[2]

But in the case of an injury to a passenger by the derailment of a train, or such like cause, the passenger makes a *prima facie* case on establishing the injury and the accident causing the same, and before the railroad company can escape liability therefor, it must appear that the accident happened from causes beyond its control, and to which neither its own negligence nor that of its employees or the

218; Murphy v. Atlanta, etc., R. Co., 89 Ga. 832; 15 S. E. Rep. 774.
[98] Sawyer v. Hannibal; etc., R. Co., 37 Mo. 240.
[99] McPadden v. New York, etc., R. Co., 44 N. Y. 478.
[1] Connelly v. Manhattan R. Co., 68 Hun (N. Y.) 456.
[2] Gillispie v. St. Louis, etc., R. Co., 6 Mo. App. 554.

manufacturer of its appliances contributed, or otherwise it will be held responsible for the injury.[3]

[3] Carroll v. Staten Island R. Co., 58 N. Y. 126; 65 Barb. 32; 7 Am. Ry. Rep. 25.

"A common carrier of passengers must exercise the utmost care, diligence, and foresight of a very cautious person, and is responsible for any injury to a passenger except that occasioned by inevitable casualty or some other cause which human foresight could not prevent." Kline v. Santa Barbara Consol. Ry. Co. (Cal. 1907), 90 Pac. Rep. 125.

"Plaintiff, while riding in the caboose of a freight train, was injured by a derailment of the train. The train had previously encountered a hard rain, with high winds, and at the place where it was wrecked it encountered a cyclone which passed over the right of way; its path extending from 250 to 400 yards in width and 7 or 8 miles in length. The cyclone unroofed, wrenched from their foundations, and destroyed houses, and its force stopped the train, wrenched and lifted the cars from their trucks, and hurled one of them a distance of 150 feet into a field beyond, and when it struck the ground whirled it around like a top. Only the engine and three heavy iron-tanked oil cars remained on the track. *Held*, that the wreck was the result of an act of God, for which the carrier was not responsible." Galveston, etc., Ry. Co. v. Crier (Tex. Civ. App.), 100 S. W. Rep. 1177.

In Sullivan v. Ry. Co., 133 Mo. 1, a damage suit was brought by plaintiff, a passenger on one of defendant's street cars, because a fellow passenger carelessly threw a lighted match on her dress and she was seriously burned thereby. No such accident, it seems, had ever occurred on *a car before*. And it was ruled that the defendant was not guilty of negligence on account of the occurrence mentioned, because *it could not have been foreseen* that *such an accident would have occurred*, and therefore, could not have been provided against, the court remarking: "Nor could it be expected that the proprietor of this car on a summer day would have anticipated that one of its passengers would be burned in this way. The most prudent man would never have thought of such an accident, nor have furnished such a car in such weather with fire extinguishers."

CHAPTER XXII.

THE ROADBED AND TRACK.

§ 593. **Duty regarding generally.** — A railroad company, in engaging in the business of a common carrier of passengers, undertakes that its track and roadbed is in good traveling order and fit for use and if an injury results to a passenger from an imperfection of the track or roadbed, the railroad

910

company will be liable, unless the imperfection was of a character in no degree attributable to its negligence.[1]

The duty applies generally to the company's roadbed, track and culverts and in the construction of the track and bridges, railroad companies engaging in the business of carrying passengers are held to that degree of care and foresight which will avoid such dangers as can be reasonably foreseen, or ascertained by competent and skillful engineers, as liable to result from rainfalls and freshets, incident to the particular locality through which the railroad is constructed.[2]

The standard of care and diligence required as to the track and roadbed of the carrier does not depend upon the pecuniary condition of the railroad company or the amount of its revenues, but the law exacts of the carrier, regardless of the remunerative character of its business, the duty of providing a track, roadbed and appliances reasonably safe for the business in which it is engaged, and which will protect the lives and limbs of the persons which it agrees to transport, with a reasonable degree of safety,[3] and, indeed, anything less would be to leave the lives of persons in the hands of the reckless and unprotected against the negligent and incautious.[4]

[1] Nashville, etc., R. Co. v. Messino, 1 Sneed (Tenn.) 220; Sullivan v. Philadelphia, etc., R. Co., 30 Pa. St. 234; Pennsylvania R. Co. v. McKinney, 124 Pa. St. 462; 37 Am. & Eng. R. Cas. 153; Gonzales v. New York, etc., R. Co., 39 How. Pr. (N. Y.) 407.

[2] Libbey v. Maine Central R. Co., 85 Me. 34; 26 Atl. Rep. 943; 58 Am. & Eng. R. Cas. 81; International, etc., R. Co. v. Halloren, 53 Texas 46; 37 Am. Rep. 744; 3 Am. & Eng. R. Cas. 343.

[3] Taylor v. Grand Trunk R. Co., 48 N. H. 304.

[4] Tuller v. Talbot, 23 Ill. 357; Ingalls v. Bills, 9 Metc. (Mass.) 1, 15; Bowen v. Railroad Co., 18 N. Y. 410; Libbey v. Maine Central R. Co., 85 Me. 34; 26 Atl. Rep. 943; 58 Am. & Eng. R. Cas. 81.

The same duty which requires the carrier to provide safe cars, engine and other appliances, necessitates the construction and maintenance of safe roadbed, track, cross-ties, rails, bridges, culvert and other arrangements for the safe running of the cars and engines. Palmer v.

§ 594. **Degree of care required.**— Carriers of passengers are required to use the utmost human sagacity and foresight, in the construction of their roads, tracks, bridges and other arrangements, to prevent accidents to their passengers [5] and they are held to the most exact care in the repair and care of their track and bridges, to the end that the lives of persons who entrust themselves to their care may be safeguarded as far as possible.[6]

The railroad company is bound to furnish for its passengers a reasonably safe and sufficient track and equipments, and to maintain them in a reasonably safe condition, so far as can be provided by the utmost human skill, diligence and foresight, and it is liable to a passenger for slight negligence in this respect, causing injury.[7]

The carrier is also held to the utmost care in the removal of obstructions and the repair of its bridges and switches and all other matters properly pertaining to the safety and condition of its track.[8]

While the railroad company is not an insurer of the safety of its passengers, it is bound to use a high degree of skill and

Delaware, etc., R. Co., 46 Hun 488; 120 N. Y. 170; 30 N. Y. S. R. 817; Seybolt v. New York, etc., R. Co., 95 N. Y. 562; McCafferty v. Pennsylvania R. Co., 193 Pa. St. 339; 44 Atl. Rep. 435; McAfee v. Vicksburg, etc., R. Co., 42 La. Ann. 790; 7 So. Rep. 720; Persching v. Chicago, etc., R. Co., 71 Iowa 561; 32 N. W. Rep. 488.

The impoverished condition of the road was held to be no defense to a suit of a passenger for injury from a defective roadway, in Hansley v. Jamesville, etc., R. Co., 115 N. C. 602; 117 N. C. 565; 23 S. E. Rep. 443. 32 L. R. A. 543.

[5] Union, etc., R. Co. v. Hand, 7 Kansas 380; 1 Am. Ry. Rep. 548; Kansas, etc., R. Co. v. Miller, 2 Colo. 442; 20 Am. Ry. Rep. 245; Searle v. Kanawha, etc., R. Co., 32 W. Va. 370; 9 S. E. Rep. 248; 37 Am. & Eng. R. Cas. 179.

[6] Baltimore, etc., R. Co. v. Noell, 32 Gratt. (Va.) 394; Virginia, etc., R. Co. v. Sangor, 15 Gratt. (Va.) 230.

[7] St. Louis, etc., R. Co. v. Mitchell. 57 Ark. 418; 21 S. W. Rep. 883.

[8] Carrico v. West Virginia, etc., R. Co., 35 W. Va. 389; 14 S. E. Rep. 12; 52 Am. & Eng. R. Cas. 393.   .

vigilance to guard against accidents, and a latent defect which will relieve it from liability is such only as no reasonable degree of skill and foresight could guard against or discover.[9]

The company owes a higher duty to its passengers than mere ordinary care, in the maintenance and construction of its tracks; it is bound to exercise the highest degree of practicable care, not the utmost possible precaution that might be imagined, but the highest care and best precautions known to practical use, and which are consistent with the mode of transportation adopted.[10]

§ 595. Inspection of track.— It is an essential part of the legal obligation of a carrier toward its passengers, to exercise due care to discover, by inspection and examination, a defect in its railroad track,[11] and it is bound to keep itself informed as to the condition of its track and to know whether

[9] Palmer v. Delaware, etc., Co., 120 N. Y. 170; 46 Hun 486; 11 N. Y. S. R. 872; 24 N. E. Rep. 302; 44 Am. & Eng. R. Cas. 298.

[10] Southern Kansas R. Co. v. Walsh, 45 Kansas 653; 26 Pac. Rep. 45; 47 Am. & Eng. R. Cas. 493.

"The keeping of railroad tracks in such a condition that the trains can be operated over them in the usual and customary way in which the same are operated is not the test of the degree of care required of the railroad, but it is bound to the highest degree of care in keeping its tracks in condition for the operation of its trains." St. Louis, etc., R. Co. v. Boyer (Tex. Civ. App. 1906), 97 S. W. Rep. 1070.

For approved instruction holding the carrier liable for failure to use the highest practical degree of care, skill and diligence in furnishing safe roadway, track and embankments, but not for the highest degree of care the human mind can conceive of, nor such care as would render the transportation of passengers absolutely without risk, or such as would drive the carrier out of business, see Railroad Co. v. Crumpley, 122 Fed. Rep. 425; 59 C. C. A. 51.

[11] Furnish v. Missouri Pacific Ry. Co., 102 Mo. 438; 13 S. W. Rep. 1044; International, etc., R. Co. v. Halloren, 53 Texas 46; 37 Am. Rep. 744; 3 Am. & Eng. R. Cas. 343.

or not it is in a fit condition for the safe passage of its trains.[12]

It is the duty of the railroad company to furnish a safe roadway or as safe as due prudence can make it, and for this purpose to keep all portions of its track in repair and so watched and tended as to insure the safety of all persons who may be upon the trains operated by such company, in so far as proper care and prudence may safeguard its passengers and this is a continuing duty owing by the railroad company to its passengers.[13]

In order to be assured that its line of road is in a reasonably safe condition, the railroad company must make frequent inspections of its roadbed and track, such as can be consistently done with the conduct of its business [14] and under circumstances of more than ordinary peril to its passengers, the carrier should inspect its track with more than ordinary promptitude, at such places as are most liable to injury by storm or flood.[15]

Every portion of the track, exposed to flood, or known to be likely to sustain damage thereby, ought to be examined after every storm, before a train carrying passengers is allowed to pass over such portion of track and if this is not done and an injury to a passenger results by a derailment of a train, the railroad company would be held liable for negligence.[16]

Nor would it be a defense by a railroad company, sued by a passenger who had sustained injury on account of a defective track, for it to show that the track looked to be in a

[12] Toledo, etc., R. Co. v. Apperson, 49 Ill. 480.

[13] East Tennessee, etc., R. Co. v. Gurley, 12 Lea (Tenn.) 46; 17 Am. & Eng. R. Cas. 568.

[14] Libby v. Maine Central R. Co., 85 Me. 34; 26 Atl. Rep. 943; 58 Am. & Eng. R. Cas. 81.

[15] Libby v. Maine Central R. Co., *supra.*

[16] Hardy v. North Carolina R. Co., 74 N. Car. 734.

good or safe condition, for it is' the duty of the company to exercise care and skill to discover defects in its track, regardless of whether the track looked all right or not. In other words, it is not excused in acting on mere appearances, but must show diligence to discover defects.[17]

§ 596. **Care such as used by cautious persons.** — The rule is

[17] Chicago, etc., R. Co. v. Lewis, 145 Ill. 67; 33 N. E. Rep. 960; 58 Am. & Eng. R. Cas. 126. But, see where rail broke from frost and this defect was not apparent, but rail looked all right, on inspection and this was held to be a defense. Missouri Pacific Ry. Co. v. Johnson, 72 Texas 95; 10 S. W. Rep. 325; 37 Am. & Eng. R. Cas. 128.

In Chicago, etc., R. Co. v. Lewis (145 Ill. 67; 33 N. E. Rep. 960; 58 Am. & Eng. R. Cas. 126), Shope, J., speaking for the court, said: "It is next insisted that the court erred in refusing the eleventh instruction asked by appellant. This instruction was properly refused, for the reason that it told the jury that if the track was 'apparently' good and safe, and the train was in charge of an experienced engine driver and conductor, and was well and carefully managed, appellant was not liable. It is not enough that the track was 'apparently' in good and safe condition. If there were defects rendering it unsafe, which by the exercise of care and skill, might have been discovered, it was the duty of appellant to have discovered them, and thus to have avoided danger to its passengers."

But speaking for the Supreme Court of Texas, Gaines, J., in Missouri Pacific Ry. Co. v. Johnson (72 Texas 95; 10 S. W. Rep. 325; 37 Am. & Eng. R. Cas. 128), said, in regard to the inspection of a rail broken by a sudden frost: "If the break in the rail caused the injury and was a sudden fracture, brought about by cold weather, which the company did not have time to discover, and if defects in the track did not contribute to it, then the company was not liable, provided the rail, before the accident, was such as a person of competent skill might reasonably presume, upon inspection, to be free from liability to fracture." The railroad company, however, was held liable, upon a remittitur of exemplary damages.

The liability of a railroad company for an injury to a passenger applies as well to a track *leased* by it, and which it is using with its trains, as to a railroad track owned by it, and it is in duty bound to inspect the one, just as often as it would be the other. Wisconsin, etc., R. Co. v. Ross, 142 Ill. 9; 31 N. E. Rep. 412; 43 Ill. App. 454; 53 Am. & Eng. R. Cas. 73; Philadelphia, etc., R. Co. v. Anderson, 94 Pa. St. 351; 39 Am. Rep. 787; 6 Am. & Eng. R. Cas. 407.

announced in a number of cases, that in the care of the roadbed and track and the culverts and bridges of a railroad used
for the conveyance of passengers, the railroad company is
bound to furnish a reasonably safe and sufficient track and
equipments so far as can be provided by the utmost human
skill, diligence and foresight, which is such care and skill
as is exercised by a very cautious person under like circumstances.[18]

In a Missouri case,[19] where an instruction had been given
by the trial court in practically the language of the above
paragraph, the measure of care it imposed on the railroad
company was approved by the Supreme Court, in an opinion
by Judge Barclay, wherein the following language was used:
" When a passenger commits his person to a carrier for hire
for transportation by railroad, over rivers, across mountains,
through cities, in the night — it may be while asleep, at a
speed expressive of the progress of the age in which we live,
he may justly demand the exercise of such care on the part
of the carrier, against disaster, as in the nature of things
such undertaking would imply. That degree of care has
generally been defined in language such as was used in the
instruction before us."

Of course if a railroad company should fail to employ competent and skilled engineers and surveyors to construct its
track, or to keep it in repair, after its construction, so as to
avoid such dangers as might reasonably be apprehended, it
would not be fulfilling the full measure of its duty toward

18 Leslie v. Wabash, etc., R. Co., 88 Mo. 50; Dougherty v. Missouri,
etc., R. Co., 97 Mo. 647; 11 S. W. Rep. 251; 8 S. W. Rep. 900; 81
Mo. 325; 51 Am. Rep. 239; Pennsylvania R. Co. v. Roy, 102 U. S.
451; White v. Boston, etc., R. Co., 136 Mass. 321; Pennsylvania, etc.,
R. Co. v. Anderson, 94 Pa. St. 351; Caldwell v. Steamboat Co., 47
N. Y. 282; Miller v. Steamship Co., 118 N. Y. 200.

19 Furnish v. Missouri Pacific Ry. Co., 102 Mo. 438, 451; 13 S. W.
Rep. 1044.

the traveling public, as declared in the adjudicated cases on this duty owing to the passenger, and where freshets or rain-falls are apt to wash out the track or roadbed this must be anticipated and guarded against, or a liability will be held to result from an injury to a passenger from such a cause.[20]

§ 597. **Care in selecting materials.**— While a railroad company must do all that human care, vigilance and fore-sight can reasonably accomplish, consistent with the practical operation of its road, in providing safe tracks and roadbed for the use of its trains, it does not absolutely insure its pas-sengers against injury and though liable for an injury to a passenger, due to its negligence, it is not responsible for an accident due to a hidden defect in materials that have been used for cross-ties or rails, if the defect could not, by the ex-ercise of a very high degree of care and diligence, have been detected.[21]

The carrier is therefore held to exercise a sufficient degree of care in the selection of plans and materials for the con-struction of its track and roadbed, if it selects such plans and materials as are in general use and have been found suffi-cient, in the past, by the best and most skillfully conducted railroads.[22]

§ 598. **Liability for injuries caused by defective track.**— The carrier is responsible for accidents caused by a defective railroad track, in case of an injury to a passenger.[23]   It is the legal duty of the passenger carrier to have a good, sub-stantial and safe roadway and track for the use of the trains,

[20] Libbey v. Maine Central R. Co., 85 Me. 34; 26 Atl. Rep. 943.

[21] St. Louis, etc., R. Co. v. Moore, 14 Ill. App. 510.

[22] Pershing v. Chicago, etc., R. Co., 71 Iowa 561; 32 N. W. Rep. 488; 34 Am. & Eng. R. Cas. 405.

[23] Wisconsin, etc., R. Co. v. Ross, 142 Ill. 9; 31 N. E. Rep. 412; 43 Ill. App. 454; 53 Am. & Eng. R. Cas. 73.

and in case of a default in this duty, in consequence of which
a passenger sustains an injury, this will be sufficient evidence
of negligence to justify a verdict for damages in favor of the
injured passenger.[24]

Where two railroad tracks are constructed so close together that on account of the sunken rail in one of the tracks,
the cars on the two tracks, in passing each other, are liable
to collide and in consequence of such an accident, a passenger
is injured, the railroad company will be held liable.[25]

But a railroad company is only required to furnish for the
use of its trains, a reasonably good track and not one that is
perfectly safe, for this would make of it an absolute insurer.[26]   The railroad company, however, is bound to the
exercise of a high degree of care to maintain its track and
roadbed in a reasonably safe condition for the use of its passenger trains, and while a passenger assumes the risk of
injury due to the particular mode of conveyance in which
he takes passage, a passenger on a freight train has the same
right to expect a reasonably safe track and roadbed that a
passenger on a regular passenger train has.[27]

[24] Florida, etc., R. Co. v. Webster, 25 Fla. 394; 5 So. Rep. 714.

[25] Gray v. Rochester City R. Co., 61 Hun 212; 15 N. Y. Supp. 927;
40 N. Y. S. R. 715.

[26] Pattee 'v. Chicago, etc., R. Co., 5 Dakota 267; 38 N. W. Rep. 435;
34 Am. & Eng. R. Cas. 399.

[27] Ohio Valley R. Co. v. Watson (Ky.), 21 S. W. Rep. 244; 58
Am. & Eng. R. Cas. 418.

"The testimony of a passenger that his and three other cars left
the track suddenly and turned over, injuring him, shows a defect
in the rails, or wheels of the cars, at the time of the accident, and
requires the carrier to explain the accident in order to escape liability."
Brown v. Yazoo, etc., R. Co. (Miss. 1906), 41 So. Rep. 383.

Where the rails of a track are displaced by a wrongdoer, not in any
way connected with the railroad company, just before the arrival of a
train, to cause a wreck, the company is not liable. Deyo v. New
York, etc., R. Co., 34 N. Y. 9; Baltimore, etc., R. Co. v. Herold, 74
Md. 510; 22 Atl. Rep. 323; 14 L. R. A. 75.

§ 599. **Negligence presumed from defective roadway.**— In a Pennsylvania case,[28] it was adjudicated that where a casualty occurs, by reason of any defect in the roadway of a railroad company, resulting in the injury of a passenger, the presumption of negligence arises against it and to escape the legal consequences of such presumption it is incumbent on the railroad company to show that it was free from negligence causing the injury.

A similar exposition of the law was applied in a Missouri case wherein Judge Gantt, speaking for the Supreme Court,[29] said: " When the passenger suffers injury by the breaking down or overturning of the coach, the *prima facie* presumption is, that it was occasioned by some negligence of the carrier and the burden is cast upon the carrier to rebut and establish that there has been no negligence on its part and that the injury was occasioned by inevitable accident or by some cause which human precaution and foresight could not have averted."

A derailment occurring from some defect in the roadway was considered by the Arkansas Supreme Court,[30] with reference to the rule *res ipsa loquitur,* and it was also held to apply to such an injury, the court saying: " The mere fact that the appellee was injured, without more, was not suf-

[28] Clow v. Pittsburg Traction Co., 27 Atl. Rep. 1004.

[29] Clark v. Chicago, etc., R. Co., 127 Mo. 208; 29 S. W. Rep. 1013; citing Furnish v. Missouri Pacific Ry. Co., 102 Mo. 348; 13 S. W. Rep. 1044; Lemon v. Chanslor, 68 Mo. 340.

[30] St. Louis, etc., R. Co. v. Mitchell, 21 S. W. Rep. 883. See, also, on this presumption, in this class of accidents, Holbrook v. New York, etc., R. Co., 12 N. Y. 236; Arkansas, etc., R. Co. v. Timmonds, 51 Ark. 459; 40 Am. & Eng. R. Cas. 698; Little Rock, etc., R. Co. v. Hopkins, 54 Ark. 213; Sullivan v. Pennsylvania R. Co., 30 Pa. St. 239; Central, etc., R. Co. v. Freeman, 75 Ga. 338; Berry v. Missouri Pacific Ry. Co., 124 Mo. 224, covering over 100 pages; 25 S. W. Rep. 229; Philadelphia, etc., R. Co. v. Anderson, 44 Am. & Eng. R. Cas. 345; Kansas City, etc., R. Co. v. Stoner, 52 Am. & Eng. R. Cas. 462; Louisville, etc., R. Co. v. Miller (Ind.), 58 Am. & Eng. R. Cas. 304.

ficient to raise a presumption of negligence on the part of the railway company. But the derailment of the car, and its overturning, and the injury to appellee thereby, being in the usual course, a logical inference of negligence might be drawn therefrom; hence they were sufficient to cast upon the appellant the burden of proving that the injury was not caused by any want of care on its part. In such a case the maxim *res ipsa loquitur* applies."

§ 600. **Condition of rails and cross-ties.**— The duty of the carrier with reference to the condition of its rails and cross-ties, used to construct its track, has been specifically passed upon by one court, where the subject came before it and it was held that the carrier was under the legal duty to provide sound cross-ties and that the rails should be strong and securely laid and for an accident resulting from unsound cross-ties or insecure rails, the carrier would be liable to respond in damages.[31] It is also held, where the ties are unsound and the rails are insecurely fastened thereto, that the railway company will be held guilty of negligence, regardless of the fact that it establishes a recent inspection of its track. When such a condition exists, it is apparent that it ought to be disclosed by a reasonably careful inspection of the track and if it was not, the inspection would be no defense.[32]

It is also held to be negligence on the part of a railroad company to so lay its cross-ties and rails that the rails will be subject to displacement, caused by the expansion and contraction, by hot and cold weather.[33] A verdict will not be disturbed, where it is shown that rails of different lengths

[31] McFee v. Vicksburg, etc., R. Co., 42 La. Ann. 790; 7 So. Rep. 720.
[32] Chicago, etc., R. Co. v. Lewis, 145 Ill. 67; 33 N. E. Rep. 960; 58 Am. & Eng. R. Cas. 126.
[33] Reed v. New York, etc., R. Co., 56 Barb. (N. Y.) 493.

were used in the construction of a railroad track and short pieces of rails used at intervals, to supply rails of the ordinary length.[34] And where it was shown that rails of shorter lengths would not pass trains smoothly over the joints, unless so laid as to be liable in hot weather to displacement, then they should be so arranged as not to be subject to such displacement and rails of the proper length used, or this would enable an injured passenger to successfully charge the carrier with negligence.[35]

§ 601. **Care of embankments and cuts.**—Where the facts and circumstances connected with an accident on a railroad train, whereby a passenger is injured, show that it happened from a washing away of the roadbed, occasioned by the pressure of water against an embankment therein, the presumption of negligence arises against the railroad company and it will have the burden of showing that the washout was due to the act of God, or it will be liable for the injury.[36] The mere proof that a passenger was injured by reason of a part of an embankment being washed away, which was so constructed as not to resist the action of water, is, of itself proof of negligence sufficient to render the carrier liable.[37] Nor would this *prima facie* case be overcome or disproven or the company relieved of liability, in such a case, by establishing the fact that its railroad was constructed under the supervision of a competent and skilled engineer.[38]

The failure to construct the banks of a cut so that they will not slide, by reason of the action of ordinary causes or

[34] Florida, etc., R. Co. v. Webster, 25 Fla. 394; 5 So. Rep. 714.

[35] Reed v. New York, etc., R. Co., 56 Barb. (N. Y.) 493.

[36] Brehm v. Great Western R. Co., 34 Barb. (N. Y.) 256; Holbrook v. Utica, etc., R. Co., 12 N. Y. 236.

[37] Kansas Pacific R. Co. v. Lundin, 3 Colo. 94.

[38] Philadelphia, etc., R. Co. v. Anderson, 94 Pa. St. 351; 39 Am. Rep. 787; 6 Am. & Eng. R. Cas. 407.

sources and to properly inspect them, so as to prevent injury
by running trains along such banks, when in an unsafe condition, is also held to be such negligence as to entail a liability on the railroad company for an injury to a passenger,
caused by the banks of such a cut giving way to the action
of water.[39]   To allow a break in an embankment, caused
by a heavy rainfall, to remain open for ten hours without
placing a guard at or near the place to warn passing trains
of the danger, was also held to be negligence, in a North
Carolina case.[40]

And where the *prima facie* case of an injured passenger,
caused by a derailment due to an embankment giving way,
is sought to be explained by the railroad company, by showing
that the flood causing the washout resulted from an unusual
rainfall, it is generally held to be an issue for the jury to
determine whether or not the embankment was so constructed,
as in the light of the surrounding conditions it ought to have
been constructed.[41]

§ 602. **Failure to fence track.**— The police regulation of
many of the States, requiring railroad companies to fence
their tracks, is intended not only to prevent injury to stock
that may come upon the railroad track, but also for the protection of passengers and employees, by preventing the derailment of the train.[42]

[39] Gleeson v. Virginia Midland R. Co., 140 U. S. 435; 11 Sup. Ct.
Rep. 859; 47 Am. & Eng. R. Cas. 513.

[40] Hardy v. North Carolina R. Co., 74 N. Car. 734; 13 Am. Ry.
Rep. 121.

[41] Texas, etc., R. Co. v. Barron, 78 Texas 421; 14 S. W. Rep. 698;
Brehm v. Great Western R. Co., 34 Barb. (N. Y.) 256.

[42] Donegan v. Erhardt, 119 N. Y. 468; 42 Am. & Eng. R. Cas. 580;
Jones v. Seligman (N. Y.), 3 Am. & Eng. R. Cas. 236; Tracy v. Troy,
etc., R. Co., 38 N. Y. 433; 55 Barb. 529; Shepard v. Buffalo, etc., R.
Co., 35 N. Y. 641; Corwin v. New York, etc., R. Co., 13 N. Y. 42;
Graham v. Delaware, etc., Co., 46 Hun (N. Y.) 386; Buxton v. North-

It is held, in Wisconsin,[43] that one object of statutes imposing such a duty upon railroad companies is for the safety of passengers and that proof of the fact that a passenger was injured as a result of the failure on the part of a railroad company to fence its track, as required by statute, is sufficient proof of negligence to render the company liable.

And it is also held, in Indiana,[44] that the failure to fence, in case of a resulting injury to a passenger, establishes a *prima facie* case of negligence on the part of the railroad company and if the failure to fence is shown to have been the proximate cause of the injury, the right of the injured passenger to recover is clear and complete.

But this is not a universal rule and the duty to fence is held not to obtain, as to persons already on the line of the railroad, but only to apply to persons off the line of railroad, to prevent them from getting upon the track.[45] Accordingly, it is held, in one case,[46] that if a passenger, in

eastern R. Co., 3 Q. B. 549; Brown v. New York, etc., R. Co., 34 N. Y. 404; Lackawanna, etc., R. Co. v. Chenoweth, 52 Pa. St. 382; Sullivan v. Philadelphia, etc., R. Co., 30 Pa. St. 234; Riggs v. St. Francois, etc., R. Co., 120 Mo. App. 335; 96 S. W. Rep. 707.

[43] Blair v. Milwaukee, etc., R. Co., 20 Wis. 254.

[44] Louisville, etc., R. Co. v. Hendricks, 128 Ind. 462; 28 N. E. Rep. 58.

[45] Harrold v. Great Western R. Co., 14 L. T. 440.

[46] Harold v. Great Western R. Co., *supra*.

In Brown v. New York, etc., R. Co. (34 N. Y. 404), where a passenger was injured by a collision with cattle on the track, the court declared that as the railroad company was bound to use the highest degree of care and foresight to secure the safety of its passengers, they were entitled to have the statutory duty toward fencing the track, to keep cattle off the track, complied with.

And see, also, Fordyce, Receiver, v. Jackson, 56 Ark. 594; 20 S. W. Rep. 528; Texas, etc., R. Co. v. Thompson (Texas), 77 S. W. Rep. 439; Chicago, etc., R. Co. v. Elder, 149 Ill. 173; 36 N. E. Rep. 565; Indianapolis, etc., R. Co. v. Hendricks, 128 Ind. 462; 28 N. E. Rep. 58.

In Blair v. Milwaukee, etc., R. Co. (20 Wis. 254), it was held that proof of the fact that a passenger was injured by failure to fence the track and keep cattle off established a case entitling him to recover.

getting out of a carriage, which had stopped further away than the station platform, falls from an embankment to the roadway beneath, owing to the absence of a fence on the top of the embankment, the railroad company would not be liable for his injury.

§ 603. Duty to provide against ordinary rainfall.—In a Texas case,[47] it was held that a railroad company could not defend itself against a claim for damages resulting from insufficient water ways by showing that the flood which caused the injury had been of very infrequent occurrence; but that, in order to excuse itself, it must show that it was such an extraordinary flood as had not occurred in the locality in the memory of persons there living.

In Lackawanna, etc., R. Co. v. Chenoweth (52 Pa. St. 382), it was held that while the provision as to fencing the track was not enacted to protect passengers, the railroad company assumed all the risk of a failure to fence its track and an injured passenger could take advantage of its failure and establish negligence by proof of the fact.

But the rule is held in some cases, not to extend to employees, injured by a collision with cattle on the track, due to a failure to fence. Langlois v. Buffalo, etc., R. Co., 19 Barb. (N. Y.) 364; Cowan v. Union Pacific R. Co., 35 Fed. Rep. 43; Sweeny v. Central Pacific R. Co., 8 Am. & Eng. R. Cas. 151; Magee v. Northern Pacific R. Co., 78 Cal. 430; Prather v. Richmond, etc., R. Co., 80 Ga. 427.

In Missouri, the duty to fence is held to apply not only to adjoining owners, but for the benefit of the general traveling public also. Riggs v. St. Francois, etc., R. Co., 120 Mo. App. 353; 96 S. W. Rep. 707; Robinson, etc., R. Co. v. Railway, 57 Mo. 494; Jackson v. St. Louis, etc., R. Co., 43 Mo. App. 324.

" The object of the statute is to afford protection to private property, as well as to passengers on trains." Judge Henry, in Rozzelle v. Hannibal, etc., R. Co., 79 Mo. 351.

See, also, Madison v. Missouri Pacific Ry. Co., 60 Mo. App. 509; Dickson v. Omaha, etc., R. Co., 124 Mo. 140; 27 S. W. Rep. 476; 25 L. R. A. 320; 46 Am. St. Rep. 429; Atchison, etc., R. Co. v. Reesman, 60 Fed. Rep. 370; 9 C. C. A. 20; 23 L. R. A. 768; Oyler v. Quincy, etc., R. Co., 113 Mo. App. 375; 88 S. W. Rep. 162.

[47] Gulf, etc., R. Co. v. Pomeroy, 67 Texas 498; 3 S. W. Rep. 722.

This is likewise the holding of the United States Supreme
Court in a very able opinion,[48] wherein the rule is laid down
that a railroad company is required to so construct its roadbed and track as to avoid those dangers which it could be
reasonably foreseen by competent and skillful engineers might
result from the ordinary rainfall and freshets peculiar to the
particular section in which it is constructed. And a similar rule has been applied in those States where the question
has been adjudicated.[49]

§ 604. **Extraordinary floods.**— If railroad companies were
compelled, in the construction of their tracks and roadbeds,
to provide against the consequences of extraordinary storms
or floods it could, as remarked in one case,[50] with equal pro-

[48] Gleeson v. Virginia Midland R. Co., 140 U. S. 435; 11 Sup. Ct.
Rep. 859; 47 Am. & Eng. R. Cas. 513.

[49] Libby v. Maine Central R. Co., 85 Me. 34; 26 Atl. Rep. 943; 58
Am. & Eng. R. Cas. 81; International, etc., R. Co. v. Halloren, 53
Texas 46; 37 Am. Rep. 744; 3 Am. & Eng. R. Cas. 343.

In International, etc., R. Co. v. Halloren, *supra*, the accident resulted
from a washout, caused, as witnesses testified, by "the hardest rain
at and about the locality of the accident, which any of the witnesses
had ever seen in that part of the country." The defendant's section
boss had passed over the track but a short time before the accident
and found the track in safe condition. The accident occurred at night.
The court held that under this state of facts, the court should have
charged the jury that the company was not responsible, unless those
in charge of the train knew of the washout.

The liability for an accident due to the washing away of a culvert,
depends upon the question of due care in the construction of the
culvert, as held in Texas. Bonner v. Wingate, 78 Texas 333; 14 S. W.
Rep. 790. See, also, where the test of reasonable care was applied
to a track, in Pattee v. Chicago, etc., R. Co., 5 Dakota 267; 38 N. W.
Rep. 435.

Floods in a locality noted for heavy rains and floods, cannot be said
to be inevitable, so as to relieve a railroad company from resulting
damages. Cobb v. St. Louis, etc., R. Co., 149 Mo. 609; 50 S. W.
Rep. 894.

[50] Nashville, etc., R. Co. v. David, 6 Heisk. 261; Ellet v. St.

priety be required that they should provide against a flood, such as the deluge in the days of Noah.[51]   The law does not place such a hardship upon carriers of passengers, for this would be to make of them absolute insurers of the passengers' safety.

It is therefore not negligence on the part of a railroad company, in the construction of its track and roadbed, to fail to provide against such extraordinary and unprecedented floods, or other inevitable casualties, caused by the hidden forces of nature, unknown to common experience and which could not have been reasonably anticipated by that degree of engineering skill and experience required in the prudent construction of a railroad.[52]   Negligence can never be predicated of an act which could not, by reasonable care or foresight have been anticipated and negligence lies at the basis of the carrier's liability.[53]

A railroad company is not liable to a passenger for an injury caused by a train turning over, due to a defect in the track, caused by a violent storm, in the absence of proof that the engineer had reason to expect that the track was out of order and that he failed to test it.[54]   And if the real cause of the injury to a passenger is a sudden and unusual rain storm, which washed away the roadbed, the negligence of the carrier, which only remotely and indirectly

Louis, etc., R. Co., 76 Mo. 520; 12 Am. & Eng. R. Cas. 183; Pittsburg, etc., R. Co. v. Gilliland, 56 Pa. St. 445.

[51] No reported cases of damage suits growing out of this flood, have been called to the attention of the author.

[52] Libby v. Maine, etc., R. Co., 85 Me. 34; 26 Atl. Rep. 943; 58 Am. & Eng. R. Cas. 81.

[53] In such a case, says Bramwell, B., in Cornman v. London, etc., R. Co. (4 Hurl. & N. 781, 786), " it is always a question whether the mischief could have been reasonably foreseen. Nothing is so easy as to be wise, after the event."

[54] Ellet v. St. Louis, etc., R. Co., 76 Mo. 518; 12 Am. & Eng. R. Cas. 183.

contributed to the injury, will not establish a liability, nor can a liability be predicated upon the mere failure of the embankment to withstand a flood of water, shown to be unusual or extraordinary.[55]

It is generally a defense to an action shown to have resulted from an extraordinary flood, that the roadbed and track were inspected immediately, or a short time prior to the flood and that same were in good condition and that the accident followed in such a short time that another inspection or examination would not, in the exercise of due care, be due from the railroad company.[56] And if it appears, from the evidence of the plaintiff that the injury sued for was caused by an extraordinary flood, then the plaintiff is generally required to go further and show that the negligence of the railroad company combined with such cause to produce the injury, or that after the flood, by exercising due care, the accident could have been avoided.[57]

[55] Gillespie v. St. Louis, etc., R. Co., 6 Mo. App. 554.

[56] International, etc., R. Co. v. Halloren, 53 Texas 46; 37 Am. Rep. 744; 3 Am. & Eng. R. Cas. 343.

[57] Gillespie v. St. Louis, etc., R. Co., 6 Mo. App. 554.

Speaking of the effect on the defense of *vis major*, and the plaintiff's contention that the fact that the roadbed had been washed away by the flood or a "heavy" rain storm, was some evidence of negligence, as set forth in the instruction of the court, Judge Hayden, speaking for the St. Louis Court of Appeals, said: "It may be fairly said that any elevated embankment or roadbed of any kind, however well-built, would be liable to be washed away by a 'heavy flood' if the flood was heavy enough. The mere liability to be washed away thus predicable of every roadbed certainly cannot render immaterial the suddenness and overpowering force which the law puts as a risk upon the passenger." Gillespie v. St. Louis, etc., R. Co., 6 Mo. App. 560.

It is error to charge that bridges should be built so as to permit the safe passage of trains in time of high water, as this practically places the responsibility of an insurer on the carrier. San Antonio, etc., R. Co. v. Lynch (Texas), 55 S. W. Rep. 517; Stober v. St. Louis, etc., R. Co., 91 Mo. 509; 4 S. W. Rep. 389.

If sufficient time has elapsed following a flood which has washed

§ 605. **Duty as to bridges and trestles.**— The duty of a carrier of passengers is not discharged by the purchase from a reputable manufacturer, of the material used in the construction of its bridges, but it is also incumbent on the railroad company to carefully and skillfully test and inspect the materials before using them and to make constant inspections while the materials are in use.[58]

The railroad, however, must have some care or control over the bridge, before it will be held negligent in the use thereof and if a railroad company uses a bridge, which was built by the State, as a part of a highway, according to approved plans, prepared by skillful architects and officers of the State, this will not be held to be an appliance over which it has the right of control, so as to render it liable for an injury to one of its passengers, caused by a defect in the device for raising and lowering the bridge, which, although discoverable in the manufacture, was not apparent by ordinary observation.[59]

It is held, in an Illinois case,[60] that a passenger cannot recover damages for an injury sustained by the giving way of a trestle, where the evidence showed that the giving way of the trestle was due to an unprecedented or unusual rainfall just before the accident and there was a total absence of evi-

out a railroad bridge, to have enabled the railroad company to have placed a watchman near the bridge to prevent trains using it, the railroad company will be held liable for the negligence in failing to discover the wrecked bridge, the same as it would have been had its negligence originally occasioned the break in the bridge. Louisville, etc., R. Co. v. Thompson, 107 Ind. 442.

[58] Louisville, etc., R. Co. v. Snyder, 117 Ind. 435; 20 N. E. Rep. 284; 3 L. R. A. 434; 37 Am. & Eng. R. Cas. 137; Kansas Pacific R. Co. v. Miller, 2 Colo. 442; 20 Am. Ry. Rep. 245.

[59] Birmingham v. Rochester City, etc., R. Co., 137 N. Y. 13; 32 N. E. Rep. 995; 58 Am. & Eng. R. Cas. 134.

[60] Wabash, etc., R. Co. v. Koenigsam, 13 Ill. App. 505.

dence of negligence on the part of the railroad company, and a similar rule is announced in a Virginia case.[61]

In case of an injury to a passenger, caused by the breaking of a bridge or trestle, it is a question for the jury whether or not the railroad company engaged the services of a competent engineer who adopted the best methods and materials in the construction of the bridge. If the railroad company did this, it is not liable; but the mere fact that it engaged the services of such a person will not relieve it from the consequences of an accident due to a deficiency in the work.[62]

§ 606. **Inspection of bridges.**— Speaking of the duty of a railroad company to inspect its bridges, after an unusually high storm and flood, to prevent injury to a passenger — an expressman, injured by falling, with his car, through a bridge, which had been damaged by the storm — the Supreme Court of Missouri, in a recent case,[63] speaking through Judge Sherwood, used this language: " Here all the testimony shows, beyond dispute, that the bridge was unsafe; that the stream which it spanned was a turbulent and dangerous stream, subject to sudden floods, which frequently destroyed portions of the bridge; and that the only safe bridge which could be built at the location described in the

[61] Richmond, etc., R. Co. v. Moffett, 88 Va. 785; 14 S. E. Rep. 370.
[62] Grote v. Chester, etc., R. Co., 2 Exch. 251; 5 Railw. Cas. 649.
In the absence of evidence that the safety of a bridge may depend upon a single iron rod, it is error to charge the jury that a defect in such a rod that could not be discovered by a careful inspection would not establish negligence. Bedford, etc., R. Co. v. Rainbolt, 99 Ind. 551; 21 Am. & Eng. R. Cas. 466.
It is no defense to the presumption of negligence arising from a broken bridge and an injury to a passenger, that the most improved plans were followed in the construction of the bridge. Louisville, etc., R. Co. v. Pedigo, 108 Ind. 481; 8 N. E. Rep. 627; 27 Am. & Eng. R. Cas. 310. Nor is lack of funds to build a better bridge a defense. Oliver v. New York, etc., R. Co., 1 Edm. Sel. Cas. (N. Y.) 589.
[63] Cobb v. St. Louis, etc., R. Co., 149 Mo. 628; 50 S. W. Rep. 894.

pleadings, was one built after the manner heretofore described. And it was the plain duty of the defendant, in order to exercise ordinary care, to build a safe bridge at the point indicated; as defendant from long experience knew the dangerous character of the stream and its liability to sudden rises. Knowing these facts, knowing that a great rise had occurred in the stream the night before, and not knowing whether or not a heavy rain had fallen after that, between midnight and morning (although that was the fact), it was defendant's bounden duty to make examination of the bridge the next morning and ascertain, before it attempted to cross with its train load of people, that the bridge was not only safe in external appearance, but that a bent of the bridge had not been swept out the night before."

§ 607. **Care of switches.**— A railway switch which is either defectively constructed or out of repair, is necessarily dangerous to the lives of passengers transported over that portion of the railroad where the switch is located and where it must be used to regulate the movement of passenger trains, a company using such an appliance will be held guilty of such actionable negligence as to enable a passenger to recover damages, in case of injury sustained from such a cause.[64]

And where the railroad that owns and maintains the switch, permits the trains of another railroad company to use its tracks under a traffic arrangement, and the owner of the road employs the men who look after the switch, it will be liable for the injuries received by the passenger of the other railroad company, which used the track and switch for a consideration paid to the owner thereof.[65]

[64] Stodder v. New York, etc., R. Co., 50 Hun (N. Y.) 221; 19 N. Y. S. R. 772; 121 N. Y. 655.

[65] Stodder v. New York, etc., R. Co., *supra*.

" Where a passenger was injured as the result of a collision between a passenger train and a freight train standing on a siding resulting

§ **608. Derailment establishes prima facie case.** — Proof by a passenger of a derailment of a train on which he was riding together with a resulting injury, from such cause, is generally held to establish a *prima facie* case of negligence on the part of the carrier, in failing to maintain a reasonably safe track or roadbed.[66]

In one case,[67] where this question was adjudicated, the plaintiff, when within a mile of her destination, was injured as a result of a derailment of her train, the locomotive leaving the track and all the cars turning over on the side. The south rail, at the point where the locomotive left the track, was bent inwardly toward the north rail and a number of ties were broken off and splintered, some of them being rotten and decayed. On this common knowledge of the conditions usually accompanying such wrecks, it was held by the court that the plaintiff had established a *prima facie* case and that on failure on the defendant's part to satisfactorily explain the cause of the derailment, a recovery for the plaintiff would be permitted to stand, as the fact of the derailment and the condition of the railroad track showed evidence of the defendant's negligence in failing to maintain a reasonably safe track and roadbed. And this decision is but one of a large number affirming the same rule.[68]

from an open switch, the burden was on the carrier to prove that the collision was the result of some unavoidable accident." Southern Ry. Co. v. Brewer (Ky. 1907), 105 S. W. Rep. 160.

[66] Hipsley v. Kansas City, etc., R. Co., 88 Mo. 348; 27 Am. & Eng. R. Cas. 287; Breen v. New York, etc., R. Co., 109 N. Y. 297; Seybolt v. New York, etc., R. Co., 95 N. Y. 562. In Furnish v. Missouri Pacific Ry. Co. (102 Mo. 353), Judge Barclay, speaking for the court, said: "It might be more accurate to say, in proper form for the purposes of a jury trial, that the fact of the derailment of the car and of plaintiff's injury thereby, makes out a *prima facie* case of defendant's negligence, which unexplained, would justify a recovery."

[67] Furnish v. Missouri Pacific Ry. Co., 102 Mo. 348; 13 S. W. Rep. 1044.

[68] Logan v. Metropolitan R. Co., 183 Mo. 582; 82 S. W. Rep. 126;

§ 609. Landslide raises no presumption of negligence.—
The question whether or not a landslide upon a railroad
track, çausing a derailment of a train and resulting in an
injury to a passenger, would raise a presumption of negligence on the part of the railroad company was squarely

Smith v. Chicago, etc., R. Co., 108 Mo. 243; 18 S. W. Rep. 971; Olsen
v. Citizens Ry. Co., 152 Mo. 426; 54 S. W. Rep. 470; Malloy v. St.
Louis, etc., R. Co., 173 Mo. 75; 73 S. W. Rep. 159; Clark v. Chicago,
etc., R. Co., 127 Mo. 208; 29 S. W. Rep. 1013; Shouler v. Omaha, etc.,
Ry. Co., 87 Mo. App. 624; Gleeson v. Virginia Midland R. Co. (by
Justice Lamar), 140 U. S. 435, 445; 35 L. Ed. 458; Virginia Central
R. Co. v. Sanger, 15 Gratt. 237; Bennett v. Louisville, etc., R. Co.,
102 U. S. 577; 26 L. Ed. 235; McElroy v. Nashua, etc., R. Co., 4
Cush. 400; Kearney v. London, etc., R. Co., L. R. 6 Q. B. 759; Goodloe
v. Metropolitan R. Co., 120 Mo. App. 194; Mefford v. Missouri, etc.,
R. Co., 121 Mo. App. 647; Ohio & Mississippi R. Co. v. Voight, 122
Ind. 288.

"It is a sufficient allegation of negligence in an action for injury
to a passenger to allege that the train on which he was a passenger
was derailed." Galveston, etc., Ry. Co. v. Garcia (Tex. Civ. App.
1907), 100 S. W. Rep. 198.

"That a passenger was injured by the derailment of the locomotive,
caused by a collision with standing cars, cast the burden on the railroad company of showing that it exercised the highest · practicable
degree of care." Mitchell v. Chicago, etc., Ry. Co. (Iowa 1908), 114
N. W. Rep. 622.

"Where a passenger on a car was injured by the derailment of
the car, it raised a presumption of negligence on the part of the
carrier." Braun v. Union Ry. Co. (N. Y. Supp. 1906), 100 N. Y. S.
1012.

The fact of a derailment, together with an injury to a passenger,
was held to raise the presumption of negligence of the carrier, in the
following cases: Louisville, etc., R. Co. v. Miller, 141 Ind. 533; 37
N. E. Rep. 343; Cleveland, etc., R. Co. v. Newell, 104 Ind. 264; Albion,
etc., Co. v. DeNobra, 72 Fed. Rep. 739; 44 U. S. App. 347; 19 C. C. A.
168; 3 Am. & Eng. R. Cas. (N. S.) 564; St. Louis, etc., R. Co. v.
Mitchell, 57 Ark. 418; 21 S. W. Rep. 883; Atchison, etc., R. Co.
v. Elder, 57 Kansas 312; 46 Pac. Rep. 310; Chicago, etc., R. Co. v.
Zernecke, 59 Neb. 689; 82 N. W. Rep. 26; Louisville, etc., R. Co. v.
Jones, 108 Ind. 551; Seital v. Middlesex, etc., R. Co., 109 Mass. 398;
Alabama, etc., R. Co. v. Hill, 93 Ala. 514; 9 So. Rep. 722; 47 Am. &
Eng. R. Cas. 500; Higgins v. Hannibal, etc., R. Co., 36 Mo. 418;

considered by the Supreme Court of Pennsylvania,[69] and the conclusion was reached that no presumption would arise from an injury shown to be due to such a cause.

In considering this phase of the case, the court said: "Authority need scarcely be cited that where an injury occurs to a passenger in consequence of something done or not done, connected with the appliances of transportation, there arises the presumption of negligence, which the carrier is required to rebut. This presumption necessarily arises from the contract of carriage, under which the passenger passively trusts himself to the safety of the carrier's means of transportation, and to the skill, diligence and care of his servants, and by which the carrier, in consideration of the fare, undertakes to carry safely, and, to do so, to furnish the best means and appliances for the purpose, and competent, skillful and diligent servants. An accident connected with them

Dimmitt v. Hannibal, etc., R. Co., 40 Mo. App. 654; Meador v. Missouri, etc., R. Co., 62 Kansas 865; 61 Pac. Rep. 442; Andrews v. Chicago, etc., R. Co., 86 Iowa 677; 53 N. W. Rep. 399; 52 Am. & Eng. R. Cas. 252.

When in the trial of an action for damages by a passenger, it is shown that the injury was due to a derailment caused by a bad roadway, bridge, culvert, ties, rails or fastenings, the presumption of negligence obtains. Pershing v. Chicago, etc., R. Co., 71 Iowa 561; 32 N. W. Rep. 488; Arkansas, etc., R. Co. v. Griffith, 63 Ark. 491; 39 S. W. Rep. 550.

But even in the case of a broken trestle, if there is no negligence shown at the trial, or it appears that the accident was without neglect, no recovery can be permitted to stand. Wabash R. Co. v. Koenigsam, 13 Ill. App. 505; Houston, etc., R. Co. v. Norris (Texas), 41 S. W. Rep. 708.

[69] Fleming v. Pittsburg, etc., R. Co., 27 Atl. Rep. 858, distinguishing Sullivan v. Pittsburg, etc., R. Co., 30 Pa. St. 234; Gleeson v. Virginia, etc., R. Co., 140 U. S. 435; 35 L. Ed. 458; Spear v. Pennsylvania R. Co., 119 Pa. St. 68.

The same rule obtains as to snow slides in a section of the country where they have not been known before. Denver, etc., R. Co. v. Pilgrim, 9 Colo. App. 86; 47 Pac. Rep. 657; Colorado Midland, etc., R. Co. v. Andrews, 11 Colo. App. 205; 53 Pac. Rep. 518.

raises the presumption that they were not such and that the carrier was guilty of negligence. But if the accident has no connection with the appliances or machinery — if it is disconnected with the operation of the business of the carrier so as not to involve the safety or sufficiency of the instrumentalities, or the negligence of his servants — no such presumption arises, and the burden of proof to show negligence is upon the plaintiff, who avers it."

§ 610. **Landslide, due to ordinary rain.**— In a well-considered case [70] decided by Justice Lamar, of the United States Supreme Court, the injury to a postal clerk — held to occupy the same status as that of any other passenger — was due to a landslide which occurred in a railway cut, causing the partial derailment of the train. Defense was made by the railway company that the landslide was due to the act of God, in that it was a sudden slide, caused by the vibration of the train itself and by an unprecedented rainfall, that weakened the earth banks of the cut, which a short time before the accident were in a safe condition. Considering the evidence along with this defense, the court observed: "There was no evidence that the rain was of extraordinary character, or that any extraordinary results followed it. It was a common, natural event; such as not only might have been foreseen as probable, but also must have been foreknown as certain to come. Against such an event it was the duty of the company to have guarded. Extraordinary floods, storms of unusual violence, sudden tempests, severe frosts, great droughts, lightnings, earthquakes, sudden deaths and illnesses, have been held to be acts of God, but we know of no instance in which a rain, of not unusual violence, and the

70 Gleeson v. Virginia Midland R. Co., 140 U. S. 435, 445; 35 L. Ed. 458, 463.

probable results thereof, in softening the superficial earth, have been so considered. * * *

"This view of the obligation of the company, of course makes it immaterial that the slide was suddenly caused by the vibration of the train itself. It is not a question of negligence in failing to remove the obstruction, but of negligence in allowing it to get there."

But of course if the rainfall or other cause of the landslide occasioning the injury to the passenger had been of such unusual character as to have come within the definition of an act of God, the defense of the railway company, within the rule established by other decisions of the same court, would have obtained.[71]

§ 611. **Obstructions on or near the track.**— The duty of a railroad company to employ the utmost care and diligence in guarding the safety of its passengers creates the obligation to provide as far as extreme caution can do so, against obstructions on or near the track, by which injury is likely to result to the persons whom it transports.[72]

When a passenger is injured by any such obstruction along the line of the railroad, the burden is cast upon the railroad company to prove that the accident was the result of the plaintiff's own negligence, or that the most thorough and perfect diligence could not have foreseen and prevented the injury. Neither can the carrier relieve itself from liability in regard to the condition of its roadbed or track, by undertaking to confide these duties, which it owes, in law, to its passengers or to other agents or contractors, for this is one of

[71] Memphis, etc., R. Co. v. Reeves, 77 U. S. (10 Wall.) 176; 19 L. Ed. 909, 913; Gillespie v. St. Louis, etc., R. Co., 6 Mo. App. 564; McClary v. Sioux City R. Co., 3 Neb. 44; LeBarron v. East Boston Co., 11 Allen 316.

[72] Virginia, etc., R. Co. v. Sanger, 15 Gratt. (Va.) 230.

the nondelegable duties that the law will not permit the carrier to delegate to irresponsible parties.[73]

A passenger injured by a coal bin, constructed so near the railroad track, as to strike a passenger standing on a car step; [74] one injured by a piece of a railroad gate, projecting through a car window [75] and the case of a passenger sustaining injury by reason of the failure of the carrier to cut the timber or bushes alongside the track,[76] are familiar instances of the application of the rule of liability set forth in this section.

§ 612. **Rock falling on track.**— Under the rule requiring the carrier to keep the railroad track free from obstructions, the Supreme Court of Virginia [77] considered the liability of the railroad company for an injury to a passenger, caused by rock getting on the track, which had been piled up alongside the track, to be used as ballast. In the course of its opinion the court said: " Combining in themselves the ownership, as well of the road as of the cars and locomotives, they are bound to the most exact care and diligence, not only in the management of the trains and cars, but also in the structure and care of the track, and all the subsidiary arrangements necessary for the safety of the passengers. And as accidents as frequently arise from obstructions on the track, as perhaps from any other cause whatever, it would seem to follow, obviously, that there is no one of the duties

[73] Carrico v. West Virginia, etc., R. Co., 35 W. Va. 389; 14 S. E. Rep. 12; 52 Am. & Eng. R. Cas. 393.

[74] Dickinson v. Port Huron, etc., R. Co., 53 Mich. 43; 18 N. W. Rep. 553; 21 Am. & Eng. R. Cas. 456.

[75] Tyrrell v. Eastern R. Co., 111 Mass. 546.

[76] Louisville, etc., R. Co. v. Ritter, 85 Ky. 368; 3 S. W. Rep. 591; 28 Am. & Eng. R. Cas. 167.

[77] Virginia Central R. Co. v. Sanger, 15 Gratt. (Va.) 230. See, also, McElroy v. Nashua, etc., R. Co., 4 Cush. 400; Bennett v. Louisville, etc., R. Co., 102 U. S. 577; 26 L. Ed. 235.

of a railroad company more clearly embraced within its
warranty to carry their passengers safely, as far as human
care and foresight will go, than the duty of employing the
utmost care and diligence in guarding their road against such
obstructions."

§ 613. **Collision due to slippery rails.**— The Missouri
Court of Appeals, at Kansas City, recently had before it the
decision of a cause, wherein the railroad company set up as
a defense to the action of a passenger, for an injury due to
a collision, that the collision was caused by the slippery condition of its railroad track, which prevented the stopping of
the car in time to avoid the collision. The fact of the collision, with the accompanying injury to a passenger, was held
sufficient not only to carry the issue of negligence past the
trial judge, to the jury, but to raise a presumption of negligence which would become conclusive, in the absence of an
explanation thereof, consistent with right action on the part
of the carrier and the fact that the railroad track was slippery and that this condition may have contributed to the
collision, was held to be no excuse, since the railroad company, in the exercise of due care, as a cautious man in the
same business, ought to have anticipated such a condition and
used care to guard against it, in the management of its trains
or cars.[78]

§ 614. **Broken rail — When evidence of negligence.**— It
is held, in New York,[79] that a railroad company is not responsible for an injury to a passenger, due to a derailment of
a train, caused by the sudden breaking of a good, solid rail,
which would stand the test of a careful examination, where

[78] Goodloe v. Metropolitan R. Co., 120 Mo. App. 194, 200.
[79] McPadden v. New York, etc., R. Co., 44 N. Y. 478. See, also,
Beers v. Housatonic R. Co., 19 Conn. 566; Frink v. Potter, 17 Ill. 406.

the breaking of the rail was due to the extreme cold weather, and there was a total absence of evidence at the trial,to show any negligence whatever on the part of the railroad company, as the roadbed, track, ties and all the conditions of the track, immediately after the injury and derailment were found to be in first class condition.   A similar rule was announced in a Canadian case,[80] and it was held that there was no liability for a derailment of a passenger train, caused by the sudden breaking of a good, sound rail, properly laid down, on good solid ties and on a properly constructed roadbed, where the only reasonable explanation of the breaking of the rail was the sudden rise in the temperature and the extreme cold that prevailed immediately before the casualty.

But in order to relieve the railroad company, even in the case of the breaking of an otherwise sound rail, it ought to be shown that it was properly laid down and laid upon a properly constructed roadbed and upon solid or reasonably safe ties, for if a broken rail is found to have been improperly laid down,[81] or a defective rail spliced and laid upon a sharp curve, or a lighter rail substituted for a heavier rail, where good railroading would demand a rail of heavier weight, then this circumstance, coupled with the derailment and the injury to a passenger, would be sufficient evidence of negligence on the part of the railroad company, to send the case to the jury.[82]

[80] Canadian, etc., R. Co. v. Chalifoux, 22 Can. S. C. 721.

[81] Pittsburg, etc., R. Co. v. Williams, 74 Ind. 462; 3 Thompson on Neg., § 2811; McCafferty v. Pennsylvania, etc., R. Co., 193 Pa. St. 339; 44 Atl. Rep. 435.

[82] McCafferty v. Pennsylvania, etc., R. Co., 193 Pa. St. 339; 44 Atl. Rep. 435; Peoria, etc., R. Co. v. Reynolds, 88 Ill. 418.

A wreck caused by the sudden breaking of a good-looking railroad rail, calculated to stand the test of a proper examination, by cold weather, is not a cause for which the railroad company is liable in damages. Missouri, etc., R. Co. v. Johnson, 72 Texas 95; 10 S. W. Rep. 325.

§ 615. **Spread or bent rail, causing derailment.**— While a mere derailment of a railroad train, coupled with an injury due to such derailment by a passenger on such train, will ordinarily establish a *prima facie* case on the part of the passenger, sufficient to shift the burden of proof from the plaintiff to the defendant, or to justify a recovery on the part of the passenger for the injury sustained, in the absence of explanation of the derailment by the carrier, consistent with a cause for which it would not be responsible, if the evidence of the plaintiff goes further and shows the cause of the derailment and this develops to be due to a condition which would not render the railroad company liable, then the *prima facie* case of the plaintiff is overcome and the same result follows as to a right of recovery based upon a specific ground of negligence, which the evidence fails to establish.

This is illustrated by the recent decision of the Arkansas Supreme Court,[88] in the case of an injury to a passenger, caused by a derailment of the train on which he was riding. The plaintiff predicated a right of recovery upon the specific ground of negligence in permitting a spread or bent rail to remain in the railroad track, which occasioned the derailment of the train and the trial court, in its charge to the jury, told them that if they found that there was a spread or bent rail, at the time and place of the derailment that they might infer negligence from that fact and the burden of disproving it was then cast upon the defendant. This was held to be error, prejudicial to the railroad company, since it assumed that any spread or bend in the rail would be negligence, without regard to its sufficiency to cause the derailment of a car, or otherwise affect the safety of a train.

§ 616. **Duty to keep track in repair.**— Railroad companies are not liable for injuries resulting to their passengers from

[88] Arkansas Midland R. Co. v. Canman, 52 Ark. 517.

939

unexpected and unforeseen contingencies, which could not reasonably have been provided against, such as unprecedented storms, floods, or other inevitable casualties, caused by the hidden forces of nature, unknown to common experience and which could not reasonably have been anticipated by that degree of engineering skill required in the prudent construction of railroad tracks, [84] but a spell of wet weather, following an ordinary snow storm, does not come within this exception to the rule of liability and will not relieve the railroad company from an injury to a passenger from a failure to keep its roadbed in repair, after such an ordinary course of nature.[85]

And if a railroad track is permitted to remain out of repair and pieces of broken rails are used to supply the place of a defective rail, laid upon rotten ties and in running a train over such a defective track, at a speed of from twenty-five to thirty miles an hour, a wreck occurs, injuring a passenger, the carrier will be held liable for negligence in failing to keep its track in repair.[86]

§ 617. Care of double track roads.—Where a railroad company constructs a double track railroad and the rails are apt to be pushed out of position by the expansion caused by the heat or the cold, or by its custom of running the trains only one way over each of said double tracks, it is the duty of the railroad company to properly guard against this result, either by so fastening the rails to the cross-ties that

[84] Libbey v. Maine Central R. Co., 85 Me. 34; 26 Atl. Rep. 943; 58 Am. & Eng. R. Cas. 81.

[85] Missouri Pacific Ry. Co. v. Johnson, 72 Texas 95; 10 S. W. Rep. 325; 37 Am. & Eng. R. Cas. 128.

[86] Peoria, etc., R. Co. v. Reynolds, 88 Ill. 418; 21 Am. Ry. Rep. 324.

Upon evidence of subsequent repairs, as showing defective condition of track, on prior occasion, see Stewart v. Everts, 76 Wis. 35; 44 Am. & Eng. R. Cas. 313, and note and cases cited, on page 318.

they will not be pushed out of position, or by running the trains both ways on the same track.[87]

In a New York case,[88] a railway company was sued for an injury to a passenger, occurring on a double track railroad, caused by a derailment due to the rails becoming displaced. Some of the evidence, at the trial, tended to show that the displacement of the rails was caused by the expansion and contraction caused by heat and cold, while other evidence tended to show that the rails were shoved forward out of position, due to running the trains only one way over the track. The court held that it was immaterial which of these two causes may have contributed to bring about the condition of the track that existed at the time of the derailment and injury to the plaintiff, as either or both only showed a defective track, which might have been avoided by the defendant, by the exercise of a proper degree of care, and that it was liable for the injury to the passenger.

§ 618. **Acts of public enemy.**— Acts of a public enemy, which may result in the demolition of a railroad track or roadbed, causing injury to a passenger, when unmixed with some negligent act on the part of the railroad company, will not furnish the basis for a cause of action, on the part of the injured passenger, as railroad companies are not liable for acts of the public enemy,[89] any more than they are for mere accident, or misadventure, or some sudden convulsion of nature, or an unknown or unforeseen destruction of some part of the roadbed or track, to which no act of negligence, or any want of care or diligence has contributed.[90]

[87] Reed v. New York, etc., R. Co., 56 Barb. (N. Y.) 493.

[88] Reed v. New York, etc., R. Co., *supra*.

[89] Sawyer v. Hannibal, etc., R. Co., 37 Mo. 240.

[90] Libby v. Maine Central R. Co., 85 Me. 34; 26 Atl. Rep. 943; 58 Am. & Eng. R. Cas. 81; International, etc., R. Co v. Haloren, 53 Texas 46; 37 Am. Rep. 744; 3 Am. & Eng. R. Cas. 343.

In a suit by a passenger on a train, therefore, for injuries occasioned by the cars being thrown into a chasm, occasioned by the burning of a bridge, by the public enemy, during the late war,[91] where the agents and employees of the railroad were prevented from receiving notice of the fact of the defect in the road, by being driven off or overawed by the enemy, it was held proper for the trial court to instruct the jury that the railroad company would not be liable for the injury, unless its employees in charge of the train were negligent in failing to ascertain the damage to the bridge and the accident was caused by this neglect on their part.[92]

[91] This casualty occurred during the war of the rebellion, on September 3, 1861, by the burning of the bridge across the Platte River, in Buchanan County, Missouri.

[92] In the course of his opinion in Sawyer v. Hannibal, etc., R. Co. (37 Mo. 257), Judge Holmes, said: "It is clear from the evidence that there was no other defect or insufficiency in the bridge or the railroad than what arose from the fact that the bridge had been burned down by the public enemy, a few hours previous to the passing of the train. The accident happening solely in consequence of the bridge having been destroyed in this manner, it is plain that this is not what is ordinarily understood by a defect or insufficiency in a railroad. The question of negligence that was really in issue in this train, must be regarded as having reference solely and exclusively to the acts and conduct of the officer who had charge of the train upon that occasion."

CHAPTER XXIII.

§ 619. **Duty regarding generally.**— Passenger carriers are required to provide reasonable accommodations at their stations for passengers who have occasion to travel on their roads and to keep in a safe condition for the use of their patrons, all portions of their stations and platforms, to which the traveling public are invited, or to which they would naturally resort, as well as all portions of the station grounds, reasonably near to the platforms, where those taking trains, or being discharged therefrom, would ordinarily go.[1]

Platforms should be provided for the landing of passen-

---

[1] Stewart v. International, etc., R. Co., 53 Texas 289; 2 Am. & Eng. R. Cas. 497; Keefe v. Boston, etc., R. Co., 142 Mass. 251; 7 N. E. Rep. 874; 27 Am. & Eng R. Cas. 137. For injury to passenger from falling over mail sacks thrown on platform by mail clerk, see Sargent v. St. Louis, etc., R. Co., 114 Mo. 348; 21 S. W. Rep. 823.

gers leaving the carrier's trains and for those desiring to take the trains at the stations, and safe and proper means of ingress and egress to and from the trains, platforms and stations, and the approaches thereto, should be maintained.[2]

Railroad companies should so arrange their station grounds that passengers who get off the trains at the depots or places provided to alight, may leave the cars without danger and reasonably safe passageways or approaches should be provided leading to and from the station and platform, so passengers invited to get on or off the trains may do so without danger to life or limb.[3]

But the carrier is not bound to insure its passenger a safe exit from the depot or platform, across its right of way, until he shall have passed off of its property; it is required only to furnish a reasonably safe passageway to and from its trains and it is under no legal obligation to see personally to the safe exit or entry of its passengers, providing a reasonably safe way is provided for their use.[4]

[2] Moses v. Louisville, etc., R. Co., 39 La. Ann. 649; 2 So. Rep. 567; 30 Am. & Eng. R. Cas. 556.

[3] Central R. Co. v. Thompson, 76 Ga. 770; Knight v. Portland, etc., R. Co., 56 Me. 234.

[4] Central R. Co. v. Thompson, supra.

The failure to maintain reasonably safe waiting rooms, platforms and approaches thereto, by which passengers sustained injuries, was the ground of negligence set up, in the following cases: Dodge v. Boston, etc., Co., 148 Mass. 207; 19 N. E. Rep. 373; Gilmore v. Philadelphia R. Co., 154 Pa. St. 375; 25 Atl. Rep. 774; Archer v. New York, etc., R. Co., 106 N. Y. 589; 13 N. E. Rep. 318; Chewning v. Ensley R. Co., 100 Ala. 493; 14 So. Rep. 204; Pennsylvania R. Co. v. Marion, 123 Ind. 415; 23 N. E. Rep. 973; 7 L. R. A. 687; New York, etc., R. Co. v. Doane, 115 Ind. 435; 1 L. R. A. 157; Merwin v. Manhattan R. Co., 48 Hun 608; 113 N. Y. 659; Collins v. Toledo, etc., R. Co., 80 Mich. 390; Union Pacific R. Co. v. Evans, 52 Neb. 50; 71 N. W. Rep. 1062; Delaware, etc., R. Co. v. Trautwein, 52 N. J. L. 169; 19 Atl. Rep. 178; 41 Am. & Eng. R. Cas. 187; Christie v. Chicago, etc., R. Co., 60 Minn. 161; 63 N. W. Rep. 482; Philadelphia, etc., R. Co. v. Anderson, 72 Md. 519; 20 Atl. Rep. 2; 8 L. R. A. 673.

§ 620. **Degree of care required.**— A carrier of passengers by steam is required to exercise a very high degree of care in the maintenance of a safe roadway, track, cars, bridges and other appliances used in the transportation of its passengers, for such powerful engines of commerce entail the greatest hazard in their use, and the slightest negligence is apt to produce extreme peril; but the reason for the rule requiring such a high or extraordinary degree of care, ceases with the removal of the risk occasioning the rule itself and since depots or station grounds, in themselves, are no more dangerous places than other similar character of real property, the rule of law requiring the extreme degree of care in the safety of roadway, engines, cars and such appliances, does not apply with reference to the carrier's stations and approaches thereto, but the law is satisfied if such as are reasonably safe are provided for the use of passengers.[5] The passenger's detention at a station or his exit to his train is not attended with the same degree of hazard as the journey on the train and the duty of the carrier is lessened to that of a reasonable degree of care for the protection of its passengers at its stations or on its station grounds.[6]

But at a station where a great many trains are daily passing, as this would render the approaches to the station very dangerous, the railroad company will be held remiss in the performance of its duty, if it fails to adopt any precautions to prevent injury to passengers from passing trains.[7] The law requires of the carrier that its passengers shall have the benefit of reasonable care for their protection, while on its station grounds, and that they shall not be exposed to a peril of which it was or ought to have been aware, and if the carrier is remiss in this duty for the protection of its passen-

[5] Taylor v. Pennsylvania R. Co., 50 Fed. Rep. 755.

[6] Moreland v. Boston, etc., R. Co., 141 Mass. 31; 6 N. E. Rep. 225.

[7] Wallace v. Wilmington, etc., R. Co. (Del.), 18 Atl. Rep. 818.

II—8

gers at its stations, and the injury results from a cause which could reasonably have been anticipated as likely to produce injury, the carrier will be liable for damages.[8]

§ 621. **Waiting rooms for passengers.**— Where the business of a carrier is of sufficient importance, at a given station, to justify the same, waiting rooms for passengers should be maintained, in a reasonably safe and comfortable condition for the use of the passengers.[9] A passenger injured as a result of a failure, on the carrier's part, to maintain its station in a reasonably safe condition, is entitled to recover damages therefor.[10] Thus, one injured by falling, or being thrown, by a defective and dangerous door mat, which had been dangerous for some time, placed in front of a station door, where a passenger was apt to use it, was held

[8] Carpenter v. Boston, etc., R. Co., 97 N. Y. 494; 49 Am. Rep. 540; 21 Am. & Eng. R. Cas. 331.

The company was held liable for a failure to use *reasonable care*, only in the maintenance of stations and grounds, in the following cases: Kelly v. Manhattan R. Co., 112 N. Y. 443; 20 N. E. Rep. 383; 3 L. R. A. 74; Robertson v. Wabash R. Co., 152 Mo. 382; 53 S. W. Rep. 1082; Moreland v. Boston R. Co., 141 Mass. 31; 1 N. E. Rep. 909; Pennsylvania R. Co. v. Hammill, 56 N. J. L. 370; 29 Atl Rep. 151; 24 L. R. A. 531; Chicago, etc., R. Co. v. Scates, 90 Ill. 586.

But this rule is not of universal application and it is held in the following cases that the same degree of care is required in the maintenance of safe grounds and depots that is required in the case of roadway, tracks and trains, etc.: Franklyn v. Southern R. Co., 85 Cal. 63; Johns v. Charlotte, etc., R. Co., 39 So. Car. 162; 17 S. E. Rep. 698; 20 L. R. A. 520; Gulf, etc., R. Co. v. Butcher, 83 Texas 309; 18 S. W. Rep. 583; Missouri, etc., R. Co. v. Wortham, 73 Texas 25; 10 S. W. Rep. 741. The reason of the rule and the weight of authority, however, are as stated in the text.

[9] "A railroad must maintain its stations and platforms in a reasonably safe condition for passengers taking passage on its trains or coming to the stations for that purpose." Cincinnati & T. P. Ry. Co. v. Giboney (Ky. 1907), 100 S. W. Rep. 216.

[10] 3 Thompson on Negligence, § 2683, and cases cited.

entitled to recover for such an injury.[11] A passenger injured by the use of a defective chair in a waiting room, where the defect in the chair had continued for a time sufficient to charge the railroad company with notice of the defect, was also held entitled to recover therefor.[12] And the railroad company will be liable for the communication of an infectious disease, such as smallpox, by the presence of the germs of such a disease in its waiting rooms, where passengers are required to wait for their trains.[13] Nor could the carrier avoid the responsibility for an unsafe and dangerous waiting room, by the fact that it was leased from another company, which had obligated itself to maintain the same in a safe condition for the use of the lessee's passengers, for having invited its passengers to enter such a station, the law would create a corresponding obligation on the carrier, to maintain it in a reasonably safe condition.[14]

But a carrier will not be liable in the absence of a defective condition of its station, superinduced by its negligence,

[11] "A railroad company which is negligent in maintaining a defective door mat at its depot is liable for injuries sustained by a person who is injured by being caught and thrown by such mat, though the injured person was not a passenger, but came to the depot to bid a departing passenger good-bye." Galveston & S. A. Ry. Co. v. Matzdorf (Tex. Civ. App. 1908), 107 S. W. Rep. 882.

[12] Texas, etc., R. Co. v. Humble, 97 Fed. Rep. 837.

[13] "A carrier is liable in damages for the communication of smallpox by a ticket agent to a passenger buying tickets from him, where the agent knows he is infected." Missouri, K. & T. Ry. Co. v. Raney (Tex. Civ. App. 1907), 99 S. W. Rep. 589.

[14] "Where a carrier held out a station as a proper place for its passengers to go for the purpose of taking its cars, and the passengers had the right to regard themselves as having come to the station by its invitation, the carrier, though not controlling the station, but using it for his own benefit under an agreement with a lessee thereof, was liable to the passengers for injuries caused by defects in the rules regulating the use of the station, rendering the details of the agreement with the lessee inadmissible." Kuhlen v. Boston, etc., Ry. Co. (Mass. 1907), 79 N. E. Rep. 815.

or want of ordinary care and the mere fact that a passenger
sustains an injury by the sudden shutting of the doors of a
station waiting room, where the doors are not in a dangerous
or defective condition, will not render the carrier liable for
such an injury.[15] And where the doors opening from a
waiting room are labeled, respectively, " Basement " and
" Toilet," a passenger who through mistake opens the door
to the basement, thinking he is going into the toilet room, as
a result of which he falls down the stairs into the basement
and sustains injury, cannot recover, since there is no negligent act on the part of the carrier, as a basis of the cause of
action, but the injury is due to the passenger's own mistake in entering the wrong door.[16]

§ 622. **Failure to heat waiting room.**—Not only by the
common law, but by statutes, in many States, railroad companies are required to keep their waiting rooms heated in
cold weather, so as to avoid injury to passengers required to

[15] " In an action against a carrier for injuries, plaintiff alleged that
while passing through the doors of defendant's station, which were
opened in the usual manner, 'said doors, without notice or warning
to plaintiff, suddenly closed, and plaintiff was crushed between the
same,' and that she suffered certain specified injuries. *Held*, that the
petition does not state a cause of action, as there is no allegation that
the injuries resulted from defendant's negligence, and there is no necessary presumption of negligence from the facts stated." Rawson v.
Kansas City Ry. Co. (Mo. App. 1908), 107 S. W. Rep. 1101.

[16] " Where doors in a passenger waiting room were respectively labeled
'Basement' and 'Toilet,' and plaintiff, a passenger, intending to enter
the toilet, by mistake opened the basement door, and was injured by
falling downstairs, the door and stairs being necessary for the convenient use of the station, the carrier was not negligent in failing to
keep the door locked." McNaughton v. Illinois Cent. R. Co. (Iowa
1907), 113 N. W. Rep. 844.

The fact that plaintiff was injured by a screw eye, in a station door,
which was used to fasten the door back, did not establish that the
door was negligently constructed. Graeff v. Philadelphia, etc., R. Co.
(Pa.), 28 Atl. Rep. 1107; 58 Am. & Eng. R. Cas. 431.

wait for their trains.[17]   Where the weather is sufficiently cold to require a fire in a waiting room, a failure to maintain such fire, or to cause the room to be comfortably heated, will render the carrier liable in case of an injury to a passenger as a result of the failure to heat the waiting room, in accordance with the duty on the part of the carrier.[18]

A railway company has been held liable for a severe cold, contracted by a passenger, as a result of waiting in an insufficiently heated waiting room.[19]   If the condition of the waiting room is the proximate cause of the contraction of pneumonia, by a passenger, the carrier will be held liable therefor,[20] and where it can be shown that the cause of a passenger going into consumption was naturally and prob-

[17] "Under Ky. St. 1903, § 784, providing that railroad companies shall keep their waiting rooms comfortably warm in cold weather, and also at common law, railroad companies are liable for any injuries sustained because of failure to maintain a fire in the waiting room, if necessary to make it comfortable." Cincinnati, etc., Ry. Co. v. Mounts (Ky. 1907), 104 S. W. Rep. 748.

[18] *Ante idem.* "In an action against a carrier, evidence *held* sufficient to show that illness experienced by a passenger was due to defendant's negligence, whereby the passenger was exposed to inclement weather, owing to a station being closed and to her being compelled to wait in an insufficiently heated waiting room." International, etc., R. Co. v. Johnson, 95 S. W. Rep. 595.

[19] "In an action by a passenger, it appeared that when she was admitted to the waiting room her train was due by schedule in a few minutes, and that she had not been advised that the train was late, or, if late, that she could assume that it would not arrive at any time. The train did not arrive for an hour, and she contracted an illness owing to the lack of a fire in the station. *Held,* that the fact that every other passenger in the party of which plaintiff was a member suffered in some degree from the cold and exposure, but that no other person became ill therefrom, was not relevant." International, etc., R. Co. v. Johnson (Tex. Civ. App. 1906), 95 S. W. Rep. 595.

[20] "If the condition of a carrier's waiting room was the proximate cause of a passenger contracting pneumonia, the carrier is liable in damages." St. Louis, etc., R. Co. v. Hook (Ark. 1907), 104 S. W. Rep. 217.

ably caused by a cold contracted while waiting for a train, in a cold waiting room, the carrier will be held liable in damages for the death of the passenger so exposed.[21]

But of course, in any case, it must be definitely shown that the injury to the passenger resulted from a failure on the carrier's part to properly heat its station, before it can be held in damages on this ground for having caused the injury.[22]   And where a statute only required the carrier to have its station opened and warmed for an hour before the arrival and departure of a train and the station was so opened, it is not answerable to a passenger who arrived before the station was so opened and who was injured by the cold, while waiting for the station to be opened.[23]

§ 623. **Duty regarding toilet rooms.**— Although it has been held, in England, that there is no duty placed by law upon the carrier of passengers, by steam, to provide suitable water-closets for use by its guests and that it is beyond the power of the railroad commissioners to order free closets constructed and maintained by the passenger carrier,[24] this decision is not followed, in a Texas case,[25] but the railroad

---

[21] "Where the negligence of a carrier in failing to properly warm a wating room produced a condition of health in a passenger obliged to wait in such room rendering the passenger susceptible to tuberculosis, and as a natural and probable consequence she became affected with the disease and died thereof, the carrier was liable." Chicago, etc., Ry. Co. v. Groner (Tex. Civ. App. 1906), 95 S. W. Rep. 1118.

[22] St. Louis, etc., R. Co. v. Hook (Ark.), 104 S. W. Rep. 217.

[23] "Where a railroad, in compliance with the express requirements of Rev. St. 1895 (art. 4521), opened its station one hour before the departure of a train, it was not liable to a prospective passenger for injuries and suffering resulting to the passenger from exposure before the station was opened." Texas Midland R. Co. v. Griggs (Tex. Civ. App. 1907), 106 S. W. Rep. 411.

[24] West Hamshire Co. v. Great Eastern R. Co., 64 L. J. Q. B. (N. S.) 340.

[25] Henderson v. Galveston, etc., R. Co., 38 S. W. Rep. 1136.

company was held liable for damages for the suffering experienced by a passenger, owing to a failure to maintain a toilet room, for the use of the passengers at the station where the passenger had been discharged from the carrier's train.

Of course where toilet rooms are maintained by the carrier, the law implies the duty to maintain the same in a reasonably safe condition for the use of the passengers and for an injury to a passenger, by reason of the failure on the carrier's part to maintain a reasonably safe toilet room, the carrier will be answerable in damages.[26]

§ 624. **Station blown down by storm.**— Since there is no liability for an injury due to an action of the elements, even in the case where such injury results from a defect caused thereby in the track or roadbed, as where an unprecedented storm washes away a portion of the track or roadway,[27] there is no liability for an injury caused by the blowing away of a railroad company's station or depot, where reasonable care and caution was used in the erection of the depot,[28] for if such injury could not have been anticipated, where extraordinary care is exacted, under the circumstances, there is small room for holding that it ought to have been foreseen, in a case where only reasonable or ordinary care is demanded of the carrier.

[26] Jordan v. New York, etc., R. Co., 165 Mass. 346; 43 N. E. Rep. 111; 32 L. R. A. 101.

[27] International, etc., R. Co. v. Haloren, 53 Texas 46; 37; Am. Rep. 744; Ely v. St. Louis, etc., R. Co., 77 Mo. 34.

[28] Pittsburg, etc., R. Co. v. Brigham, 29 Ohio St. 374. In this case the trial court charged the jury that the railway company was "bound to guard against all storms which can reasonably be anticipated." This was held to be error, by the higher court. Of this instruction, Judge Thompson, says: "The instruction condemned is absolutely unexceptionable" (3 Thompson on Neg., note to § 2680), but the conclusion of the court as to the instruction seems proper, and, manifestly, the result of the decision is eminently right.

It is therefore held, in an Ohio case,[29] that a railroad company is not liable for an injury caused by the blowing down of its station, if the railroad company used reasonable or ordinary care in the erection and construction of the station, for ordinary care, under the circumstances, would not compel the carrier to guard against all storms that might occur, nor would reasonable diligence require it to anticipate that an unusual event, such as a storm sufficient to blow down a reasonably strong building, would occur, as such storms are not the usual, but the unusual thing, and only that which is apt to occur would be anticipated.

§ 625. **Failure to light station and platform.**— It is the legal duty of a railway company to furnish sufficient lights at night, to securely guide the steps and the way of the passengers as well as to light the places where employees are required to work, in connection with their duties toward the passengers of the railroad company, and this duty is violated by a railway company which, for any reason, leaves coaches of a passenger train outside the station grounds, at a place where the lights of the city, intended to light up the place, are so obstructed as to make it dark at and about the place where the train is placed.[30]

If a passenger is injured, while attempting to reach a sleeping car, by the only approach to be used for that purpose, because of the fact that the station grounds of the railroad company were not sufficiently lighted to enable him to safely reach his destination, the company would be liable.[31] The obligation to sufficiently light the station and grounds, includes the duty to light the place where cars are stopped

---

[29] Pittsburg, etc., R. Co. v. Brigham, *supra*.

[30] Moses v. Louisville, etc., R. Co., 39 La. Ann. 649; 2 So. Rep. 567; 30 Am. & Eng. R. Cas. 556; Alexandria, etc., R. Co. v. Herndon, 87 Va. 193; 12 S. E. Rep. 289.

[31] Moses v. Louisville, etc., R. Co., *supra*.

at night, to enable the passengers to reach the dining hall of the railroad company and to enable them to safely re-enter the cars, and for a failure to discharge such duty the company would be liable,[32] as it would for a failure to properly light a trestle used as an approach to its station grounds, whereby a passenger sustained injury, for in maintaining such a structure for use by passengers, the railroad company impliedly invites them to use the same and there is a corresponding obligation to make it reasonably safe for the use intended.[33]

[32] Peniston v. Chicago, etc., R. Co., 34 La. Ann. 777.

[33] Johns v. Charlotte, etc., R. Co., 39 So. Car. 162; 17 S. E. Rep. 698; 58 Am. & Eng. R. Cas. 175.

"Where a railroad, either for its own or for the convenience of its patrons, establishes quasi-depots or stopping places, it must make them safe by providing lights at night." Wagner v. Atlantic Coast Line R. Co. (N. C. 1908), 61 S. E. Rep. 171.

"In an action against a railway company for injury to an alighting passenger, the question whether the station and platform were sufficiently lighted is ordinarily for the jury." Merryman v. Chicago Great Western Ry. Co. (Iowa 1907), 113 N. W. Rep. 357.

"The duty of a common carrier sufficiently to light its depot is not excused by the fact that there is no system of public lighting in the municipality in which it is located." Toledo & W. R. Co. v. Stevenson, 122 Ill. App. 654.

The railroad company's failure to keep its station and platform or premises lighted at night, was the ground of complaint, in the following cases, where passengers were injured, viz., Louisville, etc., R. Co. v. Treadway, 142 Ind. 475; 40 N. E. Rep. 807; Fullerton v. Fordyce, 144 Mo. 519; 44 S. W. Rep. 1053; 10 Am. & Eng. R. Cas. (N. S.) 729; McDonald v. Illinois R. Co., 88 Iowa 345; 55 N. W. Rep. 102; Alabama, etc., R. Co. v. Arnold, 84 Ala. 159; 5 Am. St. Rep. 354; Skottowe v. Oregon, etc., R. Co., 22 Oregon 430; 30 Pac. Rep. 222; 16 L. R. A. 593; Stafford v. Hannibal, etc., R. Co., 22 Mo. App. 333; Waller v. Missouri Pacific Ry. Co., 59 Mo. App. 410; Missouri Pacific Ry. Co. v. Neiswanger, 41 Kansas 621; 21 Pac. Rep. 582.

In Gerhart v. Wabash Ry. Co. (110 Mo. App. 105), where a passenger fell from an unlighted station platform, that had no railing, Judge Ellison, for the court, said: "It was the duty of defendant to have its platform lighted so that passengers discharged from cars

953

§ 626. **Defective platforms, generally.**— It is the duty of a railroad company to provide platforms, or suitable substitutes therefor, at all stopping places where it is accustomed to receive and discharge passengers and a failure to discharge this duty is such negligence as to render the company liable in case of an injury due to such a source.[34] In case of an injury to a passenger from falling into a hole in a station platform, the railway company would be liable, if it had permitted the hole to remain a length of time that would have enabled it, by due care, to have discovered the presence of the hole and in such a case it would be error to charge the jury that the railway company was not liable, unless it "failed to use ordinary care" after being aware of plaintiff's presence, for the negligence consisted in allowing the hole to remain in the platform and this was the cause of the injury, whether that was before or after the danger to the plaintiff was known.[35]

But the law does not require a station platform to conform to any particular design, or to come within any special distance of the cars, if it is such as is customarily constructed. And where a passenger was injured by stepping between the platform and the car step and the evidence showed that it was eleven inches from the platform to the

could proceed with safety, in the exercise of care, along the usual course taken by passengers, to where they would leave the platform." Nor was it held to affect this duty on the part of the railroad company, that the train on which the passenger had been carried, was a special train.

See, also, as to recognition of duty to keep platform lighted, at night, Sargent v. St. Louis, etc., R. Co., 114 Mo. 348; 21 S. W. Rep. 823; 19 L. R. A. 460; 58 Am. & Eng. R. Cas. 184; Fordyce v. Merrill, 5 S. W. Rep. 329; Beuneman v. Railroad Co., 20 N. W. Rep. 379; Hutchinson on Carrier's (2 ed.), §§ 518, 519; Nicholson v. Lancashire, etc., R. Co., 3 H. & C. 534; 34 L. J. Ex. 84; 12 L. T. 391.

[34] Ensley R. Co. v. Chewning, 93 Ala. 24; 9 So. Rep. 458; 50 Am. & Eng. R. Cas. 46.

[35] Louisville, etc., R. Co. v. Wolfe, 80 Ky. 82.

car step and the lower step was eight inches below the top
of the platform and it was one foot and seven inches therefrom and the second step was about four inches below the
platform and about two feet therefrom, and the passenger
stepped on the second step and then onto the platform, without holding onto the iron rail at the side of the steps, and
without looking where he stepped, the court held that plaintiff was not entitled to recover for the injuries so received.[36]

[36] Laflin v. Buffalo, etc., R. Co., 106 N. Y. 136; 30 Am. & Eng. R.
Cas. 596.

"In an action for injuries to a passenger while alighting from
defendant's train, evidence of the condition of the pavement where
defendant alighted, four or five weeks after the accident, tending to
show the existence of lumps of coal and clinkers, should be excluded."
Missouri, etc., Ry. Co. v. Dunbar (Tex. Civ. App. 1908), 108 S. W.
Rep. 500.

An injury to a passenger due to a failure to provide a reasonably
safe platform at the carrier's station, was held to give a cause of
action, in the following cases: Fullerton v. Fordyce, 121 Mo. 1; 25
S. W. Rep. 587; 144 Mo. 519; 44 S. W. Rep. 1053; 10 Am. & Eng. R.
Cas. (N. S.) 729; Toledo, etc., R. Co. v. Wingate, 143 Ind. 125;
37 N. E. Rep. 274; Gulf, etc., R. Co. v. Buchter, 83 Texas 309; 18
S. W. Rep. 583; Keefe v. Boston, etc., R. Co., 142 Mass. 251; St.
Louis, etc., R. Co. v. Barnett, 65 Ark. 255; 45 S. W. Rep. 550;
Illinois, etc., R. Co. v. Davidson, 76 Fed. Rep. 517; 46 U. S. App. 300;
Robertson v. Wabash Ry. Co., 152 Mo. 382; 53 S. W. Rep. 1082.

In Barth v. Kansas City, etc., R. Co. (142 Mo. 536; 44 S. W. Rep.
778), the distance between the railing and the steps of the car was
twenty-six inches and it was held to be a jury issue, whether or not
this was a negligently constructed platform.

See, also, Evans v. Interstate Transit Co., 106 Mo. 594.

"A railroad company was liable for injuries to one of its passengers,
sustained after alighting from a train at a station by slipping down
an incline on a platform leading to the waiting room, because of the
failure of the railroad to use ordinary care to keep it in safe condition
for the use of passengers, or to warn them that it was not a proper
way for them to take in going to and from the train, though another
and safe way to the waiting room had been provided by the company,
where the platform on which the injury occurred was usually used by
passengers going to and from the train, and where such use had
been continued for such a length of time that the railroad company

§ 627. **Collisions with baggage trucks.**— The care exacted
by the law on the part of the carrier, to avoid injury to its
passengers, includes the duty to exercise reasonable care to
avoid striking passengers with baggage trucks, or similar
vehicles used on the station platform, where passengers are
allowed or invited to congregate to take cars, or to alight from
their trains.

Nor would it be essential in each case, to establish that the
one in charge of the truck was a regular employee of the
railroad company, for it is liable for the negligent injury
of a passenger by being struck by a baggage truck, in the
hands of one whom it has permitted for a considerable length
of time to use such truck on its platform, as where it has
permitted a news agent to take papers from the station to the
mail car, on a baggage truck, at a time when passengers are
congregated on the platform, as a result of which a passenger sustains an injury,[37] and in an action for a personal injury to a passenger, by being struck by a baggage truck,
while walking along the platform of a station, after alighting from a train, the issue whether or not the passenger
backed against the truck, or was negligently struck by the
truck and whether the passenger or the employee of the company, who was handling the truck, was in the exercise of due
care, are proper issues of fact the jury should decide.[38]

necessarily knew of the use." Judgment (Civ. App. 1907), 103 S. W.
Rep. 695, affirmed; Missouri, etc., Ry. Co. v. Criswell (Tex. 1908), 108
S. W. Rep. 806.

[37] A railroad company which customarily permits an employee of
a newspaper publisher to take the papers from the station gate to
the mail car at a time when passengers are hurrying to and fro on
the platform is held, in Mangum v. North Carolina R. Co. (N. C.), 58
S. E. Rep. 913; 13 L. R. A. (N. S.) 589, to be liable for his negligent
use of the truck on which they are carried, which results in injury to
a passenger.

[38] Keefe v. Boston, etc., R. Co., 142 Mass. 251; 7 N. E. Rep. 874;
27 Am. & Eng. R. Cas. 137.

§ 628. **Passenger struck by mail sacks.**— Where mail sacks are customarily discharged upon a passenger platform, it is the duty of the railroad company to guard against injuries to passengers by reason of the presence of such mail bags and the duty is held to extend to every part of the platform, where passengers are invited or allowed to go.[39]

A company that had notice of the habit of the mail agents, in the employ of the government, to throw mail sacks full of mail out of trains, on a platform where passengers were congregated, was held liable for an injury to a passenger, by being struck by a mail sack so thrown from a train, in a New York case,[40] where the evidence showed that no diligence had been used to try to prevent this dangerous custom, and a similar conclusion, as to the railroad company's liability, was reached, in a Massachusetts case.[41]

But, as aptly observed, in a Missouri case,[42] by Judge Black, for the Supreme Court, "Persons going to and from trains must know that depots are more or less crowded on such occasions; that at small stations baggage is handled on trucks on the platform and that there is always more or less confusion. Common prudence dictates that passengers should, at such times and places, look where they are stepping and be observant of what is going on around them. The care of the passenger must be suited to the surroundings, for this is but ordinary care." And in this case, where a female passenger was injured by falling over mail sacks, thrown upon an unlighted platform, it was held error for

[39] Sargent v. St. Louis, etc., R. Co., 114 Mo. 348; 21 S. W. Rep. 823; 19 L. R. A. 460; 58 Am. & Eng. R. Cas. 184; Ohio, etc., R. Co. v. Simms, 43 Ill. App. 260.

[40] Carpenter v. Boston, etc., R. Co., 97 N. Y. 494; 49 Am. Rep. 540; 21 Am. & Eng. R. Cas. 331.

[41] Snow v. Fitchburg, etc., R. Co., 136 Mass. 552; 49 Am. Rep. 40; 18 Am. & Eng. R. Cas. 161.

[42] Sargent v. St. Louis, etc., R. Co., 114 Mo. 348; 21 S. W. Rep. 823; 19 L. R. A. 460; 58 Am. & Eng. R. Cas. 184.

the court to charge the jury that plaintiff was entitled to assume that the platform was free from such obstructions, unless she had been warned by the employees of the railroad company, as this practically absolved her from all duty to care for her own safety.[43]

§ 629. **Defects in premises near stations.**— Premises of a railroad company, adjoining a station where passengers are taken on or put off of trains, ought to be maintained in a reasonably safe condition, so that passengers passing over such premises will not receive injuries.

A railroad company is negligent if it stops a train over an open ditch, waiting for another train to pass, for a half hour or such period of time, where the existence of the ditch was known to the conductor of the train, and a passenger who fell into the ditch, while carefully attempting to leave the train, is entitled to recover damages for an injury so received.[44] And if a passenger is carried past his station and put off at a place where it is dangerous for him to pass along the railroad company's premises, back to the station, without any warning of the danger being given him, by the employees of the railroad company, it will be answerable for any injuries he may receive.[45]

But a railroad has a legal right to presume that passengers will not attempt to get on or off of the trains, except at places that the company may designate for that purpose and it is not the duty of the company to keep its track clear for the

[43] Sargent v. St. Louis, etc., R. Co., 114 Mo. 356.

[44] Montgomery, etc., R. Co. v. Boring, 51 Ga. 582. A passenger is entitled to rely on the safety of the premises at any place where he may be asked to leave a train. Baltimore, etc., R. Co. v. State, 60 Md. 449; 12 Am. & Eng. R. Cas. 149; Hulbert v. New York, etc., R. Co., 40 N. Y. 145.

[45] New York, etc., R. Co. v. Doane, 115 Ind. 435; 17 N. E. Rep. 913; 7 Am. St. Rep. 451; 1 L. R. A. 157; 37 Am. & Eng. R. Cas. 87.

benefit of those who may pursue the cars when leaving the station and if a passenger is injured by attempting to mount a train at a point beyond that designated as the proper place for passengers to get on the trains, owing to an obstruction on the premises, the railroad company would not ordinarily be liable for such an injury, for the law would not charge it with knowledge of the fact that such a place would be used by a passenger for such a purpose and reasonable care would not compel it to take such notice.[46]

§ 630. **Approaches and passageways.**— The duty of maintaining the grounds around the carrier's station in a reasonably safe condition, applies to all portions of the premises of the railroad company that will be used by the carrier's passengers, whether in approaching the station, or while embarking or disembarking from the cars.

Reasonable care should be used to provide safe passageways to and from the station and cars [47] and the duty in this regard corresponds to that owing by municipal corporations with respect to its sidewalks and streets used by the traveling public.[48]

A failure to provide a safe passageway was held to give a cause of action where an injury resulted on a way leading from a train to a telegraph office; [49] on a way leading from

---

[46] Perry v. Central R. Co., 66 Ga. 746.

A passenger, injured as a result of falling over rubbish, at a place where he was put off the train, was held entitled to recover damages in England. Bridges v. North London R. Co., 43 L. J. Q. B. 151; L. R. 7 Q. B. 213; 23 W. R. 62; 30 L. T. 844.

[47] Redner v. Lehigh, etc., R. Co., 148 N. Y. 733; 73 Hun 562; East Tennessee, etc., R. Co. v. Watson, 94 Ala. 634; 10 So. Rep. 228; Gilmore v. Philadelphia, etc., R. Co., 154 Pa. St. 375; 25 Atl. Rep. 774; Flanagan v. Philadelphia, etc., R. Co., 181 Pa. St. 237; 37 Atl. Rep. 341; Texas, etc., R. Co. v. Orr, 46 Ark. 182.

[48] O'Reilly v. Long Island R. Co., 44 N. Y. Supp. 264; 15 App. Div. 79.

[49] Clussman v. Long Island R. Co., 9 Hun 618; 73 N. Y. 606.

the cars to an eating house;[50] to the approaches to the station and platform;[51] for an injury on falling from a plank, used, instead of steps, to approach the platform;[52] an injury caused by falling into a hole in a passageway to a station,[53] or the dangerous condition of an elevated walk, to a landing;[54] to an injury caused by a defective bridge, which it was necessary to cross, in reaching the station,[55] and a female passenger, injured by reason of an unsafe passageway, leading to a baggage room of the carrier, was also held entitled to recover damages for injuries received thereby.[56]

But as to that portion of the carrier's premises not intended for the use of passengers, and as to which there is no express or implied invitation to them to use, there is no duty to keep passageways in repair, nor is the carrier bound to anticipate that such ways will be used by a passenger, in order to reach the station by a "short cut," instead of using the customary way intended for use by passengers.[57]

[50] Peniston v. Chicago, etc., R. Co., 34 La. Ann. 777; 44 Am. Rep. 444.

[51] Union Pacific R. Co. v. Evans, 52 Neb. 50; 71 N. W. Rep. 1062.

[52] Collins v. Toledo, etc., R. Co., 80 Mich. 390; 45 N. W. Rep. 178.

[53] Green v. Pennsylvania R. Co., 36 Fed. Rep. 66.

[54] Skottowe v. Oregon, etc., R. Co., 22 Oregon 430; 30 Pac. Rep. 222; 16 L. R. A. 593.

[55] East Tennessee, etc., R. Co. v. Watson, 94 Ala. 634; 10 So. Rep. 228.

[56] Exton v. Central R. Co., 63 N. J. L. 356; 46 Atl. Rep. 1099.

[57] Longmore v. Great Western R. Co., 19 C. B. (N. S.) 183.

"It is the duty of a carrier of passengers to maintain a stairway used by outgoing passengers in making an exit to the street in a reasonably safe condition for travel; and if it allows the steps to become covered with a thin coating of mud, whereby the steps become slippery and unsafe, it fails to perform its duty." MacLaren v. Boston Elevated Ry. Co. (Mass. 1908), 83 N. E. Rep. 1088.

"The presence of a piece of tobacco on a stairway leading to a railroad station, upon which a passenger stepped and fell, is not, in the absence of evidence to indicate that the railroad had a reasonable opportunity to discover and remove it, sufficient to charge the railroad with negligence." Kaplowitz v. Interborough Rapid Transit Co., 103 N. Y. S. 721.

§ 631. **Placing cars across approach to station.**— Where a railroad company runs a freight train between a passenger train and a station and then cuts the train in two, leaving stationary cars so placed as to obstruct access to the station, it must use due care to prevent injury to its passengers, who have a right to use the approach to the station and for a failure to give warning of the movement of cars, as a result of which a passenger is injured, the company would be liable.[58] In a recent Kentucky case,[59] where access to the station was obstructed by a train of stationary cars, on a cold day, and the passenger was injured by contracting a severe cold, while waiting for the cars to be removed, so she could reach the station, a verdict in her favor, was upheld by the Court of Appeals, as the railroad company was held to be negligent in thus blocking the approach to its station, for an unreasonable time, by stationary cars.

"In an action for injuries sustained by an outgoing passenger by slipping on depot steps, whether the steps were muddy and slippery, and unsafe to travel on, *held*, under the evidence, for the jury." MacLaren v. Boston Elevated Ry. Co. (Mass. 1908), 83 N. E. Rep. 1088.

Failure to maintain a reasonably safe approach to a station, was the ground of liability, in Little Rock, etc., R. Co. v. Cavenesse, 48 Ark. 106; 2 S. W. Rep. 505; and Stewart v. International, etc., R. Co., 53 Texas 289; 2 Am. & Eng. R. Cas. 497.

[58] Louisville, etc., R. Co. v. Thompson, 64 Miss. 584; 1 So. Rep. 840; 30 Am. & Eng. R. Cas. 541.

[59] In Louisville, etc., R. Co. v. Dougherty (108 S. W. Rep. 336), the Kentucky Court of Appeals upheld a judgment for $1,500 against a railroad company for injuries sustained by a passenger from exposure to cold while waiting for a train to be moved which obstructed access to the depot. On a bitter cold morning the plaintiff went to the defendant's station to take a train and found a freight train blocking her way to the depot, by reason of which she was compelled to stand for half an hour in the cold and suffered injury to her health. The only nearby place where she could have found shelter was a store which, to her knowledge, had the reputation of being a place that a modest woman could not with propriety enter, and the court held that, such being the case, she owed no duty to enter the store, and the railroad was liable for the damages sustained by the plaintiff.

And in a Massachusetts case,[60] where an iron truck was placed across the approach to a station, and a passenger arriving on a train, attempted to pass over such truck, and sustained an injury, it was held to be a jury issue whether or not, under the circumstances, the railroad company was in the exercise of reasonable care in thus obstructing the access to its station and also whether the passenger exercised due care for her own safety, in thus passing over the obstruction in her path.

§ 632. **Running engine or cars between passenger train and station.**— The ordinary rule of "look and listen," before crossing a railroad track, is held, in a recent Kansas case,[61] not to apply, where a railroad company stops a passenger train at a place where other tracks are between it and the depot platform, since, under such circumstances, it is held, the company's passengers have a right to assume that they would be protected from moving trains of cars, while going to or from the station. This decision is perhaps with the great weight of authority on this question,[62] and for any unwarranted movement of engines or trains on the tracks intervening, between the passenger's train and the station, whereby a passenger sustains injury, the railroad company

[60] Bethmann v. Old Colony R. Co., 155 Mass. 352; 29 N. E. Rep. 587.

[61] Atchison, etc., R. Co. v. McElroy, 91 Pac. Rep. 785; 13 L. R. A. (N. S.) 620.

[62] Denver, etc., R. Co. v. Hodgson, 18 Colo. 117; 31 Pac. Rep. 954; Chicago, etc., R. Co. v. Lowell, 151 U. S. 209; 38 L. Ed. 131; Reading v. Central, etc., R. Co., 68 N. J. L. 643; 54 Atl. Rep. 431; Warner v. Baltimore, etc., R. Co., 168 U. S. 339; 42 L. Ed. 491; St. Louis, etc., R. Co. v. Johnson, 59 Ark. 122; 26 S. W. Rep. 593; Pennsylvania R. Co. v. White, 88 Pa. St. 327; Wheelock v. Boston, etc., R. Co., 105 Mass. 203; Atlantic City R. Co. v. Goodin, 62 N. J. L. 397; 42 Atl. Rep. 333; 72 Am. St. Rep. 652; 45 L. R. A. 673; Brassell v. New York, etc., R. Co., 84 N. Y. 241; Atchison, etc., R. Co. v. Shean, 18 Colo. 368; 33 Pac. Rep. 108; 20 L. R. A. 729.

would generally be held liable therefor,[63] as it is held to be negligence to move a train or car at a rapid speed, along a track intervening between a station and a train where passengers are being discharged, without notice or warning of the danger.[64]

But the rate of speed would necessarily determine the negligence of the railroad company, in such a case and if due warning of the movement of a car or engine was given to passengers and the train or engine was not moved at a rapid rate of speed, but slowly, and a proper lookout maintained, the railroad company would not ordinarily be held negligent [65] and a passenger is not justified in shutting his eyes at such a place of danger and walking ahead on the assumption that no trains will be moved on the tracks intervening between the station and his train, and if an injury is sustained by reason of a want of due care on the passenger's part, no recovery could be had therefor.[66]

[63] Imhoff v. Chicago, etc., R. Co., 22 Wis. 681; Armstrong v. New York, etc., R. Co., 66 Barb. 437; 64 N. Y. 635; Hirsch v. New York, etc., R. Co., 6 N. Y. Supp. 162; 53 Hun 633; 125 N. Y. 701.

[64] Robostelli v. New York, etc., R. Co., 33 Fed. Rep. 796; 34 Am. & Eng. R. Cas. 515; Denver, etc., R. Co. v. Hodgson, 18 Colo. 117; 31 Pac. Rep. 954.

[65] Goldberg v. New York, etc., R. Co., 133 N. Y. 561; 30 N. E. Rep. 597; 44 N. Y. S. R. 71.

[66] Connolly v. New York, etc., R. Co., 158 Mass. 8; 32 N. E. Rep. 937. "A petition alleged that plaintiff was a passenger and left the waiting room in a station to board the train; that the passageway was not more than three feet wide, upon which were several baggage trucks on which negroes were seated, compelling plaintiff to pass between the trucks and the edge of the passageway next the track; that in so doing an engine of defendant approached her from the rear without any signal and struck petitioner on the back, knocking her down, and inflicting the injuries complained of; that the engine was running at a dangerous rate of speed, and that the employees in charge failed to keep a proper lookout. Held to state a good cause of action." Georgia R., etc., Co. v. Lloyd (Ga. 1907), 59 S. E. Rep. 801.

§ 633. Injuries by falling into cattle guards.— A railroad company should not permit cattle guards to be maintained on the premises near its station, where passengers are apt to fall into same and if a company maintains a cattle guard at a place where a passenger on being discharged from a train, is apt to fall into such a trap, it can be held liable for the damages resulting from such an injury.

It was accordingly held, in a New York case,[67] that a railroad company was liable for the death of a female passenger, caught in a cattle guard and struck by a passing train, where the cattle guard was maintained near a public highway, leading from the place where the passenger was discharged from her train and it had been permitted to fill up with snow, until the presence of the guard was not perceptible. And a similar liability was recognized, in a Wisconsin case,[68] in favor of a passenger, who on a dark night, was permitted to approach a caboose, placed at a distance from the station, without warning of the cattle guard. And, likewise, in a Missouri case,[69] the company was held liable for an injury to a passenger put off of his train at a distance from the station, who fell into a cattle guard or trestle, in an attempt to reach the station.

. But unless the railroad company has reason to believe that passengers will use that portion of its premises away from its station, there is no duty to remove cattle guards or to give warning of their presence and if a passenger leaves a train, stopped to permit another train to pass, on a dark night, without notice to the employees of the railroad company that he intends to take such course, he cannot recover

[67] Hoffman v. New York, etc., R. Co., 75 N. Y. 605; 13 Hun 589.

[68] Hartwig v. Chicago, etc., R. Co., 49 Wis. 358; 5 N. W. Rep. 865; 1 Am. & Eng. R. Cas. 65.

[69] Winkler v. St. Louis, etc., R. Co., 21 Mo. App. 99, quoted in Adams v. Missouri Pacific Ry. Co., 100 Mo. 555; 12 S. W. Rep. 637; 41 Am. & Eng. R. Cas. 105.

for an injury received by falling into a cattle guard, for his conduct in leaving the train could not, reasonably, have been anticipated on the part of the railroad company and there is no failure to discharge its duty toward such a passenger, as a basis for its liability.[70]

[70] Frost v. Grand Trunk R. Co., 10 Allen (Mass.) 387.

CHAPTER XXIV.

CARS, ENGINES AND APPLIANCES.

§ 634. **Care to provide.**— A carrier, in the conduct and management of its passenger business, must provide cars, engines and appliances that are reasonably safe for the use of their patrons, and as to all the appliances made use of by it for passenger business, it is bound to exercise the highest degree of care and diligence for the convenience and safety of its passengers, that is reasonably consistent with the practical conduct of the business and it is liable for the slightest

966

negligence in this regard.[1] The obligation imposed on railroads, with respect to passengers, is that their cars, engines and appliances shall be suitable, sufficient and as safe as care and skill can make them.[2] And this duty and obligation exists not only in respect to the vehicles used by the railroad company, but to every means and instrument used or embraced by the carrier in the transportation of its passenger and this duty extends throughout the entire journey of the passenger.[3]

But while required to provide for the safety of their passengers all such things as are reasonably consistent with the business and appropriate to the means of conveyance employed, railroad companies are not required, in order to insure the safety of their cars or appliances, to incur such expense as would render the business of carrying passengers wholly impracticable,[4] nor are they bound to have their cars or appliances constructed of the " most perfect material," or "in the most perfect manner in which care and diligence can suggest," in the transaction of the business.[5]

[1] Pershing v. Chicago, etc., R. Co., 71 Iowa 561; 32 N. W. Rep. 488; 34 Am. & Eng. R. Cas. 405; Chicago, etc., R. Co. v. Reilly, 40 Ill. App. 416; Eureka Springs R. Co. v. Timmons, 51 Ark. 459; 11 S. W. Rep. 690; 40 Am. & Eng. R. Cas. 698.

[2] Nashville, etc., R. Co. v. Jones, 9 Heisk. (Tenn.) 27; 19 Am. Ry. Rep. 261; Taylor v. Pennsylvania R. Co., 50 Fed. Rep. 755.

[3] McLean v. Burbank, 11 Minn. 277; Jacobus v. St. Paul, etc., R. Co., 20 Minn. 125.

[4] Arkansas Midland R. Co. v. Canman, 52 Ark. 517; 13 S. W. Rep. 280; Indianapolis, etc., R. Co. v. Horst, 93 U. S. 291.

[5] Yerkes v. Keokuk, etc., Co., 7 Mo. App. 265.

"A common carrier of passengers is bound to provide safe cars, keep them in good repair, and do all things reasonably necessary to secure safe transportation of passengers from place to place and their safe departure from the cars after reaching their destination." Smithers v. Wilmington City Ry. Co. (Del. Super. 1907), 67 Atl. Rep. 167.

"In an action for injuries to a female passenger as she was alighting from a train, the court charged that it was defendant's duty to exercise great care in providing ' safe means ' for passengers to alight,

§ 635. Rule applied by Supreme Court.— Considering the degree of care required by a railroad company, in furnishing cars and appliances, for the use of its passengers, Justice Harlan, for the United States Supreme Court,[6] used this language: " The carrier, is required, as to passengers, to observe the utmost caution, characteristic of very careful, prudent men. He is responsible for injuries received by passengers, in the course of their transportation, which might have been avoided or guarded against, by the exercise upon his part, of extraordinary vigilance, aided by the highest skill. And this caution and vigilance must necessarily be extended to all the agencies or means employed by the carrier in the transportation of the passenger. Among the duties resting upon him is the important one of providing cars and vehicles adequate, that is, sufficiently secure, as to strength and other requisites, for the safe conveyance of passengers. That duty the law enforces with great strictness. For the slightest negligence or fault in this regard, from which injury results to the passenger, the carrier is liable in damages. These doctrines, to which the courts, with few exceptions, have given a firm and steady support, and which it is neither wise nor just to disturb or question, would, however, lose much, if not all, of their practical value, if carriers are permitted to escape responsibility, upon the ground

and that if defendant negligently and carelessly failed to provide safe means for passengers to alight, and by reason thereof plaintiff was injured, she was entitled to recover. *Held*, that the term ' safe means ' was not alone referable to defendant's failure to provide a step for plaintiff to alight, as alleged, of which there was no proof, but was also applicable to the alleged negligence of defendant's negro porter in jerking her from the train while assisting her to alight." Texas & P. Ry. Co. v. Beezley (Tex. Civ. App. 1907), 101 S. W. Rep. 1051.

6 Pennsylvania R. Co. v. Roy, 102 U. S. 451; 12 Otto 451; 26 L. Ed. 141. See, also, The New World v. King, 16 How. 469; Stokes v. Saltonstill, 13 Pet. 181; New Jersey, etc., R. Co. v. Pollard, 89 U. S. 341; 22 L. Ed. 877; 22 Wall. 341; Philadelphia, etc., R. Co. v. Derby, 14 How. 468; 14 L. Ed. 502.

that the cars or vehicles used by them and from whose in-
efficiency injury has resulted, to the passenger, belonged to
others."

§ 636. Duty may be enforced by mandamus.— The *quasi*-
public character of the duty on the part of railroad companies to provide reasonably safe rolling stock, cars, engines
and other appliances, and the power of the State in the interest of the traveling public, to compel the proper performance of this duty, to further the interests of the traveling
public of the State, was recently the subject of inquiry by
the Supreme Court of Florida, where a mandamus proceeding was instituted at the relation of the State, to compel the
railroad company, in the interest of the safety of its patrons,
to provide additional rolling stock.

The court, after a careful consideration of the rights of
the railroad company and those of the general public, concluded that the duty of providing a reasonably safe roadbed,
track, equipment and facilities and of maintaining and operating the property in a proper condition for rendering
safe, prompt and adequate service to the traveling public,
without unjust discrimination, could be enforced by the
courts, by the proceeding by mandamus, in a proper case,
upon the relation of the attorney-general, in the absence of
some other adequate remedy provided for by the legislature.
The decision is an interesting exposition of the law upon this
novel proposition and may be read with interest and profit.[7]

[7] See State *ex rel.* Ellis v. Atlantic Coast Line R. Co., 53 Fla. 650;
44 So. Rep. 213; 13 L. R. A. (N. S.) 320, where it is held that the
duty of providing a reasonably safe and sufficient roadbed, track, equipment, and facilities, and of maintaining and operating the property in
a proper condition for rendering safe, prompt, and adequate service,
without unjust discrimination, may be enforced by mandamus in a
proper case upon the relation of the attorney-general, when no other
adequate remedy is provided by law.

§ 637. **Inspection of cars and engines.**— Whether the system and manner of examining the cars and appliances of a railroad company is all that may be required of the carrier, cannot be determined by any rule of law to be applied by the courts, under a given state of facts, but the question is necessarily one of fact for the jury to determine, under proper instructions from the court.[8]   In a suit by a passenger, to recover damages for injuries due to an unsafe car or other appliance, a charge which declares that it is the duty of the carrier to inspect its trains and cars, is not erroneous, when the injuries are alleged to be due to a failure on its part to furnish safe cars for traveling purposes, for the duty of inspection, as applied to cars and engines in use by a carrier, is one of the nondelegable duties imposed by law on the carrier, for the safety of the passengers.[9]

The requirement as to the frequency with which the inspections ought to be made, to bring the carrier's conduct up to the full measure of the legal requirement, is necessarily dependent upon the liability of impairment and the consequences which may be apprehended from a defective condition of the car or appliance.[10]   An appliance not subject to much use or wear, or not likely to produce injury, even if found in a defective condition, is not required to be inspected with such frequency as one liable to be more dangerous when out of repair, or more apt to become defective from the use to which it is put. No such minute examination of car trucks, for instance, is required, as would defeat the purpose of through traffic and if a defect is discovered in a truck, no minute examination of the whole truck is required, for the

[8] Palmer v. Delaware, etc., Co., 120 N. Y. 170; 24 N. E. Rep. 302; 30 N. Y. S. R. 817; 46 Hun 486; 11 N. Y. S. R. 872; 44 Am. & Eng. R. Cas. 298; Schneider v. Second Avenue R. Co., 39 N. Y. S. R. 370.

[9] Texas, etc, R. Co. v. Suggs, 62 Texas 323; 21 Am. & Eng. R. Cas. 475.

[10] Palmer v. Delaware, etc., Co., *supra*.

reason that the effect of the defect might not necessitate an examination of the rest of the truck.[11]

§ 638. **Obligation assumed by company furnishing motive power.**— It would seem, upon principle, that a company furnishing the motive power and moving the cars of another railroad company, used for passenger traffic, for so much a car, or any other consideration agreed upon, would come within the rule making the carrier of passengers liable for a failure to exercise the very high degree of care that obtains in any other case,[12] and this is the rule adopted in some cases, as to terminal or other companies that receive on their tracks the cars or trains of other railroad companies and place them under the control of their own employees or agents and by means of their own locomotives, transport them to a given destination. All such companies are held to be common carriers of passengers and to assume the relation with all its accompanying liabilities.[13]

But this rule is not of universal application, and the fed-

[11] Richardson v. Great Eastern R. Co., 24 W. R. 907; L. R. 1 C. P. D. 342; 35 L. T. 351; International, etc., R. Co. v. Haloren, 53 Texas 46; 37 Am. Rep. 744; 3 Am. & Eng. R. Cas. 543.

Judge Thompson complains of the decision of the court, in Proud v. Philadelphia, etc., R. Co. (64 N. J. L. 702; 46 Atl. Rep. 710), holding that a railroad company, while bound to inspect its trains, need not keep up a continuous inspection or to know, at each moment the condition of every part of the train. This decision but bespeaks the practical rule, without gloss or glamour. It would be an impossibility for a railroad company to know, at each minute, the exact condition of a moving train and for this reason, as the law does not require the impossible, the rule is sound. See Palmer v. Pennsylvania R. Co., 111 N. Y. 488; 18 N. E. Rep. 859; 2 L. R. A. 252; 3 Thompson on Neg:, § 2786, p. 252.

[12] Schopman v. Boston, etc., R. Co., 9 Cush. (Mass.) 24; Philadelphia, etc., R. Co. v. Derby, 14 How. (U. S.) 468; Thompson, Carr. Pass., §§ 31, 175.

[13] Schopman v. Boston, etc., R. Co., 9 Cush. (Mass.) 24; Philadelphia, etc., R. Co. v. Derby, *supra*.

eral court has held that a railroad company that furnishes only the motive power to other railroads, not chartered to act as a common carrier of passengers, but engaged only in the business of hauling the passenger trains of various railroads across a bridge and through a tunnel, to a depot, is responsible only for a failure to exercise ordinary care and diligence in the handling of such trains, regardless of the degree of care exacted from the original company, whose trains are handled by it and which bears the relation of carrier toward its passengers.[14]

§ 639. **Duty to adopt new improvements.**— Carriers of passengers are bound to keep pace with science, art and modern improvements, in supplying safe vehicles, and they must adopt the most improved modes of construction and the most approved appliances of safety in the use of railroads. They are not excused from the use of all known tests of safety reasonably practicable in the improvements of their cars and appliances, nor is it material, when the vehicle has ceased to be up to the proper standard, that it was originally constructed by a competent and skilled manufacturer.[15] Railroad companies are bound to adopt every precaution which skill, care and foresight can provide and to exercise due care and caution in adopting new improvements, to secure additional protection for their passengers. If a defect exists, which could have been remedied by the adoption of a known scientific invention, or approved improvement, it is the duty of the carrier to employ such means, although it may not be in general use by railroad companies.[16]

But carriers are not required to adopt every new invention

[14] Keep v. Union, etc., R. Co., 9 Fed. Rep. 625; 3 McCrary (U. S.) 208. The soundness of this ruling is questioned by Judge Thompson. 3 Thompson, Neg., § 2808, p. 275.

[15] Treadwell v. Whittier, 80 Cal. 574; 22 Pac. Rep. 266.

[16] Caldwell v. New Jersey S. Co., 47 N. Y. 282.

and it is sufficient if they conform to such machinery and appliances as are in ordinary use by careful railroad companies and which have been approved by the prudent companies, engaged in a similar business.[17] The newest inventions are not always the safest appliances, and the mere adoption of the newest, if it is not the safest, might, of itself, furnish ground for a charge of negligence on the part of the carrier. The law, therefore, does not require the adoption of all the latest improvements, but that such, in kind and quality, as are approved by other prudent carriers, shall be adopted, to enable them, similarly situated, the better to perform their duties to the traveling public.[18] And, generally, the question whether or not the adoption of an appliance is a necessity for enhancing the safety of passengers, is an issue of fact for the jury.[19]

§ 640. **Liability for defective cars or appliances.**— The law requires the passenger carrier to furnish sufficiently safe cars and appliances to secure the safety of passengers, by the exercise of the utmost care and skill in their construction, whether it constructs them itself, or employs others to do so. It is not enough to show that reputable manufacturers were employed to construct the cars, but the carrier must see that the manufacturer not only possessed the requisite capacity and skill, but that such skill was actually exercised, in the construction of the coach or appliance.[20] The

[17] Louisville. etc., R. Co. v. Jones, 83 Ala. 376; 3 So. Rep. 902; 34 Am. & Eng. R. Cas. 417.

[18] Wallace v. Wilmington, etc., R. Co. (Del.), 18 Atl. Rep. 818.

[19] Hegeman v. Western R. Co., 13 N. Y. 9; 16 Barb. 353.

[20] Hegeman v. Western R. Co., 13 N. Y. 9; 16 Barb. 353; Holton v. London, etc., R. Co., 1 C. & E. 542; Taylor v. Grand Trunk R. Co., 48 N. H. 304; Gonzales v. New York, etc., R. Co., 39 How. Pr. (N. Y.) 407; Sullivan v. Philadelphia, etc., R. Co., 30 Pa. St. 234.

carrier is accordingly held responsible for the use of a defective car, occasioning injury to a passenger.[21]

The use of defective cars, with knowledge of their condition, is inconsistent with the degree of care required of a carrier of passengers and an instruction to that effect is proper, it being left to the jury, ordinarily, to determine whether or not the given car was defective and, if so, whether or not the carrier knew of the defect.[22] While the carrier is not an insurer, the courts hold it to the utmost diligence in the construction of its cars and appliances, used in the service for transportation of passengers.[23]

If an injury to a passenger occurs by the breaking of a bolt, whereby the rear wheels of a car were separated from the car, this would be sufficient evidence of negligence to establish a *prima facie* case, in favor of the injured person, and it would not necessarily constitute a conclusive defense to the action that the carrier had caused the car to be properly inspected and that no indication of any defect therein was open to careful observation.[24]

§ 641. **Injury from defect in, establishes prima facie case.** — Since the carrier is bound to exercise the utmost care and diligence in the use of cars and engines and other appliances, used in its passenger business, and it is responsible in law for the slightest neglect in this particular, in case of an injury caused thereby to a passenger, when an accident and injury are proved, resulting from the breaking of the carrier's cars or appliances, a want of road-worthiness, or insufficiency of construction or equipment, or other like ac-

[21] East Line R. Co. v. Smith, 65 Texas 167; Gulf, etc., R. Co. v. Ryan, 69 Texas 665; 7 S. W. Rep. 83; 33 Am. & Eng. R. Cas. 289.

[22] East Line R. Co. v. Smith, 65 Texas 167.

[23] Carroll v. Staten Island R. Co., 58 N. Y. 126; 65 Barb. 32; 9 Am. Ry. Rep. 486.

[24] Germain v. Montreal, etc., R. Co., 6 Low. Can. 172.

cidents occurring on the road, the law will imply some degree of negligence from these facts, for from their very nature they may be taken as affirmatively importing at least that slightest degree of negligence or unskillfulness which will be sufficient to render a carrier liable for an injury to a passenger.[25]

But this rule has no application where the injury to the passenger is occasioned by an outside agency and without fault on the part of the carrier. In such case, a recovery can only be had, upon proof of negligence on the carrier's part.[26]

§ 642. **Latent defects in.**— While the rule is stated to be that a railroad company contracts, with its passengers, not only for its own skill, but for that of the manufacturer, as well, from whom it has purchased its cars and appliances,[27] it is not held to warrant its cars or appliances and companies buying rolling stock from reputable manufacturers are not chargeable with negligence in accepting material on such

[25] Schultz v. Pacific R. Co., 36 Mo. 13. This case is overruled, in so far as it recognized a transmission of a right to sue for the death of an employee, due to the negligence of a coemployee, under the Missouri death statute, in Porter v. Hannibal, etc., R. Co., 64 Mo. 112, which latter case is affirmed by the Missouri decisions, in a complete line, on this point, culminating with the case of Strottman v. St. Louis, etc., R. Co., 109 S. W. Rep. 769. But the Schultz case, on the proposition announced in the text is approved, in the later cases. Furnish v. Missouri Pacific R. Co., 102 Mo. 438; Dougherty v. Missouri R. Co., 81 Mo. 325; Hipsley v. Kansas City, etc., R. Co., 88 Mo. 348; 27 Am. & Eng. R. Cas. 287; Hite v. Metropolitan R. Co., 130 Mo. 137; 31 S. W. Rep. 262; 32 S. W. Rep. 33; 51 Am. St. Rep. 555; Breen v. New York, etc., R. Co., 109 N. Y. 297; Seybolt v. New York, etc., R. Co., 95 N. Y. 562.

[26] Hite v. Metropolitan R. Co., 130 Mo. 138; 31 S. W. Rep. 262; 51 Am. St. Rep. 555; Smith v. Minneapolis, etc., R. Co., 32 Minn. 1; Pennsylvania R. Co. v. Gibson, 96 Pa. St. 83.

[27] Birmingham v. Rochester, etc., R. Co., 37 N. Y. S. R. 317; 59 Hun 583; 14 N. Y. Supp. 13.

inspection as is usual and practicable, without discovering any latent defects.[28]

In the case of an injury to a passenger, resulting from the breaking of a car wheel to a coach, if it appears that the wheel was made by one of the most skillful manufacturers of car wheels and had been thoroughly tested by skillful and experienced men and no defects perceived and such wheels were in extensive use, the railroad company cannot be held liable for negligence.[29]

And where an injury is due to a defect in a car, but the facts show that it was a latent defect and the evidence is as consistent with proper care, on the carrier's part, as with negligence, a nonsuit ought to be directed.[30]

§ 643. **Carrier's responsibility for negligence of manufacturer.**— While the courts and text writers, generally, who assert that the carrier ought to be held responsible, in case of an injury to a passenger, due to a latent defect or flaw in a manufactured appliance, concede that the basis of the carrier's liability is some act of personal negligence on the part of the carrier, it is none the less maintained, by respectable courts [31] and text writers [32] that both reason and authority favor the rule of holding the carrier liable for an injury due to a latent defect which no degree of care on its part could discover, if the defect ought to have been discov-

[28] Grand Rapids, etc., R. Co. v. Huntley, 38 Mich. 537; Richardson v. Great Eastern R. Co., L. R. 1 C. P. D. 342; Alden v. New York, etc., R. Co., 26 N. Y. 102; Meier v. Pennsylvania R. Co., 64 Pa. St. 225; Redhead v. Midland R. Co., 8 B. & S. 371; 36 L. J. Q. B. 181; L. R. 2 Q. B. 412; 15 W. R. 831; 16 L. T. 485.

[29] Toledo, etc., R. Co. v. Beggs, 85 Ill. 80.

[30] Gilbert v. North London R. Co., 1 C. & E. 31.

[31] Hegeman v. Western R. Co., 16 Barb. (N. Y.) 353; 13 N. Y. 9; Pittsburg, etc., R. Co. v. Nelson, 51 Ind. 150.

[32] 3 Thompson on Neg., § 2805; 2 Hutchinson on Carr. (3 ed.), § 909.

ered by the highest degree of care on the part of the manufacturer.

The theory of the law, as applied by those courts and text writers, asserting this extreme liability of the carrier, is that the negligence of the manufacturer is the negligence of the purchaser, in case the latter is a railroad company. This rule of law applies in no other vocation and is extended to no other class of litigants. It is a fiction, at the outset, to charge a manufacturer with negligence in failing to discover a flaw in an appliance disclosing no flaw, when subjected to careful inspection, and it is a double fiction to impute such imputed negligence to one in no way responsible therefor. An event that cannot be anticipated is never held to be the result of a negligent act, yet, in this instance, an event that could not be anticipated is held to be negligence, on the carrier's part. This is making an absolute insurer of the carrier, although it is conceded it is not an insurer. It is also predicating a liability on negligence, where none in fact exists.

Of course it is important to safeguard and protect the passenger, as far as sound principles of law will permit him to be safeguarded, but no further. He ought not to be insured, when the undertaking is only to indemnify him for the result of negligent acts.

Like the rule of comparative negligence, which had its origin in a mistaken holding of a court,[33] this rule making the carrier liable for the negligence of the manufacturer in failing to discover latent defects in cars or appliances, also owes its origin to an ill considered case.[34] In the State where it was delivered, it has been limited and reviewed,[35]

[33] 1 Thompson on Negligence, § 270.
[34] Hegeman v. Western R. Co., 13 N. Y. 9.
[35] Caldwell v. New Jersey R. Co., 47 N. Y. 282; Carroll v. Staten Island R. Co., 58 N. Y. 126; McPadden v. New York, etc., R. Co., 44 N. Y. 478.

and in other jurisdictions denied as unsound.[36] While not defending it on principle, some text writers have announced the doctrine, as a good one, from a policy standpoint,[37] and this has caused other courts to quote it approvingly.[38] .

§ 644. No liability, on principle, without personal negligence of carrier.—While not unmindful of the respectable authorities that maintain the opposite and assert that the carrier is responsible for the negligence of a manufacturer of a car or appliance, in failing to subject it to such tests as will disclose the presence of a latent defect,[39] the rule is believed to be, according to sound principles of the law, that no such responsibility exists on the part of a carrier, whether it is a railroad company, or a private individual, for such a defect in an appliance, purchased from a reputable manufacturer and subjected to careful tests by the railroad company, or other purchaser.

Discussing this subject, according to the undertaking of the carrier, as recognized by the decisions and according to sound principles, the Supreme Court of Tennessee, in a logical decision,[40] by Nicholson, C. J., said: " The legitimate obligation imposed upon the company by its contract with a passenger, or employee, is, that its engine and apparatus are then suitable, sufficient, and as safe as care and skill can

[36] Meier v. Pennsylvania R. Co., 64 Pa. St. 225; Frederick v. Northern R. Co., 157 Pa. St. 103; Grand Rapids, etc., R. Co. v. Huntley, 38 Mich. 537; Nashville, etc., R. Co. v. Jones, 9 Heisk. (Tenn.) 27.

[37] See Thompson and Hutchinson, *supra.* Hutchinson cites Meier v. Pennsylvania R. Co., as following this case, when it expressly refuses to do so. Hutchinson on Carr. (3 ed), § 909, p. 1018.

[38] Alden v. New York, etc., R. Co., 26 N. Y. 102. The first case, where this ill-advised decision was rendered, was by a divided court, Marvin and Denio, JJ., dissenting. Hegeman v. Western R. Corp., 13 N. Y. 9.

[39] Hegeman v. Western R. Corp., 13 N. Y. 9; 3 Thompson on Neg., § 2805; 2 Hutchinson on Carr. (3 ed.), § 909.

[40] Nashville, etc., R. Co. v. Jones, 9 Heisk. (Tenn.) 27.

make them, and that the company will be responsible. for any injury resulting from defects therein, which might have been discovered by the company or its agents, by the proper care and skill, in the application of the ordinary and approved tests. If the defects are such that they could not be discovered by the company or its agents, after a careful and skillful application of the ordinary and approved tests, then the company cannot be held responsible, although it may appear that the defects might have been discovered by the manufacturer by applying proper tests. We hold it unreasonable to· assume that the company not only contracts to be responsible for its own negligence but also for that of the manufacturers."

The Supreme Courts of Pennsylvania,[41] Michigan,[42] Indiana,[43] and other States have announced practically similar views upon the liability of the carrier for injuries due to undiscovered and undiscoverable defects in cars and appliances purchased from reputable manufacturers, and this is believed to be the rule more consistent with sound principles and property rights and the undertaking of the carrier, as recognized by all the authorities, in all other instances.

§ 645. **Vehicles or cars owned by others.**— If the carrier were permitted to avoid the effects of injuries due to unsafe appliances or to the defective construction of cars operated by it, merely because they belonged to other companies, it

[41] Meier v. Pennsylvania R. Co., 64 Pa. St. 225; Frederick v. Northern R. Co., 157 Pa. St. 103.

[42] Grand Rapids, etc., R. Co. v. Huntley, 38 Mich. 537.

[43] Grand Rapids, etc., R. Co. v. Boyd, 65 Ind. 526.

As pertinently remarked by the Supreme Court of Maine, in a leading case, in all these cases where the negligence is predicated on the discovery of the fact, after the event, producing the injury: "It is easy to be wise, after the event," and a negligent inspection, on the part of a manufacturer can always be established, by experts. Libby v. Maine, etc., R. Co., 85 Me. 34; 26 Atl. Rep. 943; 20 L. R. A. 812.

would be difficult, in each case, to establish a liability for an injury that the carrier ought to bear, hence it is generally held to be immaterial what company owned the car in which an injury is sustained, if it is due to an original imperfection in the car, or to a lack of care in the repair of the appliances therein, the carrier using the car at the time of the injury is liable therefor.[44]

Sleeping cars are very generally owned by other companies than the carrier engaged in the transportation of passengers from place to place, by rail, yet, if the railroad company permits one of its passengers to enter a sleeper and he sustains an injury due to a defect in the construction of the car or its appliances, or to an unsafe operation of the car, as a part of the train, on which the passenger is being conducted, the railroad company will be liable for such an injury, to the same extent as if it owned the sleeping car, wherein the injury was sustained.[45]

But in case of an injury to a passenger on a sleeping car, a distinction is to be recognized between the duty of the railroad company, in so far as its own negligence may enter into the cause of the injury, and that of the sleeping car company that owns the car, for while the railroad company, as between itself and the passenger, cannot shift its responsibility to the sleeping car company, yet the carrier's duties relate only to safe transportation and will not be held to include the duty of providing dressing rooms or other conveniences in the sleeper, which pertain to the obligations of the sleeping car company exclusively.[46]

[44] Hannibal, etc., R. Co. v. Martin, 111 Ill. 219; Nashville, etc., R. Co. v. Carroll, 6 Heisk. (Tenn.) 347; Stoddard v. Boston, etc., R. Co., 181 Mass. 422; 63 N. E. Rep. 927; 2 Hutchinson on Carr. (3 ed.), § 916, p. 1028, and cases cited.

[45] Pullman Co. v. Norton (Texas), 91 S. W. Rep. 841; Robinson v. Wabash, etc., R. Co., 135 Mich. 254; 97 N. W. Rep. 689.

[46] Ozanne v. Illinois, etc., R. Co., 151 Fed. Rep. 900.

§ 646. Must provide safe place for passenger to ride.— It is held, in a New York case,[47] that the stoppage of a passenger train, at a regular station on the line of a railroad company, is an invitation to the public to take passage thereon and the sale of a ticket for the train will bind the company operating it to furnish the passenger using the ticket a safe and secure place to ride. Proof of the failure on the part of the carrier to furnish such a safe place to ride, whereby a passenger is obliged to ride in an unsafe place, furnishes evidence of the negligence on the part of the carrier, for which a recovery might be permitted, in case of the injury of the passenger due to such cause.[48]

The same rule is stated somewhat differently, in another case,[49] where the court held that when a carrier accepted the fare from a passenger, without any restriction in the contract of carriage, as to the place or mode of carriage, the carrier is bound to furnish the passenger with a safe and comfortable vehicle and a safe and comfortable place or position in the car and so to transport the passenger that he shall not sustain injury from any fault or neglect of the carrier and in case of an injury to the passenger, due to the

"Plaintiff, a passenger in a sleeping car on defendant's railroad, was thrown down while in the ladies' dressing room, by the swing of the car as the train passed around a curve going at its ordinary speed. The car was constructed according to patterns uniformly used by the makers, which was considered the best, but the ladies' dressing room was not equipped with handholds affixed to the walls, nor with any seat or chair. Cars of the type in question had been operated for years with safety, and plaintiff's injury was the first of its kind that the sleeping car company had ever known. *Held*, that the failure to equip the dressing room with seats and handholds did not constitute negligence *per se*." Ozanne v. Illinois Cent. R. Co. (U. S. C. C., Ky., 1907), 151 Fed. Rep. 900.

[47] Werle v. Long Island R. Co., 98 N. Y. 650; 21 Am. & Eng. R. Cas. 429.

[48] Werle v. Long Island R. Co., *supra*.

[49] Hadencamp v. Second Avenue R. Co., 1 Sweeney (N. Y.) 490.

fault or neglect of the carrier, provided the passenger occupies as safe a place as he can and conducts himself with due care, in the place to which he is assigned, the carrier is responsible.

§ 647. **Duty to heat coach — Other accommodations.**— The carrier is under the obligation to provide for the heating of its coaches in cold weather, so as to avoid exposing its passengers to the cold,[50] and to supply retiring places for the convenience of the passengers,[51] drinking water,[52] lights for its coaches,[53] and such other conveniences and comforts as are generally and customarily supplied by railroad companies for the use of passengers, and for an injury to a passenger resulting from a failure to supply such conveniences, the carrier will be liable in damages.

But before a liability would be recognized for such cause, the failure of the company to supply such conveniences or appliances must be the proximate cause of a personal injury to the passenger and it must not be a case of mere incon-

"A carrier of passengers is not allowed to overcrowd its vehicles or cars, and a passenger who goes on a train for passage is not negligent in occupying a position in the baggage compartment of a combination car where there are no unoccupied seats in the passenger compartments or coaches." Lane v. Choctaw, etc., R. Co. (Okl. 1907), 91 Pac. Rep. 883.

"Where a railroad company makes no provision for assisting passengers to seats when necessary, a person accompanying a passenger needing such assistance may enter the train for that purpose, and may rely upon information furnished by a brakeman stationed at the steps to assist passengers getting on and off the train as to the time the train will remain at the station." St. Louis Southwestern Ry. Co. v. Cunningham (Tex. Civ. App. 1907), 106 S. W. Rep. 407.

[50] Missouri, etc., R. Co. v. Byrd (Texas), 89 S. W. Rep. 991; St. Louis, etc., R. Co. v. Haney (Texas), 94 S. W. Rep. 386; 2 Hutchinson on Carr. (3 ed.), § 922, and cases cited.

[51] Wood v. Central, etc., R. Co., 84 Ga. 363; 10 S. E. Rep. 967.

[52] Hunter v. Railroad Co. (S. Car.), 51 S. E. Rep. 860.

[53] Hutchinson on Carr. (3 ed.), § 922, p. 1035, and cases cited.

venience, as distinguished from a physical injury, due to such a cause. The passenger cannot recover damages for a failure to supply a coach with a water-closet, unless he sustained a physical injury thereby,[54] and since the carrier by freight train is not required to furnish the same conveniences as those used on a passenger train, and the passenger assumes the risk of injury due to a lack of such conveniences ordinarily found in such conveyances, the passenger cannot recover damages for a failure to provide a closet in a caboose, as a result of which an injury was sustained.[55]

But in the case of transportation by passenger coaches, it is held that the same high degree of care is to be exercised in providing those necessary appliances for the convenience and comfort of the passengers, as obtains in other cases and for an injury from a failure to have a coach properly heated, the carrier would be liable.[56]

[54] Henderson v. Texas, etc., R. Co., 42 S. W. Rep. 1030.

[55] Rodgers v. St. Louis, etc., R. Co. (Ark.), 89 S. W. Rep. 468; 1 L. R. A. (N. S.) 1145.

[56] International, etc., R. Co. v. Harrison, 97 Texas 611; 80 S. W. Rep. 1139.

"While a carrier as between itself and the passenger cannot transfer or shift its duty to a sleeping car company whose cars it hauls, yet the carrier's duties relate to safe transportation, and do not include the duty to provide dressing rooms for passengers." Ozanne v. Illinois Cent. R. Co. (U. S. C. C., Ky., 1907), 151 Fed. Rep. 900.

"A white female passenger sustained injuries in consequence of the failure of the carrier to heat its coach. The smoking and colored coaches and a sleeper were warm. It was not shown that the passenger knew that there was a sleeping car attached to the train, or that the other two coaches were warm. No one, in answer to her complaints, told her to go into other cars because they were warm. She could not, without violating the law, go into the negro coach, and females were not expected to occupy the smoking car. Held insufficient to raise the issue of contributory negligence of the passenger in failing to go into another coach." Texas & N. O. R. Co. v. Harrington (Tex. Civ. App. 1906), 98 S. W. Rep. 653.

"In an action for injuries to a passenger on a freight train while attempting to alight to respond to a call of nature, the absence of a

§ 648. **Injuries from failure to light coaches.**— In a reported case,[57] which arose in New York, a passenger in a sleeping coach was injured, while groping around in the dark, looking for the water-closet, which he could not find on account of the failure of the sleeping car company to keep that portion of the car lighted. It was held that it was not necessarily negligence on the part of the passenger to grope around in the dark, knowing that the locality of the car was insufficiently lighted, as he had a right to rely upon the performance of this duty by the carrier and the question of whether or not this portion of the car ought to have been kept lighted, to avoid such injuries, was held to be a question of fact for the jury, in view of all the facts and circumstances in evidence.

It was also held, by the federal court, that where a railroad company provides vestibuled coaches, it is required to keep the platform of such coaches reasonably lighted, to prevent a passenger, whom it impliedly invites to use the vestibule, from falling off and sustaining injuries.[58]

§ 649. **Car windows and doors.**— It is the duty of the carrier to provide cars with reasonably safe doors and windows, as these are constructed for the use of passengers and are apt to be used by them at any time. In case of an injury to a passenger, caused by a defect in a door or window, which

water-closet in the caboose may be considered, in passing on the question whether the employees in charge of the train were bound to know that the passenger would be likely to leave the car at stops, and would be negligent if they failed to warn him of the dangerous position of the car at stops." International & G. N. R. Co. v. Cruseturner (Tex. Civ. App. 1906), 98 S. W. Rep. 423.

[57] Piper v. New York, etc., R. Co., 76 Hun 44; 59 N. Y. S. R. 629; 27 N. Y. Supp. 593.

[58] Bronson v. Oakes, 76 Fed. Rep. 734; 40 U. S. App. 413; 22 C. C. A. 520.

could have been discovered by a reasonable inspection, the carrier will be held liable.[59]

In one Pennsylvania decision [60] it was held that no car was road-worthy if the windows were not so constructed as to prevent the passengers from putting their arms through them on a narrow board, but this decision does not seem to be supported by either reason or authority. A carrier is not bound to place its passengers in strait-jackets, or to provide such bars or appliances as will prevent them from placing their arms or hands in dangerous places, or to prevent them from protruding their bodies outside of car windows, as the carrier has the same right that any natural person has, to presume proper conduct on the part of its passengers. It is accordingly held, in another Pennsylvania case,[61] that

[59] Texas, etc., R. Co. v. Smith (Texas), 10 Am. Neg. Cas. 326; Leyh v. Newburgh, etc., R. Co. (N. Y.), 6 Am. Neg. Rep. 361. For injuries due to defective car windows, see Och v. Missouri, etc., R. Co., 130 Mo. 27; 31 S. W. Rep. 962; 36 L. R. A. 442; Alberti v. New York, etc., R. Co. (N. Y.), 9 Am. Neg. Cas. 664; Richards v. Great Eastern R. Co., 28 L. T. 711; Murray v. Metropolitan R. Co., 27 L. T. 762; Kelly v. New York, etc., R. Co., 109 N. Y. 44; 15 N. E. Rep. 879.

[60] Pennsylvania R. Co. v. Kennard, 10 Am. Neg. Cas. 151.

[61] Missimer v. Philadelphia, etc., R. Co., 17 Phila. (Pa.) 172.

"Where a carrier provided vestibules for its passenger cars, it thereby impliedly invited its passengers to pass to and fro to such portions of the train as they were entitled to occupy according to the grade of their transportation, and was thereby bound to maintain such vestibules in a reasonably safe condition." Wagoner v. Wabash R. Co. (Mo. App. 1906), 94 S. W. Rep. 293.

"In an action for injuries to a passenger whose fingers were crushed by the closing of a car door, the evidence *held* sufficient to warrant a finding that the latch used to hold the door open was defective." Missouri, etc., Ry. Co. v. Perry (Tex. Civ. App.), 95 S. W. Rep. 42.

While the carrier is generally not liable for an injury to a passenger, due to the sudden closing of a door, or window, in a coach (2 Hutchinson on Carr., 3 ed., 927), which could not have been foreseen as likely to occur, if the passenger is not allowed time to enter the train and by the too hasty starting of the train, his hand is caught in the door, which was not securely fastened and it is injured, he can recover. Poole v. Georgia, etc., R. Co., 89 Ga. 320; 15 S. E. Rep. 321.

it is not the duty of the carrier to place screens at the windows of its cars, either to prevent passengers from putting their heads or arms out, or to protect them against missiles thrown by persons outside the car, over whom the railroad company has no control, since an injury due to the wrongful act of either the passenger or a third person, is not, in due care, to be anticipated on the part of the carrier.

§ 650. **Defective baggage racks, chandeliers, etc.**— As it would be negligence almost amounting to wantonness to permit railroad companies to leave defective baggage racks, ventilating windows, lamp shades or gas fixtures so defectively attached to the car as to be liable to fall upon passengers, not looking or anticipating such unexpected substances to strike them, carriers are very generally held liable for such injuries, when the evidence shows that the appliance was in a defective condition, which could have been ascertained by a reasonably careful inspection, prior to the acci-

There is generally no liability for injuries from closing doors on a passenger's hand, whether the act of closing the door is that of another passenger, or of an employee of the carrier, as such things are not to be anticipated by the carrier, but are mere accidents, which cannot be guarded against. 2 Hutchinson on Carr. (3 ed.), § 927, p. 1043.

But if vestibuled doors are provided and are not kept in repair, but owing to a defect in such a door, it either stands open and a passenger falls from the train thereby, or it closes, without warning, on his hand, the carrier is liable, as for neglect in repairing any other appliance or part of its vehicle. Crandall v. Minneapolis, etc., R. Co. (Minn.), 105 N. W. Rep. 185; Robinson v. United States, etc., Ass'n, 132 Mich. 659; 94 N. W. Rep. 211; 102 Am. St. Rep. 436; 2 Hutchinson on Carr. (3 ed.), § 927, p. 1044, and cases cited.

The railroad company was held to be under no duty of warning passengers of the danger of protruding their bodies or limbs out of car windows, and of the probability of being struck by obstructions, in Miller v. St. Louis, etc., R. Co. (5 Mo. App. 471), where Bakewell, J., said: "Was the conductor bound to warn plaintiff not to put his elbow out, if he saw it on the sill of the window? Or was he bound to watch, to see that all passengers kept their elbows inside the car? We think not." (5 Mo. App. 480.)

dent,[62] nor would the plaintiff, generally, be required to establish the defective condition of the appliance by stronger
evidence than the fact of the injury resulting from the falling of such an appliance, for the rule res ipsa loquitur would
apply, in such a case.[63]

Accordingly, it was held, in a Massachusetts case,[64] where
the plaintiff, a passenger on the defendant's road, was injured
by the falling of a porcelain lamp-shade, attached to the up-
per portion of the car, that the fact that the shade fell was
alone sufficient to authorize the jury in finding that it was in
an unsafe condition prior to the injury, owing to the defendant's negligence.

§ 651. Platforms and steps to cars.— A railroad company
is bound to provide, for the use of its passengers, in entering
and leaving its cars, platforms and steps as safe as the high
degree of care, required in similar instances of such carriers, will make them, nor has it satisfied the requirements
of the law to provide safe platforms and steps for the use
of the passengers, when it has provided such as are ordinarily provided for similar cars on similar roads, in the locality where the railroad is operated.[65]

[62] Murray v. Metropolitan R. Co., 27 L. T. 762; Kelly v. New York,
etc., R. Co., 109 N. Y. 44; 15 N. E. Rep. 879; Och v. Missouri, etc.,
R. Co., 130 Mo. 27; 31 S. W. Rep. 962; 36 L. R. A. 442

[63] White v. Boston, etc., R. Co., 144 Mass. 404; 11 N. E. Rep. 552;
30 Am. & Eng. R. Cas. 615.

[64] White v. Boston, etc., R. Co., supra. In this case, the court said:
"If the shade was defective and unsafe, the question whether it was
in that condition through the negligence of the defendant, would
be for the jury, and the fact that it broke and fell from the use for
which it was intended, would be evidence that it was defective and
unsafe, and if not explained or controlled, would be sufficient evidence
to authorize the jury to find that the defendant was negligent in
regard to it." Citing, Kendall v. Boston, 118 Mass. 234; Field v.
Middlesex R. Co., 109 Mass. 398.

[65] Dougherty v. Kansas City, etc., R. Co., by Judge Robinson, 128
Mo. 33; 30 S. W. Rep. 317; 49 Am. St. Rep. 536.

But, as in the case of other appliances, in connection with the business of passenger transportation, railroad companies do not absolutely warrant the safety of the platforms and steps to their cars, but are responsible only for a failure to exercise the highest degree of care to maintain them in a reasonably safe condition.[66] The carrier is not required to furnish portable steps for the use of its passengers, on entering or leaving its cars; [67] nor is it bound to provide a chain and place it across the rear end of the platform to a caboose, on which passengers are allowed to ride, to prevent them from falling off.[68]

[66] Chicago, etc., R. Co. v. Hazzard, 26 Ill. 373; Sargent v. St. Louis, etc., R. Co., 114 Mo. 348; 21 S. W. Rep. 823; 19 L. R. A. 460; Kelly v. New York, etc., R. Co., 112 N. Y. 443.

[67] Young v. Missouri Pacific Ry. Co., 93 Mo. App. 267. Judge Smith, in this case, said: "If it did furnish such steps, it was but a self-imposed duty, for the violation of which there could, of course, be no liability." Barney v. Hannibal, etc., R. Co., 126 Mo. 372, 392; 28 S. W. Rep. 1069; 26 L. R. A. 847.

[68] Chicago, etc., R. Co. v. Hazzard, 26 Ill. 373; Lusby v. Atchison, etc., R. Co., 41 Fed. Rep. 181; 41 Am. & Eng. R. Cas. 93.

In Chicago, etc., R. Co. v. Hazzard (26 Ill. 373), the court said: "The care required is not that care without which accidents will not happen; as, for example, after a passenger is received on board, he would be safer — less liable to accident — if locked up in the car, or chained to one of the seats or other fixture so as to deprive him of locomotion, moving from car to car. This would be the very utmost degree of care and caution, but that is not required."

A platform to a car which had protruding iron flanges, over which a passenger stumbled and fell, was held to be a defectively constructed platform, in Chicago, etc., R. Co. v. Gates, 162 Ill. 98; 61 Ill. App. 211.

And a platform, with coupling pin projecting above the surface, on which a passenger's dress caught and threw her, was held to be a defective platform, in Illinois, etc., R. Co. v. O'Connell, 160 Ill. 636; 43 N. E. Rep. 704.

"When a station platform is so much below the level of the lower steps of the car as to make it unsafe for passengers to alight without an intermediate stool or steps, the carrier must provide one, but need not assist the passengers in alighting." Merryman v. Chicago Great Western Ry. Co. (Iowa 1907), 113 N. W. Rep. 357.

"Where, owing to the varying widths of a railroad company's cars,

§ 652. Condition of car wheels.— It has been held, in England,[69] that a railroad company is not liable for an in-

the space between the platform of a car and the station platform varied, it was the duty of the railroad company to use reasonable care to prevent accident by giving warning to one moving in the midst of a crowd of passengers seeking to board one of the narrower cars of the space between the platforms of the car and station." Woolsey v. Brooklyn Heights R. Co. (N. Y. Supp. 1908), 108 N. Y. S. 16.

"Where a passenger, in attempting to board a train, slipped and fell by reason alone of the icy condition of the car steps, the fact that the railroad company may also have been negligent in not providing a portable step is not a ground of recovery." Ft. Worth, etc., Ry. Co. v. Work (Tex. Civ. App. 1907), 100 S. W. Rep. 962.

"Where a passenger was injured by falling from the icy platform and steps of a railroad car, the carrier was not chargeable with negligence merely because vestibuled cars were not provided." Haas v. St. Louis & S. F. R. Co. (Mo. App. 1908), 106 S. W. Rep. 599.

"Where a plaintiff was injured while alighting from a passenger coach by her heel catching in the step, and the negligence alleged was the height of the step from the ground, and there was no evidence that the height was unusual, no negligence of defendant was shown." Traphagen v. Erie R. Co. (N. J. 1906), 64 Atl. Rep. 1072.

"A boy passenger riding on the platform and a defective step of a railway car assumed the risk of injury through such step, and the swaying of the train caused by defective track and roadbed, if he knew the step was defective and that the car was swaying, unless he was insufficiently intelligent to be able to understand the danger of so riding." Walling v. Trinity & Brazos Valley Ry. Co. (Tex. Civ. App. 1907), 106 S. W. Rep. 417.

"A woman carrying a baby, having boarded defendant's train, was about to enter the smoking car, when the brakeman told her to cross quickly over into another car, and in attempting to do so she fell between the cars and was injured. Plaintiff testified that the child prevented her from seeing the space between the platforms, and defendant's evidence showed that the curves of the platform were determined by the shortest curve at which it was necessary for the cars to pass, and that the best device known for covering the space between the cars had proved impracticable. *Held*, that there was no negligence on the part of the defendant; it not having been bound to warn the passenger or to assist her in crossing." Hawes v. Boston Elevated Ry. Co. (Mass. 1906), 78 N. E. Rep. 480.

[69] Redhead v. Midland R. Co., 8 B. & S. 371; 36 L. J. Q. B. 181; L. R. 2 Q. B. 412; 15 W. R. 831; 16 L. T. 485, affirmed on appeal, in 9 B. & S. 519; L. R. 4 Q. B. 379; 38 L. J. Q. B. 169; 20 L. T. 682;

jury to a passenger, due to a latent defect in a car wheel, which no amount of care or skill could discover.

This holding is in accord with the principle of the law underlying the carrier's liability to passengers, from such causes resulting in injuries, for an accident caused by a latent defect in the wheel of a passenger coach, which no care could detect, ought not to subject the railroad company to a liability, since it does not absolutely warrant the road-worthiness of its vehicles, but it is only bound to use the utmost care and vigilance to see that they are sufficient and maintained in a safe condition for use.[70]

But where, in an action for an injury to a passenger, the evidence tends to show the negligence on the part of the railroad company, in running the train at a high rate of speed, over a defective track and roadbed and that one of the coaches had a cracked car wheel, which had not been carefully inspected, this will be sufficient evidence upon which to predicate a verdict for the injured passenger and a judgment on such a verdict ought not to be set aside upon the ground that it has no substantial evidence to support it.[71]

§ 653. **Insufficient car axles.**— In a New York case [72] it was decided that a carrier of passengers was liable for an injury to a passenger caused by a defective car axle giving way, although the defect in the axle could not have been discovered by any practical test or examination of the axle, prior to the accident. This decision followed an earlier case

17 W. R. 737; followed, in Searle v. Laverick, L. R. 9 Q. B. 122; 43 L. J. Q. B. 43; 30 L. T. 89; 22 W. R. 367.

[70] Redhead v. Midland R. Co., *supra;* Blamires v. Lancashire, etc., R. Co., 42 L. J. Ex. 182; L. R. 8 Ex. 283.

[71] Texas, etc., R. Co. v. Hamilton, 66 Texas 92; 26 Am. & Eng. R. Cas. 182. See, for case holding that it was jury issue whether drive wheel of engine had been properly inspected, Manser v. Eastern, etc., R. Co., 3 L. T. 585.

[72] Alden v. New York, etc., R. Co., 26 N. Y. 102.

in New York,[73] holding that a railroad company was liable for an injury to a passenger, by the breaking of a car axle, purchased from reputable and practical manufacturers, although the defect could not be discovered by an external examination, provided it might have been known by a vigilant examination, during the process of manufacture.

This former decision has been criticised in a Tennessee case;[74] disapproved in a Pennsylvania decision;[75] reviewed by the New York court,[76] and limited in its application by later cases in New York.[77]

As the practical effect of the decision is to make of the carrier an insurer of the safety of the passengers transported by it and the liability is made to depend upon a mere defect and injury, in the face of proof of a want of all negligence, it ought not to be generally followed, because not in harmony with the settled principles of the law, as generally followed and announced by the courts.

The better rule and the one more in accord with the principles of the law, applicable to the subject of the carrier's liability, in such cases, is that the railroad company is not liable to passengers for injuries resulting from latent defects in parts of the car, which human knowledge, skill and foresight cannot provide against. And if a passenger is injured by the breaking of an axle, made by the most proficient manufacturer of such appliances, of the best material and apparently in good condition, the roadbed and track being sound and the train running at a proper rate of speed, there is no liability for an injury to the passenger, due to such cause, as there is a total absence of the basis for such liability, in

[73] Hegeman v. Western R. Co., 13 N. Y. 9. See, also, Sharp v. Gray, 9 Bing. 457; 2 M. & S. 621.

[74] Nashville, etc., R. Co. v. Jones, 9 Heisk. (Tenn.) 27.

[75] Meier v. Pennsylvania R. Co., 64 Pa. St. 225.

[76] Caldwell v. New Jersey S. Co., 47 N. Y. 282.

[77] McPadden v. New York, etc., R. Co., 44 N. Y. 478; Carroll v. Staten Island R. Co., 58 N. Y. 126.

that no negligence is shown.[78]   But if the employees of the
railroad company have made a proper inspection of such an
appliance as a car axle and an accident afterwards ensues,
whereby a passenger is injured, it does not follow, necessarily, that there is no negligence, upon which a recovery
can stand, for it is none the less a fact for the jury to decide,
whether or not the inspection was carefully or improperly
made and the defect, if any existed, could have been discovered by a reasonably careful inspection.[79]

§ 654. **Defective brakes.**— In an action for damages for
an injury by reason of a defective brake on one of the cars
in the train, where the accident and injury occurred at night
and during a heavy storm, it is proper for the court to charge
the jury that the railroad company would be liable if the
injury was due to a brake " which was out of order, or not
in reasonable repair, or not reasonably safe for the occasion,"
since the company is required to furnish a brake sufficient
for stormy weather, as well as one sufficient for fair weather,
otherwise passengers would be left without efficient safeguards. at the time when they are most needed.[80]   And an

[78] Meier v. Pennsylvania R. Co., 64 Pa. St. 225; Fredericks v.
Northern, etc., R. Co., 157 Pa. St. 103; Philadelphia, etc., R. Co. v.
Anderson, 94 Pa. St. 351; 39 Am. Rep. 787; 6 Am. & Eng. R. Cas. 407.
[79] Thacher v. Great Western R. Co., 4 U. C. C. P. 543.
But for an injury due to the breaking of a car axle, which had been
carefully selected, after the train had rounded a six degree curve,
where no defects were apparent in the axle, there was held to be no
liability, in Dube v. The Queen, 3 Can. Exch. 147.
Injuries to passengers were due from the breaking of defective car
axles, in the following cases: Frink v. Potter (Ill.), 9 Am. Neg.
Cas. 200; Indianapolis, etc., R. Co. v. Boyd, 9 Am. Neg. Cas. 289;
Chicago, etc., R. Co. v. Voight, 9 Am. Neg. Cas. 291; Pennsylvania R.
Co. v. Newmeyer (Ind.), 9 Am. Neg. Cas. 291; Ingalls v. Bills (Mass.),
9 Am. Neg. Cas. 426; Minneapolis, etc., R. Co. v. Huntley (Mich.),
9 Am. Neg. Cas. 472.
[80] Mackey v. Baltimore, etc., R. Co., 8 Mackey (D. C.) 282.

injury due to a defective brake wheel, whereby a passenger sustains damages, without his fault, will constitute a cause of action against the railroad company operating the car with the defective brake wheel.[81]

But where mixed trains, consisting of passenger and freight cars are run, and the use of such trains is not forbidden by law, air brakes will not be required, unless it is shown to be practicable to use such brakes on trains of this character and the use of such brakes is necessary to protect passengers from injury.[82]

§ 655. Injury due to defective couplings.— As the policy of the law, for the protection of the citizen, is to hold the carrier of passengers responsible for the highest possible degree of care and foresight in providing appliances over which the passenger has no control or right of inspection, and in case of an injury to a passenger, to compel restitution in damages, if the injury is due, in any degree, to the negligence on the part of the carrier, this rule could not be applied, in case of an injury to a passenger caused by a defect in the carrier's appliances, to a case where the necessity for such a rule is more apparent than in that of an injury due to

[81] Cleveland, etc., R. Co. v. McHenry, 47 Ill. App. 301.

[82] Arkansas Midland R. Co. v. Canman, 52 Ark. 517; 13 S. W. Rep. 280.

For injury to passenger on car platform, owing to failure of brake to work, going down steep grade, where carrier held liable, see Burns v. Bellefontaine Ry. Co., 50 Mo. 139; 4 Am. Neg. Cas. 477.

And for injury to passenger caused by jumping off train, when air brake failed to work, see Porter v. Railroad (Mich.), 4 Am. Neg. Cas. 96.

" Where a railway company relies on an inspection of brakes as a defense to an action for injuries to a passenger, in a collision caused by alleged defective brakes, the inspection must be shown to be as thorough as the dangers incident to the business make necessary." Rouston v. Detroit United Ry. (Mich. 1908), 115 N. W. Rep. 62.

defective couplings between the coaches of a train.[83]   This is a frequent source of injury to passengers, standing or stepping upon the platforms of cars, and such appliances are located where no degree of care on the passenger's part would bring him in contact with the appliance and the necessity for such frequent use of couplings, in the movement of cars and trains, ought to require the courts to compel railroads to use the highest degree of care in the selection and care of these appliances.[84]

If a passenger is injured, while passing from one coach to another, in a passenger train, caused by the giving way of a coupling between the coaches, the railroad company ought to be held liable for the injury, if there is a defective coupling which could have been detected by the most careful examination, for this is not a visible risk which the passenger would assume.[85]   But if the railroad company has used the best automatic couplers, equipped with air brakes, and no defect could be discovered therein, by ordinary care, but a passenger was injured as a result of the coaches coming apart, without any apparent cause therefor, the company would not be liable, in the absence of some showing of negligence to rebut this defense of ordinary care and diligence on its part.[86]

§ 656. **Duty to provide spark arresters.**— The duty of railroad companies, operating their trains by means of steam,

[83] Goodrich v. New York, etc., R. Co., 116 N. Y. 398; 22 N. E. Rep. 397.

[84] Costikyan v. Rome, etc., R. Co., 12 N. Y. Supp. 683.

[85] Costikyan v. Rome, etc., R. Co., 12 N. Y. Supp. 683.

[86] Holland v. St. Louis, etc., R. Co., 105 Mo. App. 117; 79 S. W. Rep. 508.

" Where a passenger injured by the breaking of a defective coupling and the parting of the train, showed that an inspection of the coupling might have disclosed the defect, the company was required to show that it made an inspection, and a failure to do so warranted a recovery." Galveston, etc., Ry. Co. v. Young (Tex. Civ. App. 1907), 100 S. W. Rep. 993.

to provide spark arresters, to prevent injury to their passengers by escaping sparks and cinders, has been before the courts and it is held to be an affirmative duty on the part of carriers to provide such appliances, in order to protect passengers from such accidents.[87] As in the case of other similar appliances, the duty is not to provide the best or safest spark arrester that may have been invented or placed on the market,[88] but to provide one that is reasonably sufficient for the purpose and to keep it in repair, the same as the carrier is required to maintain its other appliances in repair, for the protection of its passengers.[89]

Of course there is more or less chance of a spark or cinder resulting in injury to a passenger, not only because of the fact that such cinders are usually cold, before going a very long distance, and also because it is more or less a chance if a live spark happens to enter a passenger's eye, so although an engine emits sparks, it cannot well be said that the company was negligent in not anticipating that the unusual circumstance should have been anticipated, that the spark, thus emitted, would enter the eye of the passenger. All such conclusions depend so entirely upon the element of chance that it seems like basing a liability upon a fictitious basis to hold the company for negligence in any case, for an injury due to such a cause, since carriers are not held liable for accidents.

In a recent Kansas case, it was held that a railroad company was not liable for an injury to a passenger, caused by a spark or cinder flying into his eye, where it appeared

[87] St. Louis, etc., R. Co. v. Parks, 97 Texas 131; 76 S. W. Rep. 740; 90 S. W. Rep. 343; Missouri, etc., R. Co. v. Mitchell (Texas), 79 S. W. Rep. 94; 2 Hutchinson on Carr. (3 ed.), § 912, p. 1022, and cases cited.

[88] St. Louis, etc., R. Co. v. Parks, *supra*.

[89] See chapter, Various Duties of the Railroad Company; 2 Hutchinson on Carr., § 912, p. 1022.

that the locomotive was in good repair and equipped with the best known spark arrester, and the engine was handled by a competent engineer and there was no other act from which it could be said the carrier was negligent.[90]

[90] Kansas City, etc., R. Co. v. Orton, 67 Kansas 848; 73 Pac. Rep. 63.

CHAPTER XXV.

NEGLIGENCE IN THE EQUIPMENT AND OPERATION OF TRAINS.

§ 657. Care in equipment and operation of trains, generally.— In the equipment and operation of its passenger trains, a railroad company is held to a very high degree of care. for the protection and safety of the passengers transported and is answerable for any negligence, in this particu-

997

lar, whereby a passenger is injured.[1] The cases on personal injuries due to failure on the carrier's part to properly equip or operate its trains, use various terms, as expressive of the high degree of care to be exacted of the carrier and in some it is held to be the "highest degree of care" for the safety of the passenger;[2] in others,[3] "the utmost care" and in still others,[4] the "utmost human skill, diligence and foresight" for the safe transportation of the passenger. These various terms are practically of the same import and evince the disposition on the part of the courts to hold the carrier, in the equipment and management of its trains, to the high degree of care and caution. such as would be exercised by a very cautious person.[5]

But the carrier does not insure the safety of the passengers, against injury from any particular cause,[6] and it does not owe to the passengers, the "utmost care that human

[1] Huelsenkamp v. Citizens R. Co., 37 Mo. 537; 90 Am. Dec. 399; Lemon v. Chanslor, 68 Mo. 340; 30 Am. Rep. 799; Dougherty v. Missouri, etc., R. Co., 81 Mo. 325; 51 Am. Rep. 239; 97 Mo. 647; 11 S. W. Rep. 251; Furnish v. Missouri Pacific Ry. Co., 102 Mo. 438; 13 S. W. Rep. 1044; 22 Am. St. Rep. 781; Clark v. Chicago, etc., R. Co., 127 Mo. 197; 29 S. W. Rep. 1013; Baltimore, etc., R. Co. v. Noell, 32 Gratt. (Va.) 394; McElroy v. Nashua, etc., R. Co., 4 Cush. (Mass.) 400; Searle v. Kanawha, etc., R. Co., 32 W. Va. 370; 9 S. E. Rep. 248; 37 Am. & Eng. R. Cas. 179.

[2] Tillman v. St. Louis Transit Co., 102 Mo. App. 553; 77 S. W. Rep. 320.

[3] Fillingham v. St. Louis Transit Co., 102 Mo. App. 573; 77 S. W. Rep. 314.

[4] Lemon v. Chanslor, 68 Mo. 340; 30 Am. Rep. 799; Coudy v. St. Louis, etc., R. Co., 85 Mo. 79; Dougherty v. Missouri, etc., R. Co., 81 Mo. 325; 51 Am. Rep. 239. But an instruction in this extreme form, was held bad, in Dougherty v. Missouri, etc., R. Co., 97 Mo. 667, on rehearing; 11 S. W. Rep. 251.

[5] Wilburn v. St. Louis, etc., R. Co., 48 Mo. App. 224; O'Connell v. St. Louis, etc., R. Co., 106 Mo. 482; 17 S. W. Rep. 494.

[6] Gilson v. Jackson County R. Co., 76 Mo. 282; Leslie v. Wabash R. Co., 88 Mo. 50; Hite v. Metropolitan, etc., R. Co., 130 Mo. 132; 31 S. W. Rep. 262; 51 Am. St. Rep. 555.

imagination can conceive," although it does owe them care of a very high degree, to avoid injuries due to a failure to properly equip and manage its trains.[7] Accordingly, it is held that a charge to the jury that the carrier owed to its passengers such care and foresight as is "reasonably practicable," is sufficient, and the defendant should not be required to exercise the "utmost practicable human skill, diligence and foresight."[8] However, an instruction that the carrier ought to exercise, in the transportation of its passengers, in the equipment and management of its cars, "the highest degree of care which could ordinarily be expected of very prudent persons under the like or similar circumstances," has been approved.[9]

§ 658. **Rules and regulations governing passengers.**— Passenger carriers may adopt such rules and regulations for the management of their trains and passenger business. as are reasonable and calculated to promote the interests of the

[7] Magrane v. St. Louis, etc., R. Co., 183 Mo. 119; 81 S. W. Rep. 1158.

[8] Feary v. Metropolitan Ry. Co., 162 Mo. 75; 62 S. W. Rep. 452.

[9] Muth v. St. Louis, etc., R. Co., 87 Mo. App. 422.

A passenger injured by the negligence of employees handling a train, is entitled to damages, although they did not know he was in the car. Way v. Chicago, etc., R. Co., 73 Iowa 463; 35 N. W. Rep. 525; 34 Am. & Eng. R. Cas. 286. And see, Louisville, etc., R. Co. v. Ballard, 85 Ky. 307; 3 S. W. Rep. 530; 7 Am. St. Rep. 600; 28 Am. & Eng. R. Cas. 135.

A trial court should not hold the railroad company to be negligent for failing to provide a brakeman for each car in its train. Dinwiddie v. Louisville, etc., R. Co., 9 Lea (Tenn.) 309; 15 Am. & Eng. R. Cas. 483.

It is held negligence to fail to provide different kinds of uniforms and lanterns for conductors and station masters, in Kansas City, etc., R. Co. v. Sanders, 98 Ala. 293; 13 So. Rep. 57; 58 Am. & Eng. R. Cas. 140.

The duty of the carrier, with reference to the equipment of its trains and the care to be exercised in the management of the trains, is the same. Evers v. Wiggins, etc., Co., 116 Mo. App. 130; 92 S. W. Rep. 118.

company and of the traveling public,[10] and rules governing the management of trains,[11] for the conduct of the employees on a train and also for the conduct of the passengers being transported,[12] providing for the safety of passengers,[13] for the manner of transporting the passengers,[14] respecting the mode of performing the duties of a passenger carrier,[15] the admission of passengers to the trains of the carrier,[16] and governing the classification of their business,[17] will be upheld by the courts, provided all such rules are reasonable and do not subject the passenger to unnecessary annoyance or hazard.[18]

The reasonableness of a given rule, in the absence of particular facts and circumstances, as to its application,[19] would be ordinarily a question of law for the court,[20] but under cer-

[10] Boster v. Chesapeake, etc., R. Co., 36 W. Va. 318; 15 S. E. Rep. 158; 52 Am. & Eng. R. Cas. 357.

[11] Wightman v. Chicago, etc., R. Co., 73 Wis. 169; 40 N. W. Rep. 689; 2 L. R. A. 185; Britton v. Atlanta, etc., R. Co., 88 N. Car. 536; 43 Am. Rep. 749; 18 Am. & Eng. R. Cas. 391.

[12] Crawford v. Cincinnati, etc., R. Co., 26 Ohio St. 580; Chicago, etc., R. Co. v. McLally, 84 Ill. 109; 16 Am. Ry. Rep. 425.

[13] Florida, etc., R. Co. v. Hirst, 30 Fla. 1; 11 So. Rep. 506; 52 Am. & Eng. R. Cas. 409.

[14] Avery v. New York, etc., R. Co., 121 N. Y. 31; 24 N. E. Rep. 20; Gray v. Cincinnati, etc., R. Co., 11 Fed. Rep. 683.

[15] Johnson v. Concord R. Co., 46 N. H. 213.

[16] Northern, etc., R. Co. v. O'Connor, 76 Md. 207; 24 Atl. Rep. 449; 16 L. R. A. 449; 52 Am. & Eng. R. Cas. 176.

[17] Farber v. Missouri Pacific Ry. Co., 116 Mo. 81; 22 S. W. Rep. 631.

[18] Central, etc., R Co. v. Strickland, 90 Ga. 562; 16 S. E. Rep. 352; 52 Am. & Eng. R. Cas. 216; Eddy v. Rider, 79 Texas 53; Norfolk, etc., R. Co. v. Wysor, 82 Va. 250; 26 Am. & Eng. R. Cas. 234·

[19] Pittsburg, etc., R. Co. v. Lyon, 123 Pa. St. 140; 16 Atl. Rep. 607; 37 Am. & Eng. R. Cas. 231.

[20] South Florida R. Co. v. Rhodes, 25 Fla. 40; 5 So. Rep. 633; 3 L. R. A. 733; 37 Am. & Eng. R. Cas. 100; Chilton v. St. Louis, etc., R. Co., 114 Mo. 88; 21 S. W. Rep. 457. And it is held error to submit the issue to the jury, in Avery v. New York, etc., R. Co., 121 N. Y. 31; 24 N. E. Rep. 20; St. Louis, etc., R. Co. v. Adcock, 52 Ark. 406; 12 S. W. Rep. 874; 40 Am. & Eng. R. Cas. 682; Illinois R. Co. v.

tain circumstances it is held to be a mixed question of law and fact.[21]

§ 659. **Passenger's notice and violation of rules.**— Passengers are not presumed to be acquainted with the secret rules of the carrier to its employees, governing the conduct of its passenger business,[22] and before a rule will be binding on a passenger, it must be brought home to him,[23] but it is the duty of the passenger to inform himself of the reasonable rules and regulations of the carrier, governing the conduct of its business and for the safety of the passenger [24] and if the passenger's rules —such as the familiar one. that passengers must not stand on the platforms of cars — are posted in conspicuous places where the passengers could see them, they will be presumed to have had notice of such rules and must assume the burden of proof, when it is alleged that they did not have such notice.[25]

Passengers are required to observe and comply with the reasonable rules, adopted by the carrier for their protection and the management and operation of the train, and if they

Whitmore, 43 Ill. 420; Morris, etc., R. Co. v. Ayres, 29 N. J. L. 393; Hoffbauer v. Davenport, etc., R. Co., 52 Iowa 342; 3 N. W. Rep. 121.

[21] Bass v. Chicago, etc., R. Co., 36 Wis. 450; 9 Am. Ry. Rep. 101; Brown v. Memphis, etc., R. Co., 4 Fed. Rep. 37.

"A rule requiring the expulsion from a car of a passenger who refuses to either pay his fare or produce a proper transfer ticket showing his right to ride on the car is a reasonable one." Norton v. Consolidated Ry. Co. (Conn. 1906), 63 Atl. Rep. 1087.

[22] Georgia, etc., R. Co. v. Murden, 86 Ga. 434; 12 S. E. Rep. 630; Lake Shore, etc., R. Co. v. Rosenzweig, 113 Pa. St. 519; 6 Atl. Rep. 545; 26 Am. & Eng. R. Cas. 489.

[23] Norfolk, etc., R. Co. v. Wysor, 82 Va. 250; 26 Am. & Eng. R. Cas. 234; Hufford v. Grand Rapids R. Co., 64 Mich. 631; 31 N. W. Rep. 544.

[24] Southern, etc., R. Co. v. Kinsdale, 38 Kansas 507; 16 Pac. Rep. 937; 34 Am. & Eng. R. Cas. 256; Atchison, etc., R. Co. v. Gants, 38 Kansas 608; McRea v. Wilmington, etc., R. Co., 88 N. Car. 526; 43 Am. Rep. 745; 18 Am. & Eng. R. Cas. 316.

[25] Macon, etc., R. Co. v. Johnson, 38 Ga. 409.

fail to do so, after notice to them of the existence of the rule, in case of an injury, brought about in part because of such violation of the rule of the carrier, the passenger would be without remedy.[26]

§ 660. **Duty to employ competent employees.**— Even as to its own employees, the railroad company owes the obligation to employ a sufficient number and competent employees, so as to conduct its business with reasonable safety.[27] This duty applies, with even stronger reason, in favor of a passenger and it is just as essentially the duty of a carrier to

[26] Crawford v. Cincinnati, etc., R. Co., 26 Ohio St. 580; 13 Am. Ry. Rep. 387; Boster v. Chesapeake, etc., R. Co., 36 W. Va. 318; 15 S. E. Rep. 158; 52 Am. & Eng. R. Cas. 357.

"To absolve itself from liability for injuries to a passenger riding in its baggage car, the carrier must adopt and post in a conspicuous place in its passenger cars printed rules and regulations forbidding or warning passengers not to ride in such baggage car." Lane v. Choctaw, etc., R. Co. (Okl. 1907), 91 Pac. Rep. 883.

"Regulations of a carrier as to which platform shall be used for the purpose of alighting, which are in the form of instructions to its trainmen, are not binding upon a passenger, if not known to him." Harley v. Aurora, etc., Ry. Co., 128 Ill. App. 643.

"In an action for injuries to a passenger, the admission of the rules of the company, prescribing the duties and powers of its servants, is erroneous, where it does not appear that the plaintiff knew of the existence of such rules or relied or acted thereon." Illinois Cent. R. Co. v. Downs, 122 Ill. App. 545.

"Where, in an action for personal injuries sustained by a passenger, the carrier desires to avail itself of its rules and regulations relating to passengers and a violation thereof by the passenger, the same must be pleaded." Lane v. Choctaw, etc., R. Co. (Okl. 1907), 91 Pac. Rep. 883.

"Though a railway company had a rule prohibiting the carriage of passengers on its freight trains without special authority, where plaintiff did not know of such rule, and was on the train by consent of the conductor, and the company knew or should have known that this rule was generally violated and did not object, it was liable for his negligent injury." St. Louis Southwestern Ry. Co. v. Morgan (Tex. Civ. App. 1906), 98 S. W. Rep. 408.

[27] See chapter, Various Duties of the Employer.

employ a sufficient number and competent employees to manage and operate its trains, as it is to provide safe cars, engines and appliances for the transportation of its passengers and it should be held to a high degree of care in this particular, and failing therein, in case of injury to a passenger, the carrier is liable in damages.[28]

Speaking of the duty to employ a sufficient number and competent employees, to safely manage the car or train on which an injured passenger was riding, Judge Gantt, for the Missouri Supreme Court recently said, in approving the instruction that had been given on this issue, in the trial court: " The additional objection that it required defendant to have skillful employees is without merit. The law exacts that a company, using appliances which will naturally prove very dangerous, if not handled skillfully, shall have competent servants in charge thereof." [29]

§ 661. **Excessive rate of speed.**—Where the speed of trains is not regulated by statute or ordinance, unless in exceptional cases, the existence of a high rate of speed does not argue a fault on the part of the railroad company, as the reasonable rule is that the highest rate of speed is proper and legitimate which is consistent with the safety of the passengers transported.[30]

A company has the lawful right to run its trains at such times, on such terms, and at such increased rates of speed, within the limits of prudence and safety to its passengers, as the necessities or convenience of its business may require, and it is erroneous to assume that the running of special

[28] Evers v. Wiggins Ferry Co., 116 Mo. App. 130; 92 S. W. Rep. 118; Olsen v. Citizens Ry. Co., 152 Mo. 426; 54 S. W. Rep. 470.

[29] Olsen v. Citizens Ry. Co., 152 Mo. 431; 54 S. W. Rep. 470.

[30] Houston v. Vicksburg, etc., R. Co., 39 La. Ann. 796; 2 So. Rep. 562; 34 Am. & Eng. R. Cas. 76; Gonzales v. New York, etc., R. Co., 39 How. Pr. (N. Y.) 407; Terry v. Jewett, 78 N. Y. 338.

trains, or the running of trains at an increased rate of speed, is negligence on the part of the carrier.[31]

A railroad company owes the duty to the public to make velocity of locomotion compatible with safety, so far as this can be effected by care and skill. It is the implied condition of the contract of carriage, that a passenger shall not be placed in jeopardy of life or limb by even the slight negligence of the railroad company. The sense of the company's responsibility for injuries due to its negligence is the strongest assurance that the public can have of a safe performance of the contract, and the rule of liability should be strictly enforced to this end,[32] but the courts should not be vindictive in the administration of the law toward any particular class or against any particular litigant and negligence should always be held to be the basis of the liability, in each case.

A high rate of speed is not negligence, on the part of a railroad company, if the conditions of the roadway and the cars and appliances used will permit it without increasing the peril of the passenger and in determining whether or not a given rate of speed, maintained by a certain train, is a negligent operation of the road by the carrier, the character of the roadway, the grades and curves, the road-worthiness of the train and various other conditions necessarily affecting the question of safety in running at such a rate of speed, should be taken into consideration.[33]

[31] East Tennessee, etc., R. Co. v. Winters, 85 Tenn. 240; 1 S. W. Rep. 790.

[32] Black v. Carrollton, etc., R. Co., 10 La. Ann. 33.

[33] Chicago, etc., R. Co. v. Lewis, 145 Ill. 67; 33 N. E. Rep. 960; 58 Am. & Eng. R. Cas. 126.

"The fact that a train is running at a high rate of speed is not negligence, where the condition of the track and roadbed and the character of the engine and equipment are such that that speed may be safely maintained." Illinois Cent. R. Co. v. Porter (Tenn. 1906), 94 S. W. Rep. 666.

"Whether a given rate of speed constitutes negligence of a carrier depends on the surrounding circumstances of each case." Elgin, etc., Traction Co. v. Wilson, 120 Ill. App. 371, judgment affirmed, 75 N. E. Rep. 436; 217 Ill. 47.

Where the evidence showed that at the place where a derailment occurred, the ties were rotten and the spikes loose, so as to endanger a train operated at a high rate of speed, it was held proper to charge the jury that to entitle the plaintiff to recover it must be shown that the train was run at a high rate of speed, or at a speed so great as to constitute negligence, considering the condition of the track and train. Chicago, etc., R. Co. v. Lewis, 145 Ill. 67; 33 N. E. Rep. 960; 58 Am. & Eng. R. Cas. 126; Indianapolis, etc., R. Co. v. Hall, 106 Ill. 371.

It was lfeld to be negligence to run a train at a high rate of speed, at a place known to be frequented by cattle, without some precaution to keep the cattle off the track, in Brown v. New York, etc., R. Co., 34 N. Y. 404.

In Houston v. Vicksburg, etc., R. Co. (39 La. Ann. 796; 2 So. Rep. 562; 34 Am. & Eng. R. Cas. 78), Todd, J., speaking for the court, said: "A high rate of speed has always been a great *desideratum*, and engineering skill has been taxed to the utmost, to attain it; and we conceive the reasonable and established rule on this subject to be, that no conceivable rate of speed, consistent with the safety of passengers, is negligence *per se*."

An instruction that the mere speed of a train and the fact that it was behindhand are not, *per se*, evidence of negligence, is held to be proper, in New York, etc., R. Co. v. Kellams (Va.), 32 Am. & Eng. R. Cas. 114.

It is now settled law that no rate of speed in crossing a public highway, in the absence of statute or ordinance, will constitute negligence on the part of a railroad company. Reading, etc., R. Co. v. Ritchie, 102 Pa. S. 425; 19 Am. & Eng. R. Cas. 267; Powell v. Missouri Pacific R. Co., 76 Mo. 80; 8 Am. & Eng. R. Cas. 467; Goodwin v. Chicago, etc., R. Co., 75 Mo. 73; 11 Am. & Eng. R. Cas. 460; Wallace v. St. Louis, etc., R. Co., 74 Mo. 594; Hite v. Metropolitan Ry. Co., 130 Mo. 132; 31 S. W. Rep. 262; 51 Am. St. Rep. 555; Fanning v. St. Louis Transit Co., 103 Mo. App. 151; 78 S. W. Rep. 62; Artz v. Chicago, etc., R. Co., 44 Iowa 284; Chicago, etc., R. Co. v. Harwood, 80 Ill. 88; Cohen v. Eureka, etc., R. Co., 14 Nev. 376; Grand Rapids, etc., R. Co. v. Huntley, 38 Mich. 537; Telfer v. Northern, etc., R. Co., 30 N. J. L. 188; Grows v. Maine, etc., R. Co., 67 Me. 100; Terre Haute, etc., R. Co. v. Clark, 73 Ind. 168; 6 Am. & Eng. R. Cas. 84; Commonwealth v. Fitchburg, etc., R. Co., 126 Mass. 472; Warner v. New York, etc., R. Co., 44 N. Y. 465.

§ 662. **Injury from negligent delay in transportation.**— It seems doubtful if mere delay in the transportation of a passenger, unaccompanied by other circumstances or conditions, contributing to personal injury of the passenger, could ever furnish the basis for a charge of negligence directly contributing to produce the injury of a person, for which the railroad company would be answerable, for delays, from unavoidable causes, are customary, in the transportation of passengers by all kinds of trains and there is nothing in the fact of a delay which could cause personal injury, without accompanying conditions, affecting the health or personal safety of the passenger.

However, in a late Missouri case,[34] where a passenger

But running a train at a high or dangerous rate of speed, at a place where the track was known, or might by due diligence have been known to be dangerous or unsafe, was held to be negligence, in Chicago, etc., R. Co. v. Lewis, 145 Ill. 67; 33 N. E. Rep. 960; 58 Am. & Eng. R. Cas. 126; Cleveland, etc., R. Co. v. Newell, 75 Ind. 542; 8 Am. & Eng. R. Cas. 377; Missouri Pacific Ry. Co. v. Collier, 62 Texas 318; 18 Am. & Eng. R. Cas. 281; Chicago, etc., R. Co. v. Reynolds, 88 Ill. 418; White v. Milwaukee, etc., R. Co., 61 Wis. 536; 18 Am. & Eng. R. Cas. 213.

Rounding a sharp curve, at a high rate of speed, may be evidence of negligence, sufficient to charge a carrier, for an injury to a passenger, in being thrown from a car. Busch v. St. Paul, etc., R. Co. (Minn), 55 N. W. Rep. 87; Gidionsen v. Union Depot R. Co., 129 Mo. 392; 31 S. W. Rep. 800.

And it is held competent to give opinion evidence as to speed of train, in Galveston, etc., R. Co. v. Welsh (Texas), 22 S. W. Rep. 957; Sears v. Seattle, etc., R. Co. (Wash.), 33 Pac. Rep. 390.

It was held, in a New York case, that if a community for a considerable length of time, consents or acquiesces in a given rate of speed for a railroad train, and no injury has resulted, this is evidence of a proper rate, in case of an injury. Wilds v. Hudson River R. Co., 29 N. Y. 315, 326. But this rule is criticised by an Indiana judge. Cleveland, etc., R. Co. v. Newell, 75 Ind. 542; 545. And also by Judge Thompson. 3 Thompson on Neg., note to page 299, § 2828.

[34] "Where there was such negligent delay in the transportation of a freight train that one who had taken passage thereon for a distance of 60 miles was obliged to pass the night in a car, whereby he sustained

was being transported by freight train and in a distance of only sixty miles, there was a negligent delay of twenty-four hours, and the passenger was compelled to pass the entire night in a cold car, as a result of which he sustained injuries, it was held that the carrier was liable for the injury.

And in a Texas case,[35] where a passenger was negligently delayed, in a very warm and uncomfortable place, for a period of three hours, and as a result of her weak and debilitated condition, contracted an additional illness, it was held that the delay was the proximate cause of her injury and the carrier might be made to respond in damages therefor.

It will be noticed that in both these cases the liability is rather made to depend upon the failure of the carrier to heat the car in which the passenger was required to spend the night, or to furnish fans or other customary accommodations, to relieve the passenger from the extreme heat prevailing, and this was the basis of the neglect upon which the liability was made to depend. It would ordinarily be a difficult thing to find delays without such inconveniences, and the fact of the delay, if it can be made to appear as a controlling factor, in the causes contributing to the injury of the passenger, ought, of course, to be shown to be a negligent delay, and not merely such a delay as would ordinarily

injuries from exposure to cold, the carrier was liable for such injuries." Green v. Missouri, etc., Ry. Co. (Mo. App. 1906), 97 S. W. Rep. 646.

"The fact that a passenger is riding on a freight train does not relieve the carrier of liability for injuries to him owing to negligent delay in transportation." Green v. Missouri, etc., Ry. Co., 97 S. W. Rep. 646.

[35] "Where a passenger, because of a recent surgical operation, was weak, debilitated, and naturally very susceptible to extreme heat, a negligent delay without notice to her, of the train for three hours in a very warm and close place, without the proper and usual accommodations furnished by railways, was the natural and probable cause of her injuries." Gulf, etc., Ry. Co. v. Redeker (Tex. Civ. App. 1907), 100 S. W. Rep. 362.

be likely to occur in a well-regulated railroad, properly equipped.

§ 663. **Injuries from exposure to weather.**— A passenger carrier, in a recent Missouri case,[36] is held bound to take notice that inclement weather will injuriously affect a passenger's health, and if it fails to adopt such precautions as will protect its passengers from the weather, it is answerable for any damages that may result, and it is not essential that it should have understood just what form the injury is likely to assume. A railroad company was held liable for an injury to a passenger, riding in a box car, where the injury resulted from a delay incurred in the transportation and no means were provided to protect him from the inclement weather.[37] A similar injury from inclement weather was held to be a proper element of damage sustained by a passenger, in New York;[38] a like recovery was upheld, in Mississippi,[39] and it may be stated as the general rule that such damages are recoverable for injuries to a passenger, where the negligence of the carrier may be said to be the proximate cause of such injury.[40]

§ 664. **Unusual jerks or jars, in starting or stopping passenger trains.**— The sudden violent motion, resulting in the jerking of a passenger train, either in starting the train,[41]

[36] Green v. Missouri, etc., Ry. Co., 121 Mo. App. 720; 97 S. W. Rep. 646.

[37] Green v. Missouri, etc., Ry. Co., *supra.*

[38] Williams v. Vanderbilt, 28 N. Y. 217; Weed v. Railroad Co., 17 N. Y. 362.

[39] Mobile, etc., Ry. Co. v. McArthur, 43 Miss. 180.

[40] Norfolk, etc., Ry. Co. v. Lipscomb, 90 Va. 137; International, etc., Ry. Co. v. Harder (Texas), 81 S. W. Rep. 356; Galveston, etc., Ry. Co. v. Tuckett (Texas), 25 S. W. Rep. 150; Coleman v. Charleston, etc., Ry. Co., 138 N. Car. 354.

[41] Kentucky, etc., Co. v. Quinkert, 2 Ind. App. 244; 28 N. E. Rep. 338.

or the jolting or jarring of the train, in suddenly bringing it to a stop,[42] resulting in the injury to a passenger on such train, may or may not constitute negligence, according to the facts and circumstances attending the case.

The duty of the carrier, with reference to the sudden starting of its passenger trains, was recently stated by the Supreme Court of Missouri,[43] as follows: "A common carrier of passengers is bound to allow its passengers reasonable time to enter and leave its cars, and while it may start, before a passenger has been seated, it must exercise the highest degree of care that prudent and cautious persons would use and exercise under similar or the same circumstances in starting its cars, so as not to suddenly jerk or jar him and thereby injure him."

And the same rule is applied to the carrier, in stopping its trains, by the Kansas City Court of Appeals, in a recent case,[44] wherein it is said, after quoting the above statement of the law, by the Supreme Court: "And, of course, the same rule is applicable where a train has stopped and a passenger is in the act of leaving one of its coaches."

If the sudden jolting or jarring of a passenger train is due to a cause over which the carrier had control, it will furnish evidence of negligence on its part, in case a passenger sustains an injury thereby, whether the jolting is due to the striking of an obstruction on the track; [45] backing other cars

[42] Coudy v. St. Louis, etc., R. Co., 13 Mo. App. 587; 85 Mo. 79.

[43] Decision by Judge Gantt, Barth v. Kansas City, etc., R. Co., 142 Mo. 550; 44 S. W. Rep. 778. And see, also, Dougherty v. Missouri Pacific Ry. Co., 9 Mo. App. 478, by Judge Thompson; Dougherty v. Missouri, etc., R. Co., 97 Mo. 647; 8 S. W. Rep. 900; 11 S. W. Rep. 251; Jacquin v. Grand Avenue R. Co., 57 Mo. App. 320; Jackson v. Grand Avenue Ry. Co., 118 Mo. 199; 24 S. W. Rep. 192; Gilson v. Jackson County Ry. Co., 76 Mo. 282.

[44] Moorman v. Atchison, etc., R. Co., 105 Mo. App. 711, 719; 78 S. W. Rep. 1089.

[45] Burke v. Manchester, etc., R. Co., 18 W. R. 694; 22 L. T. 442.

against the car in which the passenger is located,[46] or striking such car, with unusual force, with a switch engine,[47]
under the control of the carrier or its employees.

[46] Quackenbush v. Chicago, etc., R. Co., 73 Iowa 458; 35 N. W.
Rep. 523; 34 Am. & Eng. R. Cas. 545.

[47] East Line, etc., R. Co. v. Rushing, 69 Texas 306; 6 S. W. Rep.
834; 34 Am. & Eng. R. Cas. 367.

" Where a passenger alighted from a train while it was standing at
a water tank and subsequently boarded it while it was moving, and
just after he boarded it, and while he was standing on the steps of a
car, he was thrown therefrom by a sudden jolt of the train, there
was no negligence. authorizing a recovery for his injuries." Winchell
v. New York Cent. & H. R. R. Co. (N. Y. Supp. 1907), 105 N. Y. S. 425.

The sudden jerking of a train backward, while passengers are
leaving cars, was held negligence, in Sauter v. New York, etc., R. Co.,
66 N. Y. 50; 6 Hun 446.

One injured by a sudden acceleration of speed, after invited to alight,
by an employee, was held entitled to recover, in Smith v. Chicago, etc.,
R. Co., 108 Mo. 243; 18 S. W. Rep. 971; 52 Am. & Eng. R. Cas. 483;
London, etc., R. Co. v. Hellawell, 26 L. T. 557; Louisville, etc., R. Co.
v. Wood (where conductor helped passenger to alight), 113 Ind. 544;
14 N. E. Rep. 572; 16 N. E. Rep. 197; Wood v. Lake Shore, etc., R.
Co., 49 Mich. 370; 13 N. W. Rep. 779; 8 Am. & Eng. R. Cas. 478;
Milliman v New York, etc., R. Co., 66 N. Y. 642; 4 Hun 409; Norfolk,
etc., R. Co. v. Prinnell (Va.), 3 S. E. Rep. 95; 30 Am. & Eng. R.
Cas. 574; Pennsylvania R. Co. v. Aspell, 23 Pa. St. 149; McNulta v.
Ensch, 134 Ill. 46; 24 N. E. Rep. 631.

And for an injury resulting from the sudden starting of a train
while plaintiff was getting aboard, see Galveston, etc., R. Co. v. Cooper,
2 Texas Civ. App. 42; 20 S. W. Rep. 990; Montgomery, etc., R. Co. v.
Stewart, 91 Ala. 421; 8 So. Rep. 708.

" It was the custom of a railway company to slow down its trains
before reaching a crossing, and either to come to a full stop at the
crossing or run slowly over it. Persons intending to take passage on
its trains at the crossing usually grasped the handrail on a coach, and
walked along with the train, and boarded the car at the moment of
stopping. A person went to the crossing, intending to take passage on
a train which slowed down before reaching the crossing. He caught
the handrail of a coach, and while holding onto the rail and walking
along with the train, intending at the moment of its stopping to step
onto the steps of the coach, the train was suddenly jerked forward, and
he was thrown to the ground. *Held*, that he was not entitled to recover
for the injury sustained, without showing that he was seen by an

§ 665. **Same — Injury from, establishes prima facie case.**—
Where a passenger on a regular passenger train is injured
by a sudden jerk, jolt, or jar, of such unusual force or suddenness as to be out of the ordinary, and not such as usually
results from the careful operation of a passenger train, this is
held to establish a *prima facie* case against the carrier and to
shift the burden to the carrier of establishing that the injury
was not due to any negligence on its part. In other words,
the rule *res ipsa loquitur* applies to such an injury.[48]

Upon the propriety of giving an instruction to the jury
that the burden of explaining an injury to a passenger — who
had arisen from his seat in a passenger car to recover a
bundle that had fallen to the floor — thrown to the floor and
through an open door in the coach, by a sudden and unusual
jerking of the train, Judge Norton, speaking for the Missouri Supreme Court,[49] said: "The instruction, we think,
is sustained by the authorities, which hold that when an

employee in charge of the train." Collins v. Southern Ry. Co. (Miss.
1906), 42 So. Rep. 167.

"Where, in an action for injuries to a passenger in a collision caused
by backing of cars against a standing caboose in which plaintiff was
sitting, there was evidence that plaintiff had gone into the car with
knowledge of the carrier's servant, an instruction that if the train
of cars including the caboose was not coupled to the engine, the plaintiff
was on the car at the time of the injury in his own wrong, and could
not recover, was erroneous as making defendant's liability exclusively
depend on whether the caboose, when plaintiff got into it, was
coupled to the engine." Miller v. Atlanta, etc., R. Co. (N. C. 1906),
55 S. E. Rep. 439.

[48] Coudy v. St. Louis, etc., R. Co., 13 Mo. App. 587; 85 Mo. 79, 1. c.
85; Dougherty v. Missouri Pacific Ry. Co., 9 Mo. App. 478; Scott v.
Dock Co., 11 Jur. N. S. 1108; Meier v. Philadelphia, etc., R. Co., 64
Pa. St. 225; Stokes v. Saltonstall, 13 Peters 181; New Jersey, etc.,
R. Co. v. Pollard, 22 Wall. (U. S.) 341; 22 L. Ed. 877; Hite v.
Metropolitan Ry. Co., 130 Mo. 138; 32 S. W. Rep. 33; 51 Am. St.
Rep. 555; Barth v. Kansas City, etc., R. Co., 142 Mo. 536; 44 S. W.
Rep. 778; Moorman v. Atchison, etc., R. Co., 105 Mo. App. 711; 78
S. W. Rep. 1089.

[49] Coudy v. St. Louis, etc., R. Co., 85 Mo. 89.

injury is shown to have been occasioned by an error of the carrier or his servants, in operating the instrumentalities employed in the business of carrying, a presumption of negligence arises against the carrier which casts on him the burden of showing that the accident happened, notwithstanding the exercise on his part of the high degree of care which the law imposes upon him."

But the rule thus announced, as to injuries due to sudden jerks, jolts, or jars, in the operation of a passenger train, has no application, where the injury is occasioned by a jar, or jerk, due to some outside agency and without any fault on the part of the carrier. In such a case no recovery can be had, unless the plaintiff goes further than establishing the mere fact of an injury due to a jolt, or jar, for he must also show that it was occasioned by the actual neglect on the part of the railroad company.[50]

§ 666. Same — Injury to feeble passenger by jerk or jolt.

[50] Smith v. Milwaukee, etc., R. Co., 32 Minn. 1; Pennsylvania R. Co. v. Gibson, 96 Pa. St. 83; Hite v. Metropolitan Ry. Co., 130 Mo. 138; 32 S. W. Rep. 33; 51 Am. St. Rep. 555.

In New Jersey, etc., R. Co. v. Pollard (22 Wall. 341; 22 L. Ed. 877), plaintiff, a married woman, was standing in the aisle, braced against the seats with her knees, fixing her little girl's hair; the train had just arrived at Jersey City and passengers were getting off the train, when a sudden jerk or jolt threw the plaintiff back, so that her spine struck the arm of the seat and she was severely injured. The trial court charged the jury that the facts made a *prima facie* case of negligence and this was approved, in a decision by Chief Justice Waite.

In Moorman v. Atchison, etc., R. Co. (105 Mo. App. 711; 78 S. W. Rep. 1089), the passenger was in the act of alighting, when he sustained an injury by a forward lurch of the car and the court held that this was of itself, sufficient to send the case to the jury, on the question of defendant's negligence in thus jerking the car in which plaintiff was riding, under the rule that where the vehicle is under the management and control of the carrier and the accident is such as, according to the usual course of events, it will not occur, then negligence may be inferred, in the absence of an explanation of the cause.

— As to all of its passengers, a railroad company, receiving persons in any of its cars, for transportation, before making up its trains, owes them the duty to make up its trains, and to couple, manage and control its cars and engines in such a careful, skillful and prudent manner as to carry and protect its passengers and it will be liable for an injury to any of its passengers resulting from a neglect of this duty, whether the injured passenger is strong and robust or in feeble health.[51]

But the obligation of the carrier extends not only to exercising such care and caution as will avoid injury to persons on its trains in good health, or robust physical condition; it must also exercise a degree of care sufficient to avoid injury to passengers whom it has agreed to carry, although they may not be in ordinary physical condition, but in feeble health.[52] Accordingly, if a passenger is permitted to enter the carrier's car, for transportation to a given point, who is not in ordinary physical condition, but is feeble, as a result of recent sickness, and such passenger is injured by a jolt or jerk, caused by the striking of the car in which he was riding, by a switch engine, as a result of which he was thrown against a seat in the car, this is sufficient evidence of negligence on the carrier's part, upon which to base a verdict in favor of such injured passenger, although a robust

[51] Hannibal, etc., R. Co. v. Martin, 111 Ill. 219; 11 Ill. App. 386; Choate v. Missouri Pacific Ry. Co., 67 Mo. App. 105.

[52] Fortune v. Missouri R. Co., 10 Mo. App. 252; Ridenhour v. Kansas City, etc., R. Co., 102 Mo. 270; 13 S. W. Rep. 889; Shareman v. Transit Co., 103 Mo. App. 515; 78 S. W. Rep. 846. An instruction that the carrier was negligent in starting a train, before an old, blind passenger could reach her seat, if she was given no assistance by a brakeman, who knew her condition, was approved, in Hanks v. Chicago, etc., R. Co., 60 Mo. App. 274, as it was held to be the duty to exercise greater care toward such a passenger than others, not under such disability. But this is not true, if no notice of the disability is brought home to the carrier. Mathew v. Wabash R. Co. (Mo.), 78 S. W. Rep. 271.

person, under the same conditions, may have escaped the injury sustained.[53]

§ 667. Same — Jerks and jolts during transit.— Even as to jerks and jolts in the management of passenger trains, a different rule of liability seems to obtain, on the part of the carrier, as to jerks or jars, while passengers are alighting from or boarding a train, and those incident to the usual operation of the train, while in transit, due to increased speed or the rounding of curves, such as are usual on all railroad tracks.   This rule results from a consideration of the relation of the carrier toward its passengers and the risks necessarily assumed by the latter, for since the carrier is not an insurer of the safety of the passenger, it is not liable for an injury occurring during the existence of the relation, when all reasonable care and skill has been used.

It is accordingly held, in a Missouri case,[54] that a passenger on a passenger car, who was injured by being thrown off the car, while rounding a curve, on account of a sudden jerk or jolt, could not recover damages from the carrier, where the evidence showed that the passenger knew of the greater speed required to round the curve and there was no negligence established, either in the condition of the roadway, or the appliances or vehicles used, or the acts of the employees in charge of the car, but it appeared that such jerks are usual in rounding such curves and that engineering skill has not been able to avoid such things, but that they were incidental to all cars, run at the rate of speed at which the car was being operated when the injury to the plaintiff occurred.

[53] East Line, etc., R. Co. v. Rushing, 69 Texas 306; 6 S. W. Rep. 834; 34 Am. & Eng. R. Cas. 367.

[54] Hite v. Metropolitan, etc., R. Co., 130 Mo. 132; 31 S. W. Rep. 262; 32 S. W. Rep. 33; 51 Am. St. Rep. 555.

But while damages are not allowed for jerks or jolts occasioning injury, in the absence of negligence on the carrier's part, due to the mere acceleration of the speed of the train, or the sudden rounding of a curve in a properly constructed track,[55] this would not be true as to a jerk or jolt, occasioned by the negligence of the employees operating the train, and although a passenger might be held negligent in riding on the platform of a car, if the employees in charge of the engine, with notice of the dangerous position assumed by such passenger, suddenly moved the train forward with such momentum as to throw him off the platform and seriously injure him, this would be held such an act of negligence as to render the carrier liable.[56]

[55] Bartley v. Metropolitan, etc., Ry. Co., 148 Mo. 124; 49 S. W. Rep. 840, and cases cited.

[56] Montgomery, etc., R. Co. v. Stewart, 91 Ala. 421; 8 So. Rep. 708.

In Hite v. Metropolitan Ry. Co. (130 Mo. 140; 32 S. W. Rep. 33; 51 Am. St. Rep. 555), Judge Burgess, for the Missouri Supreme Court, said: " There was no defect in the appliances by which the cars were operated, or in the construction of the road, nor was there any negligence or carelessness on the part of those in control of the car at the time of the injury. Whatever presumption of negligence there was arising from the injury, and the lurch or jerk in the cars, at the time, was completely overcome by the evidence, which showed that all reasonable skill and care had been employed by defendant."

In the case of injuries to passengers in passenger coaches, caused by the shunting of other cars against those in which the passengers are located, causing such a jolt or jar, as to throw passengers down, or from the car, the railroad companies have been held liable in the following cases: Gardner v. Waycross R. Co., 94 Ga. 538; 19 S. E. Rep. 757; Everett v. Oregon, etc., R. Co., 9 Utah 340; 34 Pac. Rep. 289; Moore v. Saginaw, etc., R. Co., 115 Mich. 103; 72 N. W. Rep. 1112; Kansas City, etc., R. Co. v. Campbell, 6 Kansas App. 417; 48 Pac. Rep. 817.

" In an action against a railway for personal injuries to a passenger, where negligence of the defendant's servants is alleged in failing to keep the plates over the bumpers between passenger cars, and in backing the engine violently against the coaches while passengers were entering, the question of negligence was properly submitted to the jury." St. Louis, etc., R. Co. v. Snell (Ark. 1907), 100 S. W. Rep. 67.

§ 668. **Formation of mixed trains — Statutes controlling.—**
A passenger taking transportation on a mixed train is bound
by the same rule of law that applies to a freight train, and
such passenger is held to assume the risk of injury from
the jerks or jars, incident to the careful and proper operation of the train, to the same extent that a passenger assumes such risks as are incident to the method of conveyance
selected and the inconveniences in riding on a freight train.[57]

But under a statute regulating the formation of mixed
trains, such as the Indiana statute,[58] which provides that in
the formation of such trains, carriers cannot place freight,
lumber, merchandise or baggage cars in the rear of passenger coaches, if a passenger sustains injury because of a violation of such a statute, the carrier must respond in damages
to the injured passenger, or his representative, in cases
where the violation of the statute is the proximate cause of
the injury sued for.[59]

"Where the engineer of a passenger train failed to obey an order
to stop at a station where plaintiff, a passenger on the train, alleged
it was to meet and pass a train going in the opposite direction, whereupon the conductor suddenly and violently stopped the train by the
application of the air from the rear, throwing plaintiff against one
of the seats and injuring her, defendant, though chargeable with negligence in passing the station, in violation of the order, causing the
necessity for the sudden and violent stoppage in order to prevent
collision, was not negligent in making the stop for the purpose." Todd
v. Missouri Pac. Ry. Co. (Mo. App. 1907), 105 S. W. Rep. 671.

[57] Arkansas, etc., R. Co. v. Canman, 52 Ark. 517; 13 S. W. Rep. 280;
Oviatt v. Dakota, etc., R. Co., 43 Minn. 300; 45 N. W. Rep. 436.

[58] Burns' Ann. St. Ind. 1901, § 5191.

[59] "Burns' Ann. St. 1901, § 5191, provides that, in forming a passenger train, baggage, freight, merchandise, or lumber cars shall not
be placed in rear of passenger cars. A combination smoking and
baggage car, with one end not vestibuled, and designed to be placed
next to the engine, was placed behind a passenger coach, and plaintiff,
in passing through the train, fell or was thrown overboard through the
unprotected space. *Held*, that such a car was within the prohibition,
and the company in disregarding the statute was guilty of negligence."

A passenger in a passenger coach, attached to a freight train, is not to be judged by the same harsh rules as govern the operation of an exclusive freight train carrying passengers, as held in a recent Arkansas case,[60] for while jerks and jars are held to be so customary in the operation of freight trains as to render it negligence on the part of a passenger to stand in a caboose, while switching is being done, in this case, it was held, by the Arkansas court, that it was not necessarily negligence for a passenger to stand in a coach, attached to a freight train, and injured by a jar caused by the bumping of the cars against the coach in which she stood.

§ 669. **Care toward passengers on freight trains.**— A railroad company, undertaking to carry passengers for hire, upon freight trains, owes them the same duty, as to care, which the law exacts of it as to passengers transported on passenger trains, the only difference being that the passengers on freight trains assume those dangers or perils which are necessarily incident to that mode of conveyance.[61]

It is therefore held, in a Missouri case,[62] that it is not error to instruct that the same care is owing to the passenger as would be due him, were he riding on a passenger

Pittsburgh & St. L. Ry. Co. v. Schepman (Ind. App. 1907), 82 N. E. Rep. 998.

[60] "The mere fact that a woman passenger who had boarded the passenger coach of a mixed train at the station platform went to the front end of the coach to get a drink of water while the coach was standing and while switching was being done by the engine for the purpose of making up the train did not make her guilty of contributory negligence as a matter of law." St. Louis, etc., Ry. Co. v. Billingsley (Ark. 1906), 96 S. W. Rep. 357.

[61] McGee v. Missouri Pacific Ry. Co., 92 Mo. 208; 4 S. W. Rep. 739; 1 Am. St. Rep. 706; Whitehead v. St. Louis, etc., R. Co., 99 Mo. 263; 11 S. W. Rep. 751; 6 L. R. A. 409; Wait v. Omaha, etc., R. Co, 165 Mo. 612; 65 S. W. Rep. 1028.

[62] Fullerton v. St. Louis, etc., R. Co., 84 Mo. App. 498.

train, or, in other words, that the carrier is liable for a failure to exercise "the utmost care and skill, which prudent men would use in like business and under like circumstances, to safely transport plaintiff to his destination." [63]

But while the responsibility of a railroad company for the safe transportation of passengers on freight trains, is not restricted or lessened, and the same degree of care is required in the management of such a train when carrying passengers, as in the operation of an exclusive passenger train, yet a passenger on a freight train is charged with knowledge of and he assumes the increased hazards, incident to that mode of travel,[64] and he accepts passage with notice that the train is not equipped with all the safeguards provided for passenger trains and the risks of injury due to this fact.[65]

[63] Practically the same kind of an instruction is, however, disapproved, on rehearing, in Dougherty v. Missouri, etc., R. Co., 97 Mo. 667; 11 S. W. Rep. 251.

[64] Portuchek v. Wabash R. Co., 101 Mo. App. 52; 74 S. W. Rep. 368.

[65] Erwin v. Kansas City, etc., R. Co., 94 Mo. App. 289; 68 S. W. Rep. 88.

"The fact that it was customary for the employees of a carrier, in the operation of its freight trains, to act as was done at the time a passenger on a freight train was injured did not relieve the carrier of the duty of exercising the degree of care imposed on it by law, under the circumstances existing at that time." International, etc., R. Co. v. Cruseturner (Tex. Civ. App. 1906), 98 S. W. Rep. 423.

"Where a passenger was injured in a freight car, it was error to instruct that if he took no precaution to protect himself against the jar ordinarily incident to an approaching coupling 'which he knew or in the exercise of ordinary care ought to have known, was about to occur from said coupling,' he could not recover." Hardin v. Ft. Worth, etc., Ry. Co. (Tex. Civ. App. 1907), 100 S. W. Rep. 995.

When a railroad company receives and undertakes to carry a passenger on a freight train, it is bound to all the obligations of a passenger carrier, except in so far as this is affected by the method of conveyance used. Jones v. Wabash Ry. Co., 17 Mo. App. 158; Ohio, etc., R. Co. v. Dickerson, 59 Ind. 317; New York, etc., R. Co. v. Doane, 115 Ind. 435; 17 N. E. Rep. 913; 7 Am. St. Rep. 451; 1 L. R. A. 157; Pennsylvania R. Co. v. Newmeier, 129 Ind. 401; 28 N. E. Rep. 860;

§ 670. **No negligence inferred from jolts or jerks on freight trains.**— It is a matter of common knowledge that jolts and jerks are usual incidents in the operation of freight trains and therefore negligence cannot be inferred from the mere fact that a passenger's injury resulted from a jar, caused by the sudden stopping of such a train. In other words, a jar, or jerk, in a freight train, is not, of itself, evidence of negligence.[66]

Illustrative of this rule, in a recent Missouri case,[67] the freight train was very long and was slowly approaching, on an up grade, a station where it was to take in another

52 Am. & Eng. R. Cas. 454; Guffey v. Hannibal, etc., R. Co., 53 Mo. App. 462; Whitehead v. St. Louis, etc., R. Co., 99 Mo. 263; 11 S. W. Rep. 751; 39 Am. & Eng. R. Cas. 410; McGee v. Missouri Pacific Ry. Co., 92 Mo. 208; 4 S. W. Rep. 739; Tibby v. Missouri Pacific Ry. Co., 82 Mo. 292; Missouri Pacific Ry. Co. v. Holcomb, 44 Kansas 332; 24 Pac. Rep. 467; 44 Am. & Eng. R. Cas. 303; Perkins v. Chicago, etc., R. Co., 60 Miss. 726; 21 Am. & Eng. R. Cas. 242; Indianapolis, etc., R. Co. v. Horst, 93 U. S. 291; Chicago, etc., R. Co. v. Arnol, 144 Ill. 261; 33 N. E. Rep. 204; 58 Am. & Eng. R. Cas. 411; Crine v. East Tennessee, etc., R. Co., 84 Ga. 651; 11 S. E. Rep. 555; Ohio, etc., R. Co. v. Watson (Ky.), 21 S. W. Rep. 244; 58 Am. & Eng. R. Cas. 418.

But a passenger in using this mode of conveyance is held to assume all the risks necessarily incident to that mode of conveyance, in the following cases: Portuchek v. Wabash R. Co., 101 Mo. App. 52; 74 S. W. Rep. 368; Wait v. Omaha, etc., R. Co., 165 Mo. 612; 65 S. W. Rep. 1028; Hedrick v. Missouri Pacific Ry. Co., 195 Mo. 104; 93 S. W. Rep. 268; Pennsylvania R. Co. v. Newmeyer, 129 Ind. 401; 28 N. E. Rep. 860; 52 Am. & Eng. R. Cas. 454; Woolery v. Louisville, etc., R. Co., 107 Ind. 381; 8 N. E. Rep. 226; 57 Am. Rep. 114; Louisville, etc., R. Co. v. Bisch, 120 Ind. 549; 33 N. E. Rep. 204; 41 Am. & Eng. R. Cas. 89; Wallace v. Western, etc., R. Co., 98 N. Car. 494; 4 S. E. Rep. 503; 2 Am. St. Rep. 346; 34 Am. & Eng. R. Cas. 553.

66 Chicago, etc., R. Co. v. Hazzard, 26 Ill. 373; Guffey v. Hannibal, etc., R. Co., 53 Mo. App. 462; Hedrick v. Missouri Pacific Ry. Co., 195 Mo. 104; Portuchek v. Wabash R. Co., 101 Mo. App. 52; 74 S. W. Rep. 368; Wait v. Omaha, etc., R. Co., 165 Mo. 612; 65 S. W. Rep. 1028; Chicago, etc., R. Co. v. Arnol, 144 Ill. 201; Olds v. New York, etc., R. Co., 172 Mass. 72; Erwin v. Kansas City, etc., R. Co., 94 Mo. App. 289; 68 S. W. Rep. 88.

67 Hedrick v. Missouri Pacific Ry. Co., 195 Mo. 104.

car. Plaintiff was riding in the caboose, on a drover's pass, and went to the rear of the car with a view to getting off to assist in putting his stock in the car, when the engine stopped suddenly and the rebound, from taking up the slack, violently jerked the caboose and threw plaintiff down and injured him. There was no evidence of any negligence on the defendant's part, or on the part of any of its employees, except that the train stopped very suddenly and it did not appear that the stopping of the engine, in the usual way, would not have occasioned the lurch, in a train the length of the train on which the plaintiff was riding, so the court held that the rule *res ipsa loquitur* did not apply to such a case, since there was nothing that tended to show negligence on the defendant's part and the plaintiff was denied a recovery.

This decision is in accord with the weight of authority on this question, for not only in Missouri,[68] but in Illinois [69] and other States,[70] a similar rule is applied as to injuries

[68] Wait v. Omaha, etc., R. Co., 165 Mo. 612; 65 S. W. Rep. 1028.

[69] Chicago, etc., R. Co. v. Arnol, 144 Ill. 201.

[70] Olds v. New York, etc., R. Co., 172 Mass. 72.

In Hedrick v. Missouri Pacific Ry. Co. (195 Mo. 123; 93 S. W. Rep. 268), Judge Gantt, speaking for the Supreme Court of Missouri, said: " If the plaintiff can recover on the facts elicited in this case, it must be upon the one proposition that the jerk or jar caused by the train stopping, was *ipso facto*, negligence. We know of no case that would justify us in so holding. The jar was the natural result of the stopping of a long train of freight cars, and the giving out of the slack. When it is considered that it is a matter of common knowledge that in the movement of trains, there is more or less jolting and jarring, incident to the starting and stopping of the train, and that, so far, human skill and ingenuity has not been able to prevent this entirely, it cannot be said, as a matter of law, that negligence can be predicated upon the mere fact that the jolt or jerk results from the stopping of a long freight train. It is well settled that negligence cannot be presumed, when nothing is done out of the usual course of business, unless the course is improper."

In Erwin v. Kansas City, etc., R. Co. (94 Mo. App. 289; 68 S. W.

due to sudden jerks and jolts in freight trains, and the mere fact of an injury due to such a usual movement of

Rep. 88), Judge Bland, speaking for the St. Louis Court of Appeals, said: "When the fact that there is more or less jerking and jolting incident to the operation of a freight train — a matter of common knowledge — is taken into view, negligence cannot be inferred from the mere fact that the plaintiff was injured by a jar occasioned by the stopping of the train."

In Portuchek v. Wabash R. Co. (101 Mo. App. 54; 74 S. W. Rep. 368), Judge Reyburn made a like observation for the same court, as follows: "It is not to be expected that there would be the same exactness in drawing up to a station by a freight train, as by a train devoted to passenger service, and precisely the same degree of care exercised in the operation of both, may produce different results respecting the safety of the passengers, from the dangers inseparably connected with the conduct of one train and not with the other, and this the public presumably understands and conducts itself accordingly and such inherent hazards, the passenger is held to assume, in taking the freight train."

See, also, to same effect, Saxton v. Missouri Pacific Ry. Co., 98 Mo. App. 494; 72 S. W. Rep. 717; Guffey v. Hannibal, etc., R. Co., 53 Mo. App. 462; Wait v. Omaha, etc., R. Co., 165 Mo. 612; 65 S. W. Rep. 1028; Whitehead v. St. Louis, etc., R. Co., 99 Mo. 263; 11 S. W. Rep. 751; 6 L. R. A. 409; McGee v. Missouri Pacific Ry. Co., 92 Mo. 208; 4 S. W. Rep. 739; 1 Am. St. Rep. 706; Wagner v. Missouri Pacific Ry. Co., 97 Mo. 512; 10 S. W. Rep. 486; 3 L. R. A. 156; Hays v. Wabash Ry. Co., 51 Mo. App. 438; Ohio, etc., Ry. Co. v. Dickerson, 59 Ind. 317; Chicago, etc., R. Co. v. Arnol, 144 Ill. 261; Olds v. New York, etc., R. Co., 172 Mass. 72.

In Olds v. New York, etc., R. Co. (172 Mass. 72), Knowlton, J., speaking for this able court, said: "Persons taking passage upon freight trains, or in a caboose or car attached to a freight train, cannot expect or require the conveniences or all of the safeguards against danger that they may demand upon trains devoted to passenger service, and are accordingly held to have accepted the accommodation provided by the company, subject to all the ordinary inconveniences, delays and hazards incident to such trains, when made up and equipped in the ordinary manner of making up and equipping such trains, and managed with proper care and skill."

See, further, on the different measure of liability in case of accidents from incidents of riding on freight trains, as compared to passenger trains, Smotherman v. St. Louis, etc., R. Co., 29 Mo. App. 265; Harris v. Hannibal, etc., R. Co., 89 Mo. 233; 1 S. W. Rep. 325; 58 Am. Rep. 111; Minock v. Minneapolis, etc., R. Co., 97 Mich. 425.

1021

these trains, raises no presumption of negligence on the carrier's part.

` § 671. **Duty to give signals.**— Passengers on a train are not included in either the letter or spirit of a statute requiring the sounding of the whistle or ringing of the bell, on crossing highways, or approaching stations, and the failure to comply with such a statute is not, ordinarily, negligence which a passenger on the train can take advantage of when suing for damages for personal injuries, to which the failure to ring the bell or sound the whistle could have had no tendency to contribute.[71]

In an Alabama case,[72] it was held to be negligence to fail to sound the whistle or to ring the bell, on leaving a station, as required by the statute of the State, which passengers or the public generally could take advantage of, but this failure would not excuse a passenger, in boarding the train, while the train was moving, from his own contributory negligence, although the failure to sound the whistle before the train started to move, was negligence on the part of the railroad company.

The object of giving signals before starting passenger trains is to enable tardy passengers to safely board the train before it pulls out and this duty, recognized by the court in Georgia,[73] was said to be imposed to prevent passengers from being left, on account of their own tardiness, and whether or not the signals are given loud enough to be heard by passengers and the question of whether or not the injury to the passenger was due to the failure to properly

---

[71] Malcolm v. Richmond, etc., R. Co., 106 N. Car. 63; 11 S. E. Rep. 187; 44 Am. & Eng. R. Cas. 379; Alabama, etc., R. Co. v. Hawk, 72 Ala. 112; 47 Am. Rep. 403; 18 Am. & Eng. R. Cas. 194.

[72] Central, etc., R. Co. v. Letcher, 69 Ala. 106; 12 Am. & Eng. R. Cas. 115.

[73] Central, etc., R. Co. v. Perry, 58 Ga. 461; 16 Am. Ry. Rep. 122.

give the signals, or to his own want of ordinary care, in boarding the train, are generally issues of fact for the jury, in case the evidence is conflicting.[74]

§ 672. **Running trains too close together.**— As the most serious consequences might result from the operation of passenger trains with a very few minutes between the scheduled time for the running of such trains and it is the duty of the railroad company to avoid the operation of trains in a manner likely to produce collisions, it is generally held that some system or schedule time for the running of trains must be adopted, to prevent collisions and the operation of trains with only a short interval between them, or starting the second train before the first has had sufficient time to clear a distance so that the second train can be safely operated, is carelessness, which the rules of most carefully conducted railroads attempt to prevent.[75]

The operation of a train on the same track that is used by another train, which is started without sufficient time to enable the first train to clear a reasonable distance, so as to prevent accidents, especially where the first train is operated in the nighttime and without signals to prevent a rear end collision, is held to be negligence, as matter of law, in Missouri.[76]

[74] Central, etc., R. Co. v. Perry, *supra*.

Running a caboose, in which passengers are located, in the night time, on a track where another train is following close behind the caboose, without any signal or light on the caboose, is negligence, as squarely held, in a Missouri case. Fleming v. Kansas City, etc., R. Co., 89 Mo. App. 129.

And it is negligence to permit a train to stand on a railroad track, where it is apt to be struck by another train, whether at a crossing, or elsewhere, without putting out a flag, or adopting any other means of signaling, to avoid a collision. Clark v. Chicago, etc., R. Co., 127 Mo. 197; 29 S. W. Rep. 1013.

[75] Gonzales v. New York, etc., R. Co., 39 How. Pr. (N. Y.) 407; Fleming v. Kansas City, etc., R. Co., 89 Mo. App. 129.

[76] Fleming v. Kansas City, etc., R. Co., 89 Mo. App. 129.

And it is likewise held to be negligence, giving a right of action, in case of an injury resulting therefrom, for a railroad company to so arrange its time-table that within one minute from the time that an accommodation train is to leave a station, an express train, running at the rate of thirty miles an hour, according to scheduled time, is due at the same place.[77]

§ 673. **Operating trains out of time.**— The employees running a passenger train and those directly connected with the management of the train, are bound to know and inform themselves of the time that other trains are liable to meet and pass the train they are operating, or when they will reach or pass certain stations. And it is the duty of all such employees, if trains are running out of their regular scheduled time, to be on the lookout for all such trains and give timely notice of meeting any trains out of time. A failure to use a high degree of care and diligence on the part of such employees, in this particular, in case of an injury to a passenger due to such a cause, is held to be negligence on the part of the railroad company.[78]

But it is not necessarily negligence to run a hand car over a railroad track when a train that has the right of way is past due, even though more than ordinary danger is incurred thereby.[79] It is frequently necessary, to avoid graver dangers, that trains be run out of time and this is customary and no presumption of negligence will result from this course, where due regard is had to the running time of the various trains and extreme care taken to avoid collisions or other accidents. The proper measure of care must be exercised, however, both with a view to the safety of the em-

[77] Gonzales v. New York, etc., R. Co., 39 How. Pr. (N. Y.) 407.

[78] Gonzales v. New York, etc., R. Co., 39 How. Pr. (N. Y.) 407; Fleming v. Kansas City, etc., R. Co., 89 Mo. App. 129.

[79] Campbell v. Chicago, etc., R. Co., 45 Iowa 76.

ployees operating the various trains or vehicles on the same track, when running out of their regular time, and with a due regard to the protection of the passengers on the trains run on the same track, and a failure to exercise such care, if an accident results therefrom, is presumptive evidence of negligence in the case of the passenger. [80]

§ 674. **Collisions of trains on same track.**— It is negligence, for which a carrier will be held responsible to an injured passenger, to so operate its trains on the same track that they will be likely to collide, and the highest degree of care consistent with that which prudence in the business would suggest, is exacted of the carrier to avoid such collisions.

It was held, in an Indiana case,[81] that it was negligence to operate a train, up a steep grade, on a track with many curves, only eight minutes behind a long freight train, with no signals or other means to avoid a collision between the two; it is negligence to operate two trains on the same track, the one following the other, with only a short interval between the two, without adopting some means to prevent collision between the two; [82] a company is held liable for a collision between a caboose, operated on the same track, at night, with another train approaching from the rear, when no signals or lights are placed upon the caboose; [83] and the United States Supreme Court held, in a leading case,[84] by

[80] See chapter, Demonstrative Evidence of Negligence, rule *res ipsa loquitur.*

[81] Louisville, etc., R. Co. v. Taylor, 126 Ind. 126; 25 N. E. Rep. 869.

[82] Louisville, etc., R. Co. v. Long (Ky.), 22 S. W. Rep. 747.

[83] Fleming v. Kansas City, etc., R. Co., 89 Mo. App. 129.

[84] Farlow v. Kelly, 108 U. S. 288; 2 Sup. Ct. 555; 11 Am. & Eng. R. Cas. 104.

Nor is it true that any less degree of care is exacted in the operation of cars on switches, than on main lines. In Fleming v. Kansas City, etc., R. Co. (89 Mo. App. 129), Judge Broaddus, speaking for the Kansas City Court of Appeals, said: "Even if its business may properly be termed a 'switching business' it would not be exonerated from

Chief Justice Waite, that it was culpable carelessness for a carrier to leave a freight car on a switch track, in such a

those precautions for safety that are usually employed by railroads doing that kind of business. We have yet to learn that railroad companies use less caution while operating their trains on switches, than at other places, and if such be the fact, it is none too soon for the courts to condemn such practice."

An engineer is held properly excusable for jumping from his engine in the emergency, but this is not an excuse for the carrier, for his original negligence in failing to avoid the collision, in Bunting v. Hogsett, 139 Pa. St. 363; 21 Atl. Rep. 31; 48 Am. & Eng. R. Cas. 87.

Carrier held liable for collision, in Treux v. Erie R. Co., 4 Lans. (N. Y.) 198. But for collision caused by engine, left on side track, being run onto main track, when cause of its doing so is not explained, and that this is no evidence of negligence in causing a collision, see, Mars v. Delaware, etc., R. Co., 54 Hun 625; 28 N. Y. S. R. 228; 8 N. Y. Supp. 107. And see, International, etc., R. Co. v. Gray, 65 Texas 32; 27 Am. & Eng. R. Cas. 318.

A railroad company, allowing third persons to leave loaded coal cars on a side track, so close as to cause a collision with a moving train, was held liable, in Georgia, etc., R. Co. v. Underwood, 90 Ala. 49; 8 So. Rep. 116; 44 Am. & Eng. R. Cas. 367.

But a railroad company was held not liable for the effects of a collision brought about by another company, having statutory running privileges on its track, in Wright v. Midland R. Co., 42 L. J. Ex. 89; L. R. 8 Ex. 137; 21 W. R. 460; 29 L. T. 436.

"In an action by a passenger for personal injuries sustained in a collision of two of defendant's trains, an instruction that the burden of overcoming the presumption of negligence arising from the evidence of the occurrence of an accident and the injury to the passenger is upon the carrier, and that, where the evidence shows that the injury to a passenger is brought about by a collision between said train and another train of the same company, the evidence is sufficient to warrant the finding that the carrier was guilty of negligence, is not erroneous when taken in connection with the cause at issue, though the first clause alone is broader than it in fact should be." New York, etc., R. Co. v. Callahan (Ind. App. 1907), 81 N. E. Rep. 670.

"In an action by a passenger for personal injuries sustained in a collision of two of defendant's trains, a complaint which alleges that the collision occurred wholly on account of the negligence of the defendants in the construction. equipment. operation, and control of the railway, and the trains thereon. sufficiently charges acts of negligence." New York, etc., R. Co. v. Callahan, 81 N. E. Rep. 670.

manner that it was apt to collide with an incoming passenger train.

§ 675. **Collisions at intersection of two railroads.**— Where trains move upon intersecting lines of two railroads, it is the duty of those in control of the engines to exercise a very high degree of care to avoid collisions with other trains approaching the crossing on the other track, and the train approaching such crossing should not only be kept under control, but a proper lookout should be maintained for other trains,[85] and it is not only the duty to stop a train, when due care would require it, but if necessary, the track of the other road should be scanned,[86] and if another train has passed the danger point, the approaching train having the right of way, ought to be stopped, or both companies would be concurrently negligent,[87] in which case either of the two could be sued, or the railroads jointly held for the damages resulting from the collision.[88]

In a leading case, by the Supreme Court of Missouri,[89]

" In an action by a passenger for injuries, evidence of the condition of the cars immediately after the collision, and the efforts required to separate them, is admissible as tending to show the force of the collision, and bearing on the rate of speed." Elgin Traction Co. v. Wilson, 120 Ill. App. 371, judgment affirmed, 75 N. E. Rep. 436; 217 Ill. 47.

[85] Kansas City, etc., R. Co. v. Stoner, 51 Fed Rep. 649; 2 C. C. A. 437; 52 Am. & Eng. R. Cas. 462; 49 Fed. Rep. 209; 4 U. S. App. 109; 1 C. C. A. 231.

[86] If the safety of passengers requires it, it is held to be the carrier's duty to stop trains and send persons ahead to scan the connecting track. West Chicago R. Co. v. Martin, 47 Ill. App. 610.

[87] Pratt v. Chicago, etc., R. Co., 38 Minn. 455; 38 N. W. Rep. 356.

[88] Pittsburg, etc., R. Co. v. Spencer, 98 Ind. 186; 21 Am. & Eng. R. Cas. 478; Colegrove v. New York, etc., R. Co., 20 N. Y. 492; Wabash R. Co. v. Shacklett, 105 Ill. 364; 12 Am. & Eng. R. Cas. 106; Flaherty v. Minneapolis, etc., R. Co., 39 Minn. 328; 40 N. W. Rep. 160; 1 L. R. A. 680.

[89] Clark v. Chicago, etc., R. Co., 127 Mo. 197; 29 S. W. Rep. 1013.

it was held to constitute negligence to leave a passenger train at a railroad crossing, standing across the intersection, where the trains of the other railroad company might strike the cars, nor would it constitute a defense that the other company was negligent in running its train into such stationary train. As to this defense, Judge Gantt, for the court, said: "Here the train which stopped in a known place of danger was entirely under the control of defendant's agents and by their mismanagement they voluntarily suffered that train to stand in a position where it was liable to be struck by trains of the Wabash railroad. To escape liability on the ground of *vis major*, or the tortious act of a third person, it devolved upon defendant to show that it was guilty of no fault in falling into the danger, but all the testimony showed that defendant, with a reckless disregard of the lives of those entrusted to its keeping, placed them in a position of recognized peril. It sacrificed the lives and bodies of its confiding and sleeping passengers, to a mere matter of convenience. To escape responsibility for this, it pleads the negligence of the Wabash company, in not stopping its train, before reaching the point of intersection, forgetting, that as to its passengers, before it can avail itself of the negligent act of the Wabash, its own negligent act must not have contributed to the injury."

§ 676. **Injury from projection on passing train.**— Any carelessness, on the part of a carrier, in loading a freight train, or cars, or in failing to attend to the proper adjustment of a

The mere convenience of the railroad companies in leaving trains or cars standing on crossings, is immaterial, as compared to the safety of the passengers. Kellow v. Central, etc., R. Co., 68 Iowa 470; 23 N. W. Rep. 740; 27 N. W. Rep. 466; 21 Am. & Eng. R. Cas. 485.

The carrier is not bound to use such care as the most prudent in the business of railroading would use, to avoid a collision, but such care as the mass of prudent persons in the same business would use. Houston, etc., R. Co. v. Brin, 77 Texas 174; 13 S. W. Rep. 886.

load of lumber or other projecting substances, by which an injury is done to a passenger on another train, will render the carrier liable for the injury sustained.[90]

In a New York case,[91] the plaintiff, a passenger, was injured while seated in a car, by a bar of iron entering the car, which had been loaded onto a construction train, being pulled, on a passing track, in an opposite direction. The general rule, as to carriers, in case of an injury to a passenger, that where the means of control on the part of the carrier is exercised over the instrumentality causing injury to a passenger, and such injury occurs in an unusual manner, the passenger establishes a *prima facie* case, by proving the fact of an injury due to such a cause, was applied in this case, and in the absence of any explanation on the carrier's part, it was held that the inference would obtain that the injury resulted from the negligence and inattention of the carrier's employees, in charge of the construction train, and this was sufficient to sustain the railroad company's liability.

§ 677. **Injuries by articles thrown from train.**— Persons waiting on the platform to take passage upon a train of the railroad company, injured by any article thrown from the train by an employee of the railroad company, are entitled to recover damages, for it is held to be negligence on the part of such employees to throw articles, calculated to injure passengers or those congregated at railroad stations, from moving trains.[92]

In actions for injuries by articles thrown from moving trains, however, it is necessary, to establish a liability, to show that the article causing the injury, was actually thrown from the train by an employee of the railroad company, or

---

[90] Curtis v. Central R. Co., 6 McLean (U. S.) 401.

[91] Walker v. Erie R. Co., 63 Barb. (N. Y.) 260.

[92] 2 Hutchinson on Carr., § 1011 (3 ed.), p. 1164, and cases cited.

one standing toward it in a similar light, or that it was customary for it to permit others to throw similar articles from its trains, in a manner likely to cause injuries to its passengers.[93]

And under the Massachusetts statute,[94] exempting railroad companies from the negligence on the part of express messengers in the service of others than the railroad company, there would be no liability, on the part of the railroad company for an injury to its passenger by an express agent wrongfully throwing off a bundle which struck and injured the passenger,[95] and in the absence of such a statute, in New York, it was held, that to charge a railroad company for an injury received by a passenger, on account of being struck by a mail sack, thrown from a passing train by a mail clerk, it was necessary to establish that this was an habitual or accustomed practice on the part of mail clerks on the railroad company's trains, and that it knew of such practice, or ought to have known thereof, by reasonable care on its part, and failing to establish such conduct, likely to result in injury to the passenger, with the consent or acquiescence of the railroad company, there would be no liability for such an act.[96]

§ 678. **Care to avoid obstructions.**— The degree of care that a railroad company is bound to exercise includes the safe operation of the train on the track and a high degree

[93] *Ante idem.;* Shaw v. Chicago, etc., R. Co., 123 Mich. 629; 82 N. W. Rep. 618; 81 Am. St. Rep. 230; 49 L. R. A. 308.

[94] Massachusetts Statutes 1894, ch. 469, § 3.

[95] Winship v. Boston, etc., R. Co., 170 Mass. 464; 49 N. E. Rep. 647.

[96] Ayers v. New York, etc., R. Co., 77 Hun 414; 28 N. Y. Supp. 789. See, also, Chicago, etc., R. Co. v. Wagoner, 90 Ill. App. 556; Ayers v. New York, etc., R. Co., 158 N. Y. 254; 53 N. E. Rep. 22; Hughes v. St. Louis, etc., R. Co., 127 Mo. 447; 30 S. W. Rep. 127.

of care to avoid all obstructions likely to occasion injury to passengers.[97]

An engineer is required, on perceiving any obstruction on the track, to " use all means in his power, known to skillful engineers, in order to stop the train," unless the stopping of the train would increase the peril of passengers, when the obstruction has not been observed in time to stop the train with safety.[98]

If a derrick is constructed so close to the track as to strike a passenger standing on the platform and the railroad employees, with knowledge of the fact, fail to inform a passenger standing on the platform, of the liability to be struck by the derrick, when the car passes such an obstruction, this is sufficient evidence of negligence to make it a jury issue, whether or not the plaintiff's negligence or that of defendant caused the injury.[99]   And, likewise, a failure to give signals or to stop a train or car, in time to avoid other cars or a train, on the same track, or across the track, is negligence, as held by a Missouri court.[1]

But the duty to stop the train under all circumstances is not an absolute duty, but must be controlled by the peculiar circumstances of each case and the issue is whether or not the stopping of the train was consistent with careful railroading, or a contrary course, in the judgment of careful men, would be the safer.[2]   If a train is about to run upon an animal that is seen upon the track, the engineer is not required to reverse his engine to prevent a collision, if the rate of speed is such

[97] Cobb v. Lindell Ry. Co., 149 Mo. 135; 50 S. W. Rep. 310; Horstein v. United Ry. Cos., 97 Mo. App. 271; 70 S. W. Rep. 1105.

[98] East Tennessee, etc., R. Co. v. Deaver, 79 Ala. 216.

[99] Seymour v. Citizens Ry. Co., 114 Mo. 266; 21 S. W. Rep. 739.

[1] Horstein v. United Ry. Cos., 97 Mo. App. 271; 70 S. W. Rep. 1105; Fleming v. Kansas City, etc., R. Co., 89 Mo. App. 129; Clark v. Chicago, etc., R. Co., 127 Mo. 197; 29 S. W. Rep. 1013; Hennessey v. St. Louis, etc., R. Co., 173 Mo. 86; 73 S. W. Rep. 162.

[2] East Tennessee, etc., R. Co. v. Deaver, 79 Ala. 216.

that to do so would endanger the lives of the passengers.[3]
No duty exists to warn passengers that to protrude their
bodies or limbs from the car windows will be attendant with
danger from obstructions along the track,[4] nor is the railroad
company ordinarily liable for an injury due to a sudden
obstruction, resulting in an injury to a passenger, placed on
the track by some third person, whose act in thus occasioning
such injury could not have been reasonably expected as liable to happen.[5]

§ 679. **Injuries from collisions with cattle.**— A railway
company is bound to use the highest degree of reasonable
care and diligence to keep cattle and other stock off the
railroad track so as to prevent the derailment of the trains
and the consequent injury to passengers.   And while there
is not a conclusive presumption of negligence in every case
of injury to a passenger from cattle getting on the track,[6]
the fact that a passenger is injured by a train colliding with
a cow, which has strayed upon the track through the carelessness of the owner, will not exempt the railroad company
from liability to the injured passenger, unless it was also
free from negligence contributing to produce the injury,[7]
nor would the fact that the car was thrown off the track by

[3] Nashville, etc., R. Co. v. Troxlee, 1 Lea (Tenn.) 520.

[4] Miller v. St. Louis, etc., R. Co., 5 Mo. App. 471.

[5] Padgitt v. Moll, 159 Mo. 143; 81 Am. St. Rep. 347; 52 L. R. A.
854; 60 S. W. Rep. 121.

In Carroll v. Interstate Transit Co. (107 Mo. 653; 17 S. W. Rep.
889), the railroad company had a cattle chute near its track and
the plaintiff was injured by jumping on the rear platform of the car,
in motion, and while holding onto the iron gate that barred his
entrance to the platform of the car, until he was struck by the cattle
chute. The maintenance of the cattle chute near the track was held
not to be negligence on which the railroad company could be held
liable.

[6] Wright v. Pennsylvania R. Co., 3 Pittsb. (Pa.) 116.

[7] Card v. New York, etc., R. Co., 50 Barb. (N. Y.) 39.

1032

running over a cow unlawfully on the track, causing injury to the passenger, of itself rebut the presumption of negligence, resulting from the derailment and the injury to the passenger, since the railroad company is bound to make provisions as to all such accidents as are likely to occur, from such a customary cause.[8] It is held that the obligation as to cattle is not satisfied by the mere exercise of carefulness to keep a clear right of way, but that the employees in charge of the train ought to also keep a lookout to avoid derailments from such causes and if such precautions are not sufficient to guard against the danger, that the more effective precaution of a fence against such stock, must be resorted to.[9]

§ 680. Injury due to overloaded coach.— The reported cases upon injuries to passengers, upon railroad trains, due to the overloading of the coach, are not so numerous as in the case of negligent injuries due to the overloading of stage coaches[10] or similar conveyances, where the immediate effect of the crowded coach is to cause a breakdown and injury thus proximately resulting from the overcrowded condition of the coach.[11]

But in some of the reported cases the ground of negligence charged against railroad companies has been that the company negligently permitted its coaches to be overloaded or crowded, and this act is set up as the proximate cause of

[8] Sullivan v. Philadelphia, etc., R. Co., 30 Pa. St. 234.

[9] Fordyce v. Jackson, 56 Ark. 594; 20 S. W. Rep. 528, 597.

The railroad company was held liable to passengers, for injuries from collisions with cattle, in Chicago, etc., R. Co. v. McAra, 52 Ill. 296; Brown v. New York, etc., R. Co., 34 N. Y. 404; Patchell v. North Western R. Co., 6 Ir. C. L. 117.

[10] Israel v. Clark, 4 Esp. 259; Long v. Horne, 1 Car. & P. 612; 3 Thompson on Neg., §§ 3637, 3639, and cases cited; Maury v. Talmadge, 2 McLean (U. S.) 157, 158.

[11] Israel v. Clark, 4 Esp. 259.

the injury to the passenger. No reported cases have been found where the negligence in this respect brought about a breakdown of the coach, but in one case,[12] a railroad company was held liable for an injury to a passenger, jostled or pushed from the car platform, where he was obliged to stand, on account of the crowded condition of the car, after an invitation to get on, as there was sufficient room inside the car, which he was unable to reach on account of the crowd therein. And another case decided [13] that a railroad company was liable for an injury received by the crushing of a passenger's foot, where it had control of the approaches to its cars, used by passengers, and negligently permitted too many people to crowd upon its cars.

§ 681. Injuries from snow and ice on car platforms.— A railway company is under no obligation to remove the effects of a continuous storm of snow, sleet or rain, from the exposed platform of a car, while making its passage between stations, or at the *termini* of its route, and a passenger who has reason to know that there is snow or ice on the platform of a car which he is about to enter, and that the railroad company. has had no reasonable opportunity to effectually remove it, cannot recover damages for injuries sustained on account of a fall, caused by slipping on such a platform.[14]

Speaking of the rule governing the liability of the carrier in such a case, Ruger, C. J., speaking for the New York

12 Dennis v. Pittsburg, etc., R. Co., 165 Pa. St. 624; 31 Atl. Rep. 52.

13 Dawson v. New York, etc., Co., 52 N. Y. Supp. 133; 31 App. Div. 537.

"Whether a train was overcrowded or rules posted warning passengers not to ride in baggage cars are questions for the jury and not the court." Lane v. Choctaw, etc., R. Co. (Okl. 1907), 91 Pac. Rep. 883.

14 Palmer v. Pennsylvania R. Co., 111 N. Y. 488; 18 N. E. Rep. 859; 37 Am. & Eng. R. Cas. 150, reversing 42 Hun 656; 4 N. Y. S. R. 888; Kelly v. Manhattan R. Co., 112 N. Y. 443; 20 N. E. Rep. 383; 21 N. Y. S. R. 507.

Court of Appeals in a leading case,[15] said: " It is quite impossible to lay down any general rule applicable to all circumstances, in respect to the degree of care to be observed by a railroad corporation in the removal of ice or snow from its cars, and each case must therefore be generally determined by its own peculiar circumstances; but it is safe to say that such corporations should not be held responsible for the dangers produced by the elements until they have assumed a dangerous form, and they have had a reasonable opportunity to remove their effects."

But where the snow and ice on a car platform has existed in a dangerous condition for a length of time sufficient to enable the carrier, by the exercise of due care, to remove it, if the accumulation is in sufficient quantity to be productive of probable danger to passengers, the carrier will be held liable in case of an injury to a passenger from such a cause. And where the proof showed that plaintiff was injured by stepping from a car onto an icy platform, and that snow and ice had been forming thereon, since the day before, and that no means had been used, by sanding or placing ashes on the platform, or any other precaution taken to protect the passengers from falling thereon, this was held to be sufficient to establish a *prima facie* case of negligence on the part of the carrier and to justify a verdict for the injured passenger.[16]

[15] Palmer v. Pennsylvania R. Co., *supra*.

[16] Timpson v. Manhattan R. Co., 5 N. Y. Supp. 684.

" In an action by a passenger injured by slipping on a car platform, where plaintiff testified that she was about to alight with a grip, which she was handing to her husband, when she fell, it was not error to refuse to charge that if plaintiff could have avoided slipping by grasping the hand rail with both hands, or by grasping the hand rail on each side of the platform, or by use of some other platform, then she could not recover, provided a person of ordinary care would have attempted to so avoid slipping down, since it enunciated inconsistent theories, imposed a greater measure of care on the passenger than

§ 682. **Shutting door on passenger's hand.**— In the absence
of notice to the railway company of the danger to a passenger by the closing of the doors of its coaches, it has a right
to rely upon the fact that this customary and ordinary act
of using the doors for the purpose for which they are constructed, will not be the cause of an injury to a passenger,
who has inadvertently placed his hand upon the sill or facing of the car door.   Where an employee slammed a door to
and in doing so, without notice of the fact that a passenger's
hand was on the door facing, where it was apt to be injured,
struck and injured the hand of a passenger, who was thrown
forward by a lurch of the train, there was held to be no
evidence of negligence on the part of the railway company.[17]
But of course if the company's employees knowingly cause
such an injury to a passenger, as where an employee slammed
a door against a passenger's hand, which he ought to have
seen, by reasonable care, was in a position to sustain injury
as a result of such a careless act, the company was held
liable.[18]

In the case of an injury to an infant, the employees of
the train have a right to rely upon the care of the infant by
the parents or guardians, where they are traveling in com-

is required by law, and ignored the exact circumstances under which
the injury occurred, as testified to by plaintiff." Baltimore & A. Ry.
Co. v. Trader (Md. 1907), 68 Atl. Rep. 12.

"Where a passenger, in attempting to board a train, slipped and
fell by reason alone of the icy condition of the car steps, the fact that
the railroad company may also have been negligent in not providing
a better station platform is not a ground of recovery." Ft. Worth,
etc., Ry. Co. v. Work (Tex. Civ. App. 1907), 100 S. W. Rep. 962.

[17] Maddox v. London, etc., R. Co., 38 L. T. 458; Jackson v. Metropolitan, etc., Ry. Co., 26 W. R. 175, reversing L. R. 2 C. P. D. 125;
46 L. J. C. P. 376; 25 W. R. 661; 36 L. T. 485; L. R. 10 C. P. 49;
44 L. J. C. P. 83; 31 L. T. 475; 23 W. R. 78; Murphy v. Atlanta,
etc., R. Co., 89 Ga. 832; Coleman v. South, etc., R. Co., 4 H. & C. 699.

[18] Fordham v. London, etc., R. Co., L. R. 4 C. P. 619; 38 L. J. C. P.
324; 17 W. R. 896; L. R. 3 C. P. 368; 37 L. J. C. P. 176.

pany with older persons, and it is error to charge the jury that a railway company is liable for an injury to a child, caused by the conductor closing the door on her hand, if he could have seen her hand in danger before closing the door, as it required him to use care to see that she was not exposed to danger, which was a duty the law devolved upon the child's mother and the company would only be liable, if the conductor negligently closed the door on her hand, knowing that it was where it might be injured by so doing.[19]

[19] St. Louis, etc., R. Co. v. Rexroad (Ark.), 58 Am. & Eng. R. Cas. 615. In St. Louis, etc., R. Co. v. Rexroad, *supra*, Judge Battle, for the Supreme Court of Arkansas, said: "In the instructions given in this case, at the instance of the plaintiff, the court told the jury that if the conductor, in passing out of the car, in which plaintiff was riding, might, by the exercise of reasonable diligence, have seen her while standing at the water cooler, near the door, and, knowing that the train was about to stop, closed the door negligently or carelessly, and thereby injured her, the defendant would be liable for damages. According to this instruction, the conductor had no right to rely on the mother taking care of her child, but was bound to use reasonable diligence in seeing that she was not exposed to danger at the time she was injured. This was error, for the reasons indicated."

"A male passenger, while the train was in motion, left the day coach for the smoking car to use a closet therein. While on the platform he took hold of the knob of the door of the smoker when a porter took hold of the inside knob to leave the car. The passenger stepped aside, and the porter opened the door and passed out. The porter, though seeing the passenger, who, in order to steady himself, placed his hand on the side of the door, pulled the door shut with a jerk and injured the hand. *Held*, that the question of the negligence of the porter was for the jury." St. Louis, etc., R. Co. v. Neely (Tex. Civ. App. 1907), 101 S. W. Rep. 481.

"A passenger, whose hand was injured by having the car door shut on it, is not as a matter of law guilty of contributory negligence in disobeying a notice forbidding passengers to stand on the platform, where the train was not in motion and he was in the act of entering the car after being stopped on the platform by the conductor." Louisville & N. R. Co. v. Mulder (Ala. 1906), 42 So. Rep. 742.

"Where a railroad company provides its passenger cars with vestibule doors, it is not only answerable for the negligent acts of its servants in opening such doors and permitting them to remain so, but is also

§ 683. **Passengers injured while on roads of other railroad companies.**— If a passenger, during the course of his transportation from the place where he enters the train of the initial carrier, passes over the road of another railroad company, in the train of the original carrier, and sustains an injury on the road of such other company, by reason of the imperfect condition of the roadway or by collisions with its cars or on account of obstructions or other causes, the original carrier is liable for such injury, to the same extent as if the train had been operated for the whole distance over its own track.[20]   The carrier must be held answerable for all the agencies it employs to complete the contract of carriage, or otherwise it would be an easy matter for railroad companies to avoid the responsibility to passengers, by running their trains over the roads of other companies, and if this rule were recognized by the courts, it would be a difficult thing to establish a liability in each case.[21]   And the initial carrier using the roadway and track of another company is not only bound to see that the track is in a safe condition to enable it to safely carry its passengers, but it must also see to it that the trains of the other company owning the track, are not run so as to interfere with the safe operation of its own trains and if a collision occurs between the trains of the two companies, the passenger will not be required

responsible for its failure to exercise a high degree of care, to the end that such doors shall be closed and the vestibule rendered reasonably safe, though the doors were opened by others than its servants." Wagoner v. Wabash R. Co. (Mo. App. 1906), 94 S. W. Rep. 293.

[20] Great Western R. Co. v. Blake, 7 H. & N. 987; Candee v. Pennsylvania R. Co., 21 Wis. 582; Toledo, etc., R. Co. v. Rumbold, 40 Ill. 143; Schopman v. Boston, etc., R. Co., 9 Cush. (Mass.) 24; Pennsylvania R. Co. v. Howard, 178 U. S. 153; 44 L. Ed. 1015; Dunn v. New Jersey, etc., R. Co., 71 N. J. L. 21; 58 Atl. Rep. 164; 2 Hutchinson on Carr. (3 ed.), § 915, p. 1026.

[21] Thomas v. London, etc., R. Co., L. R. 5 Q. B. 226; Wyman v. New York, etc., R. Co., 46 Me. 162; Candee v. Pennsylvania R. Co., 21 Wis. 582.

to locate the negligence responsible for the collision, but can maintain an action against his own carrier.[22]

[22] Murray v. New York, etc., R. Co., 66 Conn. 512; 34 Atl. Rep. 506; 32 L. R. A. 539.

"Railroad companies jointly operating their roads through the agency of a lessee may be joined in one action for negligent injuries to a passenger being carried over their lines, where the negligent acts were continuous and chargeable to the common agent of the lessee." Carleton v. Yadkin R. Co. (N. C. 1906), 55 S. E. Rep. 429.

CHAPTER XXVI.

INJURIES IN BOARDING TRAINS.

§ 684. **Degree of care required.**— The same high degree of care which the law exacts of the passenger carrier, in the carriage of the passenger, to see that its roadway, track, trains and other appliances are in proper condition, to safeguard the protection of the passenger, obtains in the case of taking on the passengers, and the railroad company failing to use such a high degree of care to see that its passengers are not injured in the act of boarding its trains, due to any negligence on its part, will be compelled to respond in damages.

Speaking of this duty — to passengers in boarding cars —

1040

in a recent case,[1] the Kansas City Court of Appeals used this language: " The obligation of passenger carriers to their passengers is, as far as is capable by human care and fore-sight, to carry them safely, which extends to getting on and off their cars; or, expressed another way, they must exercise the highest degree of care of a prudent person, in view of the circumstances at the time of the injury."

And this rule is in accord with the generally recognized rule which the courts exact, for the protection of passengers in the boarding of trains, provided by the railway company, for their transportation.[2]

§ 685. Reasonable time to enter train.— It is a generally accepted rule that it is the carrier's duty to stop its trains and hold them stationary for a sufficient length of time to enable its passengers to get on the train, by the use of ordinary care on their part.[3]   Any other rule of law would

[1] This opinion is by Judge Smith. Young v. Missouri Pacific Ry. Co., 93 Mo. App. 273, 274.

[2] Clark v. Chicago, etc., R. Co., 127 Mo. 197; 29 S. W. Rep. 1013; Chicago, etc., R. Co. v. Scates, 90 Ill. 586; Langan v. St. Louis, etc., R. Co., 3 Am. & Eng. R. Cas. 368.

"Where, in an action for injuries to a passenger, plaintiff claimed that the car started suddenly while she was boarding it, an instruction submitting the question whether the car was suddenly started, and that defendant's servants knew, or by the exercise of 'proper care' should have known, that plaintiff was on the step, was not erroneous because of the phrase 'proper care,' the requisite care having been previously properly stated." Randolph v. Metropolitan Ry. Co. (Mo. App. 1907), 102 S. W. Rep. 1085.

"In an action for injuries alleged to have occurred while plaintiff was boarding one of defendant's cars as a passenger, while the car was standing at a regular stopping place for the reception of passengers, the burden was on plaintiff to prove that he was a passenger." Alabama City, etc., Ry. Co. v. Bates (Ala. 1907), 43 So. Rep. 98.

[3] Hurley v. Metropolitan Ry. Co., 120 Mo. App. 262; 96 S. W. Rep. 714; Slanahan v. St. Louis Transit Co., 109 Mo. App. 231; 83 S. W. Rep. 783; Maguire v. Transit Co., 103 Mo. App. 459; 78 S. W. Rep. 838; Bertram v. People's Ry. Co., 154 Mo. 639; 55 S. W. Rep. 1040;

subject passengers to risks of injury from moving trains or sudden jars or jolts in boarding trains, which would be productive of disastrous results to the traveling public.

Passing upon the existence of such a duty, in one Missouri case [4] it is said: " It is the law of this State that it is the duty of a carrier to stop long enough to enable its passengers to get on or off its conveyance, by the use of ordinary care or diligence." And speaking of the same obligation on the carrier's part, Judge Phillipps said: " With respect to the obligation of the defendant to the plaintiff, as a passenger, it is sufficient to say, that while it is not an insurer of the safety of passengers, it is bound by its office, as such carrier, to exercise due care and vigilance to safely transport them. It must allow reasonable time for passengers to enter and leave its cars with safety, in the exercise of ordinary care. It should give the passengers reasonable time to enter and take a seat, if there be one; and while it may start its cars before the passenger has had time to take a seat,   *   *   * it must exercise the utmost care in starting, so as not to jar or upset him." [5]

Hanks v. Chicago, etc., Ry. Co., 60 Mo. App. 280; Strayss v. Kansas City, etc., Ry. Co., 75 Mo. 185; Smith v. Chicago, etc., Ry. Co., 108 Mo. 243; 18 S. W. Rep. 971.

[4] Hanks v. Chicago, etc., Ry. Co., 60 Mo. App. 280.

[5] Dougherty v. Missouri R. Co., 81 Mo. 330.

The carrier should hold its train stationary a sufficient length of time to enable passengers to enter the cars, without starting the train, either backward or forward, and for an injury from a violation of this duty, a recovery will be allowed. Dillon v. Manhattan R. Co., 16 N. Y. S. R. 767; 49 Hun 608; 1 N. Y. Supp. 679; Falls v. San Francisco, etc., R. Co., 97 Cal. 114; 31 Pac. Rep. 901; Swigert v. Hannibal, etc., R. Co., 75 Mo. 475; 9 Am. & Eng. R. Cas. 322; Carr v. Eel River R. Co., 98 Cal. 366; 33 Pac. Rep. 213; 58 Am. & Eng. R. Cas. 239; Montgomery, etc., R. Co. v. Stewart, 91 Ala. 421; 8 So. Rep. 708; Weber v. Kansas City, etc., R. Co., 100 Mo. 194; 12 S. W. Rep. 804; 7 L. R. A. 819; 41 Am. & Eng. R. Cas. 117.

But there is no duty to hold the train stationary until a passenger

§ 686. **Failure to stop train at station.**— Passengers by railway have a right to be afforded an opportunity of getting into the cars of a train, upon which they are to take passage, from the platform of the station at which they bought their tickets, or where they have the right to expect trains to stop, from the continued course of business pursued by the carrier and for an injury from a failure to stop trains at such a

has reached a seat and seated himself. Yarnall v. Kansas City, etc., R. Co., 113 Mo. 570; 21 S. W. Rep. 1.

All that is required is to stop the trains a sufficient time to enable passengers to enter the trains and twenty to thirty minutes is ample time for this purpose, in the absence of unusual circumstances, requiring a longer time. Flint, etc., R. Co. v. Stark, 38 Mich. 714.

Failure to hold the train for a reasonable time, to enable passengers to get settled, was held to give a cause of action, in the following cases: Poole v. Chicago, etc., R. Co., 89 Ga. 320; 15 S. E. Rep. 321; McKenna v. Hudson R. Co., 64 N. J. L. 106; 45 Atl. Rep. 776; Deming v. Chicago, etc., R. Co., 80 Mo. App. 152; Macon, etc., R. Co. v. Moore, 108 Ga. 84; 33 S. E. Rep. 889; 15 Am. & Eng. R. Cas. (N. S.) 842; Barth v. Kansas City, etc., R. Co., 142 Mo. 535; 44 S. W. Rep. 778; 10 Am. & Eng. R. Cas. (N. S.) 281.

"In an action for injuries to a passenger while boarding a train, an instruction that the defendant owed to a person attempting to board its train as a passenger a duty to give a reasonably sufficient time for him to do so, and that defendant was liable for any failure to perform that duty with the high degree of care that a person of very great prudence would use, was not objectionable as placing the absolute duty upon the defendant as a matter of law to stop its trains a reasonably sufficient time to enable passengers to enter its cars." Galveston, etc., Ry. Co. v. Fink (Tex. Civ. App. 1907), 99 S. W. Rep. 204.

"A train having failed to stop at 1:45 a. m. on plaintiff's signal to take him on, plaintiff, whose home was near the station, drove across country to his store, reaching there about 8:00 a. m. The night was very cold, with a north wind and sleet, and plaintiff's only object in making the night trip was to avoid the possible loss of a few dollars by failing to open his store on time in the morning. *Held*, insufficient to justify submission to the jury of whether the company's refusal to stop the train was the proximate cause of the sickness resulting from the exposure." International, etc., R. Co. v. Addison (Tex. 1906), 97 S. W. Rep. 1037.

station, the railroad company would be liable in damages.[6]
A company selling a ticket at a way station on the line of
its railroad, is bound to stop the train, upon which passage
was intended to be taken, long enough to afford the purchaser
of the ticket reasonable time to board the train in safety,
and while he is in the exercise of due care, on his part and
failing so to do, in case of a resulting injury, there would be
a liability.[7]

But damages cannot be recovered, ordinarily, for a failure
to stop trains not regularly scheduled to stop at the station
where the passenger attempts to board the train, such as
flag stations, at which only certain trains are billed to stop
and the train in question is not one of these trains,[8] nor
can a passenger who has bought a ticket good for only such
trains as do stop at the station, complain that a train which
did not stop, was not one of the trains within the condition
of his ticket, for this condition of the contract of carriage
will be enforced by the courts, and the passenger only becomes such, as to trains that stop at the station where the
ticket was purchased.[9]

§ 687. Law exacts reasonable delay only.— The law does
not exact of a passenger carrier, in this age when rapid

[6] Hall v. McFadden, 19 New. Brun. 340.

[7] Poole v. Georgia, etc., R. Co., 89 Ga. 320; 15 S. E. Rep. 321.

[8] St. Louis, etc., R. Co. v. Berryhill, 3 Texas Civ. App. 387.

[9] Wilson v. New Orleans, etc., R. Co., 63 Miss. 352. See, also, Lake
Erie, etc., R. Co. v. People, 42 Ill. App. 387; Pittsburg, etc., R. Co. v.
Nuxum, 50 Ind. 141; 9 Am. Ry. Rep. 396; Freeman v. Detroit, etc.,
R. Co., 65 Mich. 577; 32 N. W. Rep. 833; 30 Am. & Eng. R. Cas. 623;
Burnett v. Great Northern, etc., R. Co., L. R. 10 App. Cas. 147; 54
L. J. Q. B. D. 531; 53 L. T. 507; 24 Am. & Eng. R. Cas. 647.

And for failure to stop trains at county-seat towns, as required by
Illinois statute, see Illinois, etc., R. Co. v. People, 143 Ill. 434; 33
N. E. Rep. 173; Chicago, etc., R. Co. v. People, 105 Ill. 657; 13 Am. &
Eng. R. Cas. 42.

transit is the demand of the traveling public, that a carrier shall so delay its conveyances to permit the entry of dilatory passengers, to an extent to amount to an unreasonable impediment to the general traveling public, but the passenger carrier is held to perform the full measure of the legal responsibility, in this regard, if it hold its trains for a reasonable time only, to permit passengers at its different stations to enter its trains.

Where a train has been held, for the customary period, at a station, to permit the passengers to enter the train and a passenger who had the full time to get on the train, so delayed boarding the train, that when he attempted to get on, the train had commenced to move and the conductor or train men had given him no assurance of safety in so doing, it was held that he could not hold the railway company liable for an injury so received, but that the railway company had performed its full duty in holding the train for a reasonable time and no damages could be recovered.[10]

But of course if a passenger is assured by the train men that he may attempt to board a moving train, and the speed of the train is not so great as to carry with it notice of the danger in attempting to board it, under the rule which obtains in some of the States, a recovery could be had for an injury resulting from such an attempt to board a train, even after it had been held for a reasonable time to enable passengers to get on,[11] although in New York and some other States it has been held negligence as matter of law for a passenger, under such conditions, to board a moving train, regardless of the speed at which it is moving.[12]

[10] Georgia, etc., R. Co. v. Robinson, 68 Miss. 643; 10 So. Rep. 60; Brown v. Raleigh, etc., R. Co., 108 No. Car. 34; 12 S. E. Rep. 958.

[11] Montgomery, etc., R. Co. v. Stewart, 91 Ala. 421; 8 So. Rep. 708; Chicago, etc., R. Co. v. Drake, 33 Ill. App. 114; Murphy v. St. Louis, etc., R. Co., 43 Mo. App. 351; Swigert v. Hannibal, etc., R. Co., 75 Mo. 475.

[12] Hunter v. Cooperstown, etc., R. Co., 112 N. Y. 371; Schaeffer v.

§ 688. **Appliances for boarding trains.**— A railroad company is under the duty of providing reasonably safe appliances to enable its passengers to board its trains in a reasonably safe manner, and if a passenger, acting upon a direction of an employee of the railroad company, sustains injury in the use of means not reasonably safe to enable him to board a train, or such as are not customarily in use by railroads, the railroad company making use of such unusual or improper means or appliances to enable its passengers to enter its cars, would be responsible in damages.[13]

But if the usual and customary appliances and means are being used by a passenger and such as in the past have been found reasonably safe for the purpose, then negligence can not be predicated upon the happening of such an act, for where something unusual occurs, resulting in the injury of a passenger, but such unusual occurrence is not the result of some unusual or wrongful act of the railroad company, but it has been pursuing the same course that in the past was always found reasonably safe for its passengers, then such unusual occurrence, causing the injury to the passenger, is what is termed an accident, for which the carrier is not answerable.[14]

§ 689. **Approach and ingress to train.**— It is the duty of the carrier to furnish safe and proper means of ingress to its trains, for its passengers, from its platforms or station approaches[15] and this must be done at all places where

St. Louis, etc., R. Co., 128 Mo. 64; 30 S. W. Rep. 331; Missouri Pacific Ry. Co. v. Texas, etc., Ry. Co., 36 Fed. Rep. 879.

[13] Allender v. Chicago, etc., R. Co., 43 Iowa 276; 14 Am. Ry. Rep. 443.

[14] Young v. Missouri Pacific Ry. Co., 93 Mo. App. 275.

[15] Moses v. Louisville, etc., R. Co., 39 La. Ann. 649; 2 So. Rep. 567; 30 Am. & Eng. R. Cas. 556.

the railroad company receives passengers on the line of its road.[16]

It is the duty of the company, before the departure of its passenger train, from a given station, to clear the way, by the removal of freight trains, or other dangerous obstructions, between it and the depot, so that the passenger train can be approached with safety, and if the passenger train leaves, without affording a passenger a safe means of access to it from the depot, and an injury results from this cause, the carrier would be liable therefor.[17]

It is held, in a New York case,[18] that the carrier's duty to provide a reasonably safe means of access to its trains, from its stations, was not discharged, by providing a narrow board walk, from the station platform, to the train, only three or four inches wide, for a passenger entering a car could not foresee when a person in front would suddenly stop or turn, and thus throw the passenger from such a narrow approach, as was done in this case.[19]

[16] Redner v. Lehigh, etc., R. Co., 73 Hun 562; 26 N. Y. Supp. 1050; 56 N. Y. S. R. 230.

[17] Chicago, etc., R. Co. v. Coss, 73 Ill. 394.

[18] Redner v. Lehigh, etc., R. Co., 73 Hun 562; 26 N. Y. Supp. 1050; 56 N. Y. S. R. 230. And for injury to young lady by walking off platform, in attempt to enter train, by absence of lights on platform, see Chicago, etc., R. Co. v. Trotter, 60 Miss. 442.

[19] Redner v. Lehigh, etc., R. Co., supra.

"Where a way is provided at a station for a passenger going to or from his train, he may rely on the duty of the company to keep the track clear, where passengers are passing between the train and the station." Harper v. Pittsburg, etc., R. Co., 68 Atl. Rep. 831; 219 Pa. 368.

"A passenger, who is invited by the carrier to cross a track in going to or leaving his train, is chargeable only with reasonable care, and is not necessarily guilty of contributory negligence in failing to look and listen for an approaching train before crossing; he having the right to believe that trains would be so regulated as to permit his crossing in safety." Karr v. Milwaukee Traction Co. (Wis. 1907), 113 N. W. Rep. 62.

§ 690. **Duty to furnish seat for passenger.**— Railroad companies are under the obligation to furnish seats for passengers whom they accept for transportation, and if the car is crowded, so that a passenger is not able to get a seat and he is injured as a result of a sudden start or stopping of the train, because standing and not able to find a seat, this will enter into the decision of the question of the passenger's negligence in receiving the injury.[20]

But the railroad company is not under the duty of holding its trains stationary until all its passengers have been seated, for this would entail upon them a harsh rule, variable with the slowness or swiftness of different individuals and such a rule would be calculated to retard the speed of rapid transit roads, where this inducement is a source of the principal business of railroads, in the crowded commercial centers of the country.[21]

" A railroad company placed a freight train on a switch between its depot building and a passenger train on the regular track. A passenger, intending to board the passenger train, stepped upon a flat car in the freight train directly in front of the depot building and undertook to jump from the top of it to the platform of the passenger train. His foot was caught in a stirrup in the top of the flat car, and he was injured. The flat car was not out of order. *Held,* that the passenger was, as a matter of law, guilty of contributory negligence, precluding a recovery, though the freight train should have been cut in two and a way opened for passengers to walk from the depot to the passenger train." Louisville & N. R. Co. v. Lawler (Ky. 1908), 107 S. W. Rep. 702.

[20] Louisville, etc., R. Co. v. Kelly, 92 Ind. 371; 47 Am. Rep. 149; 13 Am. & Eng. R. Cas. 1; Hardenburgh v. St. Paul, etc., R. Co., 39 Minn. 3; 38 N. W. Rep. 625; 12 Am. St. Rep. 610; 34 Am. & Eng. R. Cas. 359; Bass v. Chicago, etc., R. Co., 36 Wis. 450; 9 Am. Ry. Rep. 101; Louisville, etc., R. Co. v. Patterson, 69 Miss. 421; 13 So. Rep. 697.

[21] Yarnall v. Kansas City, etc., R. Co., 113 Mo. 570; 21 S. W. Rep. 1. In this case, on this point, Judge Sherwood, said: " It is quite clear from the testimony that the daughters of the plaintiff ' did have time to get aboard ' and even to be seated before the train started. But, under the authorities, the defendant company did not need to wait until the passengers were seated, before the cars started. As

§ 691. Moving train while passenger is getting on.— While passengers are getting on a train, it is negligence on the part of the carrier to suddenly put such train in motion, without signal, so as to endanger the safety of the passengers,[22] and a railway company is liable to a passenger who sustains injuries, caused by the employee in charge of the train putting it in motion, with knowledge that the passenger is in the act of getting on the train, notwithstanding the passenger may have remained in the waiting room an unreasonable length of time, after being notified to board the train.[23]

Nor will the fact that the conductor of a train is induced by the conduct and conversation of a passenger, to believe that he does not expect to take passage on the train, which

soon as a passenger has fairly entered the vehicle, the carrier may start, without waiting for him to reach a seat, unless there is some special reason for doing so, as in the case of a weak or a lame person, or of a passenger on the outside of a coach. And the ground of the exception must be brought to the carrier's notice or he will be justified in starting in the usual manner." Citing 2 Shearm. & Redf. on Neg. (4 ed.), § 508.

The failure to provide passengers with seats was the ground of negligence alleged as the cause of injuries received, in Oliver v. Louisville, etc., R. Co., 43 La. Ann. 804; 9 So. Rep. 431; Graham v. McNeal, 20 Wash. 466; 55 Pac. Rep. 631; 43 L. R. A. 300; 12 Am. & Eng. R. Cas. (N. S.) 149.

Following the rule announced by Judge Sherwood, in Yarnall v. Kansas City, etc., Ry. Co. (113 Mo. 570; 21 S. W. Rep. 1; 18 L. R. A. 599), it was held, in the following cases, that there was no duty on the part of the carrier, to hold a train until a passenger had found a seat, as this would be placing an unstable, variable and unreasonable impediment upon rapid transportation. Louisville, etc., R. Co. v. Hale, 102 Ky. 600; 44 S. W. Rep. 213; 42 L. R. A. 293; 10 Am. & Eng. R. Cas. (N. S.) 73; Middlesborough, etc., R. Co. v. Webster (Ky.), 50 S. W. Rep. 843; 14 Am. & Eng. R. Cas. (N. S.) 209.

[22] Keating v. New York, etc., R. Co., 49 N. Y. 673; Texas, etc., R. Co. v. Davidson, 68 Texas 370; 4 S. W. Rep. 636; Murphy v. St. Louis, etc., R. Co., 43 Mo. App. 342.

[23] Gulf, etc., R. Co. v. Fox (Texas), 6 S. W. Rep. 569; 33 Am. & Eng. R. Cas. 543; Nance v. Norh Carolina, etc., R. Co., 94 N. Car. 619.

is about to leave the station, relieve the company for injuries received by such person, in consequence of the train being started without giving him time to get on, where the conductor had actually seen him attempting to get on the train, when he gave the order to start.[24]

Starting a train, after an express [25] or implied invitation [26] to get on the train, is negligence, whether in the day or night, for the act of boarding a train, however careful the passenger may be, is accompanied with such risk as to make such inattention negligence.[27]

But if the train is moving when a passenger attempts to get on, and the speed of the train is sufficient to make such a course dangerous, and the attempt to board the train is without any invitation or direction of the railroad company's employees, it is generally held that the passenger would be guilty of negligence, barring a recovery in case of injury therefrom.[28]

[24] Swigert v. Hannibal, etc., R. Co., 75 Mo. 475; 9 Am. & Eng. R. Cas. 322.

[25] Norfolk, etc., R. Co. v. Groseclose, 88 Va. 267; 13 S. E. Rep. 454; Illinois, etc., R. Co. v. Axley, 47 Ill. App. 307; Murphy v. St. Louis, etc., R. Co., 43 Mo. App. 342, by Judge Biggs.

[26] Illinois, etc., R. Co. v. Axley, 47 Ill. App. 307.

[27] Chicago, etc., R. Co. v. Drake, 33 Ill. App. 114.

[28] Hunter v. New York, etc., R. Co., 112 N. Y. 371; McClintock v. Pittsburg, etc., R. Co., 21 W. N. C. 133; Pennsylvania, etc., R. Co. v. Aspell, 23 Pa. St. 147. See chapter, Contributory Negligence of Passengers.

Boarding a moving train, in spite of a warning by the train men, was held to be negligence, in a Missouri case, Judge Black, for the court, saying: "An instruction might well be given to the effect that if the plaintiff was warned by the men in charge of the train, not to get on, and he attempted to get on while moving, in spite of the warning, then he is not entitled to recover." Fulks v. St. Louis, etc., R. Co., 111 Mo. 343; 19 S. W. Rep. 818.

Company was held liable for starting train, while passenger was embarking, in Detroit, etc., R. Co. v. Curtis, 23 Wis. 483, and Curtis v. Detroit, etc., R. Co., 27 Wis. 158.

" A petition, in an action against a carrier for personal injuries to a

§ 692. **Boarding a moving train.**— It has been held, that an attempt to board a moving train, without the advice or direction of the railroad company's agents or employees, is negligence, which will prevent the injured person from recovering for the injury so received and also preclude his representative, in case of his death, from such an injury.[29]

But the statement that such an act is negligence, as matter of law, on the part of the passenger, does not meet with general acceptance, and the more general rule may be said to be that it will depend upon the peculiar facts of each case, whether or not the attempt to board a moving train, will be held to be a negligent act. The decisions show that an intending passenger may attempt to board a moving train and if injured in so doing may still recover and the mere act of making such an attempt is not, of itself, always negligence on his part. The speed of the train is in all cases a most important factor to be considered, and this, in connection with the conduct of the train employees and the age and activity of the traveler, as well as the health, sex and other conditions and surroundings, may properly be taken into consideration upon the solution of the question.[30]

passenger by being thrown by the sudden jerking of the train, alleged that 'just as soon as the train came to a full stop' the passenger got on, and before she could reach her seat it was started with a violent jerk. The evidence showed that the train did not come to a full stop, but the conductor jumped off and assisted the passenger to get aboard. *Held,* that there was no material variance." Feagin v. Gulf, etc., Ry. Co. (Tex. Civ. App. 1907), 100 S. W. Rep. 346.

[29] Missouri Pacific Ry. Co. v. Texas, etc., Ry. Co., 36 Fed. Rep. 879; Hunter v. Cooperstown, etc., R. Co., 112 N. Y. 371; McClintock v. Pennsylvania R. Co., 21 W. N. C. 133; Pennsylvania, etc., R. Co. v. Aspell, 23 Pa. St. 147; Schaeffer v. St. Louis, etc., R. Co., 128 Mo. 64; 30 S. W. Rep. 331.

[30] Eppendorf v. New York, etc., R. Co., 69 N. Y. 195; Filer v. New York, etc., R. Co., 49 N. Y. 47; Burrows v. Erie R. Co., 63 N. Y. 556; Hickey v. Boston, etc., R. Co., 14 Allen 429; Clotworthy v. Hannibal, etc., R. Co., 80 Mo. 220; Leslie v. Wabash R. Co., 88 Mo. 50; Doss v. Missouri, etc., R. Co., 59 Mo. 27; 21 Am. Rep. 371; Straus v. Kansas

It is therefore held to be error, in a Missouri case, to
give an instruction, making it negligence *per se,* to attempt
to board a moving train;[31] the Appellate Court of the
same State held that while it was negligence to attempt to
board a train going at a rate of from six to eight miles an
hour;[32] it could not be said, as matter of law, to be negligence
to board a train going only three or four miles an hour, the

City, etc., R. Co., 75 Mo. 185; Swigert v. Hannibal, etc., R. Co., 75
Mo. 475; Fulks v. St. Louis, etc., Ry. Co., 111 Mo. 335; 19 S. W. Rep.
818; Sly v. Union Depot Ry. Co., 134 Mo. 681; 36 S. W. Rep. 235;
Eikenberry v. Transit Co., 103 Mo. App. 442; 80 S. W. Rep. 360.

[31] Swigert v. Hannibal, etc., R. Co., 75 Mo. 475.

[32] This opinion is by Judge Biggs, of the St. Louis Court of Appeals.
Murphy v. St. Louis, etc., R. Co., 43 Mo. App. 351.

A passenger, injured in an attempt to board a moving train, was
held not entitled to recover, in Bacon v. Delaware, etc., R. Go., 143
Pa. St. 14; 21 Atl. Rep. 1002; Wabash, etc., R. Co. v. Rector, 104
Ill. 296. See, also, 3 Thompson on Neg., § 2856, and cases cited.

It was held to be negligence for a passenger to board a moving train,
in the absence of an invitation, in Knight v. Ponchartrain, etc., R.
Co., 23 La. Ann. 462; Hubener v. New Orleans, etc., R. Co., 23 La.
Ann. 492; Phillipps v. Saratoga, etc., R. Co., 49 N. Y. 177.

"It is not negligence *per se* for a passenger to board or alight from
a moving train, unless it is moving so fast as to make the danger of
boarding or alighting obvious to a person of ordinary prudence; and
ordinarily it is for the jury to determine whether the passenger's act
is negligent under all the circumstances." Gyles v. Southern Ry. Co.,
60 S. E. Rep. 433; 79 S. C. 176.

"A passenger voluntarily leaving the train at a station, knowing
that it would pull down to another platform, *held,* under the circumstances, guilty of negligence precluding a recovery for injuries sustained in attempting to regain the train." Laub v. Chicago, B. & Q.
Ry. Co. (Mo. App. 1906), 94 S. W. Rep. 550.

"Since one who unsuccessfully attempted to board a moving train,
and after hanging to a hand rail while the train ran about 800 yards,
fell, was not a passenger, he could not complain that the signal cord
was out of order, preventing the train men from stopping the train before he fell, since the company after discovering his peril was chargeable
to use only ordina-y care to avoid his injury with the means at hand."
Illinois Cent. R. Co. v. Cotter (Ky. 1907), 103 S. W. Rep. 279.

"It is not necessarily negligent to attempt to mount a slowly moving
street car." Rome Ry. Co. v. Keel (Ga. App. 1908), 60 S. E. Rep. 468.

court, on this proposition, observing: " Under the foregoing authorities we are inclined to the opinion that it is not necessarily negligence for a person to attempt to get on or off a train moving at the rate of four miles an hour. Our common knowledge and experience teaches us that, under favorable circumstances, this may be done with comparative safety. Under certain circumstances or conditions such an act might be held to be legal negligence. But, on the other hand, if it was in the daytime and there were no obstructions in the way or other hindering causes, a case would be presented in which fair inferences might be drawn both ways. It is, therefore, impossible, to formulate a rule by which all cases can be governed."

§ 693. **Same — Negligence to board train, when, on direction of conductor.**— In a leading New York case,[33] the question for decision was whether or not a passenger, killed while attempting to board a train moving at the rate of six miles an hour, when ordered to do so by the conductor, was guilty of negligence as matter of law. The majority opinion in this case was written by Justice Peckham, who said: " The important question which arises is, does a man, who is *sui juris,* and in the full possession of his faculties, with nothing to disturb his judgment, act with ordinary care, in endeavoring to board a train, moving at the rate of six miles an hour? It seems to me there can be but one answer to such a question. That it is a dangerous — a most hazardous — attempt must be the common judgment of all men. Persons are taught from their earliest youth the great danger attending upon an attempt to board or leave a train while it is in motion and no person of mature years and judgment but has the knowledge that such an attempt is dangerous

[33] Hunter v. Cooperstown, etc., R. Co., 112 N. Y. 371; 37 Am. & Eng. R. Cas. 78.

in the highest degree.   It is substantially admitted in this
case that it would have been negligence on the part of the
deceased to have made the attempt had it not been for the
request, or what is termed the direction of the conductor to
him, to get on.   It may be assumed that this direction implied
a notice to the deceased that the train would not stop at
the station, and that unless he attempted to get on while
the car was thus in motion, he would be left at the station
and compelled to take another and a later train.   It may
be assumed that in giving this direction, and in failing to
stop the train, the company was chargeable with negligence,
and yet it counts for nothing, as a justification or excuse
for the conduct of the deceased in attempting to board a
train, while thus in motion."

The Appellate Court of Missouri also held a man of
mature years guilty of negligence as matter of law, in
attempting to board a train, running from six to seven miles
an hour, in response to the direction of the conductor,[34]
and the New York case,[35] above referred to, is cited and
approved in this decision, by Judge Bond, of the St. Louis
Court of Appeals.

[34] Heaton v. Kansas City, etc., R. Co., 65 Mo. App. 479.

[35] Hunter v. Cooperstown, etc., R. Co., *supra;* 126 N. Y. 1, 2, 3,
23, 24.

The passenger is generally allowed to act upon the direction or command of an employee of a passenger carrier, in boarding a train,
without assuming the risk of obedience to such direction, and unless
the danger to be incurred is so apparent or impending as to deter a
reasonably prudent person from obeying the direction or command to
get on the train, the passenger, in case of injury, will not be denied
a recovery for an injury received while obeying a negligent direction
or command of a railroad employee.   Ephland v. Missouri, etc., R. Co.,
137 Mo. 187; 57 Mo. App. 147; 38 S. W. Rep. 926; 35 L. R. A. 109;
7 Am. & Eng. R. Cas. (N. S.) 579; Griffith v. Missouri, etc., R. Co.,
98 Mo. 168; 11 S. W. Rep. 559; Smith v. Chicago, etc., R. Co., 108
Mo. 243; 18 S. W. Rep. 971; Lent v. New York, etc., R. Co., 120
N. Y. 467; 24 N. E. Rep. 653; 31 N. Y. S. R. 538.

§ 694. **No duty to assist passenger to board train, when.**—
It is not the duty of a railway company's employees to assist
the passengers to board its cars, in all cases, for if the
ingress to a train is easy, assistance of the employees cannot
be claimed by a passenger, as a matter of right.[36]

Where this was one of the grounds of negligence relied
upon, in case of a personal injury to a passenger, the Missouri
Supreme Court, speaking by Judge Sherwood,[37] said: " In
the circumstances heretofore related, it was no part of
the duty of the defendant's employees to ' alight from said
train and assist the passengers thereon,' and negligence can
not therefore be based on such alleged failure.   When access
to the cars of a railway company is easy, as in the case at
bar, such assistance cannot be claimed as matter of right.

[36] Young v. Missouri Pacific Ry. Co., 93 Mo. App. 273; Yarnall v.
Kansas City, etc., R. Co., 113 Mo. 570; 21 S. W. Rep. 1; 18 L. R. A.
599; Hanks v. Chicago, etc., Ry. Co., 60 Mo. App. 274.

[37] Yarnall v. Kansas City, etc., Ry. Co., 113 Mo. 576, 577; 21 S. W.
Rep. 1; 18 L. R. A. 599.

Whether or not there is any duty to render assistance to a passenger in entering a train, depends upon the facts and circumstances
of each case.   Allender v. Chicago, etc., R. Co., 43 Iowa 276; 14 Am.
Ry. Rep. 443.

No duty of rendering assistance was recognized, as to a passenger
afforded a reasonable time and reasonably safe appliances and means,
in Raben v. Central Iowa R. Co., 74 Iowa 732; 34 N. W. Rep. 621;
31 Am. & Eng. R. Cas. 45.   In this case, Reed, J., said: " The contract
of the carrier is that he will carry the passenger safely and in a proper
carriage, and afford him convenient and safe·means for entering and
alighting from the vehicle in which he   carries him, but he does not
contract to render him personal service or attention beyond that."
(31 Am. & Eng. R. Cas. 49.)

"Where there were no unusual difficulties at the place of entry to a
train, and a passenger carrying a child was attended by two friends,
who could reasonably be expected to assist her, if necessary, there was
no duty devolving on the railroad company to assist her; and, where
its employee voluntarily undertook to render assistance, he was bound
to use only ordinary care." St. Louis, etc., Ry. Co. v. Green (Ark.
1908), 107 S. W. Rep. 168.

It has been ruled that it is not the duty of the employees of a railway company to assist a passenger to alight *from* a train. This was substantially the view taken by this court. And, obviously, the reasoning which denies the right of assistance to a passenger *from* a train would also deny it in getting *on* a train; the two cases cannot be distinguished, in principle."

§ 695. Same — In case of feeble or disabled passenger.— The rule of law which obtains in the case of a healthy or robust passenger, and where the access to a train or car is easy, does not apply to a feeble or disabled passenger, when the carrier's employees have notice of the disability under which the passenger is laboring, for in the case of a disabled, sick, or feeble passenger, the carrier's employees, with notice of the disability, will be guilty of negligence in failing to render assistance in boarding the train, and in case of an injury due to a failure on their part to render such assistance, the carrier could be held in damages.[38]

But even in the case of a sick or disabled passenger, there is no duty of assistance, in the absence of notice of the disability. In such cases the duty is dependent solely upon the notice to the carrier and the negligence upon the nonperformance of the ascertained duty, for without the presence of these constituent elements, liability, which is but the violation of a known duty, could not exist.[39]

[38] 2 Shearm. & Redf. on Neg. (4 ed), § 508, and cases cited: Slanahan v. Transit Co., 109 Mo. App. 228; 83 S. W. Rep. 783; Mathew v. Wabash R. Co. (Mo. App.), 78 S. W. Rep. 271; Hanks v. Chicago, etc., Ry. Co., 60 Mo. App. 274. An instruction that if the brakeman failed to properly assist a blind old lady to a seat, after notice of her disability, or if the train was started before she was seated, the defendant was negligent, was approved, in the Hank's case, *supra.*

[39] Yarnall v. Kansas City, etc., Ry. Co., 113 Mo. 578; 21 S. W. Rep. 1; 18 L. R. A. 599.

Hence it is, that even in the case of an injury to a disabled passenger, resulting from a failure on the .part of the railroad employees to render assistance in boarding a train, if notice of the fact was not brought home, either actually or constructively to the employees, no recovery could be had.[40]

§ 696. **Negligence in assisting passenger.**— Where the physical condition of a passenger is such as to require the assistance of a train man, in boarding and entering a train, it is held to be within the scope of the duties of an employee of the railroad company, to render such assistance, and if the employee is negligent in assisting the passenger, the railroad company will be liable for the damages ensuing, in case of injury to the passenger.[41]

In a Georgia case,[42] where a brakeman attempted to assist a woman to board a train, at some distance from the station platform, where the train had stopped at a low place, which made it difficult for her to step upon the platform of the car, and in trying to get on the train she was injured, the railroad company was held liable, because of the negligent way in which the brakeman had assisted her to get on the train.

But of course, as in other personal injuries, based on the negligence of the employees of a railroad company, before a recovery can be allowed, in the case of an injury alleged to be due to the negligent assistance of the employees

[40] Mathew v. Wabash R. Co., *supra;* Young v. Missouri Pacific Ry. Co., 93 Mo. App. 273. In Young v. Missouri Pacific Ry. Co. (93 Mo. App. 273), Judge Smith, for the court, said: " As bearing upon the duty of the defendant it is to be observed, that though it is disclosed by the evidence, that the plaintiff's right ankle was weak and liable to turn, this fact was in no way brought to the notice of the formers' employees, the railroad company is not liable for failure to give assistance."

[41] International, etc., R. Co. v. Anderson, 15 Texas Civ. App. 180; 53 S. W. Rep. 606.

[42] Western, etc., R. Co. v. Voils, 98 Ga. 446; 26 S. E. Rep. 483; 35 L. R. A. 655.

of a railroad company, in helping a passenger on a train, the assistance of the employee must be the proximate cause of the injury, and if, instead of this being the direct cause of an injury, the act of the passenger causes the injury, as where the employee had released the passenger at his request and he then falls under the train and is run over and killed, the railroad company would not be responsible for the injury, as the negligence of the employee in attempting to render assistance, was not the cause of the injury.[43]

§ 697. **Announcement or direction to enter train.**— A railway company may be held liable for damages caused by injuries received by passengers who are injured while they are attempting to board trains, before they are ready to be loaded with passengers, caused by the misleading announcements or directions of the employees of the railway company.[44]

Leaving a caboose on a side track open, where persons have been in the habit of boarding a caboose carrying passengers, has been held to amount to an implied invitation on the part of the railroad company, for passengers to enter such caboose;[45] but an action based on an allegation that a caboose had been drawn up ready to load passengers into and that it was negligently started while the injured passenger was getting on, is not sustained by the proof that a caboose not intended for use by passengers had been left standing on a side track for forty-five minutes before the passenger started to get on such caboose and was then started, without notice of the presence of such passenger.[46] The mere fact of a direction by an employee of the railroad company to a passenger to enter a train, is not of itself

[43] Baltimore Traction Co. v. State, 78 Md. 409; 28 Atl. Rep. 397.
[44] Flint, etc., R. Co. v. Stark, 38 Mich. 714.
[45] Illinois, etc., R. Co. v. Axley, 47 Ill. App. 307.
[46] Flint, etc., R. Co. v. Stark, 38 Mich. 714.

negligence, unless the obedience to such direction would necessarily entail some risk or danger of an injury upon the passenger directed and it must always be determined, in view of all the circumstances of a given case, whether the employee giving the directions had a right to suppose that his instructions would be understood and acted upon, in a reasonably careful manner by the passenger.[47] And while a railway company may be held liable in some cases for injuries to passengers injured by attempting to board trains, caused by misleading announcements of the company's employees, in order to recover for an injury so received it must be declared on specially [48] and a recovery cannot be upheld, on this ground of negligence, where some other ground was declared upon in the complaint.[49]

§ 698. **Same — Authority of employee on freight train must be shown.** — In the case of an invitation by an employee of a freight train, to a passenger to enter the train, the rule which obtains in the case of passenger trains does not apply, and where a negligent direction of an employee of a freight train is counted on by a passenger, as a basis of a right to recover damages for a personal injury, the plaintiff's petition should set forth the authority of the employee to give the direction to the passenger to enter the train.

In a case in Missouri,[50] where this rule of pleading was passed upon by the Court of Appeals, Judge Rombauer, for the court, said: " It will be observed that the petition fails to allege any authority, express or implied, on the part of the defendant's employees, in charge of this freight train,

---

[47] Flint, etc., R. Co v. Stark, *supra*.

[48] Flint, etc., R. Co v. Stark, *supra*.

[49] Whitehead v. St. Louis, etc., R. Co., 22 Mo. App. 60; Raming v. Metropolitan, etc., R. Co., 157 Mo. 477; 57 S. W. Rep. 268.

[50] Whitehead v. St. Louis, etc., R. Co., 22 Mo. App. 63.

to carry passengers, nor is it anywhere averred that the train was a passenger-carrying train.   *   *   *

"The petition states one of these cases,   *   *   *   where a person is carried on some conveyance, not designed for the transportation of passengers, by the invitation or sufferance of the employees, where neither a sufferance or invitation is authorized by the course of their employment.[51] *   *   * The solution of the question of liability in such a case, is not to be sought in the rule of law applicable to common carriers, but must be obtained from the principles of the law of agency.[52] This leads us to hold that the petition fails to state a cause of action and that the demurrer thereto, by way of objecting to any evidence offered in its support, should have been sustained."

§ 699. **Invitation to enter cars — Calling " All aboard "—** The customary call of the conductor of a passenger train, "all aboard," is held by the courts as tantamount to an invitation to passengers to enter the train and if such invitation is given prematurely, or at a time when it was dangerous to attempt to board the train, the carrier is held negligent therefor and in case of an injury to a passenger, who attempts to get on the train, the railroad company will be liable.[53]

[51] Snyder v. Hannibal, etc., R. Co., 60 Mo. 413; Eaton v. New York, etc., R. Co., 57 N. Y. 382.

[52] See comments of Judge Redfield, in Eaton v. Railroad, 57 N. Y. 382, in 13 Am. Law Reg. 672.

"Plaintiff, a boy of seven years old, was invited by certain of the section men to get on a hand car for a ride. The foreman ordered the man to help the boy on the car, and told him to 'hold on tight.' He held on until the car had gone 300 or 400 feet when he got dizzy, fell off, and was injured. *Held*, that he was not a passenger, but was either a licensee or a trespasser." Daugherty v. Chicago & St. P. Ry. Co. (Iowa 1908), 114 N. W. Rep. 902.

[53] Filer v. New York, etc., R. Co., 49 N. Y. 59; 68 N. Y. 124; Maher v. Central Park R. Co., 67 N. Y. 55.

The call of the conductor, in such case, may be considered as an announcement to passengers that the cars are ready and that it is safe for them to enter, unless they see something to the contrary, and such an invitation, if given prematurely, is apt to be productive of great injury to passengers and such conduct can only be held wrongful.

In a New York case,[54] where a passenger could not find a seat in the car she had entered, she was advised by a train employee that another car would be run down in a few moments where she could find a seat and upon its being run down against the car in which she had received the information, she attempted to cross onto the car so run down, on the call of the conductor, "all aboard," and in doing so, she was injured, as the car had not yet been coupled to the other car. In passing upon the case, Bradley, J., for the Appellate Court, said: "There is evidence tending to prove that at the moment the cars came together, the conductor halloed 'all aboard' and that the plaintiff and those with her heard it; and that thereupon the passengers proceeded from the platform of the car, on which she was, to pass into that ahead of it, and she followed. The evidence of such announcement of the conductor was contradicted by his evidence, and that of the brakeman. This question was one of fact for the jury; and finding, as it may now be assumed they did, that the conductor, simultaneously with the coming together of the cars, called out as before mentioned, the conclusion of the jury was permitted that it enabled the passengers to understand (unless they saw something to the contrary) that the car was ready for them to enter. And it may have been treated as an invitation to do so; and, as it was given prematurely, or before it was entirely safe to do so, it was the fault of the defend-

[54] Lent v. New York, etc., R. Co., 120 N. Y. 467; 24 N. E. Rep. 653; 44 Am. & Eng. R. Cas. 373, 377.

ant's employee, which justified the imputation of negligence against the defendant."

§ 700. Signals and warnings to passengers boarding trains.

— It is very generally held to be one of the duties of the passenger carrier, to give its passengers, through its agents, reasonable signals or warnings, of the departure of its trains, such as would ordinarily attract the attention of passengers and those interested in the movement of the trains,[55] and for an injury to a passenger, due to a failure on the part of the railroad company's employees to give its passengers clear or intelligible signals or warning, whether it was safe or not to board the train, the company would be liable.[56]

In a Wisconsin case,[57] it was held that where a passenger train was brought up to a station in such a manner as to induce passengers to believe that it was stopped for their reception, and it was started while they were getting on such train, without any signal or warning of the movement of the train, the railroad company was negligent, regardless of whether the starting of the train was necessary or not and whether the stopping of the train was for the purpose of taking on passengers or not. If the train was not ready to take on passengers, under such conditions, it was held to be the legal duty of the railroad company to have some one there

[55] Perry v. Central R. Co., 66 Ga. 746; McQuade v. Manhattan R. Co., 21 J. & S. (N. Y.) 91; 109 N. Y. 636; 16 N. E. Rep. 681; Keating v. New York, etc., R. Co., 49 N. Y. 673; 3 Lans. 469.

[56] McQuade v. Manhattan R. Co., *supra.*

[57] Curtis v. Detroit, etc., R. Co., 27 Wis. 158; 5 Am. Ry. Rep. 368, approved, in Hartwig v. Chicago, etc., R. Co., 49 Wis. 358; 1 Am. & Eng. R. Cas. 65; Duame v. Chicago, etc., R. Co., 72 Wis. 523; 40 N. W. Rep. 394; 7 Am. St. Rep. 879; 35 Am. & Eng. R. Cas. 416.

"Where a passenger knows of an opéning between the car and station platforms, the railroad company is not liable for failure to give warning thereof." Woolsey v. Brooklyn Heights R. Co. (N. Y. Sup. 1908), 108 N. Y. S. R. 16.

to warn passengers against entering the train and failing to do so, it was negligent in moving the train, while passengers were boarding the train.

§ 701. **Same — Signals by third persons.**— In an Illinois case,[58] it was held that the fact that a passenger boarding a car was injured by the starting of the car, because of a signal given by some unauthorized person, would not exempt the railroad company from liability for the injury, if the employees in charge of the car, by the exercise of due care and diligence, could have prevented the movement of the car, so as to avoid the injury to the passenger. In passing on the objection of the railroad company's counsel, that the theory of the charge of the trial court made it the duty of the conductor to countermand the signal given by the third person and that the railroad company could not be charged with the unwarranted act of a stranger, the court said: " The car or train was in control of the conductor and he was required to know, if by the exercise of due care, caution and diligence in the discharge of his duties, he could know, whether any person was attempting to get on or off his train or car, before permitting the same to start, in such a manner as would be liable or likely to injure a person so getting on or off the same. It was a duty appellant owed the public, to be discharged through its conductors, or other agents whom it might select, to afford its passengers time and opportunity to board and depart from its cars in safety. The fact, therefore, if it be conceded, that the signal for starting was given by an unauthorized person, would not exempt the railroad company from liability, if the conductor or agents of the railway company in charge, by the exercise of due care and diligence, could have prevented the moving of the car, and thereby avoided the injury."

[58] North Chicago, etc., R. Co. v. Cook, 33 N. E. Rep. 958.

§ 702. **Accidental injuries in boarding cars assumed.**— As the basis of a right of recovery, for a personal injury received in boarding a train, is the violation of some legal duty owing to the passenger by the carrier, no recovery can be had in the absence of this showing of a breach of duty, or some act of negligence, which, together with the injury to the passenger, would alone furnish a cause of action.

Negligence can never be said to exist, in any case, where the injury could not have been anticipated, by the exercise of due care on the part of the party charged therewith,[59] and hence in case of an injury to a passenger in boarding a train, if the injury is caused by an event that could not have been foreseen as probable or likely to occur, or, in other words, if the injury in boarding the train is the result of a mere accident, the railroad company will not be liable therefor.[60]

Passengers assume the risk of accidental injuries in getting on a train of cars and it has been held that a passenger cannot recover damages from the railroad company, for an injury caused by an employee slipping against him, while he was ascending the steps for the purpose of entering a car, where the falling of the employee was purely accidental and was caused by stepping from the platform rail, without intent to injure the passenger.[61]

[59] Milwaukee, etc., R. Co. v. Kellogg, 94 U. S. 469; 24 L. Ed. 256; Schaeffer v. Washington, etc., R. Co., 105 U. S. 251; 26 L. Ed. 1070.
[60] Skinner v. Atchison, etc., R. Co., 39 Fed. Rep. 188.
[61] Skinner v. Atchison, etc., R. Co., 39 Fed. Rep. 188.

CHAPTER XXVII.

§ 703. **Duty to carry to destination.**— A passenger on a railway train has a right to insist upon being carried to the place of his destination and there safely let off the train and a railway company that sells a ticket or collects fare from a passenger to a particular station on the line of its road, is under the legal duty to stop its train at such station and see that reasonable opportunity is afforded the passenger

1065

to safely alight from the train and if injury results from a breach of this duty a *prima facie* liability is established against the carrier.[1]

In a Wisconsin case,[2] a female passenger had paid her fare to a station on the defendant's railroad and a brakeman of the railroad company wrongfully compelled her to leave the train at a distance of three miles from the place of destination, at a point where she was a stranger and unacquainted with the surroundings. The exertion resulting from the walk to the station brought on severe illness, and the court held that the railroad company was liable for damages because of the negligent failure to carry the passenger to her destination.

But a railroad company, of course, is not required to stop any of its trains at stations where such trains are not scheduled to stop and a passenger who has wrongfully taken such a train may be put off at a station before the point of destination is reached, in case he knowingly took such a train, not scheduled to stop at such a station.[3] And in the case of a female passenger, put off at a station before the destination was reached, on a train not scheduled to stop at that station, no damages could be recovered for a rape committed upon the passenger, by another passenger, who disembarked at the same station, for this could not ordinarily

[1] Thomas v. Charlotte, etc., R. Co., 38 So. Car. 485; 17 S. E. Rep. 226; Lambeth v. North Carolina R. Co., 66 N. Car. 494; Pittsburg, etc., R. Co. v. Nuzum, 50 Ind. 141; Caldwell v. Richmond, etc., R. Co., 89 Ga. 550; 15 S. E. Rep. 678.

[2] Brown v. Chicago, etc., R. Co., 54 Wis. 342; 11 N. W. Rep. 356; 41 Am. Rep. 41; 3 Am. & Eng. R. Cas. 444.

" A carrier owes to its passengers the duty of doing all that human care, vigilance, and foresight can reasonably do under the circumstances, and the mode of conveyance used and the duty of the carrier in this respect is not discharged until the passenger has safely alighted from the car." Chicago City Ry. Co. v. Shreve, 128 Ill. App, 462, judgment affirmed, 80 N. E. Rep. 1049; 226 Ill. 530.

[3] Sira v. Wabash R. Co., 115 Mo. 127; 21 S. W. Rep. 905.

have been anticipated as likely to result from the act of ejecting the passenger and such wrongful act of the third person was not the direct result of the negligence of the railroad company's employees.[4]

And although a passenger takes passage upon a train regularly scheduled to stop at his destination, if the train fails to stop and the passenger, without invitation or command from the employees in charge thereof, attempts to alight from the train, while it is moving at a dangerous rate of speed, he assumes the risk of such a rash act and cannot recover damages from the railroad company, if he sustains an injury in so doing.[5]

§ 704. **Duty to announce stations.**— In order to afford passengers an opportunity to leave their trains at the destination, when the journey is completed, the courts very generally hold that the carrier must announce the name of the station upon the arrival of the train, and then stop the train a sufficient length of time to enable the passenger to safely alight.[6]

Where the ordinary signal is given on approaching a station, and it is announced in the usual manner, by the employee of the railroad company, so as to lead a passenger. to believe that the train would stop at the station called, the company cannot avoid liability for an injury to a passenger who is attempting to alight, after the train had stopped, caused by the sudden starting of the train, before he had time to get off, merely by showing that those in

[4] Sira v. Wabash R. Co., 115 Mo. 127; 21 S. W. Rep. 905.

[5] East Tennessee R. Co. v. Massingill, 15 Lea (Tenn.) 328.

[6] Louisville, etc., R. Co. v. Mask, 64 Miss. 738; 2 So. Rep. 360; Dorrah v. Illinois, etc., R. Co., 65 Miss. 14; 3 So. Rep. 36; 7 Am. St. Rep. 629; 30 Am. & Eng. R. Cas. 576; Lehman v. Louisiana, etc., R. Co., 37 La. Ann. 705; New Orleans, etc., R. Co. v. Statham, 42 Miss. 607; Nunn v. Georgia, etc., R. Co., 71 Ga. 710; 51 Am. Rep. 284.

charge of the train intended to go on further before stopping to let passengers off the train, of which no notice was given to the injured passenger.[7]

And where the conductor of a train, on a dark night, announced the approach of a station and the train came to a stop on a bridge, without notice that the station had not been reached, and a passenger, in an attempt to alight, fell and was killed, it was held that he had a right to suppose that the train had reached the station and the negligence of the railroad company was such as to warrant the submission of the case to the jury.[8]

But the mere fact that a station is called out and a train has stopped, is not necessarily evidence of an invitation to the passengers for that station to alight.[9] Whether the railroad company is guilty of any negligence in announcing the name of a station and then stopping the train short of such station, depends upon the facts and circumstances of each case.[10] And the railroad company is not responsible for the acts of third persons, not in its employ, for falsely announcing the arrival of a train at a station, whereby a passenger attempting to alight from the train, is injured.[11]

[7] McNulta v. Ensch, 134 Ill. 46; 24 N. E. Rep. 631, reversing 31 Ill. App. 100.

[8] Philadelphia, etc., R. Co. v. McCormick, 124 Pa. St. 427; 16 Atl. Rep. 848. And see, also, Columbus, etc., R. Co. v. Farrell, 31 Ind. 408.

[9] Lewis v. London, etc., R. Co., 43 L. J. Q. B. 8; L. R. 9 Q. B. 66; 22 W. R. 153; 29 L. T. 397.

[10] Central, etc., R. Co. v. Van Horn, 38 N. J. L. 133; 13 Am. Ry. Rep. 36; Memphis, etc., R. Co. v. Stringfellow, 44 Ark. 322; 51 Am. Rep. 598; 21 Am. & Eng. R. Cas. 374.

[11] Columbus, etc., R. Co. v. Farrell, 31 Ind. 408.

Announcing the name of a station is held not to be an invitation to a passenger to alight, in England v. Boston, etc., R. Co., 153 Mass. 490; 27 N. E. Rep. 1; Minock v. Detroit, etc., R. Co., 97 Mich. 425; 56 N. W. Rep. 780; Lewis v. London, etc., R. Co., L. R. 9 Q. B. 66; 43 L. J. (Q. B.) 8; 30 L. T. (N. S.) 844.

"The announcement of the next station by a porter on a railway

§ **705. No duty to awaken sleeping passengers.**— While it

passenger train, though made on the near approach to the station, is
not an invitation to a passenger to leave his seat and attempt to alight
before the train actually stops." Illinois Cent. R. Co. v. Warren
(U. S. C. C. A., Miss., 1906), 149 Fed. Rep. 658.

"A statement made by a brakeman to the passengers in a railroad
car between stations, giving the name of the 'next station,' is merely
an announcement, and not a call of the station; and, unless made when
the train is immediately approaching a station, passengers for such
station are not justified in treating it as an invitation to alight when
the train next stops." Diggs v. Louisville & N. R. Co. (U. S. C. C.
A., Tenn., 1907), 159 Fed. Rep. 97.

"Three young men traveling together were passengers on a railroad
train which approached Knoxville, Tenn., which was their destination,
after dark. The train men had announced that the next station
would be Knoxville, as required by the State statute, but had not
called the station, when the train stopped on a narrow trestle in order
to make use of a Y in turning before entering the city. The next
morning the bodies of the young men were found near together under
the trestle. Upon the trial of a consolidated action against the railroad company to recover for their deaths, there was evidence that they
left the car together, while on the trestle, and tending to show that
they fell over the edge as they stepped off. *Held*, That neither the
announcement of the name of the next station nor the stopping of
the train thereafter before it was reached was negligence, nor was
either an invitation to passengers to alight before the station was
called, which imposed on defendant the duty of warning them or rendered it liable for the deaths of plaintiffs' intestates." Diggs v.
Louisville & N. R. Co. (U. S. C. C. A., Tenn., 1907), 156 Fed. Rep. 564.

"An instruction that railway carriers of passengers must be extremely careful not to mislead passengers to believe that the halting
of the train at a station is intended as an invitation to them to
alight when it is not so intended, and, if the conduct of the carrier's
servants in managing the train is such as to create that impression
and a passenger attempts to leave the coach at a place where no
facilities are provided for doing so, and is injured, the carrier is liable, is proper." Kansas City Southern Ry. Co. v. Davis (Ark. 1907),
103 S. W. Rep. 603.

"Where plaintiff was thrown from the platform of a passenger train
by a sudden jerk before the train had arrived at its station, he could
prove that he was induced to go on the platform by a premature call
of the station by the carrier's servants." Midland Valley R. Co. v.
Hamilton (Ark. 1907), 104 S. W. Rep. 540.

is the duty of a railroad company to cause its employees to announce the names of its stations where passengers will disembark, the obligations of a carrier of passengers are so essentially different from those of an innkeeper or of a sleeping car company, that it is under no duty to awaken sleeping passengers, but it is the duty of the several passengers to keep awake, so that they will have a reasonable time to alight at their several stations, when they are called, and if a passenger attempts to alight from a moving train, after his station is passed, because he failed to hear the station announced while asleep, and injury is sustained, the railroad company is not answerable for such an accident.[12]

And even if the conductor agrees to awaken a drowsy or sleeping passenger and fails to do so, the railroad company is not answerable for this violation of his promise by the conductor, for it is a mere voluntary promise, beyond the scope of his duty as an employee of the railroad company, for which it is in no way responsible.[13]

§ 706. **Duty to stop train at station platform.**— The stopping of a passenger train out of the usual place beyond the

[12] Nichols v. Chicago, etc., R. Co., 90 Mich. 203; 51 N. W. Rep. 364; 52 Am. & Eng. R. Cas. 304. In this case, the sleeping passenger attempted to get off the train, after it had passed the station, and was thrown under the trucks and had his leg and arm crushed. In deciding that the railroad company was not liable for the injury, the court, speaking by Grant, J., said: "Under this state of facts, no liability attaches to defendant. No obligation rested upon the conductor or brakeman to awaken the plaintiff, at Otia. It was their duty to call out the station, and the duty of the plaintiff to keep awake, if he desired to alight. None of the employees of the defendant knew that the plaintiff desired to alight, or that he intended to do so. They therefore had no duty to perform towards him in assisting him to alight, or in pointing out the proper place for him to do so."

[13] Nunn v. Georgia, etc., R. Co., 71 Ga. 710; 51 Am. Rep. 284; Tillery v. Bond, 38 Fed. Rep. 825; Sevier v. Vicksburg, etc., R. Co., 61 Miss. 8; 48 Am. Rep. 74; 18 Am. & Eng. R. Cas. 245.

platform where passengers are accustomed to alight, is improper;[14] it is the duty of the employees of a train, in charge thereof, to stop the train at the station platform, for the purpose of enabling passengers to alight from the train,[15] and if the passengers are required to alight at some other place the railroad company would be liable for an injury to the passengers so received, on account of alighting at such a place.[16]

Where a train pulls up to the platform of a station, so that nothing but the forward end of the smoking car is near the platform, ladies in the rear car would not be required to pass through the smoker to alight and if, because of the position of the car in which they were riding, they sustain injuries in alighting from the train, the railroad company would be responsible therefor.[17]

But if there is nothing dangerous in the surroundings where a caboose on a freight train is stopped, to permit passengers to alight, the place where it is stopped will not occasion a liability on the part of the railroad company, merely because it was not stopped at the station, for it is not customary to stop such cars at the stations and passengers generally, taking passage upon such trains, are familiar with this fact, so if there is a clear passageway from the caboose to the platform, the fact that it is stopped a hundred or so feet therefrom, in broad daylight, will not give a cause of action to an injured passenger, as he will be pre-

[14] Flanagan v. New York, etc., R. Co., 5 Silv. Sup. Ct. (N. Y.) 495.

[15] St. Louis, etc., R. Co. v. Cantrell, 37 Ark. 519; 40 Am. Rep. 105; 8 Am. & Eng. R. Cas. 198; Memphis, etc., R. Co. v. Whitfield, 44 Miss. 466.

[16] New York, etc., R. Co. v. Doane, 115 Ind. 435; 17 N. E. Rep. 913; 1 L. R. A. 157; 7 Am. St. Rep. 451; 37 Am. & Eng. R. Cas. 87.

[17] Cartwright v. Chicago, etc., R. Co., 52 Mich. 606; 18 N. W. Rep. 380; 50 Am. Rep. 274; 16 Am. & Eng. R. Cas. 321.

sumed to take the risk of alighting at such a customary place.[18]

§ 707. **Train should be entirely stopped.**— When it is held negligence for a passenger to alight from a moving train, it would seem that it could only be held negligence on the part of the railroad company to fail to actually stop its

[18] Hays v. Wabash R. Co., 51 Mo. App. 438.

"A common carrier of persons for hire must use the utmost care and diligence for their safe carriage, and must provide everything necessary for that purpose, and exercise a reasonable degree of care and skill to announce the approach of a station where passengers are to disembark, to afford them reasonable time and opportunity under the circumstances to embark and disembark, to provide reasonable platform facilities for persons to embark and disembark with safety, to keep the station platform at night lighted in a reasonable manner, and to keep the depot and platform free from dangerous obstructions." Atchison, etc., Ry. Co. v. Calhoun (Okl. 1907), 89 Pac. Rep. 207.

"Evidence in an action against a railway company for injuries to a passenger while alighting at a station on the side of the train away from the station examined, and *held*, that the question of her contributory negligence was for the jury." Hodges v. Southern Pac. Co. (Cal. App. 1906), 86 Pac. Rep. 620.

"Where an intoxicated man was injured in alighting from a train on the side opposite the station platform, and the evidence shows that an ordinarily prudent and sober person would not have been injured under like circumstances, the company is not liable for the injury." Louisville & N. R. Co. v. Payne (Ky. 1907), 104 S. W. Rep. 752.

But a custom not to stop freight trains at the station platform, was held to be insufficient to charge a passenger with an assumption of the risk of alighting from a caboose, at a point short of the station, where he had been told to wait by the brakeman and get off at the station and as the train did not stop at the station was assisted to get off by the brakeman and was injured in doing so, for the railroad company was held liable for such an injury, in an opinion by Shiras, J., in Eddy v. Wallace, 49 Fed. Rep. 801; 4 U. S. App. 247; 52 Am. & Eng. R. Cas. 265.

"Where the carrier through its servants and agents so acts as to mislead a passenger with reference to the time, the place, and the safety of alighting, it is guilty of negligence for which a recovery will be sustained." Baltimore & O. R. Co. v. Mullen, 120 Ill. App. 88, judgment affirmed, 75 N. E. Rep. 474; 217 Ill. 203.

train to permit a passenger to alight.[19] It is accordingly held, by the New York court,[20] to be negligence on the part of a railroad company to fail to stop its train entirely, at a station to which it has sold a ticket to a passenger, in order to give reasonable opportunity for him to get off the train. And having failed to stop at the station, it is also negligence to induce a passenger to alight while the train is in motion, as a result of which an injury is sustained by the passenger.[21]

But a railroad company is not liable for an injury to a passenger, who attempts to alight from a train, before it has had time to stop; [22] and if another passenger pulls the bell cord, causing the train to start, while a passenger is alighting, the railroad company cannot be held liable for an injury so received; [23] nor would the company be liable for an injury from starting the train, after the lapse of a reasonable time for passengers to alight, when the fact that a passenger was about to then alight from the train, was not known to the railroad company's employees.[24]

§ 708. **Reasonable time to alight.**— It is the duty of a railroad company to stop its trains at all stations for a reasonable time, in order that passengers may get on and off the cars, with reasonable safety to themselves, and if it fails to do so and injury results to passengers from the

[19] Raben v. Central Iowa R. Co., 73 Iowa, 579; 35 N. W. Rep. 645; 5 Am. St. Rep. 708; 33 Am. & Eng. R. Cas. 520.

[20] Bucher v. New York, etc., R. Co., 98 N. Y. 128; 21 Am. & Eng. R. Cas. 361.

[21] Texas, etc., R. Co. v. Bingham, 2 Texas Civ. App. 278; 21 S. W. Rep. 569.

[22] Blodgett v. Bartlett, 50 Ga. 353.

[23] Mississippi, etc., R. Co. v. Harrison, 66 Miss. 419; 6 So. Rep. 319; 39 Am. & Eng. R. Cas. 449.

[24] Hurt v. St. Louis, etc., R. Co., 94 Mo. 255; 7 S. W. Rep. 1; 34 Am. & Eng. R. Cas. 422.

starting of the train while the passengers are alighting, the railroad company is held guilty of such negligence as will warrant the assessment of damages for the injury sustained.[25]

Where the train is stopped at a station to which the railroad company has undertaken to transport a passenger, if a reasonable time is not afforded the passenger to alight, and an injury is sustained by the passenger, in an attempt to alight, after the train is in motion, the railroad company would be responsible for the injury, unless the danger in attempting to alight from the train was so obvious that no reasonably prudent person would have made the attempt to alight, under the speed and at the place where the passenger tried to get off.[26]

But if the carrier of passengers by railway stops its trains

[25] Carr v. Eel River R. Co., 98 Cal. 366; 33 Pac. Rep. 213; 58 Am. & Eng. R. Cas. 239; Pennsylvania R. Co. v. Kilgore, 32 Pa. St. 292; St. Louis, etc., R. Co. v. Persons, 49 Ark. 182; 4 S. W. Rep. 755; 30 Am. & Eng. R. Cas. 567; Terre Haute, etc., R. Co. v. Buck, 96 Ind. 346; 49 Am. Rep. 168; 18 Am. & Eng. R. Cas. 234; Strauss v. Kansas City, etc., R. Co., 86 Mo. 421; 75 Mo. 185; 27 Am. & Eng. R. Cas. 170; Richmond v. Quincy, etc., R. Co., 49 Mo. App. 104; Cullar v. Missouri, etc., Ry. Co., 84 Mo. App. 340; Weber v. Kansas City, etc., Ry. Co., 100 Mo. 194; 12 S. W. Rep. 804; 18 Am. St. Rep. 541; 7 L. R. A. 819; Jackson v. Grand Ave. Ry. Co., 118 Mo. 199; 24 S. W. Rep. 102; Camell v. St. Louis Transit Co., 102 Mo. App. 198; 76 S. W. Rep. 660; Jacobson v. Transit Co., 106 Mo. App. 339; 80 S. W. Rep. 309; Reagan v. Transit Co., 180 Mo. 117; 79 S. W. Rep. 435; Peck v. Springfield Traction Co. (by Judge Ellison), 110 S. W. Rep. 659; Saeger v. Wabash R. Co. (by Judge Broaddus), 110 S. W. Rep. 686; Washington, etc., R. Co. v. Harmon, 147 U. S. 571; 13 Sup. Ct. Rep. 557; Chicago, etc., R. Co. v. Arnol, 144 Ill. 261; 33 N. E. Rep. 204; 58 Am. & Eng. R. Cas. 411; Philadelphia, etc., R. Co. v. Anderson, 72 Md. 519; 20 Atl. Rep. 2; 44 Am. & Eng. R. Cas. 345; Atchison, etc., R. Co. v. Shean, 18 Colo. 368; 33 Pac. Rep. 108; 58 Am. & Eng. R. Cas. 360; McDonald v. Long Island R. Co., 116 N. Y. 546; 22 N. E. Rep. 1068; 43 Hun 637.

[26] Central, etc., R. Co. v. Miles, 88 Ala. 256; 6 So. Rep. 696; 41 Am. & Eng. R. Cas. 150.

long enough for its passengers, by the use of reasonable expedition, to alight, then there is no cause for complaint, if an injury is subsequently sustained, in an attempt to get off of a moving train.[27]

When the train has been stopped for a reasonable time, it is no part of the duty of the employees of the railroad company to make a personal inspection, or to interrogate the passengers remaining on the train, to see if any should have alighted. The law imposes no such duty upon the passenger carrier and if it appears that other passengers, similarly situated, as to age, sex and physical condition, had ample time to alight from the train, this would furnish sufficient evidence that the injured passenger could also have safely alighted, if he had used reasonable expedition to get off the train.[28]

[27] Culberson v. Chicago, etc., R. Co., 50 Mo. App. 556.

[28] Hurt v. St. Louis, etc., R. Co., 94 Mo. 255; 7 S. W. Rep. 1; 34 Am. & Eng. R. Cas. 422.

For statement of rules for length of time to allow passengers to alight at stations, see Kellar v. Sioux City, etc., R. Co., 27 Minn. 178; 6 N. W. Rep. 486.

When the evidence is conflicting as to whether or not the passenger had time to alight, it is a question for the jury.

Pennsylvania R. Co. v. Lyons, 129 Pa. St. 113; 18 Atl. Rep. 759; 41 Am. & Eng. R. Cas. 154; Hickman v. Missouri Pacific Ry. Co., 91 Mo. 433; 4 S. W. Rep. 127.

"What is a reasonable time and opportunity for a passenger to alight safely and leave the carrier's premises is generally a question of fact for the jury." Hill v. St. Louis, etc., Ry. Co. (Ark. 1908), 109 S. W. Rep. 523.

The company's failure to afford the passenger a reasonable opportunity to alight, was the negligence complained of in the following cases: Louisville, etc., R. Co. v. Mask, 64 Miss. 738; 2 So. Rep. 360; Pennsylvania R. Co. v. Lyons, 129 Pa. St. 113; 18 Atl. Rep. 759; 41 Am. & Eng. R. Cas. 154; Madden v. Missouri, etc., R. Co., 50 Mo. App. 666; McDonald v. Long Island R. Co., 116 N. Y. 546; 22 N. E. Rep. 1068; St. Louis, etc., R. Co. v. Finley, 79 Texas 85; 15 S. W. Rep. 266; Leggett v. Western, etc., R. Co., 143 Pa. St. 39; 21 Atl. Rep. 996; Chicago, etc., R. Co. v. Byrum, 153 Ill. 131; 38 N. E. Rep. 578;

§ 709. **Sick, young, or disabled passengers.**— The fact that
a passenger is evidently very young, or very old, or decrepit,
is a circumstance that must be taken into consideration by
a carrier's employees, in the discharge of the duty to stop
the train a reasonable length of time to permit the passengers
to alight.[29]

It is not the duty of the carrier to assist its passengers
in getting on or off its cars, in all cases, but where the passenger is an infant of tender years, or is very old, or infirm,
it is the duty of the railroad company's employees to assist

Pennsylvania R. Co. v. McCaffrey, 173 Ill. 169; 50 N. E. Rep. 713;
Luse v. Union Pacific R. Co., 57 Kansas 361; 46 Pac. Rep. 768;
Smithson v. Southern, etc., R. Co., 37 Oregon 74; 60 Pac. Rep. 907;
Southern R. Co. v. Mitchell, 98 Tenn. 27; 40 S. W. Rep. 72; Ridenhour
v. Kansas City, etc., R. Co., 102 Mo. 270; 13 S. W. Rep. 889; Culbert-
son v. Chicago, etc., R. Co., 50 Mo. App. 556.

In Smith v. North Carolina R. Co. (N. C.), 61 S. E. Rep. 266, it is
held to be the duty of a carrier not only to transport passengers to
their destination, but that they must there be afforded a reasonable
opportunity to alight in safety. The court presents the law points as
follows:

"A common carrier is charged with the duty of carrying passengers
to the point of their destination, and there affording them fair and
reasonable opportunity to alight from the cars, and depart from the
train yards or depot grounds in safety.

*   *   *   *   *   *   *   *   *

"As in other duties looking to the safety of their passengers,
carriers are held to a high degree of care in respect to these obligations,
and such duties are in no sense performed by stopping before they
reach their usual place, nor in stopping before or at such place with
cars on parallel tracks, so close together that, by the projection of the
cars over the rails, passengers, in order to enter or alight from trains,
are forced into a crowded passway, where the slightest motion of either
train, or a rush of the passengers themselves, is not unlikely to result
in painful, and at times serious, or even fatal, injuries."

[29] Ridenhour v. Kansas City, etc., R. Co., 102 Mo. 270; 13 S. W.
Rep. 889; 14 S. W. Rep. 760; Fortune v. Missouri, etc., R. Co., 10
Mo. App. 253; Hannon v. St. Louis Transit Co., 102 Mo. App. 216;
77 S. W. Rep. 158.

the passenger to alight, where they have notice of the disability or infirmity.[30]

But the age or decrepitude of a passenger will not determine the time for the stopping of trains at stations, to enable passengers to alight; [31] sick persons and persons unable to care for themselves should provide proper assistance to enable them to safely travel when in a decrepit or disabled condition,[32] and, in the absence of notice of such disability, a railroad company is not answerable for a failure to hold its train stationary for such a length of time as to enable such a person to safely alight.[33]

[30] Young v. Missouri Pacific Ry. Co., 93 Mo. App. 267; Foss v. Boston, etc., R. Co. (N. H.), 47 Am. & Eng. R. Cas. 566.

[31] Toledo, etc., R. Co. v. Baddeley, 54 Ill. 19; Dawson v. Louisville, etc., R. Co. (Ky.), 11 Am. & Eng. R. Cas. 134.

[32] New Orleans, etc., R. Co. v. Statham, 42 Miss. 607; Louisville, etc., R. Co. v. Fleming, 14 Lea (Tenn.) 128.

[33] New Orleans, etc., R. Co. v. Statham, supra; Yarnall v. Kansas City, etc., R. Co., 113 Mo. 570; 21 S. W. Rep. 1.

The company's duty, with reference to holding the train, for passengers to alight, is to be considered along with the number of passengers, and the age, sex, physical infirmities, etc., of the passengers. Killian v. Georgia, etc., R. Co., 97 Ga. 727; 25 S. E. Rep. 384; Griswold v. Chicago, etc., R. Co., 64 Wis. 652; Raben v. Central R. Co., 73 Iowa 579; Washington, etc., R. Co. v. Harmon, 147 U. S. 571; 37 L. Ed. 284:

"The age of an adult passenger injured while alighting from a train in consequence of the starting thereof is not a circumstance showing negligence, in the absence of any evidence as to her physical and mental condition." Hodges v. Southern Pac. R. Co. (Cal. App. 1906), 86 Pac. Rep. 620.

"Where a passenger who, by reason of physical disability, is unable safely to leave the car unassisted, explains her condition to the conductor on surrendering her ticket, who promises to assist her, the company is negligent if such assistance is not given, and will be liable for injuries sustained in her attempt to leave the car unassisted on arrival at her destination, and failure of the company to furnish her assistance." Mercer v. Cincinnati Northern R. Co. (Mich. 1908), 115 N. W. Rep. 733; 15 Detroit Leg. N. 35.

"Plaintiff, a passenger who was unable because of physical disability to leave the car safely, secured the promise of the conductor to assist

§ 710. **Place of egress.**— A passenger carrier is under tl legal duty of providing a reasonably safe place for its pa sengers to alight from its cars, when they have reached the destination, and it is liable for an injury received by i passengers due to its failure to discharge them at a reasonab safe place.[34]

The carrier has not discharged its duty to its passenge until it has provided a reasonably safe place of exit fro the cars, and although there is one way which might taken by a passenger, which is reasonably safe, if there another way, at the place where the coach has stoppe generally taken by passengers, which is dangerous, the pi senger will not necessarily be negligent in taking the mo dangerous way to alight.[35] If the circumstances are su as to amount to an implied invitation to the passenger disembark and in doing so, because of the dangerous natu of the place, an injury results, the carrier will be lial therefor.[36] This principle is illustrated by a New Ham shire case,[37] where the rear car, in which plaintiff w

her. On arriving at her station after dark, she walked to the platform and waited some time for assistance, but it was not gi her, and a child who was with her attempted to get assistance, l failed. *Held*, that whether plaintiff was negligent in attempting alight unassisted was a question for the jury." Mercer v. Cincinn Northern R. Co. (Mich. 1908), 115 N. W. Rep. 733; 15 Detroit L N. 35.

[34] Terre Haute, etc., R. Co. v. Buck, 96 Ind. 346; 49 Am. Rep. 1(18 Am. & Eng. R. Cas. 234; Onderdonk v. New York, etc., R. Co., Hun 42; 26 N. Y. Supp. 310; 56 N. Y. S. R. 190; Lehman v. Louisia etc., R. Co., 37 La. Ann. 705; Van Ostran, v. New York, etc., R. (35 Hun 590; 104 N. Y. 683; Louisville, etc., R. Co. v. Lucas, 119 I 583; 21 N. E. Rep. 968.

[35] Missouri Pacific Ry. Co. v. Long, 81 Texas 253; 16 S. W. Rep. 1(

[36] Falk v. New York, etc., R. Co. (N. J.), 29 Atl. Rep. 157; 58 / & Eng. R. Cas. 191.

[37] Bullard v. Boston, etc., R. Co., 64 N. H. 27; 27 Am. & Eng. Cas. 117; Foss v. Boston, etc., R. Co. (N. H.), 47 Am. & Eng. Cas. 570.

riding, did not reach the platform and she was injured on leaving it by the steps, which were about three feet from the ground. The plaintiff recovered a verdict and in passing on the case the higher court said: " These facts were evidence from which a jury might find that the plaintiff exercised due care in leaving the train at the place which she knew was a bad one for alighting, and, further might find that the defendant intended she should leave at that place."

But while there is the duty of providing a reasonably safe place for passengers to leave their train, at the point of destination, on the carrier's part, this duty does not extend to an intermediate station at which the carrier has no notice the passenger wishes to alight, and as to such intermediate station, if a passenger, without notice to the carrier, alights at an unsafe place and is injured thereby, no recovery can be had.[38]

§ 711. **Safe platforms and appliances for alighting.**— A railway company should provide safe and sufficient platforms for the landing of passengers, of sufficient length to afford safe egress to passengers alighting from a train of ordinary

[38] State v. Grand Trunk R. Co., 58 Me. 176.

" Where a woman was induced to alight by the negligence of a conductor at a strange place, remote from her destination, no presumption of negligence is raised in law against the defendant from the bare fact that plaintiff sustained the injury, and the burden rests upon the plaintiff to prove the allegations of fact on which she relies for the recovery." Georgia Ry. Co. v. McAllister (Ga. 1906), 54 S. E. Rep. 957.

An interurban railroad company stopping a car for the accommodation of a passenger who desires to alight at a highway crossing is held, in McGovern v. Interurban R. Co. (Iowa, 111 N. W. Rep. 412; 13 L. R. A. (N. S.) 476), to be bound to exercise at least reasonable care to enable her to alight with as little danger as practicable; and, if the passenger is invited to alight at a place more hazardous than that at which the car might have been conveniently stopped, the carrier is held to be negligent.

length, and the passengers should be delivered on such platforms.[39]

In a Virginia case,[40] an injury was sustained by a female
passenger, who was unattended and encumbered with heavy
clothing and bundles and the train was stopped in a snow
storm, on a very dark night, at a station where there was
no platform and no assistance was afforded by the train crew,
to the passenger, in alighting. The trial court charged the
jury that if there was no platform at the station and no
assistance was rendered the plaintiff in alighting, and that
her injury was due to the absence of such platform and
lack of assistance, the plaintiff was entitled to recover and
this charge was approved by the higher court.

And the high degree of care which the carrier owes to
its passengers in alighting from its trains, does not apply
only to the necessary platforms, at stations, but includes,
also, all necessary appliances to enable the passengers to
safely alight from the cars.[41] It is negligence to permit a
wheel box to get so out of repair that it is liable to throw
a passenger to the ground, who steps on it in alighting,[42]
and evidence that no platform was furnished at the station,
but only a box, eleven inches square on top, and a little
larger at the bottom, is such evidence of a lack of care to
provide reasonably safe appliances to alight, as to charge
a carrier with negligence, in case of an injury due to such
a cause.[43]

[39] St. Louis, etc., R. Co. v. Cantrell, 37 Ark. 519; 40 Am. Rep. 105;
8 Am. & Eng. R. Cas. 198; Memphis, etc., R. Co. v. Whitfield, 44
Miss. 466.

[40] Alexandria, etc., R. Co. v. Herndon, 87 Va. 193; 12 S. E. Rep.
289; McDonald v. Chicago, etc., R. Co., 26 Iowa 124.

[41] " A railway company is charged with a high degree of care in
furnishing the safest appliances for use by passengers in alighting."
Missouri, K. & T. Ry. Co. v. Dunbar (Tex.), 108 S. W. Rep. 500.

[42] Missouri Pacific Ry. Co. v. Wortham, 73 Texas 25; 10 S. W.
Rep. 741; 3 L. R. A. 368; 37 Am. & Eng. R. Cas. 82.

[43] Missouri Pacific Ry. Co. v. Wortham, supra.

But if a railway company provides a platform and other facilities for leaving its cars, on the depot side of its track, the failure to have the opposite side prepared in like manner, cannot be regarded as negligence,[44] nor is the railroad company under any obligation to provide a portable step for the use of passengers in alighting from its cars, and if it did furnish such steps it would be a self-imposed duty, for the violation of which there could, of course, be no liability.[45]

§ 712. **Same — At flag stations.**— It frequently happens that in the operation of railroads, steps are made by trains carrying passengers at such small stations, for the accommodation of so few people, that to require all the accommodations required at more populous stations, where the business is much larger, would entail such burdens upon the railroad company that it would compel it to refuse to stop most of its trains at such stations, rather than go to the expense to fix up a station equal to such an unreasonable demand. Hence,

[44] Michigan, etc., R. Co. v. Coleman, 28 Mich. 440; 12 Am. Ry. Rep. 59.

[45] Young v. Missouri Pacific Ry. Co., 93 Mo. App. 274; Barney v. Hannibal, etc., Ry. Co., 126 Mo. 392; 28 S. W. Rep. 1069; 26 L. R. A. 847. But see, where absence of stool, held evidence of negligence. Maden v. Port Royal, etc., Ry. Co., 35 So. Car. 381; 52 Am. & Eng. R. Cas. 286.

"A railway company is charged with a high degree of care in furnishing the safest appliances for use by passengers in alighting." Missouri, K. & T. Ry. Co. v. Dunbar (Tex. Civ. App. 1908), 108 S. W. Rep. 500.

"A carrier must afford reasonable means for passengers to alight, but is guilty of no breach of duty if the construction of its car adopted is in common use and approved by experience." Traphagen v. Erie R. Co. (N. J. 1906), 64 Atl. Rep. 1072.

"In an action for injuries to a passenger while attempting to alight, resulting from the stool on which he stepped turning over, evidence was admissible which tended to show that the stool was improperly constructed, and as to the frequency with which such stools turned and caused passengers to fall." Missouri, K. & T. Ry. Co. v. Dunbar (Tex. Civ. App. 1908), 108 S. W. Rep. 500.

it is that at flag stations, where the business of the road is not sufficient to justify it, the courts relax the rule that obtains in the case of other stations and it is not negligence for the railroad company to fail to provide a platform or station for the use of passengers in alighting at such stations.[46]

In a Mississippi case,[47] a female passenger was injured as a result of getting her feet wet, in alighting from a car, at a flag station, where the water stood on the ground near the track, where she was compelled to alight, in the absence of a platform, at such station. On her complaint about the place where the car had been stopped, the conductor, forgetting his southern chivalry, replied, " No matter, it is the station "; nor did he suggest that she might pass back through the sleeper and avoid the water, but assisted her to alight in the water. Notwithstanding this lack of gentility, however, on the conductor's part, the court held that the passenger, in alighting at the flag station, assumed the risks arising from the surroundings and although she was injured as a result of getting her feet wet, she was without remedy.

§ 713. **Assisting passengers to alight.**— The law does not compel a railroad company to furnish some one to aid its passengers in alighting from its cars or to point out to them

[46] Alabama, etc., R. Co. v. Stacey, 68 Miss. 463; 9 So. Rep. 349.

[47] Alabama, etc., R. Co. v. Stacey, *supra.*

" A railroad company is not bound to stop and allow a passenger to alight, except at a regular station." Sellers v. Cleveland & St. L. Ry. Co. (Ind. App. 1907), 81 N. E. Rep. 1087.

" The failure of a railroad company to maintain a platform at a particular place, and the failure of the conductor to assist a passenger to alight there, do not show negligence, unless such place is a regular station." Sellers v. Cleveland & St. L. Ry. Co. (Ind. App. 1907), 81 N. E. Rep. 1087.

the proper places to alight,[48] where they have no knowledge of their desire or intention to do so.

It is error to instruct the jury that it is the duty of the employees of the railroad company, as matter of law, to assist the passengers to alight,[49] for there is no such duty imposed by the law, but the existence of this duty depends very largely upon the circumstances of each case.[50] A railroad company is not bound to assist a female passenger, accompanied by two small children, as matter of law, in the absence of a request for assistance [51] and even in the case of a sick or infirm passenger, if assistance is required and there is nothing in the appearance of the passenger to indicate that it is necessary, there is no obligation to render assistance, in the absence of notice of the disability or necessity therefor.[52]

But where notice of the disability or infirmity of a passenger is brought home to the employees of a railroad company and an injury results from a failure on their part to render such assistance to such a passenger as would make it reasonably safe for him to alight, the company will be liable for the injury so received,[53] and if a train is stopped

[48] Lafflin v. Buffalo, etc., R. Co., 106 N. Y. 136; 12 N. E. Rep. 599; reversing 36 Hun 638; 30 Am. & Eng. R. Cas. 596; Nichols v. Chicago, etc., R. Co., 90 Mich. 203; 51 N. W. Rep. 364; 52 Am. & Eng. R. Cas. 304; Young v. Missouri Pacific Ry. Co., 93 Mo. App. 267; Hanks v. Chicago, etc., Ry. Co., 60 Mo. App. 274; Madden v. Port Royal, etc., R. Co., 35 So. Car. 381; 52 Am. & Eng. R. Cas. 286.

[49] Simms v. South Carolina, etc., R. Co., 27 So. Car. 268; 3 S. E. Rep. 301; 30 Am. & Eng. R. Cas. 571.

[50] Memphis, etc., R. Co. v. Whitfield, 44 Miss. 466.

[51] Raben v. Central Iowa R. Co., 73 Iowa 579; 35 N. W. Rep. 645; 33 Am. & Eng. R. Cas. 520.

[52] New Orleans, etc., R. Co. v. Statham, 42 Miss. 607; Young v. Missouri Pacific Ry. Co., 93 Mo. App. 267; Hanks v. Chicago, etc., Ry. Co., 60 Mo. App. 274.

[53] Toledo, etc., R. Co. v. Baddeley, 54 Ill. 19; Thompson v. Belfast, etc., R. Co., 5 Ir. C. L. 517; Texas, etc., R. Co. v. Miller, 79 Texas 78; 15 S. W. Rep. 264; Madden v. Port Royal, etc., R. Co., 35 So. Car. 381;

at a place where it is difficult for passengers to alight, it
is held, in a Mississippi case,[54] that it is the duty of the
railroad company to render assistance in such a place.

§ 714. **Warning or instructing passengers of dangers in
alighting.**— If there is anything dangerous about the place
or appliances where a railroad company permits its passengers to alight, it ought to give reasonable warning or
direction as to the proper and safe way to alight from its
trains, for the passenger is not presumed to know of the
dangers so well as the employees of the railroad company.[55]

It has accordingly been held to be negligence not to warn

52 Am. & Eng. R. Cas. 286; Hanks v. Chicago, etc., R. Co., 60 Mo.
App. 274; Ridenhour v. Kansas City, etc., Ry. Co., 102 Mo. 270;
13 S. W. Rep. 889; Yarnall v. Kansas City, etc., Ry. Co., 113 Mo. 570;
21 S. W. Rep. 1; 18 L. R. A. 599.

[54] Memphis, etc., Ry. Co. v. Whitfield, 44 Miss. 466.

" It not being the duty of the employees of a carrier to assist a
passenger in alighting because of her sickness or other misfortune,
unless such condition is known to them, it is error to charge that it
was their duty to assist her if her feebleness was known to them, ' or
was apparent,' this implying that it was their duty to observe her
condition to see whether she needed assistance." Illinois Cent. R. Co.
v. Cruse (Ky. 1906), 96 S. W. Rep. 821.

" The action of the court in calling the attention of the jury to facts
shown in evidence in determining whether the employees of the company should have assisted the passenger to alight, and leaving it for
the jury to say whether there was negligence in not giving the passenger assistance, was proper, as the duty to assist passengers to alight
might arise under special circumstances." McGovern v. Interurban Ry.
Co. (Iowa 1907), 111 N. W. Rep. 412.

" A conductor in proffering his aid to assist a passenger to alight
from the car at her destination is acting within the scope of his
employment; so that, though there was no duty to furnish such aid,
the conductor having taken her by the arm and negligently withdrawn
the support of his hand while she was stepping down, because of which
she fell, the carrier is liable." Judgment (1905), 96 N. Y. S. 1127;
110 App. Div. 918, affirmed; Hanlon v. Central R. Co. of New Jersey,
79 N. E. Rep. 846; 187 N. Y. 73.

[55] Wilburn v. St. Louis, etc., R. Co., 36 Mo. App. 203.

passengers of the danger of alighting from the rear platform of a car; [56] it is also a breach of the carrier's duty to permit the use of a car door, not safe to be used by passengers, without warning; [57] to stop a train near an embankment, not generally used as a place for passengers to disembark from trains, on a dark night, without warning of the dangers of the place; [58] to let passengers off on a dimly lighted platform, without warning them of the dangers of a space on the platform, where the passenger was apt to fall [59] and, generally, stopping a train at any place, where it is dangerous for passengers to alight, without warning them of the danger and permitting them to do so without notice or advice, is held to be negligence,[60] for which the carrier is liable, in case of a resulting injury to the passenger.

But it cannot be said that a railroad company is negligent in failing to warn passengers about the danger of alighting at a railroad crossing, where it could not be expected that passengers would alight, but where the train was bound to stop,[61] nor would there, generally, be any duty of giving warning of an unexpected danger, to be incurred in alighting at the usual place, where proper appliances were used to facilitate the task of alighting from the train and where passengers had been accustomed to alight, by the use of ordinary care, without sustaining any injuries.[62]

[56] McDonald v. Illinois, etc., R. Co. (Iowa), 55 N. W. Rep. 102; 58 Am. & Eng. R. Cas. 263.

[57] Missouri Pacific Ry. Co. v. Long, 81 Texas 253; 16 S. W. Rep. 1016.

[58] McGee v. Missouri Pacific Ry. Co., 92 Mo. 208; 4 S. W. Rep. 739; 31 Am. & Eng. R. Cas. 1.

[59] Praeger v. Bristol, etc., R. Co., 24 L. T. 105; Cockle v. London, etc., R. Co., L. R. 7 C. P. 321; 41 L. J. C. P. 140; 27 L. T. 320; 20 W. R. 754.

[60] Cockle v. London, etc., R. Co., *supra.*

[61] Minock v. Detroit, etc., R. Co., 97 Mich. 425; 56 N. W. Rep. 780.

[62] Atlanta, etc., R. Co. v. Dickerson, 89 Ga. 455; 15 S. E. Rep. 534; Young v. Missouri Pacific Ry. Co., 93 Mo. App. 267. In this last

§ 715. **Alighting from moving train.**— In a leading Missouri case [63]— which states the general rule applying to passengers alighting from moving trains — Judge Napton, for the court, said: "Whether the attempt of the plaintiff to step from the cars when the train was in motion, was, under the circumstances of the case, such negligence as would relieve the defendant from all responsibility for accident, is a question of fact for the jury. * * * These are risks which the most prudent men will take and the plaintiff will not be barred of a recovery for his injury, if he adopted the course which most prudent men would take under the circumstances. For a person to jump from a car, propelled by steam, when it is in rapid motion, may be regarded as mere recklessness; but to step from a car not yet beyond the platform, and whose motion is so slight as to be almost or quite imperceptible, may not be negligence, and whether it is so or not, is for the jury to decide, from the physical condition of the person and all the attendant circumstances."

But other courts do not agree with the Missouri court in this rule that it is a jury issue whether or not it is negligence to alight from a moving train, and it is held, in some States, to be negligence, as matter of law, to step from a moving

case, for the court, Judge Smith said: "Where something unusual occurs, which injures plaintiff, but such unusual occurrence is not even inferentially the result of an unusual act of the defendant, and the defendant has, as far as he is concerned, been pursuing his usual course, which has theretofore been done in safety, then the unusual occurrence is what is called an accident." Citing, Guffey v. Hannibal, etc., Ry. Co., 53 Mo. App. 462; Holt v. Southwest Ry., 84 Mo. App. 462.

[63] Doss v. Missouri, etc., Ry. Co., 59 Mo. 37, 38. See, also, Loyd v. Hannibal, etc., Ry. Co., 53 Mo. 509; Waller v. Hannibal, etc., Ry. Co., 83 Mo. 608; Leslie v. Wabash R. Co., 88 Mo. 50; Sanderson v. Missouri Pacific Ry. Co., 64 Mo. App. 655; Straus v. Kansas City, etc., R. Co., 75 Mo. 185; Weber v. Kansas City, etc., Ry. Co., 100 Mo. 194; 12 S. W. Rep. 804; 7 L. R. A. 819; 18 Am. St. Rep. 541; Newcomb v. New York, etc., Ry. Co., 169 Mo. 409; 69 S. W. Rep. 348.

train, under any conditions.[64] Thus, in a New York case,[65] Andrews, J., observed: "The conclusion that it is *prima facie* dangerous to alight from a moving train, is founded on our general knowledge and common experience, and it is akin to the conclusion, now generally accepted, that it is, in law, a dangerous and therefore a negligent act, unless explained and justified by special circumstances, to attempt

[64] Morrison v. Erie R. Co., 56 N. Y. 302; Hunter v. Cooperstown, etc., R. Co., 112 N. Y. 371; 37 Am. & Eng. R. Cas. 74; Phillipps v. Rensseller, etc., R. Co., 49 N. Y. 177; McClintock v. Pennsylvania, etc., R. Co., 21 W. N. C. 133; Pittsburg, etc., R. Co. v. Aspell, 23 Pa. St. 147.

[65] Soloman v. Manhattan R. Co., 103 N. Y. 437.
The weight of judicial opinion is perhaps in favor of the ruling in this case, that getting on or off a moving train, is negligence as matter of law, as evidenced by the cases following: Boulfrois v. United Traction Co., 210 Pa. St. 263; 2 Am. & Eng. Ann. Cas. 938; Walthers v. Chicago, etc., R. Co., 72 Ill. App. 354; Chicago, etc., R. Co. v. Stewart, 77 Ill. App. 66; Southern R. Co. v. Williams (Miss.), 36 So. Rep. 394; Bacon v. Delaware, etc., R. Co., 143 Pa. St. 14; Young v. Chicago, etc., R. Co., 100 Iowa 357; Mills v. Missouri, etc., R. Co. (Texas), 57 S. W. Rep. 291; Lauterer v. Manhattan R. Co., 128 Fed. Rep. 540; Brown v. New York, etc., R. Co., 181 Mass. 365; McMurtry v. Louisville, etc., R. Co., 67 Miss. 601; Galveston, etc., R. Co. v. LeGreise, 51 Texas 189; Chaffee v. Old Colony R. Co., 17 R. I. 658; 52 Am. & Eng. R. Cas. 366; Carroll v. Transit Co., 107 Mo. 653; 17 S. W. Rep. 889.
"Where plaintiff boarded a train to assist a passenger, her jumping off after the train started was contributory negligence precluding recovery for injury." Louisville & N. R. Co. v. Wilson (Ky. 1907), 100 S. W. Rep. 290.
"A passenger who attempts to alight from a car moving at a dangerous rate of speed and is injured, is guilty of negligence directly contributing to his injury, and cannot recover." Ohio v. Metropolitan St. Ry. Co. (Mo. App. 1907), 103 S. W. Rep. 142.
"Where a passenger attempted to alight from a car moving at a dangerous rate of speed, the operators of the car were not obliged to make an effort to avert danger to him, unless they saw his situation in time to have done so, and they were not charged with the duty of discovering his peril; it not being reasonable to suppose that one would attempt to alight at such a time." Ghio v. Metropolitan St. Ry. Co. (Mo. App. 1907), 103 So. W. Rep. 142.

to cross a railroad track without looking for approaching trains. * * * If men will take hazards, they must bear the consequences of their own rashness, and it is no just reason for visiting the consequences upon another, that his negligence co-operated in producing the result."

§ 716. **Alighting from moving train presumptively negligence.**— In a New York case [66] the question was decided as to the burden of proof and the presumptive effect of the act of boarding or alighting from a moving train. The court said: " It is, we think, the general rule of law, established by the decisions in this and other States, * * * that the boarding or alighting from a moving train, is presumably and generally a negligent act, *per se,* and that in order to rebut this presumption, and justify a recovery for an injury sustained in getting on or off a moving train, it must appear that the passenger was, by the act of the defendant, put to an election between alternate dangers, or that something was done or said, or some direction was given to the passenger by those in charge of the train, or some situation created, which interfered to some extent with his free agency, and was calculated to divert his attention from the danger and create a confidence that the attempt could be made in safety."

And the cases cited by the court, in the opinion, and those decided from other States, show that this is a just conclusion from the hazardous act of boarding or alighting from a moving train, in the absence of some explanation of such an act, on the passenger's part.[67]

[66] Soloman v. Manhattan R. Co., 103 N. Y. 437.

[67] Ricks v. Georgia Southern R. Co., 118 Ga. 259; Harvey v. Easton R. Co., 116 Mass. 269.

In Fulks v. St. Louis, etc., R. Co. (111 Mo. 335; 19 S. W. Rep. 818), the court denies that the burden of proving facts that would exempt plaintiff, boarding a moving train, from the charge of negligence, is on the plaintiff. But this ruling is counter to the weight of authority

§ 717. **Same — To avoid being carried by station.**— If a passenger is carried by his station he can recover for the inconvenience, loss of time and expenses, resulting ·from the delay and for being carried past his station, but, if, instead of pursuing this course, he leaps from a rapidly moving train and sustains injury, in order to avoid being carried by the station, the passenger assumes the risk of such· a rash course and his negligence will bar a recovery.[68]

In a recent Missouri case,[69] before the Court of Appeals, it was said: " If a passenger is negligently carried beyond his stopping place, he can recover for the inconvenience, loss of time and expense of traveling back, but if he jumps or leaves the train, under circumstances which render the act imprudent, he˜ does so at his own risk and assumes the consequences of the act. The question of negligence in cases like this, must be treated as a mixed question of law and fact, the facts being left to the jury and the legal effect of them declared by the court."

But all the circumstances in each case must be fully considered in determining whether or not a passenger is guilty of negligence in alighting from a moving train that has failed to stop at his station, and it is not sound to select some . salient feature of the case and hold that this fact being present, there is negligence as matter of law, but in each case, all the facts and circumstances ought to be considered and when so considered, they should constitute a case of

on this question, as the passenger is held to have the burden of excusing this presumptively negligent act, in Browne v. Raleigh, etc., R. Co., 108 No. Car. 34; 47 Am. & Eng. R. Cas. 544; Ricks v. Georgia Southern R. Co., 118 Ga. 259; Harvey v. Easton R. Co., 116 Mass. 269; Cousins v. Lake Shore R. Co., 96 Mich. 386.

[68] Price v. St. Louis, etc., R. Co., 72 Mo. 414; Nelson v. Atlantic, etc., R. Co., 68 Mo. 593; Kelly v. Hannibal, etc., Ry. Co., 70 Mo. 604.

[69] Judge Smith, in Owens v. Wabash R. Co., 84 Mo. App. 143, 148.

negligence, or otherwise, the cause should be s⟨
the jury.[70]

**§ 718. Same — Rate of speed as determining n⟨
act.**— As the danger in alighting from a movi⟨
great or small, according to the rate of speed witl⟨
train is running, it is the most important factor ⟨
along with the physical condition and age of the⟨
in determining whether or not the act of alig⟨
a train in motion, will constitute negligence.

The Court of Appeals, in Missouri, considerin⟨
tion, held that it would not be held negligence a⟨
law, for a passenger to alight from a train mo⟨
rate of only three [71] or four [72] miles an hour, ⟨
would be negligence, as matter of law, for a p⟨
attempt to alight from a train going at a spe⟨
eight to ten miles an hour.[73] In the case refer⟨

[70] Richmond v. Quincy, etc., Ry. Co., 49 Mo. App. 10⟨
" Where the agent and employees of a railway compan⟨
failed to bring the train to a stop at a station where a⟨
entitled to leave the train, his attempt to leave it whi⟨
cannot be held to be negligence as a matter of law unle⟨
attending the attempt was so great as to be obvious to⟨
common prudence and ordinary intelligence." Turley v.⟨
Ry. Co. (Ga. 1907), 56 S. E. Rep. 748.

" Where a carrier fails to stop its train at the usual s⟨
for passengers, it should suppose that a passenger w⟨
to alight from the moving train if he could do so pr⟨
when a stranger assists the passenger in so doing, and⟨
injured, it is for the jury to determine whether the negl⟨
company or that of the assisting person was the proxin⟨
the resulting injury." Martin v. Southern Ry. Co. (S.⟨
S. E. Rep. 3; 77 S. C. 370.

[71] Dawson v. Transit Co., 102 Mo. App. 277; 76 S. W. ⟨
[72] Murphy v. St. Louis, etc., Ry. Co., 43 Mo. App. 342.
[73] Murphy v. St. Louis, etc., Ry. Co., *supra*.

It was held in the following cases that getting on or⟨
train would not be held negligence as matter of law, but⟨
would be a mixed one of law and fact, where the train⟨

court, speaking through Judge Biggs, said: "We are inclined to the opinion that it is not necessarily negligence for a person to attempt to get off a train moving at the rate of four miles an hour. Our common knowledge and experience teaches us that under favorable circumstances this may be done with comparative safety. Under certain conditions or environments such an act might be held to be legal negligence. But, on the other hand, if it was in the daytime, and there were no obstructions in the way, or other hindering causes, a case would be presented in which fair inferences might be drawn both ways. It is, therefore, impossible to formulate a rule by which all cases can be governed. Each case must stand or fall, on its own peculiar facts. * * *

very slowly, when the attempt was made: Chicago, etc., R. Co. v. Gore, 202 Ill. 192; Chicago, etc., R. Co. v. Flaherty, 96 Ill. App. 563; Baltimore, etc., R. Co. v. Kane, 69 Md. 11; Fulks v. St. Louis, etc., R. Co., 111 Mo. 335; 19 S. W. Rep. 818; Swigert v. Hannibal, etc., R. Co., 75 Mo. 475; Dister v. Long Island R. Co., 151 N. Y. 424; Creech v. Charleston, etc., R. Co., 66 So. Câr. 528; Mills v. Missouri, etc., R. Co., 94 Texas 242; Warren v. Southern Kansas R. Co., 37 Kansas 408; Johnston v. West Chester R. Co., 70 Pa. St. 257; Illinois Central R. Co. v. Glover (Ky.), 71 S. W. Rep. 630; Murphy v. St. Louis, etc., R. Co., 43 Mo. App. 342.

"The act of a passenger in alighting in the nighttime from a train which was still in motion was not negligence *per se*." Texas & P. Ry. Co. v. Whiteley (Tex. Civ. App. 1906), 96 S. W. Rep. 109.

"Whether one incumbered with bundles was negligent in alighting from a street car moving at the rate of three miles an hour *held* for the jury." Hammond, etc., Ry. Co. v. Antonia (Ind. App. 1908), 83 N. E. Rep. 766.

"In an action by a passenger for personal injury alleged to have been sustained in getting off a moving train under the direction of the train porter, the question of negligence is for the jury to determine under proper instructions." St. Louis, etc., Ry. Co. v. Leamons (Ark. 1907), 102 S. W. Rep. 363.

"It not being necessarily negligence for a passenger to alight from a moving car, even by stepping in the opposite direction to the movement of the car, a plea of contributory negligence in so doing, which does not show the speed of the car, is insufficient." Birmingham Ry. Co. v. Dickerson (Ala. 1908), 45 So. Rep. 659.

1091

All judges must admit that the speed of a train may be such that it would be foolhardy for a person under any circumstances to attempt to get on or off. But the rate of speed which will authorize a court to so direct the jury is the troublesome question. The rule is that if the train is running so fast that to get on or off would be exceedingly dangerous, then such act must be held negligent as a matter of law. * * * If to get on or off a train, running at the rate of four miles an hour, is not negligence, *per se,* would such an act be so regarded, if the train was running at twice that rate of speed? In our opinion it would be and this opinion is based on our knowledge and experience in such matters. While we are satisfied with this conclusion, yet we must confess that it has the appearance of being somewhat arbitrary. But the limit must be placed somewhere. While the Supreme Court holds that the fact that a train was in motion will not necessarily defeat a recovery, yet the intimations in many of the decisions are that the movement must be very slow and scarcely perceptible."

§ 719. **Compelling passenger to alight from train in motion.**— If a conductor or other employee of the railroad company notifies or advises a passenger to leave a train which is moving at a speed to make it dangerous for the passenger to attempt to get off the train, the railroad company will be held responsible, in case of an injury to the passenger thereby.[74]

In a Texas case,[75] on the call of a station, the train stopped and a passenger did not leave the train, until told to hurry off by the conductor, as the train was moving. Being unable to see the place where he was compelled to alight, on account of the darkness, the passenger got off at a

[74] Jones v. Chicago, etc., R. Co., 42 Minn. 183; 43 N. W. Rep. 1114; 41 Am. & Eng. R. Cas. 169.

[75] International, etc., R. Co. v. Smith, 14 S. W. Rep. 642; 44 Am. & Eng. R. Cas. 324.

point where he could not reach the ground, short of several feet, and he fell and was injured and the court held that the railroad company was liable for the injury.

But it is not every injury from alighting from a moving train, at the request of a train man, that would constitute negligence. An order or direction to a passenger to alight from a moving train, might, under the circumstances, be entirely proper. The question would depend upon the speed of the train; whether it was night or day; the situation of the ground; the presence of obstacles, or other hindering causes; the sex and age of the passenger and other circumstances affecting the risk of the undertaking.[76]

And if a passenger of mature years, with full knowledge of the surroundings and situation, attempts to get off a moving train, at a point distant from a station, for his own convenience, the mere fact that an employee of the railroad consents to the attempt to so alight, will not render the railroad company liable, in case of an injury received while attempting to get off the train.[77]

[76] In this case, a boy had asked to be let off at a coal chute and the train man told him he could safely get off a moving train. He lost his legs by complying with the direction. Judge Biggs rendered the decision for the Appellate Court and the cause was remanded for a new trial. Wilburn v. St. Louis, etc., R. Co., 48 Mo. App. 224.

[77] Chicago, etc., R. Co. v. Hazzard, 26 Ill. 373.

"Where a passenger was induced to leave the train by the negligent direction of the carrier, and he observed ordinary care in attempting to regain it, the carrier is liable for an injury received by the passenger, regardless of what other negligent cause co-operated in producing the injury." Laub v. Chicago, etc., Ry. Co. (Mo. App. 1906), 94 S. W. Rep. 550.

"A passenger is not guilty of contributory negligence in alighting from a train upon which he has been carried as a passenger at a point where he was expressly directed by the carrier to alight." Illinois Cent. R. Co. v. Johnson, 123 Ill. App. 300, judgment affirmed; 77 N. E. Rep. 592; 221 Ill. 42.

"In an action by a passenger injured while alighting from a moving train, evidence that the porter who directed plaintiff to get off the

§ 720. **Same — In front of train on parallel track.** — If a passenger, without the assistance of the carrier's employees, alights from a moving car, at a place where he is struck by an approaching engine or car, on another track, whereby he sustains injury, no recovery can ordinarily be had, for such act is held to be negligent as matter of law.[78]

In a well-considered Kansas case,[79] Horton, C. J., in disposing of the case, said: " In this case, the facts are undisputed. The negligence alleged in the petition was not proved. The car had not stopped when Dewald stepped off, and when he stepped off, it was not at the Rosedale station, nor at the place at the north end of the side track, where it was usual for the car to stop when taken back from the depot and set out on the side track. There is no evidence tending to show that the railroad company, or any of its

train at the time he did, assisted in helping passengers off at stations such as that where plaintiff alighted, was sufficient to justify a finding that it was within the scope of the porter's duty to direct passengers to alight." Texas, etc., Ry. Co. v. Whiteley (Tex. Civ. App. 1906), 96 S. W. Rep. 109.

An invitation to leave a moving train was held to relieve the passenger from the effects of his otherwise negligent act, in the following cases: Montgomery, etc., R. Co. v. Stewart, 91 Ala. 421; Chicago, etc., R. Co. v. Gore, 202 Ill. 192; Illinois Central R. Co. v. Glover (Ky.), 71 S. W. Rep. 630; Missouri, etc., R. Co. v. Forman (Texas), 46 S. W. Rep. 834; Pence v. Wabash R. Co., 116 Iowa 279; Browne v. Raleigh, etc., R. Co., 108 No. Car. 34; 47 Am. & Eng. R. Cas. 544; Dister v. Long Island R. Co., 151 N. Y. 424; Schmidt v. North Jersey R. Co., 66 N. J. L. 424.

[78] Parsons v. New York Central R. Co., 37 Hun (N. Y.) 128; Commonwealth v. Boston, etc., R. Co., 129 Mass. 500; 1 Am. & Eng. R. Cas. 457; Weber v. Kansas City, etc., Ry. Co., 100 Mo. 194; 41 Am. & Eng. R. Cas. 117; Burrows v. Erie R. Co., 63 N. Y. 556; Reibel v. Cincinnati, etc., R. Co., 114 Ind. 476; Union Pacific R. Co. v. Adams, 33 Kansas 427; 19 Am. & Eng. R. Cas. 476; Clark v. Missouri Pacific Ry. Co., 35 Kansas 350; Atchison, etc., Ry. Co. v. Townsend, 39 Kansas 115; 35 Am. & Eng. R. Cas. 352.

[79] Dewald v. Kansas City, etc., Ry. Co., 44 Kansas 586; 47 Am. & Eng. R. Cas. 557.

agents, purposely or wantonly injured the deceased. As the car had not stopped when the deceased got off, no negligence can be imputed against the railroad company or its agents, in running the engine and tender on the track parallel with the one the passenger car was on, as to the persons in that car, because it could not have been anticipated that any person in the car would be so careless or reckless as to jump off while it was moving quite rapidly and before it reached its usual stopping place. Again, it appears from the evidence, that but for the deceased's own negligence, he would not have been injured. He left the car when it was moving quite rapidly and could not have listened or looked for the approaching engine. Under such circumstances, a passenger cannot jump off a moving car, thereby placing his life and limbs in peril, and then claim to be free from fault."

But in a Missouri case,[80] where a passenger was assisted or directed to alight by the employee of the railroad company, at a place where he was struck by a passing train on a parallel track, it was held that he was not negligent, as matter of law, although he might have seen the approaching train which struck him, before he was hit by it, and thus it is that circumstances alter cases.

§ 721. **Starting train while passenger is alighting.**— If the carrier fails to stop its train at the destination of a

[80] McDonald v. Kansas City, etc., Ry. Co., 127 Mo. 38; 29 S. W. Rep. 848.

"Where passengers are alighting from a train at a point where it is necessary that they cross other tracks of the carrier, it is the duty of the operatives of a train approaching upon another track, from the opposite direction, to exercise a degree of care commensurate with the situation and the danger, and it is negligence to operate such a train at a rate of speed from 12 to 15 miles per hour at the point where such alighting passengers are required to cross, and are actually crossing." Illinois Cent. R. Co. v. Johnson, 123 Ill. App. 300, judgment affirmed, 77 N. E. Rep. 592; 221 Ill. 42.

passenger for a sufficient length of time to enable him to alight in safety, and the train is started while the passenger is in the act of alighting, whereby he is thrown down and injured, the company would be liable.[81]

And if the employees of the railroad company have reason to believe that a passenger who has reached his destination, though dilatory, may be in the act of alighting, and they cause the train to be started, without examination or inquiry, and the passenger is thereby injured, the company will be liable.[82]

But if the train had stopped for a reasonable time, to enable passengers to alight therefrom, and without any fault on the part of the employees of the railroad company, a passenger had failed to alight, and the conductor not knowing and having no reason to expect that the passenger was in the act of alighting, caused the train to start, while he was alighting, as a result of which the passenger was injured, there would be no liability.[83]

[81] Straus v. Kansas City, etc., Ry. Co., 75 Mo. 185; 6 Am. & Eng. R. Cas. 384; Jeffersonville, etc., R. Co. v. Hendricks, 26 Ind. 228; Lehman v. Louisiana, etc., R. Co., 37 La. Ann. 705; Chicago, etc., R. Co. v. Landauer, 36 Neb. 642; 54 N. W. Rep. 976; 54 Am. & Eng. R. Cas. 640.

[82] Straus v. Kansas City, etc., R. Co., 86 Mo. 421; 27 Am. & Eng. R. Cas. 170; Georgia Pacific R. Co. v. West, 66 Miss. 310; 6 So. Rep. 207.

[83] Straus v. Kansas City, etc., R. Co., 86 Mo. 421; 27 Am. & Eng. R. Cas. 170; Straus v. Kansas City, etc., Ry. Co., 75 Mo. 185; 6 Am. & Eng. R. Cas. 384.

In Anderson v. Chicago, etc., Ry. Co. (110 S. W. Rep. 650), the plaintiff was injured by the sudden starting of the train, as she attempted to step from the car steps to the platform. On the defendant's appeal from an order setting aside a verdict for the defendant, Judge Goode, for the St. Louis Court of Appeals, said:

"According to the evidence for defendant, the train stopped a little ahead of its proper stopping place, and when the conductor stepped to the station platform he signaled the engineer to back the train. It stopped the first time only a moment, and backed to the right place for passengers to get off. Just as the train started to back plaintiff came to the door of the coach and was told by one of the train crew to wait until it stopped, but she immediately proceeded down the car steps, when the porter shouted to the passengers to wait, but she either did not hear him or paid no attention to what he said, and the motion of the train threw her to the platform, where she was injured. It is conceded plaintiff's testimony supported the petition and tended to prove she was on the steps of the coach and in the act of getting off when the train moved, throwing her to the platform. But it is contended the fact plaintiff fell toward the west, while the train was backing, proves she stepped from the train while it was in motion and takes out of her testimony its probative force."

"As said, we do not regard said fact as conclusive on the issue of whether the train was moving or motionless when plaintiff stepped off; but, granting it does prove plaintiff attempted to alight while the train was moving, the question arises, would this circumstance suffice necessarily to defeat her action? In other words, should the order for new trial be reversed simply because the train was in motion when plaintiff stepped off, regardless of the rate of motion and other facts? An attempt to alight from a moving train is not negligence *per se*, but its speed of movement, the age, activity, and strength of the passenger are relevant circumstances; and there may be other relevant facts, as, for instance, that the passenger was incumbered with a valise or other burdens."

"It is negligence to start a car while a passenger is alighting therefrom at the express or implied invitation of the carrier." Burke v. Bay City Traction Co. (Mich. 1907), 110 N. W. Rep. 524.

"Though a car remained stationary for a time sufficient to have enabled a passenger to alight in safety by the exercise of reasonable diligence, this would not justify the starting of the car while she was in the very act of stepping to the street, and the carrier would be liable for resulting injuries without regard to the violence of the start." Green v. Metropolitan St. Ry. Co. (Mo. App. 1907), 99 S. W. Rep. 28.

"Where the only negligence alleged is the sudden starting of the car before plaintiff could alight, and a witness testified that plaintiff 'did not start to get off the car until the conductor had started the car,' the refusal to instruct that plaintiff could not recover if he attempted to alight while the car was in motion is error." El Paso Electric Ry. Co. v. Boer (Tex. Civ. App. 1908), 108 S. W. Rep. 199.

"In an action for injuries to a passenger by the premature starting of a train, an instruction that alighting from a moving train was not an act of negligence, unless the then conditions and circumstances made it so, of which the jury was the judge, was objectionable as misleading." Gulf, etc., Ry. Co. v. Booth (Tex. Civ. App. 1906), 97 S. W. Rep. 128.

"An instruction as to the liability of a carrier if its employees in charge of the train failed to hold it stationary long enough for plaintiff to assist his daughter into the train, but jerked it in a violent, unusual, and extraordinary manner while he was about to alight therefrom and plaintiff was thereby injured, was not defective in omitting to require a finding that the train was negligently jerked, since the facts hypothecated constituted negligence." Bond v. Chicago, etc., Ry. Co. (Mo. App. 1907), 99 S. W. Rep. 30.

"In an action for injuries to a passenger, the material issues were whether the train stopped at a station a reasonable length of time for plaintiff's wife, who was injured, to alight, and whether she was negligent in failing to use reasonable diligence to alight. The evidence showed that as soon as the train stopped plaintiff and his wife, who were sitting in the rear of the coach, got up and started out, plaintiff carrying a child. He got off safely, and deposited the child upon the platform. His wife was standing on the platform of the car with a child in her arms. Plaintiff took the child and set it down while his wife stepped down to the second step, when the train moved forward, jerking her backwards. She caught hold of the rail and jumped, to keep from falling, which caused her to alight on her left foot, injuring it. *Held*, that an instruction submitting the issue whether the train started suddenly and unexpectedly was warranted." Texas Midland R. Co. v. Ritchey (Tex. Civ. App. 1908), 108 S. W. Rep. 732.

"In an action by a passenger for injuries sustained in alighting from a train, a petition alleging that defendant frequently moved its trains at such station while passengers were alighting to get the engine in position to take water, which custom was unknown to plaintiff; that the distance from the step to the ground, which was rocky and uneven, was 25 or 30 inches and that defendant neglected to have a stool in position; that the conductor saw plaintiff descending, knew that she needed assistance, that no stool was in position on which she could alight, and neglected to give her assistance, and that by reason of either or all the acts of negligence of defendants, its agents and servants, as alleged plaintiff sustained the injuries complained of, was sufficient as against a demurrer." St. Louis Southwestern Ry. Co. v. Kennedy (Tex. Civ. App. 1906), 96 S. W. Rep. 653.

"Where plaintiff's own testimony that her injury was the result of the premature starting of defendant's car while she was attempting to alight was corroborated by physical facts, the question whether she was injured in the manner claimed, or in attempting to alight in an improper manner before the car came to a stop, as defendant claimed, and as five disinterested witnesses testified, was for the jury." Cartlich v. Metropolitan St. Ry. Co. (Mo. App. 1908), 108 S. W. Rep. 584.

§ 722. **Jerking train while passenger is alighting.**— The sudden jerking of a train, while passengers are rightfully passing out of the cars is liable to produce accidents and hence is held to be negligence by the courts.[84] In an English case,[85] the porter at a railway station opened the car door and invited a passenger to alight, while the train was yet moving slowly and while on the steps the car was suddenly jerked and started with increased speed and she was injured and the company was held liable therefor.

And it is quite generally held, in the United States, that when a station has been announced and a train is stopped at such station, passengers have a right to leave the cars, and if a passenger, while alighting, is thrown down or injured by the sudden starting or moving of the train, the passenger is not generally held to be guilty of negligence, which will prevent his recovery, but the railroad company, having violated its duty by moving the train, when the passenger had a right to assume that it would be held stationary, is guilty of negligence which will enable the injured passenger or his representatives to recover.[86]

[84] Sauter v. New York, etc., R. Co., 66 N. Y. 50; 6 Hun 446; Milliman v. New York, etc., R. Co., 66 N. Y. 642; 4 Hun 409; Wood v. Lake Shore, etc., R. Co., 49 Mich. 370; 13 N. W. Rep. 779; 8 Am. & Eng. R. Cas. 478. In this case a passenger was told the train would stop for water and when the passenger was in the act of alighting, the train suddenly started and the company was held liable.

[85] London, etc., R. Co. v. Helliwell, 26 L. T. 557.

[86] Norfolk, etc., R. Co. v. Prinnell (Va.), 3 S. E. Rep. 95; 30 Am. & Eng. R. Cas. 574; Pennsylvania R. Co. v. Aspell, 23 Pa. St. 149; McNulta v. Ensch, 134 Ill. 46; 24 N. E. Rep. 631; Louisville, etc., R. Co. v. Wood, 113 Ind. 544; 14 N. E. Rep. 572.

"Where, in an action for injuries to a passenger alleged to have been occasioned by a sudden lurch of the train as he alighted, the only evidence of contributory negligence is that plaintiff was drunk, any error in leaving to the jury to determine what was contributory negligence was against the plaintiff." Louisville & N. R. Co. v. Deason (Ky. 1906). 96 S. W. Rep. 1115.

"Where, in an action for injuries received while alighting from a

train, if the theory of plaintiff was true, the sudden movement of the
train was the proximate cause of the injury, and such act was negligence as a matter of law, where the court had submitted to the jury all
the issues of contributory negligence raised by the pleadings and
evidence, it was not error to refuse to submit as an issue whether,
'under all the circumstances of the case,' the sudden movement of
the train was negligence on the part of the defendant." Galveston,
etc., R. Co. v. Alberti (Tex. Civ. App. 1907), 103 S. W. Rep. 699.

The train was started, before the passenger had time to alight in
the following cases, with a sudden start, and the company was held
guilty of negligence in so doing: Louisville, etc., R. Co. v. Wood,
113 Ind. 544; Texas, etc., R. Co. v. Miller, 79 Texas 78; 15 S. W.
Rep. 264; Burr v. Pennsylvania R. Co., 64 N. J. L. 30; 44 Atl. Rep.
845; Macon, etc., R. Co. v. Moore, 108 Ga. 84; 33 S. E. Rep. 889;
15 Am. & Eng. R. Cas. (N. S.) 842; Texas, etc., R. Co. v. Nunn, 98
Fed. Rep. 963.

"Though a street car passenger took a transfer to another line,
justifying the assumption that she would remain in the car until the
junction with such line was reached, she still had the right to alight
at any intermediate stopping place, and if, while so alighting, the car
was started on the conductor's signal, and she was injured thereby,
and the conductor actually saw her starting to alight, or alighting
when he gave the signal, or, by the exercise of the proper care imposed upon him, should have seen her so doing, the company is liable
for her injuries, even though the signal was not given until the car
had waited a reasonable time for passengers to alight and the other
passengers had safely alighted." Farrel v. Citizens' Light & Ry. Co.
(Iowa 1908), 114 N. W. Rep. 1063.

"In an action by a passenger for personal injuries, where there was
evidence that the danger that caused plaintiff's fall was one that was
incident to the proper handling of the train, it was error to refuse
an instruction that if the jury believed that the plaintiff went upon
the platform of defendant's car while it was in rapid motion for the
purpose of alighting therefrom, and that, while on the platform, he
was thrown therefrom and injured by reason of a jerk or lurch of the
train, still plaintiff could not recover for the injuries occasioned thereby
if they were so occasioned, unless the jury believed, from the preponderance of the testimony, that the jerk or lurch was unusual or
violent and not such as was incident to the ordinary and proper
operation of the train, and unless they further found plaintiff was
not guilty of contributory negligence in going upon the platform under
the circumstances which proximately in part brought about the injuries." Houston, etc., Ry. Co. v. Johnson (Tex. Civ. App. 1907),
103 S. W. Rep. 239.

§ 723. **Starting train after reasonable time.**— Where the employees of the railroad company afford the passengers a reasonable time to leave the cars after the arrival at the end of their journey, they have the right, after the expiration of such reasonable period, to act upon the presumption that all the passengers whose place of destination is then reached, have left the cars, as is customary in such cases.[87]   And if a passenger remains in his seat after the train has stopped, and he has had a reasonable opportunity to get off the train, the conductor cannot be held negligent in then starting the train,[88] and starting the train, after such reasonable time is not *per se,* negligence.[89]

But while the employees of a train do not owe the passengers the duty to hold the train longer than a reasonable time to enable them to alight at the destination, in the absence of special circumstances requiring such longer delay, if they know, or have reason to believe, that the passenger intending to alight, from age, infirmity or other conditions existing, requires a longer time to alight than is usually required, it would be negligence to start the train until the passenger had safely alighted.[90]

§ 724. **Putting passenger off away from station.**— Where a railroad company falls short of the station, in the stopping of its train,[91] or overshoots the station,[92] and stops the train

[87] Hurt v. St. Louis, etc., R. Co., 94 Mo. 255; 7 S. W. Rep. 1; 34 Am. & Eng. R. Cas. 422; Straus v. Kansas City, etc., R. Co., 75 Mo. 185; 6 Am. & Eng. R. Cas. 384; Highland Avenue R. Co. v. Burt, 92 Ala. 291; 9 So. Rep. 410; 48 Am. & Eng. R. Cas. 56.

[88] McDonald v. Long Island R. Co., 116 N. Y. 546; 22 N. E. Rep. 1068; 43 Hun 637.

[89] Chicago, etc., R. Co. v. Landauer, 36 Neb. 642; 54 N. W. Rep. 976; 54 Am. & Eng. R. Cas. 640.

[90] Georgia Pacific R. Co. v. West, 66 Miss. 310; 6 So. Rep. 207.

[91] Adams v. Missouri Pacific Ry. Co., 100 Mo. 555; 12 S. W. Rep. 637; 41 Am. & Eng. R. Cas. 105; Eddy v. Wallace, 49 Fed. Rep. 801; 4 U. S. App. 264; 52 Am. & Eng. R. Cas. 265.

[92] Franklyn v. Southern California R. Co., 85 Cal. 63; 24 Pac. Rep. 723.   1101

at a place remote from the usual and customary place for
passengers to alight, where there are no accommodations for
the passenger, if there are especial risks and hazards which
make it dangerous for the passenger to alight at such a
place, it is the duty of the railway company to warn the
passenger thereof and to use every reasonable precaution to
avoid injury to the passenger and for a failure to adopt such
precautions, in case of a resulting injury from such causes,
the railroad company would be liable.[93]

In an Arkansas case,[94] the plaintiff was a passenger on
the defendant's railroad, from Little Rock to Knoble Station
and the train arrived at the latter station about ten o'clock
at night. Plaintiff was asleep when his train reached the
station and the train crew awakened him and told him to
hurry off the car. He stepped onto the platform, but as
the train had overshot the station, he fell and was injured
and a judgment in his favor was affirmed.

But the failure to stop freight trains at stations is not
evidence of negligence on the part of the railroad company,
as it is not generally customary to stop such trains at the
station;[95] running a train a little beyond the station before
stopping it is held not to be negligence, *per se;* nor is the
delay thereupon, for a period necessary to reverse the motion
of the train, so as to back it to the usual stopping place,[96]
and the fact that the engineer was unable to stop a train at
the usual stopping place, through the failure of the air brakes

[93] Franklyn v. Southern California R. Co., *supra;* Eddy v. Wallace,
supra; Warden v. Missouri Pacific Ry. Co., 35 Mo. App. 631; Foss v.
Boston, etc., R. Co. (N. H.), 21 Atl. Rep. 222; 47 Am. & Eng. R. Cas.
566; Thompson v. New Orleans, etc., R. Co., 50 Miss. 315.

[94] St. Louis, etc., R. Co. v. Cantrell, 37 Ark. 519; 40 Am. Rep. 105;
8 Am. & Eng. R. Cas. 198.

[95] Hemmingway v. Chicago, etc., R. Co., 67 Wis. 668; 31 N. W.
Rep. 268; 28 Am. & Eng. R. Cas. 216; Alabama, etc., R. Co. v. Car-
michael, 90 Ala. 19; 8 So. Rep. 87; 44 Am. & Eng. R. Cas. 286.

[96] Taber v. Delaware, etc., R. Co., 71 N. Y. 489; 4 Hun 765.

to work properly, is not necessarily negligence, and if the defect in the brakes is unexplained, it is fairly attributable to mere accident, if all reasonable efforts are made to stop the train.[97]

[97] Porter v. Chicago, etc., R. Co., 80 Mich. 156; 44 N. W. Rep. 1054; Reed v. Duluth, etc., R. Co. (Mich.), 59 N. W. Rep. 144; 58 Am. & Eng. R. Cas. 77; Louisville, etc., R. Co. v. Dancy (Ala.), 11 So. Rep. 796.

In Adams v. Missouri, etc., R. Co. (100 Mo. 570; 13 S. W. Rep. 509), it was held to be a jury issue whether or not a passenger, put off a train at a place distant from his station, was guilty of contributory negligence, where he attempted to ride across a bridge on a car and becoming frightened, jumped off the car and sustained the injuries sued for. It would seem, in this case, that the negligence of the railroad company had nothing to do, except remotely, with the injury sued for and this is the ground of dissent, by the minority of the court.

"Plaintiff's intestate was riding on defendant's railroad on a through ticket, which entitled him to transportation to a junction with the next connecting road. The train on which he took passage did not stop at the junction, but stopped at a station four miles north, to which the train of the connecting road also ran over defendant's track to make connection with it. Deceased was advised of such fact, and told to get off at such station, which he did, but for some unexplained reason got back on the same train and started southward. He was soon discovered by the conductor, who put him off a half mile south of the station and told him that if he would hasten back he could still catch his connecting train, which would soon follow. The place at which he was put off was between two tunnels, and he walked back through the north one, and while talking with a man whom he met, his train left the station, which was in sight and only a short distance away. He then turned southward again, walked through the first tunnel, and entered the second, which was 1,600 feet long, curving, very dark and narrow, and while in such tunnel was struck by a train and so injured that he soon died. There was no material evidence to show how he came to be struck. *Held* that, conceding that deceased was put off at a dangerous place between the two tunnels, he had passed such danger and reached a place of safety, and the proximate cause of his death was, not such negligence of the conductor, but his own voluntary act in turning back, for which defendant could not be held liable." Gwyn v. Cincinnati, etc., R. Co., 155 Fed. Rep. 88.

§ 725. **Care toward passengers alighting from freight trains.**— As in the case of other incidental risks assumed by passengers on freight trains, which are not designed nor intended for passenger service, those taking passage on this kind of conveyance, assume the risk of injuries received in alighting, caused by the lack of facilities used, providing the railroad company otherwise uses reasonable care and operates the train in accordance with the custom of ordinarily prudent companies operating such trains.[98]

This must necessarily be true, for freight trains being designed for the transportation of freight, and consisting ofttimes of a long train of cars, could not always pull up to platforms to enable passengers to alight at each station, and then do the switching necessary to enable the company to transport the freight in due time to meet the demands of its customers. The courts recognize this and do not require that stations be stopped at to enable passengers to alight from such trains.[99] The business of such trains being designed primarily for the transportation of freight and not for passengers, there is no duty to provide these trains with all the means for the safety of passengers that passenger trains have, but it is sufficient if they are handled in a reasonably prudent and careful manner and passengers are generally held to assume the risk due to the absence of such conveniences and the manner of operating trains designed for passenger service.[1]

[98] Schilling v. Winona, etc., R. Co., 66 Minn. 252; 68 N. W. Rep. 1083; Guffey v. Hannibal, etc., R. Co., 53 Mo. App. 462; Chicago, etc., R. Co. v. Arnol, 144 Ill. 261; 19 L. R. A. 313; Olds v. New York, etc., R. Co., 172 Mass. 73; 51 N. E. Rep. 450.

[99] New York, etc., R. Co. v. Doane, 115 Ind. 435; 17 N. E. Rep. 913; 7 Am. St. Rep. 451; 1 L. R. A. 157.

[1] In Schilling v. Winona, etc., R. Co. (66 Minn. 252) 68 N. W. Rep. 1083), the passenger attempted to alight from the freight train at an intermediate station and was injured, owing to the fact that the caboose was not stopped at the station and no accommodations

§ 726. **Passenger pushed from train by fellow passenger.**—
As a general rule, a railroad company is not liable for an
injury to either its employees or its passengers, on account
of an act wrongfully committed by some third party, in no
way in its employ or for whose acts it has not agreed to be
responsible, and hence a passenger cannot hold the railroad
company responsible for an injury by being pushed from
the platform of a car by a fellow passenger, unless there are
facts or conditions which would render the railroad company
liable for this act, or its own wrongful conduct combined
with that of the passenger, to produce the injury.[2]

In a Pennsylvania case,[3] which illustrates the rule, a
woman was in the act of stepping from the car steps to the
platform, in leaving the car upon which she had been transported by the railroad company, and a passenger trying to
board the car, with more or less precipitation, ran against
the plaintiff and pushed her from the car steps, as a result

were afforded for his safety in alighting. It was held that he had
no cause of action, as no duty existed to provide such accommodations
or facilities.

"Where a passenger on a freight train was warranted in assuming
that the place where the caboose stopped was the place at which she
was expected to alight, it was the duty of the carrier to stop the train
long enough for her to alight in safety, or to warn her of the danger
resulting from the further movement of the train in time to avert
injury, and it was immaterial whether the movement of the train producing injury was an incident to the ordinary operation of such trains,
or was unnecessarily violent." Southern Ry. Co. v. Burgess (Ala.
1905), 42 So. Rep. 35.

"Where in an action for injuries to a passenger on a freight train
while attempting to alight from the caboose at a place where the
train stopped, the evidence was conflicting on the issue whether the
stopping of the train with the caboose on a trestle was necessary in
the operation of the train and therefore a risk incident to travel
thereon, the issue was for the jury." International & G. N. R. Co. v.
Cruseturner (Tex. Civ. App. 1906), 98 S. W. Rep. 423.

[2] Ellinger v. Philadelphia, etc., R. Co., 153 Pa. St. 213; 25 Atl.
Rep. 1132.

[3] Ellinger v. Philadelphia, etc., R. Co., *supra*.

of which she sustained the injuries sued for. As her own testimony showed these facts and that her injury was due to the wrongful act of the other passenger in rudely pushing by her to enter the car, it was held that the railroad company was not liable for the injury.

CHAPTER XXVIII.

INJURIES TO PASSENGERS BY EMPLOYEES.

§ 727. **Ground of carrier's liability for.**— While it is very generally held, in the case of employer and employee, that the employer is not liable for an injury to a third person, due to malicious acts of the employee, outside the scope of the employment,[1] this rule is held very generally not to apply to malicious injuries inflicted upon passengers by employees of the carrier, for since the carrier is bound, by the contract of transportation to protect the passenger during the existence of the contract, from the assaults of fellow passengers or third persons which could reasonably have been anticipated, the duty is held to apply, for stronger reasons, to assaults of its own employees, and hence it is

[1] McManus v. Crickett, 1 East 106; 3 Thompson on Negligence, § 3162.

1107

quite generally held that the willfulness of the assault is
no defense, on the part of the carrier, any more than it
is that the act was disconnected from the regular duties
of the employee causing the injury.[2] In a leading case,
by the Supreme Court of Wisconsin,[3] the reason for the
rule of liability on the part of the carrier, for such acts
of its employees, is clearly presented, which is, substantially,
that the corporation could only act by its employees and
since the contract was to safely carry the passenger, if it
could be held that the corporate entity was not personally
present and consenting to the assault by the employees it
selected to perform its contract and it was not thus a party
to the breach, it would be tantamount to holding that the
very agents it selected to perform the contract could ruth-
lessly violate it and the passenger would be without redress.

The same result is reached by the Supreme Court of
Massachusetts, in a leading case,[4] where it is pointed out
that on grounds of public policy, it would not do to compel the passenger to assume the risk of assaults or malicious injuries inflicted by the carrier's employees, and that

----

[2] Philadelphia, etc., R. Co. v. Derby, 14 How. (U. S.) 468; Goddard
v. Grand Trunk R. Co., 57 Me. 202; Maleck v. Tower Grove R. Co.,
57 Mo. 18; New Orleans, etc., R. Co. v. Burke, 53 Miss. 200; Pittsburg,
etc., R. Co. v. Pillow, 76 Pa. St. 510.

[3] Craker v. Chicago, etc., R. Co., 36 Wis. 657.

[4] Bryant v. Rich, 106 Mass. 180; Goddard v. Grand Trunk R. Co.,
57 Me. 202; Ramsden v. Boston, etc., R. Co., 104 Mass. 117.

" A conductor in charge of a street car is the agent of the company.
and the power inherent in the company to expel from its cars persons
who refuse to pay the customary fare is vested in him. If by an
error in judgment he expels one who is entitled to the rights of a
passenger, the company is responsible for such error, for in legal
contemplation the company is present and is acting in the person of
its conductor." Chicago Union Traction Co. v. McClevey, 126 Ill.
App. 21.

" It is the duty of a railway company to protect a passenger from
assault by the train men." Keen v. St. Louis, etc., R. Co. (Mo. App.
1908), 108 S. W. Rep. 1125.

1108

the "carrier, rather than the passenger, ought to take the risk of such exceptional cases, the passenger being necessarily placed so much within the power of the servants."

§ 728. Liability for torts of employees, generally.— Railroad companies are responsible to passengers for the torts of the conductors and other employees of the company employed in running its trains, when such torts are committed in connection with the business entrusted to such employees and spring from, or grow immediately out of such business.[5] From this statement it results, necessarily, that the contract of carriage, on the carrier's part, guarantees immunity to the passenger from any violence at the hands of those whose duty it is to afford protection against violence by strangers.[6]

And the rule that the carriers of passengers by steam are liable for the negligent or wrongful acts of employees does not always depend upon the fact that the carrier owes a duty, or is under some obligation to the injured party, for although the injured person is not a passenger for hire, if he comes within the general class of persons to whom the duty of protection belongs, he will be entitled to recover for any injury due to the wrongful act of the carrier's employees.[7]

[5] Gasway v. Atlanta, etc., R. Co., 58 Ga. 216; 16 Am. Ry. Rep. 99.
[6] Sherley v. Billings, 8 Bush. (Ky.) 147.
[7] Johnson v. Chicago, etc., R. Co., 58 Iowa 348; 12 N. W. Rep. 329; 8 Am. & Eng. R. Cas. 206.

It is proper to instruct the jury that carriers are bound to protect their passengers from assaults by their employees, for this is a duty always due to the passenger. Louisville, etc., R. Co. v. Kelly, 92 Ind. 371; 47 Am. Rep. 149; 13 Am. & Eng. R. Cas. 1.

"A carrier is absolutely liable as an insurer for injuries to a passenger from an aggravated assault perpetrated by the carrier's conductor, followed by the passenger's arrest." Baumstein v. New York City Ry. Co., 107 N. Y. S. 23.

"A carrier is an absolute guarantor of the safety of its passengers

§ 729. **Wrongful ejection of passenger.**— Where
senger is rightfully upon the train and within th
seat where he is located when he is ejected by the e
of the railroad company, he is held, by the Suprei
of the United States,[8] to have a *prima facie* case foi
sequent wrongful ejection and his damages will
mented by any actual injuries inflicted upon hin
process of ejecting him from the train, where he he
ful right to ride.

The passenger is not bound to leave the trai
wrongfully ordered so to do, but may remain in the
demand the recognition of his rights, and if he is
in a wrongful attempt to eject him, however mist
employee of the carrier may have been in his suppo
to eject the passenger, damages may be recovered
injuries so inflicted,[9] as well as for the indignities
by reason of the assault.[10]

But if the passenger, instead of complying witl
quest of the employee to leave the train, wrongfully
the employee and then sustains an injury, due to
ployee defending himself from such wrongful as
the part of the passenger, the railroad company w

against the assaults of its employees while it is performing i
of carriage." Order (Sup. 1906), 99 N. Y. S. 936, reversed
v. New York, etc., R. Co. (N. Y. 1907), 83 N. E. Rep. 31.

The carrier by the contract of carriage assumes an absol
tion to protect passengers against the willful, as well as th
acts of its employees. Smith v. Manhattan R. Co., 45 N. Y.
New Jersey Co. v. Brockett, 121 U. S. 637; 7 Sup. Ct. Rep.

[8] New York, etc., R. Co. v. Winters, 143 U. S. 60; 36 L.
Sup. Ct. Rep. 356.

[9] Pennsylvania R. Co. v. Bray, 125 Ind. 229; 25 N. E.
Cherry v. Kansas City, etc., R. Co., 52 Mo. App. 499;
Chicago, etc., R. Co., 83 Ky. 511.

[10] Carsten v. Northern Pacific R. Co., 44 Minn. 454; 47 1
49; Delaware, etc., R. Co. v. Walsh, 47 N. J. L. 548; St.
R. Co. v. Kilpatrick, 67 Ark. 47; 54 S. W. Rep. 971; H
etc., R. Co. v. Delaney, 65 Ark. 177; 45 S. W. Rep. 351.

be liable for the injury so sustained, for the reason that the passenger, in assaulting the employee, became a trespasser, *ab initio,* and the employee was then entitled to use sufficient force to eject him.[11]

§ 730. **Ejection of sick or disorderly passengers.**— It is held to be the duty of the carrier to expel passengers infected with contagious diseases, of which it is informed,[12] and also to eject passengers whose disorderly conduct is apt to occasion injury to those traveling on the same train [13] or car, and for such reasonable force and care as may be necessary to expel such passengers, there is generally held to be no liability on the part of the carrier, for resulting injuries sustained. Of course, in the ejection of a sick passenger it would be the duty of the carrier to make the

[11] South Florida R. Co. v. Rhodes, 25 Fla. 40; 5 So. Rep. 633; 3 L. R. A. 333; Alabama, etc., R. Co. v. Drummond, 73 Miss. 813; 20 So. Rep. 7; Magee v. Oregon, etc., R. Co., 46 Fed. Rep. 734.

"Where plaintiff, while intoxicated, boarded defendant's train without intending to pay fare, defendant's employees were not bound to accept a tender of fare from a third person and suspend plaintiff's ejection, after the process of ejection had commenced." Gates v. Quincy & K. C. Ry. Co. (Mo. App. 1907), 102 S. W. Rep. 50.

"A carrier is not liable for an assault upon a passenger by one of its employees acting in self-defense." Reed v. New York & Q. C. Ry. Co., 102 N. Y. S. 19.

"Plaintiff, riding on a train without a ticket, exhibited more than the amount of the fare, but insisted on receiving his change before paying, and refused to give up the money on an offer of the conductor to accept it and then give back the change. The conductor and another employee started to remove him, when he told them to stop, and he would pay his fare. *Held* that, under the circumstances, his last promise was not a tender." Louisville, etc., R. Co. v. Cottengim (Ky. 1907), 104 S. W. Rep. 280; 31 Ky. Law Rep. 871.

[12] Connolly v. Crescent City R. Co., 41 La. Ann. 57; 5 So. Rep. 259; 3 L. R. A. 153; Paddock v. Atchison, etc., R. Co., 37 Fed. Rep. 841; 4 L. R. A. 231.

[13] Louisville, etc., R. Co. v. Logan, 88 Ky. 232; 10 S. W. Rep. 655; Sullivan v. Old Colony R. Co., 148 Mass. 119; 18 N. E. Rep. 678; Louisville, etc., R. Co. v. Johnson, 92 Ala. 204; 9 So. Rep. 269.

ejection at a proper time and place, where medical attention and accommodations could be secured,[14] and a drunken
or disorderly person ought to be ejected with due care for
his subsequent safety, and if he is put off the train at a
time or place where his subsequent injury would reasonably
be expected, in view of his helpless condition, the carrier
would be held liable for such injury.[15]

But where a sick person is broken out with an eruption
which resembles smallpox, and the employees of the carrier,
with due care for the protection of other passengers, discharge him in a careful manner, at a time and place where
proper accommodations can be secured, the fact that they
were mistaken and that the passenger did not, in fact, have
the disease, will not render the company liable for the wrongful discharge.[16]

§ 731. Injury from ejection at dangerous place.— Although
the railroad company may have the right to eject a passenger who has never had, or who has forfeited his right
to ride upon the train, yet if the employees put him off the
train at a time or place, when his injury is imminent from
a cause known to the employees, or which ought to have

[14] Paddock v. Atchison, etc., R. Co., 37 Fed. Rep. 841; 4 L. R. A. 231.
[15] Louisville, etc., R. Co. v. Johnson, 108 Ala. 62; 19 So. Rep. 511;
31 L. R. A. 372; Central R. Co. v. Glass, 60 Ga. 441; Louisville, etc.,
R. Co. v. Ellis, 97 Ky. 330; 30 S. W. Rep. 979.
[16] Paddock v. Atchison, etc., R. Co., 37 Fed. Rep. 841; 4 L. R. A. 231.
"The statute would not authorize a conductor to put off a sick
passenger vomiting or otherwise doing things a well-behaved passenger
in good health would not do, but only applies to persons who voluntarily,
or while under the influence of liquor, act in a boisterous, indecent,
and disgusting manner, to the annoyance of other passengers." Chesapeake, etc., Ry. Co. v. Crank (Ky. 1908), 108 S. W. Rep. 276.
The liability of a carrier for expulsion from its train of a passenger
in the enforcement by health officers of quarantine regulations is
denied in Baldwin v. Seaboard Air Line R. Co., 128 Ga. 567; 58 S.
E. Rep. 35; 13 L. R. A. (N. S.) 360.

been known to them, the carrier will be liable in case of the subsequent injury of the ejected passenger.[17]

Thus, if a drunken passenger is ejected at a time or place where he is apt to freeze to death;[18] where he may be drowned by falling into a pond of water,[19] or where he is apt to be struck by other trains,[20] in case of an injury from such a cause, the company will be liable therefor.

But if the condition of the drunken passenger is not such as to render him unable to take care of himself and it is not reasonably to be expected that he would receive injury from any cause likely to overtake him, it will not be held negligence to eject him at a time and place where no danger is apt to result, and if such a passenger, although intoxicated, is put off the train at a time and place when his subsequent injury could not reasonably have been apprehended, the fact that he sustains an injury later, by reason of his intoxication, will not render the railroad company liable therefor.[21]

[17] Jackson v. Alabama, etc., R. Co., 76 Miss. 703; 25 So. Rep. 353; 14 Am. & Eng. R. Cas. (N. S.) 392; Lake Shore, etc., R. Co. v. Rosenzwig, 113 Pa. St. 519; Ham v. Delaware, etc., R. Co., 155 Pa. St. 548; 20 L. R. A. 682; Union Pacific R. Co. v. Gallagher, 114 Ill. 325.

[18] Louisville, etc., R. Co. v. Sullivan, 81 Ky. 624.

[19] Gill v. Rochester, etc., R. Co., 37 Hun (N. Y.) 107.

[20] Louisville, etc., R. Co. v. Johnson, 108 Ala. 62; 19 So. Rep. 511; 31 L. R. A. 372.

[21] Brown v. Louisville, etc., R. Co. (Ky.), 44 S. W. Rep. 648; 10 Am. & Eng. R. Cas. (N. S.) 55; Roseman v. Carolina, etc., R. Co., 112 No. Car. 709; 19 L. R. A. 327.

In a Massachusetts case, a drunken passenger was ejected from a station in such a manner as to injure a woman passenger and the carrier was held liable for the injury. Gray v. Boston, etc., R. Co., 168 Mass. 20; 46 N. E. Rep. 397.

Statutes governing the places where passengers may be rightfully ejected, have been passed in many States, and it may be stated, as a general rule, that if the ejection is made in contravention of such acts, and a passenger is injured as a result thereof, there is a liability.

§ 732. Ejecting passenger from moving train.— If the employees of a railroad company eject a passenger, rightfully or wrongfully, from a train moving at a dangerous rate of speed and in consequence of such ejection the passenger sustains an injury, the railroad company would be liable for damages, for it would be held to be negligence to eject the passenger from a train moving at such a rate of speed as would be apt to injure him in alighting.[22]

For such statutes, see Statutes of California, Illinois, Massachusetts and Wisconsin.

" If a passenger is drunk and boisterous or annoys other passengers, the conductor may eject him from the train, using no more force than is necessary for that purpose." Chesapeake & O. Ry. Co. v. Robinette (Ky. 1908), 107 S. W. Rep. 763.

" In an action to recover for the death of a passenger expelled from a train at a flag station and on a stormy night, for failure to produce his ticket, where he was afterwards found dead, apparently having been killed by a locomotive, whether the employees of the carrier were guilty of negligence and whether deceased exercised due care were questions for the jury." Tilburg v. Northern Cent. Ry. Co. (Pa. 1907), 66 Atl. Rep. 846.

Drunkenness will not render the company liable for an injury to a passenger put off the train, and removed to a safe distance, merely because he afterwards gets back on the track and is hurt by a train, if there was nothing to indicate that his condition was such as to render it dangerous to leave him where he was placed. McClelland v. Louisville, etc., R. Co., 94 Ind. 276; 18 Am. & Eng. R. Cas. 260.

" In an action for the death of a passenger put off of defendant's train in a drunken condition, where the petition alleged that he was thereafter run over by another train some three or four miles from the place of expulsion, it was subject to special demurrer, as the statement of this distance negatived liability on the part of defendant." Seaboard Air Line Ry. v. Smith (Ga. App. 1907), 59 S. E. Rep. 199.

" In an action against a railroad company for the death of plaintiff's husband caused by being ejected from a train while in a helpless condition, so that he was run over by a following train, the action being based on the negligence of the employees of the first train, the fact that the evidence showed that the employees in charge of the second train used all ordinary care and diligence in trying to avoid the accident did not prevent a recovery." Macon, etc., R. Co. v. Moore (Ga. 1906), 54 S. E. Rep. 700.

[22] Hart v. West Side R. Co., 86 Wis. 483; 57 N. W. Rep. 91; South-

But the mere fact of ejecting a passenger from a moving train will not be held to be negligence *per se,* any more than it would be for the passenger to voluntarily alight from a moving train, where the place where he alights is not dangerous and the motion of the train is not sufficient to make it otherwise dangerous for him to get off the train.[23] Of course it would always be safer to stop the train before the passenger is ejected, and there is authority for the position that it should be done in every case, or a liability will result, regardless of the fact whether an injury is sustained or not;[24] but this is not in accord with the reason of the rule, for if the train is moving so slowly that an injury is not apt to result and none in fact is sustained, there is no more reason in assessing damages against the railroad company,

ern, etc., R. Co. v. Rice, 38 Kansas 398; 16 Pac. Rep. 817; Lamkin v. Vicksburg, etc., R. Co., 42 La. Ann. 997; 8 So. Rep. 530; St. Louis, etc., R. Co. v. Reagen, 52 Ill. App. 488.

[23] Southern, etc., R. Co. v. Sandford, 45 Kansas 372; 25 Pac. Rep. 891; 11 L. R. A. 432; 3 Thompson on Negligence, § 3252.

[24] Oppenheimer v. Manhattan R. Co., 63 Hun (N. Y.) 633.

A railroad company is held, in Doggett v. Chicago, B., etc., R. Co. (134 Iowa 690; 112 N. W. Rep. 171; 13 L. R. A. (N. S.) 364), not to be liable for the act of its conductor in compelling a crippled trespasser to leave a moving train, from which a person of ordinary capacity might have alighted in safety, unless he knew of the trespasser's crippled condition; and the fact that, in the exercise of ordinary care, he might have known it, is immaterial.

"Where, after an intoxicated person had boarded a car in violation of the conductor's orders, the conductor pushed him off while the train was moving and he was injured, the carrier was responsible, but only for compensatory damages for the injury sustained, unless the conductor's conduct was such as to indicate wantonness and recklessness, justifying punitive damages." Louisville, etc., R. Co. v. McNally (Ky. 1907), 105 S. W. Rep. 124.

"In an action for injuries to a passenger by being pushed from a car platform by the car porter while the train was in rapid motion, evidence *held* insufficient to warrant a finding that the porter's act was willful or other than accidental or negligent." Illinois Cent. R. Co. v. Warren (U. S. C. C. A., Miss., 1906), 149 Fed. Rep. 658.

because of the ejection, than there would be in denying a recovery for an injury to a passenger, from some negligent act of the railroad company, merely because he stepped from a slowly moving train which did not result in the injury.

§ 733. Injury from excessive force in ejecting passenger.— Notwithstanding the carrier may have the lawful right to eject a passenger, the expulsion from the carrier's train ought to be done with reasonable care for the safety of the passenger and only such force used as may be reasonably essential to expel the passenger. If, therefore, instead of using only such force as may be necessary to expel the passenger, the employees of the railroad company use such an excess of force that the passenger is injured, as a result, the company will be liable for the injury.[25]

But if the excessive force is used by the employees of the railroad company to repel force used by the passenger to resist the expulsion, or in defending themselves from the attack of the passenger, and the passenger is injured, there is no liability on the part of the railroad company,[26] for the passenger would himself be in the wrong, and having provoked the assault, the employees of the train would have the lawful right to defend themselves, and, as said in one case, in such a case the law has no scales in which to weigh the issue whether or not the force used was excessive, for it is well known that when one is engaged in self-defense, he is not engaged in an undertaking that will always permit him to act as coolly as if such an emergency did not exist.[27]

[25] Coleman v. New York, etc., R. Co., 106 Mass. 160; Chicago, etc., R. Co. v. Bills, 104 Ind. 13; Illinois, etc., R. Co. v. Davenport, 177 Ill. 110; 52 N. E. Rep. 66; Rowell v. Boston, etc., R. Co., 68 N. H. 358; 44 Atl. Rep. 488.

[26] New Orleans, etc., R. Co. v. Jopes, 142 U. S. 18; 35 L. Ed. 910.

[27] Moore v. Columbia, etc., R. Co., 38 So. Car. 1; 16 S. E. Rep. 781.

§ 734. Injury must be direct result of wrongful ejection.—
The doctrine of proximate and remote cause is peculiarly
applicable to the damages alleged to result to passengers
from their wrongful ejection from ıailroad trains, and
within the rule already discussed,[28] unless the negligence
or wrongful ejection of the passenger is directly connected
with the subsequent injuries received, there can be no recovery by the injured passenger.

Injuries from exposure to the weather, in attempting to
walk a long distance, after an ejection, were held too remote in one case;[29] where a passenger suffering from heart

"Where a conductor on a train refused to accept plaintiff's ticket,
and threatened to put him off if he did not pay his fare, and laid his
hands so heavily on plaintiff as to cause pain and tend to put him
in fear of further personal violence, it appearing that no force was
necessary, the act was excessive, and would support an inference of
malice." Glover v. Atchison, etc., Ry. Co. (Mo. App. 1908), 108 S. W.
Rep. 105.

"A railroad company is liable for damages for kicking or throwing
a trespasser off a train, or for using more force than is reasonable or
apparently necessary to eject him." Louisville & N. R. Co. v. Cottengim (Ky. 1907), 104 S. W. Rep. 280; 31 Ky. Law Rep. 871.

"Where one who boards a train, intending to ride without payment
of fare, refuses to pay fare when demanded, and the refusal is induced
by bad faith, the conductor, after attempting to eject him for non-
payment of fare, need not accept a tender of fare; but where one who
boards a train, intending to pay fare, tenders his fare after refusing
to pay, he cannot rightfully be ejected, though the tender is not
made until steps have been taken to eject him." Beck v. Quincy, etc.,
R. Co. (Mo. App. 1908), 108 S. W. Rep. 132.

"A passenger who is about unlawfully to be ejected from a traction
car cannot resist, but must either pay his fare or peaceably leave the
car; but he may recover damages for the indignity suffered in so
being required to leave the car, and likewise for any unnecessary force
that may be used in his ejection." Chicago Union Traction Co. v.
Brethauer, 125 Ill. App. 204, judgment affirmed, 79 N. E. Rep. 287;
223 Ill. 521.

[28] See chapter, Proximate and Remote Cause.

[29] Corrister v. Kansas City, etc., R. Co., 25 Mo. App. 619; Louisville,
etc., R. Co. v. Fleming, 14 Lea (Tenn.) 128.

failure was roughly removed, under the mistaken belief that he was intoxicated, and he died after being so removed, in the absence of evidence that the wrongful removal precipitated his demise, the company would not be liable; [30] the removal of a drunken passenger, in a timely and safe manner and at a reasonably safe place, will not render the company liable, if his subsequent injury could not reasonably have been anticipated, [31] nor will the railroad company be responsible for an injury received by a passenger in an attempt to walk across a trestle, after he was ejected from a train, [32] for this is the rash act of the passenger alone and could not reasonably be anticipated by the carrier.

But it has been held that the carrier ought to have foreseen the injury likely to result from the wrongful ejection of a pregnant woman at a distance from her place of destination; [33] the probable injury to a passenger, stunned by his removal from the train, at a place where he was apt to be struck by passing trains; [34] the danger to be incurred by a lone woman and a child, with considerable baggage, put off the train at a distance from her station, [35] and the injury to a passenger put off the train in very inclement weather, at a distance from any station, [36] are all held to be instances

[30] Briggs v. Minneapolis, etc., R. Co., 52 Minn. 36; 53 N. W. Rep. 1019.

[31] Roseman v. Carolina, etc., R. Co., 112 No. Car. 709; 16 S. E. Rep. 766; 52 Am. & Eng. R. Cas. 638; 19 L. R. A. 327.

[32] International, etc., R. Co. v. Folliard, 66 Texas 603.

[33] Brown v. Chicago, etc., R. Co., 54 Wis. 342; 3 Am. & Eng. R. Cas. (N. S.) 444.

[34] Cincinnati, etc., R. Co. v. Cooper, 120 Ind. 469; 22 N. E. Rep. 340; 6 L. R. A. 241.

[35] Evansville, etc., R. Co. v. Kyte, 6 Ind. App. 52; 32 N. E. Rep. 1134.

[36] Evans v. St. Louis, etc., R. Co., 11 Mo. App. 463.

"In an action by a passenger for injuries caused by falling or being thrown from the platform of a car, where the conductor had put him, an instruction fixing the liability of defendant, regardless of whether or not plaintiff exercised ordinary care to prevent the accident, was

where the wrongful ejection of the passenger is sufficiently connected with the subsequent injuries, to render the carrier liable for the damages sustained.

§ 735. **Acts within and beyond scope of employment.**—A passenger is entitled, by virtue of his contract of transportation, to protection against the misconduct or negligence of the carrier's employees. The conduct of the carrier's employees, while transacting the business of the railroad company and when acting within the general scope of their employment, is, of necessity, to be imputed to the railroad company, which constitutes them its agents for the performance of its contract with the passenger. It is immaterial that the company did not authorize or even know of the act of the employee causing injury to the passenger, or even if it disapproved or forbade it, the carrier is equally liable, if the act is done in the course of the employment.[37]

This rule is based on grounds of public policy and convenience,[38] and it applies peculiarly to carriers and passengers, for a carrier is bound, as far as practicable, to protect its passengers, while being conveyed, from violence com-

prejudicial error." Chesapeake & O. Ry. Co. v. Crank (Ky. 1908), 108 S. W. Rep. 276.

"A carrier of passengers is only liable for the direct and proximate results of the negligence complained of, or for those results which can reasonably be anticipated to flow therefrom." Illinois Cent. R. Co. v. Kerr, 125 Ill. App. 363.

"A judgment for damages against a railroad company for injury to a passenger by the negligence of an employee of the company is contrary to law, and will be reversed, where the evidence shows that such negligence was not a natural and probable proximate cause of the injury sustained, and that such injury could not reasonably have been anticipated." Florida East Coast Ry. Co. v. Wade (Fla. 1907), 43 So. Rep. 775.

[37] New Jersey Co. v. Brockett, 121 U. S. 637; 30 L. Ed. 1049.

[38] *Ante idem.* Philadelphia, etc., R. Co. v. Quigley, 62 U. S. (21 How.) 210; 16 L. Ed. 75; Higgins v. Turnpike Co., 46 N. Y. 27.

mitted by strangers and copassengers, and it under
solutely, to protect them against the misconduct o
employees while engaged in performing the contra
riage.[39]

As toward a stranger, the carrier is liable for
of its employees, only when done within the gene
of their employment; but the carrier is responsibl
malicious or wrongful acts of its employees which
injury to a passenger, whether done in the line of t
ployment or not, if performed during the discharg
duty owing by the carrier to the passenger.[40]

This is the general trend of the authorities with r
to malicious or wrongful acts of the employees of
rier toward passengers.[41]   But it is held, in New
that to entitle a passenger to recover damages for an
due to the willful misconduct of the carrier's employ
wrongful act must not only be shown but it must also
that the employee was acting, at the time, in the co
his employment.

§ 736. **What acts of employees within scope of autho**
It is frequently important to determine just what a

[39] Stewart v. Brooklyn, etc., R. Co., 90 N. Y. 591.

[40] This is Judge Ellison's language in Eads v. Metropolitan
43 Mo. App. 545.

[41] Philadelphia, etc., R. Co. v. Derby, 14 How. 468; Bryant v
106 Mass. 180; Goddard v. Grand Trunk R. Co., 57 Me. 202; Cr
Chicago, etc., R. Co., 36 Wis. 757; New Orleans, etc., R. Co. v.
142 U. S. 18; Chicago, etc., R. Co. v. Flexman, 9 Ill. App. 250.

[42] Mulligan v. New York, etc., R. Co., 129 N. Y. 506; 29
Rep. 952; 42 N. Y. S. R. 83; 53 Am. & Eng. R. Cas. 47.

"A carrier is liable for an assault committed upon a passeng
an employee of such carrier where such employee is acting with
line of his duty or within the scope of his employment; but, i
absence of proof that such employee in making such assault was i
within the line of his duty, no presumptions will be entertain
supply the absence of such proof." Chicago City Ry. Co. v. C
128 Ill. App. 528.

1120

employees, resulting in injuries to passengers, are within the scope of the employees' authority, as such. The conductor is generally held to be acting within the scope of his powers, in managing the train and its employees, controlling the conduct of passengers, and in the collection of fares and ejecting passengers and others wrongfully on the train.[43] Since it is not usual for the employer to empower inferior employees with the same authority as that possessed by those exercising superior functions, it is reasonable to suppose that the power would not be implied on the part of brakemen, or other inferior employees, to perform these functions exercised by the conductor, and many courts hold that brakemen have not the implied power to eject passengers or to perform the other functions generally exercised by the conductor, in control of the train;[44] but other courts will recognize that it is generally within the scope of the duties of a brakeman to eject passengers, or trespassers, disturbing others on the train, and hold that the railroad company is liable for injuries in so doing.[45]

And the courts of many States have held the railroad company liable for the acts of inferior employees, resulting in injuries to passengers, upon the theory that such acts were within the implied powers of the employees of the employer, and for an unauthorized act of an engineer, in throwing a chunk of coal;[46] the wrongful act of a porter,

[43] Travers v. Kansas City, etc., R. Co., 63 Mo. 421; Brown v. Hannibal, etc., R. Co., 66 Mo. 588; O'Brien v. Boston, etc., R. Co., 15 Gray (Mass.) 20; Kinsley v. Lake Shore, etc., R. Co., 125 Mass. 54; Indianapolis, etc., R. Co. v. Anthony, 43 Ind. 188.

[44] Lake Shore, etc., R. Co. v. Peterson, 144 Ind. 214; 42 N. E. Rep. 480; Farber v. Missouri Pacific Ry. Co., 116 Mo. 81; Wabash R. Co. v. Savage, 110 Ind. 156.

[45] Hoffman v. New York, etc., R. Co., 87 N. Y. 25, 30; Lang v. New York, etc., R. Co., 125 N. Y. 656; Welsh v. West Jersey R. Co., 62 N. J. L. 655; 42 Atl. Rep. 736; 15 Am. & Eng. R. Cas. (N. S.) 674; Kansas City, etc., R. Co. v. Kelly, 36 Kansas 655.

[46] Chicago, etc., R. Co. v. Doherty, 53 Ill. App. 282.

causing injury to a passenger; [47] the act of a car c
kicking a boy's hand and causing him to fall und
wheels,[48] and other similar injuries, due to the un
acts of inferior employees, have been held to be w
scope of their employment.

But where the employee clearly leaves the duti
service and pursues a private course of his own, as
baggage man, after a quarrel with a passenger, to v
personal vengeance upon him, pursued him with a
and struck him, inflicting a serious injury, it was l
the employer was not liable for the injury, as the e
was not acting within the scope of his employment.[4]

§ 737. Liability for assaults generally.— In every
of carriage, entered into between a passenger carric
passenger, there is an implied stipulation that the pa
shall be humanely treated and that the employees of t
road company, engaged in the performance of the c
contract, shall not unjustifiably assault, beat, or otl
maltreat the passenger, while the carrier sustains su
tract relations toward him, and the carrier is responsi
any breach of this implied stipulation of the conti
carriage, regardless of the motives of the employee.[50]

This rule is but the logical extension of the carrier

[47] Bayley v. Manchester, etc., R. Co., L. R. 7 C. P. 415; 1
C. P. 148; Peck v. New York, etc., R. Co., 70 N. Y. 587.

[48] Northwestern R. Co. v. Hack, 66 Ill. 238.

[49] Little Miami R. Co. v. Wetmore, 19 Ohio St. 110.

[50] Chicago, etc., R. Co. v. Barrett, 16 Ill. App. 17; McQue
Metropolitan R. Co., by Judge Johnson, 117 Mo. App. 262; I
Metropolitan R. Co., by Judge Ellison, 43 Mo. App. 536; O'B
Transit Co., 185 Mo. 263; Flynn v. Transit Co., 113 Mo. App. 1
S. W. Rep. 560; Wise v. Louisville, etc., R. Co., 91 Ky. 537; Mite
United Ry. Cos., 125 Mo. App. 1; Missouri, etc., R. Co. v. H
(Tex.), 109 S. W. Rep. 228; McLain v. St. Louis Ry. Co. (Mo. .
111 S. W. Rep. 835.

tract, for when the carrier undertakes to protect the passenger against the assaults of fellow passengers and third persons during the contract of carriage, which is a part of the contract imposed by the law, on grounds of public policy, it should, *a fortiori,* protect the passenger from the assaults of its own employees. And if this duty is not performed and this protection is not afforded the passenger, but, on the contrary, the passenger is assaulted and mistreated through the misconduct of the carrier's employees, the carrier is necessarily responsible therefor.[51]

[51] Sherley v. Billings, 8 Bush. (Ky.) 147; Winnegar v. Central Pass. R. Co., 85 Ky. 547; 4 S. W. Rep. 237; 34 Am. & Eng. R. Cas. 462.

In the absence of misconduct on the part of the passenger, it is the duty of the conductor to treat him with respect, and to protect him from insult and assault. Farber v. Mo. Pac. Ry. Co., 116 Mo. 81; 22 S. W. Rep. 631; 20 L. R. A. 350; Murphy v. St. Louis Transit Co., 96 Mo. App. 272; 70 S. W. Rep. 159; McGinnis v. Mo. Pac. Ry. Co., 21 Mo. App. 399; Eads v. Met. Ry. Co., 43 Mo. App. 536; Hutchinson on Carriers (3 ed.), §§ 980–981.

" A carrier is absolutely liable for a wrongful and unprovoked assault on a passenger on a train by a brakeman thereon." St. Louis, etc., Ry. Co. v. Dowgiallo (Ark. 1907), 101 S. W. Rep. 412.

" A conductor in charge of a passenger train has a right to defend himself from an attack by a passenger, but he has no right to strike a passenger with a pistol for the use of abusive language toward him." Coleman v. Yazoo, etc., R. Co. (Miss. 1907), 43 So. Rep. 473.

For recent decisions of the Supreme and Appellate Courts of Missouri, recognizing the right of a passenger to recover for an injury inflicted by a willful assault on the part of the employees of the carrier, see Judge Woodson's well-considered opinion, in O'Brien v. Transit Co., 110 S. W. Rep. 705, and Judge Goode's opinion, for the St. Louis Court of Appeals, in Keen v. St. Louis, etc., R. Co., 108 S. W. Rep. 1125.

" A complaint showing that plaintiff became a passenger on defendant's car, and that the servants of defendant, without cause and in violation of their duty, assaulted plaintiff, was upon a cause of action consisting of the violation of defendant's contract to carry safely." Schwartz v. Interborough Rapid Transit Co., 103 N. Y. S. 80.

" Where an intoxicated passenger, on being requested by a brakeman to deliver up a pistol which he was brandishing, gave it to his wife who placed it under her, whereupon the brakeman reached under her

§ 738. **Assaults on female passengers.**— With
female passengers, a railroad company, by implicati
contracts that they shall be protected against ob:
duct, lascivious behavior and every immodest and
approach, and if, instead of protecting female ſ
against such conduct on the part of their employees
permitted to be assaulted or approached in a lewd
ious manner, this will constitute such a violation of
of the contract of carriage as to entitle such a pas:
recover damages from the carrier.[52]

A railroad company is liable in compensatory dan
an indecent approach or assault by a conductor or.o
ployee of a train upon a female passenger,[53] and s
senger is entitled to protection, not alone from the en
of the railroad company, but from fellow passeng
turbulent and riotous and disorderly persons on the
well.[54]

But notice of the danger to the passenger from
source, or opportunity to know of such threatened

for it, it did not constitute an assault upon her." Friar v. (
N. W. Ry. Co. (Tex. Civ. App. 1907), 101 S. W. Rep. 274.

"While train men have the right, and it is their duty to
a white passenger to leave a coach set apart for negro pai
yet he having gone into it to deliver packages to a colored pɛ
and stayed there only a few minutes, and being in the act of
when the train men assaulted and ejected him, the carrier i
therefor." St. Louis, etc., Ry. Co. v. Mynott (Ark. 1907), 10!
Rep. 380.

"A railroad is liable for a rape committed on a passengɛ
brakeman." Garvik v. Burlington, etc., Ry. Co. (Iowa 190ɩ
N. W. Rep. 327.

[52] Nieto v. Clark, 1 Cliff. (U. S.) 145; Louisville, etc., R.
Ballard, 85 Ky. 307; 7 Am. St. Rep. 600; Campbell v. Pullm
Co., 42 Fed. Rep. 484; Battan v. Alabama, etc., R. Co., 77 Al
54 Am. Rep. 80; 23 Am. & Eng. R. Cas. 514.

[53] Craker v. Chicago, etc., R. Co., 36 Wis. 657; 9 Am. Ry. Re

[54] Battan v. Alabama, etc., R. Co., 77 Ala. 591; 54 Am. Rep.
Am. & Eng. R. Cas. 514.

is essential in all cases to charge the railroad company for an assault by a third person,[55] and if a female passenger is put off the train at a time and place where no such danger was threatened, with an escort of whom there was no reason to suspect such a criminal act, the railroad company would not be liable for the subsequent criminal assault upon such a passenger by her escort, for the reason that the negligence of the railroad company, even if there was a wrongful ejection of the passenger, could not be said to be the proximate cause of the injury.[56]

§ 739. **Punitive damages for insults or assaults.**— The carrier is held, in law, to be so far personally present and represented by its employees, perpetrating insult upon or assaulting passengers, as to render it liable for exemplary or punitive damages, in cases where the nature of the assault or insult is sufficiently aggravated to justify such damages.

In a leading Georgia case,[57] it was held that where a conductor of a train, without apparent provocation, rudely assaulted a passenger; used toward him grossly insulting and opprobious language and caught hold of him roughly and pulled him to the end of the car, threatening to kill him; accompanying the threat with a motion as if to draw a pistol, and spitting in his face, the railroad company was

[55] Pennsylvania R. Co. v. Hinds, 53 Pa. St. 512; Craker v. Chicago, etc., R. Co., 36 Wis. 657.

[56] Sira v. Wabash R. Co., 115 Mo. 127; 21 S. W. Rep. 905. In this case a young lady between sixteen and seventeen years, was put off the train at a station short of her destination, as her train did not stop there. The conductor was assured by a man with her that he would see her safely to a hotel. He took her to a saloon, instead, where he kept her a prisoner for five hours and criminally assaulted her. The trial court held that the railroad company was not liable for this assault and the Supreme Court, in an opinion by Judge McFarlane, affirmed this decision.

[57] East Tennessee, etc., R. Co. v. Fleetwood, 15 S. E. Rep. 778.

liable for punitive damages and it was no defense or avoidance of the right to recover such damages that the passenger had spoken insultingly of the conductor's sister-in-law, as it was not shown that such language was so recent as to have induced the conduct on the part of the conductor, while under the heat of passion.

This was the reason given by the court why the assault was not justified by the offensive language used, but in most States another and all-sufficient reason would be that words, however opprobrious, will not justify an assault, although they might justify an eviction of the passenger using offensive language in a car.[58]

But the acts on the part of the conductor, in the case referred to, were certainly sufficient, if any case can be found to justify such damages, where punitive damages ought to be allowed, and other cases cited in the note further illustrate the rule where such damages are allowed.[59]

[58] Mitchell v. United Railways Co., 125 Mo. App. 13 (by Judge Bland); 102 S. W. Rep. 661; Berryman v. Cox, 73 Mo. App. 67; Crutchen v. Big Four R. R. Co., 132 Mo. App. 311; 1 Kinkead on Torts, § 208; 1 Cooley on Torts (3 ed.), p. 289.

[59] "In an action against a railroad for wrongfully ejecting plaintiff from defendant's train, evidence that the assault on plaintiff by defendant's conductor was unprovoked, and the conduct of the conductor wanton, reckless, and malicious, justified the assessment of punitive damages." Williams v. St. Louis, etc., R. Co. (Mo. App. 1906), 96 S. W. Rep. 307.

"Where a passenger is wrongfully ejected from a train, he is entitled to recover a reasonable compensation for the indignity and mental suffering whenever such suffering is the natural and proximate result of the wrong done, if the wrong gives the party a cause of action." Lindsay v. Oregon Short Line R. Co. (Utah 1907), 90 Pac. Rep. 984.

"Where, in an action against a carrier for wrongfully ejecting plaintiff from a train, plaintiff testified that on his tendering the fare, after he had first refused to pay fare, the conductor said that it was too late, and that he had been waiting for an opportunity to expel plaintiff from the train, and the conductor testified that he had had trouble with plaintiff before about fares, and was a 'little sore' at plaintiff, and there was evidence that the conductor, after refusing to accept plaintiff's

§ 740. **Sportive acts of employees.**— The cases are not numerous, wherein the employees of the carrier have injured passengers, as a result of some sportive act not intended to cause injury, but a few of the courts have passed upon this question.

In a recent Massachusetts case,[60] a passenger was injured by the breaking of a window pane, by a missile thrown by a conductor of another car, at the party in charge of the car whereon the passenger was riding, and the railroad company was held liable for the injury. In a Missouri case,[61] where the conductor not only failed to extend protection to a passenger, but joined in an attempt to frighten him, by threats of robbing him and binding him and of killing him and throwing him from the train, as a result of which the passenger jumped from the train, the company was also held responsible.

While, of course, these injuries are analogous to injuries resulting from the malicious or wanton acts of employees of the carrier, it is none the less difficult to determine how such acts could be held to be within the scope of the duties of an employee, and for this reason it was held, in Alabama,[62] that the railroad company was not liable for an injury to a passenger, resulting from a playful attempt of an employee to strike another employee, and accidentally striking the plaintiff, who was about to embark on the train; and a

tender of fare, threw him violently off the train at a place distant from a residence or station, the question of malice on the part of the conductor was for the jury." Beck v. Quincy & C. R. Co. (Mo. App. 1908), 108 S. W. Rep. 132.

[60] Hayne v. Union Ry. Co., 189 Mass. 551; 76 N. E. Rep. 219; 3 L. R. A. (N. S.) 605.

[61] Spohn v. Missouri Pacific Ry. Co., 87 Mo. 74; 101 Mo. 417; 14 S. W. Rep. 880.

[62] Goodloe v. Memphis, etc., R. Co., 107 Ala. 233; 18 So. Rep. 166; 54 Am. St. Rep. 67; 29 L. R. A. 729.

similar rule was announced in a Mississippi case,[63] where a colored boy was so frightened by a baggage man, that he jumped from an express car and was injured, as it was held that the railroad company was not responsible, unless it was shown that the baggage man was about the business of his employer when he quit his own car and went into the express car.

. **§ 741. Communication of contagious disease.**— Where a railroad company has notice of the fact that an employee, such as a station agent, has a contagious disease, it will be liable for the communication of such disease to a passenger, where he was retained by the railroad company, in a position to come in contact with passengers, after knowledge of his disease.[64]

But although a station agent is infected with a contagious disease and while waiting on a passenger, infects him, in the sale of a ticket, the railroad company will not be liable for damages by reason of the injury to the passenger by being infected with the disease, unless the officers of the company had notice of the fact, for the company's knowledge of the diseased condition of the agent is an essential element of the charge of negligence on its part.[65]

[63] Louisville, etc., R. Co. v. Douglas, 69 Miss. 723; 11 So. Rep. 933; 30 Am. St. Rep. 582.

[64] Paddock v. Atchison, etc., R. Co., 37 Fed. Rep. 841.

[65] Long v. Chicago, etc., R. Co., 48 Kansas, 28; 28 Pac. Rep. 977; 15 L. R. A. 319; 53 Am. & Eng. R. Cas. 45.

CHAPTER XXIX.

INJURIES BY FELLOW PASSENGERS.

§ 742. **Protection from, generally.**— The duty of protection, which a carrier owes to a passenger, includes a responsibility for the unlawful acts of fellow passengers, when, by the exercise of the very high degree of care which the carrier owes to the passenger, during the transit, the wrongful acts could have been foreseen and prevented.[1]

Where the conduct of a passenger, therefore, is such as to render his presence dangerous to fellow passengers, or such as will occasion them serious annoyance or discomfort, it is not only the legal right, but the duty of the railroad company, or its employees in charge of the train, to exclude such a passenger from the train,[2] and if, instead of performing

---

[1] Texas, etc., R. Co. v. Johnson, 2 Texas Civ. App. 154.

[2] Atchison, etc., R. Co. v. Weber, 33 Kansas 543; 6 Pac. Rep. 877; 21 Am. & Eng. R. Cas. 418.

this duty, the carrier permits the unruly passenger to remain on its train until he commits some act resulting in the
injury of the other passengers, the carrier will be liable for
the injury so occasioned.[3]

§ 743. **Basis of carrier's liability in such cases.**— While
the rule is well settled that the carrier is not an insurer of
the safety of its passengers from the acts of fellow passengers, but is bound to exercise proper care and vigilance to
protect them from the wrongful acts of other passengers,
there is a difference of opinion, in the cases, as to the exact
legal principle upon which the duty of the carrier rests, some
of the cases holding that the liability depends upon the application of the maxim *respondeat superior,*[4] and others
holding that there is no such privity of contract between the
railroad company and a disorderly passenger as to render
the former liable for the acts of the latter on the principle of
respondeat superior.[5]

It would seem, upon principle, that the Pennsylvania
court[6] is right and that there is no such privity between the
carrier and a disorderly passenger, as to render the former
liable for the acts of the latter, on the principle of the

[3] Atchison, etc., R. Co. v. Weber, *supra.*

"A domestic railroad company is liable for indignities received
by a passenger from a fellow passenger on the cars of such road
operated by a lessee." Franklin v. Atlanta, etc., Ry. Co. (S. C. 1906),
54 S. E. Rep. 578, 74 S. C. 332.

"A common carrier is under the same strict obligation to protect a passenger from the negligence or willful conduct of a fellow
passenger that it is to carry him safely." Farrier v. Colorado
Springs Rapid Transit Co. (Colo. 1908), 95 Pac. Rep. 294.

[4] New Orleans, etc., R. Co. v. Burke, 53 Miss. 200; 24 Am. Rep.
689; Britton v. Atlanta, etc., R. Co., 88 No. Car. 536; 43 Am. Rep.
749.

[5] Pittsburg, etc., R. Co. v. Hinds, 53 Pa. St. 512; 91 Am. Dec.
224.

[6] Pittsburg, etc., R. Co. v. Hinds, *supra.*

maxim *respondeat superior,* but if the employees of the train failed to do all that they could to protect a passenger from the wrongful acts of disorderly persons on the train, the ground of complaint would seem to be the violation of the contract to safely carry the passenger injured and the negligence of the employees in charge of the train would be the gist of the action.

§ 744. **Degree of care exacted.**— The authorities are not agreed as to the degree of care due from the carrier toward a passenger, to protect him from injuries at the hands of fellow passengers, some of the cases — perhaps a minority — holding that the railroad company is bound to exercise the most extraordinary degree of care and skill to prevent injuries from such a source to its passengers,[7] while the weight of authority is to the effect that in guarding passengers from injuries at the hands of other passengers, the carrier is held only to the exercise of reasonable or ordinary care and diligence.[8]

As this is not an incident to ordinary travel, or an injury due to the acts of the agents or employees of the railroad company, the greater number of cases would seem to accord with the right reason of the situation, for the proposition that an extraordinary degree of care is exacted from the carrier is held not to apply to injuries received from its own premises or appliances, at the station, prior or subsequent to the journey, but such high degree of care is usually exacted only during the voyage and is held to apply only to the road-

[7] Louisville, etc., R. Co. v. Finn, 16 Ky. L. R. 57; Pittsburg, etc., R. Co. v. Pillow, 76 Pa. St. 510; 18 Am. Rep. 424; Kinney v. Louisville, etc., R. Co., 99 Ky. 59; 34 S. W. Rep. 1066.

[8] Chicago, etc., R. Co. v. Pillsbury, 123 Ill. 9; 14 N. E. Rep. 23; 5 Am. St. Rep. 483; Exton v. Central R. Co., 63 N. J. L. 356; 46 Atl. Rep. 1099; 56 L. R. A. 508; Tall v. Baltimore, etc., Co., 90 Md. 248; 44 Atl. Rep. 1007; 47 L. R. A. 120; Illinois, etc., R. Co. v. Minor, 69 Miss. 710; 11 So. Rep. 401; 16 L. R. A. 627.

bed, track, train and appliances under the care and control
of the carrier.[9]

§ 745. **Turbulent or violent passengers should be removed.**
— The law implies a contract upon the part of the carrier
fo. the protection of the party carried, from the negligence
or wanton injury by fellow passengers and for any violation of this implied contract the carrier will be liable in an
action of tort,[10] for it is everywhere agreed that carriers
must protect their passengers from injuries due to the wrongful acts of their copassengers.[11]

The carrier is bound to use the utmost practicable care
to protect those in transit from violence and insults from
those on the train, including fellow passengers. A failure
to do so will render the carrier liable for any damage
naturally and directly resulting therefrom.[12] And if it
be necessary to enable the carrier to discharge this duty,
the conductor should stop the train and summon his coemployees along with those passengers who are willing to
assist, and eject from the train any person or passenger
guilty of disorderly, insulting, or threatening conduct, and
failing to do this, in the event of an injury to a passenger
by a violent or unruly passenger, the carrier would be responsible.[13]

[9] Chicago, etc., R. Co. v. Pillsbury, *supra.*

[10] Winnegar v. Central Pass R. Co., 85 Ky. 547; 4 S. W. Rep. 237;
34 Am. & Eng. R. Cas. 462.

[11] New Orleans, etc., R. Co. v. Burke, 53 Miss. 200; 9 Am. Ry. Rep.
308; Eads v. Metropolitan R. Co. (by Judge Ellison), 43 Mo. App.
536.

[12] Spohn v. Missouri Pacific Ry. Co., 101 Mo. 417; 14 S. W. Rep.
880.

[13] New Orleans, etc., R. Co. v. Burke, *supra.*

"Where, in an action against a carrier for an assault committed
on plaintiff by another passenger, with which the conductor made no
effort to interfere, it appeared that after the difficulty, a certain person riding in the car led the assaulting party from the car, it was

§ 746. **Acts of drunken or disorderly passengers.**— While the employees of a railroad company will not be authorized to remove a passenger, merely because he may be under the influence of liquor, if there is no danger of his becoming dangerous to other passengers,[14] it is the duty of the employees of the railroad company to remove all drunken and disorderly passengers, where their conduct is such as to threaten danger to other passengers on the same train.[15]

If the employees have notice of the disorderly conduct of a passenger and fail to take any precaution to prevent an injury to other passengers, by the wrongful act of such a passenger, the railroad company will be liable to a passenger injured by the wrongful act of a drunken or disorderly passenger on the same train.[16]

But to render the carrier liable for an injury due to the wrongful act of another passenger, it must appear that the employees of the carrier had knowledge or opportunity to know of the threatened injury and that by prompt intervention, on their part, it could have been prevented or mitigated, and unless such knowledge or opportunity to know of the threatened injury is shown there is no resulting liability.[17]

not error to admit evidence to show that the former was a detective employed by the carrier." Norfolk, etc., Ry. Co. v. Birchfield (Va. 1906), 54 S. E. Rep. 879.

[14] Putnam v. Broadway, etc., R. Co., 15 Abb. Pr. (N. Y.), 383.

[15] Marquette v. Chicago, etc., R. Co., 33 Iowa, 562.

[16] Pittsburg, etc., R. Co. v. Pillow, 76 Pa. St. 510. But see, *contra*, Pittsburg, etc,, R. Co. v. Hinds (53 Pa. St. 512), holding that there is no liability for the wrongful act of disorderly passengers, because of absence of privity, essential to a liability, under rule *respondeat superior*. See, as sustaining text, St. Louis, etc., R. Co. v. Mackie, 71 Texas 491; 9 S. W. Rep. 451; 1 L. R. A. 667; 37 Am. & Eng. R. Cas. 94.

[17] Sira v. Wabash R. Co., 115 Mo. 127; 21 S. W. Rep. 905; 58 Am. & Eng. R. Cas. 538; Brown v. Chicago, etc., R. Co., 139 Fed. Rep. 972; 72 C. C. A. 20; 2 L. R. A. (N. S.) 105.

§ 747. **Discharge of firearms.**— Where a passenger enters
a car, armed with a pistol, and it is apparent that he is
turbulently disposed, either 1rom excessive drinking or otherwise, it is the duty of the conductor and employees of the
train to restrain him and disarm him or to remove him from
the train, so that he cannot injure other passengers by the
premature or reckless discharge of the pistol.[18]

If the employees of a railroad company negligently fail in
the discharge of this duty toward the passengers of their
employer, by disarming a turbulent passenger, armed with
a pistol, and likely to cause harm to the other passengers on
the train, and a passenger, in no way responsible for such
an assault upon himself, is injured by the careless or reckless discharge of a pistol in the hands of such a vicious and
turbulent passenger, the railroad company will be held liable
to the injured passenger for the injury so received.[19]

§ 748. **Acts of insane passengers.**— A common carrier is
not obliged, as a matter of law, to receive as a passenger,
an insane person, or one whose physical or mental condition
is such that his presence may cause injury or subsequent

"A carrier's employees may eject a drunken and disorderly passenger, when necessary to protect other passengers against his insults
or violence; but, if injury to another passenger could have been
avoided by requiring the drunken passenger to be and remain seated,
the carrier cannot avoid liability for the injury by the employee's
failure to perform that duty." Montgomery Traction Co. v. Whatley
(Ala. 1907), 44 So. Rep. 538.

[18] King v. Ohio, etc., R. Co., 22 Fed. Rep. 413; 18 Am. & Eng. R.
Cas. 386.

[19] Illinois, etc., R. Co. v. Minor, 69 Miss. 710; 11 So. Rep. 101;
16 L. R. A. 627; 52 Am. & Eng. R. Cas. 441.

In Tall v. Baltimore, etc., R. Co. (90 Md. 248; 44 Atl. Rep. 1007;
47 L. R. A. 120), it was decided that a carrier was not liable for the
shooting of a passenger by a fellow passenger, where the passengers
had been playing cards in the smoking room, and a quarrel arose over
the game of cards, as it could not reasonably have been foreseen that
this would occur.

discomfort to the other passengers, and the carrier has a right to exclude from its trains any one whose condition is such that a possibility of danger may be thrown upon the other passengers if he is admitted as a passenger. And where an insane person is admitted as a passenger, as soon as the railroad employees acquire notice of his condition, whether such knowledge is acquired before or at the time he becomes a passenger, or from his acts subsequent to the commencement of the journey, the railroad company is charged with the duty of exercising proper care for the protection of the other passengers upon the same train.[20]

The degree of care imposed upon the carrier, to restrain or care for an insane passenger, so as to avoid injury to other passengers, is said to be of the highest character. If the safety or comfort of the other passengers will not be imperiled, the insane person may be taken to the end of his journey, or, if the safety of other passengers demands it, he may be removed from the train at the first station, where he may be properly cared for. So long as he remains on the train, however, the company is bound to do whatever in the way of restraint or isolation is reasonably demanded, for the safety of the other passengers.[21]

In determining whether or not the railway company has adopted proper precautions to prevent injury to other passengers, by an insane passenger, it is generally an issue for the jury to decide, from all the facts and circumstances in evidence, what the situation demanded of the carrier; but if the employees of the railroad company, in the discharge of their duty, could not have reasonably anticipated that a failure to eject or restrain the insane person might result in his

[20] Meyer v. St. Louis, etc., R. Co., 54 Fed. Rep. 116; 10 U. S. App. 677; 4 C. C. A. 221; 58 Am. & Eng. R. Cas. 111.
[21] Meyer v. St. Louis, etc., R. Co., *supra.*

doing injury to his fellow passengers, their f₁
strain or eject him would not constitute neglige₁

§ 749. **Liability for assaults by fellow passe**
of the doctrine that the railroad company is bo
cise the highest practicable degree of care and
prevent injury to its passengers, during the per
the contract for transportation, arises the rule ₁
rier is likewise bound, through its employees,
a high degree of care to protect its passengers aga
from whatever sources arising, which might b₁
anticipated or naturally expected to occur, in vi₁
circumstances and the number and character of
on the train.   And if this duty is neglected a₁
ger is injured by reason of the conduct of a fello
if the injury could reasonably have been an
naturally expected, the cases are almost unanim
ing that the railroad company is responsible
injury.[23]

But a railroad company is not liable for an
passenger, caused by the wrongful act of a f₁
ger, if the circumstances are not sufficient to l
the employees of the company to have reasonabl₁

[22] Meyer v. St. Louis, etc., R. Co., *supra*.
[23] Flint v. Norwich, etc., Co., 34 Conn. 554; Mullen v. '
R. Co., 46 Minn. 474; 47 Am. & Eng. R. Cas. 649;
York, etc., R. Co., 72 N. Y. 59; Spohn v. Missouri P
87 Mo. 74; 101 Mo. 418; 14 S. W. Rep. 880; 26 Am. &
252, note; Jackson v. Missouri Pacific Ry. Co., 104 Mo.
Rep. 413; Sachrowitz v. Atchison, etc., R. Co., 37 K₁
Am. & Eng. R. Cas. 382; Holly v. Atlanta, etc., R. Co
Britton v. Atlantic, etc., R. Co., 88 No. Car. 536; 18 ₁
Cas. 391; Pittsburg, etc., R. Co. v. Pillow, 76 Pa. St. (
South, etc., R. Co., 77 Ala. 591; 23 Am. & Eng. R. Cas.
etc., R. Co. v. Pillsbury, 123 Ill. 9; 31 Am. & Eng
Felton v. Chicago, etc., R. Co., 69 Iowa 577; 27 Am. &
229; Coleman v. New York, etc., R. Co., 106 Mass. 16₁

doing injury to his fellow passengers, their failure to restrain or eject him would not constitute negligence.[22]

§ 749. **Liability for assaults by fellow passengers.**— Out of the doctrine that the railroad company is bound to exercise the highest practicable degree of care and diligence to prevent injury to its passengers, during the performance of the contract for transportation, arises the rule that the carrier is likewise bound, through its employees, to exercise a high degree of care to protect its passengers against violence from whatever sources arising, which might be reasonably anticipated or naturally expected to occur, in view of all the circumstances and the number and character of the persons on the train. And if this duty is neglected and a passenger is injured by reason of the conduct of a fellow passenger, if the injury could reasonably have been anticipated or naturally expected, the cases are almost unanimous in holding that the railroad company is responsible for such an injury.[23]

But a railroad company is not liable for an injury to a passenger, caused by the wrongful act of a fellow passenger, if the circumstances are not sufficient to have enabled the employees of the company to have reasonably anticipated

[22] Meyer v. St. Louis, etc., R. Co., *supra*.

[23] Flint v. Norwich, etc., Co., 34 Conn. 554; Mullen v. Wisconsin, etc., R. Co., 46 Minn. 474; 47 Am. & Eng. R. Cas. 649; Reeks v. New York, etc., R. Co., 72 N. Y. 59; Spohn v. Missouri Pacific Ry. Co., 87 Mo. 74; 101 Mo. 418; 14 S. W. Rep. 880; 26 Am. & Eng. R. Cas. 252, note; Jackson v. Missouri Pacific Ry. Co., 104 Mo. 452; 16 S. W. Rep. 413; Sachrowitz v. Atchison, etc., R. Co., 37 Kansas, 212; 34 Am. & Eng. R. Cas. 382; Holly v. Atlanta, etc., R. Co., 61 Ga. 215; Britton v. Atlantic, etc., R. Co., 88 No. Car. 536; 18 Am. & Eng. R. Cas. 391; Pittsburg, etc., R. Co. v. Pillow, 76 Pa. St. 510; Batton v. South, etc., R. Co., 77 Ala. 591; 23 Am. & Eng. R. Cas. 514; Chicago, etc., R. Co. v. Pillsbury, 123 Ill. 9; 31 Am. & Eng. R. Cas. 24; Felton v. Chicago, etc., R. Co., 69 Iowa 577; 27 Am. & Eng. R. Cas. 229; Coleman v. New York, etc., R. Co., 106 Mass. 160.

or foretold that the injury was apt to occur, for in such case, there is an absence of any negligence upon which to base the recovery.[24] It was accordingly held in Iowa, that a railroad company was not liable for the death of a passenger, where he was killed by being thrown from a platform car, by other passengers, when there was nothing in the conduct of the passengers at the time the train left the last station, from which the employees in charge of the train could reasonably anticipate that an assault would be committed on the deceased.[25]

§ 750. **Rape committed by fellow passenger.**— Where the conduct of the carrier's employees is such as to enable a court to say that they ought, under the circumstances of the case, to have foreseen that an assault or rape was liable to be committed upon a female passenger by a fellow passenger, the railroad company would be responsible for the injury resulting from such an act, for this would be a violation of the implied contract to protect passengers from any violence that a high degree of care could avoid, on the carrier's part.[26]

But if the circumstances connected with the assault or rape of a female passenger are not sufficient to show that the employees of the carrier ought, by the exercise of a high degree of care, to have foreseen or anticipated such a wrongful act, on a passenger's part, the carrier will not be

---

[24] Felton v. Chicago, etc., R. Co., 69 Iowa 577; 29 N. W. Rep. 618; 27 Am. & Eng. R. Cas. 229.

[25] Felton v. Chicago, etc., R. Co., *supra*.

"In an action against a railroad company by a passenger because of a violent assault made upon him by another passenger in the sight of the conductor who failed to protect him, an instruction that the passenger must be in serious danger, before the duty of the conductor to protect him against assault arises, is erroneous." Hillman v. Georgia, R. etc., Co. (Ga. 1906), 56 S. E. Rep. 68, 126 Ga. 814.

[26] Nieto v. Clark, 1 Cliff. (U. S.) 145.

answerable for such a criminal act, on the part of a fellow passenger, against a female passenger.[27]   It was accordingly held, in a Missouri case,[28] that the mere fact that a male passenger, in the hearing of the conductor of the train, offered to conduct a female passenger to a hotel, would not be sufficient to suggest to the conductor that such passenger intended the assault and ravishment of the plaintiff, so as to render the railroad company liable therefor, and although the conductor was guilty of a wrongful act in requiring the plaintiff, a young lady between sixteen and seventeen years of age, to leave the train before arrival at her destination, the subsequent rape committed on her by a male passenger, who left the train at the same station, and who decoyed her into a saloon, under the pretense of conducting her to a hotel, was not, in any sense, the direct or immediate consequence of the wrongful ejection of the female passenger, where the evidence showed that the station where she alighted was not an inappropriate or unsafe place for a youthful and inexperienced female, traveling alone, to remain between trains.

§ 751. **Altercations between employees and passengers.**—If an altercation is had between employees of the carrier and another passenger, as a result of which a passenger is injured, the carrier will be responsible in damages for the injury so inflicted, unless the employees of the carrier had taken due care to avoid injury to the injured passenger, for it is analogous to an injury by the employees of the carrier themselves and the carrier is held answerable, in all cases, for injuries of this nature.[29]

[27] Sira v. Wabash R. Co., 115 Mo. 127; 21 S. W. Rep. 905.
[28] Sira v. Wabash R. Co., *supra*.
[29] Penney v. Atlantic Coast Line R. Co., 133 No. Car. 221; 45 S. E. Rep. 563; 63 L. R. A. 497.

In a North Carolina case,[30] it was held that the employees of a train should give timely warning to the passengers about to alight from it, of the danger of possible injury in case an altercation took place between the employees and another passenger, which had resulted in the exhibition and apparent attempt to use a deadly weapon, on the part of the disorderly passenger and for a failure to so warn the passengers, in case one of their number was shot and injured in the altercation, the railroad company would be liable for this neglect to warn the passenger injured.

§ 752. **Missile thrown by fellow passenger.**— Knowledge of the probable danger of an injury to a passenger, by a missile thrown by a fellow passenger, would be necessary to charge the carrier with liability for such an injury and in the absence of such knowledge, there would generally be no liability for such an injury, due to the unexpected act of another passenger, causing such an injury, as knowledge of a passenger's danger, or of facts and circumstances from which the danger may be reasonably inferred, is necessary to fix the liability of the carrier in this class of cases.[31]

But a railroad company would be liable for an injury to a passenger by a missile thrown through the window by a fellow passenger, who had just alighted from the same train, where the employees knew that the disorderly passenger was intoxicated and had, before leaving the train, mistreated other passengers and had threatened that on arrival at his destination, he would be revenged upon other passengers, who had interfered to prevent the boisterous and disorderly conduct that he had been guilty of on the train.[32]

[30] Penney v. Atlantic Coast Line R. Co., *supra*.

[31] Jackson v. Missouri, etc., R. Co., 104 Mo. 452; 16 S. W. Rep. 413; Texas, etc., R. Co. v. Storey (Texas), 83 S. W. Rep. 852; 1 Fetter, Carr. Pass. § 98.

[32] Spangler v. St. Joseph, etc., R. Co., 68 Kansas, 47; 74 Pac. Rep. 607; 104 Am. St. Rep. 391; 63 L. R. A. 634.

§ 753. **Carrier's knowledge of threatened danger.**— To render a railroad company liable for an injury to one of its passengers, because of the wrongful act of a fellow passenger, it must be shown that its employees had knowledge or opportunity to know of the threatened injury and that by prompt intervention, it could have been avoided by them.[33] If the passenger, suing for the injury, is unable to show that the employees of the railroad company knew of the threatened injury, or that from the circumstances in connection with the accident and the character and number of the passengers on the train, they should reasonably have anticipated that the injury would result from the wrongful conduct of the passengers present, there can be no recovery.[34]

It is accordingly held, in New York,[35] that a railroad company is not liable because a drunken passenger makes a wanton and unprovoked assault upon another passenger on the same train, where there was no reason for believing that he would injure anyone and the employees had no notice that he was an unsafe and dangerous man.

In Brown v. Chicago, etc., R. Co. (139 Fed. Rep. 972; 72 C. C. A. 20; 2 L. R. A. (N. S.) 105), a railroad company was held not liable for an injury to a passenger by a missile thrown through the car window by a disorderly passenger, who had threatened to even up with the conductor, on reaching his station, as it was held that the act was unexpected and could not have been foreseen.

[33] Sira v. Wabash, etc., Co., 115 Mo. 127; 21 S. W. Rep. 905; 58 Am. & Eng. R. Cas. 538; New Orleans, etc., R. Co. v. Burke, 53 Miss. 200; 9 Am. Ry. Rep. 308.

[34] Spohn v. Missouri Pacific Ry. Co., 87 Mo. 74; 26 Am. & Eng. R. Cas. 252.

[35] Putnam v. Broadway, etc., R. Co., 15 Abb. Pr. N. S. (N. Y.) 383. See, also, Brown v. Chicago, etc., R. Co. 139 Fed. Rep. 972; 72 C. C. A. 20; 2 L. R. A. (N. S.) 105.

"A carrier is bound to protect a passenger from indignities as against a fellow passenger only where it has reason or notice to anticipate improper conduct." Franklin v. Atlanta, etc., Ry. Co. (S. C. 1906), 54 S. E. Rep. 578; 74 S. C. 332.

§ 754. **Duty of injured passenger to claim carrier's protection.**— Of course it cannot be claimed, with any authority to base such contention upon, that it is the duty of a passenger to claim protection from the employees of the carrier and in failing to do so, he forfeits his right to recover for injuries received by turbulent passengers, on the same train, for it is the duty of the carrier to protect the passenger, whether such protection is sought or not. But the injured passenger ought to be in the peace himself, and if he is not, but participates in the disturbance, or consents to the affray or injury, he is certainly not entitled to recover, under the familiar rule, *volenti non fit injuria.*

Considering this contention, in a Mississippi case,[36] Judge Woods, for the Supreme Court of Mississippi, said: "The third contention, * * * to the effect that Minor voluntarily placed himself in a position of exceptional danger, consented to the risks of the riotous conduct of his fellow passengers, and did not claim protection of the company, strongly impresses us, and, if supported by evidence, would seem to put this case without the general rule, that imposes liability upon the railroad company for injuries inflicted upon one passenger by his fellow passengers. If Minor voluntarily put himself in a position of known, apparent and exceptional danger, and took the chances of being hurt from his drunken and disorderly fellow passengers, * * * and if he continued to retain his position in the face of great danger, without any effort to avoid the same, and without any complaint to the railroad company's servants, we would be inclined to the opinion that his case was ex-

---

[36] Of course these remarks of the court are more or less outside the record, as found by the court, and hence, obiter, but at the same time, the court passed upon the defense and held that if the evidence justified it, it would be a good defense to the action. Illinois, etc., R. Co. v. Minor, 69 Miss. 710; 11 So. Rep. 101; 16 L. R. A. 627; 52 Am. & Eng. R. Cas. 441.

ceptional and not embraced in the rule announced in the case of Burke." [37]

§ 755. **Passenger with contagious disease.**— The duty of the carrier toward its passengers is not confined alone to cases where the passengers may be threatened with injury from the wrongful overt act of an insane or drunken passenger, but if the lives or health of other passengers are threatened by a person suffering from some loathsome or contagious disease, it is equally the duty of the carrier, in the care and protection of those entrusting their lives and safety to its care, to remove or restrain such person, so that the disease will not be communicated to the other passengers. [38]

It has been held that if a passenger is found to be broken out with an eruption which the best medical advice obtainable pronounces to be smallpox, and the employees of the carrier have a well-grounded and honest belief that the passenger is suffering from smallpox, then it is the duty of the employees in charge of the train to remove such a person from the train, to the end that the other passengers may not be exposed to the disease, if it should turn out that the suspected passenger had smallpox. [39]

§ 756. **Right of colored passenger to protection.**— Of course there is no reason why a carrier would have the right to distinguish between the protection that the law compels it to afford its passengers, based upon the color of the passenger, and that it has no right to refuse the same protection

[37] This case referred to by the court, is that of New Orleans, etc., R. Co. v. Burke, 53 Miss. 200; 9 Am. Ry. Rep. 308, criticised in above cited decision.

[38] Paddock v. Atchison, etc., R. Co., 37 Fed. Rep. 841; 4 L. R. A. 231.

[39] Paddock v. Atchison, etc., R. Co., *supra.*

to a colored passenger that it will be compelled to afford to a white passenger, was decided in a Georgia case.[40]

The plaintiff, a colored passenger on the defendant's train, had paid his fare and was in his proper place. During the course of his journey he was insulted, assaulted and beaten. He was cursed and abused by two drunken passengers. The conductor was appealed to and refused to interfere. Plaintiff was made to dance and sing and was subjected to many indignities. Speaking for the court, in passing upon the validity of the verdict in favor of the plaintiff, Gober, J., said: "These men, whose acts are set forth in the record, amused themselves by tormenting and insulting the plaintiff. It seems that the conductor, signaling, with a wink, was willing that it should go on. The defendant company, through its representative, forgot for a time that it had the plaintiff's money in its coffers, and was under contract and obligation to carry him safely and comfortably. It would be strange, indeed, if there were no law to extend protection to passengers under such circumstances." And the judgment of the trial court was affirmed.

[40] Richmond, etc., R. Co. v. Jefferson, 52 Am. & Eng. R. Cas. 438.

CHAPTER XXX.

§ 757. **Liability for, generally.**— It was recently decided, in a Georgia case,[1] that whenever a carrier, through its agents or employees, knew, or had opportunity to know, of a threatened injury to a passenger, from a third person, whether such person was a passenger or not, or when the circumstances were such that injury to a passenger from such a source might be reasonably anticipated, if proper precautions were not taken to prevent such an injury, the carrier would be liable for damages therefor.

But the liability of the carrier depends entirely upon the presence or absence of evidence showing that its employees either knew or ought to have known, from the attendant facts and circumstances, that injury to the passenger carried was threatened or impending, and by the exercise of the

---

[1] Savannah, etc., R. Co. v. Boyle, 115 Ga. 836; 42 S. E. Rep. 242; 59 L. R. A. 104.

1144

degree of care due from the carrier, the injury could have been guarded against.[2]

§ 758. Degree of care to prevent.

— The Supreme Court of Minnesota, in a recent case,[3] had under discussion and determination, the degree of care that a railroad company owes its passengers to protect them against injuries from the wrongful acts of strangers. A passenger in a car was injured by a stone thrown by a young man on the street, and the accident occurred during a general strike on the railroad. In deciding what degree of care the carrier owed to the injured passenger, to avoid the accident, the court said: " In our opinion it would be unjust to require a carrier of passengers, either a steam or a street railway company, to exercise the utmost care and vigilance to guard and protect passengers from criminal acts of strangers, persons not under its control, or subject to its orders, and for whose acts it is not in any way responsible. And we hold, without further discussion as respects the acts of such strangers, that carriers of passengers are liable for the exercise of ordinary care and prudence only. Such carrier is liable for all injuries resulting from the acts of strangers, which are reasonably to be anticipated, under the particular circumstances, and which ordinary care and prudence, had they been exercised, would have prevented."

This decision is quoted by the Supreme Court of Missouri [4] and the same rule is adopted in Illinois,[5] with the more flexible qualification that even as to the acts of

[2] Brown v. Chicago, etc., R. Co., 139 Fed. Rep. 972; 72 C. C. A. 20; 2 L. R. A. (N. S.) 105.

[3] Fewings v. Mendenhall, 88 Minn. 336; 93 N. W. Rep. 127; 97 Am. St. Rep. 519; 60 L. R. A. 601.

[4] Woas v. Transit Co., 198 Mo. 664; 96 S. W. Rep. 1017; 7 L. R. A. (N. S.) 231.

[5] Chicago, etc., R. Co. v. Pillsbury, 123 Ill. 9; 14 N. E. Rep. 22; 5 Am. St. Rep. 483.

strangers, the circumstances of a given case may be such as to demand the highest degree of care on the part of the railroad company, to avoid injury to its passengers.

The rule, however, should be as stated by the Minnesota court, and whether or not the facts of a given case are sufficient to show negligence, is another question. But negligence, as to acts of third parties, ought never to consist in a failure to foresee or avoid that which the most extreme degree of care could have avoided, for wrongful conduct on the part of any one is not to be anticipated and right acting and due care to avoid injury to others is the accustomed thing, and a carrier has a right to expect this conduct from strangers toward its passengers.

§ 759. **No presumption of negligence.**— In injuries due to the acts of third persons, the familiar rule that evidence of the accident resulting in an injury to a passenger, is *prima facie* proof of negligence against the carrier can have no application, because the act resulting in the injury does not arise from any act or omission on the part of the railroad company. The presumption of negligence, in such cases, arises only where the thing causing the injury complained of, was under the exclusive control of the carrier or its employees. If the wrongful act causing the injury is that of a mere stranger or third person, it is incumbent upon the passenger to prove that the carrier or its employees failed to exercise reasonable or ordinary care to prevent it.[6]

Judge Gantt, for the Supreme Court of Missouri,[7] used this language, in answering the contention that negligence should be presumed in such a case: " It is clear, in this case, that the burden of showing negligence was upon the

[6] Fewings v. Mendenhall, 88 Minn. 336; 93 N. W. Rep. 127; 97 Am. St. Rep. 519; 60 L. R. A. 601.

[7] Woas v. St. Louis Transit Co., 198 Mo. 664; 96 S. W. Rep. 1017; 7 L. R. A. (N. S.) 231.

plaintiff, and that the presumption of negligence, which arises in favor of a passenger traveling on a train, from the mere fact of an accident, has no application to a case like this. Such a presumption only arises where the injury can be reasonably attributed to some defect in track, cars, or machinery, or the conduct of the servants (employees) in charge thereof." And the Supreme Court of Pennsylvania took the same view of the subject in an early case,[8] where it was said: "If the law declares, as it does, that there is no duty resting on any person to anticipate wrongful acts in others, and to take precautions against such acts, then the jury cannot say that the failure to take such precautions is a failure in duty, and negligence. Were it worth while, abundant authority might be cited to show that the law does not require anyone to presume that another may be an ac-

---

[8] Philadelphia, etc., R. Co. v. Hummell, 44 Pa. St. 375; 84 Am. Dec. 457. See, also, Fleming v. Pittsburg, etc., R. Co., 158 Pa. St. 130; 27 Atl. Rep. 858; 22 L. R. A. 351; 38 Am. St. Rep. 835; Spencer v. Chicago, etc., R. So., 105 Wis. 311; 81 N. W. Rep. 407; Wadsworth v. Boston, etc., R. Co., 182 Mass. 572; 66 N. E. Rep. 421.

A blow from a missile to a passenger, was held not to show negligence against the carrier, in Pennsylvania R. Co. v. McKinney, 124 Pa. St. 462; 17 Atl. Rep. 14; 2 L. R. A. 820; 10 Am. St. Rep. 601; Thomas v. Philadelphia, etc., R. Co., 148 Pa. St. 180; 23 Atl. Rep. 989; 15 L. R. A. 416.

Nor is there any presumption of negligence from proof of an injury from a rock falling from a hill side, Fleming v. Pittsburg, etc., R. Co., 158 Pa. St. 130; 27 Atl. Rep. 858; 38 Am. St. Rep. 835; 22 L. R. A. 351.

Or from sawdust blowing in passenger's eye, Wadsworth v. Boston, etc., R. Co., 182 Mass. 572; 66 N. E. Rep. 421.

Or a stream of water entering a car window, injuring a passenger. Spencer v. Chicago, etc., R. Co., 105 Wis. 311; 81 N. W. Rep. 407.

But if the injury is connected with the means of transportation, or the act of the carrier's employees, the presumption obtains. As where red hot cinder enters passenger's eye, Texas, etc., R. Co. v. Jumper, 24 Texas Civ. App. 671; 60 S. W. Rep. 797.

Or a passenger is hurt by piece of coal, thrown from tender, while waiting on the platform to take a train. Louisville, etc., R. Co. v. Reynolds, 24 Ky. L. R. 1402; 71 S. W. Rep. 516.

tive wrongdoer. It is too well founded in reason, however, to need authorities. We act upon it constantly and without it there could be no freedom of action."

§ 760. Wrong must have been anticipated.— In the case of injuries to passengers by the wrongful act of other passengers, so in the case of the wrongful act of a stranger or other third person, the wrong must have been one that could have been foreseen ·or anticipated and guarded against, by reasonable diligence, on the part of the carrier, or there will be no liability for such an injury.

In an Alabama case,[9] it was held that while it is the duty of a railroad company to protect its passengers against violence or disorderly conduct on the part of passengers or strangers, when such violence or disorderly conduct may reasonably be expected and prevented, yet it is not liable in an action for damages for a wrong when it is not shown that the company had notice of any facts which would justify the expectation that a wrong would be committed, the court, in the course of its opinion, saying: "All the cases upon the subject impose the qualification that the wrong or injury done the passenger by strangers must have been of such a character as that it might reasonably have been anticipated or naturally expected to occur."

And this statement of the rule has been approved in Virginia[10] and Missouri,[11] where it was said: "It is quite generally ruled by the courts of this country, that the liability of the defendant carrier, in such a case, grows not out of the fact that the passenger was injured, but out of the

[9] Batton v. South Alabama R. Co., 77 Ala. 591; 54 Am. Rep. 80.

[10] Ball v. Chesapeake, etc., R. Co., 93 Va. 44; 24 S. E. Rep. 467; 57 Am. St. Rep. 786; 32 L. R. A. 792.

[11] Woas v. Transit Co., 198 Mo. 664; 96 S. W. Rep. 1017; 7 L. R. A. (N. S.) 231; Sira v. Wabash R. Co., 115 Mo. 135; 21 S. W. Rep. 905; 37 Am. St. Rep. 386.

failure of the carrier's servants (employees) to afford protection, after they have reasonable grounds for believing that violence to the passenger is imminent; and it is necessary, therefore, in all such cases, to bring home to the conductor or other agent or officer of the company, knowledge or opportunity to know that the injury was threatened, and to show that, by his prompt intervention, he could have prevented or mitigated it."

§ 761. **Assaults that could have been prevented.**— According to the uniform tendency of the decisions, the carrier owes to the passenger the duty of protecting him from the violence and assaults of strangers or third persons, that could have been foreseen and guarded against, by the exercise of reasonable care on its part, and it will be held responsible for the neglect of its employees in this respect, when, by the exercise of proper care, the acts of violence might have been foreseen and guarded against. Of course a railroad company is not required, in law, to furnish a police force, sufficient, in all cases, to repel all force, when unexpected and suddenly offered, but it is none the less the duty of the carrier to furnish ready help sufficient to protect the passenger from assaults from every quarter which might reasonably be expected to occur under the particular circumstances of each case.[12]

The rule is illustrated by a North Carolina case,[13] where a negro woman and her associates entered a smoking car, intended for white passengers only, and an intruder, with

[12] New Orleans, etc., R. Co. v. Burke, 53 Miss. 200; Pittsburg, etc., R. Co. v. Hinds, 53 Pa. St. 512; Flint v. Norwich Tr. Co., 34 Conn. 554; Pittsburg, etc., R. Co. v. Pillow, 76 Pa. St. 510; Southern, etc., R. Co. v. Rice, 38 Kansas, 398; 16 Pac. Rep. 817; 34 Am. & Eng. R. Cas. 316; Batton v. South, etc., R. Co., 77 Ala. 591; 54 Am. Rep. 80; 23 Am. & Eng. R. Cas. 514.

[13] Britton v. Atlanta, etc., R. Co., 88 No. Car. 536; 43 Am. Rep. 749; 18 Am. & Eng. R. Cas. 391.

drunken and disorderly passengers, assaulted her and beat her and threw her out of the car, and the employees offered no resistance and furnished no protection from the assault. Speaking for the court, Ruffin, J., said: " Circumstances such as these ought to have aroused, if they did not, the apprehension of the officer for the safety of the plaintiff, and called for his constant and watchful interposition in her behalf, in order to protect her from insult and injury. His duty at that time was made so plain that the law itself will pronounce upon his conduct and declare to be inexcusablo his negligence in sending off upon other missions every other employee of the company and betaking himself to the baggage car, during the entire stay of the train at that depot. His dalliance, too, in going to her relief, when informed of the imminence of the outrage upon her rights, manifested such an indifference, on his part, as was inconsistent with her claims and his duty."

§ 762. **Assaults that were not anticipated.**— Before the carrier will be liable for an injury to a passenger by the wrongful act of a third person, the act of the third party must be one that could have been reasonably anticipated, by due care on the part of the carrier, and unless it could have been foreseen as likely to occur, the carrier will not be liable therefor.[14]

It was accordingly held, in an Iowa case,[15] that where there was nothing to show any circumstances calculated to warn the railroad employees of the possibility of an assault on a passenger, the railroad company would not be liable therefor. A carrier would not be liable for an assault upon

---

[14] Jackson v. Missouri Pacific Ry. Co., 104 Mo. 452; 16 S. W. Rep. 413; Tall v. Baltimore, etc., Co., 90 Md. 248; 47 L. R. A. 120.

[15] Felton v. Chicago, etc., R. Co., 69 Iowa 580; 29 N. W. Rep. 618; Mullan v. Wisconsin, etc., R. Co., 46 Minn. 474; 49 N. W. Rep. 249.

a passenger, by an intruder, at a time when the train crew had left the train, at a regular station, to eat their dinner, since the assault could not reasonably have been anticipated by them,[16] nor was the presence, upon a train, of two negro tramps, stealing a ride, sufficient to cause the employees on the train to expect that such tramps were armed with deadly weapons and to anticipate that when they were brought into the train they would make a murderous assault upon a passenger, in an effort to escape.[17]

§ 763. **Injuries from stones or missiles.**— That carriers of passengers are not liable for injuries to passengers caused by stones or missiles thrown by strangers, which they have no right to anticipate, is established by a large number of well-considered cases.[18] Notice of the existence of the danger, or of facts and circumstances from which danger could be reasonably anticipated, is essential, in all such cases, to fix the liability of the railroad company, for damages in failing to guard against it.[19]

In a Missouri case,[20] where a passenger in a car was in-

16 Thweatt v. Houston, etc., R. Co., 31 Texas Civ. App. 227; 71 S. W. Rep. 976.

17 Savannah, etc., R. Co. v. Boyle, 115 Ga. 836; 42 S. E. Rep. 242; 59 L. R. A. 104.

18 Pennsylvania R. Co. v. McKinney, 124 Pa. St. 462; 17 Atl. Rep. 14; 10 Am. St. Rep. 601; 2 L. R. A. 820; Fewings v. Mendenhall, 88 Minn. 336; 93 N. W. Rep. 127; 97 Am. St. Rep. 519; 60 L. R. A. 601; Thomas v. Philadelphia, etc., R. Co., 148 Pa. St. 180; 23 Atl. Rep. 989; 15 L. R. A. 416; Woas v. St. Louis Transit Co., 198 Mo. 664; 96 S. W. Rep. 1017; 7 L. R. A. (N. S.) 231.

19 Woas v. St. Louis Transit Co., *supra.*

20 Woas v. St. Louis Transit Co., 198 Mo. 664; 96 S. W. Rep. 1017; 7 L. R. A. (N. S.) 231; Sira v. Wabash R. Co., 115 Mo. 135; 21 S. W. Rep. 905; 37 Am. St. Rep. 386; Connell v. Chesapeake, etc., R. Co., 93 Va. 44; 32 L. R. A. 792; 24 S. E. Rep. 467; 57 Am. St. Rep. 786.

The carrier was held not to be responsible for an injury to a passenger's eye, by a piece of coal striking him through an open window,

jured by a rock thrown at the motorman, who had failed to stop the car for the wrongdoer, Judge Gantt for the court, said: " It being conceded that plaintiff's injury resulted from the unlawful, wanton, and wicked act of a stranger, over whom defendant had no control, was there anything in the evidence which would justify the Circuit Court in submitting to the jury whether the defendant could have reasonably anticipated that this stranger would have hurled the rock or other missile into the car where plaintiff was seated in time for the defendant's motorman to have taken steps to prevent it ? * * * There is not the slightest pretense that this motorman had any reason to expect this party to be on the track at this place, until his car approached him; nor is there the slightest evidence that he had any right to anticipate that this stranger would violate the law by throwing a deadly missile at the motorman."

§ 764. **Throwing switch — Derailment of train.**— The rule that the negligence of the carrier must be the proximate cause of the injury to a passenger, to enable the latter to recover damages for an injury received while the relation of passenger and carrier exists, applies to an injury due to a derailment of the train, caused by some third person, wrongfully throwing a switch,[21] or interfering with the track,[22] in such manner as to cause a derailment of the train, and where it appears that the derailment results from such an intervening agency over which the carrier had no control, not-

in Pennsylvania R. Co. v. McKinney, 124 Pa. St. 462; 17 Atl. Rep. 14; 10 Am. St. Rep. 601; 2 L. R. A. 820.

Nor was the railroad company held liable for the breaking of a passenger's arm, by a missile thrown through a window, in Thomas v. Philadelphia, etc., R. Co., 148 Pa. St. 180; 23 Atl. Rep. 989; 15 L. R. A. 416.

[21] Frederics v. Northern, etc., R. Co., 157 Pa. St. 103; 27 Atl. Rep. 689; 22 L. R. A. 306; 58 Am. & Eng. R. Cas. 91.

[22] Deyo v. New York, etc., R. Co., 18 N. Y. 534; 75 Am. Dec. 258.

withstanding the general rule that a derailment establishes a *prima facie* case, or raises a presumption of negligence on the carrier's part,[23] there will be no liability, unless the carrier was negligent in failing to discover the wrongful act on the part of the wrongdoer and using due care to avoid the injury after notice of the same, or of facts which would put it on inquiry.[24]

In a Pennsylvania case,[25] a passenger was injured by the criminal act of certain parties, not connected with the railroad company, by breaking the lock to a switch and uncoupling cars which stood on the side track, thus causing loaded coal cars to run out on the main track, where a collision was caused between such cars and the train on which plaintiff was riding, but the court held that the carrier was not liable for such malicious and criminal acts of strangers, of which it had no notice. And to the same effect is a New York decision,[26] in which the rights of an injured passenger to recover from the railroad company were adjudicated and it was held that there was no liability for a derailment, caused by the culpable act of some unknown person, who had maliciously drawn the spikes which fastened the rails to the ties.

§ 765. **Obstructions on track.**— If obstructions are placed by strangers upon a railroad track, either through accident or design, the railroad company is not responsible for the consequences, unless its agents or employees have been remiss in failing to discover such obstructions.[27] It was

[23] Furnish v. Missouri Pacific Ry. Co., 102 Mo. 438, 669; 15 S. W. Rep. 315; 13 S. W. Rep. 1044; 22 Am. St. Rep. 781, 800.

[24] Frederics v. Northern, etc., R. Co., *supra*.

[25] Frederics v. Northern, etc., R. Co., 157 Pa. St. 103; 27 Atl. Rep. 689; 22 L. R. A. 306;. 58 Am. & Eng. R. Cas. 91.

[26] Deyo v. New York, etc., R. Co., 18 N. Y. 534; 75 Am. Dec. 258.

[27] Curtis v. Rochester, etc., R. Co., 18 N. Y. 534; 75 Am. Dec. 258.

held, in Pennsylvania,[28] that there was no presumption of negligence on the part of a railroad company, for an injury due to a large rock being rolled upon a track, from a hillside over three hundred feet from the cut where the rock was found, but the high degree of care exacted of railroads in the care of their track and roadbed usually is such that a *prima facie* case is established, whenever it is shown that a passenger received an injury as a result of a derailment due to an obstruction on the track.[29]

The care of the track, for the protection and safety of passengers, places the carrier under the duty of using the utmost skill and diligence to keep it free from obstructions, and when a passenger is injured by an obstruction placed on the track, the burden is said to be on the carrier to show that the most thorough diligence could not have foreseen and avoided the injury.[30]

§ 766. **Violence of intruders at railway stations.**— In an Alabama case [31] the question was decided of the liability of a railroad company for acts of violence and outrage committed in a waiting room of a railroad station, by strangers

[28] Fleming v. Pittsburg, etc., R. Co., 158 Pa. St. 130; 27 Atl. Rep. 858; 38 Am. St. Rep. 835; 22 L. R. A. 351.

[29] Virginia, etc., R. Co. v. Sangor, 15 Gratt. (Va.), 230.

[30] Carrico v. West Virginia, etc., R. Co., 35 W. Va. 389; 14 S. E. Rep. 12; 52 Am. & Eng. R. Cas. 393.

[31] Batton v. South, etc., R. Co., 77 Ala. 591; 54 Am. Rep. 80; 23 Am. & Eng. R. Cas. 514.

There was held to be no liability for an injury to a passenger in a waiting room, by a stray dog biting the passenger, in Smith v. Great Eastern, etc., R. Co., L. R. 2 C. P. 4, although the dog had torn the dress of another passenger on the platform, previous to the plaintiff's injury.

It is held in one case, in Pennsylvania, that a railroad company is never liable for the wrongful acts of strangers or third persons, unless their conduct amounts to a breach of the peace. Ellinger v. Philadelphia, etc., R. Co., 153 Pa. St. 213; 25 Atl. Rep. 1132.

or intruders, who made indecent exposures of their persons and otherwise insulted a waiting female passenger. After reviewing the evidence, which failed to disclose any notice to the employees of the railroad company of the threatened outrage or insults, Somerville, J., for the court, said: " We do not think that there is any duty to police station houses, with the view of anticipating violence to passengers, which there are no reasonable grounds to expect. This is as far as the case requires us to go. The liability of a common carrier, when receiving a passenger at a station for transportation, ought not to be greater than that of an innkeeper, who is never held liable for trespasses committed ordinarily by strangers upon the persons of his guests. There is nothing tending to prove that the company had notice of any facts which justified the expectation of such a wanton and unusual outrage to passengers. Their contract of safe carriage imposed upon the company no implied obligation to furnish a police force for the protection of passengers against such insults. It was a risk which was incidental to one's presence anywhere when traveling without a protector, and it was the plaintiff's risk, not the defendant's."

§ 767. **Acts of mob.**— It is not recognized by the courts as the duty of a railroad company to provide a police force sufficient to quell a large wayside mob, that may enter the carrier's train or its station, but passengers are generally held to take the risk of injury in such cases.[32] In a leading case, in Pennsylvania,[33] a train being stopped at a regular station of the company, a riotous crowd rushed upon the cars in such numbers as to defy the employees of the train. A fight was started in the cars, in which the plaintiff, a

[32] Pittsburg, etc., R. Co. v. Hinds, 53 Pa. St. 512; Batton v. South, etc., R. Co., 77 Ala. 591; 54 Am. Rep. 80; 23 Am. & Eng. R. Cas. 514.
[33] Pittsburg, etc., R. Co. v. Hinds, *supra.*

passenger, was injured. There was nothing to show that the employees or officers of the railroad company were fore-warned that such a crowd would board the train and the fact that the conductor knew that the crowd was composed of improper persons was not held of sufficient importance to charge the carrier with liability for their acts.

But if the carrier has notice of facts which would put it on inquiry, so that by the exercise of reasonable care, the injury from a mob may be avoided, it will be held liable for a failure to adopt such precautions as may be necessary to prevent injury from such a source.[34] Thus, in an Illinois case,[35] where a passenger train was stopped in the midst of a howling mob of strikers, to take on persons whom the mob were desirous of maltreating, the court said: "Under the circumstances, the law would charge the defendant with negligence in stopping a train filled with passengers, in the midst of a howling, revengeful, lawless mob, to take on persons whom the mob were seeking an opportunity to maltreat. Defendant ought reasonably to have anticipated that the mob would attack its train, to reach the object of their vengeance so soon as it had passed from the protection of the police, and precautionary measures should have been taken to prevent the injury to the passengers."

[34] Chicago, eac., R. Co. v. Pillsbury, 123 Ill. 9; 14 N. E. Rep. 22; 31 Am. & Eng. R. Cas. 24.

[35] Chicago, etc., R. Co. v. Pillsbury, *supra.*

Where a lawless crowd robbed a passenger, there was held to be no liability, in Weeks v. New York, etc., R. Co., 72 N. Y. 50; 9 Hun 669; 28 Am. Rep. 104, and, see, also, Cobb v. Great Western R. Co., 1 Q. B. 459; 58 Am. & Eng. R. Cas. 169.

CHAPTER XXXI.

CONTRIBUTORY NEGLIGENCE OF PASSENGERS.

1157

§ 768. **The rule, generally.**— Carriers are not liable for perils to which a passenger exposes himself by his own carelessness, rashness or folly,[1] but to recover for an injury received it is necessary that the passenger should not have been guilty of any want of ordinary care, which contributed to the injury sustained.[2]

The rule is general that the negligence of a passenger,- amounting to absence of ordinary care, for his own protection, which, concurrently with the negligence of a railroad company, directly contributes to the injury sustained, is a complete defense, whether the party could, or could not, with ordinary, or even extraordinary care, have guarded against it.[3] Though the railroad company may also have been negligent, it can still defend itself and defeat a recovery of damages by the passenger, on a showing that when the passenger was endangered by its negligence, he was also guilty of a want of ordinary care for his own protection, or that he could have avoided the consequences of the carrier's negligence, by the use of ordinary care on his part.[4]

[1] Pennsylvania R. Co. v. Aspell, 23 Pa. St. 147; St. Louis, etc., R. Co. v. Rosenberry, 45 Ark. 256; Richmond, etc., R. Co. v. Morris, 31 Gratt. (Va.) 200; Fisher v. West Virginia, etc., R. Co. (W. Va.), 19 S. E. Rep. 578; 58 Am. & Eng. R. Cas. 337.

[2] George v. St. Louis, etc., R. Co., 34 Ark. 613; 1 Am. & Eng. R. Cas. 294.

[3] Tobin v. Cable Co. (Cal.), 34 Pac. Rep. 124; 58 Am. & Eng. R. Cas. 223.

[4] Central, etc., R. Co. v. Thompson, 76 Ga. 770; Macon, etc., R. Co. v. Johnson, 38 Ga. 409.

" Where, in an action for injury to a passenger, contributory negligence is not involved in the facts alleged and proved by plaintiff, the

1158

§ 769. **Care demanded of passenger.**— It is just as much
the duty of passengers to use care to avoid injury to themselves, as it is for the railroad company to use care to
prevent injuring them, as no one is required to use greater
care to avoid injuring another than such other is to avoid
injury to himself.[5]   Carriers of passengers, of course, are
held to a very high degree of care to avoid injury to their
passengers, on account of the fact that all control and care
of the passenger is entrusted to the carrier, but it by no
means follows that all care for one's own protection is
devolved upon the carrier; the passenger is held to the
exercise of reasonable care for his own safety and if his
own want of care contributes to produce the injury, he
cannot recover.[6]   A passenger has a lawful right to rely
upon the judgment of the employees of the carrier, in the
management and operation of the train, so long as their
acts do not subject him to a danger which a reasonably
prudent or cautious man would not assume, but, if in the
course of his journey, he is subjected to such a danger,
he is guilty of negligence barring a recovery for an injury
consequent thereupon, if he fails to use reasonable care to
avoid such an injury.[7]

The passenger, while on the train, must exercise ordinary
care and prudence such as a prudent man would himself
observe, to save himself from injury, and, failing in this,
no recovery could be had for an injury directly resulting
therefrom to the passenger.[8]

burden is on the carrier to show contributory negligence." Herring
v. Galveston, etc., Ry. Co. (Tex. Civ. App. 1908), 108 S. W. Rep. 977.

[5] Pittsburg, etc., R. Co. v. Hinds, 53 Pa. St. 512.

[6] Weber v. Kansas City, etc., R. Co., 100 Mo. 194; 12 S. W. Rep.
804; 7 L. R. A. 819; 41 Am. & Eng. R. Cas. 117.

[7] Kentucky, etc., R. Co. v. Quinkert, 2 Ind. App. 244; 28 N. E.
Rep. 338; Cincinnati, etc., R. Co. v. Carper, 112 Ind. 26; Louisville,
etc., R. Co. v. Bisch, 120 Ind. 549.

[8] Hazzard v. Chicago, etc., R. Co., 1 Biss. (U. S.) 503; Mackey v.

But a passenger is only required to exercise ordinary capacity and care to protect himself from injury and the law does not exact of him all the skill and care of the most capable or ready-witted persons.[9] A passenger, engaged in going from the cars of the carrier to its eating house, is not required to exercise the same degree of care that would be exacted of a person crossing the track, under other circumstances, for he has a right to assume that the railroad company has provided a reasonably safe way, but of course he cannot recover for an injury which he could have avoided by reasonable or ordinary care, on his part.[10]

§ 770. **Passengers under disability.**— The law does not place persons laboring under such disabilities as sickness, infancy or old age, upon the plane of intoxicated persons,

Missouri Pacific Ry. Co. (U. S.), 5 McCrary, 538; Little Rock, etc., R. Co. v. Cavenesse, 48 Ark. 106; 2 S. W. Rep. 505; Jeffersonville, etc., R. Co. v. Hendricks, 26 Ind. 228.-

[9] Sheridan v. Brooklyn, etc., R. Co., 36 N. Y. 39; 34 How. Pr. 217.

[10] Atchison, etc., R. Co. v. Shean, 18 Colo. 368; 33 Pac. Rep. 108; 58 Am. & Eng. R. Cas. 360. But where a passenger steps from a car in front of another car approaching on a parallel track, which he did not stop to look for, he is held guilty of negligence, as matter of law, in Horstein v. United Railways Co. (195 Mo. 440; 92 S. W. Rep. 884), where the opinion of Judge Bland, of the St. Louis Court of Appeals, is adopted by the Supreme Court. See, also, for this opinion, 97 Mo. App. 271.

"A passenger is as much bound to use reasonable care to avoid injury as the carrier is to use the greatest degree of care to save the passenger from harm." Rehearing, 82 N. E. 1025, denied. Cleveland, etc., Ry. Co. v. Hadley (Ind. 1908), 84 N. E. Rep. 13.

"A passenger must exercise such care as persons of ordinary prudence and intelligence would exercise under the same circumstances." Pomroy v. Bangor & Aroostook R. Co. (Me. 1907), 67 Atl. Rep. 561.

"A passenger is required to exercise only ordinary care for his safety." Cleveland, etc., Ry. Co. v. Hadley (Ind. 1907), 82 N. E. Rep. 1025.

"Passengers are held to the exercise of ordinary diligence to protect themselves." Farrell v. Great Northern Ry. Co. (Minn. 1907), 111 N. W. Rep. 388.

whose disability is due to their own voluntary act, but the carrier is bound to carry the physically disabled passenger, and to use the proper degree of care to protect the known disabled persons riding on its trains, to the same extent that it is to protect the strong and able-bodied passengers. If the carrier is negligent, therefore, and a passenger laboring under physical disability is injured thereby, the carrier will be liable for the injury, even though one stronger than the injured passenger could have avoided the effect of the carrier's negligence and prevented the injury.[11]

This is certainly but common justice, as applied to the contract of transportation, undertaken by the passenger carrier, for after knowingly assuming the undertaking of safely conveying an injured or disabled or infant passenger, if the passenger is injured by the negligence of the carrier, it would be a harsh rule of law to visit such negligence upon the innocent passenger, simply because of the disability, known to the carrier, when the contract was entered into, which prevented an avoidance of the carrier's negligence. The basis of negligence — the absence of reasonable care — is lacking and there is no negligence, in such a case, on the passenger's part.

§ 771. **Must directly contribute to injury.**— The fact that a passenger who was injured by the proximate negligence of a railroad company, was himself guilty of a want of

[11] Hemingway v. Chicago, etc., R. Co., 72 Wis. 42; 37 N. W. Rep. 807. In a Texas case, an infant who did not know that the train passed the station and then backed up, and who attempted to alight, by jumping from the train on the announcement of the station, was held not negligent, as matter of law. Texas, etc., R. Co. v. Stuart, 20 S. W. Rep. 962.

It is held not to be negligence for a blind man to travel without an attendant, where this is not the cause of an injury, but only of the inability to avoid it, in St. Louis, etc., R. Co. v. Maddry, 57 Ark. 306; 21 S. W. Rep. 472; 58 Am. & Eng. R. Cas. 327.

care for his own protection, will not prevent him from recovering damages against the company, provided his carelessness did not contribute to the injury, or only remotely
contributed thereto.[12]   In other words, although a passenger,
injured by a train, may have been guilty of some negligence,
which contributed to the injury, yet if those in charge
of the train might have avoided the injury by the exercise
of ordinary care and prudence, the railroad company would
be liable, provided the negligence of the one injured was
the remote or incidental, and that of the railroad company
was the direct, cause of the injury.[13]   For instance, in an
action by a passenger for damages for an injury sustained,
while he was violating a rule of the railroad company, the
violation of the rule would not bar a recovery, unless its
disobedience contributed to the injury sustained;[14] nor
would the fact that a passenger had wrongfully boarded a
moving train, avail the railroad company as a defense, where .
she was injured by being wrongfully ejected by a brakeman,
after getting on the train.[15]

But if the negligence of the passenger contributed directly
to his injury, no recovery can be had against the carrier
for such injury, and the defendant will not be given the
benefit of the rule, as to contributory negligence, under a

[12] Central, etc., R. Co. v. Van Horn, 38 N. J. L. 133; 13 Am. Ry.
Rep. 36; McQuillen v. Central, etc., R. Co., 64 Cal. 463; 2 Pac. Rep.
46; 16 Am. & Eng. R. Cas. 353; Thirteenth, etc., R. Co. v. Boudrox,
92 Pa. St. 475; 37 Am. Rep. 707; 2 Am. & Eng. R. Cas. 30; Creed
v. Pennsylvania R. Co., 86 Pa. St. 139; Alabama, etc., R. Co. v. Hawk,
72 Ala. 112; 47 Am. Rep. 403; 18 Am. & Eng. R. Cas. 194; Shenan-
doah Valley R. Co. v. Moose, 83 Va. 827.
[13] Whalen v. St. Louis, etc., R. Co., 60 Mo. 323; 9 Am. Ry. Rep. 224.
[14] Lawrenceburg, etc., R. Co. v. Montgomery, 7 Ind. 474. See,
also, Wood v. Lake Shore, etc., R. Co., 49 Mich. 370; 13 N. W. Rep.
779; 8 Am. & Eng. R. Cas. 478; Lackawana, etc., R. Co. v. Chenewith,
52 Pa. St. 382.
[15] Reed v. Pennsylvania R. Co., 56 Fed. Rep. 184, disapproving Soloman v. Manhattan R. Co., 103 N. Y. 437; 9 N. E. Rep. 430.

charge to the jury that the negligence of the plaintiff will bar a recovery, provided the defendant has not been guilty of negligence,[16] for if the defendant can show that the negligence of the passenger contributed proximately to the injury, no action can be maintained against it therefor, although it was also negligent and its negligence concurred to produce the result complained of.[17]

§ 772. **Boarding wrong car or train.**— A passenger has been held guilty of contributory negligence, barring a recovery for his injury, where he went from the coach, in which he was riding, to the engine to get water and fell from the platform between the engine and the coach, on his return, although his fall may have been caused by a defective brake which he caught hold of, or by the negligence of the engineer, in suddenly applying the air brakes.[18] And if a passenger sustains injury while on a special train, carrying provisions and supplies to the employees of the railroad company, the fact that he was riding on this train, which was not used for the conveyance of passengers, will be proper to consider in determining the element of his contributory negligence and the liability of the railroad company for the injury to him.[19]

§ 773. **Disobedience of carrier's rules.**— All passengers are bound to observe the reasonable rules and regulations of the carrier, made for the purpose of insuring the protection and safety of the passengers, and for a violation of a known rule or regulation of this kind, in case of a resulting injury,

[16] McQuillen v. Central, etc., R. Co., 64 Cal. 463; 2 Pac. Rep. 46; 16 Am. & Eng. R. Cas. 353.

[17] Conroy v. Pennsylvania R. Co., 1 Pittsb. (Pa.) 440.

[18] McDaniel v. Highland Avenue R. Co., 90 Ala. 64; 8 So. Rep. 41.

[19] Southwestern R. Co. v. Singleton, 66 Ga. 252.

no liability will be recognized by the courts.[20]   If the passenger would hold the carrier to the full measure of its responsibility for his safe transportation, it is not asking too much of him that he conform to all the reasonable rules adopted for his own protection.[21]   It is accordingly held, that a passenger is bound to comply with all reasonable rules and regulations of the carrier for entering, occupying and leaving the cars and if by reason of a disregard of such rules, a passenger sustains injury, he cannot recover damages from the railroad company, although the carelessness of the employees of the railroad company may have combined to produce the injury sustained.[22]

But notice of the rule must be brought home to the passenger, before its violation will defeat a recovery for an injury sustained and where a passenger boarded an excursion train before the time specified by a rule of the company, the issue whether or not he had notice of the rule, in case of conflicting evidence, would be a question for the jury.[23]   The rule must also be generally enforced by the carrier, to enable it to set up the rule as a defense in an action for an injury by a passenger, and if the carrier has habitually violated the rule, it will not constitute a defense to an action by a passenger injured while violating such rule.[24]

§ 774. **Passing from one car to another.**—A passenger is generally held to be out of his place, if he assumes the risk of passing from one car to another, while a train of

[20] Baltimore, etc., R. Co. v. Leonhardt, 66 Md. 70; 5 Atl. Rep. 346; 27 Am. & Eng. R. Cas. 194.
[21] Downey v. Chesapeake, etc., R. Co., 28 W. Va. 732.
[22] Chicago, etc., R. Co. v. Reilly, 40 Ill. App. 416.
[23] Western Maryland, etc., R. Co. v. Herold, 74 Md. 510; 22 Atl. Rep. 323.
[24] Houston, etc., R. Co. v. Moore, 49 Texas 31.

cars is in motion [25] and notwithstanding the employees of
a train are negligent in the manner of operating the train,
if a passenger is injured in passing before a moving car,
or in passing from one car to another, when they are in
motion, in order to reach another car or to gain access to
another seat, he will be held negligent barring his recovery.[26]
And it is held, in Massachusetts, that if a passenger attempts
to pass from one car, while it is in motion, to another, at
the request of the conductor of the train, the passenger
will assume the risk of all injuries not due to the negligence
of the railroad company or its employees, and if the passenger, while on the platform of the car, is thrown from
the car when the train is rounding a curve, no recovery
can be had for the injury so received.[27]

But passing from one car to another on a moving train,
is not, generally, held to be contributory negligence, as
matter of law, in cases where the passenger acts upon the
request of the train employees in doing so,[28] for the passenger, in such case, is held entitled to act upon the assumption that the employees in charge of the train would not
give the order to proceed from the car, if such act were
dangerous to the passenger, and hence the obedience to the
command of a brakeman was held not to be negligence, in
an Indiana case,[29] and the issue, where the passenger acted .

[25] Willis v. Long Island R. Co., 32 Barb. 398.

[26] Baltimore, etc., R. Co. v. State, 60 Md. 449; 12 Am. & Eng. R.
Cas. 149.

[27] Stewart v. Boston, etc., R. Co., 146 Mass. 605; 16 N. E. Rep.
466; 34 Am. & Eng. R. Cas. 499; Snowden v. Boston, etc., R. Co., 151
Mass. 220; 24 N. E. Rep. 40.

[28] Davis v. Louisville, etc., R. Co., 69 Miss. 136; 10 So. Rep. 450.

[29] Louisville, etc., R. Co. v. Kelly, 92 Ind. 371; 47 Am. Rep. 149;
13 Am. & Eng. R. Cas. 1. See, also, Cincinnati, etc., R. Co. v. Carper,
112 Ind. 26; 13 N. E. Rep. 122; 31 Am. & Eng. R. Cas. 36; Cleveland, etc., R. Co. v. Manson, 30 Ohio St. 451; Hannibal, etc., R. Co.
v. Martin, 111 Ill. 219; 11 Ill. App. 386.

in response to an order of a train employee, would generally be one for the jury.[30]

§ 775. **Crossing track in front of approaching car.**— The dangers of the track are so well known by the general traveling public, that the courts, in accordance with this general knowledge on the subject, generally hold that a passenger is negligent who crosses a track at a place where no assurance of safety is given, or where the surroundings are not such as to lead him to believe he can safely do so, and if a passenger steps upon a railroad track, without looking for an approaching train or car, no recovery can be had for an injury caused by being struck by a car or engine, which could have been seen, if attention had been paid to the dangers of the surroundings.[31]

Common prudence dictates that a passenger who alights from a car, and passes behind it, in an endeavor to cross a parallel track, stop for a moment until he can have an unobstructed view of the other track, before he attempts to cross it; and if he fails to exercise that precaution, but proceeds to cross the other track, without waiting for an

---

[30] Lent v. New York, etc., R. Co., 120 N. Y. 467; 24 N. E. Rep. 653; 31 N. Y. S. R. 538; 44 Am. & Eng. R. Cas. 373.

"Where a carrier operates a train advertised as completely vestibuled in whole or in part not vestibuled, a passenger, reasonably believing from the advertisement that the train is vestibuled, and relying on that fact, and thereby induced to attempt to pass from one car to another, and injured because of the absence of the vestibule, is entitled to have the question of the carrier's negligence submitted to the jury." Judgment, 82 N. E. Rep. 998, reversed. Pittsburg & St. L. Ry. Co. v. Schepman (Ind. 1908), 84 N. E. Rep. 988.

[31] Horstein v. United Rys. Co., 97 Mo. App. 271, where the opinion by Judge Bland was adopted, in the Supreme Court, in an opinion by Judge Marshall, in 195 Mo. 440; 92 S. W. Rep. 884. See, also, Deane v. Transit Co., 192 Mo. 575; 91 S. W. Rep. 505; Moore v. Transit Co., 194 Mo. 1; 92 S. W. Rep. 390; Hafner v. Transit Co., 197 Mo. 196; 94 S. W. Rep. 291; Weller v. Chicago, etc., R. Co., 164 Mo. 198; 64 S. W. Rep. 141; 86 Am. St. Rep. 592.

unobstructed view of the track, which is not at the moment available, because of the car he has just left, and his failure so to stop contributes to his injury by a car from the other direction, no recovery can be had for the injuries so received, although no warning signals are given by the parties managing the car by which he is injured, for it is a case of mutual negligence and his conduct constitutes a want of ordinary care for his own safety.[32]

But this rule does not apply in the same strict degree, at the crossings of public streets or highways, or where persons are accustomed to be,[33] nor to a place where no obstruction to the view of the track obtains,[34] or where the passenger is expressly or impliedly given to understand that the crossing of the railroad track will not be attendant with the risk of injury from approaching cars or trains, for at such places, he has a right to rely upon the assurance which the direction of employees or the surroundings of the place suggest.[35]

[32] This is practically the language of Marshall, J., in Horstein v. United Rys. Co., *supra*.

[33] Burbridge v. Kansas City, etc., R. Co., 36 Mo. App. 669.

[34] Riska v. Union Depot R. Co., 180 Mo. 168; 79 S. W. Rep. 445. This was the distinguishing feature between this case and that of Horstein v. United Rys. Co. (195 p. 458; 92 S. W. Rep. 1002), as pointed out by the court, in the latter case.

[35] Louisville, etc., R. Co. v. Bisch, 120 Ind. 549; 22 N. E. Rep. 662; 41 Am. & Eng. R. Cas. 89.

Crossing a track, in front of a train, which was rapidly approaching, was held negligence, on the part of the passenger, in Chicago, etc., R. Co. v. Felton, 125 Ill. 458; 17 N. E. Rep. 765 (reversing 24 Ill. App. 376); 33 Am. & Eng. R. Cas. 533; Chicago, etc., R. Co. v. Dewey, 26 Ill. 255; DeKay v. Chicago, etc., R. Co., 41 Minn. 178; 43 N. W. Rep. 182; 4 L. R. A. 632; 39 Am. & Eng. R. Cas. 463; Wright v. Great Northern R. Co., L. R. 8 Ir. 257.

But if the track crossed is at the company's station, or at a place where it has permitted passengers to use the track as a passway, or by its conduct has invited them to use it, to pass over, the passenger is not held to the strict rule of duty that would obtain at other places. Mayo v. Boston, etc., R. Co., 104 Mass. 137; Rabostelli v.

§ 776. **Passengers crossing steam and street railroad tracks.**
— The cases differentiate between steam railroads and street
cars, in so far as the duty of the passenger goes, to stop,
look and listen, before stepping on the track, and while
conceding that it is contributory negligence, as matter of

New York, etc., R. Co., 33 Fed. Rep. 796; 34 Am. & Eng. R. Cas. 515;
Chicago, etc., R. Co. v. Lowell, 151 U. S. 209; 14 Sup. Ct. Rep. 281.

Where a train is stopped at a distance from the station, the passenger has a right to assume that proper precautions are adopted by the
carrier to prevent his injury by being struck by locomotives or cars,
on the track he is required to pass over, and the same rule as to looking or listening at a place where passengers were not expected to be,
would not apply to such a place. Warner v. Baltimore, etc., R. Co.,
168 U. S. 339; 42 L. Ed. 391.

"One possessing good eyesight and hearing, and familiar with the
surroundings, stepped on a railroad track with a view of crossing
the track to board a train. Before stepping on the track he did not
stop, look, or listen for a train. *Held,* that he was guilty of contributory negligence as a matter of law, though it be assumed that he
was a passenger and entitled to protection as such." Gregg v. Northern Pac. Ry. Co. (Wash. 1908), 94 Pac. Rep. 911.

"A passenger, a man of mature years, in good health, having had
considerable experience in traveling, asked for no information or
guidance as to the method of reaching a train on which he was about
to embark, though the night was dark and cloudy and the station
premises new and uncompleted. He started with others from the station, but, in buttoning his coat, fell behind them, and, on hearing
the station agent say, 'Come on,' crossed a side track, then a platform, and then passed on to the main track, erroneously believing
that the agent was on the other side of the main track, and was
struck by the coming train. The main track was straight for 900
feet, and the engine was equipped with a headlight which could be
seen 2,000 feet, and was running not more than 6 miles an hour.
The passenger at all times saw the train and its headlight, but erroneously believed that it had stopped, and stepped in front of it
while not more than 7 feet away, and did not look at the engine
while crossing. The engineer saw the passenger, and applied the
emergency brake and stopped the train within 50 or 60 feet. *Held,*
that the passenger was guilty of contributory negligence precluding
a recovery, though it be conceded that the carrier did not perform the
full measure of duty in the manner of supplying lights for its
premises." Pere Marquette R. Co. v. Strange (Ind. 1908), 84 N. E.
Rep. 819.

law, for a person to step upon a steam railroad track, without stopping, looking or listening for an approaching train, the courts of some States hold that it is not contributory negligence for a passenger to do so, with reference to street car tracks. These decisions were principally rendered in States before the modern method and means of rapid transit by electricity was in vogue and the reason for the rule does not apply to modern rapid transit street cars, as remarked in a Missouri case.[36]

Speaking of the distinction that obtains in some States, and the rule in that State, Judge Marshall, for the Supreme Court of Missouri, in the case above referred to,[37] said: "In Ohio, New York, Virginia, Illinois, New Jersey, Washington and Indiana, * * * the distinction between steam railroads and street cars obtains, or did obtain before the adoption of rapid transit, such as now exists in all large cities. Whereas, in Pennsylvania, Maryland, Oregon and Tennessee, the rule stated by the defendant obtains. The later cases in Missouri do not recognize such a distinction between steam railroads and street railroads, with respect to the obligation of the pedestrian, to look or listen for an approaching car, but the courts of this State, keeping pace with the progress of the times, recognize that there is quite as much danger to be apprehended now from stepping on the street car tracks, where the cars are run by electricity and at a rapid rate, and with great frequency and at short intervals, as there is from stepping on the steam railroad tracks, where cars do not run as often."

§ 777. **Riding on freight trains.**— The mere fact of riding on a freight train is not negligence, as matter of law, on the part of a passenger, who does not know that the em-

[36] Horstein v. United Rys. Co., 195 Mo. 457; 92 S. W. Rep. 884.
[37] Horstein v. United Rys. Co., *supra.*

ployees are violating the rules of the carrier, or exceeding their authority, in carrying passengers on such trains,[38] and a passenger who goes upon a freight train, in accordance with the directions of an employee, in good faith, to be transported to a given point, if injured because of the negligence of the employees of the train, will not be denied a recovery merely because he was riding, at the time, upon this kind of a conveyance.[39]

But a person who rides upon a freight train in violation of the rules of the railroad company, with notice that passengers are not allowed upon such trains, cannot recover for injuries due to the negligence of the employees, who took the person on the train in known violation of the employer's rules.[40]   And even though the person injured was riding in accordance with a custom to carry passengers on freight trains, as the dangers of this mode of conveyance are so well known as to be understood by the general traveling public, if, considering the risks of this mode of travel, the passenger is not reasonably careful to avoid injury, as where he stands up in a caboose, with notice of the fact that switching is being done and the car is apt to be connected with and jarred, he will be held guilty of contributory negligence barring a recovery for an injury that he would not otherwise have received, if he had been seated.[41]

[38] Alabama, etc., R. Co. v. Yarbrough, 83 Ala. 238; 3 So. Rep. 447; 3 Am. St. Rep. 715.

[39] Hanson v. Mansfield, etc., R. Co., 38 La. Ann. 111; 58 Am. Rep. 162.

[40] Whitehead v. St. Louis, etc., R. Co., 22 Mo. App. 60.

[41] Harris v. Hannibal, etc., R. Co., 89 Mo. 233; 1 S. W. Rep. 325; 27 Am. & Eng. R. Cas. 216.

"In an action for injuries to a passenger on a freight train, special findings that he was riding in the cupola of the caboose at the time of the accident, that there were seats in the caboose, that the cupola was for train men only, and that he got off before the caboose stopped, did not show him guilty of contributory negligence." Southern Ry. Co. v. Roach (Ind. App. 1906), 78 N. E. Rep. 201.

§ 778. **Care in boarding cars.**— While it is the duty of a passenger carrier to provide safe and reasonably convenient means to enable its passengers to board its trains, at the different stations along the line of its road, it is also the duty of the passenger to use the means provided with reasonable circumspection and care [42] and for an injury from a failure to do so, no recovery could be had.

If the passenger is not familiar with the manner or method of boarding the cars, inquiry should be made of the carrier's agent, or the employees of the company in charge of the train [43] and if the passenger does not accept the advice of those in the service of the company, but attempts to enter the cars while other passengers are alighting, as a result of which he is thrown from the platform and injured,[44] the result is the same as if the passenger had received the injury while violating a known rule of the carrier,[45] and no recovery can be had for the injury.

But where the passenger has acted upon the advice of the conductor of the train, in the attempt to board the car, at the time of receiving an injury, this will not be held to be negligence, as a general rule,[46] and if the passenger has used due care and caution, in boarding the train, taking into consideration the means at hand, he will not generally be denied a recovery for an injury received, while attempting to board the train, on account of his own negligence.[47]

" Whether it was contributory negligence for a passenger on a freight train to ride in the cupola of the caboose is a question for the jury to determine from all the circumstances." St. Louis Southwestern Ry. Co. v. Morgan (Tex. Civ. App. 1906), 98 S. W. Rep. 408.

[42] Keller v. Hestonville, etc., R. Co., 149 Pa. St. 65; 24 Atl. Rep. 159.

[43] Allender v. Chicago, etc., R. Co., 43 Iowa 276; 14 Am. Ry. Rep. 443; Phillipps v. Rensseler, etc., R. Co., 57 Barb. 644; 49 N. Y. 177.

[44] Hollman v. Houston, etc., R. Co., 2 Texas Unrep. Cas. 557.

[45] Drake v. Pennsylvania R. Co., 137 Pa. St. 352; 20 Atl. Rep. 994.

[46] Irish v. Northern, etc., R. Co., 4 Wash. 48; 29 Pac. Rep. 845.

[47] Curtis v. Detroit, etc., R. Co., 27 Wis. 158; 5 Am. Ry. Rep. 368.

§ 779. **Boarding train in improper manner.**— Where a passenger is injured as the result of an attempt to board a train, either in motion, or standing still, in an improper manner, this is usually held to be such an act of negligence as will prevent a recovery from the railroad company for the injury so received.

This rule is illustrated by a Missouri case,[48] where the plaintiff was injured, while attempting to board a train, passing a station at a speed variously estimated at from six to eight miles an hour. He was told by the conductor to jump on, and while young and vigorous, in boarding the train, he sprang in opposition to and not with the motion of the train, as a result of which he sustained the injuries sued for. It was held that he had no case..

It has also been held to be negligence for a passenger to attempt to board a stock car, instead of a caboose, on a moving freight train;[49] to run alongside a car and hold onto the hand rails until an obstruction is struck,[50] or a fall sustained,[51] or to attempt to mount a car, moving with rapidly increasing speed, with one's face toward the car and not looking for obstructions at the side of the railroad track.[52]

§ 780. **Entering train from wrong side.**— The employees of a passenger carrier are not negligent in failing to watch both sides of the train for passengers to board the cars, for this is such an unusual occurrence that they will not be held liable for failing to anticipate it, and if a passenger,

[48] Heaton v. Kansas City, etc., R. Co., 65 Mo. App. 479, by Judge Bond.

[49] Warren v. Southern, etc., R. Co., 37 Kansas 408; 15 Pac. Rep. 601; 31 Am. & Eng. R. Cas. 10.

[50] Phillipps v. Ransseler, etc., R. Co., 49 N. Y. 177; 3 Am. Ry. Rep. 477.

[51] McMurtry v. Louisville, etc., R. Co., 67 Miss. 601; 7 So. Rep. 401.

[52] Haldan v. Great Western R. Co., 30 U. C. C. P. 89.

in the dark, attempts to board the train on the side away from the station, without notice to the employees in charge of the train, and in so doing, sustains an injury, there can be no recovery against the railroad company.[53]

But if the railroad company has adopted the custom of permitting passengers to board its cars, at certain stations, on either or both sides of the track, and there are platforms or walks alongside the cars on both sides of the track, then a passenger will not be denied a recovery for attempting to board the cars, on the side away from the station, in accordance with this custom, if an injury is sustained, without his fault;[54] nor could the carrier set up that a passenger attempted to enter a train, on the wrong side, or at the wrong door, if the employees in charge of the train directed him to enter in the way he was attempting to enter the car, for he would not be guilty of negligence, in such a case, in relying upon the superior judgment of the employees in charge of the train.[55]

§ 781. **Boarding train at improper time.**—While it is not ordinarily held to be negligence for a passenger to enter a train of cars before the regular time for the passengers to get on the train,[56] if a passenger attempts to enter a train in the dark, at a time long before the cars are lighted or the employees are around to look after the safety of passengers and in so doing the passenger is injured, by falling between the car steps and the depot platform, no recovery

[53] Michigan, etc., R. Co. v. Coleman, 28 Mich. 440; 12 Am. Ry. Rep. 59.

[54] Phillipps v. Ransseler, etc., R. Co., 57 Barb. 645; 49 N. Y. 177; 3 Am. Ry. Rep. 477.

[55] Pitcher v. Lake Shore, etc., R. Co., 16 N. Y. Supp. 62; 33 N. E. Rep. 339.

[56] Lakin v. Oregon, etc., R. Co., 15 Oregon 220; 15 Pac. Rep. 641; 34 Am. & Eng. R. Cas. 500.

could be had for such an injury, on account of the negligence of the passenger.[57]

Nor is it always negligence, as matter of law, to attempt to board a train after a signal has been given for the starting of the train, if the train is still at rest when the attempt to enter the cars is made.[58]   But if a passenger, making such an attempt, is under the influence of intoxicating liquor, and he attempts to board a train, after a signal has been given to start the train and while making the effort to get on the train, the train is started and the passenger is injured, no recovery can be had.[59]

§ 782. **Boarding train away from station.**— The station platform and not the side track, is the proper place to board or leave a train, and if passengers, for their own convenience, attempt to board or leave a train at a side track, instead of at the regular station of the railroad company, they are generally held to assume the risk of injuries received while so doing.[60]   This is particularly true, where the railroad company has adopted rules preventing the access to its trains at other places than its regular stations, and a passenger attempting to board the train at such other place, has notice of the rule.[61]   If a person attempts to board a train, at the time it is ready to start, away from the station, the railroad company will not be liable for the injury, if his presence was not known to the employees in time

[57] Hodges v. Transit Co., 107 No. Car. 576; 12 S. E. Rep. 597.

[58] Dawson v. Boston, etc., R. Co., 156 Mass. 127; 30 N. E. Rep. 466.

[59] Houston, etc., R. Co. v. Schmidt, 61 Texas 282; 21 Am. & Eng. R. Cas. 345.

Going to a railroad yard, in the night-time, to board a train, was held to be negligence, in, Haase v. Oregon, etc., R. Co., 19 Oregon, 354; 24 Pac. Rep. 238.

[60] DeKay v. Chicago, etc., R. Co., 41 Minn. 178; 43 N. W. Rep. 182; 4 L. R. A. 632; 39 Am. & Eng. R. Cas. 463.

[61] McDonald v. Chicago, etc., R. Co., 26 Iowa 124.

to avoid the injury, by the exercise of reasonable care [62] and there is no liability for an injury to one who goes in the nighttime, to a railroad yard and attempts to board a train without notice of his presence to the employees in charge thereof.[63]

But it is not necessarily negligence, as matter of law, to attempt to board a train at other than the regular stations of the carrier; [64] where the railroad company has been in the habit of permitting its passengers to board the cars at other places than the regular stations, a passenger with such notice, will not be precluded from recovering for injuries received, on account of the negligence of the railroad company's employees, at such place.[65] A passenger injured while attempting to board a train away from the station will not be denied a recovery, if there were no rules preventing access to the train at such a place, but it was customary for passengers to follow the course taken by the injured passenger [66] and if the rules of the carrier require passengers on mixed trains to get on and off the cars at any place where they are stopped, the passenger injured while attempting to board such a train, at a distance of forty or fifty feet from the station, will not be denied a recovery, on this account.[67]

[62] Phillipps v. Northern, etc., R. Co., 41 N. Y. S. R. 780; 16 N. Y. S. 909.

[63] Haase v. Oregon, etc., R. Co., 19 Oregon, 354; 24 Pac. Rep. 238; 44 Am. & Eng. R. Cas. 360.

[64] Stoner v. Pennsylvania R. Co., 98 Ind. 384; 49 Am. Rep. 764; 21 Am. & Eng. R. Cas. 340.

[65] Keating v. New York, etc., R. Co., 49 N. Y. 673.

[66] McDonald v. Chicago, etc., R. Co., *supra*.

[67] Louisville, etc., R. Co. v. Long (Ky.), 22 S. W. Rep. 747.

And in the following cases, it was held to be negligence for a passenger, without the knowledge of the employees of the defendant, to go to a place removed from the station, to board a train. Jones v. New York, etc., R. Co., 156 N. Y. 187; 90 Hun 605; 50 N. E. Rep. 856; 41 L. R. A. 490; Foreman v. Pennsylvania R. Co., 159 Pa. St.

§ 783. **Boarding moving train.**— The general rule is that passengers who are injured while getting on or off moving trains, are held to be guilty of such negligence as will bar a recovery.[68]   Boarding or attempting to board a moving train is an improper and dangerous act and in legal contemplation, the invitation of the railroad company to its passengers, to board its trains, is withdrawn the very instant the train begins to move.[69]   If there is no evidence, therefore, of any invitation on the part of the train employees, for the passenger to board the moving train, or nothing to show that they knew of the passenger's attempt and ratified it, there can generally be no recovery for an injury received in such an attempt.[70]

And it is held in a great many well-considered cases that the mere permission or invitation on the part of the employees of the railroad company, for a passenger to do such a dangerous thing, will not excuse the negligence of the passenger, in attempting to board a rapidly moving train;[71]

541; 28 Atl. Rep. 358; St. Louis, etc., R. Co. v. Whittler, 74 Fed. Rep. 296.

In an Illinois case a passenger attempted to board a train away from the station and before it was made up, but he was held not to be negligent, as matter of law, as he was invited to do so by the employees of the train. Hannibal, etc., R. Co. v. Martin, 11 Ill. App. 386.

[68] Browne v. Raleigh, etc., R. Co., 108 No. Car. 34; 12 S. E. Rep. 958; 47 Am. & Eng. R. Cas. 544; Harvey v. Eastern R. Co., 116 Mass. 269; Missouri Pacific Ry. Co. v. Texas, etc., R. Co., 36 Fed. Rep. 879; Hays v. Wabash R. Co., 51 Mo. App. 438; Heaton v. Kansas City, etc., R. Co., 65 Mo. App. 479; Galveston, etc., R. Co. v. Le Gierse, 51 Texas 189; Spannagle v. Chicago, etc., R. Co. 31 Ill. App. 460; Soloman v. Manhattan R. Co., 103 N. Y. 437; 9 N. E. Rep. 430; 56 Am. Rep. 843; 27 Am. & Eng. R. Cas. 155; Bacon v. Delaware, etc., R. Co., 143 Pa. St. 14; 21 Atl. Rep. 1002; Cousins v. Lake Shore, etc., R. Co., 96 Mich. 386; 56 N. W. Rep. 14.

[69] Chaffee v. Old Colony R. Co., 17 R. I. 658; 24 Atl. Rep. 141; 52 Am. & Eng. R. Cas. 366.

[70] International, etc., R. Co. v. Gorman, 2 Texas Civ. App. 679.

[71] Denver, etc., R. Co. v. Pickard, 8 Colo. 163; 6 Pac. Rep. 149; 18

but if the speed of the train is not so great as to threaten immediate danger to the passenger making such an attempt, it is held, in other cases, to be a question for the jury to decide, whether, under all the circumstances, in view of the invitation, or command of the employees of the train, the passenger was negligent in making the attempt to get on the train, while it was in motion.[72]

§ 784. **Train moving slowly.**— An attempt to board a train but slightly in motion is not ordinarily held to be negligence, *per se,* on the part of a young, active passenger, unincumbered with baggage or other impediments,[73] and this

Am. & Eng. R. Cas. 284; Chicago, etc., R. Co. v. Koehler, 47 Ill. App. 147; Kansas, etc., R. Co. v. Dorough, 72 Texas 108; 10 S. W. Rep. 711.

[72] Montgomery, etc., R. Co. v. Stewart, 91 Atl. 421; 8 So. Rep. 708; Reyburn v. Central Iowa R. Co., 74 Iowa 637; 35 N. W. Rep. 606; Browne v. Raleigh, etc., R. Co., 108 No. Car. 34; 12 S. E. Rep. 958; 47 Am. & Eng. R. Cas. 544.

It was held that it was not negligence, as matter of law, for a passenger to attempt to board a moving train, which had failed to stop at a station, for him to get on: Distler v. Long Island R. Co., 151 N. Y. 424; 45 N. E. Rep. 937; 35 L. R. A. 762; Texas, etc., R. Co. v. Davison, 68 Texas 370; 4 S. W. Rep. 636; Illinois, etc., R. Co. v. Cheek, 152 Ind. 663; 53 N. E. Rep. 641; Dawson v. Boston, etc., R. Co., 156 Mass. 127; 30 N. E. Rep. 466; Birmingham, etc., R. Co. v. Clay, 108 Ala. 233; 19 So. Rep. 309.

A passenger who attempts to get on a train, moving toward an obstruction, which it is apparent he is apt to strike, is guilty of such negligence as will bar a recovery, regardless of the inducement of the train employees to board the train. Hunter v. Cooperstown, etc R. Co., 126 N. Y. 18; 26 N. E. Rep. 958; 47 Am. & Eng. R. Cas. 534.

If a passenger was warned not to attempt to get on, by the employees in charge thereof, before making the attempt to board a moving train, there can be no recovery for an injury received while so doing. Fulks v. St. Louis, etc., R. Co., 111 Mo. 335; 19 S. W. Rep. 818; 52 Am. & Eng. R. Cas. 280.

[73] Warren v. Southern Kansas R. Co., 37 Kansas, 408; 15 Pac. Rep. 601; Leslie v. Wabash R. Co., 88 Mo. 50; Doss v. Missouri, etc., R. Co., 59 Mo. 27; Wyatt v. Citizens Ry. Co., 55 Mo. 485; Strauss v. Kansas

is particularly true while the train is still at the platform of the railroad company, where there are no obstacles in the way of the passenger.[74]   And boarding a slowly moving train, at a distance from the platform, at the request of an employee of the railroad company, was held not to be negligence, as matter of law, in a Maryland case.[75]

But where the train is moving at a rate of speed which would render it a dangerous undertaking for a passenger of the age and activity of one undertaking to get on the train, then the attempt to board the train while it is in motion, will be held negligence, as a matter of law.[76]   And while it has been held that in the case of a young, active man, not incumbered by baggage or other obstacles, it will not be held negligence, as a matter of law, to attempt to board a train, running at a speed of from three to four miles an hour,[77] it has, on the other hand, been held to be negligence, *per se,* to attempt to board a train running at a speed of from four to six or eight miles an hour, although the attempt is made at the request of the train conductor.[78]

City, etc., R. Co., 75 Mo. 185; Swigert v. Hannibal, etc., R. Co., 75 Mo. 475.

[74] Fulks v. St. Louis, etc., R. Co., 111 Mo. 335; 19 S. W. Rep. 818; 52 Am. & Eng. R. Cas. 280.

[75] Baltimore, etc., R. Co. v. Kane, 69 Md. 11; 13 Atl. Rep. 387; 12 Cent. Rep. 95.

[76] Denver, etc., R. Co. v. Pickard, 8 Colo. 163; 6 Pac. Rep. 149; 18 Am. & Eng. R. Cas. 284.

[77] Murphy v. St. Louis, etc., R. Co., 43 Mo. App. 342.

[78] Hunter v. Cooperstown, etc., R. Co., 112 N. Y. 371; 19 N. E. Rep. 820; 21 N. Y. S. R. 1; 37 Am. & Eng. R. Cas. 74 (a leading case, by Judge Peckham); Murphy v. St. Louis, etc., R. Co., 43 Mo. App. 342; Heaton v. Kansas City, etc., R. Co., 65 Mo. App. 479; Denver, etc., R. Co. v. Pickard, 8 Colo. 163; 6 Pac. Rep. 149; 18 Am. & Eng. R. Cas. 284.

Boarding a slowly moving train, in compliance with the request of the conductor, was held to excuse the negligence of the passenger, in Bucher v. New York, etc., R. Co., 98 N. Y. 128; 21 Am. & Eng. R. Cas. 361; Baltimore, etc., R. Co. v. Leapley, 65 Md. 571; 27 Am. & Eng. R. Cas. 167; Lent v. New York, etc., R. Co., 120 N. Y. 467;

§ 785. Care in alighting from train.—A passenger who fails to use ordinary care to avoid injury in alighting from a train, cannot recover for an injury received, due in whole or in part to such absence of reasonable care on his part.

It is generally held to be negligence to alight at a dangerous place, in the face of warning from the employees of the train,[79] or of other passengers;[80] going to sleep until a train has started and then rushing off the train, in a manner that contributes to an injury, is negligence;[81] it is likewise negligence to alight on another track than that on which the car from which the passenger alighted stands, without stopping, or looking or listening for an approaching train,[82] and however slightly it may contribute to an injury to a passenger, if the injured passenger was intoxicated, when he sustained the injury sued for, no recovery can be had therefor, if the intoxication in part brought about the injury.[83]

44 Am. & Eng. R. Cas. 373; Filer v. New York, etc., R. Co., 59 N. Y. 351; Cincinnati, etc., R. Co. v. Carper, 112 Ind. 26; 31 Am. & Eng. R. Cas. 36; Central, etc., R. Co. v. Miles, 88 Ala. 256; 41 Am. & Eng. R. Cas. 149.

In the following cases, it was held to be negligence, as matter of law, to attempt to board a slowly moving train: West Chicago R. Co. v. Binder, 51 Ill. App. 420; Chicago, etc., R. Co. v. Scates, 90 Ill. 586; Central R. Co. v. Smith, 74 Md. 212; 21 Atl. Rep. 706; Blair v. Grand Rapids R. Co., 60 Mich. 124; 26 N. W. Rep. 855; Browne v. Raleigh, etc., R. Co., 108 No. Car. 34; 12 S. E. Rep. 958; Soloman v. Manhattan R. Co., 103 N. Y. 437; 56 Am. Rep. 843; Mills v. Missouri, etc., R. Co. (Texas), 57 S. W. Rep. 291; Harvey v. Eastern R. Co., 116 Mass. 269; Walthers v. Chicago, etc., R. Co., 72 Ill. App. 354.

79 Ohio, etc., R. Co. v. Schiebe, 44 Ill. 460.

80 Kilpatrick v. Pennsylvania R. Co., 140 Pa. St. 502; 21 Atl. Rep. 408.

81 Wilson v. New Orleans, etc., R. Co., 68 Miss. 9; 8 So. Rep. 330.

82 Gonzales v. New York, etc., R. Co., 1 J. & S. (N. Y.) 57; Horstein v. United Rys. Co., 97 Mo. App. 271; 195 Mo. 450; 70 S. W. Rep. 1105; Weller v. Chicago, etc., R. Co., 164 Mo. 180; 64 S. W. Rep. 141; 86 Am. St. Rep. 592; Culbertson v. Metropolitan R. Co., 140 Mo. 35; 36 S. W. Rep. 834.

83 Strand v. Chicago, etc., R. Co., 67 Mich. 380; 34 N. W. Rep. 712; 31 Am. & Eng. R. Cas. 54.

But it is not necessarily negligence for a passenger to fail to get off of a train, with the first lot of passengers who alight, if the attempt is made before the train has started; [84] it is not negligence for a passenger to fail to advise the employees of the train of a disability or crippled condition, which impedes the passenger's locomotion; [85] the passenger can attempt to leave a stationary train without holding on to the hand rails on the platform; [86] it is not negligence for a foreigner to fail to heed the warning of a train employee, where the warning was not understood,[87] nor can the carrier be heard to say that a passenger selected the more dangerous way of leaving a train, when its own negligence is the proximate cause of both dangers which confront the passenger.[88]

§ 786. **Alighting on wrong side of train.**—When a railroad company has provided a station and platform and other safe means of ingress and egress to and from its trains, upon one side of its track, it has, in this particular, discharged its full measure of duty toward its passengers and it is not bound to anticipate that they will, in violation of its rules, alight from the trains on the opposite side of the track, where no such facilities for alighting exist.[89]   And if a

[84] McDermott v. Chicago, etc., R. Co., 82 Wis. 246; 52 N. W. Rep. 85.
[85] McGinney v. Canadian Pacific R. Co., 7 Man. 151.
[86] McDonald v. Long Island R. Co., 116 N. Y. 546; 22 N. E. Rep. 1068.
[87] Walter v. Chicago, etc., R. Co., 39 Iowa 33; 9 Am. Ry. Rep. 78; 20 Am. Ry. Rep. 319.
[88] Delamater v. Milwaukee, etc., R. Co., 24 Wis. 578; Taylor v. Missouri Pacific Ry. Co., 26 Mo. App. 336.
" Where a person goes on a train at a station with the permission of the train men to locate his family in a sleeper, and as he starts to leave the car, while the train was moving, the brakeman tells him to hurry up, and he is thrown under the moving car and is injured, he is guilty of contributory negligence." Purvis v. Buffalo, etc., R. Co. (Pa. 1907), 68 Atl. Rep. 189; 219 Pa. St. 195.
[89] Drake v. Pennsylvania R. Co., 137 Pa. St. 352; 20 Atl. Rep. 994;

passenger, in violation of such rule, alights from the train on the side away from the station and platform, in case of a resulting injury sustained while so doing, no recovery can be had therefor.[90]

A passenger, familiar with the location and surroundings where a train is stopped, cannot recover for an injury received in alighting, in the nighttime, on the side opposite the station, when the only reason for doing so, was to save time, until the train should pull out.[91] A passenger alighting, away from the station, on a side track and struck by a train which is obscured by escaping steam from the engine, cannot recover.[92] And it is held, in Pennsylvania, that a nonsuit is properly allowed, where a passenger was injured in alighting on a side track, instead of on the station side, at the place where the train had stopped.[93]

But the fact that a passenger sustains an injury while alighting on the side opposite the station is not always held to be negligence, *per se,* but it is proper to be taken into consideration by the jury, in determining all the facts and circumstances in the case.[94] And if the railroad company has knowingly permitted its passengers, for a considerable period of time, to alight at a given station, on the side opposite the station and there is no immediate danger apparent from pursuing this course, a passenger will not necessarily be held negligent, who, in following up this custom, alights on the side opposite the station.[95]

Pennsylvania R. Co. v. Zebe, 37 Pa. St. 420; 33 Pa. St. 318; Pastoris v. Baltimore, etc., R. Co. (Pa.), 24 Atl. Rep. 283; Goldberg v. New York, etc., R. Co., 133 N. Y. 561.

[90] Drake v. Pennsylvania R. Co., *supra.*

[91] Louisville, etc., R. Co. v. Ricketts (Ky.), 19 S. W. Rep. 182.

[92] Goldberg v. New York, etc., R. Co., 54 N. Y. S. R. 90; 71 Hun 613; 133 N. Y. 561.

[93] Morgen v. Camden, etc., R. Co. (Pa.), 16 Atl. Rep. 353.

[94] McQuilken v. Central Pacific R. Co., 64 Cal. 463; 2 Pac. Rep. 46; 16 Am. & Eng. R. Cas. 353.

[95] Chicago, etc., R. Co. v. Lowell, 151 U. S. 209; 14 Sup. Ct. Rep.

§ 787. **Alighting away from station platform.**— Where a proper landing place, or platform, is provided by a railroad company, at its stations, for its passengers to alight upon, and a passenger knows of such facilities for alighting from trains, but for purposes of his own convenience attempts to alight away from the station or platform, without any direction or invitation of the employees of the train, no recovery can be had for an injury sustained while so doing, as the passenger assumes the risk of such a voluntary dangerous course.[96]

A passenger, for instance, is held to assume the risk of an injury sustained by falling off a trestle, in an attempt to alight from a train which temporarily stopped on the trestle,[97] where the employees of the train had no notice of the dangerous attempt to alight from the train at this place.

But of course if the train employees directed the passenger to alight at such a place, a different result would obtain [98] and if the station was announced and there was

281; Boss v. Providence, etc., R. Co., 15 R. I. 149; 1 Atl. Rep. 9; 21 Am. & Eng. R. Cas. 364.

"Where a passenger on a street car asked the conductor to stop at a certain street, and he said 'All right,' and upon approaching the street, the conductor closed the gates on the platform side of the car, and left the gates open on the opposite side, and then gave the signal to stop, and plaintiff, with a grip in his hand stood at the open gate and when the car slowed down as though to stop, alighted, but was thrown and injured by the car starting up at full speed, the passenger was not guilty of negligence as a matter of law." Marbourg v. Seattle, etc., Ry. Co. (Wash. 1908), 94 Pac. Rep. 649.

[96] Chicago, etc., R. Co. v. Dingham, 1 Ill. App. 162; Eckerd v. Chicago, etc., R. Co., 70 Iowa 353; 30 N. W. Rep. 615; 27 Am. & Eng. R. Cas. 114; Mitchell v. Chicago, etc., R. Co., 51 Mich. 236; 16 N. W. Rep. 388; 47 Am. Rep. 566; 12 Am. & Eng. R. Cas. 163.

[97] Nagle v. California Southern R. Co., 88 Cal. 86; 25 Pac. Rep. 1106.

[98] Hartzig v. Lehigh Valley R. Co., 154 Pa. St. 364; 26 Atl. Rep. 310; East Tennessee, etc., R. Co. v. Connor, 15 Lea (Tenn.) 254.

nothing in the surroundings to give notice of the danger of alighting away from the station, there would be a liability on the carrier's part,[99] or the question of the passenger's negligence would, at least, be a proper issue for the jury.[1]

If the surrounding circumstances are so plain and obvious as to plainly impart notice to the passenger that a station has not been reached,[2] however, or that a train has passed the station,[3] and that it is dangerous to attempt to alight from the train at the place where the train is stopped, the passenger will be held to be negligent in making such an attempt, although the station was announced, in the regular way, by the employees of the train.[4]

[99] Memphis, etc., R. Co. v. Stringfellow, 44 Ark. 322; 51 Am. Rep. 598; 21 Am. & Eng. R. Cas. 374; Texas, etc., R. Co. v. Garcia, 62 Texas 285; 21 Am. & Eng. R. Cas. 384; Pennsylvania R. Co. v. Hoagland, 78 Ind. 203; 3 Am. & Eng. R. Cas. 436; Southern Kansas R. Co. v. Peavey, 48 Kansas 452; 29 Pac. Rep. 593; McGee v. Missouri Pacific Ry. Co., 92 Mo. 208; 4 S. W. Rep. 739; 31 Am. & Eng. R. Cas. 1.

[1] Onderdonk v. New York, etc., R. Co., 74 Hun 42; 56 N. Y. S. R. 190; Foss v. Boston, etc., R. Co. (N. H.), 21 Atl. Rep. 222; 47 Am. & Eng. R. Cas. 566; Pennsylvania R. Co. v. Marion, 123 Ind. 415; 23 N. E. Rep. 973; 7 L. R. A. 687; Chicago, etc., R. Co. v. Arnol, 144 Ill. 261; 33 N. E. Rep. 204; 58 Am. & Eng. R. Cas. 411.

[2] East Tennessee, etc., R. Co. v. Holmes, 97 Ala. 332; 12 So. Rep. 286; 58 Am. & Eng. R. Cas. 252.

[3] Plant v. Midland R. Co., 21 L. T. 836; McNulta v. Ensch, 134 Ill. 46; 24 N. E. Rep. 613.

[4] Richmond, etc., R. Co. v. Smith, 92 Ala. 237; 9 So. Rep. 223; East Tennessee, etc., R. Co. v. Holmes, 97 Ala. 332; 12 So. Rep. 286; 58 Am. & Eng. R. Cas. 252; Mitchell v. Chicago, etc., R. Co., 51 Mich. 236; 16 N. W. Rep. 388; 47 Am. Rep. 566; 12 Am. & Eng. R. Cas. 163.

" The absence of the customary depot lights, which plaintiff's testator knew were maintained at the station, was not such a fact tending to suggest to plaintiff's testator that the station had not been reached as to make him guilty of contributory negligence as a matter of law in stepping from the train." Wolf v. Chicago & N. W. Ry. Co. (Wis. 1907), 111 N. W. Rep. 514.

Alighting from trains, at a distance from the regular station, at an unsafe place, such as a railroad crossing. without the direction of employees, was held negligence in the following cases: Minock v. Detroit, etc., R. Co., 97 Mich. 425; 56 N. W. Rep. 780; Harold v.

§ 788. **Alighting from moving train.**— A railroad company is not generally held liable in damages to a passenger who jumps or steps from its moving train, when there is no necessity for so doing.[5] Nor would it be a sufficient excuse to justify such rash conduct, that the passenger had been

Great Western R. Co., 14 L. T. (N. S.) 440; Jackson v. Grand Avenue R. Co., 118 Mo. 199; 24 S. W. Rep. 192.

But if the employees ask the passenger to alight, or he alights in pursuance of a long established custom, his negligence is held to be a jury issue, in the following cases: Terre Haute, etc., R. Co. v. Buck, 96 Ind. 346; 49 Am. Rep. 168; McKimble v. Boston, etc., R. Co., 141 Mass. 463; Delaware, etc., R. Co. v. Perrett, 60 N. J. L. 589; 40 Atl. Rep. 1131; Miller v. East Tennessee, etc., R. Co., 93 Ga. 630; 21 S. E. Rep. 153.

Alighting from a moving train, before it reached the station, even after announcement of the station, was held to be negligence, in the following cases: Ohio, etc., R. Co. v. Stratton, 78 Ill. 88; Adams v. Louisville, etc., R. Co., 82 Ky. 603; 21 Am. & Eng. R. Cas. 380; Armstrong v. New York, etc., R. Co., 66 Barb. 437; Central R. Co. v. Thompson, 76 Ga. 770; East Tennessee, etc., R. Co. v. Holmes, 97 Ala. 332; 12 So. Rep. 286; 58 Am. & Eng. R. Cas. 252; England v. Boston, etc., R. Co., 153 Mass. 490; 27 N. E. Rep. 1.

And in the following, it was held negligence to alight from a moving train, after it had passed the station, viz.; Little Rock, etc., R. Co. v. Tankersley, 54 Ark. 25; 14 S. W. Rep. 1099; Reibel v. Cincinnati, etc., R. Co., 114 Ind. 476; 17 N. E. Rep. 107; Illinois, etc., R. Co. v. Lutz, 84 Ill. 598; Lake Shore, etc., R. Co. v. Bangs, 47 Mich. 470; 11 N. W. Rep. 276; 3 Am. & Eng. R. Cas. 426; Nelson v. Atlantic, etc., R. Co., 68 Mo. 593; Waller v. Hannibal, etc., R. Co., 83 Mo. 608; Walker v. Vicksburg, etc., R. Co., 41 La. Ann. 795; 6 So. Rep. 916; 7 L. R. A. 111; 41 Am. & Eng. R. Cas. 172; Watson v. Georgia, etc., R. Co., 81 Ga. 476; 7 S. E. Rep. 854; Brown v. Chicago, etc., R. Co., 80 Wis. 162; 49 N. W. Rep. 807; Owen v. Great Western R. Co., 46 L. J. Q. B. D. 486; 36 L. T. 850.

[5] Whelan v. Georgia, etc., R. Co., 84 Ga. 506; 10 S. E. Rep. 1091; 44 Am. & Eng. R. Cas. 335; Tabler v. Hannibal, etc., R. Co., 93 Mo. 79; 5 S. W. Rep. 810; 31 Am. & Eng. R. Cas. 185; Fournet v. Morgan, etc., R. Co., 43 La. Ann. 1202; 11 So. Rep. 541; Gavett v. Manchester, etc., R. Co., 16 Gray (Mass.) 501; Burrows v. Erie R. Co., 63 N. Y. 556; Jewell v. Chicago, etc., R. Co., 54 Wis. 610; 41 Am. Rep. 63; 6 Am. & Eng. R. Cas. 379; Central, etc., R. Co. v. Letcher, 69 Ala. 106; 12 Am. & Eng. R. Cas. 115; Richmond, etc., R. Co. v. Morris, 31 Gratt. (Va.) 200.

negligently carried past his station, for in such event, he could recover for his loss of time and expenses of being carried back, but if he jumped or left the train under circumstances when prudence would forbid, he cannot recover for injuries so received.[6]

If the facts are not disputed and the danger of alighting would be apparent, considering the rate of speed at which the train was being run and the age and physical condition of the passenger, it is the duty of the court, as matter of law, to hold the passenger guilty of negligence in alighting from the train, under such circumstances.[7] But of course it must be made to appear that the act of the passenger, in alighting from the train in motion, was the proximate or direct cause of his injury, or, at least that it combined to produce the injury.[8] And if, instead of the act of alighting from the moving train causing the injury, the passenger was injured after safely alighting, by reason of the negligence of the railroad company, his negligence in so alighting could not be said to directly produce the injury. And where the evidence is conflicting as to whether or not the act of alighting from the train did occasion the injury and whether or not the danger of attempting to alight from a train going at the rate of speed that the train was being operated, when the passenger got off was such as to deter a reasonably prudent person from undertaking to get off of the train, the issue is properly submitted to the jury,

[6] Kelly v. Hannibal, etc., R. Co., 70 Mo. 604; Waller v. Hannibal, etc., R. Co., 83 Mo. 608.

[7] Louisville, etc., R. Co. v. Johnson, 44 Ill. App. 56; Cincinnati, etc., R. Co. v. Dufrain, 36 Ill. App. 352; Morrison v. Erie R. Co., 56 N. Y. 302; 6 Am. Ry. Rep. 166; New York, etc., R. Co. v. Enches, 127 Pa. St. 316; 17 Atl. Rep. 991; 39 Am. & Eng. R. Cas. 444.

[8] Van Ostran v. New York, etc., R. Co., 35 Hun (N. Y.) 590; 104 N. Y. 683; Little Rock, etc., R. Co. v. Tankersley, 54 Ark. 25; 14 S. W. Rep. 1099; Hickman v. Missouri Pacific Ry. Co., 91 Mo. 433; 4 S. W. Rep. 127; Lambeth v. North Carolina R. Co., 66 No. Car. 494.

under appropriate instructions from the court.[9] As determining this issue, in such a case, if the evidence shows that the conductor, or other train employee, requested the passenger to alight,[10] or if, in the act of alighting, the passenger merely selected this course in preference to some other peril, which the negligence of the railroad company subjected him to, of course this would materially modify his negligence in alighting from the moving train and lead the triers of the facts to make due allowance therefor.[11]

§ 789. Speed of train as affecting negligence in alighting.— It has been held that the question whether a passenger is guilty of negligence in alighting from a slowly moving train, depends upon the fact whether or not he has exercised the care of a reasonably prudent person in attempting to do so.[12] In other words, where the speed of the train is

[9] Louisville, etc., R. Co. v. Crunk, 119 Ind. 542; 21 N. E. Rep. 31; 41 Am. & Eng. R. Cas. 158; Bucher v. New York, etc., R. Co., 98 N. Y. 128; 21 Am. & Eng. R. Cas. 361; Western Maryland R. Co. v. Herold, 74 Md. 510; 22 Atl. Rep. 323; Tabler v. Hannibal, etc., R. Co., 93 Mo. 79; 5 S. W. Rep. 810; 31 Am. & Eng. R. Cas. 185; Doss v. Missouri, etc., R. Co., 59 Mo. 37; Enches v. New York, etc., R. Co., 135 Pa. St. 194; 19 Atl. Rep. 939; Pennsylvania R. Co. v. Marion, 123 Ind. 415; 23 N. E. Rep. 973; 7 L. R. A. 687.

[10] Highland Avenue R. Co. v. Winn, 93 Ala. 306; 9 So. Rep. 509.

[11] Pennsylvania R. Co. v. Lyons, 129 Pa. St. 113; 18 Atl. Rep. 759; 41 Am. & Eng. R. Cas. 154; Shannon v. Boston, etc., R. Co., 78 Me. 52; 2 Atl. Rep. 678; 23 Am. & Eng. R. Cas. 511.

"In an action for injuries to a passenger while alighting from a train, it was a question for the jury whether or not plaintiff was guilty of contributory negligence." Hall v. Northern Pac. Ry. Co. (N. D. 1907), 111 N. W. Rep. 609.

"Whether plaintiff, a passenger, was guilty of contributory negligence in alighting from a train, held, under the evidence, a question for the jury." Selman v. Gulf, etc., Ry. Co. (Tex. Civ. App. 1907), 101 S. W. Rep. 1030.

[12] Price v. St. Louis, etc., R. Co., 72 Mo. 414; 3 Am. & Eng. R. Cas. 365; Waller v. Hannibal, etc., R. Co., 83 Mo. 608; Cumberland Valley R. Co. v. Mangnus, 61 Md. 53; 18 Am. & Eng. R. Cas. 182; New

not such as to make it dangerous for a passenger of the age and physical condition and situated under the circumstances that the passenger is situated, to alight from the train, but if the act of alighting, under such conditions, could be safely performed, it will be a question for the jury, whether or not the passenger was negligent in alighting.[13] It is accordingly held that it is not necessarily negligent to step from a slowly moving train, if the passenger is not physically incapacitated, or otherwise disabled from safely performing such an ordinary act.[14]

But an injury resulting to a passenger from an attempt to alight from a rapidly moving train will generally be held to afford no cause of action,[15] even though the order to alight was given by an employee of the railroad company, when there was no immediate danger to the passenger from remaining on the train.[16] Just what rate of speed will constitute negligence, as matter of law, will of course depend in a measure upon the age, physical condition and activity of the passenger, as well as other surrounding circumstances. It has been held to be a jury issue, whether or not a passenger was negligent in alighting from a train moving at

York, etc., R. Co. v. Cleybourne, 69 Md. 360; 16 Atl. Rep. 208; 1 L. R. A. 541; Terre Haute, etc., R. Co. v. Voelker, 129 Ill. 540; 22 N. E. Rep. 20; 39 Am. & Eng. R. Cas. 615.

[13] Clotworthy v. Hannibal, etc., R. Co., 80 Mo. 220; 21 Am. & Eng. R. Cas. 371.

[14] Nance v. Carolina, etc., R. Co., 94 N. Car. 619; Georgia Pacific R. Co. v. West, 66 Miss. 310; 6 So. Rep. 207; Western R. Co. v. Young, 51 Ga. 489; 7 Am. Ry. Rep. 352; Filer v. New York, etc., R. Co., 49 N. Y. 47; 3 Am. Ry. Rep. 460; Nelson v. Atlantic, etc., R. Co., 68 Mo. 593; Buchner v. New York, etc., R. Co., 98 N. Y. 128; 21 Am. & Eng. R. Cas. 361; Lent v. New York, etc., R. Co., 120 N. Y. 467; 24 N. E. Rep. 653; 44 Am. & Eng. R. Cas. 373; Galveston, etc., R. Co. v. Smith, 59 Texas 406; Leslie v. Wabash R. Co., 88 Mo. 50; 26 Am. & Eng. R. Cas. 229.

[15] McLarin v. Atlanta, etc., R. Co., 85 Ga. 504; 11 S. E. Rep. 840; Houston, etc., R. Co. v. Leslie, 57 Texas 83; 9 Am. & Eng. R. Cas. 407.

[16] Southwestern R. Co. v. Singleton, 67 Ga. 306.

from four to five miles an hour.[17]   While, on the other hand, it has been held negligence, *per se,* to attempt to alight from a train traveling at a speed of from six to eight miles per hour.[18]   And, of course, if this rate of speed would render it negligence to attempt to alight from the train, it would, *a fortiori,* constitute negligence to attempt to alight from a train going at a speed of from fifteen [19] to twenty, or twenty-five miles an hour.[20]

[17] Louisville, etc., R. Co. v. Crunk, 119 Ind. 542; 21 N. E. Rep. 31; 41 Am. & Eng. R. Cas. 158; New York, etc., R. Co. v. Clourborne, 69 Md. 360; 16 Atl. Rep. 208; 1 L. R. A. 541.

[18] East Tennessee, etc., R. Co. v. Holmes, 97 Ala. 332; 12 So. Rep. 286; 58 Am. & Eng. R. Cas. 252; South, etc., R. Co. v. Schafer, 75 Ala. 136; 21 Am. & Eng. R. Cas. 405.

[19] Southwestern R. Co. v. Singleton, 66 Ga. 252; Dougherty v. Chicago, etc., R. Co., 86 Ill. 467; 17 Am. Ry. Rep. 489; Woolery v. Louisville, etc., R. Co., 107 Ind. 381; 8 N. E. Rep. 226; 57 Am. Rep. 114; 27 Am. & Eng. R. Cas. 210.

[20] Jarrett v. Atlanta, etc., R. Co., 83 Ga. 347; 9 S. E. Rep. 681.

The passenger's negligence, in alighting from a slowly moving train, was held to be a jury issue, in the following cases: Watkins v. Birmingham, etc., R. Co., 120 Ala. 147; St. Louis, etc., R. Co. v. Baker, 67 Ark. 531; 55 S. W. Rep. 941; Little Rock, etc., R. Co. v. Askins, 46 Ark. 423; Suber v. Georgia, etc., R. Co., 96 Ga. 42; 23 S. E. Rep. 387; Floytroupe v. Boston, etc., R. Co., 163 Mass. 152; 39 N. E. Rep. 797; Leslie v. Wabash R. Co., 88 Mo. 50; McDonald v. Kansas City, etc., R. Co., 127 Mo. 38; 29 S. W. Rep. 848; Richmond v. Quincy, etc., R. Co., 49 Mo. App. 104; Sanderson v. Missouri, etc., R. Co., 64 Mo. App. 655; Morgan v. Southern R. Co., 95 Cal. 501; 30 Pac. Rep. 601; Sanders v. Southern R. Co., 107 Ga. 132; Atchison, etc., R. Co. v. Hughes, 55 Kansas 491; 40 Pac. Rep. 919; Lewis v. Delaware, etc., R. Co., 145 N. Y. 508; 40 N. E. Rep. 248; Jacob v. Flint, etc., R. Co., 105 Mich. 450; 63 N. W. Rep. 502.

Where the train was moving at a rate of speed to make it obviously dangerous and the passenger was not induced to alight by the employees of the train, it was held to be negligence to alight from a moving train, in the following cases: Kilpatrick v. Pennsylvania R. Co., 140 Pa. St. 502; 21 Atl. Rep. 408; Jewell v. Chicago, etc., R. Co., 54 Wis. 610; England v. Boston, etc., R. Co., 153 Mass. 490; Nelson v. Atlantic, etc., R. Co., 68 Mo. 593; Butler v. St. Paul, etc., R. Co., 59 Minn. 135; 60 N. W. Rep. 1090; McDonald v. Boston, etc., R. Co., 87 Me. 466; 32 Atl. Rep. 1010; 2 Am. & Eng. R. Cas. (N. S.)

§ 790. **Alighting from moving train at improper time.**— A railroad company is not generally liable to a passenger injured in an attempt to alight from a moving train, where, after the station was announced, the train was held stationary for a reasonable time, but the passenger, instead of alighting then, awaited until the train had again started up.[21]   And the same result follows, if a passenger, instead of waiting for a train to stop, attempts to leave the train while it is in motion, and in so doing, receives an injury, or where the train has failed to stop a sufficient time to enable the passengers to alight and instead of waiting to have the train stopped, the passenger leaps from the train, while it is in motion.[22]

But this result does not necessarily obtain, where the train has stopped and a passenger is attempting to alight, when the train is again started, without allowing sufficient time for the passengers to alight.   If, under all the circumstances,

293; Scully v. New York, etc., R. Co., 80 Hun 197; 61 N. Y. S. R. 804; 151 N. Y. 672; 46 N. E. Rep. 1151; Victor v. Pennsylvania R. Co., 164 Pa. St. 195; 30 Atl. Rep. 381; Kansas City, etc., R. Co. v. Owens, 58 Ark. 397; 24 S. W. Rep. 1076; Schiffler v. Chicago, etc., R. Co., 96 Wis. 141; 71 N. W. Rep. 97; 8 Am. & Eng. R. Cas. (N. S.) 122; Burden v. Lake Shore, etc., R. Co., 104 Mich. 101; 62 N. W. Rep. 173; Minock v. Detroit, etc., R. Co., 97 Mich. 425; 56 N. W. Rep. 780; Savannah, etc., R. Co. v. Watts, 82 Ga. 229; 9 S. E. Rep. 129.

[21] Little Rock, etc., R. Co. v. Tankersley, 54 Ark. 25; 14 S. W. Rep. 1099; Clotworthy v. Hannibal, etc., R. Co., 80 Mo. 220; 21 Am. & Eng. R. Cas. 371; Covington v. Western R. Co., 81 Ga. 273; 6 S. E. Rep. 593; 34 Am. & Eng. R. Cas. 469; Louisville, etc., R. Co. v. Lee, 97 Ala. 325; 12 So. Rep. 48; Chicago, etc., R. Co. v. Landauer, 36 Neb. 642; 54 N. W. Rep. 976; 54 Am. & Eng. R. Cas. 640; Pennsylvania R. Co. v. Lyons, 129 Pa. St. 113; 18 Atl. Rep. 759; 41 Am. & Eng. R. Cas. 154.

[22] Jeffersonville R. Co. v. Hendricks, 26 Ind. 228; Jewell v. Chicago, etc., R. Co., 54 Wis. 610; 12 N. W. Rep. 83; 41 Am. Rep. 63; 6 Am. & Eng. R. Cas. 379; Atlanta, etc., R. Co. v. Dickerson, 89 Ga. 455; 15 S. E. Rep. 534; Morrison v. Erie R. Co., 56 N. Y. 302; 6 Am. Ry. Rep. 166; Burrows v. Erie R. Co., 63 N. Y. 556.

the passenger could reasonably conclude that he could safely alight, under such a condition, it will be a jury issue, whether or not he was negligent in attempting so to do.[23] And this would be true, particularly, in cases where the attempt to alight was made at the instance or suggestion of the employees of the train,[24] or where the motion of the train was very slow.[25]

§ 791. **Alighting on command of employees.**— A passenger who alights from a slowly moving train, at the instance or direction of the conductor, or other agent in charge of the train, on whose judgment the passenger has a right to rely, when the risk or danger of alighting is not apparent, is not chargeable with negligence, as matter of law, but it will be a question for the jury, under all the circumstances, to determine.[26] And if the employee who gives the direction is engaged in the service, upon the defendant's train, it is

[23] Louisville, etc., R. Co. v. Stacker, 86 Tenn. 343; 6 S. W. Rep. 737; 0 Am. St. Rep. 840; Carr v. Eel River R. Co., 98 Cal. 366; 33 Pac. Rep. 213; 58 Am. & Eng. R. Cas. 239; Murphy v. Rome, etc., R. Co., 32 N. Y. S. R. 381; 10 N. Y. Supp. 354; 56 Hun 645; Pennsylvania R. Co. v. Kilgore, 32 Pa. St. 292.

[24] St. Louis, etc., R. Co. v. Person, 49 Ark. 182; 4 S. W. Rep. 755; 30 Am. & Eng. R. Cas. 567; McCaslin v. Lake Shore, etc., R. Co., 93 Mich. 553; 53 N. W. Rep. 724; 52 Am. & Eng. R. Cas. 290.

[25] Ilinois, etc., R. Co. v. Able, 59 Ill. 131; 11 Am. Ry. Rep. 154; Nance v. Carolina R. Co., 94 No. Car. 619; Nichols v. Dubuque, etc., R. Co., 68 Iowa 732; 28 N. W. Rep. 44; 27 Am. & Eng. R. Cas. 183; Brooks v. Boston, etc., R. Co., 135 Mass, 21; 16 Am. & Eng. R. Cas. 345; Strauss v. Kansas City, etc., R. Co., 75 Mo. 185; 6 Am. & Eng. R. Cas. 384; Pennsylvania R. Co. v. Peters, 116 Pa. St. 206; 9 Atl. Rep. 317; 30 Am. & Eng. R. Cas. 607; Strand v. Chicago, etc., R. Co., 64 Mich. 216; 31 N. W. Rep. 184; 28 Am. & Eng. R. Cas. 213.

[26] St. Louis, etc., R. Co. v. Cantrell, 37 Ark. 519; 40 Am. Rep. 105; 8 Am. & Eng. R. Cas. 198; St. Louis, etc., R. Co. v. Rosenberry, 45 Ark. 256; Delaware, etc., R. Co. v. Webster, 6 Atl. Rep. 841; 27 Am. & Eng. R. Cas. 160; Quinn v. Manhattan R. Co., 7 N. Y. S. R. 252; Galloway v. Chicago, etc., R. Co. (Iowa), 54 N. W. Rep. 447; 58 Am. & Eng. R. Cas. 245.

generally immaterial, whether he is in sole charge of the train, or only an employee in a subordinate capacity. Accordingly, the command of the brakeman [27] is placed upon the same footing as that of the conductor of the train,[28] and the obedience to either will relieve the passenger of the charge of negligence as matter of law.

But if the train is running at a rate of speed to make it manifestly negligent for a passenger, situated as the passenger commanded to alight, is situated, or if the risk of alighting is or ought to be apparent to a man of ordinary prudence, then the command of the train employee to alight, will furnish no excuse for such a rash act, on the passenger's part and no recovery can be had for such an injury.[29] The railroad company is not responsible for the advice or directions given by other passengers and the fact that a passenger was led to alight from a moving train, on their advice, is no excuse for the passenger's negligence in so doing,[30] 'unless he was an infant, or there were other similar mollifying circumstances.[31]

However, if the command to alight is accompanied by a threat or acts on the part of the train employees, calculated to induce the passenger to attempt to alight to avoid being ejected, these circumstances, along with others, will affect

[27] Filer v. New York, etc., R. Co., 68 N. Y. 124; Galloway v. Chicago, etc., R. Co., 54 N. W. Rep. 447; 58 Am. & Eng. R. Cas. 245.

[28] Jeffersonville R. Co. v. Swift, 26 Ind. 459; East Tennessee, etc., R. Co. v. Hughes (Ga.), 17 S. E. Rep. 949; 58 Am. & Eng. R. Cas. 373.

[29] South, etc., R. Co. v. Schauffer, 75 Ala. 136; 21 Am. & Eng. R. Cas. 405; St. Louis, etc., R. Co. v. Rosenberry, 45 Ark. 256; 11 S. W. Rep. 212; Vimont v. Chicago, etc., R. Co., 71 Iowa 58; 32 N. W. Rep. 100; 28 Am. & Eng. R. Cas. 210; Bardwell v. Mobile, etc., R. Co., 63 Miss. 574.

[30] Masterson v. Macon City, etc., R. Co., 88 Ga. 436; 14 S. E. Rep. 591; Filer v. New York, etc., R. Co., 59 N. Y. 351; 7 Am. Ry. Rep. 111.

[31] Hemmingway v. Chicago, etc., R. Co., 72 Wis. 42; 37 N. W. Rep. 804; 7 Am. St. Rep. 823; 33 Am. & Eng. R. Cas. 511.

the issue of the passenger's negligence in attempting to alight.[32]

§ 792. **Jumping to avoid imminent peril.**— Where the negligence of a railroad company or its employees has placed a passenger in some sudden peril and he jumps from the train, as a reasonable measure of safety, to avoid the greater peril, the company will, generally, be held liable for the injury, even though the passenger would not have received injury if he had remained on the train.[33] If the passenger jumps from a moving train to avoid what seems an impending collision with another train, he is not chargeable with contributory negligence, if he acted as a reasonably prudent person under the same circumstances, would act, even though no collision actually occurred.[34] And if a passenger jumps from a moving car, after it has been derailed and receives injuries, it is no defense for the railroad company to set up that he would not have been injured if he had remained on the car,[35] for under such exciting conditions, the law does not hold him to the use of the best or safest course.

But if the danger of the passenger is due to his own

[32] International, etc., R. Co. v. Hassell, 62 Texas 256; 21 Am. & Eng. R. Cas. 315; Highland Avenue R. Co. v. Winn, 93 Ala. 306; 9 So. Rep. 509; Georgia, etc., R. Co. v. McCurdy, 45 Ga. 288; Baltimore, etc., R. Co. v. Leapley, 65 Md. 571; 4 Atl. Rep. 891; 27 Am. & Eng. R. Cas. 167; Jones v. Chicago, etc., R. Co., 42 Minn. 183; 43 N. W. Rep. 1114; 41 Am. & Eng. R. Cas. 169; Boggess v Chesapeake, etc., R. Co., 37 W. Va. 297; 16 S. E. Rep. 525; Bucher v. New York, etc., R. Co., 98 N. Y. 128; 21 Am. & Eng. R. Cas. 361.

[33] Southwestern R. Co. v. Paulk, 24 Ga. 356; Shannon v. Boston, etc., R. Co., 78 Me. 52; 2 Atl. Rep. 678; 23 Am. & Eng. R. Cas. 511.

[34] Baltimore, etc., R. Co. v. McKenzie, 81 Va. 71; 24 Am. & Eng. R. Cas. 395; Twomley v. Central Park R. Co., 69 N. Y. 158; 18 Am. Ry. Rep. 113; Buel v. New York, etc., R. Co., 31 N. Y. 314; St. Louis, etc., R. Co. v. Murray, 55 Ark. 248; 18 S. W. Rep. 50; 52 Am. & Eng. R. Cas. 373; St. Louis, etc., R. Co. v. Maddry, 57 Ark. 306; 21 S. W. Rep. 472; 58 Am. & Eng. R. Cas. 327.

[35] Dimmitt v. Hannibal, etc., R. Co., 40 Mo. App. 654.

negligence in assuming a dangerous position on the train, rather than to the negligence of the carrier, or its employees, and to a condition that ought not to have occasioned alarm to even a timid person;[36] or if the passenger jumps from the train, in the face of the warning and admonition of the conductor, or other employee, who assures him there is no danger, there could be no recovery for an injury due solely to such a rash act, on the part of the passenger.[37]   And if the fear of a collision from another train is brought about by an alarmed passenger, when as matter of fact, there was no cause for alarm,[38] or the fear of an injury was brought about, without cause, by other than the defendant's employees, and no danger in fact threatened the passenger, it is no excuse for the rashness in jumping from the moving train that the passenger was frightened, and the carrier would not be liable therefor, in case of a resulting injury.[39]

§ 793. Care in or about station.— A passenger awaiting the arrival of his train is bound to use reasonable care for his own protection while on the company's premises, and failing so to do, will be denied a recovery, in case of a resulting injury.

It is not negligence, however, for a passenger awaiting the arrival of a train, to leave the station and go upon that portion of the platform intended for use by passengers and if he does so, and sustains an injury by reason of the unsafe condition of the platform,[40] or by being struck by a truck,

---

[36] Galena, etc., R. Co. v. Yarwood, 15 Ill. 468.

[37] Mobile, etc., R. Co. v. Klein, 43 Ill. App. 63.

[38] Gulf, etc., R. Co. v. Wallen, 65 Texas 568; 26 Am. & Eng. R. Cas. 219.

[39] Reary v. Louisville, etc., R. Co., 40 La. Ann. 32; 3 So. Rep. 390; 8 Am. St. Rep. 497; 34 Am. & Eng. R. Cas. 277; Cousins v. Lake Shore, etc., R. Co., 96 Mich. 386; 56 N. W. Rep. 14; Western Maryland R. Co. v. Herold, 74 Md. 510; 22 Atl. Rep. 323.

[40] Fullerton v. Fordyce, 121 Mo. 1; 25 S. W. Rep. 587; 42 Am.

in the hands of an employee,[41] or by falling over an obstruction on the platform, if it is night, and he is unable to see,[42] the railroad company will generally be held liable for such an injury. Before the use of the station's facilities or platform would amount to negligence, on the part of a passenger, the danger of using same must be so apparent as to deter a reasonably prudent person.[43]

But a railroad company is only bound to provide such reasonably safe stational facilities as may be safely used by a person of good health and in good physical condition and it is not bound to provide accommodations such as may be necessary for the physically weak or sick.[44] Such persons are required to use care proportionate to their disability, unless a different degree of care is required, on account of notice of their condition, to the railroad company.[45] If the passenger fails to use due care, around the station, as where he voluntarily used an unlighted stairway, at night, when three lighted stairways were open to his use,[46] or where he stepped from the depot platform, at night, on the side, instead of on the end, where steps were provided,[47] there could, generally, be no recovery for an injury so received, as the passenger would be held guilty of contributory negligence, in pursuing such a dangerous course.

St. Rep. 516; 144 Mo. 519; 44 S. W. Rep. 1053; Gunderman v. Missouri, etc., R. Co., 58 Mo. App. 370; Robertson v. Wabash R. Co., 152 Mo. 382; 53 S. W. Rep. 1082.

[41] Chicago, etc., R. Co. v. Wooldrige, 32 Ill. App. 237.

[42] Sargent v. St. Louis, etc., R. Co., 114 Mo. 348; 21 S. W. Rep. 823; 19 L. R. A. 460; McClellan v. Long Island R. Co., 20 J. & S. (N. Y.) 22; 107 N. Y. 623; 13 N. E. Rep. 939.

[43] Ohio, etc., R. Co. v. Stansberry, 132 Ind. 533; 32 N. E. Rep. 218.

[44] Renneker v. South Carolina R. Co., 20 So. Car. 219; 18 Am. & Eng. R. Cas. 149.

[45] Renneker v. South Carolina R. Co., supra.

[46] Bennett v. New York, etc., R. Co., 57 Conn. 422; 18 Atl. Rep. 668; 41 Am. & Eng. R. Cas. 184.

[47] Forsyth v. Boston, etc., R. Co., 103 Mass. 510.

§ 794. Use of premises not intended for passengers' use.— Passengers must confine their use of the railroad company's premises to those intended for their use, or otherwise they assume the risk of using such as may not be intended for public use, for as to such portions of the carrier's property, they are licensees. only.

In a Missouri case,[48] in considering the right of a passenger injured while using the railroad company's freight platform, to recover for such an injury, the Kansas City Court of Appeals used the following language:

" It is not denied but that the defendant's passenger platform and the approaches thereto were in every respect in a reasonably safe condition, nor that in this regard it had discharged the full measure of its duty to its passengers. But it is plaintiff's insistence that the defendant's freight platform, which was a place where passengers, or those who have purchased tickets with a view to take passage on its trains, would naturally and ordinarily be likely to resort, was not in such reasonably safe condition. We can no more reasonably and fairly infer that passengers or those intending to take passage on its trains would naturally and ordinarily be likely to leave its comfortable waiting rooms or its convenient passenger platform and resort to its freight platform on the opposite side of the depot from where they enter the trains, to there wait for their arrival, than we would that persons applying at the office of a public inn for lodging would resort to its kitchen, laundry, or back yard, to there wait until the landlord puts the room assigned to them in order for their reception. We are totally unable to find any fact or circumstance in the evidence that would justify any such inference.

[48] Gunderman v. Missouri, etc., R. Co., 58 Mo. App. 370, 380, 381, citing Sweeny v. Railroad, 10 Allen 368; Zoebisch v. Tarbell, 10 Allen 385.

" If passengers, or those intending to .become passengers, while waiting for the arrival of trains, have been known, as the evidence tends to show, to go upon the defendant's freight plafform, yet, *if they went there by the mere passive acquiescence of the defendant and without a direct or implied invitation or inducement to do so, then there was no duty or obligation on the part of the defendant to keep said platform in a reasonably safe condition as to them,* for they must be held to have gone there at their own risk.   The rule is that one who enjoys a license is subject to its concomitant perils.

" *A carrier's liability in respect to the condition of its premises is neither greater nor less than that of any other person to another who by invitation or inducement, express or implied, has come upon his* premises, for the purpose of transacting business."

§ 795. **Standing or walking on or near track.**— A passenger who, in anticipation of the arrival of his train, stands between two tracks, waiting to get on the train, when it pulls into the station, injured by a coal train backing up on one track, while he is watching the other track, is guilty of such negligence as will bar a recovery for his injury.[49] And a passenger who stands upon a track looking in one direction only, for an approaching train, until he is injured by a train approaching from the opposite direction, is denied a recovery because of his own rash conduct.[50]   The railroad track is not a proper passageway for passengers to walk upon and if a passenger walking on a railroad track is struck by a train and injured his negligence will prevent

[49] McGeehan v. Lehigh Valley R. Co., 149 Pa. St. 188; 24 Atl. Rep. 205; 50 Am. & Eng. R. Cas. 32.
[50] Weeks v. New Orleans, etc., R. Co., 40 La. Ann. 800; 5 So. Rep. 72; 8 Am. St. Rep. 560; Bancroft v. Boston, etc., R. Co., 97 Mass. 275.

a recovery for such an injury.[51]   The same result obtains
in the case of an injury to a passenger injured while walking at the side of a railroad track, where trains are apt to
be run, at any time, unless from the location of the ground
or the circumstances surrounding the case, the railroad
company could be held to have extended an implied or
express invitation to its passengers to use such portion of
its premises.[52]

The same duty exists upon the part of passengers, to
look and listen for approaching trains, before stepping upon
a railroad track, that obtains in the case of other persons
and employees,[53] unless the place or locality is such a place
or locality that is used by the railroad company for a
passway, or it has led the passenger, by its conduct, to
dispense with this ordinary duty, for his own protection.[54]

§ 796. Selecting unsafe place to ride.— While it is the
duty of the railroad company to furnish safe seats or
places for its passengers to ride and the passenger is not
required to select the safest seat on the train,[55] it is none
the less the duty of the passenger to find a seat or place
to ride that is reasonably safe and if there is a safe place

[51] Louisville, etc., R. Co. v. Schmetzer (Ky.), 22 S. W. Rep. 603.

[52] Schutt v. Cumberland Valley R. Co., 149 Pa. St. 266; 24 Atl.
Rep. 305.

[53] Connolly v. New York, etc., R. Co., 158 Mass. 8; 32 N. E. Rep.
937; Weeks v. New Orleans, etc., R. Co., 40 La. Ann. 800; 5 So.
Rep. 72; 8 Am. St. Rep. 560.

[54] Atchison, etc., R. Co. v. Sheehan, 18 Colo. 368; 33 Pac. Rep. 108;
Pennsylvania R. Co. v. Keane, 41 Ill. App. 317; Philadelphia, etc., R.
Co. v. Anderson, 72 Md. 519; 20 Atl. Rep. 2; 44 Am. & Eng. R. Cas.
345; Chaffee v. Boston, etc., R. Co., 104 Mass. 108; Brassell v. New
York, etc., R. Co., 84 N. Y. 241; 3 Am. & Eng. R. Cas. 380; Parsons v.
New York, etc., R. Co., 37 Hun (N. Y.) 128; Pennsylvania R. Co.
v. White, 88 Pa. St. 327; Sanchez v. San Antonio, etc., R. Co., 3 Texas
Civ. App. 89; 22 S. W. Rep. 242.

[55] Willis v. Long Island R. Co., 34 N. Y. 670; 32 Barb. 398.

to ride and the passenger selects an unsafe place, it is no excuse for his assuming such a place, that the employees of the train knew he was there or that they had failed to drive him from such an unsafe position.[56] If the passenger, without the consent of the carrier, or its employees, selects an unsafe place to ride, or a place not intended for passengers, he assumes the risk of injury from riding in such a place and cannot hold the railroad company liable for the effect of such conduct on his part.[57]

A passenger, for instance, who voluntarily rides upon a flat car, instead of in a passenger coach, assumes the risk of injury from causes more apt to injure him while so situated, such as injury from flying sparks, or cinders; [58] but riding on a flat car, with notice or consent of the employees of the train, is not necessarily negligence, as matter of law, and where the facts are conflicting, it is held to be a jury issue.[59]

But a passenger is not necessarily negligent in failing to try to install himself in the safest seat or place in a car or on a train. The law recognizes a condition that modern society does not entirely justify, that gentlemen, from courtesy, will always concede to the ladies the safest or most desirable seats in a public conveyance and it is held not to be negligence for men to make way for ladies, if a reasonably safe place is still maintained, or to stand aside and allow ladies to assume the safer positions in public

[56] Ashbrook v. Frederick Avenue R. Co., 18 Mo. App. 290.

[57] Carroll v. Transit Co., 107 Mo. 653; 17 S. W. Rep. 889; 52 Am. & Eng. R. Cas. 273; Norfolk, etc., R. Co. v. Ferguson, 79 Va. 241; Little Rock, etc., R. Co. v. Miles, 40 Ark. 298; 48 Am. Rep. 10; 13 Am. & Eng. R. Cas. 10; Files v. Boston, etc., R. Co., 149 Mass. 204; 21 N. E. Rep. 311; Jackson v. Crilly, 16 Colo. 103; 26 Pac. Rep. 331.

[58] Higgins v. Cherokee R. Co., 73 Ga. 149; 27 Am. & Eng. R. Cas. 218.

[59] Wagner v. Missouri Pacific Ry. Co., 97 Mo. 512; 10 S. W. Rep. 486; 3 L. R. A. 156.

conveyances.[60]   With such a reward for courtesy, it would seem that it ought to be practiced more generally than it is.

§ 797. **Riding on car or engine.**— If a passenger rides at a place where he has no right to ride, under the rules of the railroad company, or in a place of great danger — as on top of a box car or caboose,[61] or on a flat car,[62] or on the engine,[63] — the mere acquiescence of the train employees in such a rash act, will not give the plaintiff, injured in such a place, any greater rights than he would otherwise have, against the railroad company, and generally, no recovery can be had by a passenger so situated.   The rule is the same, whether the passenger is one occupying the rela-

[60] Chicago, etc., R. Co. v. Fisher, 141 Ill. 614; 31 N. E. Rep. 406; 38 Ill. App. 33.

"Where plaintiff boarded the smoking car of a railroad train, and, seeing no vacant seats, stood within three inches of the door, supporting himself with his hands, while the train traveled a distance of three-fourths of a mile, and was thrown through the open door onto the platform and off the train on its crossing a switch, he was guilty of contributory negligence and could not recover for his injuries." Foley v. Boston & M. R. R. (Mass. 1907), 79 N. E. Rep. 765.

"Plaintiff's intestate, while a passenger on defendant's car, rose from her seat to attract the attention of the conductor. The car was in rapid motion and swaying violently. She stood facing the rear of the car with one hand on the back of her seat, until she was thrown to the ground, when the motion of the car was checked by the brakes. She knew that the track was uneven, and that the car for that reason was liable to sway. *Held*, that she was not in the exercise of due care, and that a verdict for defendant was properly directed." Cottrell v. Pawtucket St. Ry. Co. (R. I. 1906), 65 Atl. Rep. 269; 27 R. I. 565.

[61] It was likewise held to be negligence to ride in the cupola of a caboose, several feet above the roof of the caboose, in Tuley v. Chicago, etc., R. Co., 41 Mo. App. 432.

[62] Riding on a flat car was held to be negligence, in Higgins v. Cherokee, etc., R. Co., 73 Ga. 149; 27 Am. & Eng. R. Cas. 218.

[63] Rucker v. Missouri Pacific Ry. Co., 61 Texas 499; 21 Am. & Eng. R. Cas. 245; Downey v. Chesapeake, etc., R. Co., 28 W. Va. 732; Brown v. Scarboro, etc., R. Co., 97 Ala. 316; 12 So. Rep. 289; 58 Am. & Eng. R. Cas. 364.

tion of an employee,[64] or a third party,[65] for in either event, if the passenger prefers to ride on the engine or car, instead of inside a coach, where proper protection is afforded, the risk attending such a hazardous enterprise will be borne by the passenger alone and not by the railroad company.

§ 798. **Riding in cupola of caboose.**— The presumption of negligence on the carrier's part, from the mere fact of an injury to a passenger riding on a railroad train, does not obtain, in a case where the passenger is injured, owing to his being in a part of the car where he had no right to be, unless it is shown that he would also have been injured, if he had been in his proper place. It was accordingly held, by the St. Louis Court of Appeals, in a well-considered decision by Judge Rombauer,[66] that a passenger on a freight train, riding in a projection or cupola, several feet above the roof of a caboose, where there were no guards of any

[64] Downey v. Chesapeake, etc., R. Co., 28 W. Va. 732.

[65] Rucker v. Missouri Pacific Ry. Co., 61 Texas 499; 21 Am. & Eng. R. Cas. 245. In this case, a negro seated himself upon the pilot of the engine and told the conductor he didn't have money enough to pay his fare, to ride in the coach. He was thrown off and injured, by the engine running over a hand car, but was held to be guilty of negligence, barring a recovery. Riding on an engine, in violation of the railroad rules, was held to deny a recovery, in Chicago, etc., R. Co. v. Michie, 83 Ill. 427, and Baltimore, etc., R. Co. v. Jones, 95 U. S. 439; 24 L. Ed. 506, opinion by Justice Swayne.

A drover riding on top of a car, was held precluded from recovering for an injury received, in Little Rock, etc., R. Co. v. Miles (Ark.), 13 Am. & Eng. R. Cas. 10.

And riding on engine was held negligence, although with consent of engineer, in Daggett v. Illinois, etc., R. Co., 34 Iowa 284.

[66] Tuley v. Chicago, etc., R. Co., 41 Mo. App. 432. Judge Thompson did not concur in that portion of the opinion, holding that the plaintiff was negligent, as matter of law, in riding in the cupola of the caboose, but he placed his concurrence upon the absence of any evidence of negligence, on the defendant's part. The judgment was reversed, without remanding the cause, however, the majority of the court agreeing with the opinion of the distinguished jurist who wrote the majority opinion, holding that this was negligence, as a matter of law.

sort and which was intended for the exclusive use of the employees alone, could not recover for an injury due to being thrown from this perch by the jar caused by the caboose being struck by a switch engine, which coupled onto the caboose.

§ 799. **Standing up in car.**— While the carrier is under the duty to stop its trains a reasonable length of time, at stations, to allow its passengers to become seated and to furnish seats for its passengers, this is the extent of its duty, in this regard and if, after it has discharged its duty, in this respect, a passenger is injured by remaining standing in the car, instead of selecting a seat, on account of the starting of the train, after the usual signal, no recovery could be had for such an injury.[67]

The standing of passengers in freight cars or cabooses is usually held to be such an act of negligence, as to bar a recovery, for an injury due to the usual operation of such trains. This is because of the jars and jolts necessarily incident to such mode of travel, which is well known by the traveling public. It was accordingly held, by the Supreme Court of Missouri,[68] that no recovery could be had for an injury to a passenger in a caboose of a freight train where, at the time of the injury, the passenger was standing up in the caboose, removing his overcoat. Judge Brace, for the court, said: "He placed himself in such a position as not to be able to resist the force of the stop, which was naturally incident to the stop, fell and was injured. But for it he would have remained in his seat and in all human

[67] International, etc., R. Co. v. Copeland, 60 Texas 325.

[68] Wait v. Omaha, etc., R. Co., 165 Mo. 612; 65 S. W. Rep. 1028. See, also, Hedrick v. Missouri Pacific Ry. Co., 195 Mo. 104; 93 S. W. Rep. 268; Erwin v. Kansas City, etc., R. Co., 94 Mo. App. 289; 68 S. W. Rep. 88; Saxton v. Missouri Pacific Ry. Co., 98 Mo. App. 494; 72 S. W. Rep. 717; Guffey v. Hannibal, etc., R. Co., 53 Mo. App. 462.

probability, would have remained uninjured, as did the others in the car. For the consequences of his mistake, the defendant cannot be held liable."

But if the passenger is standing because of the absence of any seats,[69] or with the knowledge of the employees of the carrier and his injury is due to the negligence of the carrier, it is held, in some cases, to be error to instruct the jury that this conduct would constitute contributory negligence, on the passenger's part, but the issue should be submitted and decided by the jury, as any other issue of fact.[70]

[69] Wallace v. Western, etc., R. Co., 101 No. Car. 454; 8 S. E. Rep. 166; 37 Am. & Eng. R. Cas. 159.

[70] Madden v. Missouri Pacific Ry. Co., 50 Mo. App. 666; Little Rock, etc., R. Co. v. Miles, 40 Ark. 298; 48 Am. Rep. 10; 13 Am. & Eng. R. Cas. 10.

The negligence of the passenger, in standing in the aisle of a passenger coach, was held to be a jury issue, in Condy v. St. Louis, etc., R. Co., 13 Mo. App. 587; 85 Mo. 79; Morgen v. Southern, etc., R. Co., 95 Cal. 501; 30 Pac. Rep. 601; Barden v. Boston, etc., R. Co., 121 Mass. 426; Chicago, etc., R. Co. v. Arnol, 144 Ill. 261; 33 N. E. Rep. 204; 58 Am. & Eng. R. Cas. 411; Bartholomew v. New York, etc., R. Co., 102 N. Y. 716; 7 N. E. Rep. 623.

Standing up in freight car was held negligence as matter of law, in Harris v. Hannibal, etc., R. Co., 89 Mo. 233; 1 S. W. Rep. 325; 27 Am. & Eng. R. Cas. 216.

Standing in a car, near an open door, was held to be negligence, in Thompson v. Duncan, 76 Ala. 334.

But standing near an open door was held to present a jury issue, on the passenger's contributory negligence, in Condy v. St. Louis, etc., R. Co., 13 Mo. App. 587; 85 Mo. 79; Texas, etc., R. Co. v. Overall, 82 Texas 247; 18 S. W. Rep. 142.

And standing or leaning near a closed door is held not to be negligence as matter of law, in Gee v. Metropolitan, etc., R. Co., 21 W. R. 584; L. R. 8 Q. B. 161; 42 L. J. Q. B. 105; 28 L. T. 282.

"A passenger on the caboose of a local freight, whose injury is contributed to by his getting up before the train stops, may be found guilty of contributory negligence in so doing after warning, though he did not hear the conductor tell the passengers, after the train began to slow up, to keep their seats till the station was reached; there having been a notice in the car, headed in large capital letters, 'Warn-

§ 800. Standing in car while switching is being done.—
The right of an injured passenger to recover for an injury
received while he was standing in a car while switching
was being done, in violation of a printed and posted rule
of the carrier, was recently before the Court of Appeals,
of Missouri,[71] and in denying a recovery by the passenger,
so injured, Judge Bland, for the court, said:

"In respect to plaintiff's contributory negligence, the
evidence is also all one way that he is a traveling salesman,
and knew the train crew was engaged in switching at Paro-
quet, and from experience, must have known that in coupling
freight cars there is necessarily more or less jar. Seats
were provided for him, and signs were posted in the car

ing! Notice! Danger!' which forbade passengers to stand up while
the train was in motion, and he having previously frequently ridden
on local freight trains, and known that similar warnings were posted
in them." Abelson v. St. Louis, etc., R. Co. (Ark. 1907), 105 S. W.
Rep. 81.

[71] Gabriel v. St. Louis, etc., R. Co., 112 S. W. Rep. 713.

In Krumm v. St. Louis, etc., Ry. Co. (71 Ark. 590; 76 S. W. Rep.
1075), "Krumm was riding in a caboose of a freight train, and was
thrown down and injured by a collision betwen two parts of the train
which had become uncoupled. At the time of his injury Krumm was
standing near a cooler, where he had gone to get a drink, but stood
there two or three minutes waiting for the water to cool before drinking. Warning notice not to stand while the train was in motion was
posted in the caboose, but Krumm did not read it. The trial court
nonsuited him, and he appealed. Riddick, J., writing the opinion
of the court, commenting on the evidence, said: 'The notice was headed
by the words, 'Warning, Notice, Danger,' in large capital letters, and
was well calculated to attract attention. If, after having seen it,
plaintiff failed to read it, the fault was his. The rule was a reasonable
one, for it is well known that it is not practicable to operate freight
trains without occasional jars and jerks, calculated to throw down and
injure careless and inexperienced persons standing in the car. This
rule, therefore, was necessary to protect passengers on such cars from
injury. * * * We are of the opinion that the Circuit Court was
right in holding that the testimony of the plaintiff himself showed
that his injury was due to his own carelessness. The judgment is
therefore affirmed.'"

notifying him of the danger of standing in the aisle.   It is true plaintiff testified he did not see these signs, and denied that the conductor warned him, but the signs were posted in conspicuous places in the car, and plaintiff could have seen them if he had looked, and it must be held that, by providing a seat for plaintiff and posting warning signs in the car, the defendant company discharged its duty to warn him of the danger of standing in the aisle while the train was in motion, or when switching was being done, and plaintiff should be charged with notice of such danger. Indeed, from his experience as a traveling salesman, notice of the danger should be imputed to him, though he was not warned by the signs, or by the conductor, and the case falls squarely within the ruling of the Supreme Court of Arkansas in the Krumm case."

§ 801. Riding on platform of car.— For a passenger to ride upon the platform of a rapidly-moving steam car is generally held to be negligence, as matter of law, where such position contributes to an injury received, unless his presence was demanded upon the platform, because of the negligence of the carrier.[72]   A passenger riding upon the platform and thrown from the car, while the train was rounding a sharp curve in the track, was denied a recovery in one case;[73] and the negligence on the part of the passenger would be the more pronounced, where the employees of the train had requested him to be seated inside the car,[74] or

[72] Worthington v. Central Vermont R. Co., 64 Vt. 107; 23 Atl. Rep. 590; 15 L. R. A. 326; 52 Am. & Eng. R. Cas. 384; Torrey v. Boston, etc., R. Co., 147 Mass. 412; 18 N. E. Rep. 213; Ohio, etc., R. Co. v. Allender, 47 Ill. App. 484; Alabama, etc., R. Co. v. Hawk, 72 Ala. 112; 47 Am. Rep. 403; 18 Am. & Eng. R. Cas. 194.

[73] Goodwin v. Boston, etc., R. Co., 84 Me. 203; 24 Atl. Rep. 816.

[74] Louisville, etc., R. Co. v. Bisch, 120 Ind. 549; 22 N. E. Rep. 662; 41 Am. & Eng. R. Cas. 89; Graville v. Manhattan R. Co., 105 N. Y. 525; 12 N. E. Rep. 51; 34 Am. & Eng. R. Cas. 375; Fischer v. West

there were unoccupied seats in the car which the passenger could have used.[75]

But where the train is so crowded that a seat could not be had inside the car,[76] or the employees of the railroad company see a passenger on the platform and permit him to ride there, without objection,[77] it has been held that the passenger will not be guilty of negligence, as matter of law, in continuing to ride upon the platform of the car, if the danger of so riding is not so obvious as to have deterred a reasonably prudent person, which would be a jury issue.[78]

Virginia, etc., R. Co. (W. Va.), 19 S. E. Rep. 578; 58 Am. & Eng. R. Cas. 337.

[75] Memphis, etc., R. Co. v. Salinger, 46 Ark. 528; Kentucky, etc., Co. v. Quinkert, 2 Ind. App. 244; 28 N. E. Rep. 338.

[76] Willis v. Long Island R. Co., 34 N. Y. 670; Werle v. Long Island R. Co., 98 N. Y. 650; 21 Am. & Eng. R. Cas. 429.

[77] Chicago, etc., R. Co. v. Llauber, 9 Ill. App. 613; Oliver v. Louisville, etc., R. Co., 43 La. Ann. 804; 9 So. Rep. 431; 47 Am. & Eng. R. Cas. 576; Chicago, etc., R. Co. v. Fisher, 141 Ill. 614; 31 N. E. Rep. 406.

That all the seats in a car were occupied, was held not to excuse a passenger from standing on the platform, in Worthington v. Central Vermont R. Co., 64 Vt. 107; 23 Atl. Rep. 590; 15 L. R. A. 326; 52 Am. & Eng. R. Cas. 384; Camden, etc., R. Co. v. Hoosey, 99 Pa. St. 492; 44 Am. Rep. 120; 6 Am. & Eng. R. Cas. 454.

[78] Woods v. Southern Pacific R. Co., 9 Utah 146; 33 Pac. Rep. 628; Chicago, etc., R. Co. v. Fisher, 141 Ill. 614; 31 N. E. Rep. 406; Gerstle v. Union Pacific R. Co., 23 Mo. App. 361; Mitchell v. Southern Pacific R. Co., 87 Cal. 62; 25 Pac. Rep. 245.

Standing on a car platform, while switching was being done, or cars were being coupled, was held to be negligence, as matter of law, in DeMahy v. Morgen, etc., R. Co., 45 La. Ann. 329; 14 So. Rep. 61; 58 Am. & Eng. R. Cas. 448; Smotherman v. St. Louis, etc., R. Co., 29 Mo. App. 265; Rockford, etc., R. Co. v. Coultas, 67 Ill. 398.

"Where plaintiff was injured while riding on the rear bumper of a crowded car, he assumed the risk incident to that position, although his fare was accepted." Feldheim v. Brooklyn, etc., R. Co., 107 N. Y. S. 413.

"Where a man in a crowded car gives a woman his place, and stands on the front platform and is injured, he forfeits the advantage of the presumption that the accident resulted from the negligence of the company." Patterson v. Philadelphia Rapid Transit Co. (Pa. 1907), 67 Atl. Rep. 616.

"If a boy passenger on a railway train had intelligence enough to understand that it was more dangerous to ride on a car platform or on the steps than inside the car, no duty devolved upon the company to prevent him from so riding." Walling v. Trinity & Brazos Valley Ry. Co. (Tex. Civ. App. 1907), 106 S. W. Rep. 417.

"Where intestate, at the time the train on which he was a passenger ran into a washout, was riding from his own choice on a car platform which was not vestibuled, and there was ample opportunity for him to have occupied a seat in the car, and it was in the nighttime, and a severe rainstorm was either in progress or had very recently occurred, and the train was running very fast, and no one inside the car was killed, he was not, as a matter of law, guilty of want of ordinary care contributing to his own death." Miller v. Chicago, etc., Ry. Co. (Wis. 1908), 115 N. W. Rep. 794.

"A passenger on a street car was injured by being thrown from the car by a sudden lurch. The passenger at the time was standing on the front platform of the car. Prior to the accident he had experienced lurches at the place of the accident, but the shock at the time of the accident was more severe. He also knew of the defective condition of the track at the place of the accident. Held, that the passenger did not voluntarily expose himself to danger by standing on the platform; he having a right to rely on the implied contract of safe carriage." Wellmeyer v. St. Louis Transit Co. (Mo. 1906), 95 S. W. Rep. 925.

"It is not negligence as a matter of law for one to board and ride on the platform of a car." Baskett v. Metropolitan St. Ry. Co. (Mo. App. 1907), 101 S. W. Rep. 138.

"A passenger thrown from a train is not guilty of contributory negligence as matter of law because he is riding on the car platform; the cars having been so overcrowded with passengers as to make it impossible to obtain a seat in a safe place." Yazoo & M. V. R. Co. v. Byrd (Miss. 1906), 42 So. Rep. 286.

"Even if it were contributory negligence for a passenger to ride in the vestibule of a coach in a railway train, the reckless jostling of a passenger by a porter, causing the passenger to fall through an opening in the vestibule and off the train, renders the railroad company liable for the resulting damages." Chicago, etc., Ry. Co. v. Ferguson (Kan. 1906), 86 Pac. Rep. 471.

"It is not negligence per se to rise from a seat and step to the side of a slowly moving open car which is coming to a stop, for the purpose of getting on the runboard to alight when the car does stop." Davis v. Camden, G. & W. Ry. Co. (N. J. Sup. 1906), 63 Atl. Rep. 843.

"A passenger cannot be held guilty of contributory negligence as a

§ 802. Riding with limbs projecting from window.— Since the carrier provides seats for its passengers to sit in and windows for the admission of light and air, the law charges all passengers with notice of this fact and that car windows are not intended to sit in or to project portions of the passenger's bodies from.[79] It is accordingly held to be negligence for a passenger to ride with his arm, or other portion of his body projecting from an open window.[80] And in case of an injury to a passenger so riding, by being struck by an obstruction along the track,[81] such as a bridge,[82] a

matter of law in quitting his seat in a passenger coach while the train is stopping at a regular station waiting for the arrival of another train and going on the platform of the coach." Atlantic Coast Line R. Co. v. Crosby (Fla. 1907), 43 So. Rep. 318.

"The causes which may justify a passenger, without the imputation of fault on his part, as against the carrier, in leaving his seat and going outside the car and occupying temporarily a position on the platform while the cars are standing still, depend on the occasion and circumstances which induce or impel him to do so." Atlantic Coast Line R. Co. v. Crosby (Fla. 1907), 43 So. Rep. 318.

"Whether it is negligence for a passenger with the knowledge and implied assent of the train men to take a position on the car less safe than that of riding in a seat is a question for the jury." Vessels v. Metropolitan St. Ry. Co. (Mo. App. 1908), 108 S. W. Rep. 578.

"Where, in an action for injuries to a passenger, the evidence showed that while the train was in motion he left his seat and went on the platform to alight on the train coming to a stop, and that in consequence of the jerking of the train he was thrown from the platform, the refusal to charge that he was guilty of contributory negligence in getting off a moving train was proper." Forbes v. Chicago, etc., Ry. Co. (Iowa 1907), 113 N. W. Rep. 477.

[79] Moore v. Edison, etc., R. Co., 43 La. Ann. 792; 9 So. Rep. 433.

[80] Todd v. Old Colony R. Co., 3 Allen (Mass.) 18; Moakler v. Williamette Valley R. Co., 18 Oregon 189; 41 Am. & Eng. R. Cas. 135; Dunn v. Seaboard R. Co., 78 Va. 645; 49 Am. Rep. 388; 16 Am. & Eng. R. Cas. 363; Richmond, etc., R. Co. v. Scott, 88 Va. 958; 14 S. E. Rep. 763; 52 Am. & Eng. R. Cas. 405; Louisville, etc., R. Co. v. Sickings, 5 Bush. (Ky.) 1; Spencer v. Milwaukee, etc., R. Co., 17 Wis. 487.

[81] Dunn v. Seaboard, etc., R. Co., *supra*.

[82] Laing v. Colder, 8 Pa. St. 479.

water tank,[83] passing train,[84] or standing car,[85] there can generally be no recovery from the railroad company, but the negligence of the passenger will either be declared as matter of law, by the court,[86] or submitted as an issue of fact for the jury,[87] according to the rule of practice in the State where the accident occurs, or according to the positive nature of the evidence, concerning the act on the part of the passenger and the obvious nature of the obstruction causing the injury.

But while it is negligence to protrude the person from an open window, so that it will strike objects along the track, it is not generally held to be negligence to simply rest the elbow on a window sill, for this is the usual and customary thing for reasonably prudent passengers to do and in case of an injury by a falling window, due to an insufficient catch or fastening, the passenger will not be denied a recovery, merely because his arm was resting in the window.[88]

[83] Indianapolis, etc., R. Co. v. Rutherford, 29 Ind. 82.

[84] Miller v. St. Louis, etc., R. Co., 5 Mo. App. 471.

[85] Louisville, etc., R. Co. v. Sickings, *supra*.

[86] Carrico v. West Virginia R. Co., 35 W. Va. 389; 14 S. E. Rep. 12; 52 Am. & Eng. R. Cas. 393; Pittsburg, etc., R. Co. v. McClurg, 56 Pa. St. 294; Georgia, etc., R. Co. v. Underwood, 90 Ala. 49; 8 So. Rep. 116; 44 Am. & Eng. R. Cas. 367; Todd v. Old Colony R. Co., *supra*.

[87] Quinn v. South Carolina R. Co., 29 So. Car. 381; 7 S. E. Rep. 614; 1 L. R. A. 682; 37 Am. & Eng. R. Cas. 166; Pittsburg, etc., R. Co. v. Andrews, 39 Md. 329; 10 Am. Ry. Rep. 485; Moakler v. Williamette Valley R. Co., *supra*; New Jersey R. Co. v. Kennard, 21 Pa. St. 203.

[88] Farlow v. Kelly, 108 U. S. 288; 11 Am. & Eng. R. Cas. 104; Carrico v. West Virginia R. Co., *supra*; Winters v. Hannibal, etc., R. Co., 39 Mo. 468; Gulf, etc., R. Co. v. Killebrew (Texas), 20 S. W. Rep. 182.

"The unexplained falling of the window of a car soon after the passenger entered was not sufficient to charge him with knowledge that the window catch was defective, and subject him to an imputation of contributory negligence in thereafter using the window." Rehearing, 82 N. E. Rep. 1025, denied; Cleveland & St. L. Ry. Co. v. Hadley (Ind. 1908), 84 N. E. Rep. 13.

"A passenger in a railway car has the right to hoist the window

§ 803. Riding in baggage or express car.— A passenger riding in a baggage or express car, in violation of a known rule of the railroad company, cannot recover, ordinarily, for an injury received, where it appears that he would not have been injured if he had been in the proper car,[89] for in such case, the negligence is the direct cause of the injury, or contributes to bring it about.

But it is held that a passenger does not forfeit his right to recover for injuries received while riding in a baggage or express car, where his presence in the car is with the consent of the conductor or employees of the train;[90] nor would the presence of the passenger in such a car ordinarily defeat a recovery for injuries received, if the evidence shows that the injury would have resulted, if he had been in some other car,[91] such as an injury from a collision due to the negligence of the carrier or its employees, for in such case, the negligence of the passenger is not the direct cause of his injury, but the negligence of the carrier is the cause.[92]

for any proper purpose, and to assume that the catch with which it is equipped is suitable and sufficient to hold it when latched properly." Rehearing, 82 N. E. Rep. 1025, denied; Cleveland & St. L. Ry. Co. v. Hadley (Ind. 1908), 84 N. E. Rep. 13.

[89] Pennsylvania R. Co. v. Langdon, 92 Pa. St. 21; 1 Am. & Eng. R. Cas. 87; Houston, etc., R. Co. v. Clemmons, 55 Texas 88; 8 Am. & Eng. R. Cas. 396; Peoria, etc., R. Co. v. Lane, 83 Ill. 448; Kentucky, etc., R. Co. v. Thomas, 79 Ky. 160; Florida Southern R. Co. v. Hirst, 30 Florida 1; 11 So. Rep. 506; 52 Am. & Eng. R. Cas. 409.

[90] O'Donnell v. Allegheny Valley R. Co., 59 Pa. St. 239.

[91] Jones v. Chicago, etc., R. Co., 43 Minn. 279; 45 N. W. Rep. 444; 44 Am. & Eng. R. Cas. 357; New York, etc., R. Co. v. Ball, 53 N. J. L. 283; 21 Atl. Rep. 1052.

[92] Webster v. Rome, etc., R. Co., 115 N. Y. 112; 21 N. E. Rep. 725; Cody v. New York, etc., R. Co., 151 Mass. 462; 24 N. E. Rep. 402; 7 L. R. A. 843.

" Plaintiff left the passenger compartment of a carrier's combination car, in which there were empty seats, and went into the baggage compartment to talk to the baggage master. A collision occurred, in which plaintiff was thrown over a low box of fowl, causing the injuries

§ 804. **Passing between or over stationary cars.**— In an Iowa case,[93] which is of somewhat doubtful authority, it was decided that a woman could recover damages for an injury received, while perched upon the draw heads of two stationary freight cars, which were caused to collide by an engine shunting another car against them, where she was a passenger, intending to take passage upon the defendant's passenger train, and she had to cross the track and before attempting to cross over the cars, she had looked up and down the railroad track, in both directions, to see if a train was approaching. The court held that under all the circumstances in the case, her contributory negligence was an issue for the jury; but this holding is not in accord with the weight of authority on this question and it is generally held to be contributory negligence, as matter of law, for a person, without the invitation of the employees of the train, to pass between, or crawl under or over stationary cars, liable at any minute to be struck by a locomotive or car, and, generally there is no liability for an injury to a passenger, proceeding in such a reckless way to jeopardize his safety of life or limb.[94]

complained of. *Held*, that plaintiff's negligence, in changing his position in the passenger compartment and occupying an exposed position, contributed to his injury, and that he was, therefore, not entitled to recover." Bromley v. New York, etc., R. Co. (Mass. 1907), 79 N. E. Rep. 775.

[93] Allender v. Chicago, etc., R. Co., 37 Iowa 264. This case ought to be overruled.

[94] Chicago, etc., R. Co. v. Cross, 73 Ill. 394; Foreman v. Pennsylvania R. Co., 159 Pa. St. 541; 28 Atl. Rep. 358; Jones v. New York, etc., R. Co., 156 N. Y. 187; 90 Hun 605; 50 N. E. Rep. 856; 41 L. R. A. 490. Where a person attempted to pass under one of a train of freight cars, to which an engine was attached, his negligence was held to bar a recovery for an injury so received, in Smith v. Chicago, etc., R. Co., 55 Iowa 33; 7 N. W. Rep. 398. See, also, Memphis, etc., R. Co. v. Copeland, 61 Ala. 376.

1210

§ 805. **When intoxication a defense.**— The carrier is bound to use the same care to avoid injury to a drunken passenger that the law requires it to use toward a sober person,[95] and if a passenger is known to be on the platform of a moving car, in a drunken condition, so that he is apt to receive injuries that a sober passenger could avoid, it is the duty of the train employees to look out for him and to call his attention to the rules of the company, if he is not so intoxicated as to be unable to understand the danger of his surroundings,[96] and if his condition is such that he is not able to appreciate the danger, he ought to be removed from the train, if necessary, and given proper care and attention for his protection from the dangers likely to overtake a person in such condition.[97]

But where a passenger voluntarily becomes intoxicated, the law does not require of the carrier that it provide a guard, to avoid injury that his own voluntary act has exposed him to;[98] if the employees of the carrier do not know of his intoxication, only such care will be required toward him, as they would be compelled to show to a sober passenger;[99] if the injury received by such a passenger is due to his own intoxication, the carrier would not be liable therefor,[1] although the intoxication of the passenger would not be a defense, if the injury would have occurred, notwithstanding the passenger's intoxication.[2]

[95] Milliman v. New York, etc., R. Co., 66 N. Y. 642; 4 Hun 409.

[96] Fisher v. West Virginia R. Co. (W. Va.), 19 S. E. Rep. 578; 58 Am. & Eng. R. Cas. 337; McClelland v. Louisville, etc., R. Co., 94 Ind. 276; 18 Am. & Eng. R. Cas. 260.

[97] Atchison, etc., R. Co. v. Weber, 33 Kansas 543; 6 Pac. Rep. 877; 21 Am. & Eng. R. Cas. 418.

[98] St. Louis, etc., R. Co. v. Carr, 47 Ill. App. 353.

[99] Strand v. Chicago, etc., R. Co., 67 Mich. 380; 34 N. W. Rep. 712; 31 Am. & Eng. R. Cas. 54.

[1] St. Louis, etc., R. Co. v. Carr, supra.

[2] Holmes v. Oregon, etc., R. Co., 6 Sawy. (U. S.) 262; 5 Fed. Rep. 75.

§ 806. **Conduct in emergencies.**— Where a passenger is injured by the negligence of a carrier, an act done by the passenger in the face of impending danger, for the purpose of avoiding the injury, will not amount to contributory negligence, although it may, in fact, have helped to produce the injury complained of,[3] for the reason that a passenger in imminent peril, is not required by the law to exercise all the presence of mind and care of a prudent and careful man, in the face of such impending peril. The law makes allowance for the danger under which he is situated, and for the weakness of human nature and leaves the circumstances to the jury to determine whether or not the passenger acted with rashness, in view of the apprehension of danger.[4] That the liability of the carrier is not affected by the fact that the act of the passenger himself may have contributed directly to the injury, where the peril is so great as to justify it, is illustrated in a New York case,[5] where a person lost his own life in rescuing a child on the railroad track, before a moving train. It was held that he was not guilty of such rashness as to defeat a recovery for his death, although the child would have been held guilty of such negligence as would have defeated a recovery for its death.

The rule and reason therefor is clearly stated by the fed-

"That a passenger alighting from a train is drunk does not *per se* constitute contributory negligence." Louisville & N. R. Co. v. Deason (Ky. 1906), 96 S. W. Rep. 1115.

If a passenger does not appear to be so intoxicated as to be unable to care for himself, it is not necessarily negligence, on the part of the employees of the train, to permit him to remain on the platform of the car, and no recovery can be had for an injury, by his falling from the platform, while the train is rounding a curve in the track. Fisher v. West Virginia R. Co., 42 W. Va. 183; 24 S. E. Rep. 570; 4 Am. & Eng. R. Cas. (N. S.) 86; 33 L. R. A. 69.

[3] Ladd v. Foster, 12 Sawy. (U. S.) 547; 31 Fed. Rep. 827.

[4] Galena, etc., R. Co. v. Yarwood, 17 Ill. 509; Chicago, etc., R. Co. v. Trayes, 33 Ill. App. 307; Chicago, etc., R. Co. v. Cotton, 140 Ill. 486.

[5] Eckar v. Long Island R. Co., 57 Barb. 555; 43 N. Y. 502.

eral court,[6] to be, that "If a man unlawfully places another in a situation which compels him to undergo one of two hazards, and forces him to choose upon the instant, between them, he necessarily gives him the right of selection, and must be responsible for the consequences, although it may turn out that the most fortunate alternative was not adopted," and this principle applies to a passenger who may not, under the excitement of the moment incident to a sudden peril, take the safest way of avoiding the injury threatened.

§ 807. **Obeying directions of employees.**— Passengers are generally held excusable for obeying an order or direction of an employee of the carrier, employed to manage the vehicles or means of transportation, on account of the supposed superior skill and judgment of the employees, and it is not held to be negligence, on the part of the passenger, to obey such a direction, unless the danger is so imminent that no reasonably prudent person would assume it under the circumstances.[7]

It is accordingly held that a passenger is excusable for making an attempt to board a moving train on the order of the conductor, or other employee in charge of the train, although the situation of the train and the speed and sur-

[6] Saltonstall v. Stockton, 1 Taney (U. S.) 11.

The negligence of passengers, leaping from moving trains, to avoid supposed impending perils, was held to be a jury issue, in the following cases: Chitty v. St. Louis, etc., R. Co., 148 Mo. 64; 49 S. W. Rep. 868; Iron R. Co. v. Mowry, 36 Ohio St. 418; 38 Am. Rep. 597; Heath v. Glenn Falls R. Co., 90 Hun 560; 71 N. Y. S. R. 29; 36 N. Y. Supp. 22.

But if a passenger jumps, merely because some one tells him to, although the some one happens to be a brakeman of the train, if there is no real danger, no recovery can be had, for such negligent conduct, causing an injury to the passenger. McPeak v. Missouri, etc., R. Co., 128 Mo. 617; 30 S. W. Rep. 170.

[7] St. Louis, etc., R. Co. v. Baker, 67 Ark. 531; 55 S. W. Rep. 941; Indianapolis, etc., R. Co. v. Watson, 114 Ind. 20; 14 N. E. Rep. 721.

roundings make it a dangerous procedure;[8] and the same result was reached by another court, as to an attempt to alight from a moving train, on the order or direction of the employees in charge of the train.[9]

But to claim the protection of alighting from a moving train, in response to an order of a train employee it must appear that the order was immediately obeyed and if, instead of acting on the order, before the train had reached a degree of speed to render the undertaking dangerous, the passenger waited until it was unsafe to attempt to alight, the order of the employee would furnish no protection for this rashness on the part of the passenger.[10] It is also held that a passenger will not be justified in acting upon the direction of an employee not possessing the requisite power or authority to understand the risk of the enterprise;[11] and if the order is attendant with such danger as to deter any reasonably prudent person from acting upon it, the passenger will not be justified in obeying it, simply because a train employee gave the order.[12]

[8] Irish v. Northern, etc., R. Co., 4 Wash. 48; 29 Pac. Rep. 845.

[9] St. Louis, etc., R. Co. v. Cantrell, 37 Ark. 519; Boggess v. Chesapeake, etc., R. Co., 37 W. Va. 297; 16 S. E. Rep. 525.

[10] Southwestern R. Co. v. Singleton, 67 Ga. 306.

[11] International, etc., R. Co. v. Armstrong (Texas), 23 S. W. Rep. 236.

[12] Planz v. Boston, etc., R. Co., 157 Mass. 377; 32 N. E. Rep. 356; City R. Co. v. Lee, 50 N. J. L. 435; 14 Atl. Rep. 883; 7 Am. St. Rep. 798.

Where the directions given are within the scope of the employee's authority and the danger of obedience thereto is not apparent or threatening, obedience to the direction is not contributory negligence, as matter of law. Louisville, etc., R. Co. v. Bisch, 120 Ind. 549; 22 N. E. Rep. 662; 41 Am. & Eng. R. Cas. 89; Cincinnati, etc., R. Co. v. Carper, 112 Ind. 26; 13 N. E. Rep. 122; 14 N. E. Rep. 352; 31 Am. & Eng. R. Cas. 36.

It is no defense to an action for negligence on the part of employees of a train, that the passenger obeyed specific instructions of the employees, instead of general instructions to passengers. Pennsylvania R. Co. v. McClosky, 23 Pa. St. 526.

§ 808. **Recovery notwithstanding contributory negligence.**
— Although an injured passenger has, by his own negligence,
placed himself in a dangerous position, where injury is
likely to result to him, a recovery may still be had for the
injury received, if the defendant with knowledge of the
danger, failed to exercise reasonable care, by which the injury might have been avoided, unless the injury was the
result of the concurrent negligence of both parties.[13]

This rule is illustrated by the case where a passenger attempts to get on a slowly moving train and while holding
on to the railing, with notice of his condition and the danger
which confronts him, the employees of the train increase
the speed of the train, instead of promptly stopping the
train.[14]

But this rule can be reconciled with the doctrine of contributory negligence by applying it only when the defendant,
or its employees, had a clear chance to save the careless person, after the latter's negligence had ceased.[15]   And if the
negligence of the injured person not only continues up to
the time of the injury, but is also contemporaneous and co-
incident with the injury, no recovery can be had, for it is
then a case of concurrent negligence, in which case the law
affords no relief.[16]

[13] Moore v. Lindell Ry. Co., 176 Mo. 528; 75 S. W. Rep. 672
[14] Barth v. Kansas City, etc., R. Co., 142 Mo. 535; 44 S. W. Rep. 778.
[15] Shanks v. Springfield Traction Co., 101 Mo. App. 702; 74 S. W.
Rep. 386.
[16] Ries v. Transit Co., 179 Mo. 1; 77 S. W. Rep. 734; Shanks v.
Springfield Traction Co., 101 Mo. App. 702; 74 S. W. Rep. 386; Holwerson v. St. Louis, etc., R. Co., 157 Mo. 216; 57 S. W. Rep. 770; 50
L. R. A. 850.

CHAPTER XXXII.

LIABILITY OF CONNECTING CARRIERS.

§ 809. **Liability of one carrier for injury on line of another.** — Where there are several connecting lines and the plaintiff seeks to recover from one railroad company for an injury received on the line of another railroad, he is generally required to establish a contract with the line of railroad that he attempts to hold, or that it had some special interest in or control over the transportation of passengers by the line where the injury was received.[1] Nor is the sale of a through ticket by one of several connecting lines of railroad evidence of a joint contract between such railroads, whereby one of the companies will be responsible for the negligence of the other.[2]

But this rule is not of universal application and in some States, where a person contracts for transportation over a

[1] Kerrigan v. Southern Pacific R. Co., 81 Cal. 248; 22 Pac. Rep. 677; 41 Am. & Eng. R. Cas. 28.

[2] Felder v. Columbia, etc., R. Co., 21 So. Car. 35; 53 Am. Rep. 656; 27 Am. & Eng. R. Cas. 264.

1216

route composed of several railroads, for which he pays one entire sum and receives a through ticket, the contract is held to be so far entire that if no partnership or joint arrangement in fact exists, the passenger may treat the contract as joint or several, so far as the other parties are concerned.[3]

§ 810. **Liability of initial carrier.—** While one railroad company cannot be compelled to transport persons beyond its own *termini*, it is well settled that the initial carrier may lawfully contract to carry passengers over its own road and that of a connecting carrier, to a destination beyond its own route, and when such a contract is made it assumes all the obligations of a carrier toward the passenger, over the connecting line of railroad, as well as over its own.[4] And for any injury sustained on the connecting line, due to the negligence of the employees or agent of the initial carrier, the initial carrier would be liable;[5] but a company selling a through ticket over a connecting line of railroad is not liable for an injury to such a passenger on the connecting line, simply because of an arrangement whereby it receives a part of the fare paid, for the transportation of the passenger over all lines, without change of cars,[6] but the first or initial carrier is usually held to be merely the agent of the connecting lines,[7] in the absence of evidence of a partnership arrangement between the several lines.[8]

[3] Check v. Little Miami R. Co., 2 Disney (Ohio) 237.

[4] Atchison, etc., R. Co. v. Roach, 35 Kansas 740; 12 Pac. Rep. 93; 27 Am. & Eng. R. Cas. 257; Wheeler v. San Francisco R. Co., 31 Cal. 46.

[5] Griffin v. Utica, etc., R. Co., 41 Hun 448; 3 N. Y. S. R. 155.

[6] Hartan v. Eastern R. Co., 114 Mass. 44.

[7] Nashville, etc., R. Co. v. Sprayberry, 8 Baxt. (Tenn.) 341.

[8] Nashville, etc., R. Co. v. Sprayberry, *supra*.
The initial carrier was held not liable for the wrongful ejection of a passenger, by an employee of a connecting carrier, in Alabama, etc., R. Co. v. Holmes, 75 Miss. 371; 23 So. Rep. 187; 10 Am. & Eng. R. Cas. (N. S.) 270.

§ 811. **Carrier using another carrier's facilities or employees.**— Whether the company so doing is the initial or a connecting carrier of the passenger, if one railroad company uses the employees or means of transportation of another railroad company and while so doing one of its own passengers sustains an injury, the company so using the other means of transportation or employees is liable to its passenger for such injury, as it is held to have made the employees or vehicles of the other company its own, as far as its passengers are concerned and occupies the same relation toward its injured passengers as if the injury had occurred through the negligence of its own employees or the defective condition of its own appliances or means of transportation.[9]

This rule is not of universal application, however, for in an early Vermont decision,[10] Judge Redfield held that there was no responsibility on the part of the trustees of one railroad company, for an injury to their passengers, while on the road of another company, in the absence of a showing of a partnership or consolidation of interests which would render them liable for the fault or neglect of the employees of the other company.

§ 812. **Injury in car on side track of connecting road.**— The question came before the Georgia court, of the status held by

[9] Littlejohn v. Fitchburg R. Co., 148 Mass. 478; 20 N. E. Rep. 103; Atchison, etc., R. Co. v. Davis, 34 Kansas 199; Barkman v. Pennsylvania R. Co., 89 Fed. Rep. 453.

[10] Sprague v. Smith, 29 Vt. 421. See, also, for similar rule, on principle, as applied to two railroad companies, where the injury is due to the negligence of the one furnishing the facilities only. Smith v. St. Louis, etc., R. Co., 9 Mo. App. 598; 85 Mo. 418.

That a railroad company is answerable to its passengers in the same degree for the safe condition of the cars of other companies used in its trains as for its own, is held in Morgan v. Chesapeake & O. R. Co. (Ky.), 105 S. W. Rep. 961; 15 L. R. A. (N. S.) 790, notwithstanding it is required by law to take cars of connecting carriers and haul them on equal terms with its own.

a passenger who was injured in a car that had been side tracked, but not yet picked up, by the train of a carrier connecting with the road upon which the car had been transported, with the passenger in it, up to that point by the initial carrier. It was held that a passenger who has been carried on the line of a railway in a passenger car which a railroad company switches off upon the line of a connecting carrier, sustained the relation of passenger to such connecting company during the time that the car remained stationary and he was in it, if, according to the usual course of business, the connecting carrier was accustomed to receive, at once, all cars that were so delivered to it and then to immediately couple them into its own trains and transport them over its own line of railroad. And this was held to be true and the relation of passenger and carrier established, whether the passenger had, at the time of his injury, procured a ticket or paid his fare, or not.[11]

§ 813. Liability of carrier having running powers.— Where a railroad company has running powers over the line of another company, and it permits a person to travel on one of its trains, it is bound to make provision for his safety, the same as if it owned the line of road on which he traveled, although he traveled upon a ticket issued by the company owning the track.[12]

In an English case,[13] the defendant had running powers between a station on its own line and another station on the line of another railroad company, beyond the terminus of its own road. Between these two stations the profits of

[11] Chattanooga, etc., R. Co. v. Huggins, 89 Ga. 494; 15 S. E. Rep. 848; 52 Am. & Eng. R. Cas. 473.

[12] Foulkes v. Metropolitan, etc., R. Co., 5 C. P. D. 157; 49 L. J. C. P. D. 361; 42 L. T. 345; 28 W. R. 526; Hooper v. London, etc., R. Co., 50 L. J. Q. B. 103; 43 L. T. 570; 29 W. R. 241; 45 J. P. 223.

[13] Foulkes v. Metropolitan, etc., R. Co., *supra*.

the business of the two roads was divided. The plaintiff was a passenger between these two stations, on a ticket issued by the owner of the road where the injury occurred. The train on which the plaintiff traveled belonged to the defendant and it was operated by its employees. The injury was caused by the car in which the passenger traveled being unsuited to the platform of the station where the injury occurred, that was owned by the other company, but the trial court held that the defendant was liable for this injury, although it had not constructed this platform, for having permitted the plaintiff to take passage upon its own train, it was bound to make ample provision for his safety while being transported.

§ 814. **Employing another to carry out contract with passenger.**— The franchise of a railroad company is of such a public character that the law will not permit it to avoid liability to its own passengers by an attempted employment of a third person who may be entirely irresponsible, to carry out its contracts of transportation with its passengers. It is accordingly held, in a recent South Carolina case,[14] that a railroad company could not, by chartering one of its trains to a third person for a special trip, enter into such a contract with such person as would exempt it from liability for the negligence of such person toward a passenger on the train, but such third person would be held, in law, to be the agent of the carrier, and a similar rule is announced by the federal court.[15]

[14] "A railroad company cannot, in chartering one of its trains, to a third person for an excursion, enter into such a contract with such person as will exempt it from liability for negligence and willful misconduct on the ejectment of a passenger from such train, such third party being in law an agent of the railroad." Kirkland v. Charleston, etc., Ry. Co. (S. C. 1908), 60 S. E. Rep. 668.

[15] Barkman v. Pennsylvania R. Co., 89 Fed. Rep. 453.

§ 815. **Liability of owner of road or premises.**— Where a railroad company grants to another company the use of its tracks or premises, the former is liable for an injury to one of its passengers, caused by the way in which a train of cars is run, on its road, by the other railroad company.[16]

And a railroad company is liable for injuries received by a passenger at a station belonging to it, owing to the negligence of a porter on a platform which was exclusively used for the traffic of another railroad company, which had running powers over the first company's line of railroad and which had issued the ticket under which the injured passenger had traveled.[17]

§ 816. **Liability of company using another's road.**— A railroad company that operates its trains of cars over the line of railroad of another company, at the time of an accident to a passenger, is liable at common law for the injury so sustained, as the relation of passenger and carrier exists, regardless of the ownership of the road on which the injury was sustained.[18] The company using the road of another railroad company stands in the same position, toward its own passengers, as if it had been transporting them over its own road, and it will be responsible for an injury to a passenger it has agreed to transport, if, under the same circumstances, it would be liable in case it had been operating the road itself.[19]

But it is held, in a Vermont case,[20] that where a carrier

---

[16] Illinois, etc., R. Co. v. Barron, 5 Wall. (U. S.) 90; Nelson v. Vermont, etc., R. Co., 26 Vt. 717; Ohio, etc., R. Co. v. Dunbar, 20 Ill. 385; McCoy v. Kansas City, etc., R. Co., 36 Mo. App. 445.

[17] Self v. London, etc., R. Co., 42 L. T. 173.

[18] Eureka Springs R. Co. v. Timmonds, 51 Ark. 459; 11 S. W. Rep. 690; 40 Am. & Eng. R. Cas. 698.

[19] Eureka Springs R. Co. v. Timmonds, *supra.*

[20] Sprague v. Smith, 29 Vt. 421.

has the right to run its cars over the track of another company, but has no control or right over the track, aside from the running of such cars, it will not be liable for an injury to one of its own passengers, while upon the track of such other company, for an injury due entirely to the negligence of the operatives of the road, where there is no negligence on its part.

§ 817. **Liability of lessee.**— If a railroad is leased, by authority of law, in the absence of a statute imposing such liability, the lessor railroad company is not liable for an injury to a passenger caused by the negligence of the lessee in operating the road, though there be no express provision, either in the statute authorizing the lease, or in the lease itself, releasing the lessor from liability.[21]

The reason for this rule is that a railway passenger, in traveling over a leased track, has no contract relations with the lessor or any other lessee of the track than the company which carries him, and if he sustains an injury in consequence of the negligence of the lessor or of some other lessee than the one that occupies the relation of carrier toward him, his only remedy would be an action in tort, for the latter's breach of the duty it owed him to so use its property as not to cause injury to others, in the enjoyment of their legal rights.[22]

But where the lease is not authorized by law, or the law makes the lessor liable for the negligence of the lessee railroad company, it is quite generally held that the railroad company receiving the grant of its franchises from the legis-

[21] Arrowsmith v. Nashville, etc., R. Co., 57 Fed. Rep. 165; Miller v. New York, etc., R. Co., 125 N. Y. 118; 26 N. E. Rep. 35; Nugent v. Boston, etc., R. Co., 80 Me. 62; 12 Atl. Rep. 797; Virginia Midland R. Co. v. Washington, 86 Va. 629; 10 S. E. Rep. 927; 43 Am. & Eng. R. Cas. 688.

[22] Patterson v. Wabash, etc., R. Co., 54 Mich. 91; 19 N. W. Rep. 761; 18 Am. & Eng. R. Cas. 130.

lature, cannot devolve the performance of the reciprocal public duties upon another company and it remains liable for the torts of the lessee, precisely as if the lease, not authorized by law, had never been executed.[23]

§ 818. **Companies guilty of concurrent negligence.**— Of course if two or more railroad companies, using the tracks or facilities of each other, are concurrently negligent, as a result of which a passenger of either road is injured, under the familiar rule that one of two joint wrongdoers cannot claim exemption from the result of its own wrongful act, because of the negligence of another, either or both of the railroad companies will be liable to the injured passenger for the injury sustained by reason of their joint wrong.[24]

§ 819. **Stipulations limiting liability of carrier.**— There being no rule of law or public policy which compels a common carrier of passengers to assume toward a passenger the obligations of a carrier, beyond the terminus of its own line of road, the courts quite generally agree that the carrier, where it does agree to carry passengers over other roads, may, by contract, limit its own liability to acts or omissions occurring on its own line of railroad, or due to the negligence of its own employees or agents.[25]

In some jurisdictions it is held, where there is no limitation in the contract of carriage, that a carrier that undertakes to transport a passenger to a certain destination, over its own and other railroads, becomes liable for the safety of

[23] Chesapeake, etc., R. Co. v. Howard, 178 U. S. 153; Carruthers v. Kansas City, etc., R. Co., 59 Kansas 629; 54 Pac. Rep. 673; Balsley v. St. Louis, etc., R. Co., 119 Ill. 68; 8 N. E. Rep. 859; East Line, etc., R. Co. v. Lee, 71 Texas 538; 9 S. W. Rep. 904.

[24] Murray v. Lehigh Valley R. Co., 66 Conn. 512; 34 Atl. Rep. 506; 32 L. R. A. 539; Collins v. Texas, etc., R. Co., 15 Texas Civ. App. 169; 39 S. W. Rep. 643.

[25] Thompson, Carr. Pass. 403, 419, and cases cited.

the passenger throughout the entire distance he is to be transported, and where this doctrine prevails a company that sells a ticket to a point beyond its own line of road remains liable for an injury to the passenger, after the car in which he is being transported has passed onto the line of another railroad company.[26]

But even in States where this view obtains, if the passenger, by the ticket, or contract of transportation, has agreed to look only to the initial carrier, or the different carriers, for injuries that occur on their own lines of railroad, by or through the negligence of their own employees, the courts would enforce the contract and prevent an attempt to hold the initial carrier for an injury on the line of a connecting road, or *vice versa*.[27]

[26] Chollette v. Omaha, etc., R. Co., 26 Neb. 159; 41 N. W. Rep. 1106.
[27] Nashville, etc., R. Co. v. Sprayberry, 9 Heisk. (Tenn.) 852.

CHAPTER XXXIII.

§ 820. **Relation of passenger must be alleged.**— Where a person sues a railroad company for an injury received while he was a passenger on the train of the railroad company, the petition must allege the facts from which the relation arises.

If the action is for damages for an ejection, for instance, it is essential to allege that he was at the time being carried under a contract to transport him between given points on the defendant's railroad, or that he was ready and willing to pay his fare and had offered to pay same to the conductor, and if the petition fails to allege these facts, it is bad.[1]

The complaint should generally allege a contract of carriage between the injured passenger and the carrier upon a specific date, too, so that it may be seen, by the pleading,

[1] Day v. Owen, 5 Mich. 520.

1225

whether or not the injury was received while the contract was in effect, or if the contract was in existence at the date of the injuries.[2]

§ 821. **Carrier's negligence must be alleged.**— In a recent case, which came before the Kansas City Court of Appeals,[3] the question was presented whether or not, in pleading his case for a negligent injury, by the carrier, a passenger could rely upon the presumption of negligence obtaining, where an injury is shown, by reason of the carrier's appliances or roadway being defective, or whether the passenger was required to go further and allege the ultimate fact of a negligent injury, and upon the petition in which it was sought to rely upon this presumption, without setting forth the basic fact on which the cause of action rested, Judge Ellison, for the court, said: "We have not been cited to a case holding the petition to be sufficient where the facts constituting the culpability of the carrier are pleaded without a charge of negligence, and which, on their face, do not constitute or amount to negligence, by force of the statute or general law just explained. An act which does not show for itself that it is a negligent act, ought to be alleged to be negligent. * * * Conceding that facts are alleged from which a presumption of negligence arises, yet that amounts to no

[2] Conley v. Richmond, etc., R. Co., 109 No. Car. 692; 14 S. E. Rep. 303; 52 Am. & Eng. R. Cas. 490; Flint, etc., R. Co. v. Stark, 38 Mich. 714.

"A complaint for injuries to a passenger, which alleges the existence of the relation of carrier and passenger just before and at the time of the injuries, and which states that the carrier, failing in its duty to carry the passenger safely, so negligently conducted its business that by reason of such negligence the passenger received as a proximate result thereof, personal injury, states a cause of action for simple negligence, and is good as against a demurrer." Birmingham Ry., etc., Co. v. Wright (Ala. 1907), 44 So. Rep. 1037.

[3] Rawson v. Kansas City, etc., R. Co., 129 Mo. App. 613; 111 S. W. Rep. 234.

more than alleging acts which may, or may not, be negligence. It is an allegation by plaintiff that the act was negligent, unless for some reason in the carrier's knowledge it may be shown not to be. It is not the affirmative allegation of a fact, but rather it is only an allegation of matter upon which one can base a presumption. The difference is wide and substantial. If it is affirmatively alleged that an act was negligently done or omitted, no explanation can be given. It cannot be confessed and avoided. It can only be shown to be untrue. But if the act alleged is such as only raises a presumption of negligence, it may be admitted and yet explained. In an action by a passenger, the basis of the action is the negligence of the carrier, and it seems clear that a statement of the case which on its face, leaves it problematic whether there was negligence, is radically defective."

But of course it is only essential to set forth facts which show a breach of duty on the defendant's part, and if the allegation of the relation existing, and the injury sustained, will constitute an allegation of facts from which it is a necessary result that the duty owing by the carrier was violated, the passenger will generally be held to have alleged a good cause of action, although the ultimate fact that such violation constituted negligence, is omitted.[4]

§ 822. Setting out negligence of railroad company.— In an action by a passenger for injuries received through the negligence of the railroad company, the complaint of the plaintiff must charge negligence and that he was at the time without negligence, or in the exercise of due care.[5] Gen-

---

[4] In Keeton v. St. Louis, etc., R. Co. (116 Mo. App. 281; 92 S. W. Rep. 512), Judge Goode, for the St. Louis Court of Appeals, said: "There is authority for the proposition that where the acts alleged warrant the presumption of a negligent breach of duty, it is unnecessary to charge formally that they were negligently done."

[5] Cincinnati, etc., R. Co. v. Peters, 80 Ind. 168; 6 Am. & Eng. R. Cas. 126.

eral averments of negligence, however, are held to be sufficient, without defining the *quo modo,* or specifying the particular acts of diligence omitted, where simple negligence is
counted upon and the person injured was a passenger.[6]   But
if the petition fails to set up the relation occupied toward
the defendant, at the time of the injury, out of which some
duty would arise, making the acts alleged negligence, the petition is not good, as against a general demurrer.[7]   The petition, to withstand a demurrer, must set out the relation of
the plaintiff to the defendant; the circumstances out of which
the particular duty to the plaintiff arose and then facts showing a violation or breach of that duty toward the plaintiff.

§ 823. General and specific allegations of negligence.—
While it is very generally held that in setting forth his
cause of action, the plaintiff may rely upon general allegations of negligence and is not required to go further and
set up the specific acts of negligence causing his injury,[8] it
is quite generally held that where the plaintiff does set
forth specific acts of negligence, he is confined to proof of
the specific acts alleged and cannot establish his case by relying upon general acts of negligence not alleged.[9]   And even

[6] Ensley R. Co. v. Chewning, 93 Ala. 24; 9 So. Rep. 458; 50 Am. &
Eng. R. Cas. 46; Kansas City, etc., R. Co. v. Burton, 97 Ala. 240; 12
So. Rep. 88; 53 Am. & Eng. R. Cas. 115.

[7] Richmond, etc., R. Co. v. Scott, 86 Va. 902; 11 S. E. Rep. 404;
44 Am. & Eng. R. Cas. 418; Galveston, etc., R. Co. v. Thornberry
(Texas), 17 S. W. Rep. 521; Eldridge v. Long Island R. Co., 1 Sandf.
(N. Y.) 89.

"In an action for injuries to a passenger, it is sufficient to charge
negligence in general terms." Birmingham Ry., etc., Co. v. Wright
(Ala. 1907), 44 So. Rep. 1037.

[8] Gulf, etc., R. Co. v. Smith (Texas), 11 S. W. Rep. 1104; Gayle v.
Missouri Car, etc., Co., 177 Mo. 427; 76 S. W. Rep. 987; Chitty v.
St. Louis, etc., R. Co., 148 Mo. 64; 49 S. W. Rep. 868.

[9] Haviland v. Kansas City, etc., R. Co., 172 Mo. 106; 72 S. W.
Rep. 515.

though there may be general allegations of negligence, if the petition also combines specific acts of negligence, the pleader is held, in Missouri, to be confined to the specific acts of negligence alleged.[10]

But to take advantage of the departure, or the plaintiff's establishing the general acts of negligence alleged and the abandonment of the more specific allegations, the defendant must object to the evidence of the general acts of negligence, when the proof is offered, and if, instead of making such objection, the defendant meets the proof of such general charges, without objection, no objection can afterwards be heard in the higher court, because the trial court in its charge to the jury, covered the proof of the general acts of negligence, and predicated a recovery thereon.[11]

§ 824. **That plaintiff was rightfully on train.**— A petition for damages to a passenger, which fails to allege facts from which it can be logically deduced that the plaintiff, or in-

[10] Joseph v. Metropolitan R. Co., 129 Mo. App. 603; 111 S. W. Rep. 864; Spaulding v. Metropolitan R. Co., 129 Mo. App. 607; 111 S. W. Rep. 960.

[11] Dlauhi v. St. Louis, etc., R. Co., 139 Mo. 291; 40 S. W. Rep. 890; 60 Am. St. Rep. 576; 37 L. R. A. 406; Joseph v. Metropolitan R. Co., *supra*.

"Where in a personal injury action by a passenger specific injuries are alleged, recovery cannot be had for injuries not so specified." Stevens v. Kansas City Elevated Ry. Co. (Mo. App. 1907), 105 S. W. Rep. 26.

"Where, in an action for injuries of a passenger, plaintiff relied solely for a recovery on defendant's alleged negligence in suddenly stopping a train with unusual violence, which was not negligent, but properly done to avoid a collision, plaintiff could not recover for other or different causes of negligence, or on the theory of *res ipsa loquitur*." Todd v. Missouri Pac. Ry. Co. (Mo. App. 1907), 105 S. W. Rep. 671.

"The plaintiff must recover, if at all, upon his declaration; he cannot charge one species of negligence and recover upon proof of negligence of a different character." Chicago Union Traction Co. v. Lowenrosen, 125 Ill. App. 194, judgment affirmed; 78 N. E. Rep. 813; 222 Ill. 506.

jured person, was rightfully on the train, or premises, at the time of an injury to him, is fatally defective.[12]

But where a passenger sues for personal injuries received while on the cars of the defendant, it is generally sufficient to allege in the declaration that he was on the cars with the consent or permission of the defendant, or its employees in charge of the train, and from this it can be readily deduced that the plaintiff was a passenger, as matter of law, without the allegation of this conclusion from the facts alleged.[13]

But in the absence of some allegation going to show the right of the person injured upon the train, as where it was simply alleged that while on the train he was compelled by the employees of defendant, in charge of the train, to jump, as a result of which negligence he sustained the injuries complained of, it was held that the petition was fatally defective in failing to specify what right the plaintiff had on the train when the wrongful act was committed resulting in the injury.[14]

§ 825. **Negligence in assisting passenger to board train.**— While it is generally held that there is no obligation on the part of a carrier, or its employees, to assist passengers to board or alight from its trains, if this assistance is attempted to be rendered there is then the obligation, in law, to perform it with a reasonable degree of care and for an injury

---

[12] Whitehead v. St. Louis, etc., R. Co., 22 Mo. App. 60.

[13] Lammert v. Chicago, etc., R. Co., 9 Ill. App. 388.

[14] Pennsylvania, etc., R. Co. v. Dean, 92 Ind. 459; 18 Am. & Eng. R. Cas. 188.

Where the petition alleges that the plaintiff was rightfully on the train, it is not essential to set out that the injury occurred between the stations that the railroad company had agreed to carry the injured person, as this will be presumed, from the facts alleged, that the person was rightfully on the train, without setting forth the locality in question. International, etc., R. Co. v. Underwood, 67 Texas 589; 4 S. W. Rep. 216; 34 Am. & Eng. R. Cas. 570.

to a passenger, due to a lack of care on the employees assisting the passenger, an action will lie.

It was accordingly held, in a Mississippi case,[15] that a complaint which alleged that the plaintiff was at a station to be carried as a passenger; that she was weak and hardly able to walk; that the defendant's trains stopped at the station to take on passengers, and that the carrier, through its employees in charge of the train, accepted her as a passenger and transported her to her destination and received her fare, and while the employees in charge of the train were assisting her to board the train they performed the service so negligently as to injure her, stated a cause of action, and was good, as against a general demurrer.

§ 826. Injury due to bad track.— In stating a cause of action for an injury to a passenger, received while being transported, on account of the bad condition of the railroad track, it is generally sufficient to set forth the general bad condition of the track and that such condition caused the derailment or accident to the train, on which the passenger was being transported, occasioning the injury.[16] The particulars of the negligence, constituting the defective track are not essential to be alleged, but if the defendant desires more definite information as to the particular acts of negligence relied upon by the plaintiff, this could be obtained, generally, by a motion to require the petition to be made more definite and certain.[17]

[15] Williams v. Louisville, etc., R. Co., 43 So. Rep. 576.

[16] Ohio, etc., R. Co. v. Selby, 47 Ind. 471; 8 Am. Ry. Rep. 177.

[17] Ohio, etc., R. Co. v. Selby, supra.

"In an action for injuries to a person accompanying a shipment of horses, inconsistency in averments of the complaint in alleging that the train left the track by reason of rotten and defective ties permitting the rails to spread, and that the breaking of the axle of a car caused the train to leave the track, does not make the complaint bad." Southern Ry. Co. v. Roach (Ind. App. 1906), 78 N. E. Rep. 201.

§ 827. **Negligence in management of train.**— As the carrier owes, in law, the duty to the passenger to safely transport the passenger, after the commencement of the relation is undertaken, it is generally held to be a sufficient allegation of negligence for the passenger to allege that after entering the conveyance of the carrier, to be transported by it, he sustained an injury, either by reason of a collision,[18] or an assault by the employees,[19] or from some other cause where the agency connected with the injury is shown to have been under the control of the carrier.

But while it is generally held to be sufficient to so connect the carrier by general allegations of an injury received by reason of the management of the train, in which the pas-

"A petition in an action against a carrier which alleges negligence on employees in charge of the 'railroad, train and roadbed' alleges that the track was defective, though the word 'roadbed' does not include track and ties, since the word 'railroad' is broad enough to include the roadbed and the superstructure, including cross-ties, rails, and fastenings." Skiles v. St. Louis, etc., Ry. Co. (Mo. App. 1908), 108 S. W. Rep. 1082.

"In an action for an injury to plaintiff while a passenger on defendant's train which was wrecked, where the petition alleged that the negligence consisted in keeping and maintaining an unsafe and dangerous roadbed and track, and in negligent operation of the train, such charges of negligence, though general, entitled plaintiff to show any specific negligence which made the track dangerous or anything which established a negligent operation of the train." Mefford v. Missouri, etc., Ry. Co. (Mo. App. 1906), 97 S. W. Rep. 602.

"The character of an action is fixed by the allegations in the pleadings, and not by facts subsequently disclosed by the evidence; and hence, where plaintiff, in an action against a railroad for injuries, seeks to recover on the ground that the rails had not been properly spiked to the ties and the ground properly tamped, he cannot recover on other grounds." Norton v. Galveston, etc., Ry. Co. (Tex. Civ. App. 1908), 108 S. W. Rep. 1044.

18 Chattanooga, etc., R. Co. v. Huggins, 89 Ga. 494; 15 S. E. Rep. 848; 52 Am. & Eng. R. Cas. 473.

19 Pittsburg, etc., R. Co. v. Theobald, 51 Ind. 246.

senger is being conducted, it is held, in a New Jersey case,[20] not to come up to the requirement of showing that the injury is due, primarily, to the negligence of the carrier, to allege that while in a car of the carrier the plaintiff was thrown therefrom, by reason of the defendant's negligence, as this is held to be too general a description of the mode of the injury, and not sufficient to show the negligence of the carrier.

§ 828. **Failure to heat train.**— While the law recognizes the obligation on the part of the carrier to heat and render reasonably comfortable, its cars and trains, used for the transportation of passengers, it is held, in a Georgia case,[21] that the petition should set out the facts sufficiently to show whether the plaintiff was a passenger on a freight train, or a passenger train, and failing in this, that it was subject to a special demurrer — which takes the place of a motion to make the petition more definite and certain, under other

[20] Central, etc., R. Co. v. Van Horn, 38 N. J. L. 133; 13 Am. Ry. Rep. 36.

"A petition alleging that plaintiff was a passenger and had paid his fare, and that the cars were negligently kicked against the car in which he was a passenger, which threw him against the stove, breaking two of his ribs, and causing the injuries alleged and to lose the use of his left leg and to suffer great pain, states a good cause of action by which he could recover for the pain and suffering, and is sufficient to resist the general demurrer." Douglas & G. R. Co. v. Swindle (Ga. App. 1907), 59 S. E. Rep. 600.

"The complaint, charging in one place the injury to plaintiff, occasioned by collision of two trains, as resulting from the negligence of those in charge of the train on which he was a passenger, and in another place charging negligence of those in charge of both trains, permits a recovery on proof of negligence in the handling of the one train, so that a charge that, unless there was negligence of the employees in charge of both trains, which caused the injury, plaintiff could not recover, is properly refused." Central Ry. Co. v. Geopp (Ala. 1907), 45 So. Rep. 65.

[21] Atlantic Coast Line R. Co. v. Powell, 127 Ga. 805; 56 S. E. Rep. 1006.

rules of practice — and if the petition set up that complaint had been made to an agent of the carrier and a request made to have the car heated, this allegation was open to the same objection, because it failed to set out what agent of the defendant was referred to and whether or not he was connected with the operation of the train.

§ 829. **In actions for assaults.**— In an Indiana case,[22] a complaint alleged that the plaintiff, while riding upon a freight train, by the invitation and permission of the conductor, was, without being in fault, assaulted by one of the railroad company's employees, and thrown from the train and under its wheels, and that the other employees of the defendant, with knowledge of his assailant's intention, did not interfere to protect him from injury, but acquiesced in the assault, or made no objection to its continuance. This petition was held fatally defective, because it failed to allege what the assailant's duties were, or what he was engaged in at the time of the assault; because it did not allege the facts going to show that the relation of passenger and carrier existed at the time of the assault, or any facts to remove the presumption that the defendant's freight trains were engaged

[22] Smith v. Louisville, etc., R. Co., 124 Ind. 394; 24 N. E. Rep. 753.

"Where, in an action against a carrier, the ground of negligence alleged was the shoving and pushing of plaintiff off the platform of defendant's car by the porter, plaintiff would not be confined in his proof as to the effects of his injuries to the precise language of his petition." International & G. N. R. Co. v. Hugen (Tex. Civ. App. 1907), 100 S. W. Rep. 1000.

"In an action against a carrier for injuries sustained by a minor passenger, who alleged that he was pushed off the platform of a car by the porter, it was proper for plaintiff to prove that when the train reached his destination he went to the front door of the car to open it and get out, but found it locked, in order to show the exercise of reasonable diligence on his part in attempting to alight." International & G. N. R. Co. v. Hugen (Tex. Civ. App. 1907), 100 S. W. Rep. 1000.

in the transportation of freight alone, which were essential to constitute a cause of action.

§ 830. **Failure to provide facilities for alighting.**— In a Texas case,[23] the petition alleged that the carrier had failed to provide safe or proper facilities to enable the plaintiff, a passenger, to alight from its cars, and as a result of such failure the plaintiff, while endeavoring to alight, in the darkness, fell and was injured.   And in another case,[24] where it was alleged that the plaintiff was known to be a lady in delicate health and that the defendant had failed to provide a foot stool, or other device or appliance to enable her to safely alight from its car, and while attempting so to alight, she was injured, and both petitions were held to state a good cause of action.

But in a Missouri case,[25] where practically the same state of facts as in the latter case, were alleged, and a lady injured in alighting from a train, relied upon the absence of a foot stool, or other appliance, to enable her to safely alight, the Court of Appeals held that there was no duty on the part of the carrier to furnish such an appliance, and that the absence of a stool or box did not constitute negligence on its part.

§ 831. **Jerking train while passenger alighting.**— In an Indiana case,[26] in an action for an injury to a passenger while

[23] Stewart v. International, etc., R. Co., 53 Texas 289; 2 Am. & Eng. R. Cas. 497.

[24] Madden v. Port Royal, etc., R. Co., 35 So. Car. 381; 52 Am. & Eng. R. Cas. 286.

[25] Young v. Missouri Pacific Ry. Co., 93 Mo. App. 267.

[26] Kentucky, etc., R. Co. v. Quinkert, 2 Ind. App. 244; 28 N. E. Rep. 338.

"A sudden, violent, and unusual jerk of a car is not sufficient as a basis of recovery because of negligence, unless such jerk was unneces-

on one of the defendant's trains, the complaint alleged that when the train stopped at the plaintiff's destination she was notified by the employees of the train to alight and that she went upon the platform of the car for this purpose and could not alight at the place where the train had stopped, and was directed to remain on the platform, and while so situated, in the dark, with a child in her arms, without giving her time to return into the car, or to safely alight, the train was negligently started, with a violent jerk, which caused her injury. It was held that the petition stated a good cause of action and did not show any contributory negligence upon the part of the plaintiff.

§ 832. **Failure to stop train at proper place.**—While it is generally essential, in an action for being carried by one's station, to allege that the train on which the passenger was being transported was a train which regularly stopped at the station,[27] where it is alleged that the plaintiff was upon a train in pursuance of a contract of the carrier to transport him to such a station, this essential is sufficiently covered by such an allegation, and if the petition then sets forth that the passenger attempted to alight at the request of the train employees and on account of the stopping of the train at an improper and dangerous place for him to alight, he was injured while obeying such instructions, it is held to state a good cause of action.[28]

sary at the particular time and place." Augusta Ry., etc., Co. v. Lyle (Ga. App. 1908), 60 S. E. Rep. 1075.

Sudden jolts and jars in starting and stopping a freight train, which cannot be avoided in the exercise of due care, are assumed by a passenger as one of the perils of travel by that mode of conveyance. Hawk v. Chicago, etc., Ry. Co. (Mo. App. 1908), 108 S. W. Rep. 1119.

[27] Ohio, etc., R. Co. v. Hatten, 60 Ind. 12; Purcell v. Richmond, etc., R. Co., 108 No. Car. 414; 12 S. E. Rep. 954; 47 Am. & Eng. R. Cas. 457.

[28] Wilburn v. St. Louis, etc., R. Co., 36 Mo. App. 203; Evansville, etc., R. Co. v. Duncan, 28 Ind. 441.

§ 833. **Negativing contributory negligence.**— In some States it is held that the plaintiff must, in his complaint, negative the fact of his own contributory negligence, to allege a good cause of action; [29] but in other States this is held not to be essential.[30]

But of course, if the petition of the plaintiff, in stating the acts on the defendant's part, constituting the cause of action, also shows his own negligence, as a direct cause of the injury, as where he alleged an injury to his hand, which he had extended a distance of several inches from the car window,[31] or in alighting from a moving train, which was not billed to stop at the destination where the plaintiff attempted to alight,[32] as a result of which he sustained the injuries complained of, these facts, shown by the petition of the plaintiff, are held to constitute such negligence on his part as to bar a recovery.

§ 834. **Setting up limitations on liability.**— As a general rule, if the defendant, in a suit by a passenger, relies upon any special contract for a defense, whereby its general liability is limited, this is such a special defense as it will be required to be set up specially in the answer, and if it is not so pleaded, it is waived.[33]

If the rules of the carrier, as to passengers on its freight trains, place the risk of injuries received as a result of the

[29] Jeffersonville, etc., R. Co. v. Hendricks, 26 Ind. 228; Cincinnati, etc., R. Co. v. Peters, 80 Ind. 168; 6 Am. & Eng. R. Cas. 126.

[30] Lloyd v. Hannibal, etc., R. Co., 53 Mo. 509; 12 Am. Ry. Rep. 474; Petty v. Hannibal, etc., R. Co., 88 Mo. 306; Northern Pacific R. Co. v. Hess, 2 Wash. 383; 26 Pac. Rep. 866; 48 Am. & Eng. R. Cas. 91; Ohio, etc., R. Co. v. Smith, 5 Ind. App. 560; 32 N. E. Rep. 809.

[31] Richmond, etc., R. Co. v. Scott, 88 Va. 958; 14 S. E. Rep. 763; 52 Am. & Eng. R. Cas. 405.

[32] Barnett v. East Tennessee, etc., R. Co., 87 Ga. 766; 13 S. E. Rep. 904.

[33] Citizens R. Co. v. Twiname, 111 Ind. 587; 13 N. E. Rep. 55; 30 Am. & Eng. R. Cas. 616.

operation of the train, upon the passenger, these rules ought to be set up as a defense to an action by a passenger so injured.[34]   And the same is true of a special contract by the plaintiff that he would assume the risk of an injury received while engaged on a special trip, and if such contract is not urged by special plea, no evidence of the existence of the contract would generally be held competent, as this would constitute a departure, or would be outside the issue framed by the petition alleging the negligence and the simple denial of such negligence, on the defendant's part.[35]

[34] Whitehead v. St. Louis, etc., R. Co., 99 Mo. 263; 11 S. W. Rep. 751; 39 Am. & Eng. R. Cas. 410.

[35] Citizens, etc., R. Co. v. Twiname, *supra.*

The general issue in an action on the case for personal injuries does not put in issue the question as to the ownership of tracks and by whom the cars thereon are operated. Hill v. Chicago City Ry. Co., 126 Ill. App. 152.

A carrier sued for ejection of a passenger was not precluded from relying on a forfeiture of his ticket for misuse, because the conductor at the time of the ejection erroneously refused to accept the ticket because it had expired. Baltimore, etc., R. Co. v. Evans (Ind. 1907), 82 N. E. Rep. 773.

CHAPTER XXXIV.

§ 835. **On degree of care on carrier's part.**— It is proper for the court to instruct the jury that the law exacts of the carrier the highest degree of care for the protection of the passenger, in the maintenance of its roadway, track, cars and equipment, for in the case of passengers, the law requires the railroad company to exercise the highest degree of care.[1]

It is not error for the court to give to the jury a charge to the effect that the jury may determine, from the evidence, whether or not the defendant " has used that strict diligence which the law requires, in providing for the safety of its passengers," as this does not require too high a degree of care and diligence on the defendant's part.[2]

[1] Texas, etc., R. Co. v. Stewart, 1 Texas Civ. App. 642; 20 S. W. Rep. 962; Central, etc., R. Co. v. Smith, 80 Ga. 526; 5 S. E. Rep. 772; 34 Am. & Eng. R. Cas. 456; Furnish v. Missouri Pacific Ry. Co., 102 Mo. 442; 13 S. W. Rep. 1044; 22 Am. St. Rep. 781.

[2] Alabama, etc., R. Co. v. Hill, 93 Ala. 514; 9 So. Rep. 722.

But as an instruction to the effect that the greatest care and caution is exacted of the defendant, is only proper where the relation of passenger and carrier exists, it is error to give such an instruction in a case where the existence of this relation is not established by the evidence,[3] and, generally, an instruction requiring such high degree of care is only to be given in a case where the jury find, from the evidence, that the defendant was engaged in the business of transporting passengers for hire, upon a railroad operated by it.[4] An instruction that it was the duty of the defendant to "transport its passengers safely, and a failure so to do is negligence," is error, since it practically imposes upon the carrier the obligation of an insurer.[5]

[3] Frick v. St. Louis, etc., R. Co., 75 Mo. 595; 8 Am. & Eng. R. Cas. 280.

[4] Davis v. Button, 78 Cal. 247; 20 Pac. Rep. 545.
An instruction that "The law imposed upon the defendant, as a common carrier of passengers, the utmost care in carrying them safely to the place of destination, and that the absence of such care constituted negligence such as to render the carrier liable for all injuries resulting to the passenger, the passenger being free from contributory negligence," was approved, in Smith v. Chicago, etc., R. Co., 108 Mo. 243; 18 S. W. Rep. 971; 52 Am. & Eng. R. Cas. 483.

[5] International, etc., R. Co. v. Underwood, 64 Texas, 463; 27 Am. & Eng. R. Cas. 240.
In an action for injuries to an alleged passenger, an instruction setting out facts which if established, would authorize a verdict for plaintiff, is not erroneous because not in terms requiring a finding that he was a "passenger," where it requires finding of facts which would establish the relation of passenger and carrier. East St. Louis, etc., R. Co. v. Zink, 82 N. E. Rep. 283; 229 Ill. 180.
An instruction, in an action against a carrier for injuries to a passenger by the derailment of the coach, that the burden was on the carrier to prove that the coach, the engine, roadbed, tracks, and ties were reasonably safe "so far as human skill, diligence, and foresight could provide, * * * and that by the utmost human skill, diligence, and foresight is meant such skill, diligence, and foresight as is exercised by a very cautious person under like circumstances," is not erroneous, though no standard by which to measure the carrier's duty is furnished by requiring it to exercise care so far as human skill,

§ 836. **Presumption of negligence from accident.**— Upon the presumption of negligence, on the part of the carrier, which obtains in the case of a derailment of the train, on which a passenger is being conducted, resulting in injury to the passenger, the following charge to the jury has been approved, i. e., that if the jury believe from the evidence that on a date certain, the defendant was a passenger carrier, for hire, and the plaintiff on said date was being transported by it, and that, while being so transported, the passenger was injured by reason of the car in which he was riding, leaving the track, and falling down an embankment, then the burden rests on the defendant to establish to the satisfaction of the jury that the derailment was caused by inevitable accident and not from any defect or imperfection in the car or the engine by which it was drawn, or by the machinery by which it was operated, or in the roadbed, track, or ties, on the defendant's road, which could have been prevented by the utmost care, skill and diligence.[6]

§ 837. **On burden of proof.**— In a Texas case,[7] the trial court instructed the jury that the burden of proof was upon the plaintiff to show the extent of his injuries, and that he

diligence, and foresight can provide. Skiles v. St. Louis, etc., Ry. Co. (Mo. App. 1908), 108 S. W. Rep. 1082.

[6] Furnish v. Missouri Pacific Ry. Co., 102 Mo. 443; 13 S. W. Rep. 1044; 22 Am. St. Rep. 781.

In an action against a carrier for injuries to a passenger by the falling of a window of the car, where the evidence, which was not directly disputed or denied, showed that the window catch must have been weak, broken, or defective, as claimed, the court properly instructed the jury that, if the accident and resultant injury were occasioned by the defect in the appliance, a *prima facie* case of negligence as established, and it was incumbent on defendant to excuse such apparent failure of duty. Rehearing (1907) 82 N. E. 1025, denied. Cleveland, etc., Ry. Co. v. Hadley (Ind. 1908), 84 N. E. Rep. 13.

[7] Gulf, etc., R. Co. v. McMannewitz, 70 Texas 73; 8 S. W. Rep.; 34 Am. & Eng. R. Cas. 428.

was entitled to recover only for such injuries as he sustained from the accident and that he was not entitled to recover for any disease that may have proceeded from any other cause. This was held a proper charge and in accordance with the rule that the injuries must be shown to have resulted proximately from the accident, before a recovery is permitted.

And in a New York case,[8] it was also held to be a proper charge to advise the jury that the mere fact that plaintiff sustained an injury while a passenger, did not entitle him to recover, but that he was required to go further and to show that the accident and resulting injury was due to a lack of due care on the part of the railroad company, as this merely required the plaintiff to discharge the burden of proof, by connecting the accident and the injury with the negligence of the defendant.

§ 838. **Defining the term "negligence."**— As the term " negligence " is a term dependent both upon facts and law, it is generally held to be error to give an instruction, assuming that certain acts, on the part of the defendant, or its employees, will amount to actionable negligence, without giving the jury any standard by which to arrive at the correct determination of the basic fact, whether or not such acts are, or are not negligent acts. Hence, it is generally held to be proper for the court to define the meaning of the term " negligence " by proper definition, in a charge to the jury.[9]

But it is held not to be reversible error to fail to so define the term in some States.[10]

[8] Buck v. Manhattan R. Co., 32 N. Y. S. R. 51; 10 N. Y. Supp. 107.

[9] Magrane v. St. Louis, etc., R. Co., 183 Mo. 119; Casey v. Bridge Co., 114 Mo. App. 65; Johnston v. Atchison, etc., R. Co., 117 Mo. App. 308; Callahan v. Warne, 40 Mo. 131; Yarnall v. St. Louis, etc., R. Co., 75 Mo. 575; Ravenscraft v. Missouri Pacific Ry. Co., 27 Mo. App. 617.

[10] Sweeny v. Kansas City, etc., R. Co., 150 Mo. 385; 51 S. W. Rep.

§ 839. That carrier is not an insurer.— The familiar instruction that railroad companies, engaged in the transportation of persons for hire, are not insurers of the safety of their passengers, is proper to be given, in every case, of injury to a passenger, on the part of the carrier.

The form of such instructions is that "the jury are instructed that railroad companies, engaged in the transportation of persons for hire, are not insurers of the safety of their passengers, and to entitle a passenger to recover for an injury received while being transported, it devolves upon the passenger to show that the injury complained of was occasioned by the negligence of the railroad company, or its employees." [11]

§ 840. Duty toward passenger alighting.— Where the question at issue was whether the defendant, a railroad company, was negligent in stopping the cab of its freight train, near to a dangerous retaining wall, and leaving the plaintiff, who had taken passage on the train, without a light and without notice of the dangerous character of the place, it was held proper to charge the jury that — "When the defendant. brought the passenger to the place where the train was going, all that it was bound to do then was to see that he was afforded reasonable immunity from danger and reasonable protection in leaving the point where he had been landed." [12]

It is also proper to submit to the jury the issue whether or not the train was held for a reasonable time to enable passengers to alight from the train, considering the facili-

682; Linder v. Transit Co., 103 Mo. App. 574; 77 S. W. Rep. 997.

[11] An instruction in this form was approved by Judge Black, in Smith v. Chicago, etc., R. Co., 108 Mo. 243; 18 S. W. Rep. 971; 52 Am. & Eng. R. Cas. 483.

[12] Central, etc., R. Co. v. Smith, 80 Ga. 526; 5 S. E. Rep. 772; 34 Am. & Eng. R. Cas. 456.

ties afforded and the number of passengers to alight; [13] and if the jury finds from the evidence that the train was not held stationary for a time sufficient to enable the passengers to safely alight, but while the plaintiff was on the car steps the train was started and she was dragged off the platform or steps by the employees of the defendant, she is entitled to a verdict, is held to be proper, in a Missouri case.[14]

§ 841. **Safety of appliances for alighting from cars.**— Whether a railroad company has performed its duty in providing reasonably safe facilities and appliances to enable its passengers to alight from its cars, was held a jury issue, in a Texas case,[15] where the evidence showed that the carrier had furnished a box, about eleven inches square on top, and a little larger at the bottom, and the facts developed that a passenger stepping on the box would be calculated to turn it over.

But in a Missouri case,[16] upon the duty of the carrier

[13] Taber v. Delaware, etc., R. Co., 71 N. Y. 489; 4 Hun 765; Western R. Co. v. Young, 51 Ga. 489; 7 Am. Ry. Rep. 352.

[14] Owens v. Kansas City, etc., R. Co., 95 Mo. 169; 8 S. W. Rep. 350; 33 Am. & Eng. R. Cas. 524.

A charge that no duty exists toward a passenger, by a carrier, after the passenger has alighted, is error. Ormond v. Hays, 60 Texas 180.

In an action against a railroad for injuries to plaintiff while alighting from defendant's train, defendant was entitled to charges presenting its theory of the time and place at and the manner in which the accident occurred, such theory being supported by substantially all of the testimony except that of plaintiff himself. Gulf, etc., Ry. Co. v. Walters (Tex. Civ. App. 1908), 107 S. W. Rep. 369.

[15] Missouri Pacific Ry. Co. v. Wortham, 73 Texas 25; 10 S. W. Rep. 741; 3 L. R. A. 368; 37 Am. & Eng. R. Cas. 82.

[16] Young v. Missouri Pacific Ry. Co., 93 Mo. App. 274.

The attention of the Appellate Court was evidently not called to the above cited Texas case, for it is there said: "She was a passenger, alighting from the car upon which she had been traveling, to take another and to complete her trip, under her contract with the appellants. They owed her the duty of providing, *not only a reasonably safe*

to furnish a portable step to enable its passengers to safely alight from its cars, the Kansas City Court of Appeals said: "We know of no law, nor has our attention been called to any, which required the defendant to furnish portable steps for the use of its passengers in entering or leaving any of its cars. If it did furnish such steps, it was but a self-imposed duty, for the violation of which there could, of course, be no liability."

§ 842. **On contributory negligence of passenger.**— A passenger who fails or neglects to leave a car, after the train has stopped a sufficient time to enable him, by due care, to leave it, but waits until the train has started and then jumps upon the platform, after the expiration of such a reasonable time given him to alight, is guilty of negligence which will prevent a recovery for an injury so received.[17]

Where a train is not running at such a rate of speed as to make it dangerous to attempt to board or alight from the train in motion, it is proper to advise the jury that it is for them to determine whether or not, under all the facts and circumstances, the passenger was negligent in alighting from the train in motion.[18] But where, from the condition of the passenger and the speed of the train, it is manifestly a dangerous procedure for the passenger to attempt to alight, it then becomes the duty of the court to so advise the jury as matter of law.[19]

appliance for enabling her to alight, in order to make the transfer, but the safest that had been known and tested." This latter standard is manifestly too high to meet the requirements of the law, but it is none the less an expression as to a duty on the part of the carrier, to furnish an appliance or stool, to enable the passengers to alight, which was evidently overlooked by the court in Missouri.

[17] Detroit, etc., R. Co. v. Curtis, 23 Wis. 152.

[18] Louisville, etc., R. Co. v. Crunk, 119 Ind. 542; 41 Am. & Eng. R. Cas. 158.

[19] Pennsylvania R. Co. v. Lyons, 129 Pa. St. 113; 18 Atl. Rep. 759; 41 Am. & Eng. R. Cas. 154.

§ 843. **Assuming notice of danger of person injured.**— As a general rule, before the engineer, or other operator of an engine or cars on a railroad track, can be held guilty of negligence toward the person injured, since the track is fixed so that no digression can be made and the vehicles can only run on the track, while a person so located can easily step from the danger, notice of the danger to the person must be brought home to the operator of the engine or car causing the injury, or facts from which such notice could have been received in the exercise of reasonable diligence, on the

An instruction defining plaintiff's duty in entering and leaving defendant's car was not erroneous because of the use of the expression "due diligence" when in all of the instructions the terms "reasonable diligence," "ordinary care," and "reasonable care" are used synonymously. Bond v. Chicago, etc., Ry. Co. (Mo. App. 1907), 99 S. W. Rep. 30.

An instruction, in an action by a husband for injuries to his wife while a passenger, that the carrier was responsible to plaintiff if its failure to use the proper degree of care was the proximate cause of the injury, though the wife might have been guilty of negligence, unless it appeared that she could, by the exercise of ordinary care, have avoided the consequences of the negligence of the carrier, was misleading, because susceptible of the construction that plaintiff might recover notwithstanding the negligence of the wife. Texas, etc., R. Co. v. Harrington (Tex. Civ. App. 1906), 98 S. W. Rep. 653.

In an action against a carrier for personal injuries, where there was a defense of contributory negligence, an instruction which authorizes a recovery for plaintiff on facts hypothesized in it, without limiting it by reference to contributory negligence, is not reversible error, where other instructions submit the question of plaintiff's contributory negligence. Underwood v. Metropolitan St. Ry. Co. (Mo. App. 1907), 102 S. W. Rep. 1045.

An instruction, in an action for injuries to an infant while attempting to board a moving train, that in determining the issue of contributory negligence the jury should consider the infant's age, intelligence, and discretion, may be given, where there is evidence that the infant was, on account of his age, so wanting in intelligence that he could not appreciate the danger of boarding a moving train. San Antonio, etc., Ry. Co. v. Trigo (Tex. Civ. App. 1907), 101 S. W. Rep. 254.

employees in charge of the car or engine causing
r which the action is maintained.

of proving actual notice, the facts of a case
uch a condition as would, by due care, have
ce, it is error to base a charge to the jury upon
nt's liability, dependent upon actual notice to
ees in charge of the engine or car, and if such
ion is given to the jury and the facts do not war-
his would constitute reversible error, on the part
ial court, as held, in a Missouri case.[20]

44. On violation of rules.—Where there is an injury
n employee and the evidence on the part of the de-
ndant shows that the employer had a rule covering the
uty of the employee, and that the employer's rule had been
brought home to the injured employee and that the rule was
in effect and had not been complied with by the employee, at
the time of his injury, it is error on the part of the court
to refuse an instruction to the effect that the plaintiff cannot recover, if the jury finds, from the evidence, that the
rule was in effect and was known to the injured employee
and was violated at the time of the injury, in case the
violation of the rule contributed to produce the injury received.[21]

Nor would it be proper for the court to assume, as ma
ter of law, that such a rule was waived by the employer,
the proof that the rule had been violated by the employe

[20] Williams v. Kansas City, etc., R. Co., 96 Mo. 275.
[21] Francis v. Kansas City, etc., R. Co., 110 Mo. 387; Alco
Chicago, etc., R. Co., 108 Mo. 95; Schaub v. Hannibal, etc., F
106 Mo. 92; Zumwalt v. Chicago etc., R. Co., 35 Mo. App. 661;
v. Chesapeake, etc., R. Co., 37 W. Va. 524; 16 S. E. Rep. 813; I
& Eng. R. Cas. 417; Alexander v. Louisville, etc., R. Co. 83 K
Savannah, etc., R. Co. v. Folks, 76 Ga. 527; San Antonio, etc.,
v. Wallace, 76 Texas 636; 13 S. W. Rep. 565; 44 Am. & Eng.
564.

in the absence of notice of such violation to the employer's officers or agents, but on proof of such a state of facts, it ought to also submit this issue by appropriate instructions.[22]

§ 845. **Confusing recoveries under different statutes.**— It frequently happens that a plaintiff in a personal injury or death action, will confuse, in his pleading, or proof, the amount of the recovery, under different statutes, to which the proof would entitle him, and by instruction to the jury predicate a recovery under the one statute, when the proof would entitle him to a different recovery, under a wholly different statute.

That this will constitute reversible error is evidenced by the line of cases, under the death statutes of Missouri, known to the bar as the compensatory and the penalty sections of the statutes. By one of these statutes,[23] where the death is caused by common-law acts of negligence, the recovery cannot exceed the sum of five thousand dollars, and by another statute,[24] where the death is due to the negligent acts of the employees in charge of the car or engine, the fixed sum of five thousand dollars, under the statute, as it stood originally, was recoverable, as a penalty. If the plaintiff predicated his right of recovery, under the penalty section of the statute, in a case where the evidence showed that the death was due to other acts of negligence than those specified therein, this would constitute error, for it practically denied to the defendant the assessment of any less sum than that fixed by this statute, whereas, the recovery ought to have been for any sum, not to exceed this sum, where the acts of negligence were not those specified in this statute.[25]

---

[22] Alcorn v. Chicago, etc., R. Co., 108 Mo. 95; Francis v. Kansas City, etc., R. Co., 110 Mo. 387.

[23] Rev. St. Missouri, 1899, §§ 2865, 2866.

[24] Rev. St. Missouri, 1899, § 2864.

[25] Culbertson v. Railway Co., 140 Mo. 35; McKenna v. Railroad Co.,

§ 846. **Inconsistent instructions.**— It has recently been determined, in Missouri,[26] that it is reversible error to give inconsistent instructions to the jury, in a personal injury action, although the instruction given at the instance of the plaintiff may be correct and that given on behalf of the defendant may be erroneous, under the facts shown by the record, because it cannot be held which one of the two conflicting instructions the jury followed.

Speaking on this question, Judge Fox, for the Missouri Supreme Court, said, in a recent case: " Instructions numbered two and five are separate and independent declarations of law, and are directly in conflict — one of them declaring the law correctly, the other erroneously — and we are unable to say by which one the jury were guided.   This instruction constituted such error as warranted the court in granting a new trial." [27]

54 Mo. App. 161; King v. Missouri Pacific Ry. Co., 98 Mo. 235; Crumpley v. Hannibal, etc., R. Co., 98 Mo. 34; Rapp. v. St. Joe, etc., R. Co., 106 Mo. 423; Elliott v. St. Louis, etc., Ry. Co., 67 Mo. 272; Holmes v. Hannibal, etc., R. Co., 69 Mo. 536; Schlereth v. Missouri Pacific Ry. Co., 96 Mo. 509; Flynn v. Kansas City, etc., Ry. Co., 78 Mo. 195; Casey v. Transit Co., 205 Mo. 721; 103 S. W. Rep. 1146.

[26] Porter v. Missouri Pacific Ry. Co., 199 Mo. 82; Shepard v. Transit Co., 189 Mo. 362.

[27] Shepard v. Transit Co., 189 Mo. 362.

CHAPTER XXXV.

§ 847. **Liability may be confined to own line.**— A carrier may limit its liability to its own line and the courts recognize no distinction, in this regard, between the carriers of freight and the carriers of passengers.[1]

When it is expressly stipulated in the contract of transportation that the railroad company selling or issuing the transportation does so as the agent of the connecting carrier and provides that it shall not be responsible beyond its own line of railroad, each coupon of the ticket or pass becomes the separate contract of the line of railroad for which it is issued and the contract of transportation does not imply a joint obligation, resting on each of the railroad companies.[2]

[1] Gulf, etc., R. Co. v. Looney, 85 Texas 158; 19 S. W. Rep. 1039; 52 Am. & Eng. R. Cas. 197; Gulf, etc., R. Co. v. Baird, 75 Texas 263; 40 Am. & Eng. R. Cas. 160.

[2] Gulf, etc., R. Co. v. Looney, *supra.*

1250

Such limitation, if reasonable, will be binding on the passenger and the coupon or contract of each of the several connecting carriers is evidence of the passenger's right to transportation over the several lines of the different railroad companies and the liability of each is regulated and determined by the terms of such contracts and each railroad company is liable only for negligence occurring upon its own road, where this is the condition of the contract.[3]

§ 848. **Consideration for limitation of liability.**— It was held in New York, in an early case,[4] that the consideration of carrying a passenger free, or at a reduced rate, was sufficient to enable the carrier to stipulate that the passenger should travel at his own risk of accidents resulting from the negligence of the carrier's employees, for which the carrier would be otherwise responsible. This same rule was announced in two Massachusetts cases,[5] and is the basis of the principle applied by the United States Supreme Court, in recent cases.[6]

But while a reduced rate or free transportation is held to be a sufficient consideration for any reasonable condition,[7] it is not generally held that a stipulation exempting the carrier from all liability for damages resulting from the negligence of its employees is such a reasonable condition as will enable the carrier to enforce such a contract, although it may be entered into for a reduced consideration.[8]

[3] Mosher v. St. Louis, etc., R. Co., 127 U. S. 393.

[4] Bissell v. New York, etc., R. Co., 25 N. Y. 442; Wells v. New York, etc., R. Co., 24 N. Y. 181; Perkins v. New York, etc., R. Co., 24 N. Y. 196.

[5] Bates v. Old Colony R. Co., 147 Mass. 255; 17 N. E. Rep. 633; 34 Am. & Eng. R. Cas. 355; Hosmer v. Old Colony R. Co., 156 Mass. 506.

[6] Northern Pacific R. Co. v. Adams, 192 U. S. 441; 48 L. Ed. 513; Boering v. Chesapeake, etc., R. Co., 193 U. S. 442; 48 L. Ed. 742.

[7] See opinion of Judge Bliss, in Goetz v. Hannibal, etc., R. Co., 50 Mo. 472, 474.

[8] New York, etc., R. Co. v. Lockwood, 17 Wall. (U. S.) 357; Rose v.

§ 849. **Limitations must be reasonable.**— It has been many times decided that a common carrier of passengers could not lawfully stipulate for an exemption from liability, unless such exemption was just and reasonable, in the eye of the law and that it was not just and reasonable to permit it to exempt itself from the result of its own negligence or want of ordinary care and diligence.[9]

But since a railroad company is under no legal obligation to allow an express messenger to ride in the baggage car of a train, it has been held, by one of the highest authorities in the land,[10] that it is entitled to protect itself against an in-

Des Moines, etc., R. Co., 39 Iowa 246; Carroll v. Missouri Pacific Ry. Co. 88 Mo. 239; Cleveland, etc., R. Co. v. Curran, 19 Ohio St. 1; Pennsylvania R. Co. v. Henderson, 51 Pa. St. 315; Hartwell v. Northern Pacific Co., 5 Dakota 463; 41 N. W. Rep. 732; 3 L. R. A. 342; 37 Am. & Eng. R. Cas. 635; Blair v. Erie R. Co., 66 N. Y. 313.

Where transportation of a railroad employee from his home to his place of employment was not gratuitous but a part of his compensation, he was not bound by a provision of his passbook attempting to relieve the carrier from liability for injuries resulting from the negligence of the operatives of its cars. Eberts v. Detroit, etc., Ry. (Mich. 1908), 115 N. W. Rep. 43.

A contract between an employer and a carrier, releasing a carrier from liability for damages to persons transported under the contract does not release the carrier from liability to an employee of the employer; the contract being one of indemnity against liability for damages. Cleveland, etc., Ry. Co. v. Henry (Ind. App. 1907), 80 N. E. Rep. 636.

[9] New York, etc., R. Co. v. Lockwood, 17 Wall. (U. S.) 357; Atchison, etc., R. Co. v. Washburn, 5 Neb. 117; Virginia, etc., R. Co. v. Sayers, 26 Gratt. (Va.) 328; Rintoul v. New York, etc., R. Co., 21 Blatchf. (U. S.) 439; 17 Fed. Rep. 905; Eels v. St. Louis, etc., R. Co., 52 Fed. Rep. 903; Kansas City, etc., R. Co. v. Simpson, 30 Kansas 645; 46 Am. Rep. 104; 16 Am. & Eng. R. Cas. 158; St. Louis, etc., R. Co. v. Lester, 46 Ark. 236; Terre Haute, etc., R. Co. v. Sherwood, 132 Ind. 129; Peters v. Mariatte, etc., R. Co., 42 Ohio St. 275; Honeyman v. Oregon, etc., R. Co., 13 Oregon, 352; 25 Am. & Eng. R. Cas. 380; Coward v. East Tenn. etc., R. Co., 16 Lea (Tenn.) 225; 57 Am. Rep. 226.

[10] Bates v. Old Colony R. Co., 147 Mass. 255; 17 N. E. Rep. 633; 34 Am. & Eng. R. Cas. 355.

crease of its liability upon giving permission to do so, and such a condition relieving it from liability for accidents and personal injuries, is held to be neither unreasonable or against public policy.[11]

§ 850. **Contracts limiting liability for negligence.**— A carrier of passengers cannot contract so as to relieve itself from liability for an injury to a passenger from the negligence of the carrier or its employees, in the course of their employment, under the rule of public policy recognized by the great weight of authority in the United States.[12]

By the English decisions the carrier has power to provide by contract against all liability for negligence in the carriage of the passenger.[13]   And some courts in the United States,

[11] Bates v. Old Colony R. Co., *supra*.

A contract whereby a railroad employee agrees to give notice to the company within thirty days after an injury or to release it from all liability, is held to be void, under the Iowa Code (§ 2071), which gives a cause of action to railroad employees, injured as a result of the negligence of the company's agents, and makes void all contracts made in violation thereof. Mumford v. Chicago, etc., Ry. Co., 128 Iowa 685; 104 N. W. Rep. 1135. As the statute in this case only avoids contracts restricting a liability and not those providing for notice simply, this construction would appear to give the statute too broad an effect.

[12] Philadelphia, etc., R. Co. v. Derby, 14 How. (U. S.) 468; Pennsylvania R. Co. v. McClosky, 23 Pa. St. 526; Pennsylvania R. Co. v. Butler, 57 Ind. 335; Indiana, etc., R. Co. v. Mumby, 21 Ind. 48; Illinois, etc., R. Co. v. Read, 37 Ill. 484; Cleveland etc., R. Co. v. Curran, 10 Ohio St. 1; Mobile, etc., R. Co. v. Hopkins, 41 Ala. 486; Pennsylvania R. Co. v. Henderson, 51 Pa. St. 315; Gulf, etc., R. Co. v. McGowan, 65 Texas 640; 26 Am. & Eng. R. Cas. 274; Carroll v. Missouri Pacific Ry. Co., 88 Mo. 239; 57 Am. Rep. 382; 26 Am. & Eng. R. Cas. 268; Cherry v. Chicago, etc., R. Co., 191 Mo. 489; Dawson v. Chicago, etc., R. Co., 79 Mo. 296; Harvey v. Terre Haute, etc. R. Co., 74 Mo. 541; Lemon v. Chanslor, 68 Mo. 340; Sturgeon v. St. Louis, etc., R. Co., 65 Mo. 569; Rice v. Kansas, etc., R. Co., 63 Mo. 314.

[13] McCawley v. Furness R. Co., L. R. 8 Q. B. 57; Hall v. Northeastern R. Co., L. R. 10 Q. B. 437; Duffy v. Great Northern R. Co., 4 L. R.

of the highest authority, follow the English decisions and
allow railroad companies, as to passengers riding on free
transportation, to contract for exemption from all liability
for negligence.[14] Other courts concede the right to make
such exemptions in all cases of ordinary negligence, but
refuse to apply the principle to cases of gross negligence.[15]
But, as stated above, the courts of the greater number of
states in the United States, on grounds of public policy, deny
the power of railroad companies to make a valid contract exempting the carrier from liability for the negligence of its
employees in any degree.[16]

(Ire.) 178; Alexander v. Toronto, etc., R. Co., 33 U. C. 474; Northern Pacific R. Co. v. Adams, 192 U. S. 440; 48 L. Ed. 513.

[14] Welles v. New York, etc., R. Co., 26 Barb. 641; 24 N. Y. 181;
Perkins v. New York, etc., R. Co., 24 N. Y. 208; Bissell v. New York,
etc., R. Co., 25 N. Y. 442; Poucher v. New York, etc., R. Co., 49 N. Y.
263; Magnin v. Dinsmore, 56 N. Y. 168; Griswold v. New York, etc.,
R. Co. (N. Y.), 26 Am. & Eng. R. Cas. 280; Kinney v. Central R. Co.,
32 N. J. L. 409; 34 id. 513; Western, etc., R. Co. v. Bishop, 50 Ga.
465.

[15] Illinois Central R. Co. v. Read, 37 Ill. 484; Indiana, etc., R. Co.
v. Mundy, 21 Ind. 48; Jacobus v. St. Paul, etc., R. Co., 20 Minn. 125.

[16] Cherry v. Chicago, etc., R. Co., 191 Mo. 489, and cases cited.
Judge Marshall, speaking for the Missouri Supreme Court, in this case,
said: "The American rule has long been settled that a railroad company cannot, even by express contract, signed by the passenger, limit its
common-law liability for negligence, and the rule is equally as well
settled that no provision contained in the ticket will be binding upon
the passenger, whether expressly or impliedly accepted, unless such
provision is a just and reasonable one, in the eye of the law. The
reason underlying the rule is that while, ordinarily, the courts will
enforce contracts made by persons who are *sui juris*, still the public has
an interest in contracts for the carriage of passengers and the law
will require them to be just and reasonable, even if the passenger has
not so required, or had otherwise expressly agreed." (191 Mo. 518.)

If the doctrine of assumed risk has any applicability as between carrier and passenger, a passenger cannot be held to have assumed any
risk except that of accident not arising from any negligence of the
carrier. Herring v. Galveston, etc., Ry. Co. (Tex. Civ. App. 1908),
108 S. W. Rep. 977.

A common carrier cannot by contract relieve itself of the duty to

1254

§ 851. **Duty and liability toward pass-holder.**— In the absence of a stipulation affecting the carrier's duty and liability, the holder of a free pass, whether he be an employee [17] or a stranger,[18] is entitled to the same degree of care as any other passenger,[19] and in case of an injury, due to the negligence on the part of the carrier, there would be a corresponding liability.[20]

But in case one fraudulently attempts to ride on a non-transferable pass, he does not become a passenger, but is a trespasser, for whose injury the carrier would not be answerable, except for a willful or malicious injury.[21]

And where the pass contains a stipulation exempting the carrier from liability, in case it is a gratuitous pass, it is held in Canada,[22] England,[23] Connecticut,[24] Massachusetts,[25] New Jersey,[26] New York,[27] Washington,[28] and by

use ordinary care to avoid injuring persons carried on its cars with whom it was apparent its business would bring it in contact. Baker v. Boston, etc., R. Co. (N. H. 1906), 65 Atl. Rep. 386.

[17] Pembroke v. Hannibal, etc., R. Co., 32 Mo. App. 61; Ohio, etc., R. Co. v. Muhling, 30 Ill. 9; State v. Western Maryland R. Co., 63 Md. 433; 21 Am. & Eng. R. Cas. 503.

[18] Jacobus v. St. Paul, etc., R. Co., 20 Minn. 125.

[19] Jacobus v. St. Paul, etc., R. Co., *supra;* Gulf, etc., R. Co. v. McGowan, 65 Texas 640; 26 Am. & Eng. R. Cas. 274.

[20] Louisville, etc., R. Co. v. Faylor, 126 Ind. 126; 25 N. E. Rep. 869; Lemon v. Chanslor, 68 Mo. 340; Indianapolis, etc., R. Co. v. Horst, 93 U. S. 291; New York, etc., R. Co. v. Lockwood, 17 Wall. (U. S.) 357; McPheeters v. Hannibal, etc., R. Co., 45 Mo. 26.

[21] Louisville, etc., R. Co. v. Thompson, 107 Ind. 442; 8 N. E. Rep. 18; 57 Am. Rep. 120; 27 Am. & Eng. R. Cas. 88.

[22] Sutherland v. Great Western R. Co., 7 U. C. C. P. 409.

[23] McCawley v. Furness R. Co., 8 Q. B. 57; Gallin v. London, etc., R. Co., 10 Q. B. 212; Hall v. Northeastern R. Co., L. R. 10 Q. B. 437.

[24] Griswold v. New York, etc., R. Co., 53 Conn. 371; 4 Atl. Rep. 261; 55 Am. Rep. 115; 26 Am. & Eng. R. Cas. 280.

[25] Quimby v. Boston, etc., R. Co., 150 Mass. 365; 23 N. E. Rep. 205; 5 L. R. A. 846; 40 Am. & Eng. R. Cas. 693.

[26] Kinney v. Central R. Co., 34 N. J. L. 513.

[27] Bissell v. New York, etc., R Co., 25 N. Y. 442.

[28] Muldoon v. Seattle, etc., R. Co., 7 Wash. 528; 35 Pac. Rep. 422; 58 Am. & Eng. R. Cas. 546.

the United States Supreme Court,[29] to relieve the railroad company from liability for an injury due to the negligence of its employees, while such contracts are held to be void, as against public policy, in Indiana,[30] Iowa,[31] Mississippi,[32] Missouri,[33] Pennsylvania,[34] Texas,[35] and some other States.

§ 852. **Limitations in gratuitous passes.**— The Supreme Court of the United States, in a leading case,[36] where a drover had been issued a pass to enable him to accompany his cattle to market, held, in opposition to the English and

[29] Northern Pacific R. Co. v. Adams, 192 U. S. 441; 48 L. Ed. 513.

[30] Indiana, etc., R. Co. v. Mundy, 21 Ind. 48.

[31] Rose v. Des Moines, etc., R. Co., 39 Iowa 246.

[32] Illinois, etc., R. Co. v. Crudup, 63 Miss. 291.

[33] Bryan v. Missouri Pacific Ry. Co., 32 Mo. App. 228; Cherry v. Chicago, etc., R. Co., 191 Mo. 518.

[34] Buffalo, etc., R. Co. v. O'Hara, 3 Pennyp. (Pa.), 190; 9 Am. & Eng. R. Cas. 317.

[35] Gulf, etc., R. Co. v. McGowan, 65 Texas 640; 26 Am. & Eng. R. Cas. 274.

Under Const. art. 17, § 12, making railroads responsible for damages under such regulations as may be prescribed by the legislature, and Kirby's Dig., § 6773, making railroads responsible for damages to persons caused by the running of trains, a stipulation in a free pass that the passenger accepting it assumes the risk of accidents is contrary to public policy, and the passenger injured through the negligence of the carrier is entitled to recover therefor. St. Louis, etc., Ry. Co. v. Pidcock (Ark. 1907), 101 S. W. Rep. 725.

In Young v. Missouri Pacific Ry. Co. (93 Mo. App. 273), it was held, by the Kansas City Court of Appeals, that one riding on a free pass sustained all the rights of a passenger, and the following cases were cited, as authority for this position, in Missouri: Buck v. Peoples Ry., etc., Co., 46 Mo. App. 555; 108 Mo. 179; 18 S. W. Rep. 1090; Wagner v. Missouri Pacific Ry. Co., 97 Mo. 512; 10 S. W. Rep. 486; 3 L. R. A. 156; Willmott v. Consolidated, etc., Ry. Co., 106 Mo. 535; 17 S. W. Rep. 490; Jones v. St. Louis, etc., Ry. Co., 125 Mo. 666; 28 S. W. Rep. 883; 46 Am. St. Rep. 514; 26 L. R. A. 718.

[36] New York, etc., R. Co. v. Lockwood, 17 Wall. 357; 21 L. Ed. 627. See, also, Grand Trunk R. Co. v. Stevens, 95 U. S. 655; 24 L. Ed. 535.

New York cases, that the pass was not gratuitous, because it was given as one of the terms of carrying the cattle, for which he paid. The reasoning of Bradley, J., was somewhat opposed to the principles of the New York decisions, and were it not for the qualification of the broad rule announced, would seem to be utterly opposed to the New York and English rule. The court, however, in the course of the opinion, took occasion to say: "We purposely abstain from expressing any opinion as to what would have been the result of our judgment had we considered the plaintiff a free passenger, instead of a passenger for hire." In a recent decision, a stipulation in a free pass that the railway company shall not be liable to the user, "under any circumstances, whether of negligence of agents or otherwise, for any injury to the person," was held, by the same high authority, not to violate any rule of public policy and to relieve the company from liability for personal injuries, resulting from the ordinary negligence of the employees. Mr. Justice Brewer delivered the opinion of the court in this case,[37] and in the course of the opinion, said:

"In the light of this decision but one answer can be made to the question. The railway company was not, as to Adams, a carrier for hire. It waived its right as a common carrier to exact compensation. It offered him the privilege of riding in its coaches without charge if he would assume the risks of negligence. He was not in the power of the company and obliged to accept its terms. They stood on an equal footing. If he had desired to hold it to its common-law obligations to him as a passenger, he could have paid his fare and compelled the company to receive and carry him. He freely and voluntarily chose to accept the privilege offered; and, having accepted that

[37] Northern Pacific R. Co. v. Adams, 192 U. S. 441; 48 L. Ed. 513; Boering v. Chesapeake, etc., R. Co., 193 U. S. 442; 48 L. Ed. 742.

privilege, cannot repudiate the conditions. · It
benevolent association, but doing a railroad b
profit; and free passengers are not so many as
negligence on its part. So far as the element
controls, it was a contract which neither party
to enter into, and yet one which each was at
make, and no public policy was violated thereby.'

This case is controlling authority on this que
the same view of the law is taken by the courts
of the States in the United States,[38] while som
State courts hold to the opposite view that even in
tous pass, conditions exempting the carrier from t
of its own negligence are void, as against public po

[38] Union Pacific R. Co. v. Nichols, 8 Kansas 505; Kansas
Co. v. Salmon, 11 Kansas 83; Long v. Lehigh Valley R. Co.,
Rep. 870; Peterson v. Chicago, etc., R. Co. (Wis.), 32 Am
R. Cas. (N. S.) 286; Pennsylvania, etc., R. Co. v. Mahoney, 8
This question has received the consideration of many courts,
answered in different and opposing ways. The company was
liable, in Rogers v. Kennebec S. B. Co., 86 Me. 261; 25 L. R.
29 Atl. Rep. 1069; Quinby v. Boston, etc., R. Co., 150 Mass.
L. R. A. 846; 23 N. E. Rep. 205; Griswold v. New York, etc.,
53 Conn. 371; 55 Am. Rep. 115; 4 Atl. Rep. 261; Kinney v. Cei
Co., 34 N. J. L. 513; 3 Am. Rep. 265; Payne v. Terre Haute,
Co., 157 Ind. 616; 56 L. R. A. 472; 62 N. E. Rep. 472; Mul
Seattle City R. Co., 7 Wash. 528; 22 L. R. A. 794; 35 Pac. Re
10 Wash. 311; 38 Pac. Rep. 995.
This last case was decided by the Supreme Court of the St
which the federal court rendering the judgment in controvers
held. The English decisions are to the same effect. McCaw
Furness R. Co., L. R. 8 Q. B. 57; Hall v. North Eastern R. Co., L.
Q. B. 437; Duff v. Great Northern R. Co., Ir. L. R. 4 C. L. 178;
ander v. Toronto, etc., R. Co., 33 U. C. Q. 474
Ulrich v. New York, etc., R. Co., 108 N. Y. 80; 15 N. E. Rep.
Am. St. Rep. 369; Duncan v. Maine, etc., R. Co., 113 Fed. Rep. 5
[39] Among those holding that the company is responsible are:
v. Des Moines Valley R. Co., 39 Iowa 246, though that case is r
partially on a State statute; Pennsylvania R. Co. v. Butler, 57
335; Mobile, etc., R. Co. v. Hopkins, 41 Ala. 486; 94 Am. Dec.
Gulf, etc., R. Co. v. McGowan, 65 Tex. 640.

§ 853. **By printed notices.**— Common carriers of passengers cannot affect or limit their liability by merely posting notices to this effect, where no such limitation appears in

The reason usually given why the courts refuse to enforce such stipulations in gratuitous passes, is that such contracts contravene a sound public policy (Bryan v. Missouri Pacific Ry. Co., 32 Mo. App. 228). Such contracts are set aside because of the interest of the State in the lives and limbs of its citizens. This reasoning seems specious, as the contract is not that the pass-holder will be hurt or killed, or that injury will be offered him, but that, if, perchance, misfortune, from this cause, does overtake him, the carrier will not be liable. This is the condition of the contract of transportation and no consideration moves for any greater liability. In short, for the consideration of a free ride, the passenger places himself upon the same footing as an employee. The State has the same interest in the lives of employees in such vocations, that it has in the citizen riding on a free pass, for the one is generally as useful a member of society as the other, yet, under the implied contract of the common law, the employee assumed the same risk that the free passenger contracts to assume by express contract. Should not public policy apply as well to the implied contract of the employee as to the express contract of the free passenger?

In some States, such as Missouri, a little newsboy, riding by contract, is held to assume the risk (Padgitt v. Noll, 159 Mo. 143; Raming v. Metropolitan R. Co., 157 Mo. 477), and giving a reduced rate is held to be sufficient consideration for a contract exempting the railroad company from liability, on certain conditions (Goetz v. Railroad, 50 Mo. 472), and no violation of any settled or approved policy is recognized as to such members of society, yet, as to the gratuitous passenger, the reply that such conditions are in contravention of good morals, is held to prevail, over the doctrine recognized by the courts holding such contracts to be valid. The reason and weight of authority are with the text.

A carrier, carrying one gratuitously, and therefore occupying as to him the position of a mandatory, and not that of a common carrier, is liable to him, under their agreement that he shall ride at his own risk, only where injury to him is caused by its willful, reckless, wanton, or gross negligence. Marshall v. Nashville Ry., etc., Co. (Tenn. 1907), 101 S. W. Rep. 419.

A stipulation in a free pass that the carrier shall not be liable for any personal injury sustained in consequence of the negligence of its agents, or otherwise, is void, and does not prevent the passenger from

the contract of transportation,[40] but to bind
thereby, the contract must set forth the ter
tions of the contract.

A passenger is not charged with the conten
notice, posted in a conspicuous place, but wh
read, but to bind the passenger by a notice (
on the carrier's liability, it must be shown tha
understood the notice.[41]

And while it is held that a carrier has a rig
passenger by reasonable rules and regulatio
them in conspicuous places, where they will
understood by the passengers,[42] it is genera
the passenger must understand the notice bef
thereof will bind him, to the extent of limiti
tions of the carrier toward him and where the
a German, who did not understand the Eng
and the notice was posted in English, the pass
be bound by the regulations or terms of the
the carrier is able to show that he understo
as printed and posted.[43]

§ 854. Risks of riding on freight trains.— In

recovering for an assault committed by a porter of tl
veston, etc., Ry. Co. v. Bean (Tex. Civ. App. 1907), 99
[40] Macklin v. New Jersey Co., 7 Abb. Pr. N. S. (N.
[41] Macklin v. New Jersey Co., *supra.*
[42] Camden, etc., R. Co. v. Baldauf, 16 Pa. St. 67; Kc
etc., R. Co., 45 Ohio St. 284; 12 N. E. Rep. 798; 31 Am
125. Disapproved, in Indianapolis, etc., R. Co. v. All
[43] Camden, etc., R. Co. v. Baldauf, 16 Pa. St. 67.
Where a passenger rode on the front platform of
though he knew there was a sign on the car notifying
if they rode on the platform they did so at their
though there was room in the car, he is not entitled to
juries which would not have occurred if he had rid
though his fare was collected and he was not warned
Pike v. Boston Elevated Ry. Co. (Mass. 1906), 78 N. E

sengers to ride upon freight trains, a railroad company may impose such reasonable terms and conditions to the contract of transportation, as may relieve it from injuries due to the method of transportation used, and contracts compelling the passenger to assume the risks of injuries due to travel upon such means of conveyance will be enforced by the courts.[44] Indeed, without such express contracts, passengers riding upon freight trains are generally held. to assume the risk due to injuries incident to this mode of transportation.[45]

A railroad company is under no legal duty to carry passengers on freight trains, but it has the right to classify its business and to prohibit passengers entirely from riding on such trains, or to impose the terms and conditions under which passengers riding on such trains are allowed to travel thereon, and to contract for its exemption from liability and the contract will be governed by the stipulations therein, subject only to the condition that the same terms shall be impartially extended to all persons riding on such trains.[46]

§ 855. Contracts of express messengers.— It has been held, in a well-considered Massachusetts case,[47] that if an express messenger, holding a season ticket, from a company, and desiring to ride for the conduct of its business, in a baggage car, in contravention of its rules, agrees to assume all risk of injury therefrom and to hold the railroad company harmless therefor, he takes the risk of all injuries received by him while riding in the baggage car. A similar construc-

[44] South, etc., R. Co. v. Huffman, 76 Ala. 492; 52 Am. Rep. 349.
[45] Hedrick v. Missouri Pacific Ry. Co., 195 Mo. 104; 93 S. W. Rep. 268; Green v. Missouri, etc., R. Co., 121 Mo. App. 720; 99 S. W. Rep. 28.
[46] Arnold v. Illinois, etc., R. Co., 83 Ill. 273.
[47] Hosmer v. Old Colony R. Co., 156 Mass. 506; 31 N. E. Rep. 652; Bates v. Old Colony R. Co., 147 Mass. 255.

tion of the same kind of a contract was announced by a recent decision of the United States Supreme Court.[48]

Voight, an express messenger riding in a car set apart for the use of an express company, was injured by the negligence of the railway company. There was an agreement between the two companies that the former would hold the railway company free from all liability for negligence, whether caused by the negligence of the railway company or its employees. Voight, entering into the employ of the express company, signed a contract in writing, whereby he agreed to assume all the risk of accident or injury in the course of his employment, whether occasioned by negligence or otherwise, and expressly ratified the agreement between the express company and the railway company. It was held that he could not maintain an action against the railway company for injuries resulting from the negligence of its employees. Mr. Justice Shiras, who delivered the opinion of the court, reviewed many State decisions, and concluded with these words:

"Without enumerating and appraising all the cases respectively cited, our conclusion is that Voight, occupying an express car as a messenger in charge of express matter, in pursuance of the contract between the company, was not a passenger within the meaning of the case of New York C. R. Co. v. Lockwood (17 Wall. 357, 21 L. Ed. 627); that he was not constrained to enter into the contract whereby the railroad company was exonerated from liability to him, but entered into the same freely and voluntarily, and obtained the benefit of it by securing his appointment as such messenger, and that such a contract did not contravene public policy."

[48] Baltimore, etc., R. Co. v. Voight, 176 U. S. 498; 44 L. Ed. 500; 20 Sup. Ct. Rep. 385.

§ 856. **Drovers' passes.**— The United States Supreme Court, in a leading and oft cited case,[49] decided that a stock drover's pass, conditioned that the holder would waive all claims for damages for injuries due to the negligence of the employees of the carrier, was without consideration, as the holder paid a consideration for the pass and such a contract was in contravention of public policy.

This case is generally followed in the United States and all such contracts are generally held to be void. Commenting on this decision, the Supreme Court of Missouri, said: " Like stipulations and exemptions in a stock contract substantially similar were involved and passed upon by the Supreme Court of the United States, where, upon an extended review of the cases, it held that a common carrier cannot stipulate for exemption from liability from its own negligence; that the rule applied to the common carrier of goods and of passengers for hire and that a drover, transported over the railroad, upon a pass, for the purpose of taking care of his stock on the train, is a passenger for hire. We are aware that a contrary doctrine or rule has been announced in New York,[50] but this court has heretofore followed and adhered to the rule and doctrine declared in the Lockwood case." [51]

But this rule is not of universal application and it has been held, in New York,[52] where a company carries cattle

---

[49] New York, etc., R. Co. v. Lockwood, 17 Wall. 357; 84 U. S. (21 L. Ed.) 627.

[50] Bissell v. New York, etc., R. Co., 29 Barb. 602; 25 N. Y. 442.

[51] Carroll v. Missouri Pacific Ry. Co., 88 Mo. 239; 57 Am. Rep. 382; 26 Am. & Eng. R. Cas. 268. See, also, Rose v. DesMoines Valley R. Co., 39 Iowa 246; Pennsylvania R. Co. v. Henderson, 51 Pa. St. 315; Jacobus v. St. Paul, etc., R. Co., 20 Minn. 125; Gulf, etc., R. Co. v. McGowan, 65 Texas 640; 26 Am. & Eng. R. Cas. 274.

[52] Bissell v. New York, etc., R. Co., *supra.*

Where plaintiff was given a drover's pass covering return transportation, it would be presumed, in the absence of evidence to the con-

at a reduced rate and the owner free, that a pr
the contract to the effect that "the persons ridi
take charge of the stock do so at their own risk o
injury, from whatever cause" is valid and in case
to a drover riding on such a pass, due to the .
on the part of the carrier, there is no liability or
of the railroad company.

§ 857. **Contract of mail agent.**— A mail agent,
a postal car, in charge of the United States mail, is
held to be a passenger and entitled to the same
that any other passenger is entitled to.[53]

In a New York case,[54] a mail agent was kill
riding on a pass issued for his use by the railroad
and the pass contained a stipulation exempting th
from liability for any injury due to the negligenc
railroad company or its employees. The court h
the statutes of the government did not authorize i
tract to relieve the railroad company from liabi
injuries to its agents, engaged in the mail service,
carrier was liable for the death of the agent, du
negligence.

trary, that plaintiff could read, and it was his duty to read
and make himself acquainted with and comply with its c
Randolph v. Quincy, etc., R. Co. (Mo. App. 1908), 107 S.
1029.

Where the agent or the owner of the stock shipped, signed
of the injured party to a waiver of damages in the stock
contract, but this was not done by the injured person, or b
injury, but a short time before his death, this was held not t
the railroad company for damages from the injury sustaine
to the execution of the contract. Lawson v. Chicago, etc., R
Wis. 447; 24 N. W. Rep. 618; 54 Am. Rep. 634; 21 Am. &
Cas. 249.

[53] Seybolt v. New York, etc., R. Co., 95 N. Y. 562; 31 Hun
Am. Rep. 75; 18 Am. & Eng. R. Cas. 162.

[54] Seybolt v. New York, etc., R. Co., *supra.*

§ 858. **Conflict of laws.**—As in the case of other contracts, it frequently happens that a contract releasing liability on the part of the carrier, for an injury to a passenger,
is drawn in question in a State other than where the contract is executed and the question becomes important as
to what law will determine the validity of such an undertaking.   As a general rule, such contracts will be construed
as other contracts, where the validity thereof is questioned
in a State other than where the contract was executed, and
the well-settled rule that contracts void where made will
be void everywhere, and that contracts valid where made
will be valid elsewhere,[55] unless held to be contrary to the
settled policy of the laws of the State where they are attempted to be enforced,[56] applies to this species of contracts,
as to every other contract.

It was accordingly held, in Ohio,[57] where a contract was
made between the carrier and a passenger, exempting the
former from liability for an injury, in New York, where
contracts waiving damages for the carrier's negligence are
upheld, that the validity of the contract would be determined
according to the laws of New York, where the contract
would be upheld and not according to the laws of the State
of Ohio, where such contracts were held to be void, as
against public policy.

[55] Hobbs v. McLean, 117 U. S. 567; 6 Sup. Ct. Rep. 870; United
States v. Central Pacific R. Co., 118 U. S. 235; 6 Sup. Ct. Rep. 1038;
Watts v. Camours, 115 U. S. 353; 2 Parsons on Con., 712; Addison on
Con., 197; 2 Kent's Com. (12 Ed.) 477; 1 Beach, Mod. Law. Con.,
§ 584, and cases cited.

[56] Banchor v. Mansel, 47 Me. 58; Story on Con. Laws, § 244; 2
Kent's Com. 457.

[57] Knowlton v. Erie R. Co., 19 Ohio St. 260; Alexander v. Pennsylvania R. Co., 48 Ohio St. 623.

CHAPTER XXXVI.

INJURIES TO LICENSEES.

§ 859. **Who are licensees, generally.**— A license, such as will be considered here, is a permission or authority to perform some act upon or to use the premises of another, not merely by sufferance, although it may not be in pursuance of an express invitation.

The mere occasional use of railroad premises, without objection but with the passive acquiescence of the company, is not a license, unless the use is with the express or implied permission or authority of the railroad company.[1] A per-

---

[1] Palmer v. Chicago, etc., R. Co., 112 Ind. 250; Akers v. Chicago, etc., R. Co., 58 Minn. 540; 60 Am. & Eng. R. Cas. 304 Glass v. Memphis, etc., R. Co., 94 Ala. 581; 10 So. Rep. 215.

1266

missive use of the premises, on the other hand, either by express or implied authority, creates a license on the part of the person so using the premises and if the user is in connection with the business of the owner of the premises, it is more than a mere license and a greater degree of care is recognized on the part of the owner than in the case of a mere licensee, using the premises for purposes of his own.[2]

But although the person may originally enter the premises of the owner for purposes of business with the owner, if he goes outside of the line of duty or beyond that portion of the premises intended for those having such business with the owner, and remains on such portion of the premises, after his business is ended, he becomes a mere licensee and the owner is not liable by reason of any special duty toward him, if he sustains an injury on the premises.[3]

§ 860. **Duty toward licensee generally.** — Both upon principle and authority, it is sustained that one who goes upon property under a mere naked license, must enter the premises as they are and there is no responsibility on the part of the owner for the bad condition of the premises, but he is only liable where the injured person was willfully led into

[2] DeBolt v. Kansas City, etc., R. Co., 123 Mo. 496; 27 S. W. Rep. 575; Campbell v. Portland, etc., R. Co., 62 Me. 552.

[3] Heinlein v. Boston, etc., R. Co., 147 Mass. 136; McCabe v. Chicago, etc., R. Co., 88 Wis. 531; 60 N. W. Rep. 260.

Where an office for transaction of business with the public is provided by a railroad company, accessible to a street, the presence in the company's freight yard of one having business with the railroad company, is not a necessary incident of his relation toward the railroad company, and he will be regarded as a bare licensee toward whom no special duty is owing. Diebold v. Pennsylvania R. Co., 50 N. J. L. 478; 14 Atl. Rep. 576; Woolwine v. Chesapeake, etc., R. Co., 36 W. Va. 329; 15 S. E. Rep. 81; 50 Am. & Eng. R. Cas. 37; June v. Boston, etc., R. Co., 153 Mass. 79; 26 N. E. Rep. 238.

danger, or the proof shows some active wrongdoing, result-ing in the injury.[4]

The doctrine is well settled, in England, that one re-ceiving gratuitous favors from another, in the use of his property, occupies no such relation toward the owner as to create a duty to make the place any safer or better than it is when the licensee enters. To establish any duty toward the licensee, he must visit the premises upon some business with the owner, or there must be some mutuality of interest in the subject of the licensee's presence, for otherwise, he is there on his own affair.[5]

This rule seems in accord with the sound principles of the law of negligence, for to maintain an action for negli-gence, it is essential, in all cases, that there was some duty owing by the defendant toward the injured person, which was not performed and in consequence of which the injury resulted. There could be no recovery by a trespasser, based upon the unsafe condition of premises where the trespass was committed, because of the absence of the duty, upon which the right of action rests, and it is by a parity of reasoning that the courts hold that there is no liability to a bare licensee who goes upon dangerous or defective prem-ises with no other right than a naked leave or license.[6] But of course when the entry of the licensee is under an express or implied invitation, for the mutual interest or profit of both the licensee and the licensor, there is then the basis of the obligation on the owner's part, to use reasonable care for the safety of the licensee, and if there is a defect in the premises, rendering them dangerous, the owner ought to give a proper and timely warning of the

[4] Plummer v. Dill, 156 Mass. 426.

[5] Southcote v. Stanley, 1 Hurl. & N. 247.

[6] Larmore v. Crown Point, etc., Co., 101 N. Y. 391; 56 Am. Rep. 718; Roddy v. Missouri Pacific Ry. Co., 104 Mo. 234; 15 S. W. Rep. 1112; 12 L. R. A. 746; 24 Am. St. Rep. 333.

danger, or his full measure of duty toward the person invited upon the premises would not be discharged.[7]

§ 861. Duty toward licensees further considered.— There are many decisions to the effect that at places where the railroad company has permitted the use of its premises for the public to travel upon, or where, by user, an implied license to the public is held to be extended, the railroad company and its employees are held chargeable with such notice of the danger to the public, as will compel it or its employees to use ordinary care to avoid injury to the licensees so using the track or railroad premises, and for an injury due to a lack of such care, the railroad company will be liable.[8] Such. decisions are not consistent with the principles of the law governing the liability of licensors, in other than railroad cases, for if the rule as to an implied invitation is to be extended only to cases where the user is of mutual benefit to the licensor, and the licensee takes the license in all other cases, subject to its concomitant perils — which expressions are mere platitudes, if the licensor must be held to the exercise of ordinary care, in the first instance to avoid injury to the licensee — it would seem that the licensee, or one using the railroad company's property by mere passive acquiescence only, would be compelled to look

[7] Severy v. Nicherson, 120 Mass. 306; 21 Am. Rep. 514. And, see, note to 66 Cent. Law Jour. pp. 283, 284.

[8] Louisville, etc., R. Co. v. Howard, 82 Ky. 212; 19 Am. & Eng. R. Cas. 98; Davis v. Chicago, etc., R. Co., 58 Wis. 646; 17 N. W. Rep. 406; 46 Am. Rep. 667; 15 Am. & Eng. R. Cas. 424; Chicago, etc., R. Co. v. Dunleavy, 129 Ill. 132; 22 N. E. Rep. 15; 39 Am. & Eng. R. Cas. 381; Chamberlain v. Missouri Pacific Ry. Co., 133 Mo. 587; 33 S. W. Rep. 437; 34 S. W. Rep. 842; Fielder v. St. Louis, etc., R. Co., 107 Mo. 645; 18 S. W. Rep. 847; Lynch v. St. Joseph, etc., R. Co., 111 Mo. 601; 19 S. W. Rep. 1114; Smith v. Norfolk, etc., R. Co., 114 No. Car. 728; 60 Am. & Eng. R. Cas. 102; Chicago, etc., R. Co. v. Wilgus, 40 Neb. 660; 58 N. W. Rep. 1125.

out for the dangers ordinarily incident to the customary use of the property, by the owner, for in no other sense could he be held to take the license, "subject to its concomitant perils." [9]

The better rule would therefore appear to be that a railroad company owes to a licensee, using its roadway or track as a passageway, for the convenience of the public, or any portion thereof, no duty to operate its road in other than its customary method, but the persons so using the track do so at their own risk, of other than willful or wanton injuries. [10]

But of course this rule does not apply to those who come upon the premises of the railroad company for business with the carrier, for then the rule whereby an implied invitation, growing out of the mutual interest of the licensor and licensee applies, and a railway company is chargeable with the exercise of ordinary care towards all persons who may lawfully be upon its premises, transacting business with it. [11]

[9] This is the conclusion of Judge Elliott, in his excellent work on Railroads (3 Elliott on Railroads, § 1250, p. 1954).

[10] Walsh v. Fitchburg, etc., R. Co., 145 N. Y. 301; 27 L. R. A. 724; Pennsylvania R. Co. v. Meyers, 136 Ind. 242; Wright v. Boston, etc., R. Co., 142 Mass. 296; 7 N. E. Rep. 866; 28 Am. & Eng. R. Cas. 652; St. Louis, etc., R. Co. v. Fairburne, 48 Ark. 491; Central R. Co. v. Brinson, 70 Ga. 207; 19 Am. & Eng. R. Cas. 42.

[11] Spotts v. Wabash R. Co., 111 Mo. 380; 20 S. W. Rep. 190; Conlon v. New York, etc., R. Co., 74 Hun 115; 56 N. Y. S. R. 316.

A person who travels on the right of way of a railroad company not for any purpose or business connected with the railroad, but for his own mere convenience as a footway, is a trespasser, and the company owes him no duty, except to refrain from wantonly or willfully injuring him and to use reasonable care to avoid injury to him after he is discovered to be in peril. McGuire v. Chicago, etc., R. Co., 120 Ill. App. 111.

The obligation of a railroad company to trespassers and mere licensees is the same, namely, not wantonly or willfully to inflict injury, and not

§ 862. Duty to maintain premises in safe condition.— The owner of premises is generally under no legal duty to keep them in good condition for the accommodation of persons who go upon them for their own convenience merely, and where a person has a license to go upon the grounds of a railroad company, for purposes of his own, he takes them as he finds them and accepts whatever perils he incurs in the use or enjoyment of the license.[12]

Where a railroad company, therefore, permits people for their own accommodation, to pass over its lands, it is under no legal duty to keep them free from pitfalls or obstructions, which may result in injury to such a licensee,[13] and if a person, accustomed to use railroad property for his convenience, falls into an unprotected pit between the tracks and sustains injuries, there is no liability on the part of the railroad company for such an injury, as the party was, at most, a bare licensee and there being no invitation to use the premises, he took them as he found them.[14]

to injure through gross negligence evidencing willfulness. Ahern v. Chicago, etc., R. Co., 124 Ill. App. 36.

A person who is upon depot grounds in connection only with private business, and not for the purpose of taking passage upon a train of the defendant company, is merely a trespasser or licensee as to whom the company owes no other duty than not willfully or wantonly to injure. Deakin v. Illinois Cent. R. Co., 127 Ill. App. 258.

One who goes on the station grounds of a railroad company for his own convenience is there at his own risk and cannot recover for injury received because of the defective condition of the grounds. Watson v. Manitou, etc., Ry. Co. (Colo. 1907), 92 Pac. Rep. 17.

[12] Indiana, etc., R. Co. v. Barnhart, 115 Ind. 399; 16 N. E. Rep. 121; Atchison, etc., R. Co. v. Parsons, 42 Ill. App. 93.

[13] Evansville, etc., R. Co. v. Griffin, 100 Ind. 221; 50 Am. Rep. 783.

[14] Morgen v. Pennsylvania R. Co., 19 Blatch. (U. S.) 239; 7 Fed. Rep. 78.

One visiting a telegraph operator, at a railroad station, to pay a friendly visit to such operator and not on any business with the railroad company, takes the premises subject to all the risks therefrom, due to the inherently defective conditions existing. Woolwine v. Chesa-

But where the owner, by enticement, allurement or inducement, express or implied, causes another to come upon his land, he then assumes the obligation of providing for the safety and protection of the person so coming, and will be liable for an injury due to a violation of this duty, provided the inducement is equivalent to an invitation to use the land and is not simply a passive acquiescence in the use thereof.[15]

peake, etc., R. Co., 36 W. Va. 329; 15 S. E. Rep. 81; 50 Am. & Eng. R. Cas. 37. See, also, Gillis v. Pennsylvania R. Co., 59 Pa. St. 129; Sweeney v. Old Colony R. Co., 10 Allen (Mass.) 368.

A person taking a position near a mail crane, to watch it when catching the mail, assumes the risk of injury thereby. Poling v. Ohio River R. Co., 38 W. Va. 645; 18 S. E. Rep. 782.

[15] Indiana, etc., R. Co. v. Barnhart, 115 Ind. 399; 16 N. E. Rep. 121; Nichols v. Washington, etc., R. Co., 83 Va. 99; 5 S. E. Rep. 171; 5 Am. St. Rep. 257; 32 Am. & Eng. R. Cas. 27.

A boarder at the house of an employee, living in a house built by a railroad company, at a point where the crossing of the track was necessary, when injured by the negligent running of a train, was held to have a right of action, in McDermott v. New York, etc., R. Co., 28 Hun 325; 97 N. Y. 654.

In an action for injuries to a person visiting a railroad station for the purpose of sending a telephone message, by falling off a platform in the dark because there was no hand rail around the platform, *held* insufficient to show negligence on the part of the railroad company. Central of Georgia Ry. Co. v. Floyd (Ga. App. 1907), 59 S. E. Rep. 826.

The duty of a railroad company to keep in reasonably safe repair for public travel premises owned and controlled by it, situated in and around its depots and used by the public in going to and from its depots, whether on foot or in vehicles, does not extend to streets or sidewalks that are not owned or controlled by it. Webster v. Chesapeake, etc., Ry. Co. (Ky. 1907), 105 S. W. Rep. 945.

Where defendant railroad company kept and maintained a sidewalk on its right of way and over its tracks leading to its station, and permitted the walk to become defective, so that plaintiff was injured while approaching the station to assist his wife in boarding one of defendant's trains as a passenger, the railroad company was liable. Evans v. Chicago, etc., Ry. Co. (Mo. App. 1908), 109 S. W. Rep. 79.

The rule that an abutting property owner is not liable to parties injured on a defective sidewalk in front of his property does not apply to a railroad, where it maintains a station and constructs walks on

§ 863. Risks assumed by licensee.—Where a person has permission to go upon the grounds or premises of a railroad company, for purposes of his own convenience, or uses such premises by the mere acquiescence of the railroad company, he takes the premises as he finds them and accepts whatever perils he thereby incurs.[16]

For instance, where an individual is permitted to use a railroad track as a footway, he is supposed to have exercised the privilege with full knowledge of the ordinary use of the track by the railroad company and the ordinary risks attendant upon its use by foot passengers; and where such a person sues for an injury, it is error to refuse to instruct the jury that the plaintiff assumed the risk of being injured by the ordinary, or customary operations of trains, on the railroad track.[17]

§ 864. Persons working on premises of company.— A workman who goes to a railroad yard, for the purpose of doing

the grounds for the approach of the public. Evans v. Chicago, etc., Ry. Co. (Mo. App. 1098), 109 S. W. Rep. 79.

The questions what grounds are reasonably near to the depot platform, and whether persons will naturally be likely to go thereon, requiring the railroad to keep the same in a safe condition, are generally for the jury. Banderob v. Wisconsin Cent. Ry. Co. (Wis. 1907), 113 N. W. Rep. 738.

A railroad owes to one coming on its depot grounds to take leave of a passenger the duty of keeping in a safe condition all parts of its platforms and approaches thereto, to which the public naturally resort, as well as all portions of its station grounds reasonably near to the platforms, where the public would naturally be likely to go. Banderob v. Wisconsin Cent. Ry. Co., 113 N. W. Rep. 738.

One coming on the depot grounds of a railroad to take leave of a passenger sustains toward the railroad the relation of a person on its grounds by invitation, to whom it owes the duty of ordinary care. Banderob v. Wisconsin Cent. Ry. Co. (Wis. 1907), 113 N. W. Rep. 738.

16 Indiana, etc., R. Co. v. Barnhart, 115 Ind. 399; 16 N. E. Rep. 121; Stewart v. Cincinnati, etc., R. Co., 89 Mich. 315.

17 Williams v. Delaware, etc., R. Co., 18 N. Y. S. R. 857; 2 N. Y. Supp. 435.

work for the company, is not a mere licensee, as regards the amount of care due toward him, while in the discharge of his duties, but is rather occupying the status of an employee, to whom reasonable or ordinary care is owing, while engaged in the performance of his duties.[18]   An employee of one railroad company, engaged in delivering a car from his employer on the tracks of another company, in the regular course of business between his employer and the owner of the tracks, is not a mere licensee, but is entitled to be protected while engaged in his work, by the exercise of reasonable care for his protection, on the part of the employees of the other railroad company.[19]

Nor is this measure of care due only to employees, or those occupying the premises in pursuance of a contract with the owner, but if one is rightfully on the premises of the owner, as where he is engaged in the work of unloading a car,[20] he is entitled, while so engaged, to reasonable care to avoid injuring him, to the same extent as if he had been in the employ of the railroad company, whose car was being unloaded.[21]

[18] Collins v. New York, etc., R. Co., 23 J. & S. (N. Y.) 31; 8 N. Y. S. R. 164; 112 N. Y. 665; 20 N. E. Rep. 413.

[19] Turner v. Boston, etc., R. Co., 158 Mass. 261; 33 N. E. Rep. 520.

[20] Chicago, etc., R. Co. v. McDaniel, 134 Ind. 166; 32 N. E. Rep. 728.

[21] Wright v. London, etc., R. Co., 33 L. T. 830; L. R. 1 Q. B. D. 252; 45 L. J. Q. B. 570; Lovell v. Kansas City, etc., R. Co. (by Judge Johnson), 121 Mo. App. 466; 97 S. W. Rep. 193.

In an action against a railroad company to recover for the death of a person who was struck and killed by an engine while at work at a station at night unloading bedding into stock cars from a wagon, a statement made by defendant's station agent, in response to an inquiry by a fellow workman with deceased, that there was no train coming, and that they could go ahead and bed the cars, was admissible as a declaration made in the course of his duty as defendant's agent, both as evidence of a license or permission to go upon the tracks to do the work, and as bearing upon the issue of contributory negligence, and was sufficient to require the submission of such issue to the jury. Chicago, etc., Ry. Co. v. Cox (U. S. C. C. A., Mo., 1906), 145 Fed. Rep. 157.

§ 865. **Persons using premises by invitation.**— While the mere passive acquiescence of a railroad company, in the use of its premises, such as a portion of the right of way, along a railroad track, for public or private travel, does not impose upon the company the duty of providing against the dangers of accidents to those so using its property, yet, if the railroad company, directly, or by implication, induces persons to enter upon and pass over its right of way, it thereby assumes, in law, the obligation of seeing that the same is reasonably safe for the use to which it appropriates it.[22]

A railroad company, for instance, by the construction of a road crossing, may extend an invitation to the public to use such crossing for the purpose of access to the premises of others, although there is no public way beyond its own premises.[23]

But a mere permission or license for persons to cross its track is not an invitation, in law, so to do, on the part of the railroad company;[24] and whether the construction of a crossing over a track, is, of itself, such as to amount to an invitation by the company to use it, will depend upon the issue whether or not it was such a crossing as was calculated to induce the public to believe that the crossing was a public way.[25]

[22] Lake Shore, etc., R. Co. v. Bodemer, 139 Ill. 596; 29 N. E. Rep. 692; 54 Am. & Eng. R. Cas. 177.

[23] Hanks v. Boston, etc., R. Co., 147 Mass. 495; 18 N. E. Rep. 218; 35 Am. & Eng. R. Cas. 321.

[24] Wright v. Boston, etc., R. Co., 142 Mass. 296; 7 N. E. Rep. 866; 28 Am. & Eng. R. Cas. 652.

[25] Wright v. Boston, etc., R. Co., *supra.* In a well-considered Massachusetts case, the plaintiff was injured while crossing a track of the defendant. A public road came down to the track and a private crossing was used by a chemical company, across the track, but on the gate to its premises which stood open, was a sign, "No Admittance." Plaintiff drove across the track and into this gate and on returning sustained the injuries sued for. The court held there was no liability, because no breach of duty toward him, as he was a bare licensee in

§ 866. **Persons loading or unloading cars.**— The rule is quite well settled that where a railroad company places loaded cars upon a side track for the purpose of being unloaded, or an empty car, to be loaded, the owners of the freight, or their employees or agents, are held to have received an implied invitation to enter on the premises of the railroad company for this purpose, and the railroad company must not, without notice or warning, run a car or train against the car so placed.[26] Of course it is frequently essential, in the operation of a railroad, to couple to or move cars placed for purposes of loading or unloading, while the work is being performed, but in all such cases it is generally held to be the duty of the railroad company to warn those so engaged in time for them to give heed for their safety.[27]

But notice by sounding the whistle or ringing the bell is not essential, if some other equally effective notice is given, to one engaged in loading or unloading a car on a railroad track;[28] the fact that one engaged in unloading a car on a side track, has a wild horse in his team, which is easily frightened by passing trains, imposes no obligation on the part of the railroad company to so operate the trains past this point, as to prevent frightening the horse.[29] And there is generally no obligation on the part of connecting roads not

the use of the premises. Donnelly v. Boston, etc., R. Co., 151 Mass. 210; 24 N. E. Rep. 38; 42 Am. & Eng. R. Cas. 182.

[26] Gessley v. Missouri Pacific Ry. Co., 32 Mo. App. 413; Spotts v. Wabash Ry. Co., 111 Mo. 380; 20 S. W. Rep. 190; 33 Am. St. Rep. 531; Lovell v. Kansas City So. Ry. Co., 121 Mo. App. 466; 97 S. W. Rep. 193.

[27] Chicago, etc., R. Co. v. Goebel, 119 Ill. 515; Jacobson v. St. Paul, etc., R. Co., 41 Minn. 206; Ryan v. Chicago, etc., R. Co., 115 Fed. Rep. 197; St. Louis, etc., R. Co. v. Shaw, 116 Fed. Rep. 621; Galveston, etc., R. Co. v. Duncan, 88 Texas 611; Philadelphia, etc., R. Co. v. Brown, 49 U. S. App. 101; Lovell v. Kansas City So. Ry. Co., 121 Mo. App. 471; 97 S. W. Rep. 193.

[28] Conlon v. New York, etc., R. Co., 74 Hun 115; 56 N. Y. S. R. 316.

[29] Chicago, etc., R. Co. v. Clark, 2 Ill. App. 116.

1276

notified of the work of loading or unloading a car on a side track, to avoid coupling to or moving the car, on the track of the connecting road, which is used by other roads, in common with the owner of the car, but in case of an injury, due to such failure to warn the person so engaged, the owner of the car will alone be held responsible to the injured person.[30]

[30] Fletcher v. Boston, etc., R. Co., 1 Allen (Mass.) 9.

Where a railroad company places a loaded car on a side track for the purpose of being unloaded, it is negligence for it to switch cars onto the track and against the loaded car without a warning to persons unloading freight therefrom. Eckert v. Great Northern Ry. Co. (Minn. 1908), 116 N. W. Rep. 1024.

Where a car is placed on a side track by a railroad company to be unloaded, the company is bound to anticipate the presence of a person at the car, and it owes the duty of using ordinary care not to injure him, which duty does not depend upon its knowledge of his presence in the car. Dooley v. Missouri, etc., Ry. Co. (Tex. Civ. App. 1908), 110 S. W. Rep. 135.

A person unloading a car under such circumstances is under no obligation to warn the company of his presence in the car. Dooley v. Missouri, etc., Ry. Co. (Tex. Civ. App. 1908), 110 S. W. Rep. 135.

Railroad companies owe to persons engaged in the work of loading or unloading cars the duty to furnish cars in such condition that they can be used with reasonable safety, though the duty is not one to guarantee the absolute safety of appliances furnished, but only to exercise ordinary care to see that the appliances are reasonably safe and are kept so for the intended uses. St. Louis, etc., R. Co. v. Fritts (Ark. 1908), 108 S. W. Rep. 841.

Where a car was left on a siding to have a safe unloaded therefrom, a person, who went on the car to help unload it and was injured, was not a trespasser. Louisville, etc., R. Co. v. Farris (Ky. 1907), 100 S. W. Rep. 870.

Where plaintiff drove with his team to defendant railroad company's yard to unload a car of lumber, he was a licensee on the railroad premises. Cincinnati, etc., Ry. Co. v. Rodes (Ky. 1907), 102 S. W. Rep. 321.

Intestate was killed while engaged in loading a fire engine onto a flat car. After the engine had been placed thereon, intestate went on the car to fasten and protect it while in transit, and, the work not being entirely finished when the train arrived by which it was to be transported, the car was shifted to another point, where the work was

§ 867. **Persons accompanying passengers.**— It is held to be
the duty of a railroad company to maintain its station and
premises that the public are accustomed to visit, in a reasonably safe condition for the use of a guest or friend of a passenger, who visits the station with the passenger, who is
about to take passage upon a train, as the person accompanying the passenger is held to have an implied invitation to
visit the premises of the railroad company for this purpose.[31]

But this duty has been held not to extend to those at the
station at an unusual hour, for the purpose of bidding fare-
well to a person about to leave on a freight train, in charge
of live stock, for the reason that he was a passenger only in a
limited or restricted sense.[32]

§ 868. **Passenger visiting portion of premises not open to
public.**— A passenger, although upon the premises of a railroad company for the mutual benefit of himself and the com-

finished, after which the railroad engine and certain cars backed
against the car on which the engine was loaded without warning,
causing intestate to fall under the car and receive injuries resulting in
his death. *Held*, that intestate was bound to take notice of the general conditions, including the fact that the car was to be incorporated
into the train, and that the failure of the train operatives to warn
intestate that the car was about to be coupled did not constitute gross
negligence, sufficient to justify recovery for intestate's death. Nauss
v. Boston, etc., R. Co. (Mass. 1907), 81 N. E. Rep. 280.

[31] Texas, etc., R. Co. v. Best, 66 Texas 116; 18 S. W. Rep. 224.

[32] Dowd v. Chicago, etc., R. Co., 84 Wis. 105; 54 N. W. Rep. 24;
58 Am. & Eng. R. Cas. 18. The correctness of this decision, for the
reasons assigned, may well be questioned.

While persons going upon a railroad platform upon business such
as taking a train, accompanying a passenger. etc., are regarded as invited to use the platform, and as to them the company must keep its
platform in a reasonably safe condition to prevent injury, a mere
licensee must use the platform as he finds it; the company being under
a duty only to refrain from intentionally injuring him. Rowley v.
Chicago, etc., Ry. Co. (Wis. 1908), 115 N. W. Rep. 865.

pany, or on business with the railroad company, who visits a portion of the carrier's premises, not intended for public use, stands in the same relation as any other licensee, while on such portion of the carrier's premises and takes the risk of injury due to the inherently dangerous nature of the place.

Considering the right of a passenger to recover for injuries received while on the freight platform of the carrier, the Kansas City Court of Appeals [33] used this language:

"It is not denied but that the defendant's passenger platform and the approaches thereto were in every respect in a reasonably safe condition, nor that in this regard ,it had discharged the full measure of its duty to its passengers. But it is plaintiff's insistence that the defendant's freight platform, which was a place where passengers, or those who have purchased tickets with a view to take passage on its trains, would naturally and ordinarily be likely to resort, was not in such reasonably safe condition. We can no more reasonably and fairly infer that passengers or those intending to take passage on its trains would naturally and ordinarily be likely to leave its comfortable waiting rooms or its convenient passenger platform and resort to its freight platform on the opposite side of the depot from where they enter the trains, to there wait for their arrival, than we would that persons applying at the office of a public inn for lodging would resort to its kitchen, laundry, or back yard, to there wait until the landlord puts the room assigned to them in order for their reception. We are totally unable to find any fact or circumstance in the evidence that would justify any such inference.

"If passengers, or those intending to become passengers, while waiting for the arrival of trains, have been known, as the evidence tends to show, to go upon the defendant's freight platform, yet, *if they went there by the mere passive ac-*

[33] Gunderman v. Missouri, etc., R. Co., 58 Mo. App. 380, 381.

quiescence of the defendant and without a direct or implied invitation or inducement to do so, then there was no duty or obligation on the part of the defendant to keep said platform in a reasonably safe condition as to them, for they must be held to have gone there at their own risk. The rule is that one who enjoys a license is subject to its concomitant perils."

"*A carrier's liability in respect to the condition of its premises is neither greater nor less than that of any other person to another who by invitation or inducement, express or implied, has come upon his* premises, for the purpose of transacting business."

§ 869. **Persons on trains.**— A railroad company is not generally liable for an injury to one on a train, or attempting to get on a train, who has not yet assumed the relation of a passenger toward the railroad company, but like any other licensee, if the person is on the train for business of his own and not for the mutual benefit of the railroad company also, he takes the conditions as he finds them and there is no obligation to respond in damages, if he is injured by the inherently dangerous nature of the place.[34] A railroad company is not bound to hold a train, for the benefit of one who has not put himself in the relation of a passenger toward it;[35] one going on a train, to make a collection due him from the conductor of the train, is not there for business with the railroad company,[36] any more than one would be who went upon the train to sell papers to the passengers,[37] or to deliver a lunch to the conductor of the train,[38] but in

[34] Spannagle v. Chicago, etc., R. Co., 31 Ill. App. 460.

[35] Spannagle v. Chicago, etc., R. Co., *supra.*

[36] Pittsburg, etc., R. Co. v. Krause, 30 Ohio St. 222; 15 Am. Ry. Rep. 298.

[37] Fleming v. Brooklyn, etc., R. Co., 1 Abb. N. Cas. (N. Y.) 433.

[38] Wenecker v. Missouri, etc., R. Co., 169 Mo. 592; 70 S. W. Rep. 145.

all such cases, the person going on the train does so at his peril and assumes the risk of injury by the usual operation of the train.

But if the party injured on a railroad train enters the train upon a mission which can be held to be for the mutual benefit of the person injured and the railroad company, or he sustains an injury, under circumstances which can be held to create an implied invitation to him to·enter the train, then the corresponding obligation to use reasonable care to avoid his injury exists in law, and for an injury due to an absence of such care, the railroad company would be liable.[39]

[39] Lake Shore, etc., R. Co. v. Brown, 123 Ill. 162; 14 N. E. Rep. 197; 31 Am. & Eng.' R. Cas. 61.

Where plaintiff, when injured by the explosion of an engine, was riding on a freight train by permission of the conductor, and there was no evidence of wanton or willful injury, plaintiff could not recover. Vassor v. Atlantic Coast Line R. Co. (N. C. 1906), 54 S. E. Rep. 849.

One who, while in the employ of a contractor for feeding men engaged in railroad construction work, rides, with the consent, either express or implied, of the railroad company, in a caboose used in such work, is not a trespasser. Gulf, etc., Ry. Co. v. Walters (Tex. Civ. App. 1908), 107 S. W. Rep. 369.

While a railroad company does not owe a licensee riding on its train that high degree of care which it is required to exercise towards passengers, it owes him the duty of exercising ordinary care for his safety and protection from injury at the hands of its agents and employees. Gulf, etc., Ry. Co. v. Walters, 107 S. W. Rep. 369.

A railroad owes to a licensee, riding on its freight train, the duty to exercise reasonable care to avoid injuring him. Johnson v. Great Northern Ry. Co. (Wash. 1908), 94 Pac. Rep. 895.

In an action against a railroad to recover for personal injuries to a boy riding on a freight train, evidence *held* insufficient to take the question of defendant's negligence to the jury. Johnson v. Great Northern Ry. Co., 94 Pac. Rep. 895.

A railroad owes to a trespasser riding on its freight train only the duty not to wantonly or willfully injure him. Johnson v. Great Northern Ry. Co., 94 Pac. Rep. 895.

A person riding on a freight train by invitation of a brakeman, who

§ 870. No invitation implied in absence of mutual interest.
— In ascertaining the relation which an injured person bears
to the owner of premises where the injury was received, it is
generally held to be a reliable test, in determining the duty
owing by the owner, to enquire whether or not the injured
person, at the time of the injury, had business relations with
the owner of the premises, which would render his presence
of mutual advantage to the two, or whether his presence was
for his own convenience, or on business with others than the
owner of the premises. In the absence of some relation
which enures to the mutual benefit of the owner of the
premises and the injured person, or to the former alone, there
is generally held to be no implied invitation, on the part of
the owner.[40] In applying this rule, Mr. Justice Harlan,
for the United States Supreme Court, said: "It is sometimes
difficult to determine whether the circumstances make
a case of *invitation,* in the technical sense of that word, as
used in a large number of adjudged cases, or only a case of
mere license. 'The principle,' says Mr. Campbell, in his
treatise on negligence, 'appears to be that invitation is inferred
where there is a common interest or mutual advantage,
while a license is inferred, where the object is the mere
pleasure or benefit of the person using it.' " [41]

had no authority to so invite him, is a trespasser. Johnson v. Great
Northern Ry. Co., 94 Pac. Rep. 895.

[40] Benson v. Baltimore, etc., R. Co., 77 Md. 535; 26 Atl. Rep. 973;
Plummer v. Dill, 156 Mass. 426; 31 N. E. Rep. 128; 32 Am. St. Rep.
463.

[41] Bennett v. Louisville, etc., R. Co., 102 U. S. 577; 26 L. Ed. 235.
The Supreme Court of Massachusetts likewise adopted the same ruling
in the case of Redigan v. Ry. (28 N. E. Rep. 1134), wherein it said:
"The fact that the defendant made *no attempt to prevent travel
across the station grounds and platform, as a short cut between the
public streets, was not an invitation to use them for that purpose.*
Galligan v. Mfg. Co., 143 Mass. 527; 10 N. E. Rep. 171; Reardon v.
Thompson, 149 Mass. 267; 21 N. E. Rep. 369. It follows that the plaintiff's
rights are to be determined upon the theory that she was neither

§ 871. Persons having business with the carrier's employees.

— If one goes upon the premises of a common carrier, not upon any business he may have with the railroad company, but on private business with one of its employees, the status of such a person is that of a mere licensee, to whom the railroad company owes no duty other than to avoid a willful injury, because of the absence of the relation essential to the existence of some duty, on its part, toward such a person.[42]

Illustrative of this rule, is the recent Missouri case,[43] of

a trespasser nor a person induced or invited by the defendant to enter its premises, but a licensee merely, knowingly using the defendant's land and structures for a purpose solely in her own interest, for which she knew they were not intended, and entering upon them without invitation, and without right, by her voluntary act, and with the bare sufferance of the owner. The case is not one of a concealed peril or of a trap designedly laid. The exceptions do not show that the door was not easily distinguishable from the platform of which it formed a part, and the use for which it was designed must have been apparent upon inspection. The general rule is that a bare licensee has no cause of action on account of dangers existing in the place he is permitted to enter, but goes there at his own risk, and must take the premises as he finds them. Reardon v. Thompson, 149 Mass. 268; 21 N. E. Rep. 369; Parker v. Publishing Co., 69 Me. 173. No duty is cast upon the owner to take care of the licensee, or to see that he does not go to a dangerous place, but he must take his permission with its concomitant conditions and perils, and cannot recover for injuries caused by obstructions or pitfalls."

[42] Woolwine v. Chesapeake, etc., R. Co., 36 W. Va. 329; 15 S. E. Rep. 81.

[43] Wennecker v. Missouri, etc., R. Co., 169 Mo. 592, 600, 601; 70 S. W. Rep. 145.

Where intestate crossed defendant's railroad tracks in a depot yard for the purpose of conversing with persons who were loading freight cars, and later attempted to recross in front of an approaching train at a point not a public crossing, he was at most a mere licensee, as to whom the railroad company owed no duty higher than the exercise of ordinary care. Illinois Cent. R. Co. v. Willis' Adm'r (Ky. 1906), 97 S. W. Rep. 21.

The following persons have been held to be bare licensees, upon railroad premises, because having no business with the company: A boy delivering a lunch to the conductor of the train, Wennecker v.

a small boy, visiting the cars of the railroad company to deliver a lunch to the conductor of the train. In considering what, if any, duty was owing by the railroad company to the boy, to maintain a reasonably safe place for his use, while transacting his business with its employee, the court said:

" The deceased's business being with the conductor and *not with the defendant,* in our opinion, the facts fail to show that defendant owed him any other duty than as before indicated, and was under no obligation to notify him, as he approached the car, of the danger to be apprehended by him

Missouri, etc., R. Co., 169 Mo. 592; 70 S. W. Rep. 145. One paying a call upon a telegraph operator, at a railroad station, Woolwine v. Chesapeake, etc., R. Co., 36 W. Va. 329; 50 Am. & Eng. R. Cas. 37. One using the private grounds of a railroad company, to cross onto adjoining lands, injured by falling into a pit, between the tracks, Morgen v. Pennsylvania R. Co., 19 Blatchf. (U. S.) 239; 7 Fed. Rep. 78. A newsboy, going on the train, to sell his papers, Fleming v. Brooklyn, etc., R. Co., 1 Abb. N. Cas. 433. One going on a train to collect money the conductor owed him, Pittsburg, etc., R. Co. v. Krause, 30 Ohio St. 22; 15 Am. Ry. Rep. 298. One using a private crossing, to get to a chemical plant, Donnelly v. Boston, etc., R. Co., 42 Am. & Eng. R. Cas. 182. And one going to a railroad yard, to see the manager of a circus, on business, Duncan v. Chicago, etc., R. Co., 60 S. E. Rep. 189.

Where one went upon a railway train at a station for the sole purpose of purchasing fruit from a news agent, the company was not liable for his injury, resulting from his being thrown from the car by the jerking of the train, though no signal was given before the train started, since a railway company is liable to permissive licensees for wanton negligence only. Peterson v. South & W. R. R. (N. C. 1906), 55 S. E. Rep. 618.

By carrying on its cars venders of fruit, etc., for sale to passengers, a railway company does not invite the public to enter its trains at stations for the sole purpose of making purchases, and the company's failure to object to persons frequently doing so does not create more than a permissive license. Peterson v. South & W. R. R., 55 S. E. Rep. 618.

Plaintiff, having leased certain grounds to a circus, went to the railroad station, while the circus train was being unloaded, to transact

'by the running out of the slack in the train,' but if any such duty was imposed by law upon any one, it was upon Conductor Stone, for whose benefit and with whose knowledge he was on his way to the car with the lunch when he met him on the platform of the depot. This being the case, the fact that deceased was only about eleven years of age at the time of his unfortunate death, is of no significance."

§ 872. **Persons using premises for their own convenience.—** The legal distinction which exists between the obligation which is due by the owner of premises, to a mere licensee, who enters thereon, without any enticement or inducement, and the duty owing to one who enters upon lawful business, by the invitation, express or implied, of the proprietor, is well settled by the cases and the established principles of the law. The former enters at his own risk; the latter has a right to believe that, taking reasonable care of himself, all reasonable care has been used by the owner to protect him, in order that no injury may occur. There is no duty imposed by the law upon an owner or occupant of premises to keep them in suitable condition for those who come there for their own convenience merely, without any invitation express or implied and without having any business with the owner of such premises.

The reason for the distinction is manifest, for the very basis of every action for an injury to the person, is the violation of some duty owing by the party alleged to have

business between herself and the circus manager, without any reference to the railroad company or any of its employees, who had no knowledge of plaintiff's presence about the station. Plaintiff went to a part of the station not intended for passengers, and while there was injured by the negligence of the circus people while unloading the circus train. *Held*, that plaintiff was at most a mere licensee, and the railroad company, having been guilty of no willful wrong with reference to her, was not liable for her injuries. Illinois Cent. R. Co. v. Lucas, 42 So. Rep. 607.

caused the injury. Without a relation from
would spring, or be created by the law, there
negligence, or a breach of a duty that did n
consequently no liability would exist, unless
first established from which some correlative d
implied. That this is the logic of the law an
as well established as any property right recog
law, is apparent from the reasoning of the op
highest courts.[44]

[44] Barney v. Hannibal, etc., R. Co., 126 Mo. 372, 38
Missouri, etc., R. Co., 169 Mo. 592, 599, 600; Carr v. l
Ry. Co., 195 Mo. 214, 225, 227; Gunderman v. Missou
58 Mo. App. 370; Glaser v. Rothschild, 106 Mo. App.
v. Railroad Co., 9 Phila. (Pa.) 78; Chicago, etc., R.
26 Ill. App. 219; Ferguson v. Virginia, etc., R. Co.,
Donnelly v. Boston, etc., R. Co. (Mass. by Holmes,
Eng. R. Cas. 182; Wright v. Railroad Co. (Mass.), 28
Cas. 652; Cusick v. Adams (N. Y.), 21 N. E. Rep. 67
Nashville (Tenn.), 63 S. W. Rep. 231; Lochat v. Lutz (
Rep. 218; Bennett v. Butterfield, 70 N. W. Rep. 410;
Co. (Mass.), 49 N. E. Rep. 635; Beehler v. Daniels & C
512; Redigan v. Railroad Co. (Mass.), 28 N. E. Rep. 11:
276; Reardon v. Thompson, 149 Mass. 267; Manning
L. R. A. 271; De La Pena v. Railroad (Texas), 74 S
Muench v. Heineman (Wis.), 96 N. W. Rep. 800; Bentl
102 Ill. App. 166; Sterger v. Van Sticklen, 132 N. Y.
Baltimore Tr. Co., 77 Md. 535.

In the recent case of Carr v. Missouri Pacific Rai
(195 Mo. 225), Judge Burgess, speaking for the cou
distinction by use of the following language: "The
distinction between a person who comes upon a railr
at the invitation of the railroad company, or *for som*
nected with its business, and a person who goes upon
for his own convenience or pleasure. In the one case, t
to protect the person thus going upon the property of
injury, while on his premises, while as to the other, th
duty."

In Mann v. Chicago, etc., R. Co. (86 Mo. 347), wher
business with the railroad company was using a privat
was injured, the Supreme Court, in disposing of the c
any duty was owing to the injured person, said: "I

plaintiff has no right or action or standing in court. The defendant owed no duty to him, even if the crossing were defective or out of repair. * * * If the party, for whose benefit the crossing was built had, in like circumstances, been injured, a different question would, perhaps, be presented, not necessary now to be considered." Monn v. Chicago, etc., R. Co., 86 Mo. 350.

In Straub v. Soderer (53 Mo. 43), Judge Ewing delivered the opinion of the court, and in considering the duty owing to a licensee or one who occupied the relation that the plaintiff did, at the time of the alleged injury, said: "No duty is imposed by law, upon the owner or occupant, to keep his premises in a suitable condition for those who come there solely for their own convenience or pleasure, and who are not either expressly invited to enter or induced to come upon them by the purpose for which the premises are appropriated or occupied, or by some preparation or adaptation of the place *for use by customers or passengers*, which might naturally and reasonably lead them to suppose that they might properly and safely enter." Straub v. Soderer, 53 Mo. 43.

A petition, alleging that plaintiff was driving a dray in a certain town and was accustomed to meet the train on Saturdays to get laundry from a brakeman, and his practice was well known to defendant railroad company, and on the day he was injured plaintiff started to get on the freight train to get the clothes as usual, when the train suddenly started, and that his body struck a box car on a side track, whereby he was badly injured; that the car on the side track was too near the main line; that the engineer and fireman knew of such fact, and that the fireman, seeing his danger, did not signal the engineer to stop the train, or, if he did, the engineer failed to obey the signal, stated a good cause of action, whether plaintiff was a licensee or trespasser. Starr v. Southern Ry. Co. (Ga. App. 1908), 61 S. E. Rep. 735.

In Sterger v. Van Sticklen (132 N. Y. 499), it is held that "where one enters upon the premises of another as a mere licensee, without any enticement or inducement, he does so at his own risk and as to him the owner owes no duty of care or vigilance."

In Stephens v. Nichols (155 Mass. 472), "where the defendants opened *a private way, into a public street*, without putting up any sign to notify travelers that the passageway was not a public way, and the plaintiff, who was not shown to have any right in the passageway, unless as one of the public, *while on his way to premises, beyond those of the defendants, was injured by driving over a curbstone,* in the passageway, hidden by snow, no active force being used against him, it was held that the plaintiff was, at most, but a licensee, and went upon the defendant's land at his own risk."

§ 873. **Persons habitually using railroad prem**
a railroad company expressly or by clear implica
the public to use its track in a city, **town or vil**
not afterward treat one who avails himself of tl
a trespasser, but a person using the company's
such a place, is entitled to all the rights of on
upon it and may recover for an injury due to t
ordinary care, for his protection, on the part of t
company.[45]

But where pedestrians use a railroad track as a
fare, despite posted notices and other warnings for
a license for such use is not established as against tl
company,[46] and a license to walk on a railroad tr:

In Benson v. Baltimore Traction Co. (77 Md. 535), i
"where the president of a corporation, on the request of tl
of a school, gives permission to a class of thirty or mor
to visit the company's power house, for the purpose of v
examining the works and machinery therein contained, suc
are mere licensees, to whom the company is under no ob
provide against the danger of accident."

And in Traux v. Chicago, etc., R. Co. (83 Wis. 547; 53 N
842), a licensee in the use of a private railroad crossing
to come within the same rule; he was held to take the cros
found it and the company was not liable to him for injuries
because of a defect in the construction of the crossing.

In De La Pena v. Railroad (Texas, 74 S. W. Rep. 58), the
for the purpose of getting around defendant's cars, which obs
street crossing, took a path running along the right of way, u
generally used by the public with defendant's knowledge and
cence. The plaintiff fell in a hole or open ditch near the
broke his leg, but the court held that as he was a mere lice
using the path on business with the defendant, and the defends
him no duty to keep the path in a safe condition.

[45] Palmer v. Chicago, etc., R. Co., 112 Ind. 250; 14 N. E. 1
31 Am. & Eng. R. Cas. 364; Kansas Pacific R. Co. v. Pointer, 9
620; Smedis v. Brooklyn, etc., R. Co., 88 N. Y. 620; Penns
R. Co. v. Lewis, 79 Pa. St. 33; Illinois, etc., R. Co. v. D
Ky. 434; 15 S. W. Rep. 665; Clampit v. Chicago, etc., R.
Iowa 71; 50 N. W. Rep. 673; 49 Am. & Eng. R. Cas. 468.

[46] Hyde v. Missouri Pacific Ry. Co., 110 Mo. 272; 19 S. W. Re

be established by proof showing that the place was remote from any station, and that persons living near it had been in the habit of walking on it; that the railroad company's employees had seen persons walking on it and that no steps had been taken to prevent such user, as this only amounts to a mere passive acquiescence in the use of the track and does not show any invitation, either express or implied, to so use it on the part of the railroad company.[47]

§ 874. **People crossing track.**— If a person attempts to cross a railroad track, merely by the license or permission of the company, and not under circumstances from which an inducement or invitation to persons having occasion to pass thereon, to treat the same as a highway, can be inferred, no recovery can be had for an injury due to the ordinary use of the track by the railroad company, but people so using the crossing, would do so, subject to the perils incident thereto.[48] Although a railroad company has, by permitting people to repeatedly cross its tracks, at a point where there is no public right of passage, given an implied license so to do, it owes no duty of active vigilance to those using the crossing to guard them from accident. The company is not restricted by the license from the customary use of its

54 Am. & Eng. R. Cas. 157; Missouri Pacific Ry. Co. v. Brown (Texas), 18 S. W. Rep. 670; St. Louis, etc., R. Co. v. Crosnoe, 72 Texas 79; 10 S. W. Rep. 342; Illinois, etc., R. Co. v. Hetherington, 83 Ill. 510.

[47] Missouri Pacific Ry. Co. v. Brown, *supra;* Frye v. St. Louis, etc., R. Co., 200 Mo. 377; 98 S. W. Rep. 366.

Where a railroad has, by long acquiescence, licensed the public to use its station grounds for ordinary travel, the company owes a greater degree of care to persons so using its grounds than to ordinary licensees, and must conduct its business over such licensed way with the ordinary care required to avoid injuries which may be anticipated under the circumstances, including the fact of the licensed use of its grounds. Rowley v. Chicago, etc., Ry. Co. (Wis. 1908), 115 N. W. Rep. 865.

[48] Hanks v. Boston, etc., R. Co., 147 Mass. 495; 18 N. E. Rep. 218; 35 Am. & Eng. R. Cas. 321.

tracks, even though its employees in given particulars may have deviated from its usual course, with reference to those using the crossing, but all people so using the crossing are licensees simply and take the license subject to the dangers of using it.[49]   Proof that a path had existed over a track for twenty-five years, which was used by the public, without objection, was held, in a Massachusetts case,[50] not to be sufficient from which to find the railroad company had offered an inducement to use the track.   And it is generally held that a railroad company cannot be held to have acquiesced in the use of a crossing, where there is no regular road, until the company has notice of the use of the track for this purpose and ratifies such use.[51]

But if the general public, or any considerable number of people are permitted to cross the track, with the consent of the railroad company, it is the duty of the employees of the company to notify such people of the approach of trains and to be on the lookout for those using the crossing.[52]   The company is not justified, because a crossing is not a public crossing, in negligently running its trains over those who are in the habit of using the crossing.[53]   It is therefore held that a railroad company owes the duty of vigilance to ascertain the presence of those accustomed to use a switch track, in a railroad yard, for a crossing; [54] the same is true of a crossing at the junction of a public road and private

[49] Sutton v. New York, etc., R. Co., 66 N. Y. 243; Byrne v. New York, etc., R. Co., 104 N. Y. 362; 10 N. E. Rep. 539; 58 Am. Rep. 512; Harrison v. Northeastern R. Co., 22 W. R. 335; 29 L. T. 844.

[50] Wright v. Boston, etc., R. Co., 142 Mass. 296; 7 N. E. Rep. 866; 28 Am. & Eng. R. Cas. 652.

[51] Matze v. New York, etc., R. Co., 1 Hun (N. Y.) 417; 3 T. & C. 513.

[52] Louisville, etc., R. Co. v. Schuster (Ky.), 7 S. W. Rep. 874; 35 Am. & Eng. R. Cas. 407; Louisville, etc., R. Co. v. Howard, 82 Ky. 218.

[53] Gurley v. Missouri Pacific Ry. Co., 104 Mo. 211; 16 S. W. Rep. 11.

[54] St. Louis, etc., R. Co. v. Crosnoe, 72 Texas 79; 10 S. W. Rep. 342; 37 Am. & Eng. R. Cas. 313.

way, used by railroad employees, in crossing the track; [55] of
a vacant lot, adjoining a siding which is extensively used
by people in loading and unloading cars [56] and at a crossing
used for thirty years by adjoining landowners and others,
in reaching adjoining tracts of land, across the railroad
tracks.[57] In all such cases, there was held to have been

[55] Schindler v. Milwaukee, etc., R. Co., 87 Mich. 400; 49 N. W.
Rep. 670; Jones v. Grand Trunk R. Co., 18 Can. Sup. Ct. 696; 16
Ont. App. 87.

[56] Kay v. Pennsylvania R. Co., 65 Pa. St. 269.

[57] Barry v. New York, etc., R. Co., 92 N. Y. 289; 28 Hun 441;
13 Am. & Eng. R. Cas. 615; Swift v. Staten Island R. Co., 123 N. Y.
645; 25 N. E. Rep. 378.

Where there was a well-defined footpath across the track of defendant
railroad company in its yard, used for years by hundreds of people
going between the town and the shops of another railroad company,
to the knowledge of the officers and employees of defendant, there was
an implied license to so use its tracks, so that in the operation of its
trains it owed to the users of such path the same care it owed the
public at a highway or street crossing. Calwell v. Minneapolis, etc., R.
Co. (Iowa 1908), 115 N. W. Rep. 605.

It is the duty of an engineer driving an engine through a populous
street of a city, where persons on foot and in vehicles are to be expected, to keep a vigilant watch for persons not only on, but approaching,
the track, and to have the engine in reasonable control so as to stop
it if necessary, when a danger that could reasonably have been anticipated arises, and his field of observation to avoid danger is as wide as
the field which the danger created covers, and the degree of care required
is commensurate with the degree of danger. Holmes v. Missouri Pac.
Ry. Co. (Mo. 1907), 105 S. W. Rep. 624.

Where a railroad runs through a thickly populated locality, where
the frequent crossing of the track is necessary, it is its duty to keep
a lookout at that point. Duncan v. St. Louis & S. F. R. Co., 44
So. Rep. 418.

A complaint in an action against a railroad for injuring a person
at a crossing, alleging that defendant's engineer, in utter disregard for
the safety of persons passing at that point, and without giving any
signal of approach or maintaining a lookout, willfully, wantonly, etc.,
propelled an engine against plaintiff, was not sufficient to charge willful
or wanton injury. Duncan v. St. Louis & S. F. R. Co. (Ala. 1907),
44 So. Rep. 418.

One crossing a railroad track upon a pathway, not a public street,

a sufficient invitation, or inducement, to charge the railroad company with the exercise of reasonable care, to avoid injury to the people using the crossing, or private way.

§ 875. **Using railroad track as footway.**— According to the general rule of law, governing the use of all licenses merely, by the licensee, the use of a railroad track, as a footway, by pedestrians, with the company's knowledge and consent, would not bind the railroad company to the exercise of extraordinary care or caution to avoid injury to the people so using its track, but if such use would amount to a license at all, it would be upon the condition that the pedestrian should exercise ordinary care to avoid injury, or, in other words, he would take the license subject to its concomitant perils.[58]

Conduct on the part of the railroad company, amounting to an acquiescence in the use of a private crossing, would not be sufficient to create a license in the use of the track longitudinally by pedestrians.[59] A mere licensee walking on a railroad track could not recover for injuries received by a backing train, when his presence was not discovered by the employees in charge of the train in time to avoid

but which for 25 years has been used by from 25 to 75 persons daily in crossing from a street to a cotton mill, is not a trespasser, but entitled to substantially the same care and warning as though on a public crossing. Davis v. Louisville, etc., R. Co. (Ky. 1906), 97 S. W. Rep. 1122.

Where persons undertake to cross railroad tracks by passing over the grounds of a railway company, even though they do not know that they are on such grounds, they do so at their peril, notwithstanding the company had not previously seen fit to enforce its rights and prevent people from crossing there, and such company is not bound to protect or provide safeguards for such persons so using its grounds. McLain v. Chicago & N. W. Ry. Co., 121 Ill. App. 614; Gabriel v. Same, *id.*

[58] White v. Central R. Co., 83 Ga. 595; 10 S. E. Rep. 273.

[59] Richards v. Chicago, etc., R. Co., 81 Iowa 426; 47 N. W. Rep. 63; 45 Am. & Eng. R. Cas. 54.

injuring him, and this would especially be true if no notice of the use of the track for such purpose was brought home to the railroad company.[60]

But if the railroad company has, with notice of such use of its track, for a considerable period, by the general public, or any considerable number thereof, acquiesced in the use of its track by pedestrians, between given points, it is generally held to a stricter obligation to avoid injury to such persons, than if they were mere trespassers,[61] and a statute forbidding persons from walking along a railroad track, would have no bearing on a case of permissive use, by the railroad company.[62] If the track of a railroad company has been used by persons on foot, with its knowledge or acquiescence, for a considerable period, one so using the track is entitled to reasonable care to avoid injury to him.[63] Increased vigilance and precaution would be required of those in charge of trains moving in cities or towns, where people have been accustomed to travel on the track at some particular place,[64] and if a person is discovered on the track, at such a place, it is the duty of the railroad employees to use ordinary care to avoid injury to him,[65] and where the facts are conflicting it would of course be a jury issue, whether or not this was done.[66]

[60] Hagan v. Chicago, etc., R. Co., 59 Wis. 139; 17 N. W. Rep. 632; 15 Am. & Eng. R. Cas. 439; Whelen v. Chicago, etc., R. Co., 75 Wis. 654; 44 N. W. Rep. 849; 41 Am. & Eng. R. Cas. 558.

[61] Central, etc., R. Co. v. Brinson, 70 Ga. 207; 19 Am. & Eng. R. Cas. 42.

[62] Davis v. Chicago, etc., R. Co., 58 Wis. 646; 46 Am. Rep. 667; 15 Am. & Eng. R. Cas. 424.

[63] Davis v. Chicago, etc., R. Co., supra.

[64] Shelby v. Cincinnati, etc., R. Co., 95 Ky. 224; 3 S. W. Rep. 157.

[65] Gurley v. Missouri Pacific Ry. Co., 104 Mo. 211; 16 S. W. Rep. 11.

[66] Taylor v. Delaware, etc., R. Co., 113 Pa. St. 162; 8 Atl. Rep. 43; 28 Am. & Eng. R. Cas. 656.

Mere knowledge by a railroad company that pedestrians, without any public or private right of way, passed daily along its side track

§ 876. **Contributory negligence of licensee.**— Although the facts in connection with an injury to a person on railroad property may be such as to amount to the recognition of a license, on his part, to use the premises where he was injured, he is still bound to exercise ordinary care to avoid injury, and if he is walking on the track and fails to keep

and were allowed to go upon such side track, was not an express license to a pedestrian to stop on the side track at the end of a car to obtain shelter from the rain, so as to render the company liable for damages resulting from his death, caused by the backing of the engine and cars onto the side track putting in motion a number of cars thereon and causing the pedestrian to be run over. Curtis v. Southern Ry. Co. (Ga. 1908), 61 S. E. Rep. 539.

The user of a part of a railroad right of way by the public as a highway for foot passengers does not prove either an implied dedication or a prescriptive right. Manion v. Lake Erie & W. Ry. Co. (Ind. App. 1907), 80 N. E. Rep. 166.

One walking upon a street of a city, although it was used by a railroad company, was not a trespasser as between him and the company. Manion v. Lake Erie & W. Ry. Co., 80 N. E. Rep. 166.

Those in charge of a railroad train running along a street or way are bound to anticipate the presence of persons on the track and to exercise reasonable care to avoid injuring persons placed in peril. Manion v. Lake Erie & W. Ry. Co., 80 N. E. Rep. 166.

Where a railroad company permits the public to use a path through its yards, it must exercise ordinary care not to injure persons while crossing the tracks. St. Louis, I. M. & S. Ry. Co. v. Hudson (Ark. 1908), 110 S. W. Rep. 590.

Where railroad tracks in a city are habitually used for foot passage by people who may be expected thereon at any time, persons moving a train through the city must keep a lookout, and use ordinary care to avoid persons on the track, even though they are trespassers. Louisville & N. R. Co. v. Hoskins' Adm'r (Ky. 1908), 108 S. W. Rep. 305.

A railroad is bound to a greater degree of diligence in the exercise of ordinary care in the operation of a train over a track running beside a footpath than is required of a pedestrian walking along the path. Missouri, K. & T. Ry. Co. v. Brown (Tex. Civ. App. 1907), 101 S. W. Rep. 464.

If this rule would be followed by the Supreme Court of Texas, it would not perhaps be announced in any other State, for it is judicial discrimination of the most pronounced type.

a lookout for approaching trains, he can not recover for an injury so received.[67] If the injury of one accustomed to use a railroad track as a footway, was caused by the concurrent negligence of such person and the railroad employees, as where the employees failed to give notice by bell or whistle of the approach of a train and the injured person failed to look or listen for a train, which could have been seen or heard, there can be no recovery from the railroad company for an injury due to such concurrent negligence.[68]

But, if, instead of a case of concurrent negligence, the injury is due to the subsequent negligence of the railroad company's employees, as where, after discovering the injured person in a place of danger, the injury could have been avoided by the exercise of ordinary care on their part, but such care was not used, then there is generally held to be a liability, notwithstanding such prior negligence of the injured person,[69] and where the facts going to establish the negligence or the contributory negligence of the injured person are not such as to preclude every other reasonable theory of the injury, or, as more accurately stated, where reasonable minds would reach no other conclusion, the negligence

[67] McAdoo v. Richmond, etc., R. Co., 105 No. Car. 140; 11 S. E. Rep. 316; 41 Am. & Eng. R. Cas. 524.

[68] Gunther v. St. Louis, etc., R. Co., 95 Mo. 286; 8 S. W. Rep. 371; 34 Am. & Eng. R. Cas. 47; Missouri Pacific Ry. Co. v. Moseley, 57 Fed. Rep. 921; Baltimore, etc., R. Co. v. State, 69 Md. 551; 16 Atl. Rep. 212; Holwerson v. St. Louis, etc., R. Co., 157 Mo. 216; 57 S. W. Rep. 770; 50 L. R. A. 850.

[69] Valin v. Milwaukee, etc., R. Co., 82 Wis. 1; 51 N. W. Rep. 108.; Mauerman v. St. Louis, etc., R. Co., 41 Mo. App. 348; Shanks v. Traction Co., 101 Mo. App. 702; 74 S. W. Rep. 386; Ries v. Transit Co., 179 Mo. 1; 77 S. W. Rep. 734; Moore v. Lindell Ry. Co., 176 Mo. 528; 75 S. W. Rep. 672; Sullivan v. Missouri Pacific Ry. Co., 117 Mo. 214; 23 S. W. Rep. 149; Hanheide v. Transit Co., 104 Mo. App. 323; 78 S. W. Rep. 820.

of the respective parties would be a question of law for the
court, or, otherwise, an issue of fact for the jury.[70]

[70] Barton v. New York, etc., R. Co., 56 N. Y. 660; 1 T. & C. 297;
Alabama, etc., R. Co. v. Summers, 68 Miss. 566; 10 So. Rep. 63.

That defendant railroad company permitted the public, including
decedent, to use its yards as a common passageway, and thereby
obligated itself to observe ordinary care to avoid injuring them, did
not relieve decedent from the obligation to use ordinary care for his
own safety. Rich v. Chicago, etc., Ry. Co. (U. S. C. C. A., Iowa, 1906),
149 Fed. Rep. 79.

CHAPTER XXXVII.

§ 877. **Care to be observed by railroad company.**— It is the duty of a railroad company, in the operation of its trains, to use ordinary care and prudence to prevent injury to the persons of those who may be traveling upon the public highways and have occasion to cross its tracks, whether the specific duty be prescribed by statute or not. And the fact that the statute may prescribe one precaution will not relieve the railroad company from adopting others, which may be dictated by common prudence, so as to safeguard the public using the crossings over its tracks.[1]

The care and caution required of railroad companies, in the operation of their trains, is generally commensurate with the danger to persons incident to the use of crossings, and in running trains through towns and cities and over public

[1] Chicago, etc., R. Co. v. Perkins, 125 Ill. 127; 17 N. E. Rep. 1; Grand Trunk R. Co. v. Ives, 144 U. S. 408.

crossings, or in the vicinity of railroad statior
caution must be exercised, commensurate with
accidents at such places.[2]   And whether or not
exercised, in a given case, will generally be h
jury issue, where the facts are conflicting.[3]

But where a highway across a railroad track
very little used, there is a less degree of vigilar
on the part of the employees in charge of the
approaching such a crossing.[4]   In other words,
ment as to vigilance is to be measured by the
danger incurred in the use of the crossing.   Thos
of the train, are, under no circumstances, requ
ercise more than ordinary care and caution tow;
traveling with teams and wagons on a highway; 1
not required to interfere with the higher duty ov
railroad company to its own passengers,[5] and as tl
of duty is but ordinary care and caution, it is e
struct the jury that the defendant was bound, as f;
ble, to prevent injury to a person about to cross tl
front of a moving train.[6]

[2] Hicks v. Pacific R. Co., 64 Mo. 430; 17 Am. Ry. Rep. :
[3] Bailey v. New Haven, etc., R. Co., 107 Mass. 497; W
land R. Co., 57 Me. 117; Hart v. Chicago, etc., R. Co., 5(
9 N. W. Rep. 116; Macon, etc., R. Co. v. Davis, 18 Ga. (
[4] Andrews v. New York, etc., R. Co., 60 Conn. 293; 22 A·
[5] Bailey v. Hartford, etc., R. Co., 56 Conn. 444; 16 Atl
37 Am. & Eng. R. Cas. 483.
[6] Chicago, etc., R. Co. v. Dunn, 61 Ill. 385; 12 Am. R;
Aside from statutory requirements, persons handling ;
proaching crossings must use reasonable care. Elgin, etc.,
Lawlor, 82 N. E. Rep. 407; 229 Ill. 621.
If injury to one crossing a railway track was caused by a:
failure to keep a lookout, she can recover from the compai
Louisville & St. L. R. Co. v. Davis (Ky. 1908), 106 S. W
If the person in charge of an engine sees, or by the
ordinary care could see, that a team on a highway is un
and running off in the direction of the railroad crossin;
situation is such as to induce a person of ordinary p

§ 878. Reciprocal care imposed upon company and traveling public.— The rights and duties of a railroad company crossing a public crossing, in operating trains on its track, and the rights and duties of persons traveling on the highway, across the railroad track, are mutual. Both have the right to pass and both are bound to use ordinary care and diligence to avoid injury,[7] but neither is bound to exercise extraordinary care.[8] The railroad company, as the owner of its right of way, has the right to use the same, in the ordinary manner, in the operation of its trains, at highway crossings. Likewise do the public have a right of way and of passage across the tracks of the railroad company, in the ordinary manner of traveling. These rights are necessarily reciprocal and each must be exercised with reference to the other.[9]

believe there is danger of a collision at the crossing, it is his duty to exercise ordinary care to prevent such a collision. Chesapeake & O. Ry. Co. v. Pace (Ky. 1908), 106 S. W. Rep. 1176.

In determining whether or not an engineer was negligent in the handling of an engine at a highway crossing, the facts must be judged as they appeared to him, at the time, not as they appear to others, afterwards. Anderson v. New York, etc., R. Co., 60 Conn. 293; 22 Atl. Rep. 566.

One injured by the backing of a train upon him cannot sustain a charge of negligence against the road, where it does not appear that the company had notice or warning that such person was upon the track sufficiently long before the injury to form an intelligent opinion as to how the injury might be avoided and apply the means. Pittsburgh & St. L. Ry. Co. v. Puszdrakiewicz, 129 Ill. App. 295.

While the employees of a railroad company are required to exercise ordinary care for the safety of travelers while using a grade highway crossing such employees are only required not to willfully injure trespassers or mere licensees thereon. Chicago & L. Ry. Co. v. McCandish (Ind. 1907), 79 N. E. Rep. 903.

[7] Indianapolis, etc., R. Co. v. McLin, 82 Ind. 435; 8 Am. & Eng. R. Cas. 237; Pittsburg, etc., R. Co. v. Maurer, 21 Ohio St. 421; Beyel v. Newport, etc., R. Co., 34 W. Va. 538; 12 S. E. Rep. 532.

[8] Willoughby v. Chicago, etc., R. Co., 37 Iowa 432.

[9] Kelly v. Michigan, etc., R. Co., 65 Mich. 186; 31 N. W. Rep. 904; 28 Am. & Eng. R. Cas. 633.

The railroad company must use care to avoid running over some one using the crossing; care is exacted of the person using the crossing, to avoid being run over himself. In the absence of care by the railroad employees, the liability depends on an injury resulting to the traveler on the highway crossing; in the absence of care to avoid being struck by a passing train, the blame attaches to the person obstructing the crossing.[10] It is held that greater than ordinary care is to be exacted to avoid injury to passengers, accustomed to cross the railroad track, by a path on the company's grounds, appropriated to such a use,[11] and there are decisions to the effect that in a populous city, where the railroad tracks are used habitually by the traveling public, a greater degree of care is exacted from the railroad employees, to avoid injury to the public, than will be required of the traveling public using the track.[12] But as this standard of diligence would have the effect of rewarding the negligence or want of care on the part of the public — and this is the reason assigned for penalizing the negligence of railroad employees, as against the company — it is not deemed to be a sound rule, or consistent with the better doctrine, that negligence will not be divided into degrees or compared, but when the injured person was himself guilty of negligence contributing to the injury, no recovery ought to be had therefor.

It is unquestionably the duty of the employees in charge of an engine approaching a public crossing, to give proper warning and to use ordinary care to avoid injury to the traveling public, but it ought to be equally the duty of those approaching the crossing to avoid colliding with the engine.[13] The engine and train can run but on the fixed rails of the

[10] Telfer v. Northern R. Co., 30 N. J. L. 188.
[11] Whalen v. St. Louis, etc., R. Co., 60 Mo. 323; 9 Am. Ry. Rep. 224.
[12] White v. Wabash R. Co., 34 Mo. App. 57.
[13] Philadelphia, etc., R. Co. v. Hogeland, 66 Md. 149; 7 Atl. Rep. 105; Brown v. Texas, etc., R. Co., 42 La. Ann. 350; 7 So. Rep. 682.

track and it is certainly as easy for the traveler by team, or
the pedestrian, to discover the train, operated by its own
steam and making the ordinary noise of a railroad train,
as it is for the operatives of the engine to discover the team
or traveler on the highway crossing. The rule requiring
ordinary care, or that of an ordinary prudent person, ought
to bind the traveler as well as the employees of the railroad
company, to avoid injury at a highway crossing, and any
less degree of care on the part of the injured person than
that required of the railroad employees, should not be exacted.[14]

[14] Chicago, etc., R. Co. v. Fisher, 49 Kansas 460; 30 Pac. Rep. 462.

A railroad company and a traveler on a highway crossing are
charged with a mutual duty of keeing a careful lookout for danger,
and the degree of vigilance is in proportion to the known danger;
the greater the danger, the greater the care required of both. Southern Ry. Co. v. Hansbrough's Adm'x (Va. 1908), 60 S. E. Rep. 58.

The fact that a public road, treated as such by the general public
and by a railroad, was located on the railroad right of way did not
affect the reciprocal rights and duties of the public and the railroad,
though the proximity of the road to the track might affect the obligations of both on the question of the exercise of proper care. Johnson v.
Texas & G. Ry. Co. (Tex. Civ. App. 1907), 100 S. W. Rep. 206.

Use of a public highway for passage at a railroad crossing or
elsewhere is the right of all travelers in common, within the law
requiring all users to exercise reasonable care with reference to a like
use by others, so that, while the tracks are a warning to the traveler
of railway movements, the highway crossing is likewise notice to the
train operators that travelers are to be expected on the highway;
care being exacted from them commensurate with the recognizable
conditions. Southern Ry. Co. v. Fisk (U. S. C. C. A., Ill., 1908),
159 Fed. Rep. 373.

A traveler approaching a railroad crossing must exercise the same
vigilance to protect himself that the operatives in charge of an
approaching train must exercise to avoid injuring him, and a failure
to exercise such vigilance on the part of either is negligence in the
party thus failing to do his duty. Lake Shore, etc., Ry. Co. v. Brown
(Ind. App. 1908), 84 N. E. Rep. 25.

A train standing at a public crossing has no precedence over an
ordinary traveler, their rights being equal, and each is bound to act
with due regard to the other, and has a right to assume that the other

§ 879. **What constitutes a public crossing.**— A public crossing over the track of a railroad company can either result from a dedication of the ground used for the crossing, to the exclusive use of the traveling public,[15] or it may result from a user by the public, for a length of time sufficiently long to estop the railroad company from denying that it was so appropriated.[16]

In a Pennsylvania case,[17] a landowner dedicated a strip of land across a railroad track to public use as a road, and a person was injured on the crossing some ten years subsequent to the dedication and it was held that it was a public road crossing, within the contemplation of law, under the evidence in that case. In a Michigan case,[18] a highway connecting two towns crossed over the railroad track of the defendant and it had been used for twenty years and repaired by the railroad company, and it was held to be estopped to deny that it was a public crossing. So, it is held that the establishment of a flag station, at a railroad crossing, is evidence of the consent of the railroad company to the use of such crossing as a public highway.[19]

But in the absence of either a dedication or proof of a user sufficiently long to constitute the crossing a public highway, the railroad is not charged with any higher duty at such a crossing than it would owe at a merely private road crossing. A railroad company, like any private landowner, is entitled, in law, to the use of its land or other property, except at lawful crossings of public or private highways, and

will be controlled by such considerations as would influence the conduct of a man of ordinary care and prudence. Williams v. Chicago, etc., Ry. Co. (Neb. 1907), 111 N. W. Rep. 596.

[15] Pittsburg, etc., R. Co. v. Dunn, 56 Pa. St. 280.

[16] Adams v. Iron Cliff Co., 78 Mich. 271; 44 N. W. Rep. 270; 41 Am. & Eng. R. Cas. 414.

[17] Pittsburg, etc., R. Co. v. Dunn, *supra.*

[18] Adams v. Iron Cliff Co., *supra.*

[19] Webb v. Portland, etc., R. Co., 57 Me. 117.

it is not bound to guard against accidents at the crossing of an old, abandoned way, which was never legally dedicated or laid out, across its tracks.[20]

§ 880. **Care required in cities.**— The law requires of companies operating railroads over public highways or streets crossing the railroad tracks in cities, frequented by people, affirmative and active watchfulness, and the employees are charged with the duty of keeping a proper lookout for persons using the street crossings. If the failure on the part of the employees, in charge of the engine, to discover the peril of a person using the crossing and to avoid the injury, is due to their negligent omission to keep a proper lookout along the track in the direction in which the engine is moving, this will be held to be such negligence, on their part, as to render the railroad company liable for a resulting injury.[21] All statutes governing the operation of railroads in cities, for the protection of the traveling public, are generally required to be strictly complied with, or a liability will result, in case of an injury due to a violation of the statute.[22] The same degree of care is required in the use of a street laterally, which has been diverted by the railroad company, as will be required at public street crossings, for the protection of the traveling public.[23] And a greater degree of care is generally required to be exercised in running a rail-

[20] Omaha, etc., R. Co. v. Martin, 14 Neb. 295; 15 N. W. Rep. 696; 19 Am. & Eng. R. Cas. 236.

A railroad company owes to licensees crossing its track at a place used as a public crossing, though not such in fact, only the duty of using due care and reasonable diligence to avoid injuring them after becoming conscious of their peril, and is not bound to give the statutory warning of the approach of trains. Birmingham Southern R. Co. v. Kendrick (Ala. 1908), 46 So. Rep. 588.

[21] Hilz v. Missouri Pacific Ry. Co., 101 Mo. 36; 13 S. W. Rep. 946.

[22] Little Rock, etc., R. Co. v. Wilson, 90 Tenn. 271; 16 S. W. Rep. 613.

[23] Curley v. Illinois, etc., R. Co., 40 La. Ann. 810; 6 So. Rep. 103.

road train along, or across the street of a populous city, than will be necessary in approaching an ordinary crossing in the country, not so frequented by people.[24]

§ 881. **Private or farm crossings.**— Mere knowledge and passive acquiescence on the part of a railroad company, that certain persons are using a place as a crossing across its tracks, will not be sufficient to make such place a public crossing, so as to charge the railroad company with additional care, to avoid injury to persons using such a crossing; and an instruction, which assumes that the crossing would become a public crossing, because of such use, with the knowledge and acquiescence of the railroad company, is error.[25]

Nor would the crossing be changed from a private to a public crossing by mere passive use, although it was located in a town or city, where the use was for the convenience or benefit of the persons using it only, and not for the benefit of the railroad company, and the duty of using care to avoid injury to persons so using the crossing would be that of ordinary care only.[26]

That the public used steps, constructed to enable the railroad employees to go from the passenger to the freight depot, in order to shorten the distance between the station and the town, does not make the way so used a public thoroughfare, but parties using such steps, do so at their peril, as mere licensees.[27]   And even where a private crossing is constructed by the railroad company for the use of a given person, or number of persons, it is generally held that anyone else using the crossing does so at his peril and the rail-

[24] Frick v. St. Louis, etc., R. Co., 75 Mo. 595; 8 Am. & Eng. R. Cas. 280; Illinois, etc., R. Co. v. Dick, 91 Ky. 434; 15 S. W. Rep. 665; Cleveland, etc., R. Co. v. Doerr, 41 Ill. App. 530.

[25] Atchison, etc., R. Co. v. Parsons, 42 Ill. App. 93.

[26] Atchison, etc., R. Co. v. Parsons, *supra.*

[27] Illinois, etc., R. Co. v. Beard, 49 Ill. App. 232.

road owes no active duty of vigilance to avoid injury, except to those having a right to so use it.[28]

But a crossing, connecting a street, in a town, with the ground of the railroad company, generally used by those having business with the railroad company, was held to impose a duty on the railroad company to keep it in a reasonably safe condition for use by those having no business with the railroad company, in a Missouri case.[29] One using a footpath but a few feet distant from a public crossing, was held entitled to the same protection as if he had been using the crossing when injured, where the danger from the use of the crossing would be as great as it was in the use of the footpath;[30] a railroad constructing a grade crossing, in a town or city, for the use of the public, is estopped to contend that it was not a public crossing and it owes the duty of maintaining it in a reasonably safe condition for use;[31] if the crossing has been used by a given number of persons for a time sufficiently long to bring notice home to the railroad company, care proportionate to the danger in the use of the crossing, will be required on the part of the railroad company,[32] and although there is no right of way to the public to cross the track, if the use has been sufficiently prominent to charge the company with notice thereof, care proportionate to the danger ought to be exercised, to avoid injury to those using the crossing.[33]

[28] Mann v. Chicago, etc., R. Co., 86 Mo. 347.

[29] Lowenstein v. Missouri Pacific Ry. Co., 110 Mo. App. 689; 117 Mo. App. 372; 115 S. W. Rep. 2.

[30] Baltimore, etc., R. Co. v. Owings, 65 Md. 502; 5 Atl. Rep. 329; 28 Am. & Eng. R. Cas. 639.

[31] Murphy v. Boston, etc., R. Co., 133 Mass. 121; 14 Am. & Eng. R. Cas. 675.

[32] Vandewater v. New York, etc., R. Co., 74 Hun 32; 56 N. Y. S. R. 208.

[33] Barrett v. Midland R. Co., 1 F. & F. 361.

§ 882. **When railroad entitled to right of way** a sense the rights of travelers upon the public railroad company using a highway crossing, are respect to the priority of passage, the right of company is superior.[34] The right of the trave at a highway crossing of the railroad track, is sin of passage across the railroad and no individ right to commit a trespass upon the company within the limits of the highway crossing, whi tained simply for passage from one side of the the other. Any other use of the crossing is un whether such use is of the land between the tr rails or not, as the right of way and the right same is in the railroad company, when not used travel, and its use thereof is the same, at such the crossing were not there.[35]

But while the railroad company has a superio passage at crossings, the citizen still has the right track, for purposes of passage, subordinate to th the railroad company and may recover for an inj so using it, due to the negligence of the railroad or its employees.[36] The trains and teams of trav have a right to cross the railroad track and eac right to demand due care of the other; the grea of trains and the greater difficulty in stopping them, as well as the requirements of public travel thereon trains precedence over the teams of travelers on

[34] Ohio, etc., R. Co. v. Walker, 113 Ind. 196; 15 N. E. 32 Am. & Eng. R. Cas. 121; Newhard v. Pennsylvania R Pa. St. 417; 26 Atl. Rep. 105; 55 Am. & Eng. R. Cas. 258 Burlington, etc., R. Co., 38 Iowa 515.

[35] Kelly v. Michigan, etc., R. Co., 65 Mich. 186; 31 N. 904; 28 Am. & Eng. R. Cas. 633.

[36] Louisville, etc., R. Co. v. Phillipps, 112 Ind. 59; 13 N 132; 31 Am. & Eng. R. Cas. 432.

way.[37] This precedence over teams, at highway crossings, however, is granted on the condition of due and timely warning by the employees in charge of the trains of their approach to the crossings, and the right of way is not absolute, but conditional, in this regard.[38]

§ 883. Employees may assume that person will leave track, when.— No duty generally,[39] rests upon the engineer of a railroad locomotive after giving the proper signals, in respect to a traveler whom he sees approaching a railroad crossing. He is held, ordinarily, to have the right to assume that the traveler will regard the signals and will stop when he reaches the railroad, and the engineer is only called upon, in law, to act, when the traveler is so near the crossing as to be in imminent danger of a collision with the engine.[40]

[37] Morris v. Chicago, etc., R. Co., 26 Fed. Rep. 22.

[38] Indianapolis, etc., R. Co. v. McLin, 82 Ind. 435; 8 Am. & Eng. R. Cas. 237; Chicago, etc., R. Co. v. Ingraham, 33 Ill. App. 351.

The rule giving trains the right of way to cross ahead of travelers was held to apply only to regular trains, and not to a switch engine, in Northern Pacific R. Co. v. Holmes, 3 Wash. 543; 18 Pac. Rep. 76.

In the use of public streets by railroads and street cars, trains and cars have the right of way over the travelers on the highway, but in all other respects their rights to the use of the highway are equal. Pittsburgh & St. L. Ry. Co. v. Warrum (Ind. App. 1907), 82 N. E. Rep. 934.

A traveler on a public road that intersects a railway at grade is entitled to use the crossing, subject to the railroad company's superior right of way, to which when he has notice of the approach of a train he must yield. Kunz v. Oregon R. Co. (Or. 1907), 93 Pac. Rep. 141.

Where a railroad track crosses a public highway, both a traveler and the railroad have equal rights to cross, but the traveler must yield the right of way to the railroad company in the ordinary course of the latter's business. Duffy v. Atlantic & C. R. Co. (N. C. 1907), 56 S. E. Rep. 557.

[39] As the decisions at variance with this rule would indicate, "generally" would seem to be sometimes used, as Dr. Haiglester, of Charterhouse, used the same word as applicable to a boy's character, which was explained to mean "not particularly."

[40] Dyson v. New York, etc., R. Co., 57 Conn. 9; 17 Atl. Rep. 137;

1807

The courts do not require that the engineer
train shall be such an expert in psychology as
read the mind of a traveler approaching the c
be able to foretell that he will not exercise comr
prudence, for his own safety.[41]   Hence, the er
bound to anticipate that the driver of a tea.
which is seen to be slowly approaching the tra
nor is he bound to stop his train or check its s
as the team is seen, although the driver may k
reclining on the load in the wagon.   After givin
signals, the engineer has a right to assume th
will be stopped, before reaching the track,[42] a
pany could not be held negligent because he c
the engine as soon as the team and man were seen
to then stop the train.[43]

But an engineer is not held to have a right
in all cases, that persons on the track will get off
let the engine and train pass, before a collision
In the operation of trains on crowded thoroughfa
or towns, where persons are frequently met with,
be exercised as well before, as after discovering
danger.[44]   And at places where the crossing is

Wabash R. Co. v. Krugh, 13 Ill. App. 431; Ohio, etc., R. Co
113 Ind. 196; 15 N. E. Rep. 234; 32 Am. & Eng. R. Cas.
v. Maine, etc., R. Co., 77 Me. 85; 23 Am. & Eng. R. Cas. 2
Chicago, etc., R. Co., 94 Mich. 579; 54 N. W. Rep. 388;
St. Joseph, etc., R. Co., 82 Mo. App. 134; Carrier v. Miss
Ry. Co., 175 Mo. 470; 74 S. W. Rep. 1002. And this 1
to infirm or helpless persons, unless the employees on the e
of such infirmity. Candee v. Kansas City, etc., R. Co., 13
31 S. W. Rep. 1029; Jackson v. Kansas City, etc., R. Co., 15
58 S. W. Rep. 32; 80 Am. St. Rep. 650. But not to
tender age. Livingston v. Wabash R. Co., 170 Mo. 452;
Rep. 136.

[41] Boyd v. Wabash R. Co., 105 Mo. 371; 16 S. W. Rep.
[42] Indiana, etc., R. Co. v. Wheeler, 115 Ind. 253; 17 N. E.
[43] Indiana, etc., R. Co. v. Wheeler, *supra.*
[44] Georgia, etc., R. Co. v. Evans, 87 Ga. 673; 13 S. E. Rep

tensively, the assumption that all persons will use due care, is held to obtain only to a limited extent and employees are not allowed to rely thereon, to the extent of failing to use care to stop the engine, until persons are actually seen in danger on the track.[45]

§ 884. Collisions with teams, generally.— It is not the law that a railroad company is liable for a failure on the part of its employees to exercise care to stop the engine, as soon as the traveler is seen approaching the crossing, as the employees in charge of the engine have a right to act upon the presumption that the traveler will not attempt to cross in front of the engine.[46]

[45] Card v. New York, etc., R. Co., 50 Barb. (N. Y.) 39.

An instruction, limiting the right to act upon the assumption that a traveler will not attempt to cross the track, in broad daylight, so long as to allow the engine to reach a point where it cannot be controlled, or warning given, in time to prevent a collision, if the traveler continued in his course, was approved, in Heddles v. Chicago, etc., R. Co., 77 Wis. 228; 46 N. W. Rep. 115.

The employees in charge of a train may assume that a person is in possession of his faculties, and will retain his place of safety and not recklessly expose himself to danger, and, though such person gives no indication of knowledge of an approaching train, the employees are not bound to assume that he will heedlessly leave a place of safety and put himself on the track and in danger. Matteson v. Southern Pac. Co. (Cal. App. 1907), 92 Pac. Rep. 101.

An engineer, seeing a pedestrian approaching a recognized railway crossing, has the right to presume that he will stop before reaching a point of peril patent before him, in the absence of evidence showing that the pedestrian is unmindful of the approaching danger or in such a condition as not to appreciate it, and until the engineer has good reason to believe that the pedestrian will not stop before reaching a point of peril, he is not required to use proper means to prevent injuring him. Sites v. Knott (Mo. 1906), 96 S. W. Rep. 206.

A locomotive engineer has the right to assume that a person ten feet away from the track at a crossing, and not apparently deaf, will hear a whistle blown at a distance of eighty yards. Cox's Adm'r v. Louisville & N. R. Co. (Ky. 1907), 104 S. W. Rep. 282; 31 Ky. Law Rep. 875.

[46] Caldwell v. Kansas City, etc., R. Co., 58 Mo. App. 453; Guyer v.

A railroad company is not liable for striki
and horses of a traveler, upon a highway cr
injury results from accident only and is not du
gence on the part of the employees in charge
or train of cars.[47]   If the accident is due to
of the traveler to control his team, or horse,
any act on the part of the employees in charge
the railroad company is not, generally, held re:
the cause of the accident is not the negligenc
ployees.[48]   If a team can be checked more rea
engine, on approaching the crossing,.it should be
to avoid the collision with the engine, and tho
of the engine should also use due care, to avoid
Neither has the right to be on the crossing at th
and the blame for a collision ought to be visit
one whose want of care is responsible therefor.[4
always essential that an actual collision of the
the team of the traveler should occur to give
action, but if the injury is due to the negligence
road company's employees, although no actual
sults, an action can be maintained.[50]

§ 885. Striking teams that are stalled.— The r

Missouri Pacific Ry. Co., 174 Mo. 344; 73 S. W. Rep. {
etc., R. Co. v. Florens, 32 Ill. App. 365; St. Louis, et
Manley, 58 Ill. 300; Regler v. Charlotte, etc., R. Co., 94 ?
26 Am. & Eng. R. Cas. 386.

[47] Zeigler v. Northeastern R. Co., 5 So. Car. 221.

[48] Barringer v. New York, etc., R. Co., 18 Hun (N. Y.
rule is not followed, in Missouri, by the Kansas City Court
but a frightened horse, which occasioned the injury, 1
excuse the otherwise lack of care, on the part of the tr:
the theory that the negligence of the defendant called int
uncontrolled power of the horse. Mitchell v. St. Louis,
122 Mo. App. 50.

[49] Illinois, etc., R. Co. v. Benton, 69 Ill. 174.

[50] Strong v. Sacramento, etc., R. Co., 61 Cal. 326; 8 /
R. Cas. 273.

engineer has a right to rely upon the assumption that a team
or wagon will be removed from danger, when he sees it on
or near the track, has no application to a case where a knowledge of the fact that a team is stalled, on or near the track,
is acquired by the employees in charge of an engine, in time
to have avoided the injury, by the exercise of reasonable care
on their part. It was accordingly held, in an Illinois case,[51]
that the owner of a team stalled on a track, was entitled
to recover damages for the injury to the team, where the
engineer saw the team in rounding a curve, a sufficient time
to enable him to have stopped the train and avoided the collision, but ran ahead, supposing it would be removed, by the
time the engine reached the team. And in a North Carolina
case,[52] where a portable engine was damaged by a collision
on a highway crossing and the engineer admitted that he
saw the driver of the engine waving his handkerchief a distance of six hundred yards from the crossing and that the
train could have been stopped in three hundred and fifty
yards, but he relied upon the presumption that the engine
would be removed before the crossing was reached, it was
held that the owner of the engine could recover for the injury done to the engine.

But before the railroad company would be liable for an injury to a stalled team at a highway crossing, it must be made
to appear that by reasonable care, after notice of the inability
of the team to leave the crossing, the engine could have been
stopped and the injury avoided.[53] The mere fact that the
engineer, at a distance of a mile or so, from the crossing, saw
a load of logs, to which horses were attached, standing on the
track, at the crossing, would not be sufficient to warn him

[51] Chicago, etc., R. Co. v. Hogarth, 38 Ill. 370; Chicago, etc., R.
Co. v. Gretzner, 46 Ill. 74.
[52] Bullock v. Wilmington, etc., R. Co., 105 No. Car. 180; 10 S. E.
Rep. 988; 42 Am. & Eng. R. Cas. 93.
[53] Frost v. Milwaukee, etc., R. Co., 96 Mich. 470; 56 N. W. Rep. 19.

that the load was fast upon the track, and he would not be called upon to check the speed of the train, until he was signaled to do so, or was near enough to the crossing to ascertain the danger to the team for himself.[54]

§ 886. **Frightening horses at crossings.**— Where an engineer in charge of an engine negligently stops it at a highway crossing and allows steam to be negligently emitted, the railroad company will be liable for injuries resulting from the frightening of a horse which is being lawfully driven along the highway for the purpose of crossing the track.[55]

But it must be borne in mind that the liability of the railroad company depends upon the negligent, or improper manner of handling the engine and not upon the proper handling of the engine, resulting in the frightening of horses on the highway. A railroad company has a right to make such noises as are necessarily incident to the running of its engines, and a person whose horse is injured by such noise while approaching a highway crossing, could not recover damages, unless the unnecessary noise was made by the engine, after the engineer had discovered the horse in a place of danger.[56] The railroad, with a chartered right to propel cars by steam, is not liable for injuries resulting from proper and careful exercise of the power conferred, by use of such an agency, so the liability of the railroad company, for such injuries, depends, primarily, upon the question whether or not the use of such agencies was a proper or an improper use thereof.[57] If the cause of an injury due to the act of the driver in attempting to lead the

[54] Frost v. Milwaukee, etc., R. Co., *supra.*
[55] Louisville, etc., R. Co. v. Schmidt, 8 Am. & Eng. R. Cas. 2
[56] Morgen v. Norfolk Southern R. Co., 98 No. Car. 247.
[57] Philadelphia, etc., R. Co. v. Stinger, 78 Pa. St. 219; Sta Louisville, etc., R. Co., 91 Ala. 382; Steiner v. Philadelphia, Co., 134 Pa. St. 199; 41 Am. & Eng. R. Cas. 535.

across the track, in front of a stationary engine, emitting steam, after the horse is frightened, and not to the act of the engineer, in the improper handling of his engine, of course there is no liability.[58]

The railroad company is generally liable for frightening horses, by leaving engines or cars at crossings, in violation of statutes or ordinances of a city, preventing such practices.[59] Statutes requiring signals at crossings are held, in many cases, to be as much for the protection of those using highways, near the track, as for those intending to cross the track, and for frightening horses, caused by a failure to sound the statutory signals, railroad companies are held liable in many cases.[60]

In other cases, however, such statutes are held to give no right of action for one using a road running parallel with the railroad;[61] one who had tied his team to a hitching post, near a crossing, was held not entitled to claim damages, because of the frightening of his team, due to the failure to sound the statutory signals for the crossing,[62] and it is held that the duty of giving such signals only applies to a train approaching or crossing the highway, and not to a train after having passed the highway crossing.[63]

---

[58] Louisville, etc., R. Co. v. Schmidt, *supra*.

[59] Grimes v. Louisville, etc., R. Co., 3 Ind. App. 573; 30 N. E. Rep. 200; Cleveland, etc., R. Co. v. Wynand, 134 Ind. 681; 34 N. E. Rep. 569; 55 Am. & Eng. R. Cas. 80.

[60] People v. New York, etc., R. Co., 13 N. Y. 78; Wakefield v. Connecticut, etc., R. Co., 37 Vt. 330; Pennsylvania R. Co. v. Barnett, 59 Pa. St. 259; Pollock v. Eastern R. Co., 124 Mass. 158; Texas, etc., R. Co. v. Chapman, 57 Texas 75; Ransom v. Chicago, etc., R. Co., 19 Am. & Eng. R. Cas. 16.

[61] East Tennessee, etc., R. Co. v. Feathers, 10 Lea (Tenn.) 103; 15 Am. & Eng. R. Cas. 446; Flint v. Norwich, etc., R. Co., 110 Mass. 222.

[62] St. Louis, etc., R. Co. v. Payne, 13 Am. & Eng. R. Cas. 632.

[63] Wilson v. Rochester, etc., R. Co., 16 Barb. (N. Y.) 167.
The statute requiring the blowing of a whistle or the ringing of

a bell and the checking of the speed of a train when approaching a public crossing is inapplicable where the injury occurred elsewhere than at a public crossing. Southern Ry. Co. v. Flynt (Ga. App. 1907), 58 S. E. Rep. 374.

It was held that one whose horses were frightened by the running of an engine at a greater speed than that allowed by law, could recover damages, in Chicago, etc., R. Co. v. People, 120 Ill. 667; Grand Trunk R. Co. v. Rosenberg, 9 Can. S. C. 311; 19 Am. & Eng. R. Cas. 8; 15 Am. & Eng. R. Cas. 448.

Horses frightened and injured by running on the track, at a place where the railroad company had failed to fence its track, was held to give a cause of action, in Maher v. Winona, etc., R. Co., 31 Minn. 401; 13 Am. & Eng. R. Cas. 572.

A driver, motioned by a flagman to cross the track in front of an approaching train, whereby his horses were frightened, was held not to be guilty of negligence, as a matter of law, in Buchanan v. Chicago, etc., R. Co., 35 Am. & Eng. R. Cas. 378.

Where an engine approached a crossing without the usual signal, and a driver on an empty wood wagon lost control of the team and was killed by the horses being frightened and dashing in front of the engine, it was held that he was not negligent, as a matter of law. Bates v. New York, etc., R. Co., 60 Conn. 259; 22 Atl. Rep. 538. And see, also, Central, etc., R. Co. v. Hollinshead, 81 Ga. 208; 7 S. E. Rep. 172.

In England, it is held to be negligence to emit steam at a level highway crossing, where teams are waiting to cross. Manchester, etc., R. Co. v. Fullerton, 14 C. B. N. S. 54; 11 W. R. 754.

But whether the railroad company was negligent in emitting steam, in crossing a highway, is held to be a question for the jury, in Lewis v. Eastern R. Co., 40 N. H. 187; Louisville, etc., R. Co. v. Schmidt, 134 Ind. 16; 33 N. E. Rep. 774; 55 Am. & Eng. R. Cas. 128.

It is the duty of those in charge of an engine standing still near a public crossing, over which one has started to drive, to ring the bell before moving the engine and take precautions not to strike him or frighten his horse. Atchison, etc., Ry. Co. v. Wilkie (Kan. 1907), 90 Pac. Rep. 775.

While railroad employees are not required to keep a lookout for teams near the track, they must keep a lookout to see that no one is on a crossing or about to cross, and, on seeing teams near the crossing, should make no unnecessary noise calculated to frighten them, and which might result in injury. Paris & G. N. Ry. Co. v. Calvin (Tex. Civ. App. 1907), 103 S. W. Rep. 428.

Plaintiff was not precluded from recovering from a railway company for injury caused by his horse taking fright at a box car negligently permitted to remain at a street crossing, because he attempted to drive the horse near the car after he saw it had become frightened; it not appearing that he knew it to be dangerous to do so. Ft. Worth, etc., Ry. Co. v. Morris (Tex. Civ. App. 1907), 101 S. W. Rep. 1038.

Where the conditions are such that noises incident to the operation of a railroad train would endanger a person at a crossing, which result could be avoided by temporarily suspending the noise without materially interfering with the operation of the train, ordinary care and prudence require that it be thus suspended till the danger is past. Williams v. Chicago, etc., Ry. Co., 111 N. W. Rep. 596.

To turn on the steam of a locomotive, standing at a public street crossing, without warning and without taking due precautions to discover whether there is any person on or near the crossing liable to be injured in consequence of such act, constitutes actionable negligence in the absence of special circumstances justifying the act. Williams v. Chicago, etc., Ry. Co. (Neb. 1907), 111 N. W. Rep. 596.

A railroad left its engine, under a full head of steam, projecting into a street six to ten feet, for about thirty minutes. The street was thirty-two feet wide. A traveler, while attempting to cross the street in front of the engine, was injured in consequence of his horse becoming frightened by the sudden escape of steam. *Held*, to authorize a finding that the negligent leaving of the engine in the street proximately caused the injury, and that the escape of steam was but an incident, authorizing a recovery. Fay v. Minneapolis, St. P. & M. Ry. Co. (Wis. 1907), 111 N. W. Rep. 683.

In an action against a railway company for personal injuries sustained at a crossing, if the injuries were caused by the fact that plaintiff's horse became frightened and ran into the train, the company is not liable. Cincinnati, etc., Ry. Co. v. Champ, 104 S. W. Rep. 988; 31 Ky. Law Rep. 1054.

A railway company is not legally responsible for producing unusual noises in the running of its locomotives and cars unless such noises are unnecessary. Brunswick & B. R. Co. v. Hoodenpyle (Ga. 1907), 58 S. E. Rep. 705.

Ordinarily a railroad company is not liable for injuries caused by a team taking fright at the noises incident to the ordinary operation of a train on its road. Williams v. Chicago, etc., Ry. Co. (Neb. 1907), 111 N. W. Rep. 596.

Plaintiff's horse, standing near a railroad track, was frightened by the blasts of a whistle sounded by an engine in part obstructing the highway for the purpose of calling in the brakeman. *Held* not negligence on the part of defendant to blow the whistle, and that the injuries resulting from the frightening of the horse were due to an accident without fault of any one. Berry v. Boston & M. R. Co. (Me. 1906), 66 Atl. Rep. 386.

§ 887. **Injuries due to improper appliances on cars.**— As the general traveling public has the same right to use a highway crossing over a railroad track, that the railroad company has, subject to the superior rights of the railroad, owing to the nature of the conveyances used, the interests of the general public and the other considerations above referred to, if the injury of a traveler on the highway is caused by the negligence on the part of the railroad company, in failing to adopt proper appliances to use to stop its trains, an action would accrue to the injured person, the same as if he were not a stranger or third person.[64]

It was accordingly held, in a New York case,[65] that where a traveler on a public road, crossing a railroad track, was injured by the failure of the employees to use the brakes, or owing to the absence of brakes on the car, whereby it was impossible to stop the car in time to avoid the collision, the railroad company was liable.

§ 888. **Two trains operated close together across highway.** — The general traveling public, using a highway crossing, are generally held not to have any right to say how frequently or how often the railroad company can operate its trains across the highway, for this is a matter outside the concern of the traveling public, but inside of the delegated powers of the railroad company.

The rules regulating the distance at which two trains may run on the railroad track, in the same direction, are intended solely for the protection of the employees and passengers of the railroad company and not for the benefit of the travelers upon the highways, hence, no inference of negligence can be drawn from the fact that two trains were run close together across a highway crossing, in an action to

[64] Costello v. Syracuse, etc., R. Co., 65 Barb. (N. Y.) 92; 55 N. Y. 641.
[65] Costello v. Syracuse, etc., R. Co., *supra*.

recover damages to a person for an injury received while using the crossing.[66]

But where one train is run so close behind another, as to make the statutory signals, required at the crossing, unavailing, as a means of warning a traveler on the highway, the railroad company will be held guilty of negligence in this particular, in case of an injury to a traveler on the highway, due to such a cause.[67]

§ 889. **When negligence of railroad company is a jury issue.** — Where there is a substantial conflict in the evidence upon the issue of the negligence of the railroad company in injuring a person at a crossing, it is generally held that the case should be submitted to the jury. Where the issue, for instance, is whether or not the statutory signals were given at the crossing, where the injury occurred, and the plaintiff and his witnesses testified that they had listened for the signals and none were given, while the defendant's witnesses testified that such signals were given, this is a proper case for the jury.[68] It is also held, where the evidence is conflicting as to the distance within which the engine could be stopped, after discovery of the peril to the injured person, to be a proper jury issue, whether or not the engineer or person in charge of the engine exercised due care to stop the same, after the peril was discovered.[69]

And where the issues for determination, in a crossing accident, are the rate of speed at which the engine was being operated, the length of time that warning should have been

[66] Philadelphia, etc., R. Co. v. Spearen, 47 Pa. St. 300.

[67] Chicago, etc., R. Co. v. Boggs, 101 Ind. 522; 51 Am. Rep. 761; 23 Am. & Eng. R. Cas. 282.

[68] Campbell v. New York, etc., R. Co., 49 Hun 611; 121 N. Y. 669.

[69] Swift v. Staten Island R. Co., 24 N. Y. S. R. 359; 52 Hun 614; 123 N. Y. 645; 25 N. E. Rep. 378; Spooner v. Delaware, etc., R. Co., 115 N. Y. 22; 21 N. E. Rep. 696; 41 Hun 643; 39 Am. & Eng. R. Cas. 599.

given, the distance in which the engine, with the appliances at hand, could have been stopped, in the exercise of due care, and the nature of the gates or barriers that should be used, at a crossing used as frequently as the one where the accident occurred, all such issues were held properly submitted to the jury.[70]

[70] Marks v. Fitchburg, etc., R. Co., 155 Mass. 493; 29 N. E. Rep. 1148.

What degree of care is required of a railway company to protect travelers at crossings depends upon the facts of each case and is a question for the jury. Cincinnati & T. P. Ry. Co. v. Champ, 104 S. W. Rep. 988; 31 Ky. Law Rep. 1054.

In an action for injuries at a crossing, where there is a conflict in the evidence as to whether the bell was rung, the question whether failure to ring the bell is negligence is for the jury. Crane v. Pennsylvania R. Co. (Pa. 1907), 67 Atl. Rep. 877.

In an action against a railroad for injuries sustained by plaintiff in a collision at a crossing between the vehicle in which he was riding and defendant's train, held a question for the jury whether the horse and vehicle were on the crossing, and the dangerous situation of plaintiff was or could have been discovered by the engineer when the engine first came in view, so as to have been stopped in time to prevent the collision, or whether when first seen by the engineer, the horse was standing near the crossing apparently under the control of the driver, and continued in that position until it was too late for the train to be stopped. Baker v. Norfolk & S. R. Co. (N. C. 1907), 56 S. E. Rep. 553.

In an action for injuries at a railroad crossing, questions of negligence of defendant and contributory negligence of plaintiff are for the jury. Graves v. Baltimore & N. Y. Ry. Co. (N. J. Sup. 1908), 69 Atl. Rep. 971.

Whether defendant railroad company, or its engineer, who was made a codefendant, was negligent in running its train, and whether such negligence was the proximate cause of plaintiff's injuries, were questions for the jury, so it was not error to refuse to charge that before plaintiff could recover it must be made to appear that the injury was inflicted by the willful conduct of the defendants. Southern Ry. Co. v. Reynolds (Ga. 1906), 55 S. E. Rep. 1039.

Whether decedent's failure to stop, look, and listen before attempting to cross the defendant's railroad track was the proximate cause of his death, held, under the evidence, a question for the jury. Central of Georgia Ry. Co. v. Hyatt (Ala. 1907), 43 So. Rep. 867.

Where, in an action for injuries caused by collision with a railway train at a highway crossing, the evidence was conflicting as to .whether the statutory signals were given by the company, the question was for the jury. Fitzhugh v. Boston & M. R. (Mass. 1907), 80 N. E. Rep. 792.

CHAPTER XXXVIII.

§ 890. **Liability for defective under-crossings.**— Where a railroad company either itself constructs a subway or under-crossing at a public highway, under its track, which crosses such highway on a bridge or trestle, or authorizes the construction of such a crossing, there is no reason why it should not maintain the same in a reasonably safe condition for the use of the traveling public, unless this duty is otherwise devolved by law, upon another, the same as if it had authorized or constructed the crossing of its track at grade.[1]

The duty would be the same, as to those rightfully using the premises, for the duty owing a licensee, with a right to use the premises would be the same, whether the place was at a grade crossing with the track, or below the track, except

[1] People v. New York Central R. Co., 13 N. Y. 78.

1320

as the difference in the degree of danger would affect the duty of the railroad company.

But where a railroad company constructed its track on a trestle over and along a public highway and the road commissioners changed the highway so as to run it under the trestle, without notice to the railroad company, as required by statute, to render it liable for the construction or cost of a crossing over its track, there would be no duty on the part of the railroad company to maintain or repair such a crossing and for an injury to a traveler on the highway at such an under-crossing of the railroad track, due to a defective condition of the crossing, there would be no liability.[2]

[2] Hill v. Port Royal, etc., R. Co., 31 So. Car. 393; 10 S. E. Rep. 91; 39 Am. & Eng. R. Cas. 607; 5 L. R. A. 349.

Where a road under a railroad bridge was continually and habitually used by the public, and that fact was or could by the use of ordinary care have been known by the railroad company, it owed a duty to keep the road safe, to a person using the road, regardless of whether it was a public highway or not. Missouri, etc., Ry. Co. v. Hollan, 107 S. W. Rep. 642.

One traveling on a road under a railroad bridge, commonly and habitually used by the public, with the knowledge of the railroad company is more than a licensee, and the company owes him the duty of ordinary care. Missouri, etc., Ry. Co. v. Hollan (Tex. Civ. App. 1908), 107 S. W. Rep. 642.

Where a railroad charter (P. L. 1832, p. 104, § 20), required the company to construct and keep in repair good and sufficient bridges or passages over or under the railroad where any public or other road should cross the same, the railroad company was not bound to maintain the highway under its overhead crossing in a proper state of repair. Borough of Metuchen v. Pennsylvania R. Co., 64 Atl. Rep. 484.

Where a railroad company prepared a plan for the alteration of a highway under an overhead crossing, narrowed the roadway by the construction of abutments located in the highway, and failed to properly provide for the draining thereof, the railroad company was bound to make such alterations therein as to displace the abutments from within the lines of the highway, and to properly drain the cul-de-sac formed under the bridge. Borough of Metuchen v. Pennsylvania R. Co. (N. J. Ch. 1906), 64 Atl. Rep. 484.

§ 891. **No warning necessary at overhead crossings —
Massachusetts rule.**— The reasons for the distinction requiring a warning to the public at grade and overhead crossings
was considered in a Massachusetts case, where the court used
the following language: " Where a railroad crosses a highway at grade, the law imposes upon it the duty of giving
notice to travelers of the approach of its trains.   This rule
applies, because at grade crossings the traveler on the highway and the railroad enjoy a common privilege on the highway itself and each must use such privilege with due regard
to the rights of the other.   And as a train of cars is a dangerous power, when in motion and capable of doing great
injury, a high degree of care is demanded of the railroad
in controlling it and some notice of its approach to the highway is required both by the rules of the common law and
by statute.   But where a railroad crosses a highway by a
bridge, it does not, in common with the traveler, have any
privilege in, or use of the highway itself.   Though the
track and the highway are near and adjacent to each other,
they are entirely distinct and separate.   The railroad has
no rights in the highway and consequently the same duties
are not imposed upon it that are imposed when it passes
over the highway itself in common with the traveler.   It
has the right to use its roadbed and bridge as a railroad may
use them — by running its trains at the common rate of
speed, accompanied by the usual noises attendant upon such
exercise of its right.   It is not bound, by law, to notify
the traveler of its intention to use its bridge in the ordinary
and usual manner." [8]

§ 892. **No duty to give warning at overhead crossing, in
Wisconsin.**— The Wisconsin Supreme Court has also considered the duty of the railroad company, to give notice

[8] Favor v. Boston, etc., R. Co., 114 Mass. 350; 19 Am. Rep. 364.

of the crossing of trains above streets and highways and held that no such duty existed, independently of statute, in that State. In the course of its opinion on this subject, the court said: "There is no statute and we are aware of no common-law rule, which, under such circumstances, requires railroad companies to observe these precautions to avoid accidents. If, therefore, the defendant is liable in this action, it is so because it failed to comply with the requirement of the statute prescribing its duty when its train approached the crossing of the highway." [4]

§ 893. **The reasons for the distinction considered.**— Among the well-considered authorities which hold that it is not essential, in the absence of a specific statutory provision, for railroad companies to give notice of the approach of trains, at overhead crossings, it may be well to notice another decision, which goes into the reasons for the rule. It is as follows: "It is certainly no wrong for the train to be run over such bridges in the usual and ordinary way, and even in this way, some horses going under the bridge, or being near it at the same time might be frightened by it. The train must necessarily make considerable noise going over the bridge. They can not be run without it. It is not by any means certain that a train would make less noise going over slowly, than faster. What degree of noise, must it make, to frighten horses? * * * As to ringing the bell and blowing the whistle, they are only required, if at all, in order to avoid frightening horses, and, with that view, to warn the traveler on the highway to stop. Where should he stop and how near the bridge? If near the bridge and his

---

[4] Ranson v. Chicago Ry. Co., 62 Wis. 178; 22 N. W. Rep. 147; 51 Am. Rep. 718. This case is followed and approved, in Jensen v. Chicago, etc., R. Co., 86 Wis. 589; 57 N. W. Rep. 359; 22 L. R. A. 680; and in Barron v. Wisconsin, etc., R. Co., 89 Wis. 79; 61 N. W. Rep. 303.

horse is liable to be frightened, he would be in a much more dangerous condition than if he should drive on and take his chances, for the horse, facing the train rushing over the bridge, would turn suddenly around, to escape danger and upset the carriage." [5]

§ 894. **Same — The rule in Pennsylvania.**— In a well-considered Pennsylvania case, it appeared that the plaintiffs were driving under the defendant's railroad crossing, upon a public street, when a train crossing overhead frightened their horse so that it became unmanageable and ran away, inflicting serious personal injuries and resulting in the death of one of the children. The court held that there was no liability in the case and in the course of its opinion said: " The defendant company was operating its road in a lawful manner. No defect was shown in the construction of the road. On the contrary, it was the work of competent engineers, approved by the chief engineer and surveyor of the city, and in pursuance of an ordinance of councils, expressly authorizing it. The sight and sound of a moving train always have a tendency to frighten horses. In this case the fright was occasioned by sound. We cannot measure, nor can a jury be properly allowed to measure, the amount of sound which may be made by a railroad train either in crossing bridges at overhead crossings, or at other places. The defendant road, under all the authorities, has the right to operate its road in a lawful manner; and, when it does so without negligence, and without malice, is not responsible for injuries occasioned thereby." [6]

§ 895. **A contrary doctrine recognized in Pennsylvania.**— By an earlier decision than that above referred to, in Penn-

[5] Jensen v. Chicago, etc., R. R. Co., 57 N. W. Rep. 359; 22 L. R. A. 680.

[6] Ryan v. Pennsylvania R. Co., 132 Pa. St. 304; 19 Atl. Rep. 81.

sylvania, a contrary rule was established in that State and it was held to be as much the duty of a railroad company to give notice of the approach of its trains at an overhead crossing as it was to give such notice at a grade crossing, if the crossing in each case was dangerous.[7]

The facts were that the public road crossed the bridge at a distance of nineteen feet above the track and the plaintiff while traveling over this bridge was injured as a result of a frightened horse, which took fright from the whistle of a passenger train that sounded the whistle, when directly under the horse.

In disposing of the case the court said: "The degree of care demanded of the company, in running its train, depended on circumstances, and whether it observed due care, in approaching the bridge, or was guilty of negligence in not sounding the whistle, was a question which properly belonged to the jury to decide. * * * If there was no danger to the persons and property of those who might be traveling along the public road, in running its trains, without giving any notice of their approach to the bridge, then the company is not chargeable with negligence, in not giving it. But if the danger might be reasonably apprehended, it was the duty of the company to give some notice, or warning, in order that it might be avoided."

It will be observed that the court held, in this case, that the question of the duty of the company to give notice of the approach of a train to a public crossing, was the same whether the crossing was on grade, or over or under the public road crossing, and in all such cases it was a matter for the jury to determine.

The effect of this decision is very much impaired, if not the law of the case, as therein announced, overruled, in a later case, by the same court, wherein the above decision is

[7] Pennsylvania R. Co. v. Barnett, 59 Pa. St. 259; 98 Am. Dec. 346.

distinguished and it is denied that the same rule of liability or duty extends to warnings at public road crossings,
where the road is either above or below the railroad, or on
the grade crossing with it.[8]

§ 896. **The contrary view — Cases holding warning at overhead crossing necessary.**— The above rule, exempting railroads
from the duty of giving warning of the approach of trains
at crossings, where the trains cross the highway overhead
instead of on grade, is not applied without exception and in
some of the best-considered cases, which have come to our
attention, it is held that the company must give warning at
overhead crossings, of the approach of trains the same as
at grade crossings.

The reason for this view of the company's duty is said
to be based upon the known or reasonably to be apprehended
danger from a failure to give notice of the approach of
trains, at a place where the approach of trains cannot be
seen. Or, to express it in the language of the court:
"Where the view of an approaching train is obstructed,
though the company is not required by the statute to sound
a whistle, or ring a bell, when its train approaches a highway, yet, where such appliances are available, the failure
to use them is negligence." [9]

But this rule is not followed in a later Illinois case,[10]
where the same court holds that there is no duty to give
warning of the approach of a train or engine to a highway
crossing, under a railroad bridge, but that the statute applied only to grade crossings.

[8] Farley v. Harris, 40 Atl. Rep. 798.

[9] Chicago & A. R. Co. v. Dillon, 123 Ill. 750; 15 N. E. Rep. 181;
5 Am. St. Rep. 559; Pennsylvania R. Co. v. Krick, 47 Ind. 386;
Winstanley v. Chicago, M. & St. P. R. Co., 72 Wis. 375; 39 N. W.
Rep. 856; Indianapolis R. Co. v. Hamilton, 44 Ind. 76.

[10] Cleveland, etc., R. Co. v. Halbert, 179 Ill. 196; 53 N. E. Rep. 623,
reversing 75 Ill. App. 592.

§ 897. Signals required at overhead crossings in California.
— The Supreme Court of California, in a recent decision,[11] construed the statute of that State, requiring railroad companies to give warning by bell or whistle on approaching any "street, road or highway," and held that this statute applied to an overhead bridge crossing of a highway by a railroad track, and for an injury resulting from a failure to give such warning, the railroad company was held liable.

In considering the contention that the statute did not apply to a highway crossing under the track, Lorigan, J., for the court, said: "The duty is enjoined upon the railroad to signal at a prescribed distance from 'where the railroad crosses any street, road or highway.' This is broad enough to apply at any crossing of a highway by a railroad, whether it is super, sub, or level grade. Nothing is said in the section about signaling only when the railroad crosses a highway at level grade. Nor is there anything in the section which would warrant so construing it. In fact, the language is so plain as not to be subject to construction at all. If the legislature had intended that the railroad should only give signals when crossing highways at grade, it would, as has been done in other States, have readily and clearly expressed that intention." [12]

§ 898. Warnings necessary in New York.— The rule above stated, which requires notice at overhead crossings is held to obtain in New York, under the statute of that State. The statute prescribes a penalty for running a locomotive or train of cars past a highway crossing, without giving a signal, and this is held, by an early case, to apply to an overhead crossing on a bridge.[13]

[11] Johnson v. Southern Pacific R. Co., 1 L. R. A. (N. S.) 307.

[12] The editor, in the footnote to the above decision, as annotated in 1 L. R. A. (N. S.) 307, points out the error of the court in this case, with reference to the other statutes referred to.

[13] People v. N. Y. Cent. R. Co., 13 N. Y. 78, affirming 25 Barb. 199.

§ 899. **Warning required in Kentucky.**— Th
nized in the Massachusetts and Pennsylvania
pressly repudiated in Kentucky, where the cou:
there is the same duty and liability resulting fr
to give a warning of the approach of a train at
crossing, that there is at a grade crossing.

In a Kentucky case, where the question was c
lady was thrown from her horse, which was fr
the noise of a train, on an overhead trestle.   Th
averred was the failure of the company to give r
approach of the train to the crossing.   The cou:
when a train crossed a highway on a trestle and
danger of catching a traveler on the crossing un
frightening his horse, it was necessary to give a
tice by sounding the whistle, of the approach of si

§ 900. **Warning required under Ohio statute.**—
Ohio statute, it has been held that the railroad
whose track crosses a highway on a bridge over th
must give the statutory signals, or it will be liab
of an injury to a traveler on the highway, injure
sult of such failure.

The statute provided for the giving of such s
the engine, when " approaching a turnpike, highwa:
road crossing, upon the same level therewith, an
manner, when the road crosses any other traveled
bridge or otherwise." Of course this statute was
with the evident object of requiring signals at all
crossings and the court so construed it, although
struction adopted was not so much upon the specific
of the act being construed, as the object of the statu
was held to be to prevent accidents and the construc
tended for would be too narrow in its results.[15]

[14] Rupard v. Chesapeake & Ohio R. Co., 88 Ky. 280; 11 S
70; 7 L. R. A. 316.
[15] Toledo, etc., R. Co. v. Jump, 50 Ohio St. 651; 35 N. E. 1

901. The rule followed in Tennessee.— In a well-consid-
ennessee case, the liability of a company for frighten-
rse plaintiff was driving under a trestle, from a train
assing over the trestle, was considered and the com-
s held to the duty of establishing that it was not
to give a warning, and the matter was left to the
tion of the jury to determine, under all the facts
nstances, whether or not a warning ought to have
n. The court, on this question, said: "The law
absolute duty upon the company to give notice
ticular crossing. The duty was only required, as
law, in the event the jury should find that danger
reasonably apprehended at this conjunction of un-
d overhead bridge." And because the trial court
the absolute duty, by its instructions to the jury,
efendant, to give warning at this particular cross-
d of submitting this issue to the consideration of
under all the facts and circumstances in the case,
dgment of the trial court was reversed.[16]

902. Failure to stop, look, or listen, in approaching.— The
ty of a traveler upon a public highway, in approaching a
blic crossing, on a railroad track, where such highway
s under the track of the railroad, to stop, look or listen
or an approaching train, before driving under such track,
on the highway, has recently been under consideration by
the Iowa Supreme Court,[17] and the duty is held not to ob-

[16] Louisville & Nashville R. Co. v. Sawyer, 86 S. W. Rep. 386.
In Tennessee, a statute requiring ringing of bell, or sounding of whistle, on trains approaching crossings, was held not to apply to an overhead crossing on a bridge, as no duty existed to give such warning, unless the place was otherwise dangerous. Louisville & N. Co. v. Sawyer, 86 S. W. Rep. 386.
[17] Heinmiller v. Winston, 107 N. W. Rep. 1102; 6 L. R. A. (N. S.) 150. The plaintiff in this case was a female and this may have

II—32

tain to such a highway crossing as a matter of l;
a traveler on the highway who did not stop, or l(
for a train before approaching such a crossi
guilty of negligence as matter of law. The re;
duty in the case of a grade crossing is held n
to an under-crossing of the railroad track.

In a Kentucky case,[18] it was recently held tha
familiar with a crossing under a railroad track,
built over the highway on a trestle, who appi
crossing without adopting the precaution of s;
looking or listening for an approaching train, w;
negligence as matter of law, precluding a recov
injury so received. And a Pennsylvania [19] ar
case,[20] seem to proceed upon the theory that the r
to a traveler approaching such a crossing.

As the danger to travelers upon the highway rest
the frightening of horses, is just as great in the (
in the other and the rule denying a recovery in su
based upon the want of proper care to avoid such
it would seem, upon reason, that the rule should
the one case as well as in the other.

influenced the court to mollify a rule which would seen
harsh, when applied to such a litigant.

[18] Rupard v. Chesapeake, etc., R. Co., 88 Ky. 280; 7 L.
[19] Pennsylvania R. Co. v. Barnett, 59 Pa. St. 259; 98 An
[20] Cincinnati, etc., R. Co. v. Gaines, 104 Ind. 526; 4 N.]
54 Am. Rep. 334.

CHAPTER XXXIX.

INJURIES AT DEFECTIVE CROSSINGS.

§ 903. **Duty of railroad company in maintenance of crossings.** — It is the duty of a railroad company, irrespective of statute, and upon common-law principles, to keep its road at a crossing of a highway, in a reasonably safe condition for public travel, so that a traveler on the highway, exercising ordinary care, can pass over it, in safety,[1] and for the negligent breach of this duty the railroad company must answer in damages to one who exercises ordinary care and sustains an injury from the breach of this duty by the company.[2]

[1] Gale v. New York, etc., R. Co., 76 N. Y. 594; 13 Hun 1; Cott v. Lewiston R. Co., 36 N. Y. 214; Moberly v. Kansas City, etc., R. Co., 17 Mo. App. 518; Independence v. Missouri Pacific Ry. Co., 86 Mo. App. 585.

[2] Mann v. Central Vermont R. Co., 55 Vt. 484; 45 Am. Rep. 628; 14 Am. & Eng. R. Cas. 620; Terre Haute, etc., R. Co. v. Clem, 123 Ind. 15; 23 N. E. Rep. 965; 42 Am. & Eng. R. Cas. 229; 7 L. R. A. 588.

1331

But the presumption of negligence which ol
case of an injury to a passenger, does not obtaii
of an injury to a traveler on the public highwa
railroad crossing;[3] the railroad company is oi
proof that it knowingly permitted the crossing 1
bad repair, as a result of which a traveler sustai
and. a railroad is not liable as a result of a hig
ing being out of repair, unless it had notice of s
the defect had existed for a length of time sufficie
it with notice, in law.[5]

§ 904. **Obligation extends to approaches.**— The
to a railroad crossing over a public highway are se
of the crossing proper and so essential for the
public, that the duty of maintaining the road
a safe condition for the use of the traveling pub
to extend to the approaches to the crossing, as
the crossing over the track itself, and for an inji

[3] Terre Haute, etc., R. Co. v. Clem, *supra*.
[4] Pittsburg, etc., R. Co. v. Dunn, 56 Pa. St. 280.
[5] Mann v. Chicago, etc., R. Co., 86 Mo. 347.
Where the travel does not demand it, however, there is
construct the crossing the entire width of the highwa,
Wabash R. Co., 17 Mo. App. 126.
When a grade crossing is authorized by the State, neith
road, as charged with the maintenance of the railroad hi
the town or other corporation, as charged with the mainten
carriage highway, is responsible for the dangers resulting
such a construction of the two highways. The only duty
travelers is the statutory duty of maintaining in a safe co
highway as established. Cowles v. New York & H. R. (
1907), 66 Atl. Rep. 1020, 1024; Keagy v. Same, *id.* 1024.
That an iron spike was permitted to protrude above the
a railroad highway crossing, on which spike horses would
to stumble or strike their feet while traveling over the cro
dered the crossing unsafe and constituted a breach of the
duty to keep the crossing in repair. Louisville & N. R. C(
bard (Ala. 1906), 41 So. Rep. 814.

1332

an unsafe condition of the approaches to a crossing, the railroad company will be liable, the same as if the injury occurred upon the crossing proper, over its tracks.[6]

Where the crossing is approached on a bridge, leading up to the cross-ties of the railroad track, the railroad company is required to maintain the bridge in repair, to the same extent that it would be to maintain any other approach to the track and road crossing in repair.[7] And if a bridge leading up to the crossing of a railroad track is permitted to get in bad repair, as where a hole is allowed to remain in the bridge, so that the horse of a traveler on the highway is apt to fall into the hole, in case of an injury from such a cause, the railroad company would be liable to the party sustaining the injury.[8]

[6] Failure of plaintiff, in an action against a railroad company for injury from defendant's omission to keep in repair an approach to its tracks at a public road crossing, to prove the averment of the complaint that defendant constructed the approach, is immaterial, it being defendant's duty to keep it in repair without regard to who constructed it. Southern Ry. Co. v. Morris (Ala. 1906), 42 So. Rep. 19.

[7] A bridge which runs up to the cross-ties of a railroad at a public road crossing is such an approach as the railroad company is required to keep in repair. Southern Ry. Co. v. Morris (Ala. 1906), 42 So. Rep. 19.

[8] In an action against a railroad company for injuries to plaintiff through stepping into a hole in a bridge built by defendant over a ditch on its right of way at a highway crossing, the petition alleged the existence of the highway before the construction of the railroad; that the ditch was cut at the time the railroad was built; that the bridge was constructed for the use of the public; that it was defendant's duty to restore the highway to the condition it was in before the building of the railroad or to such state as not to unnecessarily impair its usefulness, and to keep it in repair and safe condition; and that defendant failed so to do. Held that, fairly construed, the petition was not subject to the criticism that it failed to allege that when defendant constructed its road across the highway it failed to restore it to its former state, or to such state as not to unnecessarily impair its usefulness, and failed to allege that the bridge was any part of the crossing, and hence an instruction that a railroad company had the right to construct its road across any highway, but

§ 905. Liability to municipality for failure to maintain.— A railroad company which so constructs its track at the crossing of a highway as to render the highway dangerous to travelers thereon, is not only liable for an injury sustained by a traveler thereon, in consequence of the defective crossing — although he might also have a remedy against the town which was bound to keep the highway in repair [9]— but the municipality may recover against the railroad company such damages as it may be compelled to pay, by reason of the defect in the crossing, caused by the negligence of the railroad company in the construction and maintenance of its tracks thereon.[10]

And although the liability of a railroad company, for the construction of road crossings, at public highways, is imposed by statute subsequent to the grant of the charter to the railroad company, as this is a reasonable provision, based upon the police power of the State, if the railroad company subsequently fails to construct reasonably safe crossings at public streets, or to safeguard the use of its tracks, as the statute requires, and an injury to a traveler results, in consequence of its failure so to do, a municipality, rendered liable for such negligence on its part, was held entitled, in Vermont, to recover the amount of the damages it had to pay, because of such neglect of the railroad company.[11]

it is its duty to restore the highway to its former state, or to such state as not to unnecessarily impair its usefulness and to keep the crossing in repair, was warranted. St. Louis Southwestern Ry. Co. v. Smith (Tex. Civ. App. 1908), 107 S. W. Rep. 638.

When a public road or highway crosses a railroad track, the railroad company is bound to keep the approaches and the crossing in proper repair for the use of the traveling public. Louisville & N. R. Co. v. Hubbard (Ala. 1906), 41 So. Rep. 814.

[9] Gillett v. Western R. Corp., 8 Allen (Mass.) 560.

[10] Portland v. Atlantic, etc., R. Co., 66 Me. 485.

[11] Roxbury v. Central Vermont R. Co., 60 Vt. 121; 14 Atl. Rep. 92. See, also, Scanlon v. Boston, etc., R. Co., 140 Mass. 84; 2 N. E. Rep. 787.

§ 906. **When turnpike company liable for.**— Where a railroad company and a turnpike company have their respective routes located, by the charter of each company, over and across the same ground, but the charter of the railroad company is prior in point of time and hence its rights first attach to the land, although both are constructed at the same time, the turnpike company would be responsible for an injury to a traveler on the turnpike, at the railroad crossing, because of injuries due to the absence of a railing at the railroad crossing, or other safeguards, to prevent injury to travelers on the turnpike, as the duty and negligence resulting from the breach of such duty is that of the turnpike company and not of the railroad company.[12]

§ 907. **Defective under-crossing — When company not liable.**— While it may be stated, both upon reason and authority, that the liability of a railroad company for an injury due to a defective under-crossing of a public highway, which it has authorized and constructed, would not be different from that obtaining in the case of a grade or surface crossing,[13] this rule does not apply to a crossing constructed by highway commissioners, without the proper statutory notice for the construction of such crossing, and for a defective under-crossing constructed by such highway commissioners, causing injury to a traveler on such highway, the railroad company would not be liable.[14]

In a South Carolina case,[15] the railroad had built its line over and along a public road on a trestle, and the county road commissioners, without notice to the company, opened a new way under the trestle for a considerable distance

12 Zuccarello v. Nashville, etc., R. Co., 3 Baxt. (Tenn.) 364.

13 People v. New York Central R. Co., 13 N. Y. 78.

14 Hill v. Port Royal, etc., R. Co., 31 So. Car. 393; 10 S. E. Rep. 91; 39 Am. & Eng. R. Cas. 607; 5 L. R. A. 349.

15 Hill v. Port Royal, etc., R. Co., *supra.*

and changed the road to a different angle than the angle it
had formerly been laid out on. The plaintiff was injured
while driving on this new road, but it was held that the
railroad company was not liable for the injury.

§ 908. **Duty as to private crossings.**— The obligation of
railroad companies to construct crossings over its tracks, at
highway crossings, independently of statute, applies only to
public highways, opened or constructed according to law
and not to private crossings, used merely for the convenience
of the adjoining landowners, along the railroad right of
way.[16] The public use of a footway, by the acquiescence
of the railroad company, would not devolve on the railroad
company the duty of maintaining it as a public crossing, or
of keeping it open or unobstructed, for the use of those who
had thus pre-empted its right of way.[17]

But by statute in many States, railroad companies are
required to maintain not only public highways, but also
private road crossings, where necessary to enable adjoining
landowners to reach different portions of their land, or to
have an exit to a highway and where such necessity exists,
if the railroad company fails to comply with such a statute,
it would be liable to the party entitled to the maintenance
of the private way,[18] although not to one who used it for
his own convenience, without some right so to do.[19] And
it is held, in a Texas case,[20] that the railroad company would

[16] St. Louis, etc., R. Co. v. Gordon, 157 Mo. 71; 57 S. W. Rep. 742.
[17] Gurley v. Missouri Pacific Ry. Co., 104 Mo. 211; 16 S. W. Rep.
11; Berry v. Northeastern R. Co., 72 Ga. 137; 28 Am. & Eng. R.
Cas. 575.
[18] Berry v. Northeastern R. Co., *supra.*
[19] Mann v. Chicago, etc., R. Co., 86 Mo. 347.
[20] Missouri Pacific Ry. Co. v. Bridges, 74 Texas 520; 12 S. W.
Rep. 210; 39 Am. & Eng. R. Cas. 604.
In Lowenstein v. Missouri Pacific Ry. Co. (110 Mo. App. 689; 117
Mo. App. 371), plaintiff was injured while hauling hay to a private

be responsible for an injury to one received at other than a regularly established public road crossing, where it had maintained the crossing, knowing that it was in common use by the public.

§ 909. **Liability for defective or obstructed crossings.**— If a railroad company, whose tracks cross a regularly established public highway, negligently permits the crossing to become dangerous and unsafe for public travel by wheeled vehicles it will be liable for damages to a person using the crossing, while in the exercise of due care to avoid injury.[21] The liability extends not only to the crossing proper, but for any defects in the approaches,[22] or railings to the crossing, where they are required by statute;[23] the railroad company would be liable to one sustaining injury while using the crossing, on account of such neglect, whether the defect was caused by any act of the company or not, since the obligation to maintain the crossing in a safe condition is imposed upon it and it would be liable, if the defect had existed for a length of time sufficient to impart notice to it, in law.[24]

It is also held to be negligence sufficient to render a company liable for an injury, due to this cause, to allow brush or weeds, or other obstruction to remain, which will exclude the view of a railroad track, at a public crossing.[25]

hay barn, on the defendant's right of way. His action was predicated upon a right to use a private crossing, in hauling hay to one of the defendant's cars. Of course this business status, had it existed, would have amounted to an invitation to use the crossing, but as it was not shown, he was a mere licensee and no duty was due to him, with respect to maintaining a safe crossing, according to the authorities, but he assumed the risk of using the dangerous crossing, in law. See chapter, Injuries to Licensees.

[21] Tetherow v. St. Joseph, etc., R. Co., 98 Mo. 74; 11 S. W. Rep. 310.

[22] Maltby v. Chicago, etc., R. Co., 52 Mich. 108; 17 N. W. Rep. 717; 13 Am. & Eng. R. Cas. 606.

[23] Kyne v. Wilmington, etc., R. Co. (Del.), 14 Atl. Rep. 922.

[24] Oakland R. Co. v. Fielding, 48 Pa. St. 320.

[25] Indianapolis, etc., R. Co. v. Smith, 78 Ill. 112.

But even where the specific duty is imposed upon the railroad company by statute to maintain the crossing in some particular so as to be safe for the public, it is always competent for it to establish, as a defense, that this act of negligence did not occasion the injury sued for, but that it resulted from some other cause, such as the want of care of the injured person,[26] and if, at the time of an injury to the plaintiff, it appeared that the leaves were all off the trees growing on the right of way, so that no obstruction resulted in this particular, it would be error to predicate a right of recovery upon this ground of negligence.[27]   And, in any event, before the railroad company could be held guilty of negligence in allowing its right of way to be obstructed, by piling dirt from a cut along the track, or permitting weeds to grow, it would be essential to show that such obstruction would necessarily obstruct the view of a public crossing, or that it violated some other specific duty owing to the party who complained of such obstruction.[28]

[26] McKelvy v. Burlington, etc., R. Co., 84 Iowa 455; 51 N. W. Rep. 172; 49 Am. & Eng. R. Cas. 477.

[27] International, etc., R. Co. v. Kuehn, 70 Texas 582; 8 S. W. Rep. 484; 35 Am. & Eng. R. Cas. 421.

[28] Atchison, etc., R. Co. v. Parsons, 42 Ill. App. 93.

In an action for injuries to plaintiff's intestate received at a railway crossing, where it was shown that a pile of dirt obstructed the view of the tracks from the crossing, it was not error to refuse to instruct that it was the duty of intestate to exercise care commensurate with the increased danger, where it had already instructed that it was her duty to look and listen before going upon the track. Chesapeake, etc., Ry. Co. v. Wilson's Adm'r (Ky. 1907), 102 S. W. Rep. 810.

Where by leaving cars on a public crossing a railway company has obstructed the view and created an extra danger to travelers, it is bound in approaching the crossing to use extra precautions, as by less speed or increased warnings, and the fact that the crossing was on the yards of the company makes no difference. Cherry v. Louisiana, etc., Ry. Co. (La. 1908), 46 So. Rep. 596.

The mere fact that defendant railroad's train was standing across a public street and obstructing the same, so that plaintiff was obliged

§ 910. **Neglect of statutory duty regarding.**— Whenever the statute of a State in which a railroad is being operated, compels it to construct road crossings over its tracks in certain specified particulars, and it fails to do so, in case of an injury to a traveler owing to such defect in the crossing, the railroad company is generally held to be liable in damages.

The Massachusetts statute,[29] required the railroad company to " so guard and protect its rails by plank, timber, or otherwise, as to secure a safe and easy passage across its road," and this was held to impose a duty on the railroad company to plank the distance between the two tracks, in such a manner as to avoid injury to the public, and for a failure so to do, the company would be liable.[30]

Likewise, the Missouri statute,[31] requiring planks along the rails, of certain dimensions, for a distance of sixteen feet, on public roads and twenty-four feet on city streets, and prescribing other requisites for public road crossings, was held to impose the duty to put down such planking on the part of the road that was generally used by the traveling public and for a failure to place it on such portion of the road, or to maintain it in a reasonably safe condition, the railroad company would be liable, in case of an injury to a traveler from this cause.[32]

---

to. turn the runaway horse he was driving out into an alley before reaching the train, in doing which his vehicle was overturned and he was injured, did not of itself constitute negligence. Duffy v. Atlantic, etc., R. Co. (N. C. 1907), 56 S. E. Rep. 557.

A town ordinance prohibiting the blocking of street crossings by railroad companies beyond a specified time is admissible in evidence, where it is claimed that a violation of such ordinance, in connection with other acts of negligence, was the cause of the death of petitioner's decedent. Southern Ry. Co. v. Mouchet (Ga. App. 1907), 59 S. E. Rep. 927.

[29] Pub. St. Mass. ch. 112, § 124.

[30] Scanlon v. Boston, etc., R. Co., 140 Mass. 84; 2 N. E. Rep. 787.

[31] Rev. St. Mo. 1899, § 1103.

[32] Hogue v. Chicago, etc., R. Co., 32 Fed. Rep. 365.

But before a railroad company would be liable fo
injury to a traveler on a public road crossing, because
failure of such crossing to come up to the statutory req
ments, it would be necessary to show either actual or
structive notice of the failure of the crossing to com
to the statutory requirement, and a failure to repair it,
having such notice.[33]   The railroad company would n
liable for an injury to a traveler, due to other causes
that the company had failed to comply with the statu
the manner of constructing or repairing the crossing;[3]
if the defect in the crossing was due to the act of the
commissioners and not to that of the railroad compar
where the road was changed, without notice to it, an
under a narrow span of a railroad bridge, and the pl;
was injured by his buggy striking the pier or span (
bridge, there would ordinarily be no liability on the
of the railroad company.[35]

§ 911. **Raising track above street.**— In a Wisconsin
the evidence established that the railroad compan}
during the day preceding the injury to the plaintiff,
its track above the highway and had only thrown som
dirt on either side of the tracks, which would requ;
wheels of conveyances using the crossing to make a
some eight to ten inches.   The plaintiff, the following

[33] Nixon v. Hannibal, etc., R. Co., 141 Mo. 425; 42 S. W. F
[34] McKelvy v. Burlington, etc., R. Co., 84 Iowa 654; 51
Rep. 172.
[35] Hill v. Port Royal, etc., R. Co., 31 So. Car. 393; 10 S.
91; 39 Am. & Eng. R. Cas. 607; 5 L. R. A. 349.
Under Rev. St. 1895, art. 4426, requiring railroad companie;
highway crossings in repair, the failure of a railroad con
keep a highway crossing in repair is negligence *per se.*   £
Southwestern Ry. Co. v. Smith (Tex. Civ. App. 1908), 107 S.
638.
[36] Milwaukee, etc., R. Co. v. Hunter, 11 Wis. 160.

with a loaded wagon, tried to pass over the crossing and was so impeded, by reason of the new dirt on the crossing, that his team was unable to pull the load, and while stalled on the crossing a collision with an engine, which approached the crossing without signal, resulted, occasioning the injuries sued for. It was held that the plaintiff had a right to recover damages.

A similar holding was announced in a recent case in the Court of Appeals, in Missouri,[37] where the facts developed that the plaintiff, when injured, was engaged in hauling baled hay across a private crossing, approaching a railroad freight yard. The crossing plank had been removed after he had passed over the crossing in the morning and the track raised and filled in with soft ballast. He approached the crossing, sitting astride the top bale of his load of hay and the wheels struck the track on an angle and he was thrown off his load, by the wheels sinking into the soft gravel. The court held that it was a jury issue whether or not he used due care in approaching the crossing.

§ 912. **Failure to light obstructed crossing at night.**— In a Missouri case,[38] a railroad company, by permission of the city authorities of St. Louis, after repairing its railroad track, at the crossing of a much used public street, left the mud and dirt in the crossing, along its track, for a distance of ten feet long and three feet high. The plaintiff, who was riding in a buggy, approached the crossing at night and without notice of the obstruction at the road crossing, there being no light placed where the same could be seen, suffered an injury caused by the overturning of the buggy in which he rode. The plaintiff relied, for recovery, upon an ordi-

[37] Lowenstein v. Missouri Pacific Ry. Co., 110 Mo. App. 689; 117 Mo. App. 371; 115 S. W. Rep. 2.
[38] Lyon v. St. Louis, etc., R. Co., 6 Mo. App. 516, 517.

nance of the city requiring a light at night on all obstructed portions of the city streéts, and the violation of this ordinance by the railroad company. In passing on the case, and upon the admissibility of this ordinance to establish negligence against the defendant, Judge Lewis, for the Court of Appeals, said: " If the defendant's failure to perform a duty enjoined by municipal regulation, had any tendency toward causing the injury suffered by the plaintiff, this was a legitimate subject of inquiry for tracing the injury to defendant's fault; but in such an injury an essential step was to ascertain what was that duty and how was it to be performed. The ordinance furnished the only direct and proper answer." The verdict in favor of the plaintiff, in the sum of four thousand dollars, was affirmed.

§ 913. **Failure to restore crossing.**— While a railroad company, of course, in pursuance of the duty imposed upon it by law, has a right to repair a public crossing, if it fails to restore the crossing after repairing its tracks, or placing new tracks, within a reasonable time, it will be liable for an injury resulting to a traveler, exercising due care in the use of the crossing.[39]

In a Texas case,[40] the plaintiff had passed over the track in the morning and had noticed the defendant's track-laying machine a distance from the crossing. On his return, the track had been laid for a distance of some three or four hundred yards across the crossing, but only a few loose planks had been placed between the rails, which the evidence showed could have been rendered safe for use by fifteen or twenty minutes' work. In attempting to cross the track, the plaintiff was injured and it was held that it was a

[39] Dallas, etc., R. Co. v. Able, 72 Texas 150; 9 S. W. Rep. 871; 37 Am. & Eng. R. Cas. 453.

[40] Dallas, etc., R. Co. v. Able, *supra.*

proper issue for the jury to ascertain whether or not he used due care, in attempting to use the crossing in this condition.

The Missouri Court of Appeals,[41] held that it was a question for the jury whether or not the defendant had used due care in raising its track and filling it in with new ballast between the rails, and that it was also a jury issue, whether or not the plaintiff had used due care in approaching such a newly constructed crossing, while riding astride a load of baled hay, five bales high, and approaching the crossing at an angle, instead of squarely, while leaning over to watch where the wagon wheels would strike the track.

§ 914. **Changing or diverting highway crossing.**— Where a railroad company is authorized, by its charter, or the statutes of a State, to divert the location of a highway, when it is necessary in the construction of its road, the right to do so must be exercised with due regard to the public safety and the railroad company will be responsible for all injuries sustained by travelers on the highway, by reason of its failure to erect proper barriers to prevent them from driving into excavations or cuts made in the highway, where the person injured is not himself in fault.[42]

In changing or diverting a highway crossing, it is the duty of the railroad company to restore the highway in such condition as will not impair or destroy its former usefulness, and if, even after it restores a highway crossing

[41] Lowenstein v. Missouri Pacific Ry. Co., 110 Mo. App. 689; 117 Mo. App. 371; 115 S. W. Rep. 2.

Under Rev. St. 1895, art. 4426, requiring a railroad company building its road across an established highway to restore the highway to its former state, or to such state as not to unnecessarily impair its usefulness, and to keep the crossing in repair, the duty of the company to keep the crossing in repair is absolute. St. Louis Southwestern Ry. Co. v. Smith (Tex. Civ. App. 1908), 107 S. W. Rep. 638.

[42] Potter v. Bunnell, 20 Ohio St. 150; Veazie v. Penobscot, etc., R. Co., 49 Me. 119; Pittsburg, etc., R. Co. v. Moses (Pa.), 2 Atl. Rep. 188; 24 Am. & Eng. R. Cas. 295.

that it has diverted, it wrongfully encroaches upon it, or impairs its usefulness as a crossing, it will be liable to one injured as a result of such encroachment or impairment.[43]

§ 915. **When company's negligence a jury issue.**— Where the evidence is conflicting upon the issue of the performance of its duty in the construction of a railroad crossing, by a railroad company, or in the observance of care in the operation of its trains across the crossing, it is generally held to be a jury issue.

Whether or not the space between the rail and the sidewalk or planking alongside the rail is too wide, or wider than necessary to accommodate the flange of the car wheels, is held to be a jury issue, in an action for an injury due to catching the foot of a person,[44] or of a horse[45] in such a space. Whether or not it is a reasonably safe way to construct the planking alongside the rails, with a straight edge, instead of a sloping edge, so that the bottom part of the plank will touch the rail;[46] whether the duty of maintaining the crossing in a safe condition was properly discharged;[47] whether proper safeguards were adopted at the point where the injury occurred;[48] whether proper care was exercised in the construction of the crossing,[49] or due care was exercised in failing to erect guard rails for a period of three months after the road was completed,[50] are all held to be proper jury issues.

[43] Pittsburg, etc., R. Co. v. Maurer, 21 Ohio St. 421.

[44] Elgin, etc, R Co. v. Raymond, 148 Ill. 241; 35 N. E. Rep. 729.

[45] Payne v. Troy, etc., R. Co., 83 N. Y. 572; 6 Am. & Eng. R. Cas. 54.

[46] Spooner v. Delaware, etc., R. Co., 115 N. Y. 22; 21 N. E. Rep. 696; 41 Hun 643; 39 Am. & Eng. R. Cas. 599.

[47] Indianapolis, etc., R. Co. v. Love, 10 Ind. 554.

[48] Staal v. Grand Rapids, etc., R. Co., 57 Mich. 239; 23 N. W. Rep. 705.

[49] Roberts v. Chicago, etc., R. Co., 35 Wis. 679.

[50] Kyne v. Wilmington, etc., R. Co. (Del.), 14 Atl. Rep. 922.

CHAPTER XL.

§ 916. **No duty to erect gates at common law.**— By statute, in England,[1] railroads crossing a public highway on a level, were required to erect gates at the highway crossing, but this statutory provision only applied to railroad companies whose roads were constructed under parliamentary grant of powers and not to railroads owned and operated by private parties.[2] In the absence of a statute, therefore, requiring a railroad company to maintain a gate at a highway crossing over its tracks, negligence cannot be predicated on the failure so to do, in case of an injury to a person on the crossing.[3]

[1] 5 & 6 Vict., ch. 55, § 9.

[2] Matson v. Baird, 3 App. Cas. 1082; 3 Ry. & T. C. Cas. 17.

[3] Case v. New York, etc., R. Co., 75 Hun 527; 27 N. Y. Supp. 496; 57 N. Y. S. R. 653; Cummings v. Brooklyn R. Co., 104 N. Y. 669; Weber v. New York, etc., R. Co., 58 N. Y. 451.

II—33.

In some cases it is held that while raiḟroads
quired to maintain gates at all highway crossings
tion would be recognized in cases where there w₍
dangers in the use of the crossing.[4]   But in the
evidence of the amount of travel over the track
ticular crossing, or of facts showing peculiar dar
that there was a bank on one side of the track, w
exclude the view of the train, until it was with
fifty feet of the crossing, the evidence would not l
to show negligence in failing to maintain a g
evidence that twenty trains and about as many
a highway each day passed over the crossing, at
held to be insufficient to hold the railroad comp₍
negligent injury of a traveler, for the failure to
gate, where the track was in full view of the hig
distance of one hundred and fifty feet of the cr
the public authorities had never required the
maintenance of a gate at such crossing.[6]

[4] Vallance v. Boston, etc., R. Co., 55 Fed. Rep. 364; C₍
v. Boston, etc., R. Co., 101 Mass. 201.

[5] Vallance v. Boston, etc., R. Co., *supra*.

[6] Commonwealth v. Boston, etc., R. Co., *supra*.
Under Rev. Laws, ch. 111, § 191, providing that the
city or town in which a traveled place is crossed by a ra
same level may request the railroad to erect signboa
traveled place, and § 192, providing that the board, af
the railroad and hearing, may direct that gates be erect₍
crossing, and that a person be stationed there to close th
a train passes, or that a flagman be stationed at the cro
road cannot be shown to have failed to perform its duty t
or station a flagman without proof of such request. Gia
York, etc., R. Ço. (Mass. 1907), 81 N. E. Rep. 899.

Where a railroad maintained gates over a grade cro₍
not required to have a light on the arm extending over t
it being sufficient if the light necessary to enable a pers₍
ordinary care to see the arm of the gate was provided.
Covington, etc.. R. Co. (Ky. 1908), 107 S. W. Rep. 726.

Where a child ran quickly on defendant's railroad tra

§ 917. Signs should be maintained, independent of statute.

—Independent of statute it has been held that a railroad company should erect and maintain proper signs at railroad crossings and public highways so as to give notice to the public of the danger of a collision with the trains.[7]

In a Minnesota case,[8] in an action against a railroad company for damages for running over a traveler at a highway crossing, there was no signboard at the crossing to announce the danger of the track, and it was held that evidence that there was no signboard at the crossing, was proper, although there was no statute or ordinance requiring the company to have or maintain such a precaution. It was held to be a jury issue, whether or not the absence of the signboard contributed to the injury, and whether or not this constituted negligence, although the injured person was familiar with the crossing himself.

But it is generally held, even where the statute or ordinance requires a signboard, that the absence of such caution board is not the proximate cause of an injury to one familiar with the crossing, for when one has knowledge of the crossing, the board could perform no office, as this is the object of the board, to give notice.[9]

struck and killed without negligence on the part of the railroad company in the operation of the train, the railroad was not negligent in failing to fence its track to keep the child off its premises and prevent it from becoming a trespasser, there being no duty, in the absence of statute, on the part of the railroad company to build a fence or erect barriers at places other than crossings to exclude persons, whether children or adults, from its tracks. New York Cent. etc., R. Co. v. Price (U. S. C. C. A., Mass., 1908), 159 Fed. Rep. 330.

[7] Shaber v. St. Paul, etc., R. Co., 28 Minn. 103; 9 N. W. Rep. 575; 2 Am. & Eng. R. Cas. 185; Heddles v. Chicago, etc., R. Co., 77 Wis. 228; 46 N. W. Rep. 115.

[8] Shaber v. St. Paul, etc., R. Co., supra.

[9] Haas v. Grand Rapids, etc., R. Co., 47 Mich. 401; 11 N. W. Rep. 216; 8 Am. & Eng. R. Cas. 268; Field v. Chicago, etc., R. Co., 4 McCrary (U. S.) 573; 14 Fed. Rep. 332; 8 Am. & Eng. R. Cas. 425.

§ 918. City ordinance requiring maintenance of gates.—
The violation of a city ordinance requiring the maintenance
of gates at a railroad crossing, over a street of the city, is
evidence of negligence on the part of the railroad company,
and when the violation of such ordinance is directly connected with an injury to a traveler on the highway, who was
in the exercise of due care for his own safety at the time of
the injury, would establish a *prima facie* case against the
railroad company.[10]

But although a city ordinance required the gates and
the attendance thereto, by a gateman, at all times when trains
were passing, a traveler injured after the hour when he
knew the gates were not operated, could not recover, although
the ordinance was violated by the railroad company, in failing to so maintain the gates, but the violation of the ordinance
would only be evidence of the defendant's negligence and
would not, under the facts in such a case, establish a conclusive case against the railroad company.[11]   Nor could a

The absence of a signboard will not render the railroad company
liable to one who knew or ought to have known of the crossing, without
the board. Gulf, etc., R. Co. v. Greenlee, 62 Texas 344; 23 Am. &
Eng. R. Cas. 322.

But the failure to erect a signboard, when required by statute, is
prima facie evidence of negligence. Field v. Chicago, etc., R. Co.,
supra; Payne v. Chicago, etc., R. Co., 44 Iowa 236; Dodge v. Burlington, etc., R. Co., 34 Iowa 276; 5 Am. Ry. Rep. 507.

Contributory negligence will bar a recovery, although there was no
signboard erected as required by statute. Lang v. Haliday, etc., R.
Co., 49 Iowa 469.

But the absence of such board is competent, although not pleaded,
as affecting the plaintiff's care and prudence. Baltimore, etc., R. Co.
v. Whitacre, 35 Ohio St. 627; Elkins v. Boston, etc., R. Co., 115 Mass.
190.

Rev. St. 1892, § 2264, requiring signboards near crossings of highways, does not apply to the streets of an incorporated city. Seaboard
Air Line Ry. v. Smith (Fla. 1907), 43 So. Rep. 235.

[10] Rainey v. New York, etc., R. Co., 68 Hun 495; 23 N. Y. Supp. 80.
[11] Rainey v. New York, etc., R. Co., *supra.*

traveler on a city street recover damages for a personal injury received at a crossing, because of the violation of a city ordinance requiring gates at such a crossing, where the violation of the ordinance had no casual connection with the injury sued for, but in all cases, before the existence of such an ordinance and its violation give a right of action, it must have directly contributed to the injury sustained.[12]

§ 919. Open gate an invitation to cross track.— By the great weight of authority, it is held that where a railroad company provides gates, to shut the railroad track off from public travel, when the track is in use, an open gate is an invitation to the traveling public to cross the track, in the absence of circumstances, which would put the traveler on notice of the danger in so doing.[13]

[12] Jennings v. St. Louis, etc., R. Co., 99 Mo. 394; 11 S. W. Rep. 999. A municipality has power to compel a railroad company to erect and maintain safety gates at crossings, and such company is not entitled to the notice provided for by statute where it is required to place and retain a flagman at such crossing. Chicago, etc., Ry. Co. v. Averill, 127 Ill. App. 275, judgment affirmed, 79 N. E. Rep. 654; 224 Ill. 516.

Where, after an ordinance was passed, requiring a railway company to place gates at a certain crossing, the company recognized its validity by erecting the gates and partially complied with its requirements by operating them in the daytime, the question whether it was entitled to notice to erect gates after the enactment of the ordinance under Hurd's Rev. St. 1905, ch. 114, § 99, was not involved, as such notice if required had been waived. Chicago, etc., Ry. Co. v. Averill (Ill. 1906), 79 N. E. Rep. 654; 224 Ill. 516.

Where railroad crossing gates had been erected and maintained by a railroad company for some time prior to the accident, which occurred at night when the gates were up, it was no defense that the railroad company had not received notice from the city to erect and maintain such gates. Perkins v. Wabash R. Co. (Ill. 1908), 84 N. E. Rep. 677; 233 Ill. 458.

[13] Palmer v. New York, etc., R. Co., 112 N. Y. 234; Lindeman v. New York, etc., R. Co., 47 Hun 679; 11 N. Y. S. R. 837; Conway v. Philadelphia, etc., R. Co., 17 Phila. (Pa.) 71; Fitzgerald v. Long

When gates are provided by the railroad company, at street crossings, the public have a right, the gates being open, to presume in the absence of knowledge to the contrary, that the gateman is properly discharging his duty and they are not negligent in acting on this presumption that they are exposed to a danger which could only arise from a disregard of such duties.[14] In other words, all men are presumed to discharge their duty and the traveler on a public highway is not, presumptively, negligent, in acting on this legal presumption.

In an English case,[15] the absence of a gateman and the fact that a gate stood partially open, was held to be an invitation to the traveler to cross the track and notice that a train was not due. And where the statute of Maine prohibited a railroad company from operating a train across a city street, at greater speed than that fixed by law, in the absence of a flagman or a gate at the crossing, the absence of such flagman and an open gate, was held to be an invitation to cross the track and notice that a train was not due.[16] These cases illustrate the rule, as it is generally applied by the courts.[17]

Island R. Co., 21 N. Y. S. R. 942; 3 N. Y. Supp. 230; 117 N. Y. 653; 22 N. E. Rep. 1133; 27 N. Y. S. R. 980.

[14] Evans v. Lake Shore, etc., R. Co., 88 Mich. 442; 50 N. W. Rep. 386.

[15] Stapley v. London, etc., R. Co., 4 H. & C. 93; L. R. 1 Ex. 21; 11 Jur. N. S. 954; 35 L. J. Ex. 7; 14 W. R. 132; 13 L. T. 406. And see, also, North Eastern R. Co. v. Wanless, 43 L. J. Q. B. 185; L. R. 7 H. L. Cas. 12; 22 W. R. 561; 30 L. T. 275; L. R. 6 Q. B. 481. .

[16] State v. Boston, etc., R. Co., 80 Me. 430; 15 Atl. Rep. 36; 35 Am. & Eng. R. Cas. 356.

[17] Whelan v. New York, etc., R. Co., 38 Fed. Rep. 18; Cleveland, etc., R. Co. v. Schneider (Ohio), 17 N. E. Rep. 324; Central Trust Co. v. Wabash R. Co., 27 Fed. Rep. 159; Chicago, etc., R. Co. v. Boggs, 101 Ind. 522; Greany v. Long Island R. Co., 101 N. Y. 419; Owen v. Hudson River R. Co., 5 N. Y. 516; Beiseigel v. New York, etc., R. Co., 34 N. Y. 622; Dolan v. Delaware, etc., R. Co., 71 N. Y. 285; Chicago,

§ 920. **Traveler may rely upon gate, when.**— The raising or opening of a crossing gate is regarded as such an assurance of safety to the traveler upon the highway as to amount to the same thing as if the gateman had beckoned him to cross, and to this extent, the traveler is held entitled to rely upon the gates.[18]

Where a traveler is killed in driving upon a railroad track, at a highway crossing, at a place where gates are maintained, but the gateman is absent and the gates are open, it is proper for the jury to consider these facts, in connection with all the other circumstances, in determining whether or not the traveler was guilty of contributory negligence in driving on the track.[19] In the absence of circumstances showing danger to the traveler, it is generally held that he has a right to rely upon the absence of the gateman and the fact that the gates are open, and if he receives no warning and is not otherwise guilty of negligence contributing to his injury, the railroad company would be liable, if he attempted to drive across the track and received an injury, while só doing, from a moving train or engine.[20]

But where, from the facts in evidence, it is apparent that the injured traveler knew the time that a gateman left the

etc., R. Co. v. Hutchinson, 120 Ill. 589; Montgomery v. Missouri Pacific Ry. Co., 181 Mo. 477; 79 S. W. Rep. 938.

When gates at a crossing are kept closed when trains are approaching, and open when they are not, the fact that they are open is an invitation to the public to cross, and persons desiring to cross have a right to assume that they can do so without being struck by approaching trains, though they are not thereby relieved from exercising ordinary care for their own safety or from attending to other notice or warning of the approach of trains. Schulte v. Louisville, etc., R. Co. (Ky. 1908), 107 S. W. Rep. 941.

[18] Oldenburg v. New York, etc., R. Co., 124 N. Y. 414; 26 N. E. Rep. 1021.

[19] Palmer v. New York, etc., R. Co., 112 N. Y. 234; 19 N. E. Rep. 678.

[20] Central Trust Co. v. Wabash R. Co., 27 Fed. Rep. 159.

gates, at night, he would of course not be permitted to say that he relied upon the gates for protection, after the time when he knew the gates were not being operated. And where the evidence in an action for the death of a traveler on a highway crossing showed that the gates were not operated after seven o'clock in the evening, but the injury and death of the plaintiff's decedent occurred between eight and nine o'clock at night and he had notice that the gates were not operated after seven o'clock, it was held that he had no right to rely, for protection, upon the gates.[21]

§ 921. **Care exacted of traveler where gates are maintained.** — As a traveler at a highway crossing with a railroad track, is required only to exercise ordinary care, or such care as a reasonably prudent person would exercise under the same circumstances, the fact that the railroad company maintains a gateman to look after the safety of travelers on the highway crossing is a circumstance calculated to minimize the danger of the track, and hence, it is generally held, that where gates are maintained, as the danger is not so imminent, the traveler is not held to the same high degree of caution as if there were no gates at the crossing. The traveler is of course still held to the standard of ordinary caution, for his protection, but as the danger is less, the vigilance required would be proportionately less.

It is held, in New York,[22] that a traveler approaching a

[21] Rainey v. New York, etc., R. Co., 23 N. Y. Supp. 80; 68 Hun 495.

Where gates maintained across a way were closed while trains were passing only during the day, not being used after seven or eight o'clock in the evening, and no flagman was stationed there after that hour, the inference, if any, to be drawn, was that after that time such precautions were unnecessary. Giacomo v. New York, etc., R. Co. (Mass. 1907), 81 N. E. Rep. 899.

[22] Kane v. New York, etc., R. Co., 132 N. Y. 160; 30 N. E. Rep. 256; 43 N. Y. S. R. 494; 56 Hun 648; 31 N. Y. S. R. 741; 9 N. Y. Supp. 879.

highway crossing, guarded by gates, is not required to exercise the same vigilance, in looking and listening for a train or engine, that the law would require him to exercise, if there were no gates at the crossing. The degree of care to be exacted of the traveler will of course vary with the facts of each case and the dangers to be encountered at the crossing, and while the raising of the gates and a direction to come ahead, is taken as an assurance of safety,[23] if the gateman is absent and the gates are standing open, this assurance is only implied, at the best, and the traveler should not be oblivious to the dangers surrounding him.[24]

§ 922. **Open gate will not excuse traveler's negligence.**— It is held, in some cases, that an open gate is so far notice of a clear track and a safe crossing, that in the absence of circumstances imparting danger, it is not negligence in persons approaching crossings with teams to fail to stop, look and listen for a train, although the view of the track on either side of the crossing is obstructed.[25] This rule,

[23] Oldenburg v. New York, etc., R. Co., 124 N. Y. 414; 26 N. E. Rep. 1021.

[24] Lake Shore, etc., R. Co. v. Frantz, 127 Pa. St. 297; 18 Atl. Rep. 22; 39 Am. & Eng. R. Cas. 628.

The fact that safety gates maintained by a railroad company at a highway crossing are open is an implied invitation to persons traveling the highway to enter upon the crossing; and, while it does not absolve them from the duty of taking reasonable precautions to avoid injury by moving trains, it qualifies that duty to the extent that they may reasonably presume that the company's employees have performed their duty in ascertaining the safety of the crossing. Delaware, etc., R. Co. v. Larnard (U. S. C. C. A., Pa., 1908), 161 Fed. Rep. 520.

A traveler approaching a railroad crossing protected by a flagman or safety gates has the right to depend on the invitation extended to cross the tracks by signals of the flagman or the open gates; but he must exercise ordinary care for his own protection. Cross v. Illinois Cent. R. Co. (Ky. 1908), 110 S. W. Rep. 290.

[25] Cleveland, etc., R. Co. v. Schneider, 45 Ohio St. 678; 17 N. E. Rep. 321; 35 Am. & Eng. R. Cas. 334; Pennsylvania R. Co. v. Stegmeier, 118 Ind. 305.

however, is not generally followed, for it loses sight of the general rule underlying the right of the plaintiff in all personal injury actions to recover damages for an injury, that to maintain his cause of action he must be personally free from negligence directly contributing to the injury and that the negligence of the defendant alone, if the plaintiff is so negligent, will not authorize a recovery.

Considering this question, for the Supreme Court of Pennsylvania, Mitchell, J., said: "The duty to stop, look and listen is absolute and unyielding. It is for the protection of the train and its occupants, as much or more than for that of travelers on the highway and no amount of negligence on the part of defendant can absolve the plaintiff from its obligation. The fact that the safety gates were up did not and could not release the plaintiff from the necessity of observing the imperative rule for all railroad crossings." [26]

As more generally followed, the rule, therefore, is that a traveler approaching a highway crossing over a railroad track, "has no right to omit the ordinary precautions, merely because he finds the gates up," [27] but he must proceed cautiously over the track, the same as he would be compelled to do, even if signaled to cross by a flagman or watchman. The fact that gates are raised or are standing open is no excuse for a failure to stop, look and listen, but of course furnish evidence of negligence on the part of the defendant, which, if unexplained, will establish a *prima facie* case for the plaintiff, or authorize a verdict, in the absence of contributory negligence on the part of the plaintiff.[28]

[26] Lake Shore, etc., R. Co. v. Franz, 39 Am. & Eng. R. Cas. 628.

[27] Greenwood v. Philadelphia, etc., R. Co. (Pa.), 17 Atl. Rep. 188.

[28] Lake Shore, etc., R. Co. v. Franz, *supra*.

In Whelen v. New York, etc., R. Co. (38 Fed. Rep. 15), it was held that a street car driver was not necessarily negligent, as matter of law, in stopping before crossing the track, to look and listen for a train, after passing through an open gate.

§ 923. Gates should be closed when trains passing.— Where gatemen are maintained at a railroad crossing over a public highway, it is their duty to observe the railroad track and to know when trains and engines are approaching, so that it is dangerous for persons to cross the track, and when trains or engines are approaching or passing the crossing the gates should be kept closed a sufficient length of time to enable travelers on the highway to safely cross, without colliding with such train or engine.[29] For an injury due to a failure to keep the gates closed when a train was approaching, this would be held such negligence on the part of the railroad company as to entitle the injured traveler, otherwise free from negligence, to recover damages.[30]

In England, by statute,[31] railroads are required to keep gates at the end of grade crossings on the highway, closed

The fact that safety gates, which should be closed in case of danger, are standing open, does not relieve the traveler from the duty of exercising care at a railway crossing, but is to be considered by the jury in determining whether he exercised such care. Messinger v. Pennsylvania R. Co. (Pa. 1906), 64 Atl. Rep. 682.

A person is not guilty of negligence as a matter of law in entering a railroad crossing while the gates are down; but whether the act is negligence depends upon the attendant circumstances. Galveston, etc., Ry. Co. v. Walker, (Tex. Civ. App. 1908), 106 S. W. Rep. 705.

While open gates are an invitation to cross, they do not excuse a traveler approaching a railroad crossing from looking or listening where either would be effective. Shafer v. Lehigh Valley R. Co. (N. J. Supp. 1907), 66 Atl. Rep. 1072.

The fact that railroad crossings are protected by gates or a flagman does not relieve train men of the duty of exercising ordinary care in approaching crossings to prevent accident to persons at the crossings, and they must give the statutory signals, or other warning where the statutory signals are not required. Cross v. Illinois Cent. R. Co. (Ky. 1908), 110 S. W. Rep. 290.

[29] Cleveland, etc., R. Co. v. Schneider, 45 Ohio St. 678; 17 N. E. Rep. 321; 35 Am. & Eng. R. Cas. 334; Whelan v. New York, etc., R. Co., 38 Fed. Rep. 15.

[30] Cleveland, etc., R. Co. v. Schneider, *supra*.

[31] 5 & 6 Vict., ch. 55, § 9.

against all travelers and cattle, when trains are approaching
or passing the crossing, and for a violation of this statute,
resulting in injury to a traveler on such highway, a liability
would result.[32]   And independent of statute, it is held to be
negligence for a gate-keeper to leave a gate open, so that
a person sustains injury by collision with a train that he
did not see, in the exercise of due care for his own safety,[33]
since it is not only the duty of the gatemen to open the gates
for the safe passage of travelers on the highway, but to keep
the gates closed, when trains are passing.[34]

§ 924. **Negligence of gate-keeper — Motioning traveler to
cross.**— The traveling public are so far dependent upon the
acts of the gate-keeper or watchman, at a public highway
crossing a railroad track, and so far bound to obey his
directions, that if the gate-keeper or flagman is guilty of
active negligence, as where he motions the traveler to cross
the track, when it is not safe to do so, but the surroundings
are not such as to impart notice of the danger to the traveler,
and the traveler obeys the direction, this will give a cause
of action, in case of a resulting injury to the traveler.[35]

In a Massachusetts case,[36] the evidence showed that the

[32] Fawcett v. York, etc., R. Co., 16 Q. B. 610; 15 Jur. 173; 20 L.
J. Q. B. 222.

[33] Wanless v. Northeastern R. Co., 25 L. T. 103.

[34] Lunt v. London, etc., R. Co., L. R. 1 Q. B. 277; 12 Jur. N. S.
409; 35 L. J. Q. B. 105; 14 W. R. 497; 14 L. T. 225.

Where, in an action against a railroad for injuries to plaintiff's
horses and wagon through being struck by a train at a street crossing,
the only act of negligence committed was the failure of defendant's
gate watchman to close the gates, plaintiff was not entitled to recover
punitive damages. Schulte v. Louisville, etc., R. Co. (Ky. 1908), 108
S. W. Rep. 941.

[35] Bayley v. Eastern R. Co., 125 Mass. 62.

[36] Bayley v. Eastern R. Co., supra.

Where a railway maintains a watchman and gates at a crossing,
and fails to keep the same down or give proper warning when trains

deceased approached the crossing in the dusk of the evening, and just before he reached the track the gate-keeper began to close the gates and swung his lantern and shouted to the deceased to stop; the deceased stopped, but the gate-keeper immediately shouted to him to hurry up, whereupon he again started his horse, but he was struck by an engine, before he succeeded in making it across the railroad track. The court held that this constituted sufficient evidence of negligence on the part of the gate-keeper, to sustain a verdict for the representative of the deceased traveler.

§ 925. **Striking traveler with gate.**— A gateman at a highway crossing over a railroad track should so operate the gate as to avoid injuring travelers, if, by the exercise of ordinary care he can do so. And if, instead of waiting for a reasonable time, to enable travelers to pass over the crossing, he lowers the gates, so as to strike the traveler and injure him, this will be held to be the negligence of the railroad company, for which it must respond in damages.[37]

In a New York case,[38] the plaintiff, a traveler on a public

are passing, it is liable to a person injured thereby who is not guilty of contributory negligence. Louisville, etc., R. Co. v. Wilson (Ky. 1907), 100 S. W. Rep. 302.

[37] Feeney v. Long Island R. Co., 39 Am. & Eng. R. Cas. 639.

[38] Feeney v. Long Island R. Co., *supra*. In passing upon this case Vann, J., for the court, said: "It was the duty of the defendant to use due care in operating the gates so as to protect persons traveling the public highway, not only from being run over by the cars, but also against injury from the gates themselves. If, on reaching a crossing protected by safety gates, a person finds them raised and motionless, he is at liberty to go on, and, if it becomes necessary to lower the gates, while he is passing between them, it should be done with all the care demanded by the peculiar situation, and with due regard to the safety of human life. There is still less danger in passing under safety gates, as they need not be lowered rapidly, and should, at all times, be under the control of the gateman. If he

highway, approached a railroad crossing, on a rainy night, with her umbrella raised above her head. On reaching the gates she saw that they were up, and the passage seeming safe for her to cross the track, she proceeded to do so. When she was located directly between the two gates, the gateman, without warning, began to lower them, and as she was passing under the last gate it fell upon her head and injured her. The court decided that it could not be held, as a matter of law, that the plaintiff was negligent in passing under the gates without stopping to look and listen, but that it was properly a jury question to decide whether, under all the circumstances, she was guilty of contributory negligence in going upon the crossing, without stopping to look and listen.

§ 926. **Gate opened by third party.**— While an employer is not ordinarily responsible, under the doctrine of *respondeat superior,* for an act by other than an employee, because in the absence of an employment the requisite of agency on the part of the person doing the wrongful act is wanting, this rule has been so far modified in one case, when applied to the act of a stranger, in opening a crossing gate, at a railroad and highway crossing, because of the peculiar dangers of the place and the negligence of the railroad company, by way of omission, in failing to have a gateman there to look after the gate, as to render the railroad company liable for an injury to a traveler on a highway, because of the act of a stranger in leaving the crossing gates open.[39] The cross-

does his duty there is little or no danger. The plaintiff had the right to assume that the gateman would not be negligent on the occasion in question, although she was not, on this account, relieved of the necessity of exercising that degree of care that would have been used by a person of ordinary prudence, under the same circumstances."

[39] Haywood v. New York, etc., R. Co., 35 N. Y. S. R. 748; 59 Hun 617; 13 N. Y. Supp. 177; 128 N. Y. 596.

ing gates had been closed by the gateman just before the plaintiff's intestate had proceeded to use the crossing, but one of them had been raised by a woman who preceded the deceased across the track, and the absence of the gate-keeper was held to be such an act of negligence as to hold the railroad company for the death of the deceased, resulting from his attempt to use the crossing while the gate was open.[40]

§ 927. **Liability of different companies maintaining one gate.**— In a Massachusetts case,[41] the question was decided of the liability of one railroad company, employing a gate-man, for the injury to a traveler caused by the train of another railroad company using the same crossing. It appeared that the tracks of three railroad companies crossed the same street, at grade. The gates protecting the crossing were operated by a gateman and he raised and lowered the • gates when a train or engine passed on any one of the three tracks. Plaintiff was struck by a train on the track of one of these roads but did not sue the railroad company on whose track he was injured,· but sued the company employing the gateman and alleged that the gateman was negligent in raising the gate before the train on the other track had passed. There was no express contract shown in regard to the employment of the gateman by the defendant, except that the other railroad companies paid five-eighths of his wages. In the trial court, there was a nonsuit, the court holding that the railroad company whose train had caused the injury was alone liable, but the higher court held that the defendant was also liable.

§ 928. **One company using track of another company.**— It

40 Haywood v. New York, etc., R. Co., *supra*.
41 Brow v. Boston, etc., R. Co., 157 Mass. 399; 32 N. E. Rep. 362.

has been adjudicated that if one railroad company runs its trains upon the railroad track of another company, by consent, or under a traffic agreement with the owner of the road, it will be so far deemed to be the proprietor of the road, as to render it liable for injuries at crossings caused by the negligence of the gateman in charge of the gate. This holding was announced by a New Hampshire court.[42]

In an Ohio case,[43] it was also decided that if one railroad company used the railroad track and stations and crossings and gates of another railroad company, under a traffic arrangement, or for a certain per cent. of the profits of operating the trains, and maintaining the tracks, it was bound to the same care in the maintenance of gates and careful gatemen that the owner of the road would be and that it was bound to anticipate the reasonable effect of the conduct of the gatekeeper on the safety of travelers approaching and using the crossing, and to exercise care proportionate to the danger to be incurred by the traveling public. It was also held that if the defendant company, while operating the road, accepted the services of a gateman in the service of the other company, instead of employing a competent gateman of its own, he would become, for the time being, its employee and it would be responsible for the effect of his negligence. And if it had not accepted his services, so as to bind it for his acts, as its agent, it would none the less be liable for the failure to employ a competent gateman, as this is a primary duty which it could not avoid.

§ 929. **Crossing gates at private ways.**— At a merely private way, there is generally no right of action for an injury due to the inherent dangers of the way, on the part

[42] Hall v. Brown, 54 N. H. 495; 11 Am. Ry. Rep. 231.

[43] Cleveland, etc., R. Co. v. Schneider, 45 Ohio St. 678; 17 N. E. Rep. 321; 35 Am. & Eng. R. Cas. 334.

of others than those for whose benefit the way was constructed or laid out,[44] and hence, it would follow, as to all such persons using the way for their own convenience, and not upon business connected with the defendant, like any other licensee merely, they would take the crossing subject to its concomitant perils and could not recover for an injury, by reason of the defective condition of the crossing or the usual or ordinary operation of the trains thereon.[45]

But where a public highway and a private road both cross the railroad track diagonally, converging at the track, and a gate is placed by the railroad company, so as to serve both the public and the private road, a traveler on the private road, who could only cross the railroad track by means of this one gate, is regarded in the same position, with respect to the gate-keeper, as if he had been using the public road instead of the private way.[46]

[44] Mann v. Chicago, etc., R. Co., 86 Mo. 347; Straub v. Soderer, 53 Mo. 38; Carr v. Missouri Pacific Ry. Co., 195 Mo. 214; 92 S. W. Rep. 874.

[45] Mann v. Chicago, etc., R. Co., 86 Mo. 347.

[46] Lunt v. London, etc., R. Co., 1 Q. B. 277; 12 Jur. N. S. 409; 35 L. J. Q. B. 105; 14 W. R. 497; 14 L. T. 225.

In Mann v. Chicago, etc., R. Co. (86 Mo. 347), where one, without business with the railroad company, was using a private crossing and was injured, the court, in disposing of the contention that any duty was owing to the injured person, said: " In our opinion plaintiff has no right of action or standing in court. The defendant owed no duty to him, even if the crossing were defective or out of repair." * * * " If the party, for whose benefit the crossing was built, had, in like circumstances, been injured, a different question would, perhaps, be presented, not necessary now to be considered." Monn v. Chicago, etc., R. Co. 86 Mo. 350.

In Evansville, etc., R. Co. v. Griffin (100 Ind. 221), it was held that " where one permits others, for their own accommodation, to pass over his lands, he is under no legal duty to keep them free from pitfalls or obstructions which may result in injury."

In Straub v. Soderer (53 Mo. 43), Judge Ewing delivered the opinion of the court, and in considering the duty owing to a licensee, at the time of the alleged injury, said: " No duty is imposed by law, upon

§ 930. **Jury issues in actions regarding.**— It was held, in an English case,[47] to be a misconception of the law governing the liability of a railroad company, to leave to the jury the determination of the issue, whether or not, under the peculiar circumstances of the case, there was any duty upon the defendant to maintain a crossing gate at the crossing of its

the owner or occupant, to keep his premises in a suitable condition for those who come there solely for their own convenience or pleasure, and who are not either expressly invited to enter or induced to come upon them by the purpose for which the premises are appropriated or occupied, or by some preparation or adaptation of the place *for use by customers or passengers*, which might naturally and reasonably lead them to suppose that they might properly and safely enter." Straub v. Soderer, 53 Mo. 43.   ......

In Barney v. Hannibal, etc., R. Co. (126 Mo. 372, 389), the above language used by the court in Straub v. Soderer, is quoted by Judge Sherwood and approved.

Where a railroad company for many years has permitted the public without objection to cross its tracks at a certain point not in itself a public crossing, it owes the duty of reasonable care toward those using such crossing. Union Pac. Ry. Co. v. Connolly (Neb. 1906), 109 N. W. Rep. 368.

Though plaintiff, in attempting to cross railroad tracks at a private crossing, wrongfully placed himself in danger by standing on one track while waiting for a train to pass on a parallel track, forgetful of his surroundings, if the employees of an engine backing on the track on which he stood saw him, and had reasonable grounds to believe from his conduct that he was unconscious of the approaching engine and would probably not leave the track in time to avoid injury, it was their duty after such notice to use ordinary care in exercising all reasonable means at their command to avoid injuring him, and for their failure to use such care, resulting in his injury, the company is liable. Hovius v. Cincinnati, etc., Ry. Co. (Ky. 1908), 107 S. W. Rep. 214.

A person injured upon railroad tracks can predicate no right to recover upon the absence of gates at a crossing, when she has reached the place of the accident by going upon such tracks at a place where there was no street crossing, and walking upon such tracks until she reached the place of the accident. Chicago, etc., R. Co. v. Korando, 129 Ill. App. 620.

[47] Cliff v. Midland R. Co., L. R. 5 Q. B. 258; 18 W. R. 456; 22 L. T. 382.

railroad track and a public highway, as this was held to be a question of law for the court and one upon which the jury could not decide.

While this case is unquestionably rightly decided, since the duty to maintain gates did not exist at common law, but is to be imposed only when a statute or ordinance requires,[48] and a jury cannot properly determine the existence of such ordinances or laws, when a crossing gate is erected by a railroad company, then it is a proper issue for the jury to determine whether or not, under the facts in evidence, the gate was reasonably sufficient for the purpose,[49] or the maintenance of the gate and the operation thereof were properly or negligently conducted.[50]

[48] Case v. New York, etc., R. Co., 75 Hun 527; 27 N. Y. Supp. 496; 57 N. Y. S. T. 653.

[49] McKenley v. Chicago, etc., R. Co., 43 Iowa 641; 14 Am. Ry. Rep. 495.

[50] Palmer v. New York, etc., R. Co., 112 N. Y. 234; 19 N. E. Rep. 678.

In an action to recover for injuries received at a railroad crossing, where there is evidence that plaintiff stopped to look and listen eighty feet from the crossing, where people usually stop, and that at the crossing in question the safety gates were raised, the question of defendant's negligence is for the jury. Messinger v. Pennsylvania R. Co. (Pa. 1906), 64 Atl. Rep. 682.

Where a wagon is stopped at the safety gates of a grade crossing at a time when the gates were raised, and then proceeds and is struck by a train going at a rapid rate of speed, the question whether the driver of the wagon should have stopped, looked, and listened at another point is for the jury. Bracken v. Pennsylvania R. Co. (Pa. Super. Ct. 1906), 32 Pa. Super. Ct. 22.

In an action for death in a railroad crossing accident, the refusal to charge that the raising of the gates was not an invitation to pass, nor an assurance of safety, was not error; that being a question for the jury. Pulcino v. Long Island R. Co. (N. Y. Supp. 1908), 109 N. Y. S. 1076.

Where there was evidence that prior to a railroad crossing accident the gates were raised after a train had gone by, the court properly instructed that, even if the gates were up, it was the duty of deceased to use due care; but it was for the jury to say whether the gates were raised enough to warrant the deceased in believing it a declaration to him that the way was safe, and to what extent his vigilance was thereby lessened. Pulcino v. Long Island R. Co. (N. Y. Supp. 1908), 109 N. Y. S. 1076.

CHAPTER XLI.

§ 931. **Duty to employ generally.**— There is no rule of law requiring a railroad company to maintain a flagman or watchman at the crossing of its railroad track and a public street, to give notice of the movement of trains to travelers upon the highway,[1] but its only duty toward travelers on the highway is to so run and manage its trains as not to injure them while lawfully using the highway.[2] The absence of a flagman or watchman, therefore, where this is the only allegation of negligence against the railroad company, will not render the company liable for an injury to a traveler on the highway,[3] and the only outward signal required to

[1] Ernst v. Hudson River R. Co., 39 N. Y. 61; 36 How. Pr. 84; State v. East Orange, 41 N. J. L. 127.

[2] Heaney v. Long Island R. Co., 9 N. Y. S. R. 707.

[3] Schwartz v. Hudson River R. Co., 4 Robt. (N. Y.) 347.

1365

notify the travelers on the highway is the sounding of the bell and whistle,[4] It is error, therefore, to allow evidence of the absence of a flagman, in an action for injury to a traveler at a highway crossing a railway track,[5] and an instruction which tells the jury that the company is liable if it failed to maintain a flagman or watchman, if the presence of the flagman would have avoided the injury, is error.[6]

While required to take all proper precautions with reference to the movement and operation of its trains over highways, a railroad company is not required to do any act outside of this and the posting of flagmen, or watchmen, or placing of gates at the crossing, or the giving of other notice, can never be counted upon as negligence in the absence of a statute or ordinance providing for such precautions.[7]

But this rule does not obtain in England and it is held, in a few cases in that country, that while the absence of a flagman is not always evidence of negligence, but each case depends upon the facts underlying it,[8] it is also held that it is evidence of negligence for a railway company to fail to place a flagman at a crossing of a highway, where one hundred trains a day pass the highway.[9]

[4] Culhane v. New York, etc., R. Co., 60 N. Y. 133; 10 Am. Ry. Rep. 142.

[5] Sutherland v. New York, etc., R. Co., 9 J. & S. (N. Y.) 17.

[6] Carraher v. San Francisco Bridge Co., 81 Cal. 98; 22 Pac. Rep. 480; Peoria, etc., R. Co. v. Hermann, 39 Ill. App. 287. But if the defendant itself asks an instruction based on the duty of the flagman at its crossing, it is estopped to deny that one was necessary. Lake Shore. etc., R. Co. v. Johnson, 135 Ill. 641; 26 N. E. Rep. 510; 35 Ill. App. 430.

[7] Weber v. New York, etc., R. Co., 58 N. Y. 451.

[8] Stubley v. London, etc., R. Co., 4 H. & C. 83; L. R. 1 Ex. 13; 11 Jur. N. S. 954; 35 L. J. Ex. 3; 14 W. R. 133; 13 L. T. 376.

[9] Bilbee v. London, etc., R. Co., 18 C. B. N. S. 584; 11 Jur. N. S. 745; 34 L. J. C. P. 182; 13 W. R. 779; 13 L. T. 146.

And in a Michigan case,[10] while it is held that the absence
of a flagman is not evidence of negligence, it will impose
upon the railroad company the duty of adopting additional
caution, when the facts warrant it, in the absence of such
flagman, and in a Minnesota case [11] it is held that where
the injury to a traveler occurs on a much used street, in a
populous city, it is a question for the jury to determine
whether or not the presence of a flagman or watchman
would have prevented the injury.

§ 932. Not required at common law.— In a leading New
York case,[12] the question was squarely presented, whether

[10] Cooper v. Lake Shore R. Co., 66 Mich. 261; 33 N. W. Rep. 306.
See, also, Pennsylvania R. Co. v. Matthews, 36 N. J. L. 531.

[11] Bolinger v. St. Paul, etc., R. Co., 36 Minn. 418; 31 N. W. Rep.
856; 29 Am. & Eng. R. Cas. 408.

In the absence of a statute or ordinance or of a custom so to do,
it is not negligence to fail to have a flagman at a crossing, however
dangerous it may be. Welsch v. Hannibal, etc., R. Co., 72 Mo. 451;
37 Am. Rep. 440; 6 Am. & Eng. R. Cas. 75.

[12] Beisiehel v. New York, etc., R. Co., 40 N. Y. 9. See, also, Chicago,
etc., R. Co. v. Jacobs, 63 Ill. 178; McGrath v. New York, etc., R.
Co., 59 N. Y. 468; Toledo, etc., R. Co. v. Shuckman, 50 Ind. 42.

This case is followed in the later case of Weber v. New York, etc.,
R. Co. (58 N. Y. 459), where the court said: "The duty of posting
flagman or of having servants and agents, or placing gates or other
obstructions, or of giving special or personal notice to travelers at
railway crossings, can only be imposed by the legislature."

And in commenting on these cases, the Supreme Court of Missouri
in Welsch v. Hannibal, etc., R. Co. (72 Mo. 455), said: "If there
had been evidence in this case, tending to show that at such a crossing as the one where the injury occurred, the employment of a flagman
was one of the common and usual means of warning adopted by
prudent railroad companies, then the omission to have employed one
might have been negligence."

The duty of a railroad company to maintain a flagman at a highway
crossing cannot be inferred alone from the fact that it runs trains
over the crossing at a high rate of speed. Latham v. Staten Island
Ry. Co. (U. S. C. C., N. J., 1907), 150 Fed. Rep. 235.

In an action against a railroad to recover a penalty for failure to

or not the duty to employ a flagman or watchman, at a street crossing a railroad track, obtained at common law, and in determining the question the court said, after showing that no such duty was exacted by the statute: "The question remains whether the common law requires the company to warn travelers of approaching trains, by other and more effective means than the statute requires. The claim that it does, is based upon the maxim that every one must so use his own, as not to injure another. In applying the maxim, it must be borne in mind that the traveler and the railroad has each an equal right of way in the crossings derived from the same authority; the former for the purpose of travel, and the latter for running its trains. A collision is somewhat dangerous to the trains, but vastly more so to the traveler. The law imposes upon both the duty of observing care to avoid them. But the care imposed upon the company is in operating its trains, in so transacting its business, in the exercise of its right of way, as not to injure others, in the exercise of their similar rights, provided the latter exercise due care on their part. This relates to the mode of operating the trains and all other things done by the company in the transaction of its business. It does not require the company to employ men to keep travelers off its track, or to serve notices upon them that trains are approaching. Should the company do this it would relieve the traveler of all necessity of exercising care in this respect, and it would indeed be safe for him to go upon the track, having received no express warning." ·

obey an order of the county commissioners directing the employment of a watchman at a certain crossing, an objection that the complaint does not allege that defendant owned or operated tracks on the date when it was ordered by the board of commissioners to employ the watchman cannot be sustained, where the order stating that defendant owned and operated the tracks at that date was made a part of the complaint. Grand Trunk Ry. Co. v. State (Ind. App. 1907)', 82 N. E. Rep. 1017.

§ 933. Duty to maintain, may exist independent of statute.

— The duty to maintain a flagman or watchman at a street crossing is not generally held to be a negligent act, *per se,* independent of a statute imposing such a duty,[13] but where the situation of a crossing reasonably requires a railroad company to provide flagmen or gates, or some other adequate precaution, to prevent accidents, it is held, by the Supreme Court of the United States, to be its duty to provide them, whether required by statute or not.[14] An action against a railroad company cannot ordinarily be maintained on the mere fact of a failure to keep a flagman at a crossing and resulting injury therefrom. The failure to approach the crossing, with a train or engine, however, in a careful manner, connected with the failure to have a flagman at the crossing, may be taken into consideration by the jury along with any other fact or circumstance, going to show negligence on the defendant's part, and if, from all the evidence it appears that such a precaution was necessary to secure the safety of travelers on the highway, then the company will be required to adopt such precautions.[15]

But it must generally be made to appear that the nature of the crossing is such that common prudence would dictate that the company should place a flagman, or his equivalent at the crossing, before this circumstance is entitled to be held as a negligent act, on the part of the railroad company,[16] and even where a statute empowers railroad commissioners to decide upon the necessity for maintaining flag-

[13] Peoria, etc., R. Co. v. Hermann, 39 Ill. App. 287.

[14] Grand Trunk R. Co. v. Ives, 144 U. S. 408; 12 Sup. Ct. Rep. 679.

[15] Peoria, etc., R. Co. v. Hermann, 39 Ill. App. 287; Guggenheim v. Lake Shore, etc., R. Co., 66 Mich. 150; 33 N. W. Rep. 161; 32 Am. & Eng. R. Cas. 89; Heddles v. Chicago, etc., R. Co., 74 Wis. 239; 42 N. W. Rep. 237; 39 Am. & Eng. R. Cas. 645.

[16] Freeman v. Duluth, etc., R. Co., 74 Mich. 86; 41 N. W. Rep. 872; 3 L. R. A. 594; 37 Am. & Eng. R. Cas. 501; Battishill v. Humphreys, 64 Mich. 494; 31 N. W. Rep. 894; 28 Am. & Eng. R. Cas. 597.

men or watchmen at a particular railroad crossing, it must
be made to appear that such crossing is more than ordinarily
hazardous to justify a jury in finding that the railroad
company was negligent in failing to provide such flagmen
or watchmen.[17]

§ 934. **Ordinances requiring, generally.**— While it has been
held, in Ohio,[18] that a municipal corporation cannot, by
ordinance, compel a railroad company to maintain a flagman or watchman at a street crossing, to give notice to
travelers on the street of the movement of its trains, this
decision is not in accord with the weight of judicial author-

[17] Grand Trunk R. Co. v. Ives, 144 U. S. 408; 12 Sup. Ct. Rep.
679.

It is held, in Massachusetts, that the duty to maintain flagman may
exist, although no order of the Town Council is made therefor. Eaton
v. Fitchburg, etc., R. Co., 129 Mass. 364; 2 Am. & Eng. R. Cas. 183.
And see, also, New Jersey R. Co. v. West, 32 N. J. L. 91; Welsch v.
Hannibal, etc., R. Co., 72 Mo. 451; 37 Am. Rep. 440.

The failure to maintain a watchman or establish gates at a much-
used public grade crossing may be considered with other facts in
determining whether the railroad company was negligent. Davis v.
Pennsylvania R. Co. (Pa. Super. Ct. 1907), 34 Pa. Super. Ct. 388.

Where a railway crossing is unusually dangerous, the company
must employ such means as are reasonably necessary, considering its
character, to warn travelers of the approach of trains; and this duty
may require the presence of a flagman, even if the railroad commission
has not required one. Cincinnati, etc., Ry. Co. v. Champ (Ky. 1907),
104 S. W. Rep. 988; 31 Ky. Law Rep. 1054.

Where, in an action for injuries at a railway crossing, the evidence
shows that a railroad crossing was in a populous neighborhood and
was much used by the general public and the railway in the operation
of its engine, a charge predicating negligence on the failure to keep a
watchman at the crossing is proper, though there was no evidence
showing the duties of a watchman at such place, or the purpose for
which he is kept. St. Louis Southwestern Ry. Co. v. Moore (Tex.
Civ. App. 1908), 107 S. W. Rep. 658.

[18] Ravenna v. Pennsylvania R. Co., 45 Ohio St. 118; 12 N. E. Rep.
445. But see, South Covington R. Co. v. Berry, 93 Ky. 43; 18 S. W.
Rep. 1026; 50 Am. & Eng. R. Cas. 434.

ity on this subject and it is generally held to be no discrimination against a railroad company, requiring it to maintain a flagman or watchman in a populous city, at a street crossing, to give notice of the approach of its trains and cars,[19] but such legislation is quite generally upheld as a valid exercise of legislative power, in the nature of a police regulation, for the safety of persons using the streets of the city and also for the passengers on the trains of the railroad company.[20]

Where required by ordinance to maintain a flagman at a street crossing, a failure to maintain such flagman is generally held to be negligence, *per se,* on the part of the railroad company,[21] and where a flagman or watchman is maintained, as required by a valid ordinance, the negligence of the flagman or watchman is generally held to be the negligence of the railroad company employing him.[22]

But an ordinance requiring a flagman, when passed, is held to be a judicial act, imposing a pecuniary burden and loss on a railroad company, and hence it is subject to review, by the courts, in order to determine whether or not the ordinance is a reasonable and legal exercise of the legislative power, by the municipality.[23] If the crossing was not more than ordinarily hazardous, the validity of the ordi-

[19] Kentucky, etc., R. Co. v. Commonwealth (Ky.), 18 S. W. Rep. 368.

[20] State *ex rel.* Delaware, etc., R. Co. v. East Orange, 41 N. J. L. 127; Montgomery v. Missouri Pacific Ry. Co., 181 Mo. 477; 79 S. W. Rep. 930; Dickson v. Missouri Pacific Ry. Co., 104 Mo. 491; 16 S. W. Rep. 381.

[21] Murray v. Missouri Pacific Ry. Co., 101 Mo. 236; 13 S. W. Rep. 817; Pennsylvania R. Co. v. Hensil, 70 Ind. 569; 36 Am. Rep. 188; 6 Am. & Eng. R. Cas. 79; Leavitt v. Terre Haute, etc., R. Co., 5 Ind. App. 513.

[22] Dickson v. Missouri Pacific Ry. Co., 104 Mo. 491; 16 S. W. Rep. 381; Edwards v. Chicago, etc., R. Co., 94 Mo. App. 36; 67 S. W. Rep 950.

[23] State *ex rel.* Delaware, etc., R. Co. v. East Orange, 41 N. J. L. 127.

nance would be denied,[24] and, in any case, before the violation of such an ordinance could be material, in an action for an injury to a traveler on the highway, it would be essential to establish that the failure to comply with the ordinance occasioned the injury.[25]

§ 935. **Absence of, competent on issue of negligence, when.** — Although the law does not require the presence of a flagman or watchman at a crossing over a railroad track, the absence of a flagman or watchman, or any other person at the crossing, to give notice of the movement of trains, may be shown as an item of evidence to be considered by the jury, in connection with all the other evidence on the question of the defendant's negligence, in moving its trains over the crossing at the time of the injury to the plaintiff.[26] In other words, the presence or absence of a flagman is as much a part of the description of the transaction or occurrence, as any other circumstance, and the absence of a flagman, in connection with the proof of other conditions, such as the population, travel and other surroundings, is held to be competent, in some cases, to throw light upon the issue the jury is to decide, of the negligence of the defendant, in causing the injury in question.[27]

[24] Grand Trunk R. Co. v. Ives, 144 U. S. 408; 12 Sup. Ct. Rep. 679.
[25] Spilane v. Missouri Pacific Ry. Co., 135 Mo. 414; 37 S. W. Rep. 198; 58 Am. St. Rep. 580; Heaney v. Long Island R. Co., 112 N. Y. 122; 19 N. E. Rep. 422; 37 Am. & Eng. R. Cas. 529.
[26] Reid v. New York, etc., R. Co., 17 N. Y. Supp. 801; 44 N. Y. S. R. 688; 63 Hun 630; Chicago, etc., R. Co. v. Lane, 130 Ill. 116; 22 N. E. Rep. 513; 30 Ill. App. 437; Abbott v. Dwinnell, 74 Wis. 514, 43 N. W. Rep. 496; Hoye v. Chicago, etc., R. Co., 67 Wis. 1; 29 N. W. Rep. 646; Schilling v. Chicago, etc., R. Co., 71 Wis. 255; 34 Am. & Eng. R. Cas. 60; Hart v. Chicago, etc., R. Co., 56 Iowa 166; 7 N. W. Rep. 9.
[27] Brown v. Rome, etc., R. Co., 48 Hun 619; 1 N. Y. Supp. 286; 121 N. Y. 669; Chicago, etc., R. Co. v. Lane, 130 Ill. 116; 22 N. E. Rep. 513.

But the cases holding that such evidence is competent, are not unanimous, and in some cases it is held that such evidence is not competent, for any purpose, in the absence of a statute or ordinance prescribing such a duty.[28] In a New York case,[29] it is held proper, where such evidence is admitted, to charge the jury that the absence of a flagman is not proper to be considered as determining the defendant's negligence, but only as one of the surrounding circumstances, and generally, where such evidence is competent, it is held to be proper to limit the purpose of such evidence, and to advise the jury that the same cannot be considered, to determine the negligence of the defendant, but only to determine whether, in view of the absence of a flagman or watchman, the train causing the injury was moved in a reasonably cautious and careful manner.[30]

§ 936. At country road crossings.— A railroad company is not, as a matter of law, under obligation to station a flagman or watchman at a country road crossing, merely because the approach to the crossing by its track and by the

[28] Carraher v. San Francisco Bridge Co., 81 Cal. 98; 22 Pac. Rep. 480; Beiseigel v. New York, etc., R. Co., 40 N. Y. 9; Sutherland v. New York, etc., R. Co., 9 J. & S. (N. Y.) 17.

[29] Brown v. Rome, etc., R. Co., *supra*.

[30] Heddles v. Chicago, etc., R. Co., 74 Wis. 239; 42 N. W. Rep. 237; 39 Am. & Eng. R. Cas. 645.

In an action for injuries at a crossing, where plaintiff's declaration was based solely on the negligent operation of the train, and contained no averment casting on defendant a duty to use gates, or adopt any other precaution than the statutory signals, or any averment charging the company with negligence in failing to use the gates that were at the crossing, *held*, the evidence was properly admitted to show that there were gates and a gatehouse, and the gate was open and there was no gateman in attendance, it being unusual to have gatemen in the nighttime, and the evidence being admissible, not to show negligence, but to show the circumstances under which the collision occurred. Rogers v. West Jersey, etc., R. Co. (N. J. 1907), 68 Atl. Rep. 148.

highway is partially concealed by embankments, trees or other obstructions.[31] The track is itself a warning of danger and the law does not compel a railroad company to place flagmen or watchmen at all of its country road crossings to warn travelers on the highway to beware of the cars, for they are charged with notice of the danger by the track itself, which is constructed for this purpose.[32] It is not negligence, therefore, for a railroad company to fail to station a flagman or watchman at the crossing of a country road and its railroad track, in a sparsely settled section of the country, and especially would no such duty arise, when the crossing was not excluded by obstructions, but could be seen for a half mile.[33]

§ 937. At crossing of city streets.— A railroad company is not required by law to station a flagman at every street or road crossing in a city, where, in the opinion of a jury, the travel is such that ordinary prudence would require it, and it is very generally held to be error to instruct the jury that a railroad company may be found to be negligent solely on the ground of an omission to keep a flagman or watchman at a crossing of a city street, to warn travelers on the highway of the dangers of the track.[34]

[31] Haas v. Grand Rapids R. Co., 47 Mich. 401; 11 N. W. Rep. 216; 8 Am. & Eng. R. Cas. 268; Peoria, etc., R. Co. v. Hermann, 39 Ill. App. 287; Heddles v. Chicago, etc., R. Co., 74 Wis. 239; 42 N. W. Rep. 237; 39 Am. & Eng. R. Cas. 645.

[32] State v. Philadelphia, etc., R. Co., 47 Md. 76; 18 Am. Ry. Rep. 253; Maryland, etc., R. Co. v. Neubeur, 62 Md. 391; 19 Am. & Eng. R. Cas. 261.

[33] Telfer v. Northern R. Co., 30 N. J. L. 188.

[34] Beiseigel v. New York, etc., R. Co., 40 N. Y. 9; Weber v. New York, etc., R. Co., 58 N. Y. 459; Chicago, etc., R. Co. v. Jacobs, 63 Ill. 178; McGrath v. New York, etc., R. Co., 59 N. Y. 468; Toledo, etc., R. Co. v. Schuckman, 50 Ind. 42; Dyer v. Erie R. Co., 71 N. Y. 228; Buck v. Manhattan R. Co., 15 Daly (N. Y.) 276; 6 N. Y. Supp. 524; 25 N. Y. S. R. 590.

But while this rule is sound and is no doubt sustained by the weight of judicial authority, it is not of universal application. It is held, in an Iowa case,[35] that whether it can be held to be negligence for a railroad company to fail to maintain a flagman at a street crossing in a city, is to be determined from all the facts and circumstances in a case; a similar rule has been announced in a Missouri case,[36] and the Wisconsin court has gone to the extent of holding that a railroad company may be found guilty of negligence on the mere fact that a watchman or flagman was not maintained at a city street, where the evidence showed and the jury found that the operation of trains across such street was dangerous without such a precaution and that the injury would not have happened if such flagman had been maintained.[37]

§ 938. **Where crossing is unusually dangerous.**— Ordinarily the absence of a flagman or watchman at a crossing of a street or highway is no evidence of negligence on the part of the railroad company, and to make it evidence of negligence, the plaintiff must show that the nature of the crossing was such that common prudence would dictate that the company should maintain a flagman or watchman there, and before the jury will be authorized to find negligence in a failure so to do, it must generally be made to appear that the danger at the crossing was exceptional or such as to render ordinary care on the part of persons using the crossing insufficient protection against probable injury.[38]

[35] Annaker v. Chicago, etc., R. Co., 81 Iowa 267; 47 N. W. Rep. 68.

[36] Welsch v. Hannibal, etc., R. Co., 72 Mo. 451; 37 Am. Rep. 440; 6 Am. & Eng. R. Cas. 75.

[37] Kinney v. Crocker, 18 Wis. 74. See, also, Illinois Central R. Co. v. Ebert, 74 Ill. 399.

[38] Freeman v. Duluth, etc., R. Co., 74 Mich. 86; 41 N. W. Rep. 872; 3 L. R. A. 594; 37 Am. & Eng. R. Cas. 501.

But evidence that a railroad company used a much traveled street, in a populous city, for its convenience in switching cars and locomotives, and that this course of transacting its business rendered the use of the street by travelers exceptionally dangerous, will require it to exercise care proportionate to the increased danger in this use of the tracks, to avoid injury to people using the crossing, and it should maintain a flagman or watchman at the crossing, or adopt some other precaution to prevent injury to the traveling public using the street.[39]

§ 939. **Where custom binds company to maintain.**—While the law does not ordinarily exact of a railroad company the duty of placing a flagman or watchman at a street or highway, crossing a railroad track, to give notice to travelers on the highway of the dangers of trains, the railroad company, for its own convenience, may bind itself to maintain such flagman or watchman, and where it has elected to place a flagman at such a crossing and by an established custom on its part, has regularly maintained such flagman at the crossing, it will be held to have bound itself to so maintain him, or be liable for an injury received by a traveler, in his absence.[40]

And where, by such voluntary custom and practice, it has become generally known that the flagman is stationed at a certain crossing of a street, to give notice of the approach of trains, if the flagman or watchman is withdrawn from the crossing, without notice to the public using the crossing, this will be held such an act of negligence as to render the company liable, in case of an injury to a traveler on the crossing.[41]

[39] Cleveland, etc., R. Co. v. Schneider, 45 Ohio St. 678; 17 N. E. Rep. 321; 35 Am. & Eng. R. Cas. 334; Richmond v. Chicago, etc., R. Co., 87 Mich. 374; Pennsylvania R. Co. v. Matthews, 36 N. J. L. 531.

[40] Ernst v. Hudson River R. Co., 39 N. Y. 61; 36 How. Pr. 84.

[41] Ernst v. Hudson River R. Co., *supra;* Pittsburg, etc., R. Co. v. Yundt, 78 Ind. 373; 41 Am. Rep. 580; 3 Am. & Eng. R. Cas. 502.

§ 940. **Negligence of flagmen, generally.**— Although a railroad company may not have been negligent in failing to maintain a flagman or watchman at a highway crossing, yet if it does employ such flagman or watchman, his failure to perform the usual and ordinary duties of his place, may be sufficient evidence of negligence to charge the company so employing him, in case of a resulting injury to a traveler on the highway.[42]

Whether the act of the flagman or watchman, therefore, is an act of omission, or one of commission, as where he fails to give a signal, until the traveler has reached a place of danger,[43] or carelessly gives a signal, when danger is present to the traveler to obey it,[44] the railroad company employing him, will generally be held responsible for such negligent act, or failure to act on his part.[45] Of course the object of requiring a flagman at a street crossing is to prevent travelers from going on the crossing when trains are approaching and not for the purpose of giving warning of the danger, after it is too late to avoid it.[46] If a flagman at a crossing fails to notice a traveler approaching the crossing and does not give any signal of the approach of a train, until the traveler is in great danger, this is held to be such evidence of negligence as will render the railroad company liable, in case of an injury to the traveler.[47]

[42] Delaware, etc., R. Co. v. Taffey, 38 N. J. L. 525; 13 Am. Ry. Rep. 75; Kissenger v. New York, etc., R. Co., 56 N. Y. 538; 6 Am. Ry. Rep. 154; Pennsylvania R. Co. v. State, 61 Md. 108; 19 Am. & Eng. R. Cas. 326; Dolan v. Delaware, etc., R. Co., 71 N. Y. 285; Finklestein v. New York, etc., R. Co., 41 Hun (N. Y.) 34.

[43] Wilkins v. St. Louis, etc., R. Co., 101 Mo. 93; 13 S. W. Rep. 893.

[44] Sweeney v. Old Colony R. Co., 10 Allen (Mass.) 368.

[45] Dickson v. Missouri Pacific Ry. Co., 104 Mo. 491; 16 S. W. Rep. 381; Montgomery v. Missouri Pacific Ry. Co., 181 Mo. 477; 79 S. W. Rep. 930.

[46] Dickson v. Missouri Pacific Ry. Co., 104 Mo. 491; 16 S. W. Rep. 381.

[47] Edwards v. Chicago, etc., R. Co., 94 Mo. App. 36; 67 S. W. Rep. 950.

But a traveler crossing the track at a pla
dred feet from a street crossing is not entitle
the failure of a warning by the flagman at t
ing, as there is generally no duty on the p.
to give warning to those trespassing on the
than a street crossing.[48] And before the n
flagman can be made the basis of a right of 1
injured traveler on the highway, it must, in
made to appear that the negligence of such fla
that of the traveler, was the proximate cause
and in the absence of such proof, no recovery

§ 941. **Absence of flagman invitation to cro**
railroad company has habitually maintained 1
watchman, at a railroad crossing, his absence,
son having knowledge of the custom is injured
with a train, at the crossing, is generally he

[48] Spillane v. Missouri Pacific Ry. Co., 135 Mo. 414;
198; 58 Am. St. Rep. 580.

[49] Heaney v. Long Island R. Co., 112 N. Y. 122; 19 I
37 Am. & Eng. R. Cas. 529.

It is immaterial whether or not the duty to maint
has been imposed by law on a railroad. If it assume:
is bound to perform it with due care. Chicago, etc., R.
120 Ill. App. 218.

A flagman stationed at a railroad crossing must gi
proaching the crossing warning of the approach of tr
give them a reasonable opportunity to avoid being inju
Illinois Cent. R. Co. (Ky. 1908), 110 S. W. Rep. 290.

For negligence of flagman in motioning traveler in
danger, see Pennsylvania R. Co. v. Sloan, 125 Ill. 72;
37; 35 Am. & Eng. R. Cas. 440; Chicago, etc., R. Co. 1
Ill. 586; 25 N. E. Rep. 664; Peck v. Michigan, etc., R.
3; 23 N. W. Rep. 466; 19 Am. & Eng. R. Cas. 257;
New York, etc., R. Co., 61 Hun 624; 133 N. Y. 563; 1
1148; 44 N. Y. S. R. 930; Kalbus v. Abbott, 77 Wis. 6:
Rep. 810.

dence of negligence on the part of the railroad company.[50]
Like an open gate, the absence of a flagman, is generally
held to be an invitation to cross the track.[51]

In considering the effect of the absence of a flagman at a
crossing that had formerly been protected by one, in connection with the defense of contributory negligence of the plaintiff, Judge Gantt, for the Supreme Court of Missouri, in
a recent case,[52] used this language: "The action of the
defendant in maintaining a flagman at this public and much
used crossing, was most commendable, and, after the public
had become accustomed to seeing the flagman there, and advised of his duties, it cannot complain that travelers lawfully using the crossing, regulated their conduct, to some
extent upon the implied assurance that the flagman would
be there when trains were passing or approaching, and,
finding no one, when they came to the crossing, would presume no train was near. To assume otherwise would be
against all ordinary human experience. We think the fact
that the defendant voluntarily adopted the rule of maintaining the flagman there, and continued to do so until the
plaintiff and the public knew of the custom, most materially
affects the question of prudence required of plaintiff, when

[50] Burns v. North Chicago R. Co., 65 Wis. 312; 27 N. W. Rep. 43;
Chicago, etc., R. Co. v. Hutchinson, 120 Ill. 587; 11 N. E. Rep. 855; 32
Am. & Eng. R. Cas. 82; Richmond v. Chicago, etc., R. Co., 87 Mich.
374; Ernst v. Hudson River R. Co., 35 N. Y. 9; Chicago, etc., R. Co.
v. Blaul, 70 Ill. App. 518; Chicago, etc., R. Co. v. Jennings, 157 Ill.
274; 41 N. E. Rep. 629; Palmer v. New York, etc., R. Co., 112 N. Y.
234; 19 N. E. Rep. 678; Dundon v. New York, etc., R. Co., 67 Conn.
266; 34 Atl. Rep. 1041; Pennsylvania R. Co. v. Stegemeier, 118 Ind.
305; 20 N. E. Rep. 843; 10 Am. St. Rep. 136; Evans v. Milwaukee,
etc., R. Co., 88 Mich. 444; 50 N. W. Rep. 386; 14 L. R. A. 223.

[51] Chicago, etc., R. Co. v. Hutchinson, 120 Ill. 587; 11 N. E. Rep.
855; 32 Am. & Eng. R. Cas. 82; Philadelphia, etc., R. Co. v. Killipps,
88 Pa. St. 405.

[52] Montgomery v. Missouri Pacific Ry. Co., 181 Mo. 477; 79 S. W.
Rep. 930.

she reached the crossing on the night in question, and that, by its course of conduct, having invited the traveling public to expect a warning of approaching trains, it was evidence of negligence, that on the night in question, no flagman was there to warn plaintiff of the switching of cars across the street, and that plaintiff was not chargeable with gross negligence in attempting to cross the tracks in the absence of such flagman, or a signal from him not to attempt to do so." And this decision seems to be in accord with the weight of the decisions on this question.[53]

§ 942. **Backing trains across street, in absence of flagman.** — It is quite generally held to be negligence, on the part of a railroad company, to cut a car loose from a train and engine, and permit it to run across a public highway, in the absence of a flagman or watchman at the street crossing, unguarded and unattended, in such manner as to endanger a traveler passing along or across the highway.[54] Making a flying switch at a public crossing is negligence of the most aggravated kind, and cannot be excused by a rule of the

[53] Montgomery v. Missouri Pacific Ry. Co., *supra*, and cases cited.

Where a railway company had for a number of years maintained a flagman at a crossing, a person knowing that a flagman was usually stationed at such crossing had a right to rely on the presumption that he was at his post and would discharge his duty. Chicago, etc., Ry. Co. v. Wright, 120 Ill. App. 218.

The placing of gates or the stationing of flagmen at railroad crossings in a city are not duties imposed by statute or municipal ordinance on railroad companies, or voluntarily assumed by them, for the purpose of relieving the traveler on the street from taking those precautions for his own safety required by the long-settled rule of law, but as additional precautions to meet the increased peril resulting from local conditions in cities; and open gates, or a signal from a flagman to cross, do not relieve a traveler from the duty to look and listen before entering upon the tracks. Union Pac. R. Co. v. Rosewater (U. S. C. C. A., Neb., 1907), 157 Fed. Rep. 168.

[54] O'Connor v. Missouri Pacific Ry. Co., 94 Mo. 150; 7 S. W. Rep. 196; 4 Am. St. Rep. 364.

company preventing it, or by the press of business and the fact that such practice expedites the transaction of business.[55] And when cars are cut loose from a train and allowed to cross a highway of their own momentum, with no engine at either end, so that no bell can be rung or whistle sounded, the railroad company will be held negligent although there was a man stationed on the car to give notice to travelers of the danger of being struck by the car.[56]

Where a train has just passed a crossing and is to be backed down over it again, it is the duty of the railroad company to have some one in a position to prevent persons from attempting to pass over the crossing in the meantime, as the fact that a train is seen going away from the crossing, is sufficient to induce a traveler to attempt to cross the track, when there is no train coming in the opposite direction, and in the absence of some one to prevent such an attempt, or to signal the train to stop, in case of an injury to a traveler on the crossing, the company would be liable.[57]

[55] Stevens v. Missouri Pacific Ry. Co., 67 Mo. App. 356.

[56] Baker v. Kansas City, etc., R. Co., 147 Mo. 140; 48 S. W. Rep. 838; Battishill v. Humphreys, 64 Mich. 494; 31 N. W. Rep. 894; 28 Am. & Eng. R. Cas. 597.

[57] Daume v. Chicago, etc., R. Co., 72 Wis. 523; 40 N. W. Rep. 394; 7 Am. St. Rep. 879; 35 Am. & Eng. R. Cas. 416.

Where a brakeman was stationed at a crossing where a freight train had been cut in two, it was the brakeman's duty to exercise reasonable care to prevent injuring persons who might be in the act of passing over the tracks between the parts of the train. Boyce v. Chicago, etc., Ry. Co. (Mo. App. 1906), 96 S. W. Rep. 670.

Where defendant railroad company kicked certain freight cars across a public crossing likely to be used by pedestrians or vehicles at any time, without any one to control their movements or to give warning of their approach, and such cars came in contact with plaintiff's intestate as he was about to cross, whether the railroad company's act was willful or wanton was for the jury. Lacey v. Louisville, etc., R. Co. (U. S. C. C. A., Ala., 1907), 152 Fed. Rep. 134.

A railroad, when sending a car over a street crossing in its yards, must exercise ordinary care to protect persons about to use the cross-

§ 943. **When traveler may assume track is clear.**— It is a part of the duty of a watchman stationed at a public railroad crossing, to warn persons approaching the crossing, on the street, of the approach of trains or engines or cars,[58] and where a flagman, stationed at a street crossing, fails to warn a traveler on the street of the approach of a train or engine, the absence of such a signal is sufficient evidence of safety to lead the traveler to presume that the tracks are safe for him to cross.[59] The failure on the part of the watchman stationed at a city street crossing, to warn a traveler of an approaching train, is therefore evidence of negligence, which will render the railroad company liable, in case of an injury from such approaching train.[60]

But a flagman or watchman, on the end of a slowly approaching train, with the bell ringing, is held entitled to presume, when he sees a man walking soberly on or near the track, that the latter has observed the train, and, unless there is something to indicate the necessity of further notice, he will not be negligent in presuming that he will step aside and avoid the train, without additional warning.[61]

A signal to cross, however, like the absence of a signal, is sufficient to lead a traveler to believe that he can safely use a crossing, and although one on a track could see an approaching train, if he had looked in the direction, it is held, in one case, that such a traveler will not be held guilty of

ing, by some reasonable warning. Chicago, etc., Ry. Co. v. Donovan (U. S. C. C. A., Minn., 1908), 160 Fed. Rep. 826.

[58] Wilkins v. St. Louis, etc., R. Co., 101 Mo. 93; 13 S. W. Rep. 893.

[59] Chicago, etc., R. Co. v. Wilson, 133 Ill. 55; 24 N. E. Rep. 555; 42 Am. & Eng. R. Cas. 153; Chicago, etc., R. Co. v. Clough, 134 Ill. 586; 25 N. E. Rep. 664; 29 N. E. Rep. 184.

[60] Louisville, etc., R. Co. v. Webb, 90 Ala. 185; 8 So. Rep. 518; 49 Am. & Eng. R. Cas. 427; Woodley v. Baltimore, etc., R. Co., 8 Mackey (D. C.) 542; St. Louis, etc., R. Co. v. Dunn, 78 Ill. 197.

[61] Cincinnati, etc., R. Co. v. Long, 112 Ind. 166; 13 N. E. Rep. 659; 31 Am. & Eng. R. Cas. 138; Pakilinsky v. New York, etc., R. Co., 82 N. Y. 424.

contributory negligence barring a recovery for an injury received while he was obeying a signal from a flagman to cross the track.[62]

§ 944. **One company using another company's track.**— While a railroad company owning and operating its own track and railroad will generally be held negligent, giving an injured traveler a right of action, if it removes a flagman who has habitually been stationed at a street crossing, or maintains a flagman who is negligent in such manner as to injure a traveler rightfully on the highway,[63] this rule would not apply to a railroad company running its trains and engines over the road of another company, who may have been in the habit of maintaining a flagman at a street crossing.[64] And where the law does not make it the duty of the railroad company operating trains over the crossing to maintain a flagman, one company running its cars over the track of another company, has been held not liable for an injury at the crossing of a street, where no flagman was at the time, even though the evidence showed that the owner of the road was in the habit of maintaining a flagman at such crossing.[65]

§ 945. **Duty to maintain as jury issue.**— It has been held by the United States Supreme Court,[66] to be a question for

[62] Fusili v. Missouri Pacific Ry. Co., 45 Mo. App. 535.

[63] Chicago, etc., R. Co. v. Hutchinson, 120 Ill. 587; 11 N. E. Rep. 855; Montgomery v. Missouri Pacific Ry. Co., 181 Mo. 477; 79 S. W. Rep. 930.

[64] McGrath v. New York, etc., R. Co., 1 T. & C. (N. Y.) 243.

[65] McGrath v. New York, etc., R. Co., *supra*.

[66] Grand Trunk R. Co. v. Ives, 144 U. S. 408; 12 Sup. Ct. Rep. 679. See, also, Webb v. Portland R. Co., 57 Me. 117; Central Pass. R. Co. v. Kuhn, 86 Ky. 578; Lesan v. Maine, etc., R. Co., 77 Me. 85; 23 Am. & Eng. R. Cas. 245; Tierney v. Chicago, etc., R. Co., 84 Iowa 641; 51 N. W. Rep. 175; Welsch v. Hannibal, etc., R. Co., 72 Mo. 451; 37 Am. Rep. 440; 6 Am. & Eng. R. Cas. 75.

the jury, whether or not in the exercise of ordinary care, a railroad company ought to maintain a flagman or watchman at a street crossing that is especially dangerous and that the omission to so station a flagman is a proper evidential fact, in determining the negligence of the defendant.

Where such fact is held to be a proper determination for the jury it is generally held to depend upon the circumstances of the case being tried, such as the amount of business, or trains using the crossing in question, the amount of travel over the street and the obstructions that may surround the intersection of the street with the railroad track, and the issue whether or not the sounding of bell or whistle would be effective, are all proper facts to determine, in connection with the consideration of the necessity for the flagman or watchman at the given crossing.[67]

But the rule that the determination of the question whether or not a flagman or watchman was necessary at a given crossing is a proper issue for the jury is not of universal application, and in many States it is held to be an issue of law for the court,[68] and not a proper issue to submit to a jury, in any case.

[67] Lapsley v. Union Pacific R. Co., 50 Fed. Rep. 172; 51 Fed. Rep. 174.

[68] Coyle v. Long Island R. Co., 33 Hun (N. Y.) 37; Grippen v. New York, etc., R. Co., 40 N. Y. 46; Weber v. New York, etc., R. Co., 58 N. Y. 458; McGrath v. New York, etc., R. Co., 59 N. Y. 468; Houghkirk v. Delaware, etc., R. Co., 92 N. Y. 219; 44 Am. Rep. 370; Heddles v. Chicago, etc., R. Co., 74 Wis. 239; 42 N. W. Rep. 237; 39 Am. & Eng. R. Cas. 645; Winchell v. Abbott, 77 Wis. 371; Carraher v. San Francisco Bridge Co., 81 Cal. 98; 22 Pac. Rep. 480.

CHAPTER XLII.

USE OF SIGNALS AND LOOKOUTS.

§ 946. **At common law.**— In the absence of any statutory provision on the subject, it has been held that there is no duty on the part of a railroad company to cause the whistle

1385

of its engine to be sounded on approaching a public road crossing with one of its trains.[1]

And even where the statute requires that certain signals be given by an engine, in approaching a road crossing, the common law would not require that other signals, which might prove more effective, should be given in the place of those provided by the statute, but the railroad company would discharge its duty on giving the signals required by the law.[2]

But while signals are not ordinarily required, in the absence of a statute, as a special precautionary measure, the failure to ring a bell or sound a whistle as a train approaches a crossing, may be given in evidence, along with other circumstances, in a common-law action of negligence.[3]

And although a statute does not specifically require the ringing of a bell or the sounding of a whistle, on an engine approaching a highway crossing, this will not excuse the railroad company from a failure to sound the bell or blow the whistle under any and all circumstances, but if the crossing is on a sharp curve, or is otherwise dangerous, it will be held to be the duty of the railroad company to give such signals, although not required by statute.[4] This duty is held to obtain, especially, in crowded thoroughfares, such as city streets,[5] and the courts generally recognize such a duty, even in the absence of statute, when it would be the

[1] Brown v. Milwaukee, etc., R. Co., 22 Minn. 165; Spencer v. Illinois, etc., R. Co., 29 Iowa 298; Vandewater v. New York, etc., R. Co., 135 N. Y. 583; 32 N. E. Rep. 137.

[2] Beisiegel v. New York, etc., R. Co., 40 N. Y. 9.

[3] Schneider v. Missouri Pacific Ry. Co., 75 Mo. 295.

[4] Chicago, etc., R. Co. v. Dillon, 123 Ill. 570; 15 N. E. Rep. 181; Winstanley v. Chicago, etc., R. Co., 72 Wis. 375; 39 N. W. Rep. 857; 35 Am. & Eng. R. Cas. 370; Gates v. Burlington, etc., R. Co., 39 Iowa 45.

[5] Loucks v. Chicago, etc., R. Co., 31 Minn. 526; 18 N. W. Rep. 651; 19 Am. & Eng. R. Cas. 305.

only safe way of operating a train, so as to avoid injury to persons rightfully on the crossing,[6] and whether such duty does exist and whether or not the duty is properly discharged, in cases where it is recognized, if the facts are disputed, would be a jury issue.[7]

§ 947. **General duty to keep lookout.**— It is generally held to be the duty of a railroad company to keep lookouts when any of its engines are in motion, and this duty is imposed not only for the safety of the passengers and employees themselves, but to prevent injury to those who might otherwise be injured if no such precautions were observed.[8]

The duty is emphasized in places where people may be upon the track, or crossing it, and in towns or cities, where people are apt to be on the railroad track, it is held to be the duty of the engineer to keep a constant lookout to avoid injury to people crossing the track, at crossings,[9] and an en-

[6] Hermann v. New York, etc., R. Co., 137 N. Y. 558; 33 N. E. Rep. 337; Hinkle v. Richmond, etc., R. Co., 109 No. Car. 472; 13 S. E. Rep. 884.

[7] Indianapolis, etc., R. Co. v. Hamilton, 44 Ind. 76.

In the following cases it was held to be the duty of a railroad company to give warning on approaching a public highway, at common law:

Dyer v. Erie R. Co., 71 N. Y. 228; Chicago, etc., R. Co. v. Lee, 60 Ill. 501; Philadelphia, etc., R. Co. v. Killipps, 88 Pa. St. 405; State v. Philadelphia, etc., R. Co., 47 Md. 76; Artz v. Chicago, etc., R. Co., 34 Iowa 153; McGrath v. New York, etc., R. Co., 63 N. Y. 522; Webb v. Penobscot, etc., R. Co., 57 Me. 119; Peoria, etc., R. Co. v. Clayberg, 107 Ill. 644; 15 Am. & Eng. R. Cas. 356; Lynfield v. Old Colony R. Co., 64 Mass. 562; 57 Am. Dec. 124; Louck v. Chicago, etc., R. Co., 31 Minn. 526; 19 Am. & Eng. R. Cas. 305; Klanowski v. Grand Trunk R. Co., 57 Mich. 525.

[8] Bullock v. Wilmington, etc., R. Co., 105 No. Car. 180; 10 S. E. Rep. 988; 42 Am. & Eng. R. Cas. 93; Galveston, etc., R. Co. v. Hewitt, 67 Texas 473; 3 S. W. Rep. 705; Heddles v. Chicago, etc., R. Co., 74 Wis. 239; 42 N. W. Rep. 237; 39 Am. & Eng. R. Cas. 645; Chicago, etc., R. Co. v. Gomes, 46 Ill. App. 255.

[9] Halferty v. Wabash R. Co., 82 Mo. 90; Purinton v. Maine Central R. Co., 78 Me. 569; 7 Atl. Rep. 707.

gineer is negligent, as matter of law, who moves his engine
in a city or town, where people are apt to be on the track,
without keeping a constant lookout ahead.[10]

Because of the impossibility of stopping a car or engine,
in time to avoid injury, it is negligence for which the company will be required to respond in damages, in case of a
resulting injury, to move cars or engines across streets or
highways, with no lookout.[11] It is held to be negligence,
of the most aggravated character, to cut a car loose from a
train, and "shunt" it across a public highway, where people are apt to be on the crossing, without some one in charge
of the car, to keep a constant lookout to avoid injuring a
traveler on the highway,[12] and this is also true of a movement of trains or cars, backward, without someone on the
car to keep a lookout ahead.[13]

[10] Kelly v. Duluth, etc., R. Co., 92 Mich. 19; 52 N. W. Rep. 81;
Texas, etc., R. Co. v. Lowry, 61 Texas, 149.

[11] Robinson v. Western Pacific R. Co., 48 Cal. 409; Cooper v. Lake
Shore, etc., R. Co., 66 Mich. 261; 33 N. W. Rep. 306; Clampit v.
Chicago, etc., R. Co., 84 Iowa 71; 50 N. W. Rep. 673; 49 Am. & Eng.
R. Cas. 468; Cheney v. New York, etc., R. Co., 16 Hun (N. Y.) 415;
Louisville, etc., R. Co. v. Head, 80 Ind. 117; 4 Am. & Eng. R. Cas.
619; Kansas Pacific R. Co. v. Pointer, 14 Kansas, 37.

[12] O'Connor v. Missouri Pacific Ry. Co., 94 Mo. 150; 4 Am. St.
Rep. 364; 7 S. W. Rep. 106; Stevens v. Missouri Pacific Ry. Co., 67
Mo. App. 356; Baker v. Kansas City, etc., R. Co., 147 Mo. 140; 48
S. W. Rep. 838.

[13] Pinney v. Missouri, etc., R. Co., 71 Mo. App. 577.

As Shannon's Code, § 1574, subsec. 4, providing that every railroad
shall keep the engineer on the lookout ahead, and, when any obstruction appears on the road, the whistle shall be sounded, brakes put
down to stop the train, etc., is declaratory of the common law so far
as it goes, a declaration, in an action against a company for injury to
property in a collision, framed under the statute, which goes further
and includes averments of additional common-law negligence, will be
treated as one wholly under the common law. Chesapeake, etc., Ry.
Co. v. Crews (Tenn. 1907), 99 S. W. Rep. 368.

It is the grossest negligence for a railway company to back a train
through the streets of a town where children congregate without hav-

§ 948. Ordinances requiring.— Upon the same ground that statutes requiring signals by locomotives on approaching highway crossings are upheld, ·i. e., because the States have the right, under the general police power, to provide for such precautions, for the protection of the lives and limbs of the citizens, or to minimize, as much as possible, the danger of injuries from such dangerous conveyances, likely to come

ing a lookout from the forward end, and where in broad daylight a child five years old is found to have been run over and killed, and no one connected with the train was aware of the fact, it was for those who were responsible for such negligence to show that the accident was attributable to some other and excusing cause. Hollins v. New Orleans, etc., R. Co. (La. 1907), 44 So. Rep. 159.

It is negligence *per se* to back a train on a dark night over a crossing without blowing a whistle or ringing the bell or having a light on the advancing reversed car, as the railroad company must adopt some means to warn travelers of danger adequate under the circumstances. Bowles v. Chesapeake, etc., R. Co. (W. Va. 1907), 57 S. E. Rep. 131.

The fact that the engineer of a railroad train was keeping a lookout on the right-hand side of the engine, when an accident occurred, was insufficient to relieve the railroad from a charge of negligence, where, on account of a curve in the road, it was also necessary to keep a lookout at the turn on the left-hand side to protect persons passing over a crossing. St. Louis, etc., Ry. Co. v. Tomlinson (Ark. 1906), 94 S. W. Rep. 613.

A railway company is liable for injuries resulting from its failure to have its train under reasonable control in approaching a street crossing, to keep reasonable lookout for persons using the crossing, to give timely notice of the train's approach by ringing the engine's bell, to have the headlight burning, or to exercise ordinary care to prevent injury to persons using the crossing. Southern Ry. Co. v. Winchester's Ex. (Ky. 1907), 105 S. W. Rep. 167.

A railroad about to send a car over a street crossing in its yards, must use reasonable care as to persons about to use the crossing, whether strangers or employees. Chicago & St. P. Ry. Co. v. Donovan (U. S. C. C. A., Minn., 1908), 160 Fed. Rep. 826.

A railway company is not liable for injuries to one struck by a car while attempting to cross a track, for failure to keep a lookout for him, where it would have been unavailing, he having stepped immediately in front of the car from a safe place. Texas & P. Ry. Co. v. Shivers (Tex. Civ. App. 1907), 106 S. W. Rep. 894.

in contact with persons rightfully using the crossing, it is held that cities and towns have the right to adopt ordinances requiring the same or similar precautions and municipal ordinances, requiring the ringing of the locomotive bell whenever a steam engine is approaching or crossing a public street, to the end that travelers upon the street may be suitably and reasonably warned of the approach of trains, are held to be reasonable and proper regulations.[14]

§ 949. Constitutionality of statutes requiring.— It is generally held to be within the power of the different State legislatures to enact laws regulating the running of trains across public highways in the State and to make the omission to give signals and to maintain lookouts, at such crossings negligence on the part of the railroad company.[15] The right to require railroad companies to give signals in approaching highway crossings with their trains, grows out of the police power of the State, and such laws are generally upheld on this ground.[16] The charter of a railroad com-

[14] Denver, etc., R. Co. v. Ryan, 17 Colo. 98; 28 Pac. Rep. 79. The violation of city ordinances, requiring the ringing of bell, before crossing a street, was held to be negligence, *per se*, in the following cases: Hanlon v. Missouri Pacific Ry. Co., 104 Mo. 381; 16 S. W. Rep. 233; Reed v. St. Louis, etc., R. Co., 107 Mo. App. 238; 80 S. W. Rep. 919; Karle v. Kansas City, etc., R. Co., 55 Mo. 476; Stoneman v. Atlantic, etc., R. Co., 58 Mo. 503; Wallace v. St. Louis, etc., R. Co., 74 Mo. 594; Braxton v. Hannibal, etc., R. Co., 77 Mo. 455; Erwin v. St. Louis, etc., R. Co., 96 Mo. 290; 9 S. W. Rep. 577.

An ordinance which required that in driving a locomotive a bell should be rung or a whistle sounded, etc., is not applicable to a manufacturer who, for his own convenience, and the economy of moving materials and cars of his own build or construction, constructs and operates a railroad track within the limits of his private yards solely for manufacturing and moving his product. Western Steel Car & Foundry Co. v. Nowalaniak, 135 Ill. App. 137.

[15] Kiminitsky v. Northeastern R. Co., 25 So. Car. 53; Messenger v. Pennsylvania R. Co., 36 N. J. L. 407; People v. Boston, etc., R. Co., 70 N. Y. 570.

[16] Illinois, etc., R. Co. v. Slater, 129 Ill. 91; 21 N. E. Rep. 575;

pany of course confers upon it certain privileges, such as the right of eminent domain, but in the exercise of such privileges, the company is just as much subject to the general police powers of the State, such as laws requiring signals at highways, as an individual would be, under the same or similar circumstances.[17]

Statutes, therefore, requiring all railroad companies to have a bell and whistle on the engines in use on their roads, and to blow the whistle and ring the bell within a certain distance, on approaching crossings, are very generally upheld.[18]

But in some States, under the constitutional provisions of the State, statutes requiring the blowing of a whistle, or the ringing of a bell on an engine, before crossing a highway, are held to be unconstitutional, if the penalty provided for by the statute is to go to the informer, rather than to the school fund of the county where the offense was committed.[19] However, where such statutes are void in so far as they may award a part of the penalty provided for to the informer, if the rest of the statute can be clearly separated from this obnoxious provision and the statute can otherwise be upheld, that part which gives the penalty to the informer will alone be held illegal and the balance of the statute will be upheld.[20]

§ 950. **Effect of violating such statutes.**— The effect of violating the provisions of statutes requiring certain signals on approaching highway crossings is to render the company

28 Ill. App. 73; Pittsburg, etc., R. Co. v. Brown, 67 Ind. 45; Chicago, etc., R. Co. v. Fenn, 3 Ind. App. 250; 29 N. E. Rep. 790.

[17] Galena, etc., R. Co. v. Loomis, 13 Ill. 548.

[18] Pittsburg, etc., R. Co. v. Brown, 67 Ind. 45; Kiminitsky v. Northeastern R. Co., 25 So. Car. 53.

[19] Atchison, etc., R. Co. v. State, 22 Kansas 1.

[20] St. Louis, etc., R. Co. v. State, 56 Ark. 166; 19 S. W. Rep. 572; St. Louis, etc., R. Co. v. State, 55 Ark. 200.

liable for all damages sustained by individuals by reason of the failure to give such signals. Proof that signals were not given will not, of itself, entitle the injured person to recover damages, but it must also be shown that such failure occasioned the injury.[21] In other words, the meaning of such statutes is generally held to be that the failure to give the required signals will constitute negligence, and if, by reason of such failure, the person injured was not aware of the approach of the train and the injury was due, proximately, to this negligence, then the railway company is liable therefor, but otherwise not.[22]

A failure to give the statutory signals is held to be negligence, *per se,* in Missouri,[23] but the general rule is that it must not only be shown that the statutory signals were omitted, but it must also appear that this omission was the proximate cause of the injury.[24] In such States, the railway company may show, in defense of an action for damages, that the failure to give the signals was not the proximate cause of the injury,[25] for it is always true that mere negligence, followed by an injury, will not render the party sought to be charged, liable for the accident, unless it is shown that the injury was occasioned, in whole or in part, as a direct result of such negligence.[26]

[21] Stevens v. Oswego, etc., R. Co., 18 N. Y. 422.

[22] Houston, etc., R. Co. v. Nixon, 52 Texas 19.

[23] Herring v. Wabash R. Co., 80 Mo. App. 562; State *ex rel.* v. Missouri Pacific Ry. Co., 149 Mo. 104; 50 S. W. Rep. 278; Kenney v. Hannibal, etc., R. Co., 105 Mo. 270; 15 S. W. Rep. 983.

[24] Chicago, etc., R. Co. v. Harwood, 90 Ill. 425; Toledo, etc., R. Co. v. Jones, 76 Ill. 311; Parker v. Wilmington, etc., R. Co., 86 No. Car. 221; 8 Am. & Eng. R. Cas. 420; Pakalinsky v. New York, etc., R. Co., 82 N. Y. 424; 2 Am. & Eng. R. Cas. 251.

[25] Huckshold v. St. Louis, etc., R. Co., 90 Mo. 548; 28 Am. & Eng. R. Cas. 659.

[26] Atchison, etc., R. Co. v. Morgen, 31 Kansas 77; 13 Am. & Eng. R. Cas. 499; Stepp v. Chicago, etc., R. Co., 85 Mo. 229; Harlan v. St. Louis, etc., R. Co., 65 Mo. 22.

§ 951. **General object of such statutes.**— One of the main objects of all statutes imposing duties on railroad companies, in approaching public highways, to give warning by bell or whistle, is to protect human life. This policy attaches to all crossings used by the public and when notice of such use is brought home to a railroad company, it is its duty to give such warnings.[27] The purpose of giving the warning, by bell or whistle, is not only to prevent persons from driving on the track, in front of the approaching train,

Under Code 1902, § 2139, punitive damages may be awarded for willful or reckless failure to give the signals required by § 2132, at a railroad crossing, where the complaint alleges that defendant recklessly failed to give such signal. Cole v. Blue Ridge Ry. Co. (S. C. 1906), 55 S. E. Rep. 126.

It is negligence on the part of a railroad company to run its engine over a crossing used by the public without either the ringing of a bell or the sounding of a whistle, as required by Hurd's Rev. St. 1903, ch. 114, § 68; Elgin, J. & E. R. Co. v. Hadley, 122 Ill. App. 165, judgment affirmed (1906) 77 N. E. Rep. 151; 220 Ill. 462.

If a railroad company fails to comply with Ky. St. 1903, § 786, providing that locomotives shall be equipped with bells and steam whistles, and that they shall be rung and sounded outside incorporated cities and towns at a distance of at least 50 rods from a grade highway crossing at which a signal board is required to be maintained, and shall be continuously sounded until the engine has reached the crossing, and a person is injured as a result thereof, the failure is negligence for which recovery may be had. Louisville & N. R. Co. v. Joshlin (Ky. 1908), 110 S. W. Rep. 382.

Failure of those in charge of a train to ring a bell or to sound a whistle at a distance of 80 rods from the place where a railroad crosses any road or street, and to keep ringing the bell or sounding the whistle until it shall have crossed, as required by statute, is negligence. St. Louis, etc., Ry. Co. v. Tomlinson (Ark. 1906), 94 S. W. Rep. 613.

The statutory duty to ring the engine bell or blow the whistle at a crossing is imperative, and failure to comply with it is negligence on the part of the railway company, even though it may have adopted other means of warning, less effective than gates or flagmen. Cincinnati & T. P. Ry. Co. v. Champ (Ky. 1907), 104 S. W. Rep. 988; 31 Ky. Law Rep. 1054.

[27] Missouri Pacific Ry. Co. v. Lee, 70 Texas 496; 7 S. W. Rep. 857; 35 Am. & Eng. R. Cas. 364; International, etc., R. Co. v. Gray, 65 Texas 32; 27 Am. & Eng. R. Cas. 318.

but it is also to give notice to travelers on the highway, so that they may not approach within a dangerous proximity to the train and thus sustain injury by the frightening of horses, or from other cause.[28]

It is generally no defense to an action for failure to give the required signals, that the employees in charge of the engine could have given the signals, as the engines of the defendant were equipped with bells and whistles; [29] nor is it any answer to the specific mandate of the law that the injured traveler on the highway was not seen by the employees in charge of the engine, for the duty is not conditioned on the appearance of a traveler on the highway.[30]

But it is not generally required that the signals should be constantly given until the whole train has passed the crossing, and the statute is complied with, if the signals are given, until the engine has passed the crossing.[31] And where a person sees an engine on a railroad track and knows, in time to avoid an injury, that it is approaching the crossing, the railroad company will not be chargeable with negligence in failing to give the statutory signals, as the sole object of giving such signals, so far as travelers on the highway is concerned, is to give them notice of the approach of an engine or train, and when they already have this notice, the giving of signals, as to them, would be a mere useless ceremony.[32]

[28] Quigley v. Delaware, etc., R. Co., 142 Pa. St. 388; 21 Atl. Rep. 827; Voak v. Northern, etc., R. Co., 75 N. Y. 320; Harty v. Central R. Co., 42 N. Y. 471; Chicago, etc., R. Co. v. Boggs, 101 Ind. 522; 51 Am. Rep. 761; 23 Am. & Eng. R. Cas. 282; Ransom v. Chicago, etc., R. Co., 62 Wis. 178; 22 N. W. Rep. 147; 51 Am. Rep. 718; 19 Am. & Eng. R. Cas. 16.

[29] State ex rel. v. Missouri Pacific Ry. Co., 149 Mo. 104; 50 S. W. Rep. 278.

[30] Hilz v. Missouri Pacific Ry. Co., 101 Mo. 36; 13 S. W. Rep. 946.

[31] Bell v. Hannibal, etc., R. Co., 72 Mo. 50.

[32] Pakalinsky v. New York, etc., R. Co., 82 N. Y. 424; 2 Am. & Eng. R. Cas. 251.

§ 952. **What trains required to give signals, generally.**—
The statutory precautions, with reference to the giving of
signals, on trains approaching highway crossings, intended
for the prevention of accidents at crossings, are generally
held to apply indifferently to all trains impelled by steam
power, whether moving backward or forward, or by means
of an engine placed in front or at the rear of the train, or
at some intermediate point.[33] And the statute requires the
giving of the signals, generally, whether the train commences
to move within the distance named in the statute, or beyond
it, for quite frequently, trains standing nearer the crossing
than the statutory distance named, will approach the crossing with much less noise than those coming from a greater
distance from the crossing, and the necessity of notice, in
such case, is greater than if they had been operated for a
greater distance.[34]

But of course a train running without an engine is not
required to give the statutory signals, when it is run over
a crossing, without the engine, in making up the train, or
switching, preliminary thereto, as it would be impossible to
give such signals when no engine was attached to the
train.[35] Those in charge of such a train, however, will not
be relieved of the duty of adopting some other precaution to
prevent injury to travelers on the highway, and if no other
signals are provided, or no one stationed at the crossing, or
on the train, to prevent injury to those using the crossing,
the company would be liable, in case of an injury traceable
to such a cause.[36]

[33] Little Rock, etc., R. Co. v. Wilson, 90 Tenn. 271; 16 S. W. Rep. 613.
[34] Lake Shore, etc., R. Co. v. Johnson, 135 Ill. 641; 26 N. E. Rep.
510; 35 Ill. App. 430; Texas, etc., R. Co. v. Bailey, 83 Texas 19; 18
S. W. Rep. 481; Cahoon v. Chicago, etc., R. Co., 85 Wis. 570; 55 N. W.
Rep. 900.
[35] Ohio, etc., R. Co. v. McDonald, 5 Ind. App. 108; 31 N. E. Rep. 836.
[36] Ohio, etc., R. Co. v. McDonald, *supra.*
The duty of giving signals applies as well to trains run on side

§ 953. **Failure to signal, at crossing, negligence.**— It is very generally held to be the duty of those in charge of an engine approaching a highway crossing, to give timely warning by bell or whistle, of its approach to the crossing, or to a public road, and a failure to perform this duty is negligence, and the right of an injured traveler to recover for an injury at such crossing, depends upon the facts connected with such injury.[37]

Where those in charge of a train of cars, or of an engine, approach a railroad crossing, without the signals required by statute or ordinance, they are generally held to be guilty of such negligence as will render the company liable to one who, without concurring negligence, is injured while attempting to cross the track.[38]

tracks, as to trains run on the main track. Brown v. Griffin, 71 Texas 654; 9 S. W. Rep. 546; Roberts v. Alexandria, etc., R. Co., 83 Va. 312; 2 S. E. Rep. 518.

And the duty extends likewise to wild trains, as well as to those regularly operated. Lyman v. Boston, etc., R. Co. (N. H.), 20 Atl. Rep. 976; 45 Am. & Eng. R. Cas. 163.

Shannon's Code Tenn., § 1574, subsec. 4, which requires every railroad company to keep some person on the locomotive always on the lookout ahead and to sound the whistle, apply the brakes, and employ every means to stop the train when any person, animal or other obstruction appears upon the road, does not apply to a train which became uncoupled on a side track in depot grounds and was backing up to recouple. Payne v. Illinois Cent. R. Co. (U. S. C. C. A., Tenn., 1907), 155 Fed. Rep. 73.

[37] Eskridge v. Cincinnati, etc., R. Co., 89 Ky. 367; 12 S. W. Rep. 580; 42 Am. & Eng. R. Cas. 176; Cincinnati, etc., R. Co. v. Butler, 103 Ind. 31; 2 N. E. Rep. 138; 23 Am. & Eng. R. Cas. 262; Petty v. Hannibal, etc., R. Co., 88 Mo. 306; 28 Am. & Eng. R. Cas. 618; Renwick v. New York, etc., R. Co., 36 N. Y. 132; Murray v. Missouri Pacific Ry. Co., 101 Mo. 236; 13 S. W. Rep. 817; Ohio, etc., R. Co. v. Reed, 40 Ill. App. 47; Bitner v. Utah, etc., R. Co., 4 Utah 502; 11 Pac. Rep. 620; Olsen v. Oregon, etc., R. Co., 9 Utah 129; 33 Pac. Rep. 623; Terre Haute, etc., R. Co. v. Voelker, 129 Ill. 540; 22 N. E. Rep. 20; 39 Am. & Eng. R. Cas. 615; Reed v. Chicago, etc., R. Co., 74 Iowa 188; 37 N. W. Rep. 149; Huckshold v. Hannibal, etc., R. Co., 90 Mo. 548; 2 S. W. Rep. 794; 28 Am. & Eng. R. Cas. 659.

[38] Baltimore, etc., R. Co. v. Walborn, 127 Ind. 142; 26 N. E. Rep.

But the breach of their duty, by the employees of the railroad company, in the giving of signals at the road crossing, does not dispense with the necessity of due care on the part of the traveler approaching the crossing, and if he could, by reasonable care on his part, have seen the train, although no signals were given, he will generally be held to be negligent too.[39] A failure to ring the bell or sound the whistle never raises a presumption that this was the cause of the injury, as the omission of these signals is no more nor less than negligence, like the breach of any other duty. The division of negligence into degrees, or classes, is generally disapproved by the ablest courts and writers, and a failure to give signals is only negligence; no more; no less.[40]

§ 954. Failure to signal — When traveler may assume track is clear.— One approaching a railroad crossing has a right

207; Hughes v. Chicago, etc., R. Co. (Iowa), 55 N. W. Rep. 470; Gratiot v. Missouri Pacific Ry. Co., 116 Mo. 450; 21 S. W. Rep. 1094; 55 Am. & Eng. R. Cas. 108; Hoye v. Chicago, etc., R. Co., 62 Wis. 666; 23 N. W. Rep. 14; 19 Am. & Eng. R. Cas. 347.

[39] Beyel v. Newport, etc., Co., 34 W. Va. 538; 12 S. E. Rep. 532.

[40] Bellefontaine R. Co. v. Hunter, 33 Ind. 335.

Though the lowering of gates across a street, where a railroad company is required to maintain them by ordinance, is notice that it is dangerous to cross, it does not excuse the railroad for failure to give the signals required by Civ. Code 1902, §§ 2132, 2139, at least 30 seconds before a train is moved. Weaver v. Southern Ry. Co. (S. C. 1907), 56 S. E. Rep. 657; 76 S. C. 49.

Failure to give the statutory signals, at a highway crossing, was held to be negligence *per se*, in the following cases: Voak v. Northern, etc., R. Co., 75 N. Y. 320; Gates v. Burlington, etc., R. Co., 39 Iowa 45; Philadelphia, etc., R. Co. v. Stinger, 78 Pa. St. 219; Paducah, etc., R. Co. v. Hoehl (Ky.), 12 Bush. 41; Renwick v. New York, etc., R. Co., 36 N. Y. 132; Peoria, etc., R. Co. v. Stiltman, 88 Ill. 529; Ellert v. Green Bay R. Co., 48 Mo. 606.

But the failure to give such signals was held not to be necessarily negligence in the following cases: Chicago, etc., R. Co. v. Van Patten, 64 Ill. 510; Toledo, etc., R. Co. v. Jones, 76 Ill. 311; Barrenger v. New York, etc., R. Co., 18 Hun 398; Cosgrove v. New York, etc., R. Co., 18 Hun 329.

to presume that the railroad company will obey the law in notifying him of the approach of its train, by ringing the bell or sounding the whistle, within the required distance, before the crossing is reached, as required by the statute.[41] The omission of the railroad employees to ring the bell or sound the whistle, as required by law, is held to be an assurance of safety to one on the highway, and such failure will have an important bearing upon the conduct of the traveler on the crossing, in estimating the amount of care required of him.[42] In such case, the traveler is not bound to be on the alert, or to exercise the same degree of care he would if he knew that a train was approaching.[43] When a traveler, by reason of the railroad company's failure to give the statutory signals, is led into a place of danger, so that his life is jeopardized and finally lost, his lack of vigilance, under the circumstances, will not generally be held to be negligence, as a matter of law, but his conduct will be a proper circumstance to go to the jury, in determining his negligence.[44]

A traveler on a highway is held to be entitled to assume that the track is clear and that no train is approaching, when no flag is presented and no whistle or bell is sounded, to announce the approach of a train.[45]

But where the statutory signals are given, the employees of the railroad company have the same right to assume that the signals will be heeded and that a traveler on the highway will not become so engrossed in his own surroundings

[41] Petty v. Hannibal, etc., R. Co., 88 Mo. 306; 28 Am. & Eng. R. Cas. 618.

[42] Rodrian v. New York, etc., R. Co., 28 N. Y. S. R. 625; 7 N. Y. Supp. 811.

[43] Beisegel v. New York, etc., R. Co., 34 N. Y. 622; Ernest v. Hudson River R. Co., 35 N. Y. 9; 32 How. Pr. 61.

[44] Hendrickson v. Great Northern R. Co., 49 Minn. 245; 51 N. W. Rep. 1044.

[45] Beisegel v. New York, etc., R. Co., *supra.*

or thoughts, that he will proceed, in the face of the danger signals, upon the crossing, in front of the approaching train.[46]

§ 955. **Kind of signals to be given.**— Where the statute does not specify the kind of signals to be given, the railroad company is required to give the kind of signals that are usual and customary.[47]

Where the law requires a signal by bell, hung on the engine, a signal in this way is sufficient and it is not necessary that the injured traveler should have heard it, to relieve the company from liability, for a collision on a crossing.[48] When the company complies with the statute, by causing the bell or whistle to be sounded, it is not essential that it should have a bell or whistle which can be heard by all men, for if the bell is ordinarily sufficient to give notice to those with normal hearing, this is a compliance with the statute.[49]

Where the bell is sounded or the whistle rung — when either is sufficient — the engineer is held to have complied with the statute and no liability generally is held to result, from a failure to make the signals heard, where they are such as are customarily given.[50]

But the signals must generally be sounded at the proper distance and in the usual way, to relieve the company from liability for failure to signal, in case of a resulting collision at a crossing.[51] The bell should generally be rung, not only

[46] Stepp v. Chicago, etc., R. Co., 85 Mo. 229.

[47] Paducah, etc., R. Co. v. Hoehl, 12 Bush. (Ky.) 41; 18 Am. Ry. Rep. 338.

[48] Grippen v. New York, etc., R. Co., 40 N. Y. 34.

[49] Houghkirk v. New York, etc., R. Co., 92 N. Y. 219; 44 Am. Rep. 370; Solen v. Virginia, etc., R. Co., 13 Nev. 106; Heaney v. Long Island R. Co., 112 N. Y. 122; 19 N. E. Rep. 422.

[50] Toledo, etc., R. Co. v. Goddard, 25 Ind. 185.

[51] Louisville, etc., R. Co. v. Goetz, 79 Ky. 442; 42 Am. Rep. 227; 14 Am. & Eng. R. Cas. 627.

in approaching the crossing, but so long as there is danger of encountering travelers on the track,[52] and if this obligation is not performed, in a reasonable manner, it is generally held sufficient evidence of negligence to support a verdict.[53]

§ 956. **When statute is in the alternative.**— Where the statute only requires that either a bell must be rung, or a whistle sounded, on approach to highway crossings, then it is error for the trial court to submit the cause to the jury, under instructions making the railroad company guilty of negligence if it failed to do either and a verdict so obtained would be set aside.[54]

[52] Whiton v. Chicago, etc., R. Co., 2 Biss. (U. S.) 282; Kenney v. Hannibal, etc., R. Co., 105 Mo. 270; 15 S. W. Rep. 983; Chicago, etc., R. Co. v. Wilson, 133 Ill. 55; 24 N. E. Rep. 555; 42 Am. & Eng. R. Cas. 153.

[53] Crawford v. Delaware, etc., R. Co., 13 N. Y. S. R. 298.

There is no duty to continue giving signals, after train has passed the crossing, in Missouri. Zimmerman v. Hannibal, etc., R. Co., 71 Mo. 476; 2 Am. & Eng. R. Cas. 191.

The Missouri statute requires signal by bell or whistle 80 rods from crossing. R. S. Mo. 1899, § 1102, Ann. St. 1906, p. 938; Day v. Missouri, etc., R. Co., 112 S. W. Rep. 1019.

This distance need not be curved, as the track, but may be on a straight line. Andrews v. New York, etc., R. Co., 60 Conn. 293; 22 Atl. Rep. 566.

The Massachusetts statute (Act 1874, ch. 372, as amended) gives cause of action for failure to ring bell or sound whistle, in approaching crossing. Fuller v. Boston, etc., R. Co., 133 Mass. 491; 14 Am. & Eng. R. Cas. 495.

And the New Jersey statute requires signal by bell or whistle, 300 yards from crossing. New York, etc., R. Co. v. Leamen, 54 N. J. L. 202; 23 Atl. Rep. 691.

Testimony as to what kind of whistle was blown at the whistling post is admissible in a railroad crossing collision case. Southern Ry. Co. v. Hobbs (Ala. 1907), 43 So. Rep. 844.

[54] Ohio, etc., R. Co. v. Reed, 40 Ill. App. 47; Tyler v. Old Colony R. Co., 157 Mass. 336; 32 N. E. Rep. 227; Turner v. Kansas City, etc., R. Co., 78 Mo. 578; 19 Am. & Eng. R. Cas. 506; Barr v. Hannibal,

And where the statute only requires the signals, in the alternative, if an injured person pleads in one count, that the whistle was not sounded, and in the other that the bell was not rung, as these allegations, in the separate counts, do not preclude the presumption of a compliance with the statute, both counts will be held bad pleading.[55] And if the statute only requires the bell to be rung on approaching the crossing in a city street, it is error to predicate a recovery on a failure to do both.[56]

But although the statute may provide for either method of signaling and a charge to the jury gives a right of recovery, on a failure to do both, while such charge would be erroneous in omitting the alternative method of complying with the statute, as where it predicated a recovery if the whistle and bell were not sounded, this would be harmless error, where the evidence showed that neither method of signaling was adopted.[57]

§ 957. **When view of track is obstructed.**— It is generally held that if a railroad company has made an otherwise comparatively safe crossing dangerous, by the placing of cars in such position as to obstruct the view of the track, it is bound to use precautions commensurate with the increased danger and to give such signals as will be sufficient to advise travelers of approaching trains.[58]

etc., R. Co., 30 Mo. App. 248; Terry v. St. Louis, etc., R. Co., 89 Mo. 586; 1 S. W. Rep. 746; Kenney v. Hannibal, etc., R. Co., 105 Mo. 270; 15 S. W. Rep. 983; McCormick v. Kansas City, etc., R. Co., 50 Mo. App. 109; Spicer v. Chesapeake, etc., R. Co., 34 W. Va. 514; 12 S. E. Rep. 553; 45 Am. & Eng. R. Cas. 28.

[55] Terry v. St. Louis, etc., R. Co., 89 Mo. 586; 1 S. W. Rep. 746.

[56] Coffin v. St. Louis, etc., R. Co., 22 Mo. App. 601.

[57] East Tennessee, etc., R. Co. v. Deaver, 79 Ala. 216.

The statute providing for the giving of signal by bell or whistle, it is error to instruct that both should be given, or that the company should signal by bell " and " whistle. St. Louis, etc., R. Co. v. State, 22 S. W. Rep. 918.

[58] Funston v. Chicago, etc., R. Co., 61 Iowa 452; 16 N. W. Rep. 518;

If a bell or whistle will not give sufficient warning of the approach of trains to a crossing, because of a high bank obstructing the track, then other signals will be required.[59] And if a train is operated in a cut, with flat cars, which cannot be seen above the banks of the cut, which is constructed on a curve, it is generally held to be negligence to operate the train, by merely giving notice by bell, if the whistle would more adequately inform travelers on the highway of the approach of the train.[60] And, of course, if the travel over the highway or street is considerable, as in cities or towns, then the duty of giving signals which will prevent a collision with travelers on the street, is all the more imperative in case of an obstructed track, because of the increased travel on the highway.[61]

14 Am. & Eng. R. Cas. 640; New York, etc., R. Co. v. Randel, 47 N. J. L. 144; 23 Am. & Eng. R. Cas. 308; Peoria, etc., R. Co. v. Stillman, 88 Ill. 529; 21 Am. Ry. Rep. 352; Houston, etc., R. Co. v. Wilson, 60 Texas 142; Anderson v. New York, etc., R. Co., 53 Hun 633; 125 N. Y. 701; 34 N. Y. S. R. 1012; Wilton v. Northern R. Co., 5 Ont. 490.

[59] Roberts v. Chicago, etc., R. Co., 35 Wis. 679.

[60] Chicago, etc., R. Co. v. Triplett, 38 Ill. 482; Richmond, etc., R. Co. v. Johnson, 89 Ga. 560; 15 S. E. Rep. 908; Indianapolis, etc., R. Co. v. Staples, 62 Ill. 313; 7 Am. Ry. Rep. 365.

[61] Bleyle v. New York, etc., R. Co., 46 Hun 675; 113 N. Y. 626; 20 N. E. Rep. 877; 22 N. Y. S. R. 993; Philadelphia, etc., R. Co. v. Stinger, 78 Pa. St. 219.

When a railway company operates its trains over a highway crossing at grade in a municipality where buildings are so situated as to obscure the approach of trains, it is charged with the duty of exercising care commensurate with the danger there existing, in the operation of trains and the giving of signals by bell and whistle, but it is not the insurer of the safety of travelers using the crossing, though in so doing they exercise ordinary care. Weaver v. Columbus, etc., Ry. Co. (Ohio 1907), 81 N. E. Rep. 180.

The care required of a company to provide safeguards at a crossing must be commensurate with the danger, and where it has created an extraordinary danger it is required to exercise extraordinary care; but it is not required by the law that the means adopted should prove effective. Cincinnati & T. P. Ry. Co. v. Champ, 104 S. W. Rep. 988; 31 Ky. Law Rep. 1054.

§ 958. **Giving signals at improper place.**— The question was presented, in a Connecticut case,[62] whether or not it is a substantial compliance with the statute requiring signals at a distance of eighty rods from the crossing, to give such signals at a greater distance. The whistle was sounded at a distance of four hundred feet short of the signal post and was not sounded again, although the bell was kept ringing until the crossing was reached. The plaintiff's intestate was approaching the crossing, when the whistle was sounded and was soon after struck and killed, and it did not appear that he heard the whistle, although it could have been heard, but the wind was unfavorable to convey the sound to him. The trial court held the engineer guilty of negligence, solely on account of the failure to sound the whistle at the proper place and this holding was affirmed by a divided court.

In a Texas case,[63] however, this question was not decided in the same way, and it was held that the statute of that State, which provides that the whistle must be sounded at

In an action against a railroad company to recover damages for the death of a boy between thirteen and fourteen years of age, at a public grade crossing in a town, the case is for the jury where the evidence tends to show that the crossing was a dangerous one; that there was no watchman stationed or gates maintained at it, and that the train was run at a high rate of speed without bell rung or whistle blown, or other signal given of the approach of the train. Davis v. Pennsylvania R. Co., 34 Pa. Super. Ct. 388.

[62] Bates v. New York, etc., R. Co., 60 Conn. 259; 22 Atl. Rep. 538,
[63] Texas, etc., R. Co. v. Bryant, 56 Fed. Rep. 799.

Except in the case of a sudden emergency, the fact that the engineer was otherwise engaged, is no excuse for failure to give the statutory signals. Petrie v. Columbia, etc., R. Co., 29 So. Car. 303; 7 S. E. Rep. 515; 35 Am. & Eng. R. Cas. 430.

And, generally, where the statute prescribes a certain thing to be done, a failure to do it, is held to be negligence, as the standard of diligence is the command of the statute and it is no excuse to fail to comply therewith, as a less degree of care is not sufficient, as a substantial compliance, or this is the reasoning of the United States Supreme Court, on this question. Deserant v. Coal, etc., R. Co., 178 U. S. 409; 44 L. Ed. 1127.

least eighty rods from the crossing of all highways, was sufficiently complied with, where the whistle was blown at a greater distance than eighty rods, if it could have been heard by a person of ordinary hearing, whether the injured person actually heard it or not.

§ 959. **When other precautions required.**— It is held in some States, that although the statutory signals are given by the employees of a railroad company on approaching a highway crossing, it will not be enough to relieve the company from all liability for an injury caused by a collision on the highway, if, under the peculiar circumstances or surroundings, other precautions ought to have been adopted also.[64] For instance, it is held that the railroad company does not discharge its whole duty by merely ringing the bell, or sounding the whistle, where the speed of the train is such as to render it impossible to hear the signals, on the approach to the crossing.[65] And, in line with these decisions, it is held that the jury can decide whether or not other or additional precautions were essential, to avoid the injury, although the statutory signals were given.[66]

But these cases do not perhaps agree with the great weight of judicial opinion on this question, and where a statute requires certain precautions of railroad companies on approaching the highway, this is held to be exhaustive and

[64] Dyer v. Erie R. Co., 71 N. Y. 228; Morris v. Chicago, etc., R. Co., 26 Fed. Rep. 22; Webb v. Portland R. Co., 57 Me. 117; Linfield v. Old Colony R. Co., 10 Cush. (Mass.) 562; New York, etc., R. Co. v. Randel, 47 N. J. L. 144; 23 Am. & Eng. R. Cas. 308.

[65] Bleyle v. New York, etc., R. Co., 11 N. Y. S. R. 585; 46 Hun 675; 113 N. Y. 626; 20 N. E. Rep. 877; Bates v. New York, etc., R. Co., 60 Conn. 259; 22 Atl. Rep. 538; Richardson v. New York, etc., R. Co., 45 N. Y. 846.

[66] Finklestein v. New York, etc., R. Co., 41 Hun (N. Y.) 34; 2 N. Y. S. R. 680; Byrne v. New York, etc., R. Co., 104 N. Y. 362; 10 N. E. Rep. 539.

exclusive, unless otherwise provided and the statute is taken to define the whole of the ordinary duty of the railroad company in such cases.[67]   In other words, the familiar rule, *expressio unius,* is held to apply to the construction of such statutes and the method prescribed dispenses with other acts not specified.[68]   So, it is held, in an Illinois case,[69] that if

[67] Dyson v. New York, etc., R. Co., 57 Conn. 9; 17 Atl. Rep. 137.

[68] This rule was applied by the Missouri court, in an able opinion by Judge Sherwood, in Heidelberg v. St. Francois County (100 Mo. 74), as follows:

"When special powers are conferred, or where a special method is prescribed for the exercise and execution of a power, this brings the exercise of such power within the purview of the maxim *expressio unius,* etc., and *by necessary implication forbids and renders nugatory the doing of the thing specified, except in the particular way pointed out.*"

[69] Chicago, etc., R. Co. v. Dougherty, 110 Ill. 521; 17 N. E. Rep. 1; 19 Am. & Eng. R. Cas. 292. And see, also, New York, etc., R. Co. v. Leahman, 54 N. J. L. 202; 23 Atl. Rep. 691.

Where, in an action for death at a railroad crossing the only negligence charged in the pleadings was the failure to ring a bell or blow the whistle as the train approached the crossing, plaintiff was not entitled to have the question whether defendant was bound to use extra precautions for safety of travelers on the crossing because of its unusually dangerous character, submitted to the jury. Holmes v. Pennsylvania R. Co. (N. J. 1907), 66 Atl Rep. 412.

If a railroad knew or should have known that a crossing was unusually dangerous, and that the statutory signals and warnings were not sufficient to give reasonable notice of the approach of trains to the traveling public, it was its duty to use such other means to prevent injury to travelers as in the exercise of a reasonable judgment by ordinarily prudent persons might be considered necessary; and if the railroad neglected the statutory signals or such other signals as were so reasonably necessary, thereby causing the death of plaintiff's decedent, it was liable. Louisville & N. R. Co. v. Lucas' Adm'r (Ky. 1906), 98 S. W. Rep. 308.

Where a traveler was injured at a crossing, it is not a conclusive answer for the railroad to say that the bell was rung or the whistle sounded, unless it appears that under the circumstances the signal was sufficient to give timely notice to travelers approaching on the highway. Bickel v. Pennsylvania R. Co., 66 Atl. Rep. 756; 217 Pa. St. 456.

Where a street crossing over railroad tracks is used by many persons,

a railroad company has the bell or whistle, required by the statute, and the proper signal is given on the approach of a train, then, so far as signaling for a public crossing is concerned, the railroad company is without blame, whether or not the signal given is observed or heeded, by the traveler on the highway.

§ 960. **Statutes apply to what roads.**— Statutes requiring signals, by bell or whistle, on approaching road crossings, apply generally, to railroad companies organized before the statute, as well as to those organized after the law is enacted, for the doing of these things, for the protection of the lives and limbs of the citizen, does not depend, in any measure, on the date of the organization of the corporation operating the railroad.[70]

The legislatures of the different States are generally held to have the power to impose such duties upon all railroads operating in the State, without regard to the date of the organization of the corporation, for the right to impose such duties grows out of the police power of the State.[71]

Nor is it essential that the company operating the railroad and failing to give the statutory signals, should be

and is more than ordinarily dangerous to such persons, the company, in addition to the usual signals, must provide such signals as are reasonably necessary to give notice of a train's approach to the crossing. Southern Ry. Co. in Kentucky v. Winchester's Exec. (Ky. 1907), 105 S. W. Rep. 167.

The failure of an engine crew to use ordinary care as to giving warning signals on the approach of a crossing is negligence for which the railroad company is liable. The statutory requirement as to crossing signals is not exclusive. Wheeling & L. E. Ry. Co. v. Parker (Ohio C. C. 1906), 29 Ohio Cir. Ct. R. 1.

[70] Galena, etc., R. Co. v. Loomis, 13 Ill. 548; Western Union R. Co. v. Fulton, 64 Ill. 271; Indianapolis, etc., R. Co. v. Blackman, 63 Ill. 117.

[71] Illinois, etc., R. Co. v. Slater, 129 Ill. 91; 21 N. E. Rep. 575; 28 Ill. App. 73.

the owner of the roadbed or equipment in use, when the statute was violated, for if the company sued was engaged in operating the railroad, it will be within the terms of such a statute, as much so as if it had been the "owner" of the railroad.[72] And a dummy road, operating its cars by use of a steam engine across a highway, was held, in Tennessee, to be as much within the terms of a statute requiring signals at road crossings, as a regular steam railroad.[73]

§ 961. **What are public highways, generally.**— Where the evidence tends to show that a public road has been traveled for a period of ten or fifteen years, it is generally held to be a sufficient showing of a "traveled public road," within the meaning of a statute requiring signals at a crossing of such road and a railroad track.[74] And where there has been such a user of a road or highway by the public and it has either been kept in repair or taken in charge by the public authorities, the fact that they may have failed to perform their duty, with reference to the repair of the way, will not affect the mandate of the statute that it shall nevertheless be deemed a public highway, so as to require signals at crossings by approaching trains.[75]

The duties imposed by statutes requiring signals at public road crossings, are generally held to apply to streets in towns and cities, as well as to public traveled highways in the country,[76] but whether or not such application of the given statute will obtain, depends upon the particular lan-

[72] State v. St. Joseph, etc., R. Co., 46 Mo. App. 466.

[73] Katzenberger v. Lawo, 90 Tenn. 235; 16 S. W. Rep. 611; 50 Am. & Eng. R. Cas. 443.

[74] State v. St. Joseph, etc., R. Co., 46 Mo. App. 466.

[75] Lewis v. New York, etc., R. Co., 123 N. Y. 496; 26 N. E. Rep. 357; 52 Hun 614.

[76] Western, etc., R. Co. v. Atlanta, 74 Ga. 774; 19 Am. & Eng. R. Cas. 233; Mobile, etc., R. Co. v. Davis, 130 Ill. 146; 22 N. E. Rep. 850; 42 Am. & Eng. R. Cas. 70.

guage of the statute, and in New York,[77] and some other States,[78] the statutes requiring signals at road crossings are held not to apply to streets in towns or cities.

But although a highway or street has been regularly laid out, across a railroad track, if the statute requires notice of such fact, a railroad company would not be held to have violated the statute, with reference to the giving of signals at such road crossing in the absence of a notice of the completion of the road or street.[79]

And where the language of the statute is that signals will be required only at " traveled public roads or streets," the railroad company is under no duty to give such signals at a road or street which has never been traveled, and which is not capable of being traveled by teams and conveyances.[80]

[77] Bleyle v. New York, etc., R. Co., 11 N. Y. S. R. 585; 46 Hun 675; 113 N. Y. 626; 20 N. E. Rep. 877.

[78] Missouri Pacific Ry. Co. v. Peirce, 33 Kansas 61; 5 Pac. Rep. 378; 19 Am. & Eng. R. Cas. 318; Louisville, etc., R. Co. v. French, 69 Miss. 121; 12 So. Rep. 338; Mayer v. New York, etc., R. Co., 132 N. Y. 579; 29 N. Y. S. R. 183.

[79] Ewan v. Chicago, etc., R. Co., 38 Wis. 613; Cordell v. New York, etc., R. Co., 64 N. Y. 535.

[80] Byrne v. New York, etc., R. Co., 94 N. Y. 12.

A private stop, to enable persons to get on or off trains, is not " a depot or crossing," requiring signals, within the Alabama law. Cook v. Central R. Co., 67 Ala. 533.

For right of company to defend an action for injury at a crossing, on account of the avenue not being a public highway, in Illinois, see Chicago, etc., R. Co. v. Dillon, 123 Ill. 570; 15 N. E. Rep. 181; 32 Am. & Eng. R. Cas. 1.

Proof that a highway has been worked by the public authorities, is *prima facie* evidence that it is a public highway. Illinois Central R. Co. v. Benton, 69 Ill. 174.

In Tennessee, it is held to be no defense to an action for failure to give signals at streets in a city, that the municipality made it a misdemeanor to give such signals, by bell or whistle. Katzenberger v. Lawo, 90 Tenn. 235; 16 S. W. Rep. 611; 50 Am. & Eng. R. Cas. 443.

Rev. Laws, ch. 111, § 188, provides that the bell of an engine shall be rung or its whistle blown where the railroad crosses on the same level any highway, townway, or traveled place at which a signboard

§ 962. **Signals not required at private crossings, generally.** — Railroad companies are not generally required to give statutory signals on approaching the crossing of private ways, where they have not been accustomed so to do.[81]

But where those engaged in the operation of the trains have been accustomed to give warning of the approach of trains at private crossings and thereby those using such crossings are induced to believe that such signals will be given and they are not given, and one who relied upon the giving of such accustomed signals was injured, because of the failure to give such signals, the railroad company would be held liable for the injury.[82]

And although the crossing is not a public traveled way, if the public have, for a long time, crossed the track at a given crossing, and the railroad company has acquiesced in the use of such crossing, this is held, in many cases, to amount to such an implied license to use the track to cross at that place, as to raise, in law, the duty to exercise reasonable care to avoid injury to those using the crossing, and, in a given case, signals might be required at such a private crossing.[83]

is required to be maintained by §§ 190 and 191. Section 190 requires a signboard to be maintained at any highway or townway where a railroad crosses at the same level. *Held*, that a way being a highway within the meaning of Rev. Laws, ch. 111, §§ 188, 190, the failure to ring the bell or sound the whistle at a crossing thereon was of itself evidence of negligence. Giacomo v. New York & H. R. Co. (Mass. 1907), 81 N. E. Rep. 899.

[81] Johnson v. Louisville, etc., R. Co. (Ky.), 13 Am. & Eng. R. Cas. 623; Locke v. St. Paul, etc., R. Co., 15 Minn. 350; Maxey v. Missouri Pacific Ry. Co., 113 Mo. 1; 20 S. W. Rep. 654; Annapolis, etc., R. Co. v. Pumphrey, 72 Md. 82; 19 Atl. Rep. 8; 42 Am. & Eng. R. Cas. 599; Georgia, etc., R. Co. v. Cox, 61 Ga. 455; Sanborn v. Detroit, etc., R. Co., 91 Mich. 538; 52 N. W. Rep. 153; 50 Am. & Eng. R. Cas. 114; Bennett v. Grand Trunk R. Co., 3 Ont. 446; 13 Am. & Eng. R. Cas. 627.

[82] Blackwell v Lynchburg, etc., R. Co., 111 No. Car. 151; 16 S. E. Rep. 12; Vandewater v. New York, etc., R. Co., 135 N. Y. 583; 32 N. E. Rep. 636; 49 N. Y. S. R. 55.

[83] Byrne v. New York, etc., R. Co., 104 N. Y. 362; 10 N. E. Rep.

539; Owens v. Pennsylvania R. Co., 41 Fed. Rep. 187; Cranston v. New York, etc., R. Co., 32 N. Y. S. R. 592; 57 Hun 590; 125 N. Y. 724.

A railroad company is not required to sound the whistle, ring the bell, or give other notice of the approach of its engine to a private crossing located in a sparsely settled neighborhood in the country. Hoback's Adm'r v. Louisville, H. & St. L. Ry. Co. (Ky. 1907), 99 S. W. Rep. 241.

The failure of a railway company to give the usual signal upon approaching a station on its road about one thousand seven hundred or one thousand eight hundred feet from a private crossing, where, had the signal been given, it might have been heard, is not evidence of negligence in an action to recover damages for an injury inflicted at such private crossing, the railway company being under no obligation to give a signal at private crossings. Annapolis, W. & B. Ry. Co. v. State (Md. 1906), 65 Atl. Rep. 434.

Civ. Code 1895, § 2222, requires railroads to set a post 400 yards from each road crossing, and declares that the engineers of trains approaching the crossing shall blow the whistle until the locomotive arrives at the public road, and shall simultaneously check and keep checking the speed thereof so as to stop in time, should any person or thing be crossing the track on such road. *Held*, that such section did not require the blowing of a locomotive whistle before reaching a crossing which was not a public road crossing. McCoy v. Central of Georgia Ry. Co. (Ga. 1908), 62 S. E. Rep. 297.

A railroad company is not exempt from liability for killing a pedestrian because she was at a private crossing and was not going to its station, where the crossing is in a town where the presence of persons on the track is to be anticipated, and where it is required to keep a lookout for them and give adequate notice of the approach of a train. Louisville & N. R. Co. v. McNary's Adm'r (Ky. 1908), 108 S. W. Rep. 898.

Signals or lights or watchmen are not required on a backing train otherwise than at public crossings to warn trespassers using the track for their own convenience as a footpath. Melton v. Chesapeake & O. Ry. Co. (W. Va. 1908), 61 S. E. Rep. 39.

Where the public were allowed by a railroad to use a track for passage to and from a depot, and the use was notorious and had prevailed for a long time, the railroad owed the public the duty of operating its cars over the track with due care for the safety of any persons who might happen to be there, and such duty involved the anticipation that persons might undertake to use the track at any moment. International & G. N. R. Co. v. Howell (Tex. Civ. App. 1907), 105 S. W. Rep. 560.

A road made on the company's land, for ingress to the depot, is

§ 963. **Mutual care required of traveler and railroad company.**— The obligations and the rights and duties of railroad companies and travelers on the public highways, are mutual and reciprocal and no greater degree of care is required of the one than of the other. The preference given to the train, of the right of way in the use of the crossing, does not impose upon a traveler using the highway the whole duty of avoiding a collision.[84]

Those in charge of engines passing over public highways, are bound not only to sound the whistle or ring the bell, but to keep a lookout for travelers on the road crossing and a failure to do either, in a given case, may amount to negligence, giving a right of action, in case of a resulting injury therefrom, but this does not, on the other hand, relieve the traveler of active vigilance to avoid a collision with the train, and although the railroad company has failed to discharge its duty in this regard, if he is likewise remiss in the performance of his duty, there could be no recovery.[85] The train has the preference of the right of way, because of the necessary momentum of the train, in full speed, and the necessities of railroad travel, over that of private vehicles,

not a "traveled public road," within the Missouri statute, so that signals will be required. Bauer v. Kansas, etc., R. Co., 69 Mo. 219; Hodges v. St. Louis, etc., R. Co., 71 Mo. 50.

A private way, used in a railroad yard, although for a long time, is not a "public traveled way," at which signals are required, by the Missouri statute. Gurley v. Missouri Pacific Ry. Co., 104 Mo. 211; 16 S. W. Rep. 11.

But where the road crossing was planked as required by the statute, by the railroad company, it is estopped to deny that it is a "public traveled way." Russell v. Atchison, etc., R. Co., 70 Mo. App. 88.

A discontinued townway, although still used by abutting owners, is not such a traveled way, as to require signals, in Massachusetts. Coakley v. Boston, etc., R. Co., 33 N. E. Rep. 930.

[84] Continental, etc., R. Co. v. Stead, 95 U. S. 161; Olsen v. Oregon, etc., R. Co., 9 Utah 129; 33 Pac. Rep. 623.

[85] Chicago, etc., R. Co. v. Cauffman, 38 Ill. 424; Lehigh Valley R. Co. v. Brandmaier, 113 Pa. St. 610; 6 Atl. Rep. 238.

but it must give due warning of its approach to the highway crossing, and failing so to do, those in charge of the train are generally held negligent.[86]   If the crossing is well known to be an unusually dangerous crossing, a greater degree of care is required, both from the employees of the railroad company and from the travelers using such highways, than at ordinary crossings where the danger is not so great.[87]

§ 964. **Who may complain of failure to give signals.**— The duty of railroad companies to ring a bell or sound a whistle, on a train approaching a highway crossing, is intended for the benefit or protection of travelers upon the public highway, and also for the passengers on the trains, and the place usually indicated for the giving of such signals is at or near the intersection of the railroad track and the highway.[88] Such statutes are intended to provide a warning only to persons using or about to use the crossing of the track over the highway, but it does not follow, necessarily, that no signals, except those named in the statute, are to be given.[89] Persons using the crossing, or those approaching and expecting to use it, are held to be entitled to receive the statutory signals, as well as those at or near the crossing, if so situated as to be subject to receive an injury by a passing train.[90]   And the failure to give the required signals can be taken advantage of by one whose horse is frightened, by the near approach of the train, because of the failure to sooner discover the train, as well as by those crossing the track, on the highway.[91]

[86] Continental, etc., Co. v. Stead, 95 U. S. 161.

[87] Wabash R. Co. v. Wallace, 110 Ill. 114; 19 Am. & Eng. R. Cas. 359.

[88] Williams v. Chicago, etc., R. Co., 135 Ill. 491; 26 N. E. Rep. 661; 32 Ill. App. 339.

[89] Burger v. Missouri Pacific Ry. Co., 112 Mo. 238; 20 S. W. Rep. 439.

[90] Wakefield v. Connecticut, etc., R. Co., 37 Vt. 330.

[91] Grand Trunk R. Co. v. Rosenberger, 9 Can. Sup. Ct. 311; 8 Ont. App. 482; 32 U. C. C. P. 349; 19 Am. & Eng. R. Cas. 8.

But the failure to comply with the statute will generally give no right of action to one hurt at a distance from a highway crossing, since the statute does not require that such warnings shall be continued between crossings, but only that they be given until the engine has passed the crossing.[92] Nor does the duty of giving statutory signals on the approach of a highway, have any application to a person situated in the middle of a train and between two cars, but the duty applies to those only crossing or intending to cross the highway, or those so situated near it, as to be entitled to the warning, because of their close proximity thereto.[93]

§ 965. Persons walking on or along track.— Statutes re-

[92] Bell v. Hannibal, etc., R. Co., 72 Mo. 50; 4 Am. & Eng. R. Cas. 580.

[93] Burger v. Missouri Pacific Ry. Co., 112 Mo. 238; 20 S. W. Rep. 439.

Shannon's Code Tenn., § 1574, subd. 4, provides that when any person or other obstruction appears on a railroad the alarm whistle shall be sounded, the brake put down, and every possible means employed to stop the train and prevent an accident. *Held*, that in order to recover for the death of a person under such act, it must be proved that decedent appeared on the road in front of the engine, as an obstruction thereto, and that the engineer failed to sound the alarm, put down the brakes, and employ every possible means to stop the train and prevent the accident. Virginia, etc., Ry. Co. v. Hawk (U. S. C. C. A., Tenn., 1908), 160 Fed. Rep. 348.

Since Civ. Code 1896, § 3440, requires a warning to be given by trains only on approaching public crossings, the complaint, while alleging that the cars were left on a street, was defective in not averring that plaintiff was injured at the intersection of the street with the track, since the cars might have been lying in the street, parallel therewith; it not appearing that they were moved across a public crossing. Birmingham Southern R. Co. v. Kendrick (Ala. 1908), 46 So. Rep. 588.

Railroads are not required, where the crossing law does not apply, to give any warning signal to travelers on adjacent highways of the approach of a train, nor are they required to keep any lookout for such travelers. Southern Ry. Co. v. Flynt (Ga. App. 1907), 58 S. E. Rep. 374.

quiring a bell to be rung or a whistle sounded on trains before reaching highway crossings are generally held to be intended for the protection of travelers using or about to use the crossings only and not to refer to persons injured while on the track, walking lengthwise with it,[94] or to persons traveling parallel with the track, either riding or walking.[95]

But this rule is not of universal application, and while it is conceded, by a Georgia decision,[96] that such statutes are primarily for the benefit of those using the crossings of highways, and not for those walking on the track, or along it, relatively to the latter, a failure to give the statutory signals is held to be some evidence of negligence, to be considered by the jury. And it is held to be improper to charge the jury that those walking on the track or along it, are not entitled to signals, by bell or whistle, but that such signals are required to be given only for those crossing the track at highways, as this is too broad, without some explanation or qualification, made necessary, in the absence of other instructions qualifying it.[97]

§ 966. Persons who know train approaching not entitled to.

— As the principal object in requiring signals, by bell or

[94] Chicago, etc., R. Co. v. McKnight, 166 Ill. App. 596; O'Donnell v. Providence, etc., R. Co., 6 R. I. 211; Randall v. Baltimore, etc., R. Co., 109 U. S. 478.

[95] East Tennessee, etc., R. Co. v. Feathers, 10 Lea (Tenn.) 103; 15 Am. & Eng. R. Cas. 446; Louisville, etc., R. Co. v. Lee, 47 Ill. App. 384.

[96] Central, etc., R. Co. v. Raiford, 82 Ga. 400; 9 S. E. Rep. 169; 37 Am. & Eng. R. Cas. 481.

[97] Georgia, etc., R. Co. v. Daniels, 89 Ga. 463; 15 S. E. Rep. 538.

Where one reaches a public crossing over a railroad by walking on the right of way between the tracks, it does not deprive him of the safeguards demanded of the company for a person crossing the railroad on such public crossing. Bowles v. Chesapeake & O. R. Co. (W. Va. 1907), 57 S. E. Rep. 131.

whistle, on approaching highway crossings, is to inform travelers on the highway of an approaching train, or engine, and this is the sole object, so far as a traveler on the highway is concerned, there can generally be no complaint on the part of a person who already knew that a train was approaching, in time to avoid an accident thereby, that no notice by bell or whistle was given. If the traveler sees or knows of the approaching train, in time to avoid the collision, the object of ringing the bell or sounding the whistle is already subserved, and the failure to perform such acts, or either of them, could not be said to be the proximate cause of an injury, under such circumstances.[98]

But although the evidence might show that an injured traveler at a highway crossing had notice of the approach of a train, if the evidence on other phases of the case, going to show the defendant's negligence, is conflicting, as where it is an open question if the knowledge of the approach of the train was in time to have avoided the injury, it is error for the trial court to tell the jury that they should not consider the failure to sound the whistle or ring the bell, in determining the question of the defendant's negligence, as this, like any other omission of duty, on the defendant's part, is always a relevant fact, that may be properly considered, in determining the issue of the defendant's negligence.[99]

[98] Chicago, etc., R. Co. v. Bell, 70 Ill. 102; Atchison, etc., R. Co. v. Walz, 40 Kansas 433; 19 Pac. Rep. 787; State v. Baltimore, etc., R. Co., 69 Md. 339; 14 Atl. Rep. 688; 35 Am. & Eng. R. Cas. 412; Telfer v. Northern R. Co., 30 N. J. L. 188; Houston, etc., R. Co. v. Nixon, 52 Texas 19; Saldana v. Galveston, etc., R. Co., 43 Fed. Rep. 862.

[99] McDonald v. International, etc., R. Co. (Texas Civ. App.), 20 S. W. Rep. 847, reversed in 86 Texas 1, cited below.

Where intestate had full knowledge that the train by which he was struck was approaching before he went onto the track in front of it, it was immaterial whether the statutory provision requiring the whistle to be blown and the bell rung was complied with. Illinois Cent. R. Co. v. Willis' Adm'r (Ky. 1906), 97 S. W. Rep. 21.

Where, however, it clearly appears that the injured traveler saw the engine in ample time to have avoided the collision, then it is proper for the court to tell the jury that a failure to ring the bell or sound the whistle, is not negligence, as to such a traveler.[1]

§ 967. **Trespassers and others on railroad track.**— As a general rule, statutes requiring signals to be given at a specified distance before trains reach highway crossings, are held not to apply to persons walking upon the track, between where the signal is required to be given and the crossing, and a railroad company cannot be charged with negligence in failing to give such warning, as to them.[2]

Nor is it competent to charge the railroad company with such an implied duty, by proof of the fact that other persons than the injured one, had also used the track as a passway or footpath, for all that this would establish would be that an implied license was granted to so use it, which would impose no duty as to active vigilance upon the company.[3] It is held in Pennsylvania,[4] that one not upon a crossing rightfully is not entitled to the signals provided by the statute, but this decision is perhaps not in line with the weight of authority on this subject, as the law does not distinguish between those wrongfully and rightfully on the track, at highway crossings.

It is generally held to be the duty of an engineer to give signals at crossings, or other places where the public have a right to be on the track, and this duty extends even to a trespasser on the track, if no signals were given, after his presence was discovered, or there are facts going to show

[1] McDonald v. International, etc., R. Co., 86 Texas 1; 22 S. W. Rep. 939; 55 Am. & Eng. R. Cas. 280.

[2] Harty v. Central R. Co., 42 N. Y. 468.

[3] Matze v. New York, etc., R. Co., 1 Hun (N. Y.) 417; 3 T. & C. 513.

[4] Pittsburg, etc., R. Co. v. Evans, 53 Pa. St. 250.

wantonness or willfulness in the infliction of the injury.[5]

But where a person is seen walking on one track and a train is approaching on another parallel track, there is no duty, on the part of the employees in charge of the engine to give warning by bell or whistle, and if such a person suddenly steps onto the track on which the train is approaching, in front of the engine, so that no time elapsed to enable those in charge of the engine to stop it, the company will not be chargeable with negligence in failing to give a signal.[6]

§ 968. Injuries near crossings.— Where a statute requires signals at crossings of highways only, a failure to give them at a distance from the crossing will not generally be held to be the proximate cause of an injury to a pedestrian on the track, at such a place.[7]   And, generally, before one in the vicinity of, but not intending to use a crossing, can hold the railroad company liable for a failure to give statutory signals, the liability must grow out of peculiar facts and

[5] Shelby v. Cincinnati, etc., R. Co., 85 Ky. 224; 3 S. W. Rep. 157.

[6] Harty v. Central R. Co., 42 N. Y. 468.

A complaint against a railroad company and a conductor of a freight train to recover for being knocked down by moving cars, alleged that the individual defendant was a conductor on a freight train which inflicted the injury, and had charge thereof when plaintiff was injured while attempting to drive some calves across the track, and that defendants were negligent in failing to ring the bell or sound the whistle of the locomotive, or to place some person in charge of the car keeping a lookout which was being "kicked" backward on the switch and caused the injury to plaintiff. *Held*, that though the cause of action was imperfectly stated, yet it stated a cause of action against both defendants for joint or concurrent negligence. St. Louis Southwestern Ry. Co. v. Adams (Ark. 1908), 112 S. W. Rep. 186.

One walking on the track was held not entitled to receive the statutory signals, in Harty v. Central R. Co., 42 N. Y. 468.

Nor was one walking at the side of the track, in Chicago, etc., R. Co. v. Dickson, 88 Ill. 431.

[7] Pike v. Chicago, etc., R. Co., 39 Fed. Rep. 754.

circumstances by reason of which the injured party had a right, in the exercise of ordinary care, to rely upon and wait for the signals, and making an omission to give them negligence.[8]

But while statutory provisions requiring signals at crossings are intended to protect life and property at the crossings, yet, if an accident takes place just beyond the crossing, the fact that the requirement of the statute was disregarded, is held, in some cases, to be competent, in determining the question of negligence on the part of the railroad company.[9]

§ 969. Frightening horses by failure to give signals.— If a train or engine approaches a highway crossing, at grade, without giving the signals required by law, it is generally held to be such negligence as will render the railroad company liable for an injury to a person injured thereby, al-

[8] Maney v. Chicago, etc., R. Co., 49 Ill. App. 105.

[9] Western, etc., R. Co. v. Jones, 65 Ga. 631; 8 Am. & Eng. R. Cas. 267; Georgia, etc., R. Co. v. Williams, 74 Ga. 723; East Tennessee, etc., R. Co. v. Markens, 88 Ga. 60; 13 S. E. Rep. 855; Toledo, etc., R. Co. v. Foster, 43 Ill. 415.

Plaintiff alleged that her deceased husband was using the right of way longitudinally at a place which was much used by the public, and was struck by defendant's train as he stooped down to tie his shoe. The only negligence charged was failure to observe Code, § 2222, as to checking speed of the train and ringing the bell on approaching the crossing. The petition alleged that deceased was thirty feet beyond the crossing. *Held*, that the failure was not negligence, *per se*, and the complaint stated no cause of action. Georgia R. Co. v. Williams (Ga. App. 1907), 59 S. E. Rep. 846.

Where a traveler was injured while crossing a railroad track, and the injury would have been avoided by the exercise of care on the part of the train operatives, the mere fact that the traveler deviated from the street or highway boundary line at the crossing, without obscuring his purpose of crossing or making such care unavailable for his protection, did not absolve the railroad company from its liability for negligence. Southern Ry. Co. v. Fisk (U. S. C. C. A., Ill., 1908), 159 Fed. Rep. 373.

though the injury results, not from a collision with the train or engine, but from the horse being driven, becoming frightened, where it appears that the fright of the horse might have been prevented, if the signals had been given, as required.[10]

If a driver on the highway does not discover the approach of a train, by reason of the failure to give the proper signals, and his horse becomes unmanageable and rushes upon the track, the railroad company will not be relieved from liability, if the fright of the horse and its unmanageable state was occasioned by the near approach of the train and the nearness of the train was, in turn, due to the failure to give the statutory signals.[11]

And in a large number of cases the railroad company is held liable for injuries due to frightened horses, by the failure to give signals, on approaching highway crossings, whether the team so frightened was on or approaching the crossing, or not. Where such rule prevails, if the horse of a traveler proceeding on a highway parallel to the railroad track, becomes frightened by reason of the failure of the engineer to cause proper signals to be given, a right of action would accrue, in case of an injury due to such fright.[12]

But of course, before a failure to signal will give a right of action for an injury alleged to have been sustained from the fright of horses, it must be made to appear that the injury was due proximately to such failure to signal, on the part of those in charge of the engine.[13] Nor will the blow-

[10] Norton v. Eastern R. Co., 113 Mass. 366; Philadelphia, etc., R. Co. v. Hoagland, 66 Md. 149; 7 Atl. Rep. 105; Green v. Eastern R. Co., 52 Minn. 79; 53 N. W. Rep. 808; Grand Trunk R. Co. v. Sibbald, 20 Can. Sup. Ct. 259; 18 Ont. App. 184.

[11] Cosgrove v. New York, etc., R. Co., 87 N. Y. 88; 41 Am. Rep. 355; 6 Am. & Eng. R. Cas. 35; Texas, etc., R. Co. v. Chapman, 57 Texas 75; Quigley v. Delaware, etc., Co., 142 Pa. St. 388; 21 Atl. Rep. 827; Vanwort v. New Brunswick, etc., R. Co., 27 N. Brun. 59.

[12] Ransom v. Chicago, etc., R. Co., 62 Wis. 172; 22 N. W. Rep. 147; 51 Am. Rep. 718; 19 Am. & Eng. R. Cas. 16.

[13] East Tennessee, etc., R. Co. v. King, 81 Ala. 177; 2 So. Rep. 152;

ing of the whistle give a right of action, in case of an injury
due to a runaway horse, where the engineer whistled as
soon as he saw the horse and this was the natural and
ordinary thing to do, on approaching the crossing.[14]

§ 970. **No duty to check speed, after giving signals.**—
Where a railroad company has caused the proper statutory
signals to be given, on the approach of a train to an ordinary
grade crossing, in the country, it is not required to slow up
the train, or come to a stop, until a traveler on the highway shall come to a realization of his danger, or heed the
warning given him, where he has an opportunity to hear
and see the train and there is nothing to prevent him from
hearing it, or from seeing it as it approaches the crossing.[15]

31 Am. & Eng. R. Cas. 385; Central R. Co. v. Brinson, 70 Ga. 207;
19 Am. & Eng. R. Cas. 42; Chicago, etc., R. Co. v. Van Patten, 64
Ill. 510; Toledo, etc., R. Co. v. Cline, 135 Ill. 41; 25 N. E. Rep. 846;
45 Am. & Eng. R. Cas. 150; Artz v. Chicago, etc., R. Co., 34 Iowa
153; 5 Am. Ry. Rep. 169; Texas, etc., R. Co. v. Wright, 62 Texas 515;
23 Am. & Eng. R. Cas. 304.

[14] Shaffert v. Chicago, etc., R. Co., 62 Iowa 624; 17 N. W. Rep. 893.

If plaintiff before undertaking to cross railroad tracks at a street
crossing exercised reasonable and ordinary care, and if, after the
engineer or fireman on an approaching engine applied steam to the
engine, the horse plaintiff was driving became frightened and stood
upon the track on which the engine was moving, and plaintiff attempted
to urge the horse forward, but could not do so, the company's employees
were bound to keep a lookout and to ascertain whether the crossing
was clear, and if they failed to do so, and plaintiff was injured in
consequence, without any fault on her part, the company is liable.
Zipperlen v. Southern Pac. Ry. Co. (Cal. App. 1908), 93 Pac. Rep. 1049.

In an action for injuries at a crossing which the person injured
was approaching with restive horses, it is for the jury to determine
whether the railroad company gave proper signals at a point where
the driver would have heard them in time to save himself from being
placed in a dangerous position. Bickel v. Pennsylvania R. Co., 66
Atl. Rep. 756; 217 Pa. St. 456.

[15] Newhard v. Pennsylvania R. Co., 153 Pa. St. 417; 26 Atl. Rep.
105; 55 Am. & Eng. R. Cas. 258; Arnold v. Pennsylvania R. Co.,
115 Pa. St. 135.

If the duty existed, to slow down trains, or stop engines after giving the statutory signals, at all road crossings, where nothing appeared to indicate that the warning signals were not heard or understood, the travel upon railroads would be unnecessarily slow and the business of railroading would be greatly injured.

The engineer in charge of an engine approaching a grade crossing, therefore, has a right to assume that his signals were heeded by a traveler approaching the crossing, and he has a right to expect that he will stop, according to the known custom, until the train has passed, and no duty exists to slow down or stop the train, until the danger of the traveler is apparent, or it is evident that the signals are not heeded.[16]

§ 971. **Burden of proof.**— In most of the States where the statutes require signals to be given on the approach of a locomotive to a highway crossing, the burden of establishing that signals were not given is held to be on the plaintiff, since he holds the affirmative of the issue.[17] Where such rule obtains, it is held to be error for the trial court to instruct the jury that the burden of proof is on the railroad company, to show that an accident at the crossing did not result from a failure to give the statutory signals.[18] This would seem to be in accord with the reason of the rule, for in all cases of negligence, it is the duty of the plaintiff to prove his case, and not only to establish the given duty, but the breach thereof, by defendant, as essentials of his right of action, in the first instance.

But this rule that the burden is on the plaintiff is not without exception and in some States it is held to be on the

---

[16] Chicago, etc., R. Co. v. Lee, 68 Ill. 576.

[17] Ohio, etc., R. Co. v. Reed, 40 Ill. App. 47; Wabash R. Co. v. Hicks, 13 Ill. App. 407; Becht v. Corbin, 92 N. Y. 658.

[18] Peoria, etc., R. Co. v. Foltz, 13 Ill. App. 535; Chicago, etc., R. Co. v. Adler, 56 Ill. 344; 3 Am. Ry. Rep. 278.

railroad company to establish that it did give the signals. In other words, it is held, in some States, such as Missouri [19] and Alabama,[20] that the railroad company must establish

[19] Crumpley v. Hannibal, etc., R. Co., 111 Mo. 152; 19 S. W. Rep. 820; Coffin v. St. Louis, etc., R. Co., 22 Mo. App. 601; Day v. Missouri, etc., R. Co. (by Judge Johnson), 112 S. W. Rep. 1019.

"Rev. St. 1899, § 1102 (Ann. St. 1906, p. 938), requires operators of locomotives to signal for country road crossings by ringing the bell for a distance of eighty rods from the crossing, or by sounding the whistle at least eighty rods therefrom, and makes the railroad company liable for all damages sustained at the crossing when neither precaution is taken, but provides that the company may show that the failure to signal as required was not the cause of the injury. *Held*, that neglect to give the signal is made *prima facie* evidence that the negligence was the direct cause of the injury, where a plaintiff is injured by a collision at a public road crossing, but th· presumption may be overcome, and, where it appears that the failure to signal was not a producing cause, plaintiff cannot recover by reason of the failure, and, where defendant's evidence, while tending to overthrow the presumption, is opposed by facts adduced by plaintiff showing that failure to signal was the proximate cause, the issue is for the jury."

Since Rev. St. 1899, § 1102 (Ann. St. 1906, § 938), providing that a railroad shall be liable for damages sustained at a crossing, when the bell on the engine shall not be rung, but it may know that the failure to ring the bell was not the cause of the injury, makes proof of an accident at a crossing and the failure to ring the bell sufficient for a *prima facie* case, and throws on the railroad the burden of proving that the accident was not the result of a failure to ring the bell, an instruction, in an action against a railroad for the death of a pedestrian at a crossing, based on the failure of the railroad to ring the bell, that, before plaintiff could recover, the jury must find that she proved the facts in support of her case by a preponderance of the evidence, was erroneous, warranting the granting of a new trial after verdict for the railroad. McNulty v. St. Louis & S. F. R. Co. (Mo. 1907), 101 S. W. Rep. 1082.

[20] Day v. Missouri, etc., R. Co., *supra;* South,.etc., R. Co. v. Thompson, 62 Ala. 494; Georgia Pacific R. Co. v. Blanton, 84 Ala. 154; 4 So. Rep. 621.

Rev. Laws, ch. 111, § 268, provides that if a person is injured by collision at a railroad crossing, and the corporation has neglected to give signals required by § 188, which contributed to the injury, the corporation shall be liable, unless the person injured has been grossly or willfully negligent, which also contributed to the injury. *Held,* that the signals were given, where an injury occurs at a crossing of a highway, and proof that no signals were given raises the presumption, against the company, that this was the proximate cause of the injury to the traveler.

that where plaintiff was injured at a crossing, by defendant's failure to give statutory signals, the burden of proof of plaintiff's negligence was on defendant. Kelsall v. New York & H. R. Co. (Mass. 1907), 82 N. E. Rep. 674.

Where a railroad fails to comply with the signal statute when approaching a crossing, and a person is killed there by the train, the noncompliance is presumed to be the negligence which caused the death, unless it is shown to have been caused in some other manner. Drawdy v. Atlantic Coast Line R. Co. (S. C. 1907), 58 S. E. Rep. 980.

In an action for injuries to plaintiff in a collision at a railroad crossing, plaintiff established a *prima facie* case when she proved her injury and a violation of Rev. St. 1899, § 1102, requiring the giving of certain crossing signals, etc. Stotler v. Chicago & A. Ry. Co. (Mo. 1906), 98 S. W. Rep. 509.

In order to recover for the negligence of a railroad company in running its engine over a crossing used by the public without the ringing of a bell or the sounding of a whistle, it must be shown that such failure was the proximate cause of the injury. Elgin, J. & E. R. Co. v. Hoadley, 122 Ill. App. 165, judgment affirmed (1906), 77 N. E. Rep. 151; 220 Ill. 462.

In an action for injuries at a crossing, the burden is on defendant to make it affirmatively appear that the injury was the result of contributory negligence of the person injured. Central of Georgia Ry. Co. v. North (Ga. 1907), 58 S. E. Rep. 647.

In order to recover for injuries resulting from a collision at a highway crossing, alleged to have been caused by defendant's failure to give proper signals on approaching the crossing, its failure to do so must have been the proximate cause of the injuries. Kujawa v. Chicago & St. P. Ry. Co. (Wis. 1908), 116 N. W. Rep. 249.

The burden of proof of all the elements of a right of action under such act is on plaintiff. Virginia & S. W. Ry. Co. v. Hawk (U. S. C. C. A., Tenn., 1908), 160 Fed. Rep. 348.

The burden of proof, under statute, for failure to give the signals, by bell or whistle, at a road crossing, is held to be shifted to the defendant, under the Missouri statute. Crumpley v. Hannibal, etc., R. Co., 19 S. W. Rep. 820.

But under the Massachusetts statute, the burden of proof is held to be on the plaintiff. Hubbard v. Boston, etc., R. Co., 34 N. E. Rep. 459.

§ 972. **Negative and positive evidence to establish.**— In an action for an injury due to a failure of a railroad company to cause the statutory signals to be given at a railroad crossing, the failure to give such signals may be established by other than positive and direct testimony.[21]   If a person, at or near a crossing, was conscious and in possession of all his senses, and he swears that he did not hear the signals given, then, if he was in a position to hear the signals, this is evidence sufficient to go to the jury, upon the issue whether or not signals were, in fact, given.[22]   Indeed, there may be cases where a jury should give greater credence to negative than to positive evidence, respecting the giving of signals, and where witnesses near at hand and in a position to see and hear, testify that no such signals were given, they may be believed, as against others, who state that the signals were given.[23]

But negative evidence, or the evidence of witnesses who did not hear a signal, is not entitled to the same degree of weight with affirmative evidence of other witnesses that a signal was given, where the witnesses are disinterested and both are situated practically in the same position.[24]   The burden of establishing that the signals were not given, is on the plaintiff in the law suit and it is generally held not to be sufficient to establish by one or more witnesses that

[21] Illinois, etc., R. Co. v. Slater, 129 Ill. 91; 21 N. E. Rep. 575. Where the plaintiff was in the possession of his faculties and exercising due care, it may be presumed that his injury was due to a failure to give the signals, in Illinois. Chicago, etc., R. Co. v. Lee, 68 Ill. 576. Proof of a customary failure to ring the bell was held competent, in a Texas case, upon the issue whether or not the signals were given at the time of the injury. International, etc., R. Co. v. Keuhn, 2 Texas Civ. pp. 210; 21 S. W. Rep. 58.

[22] McCormick v. Kansas City, etc., R. Co., 50 Mo. App. 109.

[23] Chicago, etc., R. Co. v. Cauffman, 38 Ill. 424.

[24] Wabash R. Co. v. Hicks, 13 Ill. App. 407; Chicago, etc., R. Co. v. Robinson, 106 Ill. 142; 19 Am. & Eng. R. Cas. 396.

they did not hear the signals, without a further showing that they were in a position to have heard the signals, if they had been given.[25] And where the whole train crew testified, without dispute, that the signals were given, the evidence of one or two people, situated at a distance from the crossing, who had casually noticed the train, but did not hear the signals, is held, at best, to be a mere scintilla of evidence and not sufficient to justify a submission of this issue to the jury.[26]

§ 973. **Instructions concerning duty of.**— While negligence is always a question for the jury, where the facts are disputed and the conclusion as to this question generally depends upon different facts and circumstances, where a given statute makes a certain act essential, it is generally held that a failure to do such act is negligence, and it is proper for a court to so advise the jury, by proper instruction. This rule applies to a failure to ring the bell on approach-

[25] Ohio, etc., R. Co. v. Reed, 40 Ill. App. 47; Bleyle v. New York, etc., R. Co., 11 N. Y. S. R. 585; 46 Hun 675; 113 N. Y. 626; 20 N. E. Rep. 877.

[26] Bohan v. Milwaukee, etc., R. Co., 61 Wis. 391; 21 N. W. Rep. 241; 19 Am. & Eng. R. Cas. 276; Ellis v. Great Western R. Co., L. R. 9 C. P. 551; 43 L. J. C. P. 304; 31 L. T. 874.

Where it was admitted that signals were not given on the train approaching the crossing, and the pedestrian was familiar with the crossing, the exclusion of evidence whether the bell could be heard at the pedestrian's residence was proper. Matteson v. Southern Pac. Co. (Cal. App. 1907), 92 Pac. Rep. 101.

In an action against a railroad company for injuries by collision at a grade crossing, evidence *held* sufficient to raise an inference that, if the statutory signals had been given as a train approached the crossing, the witnesses would have heard them. Rogers v. West Jersey & S. R. Co. (N. J. 1907), 68 Atl. Rep. 148.

Where a witness testifies that he was near a railroad crossing and was listening for an approaching train, and that he heard no whistle, his testimony, if believed, is proof that no whistle was sounded. Schwarz v. Delaware, L. & W. R. Co. (Pa. 1907), 67 Atl. Rep. 213.

ing a highway crossing, and it is no invasion of the province of the court to advise the jury that a failure to ring the bell, on approaching a highway crossing, is negligence.[27]

An instruction that it was the duty of the engineer to continuously ring the bell, within the statutory distance, until the crossing was reached, was held to be a proper charge, in one case;[28] but in another case, it was held not to be incumbent on the engineer to continuously ring the bell, on approaching the crossing, if no danger of a collision seemed imminent, and no harm to so advise the jury.[29]

But an instruction that it was the duty of the railroad company, in the operation of the engine which injured the plaintiff, across the highway crossing, in question, to give such signals as would apprise " all, of the danger of crossing the railroad track," is too broad, for if the statutory signals are given, whether " all " hear and are apprised of the approach of the train, is a duty imposing a harder burden on the defendant than the law exacts.[30]

[27] Atlanta, etc., R. Co. v. Wyly, 65 Ga. 120; 8 Am. & Eng. R. Cas. 262.

[28] Smedis v. Brooklyn, etc., R. Co., 88 N. Y. 13; 8 Am. & Eng. R. Cas. 445; Louisville, etc., R. Co. v. Gardner, 1 Lea (Tenn.) 688.

[29] Moran v. Nashville, etc., R. Co., 2 Baxt. (Tenn.) 379.

[30] Wabash R. Co. v. Coble, 113 Ill. 115.

An instruction, in an action for injuries at a railroad crossing, predicating negligence on the starting of an engine, the sounding of the whistle, and the escape of steam, which caused a team to run away, confining the noises to the time plaintiff was in the act of crossing the track, with the knowledge of the operatives of the engine, is sustained by the evidence that the engine was stopped to let the team cross, and that the team did start to cross, but before it cleared the track the plaintiff started the engine without actually knowing that the team had cleared the track, and the further fact that plaintiff was picked up only thirty feet from the track on being thrown from the wagon, and that another team which had started to cross in the rear of plaintiff's team was cut off by defendant's engine before it had crossed. St. Louis Southwestern Ry. Co. v. Moore (Tex. Civ. App. 1908), 107 S. W. Rep. 658.

An instruction given in an action to recover for injuries arising

§ 974. **Jury issues regarding.**— Whether the failure to ring the bell or sound the whistle on a locomotive, in ap-

from the alleged failure of the defendant company to ring a bell or sound a whistle, as required by law, is erroneous, which directs a verdict in favor of the plaintiff without proof that the plaintiff was in the exercise of due care. Chicago, M. & St. P. Ry. Co. v. Gill, 132 Ill. App. 310.

In an action against a railroad for injuries at a street crossing, an instruction that it is the duty of those operating an engine in a city along a public street to keep a lookout for persons going along such street, and on seeing that any person is in imminent danger of being injured to use all means at hand to avoid the injury, was not misleading, as assuming that an actual lookout is necessary to the exercise of ordinary care by employees in operating trains, in view of a further charge that if the jury found that those operating the engine failed to exercise ordinary care to keep a lookout in the direction the engine was moving to prevent injuries to persons going along the street, and that the same was negligence, and that such negligence, if any, was the proximate cause of the injury, etc., to find for plaintiff. Texas Mexican Ry. Co. v. De Hernandez (Tex. Civ. App. 1908), 108 S. W. Rep. 765.

An instruction was not erroneous for not including the element that the jury must find that the failure of the train operatives to give signals was the cause of the injury, where the instruction was not given with a view to specify all the elements which plaintiff must prove to entitle him to recover, but was designed to inform the jury that, if plaintiff found himself in a perilous position by reason of the failure of defendant to give the statutory signals, and while endeavoring to extricate himself from his perilous position, he acted as a reasonably prudent man would act, he might recover. Illinois Southern Ry. Co. v. Hamill, 80 N. E. Rep. 745; 226 Ill. 88.

Though Shannon's Code (Tenn.), §§ 1574, 1575, making a railroad company that fails to keep some one on the locomotive always on the lookout liable for damages resulting from collisions, does not apply to the making up of trains and other necessary switching in the company's yards, yet, where there was no evidence that the injury complained of happened in the company's yards, it was not error to instruct that the company would be liable for violation of the statute. Alabama Great Southern R. Co. v. Hardy (Ga. 1908), 61 S. E. Rep. 71.

In an action against a railroad for injuries to a person, at a foot crossing, in a thickly populated part of a town, a charge that the railroad was under no duty to sound the whistle while approaching the path across the track, was erroneous, as invading the province of the jury. Duncan v. St. Louis & S. F. R. Co. (Ala. 1907), 44 So. Rep. 418.

proaching a highway crossing, was the proximate cause of
an injury to the plaintiff, or person injured, is generally held
to be an issue of fact for the jury to determine.[31]   The failure to signal, of itself, will not justify a verdict, but it is
only when such failure occasioned the injury sued for, and
whether this is true, or not, is an issue of fact in most
cases.[32]

And where the evidence is conflicting as to whether or
not signals were given, in approaching a crossing, it is likewise held to be an issue for the jury to determine, whether
or not such signals were in fact given,[33] and, if given,
whether or not they were properly given.[34]

It is not, however, for the jury to determine what signals
were required to be given, in each case, as this is an issue of
law for the court, and a general submission of this question
to the jury is held to be error.[35]

[31] Illinois, etc., R. Co. v. Benton, 69 Ill. 174; McCormick v. Kansas
City, etc., R. Co., 50 Mo. App. 109; Sauerborn v. New York, etc., R.
Co., 23 N. Y. Supp. 478; 52 N. Y. S. R. 784; 141 N. Y. 553; Calhoun
v. Gulf, etc., R. Co., 84 Texas 226; 19 S. W. Rep. 341; Chicago, etc.,
R. Co. v. Wilson, 133 Ill. 55; 24 N. E. Rep. 555; Western, etc., R.
Co. v. Jones, 65 Ga. 631; 8 Am. & Eng. R. Cas. 267.

[32] Indianapolis, etc., R. Co. v. Blackman, 63 Ill. 117; 7 Am. Ry.
Rep. 56; Maney v. Chicago, etc., R. Co., 49 Ill. App. 105; Chicago,
etc., R. Co. v. Dovorak, 7 Ill. App. 555; Chicago, etc., R. Co. v. Logue,
47 Ill. App. 292.

[33] Chicago, etc., R. Co. v. Custer, 22 Ill. App. 188; Cleveland, etc.,
R. Co. v. Richey, 43 Ill. App. 247; McCormick v. Kansas City, etc., R.
Co., 50 Mo. App. 109; Beckwith v. New York, etc., R. Co., 54 Hun
(N. Y.) 446; 125 N. Y. 759; Mobile, etc., R. Co. v. Davis, 130 Ill. 146;
22 N. E. Rep. 850; 42 Am. & Eng. R. Cas. 70; Lee v. Chicago, etc.,
R. Co., 80 Iowa 172; 45 N. W. Rep. 739; 45 Am. & Eng. R. Cas. 157;
Annaker v. Chicago, etc., R. Co., 81 Iowa 267; 47 N. W. Rep. 68.

[34] Paducah, etc., R. Co. v. Hoehl, 12 Bush. (Ky.) 41; 18 Am. Ry.
Rep. 338.

[35] Dyer v. Erie R. Co., 71 N. Y. 228.
In an action against a railroad for injuries, a charge that the failure
to blow the whistle after the engineer discovered the injured person,
does not of itself constitute such negligence as will authorize a verdict

for the injured person was erroneous, as invading the province of the jury. Duncan v. St. Louis & S. F. R. Co. (Ala. 1907), 44 So. Rep. 418.

In an action for injuries to a boy at a railroad crossing, evidence examined, and *held* that the question of defendant's negligence and plaintiff's contributory negligence was for the jury. Meyers v. Central R. Co., 67 Atl. Rep. 620; 218 Pa. St. 305.

In an action for death at a railroad crossing, evidence that the bell was not rung *held* insufficient to require submission of such issue to the jury. Holmes v. Pennsylvania R. Co. (N. J. 1907), 66 Atl. Rep. 412.

CHAPTER XLIII.

§ 975. **Common-law duty regarding.**— In the absence of statute, or municipal regulation preventing it, trains may be run over highway crossings at any rate of speed which is reasonably safe to the passengers being conveyed.[1]

At common law the rule is that the railroad company is under the duty of using ordinary care and prudence, at all times, to prevent unnecessary risk or hazard to the traveling public,[2] but the common law did not fix any definite rule as to the rate of speed of trains at crossings. The weight of authority is that trains may be run, in the absence of statute or ordinance, limiting the rate of speed, at any speed that is

[1] Chicago, etc., R. Co. v. Florens, 32 Ill. App. 365; Chicago, etc., R. Co. v. Lee, 68 Ill. 582.

[2] Lapsley v. Union Pacific R. Co., 50 Fed. Rep. 172; 51 Fed. Rep. 174.

1430

consistent with the passengers' safety, but as to the rate of speed at crossings, the question depends more or less upon the character of the crossing and the number of people ordinarily using it.[3]

The question of negligence at common law, is dependent, therefore, upon the surrounding facts and circumstances, in each case, in determining what rate of speed at crossings will be held negligence and while excessive speed would not be held consistent with the exercise of due care, at a much traveled crossing in a city, such speed, in a sparsely settled community, or on a country road crossing, would not be held to be excessive, and in this respect the question of negligence *vel non,* under the rules of the common law, cannot be said to depend upon any particular rate of speed.[4]

§ 976. Constitutionality of statutes regulating.— Unlimited discretion, in the regulation of the speed of trains, is not conferred by the State on the railroad corporation, by its charter. Among the rights reserved by the State is the right to regulate the construction of crossings over highways and the passage of trains over such crossings and through cities and villages, where the lives of citizens are constantly placed in imminent danger from the rapid speed of railway trains.[5]

A statute regulating the speed of trains at highway and street crossings, therefore, requiring guards to be placed at bridges and other points of danger, for the safety of the passengers on the trains and the travelers on the thoroughfares in the State, is held to be a constitutional exercise of the police power of the State.[6]

[3] East Tennessee, etc., R. Co. v. Deaver, 79 Ala. 216.

[4] Western R. Co. v. Sistrunk, 85 Ala. 352; 5 So. Rep. 79.

[5] Toledo, etc., R. Co. v. Deacon, 63 Ill. 91; 7 Am. Ry. Rep. 150; Chicago, etc., R. Co. v. Chicago, 140 Ill. 309; Lake Shore, etc., R. Co. v. Cincinnati, etc., R. Co., 30 Ohio St. 604.

[6] Ohio, etc., R. Co. v. McClelland, 25 Ill. 140.

§ 977. **Ordinances regulating.**— While the law does not prescribe the rate of speed that trains may be operated outside of cities and towns, over highway crossings, and in the absence of statutory or municipal regulation, no rate of speed is held to be negligence, *per se*,[7] the rule is different where there is a valid ordinance regulating the rate of speed at which trains may be operated over crossings in a city or town, and where a city ordinance, duly authorized by law, expressly requires railroad trains passing through the city limits to observe a certain rate of speed, a failure to comply therewith is held to be negligence, *per se*.[8]

An ordinance prohibiting the backing of an engine, at a

The protection of life and property on a highway where it is crossed by a railroad is the purpose of Civ. Code 1895, § 2222, requiring an engineer to check a locomotive at a crossing so as to stop in time should any person be crossing the same, and whether a person on the crossing is in actual motion or temporarily standing does not make two such distinct situations that that section applies only for the protection of persons in the one and not in the other. Central of Georgia Ry. Co. v. Motz (Ga. 1908), 61 S. E. Rep. 1.

St. 1898, §§ 1809, 1819, limiting the speed of trains in cities and villages, and imposing penalties for violations thereof, are penal, and must be strictly construed, and should be so construed as not to give cumulative penalties, unless the legislative intent to the contrary is clear. State v. Wisconsin Cent. Ry. Co. (Wis. 1907), 113 N. W. Rep. 952.

Failure to observe statutory requirements as to checking speed of train and ringing bell at street crossing is not negligence as to a person on the track not at a crossing. Georgia R., etc., Co. v. Williams (Ga. App. 1907), 59 S. E. Rep. 846.

[7] Goodwin v. Chicago, etc., R. Co., 75 Mo. 73; Powell v. Missouri Pacific Ry. Co., 76 Mo. 80.

[8] Karle v. Kansas City, etc., R. Co., 55 Mo. 476; Wallace v. St. Louis, etc., R. Co., 74 Mo. 594; Braxton v. Hannibal, etc., R. Co., 77 Mo. 455; Eswin v. St. Louis, etc., R. Co., 96 Mo. 290; 9 S. W. Rep. 577; Kelly v. Missouri Pacific Ry. Co., 101 Mo. 67; 13 S. W. Rep. 806; 8 L. R. A. 783; Gratiot v. Missouri Pacific Ry. Co., 116 Mo. 450; 21 S. W. Rep. 1094; 16 L. R. A. 189; Graney v. St. Louis, etc., R. Co., 38 S. W. Rep. 989; 140 Mo. 89; 41 S. W. Rep. 246; 38 L. R. A. 633; 157 Mo. 666; 57 S. W. Rep. 276; 50 L. R. A. 153.

greater speed than four miles an hour, inside the city limits, has been upheld, as a valid police regulation; [9] an ordinance preventing a greater speed limit, inside the city limits, than six miles an hour has been upheld by the courts,[10] and a municipal regulation preventing a greater speed than eight miles an hour has also been upheld. And where an injury to a traveler results at a street crossing, in a city with an ordinance preventing excessive speed of trains, it is always competent evidence, tending to show negligence on the part of the railroad company, that the train which occasioned the injury was being operated at a rate of speed beyond that fixed by the ordinance,[11] and whether or not this rate was the cause of the injury and if the ordinance had been observed, the accident could have been avoided, will generally be held to be an issue for the jury.[12]

But while a traveler on a street crossing of a city is entitled to recover for an injury received at a crossing, where there was an ordinance limiting the rate of speed, which was being violated at the time of the injury, if it is shown that the violation of the speed ordinance occasioned the injury,[13] it is only where this appears, that the plaintiff establishes a case sufficient to entitle him to damages, and the fact that a train was violating a municipal ordinance, at the time of injury to a traveler, will not of itself establish a right of recovery, unless it also appears that the injury would not have occurred, unless the ordinance had been violated.[14]

[9] Louisville, etc., R. Co. v. Webb, 90 Ala. 185; 8 So. Rep. 518; 49 Am. & Eng. R. Cas. 427.

[10] Keim v. Union Ry. Co., 90 Mo. 314; 2 S. W. Rep. 427.

[11] Meek v. Pennsylvania R. Co., 38 Ohio St. 632; 13 Am. & Eng. R. Cas. 643.

[12] Dahlstrom v. St. Louis, etc., R. Co., 108 Mo. 525; 18 S. W. Rep. 919.

[13] Gratiot v. Missouri Pacific Ry. Co., 116 Mo. 450; 21 S. W. Rep. 1094; 16 L. R. A. 189.

[14] Philadelphia, etc., R. Co. v. Stebbing, 62 Md. 504; 19 Am. & Eng. R. Cas. 36.

§ 978. **General observations concerning.**— There is always room for emphasizing, before the jury, the very dangerous character of a rapidly moving train, but the law allows it and has imposed what the legislature considered sufficient safeguards against danger from it. On the other hand, nothing could be more dangerous than the irregular running of fast trains over highway crossings. Reliability in the movement of trains is essential for the protection of the numerous lives of people on the trains themselves, which usually exceeds the number met with at the numerous highway crossings intersected by the railroad. Time lost by slowness at one place must usually be made up at some other place, and

Evidence that a city ordinance forbade trains to be run at a higher rate of speed than five miles an hour may be considered in ascertaining whether or not the train was being negligently run, but such an ordinance is not in itself evidence of negligence. Bracken v. Pennsylvania R. Co., 32 Pa. Super. Ct. 22.

Where a train is running twenty-five miles an hour within the city limits, in violation of ordinances, but slows up to five miles an hour, and then strikes a person walking on the track, the excessive speed is not the proximate cause of the injury. Holland v. Missouri Pac. Ry. Co. (Mo. 1908), 109 S. W. Rep. 19.

In an action for injuries at a railroad crossing, a paragraph of the complaint charging negligence in that defendant approached the crossing with its engine at a high and dangerous rate of speed, in violation of an ordinance of the town, and that plaintiff was injured, was fatally defective when it did not allege that defendant's negligence was the proximate cause of the injury. Lake Erie, etc., R. Co. v. Moore (Ind. App. 1907), 81 N. E. Rep. 85.

It will be presumed that ordinances regulating speed of trains within a city are reasonable, and, in an action for an injury resulting from a violation of such ordinance, it is not necessary for plaintiff to state in the complaint that the ordinance in question was suitable to the place where the injury occurred. Kunz v. Oregon R., etc., Co. (Or. 1908), 94 Pac. Rep. 504.

The violation by a railroad company of an ordinance regulating the speed of trains is not conclusive evidence of negligence, but in an action for an injury at a crossing it is to be submitted to the jury as a circumstance from which negligence may be inferred. Erie R. Co. v. Farrell (U. S. C. C. A., N. Y., 1906), 147 Fed. Rep. 220.

any considerable loss always adds to the danger from the operation of the train. Persons at crossings can usually inform themselves of the time and condition of passing over the railroad track and accidents do not often happen when both parties are reasonably cautious. Hence, it is, that the law does not place any restriction upon the rate of speed at which trains may be run across the country and over highway crossings, and trains are not required to slow down or stop at such places and where the statutory signals are given no rate of speed, in itself, is held to be negligence.[15]

If the statutory precautions are taken at crossings of highways a railroad company is not ordinarily negligent in operating a train at an excessive rate of speed, for ordinarily where gates, flagman, or signals are given, this is sufficient to avoid an injury at a crossing, regardless of the rate of speed, unless it is in a thickly settled community.[16]

But a railroad company will be held negligent, in operating a train over a highway crossing at an excessive rate of speed, in the absence of the other precautions required by law.[17] If there is imminent danger of a collision at a crossing, which might have been avoided by slowing down the train, the engineer cannot be justified in failing to do so, by the plea that the traveler should have kept out of the way,[18] and ordinary care will usually be held to require that the speed of the train should be slackened, whenever there is great danger to the traveling public from an excessive rate of speed or when the locomotive, by due care, could have been

[15] Warner v. New York, etc., R. Co., 44 N. Y. 465; Black v. Burlington, etc., R. Co., 38 Iowa 515; Klanowiski v. Grand Trunk R. Co., 64 Mich. 279; 31 N. W. Rep. 275.

[16] Pennsylvania R. Co. v. Coon, 111 Pa. St. 430; 3 Atl. Rep. 234; Moore v. Philadelphia, etc., R. Co., 108 Pa. St. 349.

[17] Thayer v. Flint, etc., R. Co., 93 Mich. 150; 53 N. W. Rep. 216.

[18] Strong v. Sacramento, etc., R. Co., 61 Cal. 326; 8 Am. & Eng. R. Cas. 273.

stopped, after the danger to the traveler was apparent and the injury avoided.[19]

§ 979. **Ordinary care required.**— Independently of statute, limiting the speed of trains at highway crossings, the speed must nevertheless be consistent with the care and prudence required of careful railroad management and with that degree of care and prudence required to be exercised for the safety of the lives and limbs of persons rightfully approaching and traveling over the railroad track on the highway in question.[20]

Regardless of a statute or ordinance on the subject, therefore, the speed of railroad trains, at crossings, may be held to be negligence, if excessive, and if a collision is caused thereby, the railroad company would be liable for the damages resulting.[21]

But whether or not a given rate of speed would be deemed excessive would depend upon a full consideration of all the facts and circumstances in evidence.[22] As a general rule, negligence cannot be inferred from the speed of a train, alone, unconnected with other facts or circumstances, and a railroad company is not bound to slacken the speed of a train in a much used crossing in a city, unless there are no other safeguards provided and the crossing is a dangerous one, in itself.[23] There is, therefore, no limit to the speed

[19] Moore v. Central R. Co., 47 Iowa 688, where it was held that ordinary care would require the checking of a hand car, where the traveler was seen approaching the highway, although he had not entered upon the track, at the crossing. See, also, Augusta, etc., R. Co. v. McElmurray, 24 Ga. 75.

[20] Guggenheim v. Lake Shore, etc., R. Co., 66 Mich. 150; 33 N. W. Rep. 161; 32 Am. & Eng. R. Cas. 89.

[21] Massoth v. Delaware, etc., Co., 64 N. Y. 524.

[22] Massoth v. Delaware, etc., Co., *supra;* Salter v. Utica, etc., R. Co., 88 N. Y. 42; 8 Am. & Eng. R. Cas. 437.

[23] Dyson v. New York, etc., R. Co., 57 Conn. 9; 17 Atl. Rep. 137.

that railroad trains are allowed to make, in the absence of
statute or ordinance, except that fixed by a careful regard
for the safety of the trains and the passengers conveyed.[24]

§ 980. **When excessive speed evidence of negligence.**— An
unlawful rate of speed over a public highway crossing is
held to be evidence of negligence sufficient to go to the jury,[25]
and proof that a train was running at a prohibited rate of
speed at a crossing, when an accident occurred, whereby a
person was injured, has been held to raise a presumption of
negligence against the railroad company, in the absence of

[24] Telfer v. Northern, etc., R. Co., 30 N. J. L. 188; Newhard v.
Pennsylvania R. Co., 153 Pa. St. 417.

Trainmen approaching crossings must use ordinary care to prevent
collisions with persons on the crossings by keeping a lookout, and
by giving reasonably sufficient signals, and by running at such rate
of speed as is reasonably consistent with the safety of such persons.
Cross v. Illinois Cent. R. Co. (Ky. 1908), 110 S. W. Rep. 290.

Plaintiff alleged that defendant's employees ran its locomotive and
cars over a public highway crossing on a certain day at a rapid rate
of speed, and thereby caused plaintiff's mules to be frightened, plunge,
and run, so that plaintiff was thrown from his wagon as he was approaching the crossing within a few feet of the track, whereby plaintiff
was seriously injured, to his damage, etc. Another count alleged that
plaintiff was riding on a wagon drawn by two mules on a highway,
and as he approached the crossing he looked and listened to discover
any danger, but discovered none until his team was very near the
track, when defendant negligently ran an engine and train at a rapid
rate of speed over the crossing, which caused plaintiff's mules to become frightened, and to run and plunge, by which plaintiff was thrown
to the ground, and seriously injured, etc. Held, that such counts were
not demurrable for indefiniteness of the negligence averred, for failure
to show how or in what manner the running of the train across the
public road at a high rate of speed caused plaintiff's mules to become
frightened and plunge, or for failure to aver that plaintiff stopped
as well as looked and listened. Nashville, etc., Ry. Co. v. Reynolds
(Ala. 1906), 41 So. Rep. 1001.

[25] Clark v. Boston, etc., R. Co., 64 N. H. 323; 10 Atl. Rep. 676; 31
Am. & Eng. R. Cas. 548; Western, etc., R. Co. v. Young, 81 Ga. 397;
7 S. E. Rep. 912; 37 Am. & Eng. R. Cas. 489.

anything to show that the accident was due to some other cause.[26]

But the rate of speed at which a train may be safely run, with reference to the safety of the passengers, cannot, in itself, be deemed negligence, as against one injured at a road crossing,[27] since an excessive rate of speed, at a highway crossing, is not, in itself, evidence of negligence, but the rate of speed may be held to be some evidence of negligence, only where it tends to make the signals, required to be given at the crossing, of no effect.[28]   An instruction that places upon the railroad company the duty of so operating its trains over road crossings as to enable it to stop its train, in case of impending danger to a traveler on the highway, is error,[29] and no presumption of negligence arises from the fact that a team and carriage was seen approaching the crossing and the engineer after discovering them, was unable to stop the engine, in the absence of other facts going to show a violation of duty toward the traveler on the highway, by the railroad employees.[30]

[26] Atchison, etc., R. Co. v. Feehan, 47 Ill. App. 66; Winstanley v. Chicago, etc., R. Co., 72 Wis. 375; 39 N. W. Rep. 856; 35 Am. & Eng. R. Cas. 370.

[27] Terre Haute, etc., R. Co. v. Clark, 73 Ind. 168; 6 Am. & Eng. R. Cas. 84.

[28] Martin v. New York, etc., R. Co., 27 Hun (N. Y.) 532; 97 N. Y. 628; Continental, etc., Co. v. Stead, 95 U. S. 161.

[29] Cohen v. Eureka, etc., R. Co., 14 Nev. 376.

[30] Telfer v. Northern, etc., R. Co., 30 N. J. L. 188.
Evidence of the speed of trains at other crossings than where the injury occurred, is generally incompetent. Aiken v. Pennsylvania R. Co., 130 Pa. St. 380; 18 Atl. Rep. 619; 41 Am. & Eng. R. Cas. 571.

Where intestate heard the train approaching, by which he was struck, and by the exercise of ordinary care could have avoided it, it was immaterial that the train was running at an excessive rate of speed. Illinois Cent. R. Co. v. Willis' Adm'r (Ky. 1906), 97 S. W. Rep. 21.

Though the speed of a locomotive when it struck decedent could not be shown alone by the testimony of the persons who saw it moving

§ 981. **When speed so great as to render signals useless.—**
If a train is being propelled at such a rate of speed as to enable it to cover the distance between a point from which
the signals for the crossing would be given and the crossing, in so short a time as to make the signals of little or no
use to one using the crossing, then a failure to give notice
at a greater distance, would be held to be negligence on the
part of the railroad company, for which there would be a
liability, in case of a resulting injury.[31]

In other words, the speed of a train should not be so
great as to render unavailing, the warning required to be
given at public crossings. This caution is especially applicable when the sound of the signals is partially obstructed
by wind or other noises, or when intervening objects prevent
those who are approaching the railroad track from seeing the
approaching train. In such cases, if an excessive rate of
speed is maintained at the crossings, watchmen should be
stationed there, or other precautions observed, to prevent
injuries to those using the crossings.[32]

§ 982. **What speed generally will be held to be excessive.—**
Unless there are special circumstances requiring a lower

after the accident, such testimony was made admissible by testimony
that a uniform speed was maintained from where the locomotive
appeared to the point where the witnesses saw it. King v. Wabash R.
Co. (Mo. 1908), 109 S. W. Rep. 671.

Where the evidence was conflicting as to the rate of speed at which
a train was running, and which struck plaintiff's intestate, and one
witness testified that it was running at the usual rate, admission of
evidence as to such usual rate was not reversible error. Louisville,
etc., R. Co. v. Goulding (Ala. 1908), 42 So. Rep. 854.

In an action for the death of a person by being struck by a train,
evidence considered, and *held* insufficient to show that at the time of
the accident, the train was running more than five miles an hour.
Holland v. Missouri Pac. Ry. Co. (Mo. 1908), 109 S. W. Rep. 19.

[31] Childs v. Pennsylvania R. Co., 150 Pa. St. 73; 24 Atl. Rep. 341.

[32] Baltimore, etc., R. Co. v. Owings, 65 Md. 502; 5 Atl. Rep. 329;
28 Am. & Eng. R. Cas. 639.

rate of speed, such as a dangerous crossing, or that the train is operated in a populous commercial center, no rate of speed, consistent with safety to the lives of the passengers and employees on the train, will be held to be negligence,[33] and the question whether or not a given rate of speed will, or will not, be held to be negligence, will therefore depend more or less, upon the surrounding circumstances.[34]

It has been held not to be negligence, *per se,* to run a train at a rate of speed of twenty-five or thirty miles an hour, across a public road, in the country.[35]   And in another case, where the signals of the train could be heard as far as a mile, it was held not to be negligence to run trains at forty or forty-five miles an hour over country road crossings.[36]   Indeed, if any other rule obtained, as this is where speed must ordinarily be maintained, to get to given destinations in time, or according to schedule, the great demand for fast trains would have to be ignored and commerce would give way to other interests.

But a speed which would not be held to be excessive, in the country, where people are seldom encountered on the crossings, might be the grossest negligence in cities, where people are congregated and frequently use such crossings. Accordingly, it is held to be negligence to operate trains over city streets, at twenty-five or thirty miles an hour,[37] and such a rate of speed, in a populous city, unaccompanied by other circumstances, may be held to be such neg-

[33] Telfer v. Northern R. Co., 30 N. J. L. 188; Chicago, etc., R. Co. v. Florens, 32 Ill. App. 365; Powell v. Missouri Pacific Ry. Co., 76 Mo. 80; Wallace v. St. Louis, etc., R. Co., 74 Mo. 594.

[34] Stepp v. Chicago, etc., R. Co., 85 Mo. 229.

[35] Goodwin v. Chicago, etc., R. Co., 75 Mo. 73; 11 Am. & Eng. R. Cas. 460; Reading, etc., R. Co. v. Ritchie, 102 Pa. St. 425; 19 Am. & Eng. R. Cas. 267.

[36] Griffith v. Baltimore, etc., R. Co., 44 Fed. Rep. 574.

[37] Central R. Co. v. Russell, 75 Ga. 810.

*lig*ence as to authorize a recovery of damages, for an injury received on account of such excessive speed.[38]

§ 983. **When special circumstances require slower trains.**— There may be special circumstances which will impose the duty on the railroad company of slacking the speed of trains, at a given time or place, as where the engineer sees that a person is crossing the track, or there were sounds or obstructions which would prevent the signals for the crossing from being readily heard or discerned.[39] In such cases, it is negligence for the railroad company to permit the train to proceed without slacking the speed of the train and for

[38] Hagan v. Philadelphia, etc., R. Co., 5 Phila. (Pa.) 179; Louisville, etc., R. Co. v. Commonwealth, 80 Ky. 143; 44 Am. Rep. 468; 14 Am. & Eng. R. Cas. 613.

A speed of from fifteen to twenty-five miles an hour by a railroad train around a very abrupt curve at a much used crossing in a city is some evidence to submit to a jury on the question of defendant's negligence. Serano v. New York Cent., etc., R. Co., 80 N. E. Rep. 1025; 188 N. Y. 156.

Where a railroad track was straight for a long distance before reaching a crossing, and a train could easily be seen from the way for several hundred feet from the crossing, and the extent of the use of the crossing did not appear, a speed of eighteen miles an hour in the nighttime could not be said to be unreasonable. Giacomo v. New York, etc., R. Co. (Mass. 1907), 81 N. E. Rep. 899.

Evidence that a train was run backward, before daylight, at a speed of thirty to forty miles an hour, without signals or other warning, and without lights, except such as are usually placed at the back end of trains, over a street crossing at which a large number of people were in the habit of crossing at that hour, but which was blocked by another train standing thereon, *held* to warrant a jury in finding that the railroad company was negligent as to one who, in attempting to go around the standing train to get over the crossing, had gone on the tracks outside the bounds of the street, and was there struck by the backing train and killed, he not being a trespasser, and that such negligence was the cause of his death. Kurt v. Lake Shore, etc., R. Co. (N. Y. Sup. 1908), 111 N. Y. S. 859.

[39] Dyson v. New York, etc., R. Co., 57 Conn. 9; 17 Atl. Rep. 137.

an injury, due to such a cause, there would be a corresponding liability.[40]

But a railroad company is not responsible for not slackening the speed of its trains at a place where a public highway crosses the track, unless there were special circumstances which would render this crossing unusually dangerous and require the slackening of the speed of the train, to avoid injury to the traveling public.[41]   And where only signals are required at a public road crossing, not otherwise dangerous, it would be error to predicate a right of recovery, on the excessive rate of speed, if the signals were given, where no special circumstances existed to justify the slowing down of the train, as this practically authorized the jury to require a different standard of diligence at crossings than that required by the legislature and enables them to hold that no defense was shown, when a full compliance with the statute had been established.[42]

§ 984. **When persons using crossings may assume speed lawful.**—Where a law limits the rate of speed that trains may be run at crossings, a person injured or killed at a crossing, must be presumed to have known the law, for all men are held to have knowledge, constructively, at least, of the law,

[40] Dyson v. New York, etc., R. Co., *supra*.

[41] Zeigler v. Northeastern R. Co., 5 So. Car. 221.

[42] Klanowski v. Grand Trunk R. Co., 64 Mich. 279; 31 N. W. Rep. 275.

The employees of a railway company running a train through a storm, such as obscures the view and deadens the sound of the train's approach, must proceed with the greatest caution, and exercise greater care than while running a train during ordinary weather. Louisville, etc., R. Co. v. Ueltschi's Ex'rs (Ky. 1906), 97 S. W. Rep. 14.

Where a train passes through a cut and emerges from a curve within a town, and so close to the station where the presence of persons on the track or about it may reasonably be expected, adequate notice of its approach should be given, and the speed be such that the lookout would not be idle. Louisville, etc., R. Co. v. McNary's Adm'r (Ky. 1908), 108 S. W. Rep. 898.

and may therefore be reasonably presumed to have acted upon the assumption that the train would be run according to law. If the train was operated at a rate of speed exceeding that provided by law, this will therefore be held to be such a circumstance, going to show negligence on the part of the railroad company, as to enable a jury to fix a liability upon it for such an injury.[43]

And a person who is about to cross a railroad track, upon a city street, where there is an ordinance limiting the rate of speed of trains within the city limits, or at street crossings, has a right to presume, until the contrary is made apparent, that the railroad company will comply with the ordinance of the city and that it will not operate its trains in violation of the ordinance.[44]

§ 985. Speed in cities.— As the danger from excessive speed of trains is greater in congested commercial centers of population than in rural districts, there is a different rule obtaining, with reference to the running of trains in the two places and in cities, where a large number of people cross the tracks or use them otherwise, it is generally held to be negligence to run a train at an excessive rate of speed, without maintaining other precautions, such as gates or watch-

[43] Langhoff v. Milwaukee, etc., R. Co., 19 Wis. 489; Haas v. Chicago, etc., R. Co., 41 Wis. 44.

[44] Correll v. Burlington, etc., R. Co., 38 Iowa 120; Ramsey v. Louisville, etc., R. Co., 89 Ky. 99; 20 S. W. Rep. 162.

One attempting to drive across a railway crossing in a town had no right to presume that an approaching train was not running in violation of a speed ordinance, where, when within from forty to sixty feet of the crossing, if she looked, she would have known it was running at a high rate of speed. Stotler v. Chicago, etc., Ry. Co. (Mo. 1907), 103 S. W. Rep. 1.

One approaching a railroad crossing is not authorized to assume that the persons operating a train will not in any way be negligent in its operation. Hutson v. Southern California Ry. Co. (Cal. 1907), 89 Pac. Rep. 1093.

men to prevent injuries.[?] If a person is injured at a street crossing in a city, by reason of the excessive speed of a train, and it appears that the injury might have been avoided but for the rate of speed at which the train was being operated, the railroad company will be held liable for damages for such an injury.[45]

Of course the failure to give the signals required by statute or ordinance would add to the negligence that might otherwise be shown by the mere fact of running a train in a city at an excessive rate of speed, and if a train in a populous city is operated over street crossings, on a down grade, without steam and without signals for the crossings of streets, this would generally be held sufficient to hold the company liable for an injury to a person on the street crossings.[47]

But of course it cannot be said to be negligence to run a train at an excessive rate of speed, even in a populous city, where proper signals are given, or gates or flagmen are maintained at street crossings and there is no ordinance preventing a high rate of speed or providing at what speed trains may be operated through the city.[48]

[45] Eskridge v. Cincinnati. etc. R. Co. 89 Ky. 367: 12 S. W. Rep. 540; 42 Am. & Eng. R. Cas. 176.

[46] Duffy v. Missouri Pacific Ry. Co. 19 Mo. App. 380.

[47] Chicago, etc., R. Co. v. Payne, 59 Ill. 534; 11 Am. Ry. Rep. 157; Chicago, etc., R. Co. v. Sullivan, 143 Ill. 48; Chicago, etc., R. Co. v. Dowd, 115 Ill. 659.

[48] Haywood v. New York, etc., R. Co. 35 N. Y. S. R. 748; 59 Hun 617; 128 N. Y. 596; 38 N. Y. S. R. 1011.

Evidence that defendant operated its train forty to fifty miles per hour over a city street crossing at which intestate was killed, in violation of a four-mile speed ordinance, held to warrant a finding that such negligence was the proximate cause of intestate's death. Wamsley v. Cleveland, etc., Ry. Co. (Ind. App. 1907), 82 N. E. Rep. 490.

A railroad company is guilty of negligence in running a train within the corporate limits of a city at a high rate of speed where it appears that at the street crossing upon which the plaintiff was injured crossing gates and gateman were maintained by such company, and

men, to prevent injuries.[45]   If a person is injured at a
street crossing in a city, by reason of the excessive speed of
a train, and it appears that the injury might have been
avoided, but for the rate of speed at which the train was
being operated, the railroad company will be held liable for
damages for such an injury.[46]

Of course the failure to give the signals required by statute or ordinance, would add to the negligence that might otherwise be shown by the mere fact of running a train in a
city at an excessive rate of speed, and if a train, in a populous city, is operated over street crossings, on a down grade,
without steam and without signals for the crossings of
streets, this would generally be held sufficient to hold the
company liable for an injury to a person on the street crossings.[47]

But of course it cannot be said to be negligence to run a
train at an excessive rate of speed, even in a populous city,
where proper signals are given, or gates or flagmen are maintained at street crossings and there is no ordinance preventing a high rate of speed or providing at what speed trains
may be operated through the city.[48]

[45] Eskridge v. Cincinnati, etc., R. Co., 89 Ky. 367; 12 S. W. Rep.
580; 42 Am. & Eng. R. Cas. 176.

[46] Duffy v. Missouri Pacific Ry. Co., 19 Mo. App. 380.

[47] Chicago, etc., R. Co. v. Payne, 59 Ill. 534; 11 Am. Ry. Rep. 157;
Chicago, etc., R. Co. v. Sullivan, 143 Ill. 48; Chicago, etc., R. Co. v.
Dowd, 115 Ill. 659.

[48] Haywood v. New York, etc., R. Co., 35 N. Y. S. R. 748; 59 Hun
617; 128 N. Y. 596; 38 N. Y. S. R. 1011.

Evidence that defendant operated its train forty to fifty miles per
hour over a city street crossing at which intestate was killed, in violation of a four-mile speed ordinance, *held* to warrant a finding that such
negligence was the proximate cause of intestate's death. Wamsley v.
Cleveland, etc., Ry. Co. (Ind. App. 1907), 82 N. E. Rep. 490.

A railroad company is guilty of negligence in running a train
within the corporate limits of a city at a high rate of speed where it
appears that at the street crossing upon which the plaintiff was injured
crossing gates and gateman were maintained by such company, and

§ 986. **Speed in towns or villages.**— As distinguished from the rule obtaining in congested commercial centers, such as cities, the rule as to the rate of speed of trains in towns and villages, which have not, by ordinance, regulated the rate of speed of trains within the limits of the town or village, may be said to be that the railroad company must operate trains in towns or villages at such a rate of speed as will conform reasonably with the surroundings and not subject the inhabitants or persons using the crossings of town or village streets, to more than ordinary danger.

Speaking of this duty, on the part of railroad companies, in the operation of trains in towns and villages, the late Judge Black, for the Supreme Court of Missouri, said: " While in the absence of municipal regulations, no rate of speed is negligence, *per se,*[49] still it does not follow that the defendant may, at all times and places, run its trains at any rate of speed. This was a proper element to be taken into consideration, in determining whether the defendant was guilty of negligence at the crossing, and this, too, without regard to the rules of the defendant. There must be a reasonable and fair regard to persons and property in running

the danger arising from the approach of such train was not made known to the plaintiff either by the lowering of the gates or the giving of any signal. Chicago, etc., Ry. Co. v. Smith, 124 Ill. App. 627; Chicago City Ry. Co. v. Same, *id.* Judgment affirmed (1907) 80 N. E. Rep. 716.

A railroad company operating a train on a city street used in common by it and pedestrians and vehicles may be required to take precautions against collisions which are not necessary when it is operating trains on its own right of way. Schwanenfeldt v. Chicago, etc., Ry. Co. (Neb. 1908), 115 N. W. Rep. 285.

It was negligence for a railroad to run trains through a city at a greater rate of speed than that prescribed by the city ordinance. Louisville, etc., R. Co. v. Christian Moehr Brewing Co. (Ala. 1907), 43 So. Rep. 723.

[49] Powell v. Missouri Pacific Ry. Co., 76 Mo. 80; Bell v. Hannibal, etc., R. Co., 72 Mo. 50; Wallace v. St. Louis, etc., R. Co., 74 Mo. 594.

through villages and over frequented public crossings, and the rate of speed must be made to conform reasonably with the surroundings." [50]

And this is the general rule on the subject, obtaining in other States, and while no rate of speed, of itself, will be held to be negligence, in the absence of ordinances preventing a high rate of speed, or when unconnected with other facts or circumstances, showing a disregard of the safety of the public, the circumstance that a train is operated at an excessive rate of speed, in a town or village, may, in connection with a failure to give the required signals, or other circumstances, show such a disregard of the safety of those using the crossings of streets, as to amount to an unreasonable rate of speed, when considered in connection with the surroundings. [51]

§ 987. **Speed of trains at country road crossings.**— There is generally held to be no obligation resting upon a railroad company, to slacken the speed of trains at public road crossings in an open level country, where the crossing is not used to any great extent by people. [52]

But of course the rate of speed at which a train is operated increases the danger to be incurred by those at public road crossings correspondingly, [53] and taken in connection with other facts and circumstances, it may be competent to establish the rate of speed at which the train was being operated over country road crossings, as a material circumstance, affecting the defendant's negligence. [54]

[50] Stepp v. Chicago, etc., R. Co., 85 Mo. 229, at page 234.

[51] Beaustrom v. Northern Pacific R. Co., 46 Minn. 193; 48 N. W. Rep. 778; Clark v. Boston, etc., R. Co., 64 N. H. 325; 10 Atl. Rep. 676; 31 Am. & Eng. R. Cas. 548.

[52] Toledo, etc., R. Co. v. Miller, 76 Ill. 278; Chicago, etc., R. Co. v. Harwood, 80 Ill. 88.

[53] Childs v. Pennsylvania R. Co., 150 Pa. St. 73; 24 Atl. Rep. 341.

[54] Stepp v. Chicago, etc., R. Co., 85 Mo. 229.

And even where there is a statute requiring the railroad company to slow down trains at crossings in cuts, or at other places, where the crossing is particularly dangerous, such as the Alabama statute,[55] this provision will only be held to apply as to such crossings as are particularly mentioned in the statute and at other road crossings, in the country, since the common law did not require any particular rate of speed, it cannot be relied upon as a ground of recovery, that the train was being operated at an excessive rate of speed, at a country road crossing, unless this is made objectionable by positive statutory enactment, free from other duties.[56]

§ 988. At dangerous crossings.— Since negligence is but the absence of care, according to the circumstances in a given case, the acts of the defendant must always be adjudged according to the apparent danger which those acts entail

[55] East Tennessee, etc., R. Co. v. Deaver, 79 Ala. 216 (Ala. Code, 1699).

[56] East Tennessee, etc., R. Co. v. Deaver, supra.

No rate of speed in a train moving in the open country is in itself negligence as to a person on a crossing, though it may become a factor, when considered with reference to the circumstances of the particular place, in determining whether due care has been exercised. Hartman v. Chicago, etc., Ry. Co. (Iowa 1906), 110 N. W. Rep. 10.

Employees in charge of a train need not slacken the speed of the train at ordinary public crossings; this being ordinarily required only at places where the population is crowded and the presence of persons on the track is to be expected. Hummer's Exec. v. Louisville, etc., R. Co. (Ky. 1908), 108 S. W. Rep. 885.

It was negligence for a railroad company to operate a passenger train at night through the country and across highways at the rate of thirty miles an hour without a headlight, and with only a red lantern hung on the tender of the engine, which was being run backwards. Gorton v. Harmon (Mich. 1908), 116 N. W. Rep. 443; 15 Detroit Leg. N. 250.

Since a higher rate of speed in the movement of cars is permissible in the open country than along the streets of a city, more caution is demanded of one crossing tracks in the country than in cities. Phillips v. Washington, etc., Ry. Co. (Md. 1906), 65 Atl. Rep. 422.

upon others. Applying this rule to the operation of trains over highway crossings, it results that if a crossing is unusually dangerous, because of obstructions, or otherwise, as the danger is correspondingly increased, trains ought, in the exercise of reasonable care, on the part of the railroad company, to be operated over such crossings at a proportionately less rate of speed than trains are operated over crossings not so dangerous.[57]

Where there was evidence, therefore, that a crossing was dangerous and was approached by a train operated at a high rate of speed, it was held that the trial court did not commit error in refusing to charge the jury that the company had discharged its full duty, on approaching the crossing with its train, in sounding the whistle or ringing the bell, at a proper distance therefrom, as the other circumstance, that the train was operated at an excessive rate of speed, at such a crossing, was also a circumstance that could properly be considered by the jury, in determining the question of the defendant's negligence.[58]

[57] Ellis v. Lake Shore, etc., R. Co., 138 Pa. St. 506; 21 Atl. Rep. 140.

[58] South, etc., R. Co. v. Thompson, 62 Ala. 494; Ellis v. Lake Shore, etc., Co., *supra*.

At exceptionally dangerous crossings, if the railroad company does not choose to have a flagman or other safety device, and the statutory signals are not sufficient, the speed of the train must be so regulated as not to unnecessarily impair the safety of persons using the highway. Cincinnati, etc., Ry. Co. v. Champ (Ky. 1907), 104 S. W. Rep. 988; 31 Ky. Law Rep. 1054.

Where, in an action against a railroad for the death of a traveler struck by a train at a crossing, the evidence showed that the highway was much traveled, and that the crossing was an unusually dangerous one, the refusal to charge that if the giving by the railroad of the statutory signals on the approach of trains is not sufficient to give reasonable notice of the approach of trains, and the railroad knew, or by the exercise of ordinary care could have known it, the railroad is required to use such other means to prevent injury to travelers at the crossing as in the exercise of a reasonable judgment might be

§ *989.* **Jury issues regarding.**— Where there is evidence that a train was being propelled at a rate of speed to make it highly dangerous to those on a public crossing over the railroad track, whether such rate of speed is prohibited by ordinance or not it was negligence on the part of the railroad company to so operate the train.[59]

It is held competent for witnesses familiar with the speed of trains, to testify that a train was going at an excessive peed, at or near the crossing, and that it failed to give the tatutory signals for the crossing, and on such evidence beg adduced, it is held to be a proper jury issue, whether not this constituted negligence.[60]

If a train is operated at a crossing in a town or city, at a te of speed prohibited by ordinance, this is generally held be sufficient evidence of negligence to warrant the submis-n of the question of the company's negligence in so op-ting the train, to the jury.[61] And where the facts and rounding circumstances in a case show that a crossing more than ordinarily dangerous, it is held to be a jury ue whether or not the circumstances were sufficient to mpel the railroad company to slacken the speed of the ain in approaching such a crossing.[62]

nsidered necessary by ordinarily prudent persons operating a train, as erroneous. Adkisson's Adm'r v. Louisville, etc., Ry. Co. (Ky. 908), 110 S. W. Rep. 284.

[59] McGrath v. New York, etc., R. Co., 1 T. & C. (N. Y.) 243; State Boston, etc., R. Co., 80 Me. 430; 15 Atl. Rep. 36; 35 Am. & Eng. R. Cas. 356.

[60] Black v. Burlington, etc., R. Co., 38 Iowa 515; Bolinger v. St. Paul, etc., R. Co., 36 Minn. 418; 31 N. W. Rep. 856; 29 Am. & Eng. R. Cas. 408.

[61] Keim v. Union, etc., R. Co., 90 Mo. 314; 2 S. W. Rep. 427; Persigner v. Wabash R. Co., 82 Mo. 197; Kendrick v. Chicago, etc., R. Co., 81 Mo. 521; Hudson v. Wabash R. Co., 32 Mo. App. 667.

[62] Zeigler v. Northeastern R. Co., 5 So. Car. 221; Heinzle v. Metropolitan R. Co., 182 Mo. 558; 81 S. W. Rep. 848.

In an action against a railway company for the death of a pedestrian at a street crossing, *held*, under the evidence, a question for the jury whether or not the speed of the train exceeded that allowed by ordinance, and the whistle was sounded and the bell rung on approaching the crossing, and whether or not the company's employees failed to use all means at hand to avert injury to decedent after discovering his peril. Galveston, etc., Ry. Co. v. Murray (Tex. Civ. App. 1907), 99 S. W. Rep. 144.

A charge that the railroad was under no duty to run its train at such rate of speed while approaching the path crossing the track, so that the train could be stopped before reaching the path if a person were discovered on the track, was erroneous, as invading the province of the jury. Duncan v. St. Louis, etc., R. Co. (Ala. 1907), 44 So. Rep. 418.

CHAPTER XLIV.

CONTRIBUTORY NEGLIGENCE OF TRAVELER ON HIGHWAY.

1451

§ 990. **General rules underlying.**— Where a traveler on
a highway takes the risk of crossing a railroad track, without
using reasonable care, and is injured, he must bear the consequence of his own imprudence.[1]

The rule of law is general that a railroad track is a place
of danger, and this rule applies as well to a side track as to a
main track.[2]

But a traveler crossing a railroad track, on a highway
crossing, whether in the country or in town, is not a trespasser, and if he is ordinarily careful in looking out for approaching trains, he cannot ordinarily be held guilty of negligence.[3] The traveler on a highway crossing has an equal
right with the railroad company, to use the crossing, and he
is also entitled to indulge the presumption that the railroad
company, in the operation of its trains, will comply with
statutes or ordinances, regulating same.[4] Any part of the

[1] Wabash R. Co. v. Hicks, 13 Ill. App. 407.

[2] Mynning v. Detroit, etc., R. Co., 59 Mich. 257; 26 N. W. Rep. 514;
23 Am. & Eng. R. Cas. 317.

[3] Glass v. Memphis, etc., R. Co., 94 Ala. 581; 10 So. Rep. 215.

[4] Jennings v. St. Louis, etc., R. Co., 112 Mo. 268; 20 S. W. Rep. 490.

street crossing may be used, in the exercise of due
the traveler is not confined to any particular porti(
street.[5] A traveler is not to be held guilty of n(
because he was struck on a street crossing, where he
due care to avoid the train standing at the crossing,
struck by a train going in another direction, wl
not signaled for the crossing,[6] and generally, to s
the traveler was guilty of negligence barring a re(
an injury received at a crossing, the railroad comp;
establish the negligence of the traveler, contributi:
injury, or must show that it was itself in the ex
due care, or that its own negligence did not caus
jury.[7]

§ 991. **Care exacted from traveler in going on tra(**
care and caution required of a person in going on a
track at a highway crossing are such reasonable
caution as a man of ordinary prudence and judgm(
exercise under similar circumstances.[8] Due and
care is required in crossing public streets, as in
transactions of life. Even on the sidewalk, espe(
voted to foot passengers, a man is bound to look wl
going, and this duty is still more imperative wh
about to cross the street where horses, wagons and (
equal rights with himself, and where each is boun(

[5] Henry v. Grand Avenue R. Co., 113 Mo. 525; 21 S. W. I

[6] New Jersey, etc., R. Co. v. West, 32 N. J. L. 91.

[7] Louisville, etc., R. Co. v. Burke, 6 Caldw. (Tenn.) 45.

[8] Wichita, etc., R. Co. v. Davis, 37 Kansas, 743; 16 Pac.
32 Am. & Eng. R. Cas. 65; Clark v. Missouri Pacific R. Co.,
354; Chicago, etc., R. Co. v. Kuster, 22 Ill. App. 188; Ho
York, etc., R. Co., 118 N. Y. 399; 23 N. E. Rep. 505; Int
etc., R. Co. v. Dyer, 76 Texas 156; 13 S. W. Rep. 377; Tuck
York, etc., R. Co., 124 N. Y. 308; 26 N. E. Rep. 916.

notice of such other's rights and to use his own with due regard thereto.[9]

Inasmuch as the exigencies of modern life, therefore, have compelled the legalizing of railroads as a means of commerce, the law imposes upon the citizen the duty of exercising the proper care and caution to avoid the danger to himself and the possible injury to those being conveyed, as passengers, likely to be caused by a collision with, or an obstruction of trains.[10]   It is accordingly held to be the duty of persons about to cross a railroad track, to look about them and see if there is danger; not to go recklessly upon the railroad track, but to take the proper precautions themselves, to avoid danger.   If a party rushes into danger, which by ordinary care he could have seen and avoided, no rule of law or justice can be invoked to compensate him for an injury he himself caused.[11]

This rule applies particularly to a crossing unusually dangerous and difficult to cross, without resulting danger, and one who is familiar with the unusual dangers surrounding an attempt to cross, at a given crossing, is held to exercise care proportionate to the probable danger to be incurred,[12] and if a person familiar with a crossing, drives so fast that he is unable to stop, after he is warned of an ap-

[9] Busby v. Philadelphia Traction Co., 126 Pa. St. 559; 17 Atl. Rep. 895; 42 Am. & Eng. R. Cas. 144.

[10] Pennsylvania R. Co. v. Righter, 42 N. J. L. 180; 2 Am. & Eng. R. Cas. 220.

[11] Lake Shore, etc., R. Co. v. Clemens, 5 Ill. App. 77; Illinois, etc., R. Co. v. Hetherington, 83 Ill. 510.

[12] Cincinnati, etc., R. Co. v. Butler, 103 Ind. 31; 2 N. E. Rep. 138; 23 Am. & Eng. R. Cas. 262; Indiana, etc., R. Co. v. Greene, 106 Ind. 279; 6 N. E. Rep. 603; 55 Am. Rep. 736; 25 Am. & Eng. R. Cas. 322; Louisville, etc., R. Co. v. Stommell, 126 Ind. 35; 25 N. E. Rep. 863.

A person attempting to cross a difficult crossing, without looking for a train, which signalled for the crossing, was held negligent barring a recovery, in Rockford, etc., R. Co. v. Byam, 80 Ill. 528.

proaching train, he cannot recover for an injury received by being struck by the train.[13]

§ 992. **Care required of persons under disability.**— The fact that a person approaching a highway crossing with a railroad track, was under physical disability, will not relieve him from the exercise of ordinary care, for, indeed, as such circumstances would render persons laboring under disabilities less able to avoid injury, they should be held to increase their vigilance, corresponding to their physical disability, in order to be held to have exercised the ordinary care that persons not so situated would be held to have exercised.   In a Missouri case,[14] where the traveler had lost an eye and the

[13] Wilds v. Hudson River R. Co., 24 N. Y. 430; Seefeld v. Chicago, etc., R. Co., 70 Wis. 216; 35 N. W. Rep. 278; 32 Am. & Eng. R. Cas. 109.

If the plaintiff was a stranger and not familiar with crossing, this is held to be an important fact, in determining the issue of his negligence, in Cohen v. Eureka, etc., R. Co., 14 Nevada 376.

Ordinary care is all that the law exacts of the traveler on the highway. This does not mean every possible precaution, but the proper inquiry is: " Did plaintiff, under the circumstances, conduct himself with that care and circumspection which should be expected of one of ordinary prudence? " McNown v. Wabash R. Co., 55 Mo. App. 585.

One crossing a street on which trains and street cars are operated is bound to know that the crossing is a place of danger, and to avoid being guilty of contributory negligence he is required to exercise such care as an ordinarily cautious person would use under similar circumstances to avoid injury. Lowden v. Pennsylvania Co. (Ind. App. 1907), 82 N. E. Rep. 941.

One approaching a railway track on a public crossing must, to be free from contributory negligence, exercise such care as an ordinarily prudent person would exercise under like conditions and similar circumstances. Louisville, etc., R. Co. v. Ueltschi's Ex'rs (Ky. 1906), 97 S. W. Rep. 14. .

One attempting to cross over a railroad track is not required to exercise extraordinary care, but is only required to exercise ordinary care, such as a person of ordinary prudence and intelligence would usually exercise under the same or similar circumstances. Chicago, etc., Ry. Co. v. Louderback, 125 Ill. App. 323.

[14] Fusili .v. Missouri Pacific Ry. Co., 45 Mo. App. 535.

train with which he collided had approached on his blind side, by way of reply to the contention that he was not negligent in failing to see the train, the court said: " If the plaintiff was under the physical infirmity stated, that imposed upon him the duty of increased vigilance, in the employment of the faculties he possessed. The general rule is that physical infirmities, of themselves, do not constitute a defense for the failure to exercise ordinary care, under· given circumstances. When one is conscious that his hearing or sight is defective, instead of exercising less, he should rather exercise greater care, in other respects. If the plaintiff had lost one of his organs of sight — if his sense of sight was impaired — it would seem that common prudence would have required that he should have exercised greater care before attempting to pass over the railroad crossing, than would have been required of one in the full possession of the faculty of sight. Persons laboring under physical disability are required to exercise what care they can, up to the measure of ordinary care, under the circumstances."

And the rule is applicable to children or infants of years of discretion and able to appreciate the danger of the track, and if a child, old enough to know the danger of so doing, runs or steps in front of an approaching train, his negligence will defeat a recovery for the injuries or death of the child so caused.[15]

But a child will not, ordinarily, be held to have been guilty of contributory negligence, in a crossing injury, although he had sufficient years and mental capacity to understand the dangers of the track, unless he also had the prudence, thoughtfulness and discretion to enable him to avoid

[15] Spillane v. Missouri Pacific Ry. Co., 135 Mo. 414; 37 S. W. Rep. 198; 58 Am. St. Rep. 580; Payne v. Chicago, etc., R. Co., 136 Mo. 562; 38 S. W. Rep. 308; Graney v. St. Louis, etc., R. Co., 140 Mo. 89; 41 S. W. Rep. 246; 38 L. R. A. 633; 157 Mo. 666; 57 S. W. Rep. 276; 50 L. R. A. 153.

the danger, such as an ordinarily prudent adult would have possessed, and he will only be held negligent, if, in view of his age, he failed to exercise the precaution which would ordinarily have been exercised by one of his years and capacity.[16]

§ 993. **Where traveler is partially blind.**— Partial blindness on the part of one about to cross a railroad track, will not excuse him from the exercise of ordinary care, but is held to impose the duty of greater caution, on his part, to avoid injury.[17]

It is accordingly held, in a Missouri case,[18] that an instruction was proper which told the jury that if the plaintiff, on account of an obstruction of the track, or the loss of an eye, could not, from where he stood, see the approaching train, then it was his duty to get where he had an unobstructed view, if there was such a place, and to look up and down the railroad track, before attempting to cross same, and if he failed to get such a view, when he could have done

[16] Graney v. St. Louis, etc., R. Co., *supra;* Thompson v. Missouri, etc., R. Co., 93 Mo. App. 548; 67 S. W. Rep. 693.

There can be no presumption that a deaf person, struck and killed by a wild engine while crossing a railroad track at a street crossing, was in the exercise of due care. Shum's Adm'x v. Rutland R. Co. (Vt. 1908), 69 Atl. Rep. 945.

Where plaintiff's intestate, a child of nine, was killed by being struck by a railroad train as she was crossing the tracks at a crossing, she was not chargeable with negligence as a matter of law, though she saw the train when she started to cross in front of it. Duggan v. Boston, etc., R. Co., (N. H. 1907), 66 Atl. Rep. 829.

A boy thirteen years of age is old enough to appreciate fully the dangerous character of a railroad crossing, and the necessity of using care for his own safety while crossing it; and therefore the rules which prevail as to adults in such cases are equally applicable to him. Gehring v. Atlantic City R. Co. (N. J. 1907), 68 Atl. Rep. 61.

[17] Mark v. Petersburg, etc., R. Co., 88 Va. 1; 13 S. E. Rep. 299; 49 Am. & Eng. R. Cas. 418.

[18] Fusili v. Missouri Pacific Ry. Co., 45 Mo. App. 535.

so, then his failure will constitute negligence on his part, preventing a recovery for an injury due to a collision with a train on the track. The plaintiff's physical infirmity was held to form a portion of the circumstances which were to determine whether or not he had exercised ordinary care in approaching the crossing as he did, and the physical infirmity was held to impose the duty of increased vigilance in the employment of his remaining faculties.[19]

§ 994. **Traveler's negligence contributing to injury bars recovery.**— A person crossing a railroad track, upon a public highway, is bound at all times to exercise ordinary care for his own safety, to avoid the cars and engines; and if he does not do so, and for that reason receives an injury, which could have been avoided by the exercise of ordinary care, on his part, then he cannot recover, although the railroad company was also negligent.[20]   Nor is there any distinction, in this regard, between the ordinary negligence of the railroad company and its gross negligence, in those jurisdictions where the law of comparative negligence does not obtain, and if a traveler on a highway, approaching a railroad crossing, neglects to take the precautions dictated by common prudence, and because of such neglect sustains an injury from a passing train, he cannot recover from the railroad company, although it may be chargeable with gross negligence.[21]

---

[19] Fusili v. Missouri Pacific Ry. Co., *supra*.

[20] Hearne v. Southern Pacific R. Co., 50 Cal. 482; 12 Am. Ry. Rep. 181; Morris v. Chicago, etc., R. Co., 26 Fed. Rep. 22; Macon, etc., R. Co. v. Wynn, 19 Ga. 440; Telfer v. Northern R. Co., 30 N. J. L. 188; Bellefontaine, etc., R. Co. v. Hunter, 33 Ind. 335; Galveston, etc., R. Co. v. Metula (Texas), 19 S. W. Rep. 376; Davey v. London, etc., R. Co., 12 Q. B. D. 70; 35 L. J. Q. B. D. 58; Taylor v. Missouri Pacific Ry. Co., 86 Mo. 457; Butts v. St. Louis, etc., R. Co., 98 Mo. 272; 11 S. W. Rep. 754; Drake v. Chicago, etc., R. Co., 51 Mo. App. 562; Chicago, etc., R. Co. v. Houston, 95 U. S. 697; Lenix v. Missouri Pacific Ry. Co., 76 Mo. 86.

[21] Grand Trunk R. Co. v. Ives, 144 U. S. 408; 12 Sup. Ct. Rep. 679; 55 Am. & Eng. R. Cas. 159.

Neither is it material, however slightly the negligence of the traveler may have contributed to bring about the injury, except in jurisdictions where the law of comparative negligence exists, for if the traveler was negligent in any degree and it contributed, however slightly, to affect the injury, there can be no recovery, although the railroad company was negligent in other respects and its negligence also concurred to produce the injury.[22]

§ 995. **Mutual care to be observed.**— As there is great danger in crossing a railroad track, even where due care is observed both by the traveler and by the railroad company, to avoid injury from passing trains, proper and reasonable care is demanded alike from those in charge of the train and engine and from the traveler on the highway. Both have the right to pass and their rights, duties and obligations are mutual and reciprocal, and the same degree of care is required of each.[23] The traveler cannot be regarded as a

[22] Owen v. Hudson River R. Co., 35 N. Y. 516; 7 Bosw. 329.

In Butts v. St. Louis, etc., R. Co. (98 Mo. 272), where the train was operated without an engine or flagman, and the deceased could have seen it approaching, if she had looked, the court, speaking through Judge Ray, said: " Such, then, being the evidence in effect and substance, in plaintiff's own behalf, it shows, we think, the existence of contributory negligence on the part of the deceased which, notwithstanding the negligence of defendant, in the said operation and management of its train, precludes a recovery on the part of the plaintiff."

And where the plaintiff failed to look or listen and the train was operated without the statutory signals, the negligence of the plaintiff was held to preclude a recovery in, Drake v. Chicago, etc., R. Co., 51 Mo. App. 562.

[23] Schofield v. Chicago, etc., R. Co., 2 McCrary (U. S.) 268; Leavenworth, etc., R. Co. v. Rice, 10 Kansas 426; Louisville, etc., R. Co. v. Goetz, 79 Ky. 442; 42 Am. Rep. 227; 14 Am. & Eng. R. Cas. 627; Whitney v. Maine, etc., R. Co., 69 Me. 208; Randall v. Richmond, etc., R. Co., 104 No. Car. 410; 10 S. E. Rep. 691; 42 Am. & Eng. R. Cas. 603; Cohen v. Eurcka, etc., R. Co., 14 Nevada 376.

trespasser, for he has a right to use the highway crossing.[24] Nor are the rights of the traveler subordinate to those of the railroad company, or superior to them, but both are equal, in law. Both parties are bound to use ordinary care — the one to avoid committing injury and the other to avoid receiving it.[25]

But while both the traveler on the highway and the railroad company have an equal right in the use of the crossing, the railroad company, in the passage of its trains, is held to have the right of way.[26] The precedence of trains, over foot or team travelers, is based upon the increased speed of the trains, the greater difficulty in stopping them and the demands of commerce by such means of transportation.[27] Hence, in determining the question of the exercise of ordinary care, on the part of the railroad company, and of the traveler on the highway, the relative rights and duties of each, viewed in the light of the difference in the means of transportation, the character of the conveyance used and the other surrounding circumstances, are to enter into the question.[28]

§ 996. Traveler's negligence must proximately contribute to injury.— The rule is, not that any degree of negligence, however slight, which may have concurred in producing the injury, will bar a recovery by the injured person, but if the

---

[24] Jennings v. St. Louis, etc., R. Co., 112 Mo. 268; 20 S. W. Rep. 490.

[25] Neither is bound to exercise extraordinary care. Willoughby v. Chicago, etc., R. Co., 37 Iowa 432; Pennsylvania R. Co. v. Krick, 47 Ind. 368; Chicago, etc., R. Co. v. Hatch, 79 Ill. 137.

[26] Ohio, etc., R. Co. v. Walker, 113 Ind. 196; 15 N. E. Rep. 234; 32 Am. & Eng. R. Cas. 121; Newhard v. Pennsylvania R. Co., 153 Pa. St. 417; 26 Atl. Rep. 105; 55 Am. & Eng. R. Cas. 258.

[27] Morris v. Chicago, etc., R. Co., 26 Fed Rep. 22.

[28] Kelly v. Michigan, etc., R. Co., 65 Mich. 186; 31 N. W. Rep. 904; 28 Am. & Eng. R. Cas. 633.

negligence of the person injured amounts to an absence of ordinary care and contributes proximately, in any degree, to the injury, there can be no recovery.[29]   Of course, if a person crossing a track is negligent and his negligence contributes at all to the injury, it would contribute proximately and directly thereto.[30]   To render the railroad company liable, therefore, for an injury at a highway crossing, if the party injured has been negligent, it should appear that the proximate cause of the injury was the defendant's omission, after becoming aware of the peril, to use a proper degree of care to avoid injuring him.   If, on discovering the danger to the traveler, it was impossible, with safety to the train and those on board, to stop the train in time to avoid the injury, the railroad company could not be held liable, unless it was guilty of negligence in the first instance, which occasioned the immediate danger to the traveler.[31]

It is accordingly not so much a question of the degree of negligence on the part of the different parties, as it is a question of the time of the negligence, in the influence it has on the cause of the injury, for if the plaintiff's negligence is contemporaneous, it could only be held to be a proximate cause of the injury, while if the defendant's negligence was subsequent to that of the plaintiff it would be held to be the proximate cause of the injury.[32]   If the immediate danger to the traveler is due to his own want of care, in

[29] Strong v. Sacramento, etc., R. Co., 61 Cal. 326; 8 Am. & Eng. R. Cas. 273; Weller v. Chicago, etc., R. Co., 164 Mo. 180; 64 S. W. Rep. 141; 86 Am. St. Rep. 592.

[30] Hearne v. Southern Pacific R. Co., 50 Cal. 482; 12 Am. Ry. Rep. 181.

[31] Maher v. Atlantic, etc., R. Co., 64 Mo. 267; 17 Am. Ry. Rep. 231; Karl v. Kansas City, etc., R. Co., 55 Mo. 484; Isabel v. Hannibal, etc., R. Co., 60 Mo. 482; Hicks v. Missouri Pacific Ry. Co., 101 Mo. 36; 13 S. W. Rep. 946.

[32] Holwerson v. St. Louis, etc., R. Co., 157 Mo. 216; 57 S. W. Rep. 770; 50 L. R. A. 850; State v. Manchester, etc., R. Co., 52 N. H. 528.

placing himself in a dangerous position, his failure to adopt the safest course to extricate himself from this danger, is no excuse.[33]   But if his dangerous position is due, primarily, to the want of care on the part of the railroad company, then his failure to pursue the safest course, after aware of his danger, under the excitement of the emergency, in which he finds himself, will not excuse the railroad company for placing him in such dangerous position.[34]

§ 997. **How far traveler may assume trains will be properly operated.**— Within reasonable limits, it is held that a traveler approaching a highway crossing, is entitled to rely upon the proper and regular operation of trains by the railway company, in accordance with the regulations of the company, brought to the attention of the traveling public and the laws and ordinances of the State or city, where the crossing is located.[35]

Under this rule of law, the traveler is held entitled to rely upon the giving of signals for the crossings;[36] that trains will be run, according to the advertised time-card or regulations of the company;[37] that the trains will not exceed

[33] Texas, etc., R. Co. v. Roberts, 2 Texas Civil App. 111; 20 S. W. Rep. 960; Quill v. New York, etc., R. Co., 16 Daly (N. Y.) 313; 32 N. Y. S. R. 612; 126 N. Y. 629.

[34] Donohue v. St. Louis, etc., R. Co., 91 Mo. 357; 3 S. W. Rep. 848; 28 Am. & Eng. R. Cas. 673.

Failure of a decedent to stop, look, and listen before attempting to cross a railroad track will not defeat a recovery, unless it contributes proximately to his death. Central of Georgia Ry. Co. v. Hyatt (Ala. 1907), 43 So. Rep. 867.

[35] Lyman v. Boston, etc., R. Co. (N. H.), 20 Atl. Rep. 976; 45 Am. & Eng. R. Cas. 163; Strong v. Sacramento, etc., R. Co., 61 Cal. 326; 8 Am. & Eng. R. Cas. 273.

[36] International, etc., R. Co. v. Graves, 59 Texas 330; Fusili v. Missouri Pacific Ry. Co., 45 Mo. App. 535.

[37] Parsons v. New York, etc., R. Co., 113 N. Y. 355; 21 N. E. Rep. 145; 48 Hun 615; 15 N. Y. S. R. 1016.

the speed limit prescribed by ordinance ; [38] that gates will not be raised, except when it is safe to cross the track,[39] or that flagmen will not be absent from the crossing, or fail to signal, except when it is safe to cross.[40]

These presumptions, however, are never to be indulged in, in the face of apparent danger, for if a traveler relies upon the presumption of safety or the running of trains in accordance with custom or habit, or a compliance with law, when he could, by looking, see the danger of acting upon such presumption, he is negligent, as matter of law.[41]

§ 998. Place of crossing track.— It has been held to be contributory negligence for a traveler on the highway to attempt to cross a railroad track, at a place where a street has not been opened, although the street may be intended to be opened there, and different people have been accustomed to

[38] Hart v. Devereux, 41 Ohio St. 565; Piper v. Chicago, etc., R. Co., 77 Wis. 247; 46 N. W. Rep. 165; Reeves v. Delaware, etc., R. Co., 30 Pa. St. 454.

[39] Chicago, etc., R. Co. v. Clough, 134 Ill. 586; 25 N. E. Rep. 664.

[40] Montgomery v. Missouri Pacific Ry. Co., 181 Mo. 491; 79 S. W. Rep. 930; Chicago, etc., R. Co. v. Hutchinson, 120 Ill. 587; 11 N. E. Rep. 855.

[41] Wabash R. Co. v. Trust Co., 23 Fed. Rep. 738; Duncan v. Missouri Pacific Ry. Co., 46 Mo. App. 207; Tyler v. Boston, etc., R. Co., 157 Mass. 336; 32 N. E. Rep. 229.

One attempting to cross railroad tracks in the face of an approaching train is justified in assuming that such train will not run at a greater rate of speed than that permitted by ordinance in force at the place of the accident. Chicago, etc., Ry. Co. v. Wilson, 128 Ill. App. 88, judgment affirmed (1907) 80 N. E. Rep. 56; 225 Ill. 50.

A traveler by a wagon approaching a point where it will be necessary to cross a railroad track laid in a public street has a right to anticipate that the train will be operated according to law, and without negligence on the part of the railroad company. Schwanenfeldt v. Chicago, etc., Ry. Co. (Neb. 1908), 115 N. W. Rep. 285.

In the absence of evidence to the contrary, a person approaching a railroad crossing in a city may presume that the railroad will not run its trains at a greater rate of speed than allowed by the city ordinance. Kunz v. Oregon R. Co. (Or. 1907), 93 Pac. Rep. 141.

disobedience would convict the traveler of negligence, as matter of law.[54]

§ 1000. **How far traveler may presume that signals will be given.**— It has been held, in a Missouri case,[55] that a traveler approaching a railroad crossing, on a highway, who does not see or hear a train, is not chargeable with negligence in assuming that the railroad company will act with appropriate care and give the proper signals for the crossing. It has been held that he is entitled to presume a compliance with municipal ordinances regulating the rate of speed that trains are operated through various cities.[56] But in other cases, in the same State, it is held that " he directly contributes to his own injury, who, paying no attention to his own safety, trusts to the obligations imposed on the company, to warn him of approaching trains." [57]

The law, as held by a New York decision,[58] no doubt lies between these two divergent views of the courts of this State for while the traveler has a right to assume that the railroad company will do its duty and ring the bell or sound the whistle, he is not relieved thereby from the duty to vigilantly use his senses and avoid danger and notwithstanding the assumption he is permitted to indulge, if he is otherwise negligent, he cannot recover.

Where the evidence is consistent with due conduct on the part of the plaintiff, it might not be amiss to charge the jury, that he had a right to assume that the railroad com-

[54] Union R. Co. v. State, 72 Md. 153; 19 Atl. Rep. 449; 42 Am. & Eng. R. Cas. 172.

[55] Tabor v. Missouri Valley R. Co., 46 Mo. 353; Kennayde v. Pacific R. Co., 45 Mo. 255. And see, Strong v. Sacramento, etc., R. Co., 61 Cal. 326; 8 Am. & Eng. R. Cas. 273.

[56] Kellny v. Missouri Pacific Ry. Co., 101 Mo. 67; 13 S. W. Rep. 806; 43 Am. & Eng. R. Cas. 186.

[57] Turner v. Hannibal, etc., R. Co., 74 Mo. 602.

[58] Shaw v. Jewett, 86 N. Y. 616; 6 Am. & Eng. R. Cas. 111.

on regular time.[49] If one, after proper signals for the cross-ing have been given, goes on the track and is injured, there can be no recovery, in the absence of some act of negligence on the part of the railroad company, which led him into danger.[50] A traveler on the highway, motioned by the flag-an at a crossing, to stay back, and to back up his wagon, innot recover, for an injury received by his violation of e flagman's signals.[51] Nor can there be a recovery for the eath of a traveler on a highway crossing, where a signal as given just before the deceased went onto the crossing, ut he ignored or disregarded the signal and drove in front f the approaching train.[52]

Some decisions, however, proceed upon the theory, that efore the traveler can be held negligent in going on the rack, in the face of a signal, it must be shown that he saw r understood the signal,[53] but these cases require the proof f a very difficult fact, especially in case of the death of the traveler and make the railroad company assume a greater burden than the law generally requires, for where the proper signals are given, this is a performance of the only duty required at highway crossings, and if the traveler was deaf or blind, there is no additional duty devolved upon the company, than to warn him and then avoid injuring him, if possible.

But it must generally be shown that the signal, if by a flagman, was where it ought to have been made and that it was a proper signal, before the giving of the signal, and its

[49] Granger v. Boston, etc., R. Co., 146 Mass. 276; 15 N. E. Rep. 619; Chicago, etc., R. Co. v. Fitzsimmons, 40 Ill. App. 360.
[50] Hinkle v. Richmond, etc., R. Co., 109 No. Car. 472; 13 S. E. Rep. 884.
[51] Diekman v. Morgen's, etc., R. Co., 40 La. Ann. 787; 5 So. Rep. 76.
[52] Fox v. Missouri Pacific Ry. Co., 85 Mo. 679.
[53] Chicago, etc., R. Co. v. Notzki, 66 Ill. 455.

to be negligence, sufficient to establish a *prima facie* case, on the part of an injured traveler, unless his own negligence proximately contributes with such negligence to affect the injury received.[62]

Speaking on this point, Judge Gantt, for the Supreme Court of Missouri, in a recent case,[63] said: "We think the fact that the defendant voluntarily adopted the rule of maintaining the flagman there and continued to do so, until plaintiff and the public knew of the custom, most materially affects the question of prudence required of plaintiff when she reached the crossing, on the night in question, and that, by its course of conduct, having invited the traveling public to expect a warning of approaching trains, it was evidence of negligence, that on the night in question, no flagman was there to warn plaintiff of the switching of cars across the street and that plaintiff was not chargeable with gross negligence in attempting to cross the track in the absence of such flagman or a signal from him, not to attempt to do so."

This case and those cited from other States,[64] proceed upon the theory that, " the flagman's duty is to know of the approach of trains and to give timely warning to all persons attempting to cross the railroad track and the public have a right to rely upon a reasonable performance of that duty."

But of course the absence of a flagman, like any other act of negligence on the part of a railroad company, will not

[62] Chicago, etc., R. Co. v. Blaul, 70 Ill. App. 518; Chicago, etc., R. Co. v. Hutchinson, 120 Ill. 587; 11 N. E. Rep. 855; Chicago, etc., R. Co. v. Jennings, 157 Ill. 274; 41 N. E. Rep. 629; Palmer v. New York, etc., R. Co., 112 N. Y. 234; 19 N. E. Rep. 678; Duncan v. New York, etc., R. Co., 67 Conn. 266; 34 Atl. Rep. 1041; Pennsylvania R. Co. v. Stegemeier, 118 Ind. 305; 20 N. E. Rep. 843; 10 Am. St. Rep. 136; Evans v. St. Paul, etc., R. Co., 88 Mich. 444; 50 N. W. Rep. 386; 14 L. R. A. 223; Jennings v. St. Louis, etc., R. Co., 112 Mo. 268; 20 S. W. Rep. 490.

[63] Montgomery v. Missouri Pacific Ry. Co., 181 Mo. 491; 79 S. W. Rep. 930, 938.

[64] Chicago, etc., R. Co. v. Hutchinson, 120 Ill. 587; 11 N. E. Rep. 855.

relieve the traveler of the duty to look out for himself, as no one has a right to rely wholly upon the care and prudence of others for his own protection from danger. And if the train could have been seen approaching or if the traveler could have heard it and failed to look or listen, then the mere fact that the flagman was absent or failed to signal him, will not excuse his otherwise negligent conduct.[65]

On this point, the decision of the Kansas City Court of Appeals, in a well-considered case,[66] is in point and it was there held that although a flagman was absent from a crossing, if the approaching train could have been seen or heard, no recovery could be had by a traveler who relied entirely on the presence of the flagman, the court, on this question, saying: " This watchman's duty was to give notice of approaching trains. It is of the same nature — performing the same office — as ringing the bell or sounding the whistle. The same rule will apply, whether the signal should come from a ringing bell, a sounding whistle or the words of caution from a flagman or the watchman. * * * Wade

[65] 2 Wood's Ry. Law, pp. 1302, 1314, and cases cited.

[66] Duncan v. Missouri Pacific Ry. Co., 46 Mo. App. 207.

Notwithstanding absence of flagman, the traveler's contributory negligence, in crossing the track, without exercising due care for his safety, was held to preclude a recovery, in Louisville, etc., R. Co. v. Webb, 49 Am. & Eng. R. Cas. 427; Sala v. Chicago, etc., R. Co., 85 Iowa 678; 52 N. W. Rep. 664; Freeman v. Duluth, etc., R. Co. (Mich.), 37 Am. & Eng. R. Cas. 501; 3 L. R. A. 594; Moore v. New York, etc., R. Co., 42 N. Y. S. R. 489; 62 Hun 621; 39 Am. & Eng. R. Cas. 628; Tyler v. Boston, etc., R. Co., 157 Mass. 336; 32 N. E. Rep. 229; Berry v. Pennsylvania R. Co. (N. J.), 26 Am. & Eng. R. Cas. 396; 4 Atl. Rep. 303.

The absence of a flagman was held to be no invitation to cross the track, in Whalen v. New York, etc., R. Co., 58 Hun 431; 35 N. Y. S. R. 556; 12 N. Y. Supp. 527.

It is error to instruct that absence of flagman is negligence, per se, as such negligence must be the proximate cause of the injury. Pennsylvania R. Co. v. Hensil, 70 Ind. 569; 6 Am. & Eng. R. Cas. 79. A negligent order of a flagman to cross, is generally held to give a cause of action. Fusili v. Missouri Pacific Ry. Co., 45 Mo. App. 535.

Duncan, the plaintiff, admits that as he approached the crossing, he saw no watchman, * * * hence he had notice that he must rely on himself for protection. He saw, too, the moving trains and was thereby put on his guard. He had notice, in fact, of all that could have been imparted to him, by the watchman, and, having such knowledge, he voluntarily put himself in a place of danger. He cannot, therefore, charge his misfortune to any omission of duty by the watchman."

§ 1002. **Open gate an invitation to cross track.**— As crossing gates are liable to be closed at any time, persons crossing the track would naturally understand that they should not linger on the track, but pass over promptly and speedily; for a person to drive in a trot, on a railroad track, therefore, when the crossing gates were up, instead of showing negligence, on his part, might be a very proper thing for him to do.[67] A traveler who goes upon a crossing when the gates are up is not by reason of this fact to be adjudged guilty of negligence barring a recovery, but an open gate, which invites passing and an unobstructed view, may be sufficient to bring the question of negligence within the province of a jury to decide, and prevent a nonsuit, or setting aside a verdict, if the jury find in favor of the traveler.[68] Some cases hold that an open gate is always an invitation to cross the track,[69] and the Illinois court has observed that to hold such conduct negligence, would be tantamount to closing the crossing entirely to the public.[70]

[67] Cleveland, etc., R. Co. v. Schneider, 45 Ohio St. 678; 17 N. E. Rep. 321; 35 Am. & Eng. R. Cas. 334.

[68] Hooper v. Boston, etc., R. Co., 81 Me. 260; 17 Atl. Rep. 64; Lindeman v. New York, etc., R. Co., 42 Hun 306; 3 N. Y. S. R. 731.

[69] Fitzgerald v. Long Island R. Co., 10 N. Y. S. R. 433; 45 Hun 591; 117 N. Y. 653.

[70] Chicago, etc., R. Co. v. Clough, 134 Ill. 586; 25 N. E. Rep. 664; 29 N. E. Rep. 184.

But a person injured when attempting to open the cross-ing gates himself, is held to have no right of action for such an injury,[71] and although an open gate may be held to be n invitation to cross, this invitation would be subject to all ʒe dangers that could be plainly seen or heard and a party ʒting upon such an invitation, if injured by such apparent ngers, would be held negligent, as matter of law.[72]

§ 1003. **The duty to stop, look and listen, generally.**— The esence of a railroad track, upon which a train may at any e pass, is notice of danger to such an extent that it is the ty of a person about to cross the track, on a public high-y, to exercise caution in so doing and to look both ways r approaching trains, if the surroundings are such as to mit of such precautions.[73] The reason for this rule which quires a traveler to stop, look and listen, before crossing a ilroad track, is, that by such action he may inform him-lf whether a train is approaching or not, the instinct of lf-preservation being sufficient to keep a person from get-

71 Wyatt v. Great Western R. Co., 6 B. & S. 709; 34 L. J. Q. B. 204.
72 Lake Shore, etc., R. Co. v. Frantz, 127 Pa. St. 297; 18 Atl. Rep. ; 39 Am. & Eng. R. Cas. 628.
73 Mann v. Belt, etc., R. Co., 128 Ind. 138; 26 N. E. Rep. 819; atta v. Chicago, etc., R. Co., 69 Mich. 109; 37 N. W. Rep. 54; Am. & Eng. R. Cas. 71; Gardner v. Detroit, etc., R. Co., 97 Mich. 0; 56 N. W. Rep. 603; Myers v. Baltimore, etc., R. Co., 150 Pa. 388; 24 Atl. Rep. 747; Ehrishman v. East Harrisburg, etc., R. ɔ., 150 Pa. St. 180; 24 Atl. Rep. 596; 51 Am. & Eng. R. Cas. 190; olland v. Missouri Pacific Ry. Co., 210 Mo. 338; 112 S. W. Rep. ʒ5; Hayden v. Missouri, etc., Ry. Co., 124 Mo. 566; 28 S. W. Rep. 74; uggart v. Missouri Pacific Ry. Co., 134 Mo. 673; 36 S. W. Rep. 20; Kelsay v. Missouri Pacific Ry. Co., 129 Mo. 362; 30 S. W. Rep. 39; Hook v. Missouri Pacific Ry. Co., 162 Mo. 569; 63 S. W. Rep. 360; Holwerson v. St. Louis, etc., R. Co., 157 Mo. 216; 57 S. W. Rep. 770; 50 L. R. A. 850; Sanguinette v. Mississippi, etc., R. Co., 196 Mo. 466; 95 S. W. Rep. 386; Stotler v. Chicago, etc., R. Co., 204 Mo. 619; 103 S. W. Rep. 1; Sims v. St. Louis, etc., Ry. Co., 116 Mo. App. 572; 92 S. W. Rep. 909.

ting in front of such a deadly vehicle, when he knows it is approaching.[74]

The rule that a person before crossing a railroad track must stop, look and listen for approaching trains, applies equally to persons walking over the track as to persons driving, and a failure to stop is not generally held to be mere evidence of negligence, but negligence, *per se*.[75] And the fact that another person who was traveling with a traveler, across a highway crossing, looked and listened for a train, but failed to see or hear it, does not establish that the injured person himself would have failed to see or hear it, if he had looked or listened himself.[76]

But the legal presumption is that a person injured at a highway crossing did stop, look and listen, and this presumption will prevail, in the absence of direct testimony on the subject.[77] The rule itself is not applied inflexibly, in all cases, without regard to age or the surrounding circumstances and conditions.[78] The obligation does not always

---

[74] Ash v. Wilmington, etc., R. Co., 148 Pa. St. 133; 23 Atl. Rep. 898.

[75] Aiken v. Pennsylvania R. Co., 130 Pa. St. 380; 18 Atl. Rep. 619; 41 Am. & Eng. R. Cas. 571; Baker v. Kansas City, etc., R. Co., 122 Mo. 533; 26 S. W. Rep. 20.

[76] Wiwirowski v. Lake Shore, etc., R. Co., 124 N. Y. 420; 26 N. E. Rep. 1023; 36 N. Y. S. R. 405.

[77] Mynning v. Detroit, etc., R. Co., 64 Mich. 93; 31 N. W. Rep. 147; 28 Am. & Eng. R. Cas. 665; Glasscock v. Central Pacific R. Co., 73 Cal. 137; 14 Pac. Rep. 518; McBride v. Northern Pacific R. Co., 19 Oregon 64; 23 Pac. Rep. 814; 42 Am. & Eng. R. Cas. 146; Pennsylvania R. Co. v. Mooney, 126 Pa. St. 244; 17 Atl. Rep. 590; 39 Am. & Eng. R. Cas. 612. But where there is affirmative evidence to the contrary, this presumption is overcome. Mynning v. Detroit, etc., R. Co., 64 Mich. 93; 31 N. W. Rep. 147; 28 Am. & Eng. R. Cas. 665. Or where, from the circumstances of the case, the conclusion is irresistible that the injured traveler did not look, or listen, as to have done so would have been to see or hear, he will be held negligent as matter of law. Kwiotkoski v. Grand Trunk R. Co., 70 Mich. 549; 38 N. W. Rep. 464.

[78] McGovern v. New York, etc., R. Co., 67 N. Y. 417; 15 Am. Ry. Rep. 119.

apply to passengers crossing a railroad track, in going from a depot to a train, or *vice versa*.[79] And while, ordinarily, a person approaching a railroad crossing should look both ways and listen, and, if necessary, stop his team and listen for an approaching train,[80] it is not necessarily the duty of a traveler to stop his team, in the absence of special circumstances requiring this precaution, but he is only required to exercise such care and caution as a reasonably prudent person would exercise under the same circumstances.[81]

§ 1004. **Care to be observed in looking and listening.**— A person approaching a highway crossing a railroad track should look and listen for approaching trains with the care and caution of an ordinarily prudent man.[82] Ordinary care in approaching a railroad crossing requires the traveler to make vigilant use of his senses; that he shall look in every direction from which danger may be apprehended and at the same time attentively listen for any signals or evidences of an approaching train.[83] Nor would ordinary care in selecting a place to look and listen, absolve a traveler from the

[79] Denver, etc., R. Co. v. Hodgson, 18 Colo. 117; 31 Pac. Rep. 954; Klein v. Jewett, 26 N. J. Eq. 474; Baltimore, etc., R. Co. v. State, 60 Md. 449; 12 Am. & Eng. R. Cas. 149.

[80] Nosler v. Chicago, etc., R. Co., 73 Iowa 268; 34 N. W. Rep. 850; Hook v. Missouri Pacific Ry. Co., 162 Mo. 569; 63 S. W. Rep. 360; Harlan v. St. Louis, etc., R. Co., 64 Mo. 480; Kelsay v. Missouri Pacific Ry. Co., 129 Mo. 362; 30 S. W. Rep. 339; Payne v. Chicago, etc., Ry. Co., 136 Mo. 562; 38 S. W. Rep. 308.

[81] Reed v. Chicago, etc., R. Co., 74 Iowa 188; 37 N. W. Rep. 149; Smith v. Citizens R. Co., 52 Mo. App. 36; Zimmerman v. Hannibal, etc., R. Co., 71 Mo. 476; 2 Am. & Eng. R. Cas. 191; Kellogg v. New York, etc., R. Co., 79 N. Y. 72; Chicago, etc., R. Co. v. Fenn, 3 Ind. App. 250; 29 N. E. Rep. 790.

[82] Norfolk, etc., R. Co. v. Burge, 84 Va. 63; 4 S. E. Rep. 21; 32 Am. & Eng. R. Cas. 101.

[83] Weber v. New York, etc., R. Co., 58 N. Y. 451.

failure to use ordinary care in approaching the crossing, after he looked and listened.[84]

The greater the danger, the more care is required by ordinary prudence on the part of the traveler and the railroad company.[85] The duty of using care is mutual upon the railroad company and the traveler, the one to avoid injury to himself and the other to avoid injuring him.[86]

The degree of care required of the traveler depends in some measure on the maturity and capacity of the individual and all of the surrounding circumstances.[87] The traveler is not required to alight from his horse or wagon and advance to the track on foot, for the purpose of making a reconnoissance of the situation afoot.[88] And while a person approaching a railroad crossing is bound to make every reasonable effort to see a train approaching, he is not, as a matter of law, bound to actually see it, unless it was apparent by looking.[89]

[84] Moberly v. Kansas City, etc., R. Co., 98 Mo. 183; 11 S. W. Rep. 569.

[85] Pittsburg, etc., R. Co. v. Yundt, 78 Ind. 373; 41 Am. Rep. 580; 3 Am. & Eng. R. Cas. 502.

[86] Eswin v. St. Louis, etc., R. Co., 96 Mo. 290; 9 S. W. Rep. 577; 35 Am. & Eng. R. Cas. 390.

[87] Swift v. Staten Island R. Co., 123 N. Y. 645; 25 N. E. Rep. 378; 33 N. Y. S. R. 604; 52 Hun 614; 45 Am. & Eng. R. Cas. 180.

[88] Strong v. Sacramento, etc., R. Co., 61 Cal. 326; 8 Am. & Eng. R. Cas. 273.

[89] Greany v. Long Island R. Co., 101 N. Y. 419; 5 N. E. Rep. 425; 24 Am. & Eng. R. Cas. 473.

Mental absorption or reverie, induced by grief or business, will not excuse the duty to look and listen. Mann v. Belt Line R. Co., 128 Ind. 138; 26 N. E. Rep. 819; Potter v. Flint, etc., R. Co., 62 Mich. 22; 28 N. W. Rep. 714.

Looking "straight ahead" is held to be such evidence of negligence on the part of the traveler, as to justify a nonsuit, in Sutherland v. New York, etc., R. Co., 9 J. & S. (N. Y.) 17; Morse v. Erie R. Co., 65 Barb. (N. Y.) 490; Nichols v. Great Western R. Co., 27 U. C. Q. B. 382.

Decedent, a man thirty-six years of age, in full possession of his fac-

§ 1005. Traveler should look in both directions.—
eler on a highway, when about to cross a railroa⸱
should keep watch in both directions for trains, alth⸱
proper signal for the crossing has been given. Ne
do this, in case of accident, is held to ·be contributor
gence on the part of the traveler, unless obstructions
a view of the track, or he had some express or imp
surances of safety, from the railroad company, whic⸱
excuse him.[90] In an Illinois case,[91] it is held to b⸱
ble negligence for any one to cross a railroad track
looking in every direction that the rails run, to ma

ulties, received fatal injuries in a collision between an autor
which he was a passenger and defendant's train at a crossing
cedent had looked at any time while the train was covering t
sand feet from the point at which it was visible from the cro⸱
must have seen the train, and an exclamation would have preve
accident. *Held*, that it was decedent's duty to look and 1
ascertain whether a train was approaching before crossing tł
and that his failure to do so was negligence as a matter
precluding recovery for his death. Read v. New York Cent. &
Co. (N. Y. Supp.), 107⸱N. Y. S. 1068.

A person approaching a railway crossing must stop, look aɪ
for approaching trains, and he must stop so near to the cross
his survey by sight and sound must so immediately precede h
to cross, as to preclude danger from approaching trains
the time he stopped, looked, and listened, and his attempt t
Central of Georgia Ry. Co. v. Barnett (Ala. 1907), 44 So. R

[90] Ormsby v. Boston, etc., R. Co., 14 R. I. 102; 51 Am. R⸱
Georgia Pacific R. Co. v. O'Shields, 90 Ala. 29; 8 So. Rep. 248
v. Balt., etc., R. Co., 128 Ind. 138; 26 N. E. Rep. 819; Tho⸱
Cleveland, etc., R. Co., 131 Ind. 492; 31 N. E. Rep. 185; Denv⸱
R. Co. v. Ryan, 17 Colo. 98; 28 Pac. Rep. 79; Chicago, etc., R⸱
Van Patten, 64 Ill. 510; Cooper v. Lake Shore, etc., R. Co., 6
261; 33 N. W. Rep. 306; Marty v. Chicago, etc., R. Co., 38 Miɴ
35 N. W. Rep. 670; 32 Am. & Eng. R. Cas. 107; Berry v. Penns⸱
R. Co., 48 N. J. L. 141; 4 Atl. Rep. 303; 26 Am. & Eng. R. Cɪ
Endress v. Lake Shore, etc., R. Co., 117 N. Y. 640; 22 N.
1130; Galveston, etc., R. Co. v. Kutac, 72 Texas 643; 11
Rep. 127.

[91] Illinois, etc., R. Co. v. Goddard, 72 Ill. 567; Garland v. C⸱
etc., R. Co., 8 Ill. App. 571.

that the track is clear.   Where there are double tracks, therefore, and trains are run one way only on each track, it is held to be contributory negligence for one who knows how the trains run, to approach the track and look but one way for the trains.[92]

But some cases hold that it is not always necessary for a traveler approaching a railroad crossing, to stop and look in both directions for approaching trains.[93]   Every case must, of course, depend more or less upon its own circumstances, and it would be unreasonable to apply such a rule, without regard to circumstances or surrounding conditions.[94]   It is held, in Missouri,[95] that it is not essential for the traveler to look constantly, in both directions.   The rule, in all its strictness, is held, in some cases, not to apply to workmen at work on or near the railroad track.[96]   In still other cases, it is held not to apply to one about to cross a city street.[97] And it may be premised, that where the evidence justifies opposing inferences or conclusions, as to the performance, by the traveler, of his duty to look, in both directions, for trains, the question is one of fact for the jury, as to whether or not he performed his duty in this respect.[98]

[92] Young v. New York, etc., R. Co., 107 N. Y. 500; 14 N. E. Rep. 434; 32 Am. & Eng. R. Cas. 130.

[93] Richmond v. Chicago, etc., R. Co., 87 Mich. 374; 49 N. W. Rep. 621; 49 Am. & Eng. R. Cas. 367; Nash v. New York, etc., R. Co., 14 N. Y. S. R. 531.

[94] Cooper v. Lake Shore, etc., R. Co., 66 Mich. 261; 33 N. W. Rep. 306.

[95] Gratiot v. Missouri Pacific Ry. Co., 116 Mo. 450; 16 S. W. Rep. 384; 49 Am. & Eng. R. Cas. 398.

[96] Noonan v. New York, etc., R. Co., 62 Hun 618; 42 N. Y. S. R. 41; 16 N. Y. Supp. 678; 131 N. Y. 594; 30 N. E. Rep. 67.

[97] Wendell v. New York, etc., R. Co., 91 N. Y. 420; Moebus v. Herrman, 108 N. Y. 349; 15 N. E. Rep. 415.

[98] Rodrian v. New York, etc., R. Co., 125 N. Y. 526; 26 N. E. Rep. 741; 35 N. Y. S. R. 814.

A traveler before undertaking to cross a railroad must look along the track in each direction for an approaching train, and if the view

§ 1006. **Failure to look and listen is negligence, when.**—
It is the duty of a traveler in the full enjoyment of his
faculties of hearing and seeing, upon a highway approaching
a railroad crossing, before he attempts to pass or drive over
the crossing, to exercise a proper degree of care and caution
and to make vigilant use of his eyes and ears for the purpose
of ascertaining whether or not a train is approaching; and
if, by the proper use of his faculties, he could have discovered the approach of a train and so have escaped injury,
and he fails to do so and is injured, he is chargeable with
contributory negligence and cannot maintain an action for
such an injury.[99] In other words, a traveler approaching
a railroad crossing is bound to know that to attempt to cross
near and in front of a moving train, involves danger; and if
he does not look and listen the court will draw the inference
that his act contributed to the injury.[1] And this rule applies although the railroad company failed to give the proper
cautionary signals, or was guilty of other acts of negligence,
concurring to cause the injury.[2] Nor will it excuse the
injured traveler that his attention was attracted by a train
on another track,[3] or that he had temporarily forgotten that

is at all obstructed, he must listen, and if he fails to do so without
a reasonable excuse, he is negligent. Kunz v. Oregon R. Co. (Or. 1907),
93 Pac. Rep. 141.

[99] Salter v. Utica, etc., R. Co., 75 N. Y. 273; Georgia Pacific R. Co.
v. Lee, 92 Ala. 262; 9 So. Rep. 230; Chicago, etc., R. Co. v. Wilson,
133 Ill. 55; 24 N. E. Rep. 555; 42 Am. & Eng. R. Cas. 153; Lang
v. Holliday Creek R. Co., 49 Iowa 469; Clark v. Missouri Pacific Ry.
Co., 35 Kansas 350; 11 Pac. Rep. 134; Wright v. Boston, etc., R. Co.,
129 Mass. 440; 2 Am. & Eng. R. Cas. 121; Cleveland, etc., R. Co. v.
Elliott, 28 Ohio St. 340; Fusili v. Missouri Pacific Ry. Co., 45 Mo.
App. 535; Holland v. Missouri Pacific Ry. Co., 210 Mo. 338; 112
S. W. Rep. 468; Hook v. Missouri Pacific Ry. Co., 162 Mo. 569; 63
S. W. Rep. 360; Hayden v. Missouri Pacific Ry. Co., 124 Mo. 566;
28 S. W. Rep. 74.

[1] Shoner v. Pennsylvania R. Co., 130 Ind. 170; 28 N. E. Rep. 616.

[2] Damrill v. St. Louis, etc., R. Co., 27 Mo. App. 202.

[3] Woodward v. New York, etc., R. Co., 106 N. Y. 369; 13 N. E.
Rep. 424; 32 Am. & Eng. R. Cas. 137.

he was in the vicinity of the crossing.[4] In other words, whenever looking or listening would have disclosed an approaching train, then the failure to look or listen is held such negligence as will bar a recovery at a highway crossing,[5] and the court may properly take the case from the jury,[6] order a nonsuit,[7] or instruct the jury that the plaintiff is not entitled to recover.[8]

But the fact that an otherwise cautious traveler had not looked for a train at the very instant of stepping upon the railroad track will not necessarily convict him of negligence, as a matter of law.[9] If the view of the track was so obstructed as to render it impossible to see an approaching train, or the acts of the railroad company had caused the traveler to expect no train at that time, it might be held a proper issue for the jury, whether or not he was negligent, under all the circumstances.[10] And where the evidence showed that the injured traveler might have seen the cars at a crossing some distance away, if he had looked, but the evidence was conflicting as to whether or not he could have discovered the cars on the track which led to the crossing, and there were other tracks on the crossing he was approaching, he was held not to be negligent as matter of law.[11]

[4] Baltimore, etc., R. Co. v. Whitacre, 35 Ohio St. 627.

[5] Davis v. New York, etc., R. Co., 47 N. Y. 400; 2 Am. Ry. Rep. 394; Boyd v. Wabash R. Co., 105 Mo. 371; 16 S. W. Rep. 909; Williams v. Chicago, etc., R. Co., 64 Wis. 1; 24 N. W. Rep. 422; 23 Am. & Eng. R. Cas. 274

[6] Straugh v. Detroit, etc., R. Co., 65 Mich. 706; 36 N. W. Rep. 161; 32 Am. & Eng. R. Cas. 164.

[7] Brooks v. Buffalo, etc., R. Co., 27 Barb. (N. Y.) 532.

[8] Schofield v. Chicago, etc., R. Co., 114 U. S. 615; 5 Sup. Ct. Rep. 1125; 19 Am. & Eng. R. Cas. 353; Gardner v. Detroit, etc., R. Co., 97 Mich. 240; 56 N. W. Rep. 603.

[9] Chicago, etc., R. Co. v. Hedges, 105 Ind. 398; 7 N. E. Rep. 801; 25 Am. & Eng. R. Cas. 550.

[10] Abbott v. Chicago, etc., R. Co., 30 Minn. 482; 16 N. W. Rep. 266.

[11] Scott v. Wilmington, etc., R. Co., 96 No. Car. 428; 2 S. E. Rep. 151. -

§ 1007. **Looking for special trains, or those out of time.**— As special trains or trains belated are apt to be run upon a railroad track, the same as those run according to regular schedule, the same duty is imposed upon the traveler at a highway crossing to look for special or irregular trains, as to look for those operated according to regular schedule.

In a Missouri case,[12] a train which injured a highway traveler, was an extra train, running at a speed of from eighteen to twenty miles an hour. The traveler had not seen it approaching, nor had he heard it coming, and the evidence showed that no signal for the crossing had been given. The court treated the duty on the part of the traveler the same as if the train had been a regular train and his contributory negligence, in failing to look for the train, was held to deny a recovery.

The fact that a train is behind time and is running faster than usual at the crossing, to make up time, is no excuse for a traveler's negligence in failing to stop, look and listen for the train, and this fact alone will not justify a recovery by an otherwise negligent traveler at a highway crossing.[13]

But it has been held, in a Michigan case,[14] that a traveler is not bound to the same degree of care where no train is due

Where a pedestrian approaching a railroad crossing attempted to cross without listening or looking for the approach of a train, and by listening the approaching train could have been heard, or by looking could have been seen, the company was not liable, though it negligently failed to give signals on approaching the crossing. Matteson v. Southern Pac. Co. (Cal. App. 1907), 92 Pac. Rep. 101.

[12] Maxey v. Missouri Pacific Ry. Co., 113 Mo. 1; 20 S. W. Rep. 654; Chicago, etc., R. Co. v. Houston, 95 U. S. 697; Durbin v. Oregon, etc., R. Co., 17 Oregon 5; 17 Pac. Rep. 5; 11 Am. St. Rep. 778; 32 Am. & Eng. R. Cas. 149; Schofield v. Chicago, etc., R. Co., 114 U. S. 615; 19 Am. & Eng. R. Cas. 353.

[13] Cincinnati, etc., R. Co. v. Howard, 124 Ind. 280; 24 N. E. Rep. 892; Schmolze v. Chicago, etc., R. Co., 83 Wis. 659; 53 N. W. Rep. 743; 54 N. W. Rep. 106.

[14] Guggenheim v. Lake Shore, etc., R. Co., 66 Mich. 150; 33 N. W. Rep. 161; 32 Am. & Eng. R. Cas. 89.

and· he has no knowledge of its approach, as he would be charged with in the case of a train running on time and when he knew of its approach. It has been said that it cannot always be held negligence for a traveler to cross a railroad track at a time when no train is due and one cannot reasonably be expected to pass, without stopping to look, or listen for a train, when no signal of its approach is given by bell or otherwise.[15] And when the track can be plainly seen for a distance sufficient to insure a safe passage if no train is in sight and it is not train time and no signals are given for the crossing, it was held, in a Kentucky case,[16] that a traveler so situated was not negligent in crossing the track, without stopping or listening for a train.

§ 1008. **Failure to look and listen not affected by company's negligence.**— As the right of a traveler upon the highway, to recover for injuries received at the crossing of a railroad track, does not exist, in cases where his own negligence concurred to occasion the injury, it is immaterial that the railroad company was also negligent, if his negligence in part contributed to the injury, for, as said by the Missouri court: " Negligence which is proximate or a cause of the injury is sufficient. It does not matter that the concurring or co-operating negligence of defendant was negligence *per se,* such as the violation of an ordinance, as in this case, or statute law." [17]

In other words, since negligence is merely a breach of legal duty, it is immaterial whether the breach consists in

[15] McGrath v. Hudson River R. Co., 19 How. Pr. (N. Y.) 211; 32 Barb. 144.

[16] Cahill v. Cincinnati, etc., R. Co., 92 Ky. 345; 18 S. W. Rep. 2; 49 Am. & Eng. R. Cas. 390.

Plaintiff was injured by a train two hours late, which failed to signal, but as he was negligent he was denied a recovery, in Howard v. Northern Central R. Co., 49 Hun 605; 1 N. Y. Supp. 528.

[17] Payne v. Chicago, etc., R. Co., 129 Mo. 419; 31 S. W. Rep. 885.

the violation of a duty imposed by common law or by statute or ordinance, the result is the same and that the one alleged to have occasioned the injury was also negligent, if the plaintiff or injured person was negligent, in a way to contribute to the injury, is immaterial, as affecting the right of recovery.[18]

One who goes upon a track at a railroad crossing, therefore, without looking or listening for a train, when by looking the approaching train could have been seen, is guilty of such contributory negligence as will preclude a recovery for an injury received, notwithstanding the negligence of the train employees, in the management or operation of the train.[19]   And if one recklessly goes upon a railroad track, without looking or listening for trains, and is killed, when by looking or listening he could have been apprised of the approach of the train, he is guilty of such contributory negligence as will preclude a recovery, in an action for his death, although the train was, at the time, running at a rate of speed forbidden by ordinance and the employees failed to ring the bell or sound the whistle for the crossing.[20]

§ 1009. **Duty to look and listen not affected by failure to give signals.**— The fact that the employees of the railroad company, in charge of its train, failed to discharge their duty in giving the customary or statutory signals for the highway crossing, will not warrant a recovery, if the injured person was also guilty of negligence in failing to look and listen for the approaching train, as he approached the crossing.[21]

[18] Chicago, etc., R. Co. v. Hedges, 118 Ind. 5; 20 N. E. Rep. 530; 37 Am. & Eng. R. Cas. 516.
[19] Butts v. St. Louis, etc., R. Co., 98 Mo. 272; 11 S. W. Rep. 754; Toledo, etc., R. Co. v. Shuckman, 50 Ind. 42; Tucker v. New York. etc., R. Co., 124 N. Y. 308; 26 N. E. Rep. 916; 36 N. Y. S. R. 272.
[20] Taylor v. Missouri Pacific Ry. Co., 86 Mo. 457.
[21] Drake v. Chicago, etc., R. Co., 51 Mo. App. 562; Mann v. Belt

Where there was a reasonable distance, before crossing the track at a highway crossing, where the traveler could have seen the approaching train, if he had stopped and listened;[22] where he failed to stop and listen at all;[23] where he stopped and looked for danger and then failed to exercise caution after this period, until he passed upon the track,[24] or where the traveler failed to exercise that degree of care which the dangerous nature of the crossing would require,[25] he will be held negligent barring a recovery, although the employee in charge of the engine failed to give the signals for the crossing and was also negligent in this particular.

§ 1010. **Failure to maintain flagman does not affect duty to look and listen.**—Although a railroad company has no flagman at a crossing of a public highway, as required by

Line R. Co., 128 Ind. 138; 26 N. E. Rep. 819; Indiana, etc., R. Co. v. Hammock, 113 Ind. 1; 14 N. E. Rep. 737; 32 Am. & Eng. R. Cas. 127; Pennsylvania R. Co. v. Rothgeb, 32 Ohio St. 66; Chicago, etc., R. Co. v. Lee, 68 Ill. 576; Union Pacific R. Co. v. Adams, 33 Kansas 427; 6 Pac. Rep. 529; 19 Am. & Eng. R. Cas. 376; Grows v. Maine, etc., R. Co., 67 Me. 100; Maxey v. Missouri Pacific Ry. Co., 113 Mo. 1; 20 S. W. Rep. 654; Stepp v. Chicago, etc., R. Co., 85 Mo. 229; Lenix v. Missouri Pacific Ry. Co., 76 Mo. 86; Caldwell v. Kansas City, etc., R. Co., 58 Mo. App. 453; Hook v. Missouri Pacific Ry. Co., 162 Mo. 569; 63 S. W. Rep. 360; Wengler v. Missouri Pacific Ry. Co., 16 Mo. App. 493; Rodrian v. New York, etc., R. Co., 125 N. Y. 526; 26 N. E. Rep. 741; 35 N. Y. S. R. 814; Cullen v. Delaware, etc., Co., 113 N. Y. 667; 21 N. E. Rep. 716; Williams v. Chicago, etc., R. Co., 64 Wis. 1; 24 N. W. Rep. 422; 23 Am. & Eng. R. Cas. 274; Ormsbee v. Boston, etc., R. Co., 14 R. I. 102; 51 Am. Rep. 354; Davey v. London, etc., R. Co., L. R. 11 Q. B. D. 213; 14 Am. & Eng. R. Cas. 650; Chicago, etc., R. Co. v. Houston, 95 U. S. 697; Pennsylvania R. Co. v. Righter, 42 N J. L. 180; 2 Am. & Eng. R. Cas. 220; Galveston, etc., R. Co. v. Kutac, 72 Texas 643; 11 S. W. Rep. 127.

[22] Louisville, etc., R. Co. v. Stommel, 126 Ind. 35; 25 N. E. Rep. 863.

[23] Gorton v. Erie R. Co., 45 N. Y. 660.

[24] Thornton v. Cleveland, etc., R. Co., 131 Ind. 492; 31 N. E. Rep. 185.

[25] Griffith v. Baltimore, etc., R. Co., 44 Fed. Rep. 574.

law, if the injured traveler on the highway could
the approaching train, if he had stopped or look
tened, a reasonable distance from the crossing,
held guilty of such contributory negligence as wil
covery for the injury so received.[26]

In an Alabama case,[27] the neglect of a person a[
a railroad crossing, on a highway, to use his sens
and hearing to guard against an approaching train
to be such contributory negligence as to prevent
for an injury from a collision with a train on th
and the fact that the railroad flagman, for the cro
sitting some ninety feet distant, with his flag ly
his lap, as the traveler on the highway observ
going onto the crossing, and that no signal was
the approach of the train, by the flagman, was h
make the question of the traveler's negligence a j

§ 1011. **Speed of train does not affect duty to lo
ten.**—It is the duty of a person about to cross
track to look in both directions for an approaching
a failure to take this precaution for his own saf
injury results, will not be excused because of the
the train which occasioned the injury may have
ning at an unusual rate of speed, or faster tha
by a city ordinance.[28]   The rule of contributory

[26] Duncan v. Missouri Pacific Ry. Co., 46 Mo. App. 198
St. Louis, etc., R. Co., 64 Mo. 480; 65 Mo. 22; Freeman
etc., R. Co., 74 Mich. 86; 41 N. W. Rep. 872; 3 L. R. A. 5
& Eng. R. Cas. 501; Moore v. New York, etc., R. Co., 42
489; 62 Hun 621; 17 N. Y. Supp. 205; Louisville, etc.,
Webb, 90 Ala. 185; 8 So. Rep. 518; 49 Am. & Eng. R.
Sala v. Chicago, etc., R. Co., 85 Iowa 678; 52 N. W. Rep.

[27] Louisville, etc., R. Co. v. Webb, 90 Ala. 185; 8 So.
49 Am. & Eng. R. Cas. 427.

[28] St. Louis, etc., R. Co. v. Mathias, 50 Ind. 65; 8 An
381; Sala v. Chicago, etc., R. Co., 85 Iowa 678; 52 N. W

14

is not changed or altered by reason of the statute or ordinance imposing the duty, on account of the violation of which the injury resulted, if the traveler's negligence in part contributed to effect the injury.[29]   The statute or ordinance limiting the rate of speed does not absolve persons approaching public railway crossings from exercising common prudence to avoid danger to themselves, nor shift the responsibility to the railroad company, should injury ensue from a failure to exercise due care.[30]

Where one could see an approaching train, therefore, for a distance of sixty or seventy rods, while he was yet six hundred feet from the track, to drive upon the track, without looking, will defeat a recovery, for an injury from a collision with the train, although the train was running at a dangerous rate of speed.[31]

But if the railroad company was guilty of running a train at a greater rate of speed than allowed by a municipal ordinance, though the traveler was guilty of contributory negligence in failing to stop and look or listen for the train, such contributory negligence would not bar a recovery, provided the traveler used due diligence to avoid the injury, after he became aware of his peril, and the employees of the railroad company, after his peril was apparent, could by the exercise of ordinary care, have avoided the injury.[32]

Taylor v. Missouri Pacific Ry. Co., 86 Mo. 457; Powell v. Missouri Pacific Ry. Co., 76 Mo. 80; 8 Am. & Eng. R. Cas. 467; Maxey v. Missouri Pacific Ry. Co., 113 Mo. 1; 20 S. W. Rep. 654; Damrill v. St. Louis, etc., Ry. Co., 27 Mo. App. 202.

[29] Schmidt v. Missouri Pacific Ry. Co., 191 Mo. 215; 90 S. W. Rep. 136; Weller v. Chicago, etc., Ry. Co., 120 Mo. 635; 23 S. W. Rep. 1061; 25 S. W. Rep. 532.

[30] Kenney v. Hannibal, etc., Ry. Co., 105 Mo. 270; 15 S. W. Rep. 983; Sweeney v. Kansas City, etc., Ry. Co., 150 Mo. 385; 51 S. W. Rep. 682; Evans v. Wabash R. Co., 178 Mo. 508; 77 S. W. Rep. 515; Ries v. Transit Co., 179 Mo. 1; 77 S. W. Rep. 734; Holland v. Missouri Pacific Ry. Co., 210 Mo. 338; 109 S. W. Rep. 19.

[31] Schofield v. Chicago, etc., R. Co., 2 McCrary (U. S.) 268.

[32] Highland Avenue R. Co. v. Sampson, 91 Ala. 560; 8 So. Rep. 778.

The defense of contributory negligence is held to be just as available where the defendant company is in violation of a speed ordinance as it is under any other circumstances, and the Missouri court has laid down and adheres to the doctrine that the statute or ordinance limiting the rate of speed does not absolve persons approaching public railway crossings from exercising common prudence to avoid danger, nor shift the responsibility to the railroad, should injury ensue from the failure to exercise such common prudence. Schmidt v. Missouri Pacific Ry. Co., 191 Mo. 215; 90 S. W. Rep. 136.

If, therefore, plaintiff's own testimony shows, or the irresistible logic of it tends to show that the deceased as he approached the track knew, or had reason to apprehend that the approaching train was being run in excess of the ordinance limit, then plaintiff cannot be held to say that deceased relied upon the speed being restrained to the ordinance limit.

We recall Holland v. Missouri Pacific Ry. Co., 210 Mo., as one of these cases where the court said under similar circumstances, at the bottom of page 350 in said opinion:

"But even if the train in question was running at the time of the accident at a rate of speed in excess of that prescribed by the city ordinance, and the defendant company was, therefore, guilty of negligence, *per se*, the conduct of the deceased in going upon the track in proximity to the approaching train, was contributory negligence on his part, which negligence was the proximate cause of the injury."

In Schmidt v. Missouri Pacific Ry. Co., *supra*, it is held that the rule of contributory negligence is not changed or abrogated by reason of the statute or ordinance imposing the duty on account of the violation of which the injury resulted. That the statute does not absolve persons approaching a public railway crossing from exercising common prudence to avoid danger, nor shift the responsibility to another should injury ensue from the failure to exercise it.

In support of this proposition we cite Green v. Missouri Pacific Ry. Co., 192 Mo. l. c. 141; 90 S. W. Rep. 805.

The Green case further holds, and also the case of Stotler v. Chicago, etc., R. Co., 103 S. W. Rep. 1; 204 Mo. l. c. 632, holds, that if one sees or has reason to believe that a train or engine on a track which he is about to cross is running at a rate of speed in excess of that permitted by the ordinance, he has no right to risk his life on the presumption that the ordinance is being observed. That there is in such case, no ground upon which to construct a rational presumption that the traveler trusted that the engineer was obeying the ordinance, see Bragg v. Metropolitan R. Co., 192 Mo. l. c. 354; 91 S. W. Rep. 527.

Travelers have no right to indulge this presumption for the further reason that when in a place of safety, if one could have looked, and he would have seen what his witnesses saw, he would, there-

§ 1012. **Duty of deaf persons or those with ears covered, to look for trains.**— Where a party who is about to cross a railroad track is deaf, and it appears that by looking, he could have seen the train, in time to have avoided the accident, it shows a great want of care for him not to have looked the more carefully, as he could not hear.[33] It is therefore held that a greater degree of care will be exacted from a deaf person, crossing a railroad track, in looking for

fore, not have had the right to act upon the presumption that the speed of the train was restrained to the ordinance limit, where he could have seen the train at least eight hundred feet away and could have definitely ascertained by looking, just what plaintiff's witnesses ascertained by looking, to-wit, that the train was running at a rate of speed not less than twenty-five miles an hour. In this connection we cite Nixon v. Hannibal, etc., Ry. Co., 141 Mo. 439; 42 S. W. Rep. 942. And if he did not see the approaching train he could of course not indulge that presumption that it would not exceed the ordinance limit of speed. Where one does not see the train at all, he has no information upon which to base any presumption. Reno v. St. Louis, etc., R. Co., 180 Mo. 483; 79 S. W. Rep. 464.

Where, in an action for injuries to plaintiff at a railroad crossing, it was reasonably certain that, if the train had been running at a speed not exceeding eight miles an hour, as required by a city ordinance, it would have missed the buggy in which plaintiff was riding and prevented the catastrophe, the proof was sufficient to justify a finding that the railroad's breach of the ordinance was the proximate cause of the accident. Stotler v. Chicago & A. Ry. Co. (Mo. 1906), 98 S. W. Rep. 509.

Where, in an action for injuries to plaintiff at a railroad crossing, plaintiff testified that he did not see the train which collided with his wagon, he cannot be heard to claim that in passing over the crossing ahead of the train he relied on a city ordinance prohibiting the operation of trains within the city where the accident occurred at more than six miles per hour. Westerkamp v. Chicago, B. & Q. Ry. Co. (Colo. 1907), 92 Pac. Rep. 687.

To authorize a recovery for a personal injury on the ground of a railroad's negligence in violating a speed ordinance, it must appear that the hurt was caused by the unlawful speed without contributory negligence of the injured person. Kunz v. Oregon R. Co. (Or. 1907), 93 Pac. Rep. 141.

[33] Illinois, etc., R. Co. v. Buckner, 28 Ill. 299.

trains, than from those whose faculties are not so impaired.[34] And if a deaf person approaches a railroad crossing and proceeds onto the track, without looking to see if a train is approaching, and is killed, in consequence, he is guilty of such contributory negligence as will bar an action for his death.[35]

And where the deafness, or partial deafness of the injured traveler, is not known to the employees of the railroad company, if the facts are such as to send the case to the jury, upon the issue of the contributory negligence of the traveler in failing to stop and look for the approaching train, the care of the employees of the railroad company will not be affected by the deafness of the traveler, not shown to have been brought to their notice and the deafness, or partial deafness of the traveler,[36] or the fact that he had his ears covered when he proceeded upon the track,[37] are circumstances for the jury to take into consideration, as establishing the contributory negligence of the traveler, in connection with his failure to look for the train.[38]

[34] International, etc., R. Co. v. Garcia, 75 Texas 583; 13 S. W. Rep. 223.

[35] Johnson v. Louisville, etc., R. Co., 91 Ky. 651; 25 S. W. Rep. 754; 13 Am. & Eng. R. Cas. 623. See, also, Purl v. St. Louis, etc., R. Co., 72 Mo. 168; Zimmerman v. Hannibal, etc., R. Co., 71 Mo. 476; 2 Am. & Eng. R. Cas. 191.

[36] Chicago, etc., R. Co. v. Triplett, 38 Ill. 482; Cleveland, etc., R. Co. v. Terry, 8 Ohio St. 570.

Where one partially deaf, passed the place where he could have seen an approaching train, by looking, and was afterwards killed, because of his failure to look for the train, it was held such contributory negligence as to prevent a recovery, in Central R. Co. v. Feller, 84 Pa. St. 226; 18 Am. Ry. Rep. 36.

[37] Elkins v. Boston, etc., R. Co., 115 Mass. 190; 7 Am. Ry. Rep. 456; Salter v. Utica, etc., R. Co., 59 N. Y. 631; Siegel v. Milwaukee, etc., R. Co., 79 Wis. 404; 48 N. W. Rep. 488.

[38] International, etc., R. Co. v. Garcia, 75 Texas 583; 13 S. W. Rep. 223; Rembe v. New York, etc., R. Co., 102 N. Y. 721; 7 N. E. Rep. 797; 2 N. Y. S. R. 498; 32 Hun 68.

§ 1013. **Duty to stop, when noise affect:**
obstructed.— In considering the duty of
highway, in approaching an obstructe‹
where noise would prevent hearing an
the late Judge Black, for the Missouri c
the crossing is obstructed from view, incr‹
quired on the part of the traveler, as we.
and if, from noise, such as a gale of wind,
a wagon, hearing is rendered difficult, the١
the duty of the traveler to stop and listen."

In a New York case,[40] where the plain:
a carryall with a large number of comp£
singing and shouting when the railroad cros.
and the plaintiff knew the crossing and k
about time for a train, and the view of ١
obstructed and the carryall failed to stop, :
the plaintiff could not recover, as his own c
ligence and that of his companions would pr‹

And the operation of a mill near a railro

In an action for death of a person struck by a
railroad crossing, evidence considered, and *held* to
tributory negligence on the part of deceased, a de‹
looking out for approaching trains as to preclude a ١
Adm'x v. Rutland R. Co. (Vt. 1908), 69 Atl. Rep. ‹

Where a deaf man approaches a railroad cros‹
required to look to the extent necessary for the exer
Osteen v. Southern Ry., Carolina Division, 57 S. E. R

Where a party approaches a crossing and wraps h;
up his head so as to protect himself from the cold or ١
to extraordinary care, as he has voluntarily diminis
for seeing or hearing a train approaching. Butterfl‹
etc., R. Co., 10 Allen 532; Elkins v. Boston, etc., R. Co.,
Stevens v. Oswego, etc., R. Co., 18 N. Y. 422; Hanover,
Coyle, 54 Pa. St. 396; Chicago, etc., R. Co. v. Still, 19 Il
etc., R. Co. v. Ebert, 74 Ill. 399; Pennsylvania R. Co.
Pa. St. 50; Roth v. Milwaukee, etc., R. Co., 21 Wis. 25

[39] Stepp v. Chicago, etc., R. Co., 85 Mo. 229.

[40] Koehler v. Rochester, etc., R. Co., 66 Hun (N.
N. Y. S. R. 619; 21 N. Y. Supp. 844.

would prevent one from hearing a train a very great distance, will not excuse the traveler from failing to look for the train.[41]

But where the traveler stops and listens for the train, although this is done at a point where his vision is obstructed by escaping steam from a factory, and the operation of the same makes such noise as to render it difficult to hear an approaching train, as this would show ordinary caution on the part of the traveler, it would be a jury issue whether or not he used such care as an ordinarily prudent person would use under the circumstances.[42]

§ 1014. **Proper place to stop, look and listen.**— Where one driving a team approaches a railroad track, he should look and listen for trains a sufficient distance from the track, so that if his horses become frightened, they may be restrained without getting on the railroad track.[43] A driver should, at the nearest and most eligible point, to the railroad track, stop his team and listen for an approaching train.[44] As to what distance from the track would be a safe place to stop and listen for trains, would depend, necessarily, on the character of the ground and the obstructions at or near the crossing, and surrounding conditions.

A traveler who failed to stop or look for a train, when within five feet of the track, when from such point, his vision of the track would have been unobstructed for a distance of two hundred and fifty feet, was held negligent.[45]

[41] Sabine, etc., R. Co. v. Dean, 76 Texas 73; 13 S. W. Rep. 45.

[42] Neiman v. Delaware, etc., R. Co., 149 Pa. St. 92; 24 Atl. Rep. 90; Alexander v. Richmond, etc., R. Co., 112 No. Car. 720; 16 S. E. Rep. 896.

[43] Rhodes v. Chicago, etc., R. Co., 58 Mich. 263; 25 N. W. Rep. 182; 21 Am. & Eng. R. Cas. 659.

[44] Moberly v. Kansas City, etc., R. Co., 17 Mo. App. 518; 98 Mo. 183; 11 S. W. Rep. 569.

[45] Gardner v. Detroit, etc., R. Co., 97 Mich. 240; 56 N. W. Rep. 603.

A traveler who failed to stop and listen for a
eighteen feet from the track, was held neg
could have seen down the track, in the direc
the train was approaching, a distance of n
feet, if he had stopped and looked.[46]   A fai
listen for a train, when it could have been se
from fifteen to thirty feet from the track,
gence, in a Missouri case.[47]   Failure to sto
of from thirty to forty feet from the track
negligence, when an unobstructed view of t
have been had from such place.[48]   And it is
proper for a traveler to stop and listen for
place as will render him within the limits of
as determined from all the facts and circum
case, and a failure to so stop and listen will
gence on his part.[49]

But a person who does stop and listen for a
necessarily be held negligent because he did 1
stop and listen at the most advantageous pla
stops from four to six rods from the crossin{
it is held, in one case, that he is not necessar
as matter of law, in failing to stop and listen a
who stopped within seventy feet of the crossing
was held not negligent, as matter of law, in f{
again, in an Iowa case.[52]   It was held not n{

[46] Urias v. Pennsylvania R. Co., 152 Pa. St. 326; 25
[47] Hayden v. Missouri, etc., R. Co., 124 Mo. 566; 28 i
[48] Huggart v. Missouri Pacific Ry. Co., 134 Mo. 673;
220; Sanguinette v. Mississippi River, etc., R. Co., 19{
S. W. Rep. 386; Schmidt v. Missouri Pacific Ry. Co.,
90 S. W. Rep. 136; Green v. Missouri Pacific Ry. Co.,
90 S. W. Rep. 805.
[49] Nosler v. Chicago, etc., R. Co., 73 Iowa 268; 34 N.
[50] Rodrian v. New York, etc., R. Co., 125 N. Y. 526; 26 }
[51] Renwick v. New York, etc., R. Co., 36 N. Y. 132; 34
[52] Lee v. Chicago, etc., R. Co., 80 Iowa 172; 45 N. W.
Am. & Eng. R. Cas. 157.

se, to stop one's team at the side of a street, instead of in the middle of the street, although the latter place would have been the best place to obtain a view of the track.[53]   And where the evidence shows that the traveler did stop and listen for a train, it is generally held, under all the evidence, a question for the jury, whether this was a proper place to listen for the cars and the traveler will not be held guilty of negligence, as matter of law, unless the evidence is all one way, to the effect that it was not a proper place to stop.[54]

[53] Scott v. Wilmington, etc., R. Co., 96 No. Car. 428; 2 S. E. Rep. 151.

[54] Smith v. Baltimore, etc., R. Co., 158 Pa. St. 82; 27 Atl. Rep. 847.

In Huggart v. Missouri Pacific Ry. Co. (134 Mo. 673), Judge Gantt, for the court, said: " It is uncontradicted and conceded that when he reached a point from thirty to forty feet from the track, a point where he was free from all danger of collision with trains upon the road, he could have seen up the track to the west a distance of six hundred and possibly a thousand feet. As a physical fact, that train was then in sight. One of two conclusions is inevitable: he either did not look and heedlessly rode upon the track and was killed, or he looked and saw the approaching train and attempted to cross ahead of it. In either case, he was guilty of such contributory negligence as bars a recovery by his widow."

And, see, also, Judge Burgess' opinion, in Sanguinette v. Mississippi River, etc., R. Co., 196 Mo. 491; 95 S. W. Rep. 386; Hayden v. Missouri, etc., R. Co., 124 Mo. 566; 28 S. W. Rep. 74; Guyer v. Missouri Pacific Ry. Co., 174 Mo. 344; 73 S. W. Rep. 584; Payne v. Chicago, etc., R. Co., 136 Mo. 562, 580; 38 S. W. Rep. 308; Lien v. Chicago, etc., R. Co., 79 Mo. App. 475; Hook v. Missouri Pacific Ry. Co., 162 Mo. 569; 63 S. W. Rep. 360.

Where the driver of a delivery wagon approaching a railroad track looked for a train while a block from the track, and not again till he drove on the track, he was guilty of contributory negligence, barring a recovery for injuries to the horse, wagon and harness from being struck by the train. St. Louis, etc., R. Co. v. Portis (Ark. 1907), 99 S. W. Rep. 66.

The duty of a traveler upon a highway before crossing a railroad to look up and down the tracks and listen for approaching trains must be performed at a time when its performance will be an efficient means of warning the traveler of his peril, if peril exists, and his failure to perform such duty is such negligence as will prevent a recovery if he is run down at the crossing, even though it be shown

1491

§ 1015. **Driving rapidly upon crossing wi**
One who drives a team at a rapid speed 1
crossing, without stopping or looking for
train, is generally held guilty of negligence
law, precluding a recovery for injuries recei
of a collision with a train on the crossing. (
right of an injured traveler to recover for in
where he had approached the crossing on a b1
Henry, for the Missouri court, in a leading

that no warning of the approach of the train was g
Atlantic City R. Co. (N. J. 1907), 68 Atl. Rep. 61.

Where the evidence is conflicting or there are i1
to be drawn both ways, from the testimony, the (
the traveler stopped, looked and listened at the pro
the jury. McGill v. Pittsburg, etc., R. Co., 152 Pa.
Rep. 540; Ely v. Pittsburg, etc., R. Co., 158 Pa. £
Rep. 970.

A traveler, familiar with the condition surrounding
ing, was injured by a train at the crossing. The trac:
above the level of the land, and was straight for eight
crossing. The traveler when thirty-five feet from the
for an approaching train, but saw none, and he did not
had at that time a clear view of the track for four hun
five feet. At thirty feet from the crossing he had a vi
for five hundred and thirty feet, and at twenty feet
open to view for one thousand and eighty-three feet. *H€*
guilty of contributory negligence as a matter of law, pre(
ery, though the company was negligent. Chicago, etc., R;
barger (Kan. 1907), 88 Pac. Rep. 531.

Where a traveler on a highway, after stopping and
approaching train at a distance of seventy-five feet from a
he could not look down the track because of an obstr(
again look or listen until he was on the main track,
struck by a train, though for at least forty feet before d
track he could have looked down the railroad a distance
hundred feet, he was held to be guilty of contributo:
precluding a recovery for his injury, even though the
negligent in failing to sound a whistle as required by ac(
827. Southern Ry. Co. v. Jones (Va. 1907), 56 S. E. Re]

55 Turner v. Hannibal, etc., R. Co., 74 Mo. 602; 6 A1

"He directly contributes to his own injury, who, paying no attention to his own safety, trusts to the obligations imposed upon the company to warn him of an approaching train. Here the plaintiff, without looking, except from a point at which he knew he could not see an approaching train, and failing to look at other points from which he could have seen it, drove, in a brisk trot, onto the track of the railroad, never having stopped to listen for an approaching train." This conduct was held negligent as matter of law, by the court.

Where the facts show that one injured at a railroad crossing, approached it at a dangerously rapid rate of speed, and that he drove upon the track, without reducing the speed of his team, when he could have heard an approaching train in time to have avoided the injury, the conclusion is irresistible that he must have seen the train and endeavored to beat it across the track, and he will therefore he held to have taken the chances of a miscalculation and to be negligent, barring a recovery for the injuries received.[56] And this would be true, whether any signals had been given for the crossing, or not, for this would only show a case of concurrent negligence on the part of the railroad company and the traveler.[57]

But where the evidence shows that the traveler was proceeding at a slow trot and that he slowed down, before driving upon the railroad track, it was held to be a proper issue for the jury, whether or not this was due care, under all

Cas. 38. Followed, in, Hixon v. St. Louis, etc., R. Co., 80 Mo. 335; Maxey v. Missouri Pacific Ry. Co., 113 Mo. 1; 20 S. W. Rep. 654.

[56] Cones v. Cincinnati, etc., R. Co., 114 Ind. 328; 16 N. E. Rep. 638. And, see, Nash v. New York, etc., R. Co., 34 N. Y. S. R. 788; 3 Silv. App. 315.

[57] Nash v. New York, etc., R. Co., *supra;* Turner v. Hannibal, etc., R. Co., *supra.*

the circumstances, and it was held **no error** '
as matter of law, that such conduct **was n**c

§ 1016. **Duty to listen, when track obstr**ı
requires a traveler on a highway to listen as
for coming trains at a railroad crossing,
vision was obstructed, is no excuse for a fai
Indeed, the fact that one is approaching a ra
with the view obstructed, does not excuse his
and listen, but it makes his duty to do so the
the view of the track is limited and partia
greater care is required, on the part of a
would be if he had an open and extende
track.[61]   One attempting to cross a railroa

[58] Richardson v. New York, etc., R. Co., 15 N. Y
N. Y. S. R. 616; 61 Hun 624.
Driving at a speed forbidden by ordinance, at the
sion between the wagon driven and a train, at a h
is such negligence as will prevent a recovery, if the
any way contributed to the injury.
Weller v. Chicago, etc., R. Co., 120 Mo. 635; 23 S. W.]
25 S. W. Rep. 532.
[59] Pennsylvania R. Co. v. Mooney, 126 Pa. St. 244; 17
39 Am. & Eng. R. Cas. 612; Gothard v. Alabama R. C(
South, etc., R. Co. v. Donovan, 84 Ala. 141; 4 So. Re]
& Eng. R. Cas. 151; Pennsylvania R. Co. v. Frana,
Terre Haute, etc., R. Co. v. Voelker, 129 Ill. 540; 22]
39 Am. & Eng. R. Cas. 615; Fletcher v. Atlantic, e(
Mo. 484; Masterson v. Chicago, etc., R. Co., 58 Mo. Ap]
v. Atchinson, etc., R. Co., 70 Mo. App. 88.
Traveler held under duty to stop, in following cases:
Louis, etc., R. Co., 71 Mo. 636; Stepp v. Chicago, etc.,]
229; Kelly v. Chicago, etc., R. Co., 88 Mo. 534; Damrill
etc., R. Co., 27 Mo. App. 202; Kelsay v. Missouri Pacifi(
Mo. 362; 30 S. W. Rep. 330; Hook v. Missouri Pacific
Mo. 569; 63 S. W. Rep. 360.
[60] Pennsylvania R. Co. v. Morel, 40 Ohio St. 338; Beye
etc., R. Co., 34 W. Va. 538; 12 S. E. Rep. 532; 45 An
Cas. 188; McBride v. Northern Pacific R. Co., 19 Oregon
Rep. 814; 42 Am. & Eng. R. Cas. 146.
[61] Atchison, etc., R. Co. v. Townsend, 39 Kansas 115; :

highway crossing, where the view of the track is obstructed, cannot recover for an injury received, if he fails to stop and look and listen for trains, before going on the track; and such failure cannot be excused by the fact that one train has just passed and another one is not expected so soon thereafter.[62]

But if, without the fault of the traveler, he is, for the time being, deprived of making full use of his eyes, and he is at a place where he can hear the ringing of the bell or the sounding of the whistle, and it is a crossing where the law requires such signals, and the traveler does listen for trains, he could not be held guilty of contributory negligence, because, without any fault on his part, he was temporarily deprived of the sense of sight, so that he could not see the approach of a locomotive on the track.[63] And if the crossing is one where a flagman or gates are maintained, as an open gate, or an absent flagman is held to be equivalent to an invitation to cross, the traveler will not be held guilty of contributory negligence, as matter of law, if he listened for a train, although he did not actually stop, at such an obstructed crossing, but his negligence will be a proper issue for the jury, under all the circumstances in the case.[64] And if the evidence for an injured traveler at an obstructed crossing, shows that he looked and listened, although he did not actually stop, he will not be held negligent, as matter of law, if different minds would reach different conclusions as

804; 35 Am. & Eng. R. Cas. 352; Cincinnati, etc., R. Co. v. Howard, 124 Ind. 280; 24 N. E. Rep. 892; Nehrbas v. Central Pacific R. Co., 62 Cal. 320; 14 Am. & Eng. R. Cas. 670.

[62] Durbin v. Oregon, etc., R. Co., 17 Oregon 5; 17 Pac. Rep. 5; 11 Am. St. Rep. 778; 32 Am. & Eng. R. Cas. 149; Clark v. Northern Pacific R. Co., 47 Minn. 380; 50 N. W. Rep. 365; Pennsylvania R. Co. v. Beale, 73 Pa. St. 504; 6 Am. Ry. Rep. 158; Kelly v. Chicago, etc., R. Co., 88 Mo. 534.

[63] Solen v. Virginia, etc., R. Co., 13 Nevada 106.

[64] Chicago, etc., R. Co. v. Adler, 129 Ill. 335; 21 N. E. Rep. 846; Cincinnati, etc., R. Co. v. Howard, 124 Ind. 280; 24 N. E. Rep. 892.

to the safety of the course pursued, but the question of his negligence, under all the circumstances, will be a proper jury issue.[65]

§ 1017. Driving rapidly on obstructed crossing.— As rapid driving in approaching a railroad crossing is not generally held to be ordinary care, because of the inability of the driver to stop the vehicle driven, in case of a rapidly approaching train, or the inability of the train employees to get the train under control, in time to avoid a collision, one who heedlessly approaches a crossing in a rapidly driven vehicle, is generally held to be guilty of such negligence as will prevent a recovery, in case of an injury due to a collision with a train.[66]

In an Iowa case,[67] where a crossing was more or less ob-

[65] Indianapolis, etc., R. Co. v. McLin, 82 Ind. 435; 8 Am. & Eng. R. Cas. 237.

There is no arbitrary rule requiring a traveler to *stop*, before attempting to cross a railroad track. If the circumstances are such that his sense of hearing can only be exercised by stopping, then he should stop, so as to be able to hear the train, or the signals. But where the conditions are such that the signals or the train can be heard, without stopping, then he need not stop. Russell v. Atchison, etc., R. Co., 70 Mo. App. 88.

Where a railroad crossing is especially dangerous, travelers must use increased care commensurate with the danger. Hummer's Exec. v. Louisville, etc., R. Co. (Ky. 1908), 108 S. W. Rep. 885.

Where the view of the track is obstructed and there is such noise, from the vehicle or other causes, as to require it, it is held to be the duty of the traveler to stop, in the following cases: Abbott v. Dwinnell, 74 Wis. 514; 43 N. W. Rep. 496; Kelly v. Chicago, etc., R. Co., 88 Mo. 534; Hook v. Missouri Pacific Ry. Co., 162 Mo. 569; 63 S. W. Rep. 360; Seefeld v. Chicago, etc., R. Co., 70 Wis. 216; 35 N. W. Rep. 278; 32 Am. & Eng. R. Cas. 109; Gothard v. Alabama, etc., R. Co., 67 Ala. 114; Baltimore, etc., R. Co. v. Hobbs (Md.), 19 Am. & Eng. R. Cas. 337; Hixon v. St. Louis, etc., R. Co., 80 Mo. 335; Brady v. Toledo, etc., R. Co., 81 Mich. 616; 45 N. W. Rep. 1110.

[66] Seefeld v. Chicago, etc., R. Co., 70 Wis. 216; 35 N. W. Rep. 278; 32 Am. & Eng. R. Cas. 109; Funston v. Chicago, etc., R. Co., 61 Iowa 452.

[67] Schafery v. Chicago, etc., R. Co., 62 Iowa 624.

structed, and a traveler on the highway, with knowledge of this fact, approached the crossing with a rapidly trotting team, he was held to have been guilty of such negligence as would bar a recovery for an injury received.

But although a traveler approaching a highway crossing does not slacken the speed of his team, but approaches the crossing on a trot, if the crossing could have been safely passed, had it been in good repair, before the approach of a train, but on account of a loose board, or other defect, the team was stalled, or prevented from going over the crossing, until too late to avoid collision with a train, then the issue of the plaintiff's negligence should be submitted to the jury.[68]

§ 1018. **When track obstructed by steam or smoke.**— When the view of a railroad track is obstructed by steam or smoke from passing trains the result is the same as if it had been obstructed from other causes, and since the view of the track cannot be had, the duty is all the more imperative to stop and listen for approaching trains. In a New York case,[69] where the plaintiff in a crossing accident attempted to avoid the effect of his failure to look for the train, by the excuse that the track was obscured by steam and smoke, the court held that it was his duty to either listen, or stop and wait until the smoke cleared away.

And in a Massachusetts case,[70] where a prospective pas-

[68] Whalen v. Arcata, etc., R. Co., 92 Cal. 669; 28 Pac. Rep. 833.

Fast driving, in approaching a crossing, was held to preclude a recovery, in, Martin v. New York, etc., R. Co., 50 N. Y. S. R. 553; 66 Hun 636; 21 N. Y. Supp. 191; Powell v. New York, etc., R. Co., 109 N. Y. 613; 15 N. E. Rep. 891; Galveston, etc., R. Co. v. Perfert, 72 Texas 344; 10 S. W. Rep. 207; 37 Am. & Eng. R. Cas. 540.

[69] Foran v. New York, etc., R. Co., 64 Hun (N. Y.) 510; 46 N. Y. S. R. 423; 19 N. Y. Supp. 417.

[70] Debbins v. Old Colony R. Co., 154 Mass. 402; 28 N. E. Rep. 274; 47 Am. & Eng. R. Cas. 531. But see, Randall v. Connecticut River R. Co., 132 Mass. 269.

senger approached a station around the end of a train standing on the siding and his view of the other track was obscured by smoke and steam, it was held that he was guilty of negligence in failing to stop and listen for the approaching train.

But as to passengers, around or near a station, there is generally held to be the duty owing, by the carrier, to avoid injury by passing trains, and the ordinary duty of the road, to stop and look and listen for approaching trains, is not enforced in all its strictness. Accordingly, it is held, in New York,[71] that a passenger was not negligent, as matter of law, in passing around a train to approach the station, but that the railroad company was negligent in operating a hand car on the adjoining track, at a rapid rate of speed, although the view of the track was obscured by steam and smoke. And the fact that steam and smoke obscured the track and prevented the sight of an approaching train, is held to be a circumstance going to show an absence of contributory negligence on the part of a traveler on the highway, in a Texas case.[72]

§ 1019. **Where track obstructed by buildings or piles of lumber.**— One who is familiar with the surroundings and approaches a railroad track in a narrow street, with buildings on either side, which will obstruct the view of the track, should stop and listen for trains a safe distance before reaching the track, and if he fails to do so, until within such a short distance of the track that an injury from a passing train cannot be avoided, he will be held guilty of negligence

---

[71] Conklin v. New York, etc., R. Co., 43 N. Y. S. R. 414; 63 Hun 628; 17 N. Y. Supp. 651; Campbell v. New York, etc., R. Co., 3 N. Y. Supp. 694; 19 N. Y. S. R. 659; 49 Hun 611; 121 N. Y. 669.

[72] Gulf, etc., R. Co. v. Anderson, 76 Texas 244; 13 S. W. Rep. 196; 42 Am. & Eng. R. Cas. 160.

barring a recovery therefor.[73] And the same rule obtains in the case of an obstruction from piles of lumber,[74] or wood,[75] and in either case a traveler will be held negligent, when his view of the track is so obscured, if he fails to stop and listen for a train, before driving up to the railroad track.

But it is held, in some cases, that a traveler on the highway cannot be held guilty of contributory negligence in failing to stop and listen for a train, when his view of the track is obstructed by a row of buildings.[76] A failure to stop until so near the track that one's team became frightened, was held not negligence, in a Minnesota case,[77] where buildings obstructed a view of the track back of the place where the team was stopped, and a railroad company was held negligent itself, in erecting obstructions on its right of way, which would obscure or obstruct the view of the track at a crossing, in an Illinois case.[78]

This decision, however, is not in accord with sound reason or the weight of authority on this question, for like any other property owner, a railroad company is held to have the lawful right to use its own land for any legitimate purpose, in the prosecution of its business, although it may obstruct the vision of those crossing its tracks. And while the existence of obstructions on the right of way might be a material circumstance as affecting the care of the railroad com-

[73] Hoffman v. Fitchburg, etc., R. Co., 67 Hun (N. Y.) 581; 51 N. Y. S. R. 245; 22 N. Y. Supp. 463.

[74] Hixson v. St. Louis, etc., R. Co., 80 Mo. 335; Henze v. St. Louis, etc., R. Co., 71 Mo. 636; Turner v. Hannibal, etc., R. Co., 74 Mo. 602.

[75] Lake Shore, etc., R. Co. v. Miller, 25 Mich. 274; 5 Am. Ry. Rep. 478.

[76] Donohue v. St. Louis, etc., R. Co., 91 Mo. 357; 2 S. W. Rep. 424; 28 Am. & Eng. R. Cas. 673.

[77] Faber v. St. Paul, etc., R. Co., 29 Minn. 465; 13 N. W. Rep. 902; 8 Am. & Eng. R. Cas. 277.

[78] Rockford, etc., R. Co. v. Hillmer, 72 Ill. 235.

pany, in the operation of trains across such an obstructed crossing, and also as affecting the care to be exercised by a traveler on such a crossing, this could not, legally, furnish any independent right of recovery of damages against the railroad company, for an injury to a traveler on the highway.[79]

§ 1020. **When track obstructed by passing trains or standing cars.**— Before crossing a railroad track, one is bound not only to stop, look and listen for a train, at a place where he can, if possible, see it approaching, but if familiar with the crossing and his view of the track is obstructed by a passing train, he should stop and remain, until his view of the track is clear, or otherwise, he is chargeable with contributory negligence.[80]   And where the view of the track is obstructed by cars standing on a side track, the duty is likewise imposed upon persons approaching the crossing of exercising a higher degree of vigilance to ascertain if it is safe to cross the railroad track.[81]   Where standing box cars on a side

[79] Cordell v. New York, etc., R. Co., 70 N. Y. 119; 18 Am. Ry. Rep. 511.

Where the view of a traveler on a highway crossing a railroad was obstructed by a rick of wood near the railroad crossing, a higher degree of care was imposed upon such traveler, than if the obstruction had not existed, the degree of caution required being in proportion to the danger caused by the obstruction. Southern Ry. Co. v. Jones (Va. 1907), 56 S. E. Rep. 155.

. A railroad was not guilty of negligence in constructing its depots and other structures at a point where they obstructed the view of the railroad from the crossing. Louisville, etc., R. Co. v. Lucas' Adm'r (Ky. 1907), 98 S. W. Rep. 308.

[80] Kraus v. Pennsylvania R. Co., 139 Pa. St. 272; 20 Atl. Rep. 993; Marty v. Chicago, etc., R. Co., 38 Minn. 108; 35 N. W. Rep. 670; 32 Am. & Eng. R. Cas. 107; Fletcher v. Fitchburg, etc., R. Co., 149 Mass. 127; 21 N. E. Rep. 302; 3 L. R. A. 743.

[81] Garland v. Chicago, etc., R. Co., 8 Ill. App. 571; Thomas v. Delaware, etc., R. Co., 19 Blatchf. (U. S.) 533; 8 Fed. Rep. 729; Stepp v. Chicago, etc., R. Co., 85 Mo. 229; Hook v. Missouri Pacific Ry. Co.,

track obstructed the view of the main track, on which a train was approaching the crossing, where a traveler was injured, in considering the duty of the traveler, under such circumstances, Judge Ray, for the Missouri Supreme Court,[82] said: "We think the law requires of him, when he cannot see the track, to listen, and, if necessary, for that purpose, to stop and listen for the train before venturing blindly upon it."

But if gates are raised, or a gateman motions a traveler to cross a track, after a train has just passed, and he is injured by another train on a different track, his negligence is held a jury issue, in a New York case.[83] If the traveler has stopped and listened for trains, at a place where his view is obstructed by standing cars, he cannot be held guilty of contributory negligence, as a matter of law, because he did not leave his team and wagon and advance to the track and reconnoiter.[84] One who listens for a train and cannot see the track, because of stationary cars, is not necessarily negligent, when no signals for the crossing have been given.[85] And where the traveler was injured by a car shunted across a crossing, without an attendant or an engine, and the traveler's view of the track was obstructed by standing cars, it was held, in a Wisconsin case,[86] to be a jury issue, whether

162 Mo. 569; 63 S. W. Rep. 360; Owens v. Pennsylvania R. Co., 41 Fed. Rep. 187.

[82] Kelly v. Chicago, etc., R. Co., 88 Mo. 534.

[83] Bond v. New York, etc., R. Co., 52 N. Y. S. R. 637; 23 N. Y. Supp. 450; 69 Hun 476.

[84] Georgia Pacific R. Co. v. Lee, 92 Ala. 262; 9 So. Rep. 230.

[85] Guggenheim v. Lake Shore, etc., R. Co., 66 Mich. 150; 33 N. W. Rep. 161; 32 Am. & Eng. R. Cas. 89; Close v. Lake Shore, etc., R. Co., 73 Mich. 647; 41 N. W. Rep. 828; 37 Am. & Eng. R. Cas. 522; Hanks v. Boston, etc., R. Co., 147 Mass. 495; 18 N. E. Rep. 218; 35 Am. & Eng. R. Cas. 321; Donnolly v. Boston, etc., R. Co., 151 Mass. 210; 24 N. E. Rep. 38; 42 Am. & Eng. R. Cas. 182; Guggenheim v. Lake Shore, etc., R. Co., 57 Mich. 488; 24 N. W. Rep. 827; 22 Am. & Eng. R. Cas. 546.

[86] Abbott v. Dwinnell, 74 Wis. 514; 43 N. W. Rep. 495. And see,

or not the traveler was guilty of contributory negligence in failing to stop and listen for the car.

§ 1021. **Track obstructed by cuts, curves, or embankments.** — Trains must be operated upon railroad tracks around curves and where the view of the track is obstructed by cuts and embankments, and the traveler who does not choose to stop and listen for the train, where he cannot see the track, because of such obstructions, must suffer the consequences of his own negligence, in case of a resulting injury.[87]

In a Michigan case,[88] which illustrates the rule, a team collided with a train at a crossing and the driver was killed. The railroad track and the highway were both below the general surface of the ground, at the crossing, and an approaching train could only be seen at intervals, by one driving toward the crossing. The driver was familiar with the crossing, but except that he checked his team, several rods from the crossing, he did not appear to have observed any further precaution. The proper signals were given by the

also, Baker v. Kansas City, etc., R. Co., 147 Mo. 140; 48 S. W. Rep. 838.

In Kelly v. Chicago, etc., R. Co. (88 Mo. 545), the court, in discussing the facts and the duty of the traveler, said: "The driver, Coleman, testifies that as he came along between the tracks he looked up and down the track to see if a train was coming and could see no train. But he also testifies that he could not see out, as the box cars on the side track prevented him from seeing. When he thus says, in such connection, that he looked up and down the track, he manifestly means, we think, that he looked in the direction he knew or supposed the track to run, in that locality, for if he could not see the train, on account of the obstruction, he could not see the track, for the same reason. The question then is, what did the law require of him in that behalf, under such circumstances. Manifestly, it then devolved on him the duty of listening."

[87] Shufelt v. Flint, etc., R. Co., 96 Mich. 327; 55 N. W. Rep. 1013.

[88] Haas v. Grand Rapids R. Co., 47 Mich. 401; 11 N. W. Rep. 216; 8 Am. & Eng. R. Cas. 268.

engine, for the crossing, and it was held that he was negligent, precluding a recovery for his death.

And crossing a railroad track, at a point where a sharp curve in the road will obstruct a view of the track, will also be held negligence, as matter of law, if the driver fails to stop or listen for an approaching train, or to adopt other precautions to avoid a collision.[89]

But where a traveler on a highway, about to cross a railroad track, at a crossing, where the track is obstructed by a curve or cut or embankment, stops and listens for a train, and just as he approaches the track, he is struck by a train which approached the crossing, without giving the statutory signals, he will not be held negligent, as matter of law.[90] And where the evidence is conflicting upon the issue whether or not the proper signals were given for a crossing, obscured by a cut or embankment, and the evidence shows that the traveler on the highway stopped and listened for the train, before driving upon the track, the question of his negligence will be a jury issue.[91]

§ 1022. **Track obstructed by weeds, brush or trees.**— The

[89] Purl v. St. Louis, etc., R. Co., 72 Mo. 168; 6 Am. & Eng. R. Cas. 27.

[90] Chicago, etc., R. Co. v. Ryan, 70 Ill. 211; Northern Pacific R. Co. v. Peterson, 55 Fed. Rep. 940; O'Toole v. Central, etc., R. Co., 12 N. Y. Supp. 347; 35 N. Y. S. R. 591; 128 N. Y. 597; Larkin v. New York, etc., R. Co., 46 N. Y. S. R. 658; 19 N. Y. Supp. 479; McNamara v. New York, etc., R. Co., 136 N. Y. 650; 32 N. E. Rep. 765; 49 N. Y. S. R. 395; Salter v. Utica, etc., R. Co., 88 N. Y. 42; 24 Hun (N. Y.) 494; 8 Am. & Eng. R. Cas. 437; Roberts v. Chicago, etc., R. Co., 35 Wis. 679; Richey v. Missouri Pacific Ry. Co., 7 Mo. App. 150; Chicago, etc., R. Co. v. Miller, 46 Mich. 532; 9 N. W. Rep. 841; 6 Am. & Eng. R. Cas. 89; Hoggart v. Evansville, etc., R. Co., 3 Ind. App. 437; 29 N. E. Rep. 941; Pittsburg, etc., R. Co. v. Martin, 82 Ind. 476; 8 Am. & Eng. R. Cas. 253; Tyler v. New York, etc., R. Co., 137 Mass. 238; 19 Am. & Eng. R. Cas. 296.

[91] Bower v. Chicago, etc., R. Co., 61 Wis. 457; 21 N. W. Rep. 536; 19 Am. & Eng. R. Cas. 301.

same rule of law applies to a case where the view of a rail-road track is obstructed by weeds, brush or trees, as where it is obstructed by any other cause, and as the obstructed track, from whatever cause, renders the crossing the more dangerous for a traveler on the highway, he must use a cor-responding higher degree of care to avoid a collision with the train and must stop and listen, if the approaching train cannot be otherwise detected.

In a recent Missouri case,[92] all previous decisions in that and other States are reviewed, where travelers were injured by contact with a train at a crossing where the track was obscured by growing weeds, grass or brush, and the court, speaking by Judge Burgess, said, in considering the duty of the traveler at such a crossing: " It appears from the evidence that after the wagon in which deceased was riding, had passed the high weeds, there was an open space of more than thirty-five feet to the railroad track. It further ap-pears that the wagon was not stopped, nor was there any evidence that any of them riding therein, * * * looked or listened for an approaching train." And adjudging upon the effect of this conduct by the deceased, the court con-tinued: " The facts disclosed by the record in this case show conclusively that Henry Sanguinette, plaintiff's hus-band, was at the time of the unfortunate occurrence, guilty of such gross negligence, contributing to his death, as to preclude her recovery."

Where the evidence shows, however, that the traveler upon

[92] Sanguinette v. Mississippi River, etc., R. Co., 196 Mo. 491, 498; 95 S. W. Rep. 386. See, also, Hayden v. Missouri, etc., R. Co., 124 Mo. 566; 28 S. W. Rep. 74; Huggart v. Missouri Pacific Ry. Co., 134 Mo. 673; 36 S. W. Rep. 220; Kelsay v. Missouri Pacific Ry. Co., 129 Mo. 362; 30 S. W. Rep. 339; Lane v. Missouri Pacific Ry. Co., 132 Mo. 4; 33 S. W. Rep. 645; 1128; Payne v. Chicago, etc., R. Co., 136 Mo. 562; 38 S. W. Rep. 308; Hook v. Missouri Pacific Ry. Co., 162 Mo. 369; 63 S. W. Rep. 360; Artz v. Chicago, etc., R. Co., 34 Iowa 153.

the highway, stopped and listened for a train, or used other precautions, equally as effective and could not see the train, on account of weeds, brush or trees growing on the right of way, or near the track, he will not be held negligent, as a matter of law, if no proper signal was given for the crossing.[93]

§ 1023. **When track obscured by dust, fog, or snow.**— It is the duty of a person intending to cross a railroad track, where he knows that trains frequently pass, to look as well as to listen, and if dust temporarily obscures his view of the track and he does not stop and wait to get a view of the track, or listen for a train, he will be held negligent, preventing a recovery for an injury received at the crossing, from a collision with a train.[94] A like rule obtains in case the view of the traveler is obscured by falling snow,[95] or by a fog,[96] and a traveler who drives or walks upon a railroad track, at a time when the view of the track is obscured by such a cause, without stopping to listen for a train, is negligent, barring a recovery for an injury received on the crossing, from a train rightfully run upon the track.

But, as in other cases where the track is obstructed, a traveler at a highway crossing has a right to act upon the presumption that the railroad company will give the proper signals for the crossing, and if the traveler is otherwise careful, the fact that the company failed to give the signals for

[93] Dimick v. Chicago, etc., R. Co., 80 Ill. 338; Chicago, etc., R. Co. v. Lee, 68 Ill. 576; Ladouceur v. Northern Pacific R. Co., 6 Wash. 280; 33 Pac. Rep. 556, 1080; Wesley v. Chicago, etc., R. Co., 84 Iowa 441; 51 N. W. Rep. 163; Boll v. Adirondack R. Co., 22 N. Y. S. R. 365; 52 Hun 610; 4 N. Y. Supp. 769.

[94] Chicago, etc., R. Co. v. Fisher, 49 Kansas 460; 30 Pac. Rep. 462; Fleming v. Western Pacific R. Co., 49 Cal. 253; 7 Am. Ry. Rep. 265.

[95] Powell v. New York, etc., R. Co., 109 N. Y. 613; 15 N. E. Rep. 891; 14 N. Y. S. R. 74; 38 Hun 640.

[96] Morris, etc., R. Co. v. Haslan. 33 N. J. L. 147; Hauser v. Central R. Co., 147 Pa. St. 440; 23 Atl. Rep. 766.

the crossing will establish a *prima facie* case and the question of the traveler's contributory negligence will be a proper issue for the jury, where he proceeded on the track, when it was obscured by snow, and the noise of the approaching train was correspondingly deadened.[97]

§ 1024. **View of track obscured by umbrella.**— The Supreme Court of Missouri, had before it, for adjudication, the right of recovery for the death of a pedestrian, upon a highway crossing, who, without stopping, or looking or listening for an approaching train, or car, stepped upon the railroad track, with an umbrella uplifted over his head, in such manner as to obscure a view of the track. The court held such conduct negligence, as matter of law, and, in passing on the case,[28] Judge Norton said: " It is, we think, manifest, that the negligence of deceased, in walking, in broad daylight, with an umbrella hoisted over him, on the railroad track, directly in front of a moving car, without looking for it, when, by looking, he could have seen its approach, was the immediate and proximate cause of his death."

Other cases, in different States, have also arisen, where travelers on the highway approach a railroad track with umbrellas raised over their heads, and without stopping or listening for a train, and such conduct is generally held to be negligence, as a matter of law, as the place is a known

---

[97] Solen v. Virginia, etc., R. Co., 13 Nevada 106.

Decedent continued to approach a railroad crossing at which he was killed, after having heard the whistle of a train, knowing that he could not see the train owing to a dense fog prevailing, and thereafter took no precautions to stop his vehicle and carefully listen for the train before permitting his son to drive on the track. *Held*, that decedent was negligent as a matter of law, and that his negligence proximately contributed to the accident. Cleveland, etc., Ry. Co. v. Houghland (Ind. App. 1908), 85 N. E. Rep. 369.

[98] Yancey v. Wabash R. Co., 93 Mo. 437, 438; 6 S. W. Rep. 272.

conveyance is negligent, if he fails to stop and look and listen for an approaching train.[4]

But failure of the driver of a covered buggy, to let down the top to his buggy, after he had stopped and listened and looked for a train, at the proper place, will not, of itself, be held to be negligence as matter of law.[5] And if the driver of a covered wagon sees an open gate, at a railroad crossing, and he stops and listens for a train, but does not alight from his wagon, he will not be held negligent, as matter of law, for driving onto the track, in case of an injury from a train which approached the crossing, without signals.[6]

[4] Terre Haute, etc., R. Co. v. Clark, 73 Ind. 168; 6 Am. & Eng. R. Cas. 84; Nash v. Richmond, etc., R. Co., 82 Va. 55; Horn v. Baltimore, etc., R. Co., 54 Fed. Rep. 301; 6 U. S. App. 381; 4 C. C. A. 346; Merkle v. New York, etc., R. Co., 49 N. J. L. 473; 9 Atl. Rep. 80.

[5] Stackus v. New York, etc., R. Co., 79 N. Y. 464; 7 Hun 559.

[6] Glushing v. Sharp, 96 N. Y. 676; 19 Am. & Eng. R. Cas. 372.

In a New Jersey case, the driver in a covered wagon had a lot of empty bottles in boxes, in the back end of the wagon, which rattled and made considerable noise. The track could not be seen until within six or seven feet of it, and the driver of the wagon was killed by a rapidly operated train. It was held that his negligence prevented a recovery for his death. Merkle v. New York, etc., R. Co., 49 N. J. L. 473; 9 Atl. Rep. 80.

In another case, the driver of a covered wagon attempted to drive across a track where a freight train was side-tracked, waiting for a passenger train to pass. He did not stop, nor look nor listen for an approaching train and was killed by a collision. It was held that his negligence prevented a recovery for his death. Horn v. Baltimore, etc., R. Co., 54 Fed. Rep. 301; 6 U. S. App. 381; 4 C. C. A. 346.

Plaintiff, with knowledge that a train was about due, approached a railroad crossing, in an inclosed milk wagon before daylight. He testified that, when one hundred and ninety feet from the track, he commenced looking toward the east and when within fifty or sixty feet he stopped, looked, and listened, but neither heard nor saw a train, though he noticed the switch and other lights between one-quarter and one-half mile east of the crossing, that he continued to look and listen, but saw

§ 1026. **Driving upon crossing on dangerously-loaded wagon.**—The Missouri Court of Appeals had before it, for decision, the case of a traveler, injured by falling from a load of loosely loaded hay, on which he was riding, while driving upon a sidling place on the crossing of the railroad right of way of the defendant.

Considering the issue of the plaintiff's negligence, the court said: "When the plaintiff, to subserve his own convenience, left the wagon way, and went upon the 'sidling' strip, he did so at his own risk. * * * No man, exercising ordinary prudence, would have attempted this without at least first descending from his lofty stand to the ground, and from there would have guided the course of his team. To remain on top of the load, while attempting to drive along the incline, was an act of the greatest imprudence, as respected his own personal safety. Though his wagon turned over, yet if he had exercised ordinary care and prudence, by alighting before driving upon the incline, he

no train until just as his horses started to cross the track, when the headlight of the locomotive approaching from the east flashed on him, and he was struck. The railroad was on a fill, and the crossing was but a short distance west of a bridge over a river. From a point twenty-five feet before reaching the track, plaintiff's view was unobstructed for an indefinite distance toward the east, and a witness who was in advance of plaintiff between one hundred and two hundred feet noticed the train approaching as he crossed the track, when it was then between a quarter and a half mile away. *Held* that, as plaintiff must have seen the train if he had looked as he testified, he was negligent as a matter of law, and could not recover. Westerkamp v. Chicago, etc., Ry. Co. (Colo. 1907), 92 Pac. Rep. 687.

Where one driving a closed milk wagon approached a railroad crossing on a dark and foggy morning, and, observing the light of a train, thought it to be the light of a station, and continued to drive his horse upon the tracks at a walk, without taking any further precautions, and a collision ensued, he was guilty of contributory negligence, precluding recovery for his death, though defendant had failed to give the statutory signals. Hamblin v. New York, etc., R. Co. (Mass. 1907), 81 N. E. Rep. 258.

would not have been hurt." And the court held that he was accordingly guilty of negligence, as matter of law.[7]

But while it would seem that another case, by the same court, would have been controlled by this decision, it was later held that a man riding astride a load of baled hay, five bales high, and who was injured by driving diagonally on a crossing he knew had been repaired with loose gravel, so that one wheel went over between the rails of the track and threw him off the load, was not necessarily guilty of negligence, as matter of law, but that it was a proper issue for the jury, whether or not, under all the circumstances, he was negligent.[8]

§ 1027. **Colliding with train on parallel track.**— Common prudence would seem to dictate that a traveler approaching a double track railroad should wait a reasonable time after the train on the track next to him has moved out, before attempting to cross the other track, so that he could have an unobstructed view of the adjoining track and see whether or not it was safe for him to cross it. A failure to exercise this precaution is held to be negligence, preventing a recovery for an injury due to a collision with a train on the other track.[9] And the result is the same, in case the train which first moves out is on the furthest track and the traveler attempts to pass before a train on the track nearest to him

[7] Meyers v. Chicago, etc., R. Co., 103 Mo. App. 268; 77 S. W. Rep 149.

[8] Lowenstein v. Missouri Pacific Ry. Co., 110 Mo. App. 689; 115 S. W. Rep. 2.

[9] Horstein v. United Rys. Co., 97 Mo. App. 271, by Judge Bland; 195 Mo. 440, by Judge Marshall; 92 S. W. Rep. 884; Weller v. Chicago, etc., R. Co., 164 Mo. 180; 64 S. W. Rep. 141; 86 Am. St. Rep. 592; Dlauhi v. St. Louis, etc., R. Co., 139 Mo. 291; 40 S. W. Rep. 890; 60 Am. St. Rep. 576; 37 L. R. A. 406; Allerton v. Boston, etc., R. Co., 146 Mass. 241; 15 N. E. Rep. 621; 34 Am. & Eng. R. Cas. 563.

has passed the crossing. If he is struck by a train on the first track, after the train he was waiting to clear the crossing, has passed, he will be denied a recovery, because of his contributory negligence.[10]

But in a Wisconsin case,[11] after a train had passed a crossing, within the view of a person intending to pass over it, under such circumstances that he had no reason to expect the approach of a train in the same direction from that in which the first train had gone, the rule which requires persons approaching crossings to look and listen for the approach of trains, was held to have no application, if the traveler was killed or injured by the backing of the second train, without warning. And in a Michigan case,[12] where a trav-

[10] Schmidt v. Philadelphia, etc., R. Co., 149 Pa. St. 357; 24 Atl. Rep. 218.

[11] Duame v. Chicago, etc., R. Co., 72 Wis. 523; 40 N. W. Rep. 394; 7 Am. St. Rep. 879; 35 Am. & Eng. R. Cas. 416. See, also, Leonard v. New York, etc., R. Co., 10 J. & S. (N. Y.) 225; Puff v. Lehigh Valley R. Co., 71 Hun (N. Y.) 577.

[12] Breckenfelder v. Lake Shore, etc., R. Co., 79 Mich. 560; 44 N. W. Rep. 957.

In Horstein v. United Rys. Co. (97 Mo. App. 271), Judge Bland, for the St. Louis Court of Appeals, said: "He moved on toward the east track, without halting or hesitating, and arrived sufficiently near that track, just in time to come in contact with the vestibule of the car. This was negligence of the most pronounced sort. It was plaintiff's duty, in the circumstances, to have stopped and waited until he could see whether or not there was an approaching car on the east track, before blindly proceeding to cross over that track," and this language is quoted and approved by the Supreme Court, in its opinion in the same case. 195 Mo. 440; 92 S. W. Rep. 884.

One who takes her stand between two tracks, without considering how near she is to the rails, and without considering the danger of being hit by a car coming on either of·the tracks, is negligent as a matter of law. Byrne v. Boston Elevated Ry. Co. (Mass. 1908), 85 N. E. Rep. 78.

Where the distance across four railroad tracks is only forty-nine feet, a traveler about to cross exercises due care if he stops, looks, and listens before venturing on the first track, and is not required to repeat the precaution with each track in succession. Cherry v. Louisiana, etc., Ry. Co. (La. 1908), 46 So. Rep. 596.

eler was injured by detached cars, on a track adjoining that whereon a train had lately stood, and the cars were set over the crossing without any warning and unattended, it was held to be a question for the jury, whether or not the traveler was in the exercise of due care, in using the crossing at the time he did.

§ 1028. **Passing under or between stationary cars.**— A train standing upon or across a highway crossing is itself evidence of danger, and in the absence of a special assurance by the employees of the railroad company that a person may safely pass between the cars, or climb under them, it will generally be held negligence to make such an attempt, and a person doing so will assume all risks of injury from a movement of the cars.[13]   And even where a person attempting to pass between or under the stationary cars of a train, is directed to do so by the employees of the train, this will not justify him in making the attempt, where the danger therefrom is obvious.[14]   It is immaterial whether or not an

Where there is an intricate combination of tracks, a person crossing the tracks is bound to exercise a degree of care commensurate with the surrounding dangers. Harlan v. St. Louis, etc., R. Co., 65 Mo. 22.

The fact that a train was not run, on regular schedule, however, is held to be a circumstance which a jury may take into consideration, in determining the plaintiff's negligence. Moberly v. Kansas City, etc., R. Co., 17 Mo. App. 518.

[13] Bird v. Flint, etc., R. Co., 86 Mich. 79; 48 N. W. Rep. 691; Andrews v. Central, etc., R. Co., 86 Ga. 192; 12 S. E. Rep. 213; 45 Am. & Eng. R. Cas. 171; Pannell v. Nashville, etc., R. Co., 97 Ala. 298; 12 So. Rep. 236; 55 Am. & Eng. R. Cas. 92; Lewis v. Baltimore, etc., R. Co., 38 Md. 588; 10 Am. Ry. Rep. 521; Howard v. Kansas City, etc., R. Co., 41 Kansas 403; 37 Am. & Eng. R. Cas. 552; O'Mara v. Delaware, etc., R. Co., 18 Hun (N. Y.) 192; Spencer v. Baltimore, etc., R. Co., 4 Mackey (D. C.) 138; 54 Am. Rep. 269; Central, etc., R. Co. v. Dixon, 42 Ga. 327; Smith v. Chicago, etc., R. Co., 55 Iowa 33; 7 N. W. Rep. 398; McMahon v. Northern R. Co., 39 Md. 438.

[14] Lake Shore, etc., R. Co. v. Pinchin, 112 Ind. 592; 13 N. E. Rep.

engine is attached to the cars, at the time of the attempt to pass between them, or climb under them, nor will it affect the right of a person guilty of such rashness, to recover for an injury received, that the train was standing across a highway and had continued to block the crossing for a length of time forbidden by municipal ordinance.[15]

But where the employees of the railroad company had directed the traveler on the highway to pass between the cars, it has been held that a recovery may be had for an injury received while so engaged, unless the risk of injury was such that a prudent man would not assume it, or the danger from the movement of the train was known to the traveler.[16] And whether a traveler on a highway who sees the first section of a severed train pass over the crossing, is negligent in attempting to cross the track, without looking or listening for the rear section of the severed train, is held to be a question for the jury, in some States.[17] And notwithstanding the contributory negligence of the traveler in attempting to pass between or under stationary cars, if the employees in charge of the train became aware of his peril in time, by the exercise of ordinary care, to avoid injuring him, but failed to do so, a recovery can be had,[18] as this

677; 31 Am. & Eng. R. Cas. 428; Renner v. Northern Pacific R. Co., 46 Fed. Rep. 344; Howard v. Kansas City, etc., R. Co., 41 Kansas 403; 21 Pac. Rep. 267; 37 Am. & Eng. R. Cas. 552.

[15] Hudson v. Wabash, etc., R. Co., 101 Mo. 13; 14 S. W. Rep. 15; Corcoran v. St. Louis, etc., R. Co., 105 Mo. 399; 16 S. W. Rep. 411; 24 Am. St. Rep. 394.

[16] Eddy v. Powell, 49 Fed. Rep. 814; 4 U. S. App. 259; 1 C. C. A. 448.

[17] York v. Maine, etc., R. Co., 84 Me. 117; 24 Atl. Rep. 790; Wilkins v. St. Louis, etc., R. Co., 101 Mo. 93; 13 S. W. Rep. 893; Baltimore, etc., R. Co. v. Fitzpatrick, 35 Md. 32; Kelly v. St. Paul, etc., R. Co., 29 Minn. 1; 11 N. W. Rep. 67; 6 Am. & Eng. R. Cas. 93.

[18] Pannell v. Nashville, etc., R. Co., 97 Ala. 298; 12 So. Rep. 236; 55 Am. & Eng. R. Cas. 92.

presents a case of subsequent proximate negligence on the part of the railroad company.[19]

§ 1029. **Crossing track in front of approaching train.**— Where a person, about to cross a railroad track, on a public highway, is apprised of the approach of a train of cars, and ventures upon the track, from a miscalculation of his danger, the error being his own, the railroad company will not be answerable for his erroneous calculation.[20]   If one sees or

[19] Holwerson v. St. Louis, etc., R. Co., 157 Mo. 216; 57 S. W. Rep. 770; 50 L. R. A. 850.

Where plaintiff, at the invitation of a brakeman, attempted to climb over a freight train to which an engine was attached, blocking a crossing at night, he assumed the risk, and could not recover for injuries sustained, in the absence of proof that those in charge of the train knew or could have known of his presence between the cars when they were moved. Southern Ry. Co. v. Clark (Ky. 1907), 105 S. W. Rep. 384.

Where plaintiff attempted at night to cross over a freight train to which an engine was attached while the train was blocking the highway crossing, and was injured by his heel becoming caught between the bumpers, he was negligent as a matter of law. Southern Ry. Co. v. Clark (Ky. 1907), 105 S. W. Rep. 384.

One attempting to pass under cars temporarily standing on a crossing and liable to be moved by a nearby engine engaged in shifting cars is guilty of contributory negligence, precluding a recovery for injuries received in consequence of the cars being moved. Jones v. Illinois Cent. R. Co. (Ky. 1907), 104 S. W. Rep. 258; 31 Ky. Law Rep. 825.

Where railroad crossings had been obstructed for an hour or more, and many persons had passed between or over the cars to the train men's knowledge, negligence in moving the train without warning did not depend on notice to the train men that the particular person injured was between or on the cars or that his position was one of peril when the train was moved. Gesas v. Oregon Short Line R. Co. (Utah 1907), 93 Pac. Rep. 274.

There is no implied assent to the crossing of a railroad track through an open space casually left between two cars pending switching, and one who attempts to make use of such opening assumes the danger, and, if killed, the company will not be liable unless after seeing the danger it could have avoided the consequences. Southern Ry. Co. v. Mouchet (Ga. App. 1907), 59 S. E. Rep. 927.

[20] Bellefontaine R. Co. v. Hunter, 33 Ind. 335; Haines v. Illinois,

hears an approaching train, he must wait for it to pass.   If he cross before the train, unless compelled to do so by an imperious necessity, his negligence is a presumption of law.[21] So, if one about to drive his team across a railroad track, sees a train approaching, and determines to try the speed of his horses against that of the engine, he does so at his peril. And if he heedlessly drives upon the track, without concerning himself to ascertain by observation, that it can be safely done, his negligence will prevent a recovery for an injury from a collision with the train.[22] If the injured traveler could have avoided the injury by exercising the opportunity to look for an approaching train, he will be regarded as having made the attempt to cross the track, after having seen the train's approach, and the law pronounces such conduct negligence.[23]

But it cannot always be held negligence to attempt to cross

etc., R. Co., 41 Iowa 227; Ernst v. Hudson River R. Co., 35 N. Y. 9; Cleveland, etc., R. Co. v. Arbaugh, 47 Ill. App. 360; State v. Maine, etc., R. Co., 77 Me. 538; 1 Atl. Rep. 673; Korrady v. Lake Shore, etc., R. Co., 131 Ind. 261; 29 N. E. Rep. 1069; Rigler v. Charlotte, etc., R. Co., 94 No. Car. 604; Baltimore, etc., R. Co. v. Maili, 66 Md. 53; 5 Atl. Rep. 87; 28 Am. & Eng. R. Cas. 628; State v. Maine, etc., R. Co., 76 Me. 357; 49 Am. Rep. 622; 19 Am. & Eng. R. Cas. 312; Tanner v. Missouri Pacific Ry. Co., 161 Mo. 497; 61 S. W. Rep. 826.

[21] Myers v. Baltimore, etc., R. Co., 150 Pa. St. 586; 24 Atl. Rep. 747; Thomas v. Delaware, etc., R. Co., 19 Blatchf. (U. S.) 533; 8 Fed. Rep. 729; Belten v. Baxter, 54 N. Y. 245; Duncan v. Missouri Pacific Ry. Co., 46 Mo. App. 198; Marland v. Pittsburg, etc., R. Co., 123 Pa. St. 487; 16 Atl. Rep. 624; Chicago, etc., R. Co. v. Bentz, 38 Ill. App. 485; Potter v. Flint, etc., R. Co., 62 Mich. 22; 28 S. W. Rep. 714; Pennsylvania R. Co. v. Righter, 42 N. J. L. 180; 2 Am. & Eng. R. Cas. 220; Gerety v. Philadelphia, etc., R. Co., 81 Pa. St. 274; 16 Am. Ry. Rep. 164.

[22] Wilds v. Hudson River R. Co., 29 N. Y. 315; Prewitt v. Eddy, 115 Mo. 283; 21 S. W. Rep. 742; Grows v. Maine, etc., R. Co., 69 Me. 412; Smith v. New York, etc., R. Co., 11 N. Y. S. R. 795; 43 Hun 679.

[23] Indiana, etc., R. Co. v. Hammock, 113 Ind. 1; 14 N. E. Rep. 737; 32 Am. & Eng. R. Cas. 127; Toledo, etc., R. Co. v. Jones, 76 Ill. 311.

a regular crossing, in front of a movin
and necessities of the occasion, and th
of knowledge of the traveler, may affe
negligence in such a case.[24] The fe
that it is not negligence, *per se,* to att
of a moving train, since it is the dail
men to do so, where there is ample ti
track.[25] It may be said that unde
whether an attempt to cross in front o:
be held negligence, will depend in soi
rate of speed of the engine and the loca
the person making the attempt.[26] Nor
gence to pass in front of a stationary tra
to indicate an intention to move the
facts are disputed as to the obvious na
be incurred, it will be held to be a jury
the person making such an attempt was
recovery for an injury received.[27]

[24] International, etc., R. Co. v. Kuehn, 2 T
S. W. Rep. 58.
[25] Thomas v. Delaware, etc., R. Co., 19 Blatc
Rep. 729.
[26] State v. Baltimore, etc., R. Co., 69 Md.
35 Am. & Eng. R. Cas. 412.
[27] Fehnrich v. Michigan, etc., R. Co., 87 Mic
890.
Where it appeared that the deceased was inf
ing an engine and train of cars approaching
across the crossing, it was held that his negli
recovery for his death, in, International, etc.,
Texas 582; 8 S. W. Rep. 484; 35 Am. & Eng.
In Missouri, it was held as far back as Kell
Co. (75 Mo. l. c. 140), that when one found it
calculation as to whether he could beat a trai
was evidenced by his making a run for it, he
ligent as not to be entitled to recover for any
race.
It has always been the law in this State tha

ligence as precludes a recovery for a person to step on a railroad track directly in front of an approaching train, and so close as to render it impossible to avoid the injury by stopping the train, and this is true even if the train was running at a rate of speed in ex-cess of the city ordinance. Tanner v. Missouri Pacific Ry. Co., 161 Mo. 497; 61 S. W. Rep. 826.

Where a traveler on a highway was injured by attempting to cross in front of a moving train, and the plea was set up that he relied upon the fact that there was an ordinance regulating the rate of speed of the train, and that the company would comply with it, the Supreme Court of Missouri replied that "He had no more right to presume that the men in charge of the locomotive would obey the requirements of the law than they had to presume that he would obey the instinct of self-preservation, and not unnecessarily thus thrust himself into danger." Kelly v. Hannibal, etc., R. Co., 75 Mo. 138; 13 Am. & Eng. R. Cas. 638. But see, Gratiot v. Missouri Pacific Ry. Co., 116 Mo. 450; 21 S. W. Rep. 1094; 55 Am. & Eng. R. Cas. 108.

That the train was exceeding a speed ordinance, is generally held no excuse for attempting to cross in front of a moving train. Studley v. St. Paul, etc., R. Co., 48 Minn. 249; 51 N. W. Rep. 115; Korrady v. Lake Shore, etc., R. Co., 131 Ind. 261; 29 N. E. Rep. 1069; Little Rock, etc., R. Co. v. Cullen, 54 Ark. 431; 16 S. W. Rep. 169.

Where, when the engineer first saw plaintiff's intestate, the train was about a quarter of a mile from the crossing at which she was killed, and she was at that time driving slowly in a one-horse vehicle toward the crossing, and was about sixty feet therefrom, and the train was running forty-five miles an hour, and she continued thus to approach the track until the train was about three hundred feet from the crossing, when she looked up and saw it and then urged her horse forward, and on seeing that she was trying to cross, the engineer put on all the braking power he had and blew the whistle, and there was nothing else he could have done to have stopped the train any quicker, the railroad company was not liable for her death. Sands v. Louisville, etc., R. Co. (Ala. 1908), 47 So. Rep. 323.

That a railway company negligently failed to signal for a highway crossing, by reason of which decedent drove his team within about two feet of the track before he discovered the train approaching at the rate of about forty-five miles an hour, that decedent could not turn the team to the right or left, and that he lost his presence of mind, and, while attempting to cross, was struck by the train, shows that his death was caused by his own negligence; it not appearing that he would not have been saved had he stopped his team when he discovered the train, or that he could not have backed the team, or that the com-

§ 1030. **Crossing in front of train, a jury issue, w**
is proper to submit to the jury the issue of the
contributory negligence in crossing a railroad track
of an approaching train, where the speed of the t

pany's negligence caused him to lose his presence of mind.
etc., R. Co. v. Abbegglen (Ind. App. 1908), 84 N. E. Rep. 5

Though the agents of a railroad company may be neglige
ning its train at a high rate of speed over a public road cr
in approaching a station where the train is to stop and in
ing a lookout, yet, if a person with knowledge of the impe
ger steps on the track and seeks to cross immediately in fi
engine and is injured, he cannot recover. Harris v. Southe
(Ga. 1907), 58 S. E. Rep. 873.

Liability of a railway company for the death of one stui
falling on a track while attempting to cross in front of
train cannot be based on a failure to give signals of
approach, where he knew the train was coming. St. Louis,
v. Ferrell (Ark. 1907), 105 S. W. Rep. 263.

Where intestate stepped on a switch track in front of
train, when but to look or otherwise to use ordinary care '
disclosed to him the train's approach, his negligence was a
ing cause of the accident, and barred a recovery unless
death would not have resulted but for defendant's negligenc
after intestate's negligence had spent its force. Teakle v.
etc., R. Co. (Utah, 1907), 90 Pac. Rep. 402.

One who, knowing that a train is rapidly approaching oi
distance away, steps onto the track just in front of i
having looked for it after passing around a car, is barri
tributory negligence, from recovery. Royster v. Souther
(N. C. 1908), 61 S. E. Rep. 179.

A person who knew that a train was approaching a cr
had ample opportunity to observe its proximity, speed, a
treme hardihood of attempting to cross in front of it. i
made the attempt and was killed. *Held*, that he was gui
tributory negligence warranting a nonsuit. Drawdy v. Atl
Line R. Co. (S. C. 1907), 58 S. E. Rep. 980.

If a pedestrian walking near a moving locomotive mov
safe place to a dangerous one so suddenly that his death
have been avoided, if an ordinance governing the speed of
had been observed, recovery for his death may not be had
cause the ordinance was violated. King v. Wabash R. Co. (
109 S. W. Rep. 071.

the distance it is from the crossing, when the attempt to cross is made, are such that it could not be held, as a matter of law, that he was negligent in making such an attempt.[28] It is usually held to be a question for the jury, whether or not the traveler was negligent in attempting to pass around or across stationary cars, when the engine was not attached to the train, and there was room sufficient to drive on the highway in front of such cars.[29] And where the evidence is conflicting as to whether or not the train was standing still, and there was an engine attached, it was held a proper jury issue, in a New York case.[30] In the case of youthful travelers, it is held to be a jury issue whether or not, under the excitement of the moment, the traveler had sufficient discretion to appreciate the danger of crossing in front of a moving train.[31] The absence of a flagman, or an open gate, at a crossing, may be sufficient inducement to cross, to make the issue of the traveler's negligence one for the jury.[32] Where the evidence shows that the traveler relied upon a compliance with a speed ordinance, by the railroad company, there is held to be an issue for the jury, as to his contributory negligence, in crossing in front of a moving train, in a Missouri case.[33] And although the traveler may have

[28] Retan v. Lake Shore, etc., R. Co., 94 Mich. 146; 53 N. W. Rep. 1094; Montgomery v. Alabama, etc., R. Co., 97 Ala. 305; 12 So. Rep. 170.

[29] Young v. Detroit, etc., R. Co., 56 Mich, 430; 23 N. W. Rep. 67; 19 Am. & Eng. R. Cas. 417.

[30] Conway v. Troy, etc., R. Co., 41 Hun (N. Y.) 639; 1 N. Y. S. R. 587.

[31] Tyler v. New York, etc., R. Co., 137 Mass. 238; 19 Am. & Eng. R. Cas. 296; Copley v. New Haven, etc., R. Co., 136 Mass. 6; 19 Am. & Eng. R. Cas. 373.

[32] Kane v. New York, etc., R. Co., 132 N. Y. 160; 30 N. E. Rep. 256; 43 N. Y. S. R. 494; 56 Hun 648.

[33] Gratiot v. Missouri Pacific Ry. Co., 116 Mo. 450; 21 S. W. Rep. 1094; 55 Am. & Eng. R. Cas. 108; Sullivan v. Missouri Pacific Ry. Co., 117 Mo. 214; 23 S. W. Rep. 149.

heedlessly entered upon the railroad track, in the path of an approaching engine, if there is substantial evidence tending to prove that the railroad company, by the exercise of ordinary care, could have discovered the impending peril in time to have avoided the injury, then the question of the traveler's negligence is held a jury issue.[34]

§ 1031. **Intoxicated person going on track.**— If a person goes on a railroad track, at a crossing or elsewhere, when so under the influence of liquor as not to be able to take care of himself, and his danger could not have been discovered by the employees in charge of the train in time to have prevented the injury, there can be no recovery from the railroad company.[35]

In a New York case,[36] the plaintiff was injured while in a buggy owned and driven by a third person. Both the plaintiff and the driver were under the influence of liquor and the driver approached the track at a rapid rate and in disregard of the signals. The trial court charged the jury, in effect, that plaintiff would not be negligent, unless he assented to the reckless driving of the person with whom he was riding, or such reckless driving was apparent to him, but this was held to be error.

In an Illinois case,[37] the ground of complaint was, that no signals for the crossing were given and the crossing was obscured by high weeds and bushes. The proof showed that

[34] Davis v. Kansas City, etc., R. Co., 46 Mo. App. 180.

When a person in crossing a railroad track, his horse being on the track, discovers an engine approaching and urges his horse forward, such act does not constitute negligence on the part of said person. Wheeling, etc., Ry. Co. v. Parker (Ohio C. C. 1906), 29 Ohio Cir. Ct. R. 1.

[35] Kean v. Baltimore, etc., R. Co., 61 Md. 154; 19 Am. & Eng. R. Cas. 321.

[36] Smith v. New York, etc., R. Co., 38 Hun (N. Y.) 33.

[37] Fulton County, etc., R. Co. v. Butler, 48 Ill. App. 301.

signals were given and a great deal of noise made by the train crossing a high bridge, a short distance from the crossing. There was also evidence that the plaintiff was under the influence of liquor when he drove upon the crossing and he was held guilty of negligence, as matter of law.

But although a person goes upon a crossing of a railroad track, in an intoxicated state, if his presence could have been discovered by the exercise of reasonable care, on the part of the railroad employees, so that the train could have been stopped and the injury avoided, notwithstanding his negligence, then the subsequent negligence of the railroad company will be held to authorize a recovery, and the prior negligence of the drunken person will not be held to bar a recovery.[38]

§ 1032. **Burden of proof on plaintiff.**—A plaintiff suing a railroad company for an injury at a crossing, holds the affirmative of the issue and has the burden of proof to establish that the injury was due to the negligence of the railroad company.[39]

And in some jurisdictions the plaintiff is also held to have the burden of proof to establish his own or the traveler's freedom from contributory negligence.[40]

[38] Kean v. Baltimore, etc., R. Co., *supra.*

Where a pedestrian, carrying a bag, deposited the bag near the track and sat down upon a tie and went to sleep, his negligence was held to bar a recovery, because of his intoxication and rash conduct, in Denman v. St. Paul, etc., R. Co., 26 Minn. 357; 4 N. W. Rep. 605. See, also, Newport News, etc., R. Co. v. Howe, 52 Fed. Rep. 362; 6 U. S. App. 172; 3 C. C. A. 121.

And the evidence of a surgeon, called immediately after an injury to an intoxicated person, that he was under the influence of liquor when he first saw him, is held competent, in, Illinois, etc., R. Co. v. Cragin, 71 Ill. 177.

[39] Lesan v. Maine Central R. Co., 77 Me. 85; 23 Am. & Eng. R. Cas. 245; Tucker v. Duncan, 4 Woods (U. S.) 652; 9 Fed. Rep. 867; 6 Am. & Eng. R. Cas. 268.

[40] Cincinnati, etc., R. Co. v. Howard, 124 Ind. 280; 24 N. E. Rep. 892.

But where there is a statute requiring a s
or whistle, by trains approaching highway (
statute is held, in some States, to shift the bu:
to the railroad company, to establish the cause
at a railroad crossing, where no statutory signa
But even where such rule obtains, the statute
change the general rule, as to the burden of ɪ
respects, so that if the plaintiff's evidence s
damages resulted from another cause than
of the railroad company, in omitting the re
at the crossing, there can be no recovery.[42]

[41] This is the rule, under the Missouri statutes. ᴵ
§ 1102; Kenney v. Hannibal, etc., R. Co., 105 Mo. 27
983; 16 S. W. Rep. 837.

[42] Kenney v. Hannibal, etc., R. Co., *supra.*
The presumption of liability imposed by statute,
that the railroad company was at the time of the ᴵ
train at an unlawful speed, is not a conclusive
upon the other hand, is a presumption fully rebutted
the injury in question was the result of the contrib
the person injured. Cleveland, etc., Ry. Co. v. ᵎ
App. 105.
Where plaintiff's intestate was struck and killed
while crossing a railroad track, the burden of proo
from contributory negligence is on plaintiff, but
that his due care should be proved by an eyewitnes:
by circumstances. Shum's Adm'x v. Rutland R.
Atl. Rep. 945.
In an action against a railroad for injuries to
by a train at a railroad crossing, the burden o
negligence is, under Acts 1899, p. 58, ch. 41, on de
Pennsylvania Co. (Ind. App. 1907), 82 N. E. Rep.
A plaintiff suing a railroad for the death of a
a train at a crossing, does not prove decedent's fɪ
utory negligence by presenting no evidence thereo
cedent's instinct of self-preservation as proof tlɪ
care. Wright v. Boston, etc., R. R. (N. H. 1907),
The burden of proving contributory negligence
in a collision at a crossing is on the railroad.
Southwestern Ry. Co. v. Boyd (Civ. App. 1907), 1ᶜ

§ 1033. **Traveler's duty not affected by company's negligence.**—As a general rule, the negligence on the part of a railroad company, will not relieve a person attempting to cross its track, from the duty of exercising ordinary care and prudence on his part to avoid injury.[43]

He directly contributes to his own injury, who, paying no attention to his own safety, trusts to the obligations imposed upon a railroad company, by law or ordinance, to warn him of an approaching train.[44]

The fact, therefore, that a train was running in a city, in violation of a speed ordinance;[45] that the train failed to stop for a reasonable time, at a station;[46] that the statutory signals were not given at the highway crossing;[47] that the flagman, required to be maintained at a crossing, was absent;[48] that the gates were up, when they should have been

Boyd v. St. Louis Southwestern Ry. Co. of Texas (Tex, 1908), 108 S. W. Rep. 813.

[43] Blaker v. New Jersey, etc., R. Co., 30 N. J. Eq. 240; 18 Am. Ry. Rep. 81.

[44] Turner v. Hannibal, etc., R. Co., 74 Mo. 602; 6 Am. & Eng. R. Cas. 38.

[45] Blanchard v. Lake Shore, etc., R. Co., 126 Ill. 416; 18 N. E. Rep. 799.

[46] McMurtry v. Louisville, etc., R. Co., 67 Miss. 601; 7 So. Rep. 401.

[47] Wabash R. Co. v. Wallace, 110 Ill. 114; 19 Am. & Eng. R. Cas. 359; Meeks v. Southern Pacific R. Co., 52 Cal. 602; 20 Am. Ry. Rep. 115; Cincinnati, etc., R. Co. v. Butler, 103 Ind. 31; 2 N. E. Rep. 138; 23 Am. & Eng. R. Cas. 262; Schaefert v. Chicago, etc., R. Co., 62 Iowa 624; 17 N. W. Rep. 893; Sala v. Chicago, etc., R. Co., 85 Iowa 678; 52 N. W. Rep. 664; Matta v. Chicago, etc., R. Co., 69 Mich. 109; 37 N. W. Rep. 54; 32 Am. & Eng. R. Cas. 71; Stepp v. Chicago, etc., R. Co., 85 Mo. 229; Petty v. Hannibal, etc., R. Co., 88 Mo. 306; 28 Am. & Eng. R. Cas. 618; Cleveland, etc., R. Co. v. Elliott, 28 Ohio St. 340; 14 Am. Ry. Rep. 123; Williams v. Chicago, etc., R. Co., 64 Wis. 1; 24 N. W. Rep. 422; 23 Am. & Eng. R. Cas. 274; Moore v. Philadelphia, etc., R. Co., 108 Pa. St. 349.

[48] Duncan v. Missouri Pacific Ry. Co., 46 Mo. App. 198; Freeman v. Duluth, etc., R. Co. (Mich.), 37 Am. & Eng. R. Cas. 501; 3 L. R. A. 594; Louisville, etc., R. Co. v. Webb, 90 Ala. 185; 40 Am. & Eng. R. Cas.

down,[49] or that the railroad company had failed to construct a sign, at the crossing, as required by law,[50] will not be held to excuse the traveler from himself exercising ordinary care to avoid injury.

§ 1034. **Injury avoidable by ordinary care.**— The plaintiff in an action to recover damages for personal injuries received while crossing a railroad track, at a highway crossing, is entitled to recover, notwithstanding the want of ordinary care on the part of the injured person, if those in charge of the train or engine could, by the exercise of ordinary care or prudence on their part, have avoided the injury.[51]

Although the plaintiff is negligent in placing himself on a track, where he is apt to be struck by an approaching train or car, the railway company will nevertheless be liable for an injury to him if the persons in charge of the engine or car either saw him, or by the exercise of reasonable care on their part could have seen him, in time to have avoided the collision.[52]

427. In this case, the syllabus is, "The neglect of a person, attempting to cross a railroad track, at the intersection of a highway, to use his senses before entering upon the track, to discover the approach of a train, is, as a matter of law, contributory negligence, which bars an action for damages, and the fact that the company's watchman failed to perform his duty, * * * does not make it a question for the jury."

[49] Greenwood v. Pennsylvania R. Co., 124 Pa. St. 572; 17 Atl. Rep. 186.

[50] Payne v. Chicago, etc., R. Co., 39 Iowa 523.

[51] Harlan v. St. Louis, etc., R. Co., 65 Mo. 22; Mauerman v. St. Louis, etc., R. Co., 41 Mo. App. 348; Rafferty v. Missouri Pacific Ry. Co., 91 Mo. 33; 3 S. W. Rep. 393; Louisville, etc., R. Co. v. Schuster (Ky.), 35 Am. & Eng. R. Cas. 407; 7 S. W. Rep. 874; Richmond, etc.. R. Co. v. Howard, 79 Ga. 44; 3 S. E. Rep. 426; Texas, etc., R. Co. v. Chapman, 57 Texas, 75; Butcher v. West Virginia, etc., R. Co., 37 W. Va. 180; 16 S. E. Rep. 457; 55 Am. & Eng. R. Cas. 181.

[52] Hickman v. Union Depot R. Co., 47 Mo. App. 65; Bullock v.

But where the testimony shows that notwithstanding the train, by which a traveler was injured at a highway crossing, was running too fast and the statutory signals for the crossing were not given, if the injury did not result proximately from the company's negligence, but from the sudden and unnecessary conduct of the plaintiff himself, in stepping upon the track, immediately in front of the train, and so near to the locomotive that it was impossible to avoid striking him, after he thus put himself in a position of danger, there could be no recovery for the injury so received.[58]

§ 1035. **When traveler's negligence a question of law for the court.**— In an action against a railroad company for an injury to a traveler at a highway crossing, where the evidence shows inexcusable negligence and carelessness on the part of the traveler, the trial court should order a nonsuit and withdraw the case from the jury.[54] If the plaintiff's own evidence shows contributory negligence, the case should be taken from the jury and a verdict for the defendant ordered, unless a nonsuit is had.[55] And if the conceded or undisputed facts show that the traveler was guilty of some act or omission which, of itself, would constitute negligence, it would be error for the court to submit the cause to the jury.[56]

Nor is it always a duty of the trial court to submit the cause to the jury, although there may be some evidence of

Wilmington, etc., R. Co., 105 No. Car. 180; 10 S. E. Rep. 988; 42 Am. & Eng. R. Cas. 93; Maryland, etc., R. Co. v. Naubauer, 62 Md. 391; 19 Am. & Eng. R. Cas. 261.

[53] Ivy v. East Tennessee, etc., R. Co., 88 Ga. 71; 13 S. E. Rep. 947; Harlan v. St. Louis, etc., R. Co., 64 Mo. 480; 17 Am. Ry. Rep. 300.

[54] Sheffield v. Rochester, etc., R. Co., 21 Barb. (N. Y.) 339.

[55] Thompson v. Flint, etc., R. Co., 57 Mich. 300; 23 N. W. Rep. 820; 23 Am. & Eng. R. Cas. 289.

[56] Hackford v. New York, etc., R. Co., 53 N. Y. 654.

due care on the part of the plaintiff, as where the traveler testified that he looked both ways for an approaching train, but the undisputed facts and the physical conditions showed that this evidence must be untrue, as to look would be to see, under the existing conditions, then the court will be justified in taking the case from the jury, notwithstanding such evidence, because of the fact that it disputes the physical facts in the case.[57]

But unless the evidence does dispute the uncontradicted physical facts, it is only when the evidence shows conclusively that the traveler was careless, that the court will be justified in taking the case from the jury.[58]   And if the fact depends upon the credibility of witnesses, or upon inferences to be drawn from the circumstances proved, about which honest men might differ, then the plaintiff has the right to have the question submitted to the jury, and their decision is conclusive, however unjust it might be.[59]

§ 1036. **When issue of, should be submitted to jury.**— Where the evidence as to the conduct of the injured traveler is conflicting,[60] or when the facts are such that reasonable men would differ upon the question,[61] whether a person, injured at a railroad crossing, by a locomotive or car, was, or was not, in the exercise of ordinary care, at the time of the injury, is generally held to be an issue for the jury to determine.[62]   And where the jury finds, on conflicting evidence,

[57] Smith v. New York, etc., R. Co., 44 N. Y. S. R. 55; 63 Hun 624; 137 N. Y. 562; Hook v. Missouri Pacific Ry. Co., 162 Mo. 569; 63 S. W. Rep. 360.

[58] Lyman v. Boston, etc., R. Co. (N. H.), 20 Atl. Rep. 976; 45 Am. & Eng. R. Cas. 163.

[59] Hackford v. New York, etc., R. Co., 53 N. Y. 654.

[60] Wichita, etc., R. Co. v. Davis, 37 Kansas 743; 16 Pac. Rep. 78; 32 Am. & Eng. R. Cas. 65.

[61] Leake v. Rio Grande, etc., R. Co., 9 Utah 246; 33 Pac. Rep. 1045.

[62] Webb v. Portland, etc., R. Co., 57 Me. 117; Mahoney v. Metropol-

that a traveler on the highway was not negligent in attempting to cross the track, this finding will not generally be disturbed, if the trial court has properly instructed the jury on the law.[63]

It has accordingly been held a proper jury issue, whether or not a child used such care as one of his years ought to have used, in attempting to cross the railroad track, at a crossing;[64] and where the train that injured the plaintiff was running in excess of the speed limit, prescribed by ordinance, it was held to be a jury issue, whether or not the plaintiff exercised due care in going on the track.[65]

itan, etc., R. Co., 104 Mass. 73; Hanson v. Minneapolis, etc., R. Co., 37 Minn. 355; 34 N. W. Rep. 223; 32 Am. & Eng. R. Cas. 13; Kenney v. Hannibal, etc., R. Co., 105 Mo. 270; 15 S. W. Rep. 983; Omaha, etc., R. Co. v. O'Donnell, 22 Neb. 475; 35 N. W. Rep. 235; Hoye v. Chicago, etc., R. Co., 67 Wis. 1; 29 N. W. Rep. 646; Parsons v. New York, etc., R. Co., 113 N. Y. 355; 21 N. E. Rep. 145; Doyle v. Pennsylvania R. Co., 139 N. Y. 637; 34 N. E. Rep. 1063; State v. Union, etc., R. Co., 70 Md. 69; 18 Atl. Rep. 1032; 42 Am. & Eng. R. Cas. 167.

[63] Delaware, etc., R. Co. v. Converse, 139 U. S. 469; 11 Sup. Ct. Rep. 569; 49 Am. & Eng. R. Cas. 323.

[64] Spillane v. Missouri Pacific Ry. Co., 111 Mo. 555; 20 S. W. Rep. 293.

[65] Gratiot v. Missouri Pacific Ry. Co., 116 Mo. 450; 21 S. W. Rep. 1094; 55 Am. & Eng. R. Cas. 108.

In an action to recover for injuries sustained at railroad crossing, where the evidence shows that plaintiff stopped, looked, and listened twenty feet from the track which permitted a view in the direction from which the engine came for six hundred feet, and that he neither saw nor heard a train, but his wagon was struck at the rear end just as it was leaving the track, the question is for the jury. Howard v. Baltimore, etc., R. Co. (Pa. 1908), 68 Atl. Rep. 848; 219 Pa. 358.

Whether reasonable care requires a traveler on a highway approaching a railway crossing to stop, look, and listen for approaching trains, or whether, having done so, he must stop, look, and listen again, or whether he may place any reliance on an absence of danger signals, or on any other circumstance, are for the jury, except in cases free from doubt. Hartman v. Chicago, etc., Ry. Co. (Iowa 1906), 110 N. W. Rep. 10.

In an action by an infant against a railroad for injuries through being struck by a locomotive while crossing defendant's track, plaintiff

1527

has the burden of proving that he was *non sui juris*. Judgment (Sup.) 103 N. Y. S. 1142, affirmed. Simkoff v. Lehigh Valley R. Co., 83 N. E. Rep. 15; 190 N. Y. 256.

Whether the presumption of due care on the part of a person killed at a railroad crossing has been rebutted is for the jury, unless the evidence to the contrary is so clear as to justify the court in holding that a verdict against defendant must be set aside as a matter of law. Unger v. Philadelphia, etc., R. Co. (Pa. 1907), 66 Atl. Rep. 235; 217 Pa. 106.

In an action by an infant over seven years old against a railroad for injuries through being struck by a locomotive while crossing defendant's track, the degree of care to be reasonably expected of plaintiff was a question of fact for the jury to determine under the circumstances and on the evidence as to his capacity and intelligence. Judgment (Sup.) 103 N. Y. S. 1142, affirmed. Simkoff v. Lehigh Valley R. Co., 83 N. E. Rep. 15; 190 N. Y. 256.

Where there is evidence that deceased stopped, looked, and listened before going on the track, but the evidence is conflicting as to where he did so, it is for the jury to determine whether he was guilty of contributory negligence. Crane v. Pennsylvania R. Co., 67 Atl. Rep. 877.

§ 1037. **What the term implies.**—Imputed negligence is the negligence of one person occurring under such conditions as to render another person legally chargeable with such negligence, the same as though it were his own. In other words, as the term itself suggests, it is the negligence of one person, imputed to another.[1]

In one sense, in every personal injury action, wherein the

---

[1] Beach, on Con. Neg. § 100, p. 129.

1529

negligence charged is that of an agent or employee of the defendant, the rule of imputed negligence is invoked and the defendant is sought to be charged, because of the relation existing which will render him legally responsible for the wrongful act of his agent, but this is not the application of the doctrine which will be considered in this chapter, for imputed negligence will here be considered only as it refers to the acts of third persons that could legally be imputed to the plaintiff, or injured person, which is more properly imputed contributory negligence, or contributory negligence that will or will not be imputed to the plaintiff, or injured person.[2]

§ 1038. **Basis of the doctrine.**— An approved text writer,[3] speaking of the subject under consideration and the reason underlying the rule, said: " The rule upon this branch of our subject is that the contributory negligence of third persons constitutes a valid defense to the plaintiff's action, only when that negligence is legally imputable to the plaintiff. There must, in order to create this imputability, be some connection, which the law recognizes, between the plaintiff and the third person, from which the legal responsibility may arise. The negligence of the third person and its legal imputability must concur. It is clear that there is no justification for the negligent misconduct of the defendant, in that some third person, a stranger, was also in the wrong. When the defendant pleads the negligence of a party other

[2] Beach, Con. Neg. § 100, p. 128; Louisville, etc., R. Co. v. Creek, 14 L. R. A. 733; Chicago, etc., R. Co. v. Wilcox, 21 L. R. A. 76; Hicks v. Citizens R. Co., 25 L. R. A. 508; Schultz v. Old Colony R. Co. (Mass.), 79 N. E. Rep. 873; 8 L. R. A. (N. S.) 597, and note. Also, paper, by Mr. John T. Marshall, in 64 Cent. Law Jour. 347, and paper by Mr. Sumner Kenner, 61 Cent. Law Jour. 244.

[3] Beach, Con. Neg., § 100, p. 129; Schultz v. Old Colony R. Co. (Mass.), 79 N. E. Rep. 873; 8 L. R. A. (N. S.) 597, and exhaustive note; Schultz v. Moon, 33 Mo. App. 329.

than the plaintiff, in bar of the action, it must appear, not only that such third person was at fault, but that the plaintiff ought to be charged with that fault."

As it is manifest that it would be unjust, according to legal principles, to hold one for the wrongful act of another in no way connected with the one charged, the rule of imputed negligence furnishes no exception to this principle, and before a plaintiff is legally to be charged with the negligence of another, there must be shown such identity between such person and the plaintiff as will render the latter responsible for his acts, in the given instance. In other words, the rule of imputed negligence is based upon the doctrine of agency, or that principle of the law which renders one responsible for the acts of another, because in the doing of the act, such other person really acts for the person sought to be charged, and unless in a given case, the negligent person could not be said to be the agent of the injured person, in the doing of the wrongful act, or they were not engaged in some joint enterprise or undertaking, or the right of action was not claimed through or under such negligent third person, then the negligence of such person will not, generally, be imputed to the injured one.[4]

§ 1039. **Imputed negligence and personal negligence distinguished.** — There is a clear distinction, noted by the cases, between the imputation, to an injured person, of the negligence of another, who may or may not be acting as his

[4] Beach, Con. Neg., § 103, p. 132, and cases cited; Minster v. Citizens Ry. Co., 53 Mo. App. 276; Becke v. Missouri Pacific Ry. Co., 102 Mo. 544; 13 S. W. Rep. 1053; 9 L. R. A. 157.

The owner of an automobile delivered it to a person not under his control or direction, under an agreement that he was to use it for hire and pay the owner the purchase price out of the money derived from its use. *Held*, that the owner was not liable for an accident caused by the person's negligence in operating the automobile. Braverman v. Hart (N. Y. Sup. 1907), 105 N. Y. S. 107.

agent, at the time of the injury, and the contributory negligence of the person injured, as affecting the right of recovery.   In the one case, the negligence of the driver would not be imputed to the injured person, in the absence of some identification, or the existence of a relation, from which agency could be predicated, while in the case of the co-operating negligence of the injured person himself, a recovery would be denied, irrespective of the negligence of the other person, upon the rule that his concurring negligence would not affect the negligence of the injured person, himself, in a suit for an injury, traceable in part to his own negligence.[5]

[5] Cincinnati, etc., R. Co. v. Howard, 124 Ind. 280; 24 N. E. Rep. 892; 19 Am. St. Rep. 96; 8 L. R. A. 593; Fechley v. Traction Co., 119 Mo. App. 358; 96 S. W. Rep. 421; Markowitz v. Metropolitan, etc., R. Co., 186 Mo. 350; 85 S. W. Rep. 351; 69 L. R. A. 389; Bresse v. Los Angeles Traction Co. (Cal.), 85 Pac. Rep. 152; 5 L. R. A. (N. S.) 1059; Colorado, etc., R. Co. v. Thomas, 33 Colo. 517; 81 Pac. Rep. 801; 70 L. R. A. 681; West Chicago, etc., R. Co. v. Dedloff, 92 Ill. App. 547; Chicago, etc., R. Co. v. Bentz, 38 Ill. App. 485; Brannen v. Kohomo, etc., R. Co., 115 Ind. 115; 17 N. E. Rep. 202; 7 Am. St. Rep. 411; Miller v. Louisville, etc., R. Co., 128 Ind. 97; 27 N. E. Rep. 339; 25 Am. St. Rep. 416; Aurelius v. Lake Erie, etc., R. Co., 19 Ind. App. 584; 49 N. E. Rep. 857; Bush v. Union Pacific R. Co., 62 Kansas 709; 64 Pac. Rep. 624; Avyln v. Boston, etc., R. Co., 105 Mass. 77; Evensen v. Lexington, etc., R. Co., 187 Mass. 77; 72 N. E. Rep. 355; Kane v. Boston, etc., R. Co., 192 Mass. 386; 78 N. E. Rep. 485; Smith v. Maine, etc., R. Co., 87 Me. 339; 32 Atl. Rep. 967; State v. Boston, etc., R. Co., 80 Me. 430; 15 Atl. Rep. 36; Louisville, etc., R. Co. v. Molloy (Ky.), 91 S. W. Rep. 685; Bricknell v. New York, etc., R. Co., 120 N. Y. 290; 24 N. E. Rep. 449; 17 Am. St. Rep. 648; Smith v. New York, etc., R. Co., 38 Hun (N. Y.) 33; Koehler v. Rochester, etc., R. Co., 66 Hun 566; 21 N. Y. Supp. 844; Miles v. Fonda, etc., R. Co., 86 Hun 508; 33 N. Y. Supp. 729; DeLoge v. New York, etc., R. Co., 92 Hun 149; 36 N. Y. Supp. 697; Zimmerman v. Union R. Co., 3 App. Div. 219; 38 N. Y. Supp. 362; . Kleiner v. Third Ave. R. Co., 36 App. Div. 191; 55 N. Y. Supp. 394; 162 N. Y. 193, 645; 56 N. E. Rep. 497; 57 N. E. Rep. 1114; Hajsek v. Chicago, etc., R. Co., 5 Neb. 67; 97 N. W. Rep. 327; Dean v. Pennsylvania R. Co., 129 Pa. St. 514; 18 Atl. Rep. 718; 15 Am. St. Rep.

The rule that an injured person is not chargeable with the
negligence of his driver, over whom no control was exercised,
has never been extended so as to relieve the injured person
from the duty to himself exercise reasonable care for his
own safety.[6] It is as much the duty of the guest or passenger, to use reasonable care to avoid injury, as it is that
of the driver, and for a failure to do so, in case of a resulting
injury, no recovery can be had.[7] The duty which the law
places on the injured person himself, is not at all affected
by the fact that no restraint or care was exercised over the
driver,[8] nor the relation of the driver toward the injured
person. The wife cannot recover if she was herself guilty
of negligence in approaching a railroad crossing, in failing
to look or listen for an approaching train, and the fact that
her husband, driving the team, was also negligent, will not
affect her right to recover; [9] a daughter, *sui juris,* riding in

733; 6 L. R. A. 143; O'Toole v. Pittsburg, etc., R. Co., 158 Pa. St.
99; 27 Am. Rep. 737; 33 Am. St. Rep. 830; 22 L. R. A. 606; Dryden
v. Pennsylvania R. Co., 211 Pa. St. 620; 61 Atl. Rep. 249; Griffith
v. Baltimore, etc., R. Co., 44 Fed. Rep. 574; 159 U. S. 603; 16 Sup.
Ct. Rep. 105; 40 L. Ed. 274; Galveston, etc., R. Co. v. Kutac, 72 Texas
643; 11 S. W. Rep. 127.

  6 Fechley v. Traction Co., 119 Mo. App. 358; 96 S. W. Rep. 421;
Holden v. Missouri, etc., R. Co., 177 Mo. 456; 76 S. W. Rep. 1045;
Sluder v. Transit Co., 189 Mo. 107; 88 S. W. Rep. 648; 5 L. R. A.
(N. S.) 186.

  In Stotler v. Chicago, etc., R. Co. (200 Mo. 107; 98 S. W. Rep.
509), a sixteen year old daughter was held not chargeable with her
mother's negligence on driving onto a railroad crossing, without looking for an approaching train. But on the appeal of the mother's
case, she was held to be precluded from recovering, because of her
own personal negligence in the case. Stotler v. Chicago, etc., R. Co.,
204 Mo. 619; 103 S. W. Rep. 1, opinion by Judge Fox.

  7 Vincennes v. Thuis, 28 Ind. App. 523; 63 N. E. Rep. 315.

  8 Missouri, etc., R. Co. v. Bussey, 66 Kansas 735; 71 Pac. Rep. 261.

  9 Willfong v. Omaha, etc., R. Co., 116 Iowa 548; 90 N. W. Rep.
358; Miller v. Louisville, etc., R. Co., 128 Ind. 97; 27 N. E. Rep. 339;
25 Am. St. Rep. 416; Toledo, etc., R. Co. v. Eatherton, 20 Ohio C. C.

a buggy with her father, cannot recover, if she was herself negligent, leading to the accident at a railroad crossing; [10] it is as much the daughter's duty to look and listen for approaching trains as it is that of the driver and for a failure to do so, no recovery could be had for an injury resulting therefrom; [11] a traveler at night, riding with a known drunken driver, is held to have been so negligent himself as to deny a recovery for an injury due to the driver's condition, [12] and, generally, the fact that the negligence of the driver of a hired vehicle will not be imputed to a passenger riding with him, when the driver has failed to stop, or look or listen for an approaching train, at a railroad crossing, will not relieve the passenger himself from the exercise of ordinary care and caution for his own protection, and if the danger is known to him, or ought, by ordinary care to have been seen, and he fails to remonstrate with the driver, or get out of the vehicle, if he has time or opportunity to do so, in case the driver fails to heed his warning, then he is held negligent himself. [13]

But contributory negligence would not be chargeable to a person injured in a collision at a crossing, with a train of cars, while such person was the guest of the owner of the vehicle in which he was riding, when the injured person had protested against proceeding to attempt to cross, after discovery of the train, but no time existed after discovery of

297; Galveston, etc., R. Co. v. Kutac, 72 Texas 643; 11 S. W. Rep. 127.

[10] Cincinnati, etc., R. Co. v. Howard, 124 Ind. 280; 24 N. E. Rep. 892; 19 Am. St. Rep. 96; 8 L. R. A. 593. But see, Stotler v. Chicago, etc., R. Co., 200 Mo. 107; 98 S. W. Rep. 509.

[11] Griffith v. Baltimore, etc., R. Co., 44 Fed. Rep. 574; 159 U. S. 603; 16 Sup. Ct. Rep. 105; 40 L. Ed. 274.

[12] Hershey v. Mill Creek Township (Pa.), 9 Atl. Rep. 452; 6 Sadler 459.

[13] Illinois, etc., R. Co. v. McLeod, 78 Miss. 334; 29 So. Rep. 76; 84 Am. St. Rep. 630; 52 L. R. A. 954.

the approaching train to spring out of the vehicle, before the occurrence of the casualty.[14] Nor will a wife, riding with her husband, holding her baby on her lap, be held negligent, as matter of law, where she had both looked and listened for a train and warned her husband about crossing without stopping, simply because she did not turn her body clear around to look for the train, which she had no reason to know was approaching,[15] and as it is a well-known fact that passengers in vehicles are prone to trust to the driver to watch for the dangers of the road, there is said to be no duty on the part of the passenger to warn the driver, as to approaching dangers, but only to warn him as to known dangers, or as to those which should reasonably have been seen and understood [16] and this is perhaps the practical construction of the rule, in such cases, for otherwise the rule requiring identification between the negligent driver and the injured person would be obviated in all cases.

§ 1040. **When cause derived from negligent person.**— Whenever the evidence in a personal injury action shows that the negligence of the injured person contributed to produce the injury, and the action is by another than the person receiving the injury, such contributory negligence on the part of the injured person is always imputable to the plaintiff.[17] In this instance there is such identity between

[14] Alabama, etc., R. Co. v. Davis, 69 Miss. 444; 13 So. Rep. 693.

[15] Lewin v. Lehigh Valley R. Co., 41 App. Div. 89; 58 N. Y. Supp. 113.

[16] See opinion of Marshall, J., in Pyle v. Clark, 75 Fed. Rep. 644; 25 C. C. A. 190; 49 U. S. App. 260; 79 Fed. Rep. 744.

[17] 1 Thompson, on Neg., § 498, p. 464; Boland v. Missouri, etc., R. Co., 36 Mo. 484; Passameneck v. Louisville, etc., R. Co., 98 Ky. 195; 32 S. W. Rep. 620; McGuire v. Vicksburg, etc., R. Co., 46 La. Ann. 1543; 16 So. Rep. 457; Cleveland, etc., R. Co. v. Crawford, 24 Ohio St. 631; 15 Am. Rep. 633; Indianapolis, etc., R. Co. v. Stout, 53 Ind. 143; Kuehn v. Missouri, etc., R. Co., 10 Texas Civ. App. 649; 32 S. W. Rep. 88.

the two persons as to affect the pla
gence on the part of the injured perso
right of action would exist only in so f
son himself would have been entitled to
so negligent that he would have had n
the injury, no cause of action would b
to the plaintiff, and he would stand in
jured person himself, so far as his r
injury is concerned.[18]

In actions under death statutes, there1
the death of husbands, or by administrate
their intestates, or by fathers or moth
minor children, as well as in other instar
son sues to recover damages for personal i
the contributory negligence of the injurec
imputed to the person suing and he is cl
consequences of such negligence, to all int
the same as the injured person would be,
his own injuries.[19]

§ 1041. **Concurrent negligence of another**
the absence of some particular relation exis
injured person and one guilty of negligence
that of the defendant to produce the injury,
gally make the negligent act of such third pe
injured person, in law, the defendant could

[18] 1 Thompson, on Neg., § 209, p. 206, and cases cite
[19] Pratt, etc., Co. v. Brawley, 83 Ala. 371; 3 So.
St. Rep. 571; 1 Thompson, on Neg., § 498, p. 465.
The contributory negligence of the wife has been
action for loss of her society, consequent upon her inj
band, under the rule of imputed negligence, althougl
force at the place of her injury relieved her of many
law disabilities and absolved the husband from liabilit
Chicago, etc., R. Co. v. Honey, 63 Fed. Rep. 39; 12 C
L. R. A. 42.

self of the negligence of the third person, for there is no rule of law which relieves one from liability for an injury to another, not himself at fault, merely because the negligence of a third person concurred with that of the defendant to produce the injury.[20]

It is well settled that when the negligence of two persons combines as the proximate cause of an injury and the injured person is himself without negligence, either or both of the joint wrongdoers may be held responsible for the result of their concurring negligence.[21]

In a recent Missouri case,[22] it was held that the negligence of the driver of a hired carriage, whether private or public, could not be imputed to the person being driven, if he did not, by some act or word, encourage the driver's special act of rashness or carelessness which resulted in his injury. And, in such case, although his injuries may have resulted from the concurrent negligence of the driver and the operator of the car with which the carriage collided, the railroad company could not excuse itself by imputing the driver's negligence to the plaintiff, as his own contributory negligence. And this decision is in accord with the great weight of authority.[23]

20 Webster v. Hudson River R. Co., 38 N. Y. 260; Sheridan v. Brooklyn, etc., R. Co., 36 N. Y. 39; 93 Am. Dec. 490; Barrett v. Third Ave. R. Co., 45 N. Y. 628; Spooner v. Brooklyn City R. Co., 54 N. Y. 230; 13 Am. Rep. 570; McMahon v. Davidson, 12 Minn. 357; Griggs v. Fleckenstein, 14 Minn. 81; 100 Am. Dec. 199; Louisville, etc., R. Co. v. Case, 9 Bush (Ky.), 728; Bartram v. Sharron, 71 Conn. 686; 46 L. R. A. 144; 43 Atl. Rep. 143; 71 Am. St. Rep. 225; Covington Tr. Co. v. Kelly, 36 Ohio St. 86; 38 Am. Rep. 558; Carlisle v. Brisbane, 113 Pa. St. 544; 6 Atl. Rep. 372; 57 Am. Rep. 483; Markham v. Houston, etc., Co., 73 Texas 247; 11 S. W. Rep. 131; New York, etc., R. Co. v. Cooper, 85 Va. 939; 9 S. E. Rep. 321.

21 Chicago, etc., R. Co. v. Harrington, 192 Ill. 9; 61 N. E. Rep. 622.

22 Sluder v. Transit Co., 189 Mo. 107; 88 S. W. Rep. 648.

23 Chicago, etc., R. Co. v. Harrington, 192 Ill. 9; 61 N. E. Rep. 622; Becke v. Missouri Pacific Ry. Co., 102 Mo. 544; 13 S. W. Rep. 1053; 9

II—45

§ 1042. **Imputation of negligence of drivers of vehicles, generally.**— One of the most frequent causes of injuries by railroads is that of the negligence of the drivers of different classes of vehicles and the consideration of the rule of imputed negligence, by the courts, is perhaps necessitated in this class of cases oftener than in any other class of personal injury cases, where the defense of imputed negligence is invoked.

In a recent carefully-considered Massachusetts case,[24] the question of when the negligence of the driver will be imputed to the injured person, is so fully answered and the law upon this subject presented in such a thorough manner, that the opinion of the court, so far as pertinent, will be quoted. After an exhaustive discussion of the authorities from all the States, the court says:

"The rule fairly deducible from our own cases, and supported by the great weight of authority by courts of other jurisdictions is that where an adult person, possessing all his faculties and personally in the exercise of that degree of care which common prudence requires under all the surrounding circumstances, is injured through the negligence of some third person, and the concurring negligence of one with whom the plaintiff is riding as guest or companion, between whom and the plaintiff the relations of master and servant or principal or agent, or mutual responsibility in a common enterprise, does not in fact exist, the plaintiff being at the time in no position to exercise authority or control over the driver, then the negligence of the driver

L. R. A. 157; Georgia, etc., R. Co. v. Hughes, 87 Ala. 610; 6 So. Rep. 413; Little Rock, etc., R. Co. v. Harrell, 58 Ark. 454; 25 S. W. Rep. 117; Tomkins v. Clay Street R. Co., 66 Cal. 163; 4 Pac. Rep. 1165; Denver City Co. v. Norton, 141 Fed. Rep. 599; 73 C. C. A. 1; Neal v. Rendall, 98 Me. 69; 56 Atl. Rep. 209; 63 L. R. A. 668; Noyes v. Boscawen, 64 N. H. 361; 10 Atl. Rep. 690; 10 Am. St. Rep. 410.

[24] Schultz v. Old Colony R. Co. (Mass.), 79 N. E. Rep. 873; 8 L. R. A. (N. S.) 597, and exhaustive note by the editor.

is not imputable to the injured person, but the latter is entitled to recover against the one but for whose wrong his injuries would not have been sustained. Disregarding the passenger's own due care, the test whether the negligence of the driver is to be imputed to the one riding depends upon the latter's control or right of control of the actions of the driver, so as to constitute in fact the relation of principal and agent or master and servant, or his voluntary, unconstrained, noncontractual surrender of all care for himself to the caution of the driver."

The Massachusetts court presents the rule, as it is generally recognized, and to render one liable for the negligence of the driver of a vehicle, in which he is traveling, either the relation of employer and employee, or principal and agent, must exist, or the parties must be engaged in a joint enterprise, whereby responsibility for each other's acts exists.[25]

§ 1043. **Negligence of drivers of public conveyances.—** Near the middle of the past century, in the celebrated English case of Thorogood v. Bryan,[26] it was held that a passenger upon the vehicle of a common carrier who sus-

[25] Cahill v. Cincinnati, etc., R. Co., 92 Ky. 345; 18 S. W. Rep. 2; 49 Am. & Eng. R. Cas. 390; Toledo, etc., R. Co. v. Goddard, 25 Ind. 185; Robinson v. New York, etc., R. Co., 66 N. Y. 11; Dean v. Pennsylvania R. Co., 129 Pa. St. 514; Masterson v. New York, etc., R. Co., 84 N. Y. 247; St. Clair, etc., R. Co. v. Eadie, 43 Ohio St. 91; Massoth v. Delaware & H. Co., 64 N. Y. 524; affirming, 6 Hun 314; Bricknell v. New York, etc., R. Co., 120 N. Y. 290; 24 N. E. Rep. 449; 30 N. Y. S. R. 932; 46 Hun 678; 42 Am. & Eng. R. Cas. 107; Hoag v. New York, etc., R. Co., 111 N. Y. 199; Stotler v. Chicago, etc., R. Co., 200 Mo. 107; 98 S. W. Rep. 509; Stotler v. Chicago, etc., R. Co., 204 Mo. 619; 103 S. W. Rep. 1; Sluder v. Transit Co., 189 Mo. 107; 88 S. W. Rep. 648, an exhaustive discussion of the rule by Judge Gantt; Fechley v. Traction Co., 119 Mo. App. 358; 96 S. W. Rep. 421; Holden v. Missouri R. Co., 177 Mo. 456; 76 S. W. Rep. 973.

[26] 65 Eng. C. L. Rep., 8 M. G. & S. 114; 8 C. B. 115.

tained an injury resulting from the conc
those in charge of the vehicle and thi
identified with the former, as to be ch
negligence and could not recover damag
gent third party. The passenger in tha
ing by omnibus to Clapton, at about 8 ·
ing and not waiting for the omnibus to ɪ
to alight, got out in the street and was ɪ
tally injured by another omnibus, going
tion. The court, as it might have done,
covery, upon the ground of the personal
decedent, but because the negligence of]
puted to him.[27] The doctrine announced
cussed case, although followed for a short ·
and the United States,[29] has now been thoɪ
in both countries, as both courts and co
nized that it was inconsistent with the ben
common law which gave an injured party
for an injury resulting directly from the ⦂
of two wrongdoers, and the effect of the de
make the innocent injured person answeraɪ
ful act of another, over whom he had and
trol whatever.[30]

[27] Coltman, J., was of opinion that deceased,
driver, by selection of the conveyance in which he
held to have participated in his negligence, and ℳ
Williams, JJ., concurred in this opinion.

[28] Armstrong v. Lancashire, etc., R. Co., 10]
both Baron Bramwell and Pollock, B., found no
Thorogood v. Bryan, although Pollock, B., rath
word "identified" as applying to the negligence o
able to the passenger, in that it ought not to be
driver was the agent of the passenger. See, als(
Junction R. Co., 3 M. & W. 244.

[29] Mooney v. Hudson River R. Co., 5 Robt. 548;]
Point, 43 Wis. 513; 28 Am. Rep. 558; Lockhart v. L
St. 151.

[30] Becke v. Missouri Pacific Ry. Co., 102 Mo. 54·

The Court of Appeals of England, finally expressly condemned the rule announced in Thorogood v. Bryan, holding,
in accordance with the preponderance of judicial and pro-
fessional opinion, in England and the United States, that

S. W. Rep. 1053; 45 Am. & Eng. R. Cas. 174; Georgia Pacific Ry. Co.
v. Hughes, 87 Ala. 610; 6 So. Rep. 413; 39 Am. & Eng. R. Cas. 674;
Elyton Land Co. v. Mingea, 89 Ala. 521; 7 So. Rep. 666; 43 Am.
& Eng. R. Cas. 309; Metropolitan R. Co. v. Powell, 89 Ga. 601;
16 S. E. Rep. 118; East Tennessee, etc., R. Co. v. Markens, 88
Ga. 60; 13 S. E. Rep. 855; Wabash, etc., R. Co. v. Shacklett,
105 Ill. 364; 44 Am. Rep. 791; Terre Haute, etc., R. Co., v. Mc-
Murray, 98 Ind. 358; 49 Am. Rep. 752; 22 Am. & Eng. R. Cas.
371; Michigan City v. Bœckling, 122 Ind. 39; 23 N. E. Rep. 518;
Larkin v. Burlington, etc., R. Co., 85 Iowa 492; 52 N. W. Rep. 480;
Louisville, etc., R. Co. v. Case, 9 Bush. (Ky.) 728; Holzab v. New
Orleans, etc., R. Co., 38 La. Ann. 185; State v. Boston, etc., R. Co.,
80 Me. 430; 15 Atl. Rep. 36; 35 Am. & Eng. R. Cas. 356; Philadelphia,
etc., R. Co. v. Hoagland, 66 Md. 149; 7 Atl. Rep. 105; Eaton v.
Boston, etc., R. Co., 11 Allen (Mass.), 500; Schindler v. Milwaukee,
etc., R. Co., 87 Mich. 400; 49 N. W. Rep. 670; Flaherty v. Minneapolis,
etc., R..Co., 39 Minn. 328; 40 N. W. Rep. 160; 1 L. R. A. 680; Alabama, etc., R. Co. v. Davis, 69 Miss. 444; 13 So. Rep. 693; Dickson v. Missouri Pacific R. Co., 104 Mo. 491; 16 S. W. Rep. 381;
Sluder v. Transit Co., 189 Mo. 107; 88 S. W. Rep. 648; Noyes
v. Boscawen, 64 N. H. 361; 10 Atl. Rep. 690; New York, etc., R.
Co. v. Steinbrenner, 47 N. J. L. 161; 23 Am. & Eng. R. Cas. 330;
Cosgrove v. New York, etc., R. Co., 87 N. Y. 88; 13 Hun 329;
Masterson v. New York, etc., R. Co., 84 N. Y. 247; 38 Am. Rep. 510;
3 Am. & Eng. R. Cas. 408; Bennett v. New York, etc., R. Co., 133 N.
Y. 563; 30 N. E. Rep. 1149; McCaffrey v. Delaware, etc., R. Co.,
137 N. Y. 568; 33 N. E. Rep. 339; 62 Hun 618; Phillipps v. New
York, etc., R. Co., 127 N. Y. 657; 27 N. E. Rep. 978; 38 N. Y. S. R.
675; Covington Transfer Co. v. Kelly, 36 Ohio St. 86; 38 Am. Rep.
558; 3 Am. & Eng. R. Cas. 335; St. Clair, etc., R. Co. v. Eadie, 43
Ohio St. 91; 54 Am. Rep. 144; 23 Am. & Eng. R. Cas. 269; Dean v.
Pennsylvania R. Co., 129 Pa. St. 514; 18 Atl. Rep. 718; 39 Am. & Eng.
R. Cas. 697; Garteiser v. Galveston, etc., R. Co., 2 Texas Civ. App. 230;
21 S. W. Rep. 631; New York, etc., R. Co. v. Cooper, 85 Va. 939;
9 S. E. Rep. 321; 37 Am. & Eng. R. Cas. 33; Little v. Hackett, 116
U. S. 366; 6 Sup. Ct. Rep. 391; Missouri Pacific Ry. Co. v. Texas
Pacific R Co., 41 Fed. Rep. 316; Union Pacific R. Co. v. Lapsley, 51
Fed. Rep. 174; 4 U. S. App. 542.

the proposition announced in that decision was essentially unjust and inconsistent with other recognized principles of law, since, while the decision stood, "no one can have gone into or have abstained from going into an omnibus, railroad or ship, on the faith of the decision." [31]   And this latter case reflects the trend of judicial expression on this case, since its publication, on both sides of the sea.[32]

§ 1044. **Persons traveling in railroad cars.**— It is now the well-established rule of law that persons traveling on a railroad who may sustain injury by the concurrent negligence of their own carrier, combined with that of a third person, will not be deprived of a recovery against either wrongdoer, because of their own carrier's negligence.   All cases which followed the rule laid down in Thorogood v. Bryan,[33] have been generally condemned with the condemnation of the rule recognized in that celebrated case.[34]

A passenger by railroad train, injured by a collision with

[31] The Bernina, L. R. 12 P. D. 58, affirmed, in L. R. 13 App. Cas. 1.

[32] Atlanta, etc., R. Co. v. Gravett, 93 Ga. 369; 20 S. E. Rep. 550; 44 Am. St. Rep. 145; 26 L. R. A. 553; Miller v. Louisville, etc., R. Co., 128 Ind. 97; 27 N. E. Rep. 339; 25 Am. St. Rep. 416; McBride v. Des Moines, etc., R. Co. (Iowa), 109 N. W. Rep. 618; Murray v. Boston Ice Co., 180 Mass. 165; 61 N. E. Rep. 1001; Schindler v. Milwaukee, etc., R. Co., 87 Mich. 400; 49 N. W. Rep. 670; Sluder v. Transit Co., 189 Mo. 107; 88 S. W. Rep. 648; 5 L. R. A. (N. S.) 186; Duval v. Atlantic Coast, etc., R. Co., 134 N. Car. 331; 46 S. E. Rep. 750; 101 Am. St. Rep. 830; 65 L. R. A. 722; Cincinnati, etc., R. Co. v. Wright, 54 Ohio St. 181; 43 N. E. Rep. 688; 32 L. R. A. 340; Central Texas, etc., R. Co. v. Gibson (Texas), 83 S. W. Rep. 862; Chicago, etc., R. Co. v. Smith, 69 Ill. App. 69; Slater v. Burlington, etc., R. Co., 71 Iowa 209; 32 N. W. Rep. 264; Kutner v. Lindell R. Co., 29 Mo. App. 502.

[33] 65 Eng. C. L. Rep. (8 M. G. & S. 114); 8 C. B. 115.

[34] The Bernina (January 24, 1887), 12 L. R. Prob. Div. 58; Little v. Hackett, 116 U. S. 366; Becke v. Missouri Pacific Ry. Co., 102 Mo. 544; 13 S. W. Rep. 1053, and cases cited: Schultz v. Old Colony, etc., R. Co. (Mass.), 79 N. E. Rep. 873, and exhaustive note by Editor of 8 L. R. A. (N. S.), p. 617.

the train of another company, could not be said to be identified with his own carrier, so that its negligence should be imputed to him, as he has no control, or management, or advisory power, even, over the carrier; he is passive, merely, in the hands of the railroad company; is wholly unable to aid it, if his aid were useful; he cannot delay or hasten the train; is not permitted to regulate any of its machinery or motive power and often, as to the selection of a carrier, must select the one upon whose trains he takes passage, or stay at home. He trusts his personal safety to the railroad company entirely and to attribute to him the negligence of its agents, would be manifestly unjust. Hence, the law exacts from the carrier whose trains carry him, the highest degree of care and attention, and of all others such reasonable care as all prudent persons are bound to bestow, and for a breach of either of these obligations, he has his action, if damages result to him.[85]

Nor is the rule different, as applied to employees of a railroad company, injured as a result of the concurrent negligence of their employer's agents and those of a third person, for a cause of action would result from such an injury, the same as if the employer's negligence had not concurred to produce the injury.[86] A decision to the contrary, in Pennsylvania,[37] was recently condemned by the Supreme Court of Illinois, and is not generally followed, since the overthrow of the early English rule on this question, as above noted.[88]

[85] Chapman v. New Haven, etc., R. Co., 19 N. Y. 341; 75 Am. Dec. 344; Webster v. Hudson R. R. Co., 38 N. Y. 260; Wabash, etc., R. Co. v. Shacklett, 105 Ill. 364; 44 Am. Rep. 791; West Chicago, etc., R. Co. v. Piper, 165 Ill. 325; 64 Ill. App. 605; 46 N. E. Rep. 186; Pittsburg, etc., R. Co. v. Spencer, 98 Ind. 186; Bunting v. Hogsett, 139 Pa. St. 363; 21 Atl. Rep. 31; 23 Am. St. Rep. 192; 12 L. R. A. 268.

[86] Chicago, etc., R. Co. v. O'Connor, 119 Ill. 586; 9 N. E. Rep. 263.

[37] Lockhart v. Lichtenthaler, 46 Pa. St. 151; Philadelphia, etc., R. Co. v. Bowyer, 97 Pa. St. 91.

[88] Chicago, etc., R. Co. v. O'Connor, 119 Ill. 586; 9 N. E. Rep. 263.

§ 1045. **Occupants of street cars.**— In
jury to the occupant of a street car, cau
collision of the street car and the car o
railroad, it is no defense in an action ag:
road company, that the street car compan
negligence contributing to the collision, f(
road company was guilty of negligence
injury, it would be no defense that it I
producing the same.[39]   In such a case, t
street car cannot be said to have or exer(
supervision over the conductor or motor
car, any more than the passenger on a ste
control the movement of the train in w]
the negligence of the agents of the stree
they were negligent, could not be impute
of the car managed by them.[40]

These cases are also expressly overruled, in Penn
v. Hogsett, 139 Pa. St. 363; 21 Atl. Rep. 31; 2:
12 L. R. A. 268.

It is held, in England, that an employee of
riding on a free pass, is affected with the negligence
train in causing a collision with a train of another
identified with such driver, as to disentitle him to
for damages against such other company, which
negligence.

Armstrong v. Lancashire, etc., R. Co., 33 L. T.
47; 44 L. J. Ex. 89; 23 W. R. 295.

[39] Georgia, etc., R. Co. v. Hughes, 87 Ala. 610
Holzab v. New Orleans, etc., R. Co., 38 La. Ann.
177; Louisville, etc., R. Co. v. Case, 9 Bush (Ky.)
Lindell Ry. Co., 142 Mo. 352; 44 S. W. Rep. 25{
Jersey, etc., R. Co., 36 N. J. L. 225; 13 Am. Rep.
Long Island R. Co., 38 Hun (N. Y.) 569; O'Toole
R. Co., 158 Pa. St. 99; 27 Atl. Rep. 737; 38 Am.
L. R. A. 606; Gulf, etc., R. Co. v. Pendry, 87 Texas
Rep. 125; 29 S. W. Rep. 1038; Whelen v. New Yor
Fed. Rep. 15.

[40] Webster v. Hudson River R. Co., 38 N. Y. 260;

Neither is a passenger in a street car, injured in a collision with another street car, by the concurrent negligence of those in charge of each car, affected by or chargeable with the negligence of the operators of the car in which he was riding; [41] nor is the rule different, in case of an injury resulting from a collision with a wagon and team, or other obstruction, negligently thrown in the way of the street car, by some third party, for in all such cases the passenger of the street car would not be legally chargeable with the negligence of the agents of the street car company, but could sue either his own carrier or the negligent third party whose team and wagon, or other obstruction, occasioned the collision. [42]

§ 1046. **Persons riding in stagecoaches.**— In a well-considered Missouri case, [43] the liability of a railroad company was considered with reference to a person riding in a public stagecoach and injured by a collision at a public crossing of a highway and the railroad. The decedent was a passenger in a public stage or hack that was struck by a train of cars of the defendant, at a public crossing, thereby overturning the coach and injuring the decedent so that he died. The defendant sought to impute the negligence of the driver of the stage to the injured passenger, but on this issue the Supreme Court said: " It is so plain that to maintain the

Haven, etc., R. Co., 19 N. Y. 341; 75 Am. Dec. 344; O'Rourke v. Lindell Ry. Co., 142 Mo. p. 352; 44 S. W. Rep. 254.

41 O'Rourke v. Lindell Ry. Co., 142 Mo. 342; 44 S. W. Rep. 254; Kuttner v. Lindell Ry. Co., 29 Mo. App. 502.

42 Bamberg v. International, etc., R. Co., 103 N. Y. Supp. 297; Hurley v. Brewing Co., 13 App. Div. (N. Y.) 167; 43 N. Y. Supp. 259; Covington Tr. Co. v. Kelly, 36 Ohio St. 86; 38 Am. Rep. 558.

43 Becke v. Missouri Pacific Ry. Co., 102 Mo. 544; 13 S. W. Rep. 1053; 9 L. R. A. 157. See, also, Brown v. New York, etc., R. Co., 32 N. Y. 597; 88 Am. Dec. 353; Landon v. Chicago, etc., R. Co., 92 Ill. App. 216.

doctrine would be to abrogate a well-so
mon law, which gives a right of action
ing directly from the joint wrongful a
against either or both of such wrongd
fect would be to make an innocent p
the wrong act of another, over whom
no control, and who is neither his serva

Neither is the negligence of the driv
coach in striking an obstruction near the
an occupant of the stagecoach; [44] nor c
denied a recovery, because of a collisioi
which he is riding with another stag
due to the concurrent negligence of both (
to have no control over the driver of
he rides, so as to make his negligence in
senger.[45]

§ 1047. **Persons riding in hired vehic**
case in the United States Supreme Cou
bility of a railroad company, for the inji
occupant of a hired vehicle, by collision at
the decedent hired an open carriage fro
keeper and the driver was sent with the car
man. The evidence tended to show that
the result of the negligence of the managers
collided with the carriage and the driver o:
former being remiss in their duty in fail
ing of the approach of the train to the cro:
ter in failing to look for the train. The
contributory negligence of the driver, wl

[44] Chamberlain v. Wheatland, 26 N. Y. S. R. 6
190; Barnes v. Rumford, 96 Me. 315; 52 Atl. Rep. 8
[45] Rigby v. Hewitt, 5 Exch. 240.
[46] Little v. Hackett, 116 U. S. 366; 29 L. Ed. 6:
391.

tended ought to be imputed to the injured occupant of the carriage, but with reference to the alleged imputed negligence of the occupant of the carriage, assuming that the driver was negligent, the trial court instructed the jury that unless the injured person interfered with the driver and controlled the manner of his driving, his negligence could not be imputed to the occupant of the carriage. This charge and the verdict and judgment against the receiver of the railroad company was approved and affirmed in the Supreme Court. This decision has been very generally followed in the different States in the United States, and it may be stated as the general rule in this country that a railroad company is liable for an injury to the occupant of a hired vehicle, resulting from a collision between its train and such vehicle, in the absence of special control of the driver by the occupant of such a vehicle, regardless of the negligence of the driver of the hired carriage.[47]

But the rule is not without limitation, in its application, and although the injured person is riding, at the time of his injury, in a hired conveyance, with a driver sent by the liveryman, yet if the injured person was riding on the seat with the driver, in an open buggy, with power to control, or in a measure prevent such reckless conduct, no recovery could be had for an injury resulting from a collision with a railroad train, at a public crossing, for the fact that the in-

[47] Sluder v. Transit Co., 189 Mo. 107; 88 S. W. Rep. 648; 5 L. R. A. (N. S.) 186; Baltimore, etc., R. Co. v. Adams, 10 App. D. C. 97; East Tennessee, etc., R. Co. v. Markens, 88 Ga. 60; 13 S. E. Rep. 855; 14 L. R. A. 281; Frank Bird Transfer Co. v. Krug, 30 Ind. App. 602; 65 N. E. Rep. 309; Bradley v. Chicago, etc., R. Co., 126 N. C. 735; 36 S. E. Rep. 181; Larkin v. Burlington, etc., R. Co., 85 Iowa 492; 52 N. W. Rep. 480; Collins v. Long Island R. Co., 29 J. & S. (N. Y.) 154; 18 N. Y. Supp. 779; Randolph v. O'Riordon, 155 Mass. 331; 29 N. E. Rep. 583; Allyn v. Boston, etc., R. Co., 105 Mass. 77; New York, etc., R. Co. v. Steinbrenner, 47 N. J. L. 161; 54 Am. Rep. 126. And the same rule is applied in England. Quarman v. Burnett, 6 M. & W. 499.

jured person was in a vehicle driven by another would not relieve him from the duty of exercising due care for his own protection.[48] Nor would there be any liability for an injury to the occupant of a hired conveyance, even where no control of the driver was possible, if the negligence of the driver was the sole cause of the collision with a railroad train, or engine, for in this case the carrier of the injured person would alone be responsible.[49] And the rule would be the same if the injured person, although riding in a hired conveyance, had control of the driver, as where he trusted the reins to a companion of his own, through whose negligence the injury resulted to him.[50]

[48] Brickell v. New York, etc., R. Co., 120 N. Y. 290; 24 N. E. Rep. 449; 17 Am. St. Rep. 648.

[49] East Tennessee, etc., R. Co. v. Markens, 88 Ga. 60; 13 S. E. Rep. 855; 14 L. R. A. 281.

[50] Flood v. London West, 23 Ont. App. Rep. 530. Distinguishing the case being considered, where the occupant of the hired vehicle was inside a closed carriage, from those cases where the negligence of the injured person co-operates to bring about the injury, Judge Gantt, for the Supreme Court of Missouri, in the case of Sluder v. Transit Co. (189 Mo. 107; 88 S. W. Rep. 648; 5 L. R. A. (N. S.) 186), said: "Plaintiff was not outside, with the driver, where he could see and advise the driver as to the crossing. He was not situated so that he could have jumped out of the carriage, after discovering his peril, on the approach of the car. From the inside of the closed carriage he could not even have communicated with the driver and directed him to stop or to rush his team, after he saw the car, or by the exercise of ordinary care under the conditions then confronting him, could have seen it in time to have averted the injury. * * * The facts of this case do not bring it within the reasoning of any of the cases which are cited as exceptions to the rule itself." Sluder v. Transit Co., 189 Mo. 143.

Where a person employs a team with a driver the relation of employer and employee does not exist, and the negligence of the driver in driving on a railway track without taking proper precautions is not imputable to the passenger.— Cotton v. Willmar & S. F. Ry. Co., 109 N. W. Rep. 835.

Where a livery team with driver is employed, the duty of caring for the safety of the passenger rests on the driver, and unless the

§ 1048. **Negligence of excursionists.**— Whatever the means of conveyance, it may be generally stated that if a party of excursionists have or retain no control over the party in charge of the vehicle used to carry the excursionists, the negligence of the party in charge of the conveyance cannot be imputed to the occupants thereof, but in case of an injury to all or any one of their number, by the joint negligence of those in charge of their conveyance and of some third party, a cause of action will lie against either of the joint wrong-doers.[51]

In a recent New York case,[52] a party of pleasure seekers had hired a tallyho coach from a liveryman, under a contract to transport them to and from a given place and send them in charge of a competent driver, and the teams and coach were under the exclusive control of the liveryman's driver, with the exception that the excursionists determined at what places the party would stop for refreshments. A collision between the coach and a railroad train occurred, in driving over the railroad track, at a highway crossing, but the court held that the negligence on the part of the driver

danger at a railroad crossing is obvious or known to the passenger, the latter may rely on the assumption that the driver will exercise proper care, unless he knows that the driver is incompetent or careless, or sees that the driver is not aware of the danger.— Cotton v. Willmar & S. F. Ry. Co. (Minn. 1906), 109 N. W. Rep. 835.

In an action for personal injuries to plaintiff while riding on a pung near a railroad track, he is not entitled to recover, if either his own negligence or that of the driver of the pung contributed to the happening of the accident.— Kane v. Boston Elevated Ry. Co. (Mass. 1906), 78 N. E. Rep. 485.

[51] In Cuddy v. Horn (46 Mich. 596; 10 N. W. Rep. 32; 41 Am. Rep. 178), excursionists drowned at sea, by reason of a collision of their vessel with another, over which they had no control, were held not chargeable with the negligence of their own crew, as they had no control over them. See, also, Koplitz v. St. Paul, 86 Minn. 373; 90 N. W. Rep. 794; 58 L. R. A. 74; Loso v. Lancaster County (Nebraska), 109 N. W. Rep. 752; 8 L. R. A. (N. S.) 618, and cases cited.

[52] Lewis v. Long Island R. Co., 162 N. Y. 52; 56 N. E. Rep. 548.

of the coach could not be imputed to
coach.   The United States Circuit Cou
Eighth Judicial Circuit, recently held
the case of a collision of a tallyho coa(
and similar decisions have been announ
tions.[54] Nor would the fact that an ii
time of the injury, was one of a numbe
on 'an excursion, in a private wagon, r(
the negligence of the driver of the wage
invited guest and had no control over the
to make one liable for the negligence of
attain a common purpose, the two must t
mon enterprise and the injured one mu
in the control, management or direction

Of course if the injured person was t
or driver, or he had supervision or contro
driver, or was co-operating in the negligen
to cause the injury, then the reasoning
would not apply, and the negligence of
would be chargeable to him.[56]

[53] Denver Tramway Co. v. Norton, 141 Fed. Re]
In this case, the court said: " Without assentir
as a general rule, that contributory negligence n
to a person riding in a vehicle, with a driver,
servant, as applied to the facts of this case, the
attributing to either of the plaintiffs any neglig
the injury. They were riding on the rear seats
seats back of the driver. They were not directin
the coach."

[54] Pere v. New Orleans, etc., R. Co., 47 La. Ann
869; Little v. Central, etc., Tel. Co., 213 Pa. St. 22(
Pitts v. New York, etc., R. Co., 79 Hun 546; 29 N

[55] Kessler v. Brooklyn Heights R. Co., 3 App.]
Supp. 799; Koplitz v. St. Paul, 86 Minn. 373; 90 !
L. R. A. 74.

[56] Denver Tramway Co. v. Norton, supra: East
Co. v. Markens, 88 Ga. 60; 13 S. E. Rep. 855; 14 L.

§ 1049. **Persons jointly engaged in common enterprise.**—
The doctrine of imputed negligence, depending, as it does,
upon the principle of agency, or identity between the negligent person and the party injured, it is well settled that
where two or more persons are jointly engaged in a common
enterprise and in furtherance of their undertaking are occupying a conveyance, in the management of which both have
equal authority or control, each will, in law, assume a responsibility for his associate's negligence, and if an injury
results to any one of the associates in such common undertaking, by reason of the negligent act of one of their number
and that of some third party, the negligence of the associate
will be imputed to all his associates and no recovery can be
had therefor.[57] To permit a person to avoid the effect of the
negligence of another, in whose negligence the injured person
thus co-operated at the time, would be to establish an exception to the general rule that no liability exists for contributory negligence on the part of the injured person, directly
concurring to produce the injury, for it is immaterial whether
the negligence of the injured person resulted solely from
his own act, or that of himself and an assistant, he cannot
avoid its effect, since the concurring negligence of another
never relieves a wrongdoer, and to exempt the injured person in such a case from the result of his own concurrent negligence, would be to establish an unwarranted exception to
the general rule, in such cases.[58]

[57] McBride v. Des Moines, etc., R. Co. (Iowa), 109 N. W. Rep. 618;
Payne v. Chicago, .etc., R. Co., 39 Iowa 523; Nesbit v. Garner, 75
Iowa 314; 39 N. W. Rep. 516; 9 Am. St. Rep. 486 · 1 L. R. A. 152;
Donnelly v Brooklyn, etc., R. Co., 109 N. Y. 16; 15 N. E. Rep. 733;
Koplitz v. St. Paul, 86 Minn. 373; 90 N. W. Rep. 794 · 58 L. R. A. 74;
Johnson v. Gulf, etc., R. Co., 2 Texas Civ. App. 139; 21 S. W. Rep.
274; Yarnold v. Bowers, 186 Mass. 396; 71 N. E. Rep. 799.

[58] This is practically the reasoning of the court in Fechley v.
Springfield Traction Co., 119 Mo. App. 366; Becke v. Missouri
Pacific Ry Co., 102 Mo. 544; 13 S. W. Rep. 1053; 9 L. R. A. 157; ·

Therefore, when one of several persons, engaged in a common enterprise, is injured or killed while driving in a wagon occupied by himself and associates, because of the negligence of a railroad company, at a public highway crossing, combined with that of the driver of the wagon, who is one of the associates in the common undertaking, there can be no recovery for the accident, as the driver is held to be the agent of the injured associate, and each of the party would be legally responsible for the acts and conduct of the rest, because of the agency existing between them.[59]

But, as remarked by Judge Bland, in a well-considered case [60] for the St. Louis Court of Appeals: "Negligence is not imputable, on the theory of joint venture, unless the relation of the parties injured in the accident is such that the negligent one might have been controlled, or at least influenced by the other." The fact that one of two partners is injured while riding in a conveyance, driven by his partner, would not affect his right of recovery, if he was free from personal negligence, where the object of the drive was not concerning any partnership business.[61] One of several employees, being carried home from work is not responsible for a collision between the hand car on which he was riding and a train on the employer's track, when he was simply obeying orders of a superior in the operation of the hand car, as he had no means of control over the hand car

Marsh v. Kansas City, etc., Ry. Co., 104 Mo. App. 577; 78 S. W. Rep. 284.

[59] Boyden v. Fitchburg, etc., R. Co., 72 Vt. 89; 47 Atl. Rep. 409; Donnolly v. Brooklyn, etc., R. Co., 109 N. Y. 16; 15 N. E. Rep. 733; Cass v. Third Avenue R. Co., 20 App. Div. 591; 47 N. Y. Supp. 356; Schron v. Staten Island R. Co., 16 App. Div. 111; 45 N. Y. Supp. 124; Payne vs. Chicago, etc., R. Co., 39 Iowa 523; McBride v. Des Moines, etc., R. Co. (Iowa), 109 N. W. Rep. 618.

[60] Baxter v. St. Louis Transit Co., 103 Mo. App. 597; 78 S. W. Rep. 70.

[61] Consolidated Traction Co. v. Hoimark, 60 N. J. L. 456; 38 Atl. Rep. 684.

and the person operating the hand car was not on an equality with the injured person. This is the rule laid down, at least, in a Texas case,[62] but it would seem that it was improperly decided, as the injured person was himself negligent in running the hand car into the approaching train, or in failure to see the train in time to avoid having to jump into a river and drown himself. In other words, it was his own act which co-operated to bring about his death, and his personal negligence concurred to produce the injury. But this case shows the extent the courts have gone where no control or influence of the driver is maintained by the injured person.[63]

[62] Garteiser v. Galveston, etc., R. Co., 2 Texas Civ. App. 230; 21 S. W. Rep. 631.

[63] The Maine Supreme Court held that where three friends, all of middle age, were riding together in a spring wagon, on a starlight night in an open wagon owned and driven by one of them, and they were run down on a railroad crossing they were all familiar with, the negligence of the driver would not be imputed to the other occupants of the wagon, as they were merely there at his invitation, and exercised no supervision or control over him. State v. Boston, etc., R. Co., 80 Me. 430; 15 Atl. Rep. 36.

In the recent case of Louisville, etc., R. Co. v. Armstrong (105 S. W. Rep. 473), the rule of imputed negligence was held applicable to the case of a person engaged in the joint business of hauling fodder with the driver of the team, and where the driver was negligent in attempting to force the team past the carcass of a horse on the railroad right-of-way, as a result of which a runaway occurred and the plaintiff was injured, this was held to be the negligence of the plaintiff also, or, in other words, the negligence of his companion was held imputed to him.

Where, while a guest of those hiring the machine and not in a position to give orders as to the speed thereof, plaintiff was injured through being thrown from defendant's automobile as the result of the negligence of defendant's chauffeur in charge thereof, he was not bound by the acts and the language of other persons in the machine in requesting the maintenance of a high rate of speed, in the absence of acquiescence therein. Rutledge v. Rambler Automobile Co., Tex. Civ. App. (1906), 95 S. W. Rep. 749.

§ 1050. **Negligence of coemployee**
negligence of a coemployee, concurrin
ployer, is never a bar to an action by
injury due to his employer's negliger
true, it is difficult to conceive how the
of a coemployee of the injured person c
effect, to discharge the joint wrongdoc
injured employee against a third per
that an injury resulted from the neglig
is always personal to the employer, and
negligence of an employee will not relie
ployer himself, it ought not to affect th
stranger to the relation.[66]

Regardless of the rule obtaining, th
of associates in a joint enterprise, or i
agency can be predicated on the part of t
or some identity is established betweer
and the injured person, where two or mo
several and distinct duties to perform,
engaged in their duties, one is injured k
of a third party, concurring with the ne
ployee, the negligence of his coemployee
to the injured employee, but the third per

[64] Cole v. Transit Co., 183 Mo. 81; 81 S. W.
v. Kansas City, etc., Ry. Co., 94 Mo. App. 215;
Browning v. Wabash Ry. Co., 124 Mo. 55; 27 S
v. Chicago, etc., Ry. Co., 54 Mo. App. 523; Fost
Ry. Co., 115 Mo. 165; 21 S. W. Rep. 916; Henr
109 Mo. 488; 19 S. W. Rep. 239; Bluedorn v. Mi
108 Mo. 439; 18 S. W. Rep. 1103; 32 Am. St. Re

[65] McCormick v. Nassau, etc., R. Co., 18 App.
Supp. 230; Chicago, etc., R. Co. v. Harrington,
Rep. 622.

[66] McCormick v. Nassau, etc., R. Co., 18 App.
Supp. 230.

for the injury, notwithstanding the concurrent negligence of the other employee.[67]

However, if, at the time of an injury to an employee, due to the combined negligence of his coemployee and a third person, the employees were engaged in a common purpose, or joint venture, so that the injured person could be said to have some control or influence over the negligent one, in the act concurring to produce the injury, then the negligence of the coemployee would be imputed to the injured employee and the negligent third party would not be liable.[68]

[67] McKernan v. Detroit, etc., Ry. Co., 138 Mich. 519; 101 N. W. Rep. 812; 68 L. R. A. 347; Baxter v. St. Louis Transit Co., 103 Mo. App. 597; 78 S. W. Rep. 70; Chicago, etc., R. Co. v. Harrington, 192 Ill. 9; 61 N. E. Rep. 622.

[68] Murray v. Boston, etc., R. Co., 180 Mass. 165; 61 N. E. Rep. 1001; Baxter v. Transit Co., 103 Mo. App. 597; 78 S. W. Rep. 70; Elyton Co. v. Mingea, 89 Ala. 521; 7 So. Rep. 666; Birmingham, etc., R. Co. v. Baker, 132 Ala. 507; 31 So. Rep. 618.

The negligence of the motorman of a street car, was held to be imputed to the conductor, where the latter had control of the motorman, in Minster v. Citizens R. Co., 53 Mo. App. 276.

But a contrary rule was announced, in New York, where there was no evidence to show that motorman did other than stop and start the car on conductor's signal, and conductor was injured by collision. Seaman v. Koehler, 122 N. Y. 646; 25 N. E. Rep. 353.

Firemen, going to fire, injured by collision with railroad train, were held not chargeable with the negligence of one of their number who drove or operated the hose cart or fire engine, in the following cases:

Birmingham, etc., R. Co. v. Baker, 132 Ala. 507; 31 So. Rep. 618; McKernan v. Detroit R. Co., 138 Mich. 519; 101 N. W. Rep. 812; 68 L. R. A. 347; Geart v. Metropolitan R. Co., 84 App. Div. 514; 82 N. Y. Supp. 1016; 177 N. Y. 535; 69 N. E. Rep. 1123; Galligan v. Metropolitan R. Co., 33 Misc. 87; 67 N. Y. Supp. 180.

But where the injured fireman knows that the orders of the driver are not to stop or slack up at railroad crossings and he rides with him, knowing he will obey these orders, he was held equally negligent with the driver, in Thompson v. Pennsylvania R. Co., 215 Pa. St. 113; 64 Atl. Rep. 323. See, also, Houston R. Co. v. Reichart, 87 Texas 539; 29 S. W. Rep. 1040.

And employees were held, not chargeable with negligence of a coemployee, in the following cases: Dickson v. Missouri Pacific Ry. Co.,

And if the employee guilty of the negligence had been constituted the agent of the injured employee, as where he appointed the coemployee to watch for backing cars while he was under a freight car, it was held, in the absence of a statute changing the common law, that the negligence of the employee placed on guard would be imputed to the injured employee under the stationary car, as the latter had made the former his agent to look for approaching cars, and his negligence was the same as that of the injured employee himself.[69]

§ 1051. Employee's negligence imputed to employer.—It is not only in cases where some third person sues the employer for an injury sustained by the negligent act of an employee, in the ordinary scope of his employment, that the negligent act of the employee is imputed to the employer, but if the latter is himself injured by an act of his employee, combined with the wrongful act of another and the employer sues to recover damages for such an injury, the negligence of his own employee will be likewise imputed to him, under the principle of agency, and he will be denied a recovery for such an injury.[70]

104 Mo. 491; 16 S. W. Rep. 381; West Chicago R. Co. v. Dougherty, 110 Ill. App. 204; 209 Ill. 241; 70 N. E. Rep. 586.

[69] Abbott v. Lake Erie, etc., R. Co., 150 Ind. 498; 50 N. E. Rep. 729.

Where plaintiff, a fireman, was riding as a passenger on a fire truck which was being driven home from a fire, and plaintiff had no control over the driver of the truck, the latter's negligence was not imputable to him. Burleigh v. St. Louis Transit Co. (Mo. App. 1907), 102 S. W. Rep. 621.

In an action against a street railroad for the death of a member of a municipal fire department, who was riding on a hose wagon, in a collision between the wagon and the car, the negligence of the driver of the wagon was not imputable to decedent. McBride v. Des Moines City Ry. Co. (Iowa, 1906), 109 N. W. Rep. 618.

[70] Pine Bluff Co. v. Schneider, 62 Ark. 109; 34 S. W. Rep. 547; 33 L. R. A. 366; Albion v. Hetrick, 90 Ind. 545; 46 Am. Rep. 230;

The rule is illustrated by a recent Missouri case,[71] \ [
the owner of a spring wagon and horse was injured in [
lision with a street car. The negligence of the employee [
ing the horse, in attempting to cross the track immedi [
in front of an approaching car, was held to be imputed t
employer, seated by his side in the wagon, and the r [
gence of the defendant alone was held not sufficient to ju [
a recovery.

But before the negligence of a driver, under such [
cumstances, will be imputed to one riding with him and [
taining injuries by reason of the combined negligence of
driver and a third person, the relation of employer [
employee must be shown, or that of principal and agen
tablished, as a matter of fact,[72] and it would not be [
cient to show that the driver of a hired conveyance tool
ders from the occupants as to when to go forward and v [
to stop, as this would not make him their employee, s [
to impute his negligence to the occupants of the h
coach.[73] If the occupants of a hired conveyance, howe [
actually do control the driver and the injury results, in [
from such supervision or control, the injury will be held
have resulted from the negligence of the occupants, as ac [
employers of the driver and no recovery can be had.[74]

Colorado, etc., R. Co. v. Thomas, 33 Colo. 517; 81 Pac. Rep. 801;
L. R. A. 681; Read v. Suburban, etc., R. Co., 115 Ga. 366; 41 £
Rep. 629; Louisville, etc., R. Co. v. Stommel, 126 Ind. 35; 25 N
Rep. 863.

[71] Markowitz v. Metropolitan Street R. Co., 186 Mo. 350; 85 S.
Rep. 351; 69 L. R. A. 389. See, also, for similar cases, Carson v. [
eral Street, etc., R. Co., 147 Pa. St. 219; 23 Atl. Rep. 369; 30
St. Rep. 727; 15 L. R. A. 257; .Smith v. New York, etc., R. Co
App. Div. 493; 38 N. Y. Supp. 666; 39 N. Y. Supp. 1119.

[72] Buckler v. Newman, 116 Ill. App. 546.

[73] Lewis v. Long Island, etc., R. Co., 162 N. Y. 52; 56 N. E.]
548.

[74] Baltimore, etc., R. Co. v. Adams, 10 App. D. C. 97.

1557

Of course the employer could never be said to be the agent
of the employee, and for an injury due to the concurrent
negligence of an employer and a third person, the employee
could generally recover.[75]

§ 1052. **Employee's negligence not imputed to employer's
guest.**— As the negligence of one person is never imputed
to another, unless some identity or agency is shown, one for
the other, the negligence of an employee will not be imputed
to the guest of the employer, riding in a wagon and injured
because of the concurrent negligence of the employee and a
railroad company, or other negligent injury caused by the
wrongful act of a third person.[76] The employer bears no
such relation toward his invited guest as to charge the latter
with the negligence of the former's employees.

Nor would it affect the result that the invited guest, injured as a result of the concurrent negligence of the employee and a third person, happened to be a member of the
employer's family, since the relation of employer and employee could not, by reason of this fact, be held to exist between himself and the employee, guilty of the negligent act,
and his negligence would not affect the injured guest's right
to recover from the negligent third person, assisting to thus
cause his injury.[77]

[75] Garteiser v. Galveston, etc., R. Co., 2 Texas Civ. App. 230; 21 S.
W. Rep. 631; Faust v. Philadelphia, etc., R. Co., 191 Pa. St. 420; 43
Atl. Rep. 329; Crawford v. Delaware, etc., R. Co., 22 J. & S. 262;
121 N. Y. 652; 24 N. E. Rep. 1092.

Where plaintiff, while riding on a truck with his employer, was injured in a collision between the truck and defendant's street car, defendant, having been negligent, could not escape liability for plaintiff's
injuries, though plaintiff's employer, who was driving the truck, was
concurrently negligent. Doctoroff v. Metropolitan St. Ry. Co. (N. Y.
Sup. 1907), 105 N. Y. S. 229.

[76] McCaffrey v. Delaware, etc., Co., 41 N. Y. S. R. 221; 16 N.
Y. Supp. 495; 137 N. Y. 568; 33 N. E. Rep. 339.

[77] Morris v. Metropolitan R. Co., 63 App. Div. 78; 71 N. Y. Supp.
321; 170 N. Y. 592; 63 N. E. Rep. 1119.

And since the imputation of negligence is confined or the employer himself, because of the relation of prir and agent existing between himself and his employ has even been held that he himself could recover dar from a railroad company for negligently causing the of his minor children, who were killed while riding wagon with an employee of the father, who had taken to ride without the parent's knowledge or consent, and ligently driven upon a railroad crossing, without lookin an approaching train of cars.[78]

§ 1053. **Persons riding in private vehicles.**— The w of authority, in the United States, favors the propos that if a person riding in a private vehicle, not his ow injured by the negligence of the driver and the concu negligence of another person, the negligence of the d will not be imputed to the injured person, unless he wa agent, in driving the vehicle, or they were jointly eng in some common object, from which the presumptio agency would be implied.[79]

[78] Faust v. Philadelphia, etc., R. Co., 191 Pa. St. 420; 43 Atl. 329.

[79] Philadelphia, etc., R. Co. v. Hogeland, 66 Md. 149; 7 Atl. 105; 59 Am. Rep. 159; Cahill v. Cincinnati, etc., R. Co., 92 Ky. 18 S. W. Rep. 2; Birmingham, etc., R. Co. v. Baker, 132 Ala. 50 So. Rep. 618; Ouverson v. Grafton, 5 N. Dak. 281; 65 N. W. 676; Hajsek v. Chicago, etc., R. Co., 68 Neb. 539; 94 N. W. 609; Pyle v. Clark, 75 Fed. Rep. 644; 25 C. C. A. 190; 45 App. 260; 79 Fed. Rep. 744; United Railroad, etc., Co. v. Bi 98 Md. 564; 56 Atl. Rep. 813; Chicago, etc., R. Co. v. Condon Ill. App. 440; Louisville, etc., R. Co. v. Creek, 130 Ind. 139; 29 Rep. 481; 14 L. R. A. 733; Chicago, etc., R. Co. v. Spilker, 134 380; 34 N. E. Rep. 218; Central, etc., R. Co. v. Gibson (Texas S. W. Rep. 862; Leavenworth v. Hatch, 57 Kansas 57; 45 Pac. 65; 57 Am. St. Rep. 309; West Chicago R. Co. v. Dedloff, 9: App. 547; Chicago, etc., R. Co. v. Wall, 93 Ill. App. 411; Lake S etc., R. Co. v. Boynton (Ind.), 43 N. E. Rep. 667; Howe v. Minnea etc., R. Co., 62 Minn. 71; 64 N. W. Rep. 102; 54 Am. St. Rep. 30 L. R. A. 684; Bricknell v. New York, etc., R. Co., 120 N. Y.

In a well-considered Georgia case,[80] it was held that one personally free from negligence, who was injured at a highway crossing by the collision of a train of cars and the vehicle in which the plaintiff was riding, would not be chargeable with the negligence of the driver, where the plaintiff exercised no supervision or control over the driver and the wagon and team did not belong to the plaintiff.

But the cases are not harmonious on this proposition and in many States the rule is laid down that a person cannot recover for injuries received while riding in a private conveyance, although no supervision over the driver or ownership of the vehicle can be charged to the plaintiff, because in such a case, if the injured person did not exercise some influence or control over the driver and permitted him to commit some negligent act, while voluntarily riding with him, the injured person ought to be chargeable with his negligence, in thus trusting himself in such a private conveyance.[81]

And of course if the injured person owned or controlled the team and wagon, or other vehicle, or the motive power by which it was run, or if the person driving it could be said to be the agent of the injured person, in so doing, the negligence of the driver would be imputed to the injured person

24 N. E. Rep. 449; 17 Am. St. Rep. 648.; Wilson v. New York, etc., R. Co., 18 R. I. 598; 29 Atl. Rep. 300; Galveston, etc., R. Co. v. Kutac, 72 Texas 643; 11 S. W. Rep. 127.

[80] Metropolitan R. Co. v. Powell, 89 Ga. 601; 16 S. E. Rep. 118. See, also, authorities *supra.*

[81] Cuddy v. Horn, 46 Mich. 596; 10 N. W. Rep. 32; 41 Am. Rep. 178; Mullen v. Owosso, 100 Mich. 103; 58 N. W. Rep. 663; 43 Am. St. Rep. 436; 23 L. R. A. 693; Lake Shore, etc., R. Co. v. Miller, 25 Mich. 274; Whittaker v. Helena, 14 Mont. 124; 35 Pac. Rep. 904; 43 Am. St. Rep. 621; Lightfoot v. Winnebago Traction Co., 123 Wis. 479; 102 N. W. Rep. 30; Olson v. Luck, 103 Wis. 33; 79 N. W. Rep. 29; Ritger v. Milwaukee, 99 Wis. 190; 74 N. W. Rep. 815; Johnson v. Superior Rapid Transit Co., 91 Wis. 233; 64 N. W. Rep. 753; Hampel v. Detroit, etc., R. Co., 138 Mich. 1; 100 N. W. Rep. 1002; 108 Am. St. Rep. 275.

and no recovery could be had, if the injury resulted in part from his negligence.[82]

§ 1054. Injured person in position to control driver.—

While the courts have refused to impute the negligence of the driver of either a public or private conveyance to an injured passenger riding with him, when the injured person was so situated as to be unable to control or influence the conduct of the driver, in the absence of a relation existing that would constitute the driver the agent of the person injured,[83] this reason would not apply where the injured person was so situated as to influence or control the driver, for in such case, it would be a case of co-operating negligence on the part of the driver and the injured person, and the fact that the driver was negligent would not excuse the injured person for his own co-operating negligence and the negligence of the driver would be held to be so ratified and affirmed and co-operated in by the injured person, if the latter was riding on the same seat with him and had the same opportunity that the driver had to discover the danger and communicate it to the driver, as to preclude a recovery for an injury alleged to be due to the concurrent negligence of the driver and another.[84]

In an instance given by one author,[85] of the driver of a team, approaching a railroad crossing, without looking to see if a train is approaching and a resulting injury to a pas-

[82] Markowitz v. Metropolitan R. Co., 186 Mo. 350; 85 S. W. Rep. 351; 69 L. R. A. 389.

[83] Baxter v. St. Louis Transit Co., 103 Mo. App. 597; 78 S. W. Rep. 70.

[84] Markowitz v. Metropolitan, etc., R. Co., 186 Mo. 350; 85 S. W. Rep. 351; 69 L. R. A. 389; Bricknell v. New York, etc., R. Co., 120 N. Y. 290; 24 N. E. Rep. 449; 30 N. Y. S. R. 932; 46 Hun 678; 42 Am. & Eng. R. Cas. 107.

[85] Thompson on Neg., § 499, p. 466.

senger riding with him, who has the same opportunity the driver had for ascertaining the presence of the train, it is asserted that the negligence of the driver would not be imputed to the injured person, but that the latter's own negligence, in the case instanced, would bar a recovery. And this same rule is laid down by the Missouri Court of Appeals, in a recent case.[86] But, as conceded by the author referred to, the negligence of the driver would be imputed in every case where the injured person was in a position to control or influence him, as held by the New York court,[87] the illustration given would bring the case within the rule where the negligence of the driver would be imputed to the passenger, for regardless of the co-operating character of the passenger's negligence, as it is the conduct of the driver alone that brings the vehicle in the position of peril and the passenger is only passive, at most, the negligence of the driver is one of the proximate causes of the injury, and the ·passenger with as much knowledge as he has, blindly trusts his safety to another, under such circumstances as ought to constitute him the passenger's agent, for with full power to influence his conduct, he restrains him not, but ratifies his negligence and co-operates therein. In such a case, the negligence of the driver ought to be squarely imputed to the passenger, without quibbling or distinction, for the fact that the injured person's negligence concurred with that of the driver is no excuse for the driver's negligence, which the passenger is, to say the least, partly responsible for.[88]

[86] Fechley v. Traction Co., 119 Mo. App. 358; 96 S. W. Rep. 421, by Judge Goode.

[87] Thompson on Neg., § 499, p. 466; Bricknell v. New York, etc., R. Co., 120 N. Y. 290; 24 N. E. Rep. 449; 30 N. Y. S. R. 932; 46 Hun 678; 42 Am. & Eng. R. Cas. 107.

[88] Markowitz v. Metropolitan, etc., R. Co., 186 Mo. 350; 85 S. W. Rep. 351; 69 L. R. A. 389; Murray v. Boston, etc., Co., 180 Mass. 165; 61 N. E. Rep. 1001; Birmingham, etc., R. Co. v. Baker, 132 Ala. 507; 31 So. Rep. 618.

§ 1055. **Guest riding in private vehicle.**— The great weight of authority supports the proposition that one riding in a private conveyance as the invited guest of the driver or owner of the vehicle, if no control or authority over the driver is exercised, in case of an injury by the combined negligence of a third party and his driver, will not be prevented from maintaining an action against the third person causing the injury, by reason of the negligence of the driver being imputed to such guest.[89]

In a recent Illinois case,[90] a person who was killed by the negligent act of the agents of a railroad train, at a high-

[89] Hot Springs, etc., R. Co., v. Hildreth, 72 Ark. 572; 82 S. W. Rep. 245; Ouverson v. Grafton, 5 N. D. 281; 65 N. W. Rep. 676; Farley v. Wilmington, etc., R. Co., 3 Penn. (Del.) 581; 52 Atl. Rep. 543; Roach v. Western, etc., R. Co., 93 Ga. 785; 21 S. E. Rep. 67; West Chicago, etc., R. Co. v. Peters, 196 Ill. 298; 63 N. E. Rep. 662; Colorado, etc., R. Co. v. Thomas, 33 Colo. 517; 81 Pac. Rep. 801; 70 L. R. A. 681; Christy v. Elliott, 216 Ill. 31; 74 N. E. Rep. 1035; 108 Am. St. Rep. 196; 1 L. R. A. (N. S.) 215; Knightstown v. Musgrove, 116 Ind. 121; 18 N. E. Rep. 452; 9 Am. St. Rep. 827; Nesbit v. Garner, 75 Iowa 314; 39 N. W. Rep. 516; 9 Am. St. Rep. 486; 1 L. R. A. 152; Bevis v. Vanceburg, etc., Co. (Ky.), 89 S. W. Rep. 126; Knox v. Boston, etc., R. Co., 185 Mass. 602; 71 N. E. Rep. 90; Howe v. Minneapolis, etc., R. Co., 62 Minn. 71; 64 N. W. Rep. 102; 54 Am. St. Rep. 616; 30 L. R. A. 684; Finley v. Chicago, etc., R. Co., 71 Minn. 471; 74 N. W. Rep. 174; Marsh v. Kansas City, etc., R. Co., 104 Mo. App. 577; 78 S. W. Rep. 284; Noonan v. Consolidated Tr. Co., 64 N. J. L. 579; 46 Atl. Rep. 770; Masterson v. New York, etc., R. Co., 84 N. Y. 247; 38 Am. Rep. 510; DeLoge v. New York, etc., R. Co., 92 Hun 149; 36 N. Y. Supp. 697; 157 N. Y. 688; 51 N. E. Rep. 1090; Flanagan v. New York, etc., R. Co., 70 App. Div. 505; 75 N. Y. Supp. 225; 173 N. Y. 631; 66 N. E. Rep. 1108; Baker v. Norfolk, etc., R. Co. (N. C.), 56 S. E. Rep. 553; Duval v. Atlantic Coast Line R. Co., 134 N. C. 331; 46 S. E. Rep. 750; 101 Am. St. Rep. 839; 65 L. R. A. 722; St. Clair, etc., R. Co. v. Eadie, 43 Ohio St. 91; 1 N. E. Rep. 519; 54 Am. Rep. 802; Wheeling, etc., R. Co. v. Suhrwiar, 67 Ohio St. 497; 67 N. E. Rep. 1100; Dean v. Pennsylvania R. Co., 129 Pa. St. 514; 18 Atl. Rep. 718; 15 Am. St. Rep. 733; 6 L. R. A. 143; Hydes Ferry Co. v. Yates, 108 Tenn. 428; 67 S. W. Rep. 69.

[90] Chicago, etc., R. Co. v. Condon, 121 Ill. App. 440.

way crossing, by the collision of a speeding train and a buggy, the team to which was driven by a friend of the injured person, with whom he was riding, was held not chargeable with the negligence of the owner of the horse and buggy, so as to preclude an action by the decedent's representatives, to recover damages for his death, and this is the generally accepted rule in such cases.[91]

Neither will the negligence of the chauffeur of an automobile, in driving the machine across a railroad track directly in front of a rapidly approaching railroad train, be imputed to a person riding in the automobile as a mere guest at the invitation of the owner or chauffeur.[92]

But, of course, to relieve the guest from the imputation of negligence on the part of the driver, in such a case, he must not have been in control of the driver at the time of the injury, or co-operating in his negligence, which brought about the accident,[93] for, as recently held by the Court of Appeals of Missouri,[94] "Few, if any, courts have held that an oc-

[91] Alabama, etc., R. Co. v. Davis, 69 Miss. 444; 13 So. Rep. 693, and cases cited.

[92] Ward v. Brooklyn Heights, etc., R. Co., 104 N. Y. Supp. 95; 115 App. Div. 104.

[93] Lake Shore, etc., R. Co. v. Boynts, 16 Ind. App. 640; 45 N. E. Rep. 812; Sluder v. Transit Co., 189 Mo. 107; 88 S. W. Rep. 648; 5 L. R. A. (N. S.) 186.

[94] Fechley v. Springfield Traction Co., 119 Mo. App. 358; 96 S. W. Rep. 421.

Where a person was injured through the negligence of a third person and the concurring negligence of one with whom she was riding as guest, the driver's negligence would not be imputed to her, where in entering and continuing in a conveyance she acted with reasonable caution, and had no ground to suspect incompetency and no cause to anticipate negligence on the part of the driver, and if the impending danger, although in part produced by the driver, was so sudden or of such a character as not to permit or require her to act for her own protection. Shultz v. Old Colony St. Ry. (Mass. 1907), 79 N. E. Rep, 873; 8 L. R. A. (N. S.) 850.

The negligence of a minor driver of a vehicle belonging to his father in approaching a railroad crossing cannot be imputed to one riding

cupant of a vehicle may entrust his safety absolutely to the driver of a vehicle, regardless of the imminence of danger or the visible lack of ordinary caution on the part of the driver to avoid harm. The law in this State and in most jurisdictions, is, that if a passenger who is aware of the danger and that the driver is remiss in guarding against it, takes no care himself to avoid injury, he cannot recover for one he receives. This is the law, not because the driver's negligence is imputable to the passenger, but because the latter's own negligence proximately contributed to his damage."

§ 1056. **When negligence of husband imputed to wife.—** The decisions of the different States are not harmonious upon the proposition whether or not the negligence of the husband, in driving, while riding in a conveyance with his wife, will be imputed to the wife, in an action by her against some third party, charged to be responsible for her injury.[95]

As a general rule, if the husband is the beneficiary, either directly or indirectly, of the damages to be recovered for the injury to his wife, as where the damages go to him, for loss of services of the wife, or are held as community property, between the husband and wife, the contributory negligence on the part of the husband would be imputed to the wife, in an action by her against one whose negligence concurred with that of her husband to cause her injury, while she was riding in a vehicle being driven by her husband.[96]

with him, as his guest. Baker v. Norfolk, etc., R. Co. (N. C. 1907), 56 S. E. Rep. 553.

[95] Reading Township v. Telfer, 57 Kansas, 798; 48 Pac. Rep. 134; 57 Am. St. Rep. 355.

[96] McFadden v. Santa Anna, etc., R. Co., 87 Cal. 464; 25 Pac. Rep. 681; 11 L. R. A. 252; Pennsylvania R. Co. v. Goodenough, 55 N. J. L. 577; 28 Atl. Rep. 3; 22 L. R. A. 460; Peck v. New York, etc., R. Co., 50 Conn. 379; Bertram v. Sharon, 71 Conn. 686; 43 Atl. Rep.

Any other view of the law would enable the husband to take advantage of his own wrong and profit by his own neglect.

It has, accordingly, been held, in Illinois,[97] that the neglect of a husband, in leaving his wife in a buggy, in proximity to a locomotive, would be imputed to the wife, where she was injured by the horse becoming frightened and throwing her from the buggy, by the blowing of the whistle and the discharge of steam from the engine. The federal courts of Iowa and Missouri have laid down similar rules and held that the negligence of the husband, in all such cases, was imputed to the wife.[98]

But the doctrine that because of the duty of a husband toward his wife, or the existence of the marital relation, his negligence will be chargeable to her, when he is at fault in driving a vehicle in which they are both riding, and she is injured by his negligence and that of another, is repudiated by the majority of the courts in the United States, in the absence of evidence to establish an agency on the part of the husband to act for the wife, in driving or managing the vehicle.[99] The wife is very generally treated the same as

143; 71 Am. St. Rep. 225; 46 L. R. A. 144; Rock Island v. Van Landschoot, 78 Ill. 485; Joliet v. Seward, 86 Ill. 402; 29 Am. Rep. 35; Carlisle v. Sheldon, 38 Vt. 440; Yahn v. Ottumwa, 60 Iowa 429; 15 N. W. Rep. 257. But, see, for case denying this rule, in Iowa, Willfong v. Omaha, etc., R. Co., 116 Iowa 548; 90 N. W. Rep. 358.

97 Toledo, etc., R. Co. v. Crittenden, 42 Ill. App. 469.

98 Morris v. Chicago, etc., R. Co., 26 Fed. Rep. 22; Huntoon v. Trumbull, 12 Fed. Rep. 844.

99 Willfong v. Omaha, etc., R. Co., 116 Iowa 548; 90 N. W. Rep. 358; Hicks v. Citizens R. Co., 124 Mo. 115; 27 S. W. Rep. 542; 25 L. R. A. 508; Chicago, etc., R. Co. v. Spilker, 134 Ind. 380; 33 N. E. Rep. 280; Miller v. Louisville, etc., R. Co., 128 Ind. 97; 27 N. E. Rep. 339; 25 Am. St. Rep. 416; Louisville, etc., R. Co. v. Creek, 130 Ind. 139; 29 N. E. Rep. 481; 14 L. R. A. 733; Lake Shore, etc., R. Co. v. McIntosh, 140 Ind. 261; 38 N. E. Rep. 476; Indianapolis, etc., R. Co. v. Johnson, 163 Ind. 518; 72 N. E. Rep. 571; Huff v. Ames, 16 Neb.

any other stranger or guest, riding with the husband, at his invitation, who does not reserve or exercise any control or supervision over him in the management of the vehicle.[1]

The wife, however, has no right to omit any prudent or reasonable effort to assure her own safety, in case of an injury while riding in a vehicle driven by her husband, and if she is personally chargeable with a want of ordinary care for her own safety,[2] or if she is engaged in a common enterprise with her husband or is in control of him or of his movements, in handling the vehicle in which they are riding, or any other facts exist, which could charge her, under the principle of agency, with the result of his acts, then his negligence will be chargeable to her, and in case of an action for an injury to her, due, in part, to his neglect, a recovery would be refused.[3]

139; 19 N. W. Rep. 623; 49 Am. Rep. 716; Hajsek v. Chicago, etc., R. Co., 68 Neb. 539; 94 N. W. Rep. 609; Munger v. Sedalia, 66 Mo. App. 629; Hedges v. Kansas City, 18 Mo. App. 62; Flori v. St. Louis, 3 Mo. App. 231; Whitman v. Fisher, 98 Me. 577; 57 Atl. Rep. 895; Neal v. Rendall, 98 Me. 69; 56 Atl. Rep. 209; 63 L. R. A. 668; Teal v. St. Paul, etc., R. Co., 96 Minn. 379; 104 N. W. Rep. 945; Finley v. Chicago, etc., R. Co., 71 Minn. 471; 74 N. W. Rep. 174; Lammers v. Great Northern R. Co., 82 Minn. 120; 84 N. W. Rep. 728; Howe v. Minneapolis, etc., R. Co., 62 Minn. 71; 64 N. W. Rep. 102; 54 Am. St. Rep. 616; 30 L. R. A. 684; Platz v. Cohoes, 24 Hun 101; 89 N. Y. 219; 42 Am. Rep. 286; Hennessy v. Brooklyn, etc., R. Co., 73 Hun 569; 26 N. Y. Supp. 321; Lewin v. Lehigh Valley R. Co., 41 App. Div. 89; 58 N. Y. Supp. 113; Galveston, etc., R. Co. v. Kutac. 76 Texas 473; 13 S. W. Rep. 327; Gulf, etc., R. Co. v. Greenlee, 62 Texas 344; Davis v. Guarnieri, 45 Ohio St. 470; 15 N. E. Rep. 350; 4 Am. St. Rep. 548.

[1] Louisville, etc., R. Co. v. Creek, 130 Ind. 139; 29 N. E. Rep 481; 14 L. R. A. 733.

[2] Hoag v. New York, etc., R. Co., 111 N. Y. 202; 18 N. E. Rep. 648.

[3] Chicago, etc., R. Co. v. Spilker, 134 Ind. 380; 33 N. E. Rep. 280. The doctrine that the negligence of the driver of a vehicle contributing to cause a collision with a locomotive is not imputable to another, riding by invitation in the vehicle, unless such person had a right or duty to influence the driver's conduct, is applicable where a wife

§ 1057. **Negligence of relatives imputed, when.**— The neglect of a relative of an injured person, in driving a vehicle in which the person injured was riding at the time of his injury, due in part to the neglect of some third person, will be imputed to the injured person whenever the relative driving or managing the vehicle could be held to be acting for the injured person, as his or her agent, in so doing, for the fact of the relationship existing would not affect the status of the parties, established by evidence from which their rights would be determined, as a matter of law, from the relation existing at the time of the injury.[4]

In the absence of a showing of agency on the part of the relative doing the driving, or managing the vehicle in which the injured person was riding, when injured, the negligence of the relative would not be imputed to the injured person. In other words, the fact of the relationship existing would not affect the legal status of the injured person at all, or charge him with the neglect of the relative doing the driving, in the absence of the relation constituting such relative the agent of the party sustaining the injury.

Accordingly, it has been held, that a parent could not be charged with the neglect of a son or daughter, with whom the parent was riding at the time of the injury;[5] the tortious act of a brother or sister is not visited upon an injured per-

---

is accompanying her husband in a buggy driven by him and a collision occurs between the buggy and a locomotive. Southern Ry. Co. v. King (Ga. 1907), 57 S. E. Rep. 687.

For the injury or death of a wife, injured by a collision with a train at a crossing, on account of the negligence of her husband, who was driving, there was held to be no liability, in Miller v. Louisville, etc., R. Co., 128 Ind. 97; 27 N. E. Rep. 339; Peck v. New York, etc., R. Co., 50 Conn. 379; 14 Am. & Eng. R. Cas. 633.

[4] Lockwood v. Belle City R. Co., 92 Wis. 97; 65 N. W. Rep. 866.

[5] Watson v. Wabash, etc., R. Co., C6 Iowa 164; 23 N. W. Rep. 380; Chicago v. McCarthy, 61 Ill. App. 300; Buckler v. Newman. 116 Ill. App. 546; Boone County v. Mutchler, 137 Ind. 140; 36 N. E. Rep. 534; Weldon v. Third Ave. R. Co., 3 App. Div. 370; 38 N. Y. Supp. 206.

son, sustaining injury through the neglect of a third person, to which the brother's or sister's wrongful act, in part, contributes; [6] a woman is not chargeable with the neglect of a daughter-in-law or son-in-law in driving in a negligent manner, in the absence of agency, on the part of the driver, to act for the mother-in-law; [7] nor is a brother-in-law or sister-in-law driving, capable by their neglect, of depriving an injured person of the right of action for an injury due in part to the wrongful act of a third person,[8] and it is held that the negligence of an uncle in driving on a street car track, will not be imputed to his nephew, sixteen years old, riding with him, in his buggy, and injured by being thrown out of the buggy, which was crashed into by a street car, that approached from the rear.[9]

[6] Lapsley v. Union Pacific R. Co., 50 Fed. Rep. 172, affirmed, in Union Pacific R. Co. v. Lapsley, on appeal, by Sanborn, J., 51 Fed. Rep. 174; 2 C. C. A. 149; 4 U. S. App. 542; 16 L. R. A. 800; Missouri, etc., R. Co. v. Thomas (Texas), 28 S. W. Rep. 139; Knapp v. Dagg, 18 How. Pr. 165; United R., etc., Co. v. Bieder, 98 Md. 564; 56 Atl. Rep. 813; Follman v. Mankato, 35 Minn. 522; 29 N. W. Rep. 317; 59 Am. Rep. 340.

[7] Johnson v. St. Paul City R. Co., 67 Minn. 260; 69 N. W. Rep. 900; 36 L. R. A. 586.

[8] Philadelphia, etc., R. Co. v. Hoagland, 66 Md. 149; 7 Atl. Rep. 105; 59 Am. Rep. 159; Baltimore, etc., R. Co. v. State, 79 Md. 335; 29 Atl. Rep. 518; 47 Am. St. Rep. 415.

[9] Peterson v. St. Louis Transit Co., 199 Mo. 331; 97 S. W. Rep. 860.

In deciding the above case, the Supreme Court of Missouri, speaking by Judge Brace, said: "The status of the plaintiff in the buggy was not that of his uncle; he was a mere passenger in the buggy, exercising no control whatever over its management or movements, and, having no right or power to do so, and upon a principle well recognized in this State, the negligence of Ole Peterson, if any, could not be attributed to him, for, as we have said, it is against both reason and authority that an innocent person should be made responsible for the wrong act of another over whom he has and exercises no control, and who is neither his servant nor his agent." Peterson v. St. Louis Transit Co., 199 Mo. 341; 97 S. W. Rep. 860.

II—47

§ 1058. **Rule as to infants non sui juris.**— In an action by
a parent or guardian of an infant of tender years, to recover
damages in his own right, for an injury to such infant, as
for a loss of the services of the child, during its minority, if
the injury to the child was in part due to the negligent
act of such parent or guardian, since it would be permitting
him to take advantage of his own wrongful act to recover
damages for the injury, the negligence of the adult in such
a case would be imputed, in law, to the infant, so as to
prevent a recovery, by the parent or guardian, for the result of his own wrong.[10] Upon this proposition the cases
all agree. A different rule obtains, however, in most of the
States, in an action for damages, for or on behalf of the
infant himself, where he is injured through the combined
negligence of his parent or guardian and some third person.

In England[11] and New York[12] the rule has been announced and followed for many years, that an infant of tender years is responsible for the parent's or guardian's negligence, when an injury results to it through the concurrent
negligence of such parent and a third person. With due
deference to precedents, which are recognized as the bul-
warks of the law, as the rule announced in these cases seems
opposed to both reason and common justice, the " New York

[10] Huff v. Ames, 16 Neb. 139; 19 N. W. Rep. 623; 49 Am. Rep.
716; Mullen v. Owosso, 100 Mich, 103; 58 N. W. Rep. 663; 43 Am.
St. Rep. 436; 23 L. R. A. 693; Chicago, etc., R. Co. v. Kowalski, 92
Fed. Rep. 310; 34 C. C. A. 1; Delaware, etc., R. Co. v. Devore, 114
Fed. Rep. 155; 52 C. C. A. 77.

[11] Waite v. Northeastern R. Co., El. Bl. & El. 719. For condemna-
tion of English rule, on this question, see Atlanta, etc., R. Co. v.
Gravitt, 93 Ga. 369; 20 S. E. Rep. 550; 44 Am. St. Rep. 145; 26 L.
R. A. 553.

[12] Hartfield v. Roper, 21 Wend. 615; 34 Am. Dec. 273; Metcalfe v.
Rochester, etc., R. Co., 12 App. Div. 147; 42 N. Y. Supp. 661; Kyne
v. Wilmington, etc., R. Co., 8 Houst. (Del.) 185; 14 Atl. Rep. 922;
State v. Boston, etc., R. Co., 80 Me. 430; 15 Atl. Rep. 36.

rule " upon this proposition, as it is often called by courts, ought not to be extended, but should be condemned in that State. To hold that a child, who is not and cannot be responsible for the danger to which it is exposed — since it has no volition in establishing the relation between itself and the person whose negligence is sought to be imputed to it — ought to be charged with the negligence of another, in exposing it to a danger it lacked the capacity to understand and the judgment to avoid, seems an extremely harsh rule of law, to be applied in such a case.[13] For this reason, a New York Court of Intermediate Appellate Jurisdiction,[14] with proper ingenuity, distinguished between the case of an injury to an infant in the sole custody of the negligent parent and an infant held in the arms of its mother, injured as a result of the negligent act of a railroad company and its father, driving a phaeton, as the court intimated that it would be preposterous to hold that the negligence of the father would not be imputed to the mother, herself, but would be imputed to the helpless infant in her arms, by a strict adherence to the rule established in that State. It is to be hoped that this object lesson, showing as it does, the harshness of the " New York rule " on this question, will ultimately lead to the abandonment of the rule now obtaining in that State.

The weight of authority in this country favors the more humane doctrine, that the negligence of the parent or guardian is not to be imputed to an infant of tender years, in-

[13] Atchison, etc., R. Co. v. Calhoun (Okla.), 89 Pac. Rep. 207; Wymore v. Mahaska County, 78 Iowa 396; 43 N. W. Rep. 264; 16 Am. St. Rep. 449; 6 L. R. A. 545.

[14] Hennessy v. Brooklyn City R. Co., 6 App. Div. 206; 39 N. Y. Supp. 805. In action for injury to the mother of the child, injured in the same accident, the court held that the mother was not chargeable with the negligence of her husband in driving the phaeton. Hennessy v. Brooklyn City R. Co., 73 Hun 569; 26 N. Y. Supp. 321; 147 N. Y. 721; 41 N. E. Rep. 723.

jured by the concurrent negligence of the parent and a third person,[15] and this rule not only comports with the obvious reason and beneficence of the situation, but is also based upon legal precedents, for it seems absurd to say that an infant, not himself capable of negligence or wrongdoing, or of legally authorizing the same, should be held, upon a fictitious theory of an implied agency, and such infant or his estate be made to suffer, because of such unauthorized act or neglect of his parent or guardian and some third person.

The result is not different if the driver of the vehicle is a stranger to the infant, instead of one standing in the relation of a parent or guardian to such infant, and for an injury to it from the combined negligence of such driver and a railroad company, the representatives of the infant or the infant itself, would not be denied a recovery upon the basis of any imputation to it of the negligence of the driver,[16] and the latter's negligence would ordinarily be an issue of fact for the jury.[17]

[15] Atlanta, etc., R. Co. v. Gravitt, 93 Ga. 369; 44 Am. St. Rep. 145; 20 S. E. Rep. 550; 26 L. R. A. 553; Hampel v. Detroit, etc., R. Co., 138 Mich. 1; 100 N. W. Rep. 1002; 108 Am. St. Rep. 275; Erie City R. Co. v. Schuster, 113 Pa. St. 412; 6 Atl. Rep. 269; 57 Am. Rep. 471; Cleveland, etc., R. Co. v. Manson, 30 Ohio St. 451; Wymore v. Mahasha County, 78 Iowa 396; 43 N. W. Rep. 264; 16 Am. St. Rep. 449; 6 L. R. A. 545; Slater v. Burlington, etc., R. Co., 71 Iowa 209; 32 N. W. Rep. 264; Battishill v. Humphries, 64 Mich. 503; 31 N. W. Rep. 894; Shippy v. Au Sable, 85 Mich. 280; 48 N. W. Rep. 584; Mullen v. Owosso, 100 Mich. 103; 58 N. W. Rep. 663; 43 Am. St. Rep. 436; 23 L. R. A. 693; Kowolski v. Chicago, etc., R. Co., 84 Fed. Rep. 586; 34 C. C. A. 1; 92 Fed. Rep. 310; Atchison, etc., R. Co. v. Calhoun (Okla.), 89 Pac. Rep. 207; Schindler v. Milwaukee, etc., R. Co., 87 Mich. 400; 49 N. W. Rep. 670.

[16] Hampel v. Detroit, etc., R. Co., 138 Mich. 1; 100 N. W. Rep. 1002; 108 Am. St. Rep. 275; Schindler v. Milwaukee, etc., R. Co., 87 Mich. 400; 49 N. W. Rep. 670.

[17] Bahrenburgh v. Brooklyn City R. Co., 56 N. Y. 652.

Upon the contention that the negligence of the mother of a sixteen-year-old girl, would be imputed to the daughter, injured as a result of the mother's having driven upon a railroad track, without looking for an approaching train, Judge Lamm, for the Supreme Court of Missouri, in Stotler v. Chicago, etc., R. Co. (200 Mo. 107; 98 S. W. Rep. 509), said: "The truth is, she was but a broken branch cast on the stream of the mother's judgment and volition, prone to be borne away on its current; and, under such circumstances, defendants cannot acquit themselves by pointing to the mother's fault; they are to be acquitted, if at all, alone upon the theory that they exercise due care themselves. * * * But we have been pointed to no soundly reasoned case going to the extent of holding that a girl of the age of Eugenia Stotler, driven by her mother upon a track (the record being silent upon her active participation in her mother's negligence) has been denied recovery under facts and circumstances such as are before us, and we take such doctrine to be bad law."

But the same court held the mother negligent, as matter of law, in driving on the railroad track, without looking or listening for an approaching train. Stotler v. Chicago, etc., R. Co., 204 Mo. 619; 103 S. W. Rep. 1, by Judge Fox.

A mother's act in permitting her child to play outdoors in the daytime, on public playgrounds, unattended, was not negligence so as to preclude recovery for injuries to such child caused by a live wire negligently left by defendants unguarded in a public place. Colorado Springs Electric Co. v. Soper (Colo. 1906), 88 Pac. Rep. 161.

Where a child in crossing a railroad track exercises the degree of care that an adult would under the same circumstances, the suggestion of negligence on the part of the parents imputable to the child is wholly negatived. Order 99 N. Y. S. 1103; 114 App. Div. 684, reversed. Serano v. New York Cent., etc., R. Co. (N. Y. 1907), 80 N. E. Rep. 1025; 188 N. Y. 156.

The negligence of a parent was held not to bar an action by a child of tender years, to sue in its own right, in the following cases: Williams v. Texas, etc., R. Co., 60 Texas 205; Albertson v. Keokuk, etc., R. Co., 48 Iowa 492; Louisville, etc., R. Co. v. Murphy, 9 Bush. (Ky.) 522; Wright v. Malden, etc., R. Co., 4 Allen 283; Pittsburg, etc., R. Co. v. Vining, 27 Ind. 573; Westbrook v. Mobile, etc., R. Co., 66 Miss. 560; 6 So. Pac. 321; Kay v. Pennsylvania R. Co., 65 Pa. St. 269; 3 Am. Rep. 628; Glassey v. Bentonville, etc., R. Co., 57 Pa. St. 172.

But in an action by the parent, for his own benefit, his negligence was held to bar the action, in the following cases: Bellefontaine, etc., R. Co. v. Snyder, 18 Ohio St. 399; 24 Ohio St. 670; O'Flaherty v. Union, etc., R. Co., 45 Mo. 70; Isabel v. Hannibal, etc., R. Co., 60 Mo. 475; Koons v. St. Louis, etc., R. Co., 65 Mo. 592; Hooker v. Chicago, etc., R. Co., 76 Wis. 542; Pittsburgh, etc., R. Co. v. Pearson,

72 Pa. St. 169; Pennsylvania R. Co. v. Böck, 93 Pa. St. 427; Smith v. Hestonville, etc., R. Co., 92 Pa. St. 450.

Contributory negligence of parents is a complete defense to an action for the alleged wrongful death of a child brought for the parents' benefit. Illinois Cent. R. Co. v. Warriner, 82 N. E. Rep. 246; 229 Ill. 91.

In the recent case of Cornovski v. St. Louis Transit Company (106 S. W. Rep 51), the Supreme Court of Missouri, in an opinion by Judge Lamm, approved an instruction that told the jury that in determining the negligence of the parents of a small child, which they had allowed to escape and go into the street, killed by a car on the defendant's railroad, the jury might take into consideration the " circumstances in life," of the parents. The cases in that State holding instructions with such a phrase proper charges to the jury were roundly criticised by the writer of the opinion, but the instruction with the criticised clause was none the less approved, because, as stated, the case was not a close one. Omitting the quotations in that part of the opinion of the court, applying to this instruction, the court, in the published opinion, said:

" Much might be said and well said against the use of the phrase ' circumstances in life ' in measuring the duty of a parent to a child where the question hinges on the parents' contributory negligence; and appellant's counsel have not been amiss or remiss in saying it. At first blush, the use of that phrase seems to involve a question of poverty or riches, of high or low social status, and to invite (or squint at the invitation of) proof of the fact in one case, that the parents are poor and needy, downcast and humble, and in another case that they are opulent and exalted, lolling in the lap of wealth and seated in a high place. Such a field of exploration in a jury trial in a negligence case is full of pitfalls and snares, insidiously appeals to class prejudice, and runs counter to the broad proposition that there is but one rule of law for the high and the low, for the rich and the poor. Doubtless the courts would shut the door on such proofs, if offered. Nevertheless, it may be said that those who of necessity are preoccupied with the toil of their own hands to earn their daily bread might not in a given case be guilty of negligence in allowing a little child to escape to the street of a city, when other persons because of other circumstances and conditions might be found by a jury to be remiss in a given case — due care being a care that adjusts itself automatically to the circumstances of the case." Dean v. Railroad, 199 Mo., loc. cit. 408; 97 S. W. Rep. 910.

" If a close case were here, we would be disinclined to follow the Czezewzka and the Levin cases. If such case were here involving a consideration of the phrase ' circumstances in life,' we would deem it

§ 1059. **When negligence imputed to children sui juris.**— The rule as to imputation of negligence to children, *sui juris,* injured when riding in a vehicle, because of the combined negligence of the driver and of some third person, is not different than the rule obtaining in the case of an adult stranger, and unless there are circumstances from which it could be found that the child had constituted the parent, guardian or driver of the vehicle its agent, or the child had itself co-operated in the negligent act of the driver which contributed to effect the injury, the negligence of the driver would not be imputed to the child, although *sui juris.*[18]

A daughter, *sui juris,* riding in a conveyance driven by her father and injured in a collision with a railroad train, is not chargeable with his neglect, in an action against the railroad company for damages for the injury, in the absence of some co-operation on her part, in his negligent act;[19] a child of seven years is held not to be chargeable with the negligence of the driver of a conveyance in which he was riding when injured;[20] a child of nine years is held not answerable for the negligence of the driver of a truck with whom he was permitted to ride;[21] the negligence of the

our duty to consider the question of its use open and serious; but in the case at bar its use must be held harmless error, if error at all. Here, there was no proof of plaintiffs' social or financial condition in life, as such. The evidence pictured to the jury the business and surroundings of plaintiffs and their home. In the evidence, the jury were told the facts upon which to base their verdict on the issue of contributory negligence. The employment and duties of the father and mother at the immediate time the child escaped to the street were before the jury."

[18] Stotler v. Chicago, etc., R. Co., 200 Mo. 107; 98 S. W. Rep. 509; Duval v. Atlantic, etc., R. Co., 134 N. C. 331; 46 S. E. Rep. 750; 101 Am. St. Rep. 830; 65 L. R. A. 722.

[19] Phillipps v. New York, etc., R. Co., 25 N. Y. S. R. 91; 6 N. Y. Supp. 621; 127 N. Y. 657; 27 N. E. Rep. 978; 38 N. Y. S. R. 675.

[20] Taylor, etc., R. Co. v. Warner (Texas), 60 S. W. Rep. 442.

[21] Robinson v. Metropolitan, etc., R. Co., 91 App. Div. 158; 86 N. Y.

driver of a sleigh is held not to be imputed to a girl of
thirteen years, riding with him by his invitation;[22] a girl
of fourteen years was held not precluded from recovering
from a railroad company for damages for an injury sustained while riding in a vehicle, as the guest of the owner,
who was admittedly negligent in approaching the crossing;[23]
and it has been held that a girl of sixteen was not chargeable
with the negligence of either her mother[24] or father,[25] in
negligently approaching a railroad crossing without looking
for trains, in the absence of some participation, by her, in
the negligent act, partly responsible for her injury.

But a child, *sui juris,* if participating in the negligent
act, contributing to cause the injury, will be denied a recovery, the same as an adult would be, in such cases.[26] A
daughter of years of discretion, who accompanies her deaf
father, to assist him in discovering approaching trains, is
held to be chargeable with his negligence in failing to look
for an approaching train, although he was driving at the
time of her injury, as she is jointly negligent with him, and
it is a case of co-operating negligence;[27] a blind son, who

Supp. 442; 179 N. Y. 593; 72 N. E. Rep. 1150. How this decision
can be reconciled with the rule, in New York, denying recovery in
the case of an infant of tender years, is apparently unexplainable.

[22] Bennett v. New York, etc., R. Co., 40 N. Y. S. R. 948; 16 N. Y.
Supp. 765; 133 N. Y. 563; 30 N. E. Rep. 1149.

[23] Hampel v. Detroit, etc., R. Co., 138 Mich. 1; 100 N. W. Rep. 1002;
108 Am. St. Rep. 275.

[24] Stotler v. Chicago, etc., R. Co., 200 Mo. 107; 98 S. W. Rep. 509;
St. Clair, etc., R. Co. v. Eadie, 43 Ohio St. 91; 1 N. E. Rep. 519; 54
Am. Rep. 802; Duval v. Atlantic, etc., R. Co., 134 N. C. 331; 46 S.
E. Rep. 750; 101 Am. St. Rep. 830; 65 L. R. A. 722.

[25] Scott v. Woods, 18 N. Y. Week. Dig. 441; Phillipps v. New York,
etc., R. Co., 25 N. Y. S. R. 91; 6 N. Y. Supp. 621; 127 N. Y. 657;
38 N. Y. S. R. 675; 27 N. E. Rep. 978.

[26] Slater v. Burlington, etc., R. Co., 71 Iowa 209; 32 N. W. Rep.
264; New York, etc., R. Co. v. Kistler, 66 Ohio St. 326; 64 N. E. Rep.
130.

[27] New York, etc., R. Co. v. Kistler, 66 Ohio St. 326; 64 N. E. Rep.
130.

DOCTRINE OF IMPUTED NEGLIGENCE.

voluntarily entrusted his safety to his father, was held chargeable with his negligence,[28] although this seems a harsh rule; a child of twelve years was held to be answerable for the negligence of a driver, in a New York case, and in some early Illinois cases,[29] mere children of eight or nine years were held to be precluded from a recovery for injuries due to the combined negligence of a driver of a vehicle in which they were riding and the wrongful act of a third person, because of the imputed negligence of the driver. But the precedents in the last two instances are not based upon sound reason and are counter to the weight of modern decisions.

[28] Johnson v. Gulf, etc., R. Co., 2 Texas Civ. App. 139; 21 S. W. Rep. 274.

[29] Toledo, etc., R. Co. v. Miller, 76 Ill. 278; Lake Erie, etc., R. Co. v. Pike, 31 Ill. App. 90.

In a recent New Jersey case, the negligence of a father in leaving a market wagon, so near a railway track, as to be struck by a passing car, was held not chargeable to his nineteen-year-old daughter, asleep on an improvised pallet in the wagon, in an action by her, for injuries sustained in the collision with the car which struck the wagon. Consolidated Traction Co. v. Behr, 59 N. J. L. 477; 37 Atl. Rep. 142.

A boy sixteen years of age was in a vehicle drawn by a horse driven by his uncle. The boy had no control over the movement of the vehicle. *Held*, that the negligence of the driver, causing a collision with a street car, was not imputable to the boy. Peterson v. St. Louis Transit Co. (Mo. 1906), 97 S. W. Rep. 860.

CHAPTER XLVI.

WHO DEEMED TRESPASSERS GENERALLY.

§ 1060. **Persons going upon railroad property.**— The proposition has been laid down by an eminent authority,[1] that " as a general rule, any one who goes upon the track or premises of a railroad company, except at a public crossing, or in a highway, without the invitation or license of the company, express or implied, is a trespasser." Under this definition one who goes upon a railroad track at other than a regular railroad crossing, and where the railroad company is required to fence its property, by statute, there being nothing to lead the railroad company to expect his presence, is held to be a trespasser.[2] One who goes upon a railroad

---

[1] 3 Elliott, on Railroads, § 1252, and cases cited.

[2] Barker v. Hannibal, etc., R. Co., 98 Mo. 50; 11 S. W. Rep. 254; 37 Am. & Eng. R. Cas. 292; Carrier v. Missouri Pacific Ry. Co., 175 Mo. 470; 74 S. W. Rep. 1002.

track at other than a highway crossing for purposes of his own convenience, is a trespasser.[3] One killed upon railroad property which is not open to the public and which is no part of a public highway, is held to be a trespasser, toward whom the company owes no duty, except to avoid wanton injury.[4] And, generally, except at stations and yards and at highway crossings, a railroad company is entitled to the exclusive use of its track and property; all persons who go thereon are trespassers and no recovery can be had for an injury to such class of wrongdoers, unless there is a wanton injury, after discovery of the presence of the trespasser.[5]

§ 1061. **Company entitled to clear track.**— Judge Lamm, for the Supreme Court of Missouri,[6] has recently, for that tribunal, so forcibly presented the reason and basis of the

[3] Candelaria v. Atchison, etc., R. Co. (N. M.), 27 Pac. Rep. 497; 48 Am. & Eng. R. Cas. 565.

[4] Collins v. New York, etc., R. Co., 24 N. Y. Supp. 1090; 55 N. Y. S. R. 82; 71 Hun 504.

[5] Houston, etc., R. Co. v. Boozer, 2 Tex. Unrep. Cas. 452. While a railroad company is chargeable with notice to guard travelers against injury at a highway crossing, and with corresponding duty in its operations there, no such notice or duty is implied in the case of a trespasser, not at or near a public way, as to whom the railroad company is only required to refrain from a willful or wanton injury. Southern Ry. Co. v. Fisk (U. S. C. C. A., Ill., 1908), 159 Fed. Rep. 373.

[6] Frye v. St. Louis, etc., Ry. Co., 200 Mo. 399, 400; 98 S. W. Rep. 566, citing Rine v. Chicago, etc., R. Co., 88 Mo. 392; Barker v. Hannibal, etc., R. Co., 98 Mo. 50; 11 S. W. Rep. 254; 37 Am. & Eng. R. Cas. 292; Sinclair v. Chicago, etc., R. Co., 133 Mo. 233; 34 S. W. Rep. 76; Reyburn v. Missouri Pacific Ry. Co., 187 Mo. 565; 86 S. W. Rep. 174.

Where there is no evidence showing permission to use the track of the company as a passageway, the necessity for the exclusive use by the company excludes any presumption of consent to its use for any other purpose. Bailey v. Lehigh Valley R. Co. (Pa. 1908), 69 Atl. Rep. 998; 220 Pa. St. 516.

rule which allows a railroad company to expect a clear track to run its trains upon, that we give the language used in the opinion: "Not only does the written law lie with that view, but such view is fortified by the reason of the thing. Thus, the right of way is acquired by purchase, or compensated for in damages, under the watchful eye of the courts, and the stringent application of constitutional and statutory safeguards, and the easement of railway companies in their tracks and rights of way, from the very necessity of the thing, is deemed, in the first instance, a paramount and exclusive one. For instance, trains run at great speed, both by day and by night. The property of shippers, the life and limbs of passengers and train men are all fettered to and bound up with the proposition that trains should have a clear track in the country and between crossings. If we gave way to any other view, we would open a flood gate for manifold wrongs, to the traveling public and public service corporations, to enter, and there would be 'fine' grinding in the mill, when the waters of that flood came in. If A and B at their own and against the defendant's will, may appropriate defendant's track for their private walking, then, by that token, they may also appropriate the track for the use of their horses, their asses, their sheep, and their swine and horned cattle. It ought not to be expected that we would so hold as to encourage a notion adding new dangers to the array now confronting train men and the traveling public, and thereby make a gazing stock of the law."

§ 1062. **Persons crossing track away from crossings.**— A railroad track is the exclusive property of the company owning it, on which no unauthorized person has a right to be for any purpose. If a person attempts to cross a track at other than the regular crossing, he does so at his own peril, unless the railroad company has consented, by acquiescence or otherwise, to the use of its track for such private purposes.[7] One injured by a train while crossing a track at a place not a highway, and where no inducement is held out to him by the company to cross, cannot maintain an action against the railroad company for the injury received.[8] The fact that others crossed the track at the same place where the plaintiff or injured person was injured, constitutes no excuse, in the absence of some invitation, express or implied, by the railroad company, to use the track for such purpose, or in the absence of proof that the place was known as a crossing.[9] And one crossing a track, in a city, at a point one hundred feet distant from the regular street crossing, at an opening in a severed train of cars, standing upon the track, is a trespasser, in the absence of evidence that such opening was made in the train for the purpose of allowing people to pass through.[10]

But a person who walks along a track laid along a public street is not a trespasser and may recover for a negligent injury, if without fault on his part.[11]   A person will not be regarded as a trespasser who is injured while crossing a track, where he had been accustomed to cross for a year or more, which fact was well known or permitted by the railroad company, or its employees.[12]   And where a railroad company has acquiesced, for a long time, in the public generally crossing its track by a trodden path, it must use reasonable care to protect a person who is crossing by such way and

[7] Galena, etc., R. Co. v. Jacobs, 20 Ill. 478.

[8] Wright v. Boston, etc., R. Co., 129 Mass. 440; 2 Am. & Eng. R. Cas. 121.

[9] Young v. Old Colony R. Co., 156 Mass. 178; 30 N. E. Rep. 560.

[10] Dahlstrom v. St. Louis, etc., R. Co., 96 Mo. 99; 8 S. W. Rep. 777; 35 Am. & Eng. R. Cas. 387.

[11] Ohio, etc., R. Co. v. Walker, 113 Ind. 196; 15 N. E. Rep. 234; 32 Am. & Eng. R. Cas. 121; Louisville, etc., R. Co. v. Phillipps, 112 Ind. 59.

[12] Illinois, etc., R. Co. v. Dick, 91 Ky. 434; 15 S. W. Rep. 665.

whether the company knew of such ᛁ
tinued for a long time, and whether or
will be held to be a jury issue, whei
flicting.[13]

§ 1063. Persons walking on tracks.·

not highways for general travel, and
matter of right, convert them into cc
except at public crossings, and then
crossing the track, with no undue tar·
tional declaration, making railroads
does not mean that they are such for ᛁ
ers.[15] The ordinary rule is, theref·
who walk on railroad tracks, at other ·

[13] Larkin v. New York, etc., R. Co., 46 N.
Supp. 479; 138 N. Y. 634; 33 N. E. Rep. 1θ
etc., R. Co., 104 N. Y. 362; Swift v. Staten
645; 33 N. Y. S. R. 604; LeMay v. Missouri
361; 16 S. W. Rep. 1049.

While a person may, for the purpose of m·
do so without becoming a trespasser, if he
along it at a place where he is not entitled to
and the company owes him no duty to k·
Birmingham Ry., etc., Co. v. Jones (Ala. 190᛬

A person is not *ipso facto*, a trespasser, 'in
railroad company, laid, upon grade, in a ·
crosses at any point where it is convenient for
going to the regular street crossing. Baltimor·
land, 176 U. S. 232; 20 Sup. Ct. Rep. 280; ·
Union, etc., R. Co., 126 Iowa, 13; 101 N. W.

Where the evidence showed that plaintiff w
he crossed was a side track, on which cars w
without bell or whistle, and the space between
to cross the track, was barely wide enough t·
through, his own negligence must be deemed
his injury. Gurley v. Missouri Pacific Ry. C᛬
W. Rep. 11.

[14] Mobile, etc., R. Co. v. Blakely, 59 Ala. 47ᛁ
[15] Hyde v. Missouri Pacific Ry. Co., 110 Mo. ᛬
54 Am. & Eng. R. Cas. 157.

or places dedicated for public use, are trespassers.[16] One walking along the track for his own convenience is a trespasser and has not the same rights as a passenger, or one using a public crossing. Mere proof of ordinary negligence will not enable him to recover for an injury on the track but he must show that the injury was wanton or willful and that he used due care for his own safety. And this rule is held to apply, although the railroad company has acquiesced in the use of its track as a footpath, for persons so using it are but licensees, without business with the company, and there is no duty owing, except not to wantonly injure them.[17] The fact that the railroad company does not actually prevent people from walking on its track, does not alter their status as trespassers, or change the relative rights and obligations of the railroad company and the people so walking.[18] The right of the public and the railroad company are equal, at street crossings; but where the track is built along the street, the right of the railroad company is superior to that of the traveling public in the use of its track.[19] And one using a railroad track, laid on the surface of the ground, in an

[16] Cook v. Central R. Co., 67 Ala. 533; Savannah, etc., R. Co. v. Meadows, 95 Ala. 137; 10 So. Rep. 141; Toomey v. Southern, etc., R. Co., 86 Cal. 374; 24 Pac. Rep. 1074; Mulherrin v. Delaware, etc., R. Co., 81 Pa. St. 375; Baltimore, etc., R. Co. v. State, 62 Md. 487; 50 Am. Rep. 233; Palmer v. Chicago, etc., R. Co., 112 Ind. 253; Central, etc., R. Co. v. Brinson, 70 Ga. 207; 19 Am. & Eng. R. Cas. 42; Masser v. Chicago, etc., R. Co., 68 Iowa 602; 27 N. W. Rep. 776; Barker v. Hannibal, etc., R. Co., 98 Mo. 50; 11 S. W. Rep. 254; 37 Am. & Eng. R. Cas. 292; Frye v. St. Louis, etc., R. Co., 200 Mo. 377; 98 S. W. Rep. 566.

[17] Illinois, etc., R. Co. v. Godfrey, 71 Ill. 500; Illinois, etc., R. Co. v. Noble, 142 Ill. 578.

[18] Blanchard v. Lake Shore, etc., R. Co., 126 Ill. 416; 18 N. E. Rep. 799.

[19] Zimmerman v. Hannibal, etc., R. Co., 71 Mo. 476; 2 Am. & Eng. R. Cas. 191; Glass v. Memphis, etc., R. Co., 94 Ala. 581; 10 So. Rep. 215.

alley, is held to be a trespasser, to whom no duty is owing, except to avoid a wanton injury.[20]

But if the track and right of way of a railroad company are habitually used by the public for a way to the city streets, and gates in the fence enable people to pass onto the right of way, one walking upon the track, on his way to the street, is not a trespasser.[21]   One is not a trespasser who for a long time has been accustomed to use the track with the railroad company's tacit permission.[22]   A passenger will not be held to be a trespasser who walks upon the railroad track, where this is the accustomed thing to do.[23]   And it is held, in a New York case,[24] that one who goes upon a railroad track in order to save the life of a young child, is not to be deemed a trespasser.

§ 1064. **Use of track by pedestrians at nighttime.**— Although the evidence in a given case might show an acquiescence or tacit permission in the use of a railroad track

[20] Montgomery v. Alabama, etc., R. Co., 97 Ala. 305; 12 So. Rep. 170; Louisville, etc., R. Co. v. Hairston, 97 Ala. 351; 12 So. Rep. 299.

[21] Lynch v. St. Joseph, etc., R. Co., 111 Mo. 601; 19 S. W. Rep. 1114.

[22] Guenther v. St. Louis, etc., R. Co., 108 Mo. 18; 18 S. W. Rep. 846.

[23] Central R. Co. v. Thompson, 76 Ga. 770.

[24] Spooner v. Delaware, etc., R. Co., 115 N. Y. 22; 21 N. E. Rep. 696; 39 Am. & Eng. R. Cas. 599.

Where one, for his own convenience, walks on the main track of a railroad, when he knows that a train is about due, without first ascertaining whether the train has in fact passed by, and fails to look and listen for an approaching train, his conduct constitutes negligence *per se*.   Chesapeake Beach Ry. Co. v. Donahue (Md. 1908), 68 Atl. Rep. 507.

Where a licensee was killed while walking along a railroad track, he was himself bound to observe a reasonable lookout for his own safety and exercise reasonable care, notwithstanding the duty imposed on the train operatives to observe a reasonable lookout to prevent injury to him.   Teakle v. San Pedro, etc., R. Co. (Utah, 1907), 90 Pac. Rep. 402.

in the daytime, sufficient to hold those so using the track to be licensees, as distinguished from trespassers, this use would not, by analogy, justify the use of the track in the night-time by pedestrians, without an express or implied consent to the use of the track at such time.

In a recent Missouri case,[25] this question was considered by the Supreme Court and where the evidence showed occasional use of the track in the daytime, but the use being made of it at the time of the injury sued for was at night, the court said: "We are pointed to no case going as far as plaintiff insists we should go, in order to sustain the judgment; and, confining our conclusions on this branch of the case to the precise facts of the record, that conclusion is that at the place Mr. Frye was struck by defendant's engine, and at the time, to-wit, in the nighttime, it was a place and a time where defendant not only had the right, but it was entitled, to expect a clear track. Hence it was a place defendant owed plaintiff no duty to look for him; and, hence, in order to recover, plaintiff must show that he was actually seen by the engineer in time to have warned him and thus avoided the injury."

§ 1065. **When company consents to general use of track.**— The authorities are generally agreed that where a railroad company consents to the general use of its track as a passway for pedestrians, it owes them the duty of keeping a lookout to avoid injuries to them, but the question is ofttimes a difficult one to determine whether or not the evidence of user by the public is sufficient to amount to a license to so use the track, or the people so using it will be held to be trespassers. The reasoning of the court as to the quantum of evidence sufficient to show such general user, as to amount

[25] This decision is by Judge Lamm and will be found to be an interesting case, ably disposed of. Frye v. St. Louis, etc., Ry. Co., 200 Mo. 405; 98 S. W. Rep. 566.

to a license, in a recent Missouri case,[26] is so pertinent that
it is given here.   Considering this question, the court, speaking through Judge Lamm, said: "In a given case there
might be such scant, or neutral evidence of public user of a
portion of a track — mere sporadic instances thereof — that
a court, as a matter of law, would determine that the employees of a railroad company charged with the running of
a locomotive engine, had no duty to look and see.   In such
case, unless they did see the dangerous exposure of a person
on the track and in time to avoid injuring him by the
use of ordinary care, the court would take the case from the
jury.   On the other hand, there might be a case where the
public user of a portion of the track by pedestrians was so
constant, so pronounced, so manifest and uncontradicted that
there could be no two opinions about it among reasonable
men, and the court, as a matter of law, might assume that
locomotive operatives owed a duty to the public to be on the
lookout there.   Then, too, there might be a case lying between said extremes and in our opinion this is one, where
the use by the public of the track was of such sort that it
became a mixed question of law and fact whether those running a locomotive engine had reason to anticipate the presence of people, and in such case that issue should be submitted to the jury, as a fact to be determined by it.   Liability, in each instance, is predicated of knowledge or notice
of the user.   Such notice may be proved by the existence
of paths, well worn by human feet, and by gaps, stiles and
gates, appurtenant to such path, by the long-continued going to and fro of people, more or less constantly, and by
the proved presence of schools, places of recreation, etc., and

[26] Eppstein v. Missouri Pacific Ry. Co., 197 Mo. 734; 94 S. W.
Rep. 967.

See, also, LeMay v. Missouri Pacific Ry. Co., 105 Mo. 361; 16 S. W.
Rep. 1049; Morgan v. Wabash R. Co., 159 Mo. 262; 60 S. W. Rep. 195;
Clem v. Wabash R. Co., 72 Mo. App. 433.

the use of the track by visiting pedestrians and habitues, all of which elements are presented in this case to an extent of such significance as made the issue, in our opinion, one for the triers of fact to decide."

But many cases hold that however general the use of a railroad track as a footway may be, unless there is evidence of consent in such use, by the railroad company, those using the track will be none the less trespassers, toward whom there is no active duty to keep a lookout to avoid injuring them.[27]

[27] Carr v. Missouri Pacific Ry. Co., 195 Mo. 214; 92 S. W. Rep. 874; Glass v. Memphis, etc., R. Co., 94 Ala. 581; 10 So. Rep. 215; Eggman v. St. Louis, etc., R. Co., 47 Ill. App. 507; Illinois, etc., R. Co. v. Hetherington, 83 Ill. 510; Spicer v. Chicago, etc., R. Co., 34 W. Va. 514; 12 S. E. Rep. 553; Finlayson v. Chicago, etc., R. Co., 1 Dill. (U. S.) 579.

In an action against a railroad company for injuries received while walking on defendant's track, an allegation in the petition, " and which track for many years pedestrians to and from the said town of C. and the said station and depot of defendant at said town of C. had been accustomed to use as a road or footpath by the forbearance and tacit consent of the defendant," sufficiently showed user of the track by pedestrians. Ahnefeld v. Wabash R. Co. (Mo. 1908), 111 S. W. Rep. 95.

Where a railway company maintains yards and switch tracks along docks and near to a much traveled thoroughfare of a city, and persons have been in the habit for a long time of walking along these tracks and up to this thoroughfare to the knowledge and with the acquiescence of the company, and without notice or warning to the contrary, a person who, while walking carefully along these tracks at a point near the thoroughfare on a dark night, is struck by a locomotive backing down upon him without warning, may recover from the company for his injuries thus sustained. Baltimore, etc., Ry. v. Campbell, 28 Ohio Cir. Ct. R. 662.

While through express train men naturally know nothing of a private path across the track near a way station, the company is charged with knowledge that at such station is a town of four hundred or five hundred people, and that its depot is approached by persons walking along the track in both directions, there being no other adequate way to get to it, and so must be held to know that this is a place at which the presence of persons on the track might reasonably be anticipated.

§ 1066. **License to use track not established by occasional user.**— That a mere occasional or special use of a railroad track will not amount to a license to the general traveling public to use it, has been decided by a Missouri case,[28] already adverted to, wherein it is said: " No cases give rise to more perplexity than cases of the character now under consideration. Men, in flippant and defiant disregard and in the teeth of the protest of railroad companies, take their lives in their hands and unconcernedly walk, in the nighttime on the piked-up paths of railroad tracks and thus seek to avoid the inconvenience of travel on dirt roads in muddy weather — applying to railroad tracks the doctrine of the right to travel *extra viam* when the roads are founderous, and, when injured, seek the courts for relief. * * * It must be evident that railroad companies are, in a sense, defenseless against such misappropriation of their tracks by footmen. They fence the right of way, they protect the track by cattle guards, and, in this instance, defendant kept up notices and signs warning the public and protesting against their use of the track. We are brought then, face to face with this asking proposition: what more can a railroad company do, or should it be required to do, to protect

Louisville, etc., R. Co. v. McNary's Adm'r (Ky. 1908), 108 S. W. Rep. 898.

In an action against a railroad for injuries to a pedestrian using the track, evidence of witnesses and photographs as to the use of the track as a roadbed by the public as pedestrians, and as to defendant's knowledge and means of knowledge of such use, was admissible to show whether or not the track was constantly used by the public, as bearing on the question whether plaintiff was a mere trespasser or a licensee. Missouri, etc., Ry. Co. v. Williams (Tex. Civ. App. 1908), 109 S. W. Rep. 1126.

[28] Frye v. St. Louis, etc., Ry. Co., 200 Mo. 402; 98 S. W. Rep. 566.

The mere passive acquiescence by a railroad company in the occasional use of its track as a footpath did not create a new duty or impose additional obligation on its part to provide against the danger of accident to trespassers walking along on the track. Chesapeake Beach Ry. Co. v. Donahue (Md. 1908), 68 Atl. Rep. 507.

itself against appropriation of its track by footmen, who are *sui juris,* than was done in the case at bar? Shall it employ armed guards? Shall it build fences that cannot be scaled, crawled through or broken down? Shall it plant spikes in its cattle guards to the danger of its own employees? Or use pitfalls? Or what can it do? We confess our inability to answer.

In our opinion, in a country district, away from congested population, under the facts of this record, defendant did all that could fairly be asked of it, when it inclosed its right of way and posted and kept up the signs shown in evidence."

§ 1067. **Persons walking on bridges or trestles.**— As a general rule, a railway company has the exclusive right to occupy, use and enjoy not only its railroad track, where constructed on the dirt embankments, but also its bridges and trestles and such exclusive right is necessary not only for the operation of the road, but for the safety of passengers and employees; and any person going upon or walking across the bridge or trestle of a railroad company, without the consent of the company, is held, in law, to be a wrongdoer, and therefore, a trespasser.[29] In a Kansas case,[30] where a woman was injured while walking across a bridge and trestle, the court, speaking through Horton, C. J., said: "Now, as the point where the plaintiff's wife was injured was not on the surface of a public highway or traveled street, but upon the trestlework or embankment of the defendant's roadbed, for all the purposes of this case, the

[29] Central, etc., R. Co. v. Vaughan, 93 Ala. 209; 9 So. Rep. 468; Mason v. Missouri Pacific Ry. Co., 27 Kansas 83; 41 Am. Rep. 405; 6 Am. & Eng. R. Cas. 1; State v. Philadelphia, etc., R. Co. (Md.), 15 Am. & Eng. R. Cas. 481; Beiser v. Chesapeake, etc., R. Co., 29 Ky. Law Rep. 249; 92 S. W. Rep. 928; Adams v. St. Louis, etc., Ry. Co., 83 Ark. 300; 103 S. W. Rep. 725.

[30] Mason v. Missouri Pacific Ry. Co., 27 Kansas 83; 41 Am. Rep. 405; 6 Am. & Eng. R. Cas. 1.

railway company had the exclusive right to occupy, use and enjoy such trestlework and embankment; therefore, the instruction that the railway company was liable only for such negligence so gross as to amount to wantonness was a correct declaration of the law to the jury. The plaintiff's wife climbed up the embankment and attempted to cross the trestlework or bridge without the consent of the company, and at her own peril, and the husband can recover only for injuries done to her for such negligence of the employees of the company as was so gross as to amount to wantonness."

But where a bridge has been habitually and constantly used for many years by people in the locality, as a footpath, without any objection or warning by the company that it should not be so used, persons walking upon it are held to be licensees, and not mere trespassers.[31]

[31] Hooker v. Chicago, etc., R. Co., 76 Wis. 542; 44 N. W. Rep. 1085; 41 Am. & Eng. R. Cas. 498.

But the mere fact that a railroad company has notice that a large crowd of picnickers are near the bridge or trestle of the railroad company will not be sufficient to charge it with notice of their intention to trespass upon its bridge and trestle, so as to obligate it to keep a lookout for them on the bridge. Smith's Adm'r v. Illinois Central R. Co., 28 Ky. Rep. 723; 90 S. W. Rep. 254.

The fact that persons walked upon a railroad trestle, however frequently, did not render them other than trespassers. Adams v. St. Louis, etc., Ry. Co. (Ark. 1907), 103 S. W. Rep. 725.

Where a railroad trestle is commonly used by the public as a footpath with the company's acquiescence, the company will be considered as having licensed the public to so use it. Texas Midland R. R. v. Byrd (Tex. Civ. App. 1908), 110 S. W. Rep. 199.

The employees of a railroad company owe to a trespasser on a trestle, only the duty to use all the means in their power, on discovery of his peril, to· avoid injuring him. Shaw v. Missouri Pacific Ry. Co., 104 Mo. 648; 16 S. W. Rep. 842; Reardin v. Missouri Pacific Ry. Co., 114 Mo. 384; 21 S. W. Rep. 731.

If a trespasser on a trestle could be discovered by the exercise of reasonable care, a failure to discover him, in time to avoid his injury,

§ 1068. **Persons on right of way.**— The right of way of a railroad company is its exclusive property, upon which no unauthorized person has a right to be. Any one who travels upon such right of way as a footway and not for any business with the railroad company is a wrongdoer and a trespasser; and the mere acquiescence of the railroad company in such user would not give the right to use the track, or create any obligation in favor of such a trespasser for special protection.[32]

But where the right of way of a railroad company has been in constant use by travelers on foot for more than twenty years, without objection, it is a question for the jury to determine whether or not the railroad company ratified such user. Such user, if acquiesced in, while not establishing a public highway upon the right of way, would relieve the persons using it, with its consent, from being treated as trespassers by the railroad company.[33]

was held sufficient to render the company liable in Clark v. Wilmington, etc., R. Co., 109 No. Car. 430; 14 S. E. Rep. 43; 48 Am. & Eng. R. Cas. 546.

[32] Baltimore, etc., R. Co. v. State, 62 Md. 479; 50 Am. Rep. 233; 19 Am. & Eng. R. Cas. 83; Masser v. Chicago, etc., R. Co., 68 Iowa 602; Toomey v. Southern Pacific R. Co., 86 Cal. 374.

[33] Davis v. Chicago, etc., R. Co., 58 Wis. 646; 17 N. W. Rep. 406; 46 Am. Rep. 667; 15 Am. & Eng. R. Cas. 424.

A person went on a railroad right of way to look for his cattle, and was struck by a train. The train approached him for more than seven hundred yards in plain view. He was in full possession of his faculties and of good hearing. *Held*, that he was a trespasser and guilty of contributory negligence as a matter of law, casting on his administrator suing for his death the burden of showing that the employees in charge of the train saw him in time to have avoided the injury and negligently failed to use proper means to do so. Chicago, etc., Ry. Co. v. Bunch (Ark. 1907), 102 S. W. Rep. 369.

Ordinarily the mere acquiescence by a railroad in the use by the public of its right of way does not amount to permission, and the public using the way are trespassers. Alabama Great Southern R. Co. v. Godfrey (Ala. 1908), 47 So. Rep. 185.

§ 1069. **Persons frequenting depot grounds or yards of the company.**— All the property of a railroad company, including its depot and adjacent yards and grounds, is its private property, on which no one is invited, or can claim a right to enter, except those who have business with the railroad.[34] If a passenger goes to a part of the premises of the railroad company, not intended for the use of the passengers, he is to be deemed a trespasser, where he could be charged with notice that he was upon private property.[35] One who seeks shelter from a storm under the roof of what had formerly been a freight house, but has been abandoned and neglected, and who sustains injury as a result of attempting to avoid the falling roof, is a trespasser.[36] And all may be classed as within this category who do not come upon the company's premises for some business with it, or those who are transacting business with the company.[37]

But one who is removing freight from a freight car is not to be deemed a trespasser, toward whom no duty is owing to avoid injuring him.[38] One who is upon the side track of a railroad company, to seek employment from a stock shipper, in feeding and watering his stock, is held to be there upon business directly connected with the operation of the road.[39] And one using a private crossing of a railroad company to haul hay to a person maintaining a hay

[34] Montgomery, etc., R. Co. v. Thompson, 77 Ala. 448; 54 Am. Rep. 72.

[35] A passenger who went, uninvited to a freight platform and was injured, was held to be a trespasser, in Gunderman v. Missouri, etc., R. Co., 58 Mo. App. 370.

[36] Lary v. Cleveland, etc., R. Co., 78 Ind. 323; 41 Am. Rep. 572; 3 Am. & Eng. R. Cas. 498.

[37] Montgomery, etc., R. Co. v. Thompson, 77 Ala. 448; 54 Am. Rep. 72.

[38] Watson v. Wabash, etc., R. Co., 66 Iowa 164; 23 N. W. Rep. 380; 19 Am. & Eng. R. Cas. 114.

[39] Shelby v. Cincinnati, etc., R. Co., 85 Ky. 224; 3 S. W. Rep 157.

barn on the company's right of way, and who ships out hay over its road, is held to have such an indirect status or business relation with the railroad company, as to entitle him to claim a duty to keep the premises in a reasonably safe condition for use.[40]

§ 1070. **Persons wrongfully upon train.**— If a person obtains entrance to a train by false representations, with the intent wrongfully to avoid paying his railroad fare, he will be deemed a trespasser, toward whom no duty will be owing, except not to wantonly injure him, and in case of an injury

[40] Lowenstein v. Missouri Pacific Ry. Co. (Mo. App.), 117 Mo. App. 371; 115 S. W. Rep. 2.

In an action against a railroad for injuries to a person visiting the depot to transact business, evidence *held* to authorize judgment for plaintiff. Central of Georgia Ry. Co. v. Hunter (Ga. 1907), 58 S. E. Rep. 154.

Where a person was injured in the nighttime while on a lawn adjacent to a depot platform, by being tripped by wires stretched across the lawn, the failure of the railroad to sufficiently light the place was material on the issue of its negligence. Banderob v. Wisconsin Cent. Ry. Co. (Wis. 1907), 113 N. W. Rep. 738.

In an action against a railroad company for personal injuries sustained by a trespasser in defendant's yards, the burden is on plaintiff to show that he was discovered by defendant's employees in time for them to have avoided the injury. Whitney v. Texas Cent. R. Co. (Tex. Civ. App. 1908), 110 S. W. Rep. 70.

A consignee engaged in unloading a car placed on an unloading track is on the railway premises by the invitation of the company, and he is not compelled to be on the lookout for unusual dangers but the employees of the company engaged in switching cars on the unloading track must give warning of the approach of cars. Lovell v. Kansas City Southern Ry. Co. (Mo. App. 1906), 97 S. W. Rep. 193.

The duty of a railroad company to anticipate the presence of persons about its stations when a train is arriving, and to exercise ordinary care for their safety, does not extend to persons passing between cars or under or over them, in the absence of an express or implied invitation on the part of the railroad company for them to do so. Brackett's Adm'r v. Louisville, etc., R. Co. (Ky. 1908), 111 S. W. Rep. 710.

from a derailment of the train, t
very instant that a person in a
fare and to comply with the reaso
operating the road, he becomes a
who entered the train as a passen
and becomes boisterous, he becom
removed from the train.[43]   A pe
pass, not transferable, issued to
represents himself to be, is a tres
a limited train, who, after notic
his station, refuses to pay his far
leave the train and take a train v
tion, is a trespasser.[45]   And a
ejected from the train and immed
trespasser, for if the first expulsioi
submit to it and depend upon
should not enter the train after fo

But one permitted to ride on a t:
permission of the conductor, is n
he may not come within the class k
person who enters the wrong train
any intent to avoid payment of his
And one who enters a train and

41 Handley v. Houston, etc., R. Co., 2
42 Lake Erie, etc., R. Co. v. Mays, 4 I
1106; Moore v. Columbia, etc., R. Co., 3
781; 58 Am. & Eng. R. Cas. 493.
43 Louisville, etc., R. Co. v. Johnson, 9:
47 Am. & Eng. R. Cas. 611.
44 Toledo, etc., R. Co. v. Beggs, 85 Ill.
45 Atchison, etc., R. Co. v. Gants, 38 K
34 Am. & Eng. R. Cas. 290.
46 North Chicago, etc., R. Co. v. Olds, 4(
47 Gradin v. St. Paul, etc., R. Co., 30 Mi
11 Am. & Eng. R. Cas. 644.
48 Lake Shore, etc., R. Co. v. Rosenzwe
Rep. 545; 26 Am. & Eng. R. Cas. 489.

there are no vacant seats, the train is going at a rapid rate of speed, is not a trespasser, because he refuses to pay his fare until a seat is provided for him, as it is the duty of the railroad company to furnish him a seat and he need not pay his fare until provided with one.[49]

§ 1071. **Persons wrongfully riding upon freight trains.**— A person wrongfully riding upon a freight car, in a freight train, is not a passenger, and the railroad company owes him no duty except to avoid a wanton injury to him.[50] One who had purchased no ticket and paid no fare, who goes to a caboose and enters it without the knowledge or consent of those

[49] Hardenberg v. St. Paul, etc., R. Co., 39 Minn. 3; 38 N. W. Rep. 625; 12 Am. St. Rep. 610; 34 Am. & Eng. R. Cas. 359.

In Lake Shore, etc., R. Co. v. Rosenzweig (113 Pa. St. 519), the court, speaking of the status of a person on a limited train, by mistake, said: "His entering the car was not like the case of a man entering the dwelling house of another unbidden. One is a public conveyance, the other is private and the occupant's home. A passenger who enters a car by mistake is not a trespasser who may be sued as such when he commits no actual injury — he has rights other than those of a trespasser."

One who seeks to board a train at a point where there is no station, and at which he had no right to be, takes his chances of injury, and cannot recover in the absence of wantonness, willfulness, or gross neglect. Ahern v. Chicago, etc., R. Co., 124 Ill. App. 36.

One who induces the conductor of a train to permit him to ride, in known violation of the company's rules, was held to be a trespasser, in McVeety v. St. Paul, etc., R. Co., 45 Minn. 268.

Persons procuring transportation by fraud were held to be but trespassers, in Louisville, etc., R. Co. v. Thompson, 107 Ind. 442; McNamara v. Great Northern R. Co., 61 Minn. 296; 63 N. W. Rep. 726; Condran v. Chicago, etc., R. Co., 67 Fed. Rep. 522; Williams v. Mobile, etc., R. Co. (Miss.), 19 So. Rep. 90.

A person who entered the train with the intention of paying his fare, but who does not do so, and when requested, fails to pay his fare, and on invitation to leave the train, refuses to leave, was held to be a trespasser, in Atchison, etc., R. Co. v. Brown, 2 Kansas App. 604; 42 Pac. Rep. 588; 2 Am. & Eng. R. Cas. (N. S.) 113.

[50] Planz v. Boston, etc., R. Co., 157 Mass. 377; 32 N. E. Rep. 356.

in charge of the train, is not a passenger, and if he sustains injury, there is no liability therefor, unless the train is a regular passenger train, or accustomed to carry passengers.[51] If a person is informed by the conductor of a freight train that the company's rules forbid passengers to ride on such train, and such person nevertheless enters the train, he is not a passenger and there is no liability, if he is injured by the mere negligence of the railroad company.[52] And the payment of fare or the offer to pay, to one known to have no authority to receive it, is not a payment that will make the person so paying, a passenger.[53]

But where by special contract for the transportation of horses, or other stock, a person is permitted to travel on a freight train, to attend to the stock, so shipped under contract, he is not a trespasser, but a passenger.[54] And a person riding on a freight train with the consent of the conductor, is not a trespasser, although the train was not intended to be operated for passengers and though the conductor was without authority to permit such person to ride.[55] This rule, however, is not of universal application, and it is held, in some jurisdictions, that a person so riding on a freight train, is a trespasser, toward whom no duty of active vigilance is due.[56]

[51] Haase v. Oregon, etc., R. Co., 19 Oregon 354; 24 Pac. Rep. 238; 44 Am. & Eng. R. Cas. 360.

[52] Gulf, etc., R. Co. v. Campbell, 76 Texas 174; 13 S. W. Rep. 19; 41 Am. & Eng. R. Cas. 100; Robertson v. New York, etc., R. Co., 22 Barb. (N. Y.) 91; Virginia Midland R. Co. v. Roach, 83 Va. 375; 5 S. E. Rep. 175; 34 Am. & Eng. R. Cas. 271; Chicago, etc., R. Co. v. Michie, 83 Ill. 427; Files v. Boston, etc., R. Co., 149 Mass. 204; 21 N. E. Rep. 311.

[53] Cleveland, etc., R. Co. v. Bertrand, 11 Ohio St. 457.

[54] Lawson v. Chicago, etc., R. Co., 64 Wis. 447; 24 N. W. Rep. 618; 54 Am. Rep. 634; 21 Am. & Eng. R. Cas. 249; Carroll v. Missouri Pacific Ry. Co., 88 Mo. 239; 57 Am. Rep. 382.

[55] Alabama, etc., R. Co. v. Yarlbrough, 83 Ala. 238; 3 So. Rep. 447; 3 Am. St. Rep. 715.

[56] Canadian Pacific R. Co. v. Johnson, 6 Montr. L. R. 213.

§ 1072. **Persons wrongfully riding on special trains, cars or engines.**— A railroad company providing sufficient trains and cars to accommodate the traveling public, has a lawful right to run extra or special trains, not open to the general traveling public, and if such trains are run, persons knowingly taking passage upon such trains are trespassers, toward whom no duty of active vigilance is due. A person riding on a pay car, without permission of the employees or officers of the railroad company, was held to be a trespasser, in one case; [57] one riding on a timber train, not used to carry passengers, and injured in a collision, was without remedy, as he was a mere trespasser upon such a train.[58] A like status attaches to one riding upon an engine, after notice that such conduct is forbidden by a rule of the railroad company.[59] And one riding a railroad velocipede without

Where plaintiff, upon the invitation of his brother, a switch brakeman, attempted to ride upon a portion of a freight train being switched in railway yards, and was injured by a sudden movement of the cars, he could not recover; he being neither a passenger nor a licensee, but a trespasser, and the brakeman having no authority as such to bind the company by any agreement for plaintiff's carriage on such train. Skirvin v. Louisville, etc., R. Co. (Ky. 1907), 100 S. W. Rep. 308.

A petition alleging that an engineer saw boys riding on an oil tank car on the narrow margin between the tank and the edge of the car and knew that their position was one of great peril and that an ordinary jerk of the car would throw them from the same, and that the engineer suddenly reversed the engine, whereby one of the boys was thrown off and run over, states a cause of action. Charleston, etc., Ry. Co. v. Johnson (Ga. App. 1907), 57 S. E. Rep. 1064.

A person who wrongfully entered a freight car, loaded with railroad iron, in a construction train, without the knowledge of the employees, was held to be a trespasser, in Berry v. Missouri, etc., R. Co., 124 Mo. 223; 25 S. W. Rep. 229.

[57] Southwestern R. Co. v. Singleton, 66 Ga. 252.

[58] Illinois, etc., R. Co. v. Meacham, 91 Tenn. 428; 19 S. W. Rep. 232.

[59] Robertson v. New York, etc., R. Co., 22 Barb. (N. Y.) 91; Chicago, etc., R. Co. v. Michie, 83 Ill. 427; Files v. Boston, etc., R. Co., 149 Mass. 204; 21 N. E. Rep. 311.

obtaining the consent of the offic
is a trespasser, and in the event
on such a vehicle of the compa₁
the injury, in the absence of ₁
causing the injury.[60]

§ 1073. **Whether children, pl
trespassers.**— Because of the pec₁
tables, constructed for the purp₀
cars, and the attractive nature of
to use them for merry-go-round₅
been held liable for injuries to ch
ing on turntables, unless reasona

[60] Craig v. Mt. Carbon R. Co., 45 Fed.
In an action against a railroad com₁
complaint simply charged that plaintiff
pose of setting a brake to prevent it fr
car which he was loading; that he wa
fendant's employees when they were one
negligently made a flying switch, wher
thirty miles an hour, collided with the b
that plaintiff was rightfully engaged in
that the circumstances were such that def
perceived that their act would put plai₁
could not escape. *Held*, that the comp
it did not show that a duty to exercise c
Judgment, 82 N. E. Rep. 1135, reverse
Yeager (Ind. 1908), 83 N. E. Rep. 742.
Where boys of immature years had]
yards, and had persistently ridden on f₁
of the employees of the company, it was
use ordinary care to prevent injuring th
stop the custom, and the fact that a boy
train and was injured did not *ipso fact*
etc., R. Co. v. Buch, 102 S. W. Rep. 12₄
Where defendant's section men neglige₁
on a hand car in a dangerous position,
off, and was injured, there was no evi₀
conduct on the part of such employees
Daugherty v. Chicago, etc., Ry. Co. (Iow₃

lock or otherwise secure the turntable, so that it could not be
pushed around.

Two conflicting and irreconcilable lines of decisions have
developed on this question, however, and the courts, as well
as the text writers, are divided as to whether any duty is owing by a railroad company toward trespassing children, playing on such machines.

The weight of authority perhaps favors the proposition
that the railroad company will be liable for an injury to a
child, received while playing on a turntable, if no reasonable
care had been used to lock or otherwise secure the turntable
against such use.[61]

The reason for the rule of nonliability, however, com-
mends itself, for not only is there an absence of any relation,
out of which a duty could arise, unless implied by law, toward a trespassing child, upon such a necessary appliance,
but the doctrine of the maxim, *Sic utere tuo ut alienum
non laedas,* ought not to be applicable, for it is only the legal
rights of others that one is bound not to disturb; there is
no rule of law that one may not use his own, in a lawful
manner, although some one else may not be wholly secure
against injury, if he wrongfully intermeddles with ones property, but the inhibition of the law extends to injuring others

[61] Sioux City, etc., R. Co. v. Stout, 17 Wall. 657; 21 L. Ed. 745;
O'Malley v. St. Paul, etc., R. Co., 43 Minn. 289; 45 N. W. Rep. 440;
Edgington v. Burlington, etc., R. Co., 116 Iowa 410; 90 N. W. Rep.
95; 57 L. R. A. 561; Nagle v. Missouri Pacific Ry. Co., 75 Mo. 653;
42 Am. Rep. 418; Kansas City, etc., R. Co. v. Fitzsimmons, 22 Kansas
686; 31 Am. Rep. 203; Chicago, etc., R. Co. v. Krahlenbuhl, 65 Neb.
889; 91 N. W. Rep. 880; 59 L. R. A. 920; Gulf, etc., R. Co. v. Mc-
Whirter, 77 Texas 356; 14 S. W. Rep. 26; 19 Am. St. Rep. 755; Ilwaco,
etc., R. Co. v. Hedrick, 1 Wash. 446; 25 Pac. Rep. 335; 22 Am. St.
Rep. 169; Ferguson v. Columbus, etc., R. Co., 77 Ga. 102; Barrett v.
Southern Pacific R. Co., 91 Cal. 296; 27 Pac. Rep. 666; 25 Am. St.
Rep. 186; Alabama, etc., R. Co. v. Crocker, 131 Ala. 584; 31 So. Rep.
561; Koons v. St. Louis, etc., R. Co., 65 Mo. 592; 1 Thompson on Neg.,
§§ 1036, 1040; 2 Wood's Ry. Law, § 321.

in their rights, not securing them
their own wrongs.[62]   And this i
number of decisions by respecta
that hold there is no liability foi
child, received while playing on
a railroad company.[63]

[62] This is the reasoning, in Deane
Knight v. Albert, 6 Pa. St. 472; 47 A
[63] Daniels v. New York, etc., R. Co.,
283; 26 Am. St. Rep. 253; 13 L. R. A.
64 N. H. 220; 9 Atl. Rep. 790; 10 Am
York, etc., R. Co., 61 N. J. L. 320; 40 .
burg, etc., R. Co., 145 N. Y. 301; 39 N.
615; 27 L. R. A. 724; St. Louis, etc.,
Am. Rep. 269; Bates v. Nashville, etc., 1
Rep. 1069; 25 Am. St. Rep. 665.

As said by Justice Holmes, when a mei
Massachusetts: "Temptation is not alv
mon law is understood by the most comp
excuse a trespass, because there is a tem
brook v. Aldrich, 168 Mass. 16; 46 N. E.
364; 36 L. R. A. 493.   And see, Pannell v.
53 S. E. Rep. 113; 4 L. R. A. (N. S.) 80

.

CHAPTER XLVII

DUTIES AND LIABILITIES TOWARD TRESPASSERS.

§ 1074. **Risks assumed by trespassers generally.**— It is so impracticable to keep trespassers off an open track that in law all who go upon it do so at their own risk. One who goes upon the tracks of a railroad company at a place not a highway crossing, for his own convenience, becomes a trespasser and assumes the risk of his conduct. The company owes to such a person no duty to facilitate his trespass or to render it safe; it is only liable for the negligence of its employees, after the presence of the trespasser on the track has been discovered.[1]

[1] Sturgis v. Detroit, etc., R. Co., 72 Mich. 619; 40 N. W. Rep. 914; Jeffersonville, etc., R. Co. v. Goldsmith, 47 Ind. 43; 8 Am. Ry. Rep. 315; Gillis v. Pennsylvania R. Co., 59 Pa. St. 129; McClaren v. In.

II—49

Between stations and public crossings a railroad track belongs exclusively to the company operating the road and all persons who walk, ride or drive thereon, are trespassers; and if such persons so walk, ride or drive thereon at the sufferance or with the permission of the company, they do so subject to all the risks incident to so hazardous an undertaking, and if they are injured by a train the railroad company is not responsible, unless the injury was wantonly or intentionally inflicted.[2]

§ 1075. **Company's duty toward trespassers generally.**— A railroad company owes no duty to a trespasser, other than not to injure him, if it knows of his presence, or sees him, in time to prevent injury.[3]   One who goes upon a railroad track at a place other than a crossing, where the railroad company is required to fence its right of way, and has so fenced it, there being nothing in the surroundings that would naturally or reasonably lead the company's employees to suspect his presence, is a trespasser, and the company owes him no duty, except not to injure him wantonly, willfully or with gross negligence, and there is no duty to look out for him.[4]

There can be no recovery for the death of a person killed while negligently on a track where the train men neither

dianapolis, etc., R. Co., 83 Ind. 319; 8 Am. & Eng. R. Cas. 217; Masser v. Chicago, etc., R. Co., 68 Iowa 602.

[2] Candelaria v. Atchison, etc., R. Co. (N. M.), 27 Pac. Rep. 497; 48 Am. & Eng. R. Cas. 565; Philadelphia, etc., R. Co. v. Hummell, 44 Pa. St. 378.

[3] Rome, etc., R. Co. v. Tolbert, 85 Ga. 447; 11 S. E. Rep. 849; Chicago, etc., R. Co. v. Hedges, 105 Ind. 398; 7 N. E. Rep. 801; 25 Am. & Eng. R. Cas. 550; Masser v. Chicago, etc., R. Co., 68 Iowa 602; 27 N. W. Rep. 776; Conley v. Cincinnati, etc., R. Co., 89 Ky. 402; 12 S. W. Rep. 764; 41 Am. & Eng. R. Cas. 537; Frye v. St. Louis, etc., Ry. Co., 200 Mo. 377; 98 S. W. Rep. 566.

[4] Barker v. Hannibal, etc., R. Co., 98 Mo. 50; 11 S. W. Rep. 254; 37 Am. & Eng. R. Cas. 292; Frye v. St. Louis, etc., R. Co., 200 Mo. 377; 98 S. W. Rep. 566.

knew of his perilous position, in time to avoid the accident, nor were reckless or wantonly negligent in not so knowing it. Simple negligence in failing to see him will not authorize a recovery when the trespasser was guilty of contributory negligence.[5]

But while the duty which a railroad company owes to a person crossing its track at other than a public crossing is not that which it owes to a person crossing at the latter point, still there is an obligation on the company to use ordinary care and prudence to protect him from injury, after discovery of his presence.[6] Railroad companies are bound to exercise their dangerous business with due care to avoid injury to others, and when they fail to do so they are liable for damages, even to a trespasser, who has not been guilty of contributory negligence.[7]

§ 1076. **Distinguished from duty owing passenger or licen-**

[5] Nave v. Alabama, etc., R. Co., 96 Ala. 264; 11 So. Rep. 391; 54 Am. & Eng. R. Cas. 151; Glass v. Memphis, etc., R. Co., 94 Ala. 581; Savannah, etc., R. Co. v. Meadors, 95 Ala. 137; 10 So. Rep. 142.

[6] Winslow v. Boston, etc., R. Co., 11 N. Y. S. R. 831; Barry v. New York, etc., R. Co., 92 N. Y. 289; Byrne v. New York, etc., R. Co., 104 N. Y. 362; 5 N. Y. S. R. 722.

[7] Houston, etc., R. Co. v. Simpkins, 54 Texas 615; 6 Am. & Eng. R. Cas. 11.

A railroad company owes no duty to a trespasser upon its right of way or tracks, except that it may not wantonly or willfully injure him. Chicago, etc., R. Co. v. Bell, 133 Ill. App. 56.

The only duty owing by a railroad company to a trespasser on its tracks, away from a public crossing, is, at the most, to do all it reasonably can to prevent injury to such trespasser after discovering his peril. Texas, etc., Ry. Co. v. Modawell (U. S. C. C. A., La., 1907), 151 Fed. Rep. 421.

A railroad company is under no obligation to stop its trains at a railroad junction merely for the benefit of a trespasser. Chicago, etc., Ry. Co. v. Moran, 129 Ill. App. 38.

To a trespasser on the track a railroad company owes no duty, except not to willfully, wantonly, or intentionally injure him. Kurt v. Lake Shore, etc., Ry. Co. (N. Y. Supp. 1908), 111 N. Y. S. 859.

see.— A railroad company is not bound to the same degree of care in regard to mere strangers or trespassers, who are unlawfully upon its premises, that it owes to passengers, or those rightfully on its premises.[8]

The obligation of the company for the safe transportation of its passengers is one arising from contract, imposing duties growing out of the relation between the parties, involving trust and confidence and requiring the exercise of the utmost diligence and care, while toward a stranger or trespasser no such relation exists. Each party, in the case of a trespasser, being in the lawful pursuit of his own business, or the lawful exercise of his own rights, is not bound by the same rigorous rule, but is required only to exercise such reasonable care to avoid injuring the other, as ordinary prudence suggests.[9] And while the carrier of passengers, for hire, must exercise the highest degree of care toward passengers who pay,[10] and ordinary care toward those rightfully on its premises,[11] ordinary care is sufficient toward trespassers after their danger is discovered,[12] as premises are not required to be kept in repair for such persons, but they assume the risk of injuries incident to the use of the property trespassed upon.[13]

But while the obligation of a railroad company to a tres-

[8] Reary v. Louisville, etc., R. Co., 40 La. Ann. 32; 3 So. Rep. 390; 8 Am. St. Rep. 497; 34 Am. & Eng. R. Cas. 277.

[9] Baltimore, etc., R. Co. v. Breinig, 25 Md. 378; Snyder v. Natchez, etc., R. Co., 42 La. Ann. 302; 7 So. Rep. 582; 44 Am. & Eng. R. Cas. 278; Barker v. Hannibal, etc., R. Co., 98 Mo. 50; 11 S. W. Rep. 254; 37 Am. & Eng. R. Cas. 292; Frye v. St. Louis, etc., Ry. Co., 200 Mo. 377; 98 S. W. Rep. 566.

[10] Higley v. Gilmer, 3 Mont. 90.

[11] Central R. Co. v. Brinson, 70 Ga. 207; 19 Am. & Eng. R. Cas. 42.

[12] Barker v. Hannibal, etc., R. Co., 98 Mo. 50; 11 S. W. Rep. 254; 37 Am. & Eng. R. Cas. 292.

[13] Carr v. Missouri Pacific Ry. Co., 195 Mo. 214; 92 S. W. Rep. 874; Sweeny v. Boston, etc., R. Co., 10 Allen 372; Cusick v. Adams, 115 N. Y. 55.

passer is not the same as that toward passengers, employees, or those having business with the railroad company, and whose presence is authorized, or even as to persons who are on its premises as a favor or gratuity to them, still, one who places himself upon railroad property in violation of a statute, does not thereby forfeit all right to have the agents and employees of the railroad company exercise some care for his personal security or life, or exempt it from liability if, by the exercise of proper precaution on its part, the casualty could have been avoided.[14]

§ 1077. **Degree of care required, toward trespassers, generally.**— A trespasser is not prevented from recovering damages for an injury received on railroad property, if the railroad company, or its employees could by ordinary care, have prevented it.[15] Employees of a railroad company in charge of its engines or cars are required to exercise ordinary care, even toward a trespasser, to avoid injuring him.[16] Although one may be improperly or unlawfully on the track of a railroad company, that fact alone will not discharge the railroad company, or its employees, from the obligation to exercise ordinary care to avoid injuring him; and where he is run . over by a train and killed, the railroad company will be responsible, if its employees could have avoided the accident by the exercise of ordinary care.[17]

[14] Savannah, etc., R. Co. v. Stewart, 71 Ga. 427; Morgen v. Wabash R. Co., 159 Mo. 262; 60 S. W. Rep. 195; Clem v. Wabash R. Co., 72 Mo. App. 433.

[15] Lay v. Richmond, etc., R. Co., 106 No. Car. 404; 11 S. E. Rep. 412; 42 Am. & Eng. R. Cas. 110.

[16] Remer v. Long Island R. Co., 1 N. Y. Supp. 124; 48 Hun 352; 15 N. Y. S. R. 884; 113 N. Y. 669; 23 N. Y. S. R. 994; 21 N. E. Rep. 1116.

[17] Isabel v. Hannibal, etc., R. Co., 60 Mo. 475; Morgen v. Wabash, etc., R. Co., 159 Mo. 262; 60 S. W. Rep. 195; Rapp v. Transit Co., 190 Mo. 144; 88 S. W. Rep. 865.

But a person using a track as a footpath for his own convenience, elsewhere than at a lawful crossing of a highway, and injured by a train while so doing, cannot recover of the railroad company, unless it was guilty of gross or wanton negligence, before his presence was discovered.[18]   One who crosses a track at a distance from a public crossing is a trespasser, in the absence of a known user of the track at such place; and the railroad company owes him no duty, except not to injure him, if, by the exercise of ordinary care, it could either have discovered his peril in time to avoid accident, or, after discovering it, could have prevented the accident.[19]

§ 1078. Liable for wanton or willful injury to trespassers.—
The fact that one is a trespasser on a railroad track does not relieve the railroad company from the obligation of exercising the degree of caution commensurate with the danger to life and limb at the point where the person was a trespasser.[20]   A trespasser on a railroad track may have redress for negligent injuries inflicted on him by being struck by

[18] Spicer v. Chesapeake, etc., R. Co., 34 W. Va. 514; 12 S. E. Rep. 553; 45 Am. & Eng. R. Cas. 28; Christy v. Chesapeake, etc., R. Co., 35 W. Va. 117; 12 S. E. Rep. 1111.

[19] Dahlstrom v. St. Louis, etc., Ry. Co., 96 Mo. 99; 8 S. W. Rep. 777; 35 Am. & Eng. R. Cas. 387.

An engineer, discovering a trespasser on the track, was not required to use all possible precautions to avert the accident, and cannot be deemed negligent because he shouted a warning, instead of sounding the danger signal; the error being one of judgment on a sudden emergency created by the negligence of plaintiff. Jones v. Sibley, etc., R. Co. (La. 1908), 46 So. Rep. 61.

Constructive knowledge by an engineer of the presence of a person in the situation of a trespasser, through the fireman's actual knowledge of his presence, is insufficient to raise a duty toward the trespasser. Seaboard Air Line Ry. v. Chapman (Ga. App. 1908), 62 S. E. Rep. 488.

[20] Crow v. Wabash, etc., R. Co., 23 Mo. App. 357.

a train, and it is no defense to the reckless striking of a trespasser, that he was loitering on the track.[21] A reckless disregard of consequences may be so great as to imply a willingness to inflict an injury such as to entitle a trespasser to recover, although there is no actual intent to harm him.[22] Although one was injured in the private yards of a railroad company, therefore, where the public were warned not to trespass, as the place was one where the public were in the habit of walking on the tracks, the company was held to owe him the duty of not wantonly and recklessly injuring him and if the employees in charge of the train saw, or by the exercise of ordinary care could have seen him, in time to have averted the injury, with due safety to the passengers on the train, the company would be responsible for the injury.[23]

But it is not the law that a railroad company is liable to a trespasser on its tracks, in the absence of any wantonness, willfulness, or gross negligence.[24] Where a person voluntarily walks upon a railroad track and is injured, away from a crossing and at a place not generally used as a passway, he will not be entitled to recover damages, in the absence of willful, wanton, or reckless conduct on the part of the rail- road company.[25]

[21] Merz v. Missouri Pacific Ry. Co., 14 Mo. App. 459.

[22] Palmer v. Chicago, etc., R. Co., 112 Ind. 250; 14 N. E. Rep. 70; 31 Am. & Eng. R. Cas. 364; Troy v. Cape Fear, etc., R. Co., 99 No. Car. 298; 6 S. E. Rep. 77; 6 Am. St. Rep. 521; 34 Am. & Eng. R. Cas. 13.

[23] Koegel v. Missouri Pacific Ry. Co., 181 Mo. 379; 80 S. W. Rep. 905; Jackson v. Kansas City, etc., R. Co., 157 Mo. 621; 58 S. W. Rep. 32; 80 Am. St. Rep. 650.

[24] Heiter v. East St. Louis, etc., R. Co., 53 Mo. App. 331; Riley v. Missouri Pacific Ry. Co., 68 Mo. App. 652.

[25] Little Rock, etc., R. Co. v. Haynes, 47 Ark. 497; 1 S. W. Rep. 774; 28 Am. & Eng. R. Cas. 572; Lake Shore, etc., R. Co. v. Boderer, 139 Ill. 596; 29 N. E. Rep. 692; 54 Am. & Eng. R. Cas. 177; Eggman v. St. Louis, etc., R. Co., 47 Ill. App. 507; Terre Haute, etc., R. Co. v. Graham, 95 Ind. 286; 48 Am. Rep. 719; 12 Am. & Eng. R. Cas. 77;

§ 1079. **Excessive speed, as evidence of willful injury to trespasser.**— The excessive speed of a train is not negligence as to one who voluntarily places himself upon the railroad track, where he has no right to be. In such cases the railroad company is not liable, unless those in charge of the train or engine, after discovery of the danger to the trespasser, could, by the exercise of proper care, have avoided the injury.[26] As to a trespasser on the track, the driving of a train at night, outside the limits of a city or town, at a very high rate of speed, cannot be regarded as negligence, sufficient to hold the railroad company liable to such tres-

Chicago, etc., R. Co. v. Hedges, 105 Ind. 398; 7 N. E. Rep. 801; 25 Am. & Eng. R. Cas. 550; Gregory v. Cleveland, etc., R. Co., 112 Ind. 385; 14 N. E. Rep. 228; 31 Am. & Eng. R. Cas. 440; Wright v. Boston, etc., R. Co., 142 Mass. 296; 7 N. E. Rep. 866; 28 Am. & Eng. R. Cas. 652; Dillon v. Connecticut River R. Co., 154 Mass. 478; 28 N. E. Rep. 899; McCreary v. Boston, etc., R. Co., 156 Mass. 316; 31 N. E. Rep. 126; Dooley v. Mobile, etc., R. Co., 69 Miss. 648; 12 So. Rep. 956.

A railroad company owes no duty of care to a trespasser on its track, except to refrain from his willful or wanton injury, and cannot be held liable for the injury of a child so trespassing, where the engineer of the train which struck him testified that he came upon the track so short a distance ahead of the engine that it was impossible to stop the train before striking him, and where the engineer's testimony was uncontradicted, except by evidence which at most could no more than raise a probability that the child had walked for some distance on the track. Grand Trunk Ry. Co. v. Flagg (U. S. C. C. A., Me., 1907), 156 Fed. Rep. 359.

A railroad company has the right to assume that a grown person, in the apparent possession of all his faculties, seen on its track will get out of the way of an approaching train, and is not liable unless, after the company in the exercise of ordinary care could have discovered that he was not going to get off the track, it could have avoided running him down. Norfolk, etc., Ry. Co. v. Dean's Adm'x (Va. 1907), 59 S. E. Rep. 389.

A railroad company is not liable for an injury to a trespasser upon its tracks unless such injury is wantonly inflicted. Janowic v. Pittsburgh, etc., R. Co., 124 Ill. App. 149.

[26] Shackelford v. Louisville, etc., R. Co., 84 Ky. 43; 4 Am. St. Rep. 189; 28 Am. & Eng. R. Cas. 591.

passer. The engineer has a lawful right to presume that he will have a clear track, at such a place.[27] And the fact that a train was run at a speed in excess of that allowed by ordinance, will not authorize a recovery for injuries received by one who, although aware of the approach of the train, crossed immediately in front of it, at a place where he had no right to be, where it appeared that the engineer, after discovering him, did all in his power to avert the accident.[28]

But to run a train at a high rate of speed, where it is known that persons are using the track, although without legal right to do so, may be evidence of such wantonness, as to hold the railroad company liable for an injury at such a place.[29] And in a death action, if it appears that at the place where the deceased was killed, many persons habitually walked on the track, and the train was running at a rate of speed in excess of that allowed by ordinance, and the engineer saw the trespasser at a distance of some six hundred feet, but did not check the speed of the train, it will be held to be a jury issue, whether or not this was such willful and wanton conduct as to justify a verdict for the plaintiff.[30]

[27] Louisville, etc., R. Co. v. Howard, 82 Ky. 212; 19 Am. & Eng. R. Cas. 98; Palmer v. Chicago, etc., R. Co., 112 Ind. 250; 14 N. E. Rep. 70; 31 Am. & Eng. R. Cas. 364.

[28] Prewitt v. Eddy, 115 Mo. 283; 21 S. W. Rep. 742; 54 Am. & Eng. R. Cas. 138.

[29] Illinois, etc., R. Co. v. Beard, 49 Ill. App. 232.

[30] Fielder v. St. Louis, etc., R. Co., 107 Mo. 645; 18 S. W. Rep. 847; 54 Am. & Eng. R. Cas. 162.

It is immaterial as to a railway company's liability for the death of one stumbling and falling on a track while attempting to cross in front of a moving train that the train was running at a negligently high rate of speed, that not being the proximate cause of the accident, and it not appearing that the result would have been different had the train been running more slowly. St. Louis, etc., Ry. Co. v. Ferrell (Ark. 1907), 105 S. W. Rep. 263.

Where a railroad company has knowledge of a trespasser or licensee

§ 1080. **Trespassers not entitled to signals.**— As a general rule a railroad company is required to ring the bell and sound the whistle of the engine, only when approaching a crossing.[31] A statute requiring the bell to be rung or the whistle sounded, on approaching a crossing, is for the benefit of those who are using the crossing and not for the benefit of trespassers at other points, and such trespassers cannot ordinarily complain of the omission to comply with the statute, even though, had the signals been given, they would have heard and been warned thereby.[32] When a person goes upon a railroad track between stations, where he has no right to be, without looking or listening for trains, he cannot recover against the railroad company, for an injury received, in the absence of willfulness, notwithstanding a failure to give the signals required by law.[33] One killed near a sharp curve was not entitled to be warned

on its tracks or notice of their expected and probable presence, the rate of speed may be negligent as to them, and whether it is negligence is a question for the jury. Rader's Adm'x v. Louisville, etc., R. Co. (Ky. 1907), 104 S. W. Rep. 774.

The running of a train in violation of city ordinances cannot alone be regarded as sufficient reason for holding that injury to a trespasser on the track was wanton or willful. Chicago, etc., Ry. Co. v. Bell, 133 Ill. App. 56.

[31] Dahlstrom v. St. Louis, etc., Ry. Co., 96 Mo. 99; 8 S. W. Rep. 777; 35 Am. & Eng. R. Cas. 387; Illinois, etc., R. Co. v. Dick, 91 Ky. 434; 15 S. W. Rep. 665; Woodward v. Kentucky C. R. Co. (Ky.), 15 S. W. Rep. 178; Eggman v. St. Louis, etc., R. Co., 47 Ill. App. 507.

[32] Toomey v. Southern Pacific R. Co., 86 Cal. 374; 24 Pac. Rep. 1074; Louisville, etc., R. Co. v. Howard, 82 Ky. 212; 19 Am. & Eng. R. Cas. 98; Shackelford v. Louisville, etc., R. Co., 84 Ky. 43; 4 Am. St. Rep. 189; 28 Am. & Eng. R. Cas. 591; Prendegast v. New York, etc., R. Co., 58 N. Y. 652; Spicer v. Chesapeake, etc., R. Co., 34 W. Va. 514; 12 S. E. Rep. 553; 45 Am. & Eng. R. Cas. 28; Casey v. Canadian Pacific R. Co., 15 Ont. 574; 37 Am. & Eng. R. Cas. 172; Dahlstrom v. St. Louis, etc., R. Co., 96 Mo. 99; 8 S. W. Rep. 777; 35 Am. & Eng. R. Cas. 387.

[33] Ivens v. Cincinnati, etc., R. Co., 103 Ind. 27; 2 N. E. Rep. 134; 23 Am. & Eng. R. Cas. 258.

by bell or whistle, under a rule of the company, requiring that the whistle be sounded before approaching all curves, as this was not intended for trespassers and it will be error for the trial court to charge the jury on the basis of a liability to sound the whistle for such curve.[34]

But the court, in the trial of a suit for the injury or death of a trespasser, on the track, away from a crossing, has a right to charge the jury that it is the duty of the railroad company to give warning by bell or whistle, immediately on discovery of the danger to such trespasser.[35] And by statute in Tennessee,[36] the engineer is required immediately on seeing a person on the track, to sound the whistle of the locomotive and use all the means in his power to stop the train, if the person does not leave the track before danger of being struck by the engine, and under such statute it is held that the engineer has no right to presume that the person will leave the track, but the duty of attempting to stop the train is imperative, immediately on discovery of the trespasser.[37]

[34] Louisville, etc., R. Co. v. Howard, 82 Ky. 212; 19 Am. & Eng. R. Cas. 98.

[35] Texas, etc., R. Co. v. Roberts, 2 Texas Civ. App. 111; 20 S. W. Rep. 960.

[36] Tenn. Code, § 1166.

[37] Hill v. Louisville, etc., R. Co., 9 Heisk. 823; 19 Am. Ry. Rep. 400. The purpose of sounding a whistle or ringing a bell upon the approach of a train to a highway crossing is to warn travelers on the highway, and there is no duty to give the crossing signals to warn a person walking on the track not at a crossing that the train is approaching the crossing, even if the engine does not have a headlight; but, while the fact that no crossing signals were given is not negligence *per se* as to such a person, it may be evidence of negligence in the operation of the train when it is run at night without a headlight and prudence requires a warning to be given. Morrow v. Southern Ry. Co. (N. C. 1908), 61 S. E. Rep. 621.

In an action for death in being struck by defendant's train while crossing the track from the depot platform, where the only act of negligence alleged was the failure of the employees in charge of the train

§ 1081. **Trespassers cannot complain of absence of flag-man.**— A requirement that a railroad company shall keep a flagman at the crossing of city streets, to give warning of the approach of trains, is intended for the protection of people crossing the tracks at the crossings of streets, and not for the benefit of people walking along the tracks, between crossings, as a footpath. The latter being trespassers, the railroad company does not owe them any duty, with respect to flagmen, at all.[38]

A railroad company, in other words, is not bound to furnish a flagman for the benefit of trespassers on its tracks, to warn them of approaching trains, but flagmen are only required for the purpose of giving warnings to those about rightfully to cross the tracks, at public crossings. As the liability toward trespassers on the track is only to give notice when their presence is actually discovered, in a place of danger, or for willful or wanton injury, after discovering them, it could not be held to be willfulness to fail to employ a flagman to warn them, at a place where they were not supposed to trespass, or even at a place where their presence might have been anticipated, for they are entitled to no signal or warning until actually found to be in a place of danger.[39]

§ 1082. **Lookout should be kept for trespassers, when.**— Ordinarily, persons in charge of a train are not bound to keep a lookout for trespassers on the track. They are not

to stop it after they saw, or by the exercise of reasonable diligence could have seen, the deceased in danger, plaintiff could not, unless the complaint was amended, avail himself of the employees' failure to ring the engine bell or blow the whistle as the train approached the depot. Edward's Adm'r v. Chesapeake, etc., Ry. Co. (Ky. 1908), 108 S. W. Rep. 303.

[38] Chicago. etc., R. Co. v. Eininger, 114 Ill. 79; 29 N. E. Rep. 196.
[39] Roden v. Chicago, etc., R. Co., 133 Ill. 72; 24 N. E. Rep. 425; 30 Ill. App. 354.

bound to anticipate such intrusion and are not liable for an injury occurring in consequence thereof, without their knowledge. The liability of the company, in such case, is only measured by the conduct of the employees, after they became aware of the trespasser.[40] A company is not bound to keep a lookout for persons trespassing in its yards, as it is for one of its own employees, or those rightfully on the premises for purposes of business with the railroad company.[41]

But railroad companies are bound to use ordinary care, prudence and foresight to avoid injury to persons on or near their tracks, and the rule of what would be regarded as ordinary care varies with reference to the facts and circumstances of a given case.[42] The facts of a given case might be such that a railroad company would be regarded as negligent for a failure to keep a lookout for persons on its track, even though such persons were trespassers.[43] While the general doctrine is that a company is entitled to a clear

[40] Terre Haute, etc., R. Co. v. Graham, 95 Ind. 286; 48 Am. Rep. 719; 12 Am. & Eng. R. Cas. 77; Masser v. Chicago, etc., R. Co., 68 Iowa 602; 27 N. W. Rep. 776; State v. Baltimore, etc., R. Co., 69 Md. 494; 16 Atl. Rep. 210; Sheffler v. Minneapolis, etc., R. Co., 32 Minn. 518; 21 N. W. Rep. 711; 19 Am. & Eng. R. Cas. 173; Williams v. Kansas City, etc., R. Co., 96 Mo. 275; 9 S. W. Rep. 573; 37 Am. & Eng. R. Cas. 329; Benson v. Central Pacific R. Co., 98 Cal. 45; 32 Pac. Rep. 809; 54 Am. & Eng. R. Cas. 126; Glass v. Memphis, etc., R. Co., 94 Ala. 581; 10 So. Rep. 215; Carrington v. Louisville, etc., R. Co., 88 Ala. 472; 6 So. Rep. 910; 41 Am. & Eng. R. Cas. 543.

[41] Rome, etc., R. Co. v. Tolbert, 85 Ga. 447; 11 S. E. Rep. 849; State v. Baltimore, etc., R. Co., 58 Md. 221; 10 Am. & Eng. R. Cas. 723; Williams v. Kansas City, etc., R. Co., 96 Mo. 275; 9 S. W. Rep. 573; 37 Am. & Eng. R. Cas. 329.

[42] St. Louis, etc., R. Co. v. Freeman, 36 Ark. 41; 4 Am. & Eng. R. Cas. 608; Troy v. Cape Fear, etc., R. Co., 99 No. Car. 298; 6 S. E. Rep. 77; 6 Am. St. Rep. 521; 34 Am. & Eng. R. Cas. 13.

[43] Troy v. Cape Fear, etc., R. Co., supra; Houston, etc., R. Co. v. Simpkins, 54 Texas, 615; 6 Am. & Eng. R. Cas. 11; Norfolk, etc., R. Co. v. Harman, 83 Va. 553; 8 S. E. Rep. 251.

track, in the operation of its trains, if there is reason to apprehend that the track may not be clear, those in charge of the train must not act upon the assumption that it will be clear.[44]   It is the duty of a railroad company, running a train within the corporate limits of a city or town, where necessity may compel or usage sanction walking upon the track, at places other than public crossings, to keep a lookout, even for trespassers.[45]   And where the railroad company is accustomed to shunt cars along the track in a city where people are accustomed to walk on the track, unattached to an engine, it is their duty to keep a lookout for people on the track and a failure to do so will be such reckless disregard of the lives and limbs of citizens as to render the company liable for an injury received by failing to adopt such precautions.[46]

[44] Frick v. St. Louis, etc., R. Co., 75 Mo. 595; 8 Am. & Eng. R. Cas. 280.

[45] South, etc., R. Co. v. Donovan, 84 Ala. 141; 4 So. Rep. 142; 36 Am. & Eng. R. Cas. 151.

[46] Savannah, etc., R. Co. v. Shearer, 58 Ala. 672; South, etc., R. Co. v. Sullivan, 59 Ala. 272.

A railroad company must use ordinary care in running its trains across and along places commonly used by the public, where the train men know thereof, to prevent injuring any one who may be so using the track. Gulf, etc., Ry. Co. v. Coleman (Tex. Civ. App. 1908), 112 S. W. Rep. 690.

In an action for injuries caused by a truck standing on defendant's platform running down the platform into a passing train by which it was thrown against plaintiff, while the company was bound to use ordinary care to prevent injury to persons using its station grounds where it had acquiesced in such use for a long period, an instruction that it was defendant's duty to keep a reasonably vigilant lookout to prevent injuries to such persons was misleading, as the phrase "vigilant lookout" is usually applied to the precaution required of train men in the operation of trains, and that question was not in issue. Rowley v. Chicago, etc., Ry. Co. (Wis. 1908), 115 N. W. Rep. 865.

The failure of a railroad company to keep a lookout and to discover a trespasser upon its tracks, or to ring a bell or blow a whistle, does not show wanton injury to a trespasser struck and killed by an en-

§ 1083. **Duty of employees, after discovery of trespasser.**—
The liability of a railroad company to a trespasser on its
track must be measured by the conduct of its employees
after they became aware of his presence there and not by
their negligence in failing to discover him, for as to such
negligence, the contributory negligence of the trespasser
would defeat a recovery.[47] The presence of a trespasser on
the track does not require the employees in charge of the
train to stop the train as soon as he is discovered or even to
check the speed, unless the circumstances show that the approach of the train is not observed, or that the person is
unable to leave the track.[48] Where the employees have
given all the usual and proper signals to warn persons on
the track of the approach of the train, they are not required
to stop the train, unless it is apparent that the person is
under some disability, or that he does not hear or compre-
hend the signals.[49] The employees of the railroad company
have a right to presume that a person will get off the track
in time to avoid injury and they are not bound to check the
speed of the train, until it appears that he cannot do so,

gine of such company. Janowicz v. Pittsburgh, etc., R. Co., 124 Ill.
App. 149.

The law imposes no duty on a railway company to keep a lookout
for trespassers in the operation of its trains; hence there can be no
recovery for an injury to a trespasser, except in case of willful or
wanton misconduct, or for negligence after discovery of the peril.
Southern Ry. Co. v. Stewart (Ala. 1907), 45 So. Rep. 51.

[47] St. Louis, etc., R. Co. v. Monday, 49 Ark. 257; 4 S. W. Rep. 782;
31 Am. & Eng. R. Cas. 424; Brown v. St. Louis, etc., R. Co., 52 Ark.
120; 12 S. W. Rep. 203; Cincinnati, etc., R. Co. v. Long, 112 Ind. 166;
13 N. E. Rep. 659; 31 Am. & Eng. R. Cas. 138; Dunkman v. Wabash
R. Co., 95 Mo. 232; 4 S. W. Rep. 670.

[48] Mobile, etc., R. Co. v. Blakely, 59 Ala. 471; Esrey v. Southern
Pacific R. Co., 88 Cal. 399; 26 Pac. Rep. 211.

[49] French v. Philadelphia, etc., R. Co., 39 Md. 574; 10 Am. Ry. Rep.
474.

or will not do so.[50]   The liability of the company therefore does not commence the moment the trespasser is seen on the track, but only when it is first discovered that he is ignorant of the approaching danger, or cannot extricate himself from it.   And if he was not discovered until too late to prevent the injury, by the use of all proper appliances, the railroad company will not be liable for the injury.[51]

But if the employees of a railroad company, in charge of a train, discover a trespasser on the track, the company will be liable, if the person was in imminent peril and its employees knew of such peril in time to have avoided the injury, by the exercise of ordinary care.[52]   If an engineer sees that a traveler on the track has placed himself in imminent peril, as where he is walking on a high trestle, which he cannot cross before overtaken by the train, he should use all the means at his command to stop the train.[53]   If the trespasser does not heed the warning, when given, the engineer should apply the brakes, if it is apparent that the person will be in imminent peril if the train is not stopped.[54] And while it is not always essential that the engine should be reversed, where other precautions were taken promptly,[55] if the trespasser was discovered a sufficient distance ahead of the train, to have enabled the engineer to stop the train, after it became apparent that he would not leave the track, the company will be liable for his injury or death, if the

[50] Sibley v. Ratcliff, 50 Ark. 477; 8 S. W. Rep. 686; 37 Am. & Eng. R. Cas. 295.

[51] Louisville, etc., R. Co. v. Black, 89 Ala. 313; 8 So. Rep. 246; 45 Am. & Eng. R. Cas. 38.

[52] Guenther v. St. Louis, etc., R. Co., 108 Mo. 18; 18 S. W. Rep. 846.

[53] Clark v. Wilmington, etc., R. Co., 109 No. Car. 430; 14 S. E. Rep. 43; 48 Am. & Eng. R. Cas. 546.

[54] Louisville, etc., R. Co. v. Coleman, 86 Ky. 556; 6 S. W. Rep. 875; 31 Am. & Eng. R. Cas. 390.

[55] Bell v. Hannibal, etc., R. Co., 72 Mo. 50; 4 Am. & Eng. R. Cas. 580.

train was not stopped, after the danger to the trespasser became apparent.[56]

§ 1084. **Duty toward children, drunken persons and persons under disability.**— A railroad company is not bound, in the absence of a statute requiring it, to fence its railroad track in order to keep children off the track. A company does not owe to a child of tender years any further or greater duty, on this account, than it owes to a person of mature years, except in so far as the infancy of the child affects the danger incurred in the trespass.[57] A company is not liable for running over a child who is using the railroad track as a playground, unless the act was done maliciously or with gross and reckless carelessness.[58] Nor does a railroad company owe any higher duty to a drunken trespasser than to a sober one, when it is without the means of determining whether he is drunk or sober.[59] If a person in

[56] Bouwmeester v. Grand Rapids, etc., R. Co., 63 Mich. 557; 30 N. W. Rep. 337; 28 Am. & Eng. R. Cas. 476.

A railroad company owes no other duty to a mere licensee upon its premises than to refrain willfully or wantonly from injuring him. Illinois Cent. R. Co. v. McMillion, 129 Ill. App. 27, 37.

A brakeman seeing a person about to cross the track behind standing cars, against which the moving car the brakeman is on is about to strike, is entitled to act on the assumption that such person will not expose himself to danger by going on the track, unless he is aware that such person is oblivious of his peril. St. Louis, etc., R. Co. v. Cain (Ark. 1907), 104 S. W. Rep. 533.

[57] Nolan v. New York, etc., R. Co., 53 Conn. 461; 4 Atl. Rep. 106; 25 Am. & Eng. R. Cas. 342; Chicago, etc., R. Co. v. Stumps, 69 Ill. 409.

[58] Morrissey v. Eastern R. Co., 126 Mass. 377; Wright v. Boston. etc., R. Co., 142 Mass. 296; 7 N. E. Rep. 866; 28 Am. & Eng. R. Cas. 652; Chicago, etc., R. Co. v. Smith, 46 Mich. 504; 4 Am. & Eng. R. Cas. 535; Hestonville Pass. R. Co. v. Connell, 88 Pa. St. 520; Duff v. Allegheny Valley R. Co., 91 Pa. St. 458; 36 Am. Rep. 675; 2 Am. & Eng. R. Cas. 1.

[59] Columbus, etc., R. Co. v. Wood, 86 Ala. 164; 5 So. Rep. 463.

II—50   1617

a state of helpless intoxication, l
the rule seems to be that the c
injury received, as a result of s
sence of willfulness or wantonn
is injured, while lying on a r
scious condition, in the absence
part of those in charge of the t
ery, whether such unconsciousne
cation or sickness, or some ot
stance or condition.[61]

But if an engineer discovers,
ness may discover, a person lyir
drunk, or sees upon the track a l
by him to be laboring under son
him insensible to danger, or ur
duty to resolve all doubts in fa
life and immediately to use ever
imperiling the lives of passenger
failure to do so, in case of an i
road · company liable for damag

[60] Illinois, etc., R. Co. v. Hutchins
Delaware, etc., R. Co., 81 Pa. St. 366;
Co., 10 Ired. (No. Car.) 402; 51 Am. D
Evans, 71 Texas 361; 9 S. W. Rep. 32
Virginia Midland R. Co. v. Boswell, 82 '
If a person in a state of helpless ir
road track, the company will not be j
him, if it can be avoided in the exerci
covery of his peril. Williams v. South
152; 11 Pac. Rep. 849.
[61] Missouri Pacific Ry. Co. v. Brown
[62] Deans v. Wilmington, etc., R. Co., 1
77; 45 Am. & Eng. R. Cas. 45; Savani
Ga. 427.
Liability to an injured idiot, who w
in a drunken condition, where he coul
time to have stopped the train, before

§ 1085. **Duty toward deaf persons on the track.**—A railroad company is not liable for the failure of its employees to stop a train in time to avoid killing a person seen on the track, there being nothing to indicate that he was not able to take care of himself, and where they made every effort to stop the train after it was apparent that he would not leave the track.[63] If the engineer, on observing a person on the track, at a place where he has no right to be, rings the bell and blows the whistle, so that any ordinary person must be aware of the approach of the train, he has a right to expect that the trespasser will leave the track; and the railroad company will not be liable for his death, even though the engineer, when he first saw him, had time to stop the train, and the trespasser was a deaf mute.[64]

But while ordinarily those operating a train have a right to assume that one walking on the track, in the direction the train is going, will step from the track, in time to avoid injury, yet if the person on the track be deaf, and that fact be known to those operating the train, they have no right to act on this assumption, but they are then required to use such diligence as will best protect him from

stationary box cars, was denied, in Daily v. Richmond, etc., R. Co., 106 No. Car. 301; 11 S. E. Rep. 320; 42 Am. & Eng. R. Cas. 124.

A railroad company is not liable for the death of a person asleep on the track, if all care was used to avoid the injury, after his danger was discovered. Rozwadosfskie v. International, etc., R. Co., 1 Texas Civ. App. 487; 20 S. W. Rep. 872; East Tennessee, etc., R. Co. v. St. John, 5 Sneed (Tenn.) 524.

But if the employees failed to take precaution, as soon as the danger was discovered, the railroad company would be liable for the death of the person asleep on the track. Mann v. Missouri, etc., R. Co. (Mo. App.), 100 S. W. Rep. 566.

63 Artusy v. Missouri Pacific Ry. Co., 73 Texas 191; 11 S. W. Rep. 177; 37 Am. & Eng. R. Cas. 288.

64 Nichols v. Louisville, etc., R. Co. (Ky.), 6 S. W. Rep. 399; 34 Am. & Eng. R. Cas. 37; Louisville, etc., R. Co. v. Cooper (Ky.), 6 Am. & Eng. R. Cas. 5; Poole v. North Carolina R. Co. (No. Car.), 8 Jones 340.

injury.[65]   With a knowledge of
trespasser, the employees in char;
a stricter measure of duty and
discharge that duty will constitu
tional killing, so as to render th
the death of a trespasser.[66]

§ 1086. **No duty to keep premi**
owner of private property is und
in a safe condition for trespass
come upon the premises, not by
plied, but for their own convenie
passer assumes all risks of dange
premises, and in order to recov
must show that the injury was
flicted, or that the owner being
vented the injury, by the exerci
the danger to the trespasser was
by the unsafe or insecure conditi
the premises without invitation, c
or pleasure, assumes the risk of a
properly incloses dangerous mac
plant, or business, is not liable fo
from meddling with such machin

[65] International, etc., R. Co. v. Smith,
R. Cas. 21.

[66] Louisville, etc., R. Co. v. Cooper,
Denson. 84 Ga. 774; 11 S. E. Rep. 103

[67] Union, etc., R. Co. v. Roark, 10 I
R. Co., 64 N. H. 220; 9 Atl. Rep. 790;
Co., 154 Mass. 349.

[68] Frost v. Eastern, etc., R. Co., sup
38; Carr v. Missouri Pacific Ry. Co., 1!

[69] Lary v. Cleveland, etc., R. Co., 78
Am. & Eng. R. Cas. 498; Collyer v. Pe
59; 6 Atl. Rep. 437.

[70] O'Connor v. Illinois Central R. Co.,
678.

will not be liable for an injury to a trespasser injured by the explosion of a torpedo on the track, with which he wrongfully meddled,[71] nor will the railroad company be responsible for an injury to a trespasser by falling into a pool of water on its private property, which it had not. fenced and not had expressly forbidden persons to enter,[72] as the trespassers, in all such cases, take the property as they find it and there is no relation out of which a duty could be implied toward them, to keep the premises in repair or in a reasonably safe condition, for trespassing.

§ 1087. **Duty toward trespassers on trains.**— In the absence of wantonness or willfulness on the part of the employees of a railroad company, toward persons trespassing on its trains, the company will not generally be held liable for an injury to such trespasser.[73]

The only duty a railroad company owes to a trespasser on one of its trains, is not to willfully or recklessly injure him, after he is discovered on the train.[74] If a person, while trying to obtain a free ride, without the consent of the railroad company or its employees, receives a personal injury, he cannot recover therefor, unless the railroad company was guilty of such gross negligence as amounts to willful misconduct.[75] Where a person clandestinely enters a box car of a freight train to beat his way over the railroad, he

[71] Carter v. Columbia, etc., R. Co., 19 So. Car. 20; 45 Am. Rep. 754; 15 Am. & Eng. R. Cas. 414.

[72] Hooper v. Johnstown, etc., R. Co., 35 N. Y. S. R. 503; 13 N. Y. Supp. 151; 59 Hun 121; 128 N. Y. 613; 28 N. E. Rep. 252.

[73] Richmond, etc., R. Co. v. Burnsed, 70 Miss. 437; 12 So. Rep. 958.

[74] Farber v. Missouri Pacific Ry. Co., 116 Mo. 81; 22 S. W. Rep. 631.

[75] Chicago, etc., R. Co. v. Mehlsack, 131 Ill. 61; 22 N. E. Rep. 812; 41 Am. & Eng. R. Cas. 60.

becomes a trespasser, and the only duty the company owes to him is not to injure him wantonly.[76]

But even though a person is known to be a trespasser on a given train, if he was permitted to enter the train with the consent of the conductor, or person in charge of the train, although he was riding in violation of the company's rules, the company will be held to owe him ordinary care and for a failure to furnish him such care in case of his injury, will be liable in damages.[77] And although a person riding unlawfully on a freight car is a trespasser, the employees of the railroad company have no right to inflict wanton or willful injury upon him.[78] Only necessary force can be used to remove a trespasser from the train, and if the employees act in a willful and wanton manner and injury to the trespasser results, the railroad company will be liable.[79]

§ 1088. **Ejection of trespassers from train.**— The conductor and employees in charge of a train have the right to eject a trespasser from the train at any suitable place, provided no unnecessary force or excessive violence is used, and if the trespasser forcibly resists, he cannot recover damages for

[76] Hendrix v. Kansas City, etc., R. Co., 45 Kansas 377; 25 Pac. Rep. 893.

[77] Whitehead v. St. Louis, etc., R. Co., 99 Mo. 263; 11 S. W. Rep. 751; 39 Am. & Eng. R. Cas. 410.

[78] Planz v. Boston, etc., R. Co., 157 Mass. 377; 32 N. E. Rep. 356.

[79] Kansas City, etc., R. Co. v. Kelly, 36 Kansas 655; 14 Pac. Rep. 172; Atchison, etc., R. Co. v. Gantz, 38 Kansas 608; 17 Pac. Rep. 54; 34 Am. & Eng. R. Cas. 290.

Where plaintiff was a trespasser on a portion of a freight train being switched in railway yards, the only duty the company owed was to avoid injuring him on discovering his peril; and, where a brakeman who invited plaintiff to ride on such a car signaled the engineer to start as plaintiff attempted to get on, the company was not liable for plaintiff's injury, where the brakeman was unable to stop the train in time to avoid the injury after discovering plaintiff's peril. Skirvin v. Louisville, etc., R. Co. (Ky. 1907), 100 S. W. Rep. 308.

the force used in overcoming his resistance, where the force used is without the intent to commit unnecessary injury. The railroad company is only liable for unnecessary force or violence, when it is wantonly or willfully exerted.[80] And if a trespasser is once ejected from a train he should submit to the ejection and rely on recovering damages, if the ejection was unlawful, and there can be no recovery where he is ejected the second time without the use of unnecessary force, although he suffers an injury therefrom.[81]

But the removal of trespassers from cars is held to be within the implied authority of the employees on the train and if they act illegally in removing a party while the train is in motion, the injured trespasser can recover damages.[82] If the employees, in the act of removing a trespasser, endanger his personal safety, as where a boy is removed from a car, in a way to make it almost certain that he would sustain an injury, the railroad company will be liable.[83]

However, the railroad company will not be liable for an injury to a trespasser, in removing him from a train, by the mere negligence of the employees, but only for an injury willfully or wantonly inflicted.[84] The mere fact of removing a trespasser from a train, while it is in motion, if it is

[80] Atchison, etc., R. Co. v. Gantz, 38 Kansas 608; 17 Pac. Rep. 54; 34 Am. & Eng. R. Cas. 290.

[81] North Chicago R. Co. v. Olds, 40 Ill. App. 421.

[82] Hoffman v. New York, etc., R. Co., 87 N. Y. 25; 41 Am. Rep. 337; 4 Am. & Eng. R. Cas. 537.

But it was held to be essential to establish the authority of the employee to remove the trespasser, in Corcoran v. Concord, etc., R. Co., 56 Fed. Rep. 1014.

[83] Kline v. Central Pacific R. Co., 37 Cal. 400; Perkins v. Missouri, etc., R. Co., 55 Mo. 201; Louisville, etc., R. Co. v. Sullivan, 81 Ky. 624; 16 Am. & Eng. R. Cas. 390.

[84] Carter v. Louisville, etc., R. Co., 98 Ind. 552; 49 Am. Rep. 780; 22 Am. & Eng. R. Cas. 360.

moving very slowly, will not be neglige
question of wantonness or willfulness
dinarily be an issue for the jury.[86]

[85] Southern Kansas R. Co. v. Sanford, 45 K
891; 47 Am. & Eng. R. Cas. 615.
[86] Southern Kansas R. Co. v. Sanford, *supra*

CHAPTER XLVIII.

CONTRIBUTORY NEGLIGENCE OF TRESPASSERS.

§ 1089. **The subject generally.**— Railroad companies are bound to exercise their dangerous business with due care to avoid injury to others, even as to trespassers on the track, but if the injured party, trespasser, employee, licensee or passenger, has, by his own negligence, contributed to the injury, he cannot lawfully recover damages.[1] It is held not to be contributory negligence, *per se,* for a person, receiving an injury from the negligence of a railroad company, to be on the track at a place where he had no right to be; but he may be guilty of such negligence, although he is at a place

[1] International, etc., R. Co. v. Jordan, 1 Texas Civ. App. 494; 10 Am. & Eng. R. Cas. 301.

1625

where he had a perfect right to
if the person neglects to use ordina
considering the time, place and c
of contributory negligence.[2]

A person who unnecessarily
track, taking no precaution to g
guilty of gross negligence and cann
jury was wantonly or recklessly in
or its employees.[3] If a man, in t
senses, chooses to walk on a rail
rails, at a time when he knows tr
going to and from his work, as w
recover for an injury from being s
his own negligence in placing hims
he was sure to be struck unless h
then failing to remove himself from
lessness as to constitute negligence
of law.[4]

§ 1090. **Care required of trespasse**
lawfully trespassing on a railroad tra
railroad company are not authorized
being on private property, on a tra
purpose which is dangerous to human
persons, and being in a place where h
a trespasser is bound to use every pr
gence, against the probability or pos
which might happen to him, while so
passer is held to a higher degree of car
own safety, than would be required o
in legal right, because a less degree of

[2] Vicksburg. etc., R. Co. v. McGowan, 62)
[3] Illinois, etc., R. Co. v. Hetherington, 83
[4] O'Donnell v. Missouri Pacific Ry. Co., 7)
[5] Finlayson v. Chicago, etc., R. Co., 1 Dill.

him by the owner of the property and he must look out for himself.[6]   If one chooses to walk on a railroad track for his convenience, without regard to the constantly moving trains, the railroad company has a right to presume that it has a clear track and proceed with its lawful business.[7]   A man walking on a railroad track, therefore, although near a public crossing, must use that degree of care to protect himself from danger which any prudent man uses under similar perilous circumstances.[8]   And where a person, not an employee of the company and against its will, and without its knowledge, goes into a yard covered with railroad tracks, which are constantly used in switching, such person is bound to use diligence commensurate with the peril in which he has placed himself, and if he fails to do this, he cannot recover for an injury that he may sustain from the running of engines and cars.[9]

§ 1091. **Negligence must be proximate cause of injury.**— As in the case of other injuries through negligence, it is generally held that to bar a recovery for an injury to a trespasser, the contributory negligence of the trespasser must be the proximate cause of the injury or a concurring proximate cause thereof.[10]   Of course if the negligence of either the plaintiff or that of the defendant is the sole cause of the injury, there is no contributory negligence in the case. There could be no contributory negligence, unless there was also negligence of the defendant, to which that of the plaintiff contributed.   Unless the negligence of defendant was the proximate cause of the injury, there would be no liability.

6 Lake Shore, etc., R. Co. v. Blanchard, 15 Ill. App. 582; Houston, etc., R. Co. v. Boozer, 2 Texas Unrep. Cas. 452.

7 Central, etc., R. Co. v. Wabash R. Co., 26 Fed. Rep. 896.

8 Georgia, etc., R. Co. v. Daniels, 89 Ga. 463; 15 S. E. Rep. 538.

9 Rome, etc., R. Co. v. Tolbert, 85 Ga. 447; 11 S. E. Rep. 849.

10 Barkley v. Missouri Pacific Ry. Co., 96 Mo. 367; 9 S. W. Rep. 793.

Unless the negligence of the plaintifl
of the injury, his action, on that gr
feated.[11]

But it is not essential that the coi
the plaintiff must be the sole proxim
to prevent a recovery on this ground,
the plaintiff concurs with that of the
injury there can be no recovery, alt
negligence of the plaintiff was not tl
of the injury.[12]   The mere fact, h
trespassing on a railroad property, at
will not prevent a recovery, if his ti
negligence, substantially contributing
if, after the trespasser is discovered i
time for the employees of the railr
saved him from injury, by exercising
they neglected to do so, it is a cas(
gence on their part, proximately causi
a case of concurrent negligence of b(
defeat a recovery for the injured tresp

§ 1092. **Failure to look and listen**
walks along a railroad track without
ordinary care to avoid injury and if h
siderable distance without looking bac
not recover for injuries sustained, in
gence by the employees of the railro;
presence and danger is discovered.[14] A

[11] Payne v. Chicago, etc., R. Co., 129 Mo. ‹
[12] Payne v. Missouri Pacific Ry. Co., supr(
[13] Daley v. Norwich, etc., R. Co., 26 Conn.
Pacific R. Co., 50 Cal. 383; 12 Am. Ry. R(
Louis, etc., R. Co., 157 Mo. 216; 57 S. W. Re]
[14] Candelaria v. Atchison, etc., R. Co., 6 ;
497; 48 Am. & Eng. R. Cas. 565; Barker

a railroad track is not free from negligence if he fails to keep watch of the movements of trains, but relies upon a rule or custom of the railroad company to give a signal of the movement of its trains.   The expectation that a signal may be given, does not relieve the person walking on the track, from the duty to keep a constant watch for his own safety.[15] And to walk upon a railroad track, without looking in both directions to discover approaching engines or trains, where the exercise of such a precaution would discover the one or the other, is such contributory negligence as will prevent a recovery, by a trespasser upon the track, unless the injury was willfully or wantonly inflicted.[16]

98 Mo. 50; 11 S. W. Rep. 254; 37 Am. & Eng. R. Cas. 292; State v. Baltimore, etc., R. Co., 69 Md. 494; 16 Atl. Rep. 210; Johnston v. Truesdale, 46 Minn. 345; 48 N. W. Rep. 1136; Lake Shore, etc., R. Co. v. Hart, 87 Ill. 529; 19 Am. & Eng. R. Cas. 249.

[15] Baltimore, etc., R. Co. v. Depew, 40 Ohio St. 121; 12 Am. & Eng. R. Cas. 64; Elliott v. Chicago, etc., R. Co., 5 Dakota, 523; 41 N. W. Rep. 758; 3 L. R. A. 363; 38 Am. & Eng. R. Cas. 62; McAdoo v. Richmond, etc., R. Co., 105 No. Car. 140; 11 S. E. Rep. 316; 41 Am. & Eng. R. Cas. 524; Syme v. Richmond, etc., R. Co., 113 No. Car. 558; 18 S. E. Rep. 114; Redmond v. Rome, etc., R. Co., 56 Hun 645; 31 N. Y. S. R. 366; 10 N. Y. Supp. 330; Schilling v. Chicago, etc., R. Co., 71 Wis. 255; 37 N. W. Rep. 414; 40 N. W. Rep. 616; 34 Am. & Eng. R. Cas. 60; Guenther v. St. Louis, etc., R. Co., 95 Mo. 286; 8 S. W. Rep. 371; 34 Am. & Eng. R. Cas. 47; Dooley v. Mobile, etc., R. Co., 69 Miss. 648; 12 So. Rep. 956; Michigan, etc., R. Co. v. Campau, 35 Mich. 468; 15 Am. Ry. Rep. 314; Lake Shore, etc., R. Co. v. Blanchard, 15 Ill. App. 582; Missouri Pacific R. Co. v. Moseley, 57 Fed. Rep. 921.

[16] Southeast, etc., R. Co. v. Stotler, 43 Ill. App. 94.

If an engine which ran over and killed decedent could not have been seen or heard, had he stopped, looked, and listened before attempting to cross the track, then the failure on his part was not the proximate cause of his death.   Central of Georgia Ry. Co. v. Hyatt (Ala. 1907), 43 So. Rep. 867.

A person on a railroad track as a trespasser, apparently in possession of his senses and faculties so that he can either see or hear the approach of a train, must listen, and, if he cannot hear, must look, for the approach of trains, and his failure to do so is negligence on his part, which at least concurs, up to the very time of the injury, with

§ 1093. **Failure to heed warnings or signals.**— If a person has notice of the approach of a train, either by word of mouth or warning from others, since this is all that signals from the engine could give him, he will generally be held negligent in remaining on the track after such notice is given him. And if, after being so notified, one has ample time to leave a railroad track and avoid a collision with an approaching train and engine, but instead of doing so, he remains on the track, after warning is thus given him, this will be held such a want of care and caution for his safety as will debar a recovery, although the employees of the railroad company were also negligent.[17]

If a person is slightly intoxicated and leaves a safe path by the side of a railroad track and proceeds to walk on the track, and after being warned by signals from the locomotive of the approach of a train, and by word of mouth by his companions, continues on the track, he is guilty of such gross negligence as will prevent a recovery for his death, caused by being struck and killed by a backing engine, there being nothing to show that the employees in charge of the engine had any notice of his presence on the track, in time to have stopped the engine, by due care on their part.[18]

that of the railway company, if there be any negligence on its part, and he must be considered in law to have brought disaster upon himself if he is injured. Beach v. Southern Ry. Co. (N. C. 1908), 61 S. E. Rep. 664, 669.

Every person who goes on a railroad track, or purposes to cross it, must use his eyes and ears to avoid injury, and every intelligent person who has arrived at years of discretion is presumed to know that it is dangerous to be on a railroad track when trains are passing to and fro, and when crossing one is expected to be vigilant and watchful of the approach of a locomotive. Holland v. Missouri Pac. Ry. Co. (Mo. 1908), 109 S. W. Rep. 19.

[17] Baltimore, etc., R. Co. v. State, 36 Md. 366; Louisville, etc., R. Co. v. Watkins (Ky.), 12 Am. & Eng. R. Cas. 89.

[18] Norfolk, etc., R. Co. v. Harman, 83 Va. 553; 8 S. E. Rep. 251.

§ 1094. **Standing on or near track.**— All persons of years of discretion are bound to know that standing on or near a railroad track is a place of danger, and whatever privilege there may have been extended to one to walk upon a track, such privilege is to be exercised at the risk of the licensee, or trespasser, at least, in so far as to require him to exercise great care, in view of the danger of the surroundings.[19] One who stands on a railroad track, in a space between two stationary cars, cannot complain if he is injured by a shunting together of the cars, unless his presence is known to the employees in charge of the engine.[20] And a like result follows from an injury due to standing too near the track, when the presence of the person is not known to the employees of the railroad company.[21] And even though the engineer sees a person on the track, whom he does not know, he is entitled to assume that the person will leave the track in time to avoid injury, and it is held, in some cases, that he is entitled to indulge this assumption, up to the last moment, and if the person is injured, the law imputes it to his own negligence and holds the company blameless.[22]

But whenever an engineer in the operation of his engine, before reaching a point, along the line of a railroad, has reasonable ground to anticipate the presence of persons on or near the track, even though they may be trespassers, then the law, through its high regard for the preservation of human life, requires him to be on the alert and to be on the lookout for persons on the track.[23]

[19] Donaldson v. Milwaukee, etc., R. Co., 21 Minn. 293; 20 Am. Ry. Rep. 15; Rheiner v. Chicago, etc., R. Co., 36 Minn. 170.

[20] East Tennessee, etc., R. Co. v. King, 81 Ala. 177; 2 So. Rep. 152; 31 Am. & Eng. R. Cas. 385; Deibold v. Pennsylvania R. Co., 50 N. J. L. 478; 14 Atl. Rep. 576.

[21] St. Louis, etc., R. Co. v. Sharp, 3 Texas Civ. App. 394.

[22] High v. Carolina R. Co., 112 No. Car. 385; 17 S. E. Rep. 79.

[23] See opinion of Judge Fox, in Fearons v. Kansas City, etc., R. Co., 180 Mo. 208; 79 S. W. Rep. 394; Chamberlain v. Missouri Pacific

§ 1095. **Walking on or near track.**— It is negligence for a person to walk upon a railroad track, whether laid in a

Ry. Co., 133 Mo. 587; 33 S. W. Rep. 437; Scullin v. Wabash R. Co., 184 Mo. 707; 83 S. W. Rep. 760; Hanlon v. Missouri Pacific Ry. Co., 104 Mo. 381; 16 S. W. Rep. 233; Levelsmeyer v. St. Louis, etc., R. Co., 114 Mo. App. 412.

Where a complaint in an action for injuries to person on tracks alleged that, when he was struck, he was standing on the right of way so near the rails that a locomotive in passing struck him, and that he was watching the operation of a steam shovel, and was unaware of the approach of the locomotive, though his view was unobstructed for a mile, and he was not an employee nor working near the rails for any one nor standing on the right of way at the invitation of defendant, the complaint is demurrable as showing plaintiff guilty of contributory negligence as a matter of law. Anderson v. Minneapolis, etc., Ry. Co. (Minn. 1908), 114 N. W. Rep. 1123.

Where deceased was a trespasser on defendant's railway track when he was struck and killed, the railroad company owed him no duty of lookout or warning, but was only required to exercise ordinary care by using all reasonable means to prevent injury to him after his peril was actually discovered. Nashville, etc., Ry. Co. v. Bean's Ex'r (Ky. 1908), 110 S. W. Rep. 328.

Where just prior to intestate's injury by being struck by a railroad train he was walking alongside the track at a place where he could not have been injured, the engineer and those in charge of the train were entitled to assume that he would not leave such place and go upon the track in front of the train. Bookman v. Seaboard Air Line Ry. (U. S. C. C. A., S. C., 1907), 152 Fed. Rep. 686.

A railroad company was not negligent as to a pedestrian struck while walking along the side of a track by a bucket attached to the side of a freight car on a passing train, where the bucket did not extend further laterally beyond the rails than types of cars in common use, and it was a general custom of defendant and other railway companies to carry such buckets attached to one of the cars to facilitate the treatment of hot boxes. Bandekow v. Chicago, etc., Ry. Co., 117 N. W. Rep. 812.

Where plaintiff was injured while standing between two cars by the sudden movement of the train, the mere fact that one of defendant's employees in charge of the train crew saw him crossing the tracks and standing near or at the cars was insufficient to charge defendant with knowledge that plaintiff was in a place of danger. Hocker v. Louisville, etc., R. Co. (Ky. 1906), 96 S. W. Rep. 526.

street or in an open field, and he who deliberately does so, is presumed, in law, to assume the risk of such conduct.[24] A trespasser walking on a railroad track, at a place where he could not be seen in time to stop the train, before he was run down, is guilty of contributory negligence, and the fact that such trespasser was intoxicated is no excuse.[25] Indeed, the negligence is the more pronounced, for one intoxicated, or under disability, to place himself in such a dangerous position, and if a person under disability, such as a crippled person, walks on a railroad track and sustains an injury as a result, his negligence will bar a recovery therefor.[26]

But walking on a railroad track, at a place where persons have habitually used the track as a passway, is not contributory negligence as a matter of law.[27] And if a person is injured at such a place and his presence could have been discovered by reasonable care, or the injury avoided, after he was discovered in a place of danger, the railroad company cannot avoid liability for the injury, by reason of the fact that the injured person was walking on the track, at the time of the injury.[28]

[24] Illinois Central R. Co. v. Hall, 72 Ill. 222; Illinois Central R. Co. v. Beard, 49 Ill. App. 232; McAlister v. Burlington, etc., R. Co., 64 Iowa 395; 19 Am. & Eng. R. Cas. 108; Lenox v. Missouri Pacific R. Co., 76 Mo. 86.

[25] Memphis, etc., R. Co. v. Womack, 84 Ala. 149; 4 So. Rep. 618; 37 Am. & Eng. R. Cas. 308; Columbus, etc., R. Co. v. Wood, 86 Ala. 164; Richards v. Chicago, etc., R. Co., 81 Iowa 426; 47 N. W. Rep. 63; 45 Am. & Eng. R. Cas. 54.

[26] Delaware, etc., R. Co. v. Cadow, 120 Pa. St. 559; 14 Atl. Rep. 450; 35 Am. & Eng. R. Cas. 405.

[27] Troy v. Cape Fear, etc., R. Co., 99 No. Car. 298; 6 S. E. Rep. 77; 6 Am. St. Rep. 521; 34 Am. & Eng. R. Cas. 13.

[28] Kansas Pacific R. Co. v. Ward, 4 Colo. 30; Alabama, etc., R. Co. v. Chapman, 80 Ala. 615; 2 So. Rep. 738; 31 Am. & Eng. R. Cas. 394. One who drives along a railroad track, at a place where he knows a train is likely to pass, is negligent. Moore v. Kansas City, etc., R. Co., 126 Mo. 265; 29 S. W. Rep. 9; Prewitt v. Eddy, 115 Mo. 283; 21 S. W. Rep. 742; Hicks v. Missouri Pacific Ry. Co., 46 Mo. App.

§ 1096. **Walking on railroad bridge or trestle.**— A person who undertakes to walk across a railroad bridge or trestle of any considerable length or height, knowing that a train is liable to approach at any time, is guilty of negligence which proximately contributes to any injury he may receive, and no recovery can be had for such an injury, unless it can be shown that it was wantonly or recklessly inflicted.[29] And if the plaintiff's own evidence shows that he was injured while walking over a bridge or trestle, crossed by a railroad track, this is ordinarily sufficient to show negligence, proximately contributory to the injury, and a nonsuit is properly granted.[30] And the fact that a railroad bridge is located

304. To stand or walk on a track, was held to be contributory negligence in Skipton v. St. Joseph, etc., R. Co., 82 Mo. App. 134.

Hitching a horse near a railroad track is negligence, if the horse is afraid of trains, and it is all the more negligent for one to run in front of a train, on the track, in an effort to save the horse. McManamee v. Missouri Pacific Ry. Co., 135 Mo. 440; 37 S. W. Rep. 119.

If a pedestrian in going on the track in front of train failed to use ordinary care, and but for this would not have been injured, there can be no recovery notwithstanding the negligence of the train men. Louisville, etc., R. C. v. McNary's Adm'r (Ky. 1908), 108 S. W. Rep. 898.

A railroad company owes a stranger walking along a railroad track no other or greater duty than to exercise ordinary care and caution in looking out for and avoiding injuring him. Holland v. Missouri Pac. Ry. Co. (Mo. 1908), 109 S. W. Rep. 19.

Plaintiff's decedent, who, after attempting to flag a fast train in the darkness, one hundred and forty yards from a station, started to walk to the station ahead of the train, and was struck and killed, was guilty of contributory negligence. Ellis v. Southern Ry. Co. (U. S. C. C. A., S. C., 1908), 163 Fed. Rep. 686.

The operators of a train, discovering a trespasser standing or walking on the track, may assume that he will get off; and they are under no duty to attempt to stop the train until they discover that he cannot or will not get off. Southern Ry. Co. v. Gullatt (Ga. 1907), 43 So. Rep. 577.

[29] Bentley v. Georgia Pacific R. Co., 86 Ala. 484; 6 So. Rep. 37; Central R., etc., Co. v. Vaughan, 93 Ala. 209; 9 So. Rep. 468.

[30] Tennenbrook v. Southern, etc., R. Co., 59 Cal. 269; 6 Am. & Eng.

in the limits of a city or town does not impose on the railroad company the duty to be on the lookout for trespassers on the bridge, where it is twenty-five or thirty feet above the grade of the street.[31] In a recent well-considered decision by the Supreme Court of Arkansas,[32] Justice Battle, for the court, said, speaking of the legal status of a person, walking on a trestle, near a town, in Arkansas: "He was at the time a trespasser on the trestle. He had no right to be there. It was constructed solely for the running of the cars and trains of the railroad company, and the fact that persons did walk upon it, however frequently, did not change its character or convert it into a highway for footmen. He was in a place of danger and so being, was guilty of contributory negligence and cannot recover damages on account of his injury, unless the train men either injured him wantonly, maliciously or intentionally, or were guilty of negligence in avoiding injuring him, after discovery of his peril."

But where a railroad bridge or trestle is commonly used by the general public as a passageway, with the knowledge and consent of the railroad company, it will be considered as having licensed the public to so use it and will owe them the duty of keeping a lookout in approaching the bridge or trestle.[33]

However, there is no presumption that the employees of the company have authority to authorize the use of a

R. Cas. 8; Evansville, etc., R. Co. v. Hiatt, 17 Ind. 102; Phillipps v. East Tennessee, etc., R. Co., 87 Ga. 272; 13 S. E. Rep. 644; 48 Am. & Eng. R. Cas. 61; Louisville, etc., R. Co. v. Cooper, 68 Miss. 368; 8 So. Rep. 747.

[31] Beiser v. Chesapeake, etc., R. Co., 29 Ky. L. R. 249; 92 S. W. Rep. 928.

[32] Adams v. St. Louis, etc., R. Co., 83 Ark. 300; 103 S. W. Rep. 725. See, also, Chesapeake, etc., R. Co. v. Barbour's Adm'r (Ky.), 92 S. W. Rep. 928.

[33] Texas Midland R. Co. v. Byrd (Texas), 90 S. W. Rep. 185.

bridge or trestle as a passway for footmen,[34] and notwithstanding the general use of a trestle or bridge by pedestrians, if a notice or warning is kept posted at either end of the bridge, persons so using it will be none the less trespassers, toward whom the only duty owing will be to avoid willful or wrongful injuries after their presence is discovered.[35]

§ 1097. **Walking on railroad track in nighttime.**— To walk along the middle of a railroad track, when it is dark, without knowing or remembering whether a train is due or not, away from a public crossing, without looking in both directions for trains and without listening attentively and anxiously for the roar and rattle of the machinery of the trains likely to be run on the track, as well as for the sound of bell and whistle, is held, in Georgia,[36] to be gross negligence. A person so trespassing on the track ought to guard against the negligence of the employees of the railroad company, if he might discover the approaching train in time to avoid the injury, and he should also anticipate that there might be negligence which he might not discover until too late to save himself from injury.[37]

And while as toward licensees and employees, rightfully

[34] St. Louis, etc., R. Co. v. Shifflett, 98 Texas 326; 83 S. W. Rep. 677.

[35] Beiser v. Chesapeake, etc., R. Co., 29 Ky. L. R. 249; 92 S. W. Rep. 928.

The fact that a railway company had permitted or acquiesced in the use of its roadbed and trestle as a footpath by the public would not excuse a person walking thereon for failure to exercise ordinary care to guard and protect himself from injury while so doing, and more diligence and caution would be required of him to constitute ordinary care than under less dangerous conditions. Texas Midland R. Co. v. Byrd (Tex. Civ. App. 1908), 110 S. W. Rep. 199.

[36] Central, etc., R. Co. v. Smith, 78 Ga. 694; 3 S. E. Rep. 397; 34 Am. & Eng. R. Cas. 1.

[37] Central, etc., R. Co. v. Smith, *supra.*

on the track, there is a duty perhaps, to furnish a headlight, as well as to give warning of the approach of trains by proper signals, this duty does not obtain, in the case of a trespasser, whose presence is not to be anticipated and there is no liability, although the engine is operated without a headlight,[38] or with a very dim headlight,[39] at the time of the injury to the nighttime trespasser on the track.

§ 1098. **Deaf person walking on track.**— It is generally held to be gross negligence for one who is deaf or hard of hearing, to walk along a railroad track, away from a public crossing, where trains are apt to pass at any minute, as the due care required to be exercised by persons in such position of danger requires a constant listening for trains, as well as a looking out for them, and where a person is not able to hear the approach of trains, he should not thus expose himself.[40] One who is partially deaf and who walks on or along a railroad track, so close as to be struck by a train, approaching him from the rear, is guilty of such contributory negligence as to defeat a recovery, in case of a resulting injury from being struck by a train, although the train employees were also lacking in the exercise of proper care and prudence to discover his presence on the track.[41] And in a Texas case,[42] where an aged man with defective hearing was killed while walking on a track, and his deafness was not known to those in charge of the train which struck him, and the employees

[38] Houston, etc., R. Co. v. Richards, 59 Texas 373; 12 Am. & Eng. R. Cas. 70.

[39] Frye v. St. Louis, etc., Ry. Co., 200 Mo. 377; 98 S. W. Rep. 566. One walking on a railroad track at night, was denied a recovery for injury by being struck by train, in Wilds v. Brunswick, etc., R. Co., 82 Ga. 667; 9 S. E. Rep. 595; Texas, etc., R. Co. v. Barfield (Texas), 3 S. W. Rep. 665.

[40] Cogswell v. Oregon, etc., R. Co., 6 Oregon, 417.

[41] Laicher v. New Orleans, etc., R. Co., 28 La. Ann. 320.

[42] Artusy v. Missouri Pacific Ry. Co., 73 Texas 191; 11 S. W. Rep. 177; 37 Am. & Eng. R. Cas. 288.

in charge of the train saw him for a considerable period before he was struck, but no effort to stop the train was made until it was within a hundred feet of the deceased, it was held that the company was not guilty of negligence and was not liable for the death, as the employees had a perfect right to assume that the deceased was in full possession of his faculties and would hear the train and leave the track, in time to avoid being killed.

§ 1099. **Lying or sitting on railroad track.**— A railroad track is such a place of danger, on account of the powerful conveyances operated at such a high rate of speed along the track, that a person who lies or sits down on the track is generally held to do so at his peril, for it is such a dangerous position to assume that his own neglect in such a dangerous place could only be held to be the proximate cause of his injury, in case of an injury from a train while in such a position.

In a North Carolina case,[48] the body of the plaintiff's intestate was found at the side of the track near a bridge, after a night train had passed. There was no direct or positive evidence as to how he was killed, but the marks on his body and other signs, tended to show that he had been sitting or lying on the end of the ties when he was struck

---

[48] Norwood v. Raleigh, etc., R. Co., 111 No. Car. 236; 16 S. E. Rep. 4.

A railroad company is not liable for the running over of one lying between the rails at a cattle guard, he being a trespasser, where ordinary care to avert the accident was exercised after discovery of his position, though he could have been discovered sooner by the exercise of proper care. St. Louis, etc., Ry. Co. v. Raines (Ark. 1908), 111 S. W. Rep. 262.

A person injured by a train while lying unconscious on a railroad track has the burden of showing negligence. Johnson v. Guffey Petroleum Co. (Mass. 1908), 83 N. E. Rep. 874; Same v. Boston, etc., R. R., *id;* Riggs v. Metropolitan Ry. Co., 115 S. W. Rep. 969.

by the train.   The court held that intestate was a trespasser and it was his duty to keep out of the way of a passing train and his failure to do so would be considered the proximate cause of his death, in the absence of evidence tending to show that the engineer could, by proper watchfulness, have seen him lying apparently insensible on the track, in time to have avoided the injury by using the appliances at his command, without jeopardizing the lives of the persons on the train.

§ 1100. **Falling asleep upon railroad track.**— As the courts of the country have never extended the common-law duty of the railroad company even toward its own employees, as to include the duty of furnishing a reasonably safe place to sleep, during hours of employment, this duty would much less be recognized in favor of a trespasser upon the railroad track, whose presence could not reasonably have been anticipated, and hence, there is generally held to be no liability for an injury to a trespasser, who has fallen asleep on the track, and sustains injury in consequence thereof, when due effort was made to avoid the injury, after his danger was discovered.[44]

In a recent Kentucky case,[45] the plaintiff and some companions, all boys about fifteen years old, had wrongfully stolen a ride on a train and then fallen asleep in the defendant's freight yard, while waiting for a freight train, to ride back.   While asleep a freight train ran over them, killing two and wounding the plaintiff, by cutting off his leg and foot.   In disposing of the case, Barker, J., for the court, said: " The evidence shows, beyond a doubt, that

[44] Williams v. Southern Pacific R. Co. (Cal.), 9 Pac. Rep. 152; Richardson v. Wilmington, etc., R. Co., 8 Rich. (So. Car.) 120.

[45] Maysville, etc., R. Co. v. McCabe, 26 Ky. L. R. 532; 82 S. W. Rep. 233.

the boys were asleep on the track, in appellant's private yard and they were therefore trespassers. Appellant owed them no duty, save to use reasonable diligence to prevent injuring them after their peril was discovered." And this decision illustrates the general rule on this subject.[46]

§ 1101. **Climbing upon cars.**— One who voluntarily and without right, gets upon a car,[47] or engine,[48] to ride, is a mere intruder or trespasser, and the railroad company owes to him no duty except the negative duty not to injure him wantonly or willfully, after his presence is discovered. And even if the employees in charge of a car,[49] or engine,[50] know of the presence of such a person thereon, and they are negligent in the management of the car, or engine, as a result of which such person sustains an injury, the railroad company will not be liable for the injury, unless the same could have been foreseen or anticipated by the employees as a probable consequence of the negligence on their part, as this

[46] Dugan's Adm'r v. Chesapeake, etc., R. Co., 24 Ky. L. R. 1754; 72 S. W. Rep. 291; Felder v. Louisville, etc., R. Co., 2 McMull (So. Car.) 403. And see, Riggs v. Metropolitan Ry. Co. (Mo.), 115 S. W. Rep. 969.

[47] St. Louis, etc., R. Co. v. Ledbetter, 45 Ark. 246.

[48] Stringer v. Missouri Pacific Ry. Co., 96 Mo. 299; 9 S. W. Rep. 905.

[49] St. Louis, etc., R. Co. v. Ledbetter, *supra*.

[50] One who got on a switch engine, at the request of the brakeman, who was not shown to have authority to invite people to ride the engine, was held not entitled to recover for an injury due to a derailment of the engine, in Stringer v. Missouri Pacific Ry. Co., 96 Mo. 299; 9 S. W. Rep. 905.

Where plaintiff was injured while climbing between the cars of a freight train standing over a highway crossing, the railroad company was not liable because plaintiff was invited to cross by a brakeman; the conductor being the representative of the railroad company in control of the train, and the brakeman having no authority to extend such invitation. Southern Ry. Co. v. Clark (Ky. 1907), 105 S. W. Rep. 384.

would not, in law, amount to willful or wanton conduct on their part.

§ 1102. **Infants climbing upon cars.**— Railroad cars are not such dangerous and attractive machines as to place any duty upon the railroad company to fence in their cars, to keep trespassing children from climbing on the cars and for an injury to a child of tender years, from climbing on cars, moving in towns or cities, or in railroad yards, the same rule obtains that applies to adult trespassers, and in the absence of a wanton or willful injury, there is no liability if a child riding the cars is injured.[51]

Speaking of the absence of a duty toward such an infantile trespasser and replying to the argument that such a child could not be held to have violated an ordinance forbidding children or others from attaching themselves to or climbing on moving cars, in towns, Judge Sherwood, for the Missouri court, in a well-decided case,[52] said: " Plaintiff being a trespasser, a violator of the law, could have no ground of recovery, based on his own dereliction. But it is claimed for plaintiff that these regulations of the law do not apply to ' babies.' While the law may not apply, in a criminal proceeding, to a child of very tender years, yet, still for the purposes of a civil action, the consequences of the unlawful act must be the same in the case of an infant, even of very tender years, as in the case of an adult. In a word, the act of an infant, in consequence of his tender years, though noncriminal, yet it is wrongful, in the sense of being an invasion of the rights of others, just as much so as though done by an adult."

[51] Chicago, etc., R. Co. v. Eininger, 114 Ill. 79; 29 N. E. Rep. 196; Barney v. Hannibal, etc., R. Co., 126 Mo. 372, 392; 28 S. W. Rep. 1069; 26 L. R. A. 847.
[52] Barney v. Hannibal, etc., R. Co., *supra.*

But if the presence of a boy is discovered on a train, and he is threatened or so mistreated that in an effort to leave the train he is injured, as where water was thrown in his face, by the employees in charge of the train, this is held to be such evidence of an intentional injury as to make the negligence of the railroad company a jury issue, in a New York case.[53]

§ 1103. **When trespasser can recover, notwithstanding his own negligence.**— Although a trespasser may have been at fault, in the first instance, in getting on the track, yet, if he makes all proper efforts to avoid injury, when the danger is apparent and the employees in charge of an approaching train fail to use all the means at their disposal, by which the injury could have been avoided, the railroad company will be responsible for the injury and the original negligence will not be held to bar a recovery.[54] If the train employees have reason to believe that a trespasser on the track is drunk, or otherwise incapacitated from avoiding the dan-

[53] Clark v. New York, etc., R. Co., 40 Hun 605; 2 N. Y. S. R. 249; 113 N. Y. 670; 21 N. E. Rep. 1116; 23 N. Y. S. R. 994.

In an action for injuries to a child received while stealing a ride on a freight car, the issue whether the person injured was of such tender age and inexperience as to be incapable of appreciating the dangers to which he exposed himself was one which should be submitted to the jury in such a manner as to permit its consideration, disconnected with the other questions regarding contributory negligence. St. Louis Southwestern Ry. Co. v. Davis (Tex. Civ. App. 1908), 110 S. W. Rep. 939.

While those in charge of trains, if they know of the actual presence of children jumping off and on the moving cars, are required not to injure them if with the means at their command they can avoid doing so, a railroad company whose lines pass through cities or other populous communities is not required to maintain a lookout there for children who are in the habit of jumping on and off the cars while in motion. Swartwood's Guardian v. Louisville, etc., R. Co. (Ky. 1908), 111 S. W. Rep. 305.

[54] Tanner v. Louisville, etc., R. Co., 60 Ala. 621.

ger, they have no right to indulge the presumption that he will get off the track, but must use ordinary care to avoid injuring him, or the railroad company will be responsible for an injury.[55]   And if the proximate cause of an injury to a trespasser on the track is the negligence of the engineer of a train, and the party injured is prevented by a providential dispensation from the use of his faculties at the time of the injury, the fact that he had been guilty of prior negligence, when no train was in view, will not constitute such contributory negligence as would prevent a recovery.[56]

But in all these cases, it is a case of subsequent negligence, amounting to wantonness, as toward trespassers, or otherwise, there would be no liability for an injury, where the prior negligence of a trespasser was conceded, for when this is true, then without wantonness, there can be no cause of action, as this is always essential, to constitute a cause of action in favor of a negligent trespasser.[57]

§ 1104. **When a question of law for the court.**— In a suit against a railroad company, for injury to a trespasser, on the track, by a moving train, where there is no conflict in the evidence, and it appears that the injury was not wanton or willful, and that the negligence of the trespasser contributed to it, the court, as matter of law, should pass upon the question of the trespasser's negligence and should direct a verdict for the defendant.[58]

[55] St. Louis, etc., R. Co. v. Wilkerson, 46 Ark. 513; Lake Shore, etc., R. Co. v. Boderer, 139 Ill. 596; 29 N. E. Rep. 692; 33 Ill. App. 479; 54 Am. & Eng. R. Cas. 177; Baltimore, etc., R. Co. v. State. 36 Md. 366; Missouri Pacific Ry. Co. v. Weisen, 65 Texas 443; Everett v. Oregon, etc., R. Co., 9 Utah, 340; 34 Pac. Rep. 289; Central, etc., R. Co. v. Vaughan, 93 Ala. 209; 9 So. Rep. 468.

[56] Houston, etc., R. Co. v. Sympkins, 54 Texas 615; 6 Am. & Eng. R. Cas. 11.

[57] Holwerson v. St. Louis, etc., R. Co., 157 Mo. 216, 244; 57 S. W. Rep. 770; 50 L. R. A. 850.

[58] Boland v. Missouri R. Co., 36 Mo. 484; Gurley v. Missouri

But when the evidence upon different material issues in a
suit for an injury to a trespasser, is conflicting, or when different conclusions can be drawn from undisputed evidence,
or the inferences to be drawn from the evidence are not certain, the issue of the trespasser's contributory negligence
should be submitted to the jury.[59]

§ 1105. **When question of fact for jury.**— Where the facts
are disputed and the evidence is conflicting, upon different
issues, the question of negligence should always be left to the
jury.[60]. And although the evidence in a record is undisputed, where it is susceptible of two inferences, the one consistent with the exercise of ordinary care and the other tending to show contributory negligence, the court should submit
the issue to the jury to decide.[61]   And if different reasonable minds would differ as to the conclusion, upon the issue
whether or not the plaintiff or injured trespasser was guilty
of contributory negligence directly affecting the injury sued
for, it is held to be a jury issue.[62]
But where the facts on the issue of the contributory negli-

Pacific Ry. Co., 93 Mo. 445; 6 S. W. Rep. 218; Hudson v. Wabash R.
Co., 101 Mo. 13; 14 S. W. Rep. 15; McClaren v. Indianapolis, etc., R.
Co., 83 Ind. 319; 8 Am. & Eng. R. Cas. 218.

[59] Drain v. St. Louis, etc., R. Co., 86 Mo. 574; Huhn v. Missouri
Pacific Ry. Co., 92 Mo. 440; 4 S. W. Rep. 937; Davis v. Kansas City,
etc., R. Co., 46 Mo. App. 180; Church v. Chicago, etc., R. Co., 119
Mo. 203; 23 S. W. Rep. 1056; Kreis v. Missouri Pacific Ry. Co., 131
Mo. 533; 33 S. W. Rep. 1150; Lamb v. Missouri Pacific Ry. Co., 147
Mo. 171; 48 S. W. Rep. 659; 51 S. W. Rep. 81.

In an action for death of a trespasser on a railroad track caused by
being struck by an engine, evidence examined, and *held* not to raise the
issue of discovered peril. Judgment, 98 S. W. Rep. 421, reversed. San
Antonio, etc., Ry. Co. v. McMillan (Tex., 1907), 102 S. W. Rep. 103.

[60] Owens v. Hannibal, etc., R. Co., 58 Mo. 386.

[61] Wentworth v. Duffy, 68 Mo. App. 513; Butts v. National Bank,
99 Mo. App. 168; 72 S. W. Rep. 1083.

[62] Dowell v. Guthrie, 116 Mo. 646; 22 S. W. Rep. 893.

gence of a trespasser are undisputed, the issue of his negligence is a question of law for the court, and it is error to submit the issue to a jury.[63] When there is no conflict in the evidence and all the causes contributing to produce the injury complained of are known, whether the given act in the chain of causation is the remote or proximate cause, is a question of law for the court.[64] Nor does a peremptory direction of a verdict in such a case usurp the province of the jury, for it is a simple pronouncement of the law upon the uncontroverted evidence. And if the facts are undisputed and such facts show that, notwithstanding the negligence of the defendant, the injury complained of would not have occurred, but for the contributory negligence of the person injured, directly tending to produce the injury, it is the duty of the court to direct the jury to find for the defendant.[65]

[63] Kelley v. Washington, etc., Co., 107 Mo. App. 490; 81 S. W. Rep. 631.

[64] Henry v. St. Louis, etc., R. Co., 76 Mo. 288; 43 Am. Rep. 762.

[65] Powell v. Missouri Pacific Ry. Co., 76 Mo. 80.

The issue of the contributory negligence of a trespasser, injured while on a railroad track, was held to be a jury issue, in the following cases: Northern Pacific R. Co. v. Amato, 49 Fed. Rep. 881; 144 U. S. 465; 12 Sup. Ct. Rep. 740; Smith v. Savannah, etc., R. Co., 84 Ga. 698; 11 S. E. Rep. 455; 42 Am. & Eng. R. Cas. 105; Crow v. Wabash R. Co., 23 Mo. App. 357; Corcoran v. New York, etc., R. Co., 19 Hun (N. Y.) 368; Remer v. Long Island R. Co., 15 N. Y. S. R. 884; 48 Hun 352; 113 N. Y. 669; 23 N. Y. S. R. 994; 21 N. E. Rep. 1116; Lay v. Richmond, etc., R. Co., 106 No. Car. 404; 11 S. E. Rep. 412; 42 Am. & Eng. R. Cas. 110; Patton v. East Tennessee, etc., R. Co., 89 Tenn. 370; 15 S. W. Rep. 919; 48 Am. & Eng. R. Cas. 581.

Where boys were known to be in a position which would become perilous by the passing of two trains, and the train men in charge of the train which had been standing at the station knew of the approach of the other train, and the train men of neither train gave them any warning, though the noise of the train starting at the station was calculated to prevent them from hearing the other, it cannot be said, as a matter of law, that there was no negligence. Central of Georgia Ry. Co. v. Motz (Ga. 1908), 61 S. E. Rep. 1.

The questions whether wires were dar
platform, and whether the railroad in t
ought to have known of the condition a
the railroad was guilty of want of ordin
wires, were material on the issue of it
the wires. Banderob v. Wisconsin Cent.
N. W. Rep. 738.

INDEX.

1647

ANNOUNCEMENT,
of train, 697.
of station, 704.

ANTICIPATED CAUSE, (See PROXIMATE CAUSE).
when liability depends upon, 28.

APPLIANCES,
safety of for jury, when, 155.
railway company furnishing to contractor, 288
obligation to repair generally, 271.
what, necessary for boarding trains, 688.
failure to discover defects in, 419.
unauthorized use of, 421.
what necessary, for alighting from trains, 711.
duty of employer to furnish, 252.
general use the test, 252.
automatic signals not required, 252.
unblocked frogs may be used when (note), 252.
unsafe hand hold, gives right of action when (note), 252.
newest need not be furnished, 253.
safest not essential, 253.
engines and cars are, 254.
scaffolds, lights and ladder as, 255.
hidden defects in, 256.

APPROACHES, (See STATIONS AND APPROACHES).
to crossings, should be maintained, 904.

APPROACHING TRAIN,
crossing in front of, 1029.

APPROXIMATE CAUSE, (See PROXIMATE CAUSE).

ARKANSAS,
statute of, establishing liability for negligence of coemployees, 514.

ASLEEP ON TRACK,
contributory negligence of trespasser in falling, 1100.

ASSAULT,
pleading action for, 829.

ASSAULT ON PASSENGERS,
rule *res ipsa loquitur* as applied to, 123.
by strangers, that could have been prevented, 761.
by strangers, that were not anticipated, 762.

II—52   1649

1652

BOARDING TRAINS (*Continued*).
on invitation, 699.
after calling " all aboard," 699.
signals and warnings to passengers in, 700.
signals by third persons to passengers, 701.
accidental injuries in, 702.

BRAKEMAN,
a coemployee with fireman and engineer, 500.
injury to, from wild engine, 363.
injury to, from defective cars, 364.

BRAKES,
injuries from defective, 654.

BREACH OF DUTY,
essential to give cause of action, 2.

BRIDGE,
crossing in front of train, 416.
injuries from failure to repair, 467.
trespasser walking on, 1096.

BRIDGES,
carrier's duty toward, 605.
inspection of, 606.
trespassers upon, 1067.
employer's duty to maintain reasonably safe, 258.
liability for injuries from defective, 259.
when low, gives right of action (note), 259.
defective overhead part of company's " ways," within meaning of
statute (note), 259.

BRIDGE WATCHER,
not coemployee with engineer, 500.

BROKEN RAIL,
causing injury to passenger, 614.

BROTHERS, (See PARTIES).
can sue for death of brothers, when, 67.

BRUSH,
obstructing track, at crossing, 1022.

BUILDINGS,
track obstructed by, at crossings, 1019.

BURDEN OF PROOF,
in crossing accidents, 1032.
instruction on, 837.
in accidents, from failure to give signals, 971.

BUSINESS OF RAILROAD,
does not affect liability, 7.

C

CABOOSE, (See CARS).
passenger riding in cupola of, 798.

CALIFORNIA,
statute of, establishing liability of railroad companies, 515.

CAR,
passing from one to another, 774.
statutory action for negligence of person controlling, 510.

CAR AXLES,
injuries from defective, 653.

CARE,
exacted of carrier in care of track, 594–597.
highest degree exacted from carrier, 577.
proportionate to mode of conveyance, must be used by carrier, 583.
absence of, constitutes negligence, when, 4.
degree of, required, by employer, 4, 10.
ordinary only, required of employer, 10.

CAR INSPECTOR,
a coemployee with other train men when, 494.

CARPENTER,
in railroad yard not coemployee of engineer, 493.

CAR PLATFORMS,
injury from snow and ice on, 681.
injury to passenger on, 651.

CARRIERS,
duty owing by, to passengers alighting from trains, 703, 726.
contracts limiting liability of, 847–858.
using another's facilities or employees, 811.
with running power on another road, 813.
employing another to transport passengers, 814.
as owner of road or premises, 815.
using another's road, 816.

[*References are to sec*

1656

COEMPLOYEES (*Continued*).
    station agent and other railway employees as, 499.
    status of various, in different departments, 500.
    negligence of, not imputed, 1050.
    . who are, when jury issue, 161.
    injury due to, for court to act on, when, 139.
    orders of, as assumed risks, 350.
    negligence of, assumed when, 354.
    negligence of, not assumed when, 386.

COLLISIONS,
    when rule *res ipsa loquitur* applies to, 116.
    caused by slippery rails, 613.
    injury from, not assumed when, 361.
    on the same track, 674.
    at intersection of two railroads, 675.
    with cattle, 679.
    when injury from, a question for court, 147.
    due to negligence of coemployees, 469.

COLORADO,
    constitution and statute of, affecting liability of railroad com-
        panies, 516.

COLORED PASSENGER,
    entitled to protection from fellow passengers, 756.

COMMON ENTERPRISE,
    imputed negligence of persons engaged in, 1049.

COMMON LAW,
    right of action, as determining jurisdiction, 41.

COMPANIES,
    using same track or train, 229.

COMPARATIVE NEGLIGENCE,
    doctrine of, not generally recognized, 443.
    based upon unnatural refinement, 443.
    the rule of, stated, 444.
    recognized, when defendant's negligence " gross," as compared to
        plaintiff's, 444.
    depends upon recognition of different degrees of negligence (note),
        444.
    applied in death cases (note), 444.
    origin of the doctrine of, 445.

CONGRESS (*Continued*).
    employer's liability act of, 544.
    safety appliance act of, 545.

CONNECTICUT,
    statute of, upon employer's liability, 517.

CONNECTING CARRIERS,
    liability of, to employees, 231.
    injury to passenger upon road of, 683.
    liability of one, for injury on line of another, 809.
    liability of initial, 810.
    using another's facilities or employees, 811.
    injury in car on side track of, 812.
    having running powers, 813.
    employing another to carry passenger, 814.
    as owner of road or premises, 815.
    using another's road, 816.
    as lessees, 817.
    concurrent negligence of, 818.
    stipulations limiting liability of, 819.

CONSIDERATION,
    of contracts limiting liability, 848.

CONSOLIDATED COMPANY,
    liability of, for torts of constituent companies, 240.

CONSTRUCTION COMPANY,
    as independent contractor, 292.

CONTAGIOUS DISEASE,
    communication of, to passenger, 741.
    communication of, by fellow passenger, 755.

CONTRACTS,
    exempting railroad company from contractor's negligence, 300.
    of employees in violation of statute, 506.
    personal injury action, may be based on, 16.
    cannot be waived, when, 18.

CONTRIBUTORY NEGLIGENCE OF EMPLOYEES, 388–442.
    explanation of the defense, 388.
    definition of, 388.
    absence of ordinary care constitutes, 389.
    mutual negligence bars recovery, 390.
    where independent cause brings about injury, 390.

1664

[*References are to sections.*]

II—53

COUPLINGS,
injuries from defective, 655.

COURSE OF EMPLOYMENT,
injury must occur in, 227.

COURT,
province of, in assessing damages, 167.

proximate cause, as issue for, when, 36.

when negligence of trespasser a question for, 1104.

issues for, generally, 130.

questions of law, proper issue for, 131.

should determine whether *prima facie* case shown, 131.

mixed questions of law and fact are for, 132.

when there is total absence of evidence of negligence, should not send case to jury, 133.

should take case from jury when no fair inference of negligence, 133.

should decide whether duty owing or not, 134.

duty of, when negligence alleged not established, 135.

should determine whether injury connected proximately with defendant's negligence when, 136.

should determine demurrer to evidence, 137.

duty of, when undisputed evidence shows contributory negligence of the plaintiff or injured person, 138.

duty of, in injuries from neglect of coemployees, 139.

duty of, where plaintiff selected more dangerous way to perform duty, 140.

should not permit jury to erect special standards for control of business, 141.

should determine necessity for rule when, 142.

should determine reasonableness of rule when, 143.

should hold that open risks are assumed, as matter of law, 144.

should determine safety of place when, 145.

should determine competency of employee when, 146.

should decide negligence in collision accidents when, 147.

duty of, where evidence disputes physical facts, 148.

determines questions of variance when, 149.

COVERED CONVEYANCE,
driving upon crossing in, 1025.

CROSSINGS, (See Defective Crossings, Grade Crossings and Overhead Crossings.)
injuries at generally, 877–889.

1668

CROSSINGS (*Continued*).

    injuries at, under rule of comparative negligence,

    injuries at, due to negligence in maintaining gates and signs, 916–930.

    injuries at, by failure to give signals, 946–974.

    injuries at, by failure to maintain flagman, 931–945.

    imputed negligence, in injuries at, 1037-1059.

    injuries at, from excessive speed of trains, 975–988.

    contributory negligence of traveler at, 990–1036.

CROSS TIES,

    carrier's duty regarding, 600.

CROSSING TRACK,

    persons engaged in, as licensees, 874.

CULVERTS,

    dangers from open, assumed, when, 342.

CUPOLA,

    passenger riding in, 798.

CUSTOMS, (See Evidence).

    when evidence of, admissible, 99.

CUTS,

    carrier's duty regarding, 601.

    obstructing track at crossing, 1021.

D

DAMAGES,

    for death of infant, 304.

    how affected by law of place of accident, 43.

    discretion of jury in assessing, 164.

    right to assess, generally, 166.

    definition of (note), 166.

    depends upon wrongful act and injury, 166.

    award of, must be founded on evidence, 166.

    accident, gives no right to, 166.

    province of court and jury in assessing, 167.

    duty to prevent or keep down, 168.

    none, for aggravation of injury by failure to employ medical aid, 168.

    augmented by unskillful treatment (note), 168.

    proximately resulting, are alone recoverable, 169.

    must be natural and proximate consequence, 169.

1670

DEATH (*Continued*).
  actions strictly construed, 42.
  local and transitory nature of action for, 40.
  law of place of accident controls when, 43.
  of foreigner, when administrator can sue for, 44.
  in foreign State, 45.
  when right to sue for, exists in either of two States, 47.
  statutes governing, need not be identical when, 48.
  no extraterritorial effect in actions for, 49.
  when statute governing, given extraterritorial effect, 50.
  penal statutes governing, 52.
  compensatory statutes governing, 52.
  limitations in actions for, 55.
  parties to action for, 56–71.
  right of recovery in deceased essential when, 57.
  actions for, due to coemployee's negligence, 507.
  of parent, damages for, 195.
  of husband, damages for, 196.
  of wife, damages for, 197.
  of child, damages for, 198.
  exemplary damages for, 200.

DEFECTS,
  evidence of notice of essential, 79.

DEFECTIVE CROSSINGS,
  care to remedy defects in, 903.
  obligation extends to approaches, 904.
  liability of municipality for, 905.
  when turnpike company liable for, 906.
  when company not liable for under crossing, 907.
  liability for private, 908.
  liability for obstructed, 909.
  neglect of statutory duty regarding, 910.
  raising track above street at, 911.
  failure to light at night, 912.
  failure to restore, 913.
  changing or diverting highway across, 914.
  when company's negligence regarding, is a jury issue, 915.

DEFENSE,
  contributory negligence as, 388.

DEFINITON,
  of demonstrative evidence, 110.

DIVISION OFFICERS,
  generally held to be vice-principals, 4

DIVISION SUPERINTENDENT,
  generally held to be vice-principal, 48

DOOR,
  shutting on passenger's hand, 682.
  injuries to passenger from, 649.

DOUBLE TRACK,
  carrier's duty toward, 617.

DRIVERS,
  negligence of, imputed when, 1042.
  of public conveyances, when negligen
  of stage coaches, when negligence impt
  of hired vehicles, when negligence imp
  of private vehicles, when negligence in

DROVER,
  as passenger, 567.

DROVERS,
  limitation of liability to, 856.

DRUNKEN PASSENGER,
  objection of, 730, 731.
  should be removed when, 746.

DRUNKEN PERSONS,
  as trespassers, 1084.
  going on track at crossing, 1031.

DUAL CAPACITY DOCTRINE,
  explained, 476.

DUE CARE,
  explained, 13.

DUST,
  obstructing track, at crossing, 1023.

DUTY,
  to injured person, must be violated, 2.
  breach of, essential to right of action, :
  imposed by statute, contributory neglig
  contract cannot affect when, 17.
  election to declare on, instead of prom
  will not control, when express contract

1674

EMPLOYER (*Continued*).

EMPLOYERS AND EMPLOYEES,

EVIDENCE (*Continued*).

FARM CROSSINGS,
injuries at, 881.

FATHER, (See PARTIES).
action by, for death of children, 62

FEDERAL EMPLOYER'S LIABILITY

FELLOW PASSENGERS,
protection from, generally, 742.
basis of liability for injuries from,
care to protect passengers from neg
should be removed, when turbulent
when drunken or disorderly, should
discharge of firearms, 747.
when insane, should be restrained,
assaults by, 749.
rape committed by, 750.
altercations between, and employees,
missile thrown by, 752.
carrier's knowledge of threatened da:
passengers should claim carrier's pr
communication of contagious disease
injury by, to colored passenger, 756.

FELLOW SERVANTS, (See COEMPLOYEE

FENCE,
injury to passenger from failure to, (

FIREARMS,
discharge of, by fellow passenger, 747
carrier not liable for use of, by fel.
747.

FIREMAN,
and brakeman coemployees, 500.

FLAG,
violation of rule requiring, by car re|

FLAGMAN,
trespasser cannot complain of absence
contributory negligence of traveler in ;
absence of, does not affect duty to lool
a coemployee of train men, 496.

FLAGMEN AND WATCHMEN,
duty to employ generally, 931.

1686

G

HIRED VEHICLES,
 imputed negligence of driver of, 1047.

HOLDING COMPANIES,
 liability of, for negligence of companies held, 242.

HORSES,
 frightening, by failure to give signals, 969.
 injuries from frightening at crossings, 886.

HOSPITAL,
 not an independent contractor, when, 299.

HUMANITARIAN DOCTRINE,
 in Missouri, 15.

HUSBAND, (See PARTIES).
 right to sue for death of wife, 61.
 damage for death of, 196.
 negligence of, imputed to wife when, 1056.

ICE,
 injury from, on car platform, 681.

ILLINOIS,
 safety appliance act of, 520.
 rule of comparative negligence in, 451.

IMMEDIATE CAUSE, (See PROXIMATE CAUSE).

IMPROVEMENTS,
 carrier's duty to adopt, 639.

IMPUTED NEGLIGENCE,
 what the term implies, 1037.
 basis of the doctrine of, 1038.
 distinguished from personal negligence, 1039.
 when cause derived from negligent person, 1040.
 concurrent negligence of another, no defense, 1041.
 to drivers of vehicles generally, 1042.
 to drivers of public conveyances, 1043.
 to persons traveling on railroad cars, 1044.
 to occupants of street cars, 1045.
 to persons riding in stage coaches, 1046.
 to persons riding in hired vehicles, 1047.
 of excursionists, 1048.
 of persons jointly engaged in common enterprise, 1049.

INDIANA,

INFANTS,

INFANTS (*Continued*).
    do not assume risks beyond scop
    do not assume risks while obeyir
    injuries to, from negligence of cc
    contributory negligence of, 313.
    contributory negligence of, a jur
    releases by, 314.

INITIAL CARRIER,
    liability of, 810.

INJURIES,
    proximate cause of various, 38.

INJURIES AT CROSSINGS,
    as affected by contributory neglig
    imputed negligence in actions for,
    from excessive speed of trains, 97¦
    from failure to give signals, 946–
    by failure to maintain flagmen, 9.
    due to negligence in maintenance o

INJURY,   ·
    nature and cause of, for jury when
    and violated right, both essential,
    and negligence in different States,
    and breach of duty both essential, :

INSANE PASSENGERS,
    care of, by carrier, 748.
    injuries to fellow passengers by, 74¦

INSANE PERSON,
    duty toward, as passenger, 586.

INSPECTION,
    of track by carrier, 595.
    of cars and engines by carrier, 637.
    of bridges, 606.
    employer's duty regarding, 266.
    of new appliances not required, 266
    extends to place of work, 266.
    must be reasonably careful, 266.
    not required of employee (note), 266
    of car wheels (note), 266.
    of hand holds (note), 266.
    by coemployees (note), 266.

INSPECTION (*Continued*).

duty of, cannot be delegated (note), 266.
of ordinary tools not required, 267.
hidden defects not disclosed by, 267.
of foreign cars, 268.

INSTRUCTIONS,

on degree of care toward passenger, 835.
on presumption of negligence from accident 836.
on burden of proof, 837.
defining negligence, 838.
that carrier is not an insurer, 839.
on duty toward passenger alighting, 840.
on safety of appliances for alighting, 841.
on contributory negligence of passenger, 842.
assuming notice of danger of person injured, 843.
on violation of rules, 844.
confusing recoveries under different statutes, 845.
inconsistent with others, 846.
upon rule of comparative negligence, 459.
on proximate cause, 31.
to passengers in alighting, 714.
upon duty to give signals, 973.

INSURANCE,

evidence of employer's incompetent, 108.

INSURER,

employer is not, 251.
instruction that carrier is not, 839.
carrier is not, 573.

INTERVENING CAUSE, (See PROXIMATE CAUSE).

what is, an, 25.

INTOXICATED EMPLOYEES,

injuries caused by, 483.

INTOXICATED PERSON,

at railroad crossing, 1031.
duty toward, as passenger, 588.

INTOXICATION,

of passenger, when a defense, 805.
as contributory negligence, 405.

INTRUDERS,

violence of, at railway stations, 766.

JURY (*Continued*).

K

KANSAS,

[References are to sections.]

1704

NOMINAL DAMAGES,
  when allowed, 172.

NONRESIDENTS, (See PARTIES).
  in actions for death, 71.

NORTH CAROLINA,
  statute upon employer's liability, 535.

NORTH DAKOTA,
  employer's liability act, 536.

NURSES,
  injuries from, within rule *res ipsa loquitur* when, 129.

O

OBSTRUCTED CROSSINGS,
  liability for injuries at, 909.
  failure to light at night, 912.
  duty to stop and listen at, 1013.

OBSTRUCTIONS,
  care to avoid, 678.
  risks from, assumed when, 326.
  injuries from, assumed when, 369.
  employee's negligence in striking, 424.
  injuries to passengers by, 611.
  placed on track by strangers, 765.
  when injuries from, gives right of action, 260.
  spouts and posts as, 260.
  must be sufficiently removed from track to permit passage of man
      on car, 260.
  caused by natural forces, should be removed, 260.
  posts as (note), 260.
  switch stand as (note), 260.
  mail crane as (note), 260.
  bridge as (note), 260.
  warehouse chute as (note), 260.
  live animals as (note), 260.

OBVIOUS RISKS,
  are assumed, 336.

OFFICERS,
  are generally vice-principals, 486.

OHIO,
  employer's liability act, 537.

PARTIES (*Continued*).

PASSAGEWAYS,

PASSENGER, (See CONTRIBUTORY NEGLIGENCE OF PASSENGER).

PROXIMATE CAUSE (*Continued*).

is that which causes injury, 22.

incidental causes are not, 22.

not nearest in time, always, 22.

instruction on (note), 22.

tests for determining, 23.

Justice Strong's statement of test (note), 23.

must have been foreseen, generally, 23.

intervening, or independent cause, not, 23.

nearness of causation, the controlling factor, 24.

agency producing, may be remote, 24.

must be individualized, 24.

concurrent cause, will not affect, when (note), 24.

distinguished from efficient intervening cause, 25.

when intervening cause is, 25.

producing other causes, 25.

producing other causes that could be foreseen (note), 25.

negligent act concurring with, 26.

two or more acts which are, 26.

not affected by concurrent, when (note), 26.

in railroad collision (note), 26.

absence of light on engine, not (note), 26.

must be wrongful and connected with injury, 27.

defendant must be author of, 27.

or one of the efficient causes, 27.

as an anticipated cause, 28.

and intervening cause, when both anticipated, 28.

rape by convict not an anticipated, 28.

rape after eviction from train, not an anticipated, 28.

when any injury resulting from, could be expected, 28.

such as ordinarily prudent person could foresee (note), 28.

aggravation of injury not, 29.

negligence of injured person as, 29.

collision with train after eviction, not, 29.

aggravation by physician not, when, 29.

last opportunity of avoiding injury as (note), 29.

negligence of physician as (note), 29.

acts in emergency as, 30.

in emergency, when no real danger threatened, 30.

instructions on, 31.

accident as, 31.

act of God, as, 31.

natural causes that could not have been avoided, as, 32.

[*References are to sections.*]

[*References are to sections.*]

1720

RISKS NOT ASSUMED (*Continued*).
   falling on icy steps (note), 364.
   dangerous working place, 365.
   caving earth bank, 365.
   injuries from low bridges, 366.
   injury from defective track, 367.
   defective roadbed (note), 367.
   running trains into open switches, 368.
   obstructions near the track, 369.
   injuries from defective cars, 370.
   defective engines, injuries from, 370.
   injuries from excessive speed, 371.
   danger must generally be appreciated, 372.
   if danger not understood, not assumed, 373.
   latent, unknown defects causing injury, 374.
   after promise to repair, 375.
   instances of risks not assumed after promise to repair, 376.
   extraordinary dangers, 377.
   dangers outside scope of employment, 378.
   dangers from orders of vice-principal, 379.
   dangers to car and track repairers, 380.
   injuries due to incompetency of employees, 381.
   under statutes denying defense of, 382.
   under statutes regulating defense, 383.
   injuries from flying particles of steel, 384.
   federal statute denying defense, 385.
   negligence of coemployees under statutes, 386.
   jury can determine what are, when, 387.

RISK OF BUSINESS,
   as affecting care and vigilance, 11.

ROADBED, (See TRACK).
   injury from, not assumed when (note), 367.

ROADBED AND TRACK,
   evidence of defects in, 82.
   at other places, 83.

ROADMASTER,
   held to be vice-principal, 486.

ROCK,
   falling on track, causing derailment, 612.

ROUNDHOUSE FOREMAN,
   not an employee with brakeman, 493.

SHOOTING,
  of passenger, by fellow passenger, 747.

SHUNTING CARS,
  risks from, assumed when, 330.

SICK PASSENGERS,
  assistance toward, in alighting, 709.

SICK PERSON,
  duty toward, as passenger, 586.

SIDE TRACK,
  injury in car on, of connecting road, 812.

SIGNAL,
  statutory action for negligence of person controlling, 511.

SIGNALS,
  injuries from observance and nonobservance of, 427.
  trespassers not entitled to, 1080.
  required at overhead crossings, when, 890–900.
  injuries to passengers by wrong, 671.
  to passengers boarding trains, 700.
  by third persons, to passengers boarding trains, 701.
  failure to give, does not affect duty to look and listen, 1009.
  how far traveler may presume that they will be given, 1000.
  failure to heed, as contributory negligence, 999.
  failure of trespasser to heed, 1093.

SIGNALS AND LOOKOUTS,
  duty to maintain at common law, 946.
  general duty to keep lookout, 947.
  ordinances requiring, 948.
  constitutionality of statutes requiring, 949.
  violation of statutes requiring, 950.
  object of statutes requiring, 951.
  what trains required to give, 952.
  failure to signal, negligence when, 953.
  traveler may assume clear track in absence of, 954.
  kind of, required, 955.
  when statute in the alternative, 956.
  when view of track is obstructed, 957.
  at improper place, 958.
  when other precautions required, 959.
  statutes requiring, apply to what roads, 960.
  what are public highways generally, 961.

STATUTES (*Continued*).
  regulating speed of trains, 976.
  requiring signals and lookouts, 949.
  effect of violating, statutes requiring signals, 950.
  object of statutes, requiring signals, 951.
  in the alternative requiring signals, 956.
  requiring signals, apply to what roads, 960.
  penal and compensatory, distinguished, 52.
  governing actions for death, construed strictly, 42.
  no extraterritorial effect given, when, 49.
  repeal of, does not affect right, when, 51.
  dangers from violating, assumed when, 356.
  denying defense of assumed risk, 382.

STATUTES REGULATING COEMPLOYEES,
  objects and reasons for such legislation, 501.
  objections to such statutes, 502.
  history of such legislation, 503.
  constitutionality of such statutes, 504.
  statute must not specialize character of employer, but nature of
      employment, to be upheld (note), 504.
  extraterritorial effect of such statutes, 505.
  contracts in contravention of, 506.
  actions for death of employees, under, 507.
  remedies under, for injuries while obeying rules or orders, 508.
  remedies under, for injuries due to negligence of superintendent,
      509.
  .controlling car, train or locomotive, 510.
  controlling any signal, point, or switch, 511.
  injured by defects in "ways, works, machinery or plant," 512.
  in Alabama, 513.
  in Arkansas, 514.
  in California, 515.
  in Colorado, 516.
  in Connecticut, 517.
  in Florida, 518.
  in Georgia, 519.
  in Illinois, 520.
  in Indiana, 521.
  in Iowa, 522.
  in Kansas, 523.
  in Kentucky, 524.
  in Louisiana, 525.

  II—57.

TRACK (*Continued*).

duty to furnish reasonably safe, cannot be delegated (note), 258.

employees may assume employer has safe (note), 258.

only reasonable care required, to maintain (note), 258.

work of laying, held to continuously change place (note), 258.

for injuries from obstructions near, 260.

carrier's duty regarding, 593.

degree of care to maintain, 594.

carrier's duty to inspect, 595.

carrier should bestow such care upon, as used by cautious persons, 596.

carrier's liability, for injuries, caused by defective, 598.

negligence presumed, from injury due to defective, 599.

condition of rails and cross-ties of, 600.

injuries from failure to fence, 602.

ordinary rainfall causing injury to, 603.

extraordinary floods, causing washouts in, 604.

bridges and trestles under, should be inspected, 606.

switches, of, causing injury to passengers, 607.

derailment caused by defect, establishes *prima facie* case, 608.

injury to, by landslide causing passenger's injury, 609.

obstructions on, causing injury to passengers, 611.

injury to passenger from rock falling on, 612.

collision due to slippery rails of, 613.

broken rail in, causing derailment, 614.

bent rail in, causing derailment, 615.

duty to keep in repair, 616.

care of double,

destruction of, by public enemy, causing injury to passenger, 618.

employee standing or walking upon, 412.

employee standing or walking near, 413.

use of, by pedestrians, 1063.

persons walking on, not entitled to signals, 965.

injury from, not assumed when, 367.

people crossing, as licensees, 874.

people using, as footway, 875.

raising above street, 911.

trespasser standing on or near, 1094.

walking on or near, 1095.

pleading injury due to bad, 826.

crossing, in front of car, 775.

TRACK REPAIRERS,

risks assumed by, 352.

TRACK REPAIRERS (*Continued*).
 are coemployees with train men at common law, 490.
 and train men as coemployees, 498.
 do not assume risks when, 380.

TRACKS,
 injuries from, assumed when, 325.

TRACK WALKER,
 and train men coemployees, 500.

TRAFFIC ARRANGEMENT,
 liability for injuries to employees, by companies engaged in, 232.

TRAIN,
 statutory action for negligence of person controlling, 510.
 employee crossing track in front of, 411.
 should be entirely stopped to let passenger alight, 707.
 crossing in front of, 1029.
 trespassers upon, 1070.
 pleading negligence in management of, 827.
 pleading failure to heat, 828.
 starting, after reasonable time for passengers to alight, 723.
 negligence in boarding, 778–782.
 negligence to board moving when, 783, 784.
 negligence in alighting from, 785–792.
 alighting in front of, on parallel track, 720.
 starting, while passenger is alighting from, 721.
 jerking, while passenger is alighting from, 722.

TRAINS,
 employees upon different, 487.
 duty toward trespassers on, 1087.
 ejection of trespassers from, 1088.
 backing, in absence of flagman, across street, 942.
 track obstructed by, at crossings, 1020.
 evidence of running of, 102.
 management of, by independent contractor, 293.
 dangers from movement of, in company yards, 328.

TRAIN DISPATCHER,
 held to be vice-principal, 488.

TRAIN SHEETS,
 as evidence, 102.

TRAVELERS,
 injuries to, by independent contractors, 296.

Lightning Source UK Ltd.
Milton Keynes UK
UKHW012017220219
337761UK00009B/332/P